AUSTRIA & SWITZERLAND

2004

PATRICK BLANCHFIELD EDITOR
CHRIS TOWNSEND ASSOCIATE EDITOR

RESEARCHER-WRITERS
BRENT A. BUTLER
ALISON GIORDANO
HELEN HUMAN
PATRICK SALISBURY
LACEY WHITMIRE

CHRISTINE PETERSON MAP EDITOR
ARIEL FOX MANAGING EDITOR

MACMILLAN

Published in Great Britain 2004 by Macmillan, an imprint of Pan Macmillan Ltd.
20 New Wharf Road, London N1 9RR
Basingstoke and Oxford
Associated companies throughout the world
www.panmacmillan.com

Maps by David Lindroth copyright © 2004 by St. Martin's Press.

Published in the United States of America by St. Martin's Press.

CONTENTS

MAPS

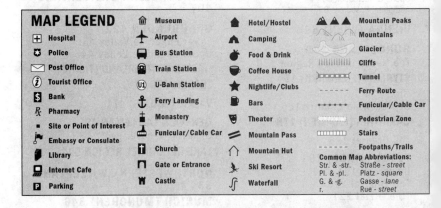

MAP LEGEND

🏛 Museum
🏨 Hotel/Hostel
⛰⛰⛰ Mountain Peaks

✚ Hospital
✈ Airport
🏕 Camping
Mountains

🆘 Police
🚌 Bus Station
🍴 Food & Drink
Glacier

✉ Post Office
🚉 Train Station
☕ Coffee House
Cliffs

ⓘ Tourist Office
Ⓤ U-Bahn Station
★ Nightlife/Clubs
Tunnel

$ Bank
⚓ Ferry Landing
🍺 Bars
Ferry Route

℞ Pharmacy
Monastery
Theater
Funicular/Cable Car

■ Site or Point of Interest
Funicular/Cable Car
Mountain Pass
Pedestrian Zone

Embassy or Consulate
✝ Church
Mountain Hut
Stairs

Library
Gate or Entrance
Ski Resort
Footpaths/Trails

Internet Cafe
Castle
Waterfall

P Parking

Common Map Abbreviations:
Str. & -str.   Straße - street
Pl. & -pl.   Platz - square
G. & -g.   Gasse - lane
r.   Rue - street

HOW TO USE THIS BOOK

COVERAGE. Welcome to *Let's Go: Austria and Switzerland 2004!* We'll be your guide to all things Austrian and Swiss, from alphorns and cheese to Mozart and the Zillertal. In this book, Austria precedes Switzerland, and each country is broken down into regions that are covered in chapters that move in a clockwise direction geographically. As in real life, Liechtenstein is sandwiched between Austria and Switzerland. Black tabs on the side of each page should help you navigate your way, and an extensive index (see p. 564) is always there to fall back on.

LISTINGS. Unless otherwise noted, our researchers list establishments in order of value from best to worst. Our absolute favorites are awarded the Let's Go thumbpick (⬛). These are also listed under "thumpicks" in the index. Since best value does not always mean the cheapest prices, we indicate a restaurant or lodging's relative price by means of price ranges ranked ❶ to ❺ (see pages X-XI).

FEATURES. In addition to providing up-to-date coverage, *Let's Go: Austria and Switzerland 2004* also includes off-the-beaten-track prose detours on items of unique interest to travelers in Austria and Switzerland. Painstakingly compiled by researchers in the field, these features range from information on hidden deals like sleeping in a Swiss barn (see p. 412) to spotlights on local cuisine like *Sacher Torte* (see p. 76) to interviews with vivid locals and the lowdown on regional legends and festivals.

ALTERNATIVES TO TOURISM. A rise in tourism over the last few decades has had some alarming effects on tourist destinations. To help preserve the places we visit, and to encourage responsible travel that is sensitive to the culture, environment, and economy of the destination, *Let's Go* guides now include a chapter providing volunteer abroad, study abroad, and work abroad options (see p. 59).

SCHOLARLY ARTICLES. To further aid travelers in understanding the destinations they visit, *Let's Go* solicits experts for in-depth treatments of regional political and cultural issues. This year's article, by film scholar Mattias Frey, details cutting-edge developments in Austrian cinema (see p. 84).

LANGUAGE ISSUES. Switzerland is a country of four languages and confusing dialects, and though your English may carry you through Vienna and Salzburg, at some point you may be at a loss for words (in a bad way) in Austria as well. To better aid you, this book's appendix (see p. 557) contains a chart of useful phrases in German, French, and Italian. Places that have names in more than one language appear in the text and maps with the more commonly-used name first; when place names differ from their common English names, the English word is listed in parentheses as appropriate. For convenience, common foreign words (like *Altstadt*, *vielle ville*, and *città vecchia*—all of which mean 'old town') are translated when first introduced, and italicized throughout.

SOLO TRAVELERS. Unless otherwise stated, we assume that our reader is a solo traveler. Accommodations and transportation information in this guide is therefore geared toward options for the solo traveler; transportation prices are one-way unless otherwise noted. Nonetheless, we also report on accommodations for travelers in larger groups wherever it's feasible.

A NOTE TO OUR READERS

The information for this book was gathered by *Let's Go* researchers from May through August of 2003. Each listing is based on one researcher's opinion, formed during his or her visit at a particular time. Those traveling at other times may have different experiences since prices, dates, hours, and conditions are always subject to change. You are urged to check the facts presented in this book beforehand to avoid inconvenience and surprises.

RESEARCHER-WRITERS

Brent A. Butler   *Carinthia, Tyrol, Vorarlberg, Liechtenstein*

An energy systems planner dedicated to environmental protection, Brent was the perfect choice to research Austria's mountains. An avid cyclist, sailor, and hiker, he ensured that mountain adventurers in western Austria would not be lead astray. But Brent is not only an outdoorsman. Making friends all across Austria, he expanded accommodations and nightlife sections, while still researching everything else down to the finest detail.

Alison Giordano   *Vienna, Burgenland, Upper Austria, Lower Austria*

As a young actress thrilled to experience the culture of a cosmopolitan city, Alison sparkled with vitality from beginning to end. These were heady times, but she refused to let it go to her head, channeling her energy into an indefatigable work ethic and revamping the Vienna coverage in a way we wouldn't have thought possible. Reading Alison's honest, thoughtful prose, it's hard to imagine that even native Viennese might know their city better than she.

Helen Human   *Salzburger Land, Styria*

Undaunted by the biggest heat wave Europe has seen in years, Helen took to her itinerary with ease. A devoted fan of *The Sound of Music*, she researched Salzburg's old-world charm with wide eyes. Falling into the steady rhythm of travel between small towns, she explored the lakes of the Salzkammergut and the wine country of Styria. Heading south for the home stretch, Helen unlocked Graz's secrets with impressive insight and efficiency.

Patrick Salisbury   *Francophone Switzerland, Ticino, Bernese Oberland*

An avid hiker and rower, Patrick took the Swiss Alps in hand and did not let go until they had submitted. Though we cringed a little to hear of his paragliding exploits and (thankfully unfulfilled) plans to bungee jump, any traveler blazing an independent trail through Switzerland's wilder side can find a kindred spirit in Patrick. With an eye for subtle *reportage* and a keen awareness of the *Let's Go* style, Patrick tore through Switzerland like a pro.

Lacey Whitmire   *German-speaking Switzerland*

Armed with an iron-clad mastery of Swiss German, an unflagging optimism, and an uncanny ability to accquire friends along her way, Lacey and her bubbly phone calls regularly brightened the week of the A&S team. A supreme pleasure to read, Lacey's correspondences included not only sterling copy and fabulously engaging Feature narratives, but the odd bottle of *Appenzellerbitter*, and served to remind us all, however vicariously, of the joy of traveling.

CONTRIBUTING WRITERS

Mattias Frey researched Vienna for *Let's Go: Austria & Switzerland 2002* and has contributed to editions of *Let's Go: Germany*. He is now a free-lance film critic in Berlin.

ACKNOWLEDGMENTS

LET'S GO

Team A&S thanks: Liz, for serendipitously competent disaster relief. The rest of the Axis Lounge, with whom we have shared so much. Prod, the MEs, and Jeff and Julie, for putting up with our problems, frustrations, and questions, and for showing us the way.

Team A&S does not thank: Our spontaneously disappearing Bookfile, wherever it may be.

Patrick Blanchfield thanks: Chris, for your dedication, professionalism and talent. Ariel, for your guidance and kind patience. Christine, for the maps. Countless other folk who make *Let's Go* what it is. And, of course, my RWs: you are my children. Beyond the office, Chris Reisig, for another summer as a bastion of sanity and dear friendship. Kevin and Jacob, too. Robin and Catherine, highlighters and so much more. All, and my family—how could I thank any of you enough, in any one place, for any one thing?

Chris Townsend thanks: Ariel, Patrick, and Christine, of course. Without you guys...you know. And our wonderful RWs, who braved glaciers, slept in hay, and worked without sleep. They dealt with broken laptops, sweltering heat, unfriendly hostel owners, "theoretical" train vouchers, and impossible bus connections, all just to put the A and the S in A&S. Mac, for good times, an education in good whiskey, and fine Indian cuisine. Eddie and Steven, for the 4th, the Cape, and so much else. McSloot, McB, Dave-mon, and the #38 girls, for one hell of a summer. Paul and John, for our conquest of the White Mountains (Sliding Board never stood a chance). Carrie, for the Rocky Mountains. Mom and Dad, for being awesome.

Christine Peterson thanks: Thanks to Brent, Ali, Helen, Pat and Lacey for all their beautiful maps, and to Pat and Chris for pulling through the editing despite the technical difficulties. Thanks also to all the folks in Mapland, especially Nathaniel and Lizzie.

Editor
Patrick Blanchfield
Associate Editor
Chris Townsend
Managing Editor
Ariel Fox
Map Editor
Christine Peterson
Typesetter
Dusty Lewis

Publishing Director
Julie A. Stephens
Editor-in-Chief
Jeffrey Dubner
Production Manager
Dusty Lewis
Cartography Manager
Nathaniel Brooks
Design Manager
Caleb Beyers
Editorial Managers
Lauren Bonner, Ariel Fox,
Matthew K. Hudson, Emma Nothmann,
Joanna Shawn Brigid O'Leary,
Sarah Robinson
Financial Manager
Suzanne Siu
Marketing & Publicity Managers
Megan Brumagim, Nitin Shah
Personnel Manager
Jesse Reid Andrews
Researcher Manager
Jennifer O'Brien
Web Manager
Jesse Tov
Web Content Director
Abigail Burger
Production Associates
Thomas Bechtold, Jeffrey Hoffman Yip
IT Directors
Travis Good, E. Peyton Sherwood
Financial Assistant
R. Kirkie Maswoswe
Associate Web Manager
Robert Dubbin
Office Coordinators
Abigail Burger, Angelina L. Fryer,
Liz Glynn
Director of Advertising Sales
Daniel Ramsey
Senior Advertising Associates
Sara Barnett, Daniella Boston
Advertising Artwork Editor
Julia Davidson, Sandy Liu
President
Abhishek Gupta
General Manager
Robert B. Rombauer
Assistant General Manager
Anne E. Chisholm

ABOUT LET'S GO

GUIDES FOR THE INDEPENDENT TRAVELER

Budget travel is more than a vacation. At *Let's Go*, we see every trip as the chance of a lifetime. If your dream is to grab a knapsack and a machete and forge through the jungles of Brazil, we can take you there. Or, if you'd rather enjoy the Riviera sun at a beachside cafe, we'll set you a table. If you know what you're doing, you can have any experience you want—whether it's camping among lions or sampling Tuscan desserts—without maxing out your credit card. We'll show you just how far your coins can go, and prove that the greatest limitation on your adventure is not your wallet, but your imagination. That said, we understand that you may want the occasional indulgence after a week of hostels and kebab stands, so we've added "Big Splurges" to let you know which establishments are worth those extra euros, as well as price ranges to help you quickly determine whether an accommodation or restaurant will break the bank. While we may have diversified, our emphasis will always be on finding the best values for your budget, giving you all the info you need to spend six days in London or six months in Tasmania.

BEYOND THE TOURIST EXPERIENCE

We write for travelers who know there's more to a vacation than riding double-deckers with tourists. Our researchers give you the heads-up on both world-renowned and lesser-known attractions, on the best local eats and the hottest nightclub beats. In our travels, we talk to everybody; we provide a snapshot of real life in the places you visit with our sidebars on topics like regional cuisine, local festivals, and hot political issues. We've opened our pages to respected writers and scholars to show you their take on a given destination, and turned to lifelong residents to learn the little things that make their city worth calling home. And we've even given you Alternatives to Tourism—ideas for how to give back to local communities through responsible travel and volunteering.

OVER FORTY YEARS OF WISDOM

When we started, way back in 1960, Let's Go consisted of a small group of well-traveled friends who compiled their budget travel tips into a 20-page packet for students on charter flights to Europe. Since then, we've expanded to suit all kinds of travelers, now publishing guides to six continents, including our newest guides: *Let's Go: Japan* and *Let's Go: Brazil*. Our guides are still annually researched and written entirely by students on shoe-string budgets, adventurous travelers who know that train strikes, stolen luggage, food poisoning, and marriage proposals are all part of a day's work. Even as you read this, work on next year's editions is well underway. Whether you're reading one of our new titles, like *Let's Go: Puerto Rico* or *Let's Go Adventure Guide: Alaska*, or our original best-seller, *Let's Go: Europe*, you'll find the same spirit of adventure that has made *Let's Go* the guide of choice for travelers the world over since 1960.

GETTING IN TOUCH

The best discoveries are often those you make yourself; on the road, when you find something worth sharing, please drop us a line. We're Let's Go Publications, 67 Mt. Auburn St., Cambridge, MA 02138, USA (feedback@letsgo.com).

For more info, visit our website: www.letsgo.com.

PRICE RANGES>>AUSTRIA & SWITZERLAND

Our researchers list establishments in order of value from best to worst; our favorites are denoted by the Let's Go thumbs-up (☒). Since the best value is not always the cheapest price, we have incorporated a system of price ranges for quick reference. Our price ranges are based on a rough expectation of what you will spend. For **accommodations,** we base our price range off the cheapest price for which a single traveler can stay for one night. For **restaurants** and other dining establishments, we estimate the average amount that you will spend in that restaurant. The table below tells you what you will *typically* find in Austria & Switzerland at the corresponding price range; keep in mind that a particularly expensive ice cream stand may still only be marked a ❷, depending on what you will spend.

ACCOMMODATIONS	RANGE	WHAT YOU'RE *LIKELY* TO FIND
❶	under €15/ 23SFr	Camping; Most HI and university dorm rooms, expect bunk beds and a communal bath; you may have to provide or rent towels and sheets.
❷	€16-25/24-54SFr	Upper-end hostels or small hotels. You may have a private bathroom, or there may be a sink in your room and communal shower in the hall.
❸	€26-34/55-85SFr	A small room with a private bath. Should have decent amenities, such as phone and TV. Breakfast may be included in the price of the room.
❹	€35-55/86-170SFr	Similar to 3, but may have more amenities or be in a more touristed area.
❺	above €55/ 170SFr	Large hotels or upscale chains. If it's a 5 and it doesn't have the perks you want, you've paid too much.
FOOD		
❶	under €5/ 12SFr	Mostly street-corner stands, pizza places, or fast-food joints. Rarely ever a sit-down meal.
❷	€6-10/ 13-23SFr	Sandwiches, appetizers at a bar, or low-priced entrees. You may have the option of sitting down or getting take-out.
❸	€10-16/ 24-37SFr	Mid-priced entrees, possibly coming with soup or salad. You'll probably have a waiter, so factor in the tip.
❹	€17-25/ 38-52SFr	A somewhat fancy restaurant. Few restaurants in this range have a dress code, but some may look down on t-shirt and jeans.
❺	above €26/ 53SFr	Complicated food, a stocked wine list, and a swank atmosphere. Dress well; there may be someone in the bathroom to hand you little towels.

Austria and Switzerland: Chapter Divisions

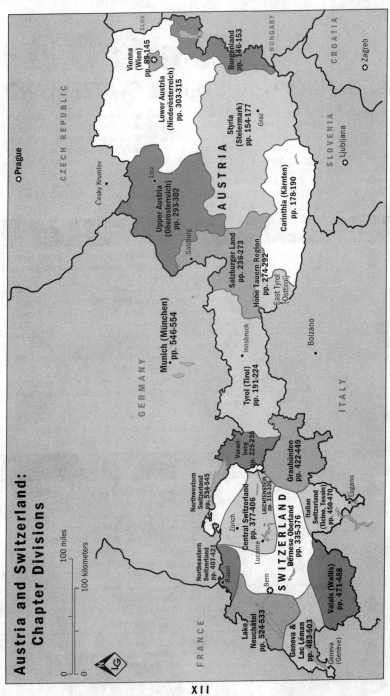

100 miles

100 kilometers

CZECH REPUBLIC

GERMANY

FRANCE

ITALY

SLOVENIA

HUNGARY

CROATIA

SLOV

Prague

Český Krumlov

Linz

Salzburg

Innsbruck

Bolzano

Graz

Ljubljana

Zagreb

Zürich

Lucerne

Bern

Basel

Geneva (Genève)

Lugano

AUSTRIA

SWITZERLAND

LIECHTENSTEIN

Vienna (Wien) pp. 89–145

Lower Austria (Niederösterreich) pp. 303–315

Upper Austria (Oberösterreich) pp. 293–302

Burgenland pp. 146–153

Styria (Steiermark) pp. 154–177

Carinthia (Kärnten) pp. 178–190

Salzburger Land pp. 236–273

Hohe Tauern Region pp. 274–292

East Tyrol (Osttirol)

Munich (München) pp. 546–554

Tyrol (Tirol) pp. 191–224

Vorarl-berg pp. 225–235

Graubünden pp. 422–449

Northwestern Switzerland pp. 534–545

Central Switzerland pp. 377–406

Northeastern Switzerland pp. 407–421

Italian Switzerland (Ticino, Tessin) pp. 450–470

Bernese Oberland pp. 335–376

Valais (Wallis) pp. 471–488

Lake Neuchâtel pp. 524–533

Geneva & Lac Léman pp. 483–503

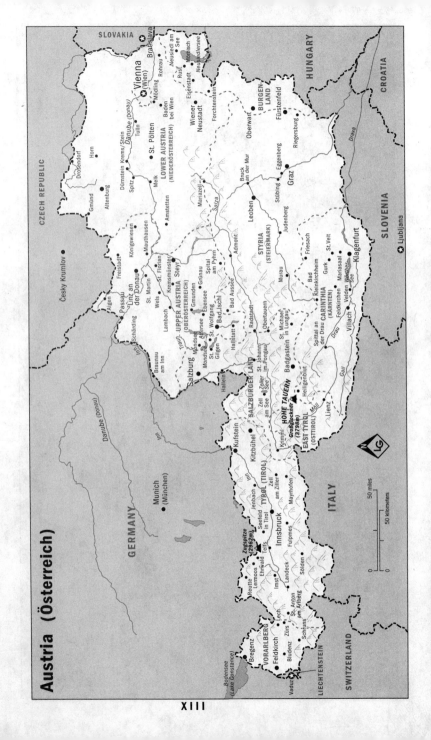

Austria (Österreich)

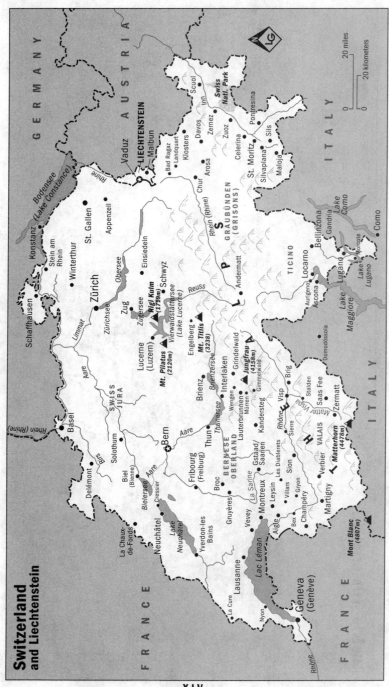

Switzerland
and Liechtenstein

GERMANY

AUSTRIA

FRANCE

ITALY

N

LG

20 miles

20 kilometers

Bodensee (Lake Constance)

Rhine

Vaduz
LIECHTENSTEIN
Malbun

Konstanz
Stein am Rhein
Schaffhausen

St. Gallen
Appenzell
Bad Ragaz
Landquart
Klosters
Scuol
Swiss Natl. Park
Zernez
Inn

Winterthur

Zürichsee
Obersee
Einsiedeln

Arosa
Davos
Pontresina
Celerina
St. Moritz
Silvaplana
Sils
Maloja

Limmat
Zürich
Zug
Zugersee
Schwyz
Rigi Kulm (1798m)

Chur

GRAUBÜNDEN (GRISONS)

Rhein (Rhine)

Lucerne (Luzern)
Mt. Pilatus (2120m)
Vierwaldstättersee (Lake Lucerne)
Reuss

Andermatt

P

L

S

TICINO

Bellinzona
Locarno
Ascona
Lake Maggiore
Aurigeno
Lake Lugano
Lugano
Gandria
Lake Como
Como
Morcote
Lugano

Engelberg
Mt. Titlis (3238)

Grindelwald
Jungfrau (4158m)
Gimmelwald
Wengen
Mürren
Lauterbrunnen

Brienz
Brienzersee
Interlaken
Thunersee
Thun

Domodossola

Brig
Visp
Stalden
Saas Fee
Zermatt
Matterhorn (4478m)

ITALY

SWISS JURA

Aare

Basel
Rhein (Rhine)
Birs

Solothurn
Biel (Bienne)
Cressier
Bielersee

Delémont

La Chaux-de-Fonds
Neuchâtel
Lake Neuchâtel

Bern

Fribourg (Freiburg)
Broc
Gruyères
La Sarine
Vevey
Montreux
Lac Léman

BERNESE OBERLAND

Kandersteg
Gstaad/Saanen
Les Diablerets
Sion
Sierre

VALAIS
Matter Vispa
Rhône

Verbier
Martigny
Mont Blanc (4807m)

Yverdon-les-Bains
Lausanne
La Cure
Nyon
Geneva (Genève)

Villars
Leysin
Bex
Aigle
Gryon
Champéry

Rhône

FRANCE

ITALY

XIV

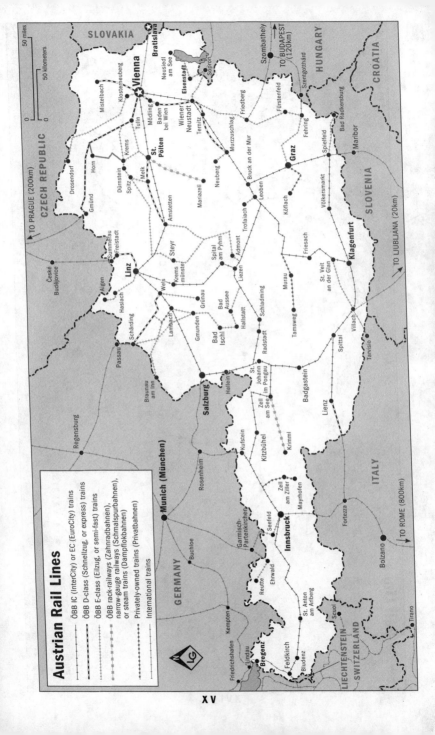

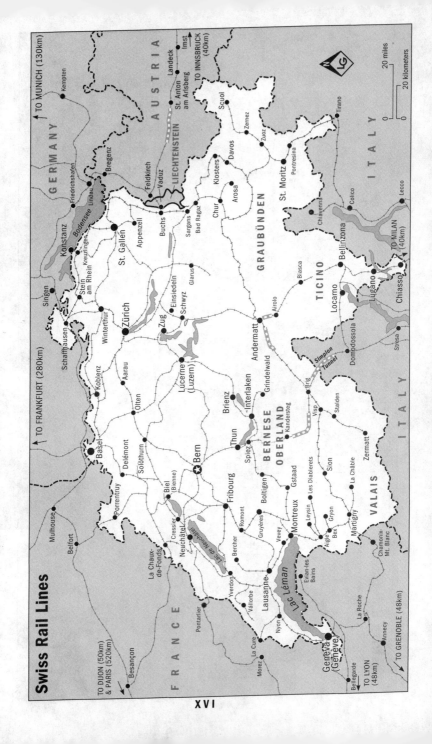

Swiss Rail Lines

DISCOVER AUSTRIA & SWITZERLAND

Austria and Switzerland are an adventurer's paradise, with infinite opportunities for pulse-quickening exploits. Mountain climbing, paragliding, and canyoning, along with unparalleled opportunities for hiking and skiing, provide exposure to an outdoors that has awed visitors for centuries. Though scenic beauty is ample explanation as to why Austria and Switzerland draw millions of tourists each year, it would be wrong to assume that this alone accounts for their popularity. Between each glorious summit and breathtaking alpine trail are world-class cities such as Vienna, Salzburg, Geneva and Zurich, which showcase many of Europe's most prized artistic, musical, and architectural treasures. Smaller cities like Klagenfurt, Hallstatt, and Lucerne, as well as countless picturesque hamlets, add to the countries' allure with their captivating *Altstädte* (old towns) and quaint charms. Linking everything is a dense network of carefully coordinated trains and well-tended budget accommodations, all of which help thrifty travelers explore on schedule and in comfort.

FACTS AND FIGURES

CAPITAL OF AUSTRIA: Vienna

POPULATION: 8,120,000

LIFE EXPECTANCY: Men 75, women 81

LAND AREA: 83,857sq. km (32,377 sq. mi.)

LANGUAGE: German

RELIGION: 78% Catholic, 5% Protestant, 17% Muslim and other

CAPITAL OF SWITZERLAND: Bern

POPULATION: 7,444,000

LIFE EXPECTANCY: Men 77, women 83

LAND AREA: 41,285 sq. km (15,941 sq. mi.)

LANGUAGES: German, French, Italian, and Romansch

RELIGION: 46% Catholic, 40% Protestant, 14% other

WHEN TO GO

Everything has its season in Austria and Switzerland, so determine what your primary interests are when deciding when to travel. Outdoor enthusiasts should know that December to March is peak ski season, while July and August are ideal for hiking. In ski country, lodgings are scarcer and more expensive in winter, while cities see increased prices during the summer; rooms can be harder to come by if you don't have a reservation. The cheapest time to go is in the shoulder season (May-June, September-October) when there is the added benefit of milder weather. However, many mountain towns throughout Austria and Switzerland shut down completely in May and June so that the hostel owners can take a break from providing vacations for others. Christmastime is particularly magical in Austria—entire towns are decorated for the holidays and *Christkindlmarkets* selling handmade ornaments, toys, and nutcrackers spring up in the central squares. If you're a music or theater fan, be aware that the Vienna State Opera, the Vienna Boys' Choir, and major theaters throughout Austria and Switzerland don't have any performances during July and August.

A LEGACY OF CULTURE

Thanks to the Imperious Hapsburgs and the smart banking of the savvy Swiss, the two nations have amassed an impressive collection of masterpieces in their museums. **Vienna** has classically reigned supreme as far as paintings are concerned: one of the four largest art collections in the world, collected and commissioned by the Habsburgs, is now stored in the **Kunsthistorisches Museum** (p. 134). The **Österreichische Galerie** assembles, among other pieces, great works from the Viennese artistic explosion at the beginning of the 20th century, including Klimt's *The Kiss*. The hip, contemporary side of Viennese culture is stored in the **Museums-Quartier,** a massive complex of museums and restaurants that opened its doors to rave reviews in 2001. Housing the **ZOOM Kindermuseum** for the under-12 set, as well as a dance performance center, gardens, and a pedestrian mall, this giant arena explores culture in all directions. To see where art was made—rather than stored—head to **Mozarts Wohnhaus** (p. 251) in **Salzburg.** On the way to Salzburg take a virtual flight at the **Ars Electronica** in **Linz** (p. 298).

In Switzerland, don't miss the **Kunsthaus Zürich** (p. 389), which juxtaposes well-known masterpieces with cutting-edge art, or the **Oskar Reinhart Collections** in **Winterthur** (p. 394), where the buildings are as beautiful as the works by Daumier and Picasso within. A trip to **Lausanne** is worthwhile in part because of the haunting works in the **Collection de l'Art Brut** (p. 509), which reveal the unexpected wells of artistic potential locked in the minds of the peasant, the criminal, and the insane. For the young and noisy at heart, the clanging, hands-on, futuristic sculptures in the **Museum Jean Tinguely** are an irresistible draw to **Basel** (p. 541).

RELIVING HISTORY

Centuries of serfdom, feudalism, and imperial power-mongering have left their mark on the landscapes of Austria and Switzerland. Crumbling castles, elaborate palaces, and medieval inner cities will transport you back in time. In Austria, explore the ruins of **Burg Dürnstein** (p. 308), where Richard the Lionheart was held for ransom; hike up to **Burg Hochosterwitz** (p. 184) along spiraling outer fortifications; or shiver in the *Hexenzimmer* (Witches' Room) of **Burg Kronegg** in Riegersburg (p. 168), built on a barren cliff of volcanic rock. If you're looking for something a little more ornate, the hulking and yellow **Benediktinerstift** of Melk (p. 308) takes the prize for ecclesiastical Baroque splendor. Vienna and Salzburg hold the lion's share of Austria's palaces—among the most impressive are **Lustschloß Hellbrunn** (p. 256), which boasts hilarious *Wasserspiele* (water games) in its gardens, and the delicate, mirrored **Schloß Schönbrunn** (p. 130).

In Switzerland, the **Château de Chillon** in Montreux (p. 501) is the subject of a famous poem by Lord Byron, while the **Castello di Montebello** in Bellinzona (p. 453) boasts a working drawbridge. The lavishly carved, gilt-wood library of the Benedictine monks in **St. Gallen** (p. 413) is also a masterpiece. To complete the medieval experience, visit the town of **Stein am Rhein** (p. 411), or wander the labyrinthine streets of Switzerland's **Bern** (p. 335). Then, relive country life at the **Freilichtmuseum Ballenburg,** a park and open-air museum where over 100 historic homes from across Switzerland have been transported to recreate 13 different villages, on a terrific daytrip from **Brienz** (p. 349).

THE BEATEN PATH...

The backpacker's world is a remarkably small one, concentrated around large hostels in strategic locations throughout Austria and Switzerland. If you want to follow the beaten path and go with the partying crowd, Switzerland's backpacker mecca is in **Interlaken** (p. 352), which boasts a dizzying aggregation of hostels and a year-round crowd of young, English-speaking travelers seeking adrenaline rushes of every sort imaginable. Other Swiss hot spots are **Zermatt** (p. 471), **Zurich** (p. 471), **Montreux** (p. 512), and **Geneva** (p. 489). In Austria, nothing can touch **Vienna** and its vast array of accommodations (p. 103) for backpacker-congregating, though **Innsbruck** (p. 191) and **Salzburg** (p. 237) are solid rivals.

...AND THE ROAD LESS TRAVELED

If you didn't come to hang out with the same English-speaking backpackers every night, head for the handful of smaller backpacker resorts/hostels hidden in the hills. Switzerland has a number of these getaways, including the **Swiss Alps Retreat** in Gryon (p. 522), the ultra-friendly **Hiking Sheep Guesthouse** in Leysin, and the adventure-oriented **Swiss Adventure Hostel** in Boltigen. Austria has the **Treehouse** hostel in Grünau (p. 267) and the gorgeous **Schloß Röthelstein** in Admont (p. 169). More comfortable and service-oriented than mainstream hostels, they offer the opportunity to get to know both the owners and the countryside well. *Privatzimmer* are a widespread option for experiencing Austrian and Swiss hospitality away from the crowds of travelers. Try quiet, gorgeous towns like **Sölden** (p. 180) and **Lech** (p. 279) in Austria or **Guarda** (p. 380) or **Cressier** (p. 450) in Switzerland for a laid-back glimpse of everyday life in the two countries.

■ LET'S GO PICKS

BEST PLACE TO THROW YOURSELF OFF A CLIFF: If the bungee options in Interlaken (p. 352) don't cut it, head to **Val Verzasca** (p. 454) near Locarno for the highest bungee jump in the world.

NICEST PEOPLE THIS SIDE OF THE ALPS: Andi and Joy, owners of **Pension Sinilill** (p. 283), tell stories of Austrian swimming championships and Filipino cock-fighting on their warm hearth.

BEST MEETING OF MATTER AND ENERGY: Brush up on quantum mechanics at **Einstein's House** (p. 312).

MOST FRAGRANT TIMEPIECE: Smell the roses and check the time at the flower clock in the **Theresiengarten**.

BEST BUS RIDE ON EARTH: Spend 5hr. gawking from a bus on the ride down the **Großglocknerstraße** (p. 277).

BEST PLACE TO FRESHEN UP: Cleanse yourself at the **Museum of Historical Sanitary Objects** (p. 215), host to assorted bathtubs and toilets.

BEST OPERA WITHOUT RED VELVET: Every July and August the **Bregenzer Festspiele** (p. 225) stages world-class opera, floating on the *Bodensee*.

BEST LIGHTING EFFECTS IN A BATHROOM: The *pissoir* at the **Hotel Goldener Löwe** illuminates (so that you can let the waterfall on the wall inspire you). You get less help in the bathroom at the **Funny Farm** (p. 321), where the only light is a blacklight (wear lots of white—the only other light comes from the disco ball on the ceiling).

BEST PLACE TO WATCH MEN IN TIGHTS: Wow yourself at the **Vienna Staatsoper ballet**, home to one of the world's most prestigious companies.

SUGGESTED ITINERARIES

BEST OF AUSTRIA

imposing ruins of Schloß Dürnstein loom over the valley as you make your way along the Danube river, past **Krems** and **Stein,** to **Vienna** (p. 89) itself, the former Imperial headquarters. The magic of Strauss's waltzes and the thunder of Beethoven's symphonies resonate through Vienna's Baroque buildings. From the stately Staatsoper to the glittering Musikverein, the majestic Hofburg to Otto Wagner's simple Kirche am Steinhof, Vienna's attractions provide sensory stimulation galore.

BEST OF AUSTRIA (MIN. 2 WEEKS)

For the best nature and culture Austria has to offer, start your journey in **Bregenz** (p. 225), capital city of Vorarlberg. Spend a day in the city, on the shores of Europe's largest freshwater lake. Then spend another day poking around the rolling hills of the Bregenzerwald. Take a train ride through gorgeous Alpine scenery on the way to **Innsbruck** (p. 191). Wander through the old-world charm of the Hapsburg Empire's legacy in the morning and take a daytrip to Schloß Ambras in the afternoon. After that, explore the Hohe Tauern National Park from **Zell am See** (p. 282). Take one day to visit the Krimml Waterfalls, and another to admire the dramatic mountain scenery on the Großglockner Hochalpenstraße. Descend from the mountains and head north to the hills of Salzburger Land. While it may be crowded with tourists, the **Salzburg** (p. 237) of Maria von Trapp and Mozart is not to be missed. Once one of the most powerful religious centers in Europe, this city boasts an impressive collection of worthy sights that remain from its cultural heyday. **Hallstatt** (p. 258), balanced between cliffs and a lake, is of historical interest as a cradle of European civilization, and of immediate interest for its stunning hiking and ice caves. Don't forget to sneak down to **Graz** (p. 154), Austria's second-largest city. This vibrant university town hosts a variety of entertainment venues from opera to musical festivals. Don't miss the Schloßberg (castle mountain) for a bird's-eye view of the city. Make your way up to **Melk** (p. 308) for its unmistakable yellow abbey perched high on a hill. Save an afternoon for the Renaissance courtyard, Romanesque fortress, and Gothic chapel at Schloß Schallaburg, only 5km away. The

BEST OF SWITZERLAND

BEST OF SWITZERLAND (MIN. 2 WEEKS)

Spend your first day or two strolling the quiet squares around John Calvin's Cathédrale de St. Pierre in **Geneva** (p. 489), acquainting yourself with this international city and symbol of diversity for a quadrilingual nation. Make sure to check out the bohemian artist community called Artamis, as well as the UN and WTO buildings on International Hill. Now head west to the mighty Alps in **Zermatt** (p. 471), home of the Matterhorn and a number of other towering peaks. The number of hikes and ski trails within walking distance of the town is unparalleled. Time your stay to see the annual Jazz Festival from late July to early August in **Montreux** (p. 512). The festival attracts headlining acts and street-corner musicians from all over the world, creating an energetic, cosmopolitan atmosphere. Head north to lakeside **Neuchâtel** (p. 524), both for its own culinary delights and as a gateway to wine-tasting in tiny **Cressier** (p. 528). Then, step east to **Fribourg,** a refined, multilingual city that provides an easy daytrip to cheese-producing **Gruyères.** Take a break from the city scene with a few days in the **Jungfrau Region.** Skydive, bungee-jump, and river raft your way to adrenalin-pumping happiness in **Interlaken** (p. 352), the adventure capital of the world. For quieter thrills, head south into the small mountain towns. Make the expensive-but-worth-it daytrip to the **Jungfraujoch** (p. 362), appropriately dubbed the "top of Europe." To ease off your mountain high, let nearby **Lucerne** (p. 396) intrigue you with its *Altstadt*, museums, clear blue lake, and looming twin peaks. Then take the train to **Zurich** (p. 377) and explore one of the world's most influential banking centers, where Ulrich Zwingli and the Dadaists once tormented revolutions. Then get into hiking mode as you approach **Appenzell**, where down-home Swiss countryside hospitality welcomes you into peaceful forests, flowered meadows, and jagged mountains. To warm up from the crisp mountain air, head for the Mediterranean climate and Italian flair of **Locarno** (p. 454). Take a ferry ride on the calm waters of warm *Lago Maggiore*, and make a visit to the 500-year-old orange-yellow Franciscan monastery.

HIKING THE ALPS (MIN. 2 WEEKS)

Test out your trail legs on the paths that extend from **Zermatt** (p. 471). The town's most exciting hikes lead to spectacular views of (or hikes on) the Matterhorn (4199m). In close proximity are several of the highest mountains on the continent. In central Switzerland, unspoiled **Kandersteg** (p. 370) has hikes to glaciers and high-lying glacial lakes like Öschinensee. From there, take a train to **Interlaken** and head into the **Jungfrau region** (p. 359). Cliff-walled valleys allow for both level and extremely steep hikes. **Lauterbrunnen** is

near a number of prominent waterfalls, and each tiny village affords hikes near the imposing Jungfrau (4158m), Mönch (4099m), and Eiger (3970m), the last of which remains one of the most legendary mountaineering challenges in the world. To get away from any hint of a resort, head for rustic **Appenzell**, where a network of country guesthouses will warm any hiker's heart (and stomach). Heading south to the wildest canton in the country, Graubünden, will bring more splendid isolation in the **Swiss National Park** (p. 436). There is less human presence here than almost anywhere else in the two countries. Nature lovers will appreciate the unspoiled wildlife, and hard-core hikers can select between a variety of difficult hikes.

On your way to Austria, make a stop in **Upper Liechtenstein** (p. 319). Above the prince's palace spread craggy peaks on open ridges that afford views into Austria, Switzerland, and Germany.

In Austria, head straight for dramatic scenery in the rugged mountains of the **Ötztal** (p. 221). Trails lead through steep green forests that turn into sweeping Alpine panoramas. Moving eastward, you'll run into the **Hohe Tauern National Park** (p. 274), the largest national park in Europe. Countless paths lead through meadows and over glaciers beneath towering summits. **Zell am See** to the north and **Lienz** to the south are bases for exploration; travel between them on the **Großglocknerstraße** (p. 277), arguably the most dramatic mountain road in Europe, if not the world. For the best Hohe Tauern hiking, stay in **Heiligenblut** (p. 279) beneath the *Großglockner* (3798m), Austria's highest mountain. Finish in **Hallstatt** (p. 258). Hiking here leads past waterfalls

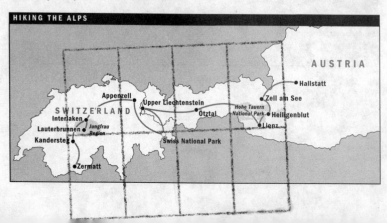

HIKING THE ALPS

AUSTRIA

Hallstatt

Appenzell

Upper Liechtenstein

Zell am See

SWITZERLAND

Hohe Tauern
National Park

Heiligenblut

Interlaken

Ötztal

Lauterbrunnen   Jungfrau
                 Region

Lienz

Kandersteg

Swiss National Park

Zermatt

DISCOVER

and the lush foliage and chalk cliffs of the Dachstein range.

ALPINE SKIING (MIN. 3 WEEKS)

You could land just about anywhere in Switzerland or Austria in the winter and have a fabulous skiing experience. A number of glaciers offer the opportunity for skiing year-round, even in August. It's important to differentiate between the fancier resorts and simpler ones—discerning travelers will find great skiing for their money *and* the chance to glimpse some famous faces. One good place to start is **Kitzbühel** (p. 206), where downhill skiing was actually invented in 1892—plan carefully to avoid, view, or participate in the gigantic annual Hahnenkamm World Cup race. On your way west stop in **Mayrhofen** (p. 219), where even August finds skiers on the glacier in **Hintertux**. The next major resort valley to the west is the **Ötztal** (p. 221), which has a more down-to-earth feel while still providing plenty of high-quality snow and slopes. From there, head into the **Arlberg** region, one of the world's most legendary resort areas. The center of the area is **St. Anton** (p. 213), which hosted the 2000 World Championships and is usually considered the birthplace of modern skiing. From there, it's an easy train ride

to **Innsbruck** (p. 191), home of the 1964 and 1976 Winter Olympics for good reason. Shuttles run to snow-covered mountains, even in summer.

Hopping the border to Switzerland, glitzy **St. Moritz** (p. 446) is a familiar name in any skiing household, particularly the royal families of Britain and Hollywood. From there, head to central Switzerland and the **Jungfrau Region** (p. 359) just south of the mega-resort town of **Interlaken.** The little towns wedged between big mountains provide reasonably-priced skiing that will challenge skiers of all levels. Moving to the southwest, you'll run across thriving **Gstaad** and **Saanen** (p. 372), an international resort magnet. Gstaad is covered in movie-star glitz, while Saanen is down-to-earth. Both are especially suited for intermediates. French Switzerland does its best to compete with **Les Diablerets** (p. 519), where snowboarders and younger crowds flock, even in summer when glacier skiing draws the crowds. Finally, make sure to take the cog railway up to **Zermatt/Saas Fee** (p. 478), the ski paradise in southwestern Switzerland. Nearby is **Martigny** (p. 485), one of Europe's premier resorts, with more than enough size, snow, and challenge to back up its lofty reputation.

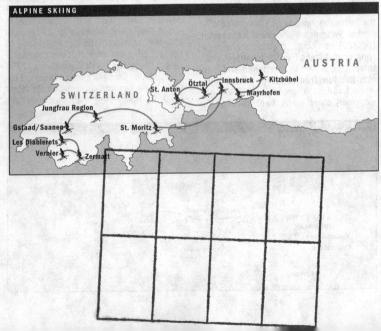

ALPINE SKIING

ESSENTIALS

FACTS FOR THE TRAVELER

 ENTRANCE REQUIREMENTS.
Passport (p. 9). Required of all foreign visitors.
Visa (p. 9). Required only for a continuous stay of more than three months.
Work Permit (p. 9). Required to work in Austria or Switzerland.
Driving Permit (p. 47). Required of all those planning to drive.

EMBASSIES & CONSULATES

All diplomatic missions are embassies unless otherwise indicated.

AUSTRIAN CONSULAR SERVICES ABROAD

Australia: 12 Talbot St., Forrest, **Canberra** ACT 2603 (☎00 6295 1533; www.austri-aemb.org.au). Consulates in **Adelaide, Brisbane, Melbourne, Perth,** and **Sydney.**

Canada: 445 Wilbrod St., **Ottawa,** ON K1N 6M7 (☎613-789-1444; www.austro.org). Consulates in **Montreal, Toronto, Vancouver, Halifax, Calgary, Regina,** and **Winnipeg.**

Ireland: 93 Ailesbury Court, **Dublin** 4 (☎(01) 269 45 77 dublin-ob@bmaa.gv.at).

New Zealand: Consulate, Level 2, Willbank House, 57 Willis St., **Wellington** (☎04 499 63 93; fax 499 6392); another consulate in **Auckland.**

South Africa: 1109 Duncan St., Momentum Office Park, Brooklyn, **Pretoria** 0011 (☎(012) 45 29 155; fax 46 01 151); during sessions of Parliament (Jan.-June), embassy is based in **Cape Town,** Standard Bank Centre, 1001 Main Tower, Hertzog Blvd., Cape Town 8001. Consulates in **Cape Town** and **Johannesburg.**

UK: 18 Belgrave Mews West, London SW1 X 8HU (☎020 7235 3731; www.austria.org.uk). Consulates in **Birmingham, Edinburgh, Hamilton.**

US: 3524 International Ct. NW, **Washington, D.C.** 20008-3035 (☎202-895-6700; obwas@sysnet.net). Consulates in **Chicago, Los Angeles,** and **New York.**

SWISS CONSULAR SERVICES ABROAD

Australia: 7 Melbourne Ave., Forrest, **Canberra** ACT 2903 (☎(02) 6273 3977; vertretung@can.rep.admin.ch). Consulates in **Melbourne** and **Sydney.**

Canada: 5 Marlborough Ave., **Ottawa,** ON K1N 8E6 (☎613-235-1837; vertretung@ott.rep.admin.ch). Consulates in **Montréal, Québec, Toronto,** and **Vancouver.**

Ireland: 6 Ailesbury Rd., Ballsbridge, **Dublin** 4 (☎(01) 353 1218 6382; vertretung@dub.rep.admin.ch).

New Zealand: Consulate, 22 Panama St., Panama St., **Wellington** 6001 (☎(04) 472 15 93 or 472 15 94; fax 499 63 02); also a consulate in **Auckland.**

South Africa: P818 George Ave., Arcadia 0083, 0001 **Pretoria** (☎(012) 430 67 07; vertretung@pre.rep.admin.ch); during sessions of Parliament (Jan.-June), the embassy is based in **Cape Town,** P.O. Box 1546, Cape Town 8000 (☎(021) 418 36 69; fax 418 15 69). Consulates in **Cape Town, Durban,** and **Johannesburg.**

UK: 16-18 Montague Pl., **London** W1H 2BQ (☎(020) 76 16 60 00; swissembassy@lon.rep.admin.ch). Consulates in **Belfast, Edinburgh, Manchester, Guernsey** and **Warwick/Bermuda.**

US: 2900 Cathedral Ave. NW, **Washington, D.C.** 20008-3499 (☎202-745-7900; www.swissemb.org). Consulates in **Atlanta, Boston, Chicago, Houston, Los Angeles, New York,** and **San Francisco.**

CONSULAR SERVICES IN AUSTRIA

Foreign embassies are based in Vienna. Look in the Vienna telephone book under *Botschaften* (embassies) or *Konsulate* (consulates). For more info, see p. 101.

Australia: IV, Mattiellistr. 2 (☎(01) 513 16 56; www.australian-embassy.at).

Canada: I, Laurenzerberg 2 (☎(01) 531 38 30 00; www.kanada.at).

Ireland: I, Rotenturmstr. 16-18 5th Floor (☎(01) 715 42 46; vienna@iveath.irlgov.ie).

New Zealand: The New Zealand embassy in **Berlin,** Germany has responsibility for Austria. Friedrichstr. 60, 10117 Berlin (☎(030) 20 62 10; nzemb@t-online.de). **Consulate, Vienna,** XIX, Springsiedelg. 28 (☎(01) 318 85 05; p.sunley@aon.at).

South Africa: XIX, Sandg. 33 (☎(01) 320 64 93; www.southafrican-embassy.at).

UK: III, Jauresg. 10 (☎(01) 716 13 51; www.britishembassy.at).

US: IX, Boltzmanng. 16 (☎(01) 313 39; www.usembassy-vienna.at).

CONSULAR SERVICES IN SWITZERLAND

Nearly all foreign embassies in Switzerland are located in Bern.

Australia: Consulate: Geneva, Chemin des Fins 2, Case Postale 172, Geneva 1211 (☎(022) 799 91 00; mission.australia@ties.itu.int).

Canada: Kirchenfeldstr. 88 (☎(031) 357 32 00; bern@dfait-maeci.gc.ca).

Ireland: Kirchenfeldstr. 68 (☎(031) 352 14 42; irlemb@bluewin.ch).

New Zealand: The New Zealand embassy in **Berlin,** Germany has responsibility for Switzerland. Friedrichstr. 60, 10117 Berlin (☎(030) 20 62 10; nzemb@t-online.de). Consulate: **Geneva,** Chemin des Fins 2, 1218 Grand Saconnex (☎(022) 929 03 50; mission.nz@itu.ch).

South Africa: Alpenstr. 29 (☎(031) 350 13 13; www.southafrica.ch).

UK: Thunstr. 50 (☎(031) 359 77 00).

US: Jubiläumstr. 93 (☎(031) 357 70 11; www.usembassy.ch).

NATIONAL TOURIST OFFICES ABROAD

AUSTRIAN NATIONAL TOURIST OFFICES

Australia and New Zealand: 1st Floor, 36 Carrington St., **Sydney** NSW 2000 (☎(02) 2299 3621; fax 2299 3808).

UK and Ireland: 14 Cork St. GB-**London** W13N3 (☎(020) 76 29 04 61; info@anto.co.uk).

US and Canada: 500 Fifth Ave., Suite 800, P.O. Box 1142, **New York,** NY 10110 (☎212-944-6885; fax 730-4568).

SWISS NATIONAL TOURIST OFFICES

UK: Swiss Centre, Swiss Court, **London** W1V 8EE (☎0171 734 1921).

US and Canada: 608 Fifth Ave., **New York,** NY 10020 (☎877-794-8034; 212-757-5944; info.usa@switzerland.com); additional offices in **San Francisco** (☎415-362-2260) and **Los Angeles** (☎310-640-8900). In **Canada** call toll-free ☎800-002-0030 to be transferred to New York. Elsewhere internationally, call toll-free ☎877-794-8037.

DOCUMENTS & FORMALITIES

PASSPORTS

REQUIREMENTS. Citizens of Australia, Canada, New Zealand, South Africa, the UK, and the US need valid passports to enter Austria or Switzerland and to re-enter their own country, and can stay three months without a visa. If you apply for a visa, make sure your passport is valid for at least three months longer than the visa, or you could face a fine upon returning with an expired passport.

NEW PASSPORTS. Citizens of Australia, Canada, Ireland, New Zealand, the United Kingdom, and the United States can apply for a passport at any post office, passport office, or court of law. Citizens of South Africa can apply for a passport at any Home Affairs office. Any new passport or renewal applications must be filed well in advance of the departure date, although most passport offices offer rush services for a very steep fee. Be aware that after April 8, 2004, US embassies and consulates will no longer issue American passports abroad. Applying for a passport in a foreign consulate will take longer, because it needs to be printed in the US.

PASSPORT MAINTENANCE. Photocopy the page of your passport with your photo, passport number, and other identifying information, as well as any visas, travel insurance policies, plane tickets, or traveler's check serial numbers. Carry one set of copies in a safe place, apart from the originals, and leave another set at home. If you lose your passport, notify the local police and the nearest embassy or consulate of your home government immediately. In an emergency, ask for immediate temporary traveling papers that will permit you to re-enter your home country—in most cases, consulates can only issue temporary passports, which cannot be extended. More detailed info regarding lost and stolen passports is available at www.usembassy.it/cons/acs/passport-lost.htm.

Your passport is a public document belonging to your nation's government. You may have to surrender it to a foreign government official, but if you don't get it back, inform the nearest diplomatic mission of your home country.

VISAS, INVITATIONS, & WORK PERMITS

VISAS. Citizens of Australia, Canada, Ireland, New Zealand, South Africa, the UK, and the US do not need visas to visit Austria or Switzerland. For more detailed information about which nationalities require visas, visit either the Austrian Embassy web site (www.bmaa.gv.at/embassy/uk/index.html.en) or the Swiss Embassy web site (www.swissemb.org).

WORK PERMITS. Admission to Austria or Switzerland as a visitor does not include the right to work, which is authorized only by a work permit. Studying in either country requires a special visa. For more information, see the Alternatives to Tourism chapter (p. 59).

IDENTIFICATION. When you travel, always carry two or more forms of identification on your person, including at least one photo ID; a passport combined with a driver's license or birth certificate is usually adequate. Many establishments, especially banks, require several IDs in order to cash traveler's checks. Never carry all your forms of ID together; split them up in case of theft or loss.

ESSENTIALS

 ONE EUROPE. The idea of European unity has come a long way since 1958, when the European Economic Community (EEC) was created to promote solidarity and cooperation between founding states. The EEC has become the European Union (EU), with political, legal, and economic institutions spanning 15 member states: Austria, Belgium, Denmark, Finland, France, Germany, Greece, Ireland, Italy, Luxembourg, The Netherlands, Portugal, Spain, Sweden, and the UK.

What does this have to do with the non-EU tourist? Well, 1999 saw **freedom of movement** established across 14 European countries—the entire EU minus Denmark, Ireland, and the UK, but plus Iceland and Norway. This means that border controls between participating countries have been abolished and visa policies harmonized. While you're still required to carry a passport (or government-issued ID card for EU citizens) when crossing a border, once you've been admitted into one country, you're free to travel to all participating states. Britain and Ireland have also formed a **common travel area,** abolishing passport controls between the UK and the Republic of Ireland, meaning that the only times you'll see a border guard within the EU are traveling between the British Isles and the Continent—and of course, in and out of Denmark. For more important consequences of the EU for travelers, see **The Euro** (p. 13) and **European Customs** (p. 11).

TEACHER, STUDENT, & YOUTH IDENTIFICATION. The **International Student Identity Card (ISIC),** provides discounts on transport and accommodations, access to a 24hr. emergency help-line for medical, legal, and financial emergencies (in North America call ☎877-370-ISIC (877-370-4742), elsewhere call US collect +1 715-345 0505), and insurance benefits for holders of US-issued cards. Many student travel agencies issue ISICs, including STA Travel in Australia and New Zealand; Travel CUTS in Canada; USIT in the Republic of Ireland and Northern Ireland; SASTS in South Africa; Campus Travel and STA Travel in the UK; and Council Travel (www.counciltravel.com/idcards/default.asp) and STA Travel in the US (see Budget and Student Travel Agencies, p. 35). The card is valid from September of one year to December of the following year and costs US$22. Applicants must be degree-seeking students of a secondary or post-secondary school and must be at least age 12. Because of the proliferation of fake ISICs, some services (particularly airlines) require additional proof of identity, such as a school ID or a letter attesting to your student status, signed by your registrar and stamped with your school seal.

The **International Teacher Identity Card (ITIC)** offers the same insurance coverage and similar but limited discounts. The fee is AUS$13, UK£6.50, or US$22. For more info, contact the **International Student Travel Confederation (ISTC),** Herengracht 479, 1017 BS Amsterdam, Netherlands (☎31 (20) 421 28 00; www.istc.org). The **ISTC** issues a discount card to travelers who are 26 or under, but are not students. This one-year **International Youth Travel Card** (IYTC; formerly the GO 25 Card) offers many of the same benefits as the ISIC (US$22).

If you are an ISIC card carrier, you can activate your ISIC's ISIConnect service, a new integrated communications service (powered by eKit.com). With ISIConnect, one toll-free access number (in Austria ☎0800 29 10 18, in Switzerland 0800 89 73 06) gives you access to several different methods of keeping in touch via phone and Internet, including a reduced-rate international calling plan that treats your ISIC card as a universal **calling card;** a personalized **voicemail** box accessible from pay phones anywhere in the world or for free via Internet; **faxmail** service for sending and receiving faxes via email, fax machines, or pay phones; various **email** capabilities, including a service that reads your email to you over the phone; an online **"travel safe"** for storing (and faxing) important documents and numbers; and a 24hr. **help line** (via phone or email at ISIConnect@ekit.com) offering assistance and medical and legal referrals. To activate your ISIConnect account, visit the service's web site (www.isiconnect.ekit.com) or call the customer service number of your home country: in Australia ☎800 11 44 78, in Canada 877-635-3575, in Ireland 800 55 51 80 or 800 57 79 80, in New Zealand 0800 00 67 31, in South Africa 0800 99 29 21 or 0800 99 72 85, in the UK 0800 376 23 66 or 0800 731 56 64, and in the US 800-706-1333.

CUSTOMS

Austria and Switzerland prohibit or restrict the importation of firearms, explosives, ammunition, fireworks, booby traps, controlled drugs, most plants, lottery tickets, most animals, pornography, and items manufactured from protected species (e.g. ivory or fur). To avoid hassles about prescription drugs, ensure that your bottles are clearly marked and carry a copy of the prescription. Duty-free allowances were abolished for travel between EU member states on July 1, 1999, but still exist for those arriving from outside the EU. Keeping receipts for purchases made abroad will help establish values when you return.

 EUROPEAN CUSTOMS. Goods, as well as people, are permitted freedom of movement in the EU. This means that there are no customs controls at internal EU borders (i.e., you can take the blue customs channel at the airport), and travelers are free to transport whatever legal substances they like as long as it is for their own personal (non-commercial) use—up to 800 cigarettes, 10L of spirits, 90L of wine (60L of sparkling wine), and 110L of beer. You should also be aware that duty-free has been abolished for travel between EU member states; however, travelers between the EU and the rest of the world still get a duty-free allowance when passing through customs.

 ADDITIONAL CUSTOMS RESOURCES:
Australia: Australian Customs National Information Line (in Australia call ☎(01) 30 03 63, elsewhere call ☎+61 (02) 6275 6666; www.customs.gov.au).
Canada: Canadian Customs, 2265 St. Laurent Blvd., Ottawa, ON K1G 4K3 (☎800-461-9999 (24hr.) or 613-993-0534; www.revcan.ca).
Ireland: Customs Information Office, Irish Life Centre, Lower Abbey St., Dublin 1 (☎(01) 878 8811; www.revenue.ie).
New Zealand: New Zealand Customhouse, 17-21 Whitmore St., Box 2218, Wellington (☎(04) 473 6099; www.customs.govt.nz).
South Africa: Commissioner for Customs and Excise, Private Bag X47, Pretoria 0001 (☎(012) 314 9911; www.gov.za).
United Kingdom: Her Majesty's Customs and Excise, Passenger Enquiry Team, Wayfarer House, Great South West Rd., Feltham, Middlesex TW14 8NP (☎(020) 8910 3744; www.hmce.gov.uk).
United States: US Customs Service, 1330 Pennsylvania Ave. NW, Washington, D.C. 20229 (☎202-354-1000; www.customs.gov).

MONEY

CURRENCY & EXCHANGE

Austria formerly used the *Schilling* as its unit of currency; now, as a member of the European Union, it has completely switched over to the euro. The **euro (EUR €)** is divided into 100 cents. Denominations for coins are 1, 2, 5, 10, 20, and 50 cents and 1 and 2 euros, while bills are available in amounts of 5, 10, 20, 50, 100, 200, and 500 euros. In Austria, railroad stations, airports, hotels, and most travel agencies offer exchange services, as do banks and currency exchanges.

The Swiss monetary unit is the **Swiss Franc (SFr),** which is divided into 100 *centimes* (called *Rappen* in German Switzerland). Coins are issued in 5, 10, 20, and 50 centimes and 1, 2, and 5 Swiss Francs; bills come in denominations of 10, 20, 50, 100, 500, and 1000 Swiss Francs. Currency exchange is easiest at ATMs, train stations, and post offices, where rates are close to bank rates but commissions are smaller.

The currency chart below is based on August 2004 exchange rates between local currency and US dollars (US$), Canadian dollars (CDN$), British pounds (UK£), Australian dollars (AUS$), New Zealand dollars (NZ$), South African Rand (ZAR), Czech crowns (Kč), Hungarian forints (FT), and European Union euros (€). Check a large newspaper or the web (e.g. http://finance.yahoo.com or www.bloomberg.com) for the latest exchange rates.

As a general rule, it's cheaper to convert money in Austria or Switzerland than at home. Bring an ATM card and start your vacation without languishing in lines. Travelers from the US can get foreign currency from the comfort of home: **International Currency Express** (☎888-278-6628) delivers foreign currency or traveler's checks in two days (US$12) at competitive exchange rates.

Currency exchange kiosks and change machines should be your last resort when you need local funds. Most have unfavorable rates and charge hefty commissions. Banks, post offices, and small train stations often have better rates, but ATMs and credit cards are your best bet, since you'll profit from their low corporate rates (see p. 14). The only drawback to ATMs is the transaction fee that some banks charge—be sure to check what the fee is with your bank at home. If you need to change cash or traveler's checks, take the time to compare the rates offered by different banks and kiosks (*Wechselstube* in German, *bureau de change* in French, *cambio* in Italian). A good rule of thumb is to only go to banks or kiosks with at most a 5% margin between their buy and sell prices. Since you lose money with each transaction, convert in large sums (unless the rate is unfavorable).

EURO		
US$1 = €1.06		€1 = US$0.43
CDN$1 = €0.691		€1 = CDN$1.45
AUS$1 = €0.607		€1 = AUS$1.65
NZ$1 = €0.517		€1 = NZ$1.53
ZAR1 = €.107		€1 = ZAR9.33
10Kč = €0.32		€1 = Kč30.7
100FT = €0.4123		€1 = 242.56FT

SWISS FRANC	US$1 = 1.66 (SFR/CHF)	1SFR = US$0.60
	€1 = 1.52SFR	1SFR = €.66
	CDN$1 = 1.09SFR	1SFR = CDN$0.92
	AUS$1 = 0.88SFR	1SFR = AUS$1.14
	NZ$1 = 0.72SFR	1SFR = NZ$1.38
	ZAR1 = 0.20SFR	1SFR = ZAR4.94
	10Kč = 0.45SFR	1SFR = Kč22.31
	100FT = 0.61SFR	1SFR = 164.98FT

TRAVELER'S CHECKS

Traveler's checks (American Express and Visa are the most recognized) are one of the safest means of carrying funds. Several agencies and banks sell them for a small

 THE EURO Since 1999, the official currency of 11 members of the European Union—Austria, Belgium, Finland, France, Germany, Ireland, Italy, Luxembourg, The Netherlands, Portugal, and Spain—has been the **euro.** (In January 2001, Greece was admitted as well.) The exchange rate between euro-zone currencies was permanently fixed on January 1, 1999 at 1 EUR = 1.96DM (German marks) = 6.56F (French francs) = 1936.27L (Italian lire) = 13.76AS (Austrian Schillings). For more info, see www.europa.eu.int.

commission. Each agency provides refunds if checks are lost or stolen, and many provide other services, such as toll-free refund hotlines, emergency message services, and stolen credit card assistance. If you're ordering checks, do so well in advance, especially when requesting large sums. You can get traveler's checks in most currencies, including Swiss Francs and euros.

In order to collect a **refund for lost or stolen checks,** keep your check receipts separate from your checks and store them in a safe place or with a traveling companion. Record check numbers when you cash them, leave a list of check numbers with someone at home, and ask for a list of refund centers when you buy your checks. Never countersign your checks until you are ready to cash them, and always bring your passport with you when you plan to use the checks.

American Express: Checks available with commission at select banks, at all AmEx offices, and online (www.americanexpress.com; US residents only). American Express cardholders can also purchase checks by phone (☎888-269-6669). Checks available in US, Australian, and Canadian dollars, British pounds, euros, and Swiss Francs. *Cheques for Two* can be signed by either of 2 people traveling together. For purchase locations or more information contact AmEx's service centers: in the US and Canada ☎800-221-7282, in the UK 0800 587 6023, in Australia 800 68 80 22, in New Zealand 0508 555 358, elsewhere in the US collect +1 801-964-6665. For general assistance, or to report stolen or lost checks, call ☎0800 232 340 in Austria, or 0800 255 200 in Switzerland.

Travelex/Thomas Cook MasterCard: In the US and Canada call ☎800-223-7373, in the UK (0800) 62 21 01, in Austria (0800) 29 62 66, in Switzerland (0800) 55 01 30. Checks available in 13 currencies, including Swiss Francs, at 2% commission. Thomas Cook offices and *Sparkasse* banks in Austria cash Thomas Cook traveler's checks commission-free.

Visa: Checks available (generally with commission) at banks worldwide. In the US call
☎800-227-6811, in the UK (0800) 89 50 78, elsewhere call UK collect +(44) (020)
79 37 80 91. For general information, or to report lost or stolen cards, call: in Austria
(0800) 29 61 02, in Switzerland (0800) 55 84 50.

CREDIT, DEBIT, & ATM CARDS

Major credit cards such as **MasterCard** (a.k.a. EuroCard or Access in Europe) and
Visa (a.k.a. Carte Bleue or Barclaycard) are the most welcomed, and can be used to
obtain advances in euros or Swiss Francs from some banks and teller machines.
American Express cards also work in some ATMs, as well as at AmEx offices and
major airports. Many credit cards offer insurance or emergency assistance.

ATMS AND PIN NUMBERS. All automatic teller machines require a 4-
digit **Personal Identification Number (PIN).** You must ask your credit card company to assign you one before you leave. Without a PIN, you will be unable to
withdraw cash with your credit card abroad. There are no letters on the keypads
of European ATMs, so work out your PIN numerically: ABC correspond to 2, DEF
to 3, GHI to 4, JKL to 5, MNO to 6, PQRS to 7, TUV to 8, and WXYZ to 9. If you
lose your card, call for help at the following toll-free numbers, all of which have
English-speaking operators: **MasterCard** (Austria ☎(0800) 21 82 35, Switzerland (0800) 89 70 92); **Visa** (Austria ☎(0600) 67 04, Switzerland (0800) 89
27 33); **American Express** (call the US collect ☎+1 301-731-5724).

Transaction fees for all credit card advances (up to US$10 per advance, plus 2-
3% extra on foreign transactions after conversion) tend to make credit cards a more
costly way of withdrawing cash than ATMs or traveler's checks, and not all banks
will be willing to let you buy euros or Swiss Francs on credit. In an emergency,
however, the transaction fee may be worth it. To be eligible for an advance, you'll
need to get a **Personal Identification Number (PIN)** from your credit card company
(see ATMs and Pin Numbers, p. 14). It's also a good idea to call your credit card
company and let them know you'll be using your card abroad, as some companies
initiate security measures, such as freezing cards, when spending patterns change.

CREDIT CARD COMPANIES. Visa (US ☎800-336-8472) and **MasterCard** (US ☎800-
307-7309) are issued in cooperation with banks and other organizations. **American
Express** (US ☎800-843-2273) has an annual fee of up to US$55. AmEx cardholders
may cash personal checks at AmEx offices abroad, access an emergency medical
and legal assistance hotline (24hr.; in North America call ☎800-554-2639, elsewhere
call US collect +1 715-343-7977), and enjoy American Express Travel Service benefits (including plane, hotel, and car rental reservation changes; baggage loss and
flight insurance; mailgram and international cable services; and held mail). The **Discover Card** (US ☎800-347-2683, elsewhere call US +1 801-902-3100) offers small
cash-back bonuses, but it may not be readily accepted in Austria and Switzerland.

CASH CARDS AND ATM CARDS. Cash or debit cards—often called ATM (Automated Teller Machine) cards—can be used throughout Austria and Switzerland.
ATMs get the same wholesale exchange rate as credit cards, but there is often a
limit on the amount of money you can withdraw per day (usually about US$500),
and computer networks sometimes fail. There is typically also a surcharge of $1-5
for each withdrawal. The two major international money networks are **Cirrus** (US
☎800-424-7787) and **PLUS** (US ☎800-843-7587). Look for signs reading "Bankomat"
with a green or blue "B," and compare the symbols on the back of your card with

those above the machine to find out which machines your card will work in. **Visa TravelMoney** is a system allowing you to access money from any Visa ATM, common throughout Austria and Switzerland. You deposit an amount before you travel (plus a small administration fee), and you can withdraw up to that sum. The cards, which give you the same favorable exchange rate for withdrawals as a regular Visa, are especially useful if you plan to travel through many countries. Obtain a card by either visiting a nearby Thomas Cook or Citicorp office, or by calling toll-free (US ☎877-762-3227; minimum US$300 deposit, US$15 activation fee).

GETTING MONEY FROM HOME

If you run out of money, the easiest solution is to have someone make a deposit to your credit card or cash (ATM) card. Otherwise consider the following options.

WIRING MONEY. It is possible to arrange a **bank money transfer,** which means asking a bank back home to wire money to a bank in Austria and Switzerland. This is the cheapest way to transfer cash, but it's also the slowest, usually taking several days or more. Travelers from the US, Canada, and the UK can wire money abroad through **Western Union' s** international money transfer services. In the US call ☎800-325-6000, in Canada 800-235-0000, in the UK (0800) 83 38 33. In Austria call (01) 514 00 29 86, in Switzerland call the office in Zurich at (0800) 81 10 99. The rates for sending cash are generally US$10-11 cheaper than with a credit card, and the money is usually available at the place you're sending it to within an hour. To locate the nearest Western Union location, consult www.westernunion.com.

US STATE DEPARTMENT (US CITIZENS ONLY). In emergencies, the US State Department will forward money within hours to the nearest consular office, which will disburse it according to instructions for a US$15 fee. If you wish to use this service, contact the Overseas Citizens Service division of the US State Department (☎202-647-5225; nights, Sundays, and holidays 202-647-4000).

COSTS

If you stay in hostels and prepare most of your own food, expect to spend anywhere from US$45 to US$75 (61-102SFr; €40-66) per person per day in Switzerland, slightly less in Austria. **Accommodations** start at about US$16 (22SFr) per night for a hostel in Switzerland and US$10 (€9) in Austria, while a basic sit-down meal usually costs around US$12 (16SFr; €11).

TIPPING

There is technically no need for **tipping** in Switzerland, as gratuities are already automatically factored into prices; in Austria, menus will say whether service is included (*Preise inclusive* or *Bedienung inclusiv*); if it is, you don't have to tip. If it's not, leave a tip up to about 10%. It is considered polite, however, in both Austria and Switzerland to round up your bill to the nearest euro or 1 or 2 Francs as a nod of approval for good service; tell the waiter or waitress how much you want back from the money you give. If you just say "*Danke,*" the waiter/waitress will most likely assume that you intend for him/her to keep the change. Austrian restaurants expect you to seat yourself, and servers will not bring the bill until you ask them to do so. Say "*Zahlen bitte*" (TSAHL-en BIT-uh) to settle your accounts. Don't leave tips on the table. Be aware that some restaurants charge for each piece of bread that you eat during your meal.

TAXES

No taxes are added to purchases made in **Switzerland.** In **Austria,** there is a 10% to 20% value added tax (VAT) on all books, clothing, souvenir items, art items, jewelry, perfume, cigarettes, alcohol, etc. Tourists must pay this tax at the time of purchase, but may get the tax refunded later if the amount of purchase is €75 (about US$70) or greater at a particular store. To get the refund, fill out the Austrian Form U-34 (the "Global Refund Cheque"), available at most stores, and an ÖAMTC quick refund form to get a check at the airport or train station. Make sure the store affixes their store identification stamp to the forms at the time of purchase. When you leave the country, go to the VAT or Customs office (located in the airport or train station) to get your form validated for the amount of the refund, which can be cashed in the airport or station. Unfortunately, only non-EU citizens can claim the VAT refund.

SAFETY & SECURITY

PERSONAL SAFETY

EXPLORING. Austria and Switzerland are relatively safe countries, so most safety and security concerns can be resolved by using common sense. In general, safety means not looking like a target. The gawking camera-toter is a more obvious target than the low-profile traveler, so avoid unwanted attention by trying to blend in. Familiarize yourself with your surroundings before setting out; if you must check a map on the street, duck into a café or shop. If you are traveling alone, be sure that someone at home knows your itinerary, and never admit that you're traveling alone. When you arrive in a new city, find out what areas to avoid from tourist information or the manager of your hostel. Stick to busy, well-lit streets. Whenever possible, *Let's Go* warns of unsafe neighborhoods and areas, such as drug hangouts. The American Society of Travel Agents provides extensive information at their web site (www.astanet.com), including a section on *Travel Safety*.

EMERGENCY TELEPHONE NUMBERS	**Police:** Austria ☎ **133.** Switzerland ☎ **117.** **Ambulance:** Austria and Switzerland ☎ **144.** **Fire:** Austria ☎ **122.** Switzerland ☎ **118.**

SELF DEFENSE. There is no sure-fire way to avoid all the threatening situations you might encounter when traveling, but a good self-defense course will give you concrete ways to react to unwanted advances. **Impact, Prepare,** and **Model Mugging** can refer you to local self-defense courses in the US (☎ 800-345-5425). Visit the web site at www.impactsafety.org/chapters for a list of nearby chapters. Workshops (2-3hr.) start at US$50; full courses run US$350-500.

DRIVING. Driving in Austria and Switzerland is a pleasant but expensive proposition. The roads are well maintained with the money drivers pay for the right to drive here (they won't even let you on the Autobahn in Switzerland without a permit sticker). Be sure to observe the speed limit and don't drive drunk—the Austrian and Swiss police will not hesitate to take away your license and your car if you have any alcohol in your blood. Study route maps before you hit the road; depending on the region, some roads have poor (or nonexistent) shoulders, few gas stations, and roaming animals. Twisting mountain roads may be closed in winter but, when open, require particular caution. Learn the **Alpine honk:** when going blind around an abrupt turn, stop and give the horn a toot before proceeding. Shift to low gear, drive slowly, brake occasionally, and **never pass anyone.**

For long drives in desolate areas, invest in a cellular phone and a roadside assistance program (see p. 46). Park your vehicle in a garage or well-traveled area, and use a steering wheel locking device in larger cities. Hide baggage in the trunk, and if the tape deck or radio is removable, hide it in the trunk as well, or take it with you. **Sleeping in your car** is one of the most dangerous (and often illegal) ways to get your rest, second only to sleeping in the open. If your car breaks down, wait for the police to assist you. *Let's Go* does not recommend **hitchhiking,** particularly for women—see **By Thumb,** p. 50, for more information.

TRAVEL ADVISORIES. The following government offices provide travel information and advisories by telephone, by fax, or via the web:

Australian Department of Foreign Affairs and Trade: ☎ 13 00 555135; faxback service 02 6261 1299; www.dfat.gov.au.

Canadian Department of Foreign Affairs and International Trade (DFAIT): In Canada and the US call ☎ 800-267-8376, elsewhere call +1 613-944-4000; www.dfait-maeci.gc.ca. Call for their free booklet, *Bon Voyage...But.*

New Zealand Ministry of Foreign Affairs: ☎ 04 439 8000; www.mft.govt.nz/travel/index.html.

United Kingdom Foreign and Commonwealth Office: ☎ 020 7008 0232; www.fco.gov.uk.

US Department of State: ☎ 202-647-5225; faxback service 202-647-3000; http://travel.state.gov. For *A Safe Trip Abroad,* call 202-512-1800.

TERRORISM. In light of the September 11, 2001 attacks on the United States, awareness of terrorist threats has heightened across Europe. Austria and Switzerland enjoy a relatively safe existence, but it is important to remain alert to potential dangers, particularly in major cities and tourist destinations. Report suspicious persons and unattended luggage or packages to proper authorities. Always familiarize yourself with the exits in crowded and public locations, such as in theaters, stadiums, and museums. Be patient with security-related transportation delays when flying in and out of the United States and in train stations. Do not talk about bombs or terrorism in airports, even in jest or casual conversation, as airport security have been instructed to question and detain individuals who do so.

FINANCIAL SECURITY

PROTECTING YOUR VALUABLES. Although Austria and Switzerland have low crime rates, thieves are happy to relieve ignorant tourists of their money. Be on the alert, particularly in crowds. Beware of classic scams: sob stories that require money, distractions that allow enough time to steal your bag, and little kids with big newspapers. To prevent easy theft, don't keep all your valuables (money, important documents, etc.) in one place. **Photocopies** of important documents allow you to recover them in case they are lost or filched. **Don't carry your wallet or money in your back pocket.** Never count your money in public and carry as little as possible. If you go to ATMs, avoid them in poorly lit or deserted areas and don't go at night. If you carry a purse, buy a sturdy one with a secure clasp, and carry it crosswise on the side away from the street with the clasp against you. Secure packs with small combination padlocks that slip through the two zippers. A **money belt** is the best way to carry cash; you can buy one at most camping supply stores. A nylon zippered pouch with a belt that sits inside the waist of your pants or skirt combines convenience and security. A **neck pouch** is an equally safe way to carry money, though less accessible. Refrain from pulling it out in public; if you must, be very discreet. Avoid keeping anything precious in a waist-pack: your valuables will be highly visible and easy to steal. Keep some money separate from the rest to use for emergencies or in case of theft.

In public, watch your belongings at all times. Beware of con artists and **pickpockets** on the street and on public transportation (although neither Austria nor Switzerland has a big problem with street crime). On buses and trains, keep your bag close to you; don't check your baggage on trains, don't trust anyone to "watch your bag for a second," and don't ever put it under your seat in train compartments. If you take a **night train,** either lock your bag to the luggage rack or use it as a pillow. In your hostel, if you can't lock your room, lock your bag in lockers or at the train station (you'll need your own **padlock**).

DRUGS & ALCOHOL. Drugs can easily ruin a trip. Every year thousands of travelers are arrested for trafficking or possession of drugs or for simply being in the company of a suspected user. Marijuana, hashish, cocaine, and narcotics are illegal in Austria and Switzerland, and the penalties for illegal possession of drugs, especially for foreigners, range from stern to severe. You may be imprisoned or deported, and a meek "I didn't know it was illegal" will not suffice. It is not unknown for a dealer to increase profits by first selling drugs to tourists and then turning them in to authorities for a reward. Even such reputedly liberal cities as Vienna, Salzburg, and Zurich take an officially dim view of befuddled drug-buying tourists. The worst thing you can possibly do is carry drugs across an international border—not only could you end up in prison, you could also be hounded by a "Drug Trafficker" stamp on your passport for the rest of your life. If you are arrested, all your home country's consulate can do is visit, provide a list of attorneys, and inform family and friends. Remember that you are subject to the laws of the country in which you travel, not to those of your home country, and it is your responsibility to familiarize yourself with these laws before leaving. Police officers, members of the *Polizei* or *Gendarmerie,* typically speak little English.

Imbibing **alcohol** in Austria and Switzerland is generally trouble-free—beer is more common than soda, and a lunch without wine or beer is unusual. In both Austria and Switzerland, you must be 16 to drink legally. In Switzerland you can only be arrested for being drunk in public if you cause harm to others.

HEALTH

Common sense is the simplest prescription for good health while you travel. Travelers complain most about their feet and stomachs, so take precautionary measures: drink lots of fluids to prevent dehydration and constipation, wear sturdy, broken-in shoes and clean socks, and use talcum powder to keep your feet dry.

BEFORE YOU GO

In your **passport,** write the names of any people you wish to be contacted in case of a medical emergency, and also list any **allergies** or medical conditions you want doctors to be aware of. Allergy sufferers might want to obtain a full supply of any necessary medication before the trip. Matching a prescription to a foreign equivalent is not always easy, safe, or possible. Carry up-to-date, legible prescriptions or a statement from your doctor stating the medication's trade name, manufacturer, chemical name, and dosage. While traveling, be sure to keep all medication with you in your carry-on luggage. Preparation can help minimize the likelihood of contracting a disease and maximize the chances of receiving effective health care in the event of an emergency. Leave all medication in original, labeled containers. What is legal at home may not be legal abroad; check with your doctor or the appropriate foreign consulate to avoid nasty surprises. For tips on packing a basic **first-aid kit,** and other health essentials, see p. 23.

IMMUNIZATIONS & PRECAUTIONS. Take a look at your immunization records before you go. Travelers over two years old should be sure that the following vaccines are up to date: MMR (for measles, mumps, and rubella); DTaP or Td (for diphtheria, tetanus, and pertussis); OPV (for polio); HbCV (for haemophilus influenza B); and HBV (for hepatitis B). For recommendations on immunizations and prophylaxis, consult with the CDC (see below) in the US or the equivalent in your home country, and ask a doctor for guidance.

USEFUL ORGANIZATIONS & PUBLICATIONS. The US **Center for Disease Control and Prevention** (CDC; ☎877-FYI-TRIP/877-394-8747; www.cdc.gov/travel) maintains an international fax information service and an international travelers' hotline (☎404-332-4559). The CDC's comprehensive booklet *Health Information for International Travel*, an annual rundown of disease, immunization, and general health advice, is free online or US$25 via the Public Health Foundation (☎877-252-1200). Consult the appropriate government agency of your home country for consular information sheets on health, entry requirements, and other issues for various countries (see Travel Advisories, p. 17). For quick information on health and other travel warnings, call the **Overseas Citizens Services** (US ☎202-647-5225; after-hours 647-4000) or contact a passport agency or diplomatic mission abroad. US citizens can send a self-addressed, stamped envelope to the Overseas Citizens Services, Bureau of Consular Affairs, #4811, US Department of State, Washington, D.C. 20520. For information on medical evacuation services and travel insurance firms, see the US government's web site at http://travel.state.gov/medical.html or that of the **British Foreign and Commonwealth Office** (www.fco.gov.uk).

For detailed information on travel health, including a country-by-country overview of diseases, try the **International Travel Health Guide,** by Stuart Rose, MD (Travel Medicine, US$12.95; individual chapters available for free download at www.travmed.com). For general health info, contact the **American Red Cross** (check www.redcross.com for regional branch 800-numbers). A good book to pick up is *Doctor's Guide to Protecting Your Health Before, During, and After International Travel.* (Pilot Books US$20).

MEDICAL ASSISTANCE ON THE ROAD. Medical care in Austria and Switzerland is generally excellent. Most doctors and pharmacists speak at least some English. If you are concerned about being able to access medical support while traveling, there are special support services you may employ. The *Med-Pass* from **GlobalCare, Inc.,** 6875 Shiloh Rd. East, Alpharetta, GA 30004, USA (☎800-860-1111; www.globalems.com), provides 24hr. international medical assistance, support, and medical evacuation resources. The **International Association for Medical Assistance to Travelers,** 417 Center Street, Lewiston NY 14902 in the US, 1287 St. Clair Av. West, Suite #1, Toronto M6E 1138 in Canada (**IAMAT;** US ☎716-754-4883, Canada 416-652-0137; www.iamat.org) has free membership (though a donation is encouraged), lists English-speaking doctors worldwide, and offers detailed info on immunization requirements and sanitation. If your regular **insurance** policy does not cover travel abroad, consider purchasing additional coverage.

Those with medical conditions (diabetes, allergies to antibiotics, epilepsy, heart conditions) may want to obtain a stainless-steel **Medic Alert** ID tag (first year US$35, annually thereafter US$20), which identifies the condition and gives a 24hr. collect-call number. Contact the Medic Alert Foundation, 2323 Colorado Ave., Turlock, CA 95382, USA (☎888-633-4298; www.medicalert.org).

ONCE IN AUSTRIA & SWITZERLAND

ENVIRONMENTAL HAZARDS

Heat exhaustion and dehydration: Heat exhaustion can lead to fatigue, headaches, and wooziness. Avoid it by drinking plenty of fluids, eating salty foods (e.g. crackers), and avoiding dehydrating beverages (e.g. alcohol, coffee, tea, and caffeinated soda). Continuous heat stress can eventually lead to heatstroke, signaled by a rising temperature, severe headache, and cessation of sweating. Victims should be cooled off with wet towels and taken to a doctor.

Sunburn: If you're prone to sunburn, bring sunscreen with you (it's often more expensive and hard to find when traveling), and apply it liberally and often to prevent burns and reduce the risk of skin cancer. If you are planning on spending time near water, in the mountains, or in the snow, you risk getting burned, even through clouds. If you get sunburned, drink more fluids than usual and apply calamine or an aloe-based lotion. Be aware that UV rays are stronger at higher elevations; invest in a stronger SPF.

Hypothermia: A rapid drop in body temperature is the clearest sign of overexposure to cold, but by the time such obvious symptoms arise, it is often too late to prevent death. Victims may also shiver, feel exhausted, have poor coordination or slurred speech, hallucinate, or suffer amnesia. A very common and particularly devastating symptom is confusion. Most hypothermia victims die from a fall or another secondary cause as a result of poor decision-making, rather than from the condition itself. Further, in later stages of hypothermia, victims generally have the sensation that they are too hot, and ironically shed clothes to stay cool. *Do not let hypothermia victims fall asleep,* or their body temperature will continue to drop and they may die. Warm victims slowly so they do not go into shock. To avoid hypothermia, keep dry, wear layers, stay well-fed and hydrated, and stay out of the wind.

Frostbite: When the temperature is below freezing, watch out for frostbite. If skin turns white, waxy, and cold, do not rub the area. Drink warm beverages, get dry, and slowly warm the area with dry fabric or steady body contact until a doctor can be found.

High altitude: Spending time at severe altitudes can cause fatigue, nausea and headaches. Though visiting the vast majority of Switzerland and Austria should pose no problem to the average traveler, allow your body a couple of days to adjust to less oxygen before exerting yourself, and avoide smoking or medication that may affect breathing (many sleeping pills do this). Diamox, a prescription drug that combats altitude sickness, should be considered only by those intending to do intensive mountaineering—talk to a doctor about possible side-effects and its appropriateness for your plans.

INSECT-BORNE DISEASES

Many diseases are transmitted by insect (mainly mosquitoes, fleas, ticks, and lice). Be aware of insects in wet or forested areas, especially while hiking and camping; wear long pants and long sleeves, tuck your pants into your socks, and buy a mosquito net. Use insect repellents such as DEET and soak or spray your gear with permethrin (licensed in the US for use on clothing). **Ticks**—responsible for Lyme and other diseases—are a concern in rural and forested areas, particularly in the Danube delta in Austria and in the Winterthur region in Switzerland.

Tick-borne encephalitis: A viral infection of the central nervous system transmitted during the summer by tick bites (primarily in wooded areas) or by consumption of unpasteurized dairy products. Symptoms range from nothing at all to headaches and flu-like symptoms to swelling of the brain (encephalitis). The risk of contracting the disease is relatively low, especially if precautions are taken against tick bites.

Lyme disease: A bacterial infection carried by ticks and marked by a circular bull's-eye rash of 2 in. or more. Later symptoms include fever, headache, fatigue, and aches and pains. Antibiotics are effective if administered early. Left untreated, Lyme disease can cause problems in joints, the heart, and the nervous system. If you find a tick attached to your skin, grasp the head with tweezers as close to your skin as possible and apply slow, steady traction. Removing a tick within 24 hours greatly reduces the risk of infection.

FOOD- & WATER-BORNE DISEASES

Prevention is the best cure: be sure that your food is properly cooked and the water you drink is clean. Though health regulation in Austrian and Swiss restaurants impose a high standard, watch out for food from markets or street vendors that may have been cooked in unhygienic conditions. Other culprits are raw shellfish, unpasteurized milk, and sauces containing raw eggs. When hiking, resist the temptation to drink from pristine-looking Alpine streams; even glacial runoff can be a home for bacteria. Instead, buy bottled water, or purify your own water by bringing it to a rolling boil or treating it with **iodine tablets**; note, however, that some parasites such as *giardia* have exteriors that resist iodine treatment, so boiling is more reliable. Always wash your hands before eating or bring a quick-drying purifying liquid hand cleaner.

Mad Cow Disease: Bovine spongiform encephalopathy (BSE), better known as Mad Cow Disease, is a chronic degenerative disease affecting the central nervous system of cattle that broke out in alarming numbers of cattle in 2001 and 2002. The human variant is called Creutzfeldt-Jakob disease (nvCJD), and both forms of the disease involve invariably fatal brain diseases. Information on nvCJD is not conclusive, but the disease is supposedly caused by consuming infected beef; however, the risk is very small (around 1 case per 10 billion servings of meat). It is believed that consuming milk and milk products does not pose a risk.

Traveler's diarrhea: Results from drinking untreated water or eating uncooked foods; a temporary (and fairly common) reaction to the bacteria in new food ingredients. Symptoms include nausea, bloating, and malaise. Try quick-energy, non-sugary foods with protein and carbohydrates to keep your strength up. Over-the-counter anti-diarrheals (e.g. Imodium) may counteract the problems, but can complicate serious infections. The most dangerous side effect is dehydration; drink 8 oz. of water with half tsp. of sugar or honey and a pinch of salt, try uncaffeinated soft drinks, or munch on salted crackers. If you develop a fever or your symptoms don't go away after 4-5 days, consult a doctor. Consult a doctor for treatment of diarrhea in children.

Parasites: Microbes, tapeworms, etc. that hide in unsafe water and food. **Giardiasis,** for example, is acquired by drinking untreated water from streams or lakes all over the world. Symptoms include swollen glands or lymph nodes, fever, rashes or itchiness, digestive problems, eye problems, and anemia. Boil water, wear shoes, avoid bugs, and eat only cooked food.

OTHER INFECTIOUS DISEASES

Rabies: Transmitted through the saliva of infected animals; fatal if untreated. By the time symptoms appear (thirst and muscle spasms), the disease is in its terminal stage. If you are bitten, wash the wound thoroughly, seek immediate medical care, and try to have the animal located. A rabies vaccine, which consists of 3 shots given over a 21-day period, is available but only semi-effective.

Hepatitis B: A viral infection of the liver transmitted via bodily fluids or needle-sharing. Symptoms may not surface until years after infection. Vaccinations are recommended for health-care workers, sexually-active travelers, and anyone planning to seek medical treatment abroad. The 3-shot vaccination series must begin 6 mo. before traveling.

Hepatitis C: Like Hep B, but the mode of transmission differs. IV drug users, those with occupational exposure to blood, hemodialysis patients, and recipients of blood transfusions are at the highest risk, but the disease can also be spread through sexual contact or sharing items like razors and toothbrushes that may have traces of blood on them.

AIDS, HIV, & STDS

AIDS and HIV are as common in Austria and Switzerland as in the rest of Western Europe. For more detailed information on **Acquired Immune Deficiency Syndrome (AIDS)** in the two countries, call the **US Centers for Disease Control's** 24hr. hotline at ☎800-342-2437, or contact the **Joint United Nations Programme on HIV/AIDS (UNAIDS),** 20 Av. Appia 20, CH-1211 Geneva 27, Switzerland (☎+41 (22) 791 36 66; fax 791 41 87).

Sexually transmitted diseases (STDs) such as gonorrhea, chlamydia, genital warts, syphilis, and herpes are easier to catch than HIV and can be just as deadly. **Hepatitis B** and **C** are also serious STDs (see Other Infectious Diseases, above). Though condoms may protect you from some STDs, oral or even tactile contact can lead to transmission.

WOMEN'S HEALTH

Women traveling in unsanitary conditions are vulnerable to **urinary tract** and **bladder infections,** common bacterial diseases that cause a burning sensation and painful and sometimes frequent urination. To try to avoid these infections, drink plenty of vitamin-C-rich juice and plenty of clean water, and urinate frequently, especially right after intercourse. If symptoms persist, see a doctor.

Since **tampons, pads,** and reliable **contraceptive devices** are sometimes hard to find when traveling and your preferred brand will rarely be available, bring supplies with you.

FURTHER READING: WOMEN'S HEALTH.
Adventures in Good Company: The Complete Guide to Women's Tours and Outdoor Trips, by Thalia Zepatos (US$17).
Handbook for Women Travellers, by Maggie and Gemma Moss, Piaktus Books (US$15).

PACKING

Pack lightly: lay out what you absolutely need, then take half as many clothes and twice as much money. If you plan to do a lot of hiking, also see the section on **Camping and the Outdoors,** p. 27.

LUGGAGE. If you plan to cover most of your itinerary by foot, a sturdy **frame backpack** is unbeatable. (For the basics on buying a pack, see p. 29.) Toting a **suitcase** or **trunk** is fine if you plan to live in one or two cities and explore from there, but not a good idea if you're going to be moving around a lot. In addition to your main piece of luggage, a **daypack** (a small backpack or courier bag) is a must.

CLOTHING. No matter when you're traveling, it's always a good idea to bring a **warm jacket** or wool sweater, a **rain jacket** (Gore-Tex® is both waterproof and breathable), sturdy shoes or **hiking boots,** and **thick socks. Flip-flops** or waterproof sandals are must-haves for grubby hostel showers. You may also want to add one outfit beyond the jeans and t-shirt uniform, and maybe a nicer pair of shoes if you have the room. If you plan to visit any religious or cultural sites, remember that you'll need something besides tank tops and shorts to be respectful in more formal settings.

SLEEPSACK. Some hostels require that you provide your own linen or rent sheets from them. Save cash by making your own sleepsack: fold a full-size sheet in half the long way, then sew it closed along the long side and one of the short sides.

CONVERTERS & ADAPTORS. In Austria and Switzerland electricity is 220V AC (240V in Britain and Ireland), enough to fry any 110V North American appliance. You can get an **adapter** (which changes the shape of the plug) and a **converter** (which changes the voltage) at a hardware store. **Americans** and **Canadians** should buy an adapter and a converter. Don't make the mistake of using only an adapter. **New Zealanders** and **South Africans** (who both use 220V at home) as well as **Australians** (who use 240/250V) won't need a converter, but will need a set of adapters to use anything electrical.

FIRST-AID KIT. For a basic first-aid kit, pack: bandages, pain reliever, antibiotic cream, a thermometer, a Swiss Army knife, tweezers, moleskin, decongestant,

---

PACKING LIGHT, THE AUSTRIAN WAY In the summer of 1870, Austrian climbing legend Hermann von Barth took to the hills of the Karwendel Range in Tyrol and climbed no fewer than 88 peaks, 12 of which were first-ever ascents. His luggage consisted simply of a drinking cup, binoculars, smelling salts, a lighter, a can of paint and a paintbrush to paint his name on each peak, and a bottle of poison in case he fell and wasn't able to rescue himself. He never fell.

---

motion-sickness remedy, diarrhea or upset-stomach medication (Imodium or Pepto Bismol), an antihistamine, sunscreen, insect repellent, and burn ointment.

IMPORTANT DOCUMENTS. Don't forget your passport, traveler's checks, ATM and/or credit cards, and adequate ID (see p. 9). Also check that you have any of the following that apply to you: a hosteling membership card (see p. 25); driver's license (see p. 9); travel insurance forms; and a rail or bus pass (see p. 39).

USEFUL THINGS TO BRING:

First-aid kit: (see p. 23), and medications and vitamins (see Health, p. 18)
Laundry supplies: travel clothesline and small carton of detergent.
Shower supplies: towel, shampoo, slippers for the shower, and soap.
Personal hygiene supplies: deodorant, tampons, razors, tweezers, and condoms.
Sealable plastic bags for damp clothes, food, shampoo, and other spillables.
Money belt for carrying valuables and a small calculator for currency conversion.
Useful items: travel alarm clock, water bottle, needle and thread, safety pins, umbrella, sunscreen, sunglasses, sun hat, insect repellent, padlock, earplugs, flashlight, compass, string, and electrical tape (for repairing tears).

ESSENTIALS

ACCOMMODATIONS

Accommodations in Austria and Switzerland are usually clean, orderly, and expensive. Always ask if your lodging provides a **guest card** *(Gästekarte)*. Guest cards grant discounts on local sports facilities, hiking excursions, town museums, and public transportation. In Austria, the tax that most accommodations slap on bills funds these discounts—take advantage of them to get your money's worth.

Most local tourist offices distribute extensive listings (the *Gastgeberverzeichnis*), and many will reserve a room for a small fee. National tourist offices can also supply more complete lists of campsites and hotels. Be aware that *Privatzimmer* and *Pensionen* may close their doors without notice; it's best to call ahead.

HOSTELS

 A HOSTELER'S BILL OF RIGHTS. Unless we state otherwise, you can expect that every hostel has: no lockout, no curfew, free hot showers, secure luggage storage, and no key deposit.

Hostels (*Jugendherbergen* in German, *Auberges de Jeunesse* in French, *Ostelli* in Italian) are the hubs of the gigantic backpacker subculture that rumbles throughout Europe every summer, providing innumerable opportunities to meet travelers from all over the world. Hostels generally offer dorm-style accommodations, often in single-sex large rooms with bunk beds, although some hostels do offer private rooms for families and couples. They sometimes have kitchens and utensils for your use, bike or moped rentals, storage areas, and laundry facilities. There can be drawbacks: some hostels close during certain daytime "lockout" hours, have a curfew, don't accept reservations, impose a maximum stay, or, less frequently, require that you do chores. In Austria and Switzerland, a dorm bed in a hostel averages around US$12-20. Check out the **Internet Guide to Hostelling** (www.hostels.com), which provides a directory of hostels from around the world in addition to oodles of information about hostelling and backpacking worldwide. **Eurotrip** (www.eurotrip.com/accommodation/accommodation.html) has information and reviews on budget hostels and several international hostel associations.

> **LOCAL HI ORGANIZATIONS.** To join HI, contact:
>
> **Australian Youth Hostels Association (AYHA),** Level 3, 10 Mallett St., Camperdown NSW 2050 (☎(02) 9565 1699; www.yha.org.au). AUS$52, under 18 AUS$16.
>
> **Hostelling International-Canada (HI-C),** 205 Catherine St., Ottawa, ON K2P 1C3 (☎613-237-7884; www.hostellingintl.ca). CDN$35, under 18 free.
>
> **An Óige (Irish Youth Hostel Association),** 61 Mountjoy St., Dublin 7 (☎01 830 4555; www.irelandyha.org). IR£15, under 18 IR£7.5.
>
> **Youth Hostels Association of New Zealand (YHANZ),** P.O. Box 436, 193 Cashel St., 3rd Floor Union House, Christchurch 1 (☎03 379 99 70; www.yha.org.nz). NZ$40, under 18 free.
>
> **Hostels Association of South Africa,** 3rd fl. 73 St. George's House, Cape Town 8001 (☎021 424 2511; www.hisa.org.za). R55, under 18 R30.
>
> **Youth Hostels Association (England and Wales) Ltd.,** Trevelyan House, Dimple Rd., Matlock, Derbyshire DE4 3YH, UK (☎01629 59 26 00; www.yha.org.uk). UK£13, under 18 UK£6.50, families UK£26.
>
> **Hostelling International Northern Ireland (HINI),** 22 Donegall Rd., Belfast BT12 5JN (☎02890 31 54 35; www.hini.org.uk). UK£10, under 18 UK£6.
>
> **Hostelling International-American Youth Hostels (HI-AYH),** 733 15th St. NW, #840, Washington, D.C. 20005 (☎202-783-6161; www.hiayh.org). US$25, under 18 free.

Many HI hostels accespt reservations via the **International Booking Network** (www.hostelbooking.com) for a nominal fee. In addition, the HI webpage (www.iyhf.org) has information on the IBN as well as the web addresses and phone numbers of all national associations and can be a great place to begin with researching hosteling in a specific region.

Switzerland also has the smaller, more informal **Swiss Backpackers (SB)** organization. SB is an organization of 26 hostels that appeal to the young, foreign traveler interested in socializing. The neon-colored, all-English web site lists the hostels and also has a wealth of general information on backpacking, and specific information on adventure activities in Switzerland (www.backpacker.ch).

OTHER ACCOMMODATIONS

YMCA AND YWCAS. Not all **Young Men's Christian Association (YMCA)** locations offer lodging; those that do are often located in urban downtowns, which can be convenient but a little gritty. YMCA rates are usually lower than hotel rates but higher than hostel rates and may include the use of TV, air conditioning, pools, gyms, access to public transportation, tourist information, safe deposit boxes, luggage storage, daily housekeeping, multilingual staff, and 24hr. security. Many

YMCAs accept women and families (group rates are often available), but some will not lodge people under 18 without parental permission. Free booking is offered on the Travel Y's website (www.travel-ys.com).

HOTELS. Hotels are expensive in Austria (singles €40-100; doubles €70-250) and exorbitant in Switzerland (singles 50-75SFr; doubles 80-150SFr). Switzerland has set the international standard for hotels; even 1-, 2-, and 3-star accommodations tend to be nicer than their counterparts in other countries. The cheapest hotel-style accommodations have **Gasthof** or **Gästehaus** in the name; **Hotel-Garni** also means cheapness. Continental breakfast *(Frühstück)* is almost always included.

PRIVATE ROOMS & PENSIONS. Renting a **private room** *(Privatzimmer)* in a family home is an inexpensive and friendly way to house yourself. Such rooms generally include a sink and use of a toilet and shower. Many places rent private rooms only for longer stays, or they may levy a surcharge (10-20%) for stays of less than 3 nights. *Privatzimmer* start at 25 to 60SFr per person in Switzerland. In Austria, rooms range from €18-30 a night. Slightly more expensive, **pensions** *(Pensionen)* are similar to the American and British notion of a bed-and-breakfast. Generally, finding rooms for only one person might be difficult, especially for one-night stays, as most lodgings have rooms with double beds *(Doppelzimmer);* single travelers can get these rooms if they pay a bit more. Continental breakfast is *de rigueur;* in classier places, meat, cheese, and an egg will grace your plate and palate. Contact the local tourist office for a list of private rooms and *Pensionen*.

UNIVERSITY DORMS. Some **colleges and universities** (see Vienna: Accommodations, p. 103), open their residence halls to travelers when school is not in session—some do so even during term-time. Rates tend to be low, and many offer free

ESSENTIALS

local calls. *Let's Go* lists colleges that rent dorm rooms among the accommodations for appropriate cities. College dorms are popular with many travelers, especially those looking for long-term lodging, so reserve ahead.

HOME EXCHANGE & RENTALS. Home exchange offers travelers various types of homes (houses, apartments, condominiums, villas, even castles in some cases), plus the opportunity to live like a native and cut down on accommodation fees. For more information, contact **HomeExchange.com** (US ☎800-877-8723; www.homeexchange.com), or **Intervac International Home Exchange** (in **Austria,** call Hans and Ingeborg Winkler (☎/fax (0423) 238 3388; intervac.at@utanet.at); in **Switzerland,** call Claudia and Iso Niedermann (☎/fax (071) 944 27 79; www.intervac.com). **Home rentals** are more expensive than exchanges, but can be cheaper than comparably serviced hotels. Both home exchanges and rentals often including kitchen, maid service, TV, and telephones, and are ideal for families or travelers with special dietary needs.

FURTHER READING: ACCOMMODATIONS
Europe the European Way: A Traveler's Guide to Living Affordably in the World's Great Cities. Globe Pequot Press (US$14).

CAMPING & THE OUTDOORS

CAMPING

Camping is an inexpensive way to tour Austria and Switzerland. Be prepared, though, as most campsites are not isolated areas; they are large plots that are more often filled with RVs than tents. Camping in Austria and Switzerland is less about getting out into nature and more about having a cheap place to sleep. Almost all campsites are in valleys near towns, although many are perched underneath impressive mountains. Most sites are open in the summer only, but some sites are specifically set aside for winter camping. In Switzerland, prices average 6-9SFr per person, and 4-10SFr per tent site. In Austria, prices run €4-6 per person and €4-8 per tent (plus tax if you're over 15), making camping only sometimes cheaper than hosteling.

Unlike in the United States, camping outside of established campsites in the backcountry is almost never allowed, and violators may be subject to steep fines. Backcountry hikers and mountaineers can resort to the famously well-maintained system of mountain huts *(Hütten)*, which are strategically positioned throughout the Alps to serve all needs outside of an emergency high-mountain bivouac *(Biwak)*. Huts in Austria range from rustic, spartan high-altitude shelters to sprawling affairs with full-service restaurants. A bed generally costs no more than €20, or €10 with ÖAV membership, and often can be substantially cheaper, especially if you are willing to sacrifice a bit of comfort. In Switzerland huts are listed from those in *Kategorie 1* (large huts with many amenities) to *Kategorie 3* (primitive structures or bivy shelters). Swiss huts run about 30SFr for adults, with discounts for SAC members, children, and young adults. Many huts in both countries offer meals in an in-house restaurant; travelers can choose to pay for meals separately, or pay one price for half-board *(Halbpension)*, including bed, breakfast, or dinner.

Both countries have well-developed Alpine Clubs, listed below under Hiking.

HIKING

Austria and Switzerland are renowned for their hiking, with paths ranging from simple hikes in the Swiss Jura and the wine valleys of eastern Austria to ice-axe-wielding expeditions over glaciers to the towering peaks of the Berner Oberland, Valais, and the Hohe Tauern. Nearly every town and city in the two countries has a series of trails in its vicinity shown on maps available at the local tourist office.

Free hiking **maps** are available from even the most basic tourist office, but for lengthy hikes every hiker should have a topographic map of no more than 1:50,000 scale. In Austria and Switzerland two companies make these maps: **Freytag-Berndt** and **Kümmerly-Frey** (maps about US$10). These maps are available in kiosks, bookstores, and tourist offices all over Austria and Switzerland, and from **Pacific Travellers Supply**, 12 W. Anapamu St., Santa Barbara CA 93101, USA (☎805-963-4438; www.pactrav.com).

Hiking trails are marked by signs indicating the time to nearby destinations, which may not assume your particular level of expertise and endurance. ("Std." is short for *Stunden*, or hours.) Usually trails will also be marked with either a red-white-red marker, or a blue-white-blue marker. The blue marker, or any trail marked *"Für Geübte,"* means that mountaineering equipment is needed, while the red markers line paths that require no more than sturdy boots and hiking poles. Most mountain hiking trails (unless you have specialized equipment) and mountain huts are open only from late June to early September because of snow cover that lasts into the summer.

 BACKCOUNTRY USE IN AUSTRIA AND SWITZERLAND. Be aware that backcountry camping is prohibited in public areas in both countries. Travelers planning **overnight hikes** must stay in the Alpine huts described above. Sleeping in one of these huts helps to preserve the fragile Alpine ecosystem, and it is generally safer for you—when you leave, you are expected to list your next destination in the hut book—thus alerting search-and-rescue teams if a problem should occur.

Österreichischer Alpenverein (ÖAV) (Willhelm-Greil-Str. 15, A-6010 Innsbruck (☎(0512) 595 47; www.oeav.at). Maintains most mountain huts across Tyrol and throughout Austria. Third-party insurance, accident provision, travel discounts, and a wealth of maps and mountain information are also included with membership. €41; students 27 and under, juniors age 19-25, seniors 61 and over, €30; children 18 and under €14.

Schweizer Alpen-Club/ Club Alpin Suisse (SAC-CAS), Sektion Bern, Monbijoustr. 61, CH 3007, Bern (☎(031) 370 18 18; fax 370 18 00). Maintains a large number of the Alpine huts in Switzerland. Organized as a federation of smaller clubs, so membership is through a particular town or region's branch. Cost and member privileges vary by branch.

Naturfreunde (Austria ☎(01) 892 35 34, www.naturfreunde.at; Switzerland (☎(031) 306 67 68, www.naturfreunde.ch) also maintains a number of huts and coordinates activities in a wide range of outdoor sports.

WILDERNESS SAFETY

Stay warm, stay dry, and stay hydrated. On any hike, you should pack enough equipment to keep you alive should disaster strike. This includes raingear, hat and mittens, warm clothes, a first-aid kit, a headlamp or flashlight, a reflector, a whistle, high energy food, and extra water. Dress in layers of **synthetic materials** designed for

> **FURTHER READING: HIKING.**
> *100 Hikes in the Alps*, by Vicky Spring (US$15).
> *Walking Austria's Alps: Hut to Hut*, by Jonathan Hurdle (US$11).
> *Walking Switzerland the Swiss Way*, by Marcia and Philip Lieberman (US$13).
> The "Swiss Way" refers to hiking hut-to-hut.
> *Walking in the Alps*, by Kev Reynolds (US$23). A comprehensive reference for more serious hikers, not intended as a travel guide.
> *Swiss-Bernese Oberland*, by Philip and Loretta Alspach (US$17).
> *Walking Easy in the Austrian Alps* and *Walking Easy in the Swiss Alps*, by Chet and Carolee Lipton (US$15).

the outdoors, or **wool.** Pile fleece jackets and Gore-Tex® raingear are good choices. Never rely on cotton (the "death fabric") for warmth. Make sure to check all equipment for any defects before setting out. See **Camping and Hiking Equipment,** below, for more information.

Check **weather forecasts** and pay attention to the sky. Don't hike when visibility is low or the weather looks iffy. Whenever possible, let someone know when and where you are going hiking. Do not attempt a hike beyond your ability—you may be endangering your life. Of particular concern in Austria and Switzerland is **glacier hiking.** Never hike over glaciers alone; snow-covered crevasses in glaciers have swallowed many an unsuspecting hiker. See **Health,** p. 18, for information about outdoor ailments such as heatstroke, hypothermia, rabies, and insects, as well as basic medical concerns and first-aid. For more information, consult *How to Stay Alive in the Woods*, by Bradford Angier (US$89).

CAMPING & HIKING EQUIPMENT

WHAT TO GET...

Purchase equipment before you leave so that you'll know exactly what you have and how much it weighs. Spend some time examining catalogs and talking to knowledgeable salespeople. Camping equipment is generally more expensive in Australia, New Zealand, and the UK than in North America.

Sleeping Bag: Most good sleeping bags are rated according to the lowest outdoor temperature at which they will keep you warm. ("summer" means 30-40°F at night and "four-season" or "winter" generally means below 0°F). Sleeping bags are made either of down (warmer and lighter, but more expensive, and miserable when wet) or of synthetic material (heavier, more durable, and warmer when wet). Prices vary, but might range from US$60-210 for a summer synthetic to US$250-600 for a good down winter bag. For **sleeping bag pads** you can choose from foam pads (US$10-20) or air mattresses (US$15-50). Both types cushion your back and neck and insulate you from the ground. Therm-A-Rest brand self-inflating sleeping pads are part foam and part air-mattress that partially inflate upon unrolling (US$40-200). Bring a **"stuff sack"** or plastic bag to store your sleeping bag and keep it dry.

Backpack: If you intend to do a lot of hiking, you should have a frame backpack. **Internal-frame packs** mold better to your back, keep a lower center of gravity, and can flex to allow you to hike difficult trails. Make sure your pack has a strong, padded hip belt, which transfers the weight from the shoulders to the legs. Any serious backpacking requires a pack of at least 3000 cubic in. (12,000cc). Sturdy backpacks cost anywhere from US$125-420. Before you buy any pack, try it on and imagine carrying it full; fill it with something heavy and walk around the store to get a sense of how it distributes weight. A **waterproof backpack cover** will prove invaluable. Otherwise, plan to store all of your belongings in plastic bags inside your backpack.

Boots: Be sure to wear hiking boots with good **ankle support** regardless of the terrain you are hiking. Your boots should fit snugly and comfortably over a pair of wool socks and a thin liner sock. If you're planning on doing any serious hiking, your boots should be waterproof Gore-Tex® or a similar fabric. In addition, the fewer seams a boot has the more waterproof it will be—the best hiking boots are solid leather. Break in boots for several weeks before setting out. Days of tough hiking may still yield painful and debilitating blisters; **moleskins** (moleskins at most pharmacy stores) are good first aid for raw feet.

Tent: The best tents are free-standing (with their own frames and suspension systems), set up quickly, and require staking only in high winds. Low-profile dome tents are generally the best in trying weather conditions. Tents are rated by the number of seasons; "winter/mountaineering" or "4-season" is a must if you plan to backpack in the winter, as they are warmer, sturdier, and shed snow more easily. They are also heavier and more expensive, so if you hike predominantly in the summer, consider a "3-season" tent. There are also "convertible" tents from which you can remove pieces to turn it from a 4-season into a 3-season. Good 3-season tents start at US$200, 4-season at US$450. Seal the seams of your tent with waterproofer, and make sure it has a rain fly. A **battery-operated lantern**, a **plastic groundcloth**, and a **nylon tarp** are also useful.

Other Necessities: The **raincoat** and **rainpants** combination is far superior to a poncho. Ideal is a fabric such as Gore-Tex® that is both waterproof and breathable. **Synthetic materials,** like polypropylene or 100% polyester tops, socks, and long underwear, along with a pile ("fleece") jacket, will keep you warm even when wet. When camping in autumn, winter, or spring, bring along a **"space blanket,"** which helps you retain your body heat and doubles as a groundcloth (US$5-15). Hard plastic **water bottles** (such as those made by Nalgene®) keep water cooler than metal ones do, and are virtually shatter- and leak-proof. Large, collapsible **water sacks** will significantly improve your lot in primitive campgrounds and weigh practically nothing when empty. Except in very high alpine environments, **water-purification** is a must. Polar Pure produces bottled iodine solution that can purify up to 2000L water ($10). If you can't stand the taste of iodinated water, portable filters are available for $50-200. Even with treatment, only use water sources where water is running and looks clear and clean. If you want to cook your own food, you'll need a **camp stove.** It is best to get a stove that can run on kerosene fuel, which unlike other fuel types is widely available in both Europe and North America. For backpacking, a lightweight design with a detachable fuel source and a windscreen is ideal. A **first aid kit, Swiss Army knife, insect repellent, headlamp,** and **waterproof matches** are other essential camping items.

...AND WHERE TO BUY IT

The mail-order/online companies listed below offer lower prices than many retail stores, but a visit to a local camping or outdoors store will give you a good sense of the look and weight of certain items.

Campmor, P.O. Box 700, Upper Saddle River, NJ 07458, USA (☎888-226-7667, elsewhere call US +1 201-825-8300; www.campmor.com).

Discount Camping, 880 Main North Rd., Pooraka, South Australia 5095, Australia (☎(08) 82 62 33 99; www.discountcamping.com.au).

Eastern Mountain Sports (EMS), 327 Jaffrey Rd., Peterborough, NH 03458, USA (☎888-463-6367 or 603-924-7231; www.shopems.com).

Mountain Designs, P.O. Box 1472, Fortitude Valley, Queensland 4006, Australia (☎(07) 32 52 88 94; www.mountaindesign.com.au).

Sierra Trading Post, 5025 Camptstool Rd., Cheyenee, WY 82007, USA (☎800-713-4534; www.sierratradingpost.com).

Recreational Equipment, Inc. (REI), Sumner, WA 98352, USA (☎800-426-4840 or 253-891-2500; www.rei.com).

YHA Adventure Shop, 14 Southampton St., London WC2E 7HA, UK (☎(020) 78 36 85 41; www.yhaadventure.com). The main branch of one of Britain's largest outdoor equipment suppliers.

SKIING

The fact that four Winter Olympics (St. Moritz 1928 and 1948, Innsbruck 1964 and 1972) have been held in Australia and Switzerland is no accident—the skiing in these two countries is easily among the best in the world. An Austrian, Matthias Zdarsky, wrote the world's first instructional book on skiing in 1897 and organized the world's first slalom race in Lilienfeld in 1905. St. Anton is often credited as the "birthplace of modern skiing," center for the world's first ski club in 1901. Kitzbühel is home to what is probably the world's most famous ski race, the Hahnenkamm. Swiss resorts such as Verbier and Zermatt are meccas to diehard skiers because of their challenging runs, wild vertical drop, and overall vastness.

Skiing in the Alps deserves its excellent reputation for a number of reasons. Many travelers are drawn to the old-school charm of the small Alpine villages that predate accompanying resorts by centuries. Vertical drop is higher in the Alps than at almost any resort in North America, and the weather is often both more consistent and gentler. Expert skiers can find some of the most difficult terrain anywhere in the world, along with the freedom to explore at will. "Off piste" skiing still only exists in its true form in Europe, where resorts allow people to ski wherever they please as long as they take responsibility for their actions (and foot the bill for rescue, if necessary). Most alpine skiing is above the timber line, so even the not-so-adventurous can ski thousands of vertical feet without ever losing sight of sweeping 180-degree panoramas. In addition, a number of resorts offer year-round skiing on glaciers. In Austria, these include Stubai (near Innsbruck), Hintertux (near Mayrhofen), and Obergurgl (in the Ötztal). In Switzerland, summer glacier skiing exists in Zermatt, Saas Fee, and Les Diablerets.

Many mountain towns in Austria and Switzerland sleep through most of the year, but come alive during the winter months. If you go, make sure to book your vacation at least a month or two in advance, or you may not find a place to stay. Typically, accommodations in winter are booked in blocks of a week, usually between two Saturdays. High season is normally in the weeks around Christmas and New Year's, and from February to March. Tourist offices provide information on regional skiing as well as special deals and ski packages. Contrary to popular belief, skiing in Europe is not hideously expensive, and in many cases can be cheaper than a ski vacation in the western US. If you're especially concerned with saving money, stay away from glitzier resorts like St. Moritz, Gstaad, and Kitzbühel, among others. Destinations such as the Jungfrau Region in Switzerland and the Ötztal in Austria still offer excellent skiing, but without the tourist veneer.

ESSENTIALS

KEEPING IN TOUCH

BY MAIL

The postal systems of Austria and Switzerland are quick and efficient. Letters take one to three days to reach destinations within Switzerland and one to two days within Austria. Mark all letters and packages "mit flugpost" or "par avion." In all cases, include the postal code if you know it; those of Swiss cities begin with "CH," Austrian with "A."

SENDING MAIL HOME FROM AUSTRIA AND SWITZERLAND

For **airmail** transit times, see **Sending Mail to Austria and Switzerland,** below. To send a postcard or letter under 20g from **Switzerland** to an international destination within Europe costs 1.10SFr 1st ("A") class and 0.90SFr 2nd ("B") class, and to any other international destination via airmail costs 1.80SFr for A and 1.10SFr for B. Domestically, postcards require 0.90SFr for A and 0.70SFr for B. To send a postcard from **Austria** to any destination costs €0.55. A letter under 50g within Austria costs €0.75. A letter under 50g to another European country costs €1.10 (priority) or €1.00 (economy), to any other international destination costs €1.75/€1.25. Aerogrammes, printed sheets that fold into envelopes and travel via airmail, are available at post offices. Make sure to mark international mail with "Luftpost," although it's usually assumed unless otherwise specified.

SENDING MAIL TO AUSTRIA & SWITZERLAND

Mark envelopes "airmail" or "par avion" to avoid having letters sent by sea.

Australia: Allow 4-7 days for regular airmail to Austria and Switzerland. Postcards cost AUS$1, letters up to 50g cost AUS$1.65; packages up to 250g cost AUS$8, with rates for heavier packages increasing by AUS$6 every 250g.

Canada: Allow 4-7 days for regular airmail to Austria and Switzerland. Postcards and letters up to 30g cost CDN$1.25; packages ("small packages") up to 1kg CDN$21.30, up to 2kg CDN$35.55.

Ireland: Allow 5-9 days for regular airmail to Austria and Switzerland. Postcards and letters up to 25g cost €0.57 (priority) or €0.44 (economy). Packages between 500g and 1kg are €8/€4.50 1½-2kg €16/€7.80.

New Zealand: Allow 5-9 days for regular airmail to Austria and Switzerland. Postcards NZ$1.50. Letters up to 20g cost NZ$2.00. Postage for packages is on a sliding scale in increments of 10g. Minimum weight is 100g (NZ$6.02); each additional 10g adds about NZ$0.215.

UK: Allow 3-5 days for airmail to Austria and Switzerland. Postcards and letters up to 20g cost UK£0.38; rates for packages start at 100g (UK£0.92), with rates increasing about UK£0.09-0.10 for every 20g extra.

US: Allow 4-8 days for regular airmail to Austria and Switzerland. Postcards/aerogrammes cost US$0.70; letters under 1 oz. US$0.80. Packages under 1 lb. cost US$14 (Switzerland) or US$16.50 (Austria); each extra pound is between US$1.50-3.00.

RECEIVING MAIL IN AUSTRIA & SWITZERLAND

General Delivery: Mail can be sent to Austria and Switzerland through **Poste Restante** (the international phrase for General Delivery; in German **Postlagernde Briefe**) to almost any city or town with a post office. Address letters as in the following example: Napoleon BONAPARTE, *Postlagernde Briefe,* A-1010 Vienna, Austria. In Switzerland use the same formula, but have the postal code be preceded by a CH. The mail will go to a special desk in the central post office, unless you specify a post office by street address or postal code. As a rule, it is best to use the largest post office in the area, as mail may be sorted there anyway. When picking up your mail, bring a form of photo ID, preferably a passport. There is generally no surcharge; if there is a charge, it usually does not exceed the cost of domestic postage. If the clerks insist that there is nothing for you, have them check under your first name as well. *Let's Go* lists post offices and postal codes in the **Practical Information** section for each city and most towns.

American Express: AmEx's travel offices throughout the world offer a free **Client Letter Service** (mail held up to 30 days and forwarded upon request) for cardholders who contact them in advance. Address the letter in the same way shown above. Some offices will offer these services to non-cardholders (especially AmEx Traveler's Cheque holders), but call ahead to make sure. *Let's Go* lists AmEx office locations for most large cities in **Practical Information** sections; for a complete, free list, call US ☎800-528-4800.

BY TELEPHONE

CALLING HOME FROM AUSTRIA OR SWITZERLAND

A **calling card** is probably your cheapest bet. Calls are billed collect or to your account. You can frequently call collect without even possessing a company's calling card just by calling their access number and following the instructions. **To obtain a calling card,** inquire with your telephone company, or contact a national telecommunications company in your home country. To **call home with a calling card,** contact the operator for your service provider in Austria and Switzerland by dialing the appropriate toll-free access number.

Let's Go has recently partenered with ekit.com to provide a calling card that offers a number of services, including email and voice messaging. Before purchasing any calling card, always be sure to compare rates with other cards, and to make sure it serves your needs (a local phonecard is generally better for local calls, for instance). For more information, visit www.letsgo.ekit.com. You can also make international calls from pay phones, but the rates are astronomical when compared to a phonecarde.

CALLING WITHIN AUSTRIA & SWITZERLAND

The simplest way to call within the country is to use a pay phone. Most pay phones in Austria and Switzerland accept only **prepaid phone cards,** not coins. Phone cards are available at kiosks, post offices, or train stations. Rates are highest in the morning, lower in the evening, and lowest on Sunday and late at night. Dial the city code (refer to the phone code box in each city's **Practical Information**) before each number when calling from outside the city; within the city, dial only the number.

PLACING INTERNATIONAL CALLS. To call Austria or Switzerland from home or to call home from Austria or Switzerland, dial:

1. The **international dialing prefix.** To dial out of **Australia,** dial 0011; **Canada** or the **US,** 011; the **Republic of Ireland, New Zealand,** or the **UK,** 00; **South Africa,** 09; out of Austria or Switzerland, 00.
2. The **country code** of the country you want to call. To call **Australia,** dial 61; **Canada** or the **US,** 1; the **Republic of Ireland,** 353; **New Zealand,** 64; **South Africa,** 27; the **UK,** 44; Austria, 43; Switzerland, 41.
3. The **city/area code.** *Let's Go* lists the city/area codes for cities and towns in Austria and Switzerland opposite the city or town name, next to a ☎. If the first digit is a zero (e.g., 020 for London), omit the zero when calling from abroad (e.g., dial 20 from Canada to reach London).
4. The **local number.**

TIME DIFFERENCES

Austria and Switzerland are one hour ahead of Greenwich Mean Time (GMT). Both observe daylight savings time.

2 AM	5 AM	10AM	11AM	12 PM	8 PM	10PM
Vancouver San Francisco	New York Boston	London (GMT)	Austria Switzerland	Johannesburg	Sydney	Auckland

EMAIL & INTERNET

Internet access is widespread in Austria and Switzerland. You can check your email from cybercafés, which *Let's Go* lists in the Practical Information section for each city, and sometimes from universities, libraries, and hostels. Though limited free access is sometimes available in bookstores and libraries, regular Internet access isn't cheap; there is no standard price, but it tends to range from 10-15SFr per hour in Switzerland and €2-5 per hour in Austria. For a complete listing of cybercafés in Austria and Switzerland, visit www.cybercaptive.com or www.netcafeguide.com.

GETTING TO AUSTRIA & SWITZERLAND

BY PLANE

When it comes to airfare, a little effort can save you a bundle. If your plans are flexible enough to accommodate restrictions, courier fares are the cheapest. Tickets bought from consolidators and standby seating are also good deals, but last-minute specials, airfare wars, and charter flights often beat these fares. The key is to hunt around, to be flexible, and to ask persistently about discounts. Students, seniors, and those under 26 should never pay full price for a ticket.

AIRFARES

Airfares to Austria and Switzerland peak between June and August, as well as throughout the winter (particularly around Christmas time). The cheapest times to travel are fall and spring, pre- and post-ski-season. Midweek (M-Th morning) round-trip flights run US$40-50 cheaper than weekend flights, but they are generally more crowded and less likely to permit frequent-flier upgrades. Student tickets will also frequently allow free, lengthy layovers in hub cities (Paris, London, Frankfurt). Traveling with an "open return" ticket can be pricier than fixing a return date when buying the ticket. Round-trip flights are by far the cheapest; "open-jaw" (arriving in and departing from different cities) tickets tend to be pricier. Patching one-way flights together is the most expensive way to travel. Flights between capitals or regional hubs will tend to be cheaper.

If Austria or Switzerland is only one stop on a more extensive globe-hop, consider a round-the-world (RTW) ticket. Tickets usually include at least five stops and are valid for about a year; prices run US$1200-5000. Try **Northwest Airlines/KLM** (US ☎800-447-4747; www.nwa.com) or **Star Alliance,** a consortium of 22 airlines including United Airlines (US ☎800-241-6522; www.star-alliance.com).

Fares from the US to Austria and Switzerland vary tremendously depending on airfare wars and special deals. For a round-trip ticket during peak season, expect to spend anywhere from US$500-1000 versus US$300-500 during off-season.

BUDGET & STUDENT TRAVEL AGENCIES

While knowledgeable agents specializing in flights to Austria and Switzerland can make your life easy and help you save, they may not spend the time to find you the lowest possible fare—they get paid on commission. Travelers holding **ISIC** and **IYTC cards** (see p. 10) qualify for big discounts from student travel agencies. Most flights from budget agencies are on major airlines, but in peak season some may sell seats on less reliable chartered aircraft.

USIT, 19-21 Ashton Quay, Dublin 2, IR (☎01 602 1600; www.usitworld.com). Ireland's leading student/budget travel agency has 22 offices throughout Northern Ireland and the Republic of Ireland. Offers programs to work in North America.

CTS Travel, 30 Rathbone Pl., London W1T 1GQ, UK (☎020 7290 0630; www.ctstravel.co.uk). A British student travel agent with offices in 39 countries including the US, Empire State Building, 350 Fifth Ave., Suite 7813, New York, NY 10118 (☎877-287-6665; www.ctstravelusa.com).

STA Travel, 7890 S. Hardy Dr., Ste. 110, Tempe, AZ 85284, USA (24hr. reservations and info ☎800-781-4040; www.sta-travel.com). A student and youth travel organization with over 150 offices worldwide (check their web site for a listing of all their offices), including US offices in Boston, Chicago, L.A., New York, San Francisco, Seattle, and Washington, D.C. Ticket booking, travel insurance, railpasses, and more. In the UK, walk-in office 11 Goodge St., London W1T 2PF (☎0207-436-7779). In New Zealand, Shop 2B, 182 Queen St., Auckland (☎(09) 309 04 58). In Australia, 366 Lygon St., Carlton VIC 3053 (☎03 9349 4344).

Travel CUTS (Canadian Universities Travel Services Limited), 187 College St., Toronto, ON M5T 1P7 (☎416-979-2406; www.travelcuts.com). Offices across Canada and the United States in Seattle, San Francisco, Los Angeles, New York and elsewhere. Also in the UK, 295-A Regent St., London W1B 2H9 (☎0207 255 2191).

COMMERCIAL AIRLINES

The commercial airlines' lowest regular offer is the **APEX** (Advance Purchase Excursion) fare, which provides confirmed reservations and allows "open-jaw" tickets. Generally, reservations must be made seven to 21 days ahead of departure, with seven- to 14-day minimum-stay and up to 90-day maximum-stay restrictions. These fares carry hefty cancellation and change penalties (fees rise in summer). Book peak-season APEX fares early; by May you will have a hard time getting your desired departure date. Use **Microsoft Expedia** (msn.expedia.com) or **Travelocity**

ESSENTIALS

FLIGHT PLANNING ON THE INTERNET. The Internet is one of the best places to look for travel bargains. Many airline sites offer special last-minute deals on the Web. Austrian Airlines lists specials at http://airnet.aua.com/leisure/AT/framesnew/booking.htm. Other sites do the legwork and compile the deals for you—try www.bestfares.com, www.onetravel.com, www.lowestfare.com, www.orbitz.com, and www.travelzoo.com.

STA (www.statravel.com), **Council** (www.counciltravel.com), and ■ **StudentUniverse** (www.studentuniverse.com) provide quotes on student tickets, while **Expedia** (msn.expedia.com) and **Travelocity** (www.travelocity.com) offer full travel services. **Priceline** (www.priceline.com) allows you to specify a price, and obligates you to buy any ticket that meets or beats it; be prepared for antisocial hours and odd routes. **Skyauction** (www.skyauction.com) allows you to bid on both last-minute and advance-purchase tickets.

An indispensable resource on the Internet is the *Air Traveler's Handbook* (www.cs.cmu.edu/afs/cs/user/mkant/Public/Travel/airfare.html), a comprehensive listing of links to everything you need to know before you board a plane. To protect yourself, make sure that the site you use has a secure server before handing over any credit card details. Happy hunting!

(www.travelocity.com) to get an idea of the lowest published fares, then use the resources outlined here to try and beat those fares. Low-season fares should be appreciably cheaper than the high-season ones listed here.

TRAVELING FROM NORTH AMERICA

Standard commerical carriers like American (☎800-433-7300; www.aa.com) and United (☎800-241-6522; www.ual.com) will probably offer the most convenient flights, but they may not be the cheapest. You might find a better deal on one of the following airlines.

Icelandair: ☎800-223-5500; www.icelandair.com. Stopovers in Iceland for no extra cost on most transatlantic flights. New York to Frankfurt May-Sept. US$500-730; Oct.-May US$390-450. From there, a train may still be cheaper than other options. For last minute offers, subscribe to their email Lucky Fairs.

Finnair: ☎800-950-5000; www.us.finnair.com. Cheap round-trips from San Francisco, New York, and Toronto to Geneva, Munich, Vienna, and Zurich.

Martinair: ☎800-627-8462; www.martinair.com. Fly from California or Florida to Amsterdam: mid-June to mid-Aug. US$880; mid-Aug. to mid-June US$730.

TRAVELING FROM THE UK & IRELAND

Because of the many carriers flying from the British Isles to the continent, we only include discount airlines or those with cheap specials here. The **Air Travel Advisory Bureau** in London (☎020 7636 5000; www.atab.co.uk) provides referrals to travel agencies and consolidators that offer discounted airfares out of the UK.

Aer Lingus: Ireland ☎0818 365 000; www.aerlingus.ie. Return tickets from Dublin, Cork, Galway, Kerry, and Shannon to Munich and Zurich (IR£102-244).

easyJet: UK ☎0870 600 00 00; www.easyjet.com. London to Munich and Zurich (UK£47-136). Online tickets.

KLM: UK ☎0870 507 40 74; www.klmuk.com. Cheap return tickets from London and elsewhere to Munich, Salzburg, Vienna, and Zurich.

Ryanair: Ireland ☎0818 303 030, UK 0870 156 95 69; www.ryanair.ie. From Dublin, London, and Glasgow to Graz, Klagenfurt, and Salzburg. Deals from as low as UK£9 on limited weekend specials.

TRAVELING FROM AUSTRALIA & NEW ZEALAND

Qantas Air: Australia ☎13 13 13, New Zealand ☎0800 808 767; www.quantas.com.au. Flights from Australia and New Zealand to Munich, Vienna, and Zurich.

Singapore Air: Australia ☎13 10 11, New Zealand ☎0800 808 909; www.singaporeair.com. Flies from Auckland, Sydney, Melbourne, and Perth to Zurich.

Thai Airways: Australia ☎1300 65 19 60, New Zealand ☎09 377 02 68; www.thaiair.com. Auckland, Sydney, and Melbourne to Geneva, Graz, Innsbruck, Klagenfurt, Munich, Salzburg, Vienna, and Zurich.

TRAVELING FROM SOUTH AFRICA

Air France: ☎011 770 16 01; www.airfrance.com/za. Johannesburg to Basel, bern, Geneva, Munich, Vienna, and Zurich.

British Airways: ☎0860 011 747; www.britishairways.com/travel/home/public/en_za. Cape Town and Johannesburg to Geneva, Munich, Vienna, and Geneva.

Lufthansa: ☎0861 842 538; www.lufthansa.co.za. From Cape Town, Durban, and Johannesburg to Geneva, Graz, Munich, Salzburg, Vienna, and Zurich.

AIR COURIER FLIGHTS

Those who travel light should consider courier flights. Couriers help transport cargo on international flights by using their checked luggage space for freight. Generally, couriers must travel with carry-ons only and deal with complex flight restrictions. Most flights are round-trip only, with short fixed-length stays (usually one week) and a limit of one ticket per issue. Most of these flights also operate only out of major gateway cities, mostly in North America. Most flights leave from New York, Los Angeles, San Francisco, or Miami in the US; and from Montreal, Toronto, or Vancouver in Canada. Generally, you must be over 21 (in some cases 18). In summer, the most popular destinations usually require an advance reservation of about two weeks (you can usually book up to two months ahead). Super-discounted fares are common for "last-minute" flights (three to 14 days ahead).

FROM NORTH AMERICA

Round-trip courier fares from the US and Canada to Austria and Switzerland run about US$200-500. Most flights leave from New York, Los Angeles, San Francisco, or Miami in the US, and from Montreal, Toronto, or Vancouver in Canada. The organizations below provide their members with lists of opportunities and courier brokers worldwide for an annual fee. Prices quoted below are round-trip.

Air Courier Association 350 Indiana St. #300, Golden, CO 80401 (☎800-282-1202; www.aircourier.org). Ten departure cities throughout the US and Canada to Geneva and Vienna (high season US$150-360). One-year membership US$49.

International Association of Air Travel Couriers (IAATC), PO Box 980, Keystone Heights, FL 32656 (☎352-475-1584; www.courier.org). One-year membership US$45.

Global Courier Travel, PO Box 3051, Nederland, CO 80466 (www.globalcouriertravel.com). Online database. Six departure points in the US and Canada to Munich, Vienna, and Zurich. Lifetime membership US$40, 2 people US$55.

FROM THE UK, IRELAND, AUSTRALIA, & NEW ZEALAND

The minimum age for couriers from the **UK** is usually 18. **Brave New World Enterprises,** P.O. Box 22212, London SE5 8WB (www.courierflights.com) publishes a directory of all the companies offering courier flights in the UK (UK£10, in electronic form UK£8). **Global Courier Travel** (see above) also offers flights from London and Dublin to continental Europe. **British Airways Travel Shop** (☎ 0870 240 0747; www.batravelshops.com) arranges some flights from London to destinations in continental Europe (specials may be as low as UK£60; no registration fee). From **Australia** and **New Zealand, Global Courier Travel** (see above) has listings from Sydney and Auckland to Frankfurt.

STANDBY FLIGHTS

Traveling standby requires considerable flexibility in arrival and departure dates and cities. Companies dealing in standby flights sell vouchers rather than tickets, along with the promise to get to your destination (or near your destination) within a certain window of time (typically one to five days). You call in before your specific window of time to hear your flight options and the probability that you will be able to board each flight. You can then decide which flights you want to try to make, show up at the appropriate airport at the appropriate time, present your voucher, and board if space is available. Vouchers can usually be bought for both one-way and round-trip travel. You may receive a monetary refund only if every available flight within your date range is full; if you opt not to take an available (but perhaps less convenient) flight, you can only get credit toward future travel. Carefully read agreements with any company offering standby flights as tricky fine print can leave you in the lurch. To check on a company's service record in the US, call the Better Business Bureau (☎ 212-533-6200). It is difficult to receive refunds, and clients' vouchers will not be honored when an airline fails to receive payment on time.

TICKET CONSOLIDATORS

Ticket consolidators, or **"bucket shops,"** buy unsold tickets in bulk from commercial airlines and sell them at discounted rates. The best place to look is in the Sunday travel section of any major newspaper (such as the *New York Times*), where many bucket shops place tiny ads. Call quickly, as availability is typically extremely limited. Not all bucket shops are reliable, so insist on a receipt that gives full details of restrictions, refunds, and tickets, and pay by credit card (in spite of the 2-5% fee) so you can stop payment if you never receive your tickets. For more info, see www.travel-library.com/air-travel/consolidators.html.

TRAVELING FROM THE US & CANADA

Travel Avenue (☎ 800-333-3335; www.travelavenue.com) looks for the best available published fares then uses several consolidators to attempt to beat that fare. **NOW Voyager,** 74 Varick St., Ste. 307, New York, NY 10013 (☎ 212-431-1616; www.nowvoyagertravel.com.com) arranges discounted flights. Other consolidators worth trying are **Pennsylvania Travel** (☎ 877-251-6866; www.patravel.com); **Rebel** (☎ 800-227-3235; www.rebeltours.com); **Cheap Tickets** (☎ 877-377-1000; www.cheaptickets.com). Yet more consolidators on the web include **Flights.com** (www.flights.com) and **TravelHUB** (www.travelhub.com). Keep in mind that these are just suggestions to get you started in your research; *Let's Go* does not endorse any of these agencies. As always, be cautious, and research companies before you hand over your credit card number.

TRAVELING FROM THE UK, AUSTRALIA, & NEW ZEALAND

In London, the **Air Travel Advisory Bureau** (☎ (0207) 636 5000; www.atab.co.uk) can provide names of reliable consolidators and discount flight specialists. From Australia and New Zealand, look for consolidator ads in the travel section of the *Sydney Morning Herald* and other papers.

CHARTER FLIGHTS

Charters are flights a tour operator contracts with an airline to fly extra loads of passengers during peak season. Charter flights fly less frequently than major airlines, make refunds particularly difficult, and are almost always fully booked. Schedules and itineraries may also change or be cancelled at the last moment (as late as 48 hours before the trip, and without a full refund), and check-in, boarding, and baggage claim are often much slower. However, they can also be much cheaper.

Discount clubs and **fare brokers** offer members savings on last-minute charter and tour deals. Study their contracts closely; you don't want to end up with an unwanted overnight layover. **Travelers Advantage,** Trumbull, CT, USA (US$60 annual fee includes discounts and cheap flight directories; ☎877-259-2691; www.travelersadvantage.com) specializes in European travel and tour packages.

GETTING AROUND AUSTRIA & SWITZERLAND

Fares on all modes of transportation are either one-way ("single") or round-trip ("return"). "Period returns" require you to return within a specific number of days; "day return" means you must return on the same day. Unless stated otherwise, *Let's Go* always lists one-way fares. Round-trip is usually double the one-way.

BY TRAIN

European trains are generally comfortable, convenient, and reasonably swift. In fact, the train can get you to some places in Austria and Switzerland that a car cannot. Second-class travel is pleasant, and compartments (2- to 6-person) are excellent places to meet fellow travelers. Trains, however, are not always safe; lock your compartment door (if possible) and keep your valuables on your person at all times. Non-smokers probably won't be comfortable in smoking compartments, which tend to be very, very smoky. Get your stuff together a few stops before you want to get off, since trains sometimes pause only a few moments before zipping off. For longer trips, make sure that you are on the correct car, as trains sometimes split at crossroads. Towns in parentheses on schedules require a train switch at the town listed immediately before the parenthesis. You might want to ask if your route requires changing trains, as the schedules are confusing.

The **Österreichische Bundesbahn** (ÖBB), **Austria's** federal railroad, is one of Europe's most thorough and efficient. The ÖBB prints the yearly *Fahrpläne Kursbuch Bahn-Inland*, a compilation of all rail, ferry, and cable-car schedules in Austria. The massive schedule is available at any large train station, along with its companion guides, the *Kursbuch Bahn-Ausland* for international trains, and the *Internationales Schlafwagenkursbuch* for sleeping cars. Getting around **Switzerland** is also a snap. Federal **(SBB, CFF)** and private railways connect most towns and villages, with trains running frequently. The national 24hr. phone number for **rail information** is ☎ (0900) 30 03 00 and has operators who speak English, German, French, and Italian, but it costs 1.19SFr per minute. Check the web site for the federal railway system at www.sbb.ch (available in French, German, Italian, and English versions). Be aware that sometimes only private train lines go to remote tourist spots; therefore, Eurail and SwissPass may not be valid. Yellow signs announce departure times *(Ausfahrt, départ, partenze)* and platforms *(Gleis, quai, binario)*. White signs are for arrivals *(Ankunft, arrivé, arrivo)*. On major Austrian lines, make reservations at least a few hours in advance.

You can either buy a **railpass,** which allows you unlimited travel within a particular region for a given period of time, or rely on buying individual **point-to-point** tickets as you go. You can purchase individual tickets at every train station in Austria and Switzerland, at Bahn-Total service stations, at the occasional *automat*, most *Tabak* stands, and from the conductor for a small surcharge. Over 130 stations accept major credit cards as well as American Express Traveler's Cheques and Eurocheques. Most ticket validation is based on the honor system, but *Schwarzfahren* (i.e. riding without a ticket) can result in big fines, and playing "dumb tourist" probably won't work.

In Austria, children under 6 travel free, while children ages 6-12 receive a 50% discount. In Switzerland, travelers under 16 travel free with a parent with the Swiss Family Card. When traveling without a parent, children up to 16 have a 50% discount on all the offers of the Swiss Travel System.

RESERVATIONS. While seat reservations are required only for selected trains (usually on major lines), you are not guaranteed a seat without one (usually US$3-10). You should strongly consider reserving in advance during peak holiday and tourist seasons (at the very latest, a few hours ahead). You will have to purchase a **supplement** (US$10-50) or special fare for high-speed or high-quality trains such as German ICE trains. InterRail holders must also purchase supplements (US$10-25) for trains like EuroCity and InterCity; supplements are unnecessary for Eurailpass and Europass holders.

OVERNIGHT TRAINS. On night trains, you won't waste valuable daylight hours traveling and you can avoid the hassle and expense of staying at a hotel. However, the main drawbacks include discomfort, sleepless nights, and the lack of scenery. **Sleeping accommodations** on trains differ from country to country, but typically you can either sleep upright in your seat (for free) or pay for a separate space. **Couchettes** (berths) typically have four to six seats per compartment (about US$20 per person); **sleepers** (beds) in private sleeping cars offer more privacy and comfort, but are considerably more expensive (US$40-150). If you are using a railpass valid only for a restricted number of days, inspect trains schedules to maximize the use of your pass: an overnight train or boat journey uses up only one of your travel days if it departs after 7pm.

SHOULD YOU BUY A RAILPASS? Railpasses were conceived to allow you to jump on any train in Europe, go wherever you want whenever you want, and change your plans at will. In practice, it's not so simple. You still must stand in line to validate your pass, pay for supplements, and fork over cash for seat and couchette reservations. More importantly, railpasses don't always pay off. For ballpark estimates, consult the **DERTravel** or **RailEurope** railpass brochure for prices on point-to-point tickets. If you are planning to spend extensive time on trains, hopping between big cities, a railpass will probably be worth it. But in many cases, especially if you are under 26, point-to-point tickets may prove a cheaper option.

MULTINATIONAL RAILPASSES

EURAILPASS. Eurail is valid in most of Western Europe, including Austria and Switzerland. Standard **Eurailpasses,** valid for a given number of consecutive days, are best for those planning on spending extensive time on trains every few days. **Flexipasses,** valid for any 10 or 15 (not necessarily consecutive) days within a two-month period, are more cost-effective for those traveling longer distances less frequently. **Saverpasses** provide 1st-class travel for travelers in groups of two to five (prices are per person). **Youthpasses** and **Youth Flexipasses** provide parallel second-class perks for those under 26.

Passholders receive a timetable for major routes and a map with details on possible ferry, steamer, bus, car rental, hotel, and Eurostar discounts. Passholders often also receive reduced fares or free passage on many bus and boat lines.

EURAILPASSES	15 days	21 days	1 month	2 months	3 months
1st class Eurailpass	US$572	US$740	US$918	US$1298	US$1606
Eurail Saverpass	US$486	US$630	US$780	US$1106	US$1366
Eurail Youthpass	US$401	US$518	US$644	US$910	US$1126

EURAIL FLEXIPASSES	10 days in 2 months	15 days in 2 months
1st class Eurail Flexipass	US$674	US$888
Eurail Saver Flexipass	US$574	US$756
Eurail Youth Flexipass	US$473	US$622

EUROPASS. The Europass is a slimmed-down version of the Eurailpass: it allows five to 15 days of unlimited travel in any two-month period within France, Germany, Italy, Spain, and Switzerland. **First-Class Europasses** (for individuals) and **Saverpasses** (for people traveling in groups of 2-5) range from US$348/296 per person (5 days) to US$688/586 (15 days). **Second-Class Youthpasses** for those aged 12-25 cost US$244-482. For a fee, you can add **additional zones,** such as Austria/Hungary. $62 for one extra zone, $102 for two (less with the Saverpass). You are entitled to the same freebies afforded by the Eurailpass, but only when they are within or between zones that you have purchased.

SHOPPING AROUND FOR A EURAIL OR EUROPASS. Eurailpasses and Europasses are designed by the EU itself and can be bought only by non-Europeans almost exclusively from non-European distributors. These passes must be sold at uniform prices determined by the EU. However, some travel agents tack on a US$10 handling fee, and others offer certain bonuses with purchase, so shop around. Also, keep in mind that pass prices usually go up each year, so if you're planning to travel early in the year, you can save cash by purchasing before January 1 (you have three months from the purchase to validate your pass in Europe).

It is best to buy your Eurailpass or Europass before leaving; only a few places in major European cities sell them, and at a marked-up price. You can get a replacement for a lost pass only if you have purchased insurance on it under the Pass Protection Plan (US$14). Eurailpasses are available through travel agents, student travel agencies like STA and Council (see p. 35), and **Rail Europe,** 500 Mamaroneck Ave., Harrison, NY 10528 (US ☎888-382-7245, Canada 800-361-7245, UK 0990 84 88 48; www.raileurope.com) or **DERTravel Services,** whose services are available at several outfits across the US (US ☎888-337-7350; www.der.com).

INTERRAIL PASSES. If you have lived for at least six months in one of the European countries where **InterRail Passes** are valid, they are an economical option. There are eight InterRail **zones**. The **Under 26 InterRail Card** allows either 21 consecutive days or one month of unlimited travel within one, two, three, or all of the eight zones; the cost is determined by the number of zones the pass covers (UK£85-178). Passholders receive **discounts** on rail travel, Eurostar journeys, and most ferries to Ireland, Scandanavia, and the rest of Europe. Most exclude **supplements** for high-speed trains. For info and ticket sales in Europe contact **Student Travel Centre,** 21 Rupert St., 1st fl., London W1V 7FN (☎020 74 37 81 01; www.student-travel-centre.com). Tickets are also available from travel agents, at major train stations throughout Europe, or through on-line vendors (www.railpassdirect.co.uk).

DOMESTIC RAILPASSES

If you are planning to spend a significant amount of time within one country or region, a national pass—valid on all rail lines of a country's rail company—may be more cost-effective than a multinational pass. But many national passes are limited and don't provide the free or discounted travel on private railways and ferries that Eurail does. Some of these passes can be bought only in Europe, some only outside of Europe; check with a railpass agent or with national tourist offices.

NATIONAL RAILPASSES. The domestic analogs of the Eurailpass (see p. 42), national railpasses are valid either for a given number of consecutive days or for a specific number of days within a given time period. National railpasses are the way to go if you're going to be covering long distances within Austria or Switzerland. Usually, they must be purchased before you leave. Though they will usually save frequent travelers some money, in some cases you may find that they are actually a more expensive alternative to point-to-point tickets. For more information on national railpasses, check out http://raileurope.com/us/rail/passes/single_country_index.htm.

Austrian Railpass: Sold worldwide, this pass is valid for 3 days of unlimited train travel in a 15-day period on all Austrian Federal Railway lines, state, and private rail lines in Austria. Also grants a 40% discount on bicycle rental in over 130 railway stations and 50% discount on DDSG steamers between Passau and Linz and 20% on steamers between Melk, Krems, and Vienna. You can purchase up to 5 additional rail days. 2nd-class US$107, each additional day $15. Travelers ages 6-12 travel at half price. The card itself has no photo, so you must carry a valid ID in case of inspections.

VORTEILScard Senior: The ÖBB offers a discount card for women over 60 and men over 65 called the VORTEILScard Senior, available in train stations and most travel agencies. Holders get 45% off train fares, 50% if booked on the web (www.oebb.at), at ticket vending machines, or by phone (☎05 17 17). The card is also valid for 25% off selected steamers, currency exchange at half the charge, and various other benefits. Good in Austria for 1 year. €25.44, requires a photo and proof of age. Call ☎(01) 93 00 03 83 57 for more information. Operators speak German only.

VORTEILScard <26: For students under 26, offers similar benefits as the VORTEILScard Senior. Good in Austria for 1 year. €18.10, requires a photo and ISIC card for non-Austrian students. Call ☎(01) 93 00 03 64 57 for information. Operators speak German.

VORTEILScard Behinderte: For disabled travelers, offers similar benefits as the VORTEILScard Senior. Good in Austria for 1 year. €18.10, requires ID and proof of disability. Call ☎(01) 93 00 03 64 57 for information. Operators speak German only.

Swiss Transfer Ticket: Good for one round-trip to and from any entry point (airport or border crossing) to any single destination within Switzerland. Both ways must be a single day of travel, no more than a month apart. 2nd-class US$80.

Swiss Card: Same round-trip as the Swiss Transfer Ticket, plus 50% off unlimited rail and bus tickets within the month period between your entry and departure. 2nd-class $116.

SwissPass: Offers unlimited rail travel for a certain number of consecutive days: choose between 4, 8, 15, 22 day-, or 1 month-long, 1st- or 2nd-class passes. It also permits unlimited urban transportation in 36 cities, unlimited travel on some private railways and lake steamers, and 25% discounts on excursions to most mountaintops. 2nd-class 4-day passes start at US$160, 8 days at $225, 15 days at $270, 21 days at $315, and 1 month at $350.

Swiss Saver Pass: Offers the same benefits as the SwissPass at a 15% discount for groups of 2-5 adults traveling together.

Swiss Flexipass: Entitles you to 3, 4, 5, 6, or 8 days of unlimited rail travel within a 1-month period, 1st- or 2nd-class, with the same benefits as the SwissPass. 2nd-class adult passes for 3 days start at US$156, 4 days at $184, 5 days at $212, 6 days at $240, 8 days at $282.

Swiss Saver Flexipass: Offers the same benefits as the Swiss Flexipass at a 15% discount for groups of 2 or more adults traveling together.

EURO DOMINO. Like the Interrail Pass, the Euro Domino pass is available to anyone who has lived in Europe for at least six months; however, it is only valid in one country (which you designate upon buying the pass). Reservations must still be paid for separately. **Supplements** are included for many high-speed trains (e.g., German ICE). The pass must be bought within your country of residence; prices vary by country. Inquire with your national rail company for more information.

EURO-DOMINO PASS (SWITZ.)	3 days	5 days	8 days
2nd class	€101	€123	€156
2nd class youth (under 26)	€80	€100	€130

EURO-DOMINO PASS (AUSTRIA)	3 days	5 days	8 days
2nd class	€104	€130	€169
2nd class youth (under 26)	€76	€94	€112

RAIL-AND-DRIVE PASSES. In addition to simple railpasses, many countries (as well as Europass and Eurail) offer rail-and-drive passes, which combine car rental with rail-travel—a good option for travelers who wish both to visit cities accessible by rail and to make side trips into surrounding areas. Prices range per-person from $371-509, depending on the type of car. Children under the age of 11 cost $165, and to add more days costs $49-89 per day (see p. 46).

DISCOUNTED TICKETS

For travelers under 26, **BU** tickets (Billetes International de Jeunesse; operated by **Wasteels**) are a great alternative to railpasses. Available for international trips within Europe as well as most ferry services, they knock 20-40% off 1st- and 2nd-class fares. Tickets are good for 2 months after purchase and allow stopovers along the normal direct route of the train journey. Issued for a specific international route between two points, they must be used in the direction and order of the designated route and must be bought in Europe. The equivalent for those over 26, **BIGT** tickets provide a 20-30% discount on 1st- and 2nd-class international tickets. Both types of tickets are available from European travel agents, at Wasteels offices (usually in or near train stations), or directly at the ticket counter in some nations. For more info, contact **Wasteels Switzerland** (www.wasteels.ch) or **Wasteels Austria** (www.wasteelsaustria.com).

> **FURTHER READING AND RESOURCES ON TRAIN TRAVEL**
> *Thomas Cook European Timetable,* updated monthly, covers all major and most minor train routes in Europe. In the US, order it from Forsyth Travel Library (US$28; ☎800-367-7984; www.forsyth.com). In Europe, find it at any Thomas Cook Money Exchange Center. Alternatively, buy directly from Thomas Cook (www.thomascook.com).
> *Guide to European Railpasses,* by Rick Steves. Available online and by mail. (US ☎425-771-8303; www.ricksteves.com). Free; delivery $5-6.
> *On the Rails Around Europe: A Comprehensive Guide to Travel by Train,* by Melissa Shales. Thomas Cook Ltd. (US$19).
> *Europe By Eurail 2000,* by Laverne Ferguson-Kosinski. Globe Pequot Press (US$18).
> On the web: Info on rail travel and railpasses (www.raileurope.com) and point-to-point fares and schedules (www.raileurope.com/us/rail/fares_schedules/index.htm.) allow you to calculate whether buying a railpass would save you money; European railway server with links to rail servers throughout Europe (http://mercurio.iet.unipi.it/home.html).

BY BUS

Just like the railroads, the bus networks of Austria and Switzerland are extensive, efficient, and comfortable; it may be difficult to negotiate the route you need, but short-haul buses can reach rural areas inaccessible by train. Bus stations are usually adjacent to the train station. The efficient **Austrian system** consists mainly of orange BundesBuses that serve mountain areas inaccessible by train. Buy tickets at the station or from the driver. For buses in heavily touristed areas during high season (such as the Großglocknerstraße in summer), you should probably make reservations. Anyone can buy discounted tickets, valid for one week, for any particular route. Trips can be interrupted under certain conditions, depending on your ticket—be sure to ask. Small, regional bus schedules are available for free at most post offices. For more bus information, call ☎(0222) 711 01 within Austria (from outside Austria dial 1 instead of 0222) from 7am to 8pm Austrian time.

In **Switzerland,** PTT Post Buses connect rural villages and towns. SwissPasses are valid on many buses; Eurailpasses are not. Even with the SwissPass, you might have to pay extra (5-10SFr) if you're riding one of the direct, faster buses. In cities, public buses transport commuters and shoppers alike to outlying areas. Buy tickets in advance at automatic machines, found at most bus stops. The system works on an honor code and inspections are infrequent, but expect to be hit for 50-60SFr if you're caught riding without a valid ticket. *Tageskarten,* valid for 24hr. of free travel, run around 7.50SFr, but most Swiss cities are walkable.

As with railpasses, **international bus passes** typically allow unlimited travel on a hop-on, hop-off basis between major European cities. In general, these services tend to be more popular among non-American backpackers. Try **Busabout** (UK ☎020 7950 1661; www.busabout.com), which sells both two-week, consecutive-day passes (US$339, students US$309) and season passes (US$1149/1039).

BY CAR

Cars offer speed, freedom, access to the countryside, and an escape from the town-to-town mentality of trains. Unfortunately, they also insulate you from the esprit de corps of rail traveling. Although a single traveler won't save by renting or leasing a

BY CAR ■ 47

car, three or four usually will. Before setting off, know the laws of the countries in which you'll be driving (e.g., no right turn on red allowed anywhere in Austria or Switzerland). The **speed limit** in Austria is 50kph (31mph) within cities unless otherwise indicated; outside towns, the limit is 130kph (81mph) on highways and 100kph (62mph) on all other roads. In Switzerland, the speed limits are 50kph in cities, 80kph on open roads, and 120kph on highways. In both countries, all people in every car must wear **seat belts** or face heavy fines. Children under 12 may not sit in the front passenger seat unless a child's seat belt or a special seat is installed. Driving under the influence of alcohol is a serious offense—fines begin at €400 and violators may also lose their licenses. Also, when factoring in cost, be aware that gas in Europe is significantly more expensive than in the US.

The **Association for Safe International Road Travel (ASIRT;** 11769 Gainsborough Rd., Potomac, MD 20854, USA; ☎301-983-5252; www.asirt.org) can provide more specific information about road conditions. ASIRT considers road travel (by car or bus) to be relatively safe in both Austria and Switzerland. With armies of mechanized road crews ready to remove snow at a moment's notice, roads at altitudes of up to 1500m generally remain open throughout winter. (Mountain driving does present special challenges, however; see p. 16). However, many small Austrian and Swiss towns forbid cars entirely; others forbid only visitors' cars, require special permits, or restrict driving hours. EU citizens driving in Austria and Switzerland don't need special documentation—registration and license will suffice. All cars must carry a first-aid kit and a red emergency triangle. Emergency phones are located along all major highways. The **Austrian Automobile, Motorcycle, and Touring Club** (**ÖAMTC;** ☎(01) 71 19 90) provides a English-language service and sells a set of eight detailed road maps, far superior to those offered by tourist offices . The **Swiss Touring Club,** 4 Chemin de Blandonnet, 1214 Vernier, Case Postale 820 (☎(022) 417 27 27; www.tcs.ch) operates road patrols that assist motorists in need.

DRIVING PERMITS. In both Austria and Switzerland, you must be at least 18 in order to drive. If you plan to drive a car while in **Austria,** and are not a citizen of an EU country, you must have an International Driving Permit (IDP) in addition to your driver's license. Most car rental agencies in **Switzerland** don't require the permit, but it may be a good idea to get one anyway, in case you're in a situation (e.g. an accident or stranded in a smaller town) where the police do not know English. IDPs are printed in 10 languages, including German, French, and Italian.

Your IDP, valid for one year, must be issued in your own country before you depart. An application for an IDP usually needs to include one or two photos, a current local license, an additional form of identification, and a fee. To apply, contact the national or local branch of your home country's Automobile Association.

CAR INSURANCE. Most credit cards cover standard insurance. If you rent, lease, or borrow a car, you will need a **green card,** or **International Insurance Certificate,** to certify that you have liability insurance and that it applies abroad. Green cards can be obtained at car rental agencies, car dealers (for those leasing cars), some travel agents, and some border crossings. Rental agencies may require you to purchase theft insurance in countries that they consider to have a high risk of auto theft.

RENTING A CAR. To rent a car in **Austria,** you must be at least 21 for most companies (and 23 or 25 for others) and carry both an International Driver's Permit and a valid driver's license that you have had for at least one year (see p. 46). Most Austrian companies restrict travel into Hungary, the Czech Republic, Poland, and Slovakia. Rental taxes are high (21%). In **Switzerland,** the minimum rental age is 21 but also varies by company. You must possess a valid driver's license that you have had for at least one year (foreign licenses are generally valid). In both countries, drivers under 25 must often pay a daily surcharge.

Rates for all cars rented in Switzerland and Austria include an obligatory annual road toll, called a *vignette* (40SFr per year in Switzerland; €7.60 per ten days, €72.60 per year in Austria).

It is significantly less expensive to reserve a car from the US than while in Europe. Expect to pay US$200-400 per week, plus tax, for a very small car. Reserve ahead and pay in advance if at all possible. Always check if prices quoted include tax, unlimited mileage, and insurance. Ask about discounts and check the terms of insurance, particularly the size of the deductible. Ask airlines about special fly-and-drive packages; you may get up to a week of free or discounted rental.

Auto Europe (US and Canada ☎888-223-5555 or 207-842-2000; www.autoeurope.com).

Avis, (US ☎800-230-4898, Canada 800-272-5871, UK 0870 6060100, Australia 136 333; New Zealand 0800 65 51 11; www.avis.com).

Budget (US and Canada ☎800-527-0700, Quebec 800-268-8900, UK 1442 28-0181; www.budgetrentacar.com).

Europe by Car (US ☎800-223-1516 or 212- 581-3040; www.europebycar.com).

Europcar International, 3 Avenue du Centre, 78 881 Saint Quentin en Yvelines Cedex, France (☎(30) 44 90 00, US 678-461-9880; www.europcar.com).

Hertz (US ☎800-654-3001, Canada 0800-263-0600, UK 0990 99 66 99; Australia 9698 2555; www.hertz.com).

Kemwel (US ☎800-576-1590; www.kemwel.com).

LEASING. For longer than 17 days, leasing can be cheaper than renting; it is often the only option for those ages 18 to 21. The cheapest leases are agreements to buy the car and then sell it back to the manufacturer at a prearranged price. As far as you're concerned, though, it's a lease and doesn't entail enormous financial transactions. Leases generally include insurance coverage and are not taxed. The most affordable ones usually originate in Belgium, France, or Germany. Expect to pay around US$1100-1800 (depending on size of car) for 60 days. Contact **Auto Europe, Europe by Car,** or **Kemwel Holiday Autos** (see above) before you go.

ROADSIDE ASSISTANCE
In **Austria,** call ☎**120.**
In **Switzerland,** call ☎**140.**

BY AIR

Flying across Europe on regularly scheduled flights can devour your budget, but if you are short on time you might consider it. Several European airlines offer coupon packets that discount the cost of each flight leg. Most are only available as tack-ons to their transatlantic passengers, but some are available as stand-alone offers. Most must be purchased before departure. There are several useful links at http:// www.savvytraveler.com/show/marketplace/2002/20020430.shtml.

Europe by Air: www.europebyair.com. Coupons good on 24 partner airlines to 130 European cities in 27 countries. Must be purchased prior to departure; available only to non-European residents. US$99 each, excluding airport tax.

Austrian Airlines: US ☎800-843-0002; www.austrainair.com/greatdeals/ europe_airpass.html. "Discover European Airpass," offers discounted coupons (3 min., 10 max.) to American travelers for flights with AA and its partners. Transatlantic flights from New York or Washington to Vienna only; prices vary based on flight mileage, and coupons must be used within a 90-day period.

Lufthansa: US ☎800-645-3880; www.lufthansa-usa.com. "Eurofare" is available only to US travelers booked on transatlantic Lufthansa flights. Generally involves $89 flights with Lufthansa to anywhere within Europe.

BY BICYCLE

Many airlines will count your bike as your second free piece of luggage; a few charge extra (US$60-110 one-way). Many airlines sell bike boxes at the airport (US$10). Most ferries let you take your bike for free or for a nominal fee, and you can always ship your bike on trains and buses as long as there is extra room (for busy travel days, consider reserving a spot in advance). For more info, see the Swiss Federal Railway's web site (http://s26282.sbb.ch/pv/ veloselb_e.htm). *Let's Go* lists bike rental shops in the Practical Information for most cities and towns.

For info about touring routes, consult national or local tourist offices. The **Touring Club Suisse,** Chemin de Blandonnet 4, Case Postale 820, 1214 Vernier/Geneva (☎ (022) 417 27 27; www.tcs.ch), is a good source of information, offering maps, route descriptions, and mileage charts. Also check www.cycling-in-switzerland.ch for routes and travel advisories for cyclists. In Austria, **www.radtouren.at** maintains a list of long-distance bike routes (many not open to cars) throughout Austria.

If you're planning on doing long distance touring, you'll need **panniers** in which you can pack your luggage, a good **helmet** (US$25-50) and a good U-shaped **Citadel** or **Kryptonite lock** (from US$30). For equipment, **Bike Nashbar,** 6103 State Rte. 446, , Youngstown, OH 44406 (US ☎877-688-8600; www.nashbar.com), beats all competitors' offers and ships anywhere in the US or Canada. A good resource is *Europe by Bike,* by Karen and Terry Whitehall (US$15); try **Mountaineers Books,** 1001 S.W. Klickitat Way #201, Seattle, WA 98134 (US ☎800-553-4453 or 800-568-7604; www.mountaineers.org). Know how to change a tire. A few simple tools and a good bike manual will be invaluable.

If you are nervous about striking out on your own, **Blue Marble Travel** (US ☎800-258-8689 or 215-923-3788, Canada 519-624-2494; www.bluemarble.org) offers bike tours for small groups for those ages 20 to 50 through Austria. **CBT Tours,** (US ☎800-736-2453; www.cbttours.com), offers full-package seven- to 13-day biking, mountain biking, and hiking tours to Switzerland.

BY MOPED & MOTORCYCLE

If you've never been on a **moped** before, twisting alpine roads are not the place to start. However, mopeds can be put on trains and ferries, and are a good compromise between the high cost of car travel and the limited range of bicycles. Always wear a helmet and never ride with a backpack. Expect to pay about US$20-35 per day; try auto repair shops and remember to bargain. **Motorcycles** are more expensive and normally require a license, but are better for long distances. **Bosenberg Motorcycle Excursions,** Mainzer Str. 54, 55545 Bad Kreuznach, Germany (☎(49) 67 16 73 12; www.bosenberg.com) arranges tours in Austria and Switzerland and rents motorcycles (Apr.-Oct.); they have gateways in Zurich and Bern (contact the German office). Before renting, ask if the price includes tax and insurance. Avoid handing your passport over as a deposit; pay ahead of time instead. *Europe by Motorcycle*, by Gregory Frazier (Arrowstar Publishing; US$20), is helpful for planning your itinerary and making arrangements.

BY THUMB

Hitching means entrusting your life to a random person who stops beside you on the road and risking theft, assault, sexual harassment, and unsafe driving. In Austria and Switzerland, men and women traveling in groups and men traveling alone might consider hitching (called "Reisen per Autostop") beyond the range of bus or train routes. If you're a woman traveling alone or even with another woman, don't hitch. If you do decide to hitch, where you stand is vital. Hitching (or even standing) on super-highways is usually illegal: one may only thumb at rest stops or at the entrance ramps to highways. Most Europeans signal with an open hand, rather than a thumb; many write their destination on a sign in large, bold letters. Safety-minded hitchers avoid getting in the back of a two-door car and never let go of their backpacks. They will not get into a car that they can't get out of again in a hurry. If they ever feel threatened, they insist on being let off, regardless of where they are. Acting as if they are going to open the car door or vomit on the upholstery will usually get a driver to stop.

> **HITCHHIKERS BEWARE.** *Let's Go* strongly urges you to seriously consider the risks before hitching. We do not recommend it as a safe means of transportation, and none of the information presented here is intended to do so.

Most large cities in Austria and Switzerland offer a **ride service** (listed as *Mitfahrzentrale* in the **Practical Information**), a cross between hitchhiking and the ride boards common at many universities, which pairs drivers with riders. The fee varies according to destination. Be aware that not all of these organizations necessarily screen drivers and riders; ask in advance.

SPECIFIC CONCERNS

WOMEN TRAVELERS

Women travelers will likely feel safer in Austria and Switzerland than just about anywhere in the world—violent crime is rare and civility is a deeply ingrained cultural standard. It's easy to be adventurous without taking undue risks. If you are concerned, you might consider staying in hostels which offer single rooms that lock from the inside or in religious organizations that offer rooms for women only. Some travelers report that carrying pictures of a "husband" or "children" is extremely useful to help document marriage status.

When traveling, always carry extra money for a phone call, bus, or taxi. Choose train compartments occupied by other women or couples, and consider approaching older women or couples for directions if you're lost or feel uncomfortable. Look as if you know where you're going (even when you don't). Don't hesitate to seek out a police officer or a passerby if you are being harassed. Memorize the emergency numbers in places you visit, and consider carrying a whistle on your keychain. A self-defense course will both prepare you for a potential attack and raise your level of awareness of your suroundings. Also be sure you are aware of the health concerns women face when traveling. *Let's Go: Austria & Switzerland* lists emergency numbers (including rape crisis lines) in the **Practical Information** listings of most cities.

> **FURTHER READING: WOMEN TRAVELERS**
> *A Journey of One's Own: Uncommon Advice for the Independent Woman Traveler*, by Thalia Zepatos. Eighth Mountain Press (US$17).
> *Travelers' Tales: Gutsy Women, Travel Tips and Wisdom for the Road*, by Marybeth Bond. Traveler's Tales (US$8).
> *A Foxy Old Woman's Guide to Traveling Alone*, by Jay Ben-Lesser. Crossing Press. (US$11).
> *More Women Travel: Adventures, Advice & Experience*, by Miranda Davies and Natania Jansz. Penguin Books (US$16.95).

TRAVELING ALONE

There are many benefits to traveling alone, including independence and greater interaction with locals. On the other hand, any solo traveler is a more vulnerable target of harassment and street theft. As a lone traveler, try not to stand out as a tourist, look confident, and be especially careful in deserted or very crowded areas. If questioned, never admit you are traveling alone. Maintain regular contact with someone at home who knows your itinerary. For more tips, pick up *Traveling Solo* by Eleanor Berman (Globe Pequot Press, US$17) or subscribe to **Connecting: Solo Travel Network,** 689 Park Road, Unit 6, Gibsons, BC V0N 1V7 Canada (☎604-886-9099; www.cstn.org; membership US$35). **Travel Companion Exchange,** P.O. Box 833, Amityville, NY 11701, USA (☎631-454-0880, or in the US ☎800-392-1256; www.whytravelalone.com; US$48) will link solo travelers with companions with similar travel habits and interests. **Contiki Holidays** (888-CONTIKI; www.contiki.com) offers a variety of European packages designed for 18- to 35-year-olds. Tours include accommodations, transportation, guided sightseeing and some meals; most average about $65 per day.

OLDER TRAVELERS

Seniors often qualify for hotel and restaurant discounts as well as discounted admission to many tourist attractions. If you don't see a senior citizen price listed, ask and you may be pleasantly surprised. In general for Switzerland, women over 62 and men over 65 qualify as seniors; in Austria, it's women over 60 and men over 65. A **Seniorenausweis** (Senior Citizen Identification Card) entitles holders to a 50% discount on all Austrian federal trains and Bundes-Buses, and works as an ID for discounted museum admissions. The card costs €25.40, requires a passport photo and proof of age, and is valid for one calendar year. It is available in Austria at railroad stations. Both National Tourist Offices offer guides for senior citizens. Many discounts require proof of status, so prepare to be carded. Agencies for senior group travel are growing in enrollment and popularity. Here are a few:

Elderhostel, 11 Ave. de Lafayette, Boston, MA 02110, USA (☎877-426-8056; www.elderhostel.org). Organizes 1- to 4-week "educational adventures" in Austria and Switzerland on varied subjects for those 55+.

The Mature Traveler, P.O. Box 15791, Sacramento, CA 95852, USA (☎800-460-6676). Deals, discounts, and travel packages for the 50+ traveler. Subscription $30.

Walking the World, P.O. Box 1186, Fort Collins, CO 80522, USA (☎800-340-9255; www.walkingtheworld.com), organizes trips for 50+ travelers to Switzerland.

FURTHER READING: OLDER TRAVELERS

No Problem! Worldwise Tips for Mature Adventurers, by Janice Kenyon. Orca Book Publishers (US$16).

A Senior's Guide to Healthy Travel, by Donald L. Sullivan. Career Press. (US$15).

Unbelievably Good Deals and Great Adventures That You Absolutely Can't Get Unless You're Over 50, by Joan Rattner Heilman. Contemporary Books (US$13).

Have Grandchildren, Will Travel. Pilot Books (US$10).

GAY & LESBIAN TRAVELERS

Austria and Switzerland are relatively conservative countries. In the rural countryside especially, public displays of homosexuality may be unwelcome. However, more cosmopolitan and tolerant cities such as Geneva, Zurich, and Vienna have a wide variety of homosexual organizations and establishments, from biker and Christian groups to bars and barber shops. The German adjective for gay is *schwul* (sh-VOOL); for lesbian, *lesbisch* (LEZ-bisch); the collective nouns are *Schwul* and *Lesbe.* Bisexual is *bisexual* or simply *bi* (bee). In French, *homosexuelle* can be used for both men and women, but the preferred terms are *gai* (geh) and *lesbienne* (les-bee-YENN).

The age of consent in **Austria** is 18 for gay men, 14 for lesbians. **Homosexuelle Initiative (HOSI;** www.hosi.at) is a nationwide organization with offices in most cities that provides information on gay and lesbian establishments, resources, and supports, as well as publishing warnings about aggressively intolerant areas and establishments. HOSI Wien, II, Novarag. 40, Vienna (☎/fax (01) 216 66 04; www.hosiwien.at), publishes Austria's leading gay and lesbian quarterly magazine, the *Lambda-Nachrichten.* The age of consent for everyone in **Switzerland** is 16. **The Pink Cross** (office@pinkcross.ch) hosts Switzerland's nationwide lesbian, gay, and bisexual information hotline. **Rainbowline** (☎(084) 880 50 80) is in German, French, English, and Italian. **Dialogai,** headquartered in Geneva at 11-13 r. de la Navigation (mailing address Case Postale 69, 1211, Geneva 21; ☎(022) 906 40 40; www.dialogai.org), provides gay and lesbian information for French-speaking Switzerland.

Gay's the Word, 66 Marchmont St., London WC1N 1AB (☎(+44) 20 72 78 76 54; www.gaystheword.co.uk). The largest gay and lesbian bookstore in the UK, with both fiction and non-fiction titles. Mail-order service available.

Giovanni's Room, 1145 Pine St., Philadelphia, PA 19107 US (☎215-923-2960; www.queerbooks.com). An international lesbian/feminist and gay bookstore with mail-order service (carries many of the publications listed below).

International Lesbian and Gay Association (ILGA), 81 r. Marché-au-Charbon, B-1000 Brussels, Belgium (☎/fax +32 (2) 502 24 71; www.ilga.org). Not a travel service; provides political information, including homosexuality laws of individual countries.

TRAVELERS WITH DISABILITIES

Austria and Switzerland are relatively accessible to travelers with disabilities (*behinderte Reisende*). Disabled visitors to **Austria** may want to contact the Vienna Tourist Board, Obere Augartenstr. 40, A-1025 Vienna (☎(01) 211 14; www.info.wien.at), which offers booklets on accessible Vienna hotels and a guide to the city for the disabled. The Austrian National Tourist Offices in New

ESSENTIALS

> **FURTHER READING: GAY AND LESBIAN TRAVELERS**
>
> *Spartacus International Gay Guide.* Bruno Gmunder Verlag. (US$33).
>
> *Damron Men's Guide, Damron Road Atlas, Damron's Accommodations,* and *The Women's Traveller.* Damron Travel Guides (US$14-19). Call US ☎415-255-0404 or 800-462-6654, or check their web site (www.damron.com).
>
> *Ferrari Guides' Gay Travel A to Z, Ferrari Guides' Men's Travel in Your Pocket, Ferrari Guides' Women's Travel in Your Pocket,* and *Ferrari Guides' Inn Places.* Ferrari Guides (US$14-16). For more info, call ☎602-863-2408 or 800-962-2912 or visit www.q-net.com.
>
> *The Gay Vacation Guide: The Best Trips and How to Plan Them,* by Mark Chesnut. Citadel Press (US$15).

York and Vienna offer many pages of listings for wheelchair-accessible sights, museums, and lodgings in Vienna. With three days' notice, the Austrian railways will provide a wheelchair for the train. The international wheelchair icon indicates access. In **Switzerland,** disabled travelers can contact Mobility International Schweiz, Frogurbstr. 4, 4600 Olten (☎(062) 206 88 35; www.misinfothek.ch). Most Swiss buildings and restrooms have ramps. The Swiss Federal Railways have wheelchair access for most of their cars, and InterCity and long-distance express trains have wheelchair compartments.

Rail is probably the most convenient form of travel for disabled travelers in Austria and Switzerland, but you have to be willing to ask for assistance. Many trains have a special compartment reserved for disabled travelers. Guide-dog owners should inquire as to the specific quarantine policies of each destination country. At the very least, they will need to provide a certificate of immunization against rabies. Hertz, Avis, and National car rental agencies have hand-controlled vehicles at some locations. The following organizations might be of assistance:

Mobility International USA (MIUSA), P.O. Box 10767, Eugene, OR 97440, USA (☎541-343-1284 voice and TDD; www.miusa.org). Sells *A World of Options: A Guide to International Educational Exchange, Community Service, and Travel for Persons with Disabilities* (US$35).

Moss Rehab Hospital Travel Information Service (www.mossresourcenet.org). An information center on travel concerns for those with disabilities.

Society for the Advancement of Travel and Hospitality (SATH), 347 Fifth Ave., #610, New York, NY 10016 (☎212-447-7284; www.sath.org). An advocacy group that publishes the quarterly travel magazine *OPEN WORLD* (free for members, US$13 for nonmembers). Also publishes a wide range of info sheets on disability travel facilitation and destinations. Annual membership US$45, students and seniors US$30.

TOUR AGENCIES

Directions Unlimited, 123 Green Ln., Bedford Hills, NY 10507, US (☎914-241-1700 or 800-533-5343; www.travel-cruises.com). Specializes in arranging individual and group vacations, tours, and cruises for the physically disabled.

Flying Wheels Travel Service, 143 W. Bridge St., Owatonne, MN 55060, US (☎507-451-5005; www.flyingwheelstravel.com). Arranges trips for groups and individuals in wheelchairs or with other sorts of limited mobility.

ESSENTIALS

FURTHER READING: DISABLED TRAVELERS.
Resource Directory for the Disabled, by Richard Neil Shrout. Facts on file (US$45).
Wheelchair Through Europe, by Annie Mackin. Graphic Language Press (☎ 760-944-9594; http://wheelchairtravel.tripod.com; booklets US$13; on CD $20).
Global Access (www.geocities.com/Paris/1502/disabilitylinks.html) has specific links for disabled travelers in Switzerland, as well as general links.

MINORITY TRAVELERS

Although Austria and Switzerland are predominantly white, they are, as a general rule, tolerant of minority travelers. Most minority travelers will not have difficulty, though the farther you venture into the countryside, the more likely it is that you will encounter the occasional odd stare. Villagers are notoriously curious, so don't be surprised or offended if old women linger in their windows to catch a glimpse of you. In recent years, a growing population of foreign workers (particularly Turks) has felt the sting of Swiss anxiety about economic recession, but physical confrontations are rare. Anti-Semitism is not a problem affecting tourists in either country. As anywhere, however, if you feel uncomfortable in your surroundings, don't discount your instincts.

TRAVELERS WITH CHILDREN

Family vacations often require a slower pace and prior planning, but that doesn't mean they can't be done cheaply. Austria and Switzerland are decidedly family-friendly, offering transportation discounts and a plethora of attractions. Children under 6 travel free on Austrian trains and children ages six to twelve for half-price. The **Swiss Family Card** (see Railpasses, p. 43) lets children under 16 travel free with at least one parent holding a valid ticket. Children under 16 travel alone at half price.

Young children's needs can limit your choice of lodging; call ahead to make sure *Pensionen* are child-friendly. Make sure each child, no matter how young, has a valid passport. Be sure that your child carries some sort of ID in case of an emergency or if he/she gets lost, and arrange a reunion spot in case of separation when sightseeing.

FURTHER READING: TRAVELERS WITH CHILDREN.
Adventuring with Children: An Inspirational Guide to World Travel and the Outdoors, Nan Jeffrey. Avalon House Publishing (US$15).
Backpacking with Babies and Small Children, by Goldie Silverman. Wilderness Press (US$10).
Gutsy Mamas: Travel Tips and Wisdom for Mothers on the Road, by Marybeth Bond. Travelers' Tales, Inc. (US$8).
Have Kid, Will Travel: 101 Survival Strategies for Vacationing With Babies and Young Children, by Claire and Lucille Tristram. Andrews and McMeel (US$9).
Trouble Free Travel with Children, by Vicki Lansky. Book Peddlers (US$9).

RELIGIOUS CONCERNS

While the predominance of Catholics and Protestant churches make it simple for anyone of those faiths to find a place to worship, the same task can be challenging for those of other faiths.

Buddhist communities have centers in **Vienna** (Fleischmarkt 16, 1st fl., A-1010 Vienna; ☎(01) 513 38 80; bodhidharma.zendo@blackbox.at); **Innsbruck** (An der Furt 18, II., A-6020 Innsbruck; ☎/fax (0512) 36 71 13; aldo.deutsch@uibk.ac.at); and **Salzburg** (Schloßstr. 38, A-5020 Salzburg; ☎/fax (62) 74 75 16; sunyata@magnet.at).

Jehovah's Witnesses can check www.watchtower.org for more information.

Jewish visitors to Vienna can contact **The Jewish Welcome Service** (☎(01) 533 27 30). **The Jewish Community Center,** Seitenstetteng. 4, Postfach 145, A-1010 Vienna (☎(01) 53 10 40; fax 533 15 17), is a good resource for information elsewhere in Austria. Open M-Th 8am-5pm, F 8am-2pm. Switzerland has its own version, the **Federation of Swiss Jewish Communities,** Gotthardstr. 65, 8002 Zurich (☎(01) 201 55 83; fax (01) 202 16 72). Or consult *The Jewish Travel Guide,* which lists synagogues, kosher restaurants, and Jewish institutions in over 100 countries, available in Europe from Vallentine Mitchell Publishers, Crown House, 47 Chase Side, Southgate, London N14 5BP, UK (☎(020) 89 20 21 00; fax (020) 844 85 48) and in the US ($20.95) from ISBS, 5824 NE Hassalo St., Portland, OR 97213 (☎800-944-6190).

Mormons in Switzerland can visit the temple in Zollikofen, near Bern (Templestr. 2, CH-3052 Zollikofen; ☎(031) 915-5252). For Austria, www.ettl.co.at/mormon/english.

Muslims can turn to www.islam.ch (available in German, French, or Italian) for information and mosque addresses throughout Switzerland.

DIETARY CONCERNS

Vegans will likely have difficulty outside of large cities, but **ovo-lacto vegetarians** can enjoy many traditional meatless dishes. The travel section of the Vegetarian Resource Group's website (www.vrg.org/travel), has a comprehensive list of organizations and websites that are geared toward helping vegetarians and vegans traveling abroad. The website www.vegdining.com has an excellent database of vegetarian and vegan restaurants worldwide. For more information, visit your local bookstore or health food store, and consult *The Vegetarian Traveler: Where to Stay If You're Vegetarian, Vegan, Environmentally Sensitive,* by Jed and Susan Civic (Larson Publications; US$16).

Travelers who keep **kosher** should contact synagogues in larger cities for information on kosher restaurants. The Swiss National Tourist Office distributes the pamphlet *The Jewish City Guide to Basel.* Also see **Religious Concerns,** above. **Diabetic travelers** can pick up *The Diabetic Traveler* by Davida F. Kruger. American Diabetes Association ($14.95).

FURTHER RESOURCES

TRAVEL BOOK PUBLISHERS AND BOOKSTORES

Hippocrene Books, Inc., 171 Madison Ave., New York, NY 10016 (☎212-685-4371, orders 718-454-2366; www.hippocrenebooks.com). Free catalog. Publishes foreign language dictionaries and foreign language guides.

Adventurous Traveler Bookstore, P.O. Box 2221, Williston, VT 05495, USA (☎800-282-3963 or 802-860-6776; www.adventuroustraveler.com).

Bon Voyage!, 2069 W. Bullard Ave., Fresno, CA 93711, USA (☎800-995-9716, from abroad 559-447-8441; www.bon-voyage-travel.com). They specialize in Europe but have titles pertaining to other regions as well. Free catalog.

Travel Books & Language Center, Inc., 4437 Wisconsin Ave. NW, Washington, D.C. 20016 (☎800-220-2665 or 202-237-1322; www.bookweb.org). Over 60,000 titles from around the world.

THE INTERNET

> **WWW TIPS.**
> The **domain** for many Swiss web sites is .ch; Austria's is .at.
> Search for Swiss sites at **www.search.ch** and Austrian sites at **www.search.at.**

LEARNING THE ART OF BUDGET TRAVEL

How to See the World: www.artoftravel.com. A compendium of great travel tips, from cheap flights to self-defense to interacting with local culture.

Rec. Travel Library: www.travel-library.com. A fantastic set of links for general information and personal travelogues.

Backpacker's Ultimate Guide: www.bugeurope.com. Tips on packing, transportation, and where to go. Also tons of country-specific travel information.

Backpack Europe: www.backpackeurope.com. Helpful tips, a bulletin board, and links.

INFORMATION ON AUSTRIA AND SWITZERLAND

Foreign Language for Travelers: www.travlang.com. Provides free online translating dictionaries and lists of phrases in French, German, and Italian (among others).

Atevo Travel: www.atevo.com/guides/destinations. Detailed introductions, travel tips, and suggested itineraries.

Youth Hostel Listings: The official hostel web pages for Austria (www.oejhv.or.at/e-choose.htm) and Switzerland (www.jugendherberge.ch) give an overview of all hostels at a glance.

Swiss Introduction: www.myswitzerland.com. Tourism highlights, including virtual tours, hotel booking, and weather reports for Switzerland.

Austrian Introduction: www.austria.org. Official American web site for Austria with information on visas, tourism, business, and culture.

WWW.LETSGO.COM Our website, www.letsgo.com, now includes introductory chapters from all our guides and a wealth of information on a monthly featured destination. As always, our website also has info about our books, a travel forum buzzing with stories and tips, and additional links that will help you make the most of a trip to Austria and Switzerland.

ALTERNATIVES TO TOURISM

When Let's Go started out in 1961, international travel was not widespread; in 2002, nearly 700 million trips were made, projected to be a billion by 2010. This rise in tourism has created an interplay between tourists and the countries they visit. In many cases, including Austria and Switzerland, this interplay is destructive to local economies, environments, and cultures. Travelers interested in the beauty of the Alps have caused the wilderness to be less wild, glaciers to recede, and development to scar the beauty they seek. Travelers looking for Hapsburg culture and Swiss charm have found McDonald's arches incorporated into historic buildings, and a slow erosion of the unique cultures they wish to experience.

For those who would help reverse this trend, there are several ways to strengthen the local culture and environment even as you learn about it. Perhaps the easiest and most ubiquitous option for **sustainable travel** in Austria and Switzerland is study abroad. The rich historical, cultural, and intellectual tradition in these countries has today created a wealth of such options. There are an enormous number of language schools ready to teach you German, French, or Italian. Student exchange programs as well as direct enrollment in foreign universities offer travel experiences that are about as close to the local culture as can be had.

After study abroad, the most common form of alternative travel is work abroad. This option allows the traveler to become a veritable citizen of the host country and thus gain an impressive travel experience unlike any other. Unemployment in both Austria and Switzerland is quite low, and the job market is fairly ripe, especially for travelers with marketable skills. However, laws and regulations can make it difficult to successfully secure both the necessary work permits. The other major downside to working abroad is the intense amount of initiative and preparation required on the part of the traveler. If you want to work abroad in Austria or Switzerland, you will have to do your homework and be well informed.

Perhaps the purest form of sustainable travel is volunteerism, which allows you to actively make a positive difference. Volunteering as a form of travel is an option in both Austria and Switzerland, but it is a limited possibility. Both countries rank among the richest in the world per capita, and neither country has any large-scale social, political, or environmental problems. Combined with the cultural sentiment of self-reliance that has long permeated the region, these facts belie a relatively small number of volunteering opportunities. For more on volunteering, studying, and working in Austria and Switzerland and beyond, consult Let's Go's alternatives to tourism website, **www.beyondtourism.com**.

GENERAL INFORMATION

Alternatives travel options are not nearly as well delineated at it might seem. Work options are often low-paying enough that they seem like volunteer posts. Volunteer positions often require a substantial participation fee, such that they seldom seem to be true "volunteer" positions. Many databases list all types of international experiences, and sometimes what appears as a study abroad program in one database may be listed as a volunteer or work experience somewhere else. Below is a general list of sites catering to a wide variety of countries and types of experience. More specific sites are listed in the introduction to each section.

Before handing your money over to any volunteer or study abroad program, make sure you know exactly what you're getting into. It's a good idea to get the name of **previous participants** and ask them about their experiences, as some programs sound much better on paper than in reality. The **questions** below are a good place to start:

—Will you be the only person in the program? If not, what are the other participants like? How old are they? How much will you be expected to interact with them?

—Is room and board included? If so, what is the arrangement? Will you be expected to share a room? A bathroom? What are the meals like? Do they fit any dietary restrictions?

—Is transportation included? Are there any additional expenses?

—How much free time will you have? Will you be able to travel?

—What kind of safety network is set up? Will you still be covered by your home insurance? Does the program have an emergency plan?

Idealist (www.idealist.org). Perhaps the single most respected and comprehensive online resource for alternatives to tourism, this site offers general advice, listings, huge databases, and links galore. Take some time to discover all that it can provide.

UCI International Opportunities Program (www.cie.uci.edu/iop). The Center for International Education at the University of California, Irvine maintains this site, which breaks down international experience into six different categories, each sporting a large collection of very useful links.

StudyAbroad.com (www.studyabroad.com). This is not just one site, but a large complex of similar sites, each devoted to a different kind of international experience. Mostly, these sites are useful for their search engines, especially those dealing with study abroad opportunities.

GoAbroad.com (www.goabroad.com). Very similar to StudyAbroad.com, but more useful for high school students and adventure travelers.

This Alternatives to Tourism chapter is intended both to help explain how you can set up study, work, and volunteer opportunities in Austria and Switzerland, and to list a number of helpful programs and organizations. Realize, however, that even though we list specific organizations below, they are better used as guides than as necessarily the best or the only choices. Sustainable tourism is much more specific to the individual, and programs that are a good fit for one person may be an awful choice for someone else. There are tons of programs out there, and in keeping with the spirit of sustainable travel, we believe that you will be much better off, and will ultimately have a much more rewarding experience, if you explore possibilities on your own rather than never looking beyond our suggestions.

VOLUNTEERING

Volunteering abroad can be one of the most fulfilling travel experiences possible, especially if you combine it with the thrill of visiting a new place. Volunteering allows you to improve the locations you visit rather than cheapening them by spending money as a tourist or becoming yet another person contributing to the strain on the infrastructure, the private lives of the local residents, and the ecosystem. Volunteers do not drain money from the local economy like those who work abroad, nor do they divert educational resources like those who study abroad.

However, despite the virtues and personal benefits of volunteerism, such opportunities in both Austria and Switzerland are limited. There are no large-scale social issues to be addressed, and both countries cater more directly to tourism than volunteering. Austria especially has strict rules about the role of

VISA INFORMATION
Generally, visas in Austria and Switzerland are not a problem for volunteering placements. For those programs that do exist, the program usually has a special arrangement and will take care of the necessary paperwork, or will at least assist in the process. If not, it will be necessary to obtain a residence permit for either country if you are staying for longer than three months. See the **Essentials** section "Visas, Invitations, and Work Permits" (p. 9).

foreign volunteers. If you are not a citizen of the EU, it is virtually impossible to volunteer in either country without the help of a placement organization or service. Foreign volunteers in Austria and Switzerland tend to work directly for organizations that have set up programs to use short-term volunteers to complete (usually) unskilled-level work for them. These organizations arrange everything, typically including procurement of a visa, and work permit if necessary. The trade-off for this is almost invariably a big participation fee. However, the cost can be worth it for many people, as the fee usually covers airfare, living expenses, logistical details, and availability of a group environment and support system.

Your best bet when considering volunteering options is to do your homework. A first-pass search often will not unveil some of the most reputable, worthy opportunities to be found. There is a dizzying variety of web resources available, including search engines, databases, and websites that list volunteer opportunities. Try the volunteer and teach abroad mirror sites of the websites listed above under General Information (p. 59). For an incredibly comprehensive and well-chosen bibliography of volunteerism-related reading, download the PDF files at **World Volunteer Web:** www.worldvolunteerweb.org/research/bibliography.

GENERAL VOLUNTEERING

Volunteers for Peace (VFP), 1034 Tiffany Rd., Belmont, VT 05730, USA (☎ 802-259-2759; www.vfp.org). 2-3 week community service projects with international volunteers 18+ (some 15+). May-Sept., US$200 registration fee.

International Cultural Youth Exchange (ICYE), Große Hamburger Str. 30, D-10115 Berlin, GER (☎0049 30 28 39 05 50; www.icye.org). Volunteer work placements for youths age 16-30. Limited posting for Austria, but a wide variety in Switzerland. Lists both short- and long-term assignments.

AFS International, 71 West 23rd St., 17th Fl., New York, NY 10010, USA (☎212-807-8686; www.afs.org). Programs in both Austria and Switzerland. Placements with host families for students (16-18 years old) to attend schools abroad for a year, for young adults 18+ in volunteer assignments, and for teachers in volunteer educator posts.

Service Civil International/International Voluntary Service (SCI-IVS), SCI USA, 3213 W. Wheeler St., Seattle, WA 98199, USA (☎/fax 206-350-6585; www.sci-ivs.org). Arranges placement in summer volunteer work camps and middle- and long-term volunteering assignments in Austria and Switzerland. Registration fee US$175.

English Language Teaching Assistant Program (ELTAP), Division of Education, University of Minnesota, Morris, MN 56267, USA (☎320-589-6400; www.eltap.org). Assigns students and adults to posts as English teaching assistants at schools in Switzerland. $300 application fee; program fee (for 3 different 11-week programs) of $2553, which includes room, board, and social and cultural activities. Participants earn UMN course credit for their work or a certificate that can be used on resumés.

STUDYING

Study abroad programs range from basic language and culture courses to semester-long study at a university, often for credit. In order to choose a program that best fits your needs, you will want to research all you can before making your decision—determine costs and duration, as well as what kind of students participate in the program and what sort of accommodations are provided.

In programs that have large groups of students who speak the same language, there is a trade-off. You may feel more comfortable in the community, but you will not have the same opportunity to practice a foreign language or to befriend other international students. For accommodations, dorm life provides a better opportunity to mingle with fellow students, but there is less of a chance to experience the local scene. If you live with a family, there is a potential to build lifelong friendships with natives and to experience day-to-day life in more depth, but conditions can vary greatly from family to family.

The large "study" sections of the databases listed in General Information (p. 59) are helpful, especially **StudyAbroad.com.** Also try **PlanetEdu** (www.planetedu.com) for an amazing wealth of listings from a searchable database.

VISA INFORMATION

Study in **Austria** requires a residence permit *(Aufenhaltserlebnis)*. If you are a citizen of a country normally allowed free entry (see Essentials, p. 9), you can pick this up from the government once you arrive. Otherwise, you must apply in advance with the Austrian embassy in your country. To view the long list of documents necessary for the permit, visit the "Entry & Residence" section of the Austrian Exchange Service's website (www.oead.ad.at/_english/austria/options/index.html).

Study in **Switzerland** for less than three months may not require a visa or residence permit if you are a citizen of a country normally allowed free entry. If not, or the period of study is longer, you must apply for a residence permit from the Swiss embassy in your country. To obtain a permit, you must submit three copies of the permit application (available through the Swiss embassy), a copy of your passport, three passport-sized photos, and proof of your acceptance into a program of study at a Swiss institution.

In some cases, your host institution will take care of visa and residence permit applications, but usually you will be required to apply yourself, or at least pay the necessary fees. Especially in Switzerland, the application process can drag on, often for several months, so make sure to plan far in advance. Ask your host institution for their specific policy and for advice on entry and residence requirements.

UNIVERSITIES

Some American schools still require students to pay them for credits they obtain elsewhere. Most university-level study abroad programs are meant as language and culture enrichment opportunities and therefore are conducted in German or French. Still, many programs offer classes in English and basic language courses. Those relatively fluent in German, French, or Italian, on the other hand, may find it cheaper to enroll directly in a university abroad, although getting college credit may be more difficult. A particularly good resource for finding programs that cater to your interests is the **Institute of International Education** (www.iiepassport.org/webapp/controller/PassportSearchForm), which provides a searchable database with copious numbers of respectable, well-developed programs.

AMERICAN PROGRAMS

American Institute for Foreign Study, College Division, River Plaza, 9 West Broad St., Stamford, CT 06902, USA (☎800-727-2437; www.aifsabroad.com). Runs year-long, semester-long, and summer programs at the University of Salzburg for students 17 or older with proficiency in German.

Institute for the International Education of Students (IES), 33 N. LaSalle St., 15th fl., Chicago, IL 60602, USA (☎800-995-2300; www.IESabroad.org). Offers year-long and semester programs in Vienna. Internship opportunities. US$50 application fee. Scholarships available.

International Student Exchange Program (ISEP), 1616 P Street NW, Ste. 150, Washington, D.C. 20036, USA (☎202-667-8027; www.isep.org). Provides student exchanges from hundreds of schools in the US and a handful of institutions in Australia, Canada, and Great Britain to 3 universities in Switzerland and 3 universities in Austria.

School for International Training, Admissions, Kipling Rd., P.O. Box 676, Brattleboro, VT 05302, USA (☎800-336-1616 or 802-257-7751; www.sit.edu/studyabroad/europe/swiss.html). Semester- and year-long programs in Switzerland for the International Studies, Organizations, and Social Justice Program in Switzerland run US$16,045 including tuition, room, board, personal expenses, and travel cost.

Kentucky Institute for International Studies (KIIS), Murray State University, P.O. Box 9, Murray, KY 42071-0009, USA (270-762-3091; www.kiis.org). Offers summer and semester-long enrollment at their school in Bregenz, for either environmental or cultural course offerings. Course credit given through Murray State University. US$150 application fee. Program fees US$2330 (environmental) or $3350 (cultural).

Global Campus, University of Minnesota, 230 Heller Hall, 271 19th Ave. South, Minneapolis, MN 55455-0430, USA (☎612-626-9000; www.umabraod.umn.edu). Run through the UMN Office of International Programs, Global Campus sponsors a large number of study abroad opportunities (for course credit, depending on your home institution), including 7 in Austria and 3 in Switzerland.

College Consortium for International Studies (CCIS), 2000 P St. NW, Ste. 503, Washington, D.C. 20036, USA (☎800-453-6956; www.ccisabroad.org). Runs programs at Franklin College in Lugano, Switzerland and Salzburg College in Austria. Offers courses in the humanities, social sciences, and business. Summer and semester-long programs.

Central College Abroad, Box 1040, 812 University, Pella, IA 50219, USA (☎800-831-3629; www.central.edu/abroad). Offers internships, as well as summer, semester-, and year-long programs in Austria. US$30 application fee.

PROGRAMS IN AUSTRIA & SWITZERLAND

To find colleges and universities in Austria and Switzerland, head to **General Education Online** (www.findaschool.org).

Webster University, Study Abroad Office, Webster University, 470 E. Lockwood, St. Louis, MO, 63119, USA (☎800-984-6857 or 314-968-6900; www.webster.edu/worldwide_locations.html). Students from around the world can study at Webster Univer-

ALTERNATIVES TO TOURISM

sity's Geneva and Vienna campuses. Both locations offer full-degree programs or summer and semester sessions. All courses are taught in English and fully accredited.

Eidgenössische Technische Hoschschule (ETH; Swiss Federal Institute of Technology), Student Exchange Office, ETH Zentrum, CH-8092 Zurich, Switzerland (☎016 32 61 61; www.mobilitaet.ethz.ch). ETH is a member of the TransAtlantic Science Student Exchange Program (TASSEP), and therefore provides study abroad to students at specific institutions in the US, Canada, and the EU. Also separately runs bilateral exchange agreements with a list of schools in Great Britain, Canada, USA, Singapore, and Australia. Study exchanges with participating schools are generally cheap; inquire with your Study Abroad Office or Chemistry Department if your school participates in the program.

University of Fribourg, American College Program (ACP), American College Program, Admissions, Av. de Beauregard 13, Case postale 25, CH-1701 Friborg, Switzerland (☎026 300 81 90; www.unifr.ch/acp/ind.html). Available from over 100 colleges and universities in the US, the ACP allows students to take a full slate of courses at the University of Fribourg. Students can choose between fall semester, spring semester, and full-year options.

Johannes Kepler University (JKU) Linz, Altenbergerstr. 69, A-4040 Linz, Austria (☎32 24 68; www.studentjobs.jku.edu/e204/exchange/content). Semester- and year-long study available through exchange programs with participating institutions. Offers study in a fully array of academic disciplines.

European University Center for Peace Studies (EPU), Rochusplatz 1, A-7461 Stadtschlaining, Austria (☎33 55 24 98; www.aspr.ac.at/welcome.htm). Winner of the 1995 UNESCO Prize for Peace Education, EPU offers masters degrees and certificates in Peace and Conflict Resolution and Conflict Transformation.

LANGUAGE SCHOOLS

Unlike American universities, language schools are frequently independently run international or local organizations or divisions of foreign universities that rarely offer college credit. Language schools are good alternatives to university study for a directed focus on the language and an easier courseload. These can be better options for younger students who might feel uncomfortable with older students.

As with almost any form of alternative travel, careful research and prioritization are important if you want to have the best experience possible. Schools and programs vary in curriculum, cost, scholarship availabilties, makeup of student body, and location, among other factors. Look into a variety of options before choosing one. There are a number of excellent online databases to aid in your search, including **Campus Austria** (www.campus-austria.at) and the **Institute of International Education** (www.iiepassport.org/webapp/controller/PassportSearchForm).

Eurocentres, 101 N. Union St. Ste. 300, Alexandria, VA 22314, USA (☎703-684-1494; www.eurocentres.com) or in Europe: Head Office, Seestr. 247, CH-8038 Zurich, Switzerland (☎41 1 485 50 40; fax 481 61 24). Language programs (with home-stays) for beginning to advanced students for learning French at several locations in Switzerland.

National Center for Study Abroad (☎414-278-7410; www.nrcsa.com). Preregisters students for 6 schools/programs in Austria and 1 school in Switzerland (see the listing for Eurocentres, above). austrian programs are largely centered around language classes, but some include topics such as Austrian culture and history, music, and ski instructor certification. Prices and dates vary by program.

Wiener Internationale Hochschulkurse, Ebendorserstr. 10, A-1010 Vienna, Austria (☎01 405 12 54; www.univie.ac.at/wihok). Offers German courses for beginners and advanced students. Tuition for a 4-week summer course €338, accommodations €280-432; for a full semester course tuition €600; for a trimester course €245-370.

> **FURTHER READING: STUDYING ABROAD.**
> *Academic Year Abroad.* Institute of International Education Books (US$45).
> *Vacation Study Abroad.* Institute of International Education Books (US$40).
> *Peterson's Study Abroad Guide.* Peterson's (US$30).

OTHER STUDY ABROAD

There exists a wide variety of other study abroad options in Austria and Switzerland beyond programs designed specifically for college credit or for learning languages. Many schools across the country offer courses for foreign students in regionally pertinent subjects, including Austrian and Swiss culture, music, food, and history. There are also schools that offer a full curriculum of courses in many different fields, as well as schools that specialize in specific issues such as environmental education or policy advocacy. There are also schools that offer specific training in a skill or vocation, including those that train students to become hotel managers, ski instructors, and chefs, among other possibilities. Fantastic online resources include **PlanetEdu** (www.planetedu.com) and the **Austrian Press & Information Service** (www.austria.org/jan02/schools.html).

Swiss School of Hotel and Tourism Management, Comercialstraße 19, 7007 Chur, Switzerland (☎0041 812 57 06 64; www.ssh.ch/index2.html). Offers MBAs, BSs, and Swiss diplomas in tourist-industry related fields. Students must be at least 18 years old, have a high school diploma, and speak fluent English. Tuition 19,500SFr per semester.

Experiment in International Living (☎800-345-2929; www.usexperiment.org). Month-long summer programs offering high school students cross-cultural home-stays, community service, ecological adventure, and language training in Switzerland for US$4300.

WORKING

With the advent of the economic freedom associated with the European Union and the widespread proliferation of the Internet, it is becoming both easier and more common for job markets to be international, and for employers and employees to find one another from opposite sides of borders and oceans. Along with many other countries, Austria and Switzerland have seen a rise in the number of opportunities for foreign workers to find jobs within their countries.

Perhaps the easiest way to find work in Austria or Switzerland is through enrollment in a pre-designed work abroad program, similar in feel to study abroad and overseas volunteer placements. In return for rather substantial participation fees, such programs generally handle work permit paperwork, provide employees with housing and sometimes meals, and afford a ready-made social network of others who have traveled from home to work in a foreign country. For many people, especially those whose emphasis is more on short-term travel experience rather than professional advancement, these programs can be attractive options.

However, those whose primary goal is to acquire an in-depth understanding of Swiss or Austrian culture may want to look elsewhere. With the possible exception of direct enrollment in a university, no possible form of sustainable travel comes close to providing the level of cultural integration and understanding that comes with setting up your own independent work experience. Volunteer and study programs inevitably involve some insulation from the local culture, whereas working abroad generally cannot maintain nearly such a divide. As a resident working and living alongside native-born citizens, it is tough to avoid a relatively complete degree of cultural immersion, which brings with it the kind of local sensitivity that sustainable travel tries to bring about.

VISA INFORMATION

Working in **Austria** does not require a visa or work permit for EU or Swiss nationals. For everyone else, it is necessary to apply for a Type D work permit. This must be done by your employer; it is his or her duty to demonstrate that you are not filling a spot that a native Austrian could and would be willing to fill.

Working in **Switzerland** will soon be easier for EU nationals thanks to the Bilateral Agreement on the Free Movement of Persons, which first went into effect on June 1, 2002. After 12 years, all EEA (European Economic Area, of which the EU is a subset) and Switzerland citizens will be able to move freely within participating countries, with no restrictions on where they can work or live, provided they are employed. However, current restrictions are being phased out over a decade. In 2004, Europeans must still apply for a residence permit just like everyone else. In Switzerland, permits are package deals for both work and residence. Standard procedure is to first find a job, and then have your employer apply for the permit. The two most common permits for work abroad are the L permit (generally for less than a year) and the B permit (for one year; renewable). After five years of residence in Switzerland, you can apply for a C permit (permanent; holder is entitled to most privileges of Swiss citizenship).

In general, although permits may be processed quickly, both countries often have significant administrative backlogs. Don't wait until the last minute to find a job or apply for a permit; there is a fair chance that your application will be denied. If so, don't despair. With repeated attempts it's usually possible to find a way to work in Austria or Switzerland. Above all, be patient and persistent.

LONG-TERM WORK

GENERAL RESOURCES

If done independently, arranging to work in a foreign country is not an easy undertaking. Immigration laws in both Austria and Switzerland are strict enough to allow entry only for foreign workers if they are filling a position that no citizen of the country is either able or willing to fill. The first step, therefore, is to secure a job, which can be tricky from abroad. Once you have found a job, you will have to deal with the substantial amount of bureaucratic red tape involved in obtaining a work permit, an apartment, and other necessary arrangements. It is important during the process to remember that with enough persistence, there is almost always a way to eventually find employment and the necessary permits to work in Austria or Switzerland. If it doesn't work the first time, hang in there and keep trying. Do lots of research, and gain as much knowledge as possible about job markets, company hiring, and job availabilities. The listings below can be very useful in making each of these steps manageable.

Association for International Practical Training (AIPT), 10400 Little Patuxent Pkwy. Ste. 250, Colombia, MD 21044-3519, USA (☎410-997-2200; www.aipt.org). Founded in 1948 at MIT, AIPT is a tremendously helpful organization that provides cultural and career exchanges for students, professionals, and companies. Its longest running program is the International Association for the Exchange of Students for Technical Experience (IAESTE) which provides internships for students. Also helps in international job searches, and runs a service that secures work permits for US$250-400.

CDS International, 871 United Nations Plaza, New York, NY 10017-1814, USA (☎212-497-3500; www.cdsintl.org). CDS is an established non-profit providing international career development support, including a work abroad program in Switzerland for US citizens 30 and under. The program provides assistance in finding an employer and support in work authorization for a US$400 fee. Also offers internships, such as the

Culinary Arts and Hospitality Management Internship Program (www.cdsintl.org/capsin-tro.html; US$700 participation fee; open to US citizens age 21-30). CDS also provides general resources for international work experience.

StepStone, UK office: StepStone ASA, 2 Bell Court, Leapale Lane, Guildford, Surrey GU1 4LY (☎44 14 83 73 94 50; www.stepstone.com). An online database covering interna-tional employment openings for most of Europe, including Austria and Switzerland. Sev-eral seach options and a constantly changing list of openings.

INTERNSHIPS

International Association of Students in Economic and Business Management (AIESEC) (http://us.aieseconline.net). Contact info varies for each of the 43 local offices throughout the US. The "world's largest student organization." AIESEC places students in international traineeships (their word for "internship"), including positions in Austria and Switzerland. Traineeships cost $US455, not counting a US$45 non-refund-able application processing fee.

Inernational Education of Students, 33 North LaSalle St., 15th Floor, Chicago, IL 60602, USA (☎800-995-2300 or 312-944-1750; www.iesabroad.org/vienna/vienna.html). Offers a study abroad program through several universities in Vienna. Application for internships with Austrian businesses in business and teaching for stu-dents admitted to the school.

TEACHING ENGLISH

While English teachers are almost always in demand in Austria and Switzer-land, such jobs are rarely well paid, although some elite private American schools can pay competitive salaries. In most cases, you must have at least a bachelors degree to be a full-fledged teacher, although usually college under-graduates can get summer positions teaching or tutoring. Many schools require teachers to have a **Teaching English as a Foreign Language (TEFL)** certifi-cate. This does not necessarily exclude you from finding a teaching job, but certified teachers often find higher paying jobs. Native English speakers work-ing in private schools are often hired for English-immersion classrooms where no German, French, or Italian is spoken.

Placement agencies or university fellowship programs are the best resources for finding teaching jobs in Austria and Switzerland. The alternative is to make contacts directly with schools or to try your luck once you get there. If you are going to try the latter, the best time of the year is several weeks before the start of the school year. The organizations below place teachers in Austria and Switzerland.

International Schools Services (ISS), 15 Roszel Rd., Box 5910, Princeton, NJ 08543-5910, USA (☎609-452-0990; www.iss.edu/edstaff/intschoolsassisted.html). Hires teachers for 2yr. commitments at overseas schools, including a few in Austria and Swit-zerland. Candidates should have experience teaching or with international affairs.

Office of Overseas Schools, US Department. of State, Rm. H328, SA-1, Washington, DC 20522 (☎202-261-8200; www.state.gov/m/a/os/c6776.htm). Maintains a list of schools and agencies that arrange placement for Americans to teach abroad.

AU PAIR WORK

Au pairs are typically women, aged 18-27, who work as live-in nannies, caring for chil-dren and doing light housework in foreign countries in exchange for room, board, and a small spending allowance or stipend. Most former au pairs speak favorably of their experience and of how it allowed them to get to know the country without the high expenses of traveling. Drawbacks, however, often include long hours of constantly being on-duty and the somewhat low pay. In Austria and Switzerland wages range from €75-120 per week, and much of the au pair experience really does depend on with which family you're placed. The agencies below are a good starting point for looking for employment as an au pair.

Au Pair in Europe, P.O. Box 68056, Blakely Postal Outlet, Hamilton, Ontario, L8M 3M7 CAN (☎905-545-6305; www.princeent.com).

Childcare International, Ltd., (☎44 20 89 06 31 16; www.childint.co.uk).

International Au Pair Association (IAPA), Bredgade 25 H, DK-1260 Copenhagen K, Denmark (☎45 33 17 00 66; www.iapa.org).

AupairConnect, Max Global, Inc., 8370 W. Cheyenee Avenua #76, Las Vegas, NV 89129, USA (www.aupairconnect.com).

SHORT-TERM WORK

Short-term work is most easily found through established programs, although it can be managed independently as well. In Austria and Switzerland, short-term work is common in the tourism and hospitality industries. If you have ski instructor certification (usually PSIA or CSIA), you can probably find work as an instructor at a ski resort, especially if you are proficient in German or French.

International Co-operative Education, 15 Spiros Way, Menlo Park, CA 94025, USA (☎650-323-4944; www.icemenlo.com). Finds summer jobs for students in Switzerland. Costs include a US$200 application fee and a US$600 fee for placement.

Hotel Career, BEnzenbergstraße 39-47, D-40219 Düsseldorf, GER (☎49 211 938 89 70; www.hotel-career.com). A great source for finding jobs in the hotel and accommodations industry worldwide, including many listings in Austria and especially Switzerland. Offers a great search engine which, if you look around (knowledge of German is helpful), can lead you to a wide array of seasonal, year-long, and longer career-building positions. Positions suitable for a broad variety of people, from those with no experience to those with several years of experience already on their resumé.

Village Camps, Personnel Office, Dept. 1000, CH-1260 Nyon, Switzerland (☎229 90 94 05; www.villagecamps.com/personnel/about.htm). These summer camps in Leysin, Switzerland and Zell am See, Austria, for 7-18 year olds offer a number of jobs to English-speaking foreign workers. Many positions for citizens of the EU, Australia, NZ, US, Canada, and Switzerland.

FOR FURTHER READING ON ALTERNATIVES TO TOURISM

Alternatives to the Peace Corps: A Directory of Third World and U.S. Volunteer Opportunities, by Joan Powell. Food First Books, 2000 (US$10).

How to Get a Job in Europe, by Sanborn and Matherly. Surrey Books, 1999 (US$22).

How to Live Your Dream of Volunteering Overseas, by Collins, DeZerega, and Heckscher. Penguin Books, 2002 (US$17).

International Directory of Volunteer Work, by Whetter and Pybus. Peterson's Guides and Vacation Work, 2000 (US$16).

International Jobs, by Kocher and Segal. Perseus Books, 1999 (US$18).

Overseas Summer Jobs 2002, by Collier and Woodworth. Peterson's Guides and Vacation Work, 2002 (US$18).

Work Abroad: The Complete Guide to Finding a Job Overseas, by Hubbs, Griffith, and Nolting. Transitions Abroad Publishing, 2000 (US$16).

Work Your Way Around the World, by Susan Griffith. Worldview Publishing Services, 2001 (US$18).

Invest Yourself: The Catalogue of Volunteer Opportunities, published by the Commission of Voluntary Service and Action (☎718-638-8487).

AUSTRIA

The shape and size of Austria has changed so many times in its history that Oskar Bender once said, "To be Austrian is not a geographical concept but a spiritual idea." At the peak of Hapsburg megalomania, the Austrian Empire was one of the largest in history, encompassing much of Europe from Poland and Hungary in the east to The Netherlands in the west. Today it is approximately the size of Maine. Although the mighty empire crumbled during World War I, Austria remains a complex, multi-ethnic country with a unique political and cultural history. The wide range of identities within the empire continues today in the diversity of the nine provinces, or *Bundesländer,* of present-day Austria. Clockwise from the northeast, Austria's provinces are Vienna *(Wien),* Burgenland, Styria *(Steiermark),* Carinthia *(Kärnten),* Tyrol *(Tirol),* Vorarlberg, Salzburg, Upper Austria *(Oberösterreich),* and Lower Austria *(Niederösterreich).* At one time each province was an independent region but later became part of the Hapsburg lands by marriage, treaty, or trade. Today, each retains a deep-rooted character and unique dialect. The mention of Austria evokes images of onion-domed churches set against snow-capped alpine peaks, castles rising from lush meadows of golden flowers, and 10th-century monasteries towering over the majestic Danube. The mountains see tourists year-round; alpine sports dominate the winter scene, while visitors flock to the lakes in the warmer months.

LAND

Austria is a landlocked nation that shares its borders with no fewer than eight countries. It has long been a crucial cog in the machine of European commerce, thanks to the navigable Danube, the only major European river that flows east. The blue-green river has always been central to Austrian industry and aristocracy: both ruling families of early Austria, the Babenbergs and the Hapsburgs, set up residences on its shores. Now, river cruises showcase their ruined castles as well as the vineyards whose fruit sweetened the Middle Ages. The Danube's trade capabilities were enhanced in 1992 with the completion of a canal connecting the Danube to the Rhine and Main rivers, allowing the movement of barges from the North Sea to the Black Sea.

Forests and meadows cover two-thirds of Austria's total land area, and much of the country is studded with mountains. The Alps span the southern and western regions of the country, while the flatter North and East are home to most of the population. The highest point—the *Großglockner*—looms at 3798m (12,457 ft.) in the central Alps, drawing sightseers and adventure seekers. The mining of salt from vast underground deposits has also proved a valuable industry. To the Celts in 500 BC as well as many contemporary towns today, this "white gold" has been an invaluable resource on which many Austrians depend.

FLORA & FAUNA

Since much of Austria remains densely forested, you won't have to go far off the beaten path to discover the rich woodland life. The flowers aren't going anywhere, but wildlife tend to be shy, so keep voices low when you walk or hike. Though you're unlikely to see **ibex** or **marmots** unless you're hiking at high elevations, **red deer, roe deer, hare, foxes, badgers, marten,** and **pheasants** are common to the coun-

TOP TEN LIST

TOP 10 CAFÉS IN AUSTRIA

Although Vienna is the heart of Austrian café culture, many other cities (Salzburg especially) also contain a number of great cafés.

1. **Café Demel,** Vienna (p. 114). Once confectioner for the Hapsburg Imperial Court.
2. **Café Hawelka,** Vienna (p. 114). A down-to-earth family-owned-and-operated café.
3. **Café Tomaselli, Salzburg** (p. 247). A classy café in business for well over 200 years.
4. **Café Traxlmayr, Linz** (p. 296). A crowded, elegant café where you can try the city's delicious *Linzer Torte.*
5. **Café Central, Vienna** (p. 114). Former haunt of Europe's most famous writers, artists, and intellectuals.
6. **Café-Konditorei Grendler, Zell am Ziller** (p. 217). Award-winning desserts are served on the banks of a mountain river.
7. **Café Stein, Vienna** (p. 115). A busy modern alternative to the more classical cafés in Vienna.
8. **Hofgarten Café, Innsbruck** (p. 201). In the middle of Innsbruck's large public park.
9. **Café Willendorf, Vienna** (p. 113). An always-artsy, often-racy café at the heart of Vienna's gay and lesbian scene.
10. Café-Konditorei Hagmann, Krems (p. 306). Serves wonderful desserts in keeping with

try and Central Europe in general. A small bear population lives in the southern mountainous and deeply wooded regions. Lake Neusiedl, Austria's only steppe lake, hosts hundreds of bird species on reed-fringed waters. Austria's national parks, which comprise 3% of the land, are good places to spot protected wildlife.

Oak and beech trees predominate in Austria's vast forests, with fir trees at higher elevations and stone pines in the mountain regions. Colorful alpine flora blanket meadows and mountains alike, including **Edelweiss, heather, alpine rose,** and **blue gentian** (on the back of the Austrian five-cent euro piece). As a courtesy to those who come after you, take only photographs and leave only footprints.

HISTORY

IN THE BEGINNING

The first prehistoric tourists descended on Austria in the form of nomadic hunter-gatherers in about 80,000 BC, initiating the region as a popular and welcoming destination. As the nomads settled, mining salt, farming and domesticating livestock, 6km-thick glaciers crawled north, carving out the alpine valleys of postcard fame today and making room for greater habitation of Austrian lands. The 25,000-year-old carved-stone fertility goddess Venus of Willendorf (so valuable that the Natural History Museum in Vienna displays only a copy) reflects the artistic prowess of this early civilization. By 6000 BC, even the remotest areas of Austria were part of a vigorous commercial network that linked mining centers and agricultural communities, as the recent discovery of the 5300-year-old hunter-trader Ötzi proved.

As economic opportunities moved beyond salt, aggressive peoples fought for a share of wealth. In 500 BC, the **Celts** took control of the salt mines and established the kingdom of **Noricum,** which developed a relatively affluent economy based on a thriving salt and iron trade. In turn, the **Romans** conquered their Austrian neighbors to secure the Danube frontier against marauding Germanic tribes in 15 BC. One of the first Roman military posts was Vindobona, present-day Vienna.

Germanic raids finally forced the Romans to retreat from Noricum in the 5th century. Over the next three centuries, various peoples, including the Huns, Ostrogoths, and Lombards, roamed through the Austrian territories, but none established a lasting settlement. Eventually, three groups divided the region, with **Slavs** in the southwest, **Bavarians** in the north, and **Alemanni** in the south. Bavarian nobles converted peasants to Christianity in an attempt to establish law and order and create a power-base. The Archbishopric of Salzburg, created through their efforts, has remained Austria's ecclesiastical center.

HOLY ROMANS & HAPSBURGS (800-1740)

Charlemagne was the first to make Austria the barrier and meeting point between Eastern and Western Europe by conquering Bavaria in 787. After his death, the German King Otto regained control of the Holy Roman Empire, naming Margrave Liutpoldus (a.k.a. **Leopold of Babenberg**) duke of the Empire's eastern territories in 976. Leopold, a Bavarian lord, was the first ruler Austria called its own. During his reign, Austria gained its name: *Ostarrichi* (Old High German for *Österreich*), which meant "Eastern Realm" of the Empire.

The **Babenbergs**, who served as the Dukes of the Eastern Realm for the next 270 years, claimed Vienna as their home, extending their protectorate through strategic marriages. The Babenburgs made a tidy profit off of international bargains. When Duke Leopold V captured **Richard the Lionheart** on his way home from the Crusades, he chose not to give Richard over to the Holy Roman Emperor, who had put a price on the head of the English king, and instead returned Richard to England for cold, hard cash.

To the detriment of the dynasty, the last Babenberg died childless, leaving the country fragmented for 19 years. Bohemian King Ottokar II, the new Holy Roman Emperor, and the Swiss nobleman **Rudolf of Hapsburg** emerged as the major contenders for control of the Austrian lands. Rudolf had only a small plot of land in Switzerland before he beat out Ottokar in the Battle of Marchfeld in 1278, thereby claiming all of Austria and laying the foundation for six centuries of Hapsburg rule. Like their Babenberg predecessors, the Hapsburgs made every effort to increase their property through treaties and marriages, with memorable success (though they lost their original Swiss holdings after a farmers' revolution). Gradually, the Hapsburgs accumulated the various regions that make up modern Austria plus a few others. The Imperial Crown was passed down through the Hapsburg line until the collapse of the empire in the 19th century. Friedrich expanded the direct claims of the Hapsburg family by strategically betrothing his son, **Maximilian I,** to the heiress of the powerful Burgundian kingdom, giving the Hapsburgs control of much of western Europe, including The Netherlands.

Maximilian is credited with the adaptation of Ovid's couplet: *Bella gerant alii, tu felix Austria nube* ("Let other nations go to war; you, lucky Austria, marry"). Maximilian's son **Philip** married into the Spanish royal house, endowing his son, **Charles V,** with a vast empire that encompassed Austria, The Netherlands, Spain, Burgundy, Spanish America, and Italian and Mediterranean possessions. It was during Charles's reign that the Hapsburg Empire reached its height of power. However, it appears that the power was too much for Charles, who gave the Austrian empire and the crown to his brother **Ferdinand** (and the Spanish possessions to his son Philip) before retiring to the woods to become a monk in 1556. Ferdinand, despite not knowing German, Czech, or Hungarian, managed to add Bohemia and Hungary to the Hapsburg possessions, thanks to another marriage planned earlier by Maximilian.

PROTESTING CHANGE

The massive Hapsburg ship hit rough waters in the 16th and 17th centuries, when Martin Luther's Protestant Reformation swept through the Empire. By the time Ferdinand II assumed control of the Hapsburg empire in 1619, nearly nine-tenths of the population of Austria had been converted to Protestantism.

But Ferdinand II, inspired by his Jesuit education, made Austria the first battleground of the Catholic Counter-Reformation. Resistance by Protestant Bohemian nobles in Prague to Ferdinand's plans sparked Europe's **Thirty Years War** (1618-1648). The Austrian imperial troops promptly (and forcibly) converted most of the peasants back to Catholicism and chased Protestants in the upper classes off to a sympathetic Protestant Germany. This victory was followed by a greater setback at the end of the war with the **Treaty of Westphalia,** in which the Hapsburgs forfeited vast tracts of territory. While Austria recuperated, the Ottoman Turks repeatedly besieged Vienna until the French Prince Franz Eugene drove them out with a Christian relief army. In thanks for his assistance, Eugene was given **Schloß Belvedere** (see p. 131). Eugene again came through for the Hapsburgs when he led their troops to victory over the French in the **War of Spanish Succession,** which ended with a treaty giving Belgium, Sardinia, and parts of Italy to the Hapsburgs.

CASTLES CRUMBLE (1740-1900)

What the Hapsburgs gained in land they sacrificed in stability. Lacking a dominant ethnic group and having had a series of foreign leaders, the empire began to crumble in the 18th century. When **Maria Theresia** ascended to the throne in 1740, her neighbor King Friedrich the Great of Prussia seized Silesia (now southwest Poland); she spent the rest of her life unsuccessfully maneuvering to reclaim it. In the **War of Austrian Succession** (1740-1748), Maria Theresia came to be known as *Landesmutter* (mother of the people). Ironically, her relations with her own progeny weren't as successful. She married her daughter **Marie Antoinette** to the French Prince Louis XVI, a marriage that ended under the guillotine during the French Revolution. The French revolutionaries who killed her daughter soon declared war on Maria Theresia's son, **Joseph II,** who by 1792 was ruling Austria. Under the military genius of young General Napoleon Bonaparte, the Republic of France wrested Belgium and most of Austria's remaining Italian territories from the Hapsburgs. His troops even invaded Vienna, where Napoleon took up residence in Maria Theresia's favorite palace, Schönbrunn (p. 127).

Napoleon's success led to the establishment of a consolidated Hapsburg empire. In 1804, **Franz II** renounced his claim to the now-defunct Holy Roman crown and proclaimed himself Franz I, Emperor of Austria. During the Congress of Vienna, which redrew the map of Europe after Napoleon's defeat, Austrian Chancellor **Clemens Wenzel Lothar von Metternich** masterfully re-unified Austrian power. For the rest of the century, Metternich's foreign policy for Austria was dictated by a desire to maintain monarchical stability throughout Europe. Austria feared the crumbling of the Ottoman Empire to the south and the resulting creation of the new independent Slavic states in the Balkans. Metternich rightly believed that the independence of these states would encourage the Slavic people that comprised half the population of the Hapsburg Empire to fight for their own independence. In order to maintain stability within Austria, Metternich introduced harshly repressive social policies. However, like much of Europe in the first half of the 19th century, Austria is remembered more during this period for technological progress. This progress led to the rise of a stereotypically uninspired middle class, satirized in the character Papa Biedermeier by poet Ludwig Eichrocht. The term **Biedermeier** came to label the bourgeois domestic culture that flourished in this time (see p. 79).

As the Ottoman Empire disintegrated, domestic resistance to Austria's repressive social policies increased, as Metternich had feared. In 1848, students and workers built barricades, took control of the imperial palace, and demanded a constitution and freedom of the press. The revolutionary forces were divided, however, and the government was able to suppress the workers' revolution and a Hungarian rebellion. Epileptic emperor **Ferdinand I,** however, was pressured to abdicate in favor of his nephew, **Franz Josef I,** who ruled for 68 years.

Under **Otto von Bismarck,** Prussia dominated European politics and defeated Austria in 1866. The Austrian fall from power continued in 1867, when the Hungarian parliament voted to end the Austrian Empire and form the dual **Austro-Hungarian Empire,** over which Franz Josef was a figurehead. Still, non-German speakers were marginalized within the new empire until 1907, when the government ceded basic civil rights to all peoples in the Empire and accepted universal male suffrage. These concessions to the Slavic peoples of the Empire came too late. Burgeoning nationalist sentiments, especially among the Serbia-inspired South Slavs, led to severe divisions within the multinational Austro-Hungarian Empire.

THE RISE OF THE REPUBLIC

As the now-free Slavic states of the Ottoman Empire—particularly Serbia—agitated the Slavic elements within the Austro-Hungarian Empire, Franz Josef had to either quiet these forces or relinquish claims to the Slavic half of his empire. When Franz Ferdinand, the heir to the imperial throne, and his wife, Sophie, were assassinated by a young Serbian nationalist in Sarajevo in 1914, Franz Josef finally had an excuse to attack the Serbs. Austria's declaration of war set the dominos falling, and Europe tumbled into **WWI.** Franz Josef died during the war in 1916, leaving the throne to his reluctant grandnephew Charles I. Despite his valiant efforts and those of the army, declarations of independence by the Empire's non-German peoples and the desperate maneuvering of Viennese intellectuals ensured the demise of the monarchy. On November 11, 1918, Charles finally got the peace he had striven for, but only after liberals declared the first **Republic of Austria,** ending the 640-year-old Hapsburg dynasty.

Between 1918 and 1938, Austria had its first bitter taste of parliamentary democracy. After the Treaty of Versailles that ended the first World War forbade a unified *Deutsch-Österreich,* the **First Republic** suffered massive inflation and unemployment, but by the mid-1920s the Austrian government had stabilized the currency and established economic relations with neighboring states. Nonetheless, violent internal strife between political parties weakened the Republic's already shaky democratic foundation. In 1933, the weak coalition government gave way to **Engelbert Dollfuss's** declaration of martial law. In order to protect Austria from Hitler, Dollfuss entered an ill-fated alliance with fascist Italy. Two years later, just as Mussolini and Hitler made peace, Austrian Nazis assassinated Dollfuss. His successor, **Kurt Schuschnigg,** was also ultimately unable to maintain Austrian independence in the face of Nazi pressure.

WORLD WAR II & THE SECOND REPUBLIC

The First Republic ended with the Nazi annexation of Austria. On March 9, 1938, hoping to stave off a Nazi invasion, Schuschnigg called a referendum against unity with Germany, but Hitler demanded Schuschnigg's resignation. On March 12, the new Nazi chancellor invited German troops into Austria, where they met no resistance. Many Austrians believed the *Anschluß* (union with Germany) would improve their future. When the Nazis marched into Vienna on March 14, thousands cheered them on. Austria lost both its name (it became the *Ostmark,* merely the "alpine district") and its self-respect. With the exception of individual resistance fighters, cooperation with the Nazis and anti-Semitism (long an Austrian tradition) became the rule, and a failing Austrian economy began to prosper. While **WWII** raged, Austrian and German Nazis directed the construction of Mauthausen, Austria's main concentration camp, and its 49 sub-camps. An estimated 150,000 Jews, along with leading intellectuals, dissidents, handicapped persons, Gypsies, and homosexuals, were systematically tortured and murdered. One-third of the Jewish population was purged, and most others fled the country.

After Soviet troops brutally "liberated" Vienna in 1945, Allied troops divided Austria into 4 zones of occupation to re-establish an Austrian government. By April 1945, a provisional government was established with 75-year-old **Karl Renner** as president. In November, the National Assembly declared Austria's independence from Germany. Despite Russian plundering and severe famines in the late 1940s, the Marshall Plan helped to jump-start the Austrian economy, laying the foundation for Austria's present prosperity. In 1955, after **Joseph Stalin** died, Austria signed the State Treaty, under which the four powers granted Austria complete sovereignty on the condition that it remain neutral.

The State Treaty, along with the Federal Constitution of the First Republic, which was restored in 1945, formed the basis of the **Second Republic.** These documents provide for a president (head of state) who is elected to a six-year term, a chancellor (head of government), usually the leader of the strongest party, a bicameral parliamentary legislature, and powerful provincial governments. Until recently the government has been dominated by two parties, the Social Democratic Party (SPÖ), and the People's Party (ÖVP). The two parties have built up one of the world's most successful industrial economies, with enviably low unemployment and inflation rates as well as a generous, progressive welfare state.

During the 1990s, Austria moved toward closer European integration. In 1994 **Thomas Klestil** was elected on a platform of integration. In 1995 the country was accepted into the **European Union (EU),** and the Austrians accepted membership through a national referendum. Unlike some EU countries, Austria also joined the **Economic and Monetary Union (EMU),** and replaced its currency, the Austrian Schilling, with the euro in 2002.

TODAY

HAIDER & AUSTRIA'S SWING TO THE RIGHT

Austria has recently been plastered over front pages internationally, thanks to the gains made by the far-right **Freedom Party** in 1999's elections. This party is infamous primarily for its leader **Jörg Haider,** who assumed the reigns of the then-powerless party in 1986. Haider entered the public eye for his anti-immigrant stance and his numerous remarks that were sympathetic to the Nazis. He has demanded a complete ban on immigration, playing off Austrian fears of the influx of immigrants from Eastern Europe. In the November 1999 elections, Haider's party claimed 27% of the vote, second among all parties, effectively breaking up the traditional two-party lock that the Social Democratic Party and People's Party had held on the country's politics since WWII. The Social Democratic Party, which has ruled the country for decades, came in first with 33% of the vote but refused to form a coalition with Haider's party; consequently, Haider's Freedom Party formed a coalition government with the conservative People's Party in February 2000. **Wolfgang Schlüssel** of the People's Party is the chancellor of the new government, while six of the government's 12 cabinet posts are held by Freedom Party members. In Vienna, 100,000 protestors turned out on the day that the Freedom Party government was sworn in. At the same time, the 14 other nations of the **European Union** simultaneously levied unprecedented political sanctions against Austria that essentially cut off official political contact; in addition, the United States recalled its ambassador for "consultation," while the Belgian Foreign Minister called traveling to Austria "immoral." Still, when the new government was entering office, Haider and the new chancellor Wolfgang Schlüssel signed the declaration "Responsibility for Austria," which stated that the new government would work "for an Austria in which xenophobia, anti-Semitism, and racism have no place." In addition, Haider resigned from his post as president of the Freedom Party three weeks after the new government took power in February to dispel questions about his role in the government, though many have called this a purely political move.

These developments led many of the European nations to reconsider their sanctions against Austria, which were all dropped in September 2000. Many critical of the European response to the Austrian situation have claimed that the sanctions were only pushed through in the first place because the liberal Social Democratic parties that rule in a majority of the European nations wanted to protect themselves from challenges by right-wing parties in their own countries.

Regardless of the EU's motives or actions, Haider's popularity in Austria itself waned in 2001. Despite Haider's active campaigning, the Freedom Party lost 8% of the vote, giving Social Democrats an absolute majority. Haider himself was found guilty of defamation in Austrian court for various offensive comments.

PEOPLE

DEMOGRAPHICS

Austrians are fiercely proud of their culture, history, and principles. Following the longevity pattern established by Emperor Franz Joseph, Austrians enjoy a life expectancy of 78 years. The great emphasis they place on education is responsible for the literacy rate of over 98% throughout the country. Social welfare is comprehensive, and unemployment hovers at around 4%. Ethnically, the Austrian people embody the idea of the "melting pot," for although 98% of Austria's 8 million people call themselves German, nearly every Austrian has genealogical ties to at least one of the many ethnic groups once within the Hapsburg empire. As befits the erstwhile stronghold of the Counter-Reformation, 78% of Austrians are Roman Catholic, while 5% are Protestant, and 17% belong to Muslim, Jewish, Baptist, and other religious denominations.

LANGUAGE

Although German is the official language of Austria, common borders with the Czech Republic, Slovakia, Hungary, Italy, Slovenia, Liechtenstein, and Switzerland make multilingualism imperative for most Austrians. Even outside German speakers sometimes have difficulty understanding them, as the German spoken in Austria differentiates itself by accent and vocabulary from that of other German-speaking countries. Tourists eager to try out their *Deutsch* don't need to be too worried about being understood, as nearly all Austrians understand High German, but as the inhabitants of each region speak a particular dialect, it is helpful to know some general peculiarities of Austrian German. As a result of the international connections of the Hapsburg Empire, many French, Italian, Czech, Hebrew, and Hungarian words have slipped into the language (e.g. *Babuschka* for old woman). Austrians don't greet each other with the standard *Guten Tag*, opting instead for *Servus* or *Grüss Gott*. One easy way to recognize familiar words in Austrian German is to remember that Austrians add a diminutive "*erl*" (instead of the High German "*chen*" or "*lein*") to a lot of words; store clerks may ask if you want a *Sackerl* (a small bag), waiters might inquire if you would like a *Bisserl* (a little bit) more of this or that, and a young girl is called a *Mäderl*. Many vegetables have unique names in Austrian German: the German *Kartoffel* (potato) becomes *Erdapfel;* tomatoes are *Paradeiser;* corn is not *Mais* but *Kukuruz;* and green beans are *Fisoln.* Austrians mean "this year" when they say *heuer* and January when they say *Jänner.* If you get to know an Austrian well, chances are they'll say *Ferti!* or *Servus!* for goodbye.

CULTURE

FOOD & DRINK

Just as the Austrians and their language are ethnically jumbled, many of the most famous Austrian dishes are foreign in origin: *Gulasch* (stewed meat and vegetables with paprika) is Hungarian; *Knödel* (dumplings) are Bohemian; and the archetypal Austrian dish, Wienerschnitzel, probably originated in Milan. Immigrants continue to influence Austrian cooking; Turkish dishes like *Dönerkebab* are on their way to becoming an integral part of Austrian cuisine. In addition, each region of Austria contributes its own particular traditional dishes, such as Carinthian *Kasnudeln* (large cheese- or meat-filled pasta squares) or Salzburger *Nockerl* (a mountain of sweetened, baked egg whites).

Loaded with fat, salt, and cholesterol, traditional Austrian cuisine is a nightmare to cardiologists but a delight to everyone else. **Staple foods** are simple and hearty, centering around *Schweinefleisch* (pork), *Kalbsfleisch* (veal), *Wurst* (sausage), *Eier* (eggs), *Käse* (cheese), *Brot* (bread), and *Kartoffeln* or *Erdapfeln* (potatoes). Austria's most renowned dish, Wienerschnitzel, is a meat cutlet (usually veal or pork) fried in butter with bread crumbs and often served with french fries. Although schnitzel is Austria's most famous meat dish, its most scrumptious variety is *Tafelspitz*, beautifully cooked boiled beef. Soups are also an Austrian speciality; try *Gulaschsuppe* (goulash soup) and *Frittatensuppe* (pancake strips in broth).

Most of Austria's culinary inventions appear on the **dessert** cart. Tortes commonly contain *Erdbeeren* (strawberries) and *Himbeeren* (raspberries). Don't miss *Marillen Palatschinken*, a crêpe with apricot jam, or *Kaiserschmarrn*, the Kaiser's favorite (pancake bits with a plum compote). Austrians adore the sweet dessert *Knödeln*, especially *Marillenknödel* (sweet dumplings with a whole apricot in the middle), though the typical street-stand dessert is the *Krapfn*, a holeless doughnut usually filled with jam. The pinnacles of Austrian baking, however, are the twin delights of *Sacher Torte* (a rich chocolate cake layered with marmalade) and *Linzer Torte* (a light yellow cake with currant jam).

Recently, **vegetarianism** has gained popularity in Vienna, and even meaty dishes are showing the influence of a lighter, vegetable-reliant style. Vegetarians should look for *Spätzle* (a homemade noodle often served with melted cheese), *Steinpilze* (enormous mushrooms native to the area), *Eierschwammerl* (tiny yellow mushrooms), or anything with the word "Vegi" in it. Supermarket connoisseurs should have a blast with Austrian staples: yogurt (rich, almost dessert-like), the cult favorite Nutella (a chocolate-hazelnut spread), *Almdudler* (a lemonade-like soft drink), *Semmeln* (very cheap, very fresh rolls), the original *Müsli* (granola on steroids), and all kinds of chocolate, including Milka and Ritter Sport.

In the afternoon, Austrians flock to *Café-Konditoreien* (café-confectioners) to nurse the national sweet tooth with *Kaffee und Kuchen* (coffee and cake). While drinking a *Mélange*, the classic Viennese coffee with frothed cream and a hint of cinnamon, nibble on a heavenly *Mohr im Hemd*, a chocolate sponge cake topped with hot whipped chocolate, or just about anything with *Mohn* (poppy seed) in it. If you get the chance, try some steam-cooked *Buchteln* with vanilla sauce or poppy seeds.

To wash it all down, try any variety of Austrian alcoholic beverage. The most famous Austrian **wine** is probably *Gumpoldskirchen* from Lower Austria, the largest wine-producing province. *Klosterneuburger,* named for the district near Vienna where it's produced, is both reasonably priced and dry. Austrian **beers** are outstanding. *Ottakringer* and *Gold Fassl* flow from Vienna's taps, *Stiegl Bier* and *Augustiner Bräu* from Salzburg's, *Zipfer Bier* from Upper Austria's, and *Gösser Bier* from Styria's. Austria imports a great deal of Budweiser beer, but theirs is *Budvar*—the original Bohemian variety, not the chintzy American imitation. If you're looking for something to keep you up rather than put you to sleep, try a Red Bull in its country of origin.

CUSTOMS & ETIQUETTE

In general, following good manners from your own country will take you far in German-speaking ones. The rules aren't too different in Austria, although there are a few ways you can disguise your status as a tourist and impress the locals. For instance, most Germans and Austrians hold their fork in their left hand and knife in their right, but don't switch them after cutting something. While forking left-handed is hard, it can impress the locals (unless your schnitzel lands in your lap). Elbows on the table is fine; in fact, they'll look at you a little funny if you have your hands under the table or in your lap. As always, seat yourself in cafés and most restaurants. Meals in Europe are paced a bit slower, so take in the atmosphere and take your time.

THE ARTS

Ever since the wealth of the Hapsburg Empire made extensive patronage possible, Austria has maintained an impressively rich artistic tradition. Living in a country of Alpine splendor, Austrians have long sought to create beauty themselves, challenge thought, and recreate life through personal expression. Classical music evolved, devolved, and continually exploded around fresh talent in Vienna over the last three centuries. Visually, Austria's span of architectural advancements from Romanesque ruins to Hapsburg decadence to the postmodern Haas House is a continual reminder of the local innovation that has long characterized Austria.

HISTORY

Landlocked in the middle of Europe and rolling with cash, the Hapsburgs married into power and bought into art. In keeping with the cosmopolitan nature of their empire and outlook, the imperial family pursued a cultural policy that favored foreign artists over their own native sons and daughters. Building on the popularity of Baroque palaces and churches in the 17th and 18th centuries, the Empire's artists began to develop a distinct, graceful architectural style that still dominates the old centers of former Hapsburg towns across Central and Eastern Europe. Around the turn of the 20th century, Austrian artists finally got fed up with traditionalism and foreign decadence and decided to stir up the coals a bit.

ARCHITECTURE

GOLDEN ARCHES. Austria's past as an outpost of the Roman empire is still visible in the ruins of **Carnuntum** and **Vindobona** (Vienna). The influence of such classical remains can be seen in the Romanesque art and architecture of the early Middle

Ages throughout Austria: for example, in the *Riesentor* of Vienna's **Stephansdom** (see p. 118) and the cycle of frescoes in the **Nonnberg Abbey** near Salzburg (see p. 249). Ordinarily this influence takes the form of semi-circular arches, columns, and delicate metalwork, but the builders of the 8th-century **Martinskirche** of Linz actually "borrowed" Roman tombstones to fill in the walls (see p. 297). The elaborate enamel **Verduner Altar,** by the master Nicholas of Verdun, at Stift Klosterneuberg (see p. 144), is witness to the richness of art under the Babenburgs, but if it isn't rich enough for your blood, check out the 10th-century **Imperial Crown** of the Holy Roman Emperor, encrusted with cabochons and gold filigree, its shape reminiscent of Roman arches.

GOTHIC TRANSCENDENCE. The invention of flying buttresses, pointed arches, and groin vaults that came with the French Gothic style all meant that walls could be thinner, vaults could be higher, and windows could flood the whole space with light. The vast 14th-century additions to the **Stephansdom** in Vienna also show the delicate tracery and stained glass work typical of the period. Sculpture reached new heights with the intricate carvings of **Anton Pilgram** (see p. 118) and the altarpieces of **Albrecht Altdorfer** (see p. 300). Don't miss Austria's castles—these magnificent fortress-palaces, exemplified by **Festung Hohensalzburg** (see p. 248), combined the medieval desire for imposing beauty with the practical goal of imposing power.

BAROQUE EXTRAVAGANCE. Austria's preeminent Baroque architects were Johann Bernhard Fischer von Erlach, Lukas von Hildebrandt and Johann Prandtauer. **Von Erlach,** born in Graz to a sculptor father, drew up the plans for Vienna's Schönbrunn (see p. 127) and Hofburg palaces (see p. 127). His best works, however, were ecclesiastical, including the ornate **Karlskirche** in Vienna. **Von Hildebrandt** shaped Austria's more secular side. His penchant for theatricality shows up in the palace's succession of pavilions and grand views of Vienna; stone sphinxes dotting his ornamental gardens allude to Eugene's victory over the Ottomans. **Prandtauer** was a favorite of the Church. His yellow Benedictine abbey at **Melk** peers over the Danube. After beating the Turks, Prince Eugene of Savoy (see p. 71) got Prandtauer to revamp the **Schloß Belvedere** (see p. 131).

JUGENDSTIL. The early 20th century saw more streamlined ornamentations and a new ethic of function over form gripped Vienna's artistic elite. Vienna's guru of architectural modernism, **Otto Wagner,** cured the city of its "artistic hangover." His Kirche am Steinhof (see p. 126) and Postsparkasse (see p. 124) enclose fluid *Jugendstil* interiors within stark, delineated structures. Wagner frequently collaborated with his student **Josef Maria Olbrich,** notably on the Majolicahaus (see p. 125) and the Karlspl. Stadtbahn (see p. 124). Wagner's admirer **Josef Hoffmann** founded the **Wiener Werkstätte** in 1903, drawing on Ruskin's English art and crafts movement and Vienna's new brand of streamlined simplicity. Its influence later resonated in the **Bauhaus** of Weimar Germany. **Adolf Loos,** Hoffmann's principal antagonist, strongly opposed such attention to luxury. Loos once said, "Ornamentation is crime," setting himself against the Baroque grandeur that Imperial Vienna supported. Few examples of his work reside in his native city, but his notorious **Goldman and Salatsch building** (1909-1911) in the Michaelerpl. went a step beyond its aesthetic toward a more starkly functional architecture.

URBAN SOCIALISM. In the 1920s and early 1930s, the **Social Democratic** administration built thousands of apartments in large **municipal projects,** their style reflecting the newfound assertiveness of the workers' movement. The most outstanding project of the era is the **Karl-Marx-Hof** (see p. 126). The huge structure, completed in 1930, extends over 1km and consists of 1600 apartments clustered around several courtyards. The Austrian Socialist party fought a pitched battle with rightist rioters in this apartment complex before the outbreak of World War II.

The structures created by American-trained architect **Hans Hollein** recall the sprawling abandon of his training ground while maintaining the Secessionists' attention to craftsmanship and elegant detail. His exemplary contribution to Viennese **postmodern** architecture is the **Haas House** (see p. 118), completed in 1990. Controversy has surrounded the building ever since sketches were published in the mid-80s, mainly because it stands opposite Vienna's landmark Stephansdom. Examples of modern interior design include the **Restaurant Salzamt** (I, Ruprechtspl. 1) and **Kleines Café** (see p. 114), both by Hermann Czech.

FINE ARTS

BIEDERMEIER. Between the era of Napoleon and the foundation of the Republic, Austria developed a large, restless middle class. Since political expression and social critique were virtually impossible during this era, artistic expression was funneled into a narrow channel of naturalistic and applied art centered around the family circle and domestic ideals, dominated by genre, landscape, and portrait painting. The *Biedermeier* period (see p. 72) is remembered today primarily as a furniture style, but it was also an artistic movement with limited crossover into literature, characterized by a predilection for symmetries, naturalism, and harmonious detail. *Biedermeier* architecture is exemplified by the well-ordered dignity of the **Dreimäderlhaus** at Schreyvogelg. 10 in Vienna, and the best of the period's furniture is on view in the **Biedermeier Room** of the Österreichisches Museum für Angewandte Kunst (see p. 135).

ART NOUVEAU & THE VIENNESE SECESSION. In 1897, the "young" artists split from the "old," as proponents of *Jugendstil* modernism took issue with the Viennese Academy's rigid conservatism and traditional symbolism. The idea was to leave the prevailing artistic conventions behind and formulate a new way of seeing the world. **Gustav Klimt** (1862-1918) and his followers founded what is known as the **Secession** movement. They aimed to provide the nascent Viennese avant-garde with a forum in which to show their work and to make contact with foreign artists. In their revolt against the old-guard Künstlerhaus, Secessionists sought to create space and appreciation for new artistic styles, particularly their own trademark style, Art Nouveau. The effect of this freedom is apparent in Klimt's own later paintings (such as *The Kiss*), which integrate naturalistic portraits into abstractly patterned backgrounds.

EXPRESSIONISM. Oskar Kokoschka and **Egon Schiele** revolted against art in the early 20th century, seeking to present frailty, neuroses, and sexual energy. Kokoschka is often considered the founder of Viennese **Expressionism.** A renowned portraitist, he was known to scratch the canvas with his fingernails in efforts to capture the "essence" of his subjects. Similar to Kokoschka, Schiele painted with a feverish intensity in line and color. His paintings are controversial even today for their depictions of tortured figures seemingly destroyed by their own bodies or by debilitating sexuality. His figures are twisted, gnarled, and yet oddly erotic.

MUSIC

THE CLASSICAL ERA. Toward the end of the 18th century, Vienna was a musical colony. Composers hung out in salons, making fun of each other and listening to themselves play music they wrote. The popular style, now described as "Viennese Classicism," fed on itself: the more music was written, the more people wanted to write music. The first master composer of Viennese Classicism was **Josef Haydn** (1732-1809). Working for the princes of Esterhazy, Haydn created a variety of new musical forms that led to the shaping of the sonata and the symphony, structures that dominated music throughout the 19th century. Fifty-two piano sonatas, 24 piano and organ concertos, 104 symphonies, and 83 string quartets provide rich and abundant proof of his pioneering productivity. He wrote the imperial anthem, *Gott erhalte Franz den Kaiser*, in order to rouse patriotic feeling during the Napoleonic wars. After WWI, Germany adopted the melody of *Gott erhalte* for its national anthem.

The work of **Wolfgang Amadeus Mozart** (1756-1791) represents the pinnacle of Viennese Classicism. Born in Salzburg, Mozart was a child prodigy, playing violin and piano by age four, composing simple pieces by five, and performing at Europe's imperial courts by age six. In 1781 the *Wunderkind* left Salzburg for Vienna, where he produced his first mature concerti, his best-known Italian operas (including *Don Giovanni* and *La Nozze di Figaro*), and the beloved string showpiece, *Eine kleine Nachtmusik*. Throughout his life, Mozart wrote with unprecedented speed, creating 626 works of all kinds during his 35 years, always jotting down music without preliminary sketches or revisions. Unfortunately, what he produced didn't always sell. Mozart's overwhelming emotional power found full expression in his final work, the (unfinished) *Requiem*, which he continued composing until the last hours before his death, fulfilling his bitter aside to favorite student Franz Süssmayr: "You see, I *have* been writing this Requiem for myself." He was buried in an unmarked pauper's grave. Within a few decades of his death, however, Mozart was recognized once more as a master, who in Tchaikovsky's words was "the culmination of all beauty in music."

Only **Ludwig van Beethoven** (1770-1827) could compete with Mozart for the devotion of the Viennese. Born into a family of Flemish musicians in Bonn, he lived and died in Vienna. Beethoven's gifts were manifest in his piano sonatas, string quartets, overtures, and concertos, but shone most intensely in his nine symphonies, today at the core of the orchestral repertoire. His *Ninth Symphony* had an enormous cultural impact, in part because of his introduction of singers to the symphonic form—a chorus and four soloists sing the text to Friedrich Schiller's *Ode to Joy*. Beethoven's *Fidelio*, which premiered May 23, 1814, at the Kärntnertortheater in Vienna, is regarded as one of the greatest German operas. Due to increasing deafness, the composer could maintain contact with the world only through a series of conversational notebooks, which provide an extremely thorough, though one-sided, record of his conversations (including his famous emotional outpouring, the *Heiligenstadt Testament*, written in Vienna's 19th district). Music historians place Beethoven between Viennese Classicism and Romanticism.

THE ROMANTIC ERA & LATE NINETEENTH CENTURY. The music of **Franz Schubert** (1797-1828) is the lifeblood of Romanticism, a movement characterized by swelling emotion, larger orchestras, interest in the natural world, and storytelling. Born in the Viennese suburb of Lichtenthal in 1797, Schubert began his career as a chorister in the imperial Hofkapelle and later made his living teaching music. Mainly self-taught, he composed the *Unfinished Symphony* and the *Symphony in C Major*, which are now considered masterpieces but were virtually unknown during his lifetime. His lyrical genius was more readily recognized in his *Lieder*, musical setting of poems by Goethe, Schiller, and Heine. These great song cycles were made famous during musical soirées called *Schubertiaden*, which spawned a new trend of social gatherings in *Biedermeier* Vienna, featuring chamber music, readings, and alcohol. This burst of creativity was cut short by his early death from syphilis at the age of 32—he was buried next to Beethoven. Schubert's gift for pure melody lived on and was a catalyst for later musical innovations.

Like Beethoven, **Johannes Brahms** (1833-1897) straddled musical traditions. In his home near the Karlskirche in Vienna, Brahms composed his Hungarian Dances, piano concerti, and numerous symphonies, all of which were first performed by the Vienna Philharmonic. Despite his own Romantic compositions, Brahms is often regarded as a classicist who used his status and position in the

Viennese *Musikverein* to oppose Romanticism and the musical experiments of his arch-rival, **Richard Wagner.** His artistic credo, "If we cannot compose as beautifully as Mozart or Haydn, let us at least try to compose as purely," emphasized his devotion to the classical style and disinterest in modern music.

Orchestral music had mass appeal as well. Beginning with **Johann Strauss the Elder** (1804-1849), the Strauss family kept Vienna dancing for much of the 19th century. Johann Sr. composed mostly waltzes and showy pieces, including the famous *Radetzkymarsch*, which is still played every New Year by the Vienna Philharmonic. Largely responsible for the "Viennese Waltz," **Johann Strauss the Younger** (1825-1899) shone in his youth as a brilliant violinist and savvy cultural entrepreneur. The waltz became popular during the Congress of Vienna, offering a fresh exhilaration that broke free from older, more stiffly formal dances. Richard Wagner, Strauss's most famous rival, noted admiringly on a visit to the city that Viennese waltzing was "more potent than alcohol." Sensing the trend, Strauss became its master, eventually writing the *Blue Danube* and *Tales from the Vienna Woods*, two of the most recognized waltzes of all time, thereby earning the title "King of the Waltz." In his spare time he managed to produce some popular operas as well, *Die Fledermaus* being his most celebrated.

Gustav Mahler's (1860-1911) music, as a direct precursor to the Second Viennese experiments of Arnold Schönberg, incorporates fragments and deliberately inconclusive musical segments. Like modern literature, these compositions read like nostalgic remnants of a once certain and orderly world. Mahler employed unusual instrumentation and startling harmonic juxtapositions. His Eighth Symphony, called *Symphony of a Thousand*, requires an orchestra and two full choruses. Mahler's music hides formalist experimentation beneath a rich emotional beauty. His works form an integral part of the *fin de siècle* Viennese avant-garde.

THE MODERN ERA. While Mahler destabilized the conventions of composition, **Arnold Schönberg** (1874-1951) broke away from traditional harmony altogether. Originally a devotee of Richard Wagner, Schönberg rejected compositional rules that require music to be set in a tonal key and, with his 12-tone system, pursued what is generally called atonality. Some of Schönberg's most famous works are *Pierre Lunaire* and the string piece *Verklärte Nacht*. **Anton von Webern** (1883-1945) studied under Schönberg, eventually adopting and expanding his 12-tone system in music that is incredibly sparse, a sharp contrast to the lush, opulent, often overwritten music of his contemporaries. Webern drifted into obscurity and depression as the Nazis took over. While fleeing the Nazis, he was accidentally shot by US troops in Salzburg. **Alban Berg** (1885-1935), another student of Schönberg's who used a modified version of the 12-tone system, completed few works because of his obsession with ideal expression. Like Schönberg and Webern, he suffered under the Nazis as a creator of "degenerate art" and died young, in 1935.

LITERATURE

EARLY EXAMPLES. A collection of poetry dating from around 1150 and preserved in the abbey of Vorau in Styria marks the earliest known Austrian literature in German. Apart from sacred poetry, the courtly style known as *Minnesang* developed in the 12th and 13th centuries and culminated in the lyrical works of minstrel **Walther von der Vogelweide.** On a more epic scale, the **Nibelungenlied,** which dates from around 1200, is one of the most impressive heroic epics in German (also the primary source for Richard Wagner's *Ring of the Nibelungen* opera cycle). **Emperor Maximilian I** (1459-1519), nicknamed "The Last Knight," provided special support for theater and the dramatic arts during his reign. Splendid operas and pageants frequently involved the whole imperial court and led to popular religious drama that has survived in the form of rural **Passionspiele** (passion plays).

THE CLASSICAL WRITERS. Born in Vienna in 1801, **Johann Nestroy** wrote biting comedies and satires lampooning social follies. Although his name is not readily recognized by Anglophones, Nestroy is one of the canonical figures of German drama, famous for such plays as *Der Talisman* and *Liebesgeschichten und Hei-ratssachen*, as well as the *Tannhäuser* on which Wagner based his famous opera. Often called Austria's greatest novelist, **Adalbert Stifter** wrote around the same time period as Nestroy but concerned himself much more with classical *Bil-dungsroman* themes and descriptions of nature. Many of his short stories and novels, such as *Der Condor* (1840), *Die Mappe meines Urgroßvaters* (1841), and *Der Nachsommer* (1857), are classics in the canon of German literature.

A classicist with a more lyrical style, **Franz Grillparzer** penned plays about the conflict between a life of thought and a life of action. Grillparzer worked as a clerk in the Austrian bureaucracy and wrote some of his most critically acclaimed plays, such as *Des Meeres und Der Liebe Wellen* (1831), in his spare time. Most of Grill-parzer's fame came posthumously, when interest grew in his published work and the beautifully composed *Der arme Spielmann* was discovered.

FIN DE SIÈCLE. Around 1890, Austrian literature rapidly transformed in the heat of the "merry apocalypse" atmosphere that permeated society. The satires of **Karl Kraus** tried to awaken the collapsing empire's conscience, while **Sigmund Freud** analyzed its dreams. **Arthur Schnitzler** heated up the Empire's stage with bedroom scenes, while **Hugo von Hofmannsthal** staged its death by rethinking medieval and Baroque tragedies. At the Café Griensteidl, lyric poet, critic, and one-time director of the *Burgtheater* **Hermann Bahr** loosely presided over a pioneer group known as **Jung Wien** (Young Vienna), aimed at capturing the subtlest nuances of the Viennese atmosphere. Hofmannsthal walked a tightrope between Impressionism and verbal decadence, creating such exquisite pieces of drama as *Yesterday* (1891) and *Everyman* (1911) while at the same time collaborating with Richard Strauss to write librettos for, among other things, *Der Rosenkavalier*. Schnitzler, a play-wright and colleague of Freud, was the first German to write stream-of-conscious-ness prose. He skewered Viennese decadence in dramas and essays, and shocked contemporaries by portraying the complexities of erotic relationships in many of his plays, including his famous *Merry-Go-Round* (1897).

Many of Austria's literary titans, such as **Marie von Ebner-Eschenbach** and **Franz Kafka,** lived within the Hapsburg protectorate of Bohemia. Ebner-Eschenbach is often called the greatest female Austrian writer, known for her vivid individual portraits and defense of women's rights. Kafka often traveled to Vienna to drink coffee at the Herrenhof Café and swap ideas with other writers. No one else could master the surrealism of Kafka's writing, however, most famously demonstrated in *Die Verwandlung (The Metamorphosis)*, a bizarre, disorienting tale in which the narrator comes to terms with his unexpected transformation into a beetle.

The collapse of the Austro-Hungarian monarchy marked a major turning point in the intellectual and literary life of Austria. Novelists **Robert Musil** and **Joseph Roth** concerned themselves with the consequences of the empire's breakdown. Roth's novels, *Radetzkymarsch* and *Die Kapuzinergruft*, romanticize the former empire. Musil is most famous for his unfinished work in three volumes, *Der Mann Ohne Eigenschaften (The Man Without Qualities)*.

THE 20TH CENTURY. Georg Trakl's Expressionist works epitomize the early 20th-century fascination with death and dissolution; "all roads empty into black putrefaction" is his most frequently quoted line. Other Prague-born greats such as **Franz Werfel** and **Rainer Maria Rilke** shaped Austrian literature between the wars. Werfel's works investigate the dark side of the human psyche. In addition to his essays and stories, Rilke is most famous for his lyric poetry cycles the *Duino Elegies* and *Sonnets to Orpheus*. After WWII, Rilke's poetry and Kafka's oppressive parables of a cold world became models for a new generation of writers. These artistic movements owe their fascination with the unconscious to the new science of psychoanalysis launched by **Sigmund Freud.** Freud is best known for his theories of sexual repression, particularly applicable to bourgeois society, and his theories of the unconscious, which recast the literary world forever.

Contemporary Austrian literature is still affected and informed by its dark, dramatic literary tradition, but there is plenty of modern innovation as well. **Ingeborg Bachman's** stories and novels left an important legacy for Austrian feminism. One of the stalwarts of modern Austrian writing, **Thomas Bernhard** wrote *Holzfäller* (Woodcutters) and *Wittgenstein's Nephew.*

FILM

While most English speakers might not be able to name more than one Austrian actor (Arnold Schwarzenegger is easy), national filmmaking has endured a rocky tradition, alternatively thriving and waning. Emperor Franz Josef himself attended a screening in April 1896 of a short film created by the French Lumière brothers in Vienna. Inspired by Cecil B. DeMille in the U.S., the **Kolowrat** created the massive *Sodom und Gomorrha* in 1922. The addition of sound to movies allowed for W. **Forst's** 1933 invention of the Viennese musical film in *Leise flehen meine Lieder.* Anschluß in 1938 brought about the end of independent domestic film production and the consolidation of filmmakers under the Wien-Film corporation. Wien-Film was confiscated by Allied forces in 1945 and the tradition was reborn in 1946. Austrian films moved in a variety of directions, from the "woods and mountain" genre of films like *Echo der Berge* to operettas and works addressing contemporary social problems. Beginning in 1954, the illustrious *Goldene Feder* (Golden Feather) has been bestowed upon the director of the "Best Film of the Year."

THE CURRENT SCENE

Austria's rich cultural heritage has made it a draw for tourists and scholars alike, but it can also be an oppressive force, hindering the exploration of modern art and expression. Tired of Lipizzaner, chocolate and Mozart, individuals and the government alike are working to showcase the new, progressive culture and innovative art that is slowly emerging. A new exhibition in Manhattan displays the work of 100 living artists, while a brand-new Jewish theater troupe and contemporary music scene are shedding new light on creativity within Austria's borders.

SPORTS & RECREATION

Austrians take their recreation seriously; provisions for athletic funding are even written into the national constitution. This has been especially true in the intrepid spirit of mountain adventure that flows through the veins of many towns in Salzburger Land, Carinthia, and especially Tyrol, East Tyrol, and Vorarlberg. Over 450,000 Austrians belong to the Österreichische Alpenverein (ÖAV; Austrian Alpine Union), the national organization for mountain recreation and preservation. More than perhaps any other country in the world, Austria is known for its charming mountain villages, which are home to some of the world's oldest and most famous ski resorts. Austria is also renowned for its celebrated and extensive system of mountain huts, which are emulated by

Ten years ago, movie buffs would have laughed at the prospect of including Austria on a short list of exciting national cinemas. In the past, Austria has managed to produce only about 20 mediocre features per year, far fewer than European countries like France, Italy, or Germany. However, the movie world can change quickly; in terms of festival awards and critical praise, post-war Austrian cinema has never enjoyed as much renown as today. In the past three years, the Austrian film industry has experienced an incredible renaissance. With unique humor, a feisty spirit of political and aesthetic resistance, and biting self-irony, today's Austrian film scene stands at the forefront of the European cinematic landscape, from its avant-garde incarnations to its comedy offerings.

Rising Stars

Just as Canada has supplied the US with many of its finest comedians, the Austrians are generally the funniest of the German-speakers. Accordingly, comedies have have furnished Austria's burgeoning film industry with some of its largest successes. These pictures are typically stocked with comics from popular sketch comedy TV shows such as *MA 2412*. One prominent example is *Der Überfall* (The Robbery, 2001), which stars well-known comedians Roland Düringer and Josef Hader and chronicles a hold-up of a tailor's shop gone awry. In Wolfgang Murnberger's *Komm, süßer Tod* (Come, Sweet Death, 2000), Hader plays a hapless paramedic who gets mixed up in a murder mystery. *Die Gottesanbeterin* (The Praying Mantis, 2001) is a hilariously grotesque tale of a woman who sleeps and kills her way up the ladder of Austrian society. Critics tend to see these so-called "black comedies" as a typically Austrian phenomenon. The films share a morbid sense of humor and an ironic view of domestic Austrian culture.

Austrian moviemaking has flowered in more than just comedy. Michael Haneke, the country's most esteemed active filmmaker, has long been at the forefront of this upwelling. On the whole, Haneke's polemical film program attempts to lay bare the coldness of European society, challenging Hollywood's blithe treatment of violence. His controversial 1992 feature *Benny's Video* shocked crowds with its restrained, anti-psychological portrait of a teenager who kills a young girl "to see how it is." His greatest commercial success to date is *La pianiste* (The Piano Teacher, 2001), which garnered three awards at the 2001 Cannes Film Festival and went on to become a hit in arthouses worldwide. In recent years, a host of other young Austrian directors have successfully emerged on the festival circuit. Perhaps the most exciting debut in recent years was 2001's *Lovely Rita*. Directed by former Haneke scriptwriter Jessica Hausner, the film delicately sketches the downward spiral of a teenage girl from the Viennese suburbs. Deftly drawing on Haneke's intellectualism and the ambitious reach of the young director, Hausner is posied to be an important filmmaker in the future.

Documentary has potential to be another promising front for Austrian cinema. Ulrich Seidl has been at the vanguard of European documentary filmmaking for a decade. His films wander in a border zone between fact and fiction, unflinchingly capturing models, dog owners, and newspaper readers at their most disturbing. His first feature film *Hundstage* (Dog Days, 2001), an investigation into the quotidian sickness of suburban Vienna, was awarded the Special Grand Jury Prize at the 2001 Venice Film Festival. Besides Seidl's work, Austrian documentarists have reaped considerable attention for satirical pieces such as *Im toten Winkel* (In the Blind Spot, 2002), *Ausländer raus!* (Foreigners Get Out! 2002), and *Haider lebt—1 April 2021* (Haider lives, 2002).

New Wave or Zwischenhoch?

Despite the rosy state of contemporary Austrian film, the future may harbor some pitfalls. After a period of generous cultural subsidies from Social Democrat governments, federal support of film has shrunk by 40% since 1998-1999 (also the period in which many recently-screened films went into production). Moreover, several prominent Austrian directors have taken to working predominantly or exclusively abroad, including Michael Haneke (France), and Christian Frosch, Peter Kern, and Stefan Ruzowitzky (Germany). Some critics believe Austrian cinema is now experiencing merely a brief *Zwischenhoch* (high between two lows). It will take some time to ascertain whether the naysayers are correct, or if Austrian filmmaking is really at the start of something big.

Mattias Frey researched Vienna for Let's Go: Austria & Switzerland 2002 *and has contributed to* Let's Go: Germany. *He is now a free-lance film critic in Berlin.*

mountain organizations in many other parts of the world. Beyond mountains, Austria is a nation of sports and fitness enthusiasts; biking, soccer, and tennis are popular pastimes.

SKIING

The fact that two Winter Olympics (Innsbruck 1964 and 1972) have been held in Austria is no accident; its skiing is easily among the best in the world. Destinations like the Arlberg region, Innsbruck, the Zillertal, and the Ötztal have long attracted skiers from around the globe. **Kitzbühel** is home to the world's most famous and notoriously difficult ski race, the **Hahnenkamm**. Skiing is possible in summer on eight glaciers, including those near **Hintertux, Obergurgl, Zell am See,** and **Innsbruck.**

EARLY HISTORY. Austria has a long and storied skiing history. **Matthias Zdarsky** wrote the world's first instructional book on skiing in 1897 and organized the world's first slalom race in Lilienfeld in 1905. **St. Anton** is often credited as the "birthplace of modern skiing," having founded one of the world's first ski clubs in 1901. **Hannes Schneider** was a young ski intructor with St. Anton's Hotel Post when he developed the "Arlberg Technique" of alpine skiing, which is still the skiing technique taught in ski schools today. He was also instrumental in pioneering North American skiing through his work with Mt. Cranmore in New Hampshire, and teamed up with German Arnold Fanck to write 1925's *Wunder des Schnees-chuhs* (The Wonders of Skiing), which is still the best-selling ski book of all time. In 1930, **Rudolph Lettner** made a major contribution to ski technology with the invention of the metal edge for better grip and carving. Since then, the Austrians have held a reputation as the best ski engineers in the world, and much of the best ski equipment in the world, from skis to ski lifts, is still crafted in Austria.

PIONEERS ABROAD. Students of Schneider's went on to advance the sport of skiing both in Europe and North America; their efforts produced the first resort ski school in America. **Otto Lang, Otto Schneibs, Friedl Pfeifer,** and a number of others were instrumental in bringing skiing to a new continent. In addition to teaching skiing, Austrians awed Americans with their ability and fearlessness on the slopes. More than almost anyone else, **Toni Matt** will forever be an American ski legend. He came to New Hampshire in the 1930s to teach for the Hannes Schneider ski school at Mt. Cranmore, and in 1939 decided to compete in the well-known American Inferno race on Mt. Washington. Virtually unknown as a racer, Matt amazed everyone by completing the summit-to-base run (over 4000 vertical feet) in only 6 minutes 30 seconds, cutting the previous course record in half. The feat included a legendary descent of the famously difficult, near-vertical slopes of Tuckerman Ravine. Speeding into the Ravine from the summit, Toni Matt skied the headwall without making a single turn, achieving an estimated velocity of nearly 90mph.

AUSTRIA'S NATIONAL PASTIME. Austrian skiers have excelled on the slopes ever since races were first organized (by Austrians). It is mostly Austrians who populate Vienna's **Straße der Sieger** (Street of Winners), where the world's most legendary skiers are honored with bronze handprints. Much like soccer in Great Britain and baseball and basketball in America, skiing in Austria has long held the country's fascination. Generations of Austrians have grown up practicing their turns, with dreams of one day being a superstar, like **Toni Sailer** ("The Blitz from Kitz"). In 1956 he became the first of only two Olympic skiers to win gold medals in each of the three major alpine skiing categories. Most impressive were his margins of victory, the narrowest of which was a full 3½ seconds. Among many other Austrian Olympic champions, few stand out so much as **Franz Klammer** ("Kaiser Franz," "The Klammer Express"). Winner of an Olympic gold in Innsbruck in front of 60,000 adoring countrymen, he was also a five-time World Cup champion in the 1970s and 80s, and World Champion in St. Moritz in 1974. In the last decade, **Hermann Maier** ("The Herminator") has become an international ski icon, winning two World Championships and nine World Cup titles, as well as two gold medals at the 1998 Olympics in Nagano, Japan. He also survived one of the most spectacularly memorable crashes in downhill racing. Even more recently, **Stephan Eberharter** has emerged as Austria's big skiing star, with gold medals at the 2002 Olympics and the 2003 World Championships.

Not surprisingly, Austrian women have fared just as well on the international stage as the men. **Annemarie Moser-Pröll** won gold in the downhill at Lake Placid in 1980, and has 61 World Cup wins to her credit, more than any other woman in history. A close rival for "best female skier ever" is **Petra Kronberger,** who is the only skier (male or female) ever to win World Cup races in five different categories in a single season. Today, no Austrian woman's star burns quite as brightly as **Alexandra Meissnitzer,** who won in two categories at the 1999 World Championships, and took home two medals from the 1998 Olympics. She narrowly missed medals in Salt Lake City in 2002, but since she is barely 20 years old, there are plenty of opportunities still to come.

SNOWBOARDING. Although Austrians have dominated the skiing world for almost a century, they have begun to change with the times. As snowboarding has increased in popularity in America, so too have Austrians taken to it as a new form of winter recreation. Although the sport is still on the rise, remarkable young talent has already surfaced in Austria. Nicknamed "The Dominator," **Martin Freinademetz** has been at or near the top of the snowboarding slalom circuit for over a decade, with two World Championships and two World Cup titles to his credit. On the freestyle side of the sport, **Stefan Gimpl** is one of the best riders in the world, consistently defeating North American and European opponents in big air events.

MOUNTAINEERING

The longstanding Austrian passion for the outdoors is understandable given the country's topography. The Austrians are enthusiastically proud of their *Dreitausender* (three-thousand-meter peaks, similar in spirit to Colorado's "fourteeners"). Unlike in many other countries, Austrian mountains provide far more than just sightseeing. For Austrians, love of the mountains is inherently an active pursuit, especially in the high Alpine ranges in the south and west. The **Hohe Tauern National Park** straddles the border of the provinces of Carinthia, Salzburger Land, East Tyrol, and Tyrol, and encloses rugged chains such as the Glocknergruppe and the Goldberggruppe. Extreme mountaineering challenges are present on peaks like the **Großglockner** (Austria's highest mountain), whose northeast face presents a number of long and daunting icy climbs. Other ranges to the west in Tyrol, including the Stubaier Alpen, Zillertaler Alpen, and Ötztaler Alpen, include high peaks with rocky pillars, serrated ridges, snow-covered peaks, and big-mountain challenges to keep even world-class mountaineers busy.

Despite the large array of mountains at home, Austrians have long been known for pioneering climbing worldwide. In nearby Switzerland, the imposing *Eiger Nordwand* (North Face of the Eiger) was one of the world's great mountaineering challenges until it was climbed by Austrians **Anderl Heckmair, Ludwig Vörg, Heinrich Harrer,** and **Fritz Kasparek** in three to four days in 1938. Today, the world's most celebrated mountaineer is without a doubt **Reinhold Messner,** born in South Tyrol (technically in Italy but culturally still very Austrian). After completing a number of the most difficult climbs in the Alps by his early twenties, Messner was invited on a successful 1970 expedition to the Rupal Face of Pakistan's Nanga Parbat (8125m; the route has still not been repeated). He later became the first person to climb all fourteen of the world's 8000m peaks, and the second person to climb the highest peak on each continent. In 1980, without the aid of supplemental oxygen, he successfully climbed Mt. Everest alone on an extremely difficult, previously unclimbed route. After the milestone, Messner described the high-altitude experience as feeling as if "I am nothing more than a single narrow gasping lung, floating over the mists and summits."

Perhaps Messner's biggest achievement, however, is his role along with Mayrhofen native **Peter Habeler** in the development of **alpine-style climbing** on the world's highest peaks. Previously, all Himalayan climbs were attempted expedition-style, using scores of porters, weeks of time, and large amounts of money. But Messner and Habeler completed the second ascent of Pakistan's Gasherbrum I (8068m) in only three days, using a minimum of gear and food. Then, in 1978, they used the same fast-attack technique to make the first ascent of Mt. Everest (8848m) without the aid of supplemental oxygen. A flurry of media attention followed, helping to fuel a fierce debate in mountaineering circles as to the wisdom and safety of alpine-style ascents. Today, although still somewhat controversial, alpine-style is the preferred form for many important routes, and the only way in which many climbs are even feasible.

A number of other Austrians are responsible for important first ascents. Well before Habeler and Messner popularized alpine-style climbing, **Kurt Diemberger** used the approach to become the only mountaineer in the world with two first ascents of 8000m summits, climbing Broad Peak (8047m) in 1957 and Dhaulagiri (8167m) in 1960. Also on the Broad Peak team were three other Austrians, including **Hermann Buhl,** who in 1953 completed the epic first ascent of Nanga Parbat (8215m). While others on the expedition turned around due to the threat of bad weather, Buhl pushed alone to the summit and was forced to spend a night above 8000m without a tent or sleeping bag. The next day, hallucinating from the thin air and unable to eat or drink, he amazed his teammates by descending back to Camp V, alive after almost 48hr. alone at high altitude.

OTHER SPORTS

Austrians pride themselves on their fitness, with reason. National fitness campaigns are not uncommon, and the Fitness March and Fitness Run are part of the Austrian National Day. Popular sports in Austria include hiking, soccer, tennis, cycling, auto racing, and curling. The Österreichisher Fußball-Bund (ÖFB; Austrian Soccer Federation) boasts 2317 clubs and 373,300 members. **Thomas Muster** was once the top-ranked tennis player in the world, and **Jochen Rindt** was crowned Formula One champion in 1970. Austrians also take extensive *Wanderungen* (hikes)—they enjoy their country's natural beauty just as much as tourists.

HOLIDAYS & FESTIVALS

Shops and businesses are closed on national and most religious holidays. The dates for 2004 include New Year's Day (January 1st) and Epiphany (January 6th), Good Friday (April 18th), Easter Monday (April 21st), Labor Day (May 1), Ascension Day (29th), Whitmonday (June 9th), Corpus Christi (June 19th), Assumption Day (August 15), National Day (October 26), All Saint's Day (November 1), Immaculate Conception (December 8), Christmas (December 25th), and Boxing Day (December 26th). As Austria is a Catholic country, religious holidays are observed nearly everywhere, and towns and cities essentially shut down. Below are a list of holidays and festivals you'll want to participate in if you're in the neighborhood.

AUSTRIAN FESTIVALS (2004)

DATE	NAME & LOCATION	DESCRIPTION
February	Fasching, Vienna	"Carnival Season" brings waltzes, parties, and a parade the day before Lent.
mid-April to mid-May	Danube Best (Donaufestival): Krems and Korneuburg	A celebration of art, music, and theater along the Danube (Donau) River.
mid-May to mid-June	Vienna Festival (FestWochen)	Thousands descend upon the city for a celebration with theater, exhibits, and renowned orchestras.
early July	Love Parade, Vienna	Begun after the fall of the Berlin Wall, the annual festive parade celebrates love, respect, and tolerance for all.
late July to late Aug.	Salzburg Music Festival	A summer series of concerts by the Vienna Philharmonic and others.
August	Eisenstadt Fest	Freeflowing music and wine. What could be better?
Oct. 26	Austrian National Day	Commemorates formation of Austria as new independent nation after WWII.
mid-Nov. to Dec. 24th	Vienna Christmas Market (also in Salzburg)	Festive cabin-like booths are erected in front of the baroque cathedral.
December 6	Krampus (everywhere, especially small towns)	Watch out as St. Nicholas and his mischievous companion Krampus wander the streets.
December 31	New Year's, everywhere	The top draw is Vienna for the annual performance of *Die Fledermaus* at the opera.

ADDITIONAL RESOURCES

CULTURE & HISTORY

Vienna and its Jews: The Tragedy of Success, 1880s-1980s (1988). Charles E. Berkley.
The Class Art of Viennese Pastry (1997). Christine Berl.
The Fall of the House of Hapsburg (1963). Edward Crankshaw.
Vienna: Its Musical Heritage (1968). Egon Gartenberg.
Fin-de-Siècle Vienna (1961). Carl Schorske.

FICTION

The World of Yesterday (Die Welt von Gestern; 1943). Stefan Zweig.

The Metamorphosis (Die Verwandlung; 1915). Franz Kafka.
Young Törless (Die Verwirrungen des Zöglings Törless; 1906). Robert Musil.

Eyes Wide Shut (Die Traumspiele; 1900). Arthur Schnitzler.

TRAVEL BOOKS

German Survival Guide: The Language and Culture You Need to Travel With Confidence in Germany and Austria (2001). Elizabeth Bingham.

The Wines of Austria (2000). Philip Blom.
Karen Brown's Austria: Charming Inns & Itineraries (2002). Karen Brown.

Walking Austria's Alps: Hut-to-Hut (1999). Jonathan Hurdle.
Hostels Austria & Switzerland: The Only Comprehensive, Unofficial, Opinionated Guide (2002). Paul Karr.

VIENNA (WIEN)

Occupying a pivotal position between Eastern and Western Europe, Vienna is a living monument to nearly two millennia of rich history. From humble origins as a Roman camp, to Baroque glory days under the Hapsburg dynasty, to the gaslit "merry apocalypse" of its bohemian *fin-de-siècle* café culture, Vienna has often rivaled Paris, London, and Berlin in cultural and political significance. Here is where Freud grappled with the human psyche, where Mozart found inspiration for his symphonies, where Musil wrote the sprawling *Man Without Qualities*, and where Maximilian I and Maria Theresa altered the shape of European politics. Although the darker ghosts of Austria's past still lurk in the Judenplatz, location of a war-time Jewish ghetto, the city's open-mindedly cosmopolitan atmosphere shows signs of brighter developments. The MuseumsQuartier, an ultra-modern venue for architecture, film, theater, and dance, vies with a burgeoning club scene in proving that Vienna is a city still writing its own dynamic brand of history.

PHONE CODES	The **city code** for Vienna is 01 for calls placed from within Austria, 011 43 1 for calls from abroad.

SUGGESTED ITINERARIES

ONE DAY Wake yourself up with fresh coffee and a pastry at **Café Central** (p. 114), then hit the *Innenstadt*, starting with a climb up the tower of **Stephansdom** in the center of the city (p. 118). Wander along the **Ringstraße** (p. 123), which circles Vienna's medieval district and showcases architectural triumphs such as Wagner's Jugendstil *Postsparkasse* and the *Burgtheater*, plus the **Hofburg** (p. 127) and **public gardens** (p. 131). Indulge in afternoon dessert at **Demel** (p. 114), before heading to the **Spittelbergmarkt** to view local artwork and shop for gifts. Refuel near **Naschmarkt** (p. 125) for **Bermuda Dreiecke** nightlife (p. 140).

THREE DAYS Spend your first day as above, then discover how art was "made and unmade" in Vienna's world-class **art museums**, especially the **Kunsthistorisches Museum** (p. 134) or the brand-new **MuseumsQuartier** (p. 134). Eat a bite-sized lunch at Kafka's favorite restaurant, **Trzesniewski** (p. 109). Then explore outside the Ring: tour **Schloß Belvedere** (p. 131), and linger in yet another café (trust us). Take one evening to see an opera at the **Staatsoper** (p. 136), and a few hours of an afternoon to snag one of the super-cheap standing room tickets. On day three, make a vineyard visit in the **Wienerwald** (Vienna Woods) and taste new wine in the *Heurigen* (wine gardens) nestled in the suburbs of Vienna (p. 116). On your last evening, watch Vienna sparkle from the **Donauturm** (p. 132), and then walk down to the hopping boardwalk of the Danube and **Donauinsel** to dance and drink among hip Austrians in the clubs that line the river.

FIVE DAYS Tackle three of your days as above, only take time to explore different neighborhoods within the Ring—seek out the Vienna of the past near Judenplatz, Am Hof, and Freyung (p. 120). If it's Sunday, enjoy a mass sung by the **Vienna Boys' Choir** (p. 138). Then daytrip along the **Danube** between Krems and Melk (p. 304). Back in Vienna, spend a day at the delicate **Schloß Schönnbrunn** (p. 127), then (window) shop the upscale "Kaiserlich und Königlich" stores in **Kohlmarkt** (p. 119). As a final fling, return to the heart of Vienna for the spectacular evening tour of the **Stephansdom**.

Greater Vienna

SLOVAKIA

Stockerau

Wolkersdorf

Donau (Danube)

A22

Korneuburg

Ganserndorf

Tulln

Klosterneuburg

Stift Klosterneuburg

Deutsch-Wagram

Handelskai

VIENNA (WIEN)

Großenzersdorf

Purkersdorf

Donau (Danube)

Neuleng-bach

Pressbaum

Orth

A23

Fischamend

A1

Schwechat

TO CARNUNTUM (10km)

A21

Heiligenkreuz

Mödling

Schwechat

Baden bei Wien

Traiskirchen

Bruck an der Leitha

Triesting

Bad Vöslau

A2

HUNGARY

Pottenstein

Berndorf

Piesting

Ebreichsdorf

BURGENLAND

0   5 miles

0   5 kilometers

✈ INTERCITY TRANSPORTATION

BY PLANE. Vienna's airport is the **Wien-Schwechat Flughafen** (☎700 72 22 33), home of **Austrian Airlines.** (☎051 76 60; www.aua.com. Open M-F 7am-8pm, Sa-Su 8am-6pm.) A daily flight to and from **New York** and frequent flights to **Berlin, London,** and **Rome,** among other places, are available. Travelers under 25 and students under 27 qualify for discounts if they purchase tickets two weeks in advance.

The airport is far from the city center (18km), but easily accessible by public transportation. The cheapest way to reach the city is to take train S7 "Flughafen/Wolfsthal" which stops at **Wien Mitte** (trains every 15-30min. 4:59am-11:22pm, €3; Eurail not valid). There is also daily train service between **Wien Nord** or Wien Mitte and the airport (every 30min. 5:03am-10:24pm, €3). The heart of the city, Stephanspl., is a short metro ride from Wien Mitte on the U3 (Orange) line. A more convenient option is taking the **Vienna Airport Lines Shuttle Bus** (☎93 00 00 23 00; www.english.viennaairport.com/bus.html). Buses leaving the airport for the **City Air Terminal** at the Hilton opposite Wien Mitte (every 20min. 6:30am-11:10pm, every 30min. 5am-1:20am; €5.80). Buses travel to and from the airport from **Südbahnhof** and **Westbahnhof** (every hr. 5:30-8:30am and 6:55pm-12:10am, every 30min 8:25am-6:55pm). By far the easiest (and most expensive) way to and from the airport is by private airport shuttle services, such as **JetBus** (☎700 73 87 78), located just outside the baggage claim. Shuttles deliver passengers to any address in the city for staggered, though always substantial, sums of money (a ride to Wien Mitte is €25 per person). Call a day in advance to arrange pickup for a return trip. Parties of three or more get discounts when booking a return trip.

BY TRAIN. Vienna has two main train stations with international departures. The Westbahnhof is accessible by the U3 (orange) line, the U6 (brown) line, or the S7; the Südbahnhof is accessible by the U1 (red) line with a connection on the S60 or S7. For general train information (throughout Austria), call ☎05 17 17 (24hr.) or check www.oebb.at. Note that fares regularly change, so check ahead.

Westbahnhof, XV, Mariahilferstr. 132 (☎89 23 39 2). Trains from here run primarily **west**. Domestically to: **Bregenz** (8hr., 9 per day, €57); **Innsbruck** (5-6hr., every 2hr., €48.50); **Linz** (2hr., every hr., €25.50); **Salzburg** (3hr., every hr., €36.50). Internationally to: **Amsterdam** (14hr., 7:17pm, €59); **Budapest** (3-4hr., 6 per day, €37.60); **Hamburg** (9hr.; 10:17am, 7:45pm; €124.60); **Munich** (4hr., 5 per day, €63.10); **Paris** (14hr.; 8:47am, 8:21pm; €153.10); **Zurich** (9hr., 3 per day, €77.90); **Berlin** (11hr., 9:19pm, €122.24). The **information counter** is open daily 7am-10pm.

Südbahnhof, X, Wiener Gürtel 1a (☎50 53 13 2). Trains leave for destinations to the **south** and **east**. Domestically to: **Graz** (2hr., every hr. 6:04am-10:34pm, €26.90) and **Villach** (5hr., every hr. 6:04am-10:34pm, €40). Internationally to: **Berlin** (9hr., 10:25am, €87.90); **Bratislava** (1hr., 13 per day, €10.90); **Krakow** (7-8hr., 3 per day, €45.30); **Prague** (4hr., 5 per day, €45.70); **Rome** (14hr., 7:29am, €100.60); **Venice** (9-10hr., 4 per day, €71.60); and other European cities. The **information counter** is open daily in high-season 6:30am-10:00pm; in low-season 6:30am-9pm.

DISTRICT NAMES & NUMBERS: Moving roughly clockwise, Vienna's 23 districts (Bezirke) are: I, **Innenstadt**; II, **Leopoldstadt**; III, **Landstraße**; IV, **Wieden**; V, **Margareten**; VI, **Mariahilf**; VII, **Neubau**; VIII, **Josefstadt**; IX, **Alsergrund**; X, **Favoriten**; XI, **Simmering**; XII, **Meidling**; XIII, **Hietzing**; XIV, **Penzing**; XV, **Rudolfsheim Fünfhaus**; XVI, **Ottakring**; XVII, **Hernals**; XVIII, **Währing**; XIX, **Döbling**; XX, **Brigittenau**; XXI, **Floridsdorf**; XXII, **Donaustadt**; XXIII, **Liesing**.

Three stations handle mostly commuter trains. The largest is **Franz-Josefs Bahnhof,** IX, Althamstr. 10, on the tram 5. There are also two smaller stations: **Bahnhof Wien Mitte,** in the center of town, and **Bahnhof Wien Nord,** by the Praterstern on the north side of the Danube Canal. Bahnhof Wien Nord is the main S-Bahn and U-Bahn link for trains heading north, but most Bundesbahn trains go through the other stations. Some regional trains (Krems, for example) also leave from **Spittelau,** located on the U4 and U6 subway lines.

BY BUS AND BOAT. Travel by bus in Austria is seldom cheaper than travel by train; compare prices before buying a ticket. **City bus terminals** are located at Wien Mitte/Landstr., Hütteldorf, Heiligenstadt, Floridsdorf, Kagran, Erdberg, and Reumannpl. Domestic **BundesBuses** run from these stations to local and international destinations. (Local: ticket counter open M-F 6am-5:50pm, Sa-Su 6am-3:50pm. International destinations: BundesBus ☎711 01. Open 7am-10pm.)

The well-known **Donau Dampfschiffahrtsgesellschaft Donaureisen (DDSG),** I, Friedrichstr. 7 (☎58 88 00; www.ddsg-blue-danube.at), organizes cruises on the Danube, stopping at the cities of Melk, Spitz, Dürnstein, and Krems/Stein (see p. 304). The DDSG also operates hydrofoils to **Bratislava** (1½hr., Apr.-Oct. 9am; €21, round-trip €32) and **Budapest** (5½hr., April and Aug.-Nov. 9am, May-Aug. 8am, Aug.-early Sept. 1pm; €65, round-trip €89. Eurail and ISIC holders get 20% off within Austria, ages 6-15 half-price, under 6 free.)

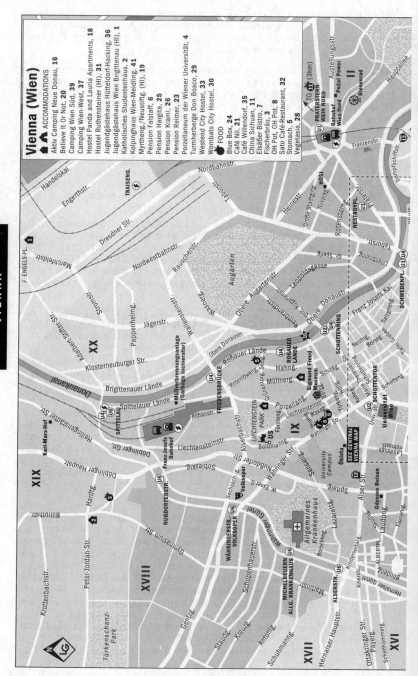

Vienna (Wien)

🏠🏕 ACCOMMODATIONS
Aktiv Camping Neue Donau, **16**
Believe It Or Not, **20**
Camping Wien Süd, **39**
Camping Wien-West, **37**
Hostel Panda and Lauria Apartments, **18**
Hostel Ruthensteiner (HI), **31**
Jugendgästehaus Hütteldorf-Hacking, **36**
Jugendgästehaus Wien Brigittenau (HI), **1**
Katholisches Studentenhaus, **2**
Kolpinghaus Wien-Meidling, **41**
Myrtheng./Neustiftg. (HI), **19**
Pension Falstaff, **6**
Pension Hargita, **25**
Pension Kraml, **26**
Pension Reimer, **23**
Porzellaneum der Wiener Universität, **4**
Turmherberge Don Bosco, **29**
Westend City Hostel, **33**
Wombats City Hostel, **30**

● FOOD
Blue Box, **24**
Café Nil, **21**
Café Willendorf, **35**
China Sichuan, **11**
Elsäßer Bistro, **7**
Fischerbräu, **3**
OH Pot, OH Pot, **8**
Sato Café-Restaurant, **32**
Stomach, **5**
Vegetasia, **28**

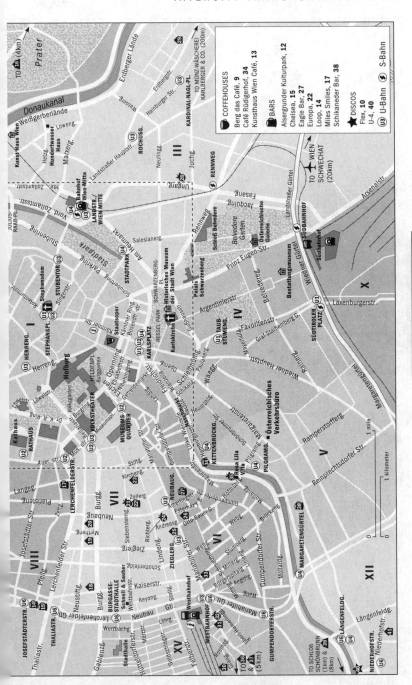

VIENNA

COFFEEHOUSES
Berg das Café, 9
Café Rüdigerhof, 34
Kunsthaus Wien Café, 13

BARS
Alsergrunder Kulturpark, 12
Chelsea, 15
Eagle Bar, 27
Europa, 22
Loop, 14
Miles Smiles, 17
Schikaneder Bar, 38

★ DISCOS
Flex, 10
U-4, 40

Ⓤ U-Bahn Ⓢ S-Bahn

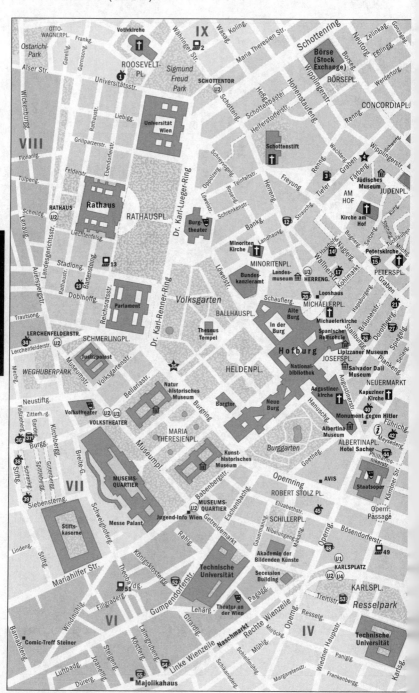

VIENNA

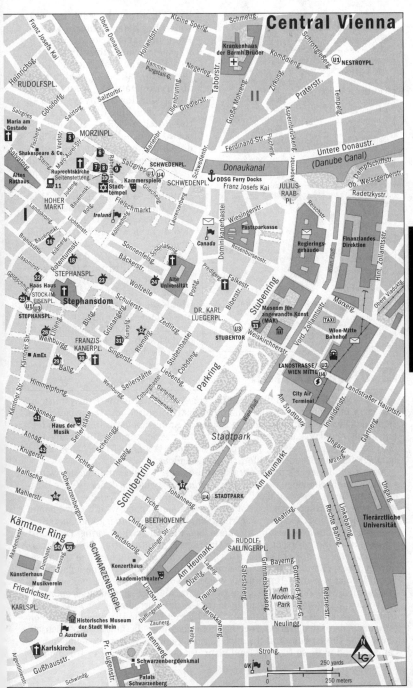

Central Vienna

Central Vienna

🏠 ACCOMMODATIONS
Hotel am Stephansplatz, 22
Hotel Imperial, 50
Hotel Zur Wiener Staatsoper, 43
Studenten Wohnheim der
  Hochschule für Musik, 41

🍴 FOOD
A Tavola, 28
Amerlingbeisl, 38
Bizi Pizza, 18
Centimeter, 39
DO&CO, 25
Inigo, 23
Konoba, 34
Levante, 17
Ma Crêperie, 24
Margaritaville, 19
Maschu Maschu, 9
Rosenberger
  Markt, 42
Smutny, 45
Trzesniewski, 21
University Mensa, 1
Wrenkh, 16
Yugetsu Saryo, 40
Zimolo, 29
Zum Mogulhof, 36

☕ COFFEEHOUSES
Café Bräunerhof, 26
Café Central, 12
Café Drechsler, 54
Café Griensteidl, 20

Café Hawelka, 27
Café MAK, 33
Café Museum, 48
Café Savoy, 55
Café Sperl, 52
Demel, 15
Hotel Imperial, 50
Hotel Sacher, 44
Kleines Café, 30

💻 INTERNET CAFES
bigNET: 11, 49 & 51
Café Einstein, 13
Café Stein, 2

🍸 BARS
Benjamin, 5
Cato, 3
Das Möbel, 37
Esterházykeller, 14
First Floor Bar, 10
Jazzland, 6
Kaktus, 8
Kunsthalle Café, 53
Mapitom der
  Bierlokal, 7
Santo Spirito, 31

⭐ CLUBS
Club Meierei, 47
Havana Club, 46
Porgy & Bess, 32
Volksgarten Disco, 35
Why Not, 4

BY CAR. From the **west**, take A1, which begins and ends in Vienna. From the **south,** take A2, or A3 to A2, which runs directly into the city. From the **east,** take A4. From the **north,** take A22, which runs along the Danube. A number of much smaller highways lead to Vienna, including Rte. 7 and 8 from the north and Rte. 10 from the south. An economical but less predictable alternative to the train is **ride-sharing. Mitfahrzentrale Wien** pairs drivers and riders over the phone. Call to see which rides are available. (☎408 22 10. Open M-Sa 7am-noon.) A ride to **Salzburg** costs €18, to **Prague** €50. Reservations two days in advance are recommended.

Although *Let's Go* does not recommend hitching, **hitchhikers** headed for Salzburg have been seen taking U4 to "Hütteldorf," from which the highway leading to the Autobahn is 10km farther. Hitchers traveling south often ride tram #67 to the last stop and wait at the rotary near Laaerberg.

✳ ORIENTATION

Vienna is divided into 23 **districts** *(Bezirke).* The first is the *Innenstadt,* or *innere Stadt* (city center), and the other districts spiral out clockwise. Street signs indicate the district number in Roman or Arabic numerals before the street and number, and postal codes correspond to the district number: 1010 for the first district, 1020 for the second, 1110 for the eleventh, etc. *Let's Go* includes district numbers for establishments before the street address.

Almost all of Vienna's major attractions are densely concentrated either within or immediately outside of **District I** (the *Innenstadt*), which is defined by the Ringstraße on three sides and the Danube Canal *(Donaukanal)* on the fourth. The **Ringstraße** (or "Ring") consists of various segments, each with its own name: Franz-Joseph-Kai, Stubenring, Parkring, Schubertring, Kärntner Ring, Opernring, Burgring, Dr.-Karl-Renner-Ring, Dr.-Karl-Lüger-Ring, and Schottenring. The **tourist office** is near the intersection of the Opernring, Kärntner Ring, and Kärntnerstraße, by the Karlsplatz U-Bahn stop. The *Innenstadt* contains all of the museums, palaces, churches, parks, cafés, restaurants, and much of the nightlife for which Vienna is known. Unfortunately, because of this impressive concentration of attractions, District I contains almost no affordable accommodations options.

Excellent alternatives can be found in the Districts surrounding the *Innenstadt.* District II is directly across the river from District I, while Districts III-IX are on the same side of the Danube. Together, they constitute the first layer of Districts beyond the tourist center of the city. Most of Vienna's budget accommodations can be found in these Districts, and many are only a short walk or U-Bahn ride from the *Innenstadt*. Although some options are somewhat isolated in residential zones, there are several prominent clusters of activity that offer more than just a place to stay. There is a wide variety of accommodations, food, and bars in **District VII**, whose offerings spill over into Districts VI and VIII, between the Westbahnhof and the *Innenstadt*. **District IX,** on the Danube just north of District I, has multiple accommodations options, food, and cafés. Further north, the **Grinzing** region of District XIX is famous for its *Heurigen* (wine taverns).

The remaining districts expand from another ring, the Gürtel ("belt"). Like the Ring, this major two-way thoroughfare has numerous segments, including Margaretengürtel, Währinger Gürtel, and Neubaugürtel. These districts are mainly outside of the main tourist attractions in the city.

▐ LOCAL TRANSPORTATION

Public transportation in Vienna is extensive and dependable; call ☎ 790 91 00 for general info. The **subway** (U-Bahn), **tram** (Straßenbahn), **elevated train** (S-Bahn), and **bus** systems operate under one ticket system. A single fare is €2 if purchased from a machine on a bus, €1.50 if purchased in advance from a machine in a station, ticket office, or tobacco shop (*Tabak* or *Trafik*). This ticket permits you to travel to any single destination in the city and switch from bus to U-Bahn to tram to S-Bahn, as long as your travel is uninterrupted. This part is tricky: to validate a ticket, punch it in the machine immediately upon entering the first vehicle. Do not stamp the ticket again when you switch trains. A ticket stamped twice or not stamped at all is invalid, and plainclothes inspectors may fine you €60 plus the ticket price. Other ticket options (available at the same places as pre-purchased single tickets) are a **24hr. pass** (€5), a **3-day "rover" ticket** (€12), a **7-day pass** (€12.50; valid M 9am-M 9am), or an **8-day pass** (€24; valid any 8 days, not necessarily consecutive; valid also for several people traveling together). The **Vienna Card** (€16.90) offers free travel for 72hr., as well as substantial discounts at museums, sights, and events, and is especially useful for non-students. If you are traveling with a child over 6, a bicycle, or a dog, you must also buy a half-price ticket (€0.80, single fare; €1.50 double fare). Children under 6 always ride free, as does anyone under 15 on Sundays and school holidays. (The pocket map available at the tourist offices lists official holidays.) You can take bicycles on all underground trains; each train restricts bikes to certain cars, marked with a bicycle symbol.

FROM THE ROAD

JAY-FINING

I know that technically jaywalking is illegal, but I can count on one hand the number of times I have seen this law observed by people who live in big American cities, let alone authorities actually enforcing it. In Vienna, however, jaywalking is a different story entirely.

I was standing at a crosswalk on one of the major streets of the city. Since there were no cars coming in either direction, I decided to walk. I had taken about three steps when the other pedestrians started yelling at me and I found myself yanked forcefully back onto the sidewalk.

Stunned, I stood patiently while I was castigated for my actions (very politely I might add; the man was concerned with my safety). During the lecture I learned that jaywalking in Vienna (and pretty much all over Austria) is finable on the spot, with a minimum penalty of €21 and in certain cases also the revocation of the perpetrator's driver's license. And foreign status will not lessen the fine—in the weeks following my little mishap I saw three tourists who were caught in the act receiving tickets along with stern talkings-to.

So, when in Vienna make sure to do as the Viennese. Look left, right, and left again, and wait for the pedestrian light to turn green.

- Alison Giordano, 2003

VIENNA

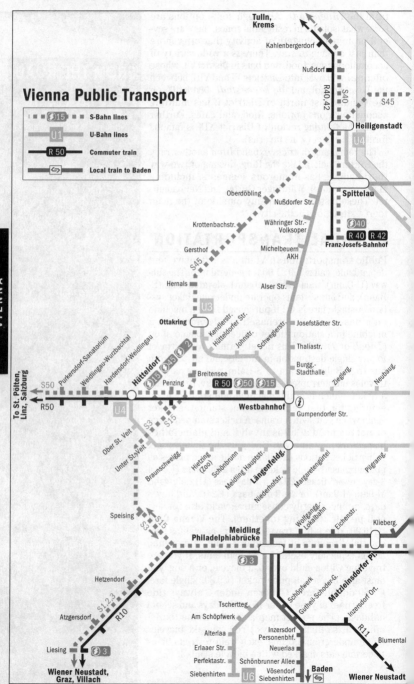

Vienna Public Transport

- ■ ■ ●15 ■ ■ S-Bahn lines
- U1 U-Bahn lines
- R 50 Commuter train
- ⟷ Local train to Baden

Tulln,
Krems

Kahlenbergerdorf

Nußdorf

R40,42

S40

S45

Heiligenstadt

U4

Oberdöbling

Nußdorfer Str.

Spittelau

Währinger Str.-
Volksoper

Krottenbachstr.

●40

R 40   R 42

Gersthof

Michelbeuern
AKH

Franz-Josefs-Bahnhof

S45

Hernals

Alser Str.

U3

Ottakring

Kendlerstr.

Hütteldorfer Str.

Josefstädter Str.

Johnstr.

Schweglerstr.

Thaliastr.

Purkersdorf-Sanatorium

Weidlingau-Wurzbachtal

Hardersdorf-Weidlingau

Hütteldorf

●15 ●15 2

Breitensee

Burgg.-
Stadthalle

Zieglerg.

Neubaug.

Penzing

R 50 ●50 ●15

To St. Pölten,
Linz, Salzburg

S50

R50

U4

S3

S15

Westbahnhof

ⓘ

Gumpendorfer Str.

Ober St. Veit

Unter St. Veit

Braunschweigg.

Hietzing
(Zoo)

Schönbrunn

Meidling Hauptstr.

Langenfeldg.

Margaretengürtel

Pilgramg.

Niederhofstr.

Speising

S3

S15

Meidling
Philadelphiabrücke

Wolfgang-
Lokalbahn

Eichenstr.

Klieberg.

●3

Matzleinsdorfer Pl.

Hetzendorf

Schöpfwerk

Guthel-Schoder-G.

Inzersdorf Ort.

Tschertteg

S1,2,3

R10

Am Schöpfwerk

Atzgersdorf

Inzersdorf
Personenbhf.

R11

Alterlaa

Blumental

Neuerlaa

Erlaaer Str.

Perfektastr.

Schönbrunner Allee

Liesing

●3

Siebenhirten

U6

Vösendorf
Siebenhirten

Baden
⟷

Wiener Neustadt

Wiener Neustadt,
Graz, Villach

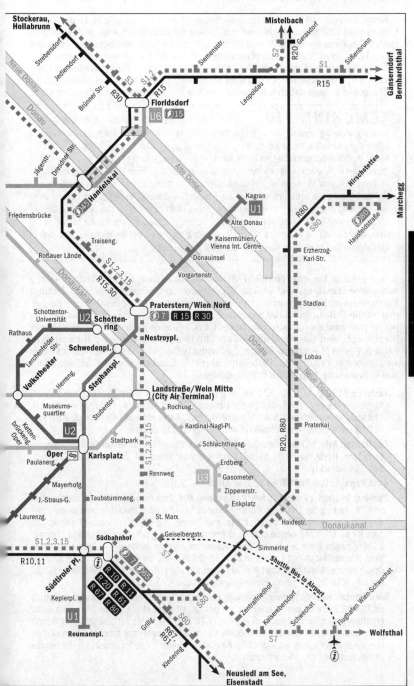

Regular trams and subway cars stop running between midnight and 5am. Beginning around 12:30am, a 'NightLine' runs along most tram, subway, and major bus routes (buses come every 30 and 50 min). In major hubs like Schottentor, some buses leave from slightly different areas than the daytime buses. "N" signs with yellow cat eyes designate NightLine stops. A complete schedule is available at bus counters in U-Bahn stations. (€1.50 for single fare; day transport passes not valid.)

The **public transportation information line** has live operators who give directions

"SMOKING PIG" Upon entering a U-Bahn station, a bubble-gum pink pig wearing nothing but a polka-dotted tie, tennis shoes, a hat, gold earrings, white gloves, and a smile poses amidst a pile of gray sand and forgotten cigarette-butts. Built like Schwarzenegger in his Mr. Olympia days, this pig (affectionately called "Hurdiwurdi" by transportation employees) occupies a number of the major U-Bahn stations of Vienna in hopes of reminding riders to finish smoking before they catch their trains. Despite the U-Bahn's no-smoking policy, "Hurdiwurdi" is not to be viewed as anti-smoking propaganda; on the contrary, it was commissioned at the behest of Casablanca, a well-known cigarette company in Austria. Painted by famous Austrian artist Deix, "Hurdiwurdi" is meant to advertise smoking as a pleasurable pastime, and one that should be resumed immediately after exiting the U-Bahn.

to any point in the city. (☎709 01 00. M-F 6:00am-10pm, Sa-Su 8:30am-4:30pm.) **Information stands** (marked with an "i") in many stations can also provide detailed instructions on how to purchase tickets, as well as an indispensable free pocket map of the U-Bahn and S-Bahn systems. A comprehensive map of Vienna's entire public transportation is also available (€1.50). Stands in the U-Bahn at Karlspl., Stephanspl., and the Westbahnhof are the most likely to have information in English. (Open M-F 6:30am-6:30pm, Sa-Su and holidays 8:30am-4pm.) Other stands are located at Praterstern, Philadelphiabrücke, Landstr., Floridsdorf, Spittelau, and Volkstheater. (Open M-F 6:30am-6:30pm.)

Taxis: (☎313 00, 401 00, 601 60, or 814 00). Stands at Westbahnhof, Südbahnhof, Karlspl. in the city center, and by the Bermuda Dreiecke for late-night revelers. Accredited taxis have yellow and black signs on the roof. Rates generally €2 plus €0.2 per km; slightly more expensive on holidays and at nights (11pm-6am).

Car Rental: Avis, I, Opernring 3-5 (☎587 62 41). Open M-F 7am-8pm, Sa 8am-2pm, Su 8am-1pm. **Hertz,** (☎70 07 32 661) at the airport. Open M-F 7:15am-11pm, Sa 8am-8pm, Su 8am-11pm.

Auto Repairs: Call **ÖAMTC** (☎120) or **ARBÖ** (☎123).

Parking: In District I, street parking is allowed M-F 9am-7pm for 1½hr. In districts II-IX and XX, parking for 2hr. max. Parking permits/vouchers are available from banks, railway stations, Vienna Line ticket offices, and *Tabaks* (€5.00). Handicapped visitors can park for an unlimited period of time in short-term parking with a valid handicap permit. 24hr. garages are open in the aforementioned districts (www.wkw.at/garagen). However, it is easiest to find parking in the Garages that line the Ringstr., including 2 by the Opera House, 1 at Franz-Josef Kai, and 1 at the Marek-Garage at Messepalast (€2.50 per day, €12.35 per week). Parking illegally risks a €25-150 fine.

Bike Rental: Rentals generally average €5 per hr. **Pedal Power,** II, Ausstellungsstr. 3 (☎729 72 34; www.pedalpower.at). €4 per hr., €17 per 4hr., €32 for 24hr. with delivery. They also offer bike tours of the city (€19-23). Discounts for students and Vienna Card holders. Open May-Oct. 8am-8pm. Check Wombats Hostel for cheap bike and in-line skate rentals. Pick up *Vienna By Bike* at the tourist office for details on the bicycle scene, including city bike information.i

CRIME IN THE CITY. Vienna is considered to be quite safe, but it is none-theless a metropolis with crime like any other, and boasts a healthy number of pickpockets. Use common sense, especially after dark. Women should not walk alone. Drug dealers congregate around the **Karlspl.** and hang around the train stations at night. Also beware of the city's small skinhead population. Avoid areas in Districts **X** and **XIV**, as well as **Prater Park.** Vienna's Red Light District covers sections of the Gürtel.

PRACTICAL INFORMATION

TOURIST & FINANCIAL SERVICES

Main Tourist Office: I, Albertinapl. (☎211 14 0, www.info.wien.at). One block up Operng. from the Opera House. The tourist office dispenses an assortment of brochures, including free city maps. The brochure *Youth Scene* provides vital information for young travelers. The office books rooms for a €3 fee plus a 1-night deposit. Open 9am-7pm.

Branch Offices:

Westbahnhof. Open 7:30am-8:40pm daily.

Highway exit "Wien Auhof," off A1. Open Easter-Oct. daily 8am-10pm, Nov.-Mar. 10am-6pm.

Highway exit "Zentrum," off A2, XI, Trierstr. 149. Open daily July-Sept. 8am-10pm; Oct. and Easter-June 9am-7pm.

North Danube Island. Open May-Sept. 10am-6pm.

Vienna International Airport, in arrival hall. Open 8:30am-9pm.

Jugend-Info Wien (Vienna Youth Information): VII, MuseumsQuartier/Babenbergerstr. 1. Take the U3 (Orange) to Volkstheater. Hip staff has information on cultural events, housing, and employment opportunities, and sells discounted youth tickets to concert events and theater productions. The indispensable *Jugend in Wien* brochure is here. Open M-Sa noon-7pm.

Österreichisches Verkehrsbüro (Austrian National Travel Office): IV, Margaretenstr. 1 (☎587 20 00; www.austria-tourism.at). Open Th 10am-6pm.

Ökista, IX, Türkenstr. 6 (☎40 14 80), specializes in student travel, tickets, and passes. Open M-F 9am-5:30pm.

Embassies: Generally, each country's embassy and consulate are located in the same building, listed under *Botschaften* or *Konsulate* in the phone book. Contact consulates for assistance with visas and passports and in emergencies.

Australia: IV, Mattiellistr. 2-4 (☎512 85 80; www.australianembassy.at).

Canada: I, Laurenzerberg 2 (☎531 38 30 00; www.dfait-maeci.gc.ca).

Ireland: I, Rotenturmstr. 16-18, 5th floor (☎71 54 24 6; vienna@iveath.irlgov.ie).

New Zealand: Consulate, XIX, Karl-Tornay-g. 34 (☎318 85 05; p.sunley@demmer.at).

South Africa: XIX, Sandg. 33 (☎320 64 93 0; www.southafrican-embassy.at).

UK: III, Jauresg. 10 (☎716 13 51 51; www.britishembassy.at).

US: IX, Boltzmanng. 16 (☎313 39; www.usembassy-vienna.at).

Currency Exchange: ATMs are your best bet. Nearly all accept Cirrus, DC, MC, V (see p. 14). **Banks** and **airport exchanges** use the same official rates. Minimum commission €12.35 for up to US$3000 traveler's checks, 1% for cash. Most are open M-W and F 8am-12:30pm and 1:30-3pm, Th 8am-12:30pm and 1:30-5:30pm. **Train station** exchanges offer long hours and a €10.91 fee for changing up to US$1000 of traveler's checks. The 24hr. exchange at the **main post office** has excellent rates and charges an €8 fee to change up to US$1100 in traveler's checks. Stay away from the 24hr. bill exchange machines in the *Innenstadt,* as they generally charge outrageous prices.

American Express: I, Kärntnerstr. 21-23, down the street from Stephanspl. (☎515 40), cashes AmEx checks for free, and Thomas Cook checks for a minimum €7 commission; sells theater, concert, and other tickets, and holds mail for 4 weeks for AmEx members. Open M-F 9am-5:30pm, Sa 9am-noon. For 24hr. refund service, call ☎0800 20 68 40.

LOCAL SERVICES

Luggage Storage: Lockers are €2 per day at all train stations.

Lost Property: Fundbüro, XVIII, Bastieng., Suite 6, 238 (☎400 080 91). For items lost on public transportation, call ☎790 94 35 00. Open M-Su 7am-9:30pm. For items lost on trains, call ☎580 03 29 96 (Westbahnhof) or 580 03 56 56 (Südbahnhof).

Bookstores: Shakespeare & Company, I, Sterng. 2 (☎535 50 53). Eclectic and intelligent. Great British magazine selection. Open M-Sa 9am-7pm. The **British Bookshop,** I, Weihburgg. 24 (☎512 19 45), has an extensive travel section. Open M-F 9:30am-6:30pm, Sa 9:30am-5pm. New branch at VI, Mariahilferstr. 4. **Comic-Treff Steiner,** VI, Barnabiteng. 12 (☎586 76 27). One of Vienna's best comic book stores. Open M-F 10am-7pm, Sa 10am-2pm.

Radio: FM4, 103.8FM. Mixes classical, oldies, and mainstream music with news updates every hr. until 7pm in English, French, and German, including the BBC World Service. "What's on in Vienna" airs at 1pm. **Radio 03,** 99.9FM Pop and rock. **Energy,** 104.2FM, and **TheMusic,** 88.6FM, both play mainstream pop.

Bi-Gay-Lesbian Organizations: The bisexual, gay, and lesbian community in Vienna is more integrated than in other Austrian cities. For the gay goings-on about town, pick up the *Vienna Gay Guide* (www.gayguide.at) from the tourist office, the monthly Viennese magazine (in German) called *Extra Connect,* or the free monthly publication *Bussi* at any gay bar, café, or club. *Falter* newspaper lists gay events in a special heading. The following organizations also sponsor events and offer help in Vienna:

Rosa Lila Villa, VI, Linke Wienzeile 102 (☎587 17 89), is a popular resource and social center for gays and lesbians whether native to Vienna or just visiting. Friendly staff speaks English and provides counseling, information, a library, and nightclub listings (see Nightlife, p. 140). Open M-F 5-8pm, gay info closed F.

Homosexuelle Initiative Wien (HOSI), II, Novarag. 40 (☎216 66 04; www.hosiwien.at). Lesbian group and phone network F 7pm. Prints *Lambda Nachrichten.* Open Tu 7-10pm (includes phone counseling). Youth Th 5pm (coming out), 7-9pm (general).

Lesbischwul und Transgender Referat (☎588 01 58 90). Gay student counseling group. F 4-6pm.

Laundromat: Most hostels offer laundry service for €4. **Schnell und Sauber,** VII, Westbahnhofstr. 60 (☎524 64 60); From Westbahnhof, take tram #18 to "Urban-Loritzpl." 6kg wash €4.50, dry €1 per 20min. Soap included. Open 24hr. **Münz-wäscherei Karlberger & Co.,** III, Schlachthausg. 19 (☎798 81 91). 7kg wash €6.50, dry €1. Soap €1. Open M-F 7:30am-6:30pm, Sa 7:30am-1pm.

Public Showers and Toilets: At Westbahnhof, in Friseursalon Navratil downstairs from subway passage. Well maintained. 30min. shower €4; with soap, towel, and shampoo €5. Showers are also available at **Jörgerbad,** XVII, Jörgerstr. 42-44, and at the airport. There are cheap pay toilets in most U-bahn stations and a special *Jugendstil* toilet in Graben (9am-7pm, requires coins).

Snow Reports: In German for Vienna, Lower Austria, and Styria ☎15 83; for Salzburg, Upper Austria, and Carinthia ☎15 84; for Tyrol and Vorarlberg ☎15 85.

EMERGENCY & COMMUNICATION

Emergencies: Police ☎133, **Ambulance** ☎144, **Fire** ☎122.

Poison Control: ☎406 43 43. Open 24hr.

Crisis Hotlines: All hotlines have English-speaking employees. **Rape Crisis Hotline:** ☎523 22 22. M 1-6pm, Tu 10am-3pm, W 1-6pm, Th 3-8pm. **24hr. immediate help:** ☎717 19. **Psychological Counsel Hotline:** ☎319 3566 or 402 7838. M-F 8pm-8am, Sa-Su 24hr.

Medical Assistance: Allgemeines Krankenhaus, IX, Währinger Gürtel 18-20 (☎404 00 19 64). **Emergency care** ☎141, **24hr. pharmacy** ☎15 50. Consulates offer lists of English-speaking physicians, or call **Wolfgang Molnar** ☎330 34 68.

Internet Access: bigNET.internet.cafe, I, Kärntnerstr. 61 (☎503 98 44); I, Hoher markt 8-9 (☎533 29 39); and the largest Internet café in Austria, Mariahilferstr., with an English-speaking staff. €3.70 per 30min; price lowers after the first 30min. **Café Stein,** IX, Währingerstr. 6-8 (☎31 97 24 19). €4 per 30min. **Café Einstein,** VIII, Rathauspl. 4 (☎405 26 26). M-F 7am-2am, Sa 10am-2am, Su 10am-midnight. **Jugend-Info des Bundesministeriums,** I, Franz-Josefs-Kai 51 (☎533 70 30). Open M-F 11am-6pm.

Post Offices: Hauptpostamt, I, Fleischmarkt 19. Vast structure contains exchange, phone, fax, and mail services. Open 24hr. Address *Poste Restante* to "LASTNAME, First-name; *Postlagernde Briefe;* Hauptpostamt; Fleischmarkt 19; A-1010 Wien." Branches throughout the city and at the train stations; look for yellow signs with the trumpet logo. **Postal Codes:** 1st district A-1010, 2nd A-1020, 3rd A-1030, etc., to the 23rd A-1230.

ACCOMMODATIONS & CAMPING

Hunting for cheap rooms in Vienna during peak tourist season (June-Sept.) can be unpleasant; write or call for reservations at least five days in advance. Otherwise, plan on calling from the train station early in the morning to put your name down for a reservation. If there are no vacancies, ask to be put on a waiting list, and inquire about alternative lodgings. Those unable to find a hostel bed should consider a *Pension*. One-star establishments are usually adequate and are most common in districts VII, VIII, and IX; singles start around €30, doubles €40.

If you're staying a longer period of time, try **Odyssee Reisen und Mitwohnzentrale,** VIII, Laudong. 7. Odyssee's staff finds apartments for €17-25 per person per night, about €90 for a week, €150 for a month. A 20% commission is charged on each month's rent. (☎402 60 61. Bring your passport to register. Open M-F 10am-2pm and 3-6pm.) **Arwag** offers similar services via the web (www.arwag.at) or through a 24hr. hotline (☎79 70 01 17). Alternatively, visit either **Österreichische Hochschüler-schaft** at Rooseveltpl. 5 or the bulletin boards on the first floor of the **Neues Institut Gebäude** (NIG building) on Universitätstr. 7 near the Votivkirche.

Whatever you do, be aware of the potentially confusing practices employed by local establishments in booking rooms (see "Open-Ended Policy," p. 105).

HOSTELS & DORMITORIES

▨ **Hostel Ruthensteiner (HI),** XV, Robert-Hamerlingg. 24 (☎893 42 02; www.hostelru-thensteiner.com). Exit Westbahnhof at the main entrance and turn right onto Maria-hilferstr.; continue until Haidmannsg. Turn left, then take the first right on Robert-Hamerlingg. and continue to the middle of the block. This top-notch hostel boasts an extremely knowledgeable, English-speaking staff; spotless rooms; a sunny, rose-filled courtyard; and amenities that include a small kitchenette with a fridge. Breakfast €2.50. Showers and sheets (except for 10-bed rooms) included. Lockers included in every room. Internet €2 for 25min. 4-night max. stay. Reception 24hr. Laundry €6. Reservations recommended, but owners often set aside beds for spontaneous arrivals. "The Outback" summer dorm €11; 4- to 10-bed dorms €10-12; singles and doubles from €18-22. AmEx/MC/V (€0.40 extra for using credit card). ❷

ACCOMMODATIONS BY LOCATION

INNENSTADT
Hotel Imperial (106) I❺
Hotel zur Wiener Staatsoper (106) I❺
Studentenwohnheim der Hochschule für Musik (107) I❸
Hotel am Stephansplatz (106) I❺

BETWEEN THE INNENSTADT AND WESTBAHNHOF
Pension Kraml (106) VI❸
Pension Hargita (106) VII❹
Myrthengasse/Neustiftgasse (105) VII❷
Lauria Apartments (106) VII❷
Hostel Panda (104) VII❷
Believe It Or Not (104) VII❷
Pension Reimerr (106) VII❹

NEAR THE WESTBAHNHOF
Wombats City Hostel (104) XIV❷
🏠 Hostel Ruthensteiner (103) XV❷
Westend City Hostel (104) VI❷

DISTRICT IX
Pension Falstafff (106) IX❹
Porzellaneum der Wiener Uni. (107) IX❸

OTHER DISTRICTS
Katholisches Studentenhaus (107) XIX❸
Jugendg. Wien Brigittenau (105) XX❷
Jugendg. Hütteldorf-Hacking (105) XIII❷
Kolpinghaus Wien-Meidling (105) XIII❷
Turmherberge Don Bosco (105) III❶
Aktiv Camping Neue Donau (107) XXII❶

OUTSIDE VIENNA
Wien-West (107) Hüttelbergstr. 80 ❶
Wien Süd (107) Breitenfurterstr. 269 ❶

Wombats City Hostel, XIV, Grang. 6 (☎897 23 36; www.wombats.at). From Westbahnhof, take the main exit and turn right onto Mariahilferstr. Continue until 152 (on the corner of Rosinag.). Turn right onto Rosinag. and continue until Grang. (2nd left). Although near the train tracks and a number of auto-body shops, this superb modern hostel compensates with a pub (8am-2am; bar closes at 11pm) and various perks, including movie screenings (every night in the cafeteria, free). Recent renovations have resulted in loft-like rooms with great views of surrounding Vienna. Breakfast €3. Shower in each room. Towels €3. Laundry €4.50. **Internet** €1 for 12 min. Bike or in-line skate rental €8 per day. 2-, 4-, and 6-bed rooms €14-36 per person. ❷

Westend City Hostel, VI, Fugerg. 3 (☎597 67 29; www.westendcityhostel.at). Located right near Westbahnhof. Exit "Äussere Mariahilfstr." and cross the large intersection, make a right on Mullerg. and a left on Fugerg. Look for the white building with vibrant purple accents. This new, large hostel lacks much in the way of character, but has comfortable beds and an ideal location. **Internet** €2.60 per 30min. Laundry €5.50. Breakfast and sheets included. Reception 24hr. Check-out 10:30am. Curfew 11:30pm. 12-bed dorms €16; 8- to 10-bed dorms €17; 4- to 6-bed €18; singles €38.50; doubles €23. ❷

Believe It Or Not, VII, Myrtheng. 10, Apt. #14 (☎526 46 58). From Westbahnhof, take U6 (brown; dir.: Floridsdorf) to "Burgg./Stadthalle," then bus #48A (dir.: Ring) to "Neubaug." Walk back on Burgg. 1 block and take the first right on Myrtheng. Ring the bell. A converted 2nd-floor apartment, this cute hostel has a kitchen and 2 co-ed bunkrooms. Sheets and lockers included. Ages 17-30. Minimum stay of 2 nights. Reception 8:15am-1pm. Check-in until 11pm. Lockout 10:30am-12:30pm. Reservations recommended. €12.25 per person; Nov.-Easter €7.50-10. ❷

Hostel Panda, VII, Kaiserstr. 77, 3rd fl. (☎522 25 55; www.lauria-vienna.at/panda). From Westbahnhof take U6 (brown; dir.: Floridsdorf.) to "Burg/Stadthalle." Take second left on Kaiserstrab. From Südbahnhof, take tram #18 to "Westbahnhof," and follow directions from Westbahnhof. Housed in an old-fashioned, semi-*Jugendstil* Austrian apartment building, this eclectic hostel has 18 mattresses packed into 2 co-ed dorms with high ceilings and art-deco lanterns. While cramped, the rooms have access to kitchen and TV. **Internet** access and laundry available at nearby businesses. Bring lock for lockers. Check-in until 11pm; lockout 10am-12:30pm; no curfew. Ages 17-30. Dorms €12.50; Nov.-Easter €9. €3.50 surcharge for 1-night stays. ❷

Myrthengasse (HI), VII, Myrtheng. 7, across the street from Believe It or Not, and **Neustiftgasse (HI)**, VII, Neustiftg. 85 (☎523 63 16; hostel@chello.at). These simple, modern hostels, both under the same management, are a 20min. walk from the *Innenstadt;* a small lounge and dining room make these hostels perfect for meeting other travelers. Breakfast, lockers, and sheets included. Lunch or dinner €5. Locks €3.65. Laundry €3.50. **Internet** access €4.36 per 30min. 5-day max. stay. Reception at Myrtheng. 24hr. Lockout 9am-2pm. Rooms separated by sex (except for families). Wheelchair-accessible. Curfew 1am. Reservations recommended; arrive by 4pm. 4- to 6-bed dorms with shower €15; 2-bed dorms with shower €17.50; Jan. 7-Mar. 17 and Nov. 11-Dec. 22 €14/€16.50. Non-members add €3.50. AmEx/MC/V. ❷

Kolpinghaus Wien-Meidling, XIII, Bendlg. 10-12 (☎813 54 87; www.kolpinghaus-wien.at). Take U6 (brown) to "Niederhofstr." Head right on Niederhofstr. and take the 4th right onto Bendlg. This well-lit, institutional hostel has 202 beds and is close to the U-Bahn. Breakfast €3.80. Showers in all rooms, bathtubs in some. Sheets included. Reception 24hr. Check-out 9am. 8- and 10-bed dorms €11.40; 4- and 6-bed dorms €12.80-14.60. AmEx/MC/V. ❷

Jugendgästehaus Wien Brigittenau (HI), XX, Friedrich-Engels-Pl. 24 (☎33 28 29; jgh.1200wien@chello.at). Take U1 (red) or U4 (green) to "Schwedenpl.," then tram N to "Floridsdorferbrücke/Friedrich-Engels-Pl." Follow the signs: it's the green building behind the tram stop, across the street and to the left of the tracks. This roomy hostel, while not centrally located, is only about a 20min. walk from the city center. Breakfast, lockers, and sheets included. Lunch and dinner €5. **Free Internet** access. Extremely wheelchair-accessible. 5-night max. stay. Reception 24hr. Lockout 9am-1pm. Reservations recommended. 24-bed dorms (men only) €12.15; 4-bed dorms €13; doubles with bath €30-34. Non-members add €3.50. AmEx/MC/V. ❷

Turmherberge Don Bosco (HI), III, Lechnerstr. 12 (☎713 14 94). Take U3 (orange) to "Kardinal-Nagl-Pl.," then take the Kardinal-Nagl-Pl. exit facing the park. Walk to the other side of the park and turn right on Erdbergstr.; Lechnerstr. is the 2nd left. The cheapest beds in town, in a former bell tower (ca.1950s). Single-sex 6- to 8-bed rooms. Curfew 11:45pm. Open Mar.-Nov. €6. ❶

Jugendgästehaus Hütteldorf-Hacking (HI), XIII, Schloßbergg. 8 (☎877 02 63; fax 87 70 26 32). From Karlspl., take U4 (green) to "Hütteldorf," take the Hadikg. exit, cross the footbridge, and follow signs to the hostel (10min.). Or take bus #53B from the side of the footbridge opposite the station. From Westbahnhof, take

FROM THE ROAD

OPEN-ENDED POLICY

I have talked to a surprising number of people who would consistently arrive at a hostel to find that their room was still occupied by the previous night's lodgers. The group would then be split up and put into different rooms, in spite of their reservations.

As I soon discovered, the "Open-Ended-Policy" is now common practice. Smaller hostels, hoping for good turnover rates, will reserve up to a predetermined percentage of the rooms they have available. However, those reservations may not guarantee a specific spot—if someone wishes to stay longer, he can simply go to the reception before check-out time and pay for another night, whether or not there are other reservations.

While this policy may seem unfair, there is a silver lining. Because the hostels do not reserve every room, there are always a few open spaces. This means that no one with a reservation is ever turned away, and people who show up in a new city on a whim can usually find a spot. Further, the policy gives the ability to extend reservations at will to get the most out of a city.

The best advice is to call ahead. If you arrive and your reservation changes from a six person room to three doubles, at least you can always be sure that you won't have to spend the night in a train station.

- Alison Giordano, 2003

S50 to "Hütteldorf." This secluded hostel has great views and is popular with school groups. Breakfast included. Lunch and dinner €5.45 each. Free luggage storage. Keycard €1.82. Reception 7am-11:45pm. Lockout 9:30am-3:30pm. Curfew 11:45pm. Discounts for groups of 18 or more. 6- and 8-bed rooms, and one 22-bed room, €13.50. Add €2.50 per person for 4-bed rooms or €5 for doubles. Non-members add €3.50. MC/V. ❷

HOTELS & PENSIONS

Check the hostels section for good deals on singles as well. When it comes to hotels, the prices are higher, but you pay for convenient reception hours, no curfews, and no lockouts.

Pension Kraml, VI, Brauerg. 5 (☎587 85 88; fax 586 75 73). Take U3 (orange) to "Zierierg.," exit onto Otto-Bauerg, take the 1st left, then 1st right. From Südbahnhof, take bus #13A to Esterhazyg. and walk up Brauerg. Near the *Innenstadt* and the *Naschmarkt,* Kraml has large airy rooms, a lounge, and cable TV. Breakfast included. 38 beds. Singles €26; doubles €48, with shower or bath €65; triples €65, with shower €85. Apartment with bath €100-115 for 3-5 people. V. ❸

Pension Hargita, VII, Andreasg. (☎526 19 28; fax 04 92). Take U3 (orange) to "Zieglerg." and take Andreasg. exit. A quiet, delightful mixture of hardwood floors, seafoam walls, and cozy beds. Breakfast €3. Reception 8am-10pm. Singles €31, with shower €50; doubles €45, with shower €52, with bath €53-60; triples €63-71. MC/V. ❹

Lauria Apartments, VII, Kaiserstr. 77, Apt. #8 (☎522 25 55). From Westbahnhof, take tram #5 to "Burgg." *The Breakfast Club* meets Vienna in this somewhat small but very comfortable cluster of apartments. Fully equipped kitchens. Sheets, lockers, and TV included. 2-night min. stay. Reception 8am-2pm. Lockout 10am-2pm; no curfew. Dorms €13; singles and student-bunk twins €35; doubles €23 per person, with shower €30; student-bunk triples €21 per person; triples €75-120. MC/V for bills over €90. ❷

Pension Reimer, VII, Kircheng. 18 (☎523 61 62; pension.reimer@aon.at), is centrally located and has huge, comfortable rooms that are cleaned continually. Breakfast included. Summer singles €38; doubles €56, with bath €64. Winter singles €31; doubles €25/30. MC/V for long stays only. ❹

Pension Falstaff, IX, Müllnerg. 5 (☎317 91 27; fax 31 79 18 64). Take U4 (green) to "Roßauer Lände." Cross Roßauer Lände, head down Grünentorg., and take the 3rd left onto Müllnerg. Medium sized rooms in a quiet location. Breakfast included. Reception 7:30am-9pm. Singles €30-33, with shower €35-40; doubles €45-66. Reduced rate (10%) for stays of 1 week or more in off-season. MC/V. ❹

Hotel Zur Wiener Staatsoper, I, Krugerstr. 1 (☎513 12 74 75; www.zurweinerstaatsoper.at). From Karlspl., exit Oper, follow Kärntnerstr. towards the city center, and turn right on Krugerstr. This hotel offers simple elegance and a prime downtown location. Singles with shower €76-95; doubles with shower €109-135; triples with shower €131-146. All prices include breakfast buffet. €4 for a safety deposit box. AmEx/MC/V. ❺

Hotel Am Stephansplatz, I, Stephanspl. 9 (☎53 40 50; www.hotelamstephansplatz.at). Take U3 (orange) to "Stephansplatz." This comfortable and elegant hotel is right in the middle of central Vienna. Inside, classy chestnut wood is complemented by oriental rugs and a colorful decorative style. Breakfast buffet included. Single with bath €105-140; double with bath €130-210. Extra person €35. AmEx/MC/V. ❺

Hotel Imperial, I, Kärntner Ring 16 (☎50 11 00; www.luxurycollection.com/imperial). Built in 1863 as the Vienna residence for the Prince of Württemberg, this opulent hotel has retained the grandeur of the Imperial era. In the heart of downtown Vienna, it is renowned for impeccable service and all the luxury amenities imaginable. Singles from €446-504; Doubles from €535-656; 1 handicap room available. AmEx/MC/V. ❺

UNIVERSITY DORMITORIES

Porzellaneum der Wiener Universität, IX, Porzellang. 30 (☎317 72 82; fax 72 82). From the Südbahnhof, take tram D (dir.: Nußdorf) to "Fürsteng." From Westbahnhof, take tram #5 to "Franz-Josefs Bahnhof," then tram D (dir.: Südbahnhof) to "Fürsteng." Primarily rents rooms for several months (up to 1 yr.) to students coming to live in Vienna, but will rent short-term to travelers if there are vacancies. Great location in the student district. No lockers. Reception 24hr. Call ahead. Singles €16-18; doubles €30-35; quads €56-64. ❸

Studentenwohnheim der Hochschule für Musik, I, Johannesg. 8 (☎514 84; fax 77 99). Head 3 blocks down Kärntnerstr. from Stephansdom and turn left onto Johannesg. Although there are families and backpackers, much of the clientele consists of music students; the former monastery has 23 practice rooms with grand pianos (€5 per hour; call in advance to reserve the concert halls). Breakfast included. Reception 24hr. Discount for groups larger than 20. Reserve well in advance. Singles €33-36; doubles 58-70; triples €66; quads €80; quints €100. Apartment (includes 2 double rooms, bathroom, kitchen, living room) €28.50 per person; entire apartment €90. ❸

Katholisches Studentenhaus, XIX, Peter-Jordanstr. 29 (☎369 55 85; fax 55 85 12). From Westbahnhof, take U6 (brown; dir.: Heiligenstadt) to "Nußdorferstr.," then bus #35A or tram #38 to "Hardtg." and turn left. From Südbahnhof, take tram D to "Schottentor," then tram #38 to "Hardtg." Enjoy the calm setting of District XIX. Reception closes at 10pm. **Free Internet** access. Call ahead. Close to Fischerbräu (see p. 111). Singles €18; doubles €30. Discounts for stays more than 1mo. ❸

CAMPING

Wien-West, Hüttelbergstr. 80 (☎914 23 14; www.wiencamping.at). Take U4 (green) to "Hütteldorf," then bus #14B or 152 (dir.: Campingpl.) to "Wien West." This convenient campground, 8km from the city center, is crowded but very clean. The campground is only 20min. from the city center and 2min. from a seemingly endless network of hiking paths through the Vienna Woods. Laundry, grocery stores, **Internet,** and cooking facilities. Wheelchair-accessible. Reception 7:30am-9:30pm. Open Apr.-Oct. €6 per person in July-Aug., €5 rest of the year; ages 4-15 €3; tent €3, camper €5. July-Aug. 2- and 4-person bungalows available for €21-25 and €31-35. Electricity €3. ❶

Wien Süd, Breitenfurterstr., 269. (☎867 36 49; www.wiencamping.at). Take the U6 (brown; dir.: Siebenhirten) to "Philadelphiabrücke" and take bus #62A to "Wien Süd." Located on the southwestern side of the city, this former imperial park encompasses vast expanses of woods and meadows. Laundry services, a café, small playground, a supermarket, and kitchen. Wheelchair-accessible. Open May-Sept. €5 per person, ages 4-15 €3; May, June, and Sept. €3.50/€3. Camper €5, tent €3. ❶

Aktiv Camping Neue Donau, XXII, Am Kleehäufel 119 (☎/fax 202 40 10, www.wiencamping.at), 4km from the city center and adjacent to Neue Donau beaches; take U1 (red) to "Kaisermühlen" then bus #91a to "Kleehäufel." Located right along the Donau, this camping site offers beach volleyball, tennis courts, waterskiing, and boat and bike rentals. Laundry, supermarket, and kitchen. Showers included. Wheelchair-accessible. Open May 14-Sept. 10 and July-Aug. 7. €5.50, children €3; May, June, and Sept. €3.50/€3. Camper €5, tent €3. ❶

VIENNA

◘ FOOD

For the Viennese, food is not mere fuel for the body—it is a multi-faceted traditional experience that begins when you wish someone *"Mahlzeit"* (roughly, "bon apetit") and ends with one of the city's renowned pastries. Be aware, though, that Viennese pastries are not only unbelievably rich, but are priced for patrons who are likewise blessed: unless you buy your sin wholesale at a local bakery, *Sacher Torte, Imperial Torte,* and even *Apfelstrudel* can cost up to €5.

Vienna's restaurants are as varied as its cuisine. *Gästehäuser, Imbiße* (food stands), and *Beisln* (small taverns or restaurants) serve inexpensive meals that stick to your ribs and are best washed down with copious amounts of beer. *Würstelstände,* found on almost every corner, provide a quick, cheap lunch (a sausage runs €2.50 or so). The restaurants downtown near **Graben** and **Kärntnerstraße** are generally expensive—a cheaper bet is the neighborhood north of the university, and near the Votivkirche (take the U2/purple to "Schottentor"), where **Universitätsstraße** and **Währingerstraße** meet. Cafés with cheap meals also line **Burggasse** in District VI. The area radiating from the **Rechte** and **Linke Wienzeile** near Naschmarkt (take U4/green to "Kettenbrückeg.") houses a range of cheap restaurants, and the **Naschmarkt** itself contains open-air stands where you can purchase fresh fruits and vegetables, bread, and a variety of ethnic food to sample while shopping at Vienna's premier flea market (Sa-Su only).

> Most places close earlier on Saturday afternoons and all day Sunday. In general, restaurants stop serving after 11pm. Some supermarkets, however, are open daily; if you're stuck without food on a Sunday, head to the one in the Westbahnhof, though prices will be slightly higher.

At Christmas time, **Christkindlmarkt** offers hot food and potent punch amid vendors of Christmas charms, ornaments, and candles. From late June to July, the **Festwochen** film festival brings international foodstuffs to the stands behind the seats (stands open daily 11am-11pm). The open-air **Brunnenmarkt** is inexpensive, and with a Turkish-style flair (take U6/brown to "Josefstädterstr.," then walk up Veronikag. 1 block and turn right). *Bäckereien* (bakeries) are everywhere (common chains include **Anker** and **Der Mann**). To combat the summer heat, look around for gelato shops that sit on nearly every corner (see "Sweet Tooth in the City," p. 112).

As for grocery stores, the lowest prices are on the shelves of **Zielpunkt, Hofer,** and **Spar.** More pricey chains include **Ledi, Mondo,** and **Renner.** Kosher groceries are available at **Kosher Supermarket,** II, Hollandstr. 10 (☎216 96 75).

RESTAURANTS

Inexpensive student cafeterias include **Vienna Technical University,** IV, Wiedner Hauptstr. 8-10 (☎586 65 02; open M-F 1-5:30pm) and **Afro-Asia Mensa,** IX, Türkenstr. 3, near the Schottentor (Prices around €4.50; open M-F 11:30am-2:30pm).

INSIDE THE RING

▨ **Ma Crêperie,** I, Grünangerg. 10 (☎512 56 87; www.macreperie.at), off Singerstr. near Stephanspl. The building has had many incarnations; it was once a burlesque theater. Sexy lighting combined with decorations retained from previous eras make this eatery captivating enough for even Al Capone (a former customer). The sensual decor complements scrumptious crêpes (€3.49-18.17). A regular menu with similar prices is also available. Try the *Himbeer* (raspberry) soda for €2. Wheelchair-accessible, with a specially designed table for the disabled. Open daily 11am-midnight. AmEx/MC/V. ❷

▨ **Smutny,** I, Elisabethstr. 8 (☎587 13 56; www.smutny.com). Exit Karlspl. onto Elizabethstr.; Smutny is directly on the right. A delicious traditional Austrian restaurant offering *Schnitzel, Gulasch,* and a €6 *Menü.* (Prices €2-7.90, AmEx/MC/V.) ❸

FOOD BY TYPE

AUSTRIAN
Smutny (108) — I ❸
Trzesniewski (109) — I, III, VI ❷
Centimeter (111) — VII, VIII, IX ❷
Amerlingbeisl (112) — VII ❷
Konoba (113) — VIII ❸
Stomach (112) — IX ❹
Fischerbräu (112) — XIX ❷

FRENCH
Ma Crêperie (108) — I ❷
Elsäßer Bistro (112) — IX ❸

VEGETARIAN
Wrenkh (110) — I ❷
Inigo (110) — I ❷
Rosenberger Markt (111) — I ❶
Café Willendorf (113) — VI ❸
Blue Box (112) — VII ❷
Amerlingbeisl (112) — VII ❷

ASIAN AND INDIAN
Yugetsu Saryo (110) — I ❹
Vegetasia (112) — III ❷
Zum Mogulhof (112) — VII ❸
China Sichuan (113) — XXII ❸

FUSION
DO&CO (109) — I ❺
Margaritaville (110) — I ❸
Wrenkh (110) — I ❷
Inigo (110) — I ❷
Vegetasia (112) — III ❷
Café Willendorf (113) — VI ❸
Blue Box (112) — VII ❷
OH Pot, OH Pot (111) — IX ❷

ITALIAN
A Tavola (109) — I ❷
Bizi Pizza (110) — I ❷
Zimolo (111) — I ❸

GREEK, TURKISH AND MIDDLE EASTERN
Sato Café-Restaurant (111) — XV ❶
Levante (110) — I, VIII ❷
Maschu Maschu (110) — I, VIII ❶
Café Nil (112) — VII ❷

CAFÉS
Kleines Café (114) — I
Café Central (114) — I
Demel (114) — I
Café MAK (114) — I
Café Hawelka (114) — I
Café Bräunerhof (114) — I
Café Museum (115) — I
Hotel Sacher (115) — I
Café Griensteidl (115) — I
Hotel Imperial (115) — I
Kunsthaus Wien Café (115) — III
Café Sperl (115) — VI
Café Drechsler (115) — VI
Café Savoy (115) — VI
Café Rüdigerhof (116) — VI
Berg das Café (115) — IX
Café Stein (115) — IX

HEURIGEN
Buschenschank Heinrich Niersche (116) — XIX
Zum Krottenbach'l (116) — XIX
Weingut Heuriger Reinprecht (117) — XIX
Franz Mayer am Pfarrplatz Beethovenhaus (117) — XIX

VIENNA

Trzesniewski, I, Dorotheerg. 1 (☎512 32 91; fax 513 95 65), 3 blocks down the Graben from the Stephansdom. A famous stand-up restaurant, this unpronounceable establishment has been serving petite open-faced sandwiches for over 80 years. A hearty lunch—6 sandwiches and a mini-beer—costs about €5. Favorite toppings include salmon, onion, paprika, and egg. Open M-F 8:30am-7:30pm, Sa 9am-5pm. **Branches** at VI, Mariahilferstr. 95 (☎596 42 91), and III, Hauptstr. 97 (☎712 99 64) in Galleria. ❷

DO&CO, I, Stephanspl. 12 (7th floor, ☎535 39 69). Set above the Stephanspl. cathedral, this modern gourmet restaurant offers both traditional Austrian as well as other international specialties like Thai noodles and Uruguay beef (main course €19-23.50). Prices are high, but so is the quality; the restaurant has an amazing view of the *Innenstadt*. Reservations recommended. Open daily noon-3pm and 6pm-midnight. V. ❺

A Tavola, I, Weihburgg. 3-5 (☎51 27 95 50; www.haslaurer.at). Take the U1 (red) or U3 (orange) to "Stephanspl." Walk down Härtnerstr. and make a left onto Weihburgg. Located in the former *Stadtkrug* (city tavern), A Tavola's romantic atmosphere draws on dimly lit vaults bathed in candlelight and Mediterranean charm. Serves a variety of homemade pasta dishes with beef, seafood, chicken, and, when in season, pheasant

ON THE MENU

VIENNA'S ORIGINAL TORTE

Viennese *Sacher Torte*, the city's renowned chocolate confection, was created by 16-year-old Franz Sacher in 1832. At the time, Sacher was studying as a pastry apprentice under the head chef for Vienna's Prince Metternich. The prince, hoping to impress his guests, commissioned the head chef to make a new pastry of exceptional sweetness. However, the head chef fell ill, and Sacher was forced to take the reigns. The result became an instant sensation the world over.

The dessert itself is an airy cake witn an apricot jam filling, coated in a creamy chocolate glaze. Cafés all over Vienna serve the dessert, generally with a side of *Schlagobers* (unsweetened whipped cream). Legal battles have ensued over claims to the "authentic" version; Demel Konditorei, one of Vienna's leading pastry houses, claims that the Sacher family sold them the recipe. However, the "Original Sacher-Torte" is made only at the Hotel Sacher, which was founded in 1876 by Franz's son Eduard. The hotel makes around 270,000 *Sacher Torten* each year, always by hand, from a recipe they claim is still a tighly-guarded secret. Thankfully, the cake can be stored for relatively long periods of time (some even say it gets better with age), allowing the famous pastry to be shipped all over the world.

(€8-16). Great selection of Italian wines by the glass (€2.72-5). Open M-Sa noon-2:30pm and 6pm-midnight. AmEx/MC/V. ❷

Levante, I, Wallnerstr. 2 (☎533 23 26; www.levante.at). Walk down Graben away from the Stephansdom, turn left onto Kohlmarkt, and right onto Wallnerstr. This Greek-Turkish franchise features streetside dining with generic fare and some vegetarian dishes. Entrees €7-12, sandwiches €3.60. **Branches** at I, Wollzeilestr. 19 (off Rotenturm, take U3 or U1 to "Stephanspl."); Mariahilferstr. 88a; and VIII, Josefstädterstr. 14 (take U2 to "Rathaus"). All open daily from 1-11:30pm. AmEx/MC/V. ❷

Margaritaville, I, Bartensteing. 3 (☎405 47 86). Take U2 (purple) to "Lerchenfelderstr." Exit onto Museumstr. and cut across the small triangular green on the left to get to Bartensteing. Authentic Tex-Mex food in a decidedly Spanish atmosphere. Entrees €8-20. Open Su-F 4pm-midnight, Sa 11am-midnight. MC/V. ❸

Yugetsu Saryo, I, Führichg. 10 (☎512 84 70). A 2min. walk from Kärntnerstr., this restaurant serves sushi galore. While the prices are high for entrees (€23-63), individual sushi rolls run €1.80-10.90. Open daily noon-2:30pm and 6-11pm. AmEx/V/MC. ❹

Wrenkh, I, Bauernmarkt 10 (☎533 15 26). This strictly vegetarian restaurant has an incredible drink selection with everything from fresh fruit juices to original, specially-designed mixed drinks (€3-8). Delicious and creative cuisine is served in a relaxed, classy atmosphere. Fare includes everything from Japanese springrolls to spinach gnocchi (€3.90-18). Open daily 11:30am-11pm. AmEx/MC/V. ❷

Maschu Maschu, I, Rabensteig 8 (☎533 29 04). In the Bermuda Dreiecke, right next to the Danube. This tiny eatery serves cheap, filling Middle Eastern falafel and shawarma (each €3). Open M-W 11:30am-midnight, Th-Sa 11:30am-3am. ❶

Bizi Pizza, I, Rotenturmstr. 4 (☎513 37 05). 1 block up Rotenturmstr. from Stephanspl. One of the best deals in the city center, Bizi whips up fresh, affordable gourmet pizza and antipasti in a great atmosphere. Pasta €5.23-6. Whole pizza €4.15-5.70. Salad bar €2.83-5.01. Open daily 10am-11:30pm. **Branches** with same hours at I, Franz-Josefs-Kai 21 (☎535 79 13) and Mariahilferstr. 22-24 (☎523 16 58); and X, Favoritenstr. 105 (☎600 50 10). ❷

Inigo, I, Bäckerstr. 18 (☎512 74 51). This popular dining spot, across from Vienna's Jesuit church, was founded by a Jesuit priest as part of a socio-economic reintegration program. It provides employment, training, and social work for 17 people who are long-term unemployed. Menu includes a diversity of international dishes and vegetarian options (€5-10) and a salad bar (€3-7). Wheelchair-accessible. Open July-Aug. M-F 8:30am-11:30pm, Sept.-June also Sa-Su 8:30am-11:30pm. AmEx/MC/V. ❷

Zimolo, I, Ballg. 5 (☎513 17 54; fax 99 78), near Stephanspl. off Weihburgg. A 2min. walk down Weiburgg. (it is somewhat hidden; walk down the lane to get to the restaurant). This sexy café has candlelit tables and a friendly staff. Serves delicious Italian dishes with an Austrian touch. Meals average €6.90-18.90. Wheelchair-accessible. Open M-Sa noon-2:30pm and 6-11pm. AmEx/MC/V. ❸

Rosenberger Markt, I, Mayserderg. 2 (☎512 34 58), off Kärntnerstr. This subterranean market offers a large selection of salad, fruit salad, waffle, antipasto, potato, and pasta bars. You pay by the size of your plate, not by weight, so pile high. Salads €2.40-6, waffles €3.60-4.30, vegetable dishes €3.60-6.90. Wheelchair-accessible. Open 11am-11pm. AmEx/MC/V. ❶

OUTSIDE THE RING

🌐 **OH Pot, OH Pot,** IX, Währingerstr. 22 (☎319 42 59); www.ohpot.at). Take U2 (purple) to "Schottentor." This adorable joint serves amazing fusion fare that draws on cuisines ranging from Chilean to Ethiopian. Try one of their filling "pots"—stew-like concoctions that come in veggie and meat varieties. (€7.80-8.60). Terrific *empanadas* (€5.20). Lunch menu (until 3pm; €5.90) comes with soup or mixed salad, choice of a "pot," and bread. Open M-F 10am-3pm and 6pm-midnight, Sa-Su 6pm-midnight. AmEx/MC/V. ❷

🌐 **Sato Café-Restaurant,** XV, Mariahilferstr. 151 (☎895 26 90). Take U3 (orange) to "Westbahnhof." Conveniently located near the Ruthensteiner and Wombats hostels, as well as family owned and run, Sato offers some of the best Turkish fare in the city at extremely low prices. The atmosphere is very relaxed and casual. Vegetarian options are available. Free bread with every meal. Excellent breakfast omelettes €2.50-3.50. Mousaka minced lamb with roasted eggplant €5. English menu available. Open daily 7am-midnight; F-Sa 9pm-4am the basement is open for drinks and appetizers. ❶

Centimeter, IX, Liechtensteinstr. 42 (☎319 84 04; www.centimeter.at). Take tram D to "Bauernfeldpl." This chain offers huge portions of greasy Austrian fare and an unbelievable beer selection (pay by the centimeter). *Schnitzel* with salad and fries €5.80. *Maß* (1L) €6. Meter (8.33L) beers €17.60. Other **branches** at VIII, Lenaug. 11 (☎405 78 08), and VII, Stiftg. 4 (☎524 33 29). Open M-F 10am-2am, Sa 11am-2am, Su 11am-midnight. AmEx/MC/V. ❷

THE LOCAL LEGEND

AUSTRIA'S MEDUSA

Above today's Zum Basilisken restaurant in Vienna (Schönlaterng. 3) is a sandstone relief depicting a story from AD 1212. Back then the restaurant was a bakery, renowned for baking the best bread in Vienna. One day a young maid discovered a horrible smell by the well. The chief baker climbed in to investigate, and briefly saw what he deemed to be an animal—medium in size, with the head of a rooster, the body of a toad, and the tail of a snake.

Word of the encounter eventually reached the Emperor's doctor, who was convinced that it was a basilisk, a mythological creature of Ancient Greece. The doctor proposed a solution: lower a person into the well, carrying a mirror. When the creature sees his own hideous reflection, he will die of shock. However, if the creature first makes eye contact with the person, it is the person who dies.

A young man named Gregor (who was in love with the maid) bravely volunteered. He was blindfolded and given a shield and a mirror, his ears sealed with wax, and his nose covered with a sash. Once he was in the well, the creature began to hiss, trying to attack as Gregor fended him off with his shield. Then, all of a sudden, the hissing ceased.

Gregor emerged deathly ill from the creature's stench. Although he later recovered, the well remains filled with stones today as a testament to his bravery.

Elsäßer Bistro, IX, Währingerstr. 32 (☎319 76 89; elaesser.bistro@aon.at). U2 (purple) to "Schottentor." In the palace that houses the French Cultural Institute. Serves wonderful and extravagant meals (around €14) and a copious selection of French wines (€3 for ¼ glass). Open M-F 11:30am-3pm and 6:30-11pm. Kitchen until 10pm. MC/V. ❸

University Mensa, IX, Universitätsstr. 7 (☎42 77 29, ext. 841), on the 7th floor of the university building, between U2 (purple) stops "Rathaus" and "Schottentor." Visitors can take the stairs from the 6th floor after a ride in the old-fashioned *Pater Noster* elevator. Typical cafeteria meals €4. Open M-F 11am-2pm. Closed July-Aug. but snack bar open 8am-3pm. ❸

Vegetasia, III, Ungarg. 57 (☎713 83 32). Take the O tram to "Neulingg." A vegetarian nirvana, this cozy Taiwanese restaurant offers tofu, *seitan,* and plenty of soy delights. Lunch buffet M-Sa €6.50. Open daily 11:30am-3pm and 5:30-11:30pm. Closed Tu evenings. AmEx/MC/V. ❷

Fischerbräu, XIX, Billrothstr. 17 (☎369 59 41). Take U6 (brown) to "Nußdorfer Str.," follow the exit sign to Währinger Gürtel. Continue until Döblinger Hauptpl., take a left, and left again onto Billrothstr. Popular spot for both young and middle-aged locals. The music in the courtyard creates pleasant ambiance for home-brewed beer (large €2.50-5), delicious veal sausage (€4.60), and chicken salad (€6.50). Open M-F 4pm-1am, Sa-Su 11am-1am. Blues brunch Sa noon-3pm. Jazz brunch Su 11am-3pm. ❷

Café Nil, VII, Siebensterng. 39 (☎526 61 65). Take tram #49 from the Volksgarten to Siebensterng. to reach this low-key Middle Eastern café. Enjoy pork-free and a number of vegetarian dishes (€6.20-12.40) with tortured intellectual types. Breakfast until 3pm. Open daily 10am-midnight. ❷

SWEET TOOTH IN THE CITY
In a city of *Schnitzel, Wurst,* and *Strudel,* it's not surprising that the lighter stuff that is Italian gelato would find such a popular home: Vienna is teeming with gelato parlors offering this smooth, mouthwatering ice cream. Look for an *Eis* shop on practically ever corner, with flavors as exotic and delicious as marscapone, tiramisu, nutella, kiwi, and mango, or the more traditional chocolate (small cones go for around €1.50; large ones for €5). Try **Eis Salon Garda,** XII, Mariahilferstr. (☎892 34 30), for artistic sundaes and some of the best cones in Vienna. Open 9:30am-11:30pm.

Blue Box, VII, Richterg. 8 (☎523 26 82; www.bluebox.at). Take U3 (orange) to "Neubaug.," turn onto Neubaug., and take your first left onto Richterg. Blue Box leads a double life: although a restaurant by day, it is a club by night, featuring an orange-filtered chandelier, black leather couches, and a distinct lack of light. Dishes are fresh and original, and DJs spin the latest trance and trip-hop. A great place to come for a late (or really late—until 5pm) breakfast. Choose from Viennese, French, or vegetarian cuisine. Entrees €3.50-7.10. Drinks €2.20-10. Open M 6pm-2am, Tu-Su 10am-2am. V. ❷

Zum Mogulhof, VII, Burgg. 12 (☎526 28 64). Ample portions of delicious Indian food served by candlelight amidst crimson carpets and velvet wallpaper—indulgence that won't strain your wallet. Vegetarian and meat dishes average €8-12. Open daily 11:30am-2:30pm and 6-11:30pm. AmEx/MC/V. ❸

Amerlingbeisl, VII, Stiftg. 8 (☎526 16 60). Take U3 (orange) to "Neubaug." and take the "Stiftg." exit. After a couple of blocks on Stiftg., enter the courtyard covered with grape vines. Laden with dark wood and sunshine, this moderately priced restaurant boasts a hydraulic-powered roof for inclement weather. Occasional live music. Entrees (including vegetarian offerings) average €6-8, late breakfast (until 3pm) €4-9.50. Open daily 9am-2am (hot food served until 1am). V. ❷

Stomach, IX, Seeg. 26 (☎310 20 99). Take tram D to "Seeg." This sophisticated establishment features first-rate Austrian cooking with a Styrian kick. If there's nice weather, eat your meal outside in a lovely courtyard. 20-something crowd. Entrees average €14. Open W-Sa 4pm-midnight, Su 10am-10pm. Reservations recommended. MC/V. ❹

Café Willendorf, VI, Linke Wienzeile 102 (☎587 17 89). Take U4 (green) to "Pilgramg." and look for the big pink building which also houses the Rosa Lila Villa, the mecca of Vienna's gay and lesbian life. This artsy café, bar, and restaurant with a vine-covered outdoor terrace serves creative vegetarian fare costing between €6.80-9, meat dishes €8.50-12.50. *Menü* €18. Relaxed atmosphere. Meals until midnight. Open M-Th 6pm-1am; F-Sa 6pm-2am. ❸

Konoba, VIII, Lerchenfelder Str., 66-88 (☎929 41 11; www.konoba.at). Take the U2 (purple) to "Lerchenfeldstr." A small, simple eatery with a waterfront atmosphere. Dalmation inspired, the food is a succulent blending of fresh fish and vegetables. Superb lobster. Entrees €6-18. Open Su-F 11am-2pm and 6pm-midnight, Sa 6pm-midnight. MC/V. ❸

China Sichuan, XXII, Arbeiterstrandbadstr. 122 (☎263 37 13; www.sichuan.at). Take the U1 (red) to "Alte Donau." The restaurant is a 10min. walk from the station. Serving authentic Chinese dishes in an authentic Oriental ambiance (complete with a pagoda and outdoor pond), China Sichuan is the perfect destination after a day swimming and sunning on the Danube. Lunch menu runs €6.90-8.72. Dinner menu €8-15. Dim-sum €3.50-4. Open daily 11:30am-2:30pm and 5:30-11pm. MC/V. ❸

⚑ CAFÉS

"Who's going to start a revolution? Herr Trotsky from Café Central?"
—Austrian general quoted on the eve of the Russian Revolution

In Vienna, the coffeehouse is not simply the place to resolve your midday caffeine deficit. For years these establishments were havens for artists, writers, and thinkers who flocked to the brooding interiors to exchange ideas and jabs at each other's work. Surrounded with dark wood and dusty velvet, they drank coffee, and stayed into the night composing operettas, writing books, and shaping modern thought. The bourgeoisie followed suit, and the coffeehouse became the city's living room, giving rise to a grand coffeehouse culture. Peter Altenberg, "the café

ONE MORE CUP OF COFFEE... Here is a quick reference guide to some of the most tempting Viennese coffees:

Mélange: espresso-like coffee with hot milk, optional whipped cream or cinnamon
Mokka: strong black coffee, much like espresso
Kapuziner: small *Mokka* with cream, sprinkled with cocoa, chocolate, or cinnamon
Verlängerte: weak coffee with cream
Fiaker: black coffee with rum
Pharisär: black coffee with rum, sugar, and whipped cream
Wiener Eiskaffee: chilled black coffee and vanilla ice cream, with whipped cream
Maria Theresa: black coffee with orange liqueur and whipped cream

writer," scribbled lines; Oskar Kokoschka grumbled alone; and exiles Lenin and Trotsky played chess. Theodor Herzl made plans here for a Zionist Israel, and Kafka came to visit the Herrenhof. The original literary café was **Café Griensteidl,** but after it was demolished in 1897 the torch passed to **Café Central** and then to **Café Herrenhof.** Cafés still exist under all these names, but only Café Central looks as it did in imperial times; today, however, it is mainly frequented by tourists.

The quintessential Viennese coffee is the *Mélange,* and you can order every kind of coffee as a *Kleiner* (small) or *Grosser* (large), *Brauner* (brown, with a little milk) or *Schwarzer* (black). Whipped cream is *Schlagobers;* if you don't like it, say *"ohne Schlag, bitte."* Choosing your coffee in Vienna requires careful study (see "One More Cup Of Coffee..." above). Decadent pastries complete the picture: *Apfelstrudl,* cheesecakes, tortes, *Buchteln* (warm cake with jam in the middle), *Palatschinken, Krapfen,* and *Mohr im Hemd* have all helped place Vienna on

THE LOCAL STORY

A FAMILY AFFAIR

Günter Hawelka is the second-generation owner of Café Hawelka (see p. 114), Vienna's first American café and one of the last old coffee houses in the city.

On the Establishment: This place was founded in 1905 during the Imperial era. When the owner fell into debt in 1939, my parents purchased the café. Unfortunately, with the start of WWII my parents had to close the café. My father went into the Army and my mother could not run the business alone—she was pregnant with me.

On reopening: My parents reopened the café in 1945, but Vienna was rife with unemployment and items like coffee, sugar, and cigarettes were only found on the Black Market; suffice it to say, our café was not doing very well.

On making the café what it is today: Fortunately my parents had a friend with a very good connection to the Allied Forces in Vienna, so they could get the best of everything—vodka from the Russians, cognac from the French, whiskey from the English, and of course, coffee and cigarettes.

On his family: My father Leopold is 92 and my mother Josefine is almost 90, but they haven't given up the place; my father works the morning shift and my mother works the night shift. I am already 63 years old, so my two sons are next in line to run the café. We want to keep it an in-the-family business.

the culinary map. The *Konditoreien*, no less traditional, focus their attention on delectables rather than coffee. To see a menu, ask for a *Speisekarte*.

INSIDE THE RING

▨ **Kleines Café,** I, Franziskanerpl. 3. Turn off Kärntnerstr. onto Weihburg. The café is located in the courtyard of the Franziskanerkirche, featuring green paneling, a low, vaulted ceiling, nightclub posters, and a few tables in the courtyard. The salads (around €6.50), the café's specialty, are veritable works of art. Open M-Sa 10am-2am, Su 1pm-2am.

▨ **Café Central,** I (☎533 37 63 24), inside Palais Fers at the corner of Herreng. and Strauchg. Café Central has surrendered to tourists because of its fame, but this mecca of the café world, with its arched ceilings and wall frescoes, is definitely worth a visit. Occasional live music. Open M-Sa 8am-10pm, Su 10am-6pm. AmEx/MC/V.

▨ **Demel,** I, Kohlmarkt 14 (☎535 17 17; www.demel.at), 5min. from the Stephansdom down Graben. The most lavish Viennese *Konditorei*, Demel was confectioner to the imperial court until the Empire dissolved. All of the chocolate is made fresh every morning. A fantasy of mirrored rooms, cream walls, and legendary desserts. Waitresses in convent-black serve divine confections (€5) that every visit to Vienna should include. Don't miss the crème-du-jour. Also serves small sandwiches and antipasti (€3). Wheelchair-accessible. Open daily 10am-7pm. AmEx/MC/V.

Café MAK, I, Stubenring 3-5 (☎714 01 21), inside the Museum für Angewandte Kunst. Take tram #1 or 2 to "Stubenring." This modern café, outfitted in funky *Bauhaus* furniture, offers a diverse menu ranging from Italian to Mexican. Peek through glass walls into the museum or dine outside among sunflowers. Students crowd the café after 10pm; techno-rave parties on Sa nights in July. Open Tu-Su 10am-2am (hot food until midnight €8-15). AmEx/MC/V.

Café Hawelka, I, Dorotheerg. 6 (☎512 82 30), off Graben, 3 blocks down from the Stephansdom. Dusty wallpaper, dark wood, and old red-striped velvet sofas make the café both down-to-earth and glorious. The Hawelkas put this legendary café on the map in 1939. Today, at 90 years and 92 years respectively, Josephine and Leopold still work in the café alongside their son (see "A Family Affair," this page). *Buchteln* (a Bohemian doughnut, fresh from the oven at 10pm) €2.80. *Mélange* €2.80. Open M and W-Sa 8am-2am, Su and holidays 4pm-2am.

Café Bräunerhof, I, Stallburgg. 2 (☎512 38 93). A delightfully shabby café in a small alley near the Hofburg with an excellent selection of newspapers. You can order bread, *Käse und Schinken* (cheese and cold cuts), and Austrian salad (€5.60-10). *Mélange* €2.80. Open M-F 7:30am-8:30pm, Sa 7:30am-6pm, Su 10am-6pm. V.

Café Museum, I, Operng. 7 (☎586 52 02), near the Opera. Head away from the *Innenstadt* to the corner of Operng. and Friedrichstr. Built in 1899 by Adolf Loos, in a plain, spacious style with striking curves, this café attracts a mixed bag of artists, lawyers, students, and chess players. Typical Austrian coffees, ranging from €2.40-8.20. Open daily 8am-midnight.

Hotel Sacher, I, Philharmonikerstr. 4 (☎514 560; www.sacher.com). Behind the opera house. This historic establishment has served world-famous *Sacher Torte* (€4.50) in stunning red style for years. While it remains elegant, casual clothing is fine. Wheelchair-accessible. Café open 11am-11:30pm; bakery open 9am-11:30pm. AmEx/MC/V. (Also see Sights: Hotel Sacher, p. 122.)

Café Griensteidl, I, Michaelerpl. 2 (☎535 26 93 2). Down the street from Café Central toward the Hofburg right in the heart of downtown. As Vienna's first literary café, Griensteidl was a meeting place for many Austrian writers, philosophers, and artists; today, it provides a relaxed café atmosphere for locals and tourists alike. Sample a wide array of ice cream, such as Griensteidl *Eiszauber* (vanilla ice cream with walnuts, apricots, chocolate, and gingerbread spices; €5.10), while scanning the selection of international newspapers. Open daily 8am-11:30pm. AmEx/MC/V.

Hotel Imperial, I, Kärntner Ring 16 (☎501 10 31 89; fax 50 11 03 55). From the Opera, turn left onto the Ring and walk 5min. This elegant café is well-decorated with chandeliers and a lovely courtyard. Serves its own insignia-stamped, marzipan-filled *Imperial Torte* (€5) to wealthy tourists without charging wealthy prices. Wheelchair-accessible. Open daily 7am-11pm. AmEx/MC/V.

OUTSIDE THE RING

▨ Café Sperl, VI, Gumpendorferstr. 11 (☎586 41 58). Take U2 (purple) to "Museumsquartier," exit to Mariahilferstr., walk 1 block on Getreidemarkt, and turn right onto Gumpendorferstr. Built in 1880, Sperl is one of Vienna's oldest and most elegant cafés. Renovations have removed a few of the original trappings, but the *fin de siècle* atmosphere remains, complimented by modern billiards tables. Coffee €2-4.50; cake €2.54-3.85. Sept.-June live piano music Sa after 5pm. Open M-Sa 7am-11pm, Su 11am-8pm; July-Aug. closed Su. AmEx/MC/V.

Café Drechsler, VI, Linke Wienzeile 22 (☎587 85 80). From Karlspl., head down Operng. and continue on Linke Wienzeile, or take U4 (green) to "Kettenbrückeng." This is the place to be the morning after. Early birds and night owls roost in this café over pungent cups of *Mokka*. Great lunch menu with huge portions and hardy food (€4.70-7.50). Open M-F 3am-8pm, Sa 3am-6pm.

Café Savoy, VI, Linke Wienzeile 36 (☎786 73 48), is a gorgeous café with dark wood and decaying gold trim. A large gay and lesbian crowd makes this a lively nightspot on weekends. Open M-F 5pm-2am, Sa 9am-2am.

Café Stein, IX, Währingerstr. 6 (☎31 97 24 19; www.cafe-stein.com), near Schottentor., has chrome seats outside (allowing you to see and be seen) and clustered tables in the smoky red-brown and metallic interior. Intimate, lively, and hip, at night it transforms into **Stein's Diner** (open M-Sa 7pm-1am). **Internet** access €3.50 per 30min. 5-11pm. Breakfast until 8pm. Open M-Sa 7am-1am, Su 9am-1am.

Kunsthaus Wien Café, III, Untere Weißgerberstr. 14 (☎712 04 97). Located in a verdant courtyard of Hundertwasser's Kunsthaus museum (see p. 24), this café serves a combination of local and vegetarian fare (€2-€18). Open daily 10am-11pm.

Berg das Café, IX, Bergg. 8 (☎319 57 20). Take U2 (purple) to "Schottentor" and take a right off Währingerstr. onto Bergg. A casual hang-out by day and super-swank gay café/bar by night, this place is always crowded. Wonderful food, desserts, and music in a relaxed atmosphere. Berg recently merged with nearby gay/lesbian bookstore **Das Löwenherz** (☎317 29 82), so you can browse during the day while you drink your *Mélange* (€2.40). Plenty of English titles. Open 10am-1am.

Café Rüdigerhof, V, Hamburgerstr. 20 (☎586 31 38). Take U4 to "Kettenbrückeng.";
Hamburgerstr. branches off from Rechte Wienzeile. In a 1902 building designed by students of Otto Wagner, this *Jugendstil* café is adorned with floral patterns and leather
couches (a gift from King Hussein to the owner) and has a large, leaf-covered garden
outside. Traditional meat and fish dishes (€5.10-7.10). Delicious iced coffee €3.50.
Open daily 10am-2am; garden open for drinks until 1:45am. AmEx/MC/V.

⚏ HEURIGEN (WINE TAVERNS)

Heurigen, marked by a hanging branch of evergreen at the door, sell wine and
savory Austrian buffet-style delicacies. The wine, also called *Heuriger,* is from the
most recent harvest and has typically been grown and pressed by the owner himself. Good *Heuriger* wine is generally white, fruity, and full of body—*Grüner
Veltliner* is a good representative of the variety; avoid reds. *Heuriger* is ordered
by the *Achtel* or the *Viertel* (eighth or quarter liter, respectively; about €2 per
Viertel). *G'spritzer* (wine and soda water, served separately, then mixed) is a
popular way of enjoying *Heuriger.* Half of the pleasure of visiting a *Heuriger,*
however, comes from the atmosphere. Worn picnic benches and old shade trees
provide an ideal spot to converse or listen to *Schrammelmusik* (sentimental folk
songs played by elderly musicians who inhabit *Heurigen*). A *Heuriger* generally
serves simple buffets (grilled chicken and pork, cabbage or corn, and pickles) that
make for inexpensive meals. Order your food inside and sit down outside; a waitress will come around to serve the wine. Those looking for some traditional fare
should order *Brattfett* or *Liptauer,* a spicy soft paprika-flavored cheese served
on *Schwarzbrot* (black bread).

Open during summer, *Heurigen* cluster together in the northern, western, and
southern Viennese suburbs, where the grapes grow. The most famous region, **Grinzing,** in District XIX, produces a uniquely strong wine. Unfortunately, those in
Grinzing (incidentally Beethoven's favorite neighborhood) are well known to tour
bus operators. You'll find better atmosphere and prices among the hills of **Sievering, Neustift am Walde** (both in District XIX), and **Neuwaldegg** (XVII). Authentic,
charming, and jolly *Heurigen* abound on Hochstr. in **Perchtoldsdorf,** just southwest of the city. To reach Perchtoldsdorf, take U4 (green) to "Hietzing" and tram
#6 to "Rodaun." Walk down Ketzerg. until Hochstr. and continue for a few minutes
to reach the *Heurigen* area. True *Heuriger* devotees should make the trip to
Gumpoldskirchen, a celebrated vineyard village with bus and train connections to
Vienna and Mödling, and on the S-Bahn line from the Südbahnhof. Most vineyard
taverns are open from 4pm to midnight; a particularly good option for a Sunday
afternoon when everything else is closed.

🏠 **Buschenschank Heinrich Niersche,** XIX, Strehlg. 21 (☎440 21 46). Take U6 (brown) to
"Währingerstr./Volksoper" then tram #41 to "Pötzleing." or bus #41A to "Pötzleindorfer
Höhe." Walk up Poltzleing. until it becomes Khevenhuller Str. and turn right onto Strehlg. On the left side of the street, hidden from tourists in the backyard of a house, this
beautiful garden overlooks the fields of Grinzing—an oasis of green grass, cheerful
voices, and relaxation in a neighborhood atmosphere. *Weiße G'spritzter* (white wine
spritzer) €1.45, 0.25L €1.89-2.03. Open M and W-Su 3pm-midnight.

🏠 **Zum Krottenbach'l,** XIX, Krottenbachstr. 148 (☎440 12 40). Take U6 (brown) to "Nußdorferstr." then bus #35A (dir.: Salmannsdorf) to "Kleingartenverein/Hackenberg."
Stretching across a sequence of terraced gardens, this *Heuriger* offers a comfortable
spot for savoring the fruit of the vine in a very traditional atmosphere in which everything
(including the light fixtures) is made of gnarled wood. Larger but more touristy and family-oriented than *Buschenschank.* 0.25L of wine about €2. Open daily 3pm-midnight.

Weingut Heuriger Reinprecht, XIX, Cobenzlg. 22 (☎32 01 47 10; reinprecht@grinz-ing.net). Take U4 (green) to "Heiligenstadt," then bus #38A to "Grinzing." This place fits the *Heuriger* stereotype on a larger scale, with endless picnic tables under an ivy-laden trellis, and *Schrammel* musicians strolling from table to table. Despite many tourists, don't be surprised to hear whole tables of Austrians break into song. There's quite a bottle opener collection near the entryway. In early June, try *Frische Erdbeerbowle*—a delectable mix of sparkling wine and strawberries (€2.20). Open Mar.-Nov. daily 3:30pm-midnight. AmEx/MC/V.

Franz Mayer am Pfarrplatz Beethovenhaus, XIX, Pfarrpl. 2 (☎370 12 87; www.mayer.pfarrplatz.at). Take U4 (green) to "Heiligenstadt," then bus #38A to "Fernsprechamt/Heiligenstadt." Walk uphill and head right onto Nestelbachg. Beethoven used to stay here back when it offered guest quarters. Festive patios vary from bustling noise to quite seclusion. Touristy. Pricey food (€4.40-18.20) but reasonable drinks at €2.20 per 0.25L. Wheelchair-accessible. Live music 7pm-midnight. Open M-F 4pm-midnight, Su and holidays 11am-midnight. MC/V.

◉ SIGHTS

Vienna's streets are by turns stately, residential, and decaying. Expect contrasts around every corner: the expanse of the Ringstraße and the narrow confines of a cobblestone courtyard, the curling flourishes of a Baroque palace and the spare lines of Socialist public housing. Grab the brochure *Vienna from A to Z* (with Vienna Card discount €4) at the tourist office. Don't miss the **Hofburg, Schloß Schönbrunn, Schloß Belvedere,** or any of the buildings along the **Ringstraße.** Those ensnared by the flowing tendrils of *Jugendstil* architecture can find many examples of it in Vienna—ask the tourist office for the *Architecture in Vienna* pamphlet, which contains photos and addresses of *Jugendstil* treasures all over town.

The range of available **tours** is overwhelming—walking tours, ship tours, bike tours, tram tours, jogging tours, and more. There are 42 themed walking tours alone, detailed in the brochure *Walks in Vienna* (free at the tourist office). Tours run about €11; some require admission fees to sites. All are worthwhile, but "Vienna in the Footsteps of *The Third Man*," which takes you into the sewers and the graffiti-covered catacomb world of the Wien River's underground canals, is one of the most unusual and exciting (bring your own flashlight). Tours on *fin de siècle* "old-timer" **trams** run May to October. (☎790 94 40 26. 1½hr. €15. Departs from Karlspl. near the Otto Wagner Pavilion Sa-Su 9:30, 11:30am, 1:30pm.) The drivers of legendary **Fiaker** (horse-drawn carriages) are happy to taxi you wherever your heart desires, but be sure to agree on the price before you set out (usually €30-35 per 20min.). There are official *Fiaker* stands in Stephanspl., Albertinapl., Heldenpl., and at the corner of Graben and Kohlmarkt. **Vienna-Bike,** IX, Wasag. (☎319 12 58), **rents bikes** (€5) and conducts 2-3hr. **cycling tours** (€20). **Bus tours** are given by **Vienna Sight-seeing Tours,** III, Stelzhamerg. 4/11 (☎712 46 83) and **Cityrama,** I, Börgeg. 1 (☎534 13). Tours start at €30. For a quick, do-it-yourself tour, take tram #1 or 2 around the Ring.

INSIDE THE RING

District I, the *Innenstadt* or *innere Stadt* (Inner city), is Vienna's social and geographical epicenter, enclosed on three sides by the broad, sweeping arc of the Ringstraße and on the northern side by the **Danube Canal.** With its Romanesque arches, Gothic portals, *Jugenstil* apartments, and modern Haas Haus, the *Innenstadt* is a gallery of architecture, perfect for sightseeing.

STEPHANSPLATZ
Take U1 (red) or U3 (orange) to "Stephansplatz."

As the heart of Vienna, Stephansplatz teems with activity in the shadow of the massive **Stephansdom**. Shops and cafés abound, providing ample opportunity for people-watching—suited professionals, political demonstrators, and camera-toting tourists all converge on the square, while students in period costumes sell tickets to Strauss or Mozart concerts.

STEPHANSDOM. Affectionately known as "Der Steffl," Stephansdom (St. Stephen's Cathedral) is Vienna's most sacred landmark, with its Gothic sculptural program and 450ft. **South Tower.** The **North Tower** was never completed; the architect met an unfortunate demise (see "A Bad Pact with the Devil," below). Take the elevator up the North Tower *(open Apr.-June and Sept.-Oct. daily 8:30am-4pm; elevator ride €3.50)* for a view of Vienna, or climb the 343 steps of the South Tower for a 360° view and close encounters with gargoyles *(open 9am-5:30pm, €2.50).*

Notable exhibits inside the cathedral include the early 14th-century Albertine choir and the Gothic organ loft by **Anton Pilgram,** so delicate in its construction that Pilgram's contemporaries warned him it would never bear the organ's weight. Pilgram replied that he would hold it up himself and carved a self-portrait at the bottom, bearing the entire burden on his back. The **high altarpiece** of the *Stoning of St. Stephen* is just as stunning. *(Cathedral tours M-Sa 10:30am, 3pm; Su and holidays 3pm. €3; in English at 3:45pm. Fantastic evening tour June-Sept. Sa 7pm; €14.)*

A BAD PACT WITH THE DEVIL In the 16th century, during the construction of the North Tower of the Stephansdom, a young builder named Hans Puchsbaum wished to marry his master's daughter. The master, jealous of Hans's skill, agreed on one condition: Hans had to finish the entire North Tower on his own within a year. Faced with this impossible task, Hans despaired until a stranger offered to help him. The stranger required only that Hans abstain from saying the name of God or any other holy name. Hans agreed, and the tower grew by leaps and bounds. One day the young mason spotted his love in the midst of his labor, and called out her name, "Maria!" With this invocation of the Blessed Virgin, the scaffolding collapsed and Hans plummeted to his death. Rumors of a satanic pact spread, and work on the tower ceased, leaving it in its present condition.

Downstairs, skeletons of thousands of plague victims fill the **catacombs.** The lovely **Gruft** (vault) stores all of the Hapsburg "innards." *(Tours M-Sa 10-11:30am and 1-4:30pm every 30min.; Su and holidays 1:30, 4:30pm every 30min. €3.)* Everyone wanted a piece of the rulers—the Stephansdom got the entrails, the Augustinerkirche got the hearts, and the Kapuzinergruft (on Neuer Markt) got the remainder. At the very top of the cathedral hangs the **bell** of the Stephansdom, the world's heaviest free-ringing bell (the whole bell moves, not just the clapper). The original bell, cast in 1711 from the metal of captured Turkish cannons, was smashed during WWII, much to the dismay of the Viennese. A series of photographs inside chronicles the process of reconstruction. The new bell has rung in every New Year since 1957.

HAAS HAUS. This controversial modern building, opposite the cathedral at Stephanspl. 12, reflects the Stephansdom in its postmodern glass and marble façade. The view is even better from inside the Haus, which has a restaurant on the top floor. Primarily a shopping center, the Haus opened in 1990 amid rumors of bureaucratic bribery and is considered something of an eyesore by most Viennese.

NEAR PETERSPLATZ
From Stephanspl., walk down Graben from Stephansdom; Peterspl. is on the right.

This tiny square off Graben is home to the Peterskirche and a good landmark from which to explore the center of Graben's *Fußgängerzone*.

GRABEN. Now closed to all traffic except feet and hooves, this boulevard was once a moat surrounding the Roman camp that became Vienna. The landscape of Graben today shows the debris of Baroque, *Biedermeier*, and *Jugendstil* efforts, which include **Ankerhaus** (#10) and the red-marble **Grabenhof** by Otto Wagner. One of the most interesting sights is the underground *Jugendstil* public toilet complex, designed by Adolf Loos. The **Pestsaüle** (Plague Column) in the square was built in 1693, to celebrate the passing of the Black Death.

PETERSKIRCHE. Construction on the church began in the 12th century, but the vast majority of Peterskirche was completed during the 1700s. A classic Baroque interior, stunning frescoes (especially in the dome), and religious martyrs encased in glass make this a sight worth seeing. *(Open daily 7am-6pm. Free.)*

KOHLMARKT. This second leg of the *Fußgängerzone* starts at the end of Graben, just past Peterskirche, and is lined with upscale shops marked "K.U.K." (Kaiserlich und Königlich), indicating that they once earned the Hapsburg seal of approval.

HOHER MARKT, RUPRECHTSPLATZ, MORZINPLATZ

From Stephanspl., walk down Rotenturmstr. and turn left onto Lichtenst., which runs into Hoher Markt. Judeng. runs from Hoher Markt to Ruprechtspl. and Morzinpl.

These three squares lie just north of Peterspl. Hoher Markt is the oldest square in town, mainly offering historical attractions, while Ruprechtspl. is home to Vienna's oldest church as well as a slew of cafés and bars in Vienna's hottest nightlife district, known as the **Bermuda Dreiecke** (see Nightlife, p. 140). Morzinpl. is a rather run-down plot of land along the Danube with a dark past.

HOHER MARKT. Both a market and execution site during medieval times, Hoher Markt was the center of the Roman encampment Vindobona. Roman ruins lie beneath the shopping arcade directly across from the fountain. *(Open Tu-Su 9am-12:15pm and 1-4:40pm. €1.80, students €0.70.)* Fischer von Erlach's Vermählungs-

---

AUSTRIAN GRAFFITI Scratched into the stones near the entrance of the Stephansdom is the mysterious abbreviation "O5." It's not a sign of hoodlums up to no good, but rather a reminder of a different kind of subversive activity. During WWII, "O5" was the secret symbol of Austria's resistance movement against the Nazis. The capital letter "O" and the number "5," for the fifth letter of the alphabet, form the first two letters of "Oesterreich." Recently the monogram has received new life; every time alleged Nazi collaborator and ex-president of Austria, Kurt Waldheim, attends mass, the symbol is highlighted in chalk. Throughout the city, "O5" has also been appearing on the sides of buildings and on flyers, protesting Jörg Haider's Freedom Party and its anti-immigrant policies.

---

brunnen (Marriage Fountain), depicting the union of Mary and Joseph, is the square's focal point. But the biggest draw is the corporate-sponsored *Jugendstil* Ankeruhr (clock). Built in 1914 by Franz Matsch, the bronze and copper timepiece has twelve 3m-tall historical figures, ranging from Emperor Marcus Aurelius to Joseph Haydn. One of statues rotates past the Viennese coat of arms each hour, accompanied by music from its era. At noon, all the figures appear. Under the walkway with the Ankeruhr is a sculptural relief depicting the signs of the Zodiac.

RUPRECHTSKIRCHE. Overlooking the Danube on Ruprechtspl., the Romanesque 11th-century Ruprechtskirche is the oldest church in Vienna. While not terribly exciting in its architecture, the church was built on the site of a Carolingian church from AD 740 and preserves the gates of the Roman settlement. Maria Theresa donated the well-clad skeleton of an early Christian martyr, which still lives in a glass case in the corner. *(Open M-W and F 10am-noon, Th 3-5pm.)*

STADTTEMPEL. Almost hidden away in Ruprechtspl. at Seitenstetteng. 2-4, the Stadttempel (City Temple) was built in 1826 following an imperial regulation that Jewish and Protestant places of worship should not have conspicuous street fronts. A sign of intolerance at the time, the regulation saved the synagogue from greater persecution. Out of Vienna's 94 synagogues, only the Stadttempel escaped Nazi destruction during *Kristallnacht* on November 9-10, 1938. It was spared because it stood on a residential block, concealed from the street. The torching of neighboring buildings damaged the synagogue, but it has been restored in Neo-Classical style. Today, an armed guard patrols the synagogue as a precaution against repeats of a 1983 terrorist attack. *(Bring your passport. Open M-Th. Free.)*

MORZINPLATZ. This largely residential area once held the Hotel Metropole, headquarters of the Gestapo, where numerous Viennese were tortured for speaking out against the *Anschluß*. The hotel was demolished in 1945; **The Monument to the Victims of Fascism** now stands in its place. Although the history of this monument is significant, travelers should be wary of traveling here, especially after dark.

NEAR JUDENPLATZ

From Stephanspl., walk down Graben. When Graben ends, go right and continue in the same direction on Bognerg. Turn right onto Seitzerg. and continue in the same direction on Kurrentg. Or, from Hoher Markt, walk down Wipplingerstr. and turn left onto Jordang.

Judenpl. was the site of the city's first Jewish ghetto, established in the Middle Ages. Wipplingerstr., which runs east-west along the square's north side, offers a number of architectural sights. The peaceful calm of the square creates an atmosphere conducive to appreciation of its sobering history.

JUDENPLATZ. Once the Jewish ghetto of Vienna, this square's focus is Rachel Whiteread's **Memorial to the Victims of the Holocaust.** The memorial, a giant inverted library made of concrete, was unveiled on the 60th anniversary of the *Kristallnacht*, Nov. 9th, 1999. Also in the square is a statue of Jewish playwright Gotthold Ephraim Lessing (1729-81). Originally erected in 1935, the statue was torn down by the Nazis; a new model was returned to the spot in 1982. The **Museum Judenplatz,** directly behind the memorial, documents the remarkable and tragic history of European Jews, with an emphasis on WWII. It also displays excavations of a synagogue built in 1294, which was burned down in the Jewish purge of 1421. (☎ 533 22 65; www.jwv.at. Wheelchair-accessible. Open M-Th and Su 10am-6pm, F 10am-2pm. €3, students € 2.50.) House #2, **Zum grossen Jordan,** bears a 16th-century relief and inscription, which at the time was meant to celebrate the medieval diaspora of Vienna's Jews.

MARIA AM GESTADE. This church's cramped position on the very edge of the old medieval town caused the nave to curve toward the south. The steep steps from the west door leading to **Tiefergraben,** a former tributary of the Danube, explain the phrase *Am Gestade* ("by the riverbank"). Maria is worthy of a complete visit, so make an appointment ahead of time in order to walk around the canopied Gothic choir of the church. *(Salvatorg. 12. Walk down Schwertg., right off Wipplingerstr., passing Judenpl. on the left. ☎ 533 95 94. Open daily 7am-6pm. Free.)*

ALTES RATHAUS. The Altes Rathaus (Old Town Hall), Wipplingerstr. 8, was occupied from 1316 to 1885, when the government moved to the Ringstr. The building is graced by a Donner fountain depicting the myth of Andromeda and

Perseus. The Altes Rathaus is also home to the tiny **Austrian Resistance Museum,** chronicling anti-Nazi activity during WWII (see "Austrian Graffiti," p. 119), and temporary exhibits. An exterior lined with Austrian flags encloses courtyards used for parties and festivals. (☎ *534 30 11 27; www.doew.at. Displays in German. Open M and W-Th 9am-5pm. Archive/library open M and W-Th 9am-5pm. Tours by appointment. Free.)*

AM HOF, FREYUNG, MINORITENPLATZ

From Stephanspl., walk down Graben. When Graben ends, turn right onto Bognerg. Am Hof will be on the right, Freyung straight ahead, and Minoritenpl. to the left (take Strauchg. off Freyung). Or, from Judenpl., take Drahtg., which runs into Am Hof.

AM HOF. What was once a medieval jousting square now houses the **Kirche am Hof** (Church of the Nine Choirs of Angels; built 1386-1662) and the black **Mariensäule** (Column to Mary). The latter was erected by Emperor Ferdinand III in gratitude to the Virgin Mary for her protection of Vienna (from the Protestant Swedes) during the Thirty Years War. A **Roman stronghold** and the **Collalto Palace** (where Mozart first performed publicly at the age of 12) surround the square. Am Hof also hosts an eclectic weekend **market.** *(Open Sa-Su 11am-1pm. Free.)*

FREYUNG. Just west of Am Hof, Freyung has the **Austriabrunnen** (Austria fountain) at its center. Freyung ("sanctuary") got its name from the **Schottenstift** (Monastery of the Scots) just behind the fountain, where medieval fugitives could claim asylum. Freyung was also used for public executions in the Middle Ages, but now the annual **Christkindlmarkt** blots out such unpleasant memories with the charm of performances, gifts, and baked goods. *(2nd Sa in Nov. through Christmas Eve open M-F 2-6:30pm, Sa-Su 10am-6:30pm.)* Three art galleries flank Freyung: the **Schottenstift Museum,** the **Kunstforum,** and **Palais Harrach.** A glass-roofed passage (adorned with chic shops) leads from Freyung to the Italianate **Palais Ferstel,** which houses one of Vienna's most cherished coffee houses, **Café Central** (see p. 114).

MINORITENPLATZ. Go down Herreng. from Freyung and take a right onto Landhausg. The square contains the 14th-century **Minoritenkirche,** whose tower was destroyed during the Turkish siege of Vienna in 1529. A mosaic copy of da Vinci's *Last Supper*, commissioned by Napoleon and purchased by Franz I, adorns the north wall of the church. (☎ *533 41 62. Open daily 9am-6pm. Free.)* On the south side of the square stands the **Bundeskanzleramt** (Federal Chancery), where the Congress of Vienna met in 1815, and where Chancellor Engelbert Dollfuss was assassinated by Nazis in 1934. (☎ *53 15 10. Open daily 9am-5pm.)*

VIENNA

UNFORGETTABLE EMPRESS Murdered by an anarchist in 1898, Empress Elisabeth (better known as Sisi) is remembered not for her untimely death, but for her legendary beauty. When she married Franz Josef in 1854, the 16-year-old Bavarian princess was considered by some to be the most gorgeous woman in Europe. But love did not flourish even in the hundreds of rooms of the Hofburg and Schönbrunn palaces—the imperial couple hated each other. Franz Josef built the Hermes Villa in the Wienerwald (Vienna Woods) for his wife's private residence. There, she unhappily wrote: "Love is not for me. Wine is not for me. The first makes me ill. The second makes me sick." In other poems, she complained about her duties as Empress, disparaged her husband, and labeled her children bristle-haired pigs. Over a century later, images of this melancholy, beautiful woman are plastered on postcards and guide books, and immortalized in various musicals and plays. A plaque on a statue of her in the Volksgarten dubs her the "unforgettable Empress Elisabeth."

MICHAELERPLATZ

Take U3 (orange) to "Herreng." Take a left onto Herreng., which leads into Michaelerpl. Or, from Minoritenpl., go back up Landhausg. and take a right onto Herreng.

Herreng., Kohlmarkt, and Schauflerg. all intersect in this prominent square, which is dominated by the Neo-Baroque, half-moon-shaped **Michaelertor,** the spectacular main gate of the Hofburg (see p. 127). In the middle of Michaelerpl. lie more excavated foundations of the Roman military camp called **Vindobona,** where Marcus Aurelius penned his *Meditations.*

MICHAELERKIRCHE. Michaelerpl. is named after this church, which occupies the block between Kohlmarkt and Hapsburgerg. The church's Romanesque foundation dates back to the early 13th century, but construction continued until 1792—note the Baroque statues over the Neo-Classical doorway. A breathtaking organ dominates the interior, while the **crypt** has a number of open coffins containing finely-clothed corpses from the 17th and 18th centuries. (☎ 533 80 00. Open May-Oct. M-F 6:30am-5pm. Tours May-Oct. 11am, 1, 2, 3, 4pm; Nov.-Apr. 11am, 3pm; call ahead for tours in English. €1.80, students €0.70.)

LOOSHAUS. On the corner of Kohlmarkt and Herreng. stands the Looshaus (now home to the Raiffeisenbank), constructed by Adolf Loos in 1910-11. Emperor Franz Josef branded it "the house without eyebrows," as a result of what he perceived to be a shocking lack of the customary Viennese window pediments. Offended by the building's modernity, the old emperor never again used the Michaelerpl. entrance to the Hofburg. (Open M-W and F 8am-3pm, Th 8am-5:30pm. Free.)

NEAR NEUER MARKT

Take U1 (red) or U3 (orange) to "Stephanspl." Walk down Kärntnerstr., away from the Stephansdom. Turn right on Donnerg., which leads into Neuer Markt. Or, from Albertina, walk down Tegetthoffstr., which runs into Neuer Markt.

Neuer Markt centers around George Raphael Donner's replica of the **Donnerbrunnen,** a graceful personification of the Danube, surrounded by the four gods who represent her tributaries, and the rivers' role in Vienna's history. The streets radiating from it lead to some of the most famous sights in Vienna. Parallel to Neuer Markt and running south toward the **Staatsoper** on Ringstraße, **Kärntnerstraße** is one of Vienna's largest pedestrian zones, lined with tourist shops and outdoor cafés. Street musicians play everything from Peruvian folk music to Neil Diamond.

KAPUZINERKIRCHE (CHURCH OF THE CAPUCHIN FRIARS). On the southwest corner of Neuer Markt. Behind its pale orange, 17th-century façade lies the **Kaisergruft** (Imperial Vault), a series of subterranean rooms filled with coffins, including remains (minus heart and entrails—see Augustinerkirche, p. 130, and Stephansdom, p. 118) of all Hapsburg rulers since 1633. Empress Maria Theresa rests next to husband Franz Stephan of Lorraine in a Rococo sepulcher surrounded by angels. (☎ 512 68 53. Open daily 9:30am-4pm; entrance until 3:40pm. Imperial Vault €4, students €3.)

HOTEL SACHER. At the end of Kärntnerstr., across from the rear of the Opera, stands the legendary Hotel Sacher. The hotel once served as a meeting place for the social and political elite to discuss affairs of state, while its *chambres separées* provided discreet locations for affairs of another sort. John Lennon and Yoko Ono awed the public by holding a press conference in one of the Sacher's suites while lying naked in bed—all, of course, in the name of peace. Today, most tourists come for the hotel's renowned *Sacher Torte* (€4.50; see p. 110).

MONUMENT GEGEN KRIEG UND FASCHISMUS. Located behind Hotel Sacher on Albertinapl., this "Memorial Against War and Fascism" was unveiled in 1988 to commemorate the suffering caused by WWII.

THE RINGSTRAßE

Trams #1 and 2 run along the Ringstr.; the U-bahn stops at its endpoints at U2 (purple): "Schottentor" and U3 (orange): "Stubentor." From Neuer Markt, take Donnerg. out of the Markt and turn right onto Kärntnerstr., which leads roughly to the middle of the Ring.

The Ringstraße defines the boundaries of the inner city, and is an historical attraction itself. After the last siege by the Ottoman Turks in 1683, city fortifications were installed around the city for protection. Then in 1857, nine years after a revolution, the military demanded that District I be surrounded by new fortifications, in response to the emerging bourgeoisie's desire for the removal of all formal barriers and for open space within the city. Imperial designers reached a compromise: the walls would be razed to make way for the 57m-wide, 4km-long Ringstraße. It would be both a pleasant, tree-studded spread of boulevard as well as a sweeping circle of road designed for the efficient transport of troops. Urban planners from all over Europe put together a group of monuments dedicated to staples of Western culture: religion, scholarship, commerce, politics, and art. In total, 12 giant public buildings were erected along the Ring. Counter-clockwise from Schottenring, they are the **Börse,** the **Votivkirche,** the **Universität,** the **Neues Rathaus,** the **Burgtheater,** the **Parliament,** the **Kunsthistorisches Museum** and **Naturhistorisches Museum,** the **Staatsoper,** the **Museum für angewandte Kunst,** and the **Postsparkasse.**

SCHOTTENRING. The first stretch of the Ring extending out from the Danube Canal, Schottenring leads past the Italianate **Börse** (stock exchange) to Schottentor, which is surrounded by university cafés, bookstores, and bars. Across Universitätsstr. rise the twin spires of the **Votivkirche,** a white Neo-Gothic cathedral. It was commissioned by Franz Josef's brother Maximilian after the Emperor survived an assassination attempt in 1853. The interior pays homage to a number of Austria's military heroes. *(Open Tu-Sa 9am-1pm and 4-6:30pm, Su 9am-1pm.)*

DR. KARL-LÜGER RING. The next stretch of the Ring runs from the university to Rathauspl. **Universität Wien** was founded in 1365, but by the 19th century, the original building had become far too small. The massive new building was built in the Italian Renaissance style to celebrate the beginning of the "Golden Age" of science. The professors, however, had hoped for a more modern building that would suggest the continuance of their own Golden Age. Inside the university is a tranquil courtyard lined with busts of departed famous professors.

DR. KARL-RENNER RING. Rathauspl. and Parliament mark this section of the Ring. The **Neues Rathaus** (town hall), with fluted arches and geraniums in the windows, honors the Flemish burghers who pioneered the idea of town halls and civic government in Europe. Opera buffs will enjoy the free nightly **Music Film Festival** (see p. 139) in July and August. *(Free tours M, W, F 1pm; meet at the blue Information booth outside.)* Across the street from the Rathaus is the **Burgtheater** (Imperial Court Theater), which has seen the premieres of some of the most famous operas and plays by Austrians, including Mozart's *La Nozze di Figaro* (The Marriage of Figaro). Inside are frescoes by Gustav Klimt, his brother, and his partner Matsch. *(☎514 44 29 55. Performance season Sept.-June. Tours in English July-Aug. M-Sa 2, 3pm; Sept.-June M-Sa 3pm. €4.50, students €2.)* Next to Rathauspl. is the **Parliament.** Decked out with winged chariots, a grand ramp leading to its columned façade, and an imposing statue of wise Athena, the Parliament invokes the great democracies of ancient Greece. *(☎40 11 00. Tours mid-Sept. to mid-July M-F 11am, 3pm; mid-July to mid-Sept. M-F 9, 10, 11am, 2, 3, 4pm; Easter holidays 11am, 3pm. €3.)*

BURGRING. On Burgring, opposite the Hofburg on either side of Maria-Theresien-Pl., stand two of Vienna's largest and most comprehensive museums, the Kunsthistorisches Museum (Museum of Art History; p. 134) and the Naturhistorisches Museum (Museum of Natural History; p. 136). When construction was complete, the builders realized with horror that Apollo, patron deity of art, stood atop the Naturhistorisches Museum, and Athena, goddess of science, atop the Kunsthistorisches Museum. Also note the statue of Empress Maria Theresa, surrounded by key statesmen and advisers. She holds the Pragmatic Sanction, which granted women the right to succeed to the throne.

OPERNRING/KÄRNTNERRING. Opernring runs from the Burggarten (see Gardens and Parks, p. 131) to Schwarzenbergstr., marked by an equestrian statue, the Schwarzenberg Denkmal. The largest feature of Opernring is the Staatsoper (State Opera; see p. 136). Built in 1869 by and for the opera-adoring public, the Staatsoper had first priority during the construction of the Ringstraße. After its destruction by Allied bombs in 1945, Vienna meticulously restored the exterior and reopened the building in 1955. Today, the Staatsoper is still at the heart of Viennese culture. You can tour the gold, crystal, and red velvet interior, but seeing an opera can be cheaper. *(Tours in English daily July-Aug. 10, 11am, 1, 2, 3, 4pm; Sept.-Oct. and May-June 1, 2, 3pm; Nov.-Apr. 2, 3pm. €5, students €2.)*

SCHUBERTRING/STUBENRING. From Schwarzenbergstr. to the Danube Canal, Schubertring borders the **Stadtpark** (see Gardens and Parks, p. 131). The **Postsparkasse** (Post Office Savings Bank), near the end of Stubenring, is Otto Wagner's greatest triumph of function over form and the most contemporary of the Ringstraße monuments. The building raises formerly concealed elements of construction (like the thousands of metallic bolts) to the level of modernist art. The interior, now a bank but still decorated in Art Noveau style, is open during banking hours. *(George-Coch-Pl. 2. Open M-W and F 8am-3pm, Th 8am-5:30pm.)*

OUTSIDE THE RING

As the city expands beyond the Ring in all directions, the distance between notable sights also expands. But what the area outside the Ring gives up in accessibility, it makes up for in its varied attractions. Some of Vienna's most famous modern architecture is outside the Ring, where 20th-century designers found more space to build. At the same time, this modern sprawl is also home to a number of startlingly beautiful Baroque palaces and parks that were once beyond the city limits.

NEAR KARLSPLATZ

Take U1 (red), U2 (purple), or U4 (green) to "Karlspl." Or, from the Staatsoper walk 2 blocks down Kärntnerstr. away from the city center, and turn left after Rechte Wienzeile.

Once a central gathering place for the Viennese, Karlspl. is now isolated behind a major traffic artery. Nonetheless, it's home to Vienna's most impressive Baroque church, the **Karlskirche**, and is surrounded by the **Musikverein** and several major museums, including the **Secession Building**, the **Künstlerhaus**, and the **Kunsthalle**.

KARLSKIRCHE. Situated in the center of the gardens, the Karlskirche is an eclectic architectural masterpiece, combining a Neoclassical portico with a Baroque dome and towers on either side. Two massive columns, covered with spiraling reliefs depicting the life of St. Carlo Borromeo ("Karl"), frame the central portion of the church. The interior is beautiful, with colorful ceiling frescoes and a golden sunburst altar. Designed by Fischer von Ehrlach and completed by his son, Johann Michael, this imposing edifice was constructed in 1793 to fulfill the promise Emperor Charles VI made to the Viennese during a plague epidemic in 1713. *(Open M-F 7:30am-7pm, Sa 8:30am-7pm, Su 9am-7pm. Free. Audio guide available, €2.)*

RESSELPARK. The park opposite Karlskirche, named for Josef Ressel (Czech-born inventor of the propeller), is tranquil and tree-shaded. The **Historisches Museum der Stadt Wien** is to the left of the Karlskirche (see Museums, p. 133), while the yellow and blue **Kunsthalle** stands out at the opposite end of the park. Across the park along Karlspl., a terrace links to the *Jugendstil* **Karlsplatz Stadtbahn Pavilions,** designed in 1899 by Otto Wagner.

SECESSION BUILDING. Northwest of Resselpark, across Friedrichstr. at #12, is the Secession Building. Its white walls, subtle decoration, and gilded dome (hence the nickname the "Golden Cabbage") are meant to clash with the Historicist Ringstraße. Otto Wagner's pupil Josef Olbrich built this *fin de siècle* monument to accommodate artists who broke with the rigid, state-sponsored Künstlerhaus. The inscription above the door reads: *Der Zeit, ihre Kunst; der Kunst, ihre Freiheit* ("To every age its art; to art, its freedom"). The Secession exhibits of 1898-1903 were led by Gustav Klimt and drew cutting-edge European artists. The exhibitions remain firmly dedicated to avant-garde art (see Museums, p. 133).

MAJOLICAHAUS. This colorful section of the Wagner Apartments, Linke Wienzeile 40, is at the "Kettenbrückeng." (U4/green) station, and a 15min. walk from Karlspl. From the Secession Building, head away from Karlspl. down Friedrichstr., which runs into Linke Wienzeile. The acclaimed *Jugendstil* Majolicahaus was a collaborative effort by Wagner and Olbrich. The wrought-iron spiral staircase is by Josef Hoffmann, founder of the Wiener Werkstätte, a communal arts-and-crafts workshop and key force in the momentum of the style. The golden neighbor of the Majolicahaus, the **Goldammer** building, is another Wagnerian mecca.

NASCHMARKT. West of Karlspl., along Linke Wienzeile, is the beginning of the Naschmarkt, a colorful food bazaar that moved from Karlspl. to its present location in the 1890s. During the week, the Naschmarkt, which derives its name from the German verb *naschen* (to nibble), presents a smorgasbord of fruits and vegetables laid out in front of bakeries, cafés, *Wurst* vendors, and cheese and spice shops. On Saturdays, it becomes a giant **flea market,** selling anything from loose junk to traditional Austrian clothing. Take heed: the early birds get the best finds. *(Open M-F 6am-6:30pm, Sa 6am-2pm.)*

THEATER AN DER WIEN. Further down Linke Wienzeile, opposite the Naschmarkt, stands the theater that hosted the premiere of Mozart's *Die Zauberflöte* (The Magic Flute) once upon a time (see p. 138). The names of the street and the theater commemorate the Wien river, which used to flow freely through Vienna, but which is now almost completely buried under city streets. *(☎ 588 300; www.musicalvienna.at. Open for performances only.)*

MUSIKVEREIN. Step across Lothringerstr. opposite Karlspl. to view the Musikverein, home of the Wiener Philharmoniker. The building's modest exterior conceals the sublime **Grosser Saal,** where the crème de la crème of the international music scene perform. Standing-room tickets offer an inexpensive way to admire both the music and the golden caryatids that line the hall (see p. 137). *(☎ 505 81 90; www.musikverein.at. Open only for performances; call ahead for prices and concert information.)*

SCHWARZENBERGPLATZ

Take tram #1, 2, D, or 71 to "Schwarzenbergpl." From Karlspl., walk down Lothringerstr. and make a left onto Schwarzenbergstr.

Schwarzenbergpl., marked by the illuminated **Hochstrahlbrunnen** (Tall Fountain), is an elongated square with a rather infamous military history. During the Nazi era, the occupied city renamed the square "Hitlerplatz"; when the Russians brutally liberated Vienna, they renamed it "Stalinplatz" and erected an enormous **Russen Hel-**

dendenkmal (Russian Heroes' Monument), a concrete colonnade behind a column bearing the figure of a Russian soldier, with a quotation from Stalin inscribed in the base. The Viennese have attempted to destroy the monstrosity three times, but the product of sturdy Soviet engineering refuses to be demolished. Vienna's disgust with its Soviet occupiers is further evident in their nickname for an anonymous Soviet soldier's grave: "Tomb of the Unknown Plunderer."

PALAIS SCHWARZENBERG. Its present location on a traffic island behind the Hochstrahlbrunnen makes it hard to believe that Palais Schwarzenberg, designed in 1697 by Fischer von Erlach's rival architect, Lukas von Hildebrandt, was once the center of a neighborhood preferred by Vienna's nobility. The palace (off-limits to the general public) is now part swank hotel, part Swedish Embassy.

ALONG THE DONAUKANAL

The Danube Canal cuts a semi-circle into the city south of the river, extending beyond the Innenstadt. Much of the area inside of the semi-circle is now taken up by parks (see Gardens and Parks, p. 131), but the outside edge of the canal provided building space for some of Vienna's great 20th-century architects to experiment with populist architecture.

HUNDERTWASSER HAUS. Fantastic Realist and environmental activist Friedensreich Hundertwasser designed Hundertwasser Haus in opposition to the aesthetic of *Rot Wien* (see Karl-Marx-Hof, below). Completed in 1985, it is a multicolored building with 50 apartments. Hundertwasser included trees and grass in the undulating balconies as a means of bringing life back to the urban "desert" the city had become; oblique tile columns and free-form color patterns also contribute to this flamboyant rejection of architectural orthodoxy. Despite hordes of visitors, Hundertwasser Haus remains a private residence. *(At the corner of Löweng. and Kegelg. Take tram N from Schwedenpl. to "Hetzg." or U3/orange to "Wien Mitte.")*

KUNST HAUS WIEN. Three blocks away at Untere Weißgerberstr. 13, is another Hundertwasser project, in this case an art museum. The bottom floor is devoted to Hundertwasser's graphic art (see Museums, p. 133), while the top floors contain controversial contemporary art exhibits (past artists include Robert Mapplethorpe and Annie Lennox). A café built along the lines of a Hundertwasser blueprint is inside (see Cafés, p. 113).

MÜLLVERBRENNUNGSANLAGE (GARBAGE INCINERATOR). Behind the "Spittelau" U-Bahn station. Hundertwasser fans will enjoy his jack-in-the-box of a trash dump. It features a smokestack topped by a golden disco ball. Hundertwasser also designed a ferry that cruises the Danube for the DDSG (see p. 91).

KARL-MARX-HOF. The most famous example of public housing built during the interwar years, Karl-Marx-Hof illustrates the ideology and aesthetic of *"Rot Wien"* (Red Vienna, the socialist republic from 1918 until the *Anschluß*). The "palace for the people" stretches out for a full kilometer, with more than 1600 identical orange-and-pink apartments. The Social Democrats used this structure as their stronghold during the civil war of 1934, until army artillery shelled the place and broke down the resistance. *(Heiligenstadterstr. 82-92. Take U4/green to "Heiligenstadt.")*

OTHER SIGHTS

KIRCHE AM STEINHOF. XIV, Baumgartner Höhe 1. Commissioned for the inmates of the state mental hospital in 1907, this unique church unites streamlined symmetry and Wagner's signature functionalism. The white walls are tiled for easy cleaning, the holy water in the basins by the door runs continuously for maximum hygiene, all corners are rounded to avoid injuries, and the pews are widely spaced to give nurses easy access to patients. The stained-glass windows were designed by Koloman Moser, a vanguard member of the Secession. (Take U2/purple or U3/

orange to "Volkstheater," then bus #48A to "Otto Wagner-Spital/Psychiatriches Zentrum." ☎91 06 01 12 04. Open M-F 8am-3pm, Sa 2:30-4:30pm. Call ahead for guided tours in English, Sa 3pm. €4.)

THE ZENTRALFRIEDHOF. The Viennese like to describe the **Zentralfriedhof** (Central Cemetery) as half the size of Geneva but twice as lively (2,500,000 people are buried here). **Tor II** (2nd Gate) is the main entrance to the cemetery, and the place to pay respects to your favorite Viennese artist: beyond it are Beethoven, Wolf, Strauss, Schönberg, Moser, and an honorary monument to Mozart; his true resting place is an unmarked pauper's grave in the **Cemetery of St. Mark,** III, Leberstr. 6-8. St. Mark's deserves a visit not just for sheltering Mozart's dust, but also for its *Biedermeier* tombstones and the wild profusion of lilac blossoms that festoon it for two weeks in spring.

Tor I leads to the **Jewish Cemetery.** Sadly, the state of the Jewish Cemetery mirrors the fate of Vienna's Jewish population—many of the headstones are cracked, broken, lying prone, or neglected because the families of most of the dead are gone from Austria. Various structures throughout this portion of the burial grounds memorialize the millions murdered in Nazi death camps.

Tor III leads to the Protestant section and the new Jewish cemetery. To the east of the Zentralfriedhof is the melancholy **Friedhof der Namenlosen** on Alberner Hafen, where the nameless corpses of people fished out of the Danube are buried. *(Tor II, the main entrance, is at XI, Simmeringer Hauptstr. 234. Take tram #71 from Schwarzenbergpl., or tram #72 from Schlachthausg. The tram stops 3 times, at each of the gates. Bus #6A also serves the other gates. You can also take S-7 to "Zentralfriedhof," which stops along the southwest wall of the cemetery.)*

◉ HAPSBURG PALACES

HOFBURG
Take tram #1 or 2 anywhere on the Ringstr. to Heldenpl., or enter from Michaelerpl.

A massive reminder of the Hapsburgs' 700-year reign, the sprawling **Hofburg** was the imperial family's winter residence. Construction on the original fortress began in 1275, but it didn't become the official dynastic seat until the mid-16th century. As few Hapsburgs were willing to live in their predecessors' quarters, hodge-podge additions and renovations continued until the end of the family's reign in 1918. Today, the complex houses several museums as well as the **Österreichische Nationalbibliothek** (Austrian National Library), the performance halls of the **Lipizzaner stallions** and the **Vienna Boys' Choir,** a convention center, and the offices of the Austrian President. It also includes the **Burggarten** and the **Volksgarten** (see Gardens and Parks, p. 131). The Hofburg is divided into several sections, including **In der Burg,** the **Alte Burg, Heldenplatz,** the **Neue Burg, Stallburg, Josefsplatz,** and **Albertina.** The museums, libraries, and apartments within the Hofburg may suit some people's tastes, but the best way to see this palatial cluster is to walk around and look up.

IN DER BURG
If you come through the Michaelertor, you'll first enter the courtyard called In der Burg (within the fortress). The central monument to Emperor Franz II isn't too exciting, but on the left is the more visually stimulating red- and black-striped **Schweizertor** (Swiss Gate), erected in 1552 and named for the Swiss mercenaries who guarded it under Empress Maria Theresa. Street musicians take advantage of the wonderful acoustics here to play melodies from the old Empire. This section of the Hofburg contains the entrances to the **Kaiserappartements** and the **Silberkammer.** *(Open daily 9am-5pm. Combined admission €7, students €6.)*

THE LOCAL LEGEND

THE CURSE OF THE LIMOUSINE

The story begins in the year 1914, when Archduke Franz Ferdinand, heir to the struggling Hapsburg throne, received an open-topped limousine as a gift from his family. Shortly thereafter, while on an official visit to Sarajevo, the Archduke and his wife were assassinated while riding through the streets in the limo, setting off the nationalistic fervor that started WWI.

After the assassination of the Ferdinands, the limousine passed into the hands of General Potiorek, a commander in the Austrian Army. Right at the beginning of the War, Potiorek suffered a humiliating defeat by the feeble and highly disorganized Serbian Army. His reputation in tatters, Potiorek returned to Vienna only to die impoverished and alone in an insane asylum. The next in line to receive the limousine was a member of Potiorek's personal staff, who owned the car for only two weeks before he lost control of the limo, ran down two peasants, and then swerved into a tree. He died instantly.

The limousine remained ownerless until the end of WWI, at which point it was purchased by a governor of Yugoslavia. After restoring the limo, the governor survived a series of accidents, the last of which cost him one of his arms. He immediately sold the limousine to a doctor.

KAISERAPPARTEMENTS (IMPERIAL APARTMENTS). On the right side of the Michaelertor is the entrance to the imperial apartments. Once the private quarters of Emperor Franz Josef (1830-1916) and Empress Elisabeth (1838-1898), neither of them spent much time in the Hofburg (or with each other, for that matter), so the rooms are disappointingly bare. Amid all the Baroque trappings, the 2 most personal items seem painfully out of place: Emperor Franz Josef's military field bed and Empress Elisabeth's wooden gym are a silent testimony to their lonely lives (see "Unforgettable Empress," p. 121).

SILBERKAMMER. on the ground floor opposite the ticket office. This vast collection of gold, silver, and porcelain once adorned the imperial table; it includes a 100ft. long gilded candelabra and the impressive **Laxemburg Goblet,** ca. 1821.

ALTE BURG

Behind the Schweizertor lies the **Schweizerhof,** the inner courtyard of the Alte Burg (Old Fortress), which stands on the same site as the original 13th-century palace. The Alte Burg houses the **Burgkapelle** and the **Weltliche und Geistliche Schatzkammer** (Secular and Sacred Treasury).

BURGKAPELLE. From the Schweizertor, make a right at the top of the stairs. This Gothic chapel is where the heavenly voices of the **Wiener Sängerknaben** (Vienna Boys' Choir) harmonize on Su and religious holidays. (☎533 99 27. Open M-Th 11am-3pm, F 11am-1pm. €2, students €1.50. Choir performs from mid-Sept. to beginning of June; call ahead to reserve a ticket; see p. 138.)

WELTLICHE UND GEISTLICHE SCHATZKAMMER.

entrance beneath the steps to Burgkapelle, through the Schweizertor and to the right. Located within are the Hapsburg jewels, the crowns of the Holy Roman and Austrian Empires, imperial christening robes, and a gorgeous, gold-painted cradle, which Maria Louisa (Napoleon's wife) gave to her infant son. The treasury also contains a "horn of a unicorn" (really an 8ft. long narwahl's horn) and a tooth reported to have belonged to John the Baptist. (Open M and W-Su 10am-6pm. €7, seniors and students €5. Free audio guide available in English.)

NEUE BURG

Built between 1881 and 1913, the Neue Burg (New Fortress) is the youngest wing of the palace, built as a last attempt on the part of the Hapsburgs to assert their imperial power. The double-headed golden eagle crowning the roof symbolized the double empire of Austria-Hungary. Planned in 1869, the intended (but never fully realized) design called for twin palaces across Heldenpl., both connected to the

Kunsthistorisches Museum and Naturhistorisches Museum by arches spanning the Ringstr. Today, the Neue Burg houses Austria's largest library, the **Österreichische Nationalbibliothek** (Austrian National Library), the fantastic **Völkerkunde Museum,** and three branches of the **Kunsthistorisches Museum** (see p. 134). *(☎ 525 244 84; www.khm.at. Open M and W-Su 10am-6pm.)*

ÖSTERREICHISCHE NATIONALBIBLIOTHEK. The Austrian National Library holds millions of books and an interesting little museum filled with ancient books written on papyrus, as well as scriptures and musical manuscripts. A reading room is open to the public; in-library use of books allowed with picture ID. *(Entrance on Heldenpl. ☎ 53 41 03 97. Open Oct.-June M-F 9am-7pm, Sa 9am-12:45pm; July-Aug. M-F 9am-3:45pm, Sa 9am-12:45pm. Museum €7.30, students €5.)*

REICHSKANZLEITRAKT (STATE CHANCELLERY WING). Standing with your back facing the red Schweizertor, the Reichskanzleitrakt is the building spanning the right length of the square. Most notable for its architecture, especially the group of buff statues on the exterior (representing the labors of Hercules). They are said to have inspired the 11-year-old Arnold Schwarzenegger, then on his first visit to Vienna, to pump *himself* up.

OTHER HOFBURG SIGHTS

HELDENPLATZ. From the Michaelertor, walk past the red Schweizertor and continue straight through the three-arched passageway. On March 15, 1938, the enormous Heldenpl. (Heroes' Square) was filled with a jubilant crowd cheering Adolf Hitler's proclamation of the *Anschluß* (the unification of Germany and Austria). The equestrian statues facing each other (both by Anton Fenkhorn) depict two of Austria's great military commanders: Prince Eugene of Savoy and Archduke Charles, whose horse rears triumphantly on its hind legs with no other support, a feat of sculpting never again duplicated. Poor Fenkhorn later went insane, supposedly due to his inability to recreate the effect.

STALLBURG (PALACE STABLES). Attached to the northeast side of the Alte Burg (to the left of the Michaelertor, if one is facing it from the outside) is the Renaissance Stallburg, the home base of the Royal Lipizzaner stallions and the **Spanische Reitschule** (Spanish Riding School). The cheapest way to catch a glimpse of the famous steeds is to watch them train. *(Mid-Feb. to June and late Aug.-early Nov. Tu-F 10am-noon, except when the horses tour. Tickets sold at the door at Josefspl., Gate 2, from about 8:30am. €11.60, children €5.)* For a more impressive (and expensive) display, you can try to attend a

The doctor enjoyed the limo for six months before he was found trapped under the car in a ditch, crushed to death. The limousine was given to a family member of the doctor, a diamond dealer, who owned the car for a year without incident. He later committed suicide.

The next victim to claim ownership of the limousine was a Swiss racecar driver—he met his demise when he crashed into a stone wall. He was thrown out of the car and over the wall, falling to his death.

At this point, now both an urban legend and an item of significant historical value, the limousine was purchased by a Serbian farmer for an astronomical sum. One day, unable to start the limo, the farmer attempted to tow the car with a horse and buggy. However, having forgotten to turn off the ignition, the limousine mysteriously started, pitched forward, and overturned the buggy, killing the farmer.

The last fatality occurred on the way to a wedding—the limousine had come into the possession of a garage owner who repaired the car to look as it did during Archduke Ferdinand's era. Trying to get to the wedding on time, the limo spun out of control on the highway, crushing most of its passengers.

Today, the limousine resides in Vienna's military history museum—no one has been brave enough to take it out for a spin.

Reitschule performance, which requires ticket reservations in writing months in advance. (☎533 90 32; www.spanische-reitschule.com. Write to: Spanische Reitschule, Michaelerpl. 1, A-1010 Wien. Mar.-June and Sept.-early Nov. Su 10:45am; Apr.-June and Sept.-Oct. Sa 10am, 1½hr. If you reserve through a travel agency, expect at least a 22% surcharge. Reservations only; no money accepted by mail. Tickets €35-150, standing room €22.) You can also learn about Lipizzaner history and training at the **Lipizzaner Museum** (see p. 136).

JOSEFSPLATZ. Just south of Stallburg, this courtyard is named after the statue of Emperor Josef II in the center. The square contains the ticket entrance for the Stallburg and the entrance to the Prunksaal (Grand Hall). Dating to 1723, the Prunksaal glitters with gilded wood, frescoes, and marble pillars, and is the secular counterpart of Fischer von Erlach's magnificent Karlskirche (see p. 124). A segment of the Nationalbibliothek, this is the largest Baroque library in Europe. Wander through the floor-to-ceiling bookcases that house over 200,000 leather-bound books (with a collection of over 2.6 million books total) and pay your respects to the 16 marble statues of various Hapsburg rulers, including Charles VI, the library's founder. (☎53 41 00; www.oub.ac.at. Prunksaal open mid-May to mid-Oct. M-W and F-Su 10am-4pm, Th 10am-7pm; mid-Oct. to mid-May M-Sa 10am-2pm. Closed first 3 weeks of Sept. €5, students €3.)

AUGUSTINERKIRCHE. High masses are held each Sunday in this 14th-century Gothic church, located in a wing attached to the Prunksaal's south side, on Josefspl. Eighteenth-century renovations (and Napoleonic flourishes) have somewhat altered the original interior. The Augustinerkirche saw the wedding of Hapsburgs Maria Theresa and Franz Stephan, and the church's **Herzgrüftel** (Little Heart Crypt) became the final resting place of their hearts. (Mass 11am. Church open M-Sa 8am-5pm, Su 11am-6pm. Free.)

ALBERTINA. Originally part Augustinian monastery, part 18th-century palace, the Albertina houses the celebrated Collection of Graphic Arts: an impressive collection of over 65,000 drawings and 1 million prints, ranging from Michelangelo to Picasso. Once the largest of the Hapsburg's residences, Albertina has undergone a series of renovations, which included restoring the original façades of the building (partially damaged during WWII) and adding a new wing for temporary exhibits. (☎53 48 30; www.albertina.at. Open M-Tu and Th-Su 10am-6pm, W 10am-9pm. Free.)

SCHLOß SCHÖNBRUNN

Take U4 (green) to "Schönbrunn." Wheelchair-accessible. www.schoenbrunn.at. Apartments open daily Apr.-June and Sept.-Oct. 8:30am-5pm; Nov.-Mar. 8:30am-4:30pm; July-Aug. 8:30am-7pm. Imperial tour €8, students €7.40. Grand Tour €10.50/€8.60. Audio guides in English included.

Named after a "beautiful brook" on the property, Schönbrunn had humble beginnings as a hunting lodge. Two earlier versions were destroyed before architect Fischer von Erlach conceived a plan for a palace befitting an emperor. Construction began in 1696, but the high costs slowed the project considerably until Maria Theresa inherited it in 1740. Under her rule, the Rococo palace that would become her favorite residence was finally completed. Its unique mustard-yellow color has been named *"Maria Theresien gelb,"* which can be seen throughout Austria. When Napoleon conquered Vienna, he acquired a fondness for the place and promptly made it his headquarters. The Grand Tour passes through the **Great Gallery,** where the Congress of Vienna danced the night away after a day of dividing up the continent, and the **Hall of Mirrors,** where the six-year-old Mozart played. The **Ceremonial Hall** includes paintings of Joseph II's wedding to Isabella of Parma. If you take the shorter Imperial Tour, you'll miss sumptuous pleasures of the palace. The Hapsburgs' suites are exquisite, trimmed in gold and silver. Also stunning are the Oriental art and rosewood paneling in the **Millions Room,** and the original red velvet bed cover in Maria Theresa's bedroom.

THE GARDENS. Equally impressive as the palace are its Imperial gardens. Designed by Emperor Josef II, the gardens extend nearly four times the length of the palace. They include a wild range of themes, from neatly ordered forests to geometric flower designs. Also featured is the massive stone **Neptunbrunnen** (Neptune Fountain), with Romanesque sculptures. *(Open daily 6am-dusk. Free.)*

On the right side of the garden is the **Palmenhaus,** an enormous greenhouse of tropical plants, and the **Schmetterlinghaus** (Butterfly House), where hundreds of butterflies flutter among the exotic flora. There is also a **maze** in whose center stand two stones that were activated by a master of Feng Shui and are said to radiate energy and harmony *(€3, students €2.50)*. The sprawling complex is crowned by the **Gloriette,** an ornamental temple serenely perched upon a hill with a beautiful view of the gardens. If you're feeling indulgent, drink a *mélange* in the temple's new café. In the summer, open-air opera is performed in the park. Built to amuse Maria Theresa's husband in 1752, the **Schönbrunn Tiergarten** (zoo) is the world's oldest menagerie, but oldest doesn't necessarily mean best or most extensive—it is basically just a side diversion within the gardens. *(Zoo open daily May-Sept. 9am-6:30pm; Feb. and Oct. 9am-5pm; Nov.-Jan. 9am-4:30pm; Mar. and Oct. 9am-5:30pm; Apr. 9am-6pm. €6.90, students €3.30, children €2.20.)*

SCHLOß BELVEDERE

Take tram D or tram #71 one stop past Schwarzenbergpl., or walk up Prinz-Eugen-Str. from Südbahnhof. Walking southeast from Schwarzenbergpl. (away from the city center), you'll find Belvedere just beyond the Schwarzenberggarten. www.belvedere.at.

Originally the summer residence of **Prince Eugène of Savoy,** one of Austria's greatest military heroes, the Belvedere has played a large role in the imperial history of Vienna. After Eugene's heirless death in 1736, his cousin sold off his possessions and Empress Maria Theresa snatched up the palace as a showroom for the Hapsburgs' art collection, opening the extensive formal gardens to the public. Though the imperial art moved to the Kunsthistorisches Museum in the 1890s, Archduke Franz Ferdinand lived in the Belvedere until his 1914 assassination. The grounds of the Belvedere, stretching from the Palais Schwarzenberg to the Südbahnhof, now contain three spectacular sphinx-filled gardens (see p. 131) and an equal number of excellent museums (see p. 134).

◪ GARDENS & PARKS

The Viennese have gone to great lengths to brighten the urban landscape with leafy green spaces. The Hapsburgs opened the city's primary public gardens, and have maintained them for centuries, until WWII after which they became public property. There are several parks along the Ring (including the **Stadtpark, Resselpark, Burggarten,** and **Volksgarten**), as well as many in the suburbs. The gardens of **Schloß Schönbrunn** and **Schloß Belvedere** (see p. 131) are particularly beautiful.

ALONG THE RING. Established in 1862, the **Stadtpark** (City Park) was the first municipal park outside the former city walls. One of Vienna's oft-photographed monuments, the gilded **Johann-Strauss-Denkmal,** occupies the center of the park and sometimes acts as a backdrop for the Vienna Boys' Choir. *(Take U4/green to "Stadtpark.")*

Clockwise up the Ring, past the Staatsoper, lies the **Burggarten** (Palace Garden), a quiet park with gorgeous greenhouses. It also contains monuments to such Austrian notables as Mozart, Emperor Franz Josef, and Emperor Franz I (Maria Theresa's husband). The **Babenberger Passage** leads from the Ring to the marble **Mozart Denkmal** (1896). Reserved for the imperial family and members of the court until 1918, the Burggarten is now a favorite destination for local residents of all ages.

The Burggarten borders Heldenpl., across from the Kunsthistorisches Museum and behind the Hofburg, which abuts the **Volksgarten** (People's Garden). Once the site of a defensive bastion destroyed by Napoleon's troops, this romantic park is now brimming with roses and romantic couples. In the center of the park is the **Temple of Theseus,** while at the north end a stark, white statue of Empress Elisabeth rests on a throne. Erected after her assassination, the plaque at the base of the statue reads: "The people of Austria erected this monument to their unforgettable Empress Elisabeth in steadfast love and loyalty" (see "Unforgettable Empress," p. 121). The best time to see visit this park is right before sunset; find a place to sit and watch as the Neues Rathaus becomes illuminated.

AUGARTEN. The Augarten, on Obere Augartenstr., northeast of downtown Vienna in Leopoldstadt, is Vienna's oldest public park. Originally a formal French garden, the Augarten was given a Baroque face-lift and opened to the public by Kaiser Josef II in 1775. Today, the Augarten is no longer as fashionable as it was in the days of Mozart and Strauss, due primarily to the ominous WWII **Flaktürme** (concrete anti-aircraft towers) that dominate the center of the park. Buildings located within the Augarten include the headquarters for the **Wiener Porzellanmanufaktur** (Vienna China Factory), founded in 1718, and the **Augartenpalais,** now a boarding school for the Vienna Boys' Choir. *(To reach the park, take tram #31 up from Schottenring or tram N to "Obere Augartenstr." and head left down Taborstr.)*

PRATER. Extending southeast from the Wien Nord Bahnhof/Praterstern, this park was a private game reserve for the Imperial Family until 1766 and the site of the World Expo in 1873. Situated in the woodlands between the Donaukanal and the river proper, the park is surrounded by ponds, meadows, and stretches of forest. The Prater is most famous for its old-school amusement park, with the stately wooden 65m-tall **Riesenrad** *(Giant Ferris Wheel; €4.50 for a 10min. ride).* Locals cherish this wheel of fortune, and when it was destroyed in WWII, the city built an exact replica, which has been turning since 1947. The area near U1 (red): "Praterstern" is the actual amusement park, which contains rides, arcades, restaurants, and casinos. Entry to the complex is free, but each attraction charges admission (€1-20). The kitschy thrill rides and wonderfully campy spook-houses are packed with children during the day, but the Prater becomes less wholesome after sundown due to the proliferation of peep shows. *(☎728 0516. www.wiener-prater.at. Open daily mid-Mar. to mid-Oct. 10am-midnight; mid-Oct. to Nov. 10am-10pm; Nov.-Feb. 10am-6pm.)*

ON THE DANUBE. The Danube's spring floods were problematic once settlers moved outside the city walls, so the Viennese stretch of the Danube was diverted into canals from 1870 to 1875 and again from 1972 to 1987. One of the side benefits of this restructuring was the creation of new recreational areas, ranging from new tributaries (including the **Alte Donau** and the **Donaukanal**) to the **Donauinsel** *(www.donauinsel.at)*, a narrow island stretching for kilometers. The Donauinsel is devoted to bike paths, soccer fields, swimming areas, boats, and summer restaurants. The northern shore of the island, along the Alte Donau, is lined with beaches and bathing areas. *(Take U1 (red; dir.: Kagran) to "Donauinsel" or "Alte Donau." Open May-Sept. M-F 9am-8pm, Sa-Su 8am-8pm. Beach admission is roughly €4.)* To catch a view of Vienna at its best, go after sundown to **Donaupark** and take the elevator up to the revolving restaurant in the **Donauturm** (Danube Tower), near the UN complex. *(Take the U1/red to "Kaisermühlen/Vienna International Center," exit towards Schüttaustr., and follow signs to the park. Tower open daily 10am-midnight. €5.20, students €4.20.)* On weekends, the brave can also bungee-jump from the 150m tower. *(Jochen-Schweizer. ☎269 62 47; www.jochen-schweizer.at. Open Sa-Su 8am-8pm. €99 Early Bird Ticket is valid for 2hr. after time of purchase; must call ahead to reserve a time.)* The area celebrates during the annual open-air **Donauinsel Fest,** which stages jazz and rock concerts and fireworks displays in late June (see Festivals, p. 139).

IN THE SUBURBS. Nearly every district in Vienna has public gardens tucked away somewhere, like the **Türkenschanz Park** in district XVIII. The garden is famous for its Turkish fountain, its pools, and its peacocks. In summer, feed the ducks or walk past the water lilies. In winter, come for sledding or ice skating. *(Take bus #40A or 10A, and enter the park anywhere along Gregor-Mendel-Str., Hasenauerstr., or Max-Emmanuelstr.)*

West of District XIII is the **Lainzer Tiergarten** (Lainz Game Preserve). Once an exclusive hunting preserve for the royals, this enclosed park has been a nature preserve since 1941. Along with paths, restaurants, and spectacular vistas, the park holds the **Hermes Villa**, a one-time retreat for Empress Elisabeth. It now houses exhibitions by the Historical Museum of Vienna, most recently one about Viennese fashion. *(Take U4 (green; dir.: Hütteldorf) to "Hietzing"; change to streetcar #60A to "Hermesstr." At the intersection, take a sharp right and walk a block to the bus stop. Take bus #60B to "Lainzer Tor." ☎804 13 24. Open Tu-Su and holidays Apr.-Sept. 10am-6pm; Oct.-Mar. 9am-4:30pm. Villa €4, students €1.50, seniors €2, family €6. F mornings free.)*

Districts XIV, XVII, XIX, and XX fade into well-tended forests that are attractive hiking destinations. The **Pötzleindorfer Park,** at the end of tram line #41 (dir.: Pötzleindorfer Höhe) from Schottentor, overlaps the lower end of the Wienerwald.

WIENERWALD. Far to the north and west of Vienna sprawl the forested hills of the Wienerwald (Vienna Woods), which extends past Baden bei Wien to the first foothills of the Alps. The woods are known for their excellent *Heurigen* and delicious white wines (see p. 116). One of the most famous and easily accessible routes into the Wienerwald is via **Kahlenberg** and **Leopoldsberg,** hills north of Vienna which provide great views of the city and direct entrance to the woods. **Kahlenberg** (484m) is the highest point of the rolling forest, with spectacular views of Vienna, the Danube, and the Alps in the distance. The Turks besieged Vienna from here in 1683, and Polish king Jan Sobieski celebrated his liberation of the city from Saracen infidels in the small **Church of St. Joseph.** *(Open daily 10am-noon and 2-5pm. To get to the Wienerwald on the tram, take tram #38 to "Grinzing," tram D to "Nußdorf," or tram #43 to "Neuwaldegg.")* For a good outlook point, climb the **Stefania Warte** tower, part of the valley's old fortifications. *(Just off the central square of Kahlenberg. Take U4/green to "Heiligenstadt" then bus #38A to "Kahlenberg," or hike up the steep 1km long Nasen Weg from the Kahlenbergdorf S-Bahn station. Open May-Oct. Sa noon-6pm, Su and holidays 10am-6pm.)*

The area around Kahlenberg, Cobenzl, and Leopoldstadt is criss-crossed by hiking paths marked with blazes. Kahlenberg and its country cemetery are within easy walking distance of the wine-growing districts of **Nußdorf** and **Grinzing.** You can follow in an early Pope's footsteps with a hike to the **Leopoldskirche,** a renowned pilgrimage site, located 1km east of Kahlenberg on **Leopoldsberg** (425m). It is on the site of a Babenberg fortress destroyed by the Turks in 1529. *(Bus #38A also runs from Kahlenberg to Leopoldsberg; 20min.)* **Klosterneuburg,** a Baroque monastery founded by Leopold (see p. 144), is a 1½hr. hike from Leopoldsberg.

🏛 MUSEUMS

All museums run by the city of Vienna are **free Friday before noon** (except on public holidays); they are marked in the tourist office's free *Museums* brochure with a red and white coat of arms. Individual museum tickets usually cost €1.50-7 less with the **Vienna Card,** though student or senior discounts are comparable (see p. 97). If you're in town for a long time, invest in the **Museum Card** (issued through the Verein der Museumsfreunde) to save a bundle on entrance fees (ask for the card at a museum ticket window). The newest additions to the museum circuit is the **MuseumsQuartier** (☎523 58 81; www.mqw.at). Originally the imperial barracks, the **Messepalast,** Museumspl., was transformed in 2001 into the **MuseumsQuartier,** a modern complex combining several previously scattered collections (see p. 134).

THE LOCAL STORY

VOLCANIC ART

Jörg Wolfert is Director of Education and Visitor Services at the Museum of Modern Art in Vienna.

This here is one of the most ambitious exhibit spaces for modern art in Europe...Both the museum and the building itself are conceptual. The building was supposed to be eight stories, but the architects were not allowed to build more than four stories above ground, so they decided to build it like a volcano, with many of the floors underground. The outside is covered with lava (basalt), and the inside has a long elevator shaft that is supposed to bring out the feel of an underground mine, like inside a volcano...Also, the dark, steel passageways are meant to make people feel they are actually walking through the inside of a volcano, and to give the idea that visiting great art should be hard work, just as it's been difficult for modern art to get here today...One problem we've had is with the limited amount of space this kind of building provides. The architects stipulated that the building is not to be altered, so when we wanted to bring two different exhibits together as one, that was a problem. They had to work out a solution that made part of the exhibits an installation piece, so that it became part of the architecture, while also connecting the exhibits. So, now we have conceptual art housed in a conceptual building.

ART MUSEUMS

■ **Österreichische Galerie** (Austrian Gallery), III, Prinz-Eugen-Str. 27 (☎ 79 55 72 61; recorded info ☎ 79 55 73 33; www.belvedere.at), in the Belvedere Palace behind Schwarzenbergpl. (see p. 131). Walk up from the Südbahnhof, take tram D to "Schloß Belvedere," or tram #71 to "Unteres Belvedere." The collection is in 2 parts. The **Upper Belvedere** (built in 1721-22) houses Austrian and European art of the 19th and 20th centuries. The highlight of the Upper Belvedere is, without a doubt, the Gustav Klimt collection, which includes his masterpiece *The Kiss*. However, the remainder of the exhibits are equally as impressive: the **Sala Terrena** is a *tour de force* of Italian sculpture, while priceless paintings by van Gogh and Egon Schiele grace the walls. The **Lower Belvedere** contains the **Austrian Museum of Baroque Art,** which showcases an extensive collection of sculptures by Donner and Maulbertsch, as well as Messerschmidt's oftentimes comical busts. David's majestic portrait of Napoleon on horseback is here, as is the **Museum of Medieval Austrian Art,** which boasts an impressive collection of Romanesque and Gothic sculptures and altarpieces. Wheelchair-accessible. Both Belvederes are open Tu-Su 10am-6pm. Last admission 30min. before closing. €7.50, students €5 (price includes both Upper and Lower Belvederes). Audio guide in Upper Belvedere €4.

Kunsthistorisches Museum (Museum of Fine Arts), I (☎ 525 240; www.khm.at). Take U2 (purple) to "Museumsquartier," U2 (purple)/U3 (orange) to "Volkstheater," or tram 1, 2, D, or J. Across from the Burgring and Heldenpl. on Maria Theresa's right. Houses the world's 4th-largest art collection, including vast numbers of 15th- to 18th-century Venetian and Flemish paintings. Must-sees include Vermeer's *Art of Painting* (room 24) and Raphael's *Madonna in the Meadow* (room 4). Ancient and classical art, including an Egyptian burial chamber, are also outstanding exhibits. Open Tu-Su 10am-6pm. Picture gallery also open Th until 10pm. Tickets €9, students and seniors €6.50. Audio guides available for €2 (1st audio guide is free). Small branches reside in the Neue Burg. Wheelchair-accessible. Open daily 10am-6pm except Tu.

Ephesos Museum exhibits the extensive findings of the Austrian excavation of classical ruins from Ephesus in Turkey, including an ancient Greek temple.

Hofjagd- und Rustkammer (Arms and Armor Collection), the world's 2nd-largest such collection.

Sammlung alter Musikinstrumente (Ancient Musical Instrument Collection). Includes Beethoven's harpsichord, Mozart's piano, and a wide array of Renaissance instruments.

MuseumsQuartier (☎ 523 58 51; www.mqw.at) is one of the 10 largest art districts in the world. Take U2 (purple) to "Museumsquartier," or U2/U3 (orange) or tram 1, 2, D, or J to "Volkstheater." Uniting Baroque architecture with ultramodern film, visual art, and performance spaces, this area offers a smattering of large museums, including:

Leopold Museum (☎52 57 00; www.leopoldmuseum.org). The world's largest Schiele collection, plus works by Klimt, Kokoschka, Gerstl, and Egger-Lienz. Open M, W-Th, Sa-Su 10am-7pm, F 10am-9pm. €9; students €5.50.

Kunsthalle Wien (☎521 89 33; www.kunsthallewien.at). Themed exhibits of international contemporary artists, from sculptors to filmmakers. Open M-W and F-Su 10am-7pm, Th 10am-10pm. Exhibition Hall 1 €6.50, students €5; Exhibition Hall 2 €5/€3.50; both €8/€6.50. Students get admission to both halls for only €2 on M. Audio guides €1.80.

Museum Moderner Kunst (Museum of Modern Art; ☎525 00; www.mumok.at). Holds Central Europe's largest collection of modern art in a brand-new building made from basalt lava. Highlights include Classical Modernism, Pop Art, Photo Realism, Fluxus, and Viennese Actionism. 20th-century masters include Magritte, Motherwell, Picasso, Miró, Kandinsky, Pollock, Warhol, and Klee. Open Tu-Su 10am-7pm; until 9pm on Th. €8, students €6.50.

Kunsthaus Wien, III, Untere Weißgerberstr. 13 (☎712 04; www.kunsthauswien.com; see p. 126). Take U1 (red) or U4 (green) to "Schwedenpl.," then tram N to "Hetzg." This museum, built by Hundertwasser, displays much of his work, as well as exhibits of contemporary art from around the world. The building lacks straight lines, which Hundertwasser called "the Devil's work", and so the floor bends and swells, creating "a melody for the feet." Open daily 10am-7pm. €8, students €6; M ½ price.

Österreichisches Museum für Angewandte Kunst (MAK; Austrian Museum of Applied Art), I, Stubenring 5 (☎71 13 60; www.mak.at). Take U3 (orange), or trams 1 or 2 to "Stubentor." A museum dedicated to the beauty of design, from the smooth curves of Thonet bentwood chairs to the intricate detail of Venetian glass. For Klimt enthusiasts, *The Embrace* is a special highlight. Recent exhibits have included photography and film by Dennis Hopper and an Andy Warhol retrospective. Open Tu 10am-midnight, W-Su 10am-6pm. €6.60, students €3.30. Tours by appointment ☎71 13 62 98; €9.90.

Akademie der Bildenden Kunst (Academy of Fine Arts), I, Schillerpl. 3 (☎588 162 25; www.akbild.ac.at). From Karlspl. turn left onto Friedrichstr., right onto Operng., and left on Lungeng. Famous for having rejected Hitler's application, the Academy offers an excellent collection, which includes several works by Peter Paul Rubens and Hieronymus Bosch's *The Last Judgment*. Wheelchair-accessible. Open Tu-Su and holidays 10am-4pm. €3.50, students €1.50. Guided tours €1.50; call ahead.

Secession Building, I, Friedrichstr. 12 (☎587 53 07; www.secession.at), on the western side of Karlspl. (see p. 125), easily distinguished by its dome of 3000 gilt laurel leaves (once derisively nicknamed the "head of cabbage"). Primarily devoted to contemporary art, although the main attraction is almost 100 years old. The work is Klimt's controversial *Beethoven Frieze*, is a 30m-long visual interpretation of Beethoven's Ninth Symphony. Pick up an English brochure for an explanation of the work's symbolism. Wheelchair-accessible. Open Tu-Su and holidays 10am-6pm, Th until 8pm. €5.50, students €3.

Salvador-Dali-Palais Surreal, I, Josefspl. 5 (☎512 25 49; www.dali-wien.at). By the Hofburg; take U3 (orange) to "Herreng." The Baroque palace of the Pallavicini family now houses a small but renowned collection of Surrealist sculptures by Dalí, including a work called *Space Elephant*, and ethereal glass sculptures. Open daily 10am-6pm. €6.50, students and seniors €3.60. AmEx/MC/V.

OTHER MUSEUMS

▨ **Haus der Musik,** I, Seilerstatte 30 (☎516 48; www.hdm.at). Near the Opera House and the Musikverein, this new, interactive science-meets-music museum will capture the imagination of people of all ages. Spanning 4 floors, the exhibits help you experience the physics of sound, learn about famous Viennese composers (each has his own room), and play with a neat invention called the Brain Opera. Admission includes the Philharmonic exhibit. Open daily 10am-10pm. €10, students €8.50.

Historisches Museum der Stadt Wien (Historical Museum of Vienna), IV, Karlspl. (☎50 58 74 70; www.museum.vienna.at), to the left of the Karlskirche (see p. 124). This collection of historical artifacts and paintings documents Vienna's evolution from a Roman encampment through the Turkish siege of Vienna to the subsequent 640 years of Hapsburg rule. Don't miss the Loos room, the *fin de siècle* art, or the 19th-century *Biedermeier* exhibits. Open Tu-Su 9am-6pm. €3.50, students €1.50. F free after 3pm.

Jüdisches Museum (Jewish Museum), I, Dorotheerg. 11 (☎535 04 31; www.jmw.at). From Stephanspl., off Graben. Jewish culture and history, including fragments of text stamped into the walls, holograms, and more traditional displays. Temporary exhibits focus on prominent Jewish figures and contemporary Jewish art. Wheelchair-accessible. Open M-W, F, Su 10am-6pm, Th and Sa 10am-8pm. €5, students €2.90.

Bestattungsmuseum (Undertaker's Museum), IV, Goldegg. 19 (☎501 95 42 27). Take tram D to "Schloß Belvedere" or U1 to "Südtirolerpl." This museum displays a morbidly fascinating (if somewhat comical) collection, including coffins with alarms (should the body decide to rejoin the living) and Josef II's proposed reusable coffin. Open M-F noon-3pm by appointment only. Free.

Freud Museum, IX, Bergg. 19 (☎319 15 96; www.freud-museum.at). Take U2 (purple) to "Schottentor," then walk up Währingerstr. to Bergg or take tram D to "Schlickg." The famed couch is not here, but Freud's former home has a smallish exhibit with some antique furniture and artifacts, like the young Freud's report cards and circumcision certificate. Open daily July-Sept. 9am-6pm; Oct.-June 9am-4pm. €5, students €3.

Lipizzaner Museum, I, Reitschulg. 2 (☎533 78 11; www.lipizzaner.at). Formerly the imperial pharmacy, the Lipizzaner is now a museum dedicated to the imperial horses, featuring paintings, harnesses, video clips, and a small viewing window through which you can glimpse the stables. Open daily 9am-6pm. €5, students €3.60. Tours €1.40; call ahead to arrange a tour in English.

Naturhistorisches Museum (Natural History Museum), I (☎52 17 70), opposite the Kunsthistorisches Museum; accessible via U2 (purple)/U3 (orange) to "Volkstheater." A substantial collection of dinosaur skeletons, meteorites, and giant South American beetles. 2 of its star attractions are man-made: a spectacular floral bouquet comprised of gemstones and a miniaturized replica of the Stone-Age beauty *Venus of Willendorf* (the original is locked in a vault). Open M and Th-Su 9am-6:30pm, Tu-W 9am-9pm. Last admission 30min. before closing. €3.50, students €1.80.

ENTERTAINMENT

While Vienna offers standard entertainment in the way of theater, film, and festivals, the heart of the city beats to music. All but a few of classical music's marquee names lived, composed, and performed in Vienna. Mozart, Beethoven, and Haydn wrote their greatest masterpieces in Vienna, creating the **First Viennese School;** a century later, Schönberg, Webern, and Berg teamed up to form the **Second Viennese School.** The Vienna **Konservatorium** and **Hochschule** are world-renowned conservatories. Also not to be missed are the various modern and classical dance groups of Vienna, in particular, the **Vienna Staatsoper Ballet.** Vienna has performances ranging from the above-average to the sublime all year long, and many are affordable to the budget traveler.

> **TO EVERYTHING THERE IS A SEASON.** Beware that Vienna's biggest cultural draws, the **Staatsoper** (State Opera), the **Wiener Philharmoniker** (Vienna Philharmonic), the **Wiener Sängerknaben** (Vienna Boys' Choir), and the **Lipizzaner Stallions** don't perform in Vienna during July and August.

OPERA

Staatsoper, Opernring 2 (www.wiener-staatsoper.at), Vienna's premier opera, performs about 300 times a year, nearly every night from Sept.-June. To get tickets:

Standing-room tickets: The cheapest way to enjoy the opera. 500 standing-room tickets are available for every performance, though you can only buy 1 per person, right before the performance. Also, realize that standing up for a 4hr. opera can be tough on the feet. While the box office opens 1hr. before curtain, those with the desire (and the stamina) should start lining up at least 1½hr. before curtain (2-3hr. in tourist season and for more popular productions) in order to get orchestra tickets. The standing line forms inside the side door on the side of the Opera by Operng. After procuring your precious ticket, hurry to a space on the rail and tie a scarf around it to reserve your spot. Casual dress, but no shorts. Balcony €2, orchestra €3.50.

Box office tickets in advance: The more secure ticket option is to purchase tickets through the official ticket offices by fax, phone, or in person; they charge no fees above the ticket price. The main ticket office is the Bundestheaterkasse, I, Hanuschg. 3, around the corner from the opera. There is also a ticket office inside the Staatsoper with the same hours (though closed Su and holidays), which also offers tours of the building year-round. Tickets may be purchased 1 month before performance. Seats €10-178, depending on location. ☎514 44 78 80; fax 514 44 29 69. Open M-F 8am-6pm, Sa-Su 9am-noon; first Sa of each month 9am-5pm.

Internet: The Bundestheaterkasse maintains a multi-lingual web site (www.bundestheater.at, also www.culturall.com) that allows you to purchase tickets in advance, view the seating plan, and check out the season schedule. However, the web is probably better used as a source of information than as a means of buying your tickets, because it charges a hefty commission (20%).

Volksoper, IX, Währingerstr. 78, specializes (not exclusively) in lighter comedic opera, operettas, and occasional musicals. As the Staatsoper was once for royalty, the "people's opera" is for the commoners. While the theater itself is less elaborate, the music is fantastic and the diversity of performances makes it a lively arts center. This opera house is a perfect choice for students—go 45min. before the show to get the best seats in the house for €7. Repertoire is diverse and includes modern operas, musicals, and dance troupes such as Alvin Ailey. Box office tickets are available at the theatre and through Bundestheaterkasse and its web site (see Staatsoper, above; www.culturall.com). Tickets range from €7-250 depending on performance and location.

Wiener Kammeroper (Chamber Opera), I, Fleischmarkt 24 (☎513 60 72; www.wienerkammeroper.at). Performs everything from classical operas to modern parodies in an open-air theater (standing tickets €7, seats €18-48). Mozart's operas are staged in the Schönbrunner Schloßpark during the summer as part of the **Klangbogen** festival (information ☎427 17; pick up a brochure at the tourist office).

ORCHESTRAS

Wiener Philharmoniker (Vienna Philharmonic; www.musikverein.at); performances in the **Musikverein,** Bösendorferstr. 12, on the northeast side of Karlspl. The Musikverein is Austria's—perhaps the world's—premier concert hall. Constructed in 1867, the building allows for unmatched acoustic perfection. The Philharmoniker's program is essentially conservative, although it occasionally includes contemporary classical music. Tickets to Philharmoniker concerts are mostly on a subscription basis and tend to sell out well in advance, but there are 3 ways to get them (it's worth it):

Musikverein box office tickets in advance: Contact the box office of the Musikverein in person or by letter. Ask about special concerts for teenagers as well. **Standing room tickets** are available from the Musikverein, but even they must be bought in advance, just like a seat. Open Sept.-June M-F 9am-7:30pm, Sa 9am-5pm. Write Gesellschaft der Musikfreunde, Bösendorferstr. 12, A-1010 Wien for more info.

Bundestheaterkasse tickets in advance: As with the Staatsoper, tickets to the Philharmoniker are offered through the Bundestheaterkasse (see Staatsoper, above).

Internet: The Philharmoniker maintains its own website (www.wienerphilharmoniker.at), which provides a full schedule, sells tickets, and provides links to sites selling tickets to Philharmoniker performances on tour and at festivals throughout the country. As always, beware of commissions!

Wiener Symphoniker (Vienna Symphony Orchestra), Vienna's second fiddle is frequently on tour, but plays some concerts at the grand, late-19th-century Konzerthaus, III, Lothringerstr. 20, just around the corner and across the river from the Musikverein. The

VIENNA

orchestra focuses on 20th-century classical music, including some ultra-modern, experimental works. The season runs Sept.-June. Get tickets and information from the Konzerthaus box office. (☎24 20 02; www.konzerthaus.at. Open M-F 9am-7:45pm, Sa 9am-1pm; June 10-Sept. 2 9am-1pm. Tickets €15-100.)

CHORAL MUSIC

Wiener Sängerknaben (Vienna Boys' Choir). Main showcase is mass every Su 9:15am (from mid-Sept. to late June only) in the **Hofburgkapelle** (U3/orange "Herreng."). Contact hofmusikkapelle@asn-wien.ac.at for info; for more on the boys' daily lives, see www.wsk.at. To get tickets to these masses:

Reserve tickets (€6-30) at least 2 months in advance; write to Hofmusikkapelle, Hofburg, A-1010 Wien, but do not enclose money. You will be sent a slip and can pick up tickets at the Burgkapelle on the F before mass 11am-1pm or 3-5pm, or before Su mass 8:15-9am.

Unreserved seats are sold in small quantity the Friday before mass 11am-1pm and 3-5pm (get in line 30min.-1hr. early), max. 2 per person. Some tickets sold early Su morning.

Standing room is free, despite rumors to the contrary, but arrive before 8am on Su.

The lads also perform every Friday at 3:30pm at the **Konzerthaus** (see Wiener Symphoniker, above) May, June, Sept., and Oct. For tickets (€28.50-32), contact Reisebüro Mondial, Faulmanng. 4, A-1040 Wien (☎58 80 41 41; ticket@mondial.at).

PREPUBESCENT PRODIGIES The 500-year-old **Wiener Sängerknaben** (Vienna Boys' Choir) functions as Austria's "ambassador of song" on its extensive international tours. Dressed in sailor suits, the boys export great works of music to the entire world. Emperor Maximilian I founded the group in 1498, Franz Schubert was a chorister, and Anton Bruckner held the post of organist and music teacher. Today, the choral music of Mozart, Hadyn, Schubert, Bruckner, and Beethoven can be heard as it was originally meant to be sung—by a boys' choir.

Sunday High Masses also occur in the major churches of the city (Augustinerkirche, Michaelerkirche, Stephansdom) and, while they don't include the Boys' Choir, they are glorious, free musical experiences (services begin at 10 or 11am, year-round), even for those who are not worshipers.

Wiener Singakademie bills itself as the oldest concert choir in Europe. Brahms was their director for the 1863-1864 season. The choir worked with some of the greatest conductors of choral music, including Mahler, Strauss, Solti, Furtwängler, and Gardiner. They perform in the Konzerthaus. See **Wiener Symphoniker, p. 137,** for ticket info.

THEATRE

In the past few years, Vienna has become a city of musicals, with productions of such Broadway favorites as *Les Misérables*. A recent fad has been creative interpretations of famous Austrians' lives, including *Elisabeth, Mozart,* and the "cyber show" *Falco*. Take U1 (red), U2 (purple), or U4 (green) to "Karlspl." to find the **Theater an der Wien,** VI, Linke Wienzeile 6, Vienna's top venue for musicals. The nearby **Raimund Theater** also shows popular musicals. Buy tickets at the box office or by phone. (☎588 85; www.musicalvienna.at. Box office open daily 10am-1pm and 2-6pm. Call in advance. €10-180.) **Vienna's English Theatre,** VIII, Josefsg. 12, presents drama in English. (☎40 21 26 00; www.englishtheatre.at. Box office M-F 10am-6pm. Tickets €15-40, student rush €9.) The **International Theater,** IX, Porzellang. 8, is also an English-language venue. (☎319 62 72. Tickets €18-25, under 26 €10.) **WUK,** IX, Währingerstr. 59, is a center for dance and concerts (☎40 12 10). Two German-language theaters are **Burgtheater** and **Akademietheater** (tickets at the **Bundestheaterkasse;** see Opera, p. 136).

FILM

Though not on the same level as Berlin or Paris, Vienna's film scene has much to offer (see "The Renaissance of Austrian Film," p. 84). Serious *cinéastes* should check out the new arenas for experimental film at the Museumsquartier. **Films** in English usually play at **Burgkino**, I, Opernring 19 (☎587 84 06; last show around 9:15pm, Sa around 11pm; also shows *The Third Man* every other Sa), **Top Kino**, VI, Rahlg. 1 (☎587 55 57; films 5:30-10pm), at the intersection of Gumpendorferstr., and **Haydnkino**, VI, Mariahilferstr. 57, near the U3/orange stop "Neubaug." (☎587 22 62; www.haydnkino.at. Last show usually around 9:30pm.) In the newspaper, films listed with "OF" after the title are shown in the original language; films listed as "OmU" are shown in the original language with subtitles. **Votivkino**, IX, Währingerstr. 12 (☎317 35 71; www.votivkino.at), near Schottentor, is an art house popular with the students and shows all films in the original language with German subtitles. **Artis Kino, Filmcasino,** and **Stadtkino** also show subtitled art and foreign films. **Künstlerhauskino**, I, Karlspl. 5 (☎505 43 28; www.k-haus.at/kino), hosts art-house film festivals (except in July). Movie tickets cost €5-10. In most Austrian cinemas you pay for an assigned seat. In summer, there are several **open-air cinemas** in the Augarten park. (Take tram #31 to "Obere Augartenstr." Shows 7, 9:30pm. €6.50.) Ask at the tourist office for details on occasional free movies in the Volksgarten. While Vienna hosts a full-sized film festival in August (see Festivals, below), the rest of the year the Austrian **Filmmuseum**, I, Augustinerstr. 1 (☎533 70 54), shows a program of classic and avant-garde films.

FESTIVALS

Vienna hosts an array of large annual festivals. The **Vienna Festival** (mid-May to mid-June) has a diverse program of exhibitions, plays, and concerts. (☎58 92 20; www.festwochen.or.at.) The Staatsoper and Volkstheater host the annual **Jazzfest Wien** during the first weeks of July, featuring many famous acts. For information, contact Jazzfest Wien (☎503 56 47; www.viennajazz.org). In addition, on the first weekend in June, most clubs and bars in Vienna host bands and DJs for **Lange Nacht der Musik**. (€15 for entrance to all events. Tickets can be purchased at any participating location or at www.events.ORF.at/langenachtdermusik.) Vienna has held the **Klangbogen** (☎427 17; www.klangbogen.at) every summer since 1952, featuring excellent concerts throughout Vienna, including **Wiener Kammeroper** (Chamber Opera; ☎/fax 513 60 72; www.wienerkammeroper.at) and performances of Mozart's operas in an open-air theater in the Schönbrunner Schloßpark. Pick up a brochure at the tourist office. From mid-July to mid-Aug., the **Im-Puls Dance Festival** (☎523 55 58; www.impuls-tanz.com) attracts some of the world's great dance troupes and offers seminars to enthusiasts. Some of Vienna's best parties are thrown by the parties (political, that is). The Social Democrats host the late-June **Danube Island Festival**, which draws millions of party-goers annually, while the Communist Party holds a **Volkstimme Festival** in mid-August. Both cater to impressionable youngsters with free rock, jazz, and folk concerts. In mid-October, the annual city-wide film festival **Viennale** kicks off. (For tickets ☎526 59 47; www.viennale.at.) In past years, the program has featured over 150 movies from 25 countries. Finally, Vienna's **Rathausplatz Music Film Festival,** July-August, in the Rathauspl. at dusk, is actually in part a culinary display from all over the world. Meanwhile, a huge screen broadcasts operas, ballets, and concerts from around the world. Come here for atmosphere and tasty treats. Also of interest to free-thinking *Let's Go* readers are two colorful parades in summer. During the first weekend of July is the **Regenbogenparade**—a predominantly gay and lesbian celebration of free love. The following weekend is another **Love Parade,** modeled after the one in Berlin, in which more than 400,000 people gather around the Prater and Donau to hear over 20 DJs spin everything from techno to trance. People are literally dancing in the streets— with clothing, without clothing, and everywhere in between.

WINTER FESTIVITIES

The Viennese don't let long winter nights go to waste. Christmas festivities begin in December with **Krampus** parties. Krampus (Black Peter) is a hairy devil that accompanies St. Nicholas on his rounds and gives bad children coal and sticks. On December 5, people in Krampus suits lurk everywhere, rattling their chains and chasing passersby, while small children nibble marzipan Krampus effigies.

As the weather gets sharper, huts of professional *Maroni-* (chestnut) roasters and *Bratkartoffeln-* (potato pancake) toasters pop up everywhere. Cider, punch, red noses, and *Glühwein* (a hot, spicy mulled wine) become ubiquitous. **Christmas markets** *(Christkindlmärkte)* open around the city. The best-known Christmas Market is probably the somewhat tacky **Rathausplatz Christkindlmarkt,** which offers, among other things, excellent *Lebkuchen* (a soft gingerbread-like cookie), *Langos* (a Hungarian round bread soaked in hot oil, garlic, and onions), and bees-wax candles. (Open daily 9am-9pm.) **Schloß Schönbrunn's** *Weihnachtsmarkt* offers old-fashioned Christmas decorations. (Open M-F noon-8pm, Sa-Su 10am-8pm.) Visit the happy **Spittelberg** market, where artists and university kids hawk offbeat creations (open M-F 2-9pm, Sa-Su and holidays 10am-9pm), or the **Weihnachtsdorf im Unicampus** (at the university campus; daily 1-10pm). The **Trachtenmarkt** shop in Schotteng. near Schottentor offers festive-ambience-soaked Christmas shopping. Most theaters, opera houses, and concert halls have Christmas programs (see p. 140). The city also turns Rathauspl. into an enormous outdoor skating rink in January and February.

The climax of the New Year's season is the **Neujahrskonzert** (New Year's concert) by the Viennese Philharmonic, broadcast worldwide. The refrain of the *Radetzkymarsch* by Strauss signals that the new year has truly begun. New Year's also brings a famously flashy **Imperial Ball** in the Hofburg. For those lacking seven-digit incomes, the City of Vienna organizes a huge chain of *Silvester* (New Year's) parties in the *Innenstadt*. Follow the **Silvesterpfad,** marked by lights hung over the street, for outdoor karaoke, sidewalk waltzing, firecrackers, and hundreds of people drinking champagne in the streets. At midnight, the St. Stephan's giant bell rings across the country, broadcast by public radio stations.

New Year's is barely over before **Fasching** (Carnival season) arrives in February and spins the city into bubbly bedlam. These are the weeks of the Viennese waltzing balls, the most famous of which, the **Wiener Opernball** (Viennese Opera Ball), draws the world's Princess Stephanies and Donald Trumps. Tickets must be reserved years in advance. For a free *Fasching* celebration, join the **carnival parade** that winds its way around the Ring, stopping traffic before Lent.

■ NIGHTLIFE

With one of the highest bar-to-cobblestone ratios in the world, Vienna is a great place to party. The *Heurigen* on the outskirts of Vienna provide an old-world Austrian way to spend an evening (see p. 116), but for a more urban night, head downtown. Take the subway (U1/red or U4/green) to "Schwedenplatz," within blocks of the **Bermuda Dreiecke** (Bermuda Triangle), so called both for the three-block triangle it covers and for the tipsy revelers who never make it home. Or, head down **Rotenturmstraße** toward Stephansdom or walk around the areas bounded by the Jewish synagogue and Ruprechtskirche. Another good zone for nightlife in the inner city is the **Bäckerstraße,** with its cellar bars. Slightly outside the Ring, the streets off Burgg. and Stiftg. in District VII and the university quarter (Districts XIII and IX) have tables in outdoor courtyards and loud, hip bars. Along the Danube is the **Donauinsel**, a boardwalk filled with cafés and clubs. Drinks are pricey but the atmosphere is consistently lively in warm weather.

Vienna's kinetic club scene rages every night of the week, later than most bars. DJs spin until dawn, and some clubs keep it going until 11am the next morning. One fact of Viennese nightlife: it starts late. Don't arrive until after 11pm. The best nights are Friday and Saturday, beginning around 1am or so. For the scoop on raves, concerts, and parties, grab the fliers at swank cafés like MAK (p. 114) or Berg das Café (p. 115), or pick up a copy of the indispensable *Falter* (€2)—it lists concerts, updates on the gay and lesbian scenes, and places that have sprung up too recently for *Let's Go* to review. Keep in mind that Vienna's club turnover is incredibly rapid, and various establishments' crowds change pretty regularly—a good clubbing strategy is to ask around and try multiple places until you find what you're looking for. Also, grab a schedule for the **Nightbus** system (see p. 100), which runs across Vienna all night after regular public transportation stops.

BARS

The term "bar" has a loose definition in Vienna. Many restaurants (see Restaurants, p. 108) live a Dr. Jekyll-Mr. Hyde existence as a place both to eat and to party.

INSIDE THE RING

Mapitom der Bierlokal, I, Seitenstetteng. 1 (☎535 43 13). Located right in the center of the Bermuda Triangle, this bar has the feeling of a *Heuriger,* with large tables clustered together in a warehouse-style interior. A great place to chat after work on F nights. Beer and Bacardi Breezers each about €3. Open daily 5pm-3am, F-Sa until 4am.

First Floor Bar, I, Seitstentteng. 5 (☎535 41 06); enter the big wooden door and walk upstairs. Somewhat hidden in the Bermuda Triangle, this swank upstairs bar offers an array of mixed cocktails (€6-7), including 8 different kinds of martinis. Great selection of Cuban cigars (€4-20). Open Su-Th 8pm-4am, F-Sa 7pm-4am. AmEx/MC/V.

Cato, I, Tiefer Graben 19 (☎533 47 90). Take U3 (orange) to "Herreng.," walk down to Strauchg., turn right, and continue on to Tiefer Graben; the bar will be on your left. A warm, cozy little bar. By the end of the night, you'll be singing right along with everyone else, thanks to friendly hostess Anna Maria. Try the *Sekte Cuvée,* an Austrian dry spirit from Burgenland (0.1L €4). Open Su-Th 6pm-2am, F-Sa 6pm-4am.

THE HIDDEN DEAL

IT'S NO FLUKE

Vienna's nightlife can be somewhat expensive—the biggest clubs often have hefty cover prices, and that doesn't even include the costs of drinks, food, and entertainment. But at club FLUC, entrance is always free.

The club is rather new, but has quickly built up a strong following among a youthful customer base. Frequented heavily by Austrians, FLUC attracts an audience with eclectic tastes that enjoys good, cutting-edge music. Despite its popularity, the place maintains a laidback, friendly (and very loud) atmosphere. Decorations are not that important; since FLUC is both free and somewhat underground, the emphasis is more on the music and the social scene than what's on the walls. Guest DJs make appearances every night, and local bands grace the stage two to three times per week. Despite the amazing frequency of performances, they are still varied; FLUC's shows range from improv to hip-hop to reggae and folk music and everything in between. A club regularly frequented by locals, FLUC is great for anyone looking to have an inexpensive night on the town, meet new people, dance, and listen to free music. Try the Czech beer "Staro Brno" (€2.40).

Praterstern 2. Take the U4 (green) to "Praterstern." FLUC is at the end of the passageway. ☎925 56 37; www.fluc.at. *Open daily 8pm-4am.*

Porgy & Bess, I, Riemerg. 11 (☎512 88 11; www.porgy.at). Take U1 (red) to "Stuben-tor," or tram 1A to "Riemerg." Unequivocally the best jazz club in Vienna, Porgy & Bess draws both Austrian and international musicians to perform within its tastefully-deco-rated walls. While jazz is the primary focus of the club, electronica spices up the pro-gram occasionally. Hip crowd primarily composed of locals, with plenty of room to sit or dance. Shows generally €15-20. Open M-Sa. 7pm-whenever, Su 8pm-whenever. MC/V.

Benjamin, I, Salzgries 11-13 (☎533 33 49). Outside the Triangle area, down the steps from Ruprechtskirche, left onto Josefs Kai, and left onto Salzgries. Dark and loud, this is a punk-rocker's heaven. Candles tilt in wax-covered wine bottles while a student crowd parties on. Tequila shot €1.60. Open daily 7pm-2am.

Kaktus, I, Seitenstetteng. 5 (☎533 19 38), in the heart of the Bermuda Triangle. Packed with beautiful 20-somethings and dripping with freely flowing alcohol, this bar offers mainstream music and attractive bartenders. Dress to impress. Beer (0.5L) €3.60. Open Su-Th 6pm-2am, F-Sa 6pm-4am. MC/V.

Jazzland, I, Franz-Josefs-Kai 29 (☎533 25 75). Near U1 (red)/U4 (green) "Schwe-denpl." Excellent live jazz of all styles wafts through the bricked interior, appealing to slightly older clientele. Music 9pm-1am. €3.60 cover. Open Tu-Sa 7pm-2am.

Santo Spirito, I, Kumpfg. 7 (☎512 99 98). From Stephanspl., walk down Singerstr. and turn left onto Kumpfg. (5min.). Opera fans will enjoy the classical music and busts on the wall of famous conductors. *Welschriesling* €3. Open M-F 6pm-2am, F-Sa 11am-3am, Su 10am-2am.

Esterházykeller, I, Haarhofg. 1 (☎533 34 82), U3 (green) to "Herrengasse," off Naglerg. One of Vienna's least expensive, most relaxed *Weinkeller*, popular with 20- and 30-somethings. Classy without being snobby. *Grüner Veltliner* wine is €2.20 for 0.25L. Open in summer M-F 4-11pm. Open in winter M-F 11am-11pm, Sa-Su 4-11pm.

OUTSIDE THE RING

☒ Das Möbel, VII, Burgg. 10 (☎524 94 97; www.dasmoebel.at). U2 (purple)/U3 (orange) to "Volkstheater." This high-ceilinged café functions as a showcase for furniture design-ers. The metal couches, car seat chairs, and Swiss-army tables rotate every 6 weeks and are well used (and purchased) by an artsy crowd. *Mélange* €2.25. Open M-F noon-1am, Sa-Su 10am-1am. MC/V usually only for furniture purchase.

Chelsea, VIII, (☎407 93 09), Lerchenfeldergürtel under the U-Bahn, between Thaliastr. and Josefstädterstr. The best place in Vienna for underground music: bands from all over Europe come to play this joint (except in summer). Techno-pop atmosphere with dancing. Cover €5-12 if a band is playing. Open daily 7pm-4am.

Loop, VII Lerchenfeldergürtel 26-27 (☎402 41 95; www.loop.co.at). Under the U-Bahn, down the street from Chelsea. While slightly more expensive, this modern, sleek bar offers a polished atmosphere bathed in the sounds of acid jazz, funk, and hip-hop. Drinks €2.60-12. Open M-W and Su 7pm-2am, Th-Sa 7pm-4am.

Schikaneder Bar, IV, Margaretenstr., 22-24 (☎585 58 88; www.schikaneder.at). Take U4 (green) to "Margaretengürtel," walk down Margaretengürtel and make a left onto Margaretenstr. (10 min.). For those interested in a very laid-back, unpretentious atmo-sphere, Schikaneder is the place to go; the main attractions are good conversation and plenty of beverages (beer starting at €2, wine by the glass €2.30). The place is packed by 9pm, so be sure to get there early. Open daily 5:30pm-4am.

Alsergrunder Kulturpark, IX, Alserstr. 4. Take U2 (purple) to "Schottentor." In the court-yard of an early 18th-century university building, the Kulturpark features not only beau-tifully landscaped grounds, but also a series of *Biergarten, Heurigen*, and bars. Frequented by late-20-somethings. Drinks around €3. Open Apr.-Oct. daily 4pm-2am.

Kunsthalle Café, IV, Treitlstr. 2 (☎586 98 64). Exit Karlspl. via "Secession/Giribaldi Park." Inside the bright yellow contemporary art museum, this chill café-by-day (with large rocky terrace for non-smokers) is filled nightly with students and the soothing sounds of funk, jazz, and blues. A great place for a chat on a warm summer night. Beer €3. Open 10am-2am or whenever the last person leaves (really). V.

Europa, VII, Zollerg. 8 (☎526 33 83; www.hinterzimmer.at). Buy a drink and strike a pose. Surrounded by concert posters and funky 70s-style neon lighting, the hip and attractive 20-something crowd hangs out late, especially after a long night of clubbing. Try a *Mai Tai* for €6.50. Open daily 9am-5am. V.

Miles Smiles, VIII, Lange G. 51 (☎405 95 17). Take U2 to "Lerchenfelderstr." Head down Lerchenfelderstr. and take the 1st right. This place has a cool, if somewhat touristy, atmosphere. The music is post-1955 jazz. Open Su-Th 8pm-2am, F-Sa 8pm-4am.

Eagle Bar, VI, Blümelg. 1 (☎587 26 61). Come to scope and be scoped. Gay men only. The young clientele is of the leather and/or denim set. Open 9pm-4am.

DISCOS & DANCE CLUBS

Flyers advertise "Clubbings"—huge, organized parties throughout the city. They're a bit like raves, only more widely attended. More information is listed in *Falter*.

▨ U-4, XII, Schönbrunnerstr. 222 (☎815 83 07; www.u4club.at). Take U4 to "Meidling Hauptstr." In the late 80s, U-4 hosted Nirvana, Mudhoney, and Hole before they were huge. These days the joint is hit-or-miss; check in advance for the theme on a given night. 2 dance areas, multiple bars. Tu Happy Hour, all night drinks from €2; Th Heaven Gay Night; Sa Boogie Night, classic funk and R&B. Cover €8. Open daily 10pm-5am.

Volksgarten Disco, I, Volksgarten (☎533 05 18). Take U2 (purple) or U3 (orange) to "Volkstheater." Hip-hop/R&B and a teenage crowd on F nights; house and a somewhat older crowd Sa. A mellower option is the adjoining Volksgarten Pavillon, a garden bar with trip-hop, trance, lounge, or house, depending on DJ and night. Cover €6-13. Open Th-Su 10pm-5am. Pavillon open daily in the summer, usually without cover.

Flex, I, Donaulände/Augartenbrücke (☎533 75 25), around the corner from the Schottenring U-Bahn station. Head toward the river and down a narrow staircase. This on-the-water club is a paradise for those tired of the Bermuda Triangle crowd. Dance, get a beer (€4), and grab a spot in the young, local scene. Or, if you're feeling adventurous, bring your own fun-in-a-bottle and sit by the river with the outside crowd. DJs start spinning at 10pm. Cover €6-10, free after 3am. Open May-Sept. daily 8pm-4am.

Havana Club, I, Mahlerstr. 11 (☎513 20 75; www.clubhavana.at). This basement salsa fest will put the rumba and Latin fire into pretty much anyone. Great on Sa nights. Salsa dancers of all levels are welcome—professionals hit center stage and amateurs line the exterior. Delicious Brazilian cocktails (€8). Open daily 8pm-2am. AmEx/MC/V.

Club Meierei, III, Stadtpark (☎710 84 00). Take U4 (green) to Stadtpark, "Heumarkt" exit. Located in the Stadtpark, Meierei has no neighbors and thus more freedom to party loudly, and is actually rented to different owners and renamed each night. Particularly good Thursday nights in its incarnation as "Club Afterwork," when it pulsates with both house and dance music. Beer €3.50. Cover €10. Open W-Sa 10pm-late.

Why Not, I, Tiefer Graben 22 (☎535 11 58). The neon interior of this gay and lesbian bar/disco offers both a meeting and greeting venue and a hip-hop subterranean blackbox dance floor. Sa is the night to be here, with drink specials from €3.50. Cover €8. Open F-Sa from 11pm. Women-only night 1 Th each month.

▶ DAYTRIPS FROM VIENNA

STIFT ALTENBURG

Stift Altenburg can be reached via the small town of Horn, which is accessible by train from Franz-Josefs Bahnhof (1½ hr, 5 per day, €12). Local bus #33 in Horn leaves for the Stift from train station (€1, every 1½ hr.). Alternatively, if weather permits, walk the picturesque 6km path from Horn to the Stift (follow the green signs).

Built in 1144, this Benedictine monastery stands out as one of Austria's most exemplary examples of Baroque architecture. Originally Gothic in style, the abbey was regularly attacked by Hussites and Swedes during the Thirty Years' War, and

THE BIG SPLURGE

GRAPE GRAZING

The Wachau wine region of Austria, home of crisp white wines and Hapsburg ruins, now has a new claim to fame: "Grape Grazing." For only €45, join **Mitch's Tours** for a day of "sipping" and "swirling" the Wachau's best wine and schnapps, while riding bikes along the Danube.

Starting at Spitz, one of the quaint towns in the heart of the Wachau, the "Grape Grazing" tour covers 20km of terrain and visits four vineyards. Participants sample six different kinds of schnapps and delight their palates with a local apricot liqueur. And there is no need to worry about drinking and riding—each grazer is encouraged to go at his or her own pace and a ferry is available for those who feel too tipsy to travel on wheels.

The tour also includes a stop for a picnic among the ruins, spectacular views of the countryside, a history lesson (in English—Mitch is Australian) and even a game of beach volleyball for those who feel so inclined.

To book a spot on a Grape Grazing tour, call ☎ *0664 435 15 90 or check online at www.mitchs-tours.com. Buses leave from Hostel Ruthensteiner and Wombat's, both in Vienna. Departure time is at 9:30am every other day, starting in the spring and running through the summer. If you go, make sure to pack a lunch, the daily essentials, and bring an extra €3 for the ferry.*

most of what is visible now dates from after Swedish soldiers sacked the monastery in 1645. Altenburg's subsequent reconstruction stands as a masterpiece of Baroque architecture, with highlights including pastel and gold frescoes of Biblical scenes, a **Bibliothek** (library), a **crypt**, and an ornate ceremonial staircase. Religious artifacts dating back to the 12th century (and which somehow survived the Swedes) are also on display. To see the crypt and library, you must take a guided tour. (☎ 02982 34 51; www.stift-altenburg.at. Stift open daily Apr.-Nov. 10am-5pm, last admission 4pm; mid-June to Aug. 10am-6pm, last admission 5pm. Tours 11am, 2, 4pm; each tour has a different theme. €7.50, students €6. Admission to the art exhibit €6, students €3. Add €1.50 for tours 9:30am, 1, 3pm.)

The region surrounding the Stift is also noteworthy for producing various rustic goods: high-quality honey, spices, tea, sheep's milk, and wool; to purchase these items, visit the Stift's **Klosterladen.** (Open Apr. 6-Nov. 1 9am-12pm, 12:45pm-5pm.) For a taste of the local wines, tour the **Altenburger Stiftskeller,** one of Austria's largest wine cellars. (Tour lasts 20-30min. €3.50). The abbey also hosts annual art exhibits and summer concerts given by the **Stift Altenburger Musikakademie.** (For concert tickets, call ☎ 02982 530 80 mid-June to Aug.; ☎ 586 19 00 from Apr. to mid-June, Sept.-Nov.; freunde.der.claviermusik@vienna.at.)

STIFT KLOSTERNEUBURG

Take S-40 from Heiligenstadt (U4/green) or Spittelau (U4, U6/red) to "Klosterneuburg-Kierling" (15min., every 30min., €1.50), or walk 1½hr. from Leopoldsberg. Exit the station, make a left and follow the signs to the Rathaus; the monastery is at the top of the hill (¼ mile).

Founded by the Babenberg Leopold III in 1114, this *Chorherrenstift* (monastery), still in use today, put the small town of Klosterneuburg on the map as the center of medieval Austrian art and culture. Expanded in 1730 by the Emperor Karl IV, the current site boasts not only the palace he built (only two of nine planned domes were completed), but also a museum and a magnificently ornate church. A tour of the Stift traces the monastery's architectural transition from Romanesque to Baroque, and includes the gold-enameled, 51-plaque **Verduner Altar,** Klosterneuburg's "most precious artwork."(Open May-Nov. Tu-Su 10am-5pm. €4.50.) Guided tours in English by advanced booking only. (☎ 02243 41 12 12; fax 411 31. Tours every hr. 10am-5pm. €5. Tour and museum combo-ticket €6.50. info@stiftklosterneuburg.at). Klosterneuburg's **Stiftsmuseum** offers an impressive collection of paintings, sculpture, tapestries, and relics from medieval and modern times. The museum also connects to the **Kaiserzim-mer,** the rooms of the adjoining palace. Their immense height, porcelain candelabras, and intricate woodwork evoke the Austria's former imperial glory. (☎02243 41 11 54; www.stift-klosterneuburg.at. Open May to mid-Nov. 10am-5pm. €4.80, seniors €3.90, students €2.90.)

CARNUNTUM

*Get to Carnuntum by S7 from Wien Nord (Praterstern) or Wien Mitte, dir.: Wolfstahl (1hr., every 30min., €6). Walk down Brukerstr. (5 min.), make a left onto Hauptstr., and continue walking for another 3 blocks; the **park/info center** is on the right. By car from Vienna: take highway A4, exit at Fischamend, and follow road B9 to Petronell-Carnuntum (30-45min.).*

Once the largest Roman outpost in the region, Carnuntum played a vital role in the Imperial defense of its Danube frontier until being conquered by Germanic tribes in the 3rd century. It's now the largest archeological site in Austria. The **Archäolo-gischer Park Carnuntum** showcases a completely reconstructed temple dedicated to the goddess Diana, the remains of houses, a highly advanced sewer system, and public baths, all dating from the 1st-3rd centuries AD. (☎21 63 33 770; www.carnuntum.com. Open daily 9am-5pm, March 29-Nov. 2. €4, students, seniors, handicapped €3. Wheelchair-accessible. Children under 6 are free. Guided tours Mar.-June and Sept.-Nov. Sat. 11am, 2pm; Su 2pm. July-Aug. M-F 10am, noon, 2pm. Prices upon request.) 20km of bike paths lead to the **Amphithe-atre Bad Deutsch-Altenburg** (site of an ancient military camp) and the **Archäologis-ches Museum Carnuntum**, which displays Austria's most extensive collection of Roman artifacts, ranging from jewelry to religious objects (Open Jan. 13-Mar. 25 and Nov. 10-Dec. 9 Sa-Su 10am-5pm, Apr.-Nov. 9 Tu-Su 10am-5pm. €4, students €3; guided tours €3. Combo museum/park ticket €8, students €6.50.)

Carnuntum also hosts annual Roman festivals, including the **Roman Athletic Com-petition** in April and the **Art Carnuntum** festival from July to August, which offers open-air cinema, theater performances, and concerts, as well as a **Roman Christ-mas market** in December (for information, call ☎02 16 33 400).

VIENNA

BURGENLAND

BURGENLAND

Just southeast of Vienna lies Burgenland, Austria's most scarcely populated province (pop. 270,000) and one of Austria's last territorial acquisitions. Until Burgenland was ceded to Austria in 1921, it was part of Hungary; in fact, it owes its name to three castles that now lie beyond its borders in Hungary. Given its history, it is not surprising that Burgenland has a Hungarian-influenced cuisine and pockets of Hungarian speakers in the more rural parts of the province. Burgenland is geographically diverse, with rolling hills and dense forests in the west, the Neusiedlersee in the northeast, and the peaks of the Rosaliengebirge on the present Hungarian border. Burgenland's gentle hills and lush river valleys give it the rich wines and *Heurigen* (cozy, vine-covered taverns) that make it world-famous. Because of the seasonal nature of many of Burgenland's delights, it's best to coordinate your visit with one of many festivals that enliven the sleepy towns.

HIGHLIGHTS OF BURGENLAND

Walk in Haydn's footsteps through the sumptuous apartments of the Hungarian Esterházy family in **Eisenstadt** (see p. 146).

Sample rich new wines in the vineyards of **Rust** (see p. 151).

Take a dip in the Neusiedlersee, then watch a floating opera in **Mörbisch**.

EISENSTADT
☎ 02682

Where I wish to live and die.
—Josef Haydn

Haydn, *Heurigen*, and Huns are the three cultural pillars of Burgenland's tiny provincial capital (pop. 12,480). As court composer for the **Esterházy** princes, **Josef Haydn** composed some of his greatest melodies here, and the town still basks in his glory. The Esterházy princes, powerful Hungarian landholders claiming descent from Attila the Hun, are to this day one of the wealthiest families in Europe. The Esterházys first settled in Eisenstadt when it was part of Hungary and decided to remain there after the change in borders. Today they own many of the region's famed vineyards, whose wines rival those from Bordeaux.

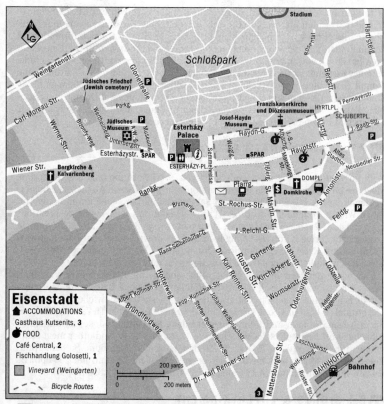

Eisenstadt

▲ ACCOMMODATIONS
Gasthaus Kutsenits, 3

🍎 FOOD
Café Central, 2
Fischhandlung Golosetti, 1

▨ Vineyard (Weingarten)

‒ ‒ ‒ Bicycle Routes

⌑ TRANSPORTATION

Eisenstadt is southeast of Vienna and west of Neusiedlersee. The easiest way to get there is by direct bus from **Südtirolerplatz** (U1/red) (1½hr., every 30min. 6am-8:45pm, fewer on weekends, €6). **Buses** run from Eisenstadt to **Rust, Mörbisch,** and **Wiener Neustadt.** The **bus station** (☎623 60) is on Dompl. next to the cathedral. Buy your ticket on the bus and tell the driver where you're going. Getting there by train is a bit complicated: from the Südbahnhof take a Regionalzug toward Deutschkreutz and change trains in tiny Wulkaprodersdorf (1¼hr., 2 per hr., €8). Another option is to take the S-bahn from the Südbahnhof (1½hr., every hr., €8) and switch trains in **Neusiedl am See,** but sit in the correct section of the train, since the train splits on its way to Neusiedl am See; one section heads to Hungary.

To get to Eisenstadt by **car,** take Autobahn A3 south from Vienna (50km). From Wiener Neustadt, take Bundesstr. 53 or Autobahn S4 east. There is an underground parking garage outside the Esterházy Palace. (Max 3 hours. Open M-F 7am-6pm, Sat. 7am-noon; 30 min €0.50.)

◪ ▣ ORIENTATION & PRACTICAL INFORMATION

Eisenstadt is centered around Hauptstr., the city's *Fußgängerzone* (pedestrian zone). Follow Bahnstr. (which becomes St. Martinstr. and then Fanny Eißlerg.) to get there from the train station. From the bus stop, walk half a block to the church.

With your back to the church, cross Pfarrg. and walk down tiny Marckingstr. to Hauptstr. Turn left and walk to the end, where Schloß Esterházy is on your right. The **tourist office** is in the right wing of the castle. The staff has information on accommodations, musical events, guided tours, and *Heurigen* in the Eisenstadt area (☎ 639 33; stadtmarketing@eisenstadt.co.at). Services in Eisenstadt include: **currency exchange** at **Bank Austria Creditanstalt** on the corner of St. Martinstr. and Dompl. (exchange costs €12.25 for up to $1,400; open M-W 8am-12:30pm and 1:30-3pm, Th 8am-12:30pm and 1:30-5:30pm); and **public bathrooms** at Dompl. and Esterházy Palace. The **post office** is on the corner of Pfarrg. and Semmelweise. (☎ 622 71. Open M-F 7am-6pm, Sa 8am-12:30pm). **Postal code:** A-7000.

![] ![] ACCOMMODATIONS & FOOD

With no youth hostel in the vicinity, *Privatzimmer* are the only budget option. Most are on the outer city limits and rent only during July and August. The hostels in **Vienna** (see p. 89) and **Neusiedl am See** (see p. 150) are cheaper and only 1hr. away. What accommodations do exist are packed in July and August; reservations are a must. At **Gasthaus Kutsenits ❸**, Mattersburgerstr. 30, a clean room is yours at a reasonable price if you're willing to walk 2km down a busy four-lane highway. From Schloß Esterházy, head down Rusterstr. to Mattersburgerstr. (☎ 635 11. Breakfast included. Rooms €20-28; discounts for multiple-night stays.)

The many **Heurigen** in Eisenstadt offer modest, affordable meals with their wines. Or, just wander along Hauptstr. and follow your nose. **Café Central ❶**, Hauptstr. 40, is a popular lunch spot offering delicious baguette sandwiches (€1.20-3.50) and strudel (€1.80) in a cool, shady enclave. (☎ 752 34. Open M-Th 7am-midnight, F-Sa 7am-2am, Su 9am-midnight.) **Fischhandlung Golosetti ❶**, Joseph-Stanislaus-Albachg. 4 off Hauptpl., sells big, cheap *Schnitzelsemmeln* and other meat sandwiches for €4-5. (☎ 629 37. Open M-Th 8am-6pm, F 7:30am-6pm, Sa 8am-1pm.) There are **Spar Markts** at Bahnstr. 16-18 (open M-F 6:45am-12:30pm and 2:30-6pm, Sa 6:45am-12pm) and Hauptstr. 13 (open M-F 7:30am-6:30pm, Sa 7:30am-5pm).

![] ![] SIGHTS & ENTERTAINMENT

SCHLOß ESTERHÁZY. Built on the footings of the Kanizsai family's 14th-century fortress, the castle-turned-palace now known as Schloß Esterházy is still owned by the family whose name it bears. Recently, the palace was actually rented out by the Austrian provincial government, which according to rumor has paid millions for maintenance of the splendid **Red Salon** during the lease. The castle has its share of history too: in the **Haydnsaal** (Haydn Hall), the famous composer conducted the court orchestra almost every night from 1761 to 1790. Since the government removed the marble floor and replaced it with a wooden one, the room is so acoustically perfect that seats for concerts in the room are not numbered—supposedly every seat provides the same quality of sound. The room is a visual symphony of red velvet, gold, oil paintings, and woodwork. *(At the end of Hauptstr. ☎ 719 30 00; www.schloss-esterhazy.at. 50min. tours Easter-Oct. daily every hr. on the hr. 9am-5pm; Nov.-Easter M-F at 10am and 2pm. €4.50, students and seniors €3.)*

HAYDN EVENTS. Catering to the town's connection with Haydn, **Haydnmatinees,** feature revolving groups of chamber musicians playing 30min. of his music. *(☎ 719 30 00. May-Aug, Th-Sa 11am in the palace. €7.50; students €5.)* The palace also hosts **Haydnkonzerte.** *(July-Aug. Th at 8pm; May-June and Sept.-Oct. Sa 7:30pm. €17-21.)* True Haydn enthusiasts can wait for The Big One: the **Internationale Haydntage** comes to town from Sept. 10-20. Held outdoors near the Schloß, it features concerts, operas, and large free video screenings of past concerts. *(Festival office ☎ 618 66; www.haydnfestival.at. Tickets €37-780.)*

THE OLD TOWN. The *Kapellmeister* had a short commute to the concert hall each day: he lived just around the corner. His modest residence is now the **Josef-Haydn Museum**, Haydng. 21, which exhibits original manuscripts and other memorabilia. *(☎ 719 39 00. www.haydn-museum.at. Open Apr.-Nov. daily 9am-5pm. Guided tours by appointment. €3, students €2.)* The *maestro* lies buried in the **Bergkirche**; from the palace, make a right on to Esterházystr. and walk two blocks. Haydn's remains were placed there in 1932 after phrenologists removed his head to search for signs of musical genius on the skull's surface. After being displayed at the Vienna Music Museum for years, Haydn's head was reunited with his body in 1954. Entrance to the *Bergkirche* includes admission to the **Kalvarienberg**, a pilgrimage annex to the church, which illustrates the 14 Stations of the Cross with hand-carved biblical figures. The rooftop stations provide a view of Burgenland. *(☎ 626 38. Open Easter-Oct. daily 9am-noon and 1-5pm. €2.50, students €1.50.)*

JEWISH MUSEUM. Eisenstadt's **Jüdisches Museum** covers the history of Jewish life in Eisenstadt and the Burgenland region. The Esterházys were known for their hospitality toward Jews, who played a major part in their rise to power. The exhibits are arranged according to Jewish holidays and contain religious items dating from the 17th century. The building contains an original private synagogue with a beautiful ark in the style of Empress Josephine as well as Gothic and Oriental murals from the early 1800s. *(Unterbergstr. 6. From the palace, make a right and then another right onto Glorietteallee, then take the first left to Unterbergstr. ☎ 651 45; www.oejud-mus.or.at/oejudmus. Open May-Oct. Tu-Su 10am-5pm. Oct.-May, reservations are necessary. €3.63, students €2.91.)* Around the corner on Wertheimerstr., near the hospital, is a **Jewish cemetery** dating back several centuries.

EISENSTADT'S JEWISH COMMUNITY The history of Jews in Eisenstadt is a tale of growth and tragic downfall. As early as 1675, Prince Paul Esterházy was moved by the plight of the persecuted Jews and decided to shelter them as *Schutzjuden* (protected Jews) on his estates. From 1732 on, the Jewish quarter of Eisenstadt formed the prosperous independent community of "Unterberg-Eisenstadt," which remained unique in Europe until 1938. In that year, the Jews of the Burgenland were among the first to be affected by the deportation orders of the Nazis. Today, only a few Jewish families remain in Eisenstadt.

FESTIVALS. Leaving Eisenstadt without sampling the wine would be like leaving Vienna without tasting *Sacher Torte*. From June 27-July 6 the **Winzerkirtag Kleinhö-flein** floods Hauptpl. with kegs, flasks, and bottles as local wineries showcase their goods. From August 21-31 is the **Festival of 1000 Wines**, when wineries from all over Burgenland crowd the palace's *Orangerie*. If you like music with your wine, visit May 23-24 when the free outdoor **Eisenstadt Fest** provides all kinds of music. At any other time of the year, fresh wine is available straight from the source in the wineries themselves. Most are small and aren't allowed to open for more than three weeks per year to sell their wine. But fear not—the wineries stagger their opening times so that wine is always available. To find out which *Buschenschenken*, or *Schenkhäuser* (wine taverns) are open, ask the tourist office for the schedule or look in the local newspaper. Most of the *Buschenschenken* are clustered in Kleinhöfler-Hauptstr.

THE NEUSIEDLERSEE REGION

Burgenland's major lake, the Neusiedlersee, is but a vestige (320 sq. km) of the water that once blanketed the whole Pannenian Plain. It's large enough that you can barely see the opposite shore, but amazingly never gets deeper than 2m. The water line recedes periodically, exposing thousands of square meters of dry land; from 1868 to 1872, the lake dried up entirely. Warm and salty, the *See* is a haven for more than 250 species of waterfowl. The tall marsh reeds that surround the lake shelter many rare plants and animals, including bugs, which can make it unpleasant to swim anywhere other than designated areas. **Storks** thrive here, and a glance of their chimney-nests is believed to bring good luck. In 1992, the lake and surrounding area were incorporated into the national park **Neusiedlersee-Seewinkel.** (☎ 021 75 34 42, www.nationalpark-neusiedlersee.org).

Cruises (*Schifffahrt*) on the Neusiedlersee allow travel between Rust, Illmitz, and Mörbisch (with bike €4.36, round-trip €7.27). **Gangl** runs boats every hr. from Illmitz to Mörbisch. (☎ 02175 21 58 or 27 94, fax 33 70; May-Oct. daily every hr. 9am-6pm, April and Oct.6-15 at 10am, noon, 2pm, and 4pm. €5.) In Mörbisch, **Schifffahrt Weisz-Sommer** cruises to Illmitz (one-way €5, roundtrip €10. ☎ 02685 83 24, fax 82 24; May-Sept. every 30min. 9am-5:30pm). For more information about the region, contact the **Neusiedlersee Tourismusbüro** at Obere Hauptstr. 24, A-7100 Neusiedl am See (☎ 86 00; www.neusiedlersee.com).

NEUSIEDL AM SEE   ☎ 02167

Less than 1hr. from Vienna by train, Neusiedl am See is the gateway to the Neusiedlersee region. The principal attraction is the lake, not the town, so consider Neusiedl a day at the beach. Proximity to the lake and its sundry water sports make Neusiedl a popular destination for families, although younger travelers should note that Neusiedl is more a place to relax with vacationing Austrian families than a place to go sightseeing.

▐▌ TRANSPORTATION & PRACTICAL INFORMATION. Trains from Vienna (Südbahnhof) and Eisenstadt arrive at Neusiedl am See's **Hauptbahnhof** (Information and ticket window open 5am-9pm. From Eisenstadt €1.50; Vienna €6.00). To town, follow Bahnstr. right onto Eisenstädterstr. (which becomes Obere Hauptstr.) and into Hauptpl. By **car** from Vienna, take A4, exit 3. From Eisenstadt, take Rte. B-50 north and Rte. B-51 east. The **tourist office** is in the *Rathaus* at Hauptpl. 1 (☎ 22 29; www.neusiedlamsee.at). Open July-Aug. M-F 8am-7pm, Sa 10am-noon and 2-6pm, Su 4-7pm; May-June and Sept. M-F 8am-noon and 1-4:30pm; Oct.-Apr. M-Th 8am-noon and 1-4:30pm, F 8am-1pm.) **Raiffeisenbank,** Untere Hauptstr. 3, has **currency exchange.** (☎ 25 64. Open M-Th 8am-12:30pm and 1:30-4pm, F 8am-12:30pm and 1:30-4:30pm.) **Luggage storage** at the train station (€2); and **emergency help** (☎ 144). **Internet** access can be found at a number of the establishments on Obere Hauptstr. and on Hauptpl. The **post office,** Untere Hauptstr. 53, is on the corner of Untere Hauptstr. and Lisztg. (Open M-F 8am-6:30pm.) **Postal code:** A-7100.

▐▌ ACCOMMODATIONS & FOOD. Heavy tourist activity, partly generated by Neusiedl's proximity to Vienna, can make finding budget accommodations tough. **Jugendherberge Neusiedl am See (HI) ❷,** Herbergg. 1, sports 86 beds in 21 quads and one double. Follow Wienerstr. and turn left onto Goldbergg. The hostel is on the corner at Herbergg. Although it's an uphill walk, the hostel is very clean and user-friendly. Amenities include a pool table, foosball, outdoor basketball court, and TV. There are showers in every room, but bathrooms are in the hall. (☎/fax 22 52. Breakfast included. Sheets €1.80. Reception 8am-2pm and 5-8pm. Reservations recommended. Open Mar.-Oct. €13-20, under 19 €11.50.) **Gasthof zur Traube ❸,**

Hauptpl. 9, has a cordial staff and pretty pink rooms and is family-friendly. (☎24 23; www.zur-traube.at. Breakfast included. €27-30 per person.) **Weinlaubengasthof Rathausstüberl ❸**, around the corner from the *Rathaus* on Kircheng. 2, is a sunny pension with two singles and 13 doubles. (☎28 83; www.rathausstueberl.at. Breakfast buffet included. Reservations recommended. €26.16-50.87 per person.) The pension also has a restaurant with a lovely shaded courtyard, great wine, and plenty of fresh fish and vegetarian dishes. The *Menü* includes soup and an entree, around €5. (Restaurant open Mar.-Dec. daily 10am-10pm.)

If the weather's nice, you can grab a picnic for the beach at the **Billa** grocery store on Seestr. (Open M-Th 7:30am-6:30pm, F 7:30am-8pm, Sa 7am-5pm.) **Rauch-kuchl ❷**, Obere Hauptstr. 57, offers *Blaufränker* red wine or other homemade specialties as well as the opportunity to hear local dialect (☎25 85. Open Tu-Sa 5-11pm). Towards the Rauchkuchl on Obere Hauptstr. 9-11 is the small wine cellar **Weinbau Mullner** (☎/fax 33 95) with a cheap and wide selection of wines, including the famous sweet **Eiswein** (€9 per bottle) made from frozen grapes. A bit difficult to find; follow the driveway up and knock for service.

⚠🎭 OUTDOOR ACTIVITIES & ENTERTAINMENT. To get to the **beach,** go to the end of Seestr. (1km), or catch the bus from the Hauptbahnhof or Hauptpl. (June-Aug., every hr. until 6pm, €2). The beach is rocky but pleasant (beach entrance: adults €2.80, 3-19 yrs. €2.20). The **Segelschule Neusiedl am See** (☎34 00 44; www.segelschule-neusiedl.at), at the docks on the far right, rents **sailboards** €11.63/€34.88/€58.14), **dinghies** (3- to 4-person boat €14.53 per hr., €43.60 per half-day, €72.67 per day), or standard **surfboards** (from €10.90 per hr.; open daily 8:30am-6pm). Close by on Seestr., find **paddleboats** (€6 per hr.), **rowboats** (€4 per hr.), and **electric boats** (€10.20 per hr.) at **Bootsvermietung Leban.**

On the first Saturday of every August, Neusiedl hosts a **Stadtfest.** The *Fußgängerzone* comes to life with food booths and music. Admission is free; contact the festival office for more information. (☎32 93; www.impulse-neusiedl.at. Open W and F 10am-noon.)

RUST ☎02685

Despite its being the smallest city in Austria (pop. 1700), Rust is a summertime haven for tourists looking to enjoy a day at the beach and some of Burgenland's best wines. Known for its sweet dessert wines (*Ausbruch*), medieval architecture, nesting storks, and prime location on the Neusiedlersee, Rust is the perfect weekend destination for students and families alike.

🚆➕ℹ TRANSPORTATION, ORIENTATION, & PRACTICAL INFORMATION. Rust lies 17km east of Eisenstadt on the Neusiedlersee. It does not have a train station, but **Post Buses** run from **Eisenstadt** (30min, several per day, €3) and **Vienna** Südtirolerpl. (1½hr., 5 per day, €9). The **bus station** is located behind the post office at Franz-Josef-Pl. 14. By **car** from Vienna, take Autobahn A3 to Eisenstadt and then Bundesstr. 52 straight into Rust. The **tourist office,** Conradpl. 1, hands out maps, plans bicycle tours, and gives information on wine tastings, the beach, and *Privatzimmer.* (☎502; info@rust.or.at. Open Nov.-Mar. M-Th 9am-noon and 1-4pm, F 9am-noon; Apr. M-F 9am-noon and 1-4pm, Sa 9am-noon; May-Sept. M-F 9am-noon and 1-5pm, Sa-Su 9am-noon; Oct. M-F 9am-noon and 1-4pm.) The **Raiffeisenbank Freistadt,** Rathauspl. 5, is the best place to **exchange money.** (☎607 05. Open M-F 8am-noon and 1:30-4pm. €1 per check plus a 1.5% commission.) There's also a 24hr. **ATM. Reisebüro Blaguss** in the *Rathaus* and **Ruster Freizeit-center** (☎595) by the beach are open late and provide emergency currency exchange. Call **taxis** at ☎06 64 18 01 80 or 066 43 00 60 66. The **post office** is open M-F 8am-noon and 2-6pm.) **Postal code:** A-7071.

⚠🏠 ACCOMMODATIONS & FOOD. If you want to stay in Rust, a *Privatzimmer* is the way to go. Reservations are strongly recommended during July and August. Be warned: prices may rise in the high season. You'll receive a warm welcome at **Gästehaus Ruth ❸**, Dr. Alfred-Ratzg. 1, where rooms with friendly service run €18-19.30 (☎/fax 68 28, gaestehausruth@utanet.at). Rust's new **Jugendgästehaus ❷**, located at Ruster Bucht 2, sits on the beachfront near tennis courts and bike paths. It boasts a warm, helpful staff and spacious, exceptionally clean rooms (☎591; www.tiscover.com/jugendgasthaus.rust. Dorms €13-27.50.) A pricier option is the four-star **Austria Trend—Seehotel Rust ❹**, Am Seekanal 2-4, will see to your every need while still maintaining a beach-and-country feel. (☎38 10; www.austria-trend.at/rus. Doubles €62-104.) For hostel prices within a 2min. walk from the lake, try **Storchencamp Rust Jugendherberge ❷**, which has clean rooms but no place to lock your belongings. From the beginning of April through October, the hostel also offers camping at the attached **Ruster Camping Platz Freizeitcenter ❶**, which has showers, laundry, a game room, a playground, and a grocery store. (☎595 or 59 52; www.gmeiner.at. Wheelchair-accessible. Reception 7:30am-10pm. Hostel €11.10-26.80, sheets €2.60. Camping €4.40-5.10, children €1.50-2.20; tent €2.40-3.20. 5min. from the beach; guests receive free entrance. Showers included.)

Vineyard-restaurants called *Buschenschenken* offer cheap snacks and superb wine; the tourist office has a list. Many are only open in the evenings. Good eats line Rathausstr., though the ravenous should seek out **Zum Alten Haus ❷**, on the corner of Feldg. and Franz-Josef-Pl., which serves up enormous portions of schnitzel and salad for only €6.50. (☎230. Open Tu-Su 9am-10pm.) **Alte Schmiede ❸**, Seezeile 24, covered by grapevines, serves traditional Austrian food with a Hungarian twist in a lively, friendly atmosphere. (☎64 18. Live music lunch and dinner. Reservations recommended. Open daily 11:30am-2pm and 5:30-10pm.) The **ADEG Markt** is at Oggauerstr. 3. (☎66 39; open M-F 7am-noon and 3-6pm, Sa 7am-noon.)

🏛☀ SIGHTS & OUTDOOR ACTIVITIES. Rust is home to Austria's only **Weinakademie** (Wine Academy) Hauptstr. 31. The institution offers courses ranging from wine cultivation to basic bartending, and holds wine tours and tastings. (☎68 53; fax 64 31. Open for wine tastings F-Su 2-6pm; daily in Sept. €11 for 10 tastes.) Many vintners (*Weinbauern*) offer wine tastings and tours of their own cellars. **Rudolf Beilschmidt**, Weinbergg. 1, has tours (☎326. May-Sept. F 5pm), as does **Weingut Marienhof**, Weinbergg. 16 (☎251. June-Sept. Tu 6pm, €4.50).

Around the corner from the tourist office, the **Fischerkirche** is the oldest church in Burgenland, dating back to the 12th century. In the 13th century, Queen Mary of Hungary donated the Marienkapelle after being rescued from the Mongols by fishermen. This interior chapel contains lovely 15th-century sculptures of the Madonna. The Romanesque and Gothic sections have also survived the Baroque remodeling fervor. (Open from Easter M-Sa 11am-noon and 2-3pm, Su 11am-noon and 2-4pm; May-Sept. M-Sa 10am-noon and 2:30-6pm, Su 2-4pm. Tours by appointment €1; call Frau Kaiser at ☎067 69 70 33 16.)

Sun worshipers can sit and splash at the **public beach** on the south shore of the Neusiedlersee. Walk down Hauptstr., take a left onto Am Seekanal, then right onto Seepromenade, which cuts through the marsh lands (about 7km) surrounding the lake. The lake has murky water, but it's OK—the muddy color comes from the shallow, easily disturbed clay bottom. The beach also has a chlorine pool, showers, lockers, restrooms, phones, water slide, and a snack bar. Keep your entrance card to exit the park. (☎591. €4 per person, after 11am €3, after 4pm €2.) Rent a **boat** from **Family Gmeiner**, next to the beach on the water's edge. (Paddleboats €6/€18; electric boats €9/€27.) The same company runs **Schiffrundfahrten** (boat tours) to Podersdorf, on the opposite shore. (☎02 66 26 83 55 38. Boats leave Rust Apr.-Oct. Th-Su

BURGENLAND

and holidays 10am, 4pm and return from Podersdorf 11am, 5pm. 4-person minimum, €19 per person.) The area is loaded with **bike trails,** covering a total of 170km. Many follow the circumference of the lake shore; others wind between towns on the Austro-Hungarian border. There are also two designated bike paths that cross the lake leading to Podersdorf and Breitenburg.

Map labels: UPPER AUSTRIA (OBERÖSTERREICH), Styria (Steiermark), Mariazell, Bad Aussee, 146, Eisenerz, 20, S6, Mürzzuschlag, TO SALZBURG (90km), Liezen, Admont, 115, Leoben, Bruck an der Mur, A9, BURGENLAND, NIEDERE TAUERN, Mur, Stubenberg am See, 54, A2, SALZBURGER LAND, SCHLADMINGER TAUERN, Stübing, Eggenberg, Badgastein, 97, Piber, Graz, Riegersburg, 65, A10, 83, Bärnbach, HUNGARY, GURKTALER ALPEN, 70, A9, 67, 76, CARINTHIA (KÄRNTEN), 98, A2, Leibnitz, 93, 93, Deutschlandsberg, Mur, 83, A2, 0 15 miles, Klagenfurt, SLOVENIA, LG, 0 15 kilometers

STYRIA (STEIERMARK)

Styria, promoted by tourist offices as "the Green Heart of Austria," is the country's second largest province. Styria has been spared the brunt of the tourist invasion prevalent elsewhere, which has allowed for the preservation of many of Southern Austria's folk traditions and ancient forests. Even its largest city, Graz, remains relatively untarnished by tourists. The crumbling medieval strongholds and stud farm for Austria's Lipizzaner stallions are among the region's most notable attractions. Famous also for its wine, Styrian vineyards are essential to any wine tour of Europe. Beyond their alcoholic spirits, Styrians are notorious for stubborn individuality and provincial pride.

HIGHLIGHTS OF STYRIA

Peruse the collected treasures of **Graz's** Landesmuseum Joanneum (see p. 162).
Marvel at a glass-blowing demonstration in **Bärnbach** (see p. 164).
Discover hidden staircases in **Admont's** Benediktinerstift (see p. 169).

GRAZ ☎ 0316

You'll definitely feel like you're in Austria's second largest city when you leave Graz's train station and enter a mob of buses, streetcars, and busy locals. For a more relaxed pace, walk just a few minutes to the pedestrian district of the old city, where locals linger over coffee in the many cafés lining the Herreng. or the narrow cobblestone Sporgasse. Graz's *Altstadt*, with winding streets, museums, and steep red-tiled roofs, is relatively tourist-free.

The two towers rising from the small mountain in the center of town commemorate the mighty fortress that withstood centuries of attacks. The mountain continued to be a refuge during war in the 20th century—the citizens of Graz hid in the

STYRIA

154

air-raid tunnels deep inside. The eastern slope of the mountain leads down into the calm Stadtpark, full of sunbathers and frisbee-throwers. In the evening, the areas around the park become a center for hip nightlife, thanks to the 42,000 students at nearby Karl-Franzens University.

■ INTERCITY TRANSPORTATION

Flights: Flughafen Graz, Flughafenstr. 51 (☎290 20), 9km from the city center. Take bus #631 from the airport into town (20min., every hr. 6:13am-11:30pm, €1.60); taxis into town cost about €14.

Trains: Trains arrive at the **Hauptbahnhof,** on Europapl., west of city center. (☎05 17 17 12, open 6am-10pm.) To: **Innsbruck** (6hr., 7per day 6:42am-10pm, €43.50); **Linz** (3½hr., every 2hr. 6:42am-6:42pm, €29.50); **Munich** via Salzburg (6¼hr., €63.10); **Salzburg** (4¼hr., 8 per day 6:42am-8pm, €36.50); **Vienna Südbahnhof** (2½hr., 16 per day 5:57am-8:57pm, €26.90); **Zurich** (10hr., 2 per day 8:42, 10pm, €74.30); **Venice** (9hr.; 2 per day 10:23am, 8:23pm; €65).

Buses: Graz-Köflach Bus (GKB), Köflacherg. 35-41 (☎59 87), runs 24hr. Buses leave from Griespl. for western Styria. The **Post Bus** office, Andreas-Hofer-Pl. 17 (☎82 76 28). Open M-F 7am-3pm. **Bundesbus** lines depart from Europapl. 5 (next to the train station) and from Andreas-Hofer-Pl.

■ ORIENTATION

Graz spreads across the Mur River in the southeast corner of Austria. The city is a gateway to Slovenia (50km south) and Hungary (70km east). Two-thirds of Graz's area consists of beautiful parks, earning it the nickname "Garden City." **Hauptplatz,** in front of the *Rathaus,* is the city center. **Jakominiplatz,** 5min. from Hauptpl., is the hub of the city's bus and streetcar system. **Herrengasse,** a pedestrian street lined with cafés and boutiques, connects Hauptpl. to Jakominipl., forming the heart of the *Fußgängerzone.* The **Universität** is tucked away past the Stadtpark, in Graz' northeast corner. The **Hauptbahnhof** lies on the other side of the river, a short ride from Hauptpl. on tram #3 or 6. To get to the city center from the train station, follow Annenstr. up and over Hauptbrücke (20min.).

■ LOCAL TRANSPORTATION

Public Transportation: For information on all local buses, trams, and trains, call **Mobil Zentrale,** Schönaug. 6 (☎82 06 06). Open M-F 9am-6pm, Sa 9am-1pm. Purchase single tickets (€1.60) and 24hr. tickets (€3.20) from the driver, booklets of 10 tickets (€12.40) or week-tickets (€7.90) from any *Tabak.* Children under 15 halfprice. Tickets are valid for all trams, buses, and the cable car and elevator that ascend the *Schloßberg;* validate them at the orange stamp box. Most trams and buses run until 11:30pm.

Taxi: Funktaxi, ☎983. **City-Funk,** ☎878.

Car Rental: Budget, Europapl. 12 (☎72 20 74; fax 72 20 76; airport ☎290 23 42).

Automobile Clubs: ÖAMTC, Conrad-von-Hötzendorf-str. 127 (☎50 40). **ARBÖ,** Kappelenstr. 45 (☎27 16 00).

Bicycle Rental: Bicycle Graz, Körösistr. 5 (☎82 13 57). 7-speed bikes €7 per day, trekking bikes €9, mountain bikes €11. Open M-F 7am-1pm and 2-6pm.

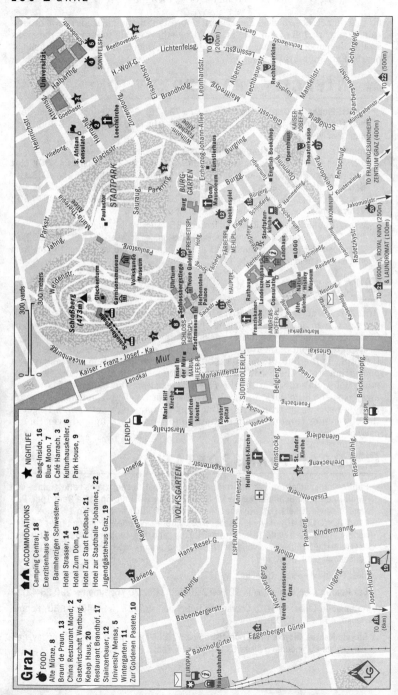

STYRIA

Graz

● FOOD
Alte Münze, **8**
Braun de Praun, **13**
China Restaurant Mond, **4**
Gastwirtschaft Wartburg, **4**
Kebap Haus, **20**
Restaurant Brandhof, **17**
Stainzerbauer, **12**
University Mensa, **5**
Wintergarten, **11**
Zur Goldenen Pastete, **10**

🛏🛏 ACCOMMODATIONS
Camping Central, **18**
Exerzitienhaus der
  Barmherzigen Schwestern, **1**
Hotel Strasser, **14**
Hotel Zum Dom, **15**
Hotel Zur Stadt Feldbach, **21**
Hotel zur Stadthalle "Johannes," **22**
Jugendgästehaus Graz, **19**

★ NIGHTLIFE
Bang-Inside, **16**
Blue Moon, **7**
Café Harrach, **3**
Kulturhauskeller, **6**
Park House, **9**

⁊ PRACTICAL INFORMATION

TOURIST & FINANCIAL SERVICES

Tourist Office: Main office, Herreng. 16 (☎807 50; www.graztourism.at), has free city maps and a city walking guide. English-speaking staff makes room reservations. **Tours** of the *Altstadt* in English start in front of the office (2hr.; Apr.-Oct. Tu-W 2:30pm; €7.50, children 6-15 €3.75). The office also offers bus tours visiting the newer parts of Graz and Schloß Eggenberg (2½hr.; Apr.-Oct. M-Tu 2:30pm; €11.50, children 6-15 €5.75). Open June-Sept. M-F 9am-7pm, Sa 9am-6pm, Su 10am-4pm, holidays 10am-3pm; Oct.-May M-F 9am-6pm, Sa 9am-3pm, Su 10am-3pm. **Branch office:** ☎807 50, in the Hauptbahnhof. Open M-W and F 8:30am-1pm and 2-5:30pm, Th 8:30am-1pm and 2-6:30pm.

Consulates: South Africa, Villefortg. 13/II (☎32 25 48). Open M 8am-noon. **UK,** Schmiedg. 10 (☎82 61 05).

Currency Exchange: Most banks open M-F 8am-noon and 2-4pm.

LOCAL SERVICES

Luggage Storage: At the station; small bag €2, medium €2.50, large €3.50.

Bookstores: English Bookshop, Tummelpl. 7 (☎82 62 66), has 2 vast floors of fiction and nonfiction. Open M-F 9am-6pm, Sa 9am-noon.

Bi-Gay-Lesbian Organizations: Verein Frauenservice Graz (Women's Information Center), Idlhofg. 20 (☎71 60 22). Office open M-F 9:30am-2:30pm, Tu 9am-5pm. Medical help available W 5-7pm. Pick up the *Genuine Gay Guide* to Styria at LOGO (see below) or at the tourist office.

Youth Organizations: Jugend Informationsservice "LOGO," Schmiedg. 23a, offers free brochures and advice for young people (☎81 60 74). Open M-F noon-5pm.

Women's Health Center: Frauengesundheitszentrum Graz, Brockmanng. 48, 3rd floor (☎83 79 98; www.fgz.co.at).

Laundromat: Putzerei Rupp, Jakominstr. 34 (☎82 11 83). 5kg load €6, soap €0.50, dryer €0.30 per 3min., centrifuge €0.50. Open M-F 8am-5pm.

EMERGENCY & COMMUNICATIONS

Emergencies: Police ☎133 (office ☎888 27 75), **Ambulance** ☎144.

AIDS Hotline: Steirische AIDS-Hilfe, Schmiedg. 38 (☎81 50 50; www.aids-hilfe.at.) Counseling available W 11am-1pm, F 5-7pm. Blood tests Tu and Th 4:30-7:30pm. Safer Sex Hotline F 7:30-8:30pm.

Pharmacy: Bärenapotheke, Herreng. 11 (☎83 02 67), opposite the tourist office. Open M-F 8am-6pm, Sa 8am-noon. AmEx/MC/V.

Hospital: Landeskrankenhaus (LKH), Auenbruggerpl. 1 (☎38 50)

Internet Access: Jugendgästehaus Graz, Idlhofg. 74 (see below). €1.50 per 20min. Open 7am-10pm. **Sit'n Surf,** Hans-Sach-g. 10 (☎81 45 65). €2.60 for 30min., €4.50 for 1hr. Open daily 8am-11pm.

Post Office: Main office, Neutorg. 46. Open M-F 7:30am-8pm, Sa 8am-noon. Cashier closes M-F at 5pm. **Branch office,** Europapl. 10, in the Hauptbahnhof. Open M-F 7am-11pm, Sa 8am-8pm, Su 1-8pm. **Postal code:** A-8010; branch office A-8020.

STYRIA

⌂ ACCOMMODATIONS

Staking out a cheap bed in Graz may require a bit of detective work, as most budget hotels, guest houses, and pensions run from €25, with cheaper options in the boondocks. Luckily, the web of local transport provides a reliable and easy commute to and from the city center. Ask the tourist office about *Privatzimmer* (€15-30 per night), especially in the crowded summer months.

▨ **Jugendgästehaus Graz (HI),** Idlhofg. 74 (☎48 76; jgh.graz@jgh.at), 20min. from the train station. Exit the station, cross the street, head right on Eggenberger Gürtel, left on Josef-Huber-G. (after the car dealership), and take a right at Idlhofg. The hostel is through a parking lot on the right. Buses #31 and 32 run from Jakominipl. (last bus around midnight). This brand-new, hotel-quality hostel has a café, restaurant, and **Internet** access (€1.50 per 20min.). Make sure your reservations are for the Jugendgästehaus and not the Jugendhotel if you want the room rates listed below. Breakfast included. Laundry €1.50, soap included; dryer €1.50. Night key available (€20 deposit). Reception 7am-11pm. 10pm-2am. 4-bed dorms €17; singles €24; doubles €40. All rooms with bath. €3 surcharge for stays of less than 3 nights. If the hostel is full, you can stay in the *Notlager* (basement rooms with hall bath) for €14.20. MC/V. ❸

Hotel Strasser, Eggenberger Gürtel 11 (☎71 39 77; fax 71 68 56), 5min. from the train station. Exit the station, cross the street, and head right on Eggenberger Gürtel; the hotel is on the left, across from the car repair shop. Airy rooms are clean and comfortable. Breakfast included. Free parking. Singles €29, with shower €36; doubles €45/€54; triples with shower €65. AmEx/DC/MC/V. ❸

Hotel Zur Stadt Feldbach, Conrad-von-Hötzendorf-Str. 58 (☎82 94 68; fax 94 68 15), 15min. walk down Jakominipl. Take tram #4 (dir.: Liebnau) or 5 (dir.: Puntigam) to "Jakominigürtel." The hotel is on the right. Rooms are plain and clean. Hall bathrooms. Breakfast €5. Reception 24hr. on 2nd floor. Singles €26, with shower €33; doubles €40/€51; triples with shower €65. ❸

Exerzitienhaus der Barmherzigen Schwestern, Marieng. 6a (☎71 60 20; fax 77 59 11 17). Walk straight out of the train station onto Keplerstr., then take a left onto Marieng. The convent will be on your right (10min.). Ring the bell marked Exerzitienhaus at the metal gate. As you might expect from a convent, the rooms are plain, clean, and quiet. Breakfast €5. Dorms €16, with shower €19; singles €23/€27. ❷

Hotel Zum Dom, Burgerg. 14 (☎82 48 00; domhotel@domhotel.co.at). From the tourist office turn right and turn left onto H-Sachs-G., and then left again onto Burgerg. The hotel will be on your left. This stylish hotel in the old city brings luxury up to date—the red carpets and chandeliers are integrated into a hip, colorful atmosphere. Every one of the spacious rooms is decorated uniquely and has a different kind of marble in each bathroom. Breakfast included. Singles €85; doubles €155, with jacuzzi €160. ❺

Hotel zur Stadthalle "Johannes," Münzgrabenstr. 48 (☎/fax 83 77 66). Take streetcar #6 from the train station or Jakominipl. to "Neue Technik." On foot from Jakominipl., head down Reitschulg., which turns into Münzgrabenstr. (15min.). Wood furniture and down comforters make these small, clean rooms comfortable. Rooms include shower, toilet, TV. Breakfast included. Singles €47; doubles €69. AmEx/MC/V. ❹

Camping Central, Martinhofstr. 3 (☎067 63 78 51 02, guenther_walter@utanet.at). Take bus #32 from Jakomininpl. to "Bad Straßgang" (15min.). Follow signs, taking the next right at the Mondo supermarket, and walk up the road. This green and conveniently-located campground includes admission to public swimming pool. Laundry €3, dryer €2. Reception 7am-10pm. Open Apr.-Oct. €13 per person, includes tent site and shower; car or camper €24 for 2 people, includes shower and electricity; additional adults €7, children 4-15 €5. Additional tax of €0.75 per person per night. ❶

◘ FOOD

Graz's student community sustains a bonanza of cheap eateries. On Hauptpl. concession stands sell *Wurst*, ice cream, and other fast food (€1.50-3) until late. Low-priced student hangouts also line Zinzendorfg. near the university. Note that most salads come dressed in the local dark pumpkin-seed oil. At **farmers' markets** on Kaiser-Josef-Pl. and Lendpl. (M-Sa 7am-12:30pm), and "Standl" on Hauptpl. and on Jakominipl. (M-F 7am-6pm, Sa 7am-12:30pm), vendors hawk various goods. There's a **SPAR** grocery store inside the train station (open daily 6am-9pm), and numerous Billas and SPARs around town.

Braun de Praun, Morellenfeldg. 32 (☎32 20 03). With over 30 menu options (€10-18) and just as many daily specials, Braun de Praun is an Austrian restaurant unafraid of a little culinary experimentation. Main dishes include curry pork with glazed banana and almond-raisin rice (€12.50) and chicken "mexicano" (€12.50), but the numerous local dishes, *Biergarten* ambience, and Lederhosen-clad waiters keep it firmly rooted in Graz. Open M-Sa 8am-2am. AmEx/MC/V. ❸

Alte Münze, Schloßbergpl. 8 (☎82 91 51). Gasthaus Alte Münze serves scrumptious Styrian specialties in a traditional setting. Excellent *Eierspatzn* (egg noodles) are €6.90 with salad. Try the local dessert *Besoffene Liesl* (*Gugelhopf* cake in apple wine; €3.30). Daily *Menü* €6.90-9.50. Open Tu-Sa 8am-11pm. ❷

Zur Goldenen Pastete, Sporg. 28 (☎82 34 16), just up the street from the Hauptpl. This deep red Gasthaus is the oldest in the city, having been built in 1575. It serves up-to-date interpretations of Austrian classics. Viennese pork cutlet €9. Most entrees cost €9-12. Open daily 11am-midnight. AmEx/MC/V. ❸

Wintergarten, Sackstr. 3-5 (☎81 16 16), in the sunny glass-topped atrium of the luxurious Erzherzog Johann Hotel, offers excellent service and gourmet entrees (€14-20). If you're ready to pull out all the stops, order their 7-course daily *Menü* (€47). Open W-Su 11:30am-2pm and 6pm-midnight. AmEx/MC/V. ❺

Stainzerbauer, Burgerg. 4 (☎82 11 06), specializes in Styrian food, but don't expect heavy plain dumplings here. Delicious dishes include *Tafelspitz* (€16.50), and roasted calf's liver with apple pieces, bacon, and polenta (€12.50), all served in the elegant atmosphere of their Renaissance courtyard decked out with fresh flowers. Open M-Sa 11am-midnight. MC/V. ❹

Restaurant Brandhof (☎84 42 55), at the corner of Gleisdorferstr. and Glacisstr., is nestled behind the opera house. The red tables in its tree-filled garden fill up in the afternoon with chatty locals enjoying its simple cuisine, like Styrian potato sausage (€5.50) and *Zwiebelrostbraten* (€8.80). Open Tu-F 10am-midnight and post-opera. ❷

Gastwirtschaft Wartburg, Halbärthg. 4 (☎32 65 20). This smoky café/bar features antique posters on the wall, filling dishes, and a student crowd. Lunch specials (€5.70) and entrees (€4-9). Open M-F 10am-2am, Sa 5pm-2am. ❷

Kebap Haus, Jakoministr. 16 (☎81 10 06), just south of Jakominipl. A superior Turkish restaurant with falafel or lamb sandwiches (take-out €2.70-3; sit down €3.10-3.90), and delicious pizzas (€5.70-6). Lunch specials include soup, entree, and salad (around €5.50). Open M-Sa 11am-midnight. AmEx/MC/V. ❷

China Restaurant Mond, Harrachg. 12a (☎35 69 79), between Café Harrach and the park. Keep both tummy and wallet bulging with the all-you-can-eat lunch buffet (M-F 11:30am-2:30pm, €5.50). A €3.80 *Menü* is also available for both lunch and dinner. Open daily 11:30am-3pm and 5:30-10pm. ❶

FROM THE ROAD

WHERE THE CITY MEETS THE COUNTRY

After two full weeks dedicated to discovering every last bit of Graz, I was walking through the downtown, tying up the loose ends in my research. Just when I thought that I had seen everything in Graz, I saw bright umbrellas in the distance, beckoning me and tempting my curiosity. Before long, I was in the middle of a farmer's market, with some 50 stands of local farmers selling their homegrown goods, including smoked meats, apples, cherries, strawberries, apricots, freshly baked loaves of bread, cakes and strudels, dried mushrooms, potatoes, zucchini and corn-preserves, oils, and juices. Walking through the shade of the tents and tables, I found myself stopping to talk in German with families proudly selling the results of their work. Each time I was greeted with an in-depth description of the item that had caught my attention.

In much of Austria, farmers' markets are a regular part of life. Almost any decent-sized town will have at least one market during the week, usually right on one of the major squares in the middle of town. As a traveler, going to these markets can be a great way to find fresh, delicious food that's cheap. Further, you are likely to get a unique insight into the pace and flavor of food and culture in the region, the kind not found in the local SPAR or Migros.

- Helen Human, 2003

University Mensa, Sonnenfelspl. 1 (☎32 33 62; fax 32 33 62 75), just east of the Stadtpark at the intersection of Zinzendorfg. and Leechg. Take bus #39 or 63 to "Uni/Mensa" for the best deal in town. Simple, satisfying *Menüs* €3.70-4.10. Large *à la carte* selection. Open M-F 9am-2:30pm. ❶

🔿 SIGHTS

THE OLD TOWN. For an entertaining way to explore Graz, try using the tourist office's free brochure, *A Short Tale of Graz.* The tourist office, a sight in and of itself, is in the **Landhaus,** the seat of the provincial government. In 1557, the building was remodeled in Lombard style by architect Domenico dell'Allio. Through the arch to the right is a striking Renaissance arcaded courtyard, where *Classics in the City* is held (see p. 163).

LANDESZEUGHAUS (PROVINCIAL ARSENAL). Anton Solar built the Landeszeughaus between 1642 and 1644. The first floor contains displays (with English translations) detailing the history of the arsenal and the series of Ottoman attacks it faced. In 1749, after the Turks had packed their cannon and gone home, the armory was to be dismantling, until an eloquent protest by Styrian nobles convinced Empress Maria Theresa to preserve it. With its massive collection of weaponry intact, the building served as a firehouse until it opened as a museum in 1882. Today, the four-story collection includes enough spears, muskets, and armor to outfit 28,000 burly mercenaries. *(Herreng. 16, next to the tourist office. ☎80 17 98 10. Open Tu-Su 10am-6pm and Th until 8pm. Tours in German, French, English at 11am, 3pm, or by appointment. €1.40. Admission with Joanneum ticket.)*

CHURCHES. The yellow Gothic **Stadtpfarrkirche** was the Abbey Church for the Dominican Order in the 16th century, and suffered severe damage in WWII. The new stained-glass windows installed in 1953 made headlines around the world; the left panel behind the high altar portrays the scourging of Christ, silently watched over by two figures bearing a resemblance to Hitler and Mussolini. The church holds **organ concerts.** *(Herreng. 23. Concerts mid-May to early Aug. Th 11:45am. Free.)*

Nearby stands Graz's **Dom** (cathedral), built in 15th-century Gothic style by Emperor Friedrich III. In 1485, the church mounted a picture on the south side of the building in remembrance of the "Scourges of God": the plague, Ottoman invasions, and locusts—holy terrors that had wiped out 80% of the population only five years prior. *(On Hofg., opposite the*

Burggarten and Burgtor. Closes 8pm. Impromptu organ music 11am-noon.) Next door is the solemn 17th-century Habsburg **Mausoleum,** an elaborate domed tomb that holds the remains of Ferdinand II. Cryptic English signs are pasted to the stone walls. Master architect Fischer von Erlach (responsible for much of Vienna's Baroque grandeur) designed the beautiful frescoes upstairs. *(Around the corner from the Dom, on Burgg. Free.)*

The 13th-century Gothic **Leechkirche** is the city's oldest structure, having been built (1202), destroyed (1250), and rebuilt (1275-1283). *(Zinzendorfg. 5, between Stadtpark and the university.)*

SCHLOßBERG. The wooded **Schloßberg** rises 123m above Graz. The hill is named for a castle which stood on it from 1125 until 1809, when it was destroyed by Napoleon's troops. Though the castle is mostly gone, the Schloßberg remains a beautiful city park. From Schloßbergpl., visitors can climb the zigzagging stone steps of the **Schloßbergstiege,** built by Russian prisoners during WWI and traditionally known as the Russenstiege (Russian steps) or the Kriegstiege (war steps). The path continues through the terraced Herberstein Gardens, a lush park with sweeping views surveying the vast Styrian plain surrounding Graz. The **Glockenturm** (bell-tower), built in 1588, is one of the few castle structures still standing, having been spared by the little emperor in return for a sizeable ransom from Graz's citizens. *(Tower open only with Schloßberg tour, see below.)* Its enormous bell (Liesl) draws a crowd with its 101 clangings (supposedly because it was forged from 101 Turkish cannon balls) thrice daily at 7am, noon, and 7pm. Next to the Liesl, you'll find the **Freilichtbühne in den Kasematten,** an outdoor theater built into the ruins of the castle foreman's massive basement. The nearby **Uhrturm** (clocktower), whose clockworks date from 1712, was originally constructed in 1265 and then rebuilt in 1569. *(North of Herreng. and Hauptpl. Tours in German or English. Apr.-mid Oct. Tu-Su every hr. 9am-5pm, meet at Glockenturm. €2.15, students and children €1.05.)*

From Schloßbergpl., the **Schloßberg Passage** burrows into the *Berg.* A network of tunnels was blasted into the hill during WWII to serve as a bomb shelter for up to 50,000 civilians. Visitors may walk through the cool, dark main passage and peer down spooky side tunnels. The largest side tunnel opens up into a large chamber, the **Dom im Berg,** which is now a popular venue for all sorts of events. *(Dom im Berg open 8am-8pm, free. The quickest way to the top of the Schloßberg is the Lift im Berg, which takes you up 77m; enter from Schloßbergpl. Or take the historic Schloßbergbahn, in operation since 1894. Both are open daily Apr.-Sept. 9am-11pm; Oct.-Mar. 10am-10pm; fare is a valid public transportation ticket or €1.50, children €0.75.)*

PARKS AND GARDENS. Down the hill on the eastern side near the Uhrturm and through the Paulustor arch is the **Stadtpark.** Graz acquired the ornate central fountain, whose eight mermaids struggle with huge spitting fish, at the 1873 Vienna World's Fair. South of the fish fountain, the Stadtpark blends into the **Burggarten,** a bit of carefully pruned greenery complementing what remains of Emperor Friedrich III's 15th-century *Burg.* His cryptic wall inscription "A.E.I.O.U." remains a mystery, varyingly interpreted as *"Austria Erit In Orbe Ultima,"* (Austria will be the Ultimate on Earth) or *"Alles Erdreich Ist Österreich Untertan"* (All on Earth is Under Austria).

OTHER SIGHTS. The magnificent **Opernhaus** was built in less than two years by Viennese architects Fellner and Helmer. *(At Opernring and Burgg., down the street from the mausoleum. ☎80 08.)* The **Glockenspiel** opens its wooden doors three times each day to reveal life-size wooden figures spinning to a slow folk song. The black-and-gold ball underneath turns to show the phases of the moon. *(Located just off Engeg. in Glockenspielpl. 11am, 3, 6pm.)*

STYRIA

🏛 MUSEUMS

The tourist office offers a handy pamphlet describing all of Graz's museums and galleries along with their locations, contact information, and prices.

LANDESMUSEUM JOANNEUM. Graz's state museum is Austria's oldest public museum. The holdings are so vast that officials have been forced to keep portions in museums scattered throughout the city. One ticket, purchased at any location, is valid for the Garrisonsmuseum, the Natural History museum, and most art museums in the city. *(For information contact Landesmuseum Joanneum, Rauberg. 10. ☎80 17 96 60; www.museum-joanneum.et. €4.30, students and seniors €2.90.)*

ART MUSEUMS. The **Joanneum** includes the **Neue Galerie,** housed in the elegant Palais Herberstein, which showcases offbeat, avant-garde 19th- and 20th-century works and paintings. *(Sackstr. 16, at the foot of the Schloßberg. ☎82 91 55; fax 81 54 01. Open Tu-Su 10am-6pm, Th until 8pm. Admission with Joanneum ticket. Tours €1.50, Tu, Th, Su at 11am, 3pm; also available in English or at other times by appointment.)* Its counterpart, located three streets behind the tourist office, is the **Alte Galerie.** This gallery presents a mid-sized collection of medieval and Baroque art, mostly of Styrian origin. Notable holdings include Lucas Cranach's *Judgment of Paris* and Jan Brueghel's copy of his father's gruesome *Triumph of Death. (Neutorg. 45. ☎80 17 97 70, fax 80 17 98 47. Open Tu-Su 10am-6pm. Tours by appointment. Admission with Joanneum ticket.)* The **Künstlerhaus,** an independent museum in the *Stadtpark,* hosts small exhibitions ranging from Tibetan artifacts to Secessionist paintings by Klimt. *(Open M-Sa 9am-6pm, Su 9am-noon. €1.60, students and children free.)*

HISTORY & SCIENCE MUSEUMS. At the **Stadtmuseum,** temporary exhibits complement the permanent third-floor display, which features 19th-century drawings of the city alongside modern photographs and a large-scale model c.1800. *(Sackstr. 18, next to the Neue Galerie at western foot of the Schloßberg. ☎82 25 80. Open Tu 10am-9pm, W-Sa 10am-6pm, Su 10am-1pm. €5, students€3, children €1.50.)* On the Schloßberg, the **Garrisonsmuseum** exhibits a modest collection of military uniforms and feathered helmets. *(☎82 73 48. Open Tu-Su 10am-5pm. €1.45, students €0.73, children €0.36. Admission with Joanneum's ticket.)* The Joanneum's scientific wing is the **Natural History Museum,** which encompasses geology, paleontology, zoology, and other -ologies. The museum has a specimen of the largest beetle species in the world, a collection of minerals and semi-precious stones, and a set of wildlife scenes. From the geology gallery, you can leave through the secret exit of the coal mine, the "Schaubergwerk." *(Rauberg. 10. ☎80 17 97 30. Open Tu-Su 9am-4pm. Admission with Joanneum ticket.)*

🎵 ENTERTAINMENT

The tourist office is a great place to find out what is giong on in Graz. Ask for a free copy of the magazine *Was ist Wo?* (in German), which details current events with prices and locations. The staff can also help you track down tickets to events.

OPERA, THEATER, & DANCE

For professional music and dance performances, Graz's neo-Baroque **Opernhaus,** at Opernring and Burgg. (☎80 08), sells standing-room tickets 1hr. before curtain call. The program includes operas and ballets of worldwide repute; for many young hopefuls, Graz is considered a stepping stone to an international career. One big show comes each July while the regular companies are on vacation. Tickets cost €10-110, but standing-room slots start at €10, and student rush tickets (26 and under) cost €6. The **Schauspielhaus** (☎80 00), the theater on Freiheitspl. (entrance on Hofg.), sells bargain seats just before showtime (daily ticket sales

10am-4pm). All tickets and performance schedules are available at the **Theaterkasse**, Kaiser-Josef-Pl. 10, at the tram stop (☎80 00; open M-F 8am-6:30pm, Sa 8a-1pm), and the **Zentralkartenbüro**, Herreng. 7, on the left inside the passage. (☎83 02 55; www.zkb.at. Open M-F 9am-6pm, Sa 9am-noon.)

FESTIVALS

Since 1985, the city has hosted its own summer festival, **Styriarte**. Concerts, mostly classical, are held daily from late June to late July in the gardens of Schloß Eggenberg, the large halls of Graz Convention Center, and the squares of the old city. Tickets are available at Palais Attems, Sackstr. 17. (☎82 50 00; fax 82 50 00 15. Open M-F 10am-6pm.) Every summer between July and August, the **American Institute of Musical Studies** transfers to Graz. Students perform works from Broadway to Schönberg on the streets and in concert halls—ask for a schedule at the tourist office. Tickets are available through the Zentralkartenburo or AIMS itself (Elisabethstr. 93; ☎32 70 66; aims@aimsgraz.at; tickets €9-37). From July to mid-August, **organ concerts** are held once a week at the Stadtpfarrkirche (Su 8pm). July and August also bring **Jazz-Sommer Graz,** a festival of free concerts. Previous years have seen jazz legends like Dave Brubek, Slide Hampton, and Dizzy Gillespie. (Contact the tourist office; concerts Th-Sa 8:30pm at Maria Hilferpl.) From late July to early August, Graz surrenders its streets to **La Strada,** the international festival of puppet and street theatre (www.lastrada.at). From late September to October, the **Steierischer Herbst** (Styrian Autumn) festival, Sackstr. 17, celebrates avant-garde art with a month of films, performances, art installations, and parties. Contact the director for details. (☎81 60 70; www.steirischerst.at.)

FILM

The award-winning movie theater **Rechbauerkino**, Rechbauerstr. 6 (☎83 05 08), occasionally screens un-dubbed arthouse films in English (€6.50, children €5.50). The **Royal Kino,** Conrad-von-Hötzendorfstr. 10 (☎82 61 33), a few blocks south of Jakominipl., shows new releases in English, without subtitles (€7.20, if you sit in one of the first 3 rows €6.20. M-W all features €5, Th-Su before 5:45pm €6.20; students Th-F €5.40, Sa-Su €6.70).

▧ NIGHTLIFE

STYRIA

After-hours activity in Graz can be found in the so-called **Bermuda Dreieck** (Bermuda triangle), in the old city behind Hauptpl. and bordered by Mehlpl., Färberg., and Prokopig. Dozens of beer gardens and bars are packed all night, every night; standard procedure is to sit outdoors until about 11pm, when ordinance requires festivities move indoors. Most university students prefer to down their beers in the pubs lining Zinzendorfg. and Halbärthg. on the other side of the Stadtpark.

> **Kulturhauskeller,** Elisabethstr. 30, underneath the *Literaturhaus*. From the Stadtpark, head straight down Elisabethstr. A young crowd demands loud, throbbing dance music, but the partying doesn't get started until 11pm on weekends. *Weißbier* €2.80. 19+. Obligatory coat check and security fee €2. Open Tu-Sa from 9pm until whenever.

> **Park House** (☎82 74 34) in the Stadtpark. From the Künstlerhaus, cross Erzherzog-Jonann-Allee and follow the stream 70m. An enclosed pavillion pumping music in a dark bar area, frequented by 18- to 30-year-olds night and day. In-house DJs nightly. Drinks €2.30-6.50. Open daily 11am-2am.

> **Bang-Inside,** Dreihackeng. 4-10 (☎71 95 49). This neon-lit gay bar turns into a pumping disco on F and Sa nights. Loud music and plenty of drinks (€3-6). Cover €3.60. Bar open W-Th and Su 9pm-2am, no cover; disco F-Sa 9pm-4am, after midnight men only.

Blue Moon, Sackstr. 40 (☎82 97 56). This local hangout just south of the Schloßberg-bahn attracts an alternative crowd of artists, musicians, and gays. Check out its cool architecture—the low curved ceilings aren't just that way for ambience; the bar is actually built back inside the mountain along a tunnel dug as an air raid shelter in WWII. Beer €2.90 and cocktails €6-7. Open daily 8pm-3am.

Café Harrach, Harrachg. 26 (☎32 26 71). A half-liter of Gösser costs €2.80 at this grad-student hangout, but this is wine-drinking country. Most everyone is tossing back white wine spritzers (€2.10) at this dark artsy café. Open M-F 9am-midnight, Sa 5pm-midnight, Su 4pm-midnight.

◪ DAYTRIPS FROM GRAZ

BÄRNBACH & THE STÖLZE GLAS-CENTER

Take the train from Graz to Köflach (50min., 8 per day 5:26am-1:40pm, €5.40). From Köflach, take the bus to the Hauptpl. in Bärnbach. Buses leave after the arrival of every train, and the bus trip is included in the train ticket as long as the total time of your trip does not exceed 2hr. From the Hauptpl., head straight on Voitsbergerstr., crossing over the stream. The Glas-Center will be on your left (3min.). By car, take A2 to Mooskirchen and follow the signs toward Voitsberg and then Bärnbach.

The sleek glass façade of the Stölze Glas-Center (Hochregisterstr. 1-3) is one many examples of the beautiful glass produced here. The center houses a **glass museum** which traces the development of glass through history and displays many interesting glass pieces, from ancient beads to modern art. A section is devoted to work produced in Bärnbach itself, including perfume bottles, lamps, and a special hand-blown 135L bottle of Almdudler. The showroom in the center has items for sale, ranging from simple ashtrays to elegant vases. Morning tours (specifc times depend on demand) showcase **glass-blowing** demonstrations. (☎03142 629 50; glas-center@stoelze.com. Open M-F 9am-5pm, Sa 9am-1pm; May-Oct. M-F 9am-5pm, Sa-Su 9am-1pm. €5.50, children €3.) The Bärnbach **tourist office** is located inside the glass center, but there is also a branch by the **Hundertwasser Church.** (☎031 42 62 00 03 39 06. Open M-F 9am-5pm, Sa-Su 9am-noon.) Free **public toilets** are on the Hauptpl. and by the church. The **post office** is on the right just up Hauptstr. from the Hauptpl. (☎629 49 13. Open M-F 8am-noon and 2-6pm.) **Postal code:** A-8572.

SCHLOß EGGENBERG

Take tram #1 (dir.: Eggenberg) to "Schloß Eggenberg" (5am-midnight). Cross the street and backtrack a quarter block, taking the first right onto Schloßstr. ☎58 32 64. Exhibits open Mar.-Nov. Tu-Su 9am-4pm. Tours in German and English Apr.-Oct. Tu-Su every hr. 10am-noon and 2-4pm. €5.70; children, students, and seniors €4.30; Prunkräume tour included. Gardens open daily Apr.-Sept. 8am-7pm, Oct.-Mar. 8am-5pm. Free with castle entrance, for gardens only €1.

West of Graz, the grandiose **Schloß Eggenberg,** Eggenberger Allee 90, contrasts sharply with its plain suburban surroundings. Built for Prince Ulrich of Eggenberg, this multi-towered palace now holds an exquisite historical coin museum, an exhibition of artifacts from antiquity, and a prehistoric museum (all open Feb.-Nov. Tu-Su 9am-5pm). The resonating bird calls and wandering peacocks give it an exotic feel. Incidentally, the last knights' tournament in Styria took place here in 1777; knights took sides based on the answer to the question "Which are prettier, blondes or brunettes?" (Really.) The guided tour of the elegant **Prunkräume**—filled with 17th-century frescoes, tile ovens, and ornate chandeliers—reveals the palace's convoluted design as a microcosm of time. Four towers symbolize the seasons, 12 gates the months, and 365 windows the days.

The **Planetensaal**, or Planet Hall, is decorated with illustrations of the days as gods, bearing a suspicious resemblance to the Eggenberger family. Especially striking is the illustration of Monday, with the image of Diana with a crescent moon in her hair. Royal blue peacocks wander freely in the game preserve.

ÖSTERREICHISCHES FREILICHTMUSEUM

The most convenient way to get to the museum is a bus that runs from Lendpl. in Graz (dir.: Gratwein; M-Sa 9am, 12:30pm) straight to the museum (return 1:23, 4:35pm; €3.20.) Trains run to Stübing from Graz every hr. (€3.20); from the Stübing train station, turn onto the main road and walk 25min. to the museum. Drivers should take A9 north and then follow the signs to the museum.

The **Österreichisches Freilichtmuseum** (Open-Air Museum), in the nearby town of **Stübing,** recreates 19th-century Austrian farm life in a quiet wooded valley. The museum consists of 90 farmhouses, barns, mills, and storehouses from all over Austria, transported plank by plank and lovingly restored into small villages by their region of origin. Especially interesting are the displays detailing how grain is farmed, how cheese is made, and how bees are kept. You can also observe the practice of traditional crafts such as wood carving and lace making. A snack bar at the midpoint of the tour serves slices of bread with various spreads, pastries, and apple wine (€1 each), all fresh from the farm. (☎ 03124 537 00. Open June-Aug. Tu-Su 9am-6:30pm, no entrance after 5pm; Apr.-May and Sept.-Oct. Tu-Su 9am-5pm, no entrance after 4pm. Exhibits in German. English guidebook €2.20. 2hr. tour in English or German Tu-Su 10:30am; €2.20. €7, students €4.50, children €3.50.)

LIPIZZANER GESTÜT PIBER (STUD FARM)

The stud farm is a 1km outside of the town of Köflach. Take the train from Graz (50min., 8 per day 5:26am-1:40pm, €5.40), then the bus to Piber. Buses leave after the arrival of every train. By car from Graz, take A2 and exit Mooskirchen, then drive through Voitsberg and Bärnbach to Piber. Signing up for the tour from the tourist office in Graz will resolve any transportation worries and guarantee an English tour (leaves Sa 2pm from the Graz tourist office, Herreng. 16; €24, children €9).

The **Gestüt Piber (Piber Stud Farm)** is the home of the world-famous **Lipizzaner** horses, whose delicate footwork and snow white coats are the pride of the Spanish Riding School in Vienna. Born either solid black or brown, they become progressively paler, reaching the pure white color sometime between the age of five and 10. The rolling green hills of Piber are home to the mares, their foals, and trained stallions in retirement. On a 1hr. tour of the stud farm, you can see the horses up close in the stables and visit the carriage house and the Lipizzaner museum in the 300-year-old Piber castle. (☎ 031 44 33 23; office@piber.com. Open Apr.-Oct. daily 9am-10:30am and 1:30-3:30pm. €10, students €5.)

TIER-UND NATURPARK SCHLOß HERBERSTEIN

Visiting Herberstein is unfortunately only practical by car, as public transportation running to the area is almost nonexistent. Take A2 from Graz heading east, exit Gleisdorf-West, then drive through Hirnsdorf and St. Johann and follow the signs toward the park (30min.). From Vienna, take A2 south to the Hartberg exit, then drive through Hartberg, Kainsdorf, Hirnsdorf, and St. Johann (1hr.). ☎ 03176 882 50; www.herbestein.co.at. Open daily mid-Mar. to early Nov. 9am-6pm; early Nov. to mid-Mar. 10am-4pm. Tours of the castle available Mar.-Oct. every hr. 11am-4pm. Call ahead for a group tour in winter. €15, students €13, children €7; price includes guided tour of the castle.

ON THE MENU

STYRIAN FOOD CHEAT SHEET

Set in a fertile valley, Graz offers fresh and delicious local cuisine unique to the Styrian region. Styrian *(Steier)* food is German, with Mediterranean and Eastern influences. Local dishes of note are *Backhenderl* (crispy fried chicken), *Sterz* (polenta) and *Wurzelfleisch* (cooked pork and vegetables). Mushrooms *(Pilze* or *Schwarmel)* are a particular specialty of the region.

Southeastern Austria is also famous for wines from the countryside. Locally produced whites— *Welschreisling, Weissburgunder, Chardonnay,* and *Sauvingnon blanc,* as well as the West Styrian *Rosé-schilcher,* are all popular selections. While in the countryside eat at a *Buschenschank* (restaurant associated with one of the wineries) to sample the cuisine outdoors, often with a beautiful view. With your wine, try ordering the local classic *Brettljause,* a cold plate with ham, sausage, pickles, cheese, and other cold fixings.

If staying in the city, there are a number of sidewalk cafés and restaurants that take advantage of the well-preserved Renaissance architecture to provide ambiance. On any given night if you wander up the alleyways in the *Altstadt* you're bound to find crowded courtyards with live music—wonderful spots to experience local flavor, in the atmosphere and on your dinner plate.

Schloß Herberstein and the surrounding estate have been in the possession of the Herberstein family ever since the year 1290. As late as 1900 the family controlled one-fifth of the state of Styria. Today they retain "just" this castle and land around it. Traditionally every Herberstein son is name Johann, and every daughter Johanna; the current generation has two Johanns and a Johanna.

The **Herberstein castle** is a fascinating mish-mash of styles—when viewed from the valley below, it appears as a stern fortress rising from the cliffs, but when approached from the top its delicate Renaissance facade makes it seem like a country palace. Tours (50min.) explore the highlights of the castle, including the cellar over the original moat and the Herberstein family museum. The **Tier- und Naturpark** (Animal and Nature Park) includes a small herd of buffalo, wolves, lions, and many other exotic animals in large outdoor pens. Some animals, including the prairie dogs and peacocks, are free to roam. For kids, there's a petting zoo and a small blue-and-white trolley which circles the park. The **historical garden** next to the castle recreates the gardens, while **Sigmund's Garden** showcases the style of gardening popular starting in the Middle Ages. On the 30min. walk that runs down to the valley past the castle, along a cool stream, and back around to the gardens, you can see striking views of the castle and enjoy the wonderfully peaceful surroundings.

STYRIAN WINE COUNTRY

Dominating the Austrian market and competitive throughout Europe, Styrian wine is known for its fruity bouquets and light quality. Try some local varieties in Deutschlandsberg and then visit the *Weinbauschulen,* where the wine is produced.

DEUTSCHLANDSBERG   ☎03462

Deutschlandsberg (pop. 8000) is a resort town tucked in the rolling hills of western Styria, and its blooming flowers and freely flowing wine make it a great place to relax. It's small enough to be quaint but large enough to offer a wealth of eating, drinking, and accommodations options. Sample the local *Schilcher* wine, a dry blush specialty. Easy connections to Graz make Deutschlandsberg an excellent daytrip, but a night in a winery guesthouse is a wonderful experience.

🚆🔧 TRANSPORTATION & PRACTICAL INFORMATION. Trains run from Graz to Deutschlandsberg (dir.: Wies-Eibiswald; 15 per day 5:26am-8:40pm, €6.80). **Buses** also run directly to Deutschlandsberg from Graz Griespl. for the same price (8 per day 6:20am-10:35pm). **By car** from Graz, take A2 to Leiboch, and from there B76 through Stainz toward Weis/Eibiswald.

To get to the **tourist office,** Hauptpl. 37, from the train station, walk straight down the stair and turn right onto Frauentalerstr., then follow the signs; the office is on your left (10min.). The staff provides a hiking and biking map (€7) for western Styria and a free map of the area around Deutschlandsberg. (☎75 20; tourismus.deutschlandsberg@utanet.at. Open Apr.-Oct. M-Tu and Th-F 9am-noon and 3-6pm, W 9am-3pm, Sa 10am-1pm; Nov.-Mar. M-F 9am-3pm, Sa 9am-noon.) There is a free public **bathroom** in the courtyard next to the tourist office, and an **ATM** at the Die Steirmärkische on the far side of the *Rathaus* from the tourist office. (Open 5am-midnight.) The pharmacy **Hirschen Apotheke,** Hauptpl. 5, is in the town center. (Open M-F 8am-12:30pm and 3-6pm, Sa 8am-noon.) The **post office** is at the corner of Fabrikstr. and Frauentalerstr. on the way from the station to the tourist office. (☎46 55 21. Open M-F 8am-12:30pm and 2-5:30pm.) **Postal code:** A-8530.

🍴🛏 ACCOMMODATIONS & FOOD. Pick up the guest information brochure at the tourist office, which includes a list of accommodations. A good choice is **Buschenschank Kästenbauer ❸,** Schloßweg 21a, situated atop a sloping vineyard. From the train station, go right, then right again onto Villenstr., cross the tracks, and go left up the footpath (20min.). Make sure to buy a bottle of the family's wine. Some of these large newly renovated rooms have balcony, and all have TV, shower, and toilet. (☎/fax 29 13. Singles €29; doubles €48. MC/V.)

The best places to eat (and drink) are the *Buschenschanken* along Schloßweg, which runs from the castle to the train station. At the top of the hill is **Stöcklpeter ❷,** Schloßweg 53. A sunny terrace with bright red tablecloths and green and yellow umbrellas offers views of the valley and castle. Traditional food (*Schweinsbraten* €5.50, grill plate €8) is best with a glass of *Schilcher* (€2.40 for 0.25L). (☎28 89. Open Tu-Sa 9am-10pm, Su until 9pm. MC/V.) A cheap and convenient option in town is **China Restaurant Peking ❷,** Hauptpl. 39, which offers filling lunch *Menüs* for €4.80-5.80. (☎26 40. Open M-Tu and Th-Sa 11:30am-2:30pm and 5-11pm.) **Gasthof Koller ❷,** Hauptpl. 10, offers lunch *Menüs* (€7.80-8.40) which are a great way to experience the local cuisine. (☎26 42. Open Tu-Sa 7am-11pm. MC/V.) You can find a **Merkur** on Frauentalerstr. (Turn left from the train station and walk 1 block. Open M-Th 8am-7pm, F 7:30am-7:30pm, Sa 7am-5pm.)

🔆 SIGHTS. The main sight in town is the **Burg Deutschlandsberg,** Burgstr. 19, a 12th-century fortress which now houses the ritzy *Burghotel* and the *Burg* museum. From the tourist office, go down the Hauptpl., take a right up Burgstr., and follow the signs—it's hard to miss. The engaging museum, which focuses on Celtic artifacts and history of the region, is a bit dry, but is revived by a lively Celtic background music and the old-world ambience of the castle. Take the stairs up to the top of the bastion for great views of the town. (☎56 02; burgmuseum@deutschlandsberg.at. Open Mar. to mid-Nov. daily 9:30am-5pm, last entry 4pm. Museum €9, students €8, children €6.) From the castle, head back to town along the Schloßstr., where a number of wineries provide excellent refreshments.

RIEGERSBURG ☎ 03153

This sleepy town, buried in the rolling green hill country east of Graz, might go unnoticed if not for its impressive castle. The **Burg Kronegg** balances on the edge of a steep cliff over vast farmland and misty hills.

▐▛ TRANSPORTATION & PRACTICAL INFORMATION. While Riegersburg is a wonderful destination, it is difficult to get there. It is most accessible on Sundays when you can take the **bus** leaving at 10:05am from the Hauptbahnhof in Graz, then the return bus leaving from Riegersburg at 5:40pm (1½hr., €8). Going on other days is feasible, but requires more precise planning because of the poor bus-train connections. Another bus from Jakminipl. runs during the week (M-F 5:30pm, Sa 12:35pm); however the return bus runs only at pre-dawn hours (5:40am). A train also runs from Graz to Feldbach (1hr., approximately every hr. from 6:18am-10:43pm, €8), where a bus to Riegersburg leaves the bus depot near the train station (20min., 4 per day M-F 6:50am-5:50pm). An €8 ticket purchased on the bus back to Feldbach (7 per day M-F 6:50am-5:50pm) is valid for train connections back to Graz (every hr. 4:20am-8:22pm). By **car,** Riegersburg is an easy 55km trip from Graz. Take A-2 and get off at the Ilz Exit, then follow the signs. The main **tourist office,** at the beginning of the trail to the castle (turn right after the Sparkasse across the Lasslhof), helps to find Pensionen and Privatzimmer. (☎86 70; www.riegersburg.com. Open M-F 11am-5pm.) If you are in Riegersburg when the tourist office is closed, pick up brochures and information at the store next door. A free public **toilet** is at the bus lot downhill from Lasslhof. An **ATM** is at Raiffeisenbank, Riegersburg 30. **Postal code:** A-8333.

▐▛ ACCOMMODATIONS & FOOD. Guesthouses in town charge €30 for doubles, while *Privatzimmer* are around €20. Be aware, there is a fee for one-night stays (€2.50-4). **Lassifhof ❸,** at the Riegersburg bus stop, is a yellow hotel with a popular bar/restaurant and an extensive art collection in the halls between the rooms. Eat some *Wienerschnitzel* with potatoes and salad (€6.20) at the restaurant downstairs or snack on *Frankfurter mit Gulaschsaft* (€3.50). (☎82 01 or 82 01. Breakfast included. Restaurant open 7am-10pm. Reception 7am-midnight. €18.50 per person, with bath and TV €27. €4 fee for 1-night stays; €4 extra for a single.) Stock up on groceries at **SPAR,** just downhill from Lasslhof on the main road. (Open M-F 6:30am-6pm, Sa 6:30am-noon.)

◪ SIGHTS: BURG KRONEGG. Riegersburg relies heavily on the revenue from tourists awestruck by the well-preserved remains of **Burg Kronegg.** Attackers never got inside, but tourists can, after tackling the steep, stone-paved path to the castle (20min.). Bring sturdy shoes and bottled water. Or you can simply turn left from the bus stop, walk up the road to the edge of town, and pay €2 to be lifted to the top by the *Seilbahn.* Lush vineyards clothe the castle slopes, while cypresses peek out in the distance. You can circle the castle and climb the *Eselstiege* (donkey stairs) by heading past the turn-off to the tourist office and turning right at the cemetery, and right at the sign to "Seilbahn Garten." As legend has it, these stairs were built when the owner of Burg Kronegg and his younger brother were feuding. The younger brother, who lived in the (now nonexistent) Schloss Lichtenegg at the base of the mountain, cut off the food and water supply to the top so that his brother had to create another way out of the castle. On your way up, look for an inconspicuous crescent moon carved into the stone wall to mark the highest point reached by invading Turks. Take a good look at the elaborate iron pattern covering the well in the castle's second courtyard—it's said that any woman who can spot a horseshoe within the design will find her knight in shining armor within a year. In the shadow of the castle chirps the **Greifvogelwarte Riegersburg,** showcasing birds of prey. *(☎73 90. Shows in German M-Sa 11am, 3pm, Su 11am, 2, 4pm. Entrance 30min. before the show. €6, students €4.)*

The castle houses two museums, which run together. The **Burgmuseum** showcases 16 of the castle's rooms, with a focus on the history of the castle and the region. Includes an exhibit on a period in the 17th century, when witch persecution in the area reached its pinnacle and also when the castle was enlarged to its present size. Several rooms are devoted to the story of Katherina "Green Thumb" Pardauff, executed in 1676 for supposedly causing flowers to bloom in the middle of winter. Also displayed is the life of the "legendary woman" Katherina Elisabeth von Gallerin, the lady castle builder/owner who outlived her three husbands. The **Weiße Saal** (White Hall), with its stucco ceiling flourishes and crystal chandeliers, works well along with the museum's video of waltzing dancers in decolleté gowns in one of the several impressive multimedia displays. The **Hexenmuseum** (Witch Museum) spreads over 12 more rooms, with an exhibit on Feldbach's witch trial (1673-1675), the biggest in Styria's history. The exhibit includes historical details explaining what lead to the witch hysteria, as well as an Iron Maiden and other artifacts from the time period. *(☎83 46. Open Apr.-Oct. daily 9am-5pm. Tours of the Burgmuseum 10am, 12:30, 3pm; of the Hexenmuseum 11am, 1:30pm. English tours available upon request. €9.50; students and children €7.)*

ADMONT ☎03613

Admont (pop. 2800), gateway to the Gesäuse alpine region, lies on the border of Styria and Upper Austria, along the Enns River. The rural town is most famous for the library in its Benedictine monastery—the largest monastic library in the world. Gorgeous mountain scenery provides an added perk on the way to the library.

▰▱ TRANSPORTATION & PRACTICAL INFORMATION. Trains run from **Selzthal,** the regional hub, to Admont (15min., 5:45am-7:23pm, €3.20). Get to Selzthal from Linz (2hr., 6:15am-4:17pm, €16.70) or Bruck an der Mur (switch trains in Leoben, trains from there are 5 per day 7:27am-3:27pm, €6.40). **Buses** to Linz depart from the post office and marketplace. For **taxis,** call ☎28 01. The Admont train station desk is open M-Sa 5:30am-7:30pm, Su 7am-7:30pm. To reach the **tourist office** from the train station, head left down Bahnhofstr., then turn right onto Haupstr. The office will be on your left after the church. Staff finds rooms free of charge and offers activity information. They also have a free map of Admont made from an aerial photograph of the town. (☎21 64; fax 36 48. Open May-Oct. M-F 8am-noon and 2-6pm, Sa 9am-noon; Nov.-Apr. M 8am-noon, Tu-F 8am-noon and 2-6pm.) **Currency exchange** and a 24hr. **ATM** are available at Raiffeisenbank, just past the tourist office on Hauptstr. (☎21 32. Open M-F 8am-noon and 2:30-4:30pm.) The Stiftsapotheke **pharmacy** is accessible through the abbey courtyard; enter by the church and turn right. (☎223 60. Open M-F 8am-noon and 2:30-6pm, Sa 8am-noon, and for emergencies. In **medical emergencies** call ☎23 47.) To reach the **post office,** head to your left from the train station—it's at the corner of Haupstr. on the way to the tourist office. (☎22 41. Open M-F 8am-noon and 2:30-5:30pm, exchange closes at 5pm.) **Postal code:** A-8911.

▰▱ ACCOMMODATIONS & FOOD. Normally one of the best places to stay in Admont is **Schloß Röthelstein,** the youth hostel located nearby in a 330-year-old castle. However, the hostel will be closed until May of 2005 for renovations. Instead, try the lovely and well-kept **Frühstückspension Mafalda ❸,** Bachpromenade 75. At the post office, turn left and cross the train tracks, then make the next two rights and cross the tracks again. Mafalda is right under the tracks, only a few minutes from the town center. (☎21 88. Breakfast, TV, and hall showers included. €20.35 per person; €21.80 for 1-night stays.) A little farther afield but with great amenities and comfortable rooms is **Gästehaus Burghart ❸**, Sonnenweg 272. Exit the tourist office and walk left down Hauptstr. At the blue "Hallenbad" sign, turn left, cross the stream, and take a right onto Wagnerstr. Continue down Wagnerstr., before going right onto Sonnenweg—the house will be down the street on the left. (☎22 59. Breakfast included. Bath and TV in room. Singles €18.17-21.80; doubles €29.07. €1.45 surcharge in winter, 20% surcharge for stays of less than 3 nights.)

There are a number of good restaurants in Admont. To get to **Gasthaus Kamper ❷**, head down Hauptstr. for several blocks; the restaurant will be on your right. Kamper offers good service, a local crowd, and large portions. (Salad bar buffet €2.30-4.50; entrees €8-12. Open Tu-Su 8:30am-midnight. AmEx/MC/V.) **Stiftskeller ❸** in the monastery, is a modern restaurant on the higher end of the prices spectrum. (☎33 54; www.stiftskeller-admont.at. 3-course *Menü* for €15-20. AmEx/MC/V.) For groceries, head to **ADEG**, across from the church. (Open M-F 7:30am-6pm, Sa 7am-noon.)

◪◨ SIGHTS & OUTDOOR ACTIVITIES. Admont is best known for its **Benediktinerstift** (Benedictine abbey), founded in 1088 and currently staffed by 26 monks. To get there, head to the church, then take a right to the courtyard behind it. The abbey's library, the largest monastic library in the world, contains over 200,000 precious leather-bound volumes as well as 1400 manuscripts, some dating back to the 8th century. With pink marble, glimmering statues, and frescoed ceilings, the building is a Baroque masterpiece. (☎231 26 01. Open Apr.-Nov. daily 10am-5pm; Dec.-Mar. Th-F 10am-noon. Guided tours 11am, 3pm; available in English if you call ahead. English info sheets €0.40. €8, students €4. Tours €1.80.)

While in Admont, you might want to try one of the leisurely hikes around the valley. An easy walk starting from the train station heads past the swimming pool and down the **Kajetan-Promenade,** where oaks over 400 years old grow, to the nature park **Eichelau** (30min.). For a longer excursion, try the 1½hr. hike on the bike path running along the river, with good views of the nearby mountains. To get to the path, head down Hauptstr. until you reach the Fleischerei. Turn right and follow signs for the R7 bike path, which eventually loops back to the beginning. The **Naturbad,** less than a 5min. walk from the train station, is a great place to swim outdoors. The non-chlorinated pool is refreshingly cool, and includes a diving board, shallow area for kids, and volleyball courts. To get there from the train station, face away from the tracks, turn left, then go right onto Friedhofsweg and follow the signs. (Open 9:30am-7pm in good weather. €2.90.)

LEOBEN ☎03842

The buckle of Austria's "Iron Belt," Leoben (pop. 30,000) lies between rolling green hills and the Mur River. Now more modern metropolis than small town, Leoben provides both a little urbanity and outdoor activities. There's also an ancient church, the Gösser beer brewery, and an idyllic city park, Am Glacis. The large town square is ringed with both elaborate old (though slightly run-down) buildings and sleek modern ones. Beyond the narrow city streets, forest trails lead into the green countryside that gave the town its name: Liubina, or "lovely region."

◪◨◫ TRANSPORTATION, ORIENTATION, & PRACTICAL INFORMATION. The train station has an **information counter.** (☎425 45, ext. 390. Open M-F 9am-6pm.) **Trains** arrive from: Graz (1hr., every 2hr. 6:42am-8pm, €9.20); Klagenfurt (2hr., every hr. 1:48am-8:30pm, €20.80); Salzburg (3½hr., 3:45am-8:19pm,

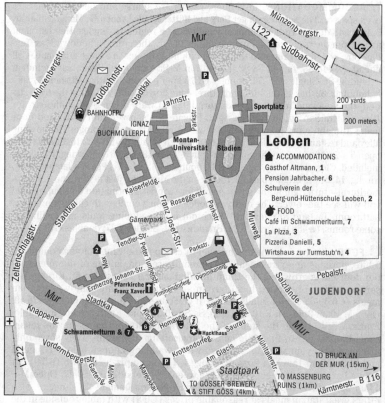

Leoben

▲ ACCOMMODATIONS
Gasthof Altmann, 1
Pension Jahrbacher, 6
Schulverein der
  Berg-und-Hüttenschule Leoben, 2
🍴 FOOD
Café im Schwammerlturm, 7
La Pizza, 3
Pizzeria Danielli, 5
Wirtshaus zur Turmstub'n, 4

€27.70), and Vienna Sudbahnhof (2hr., every 2hr. 6:57am-10:45pm, €22.30). From smaller destinations such as Mariazell, take the **bus** to Bruck an der Mur and then take the train to Leoben (15min., 1 per hr. 6:12am-12:55pm, €3.20). For local connections, the main **bus station** in Leoben is a 10min. walk from the train station; turn right onto Parkstr. from Franz Josef-Str. just before Hauptpl. Leoben is just minutes from Autobahn A9, which runs south to Graz and northwest to Steyr and Linz; take the exit for Leoben. Head straight out of the train station and cross the Mur river, and you'll be on **Franz Josef-Straße,** the main traffic artery of Leoben. Continue straight and you'll reach the center of town, the **Hauptplatz.** The **tourist office** will be on the right. (☎440 18; www.leoben.at. Open M 7am-5pm, Tu-F 7am-6:30pm, Sa 9am-12:30pm.) There are **ATMs** at the post office and Raiffeisenbank, Hauptpl. 15. (Open M-Th 8am-noon and 2-4:30pm, F 8am-noon and 2-3:30pm.) A **parking garage** is under Hauptpl. with an entrance on Langg.; turn left off Franz-Josef-Str. onto Dominikanerg. (€1.40 per hr., €13 for a whole day.) Services include: **lockers** in the train station (€2); free **public restroom** in the parking garage, accessible from the elevator in the center of Hauptpl. (open M-Sa 7am-8pm, Su 8am-6pm); **taxis** at stand by the train station (☎17 18); and **hospital** (☎401). The **post office** is at Erzherzog-Johann-Str. 17, the last right off Franz Josef Str. before Hauptpl. (☎42 47 40. Open M-F 8am-7pm, Sa 8-10am.) **Postal code:** A-8701.

⚑ ACCOMMODATIONS. in Leoben, rooms are sparse and budget rooms are even sparser. The **Schulverein der Berg-und-Hüttenschule Leoben ❸**, Max-Tendlerstr. 3, rents 48 double rooms, some of which can be rented as singles. Head straight away from the train station down Franz Josef-Str., then turn right down Max Tendler-Str., which will run into the hostel (10min.). Rooms are large and plain. Call ahead. (☎448 88; fax 44 88 83. Reception M-Sa 7am-4pm. Breakfast included, excluding Su. Singles €17.71; doubles €15.53 per person.) **Gasthof Altmann ❸**, Südbahnhofstr. 32, has 12 doubles and a three-lane bowling alley. Exiting the train station, facing away from the tracks, turn left and walk down Südbahnhofstr. for 10min.; Altmann will be on the right. Private TV, shower, and hardwood floor make Altmann more luxurious than most hotels in this price range. The bowling alley and restaurant (meals €6.50-14.50) fill with locals. (☎/fax 422 16. **Bowling alley** open Tu-Sa 10am-midnight, Su 10am-3pm. €1 for 12min. Free parking. Breakfast included. Closed late July. Singles €28; doubles €48. MC/V.) **Pension Jahrbacher ❹**, Kirchg. 14, offers bright spacious rooms on the Mur river, just next to the Schwammerlturm—turn right at the street just before tourist information on Hauptpl. and you will see the tower. The newly remodeled rooms come with chic decorations, bathroom, TV, and refrigerator. Watch out for the sloping walls and ceilings in some rooms. (☎436 00; fax 273 83. Breakfast €4. Singles €37; doubles €70.)

🍴 FOOD. Kirchg. is home to a number of cheap restaurants, or you could grab a bite, perhaps an extravagent *Eis* (-cream) creation, at one of the numerous out-door cafés crowding the Hauptpl. **Wirsthaus zur Turmstub'n ❷**, Kirchg. 7-9, serves reasonably priced local fare in an Austrian setting. Enjoy vegetarian meals (€6.50-6.90) and salads (€3-6), if you can stand a little smoke. (☎426 49. Open M 10am-2pm, Tu-F 10am-10pm, Sa-Su 10am-5pm. English menu available. AmEx/MC/V.) Climb the steps of the Schwammerlturm (named for its mushroom-like shape) to find **Café im Schwarmmelturm** at the top. They serve only drinks, so sip your wine or espresso while watching Leoben below. (Open M and W-Su 10am-1am.) **La Pizza ❷**, Langg.1, has large pizzas for two (€5-9) but only a bar at which to eat—take a pie to enjoy riverside. (☎453 47. Open M-F 11am-2pm and 5-10pm, Sa-Su 11am-10pm.) **Pizzeria Danielli ❷**, Langg. 8, also offers great Italian meals at reasonable prices (€6-8) with tables outside in the pedestrian zone and inside the decorated dining area. (Open M-Sa 10am-midnight, Su 10am-10pm.) Get some groceries at the **markets** along Franz Josef-Str.; **Billa** supermarket in the basement of the shopping arcade, Josef-Grafg. 6 (open M-W 8am-7pm, Th 7:30am-7pm, F 7:30am-7:30pm, Sa 7:30am-5pm); or the **farmers' market** on Kirchpl. (Tu and F 7am-1pm).

◉ ◪ SIGHTS & ENTERTAINMENT. Most of Leoben's attractions center around **Hauptplatz**, 10min. from the train station (cross the bridge and bear right onto Franz Josef-Str.). Sights are designated by a square sign with an ostrich eating iron horseshoes. The symbol alludes to Leoben's robust iron trade: in the Middle Ages, ostriches were thought to be capable of eating and digesting iron.

Most of the buildings on Hauptpl. are former homes of the *Hammerherren* (Hammer men)—the men who made their wealth from the iron mines in the region. The most ornate of the bunch is the 1680 **Hacklhaus**, Hauptpl. 9, which bears a dozen statues on its red-and-white facade. Justice holds a sword and a balance, Hope brandishes an anchor, and Wisdom views the world—all backwards—through the mirror in his hand. Standing guard at the center of Hauptpl. is a beautifully crafted monument erected to ward off the fires and plague that devastated much of Styria in the early 18th century. Look for St. Florian the fire-proof and St.

Rosalia the plague-resistant. Just outside Hauptpl. is the **Pfarrkirche Franz Xaver,** a rust-colored church whose elaborate interior is dominated by black-and-gold decorations. Go through the Kreuzgang to see 14 paintings of the stations of the cross.

Don't miss the chance to inspect the **Gösser brewery,** Brauhausg. 1. To get to Göss, take bus #2 from Franz Josef-Str., or walk south down Gösser Str. along the Mur in the sun (45min.). The brewery's slogan, plastered throughout Austria, is *Gut, Besser, Gösser* (Good, Better, Gösser). Examine antique brewing machinery and swill down a free stein of fresh brew. (☎20 90 58 02. Museum open Apr.-Oct. Sa-Su 9am-6pm. Tours 11am, 1, 3pm. €3.60, students €1.80.) In Göss, see Styria's oldest abbey, the **Stift Göss,** founded in 1000. (☎221 48. Open 8am-noon. Call ahead for tours.) The **Stadttheater,** Homanng. 5, is the oldest functioning theater in Austria, completed in 1790. (☎406 23 02. Advance tickets at Zentralkartenbüro, or 1hr. before performances at box office. Theater closed June-Sept.) June and July bring the **Leobener Kultursommer,** a program of theater, concerts, literary readings, and treasure hunts. Tickets at the Zentralkartenbüro in the tourist office. (Open M 9:30am-12:30pm and 3-5pm, Tu-F 9am-12:30pm and 3-6:30pm, Sa 9am-12:30pm.)

To wander away from Leoben, use hiking maps from the tourist office. A 30min. hike begins at the Stadtpark and leads to the **Massenburg ruins.** The castle was torn down in 1820, but its 13th-century gate building still stands. For a longer excursion, try the relatively easy 3hr. **hike** from the Massenburg Ruins East to the Hans Prost Haus, which offers a wonderful view of the valley.

⚄ DAYTRIP FROM LEOBEN

EISENERZ   ☎03848

Take a bus from Leoben (1 hr., 12 per day 6:30am-8:43pm, €5.40). By car, take 146 from Liezen or 115 from Leoben.

The skyline of the strip-mining town Eisenerz is dominated by the astounding *Erz*berg, an orange-and-maroon tower of stone. Supposedly, the iron was a gift from a merman who lived in a grotto not far from town. The villagers formed a clever plot to capture him, and as exchange for his release he offered them 10 years of silver, 100 of gold, or iron forever. The men chose iron, and that was the beginning of the prosperous mining center.

The **tourist office,** Freiheitspl. 7, is located in a kiosk on the main square. (☎37 00; www.eisenerz-heute.at. Open May-Oct. M-F 9am-1pm and 3-5pm, Nov.-Apr. M-F 10:30am-noon and 3-5pm.) A free **public toilet** is next to the fountain in the Bergmannpl. A youth hostel, **Jugend und Familiengastedorf Eisenerz ❸,** is scheduled to open in summer 2003. Around 5km from the city center, it will offer many amenities. (☎605 60; fax 03 16 70 83 88. €18.30 per person.)

The pyramid of the **Erzberg** is a powerful monument to mining. (From the tourist office, head straight out across Freiheitspl., turn left onto Hieflauerstr., then left again up to Bergmannpl. Continue across the square to the street branching off at the upper right, then make the next right to the Erzberg. 15min.) After donning a yellow helmet and slicker, you'll be ready for action on two possible tours. The **Schaubergwerk** takes you on a train deep inside the mountain and demonstrates how dynamite is used in mining. You'll also see mining at the entrance to the tunnels, where rock is ground in a huge mortar. The other tour is the **Hauly Abenteuerfahrt,** in which you ride up the mountain in a huge dump truck designed to transport tons of stone from the mines. A ride in one of the "largest taxis in the world" certainly provide a unique way to see Eisenerz. (☎32 00; info@abenteur-erzber.at. Open daily May-Oct.; tours 10am-

3pm. German-language tours of the Schaubergwerk 10am, 12:30, 3pm. Calling ahead for the Hauly ride is recommended. 1½hr. tour of Schaubergwerk or the 1hr. Hauly ride €13, students and children €6.50; combined ticket €22, students and children €11.)

To enjoy your natural surroundings there are a number of **hikes** from Eisenerz into the mountains. Pick up a map at the tourist office, or head straight down the road from the bus stop to a parking lot just past the hospital. In about 2½hr., you can hike from the parking lot to the Urlaubskreuz and then descend to the Leopoldsteiner See. From there you can either take the bus back to Eisenerz or return the way you came.

In winter time the Präblich ski area and its eight lifts come to life. Take the bus in the direction of Leoben; there is a shop right at the base of the main lift. Ski rental and ski courses available from the base. (☎ 066 42 06 65 20.)

MARIAZELL ☎ 03882

The little town of Mariazell, somewhat extravagantly subtitled *Gnadenzentrum Europas* (Europe's Center of Mercy), is both an active resort and pilgrimage site. While many come for lazy walks, hikes, skiing in the Bürgeralpe, or a dip in the nearby Erlaufsee, the faithful and needy come to pay homage to a shrine—the miracle-working Madonna made of linden wood. (See "Legend of Mariazell," below.)

LEGEND OF MARIAZELL In the year 1157, a monk named Magnus was sent to convert the natives of the region. Magnus rode north through Styria for days without seeing a soul. The only possessions he brought were his horse and a carved wooden statue of the Virgin Mary. When Magnus finally encountered other travelers, he was at first overjoyed, but later dismayed to find they were thieves. Just past midnight, he had a vision of the Virgin Mary sitting on the crescent moon holding the infant Jesus. She warned that he must go immediately and take with him the statue of her. He raced down the mountain with the robbers hot on his heels, only to be stopped by a wall of stone. Magnus said a prayer, and a crack opened up in the cliff just large enough so that he could slip through to safety. He emerged in a lovely green valley populated by friendly woodsmen and decided to place the miraculous statue on a tree trunk. Thus was the beginning of Mariazell as a center of mercy.

▣ TRANSPORTATION

While Mariazell may be a nice destination, it takes some determination to get there. The town is accessible from St. Pölten by the mountain **train** Mariazellerbahn (2½hr., 5 per day 7:25am-3:22pm, €11.30). However, the **train station** is actually in the neighboring St. Sebastian. From the station, face away from the tracks, turn right down Erlaufseestr., and uphill onto Wiener Str., to the town center, Hauptpl. (20min). Buses stop right near the center of town and connect Mariazell to: Bruck an der Mur (1¾hr., 5 per day 5:15am-6:15pm, €8); Graz (3hr., 4 per day 5:45am-6:10pm, €14.80); Vienna (4hr.; 5:53am, 4pm; €14.80). The **bus station** is down the steps below the post office, but for bus information, inquire in the post office or ask waiting bus drivers for times and rates. To reach Mariazell **by car** from Graz, take Rte. S-35 north to Bruck an der Mur, then Rte. S-6 to Rte. 20 north over Aflenz-Kurort and Seeberg-Sattel. From Vienna, take Autobahn A-1 west to St. Pölten, and exit onto Rte. 20 south (1hr.), over Lilienberg and Annaberg.

⚡🛈 ORIENTATION & PRACTICAL INFORMATION

The **tourist office** is at Hauptpl. 13, just uphill from the basilica. To get there from the bus stop, face away from the station and head left on Ludwig-Leber-Str., then left again on Grazer Str., and you'll get to the Hauptpl. (5min.). (☎23 66; www.mariazell.at. Open May-Sept. M-F 9am-12:30pm and 2-5:30pm, Sa 9am-12:30pm and 2-4pm, Su 10am-12:30pm; Oct.-Apr. M-F 9am-12:30pm and 2-5pm, Sa 9am-12:30pm; closed Sa-Su in Apr. and Nov.) The **train station** is at Erlaufseestr. 19. (☎22 30. Open daily 7:30am-6:20pm.) **Lockers** are available at the bus station (€1). Services include: **currency exchange** and **ATM** at the Raiffeisenbank (turn right from Wienerstr. at Hauptpl.; open M-F 8am-noon and 2-4pm, Sa 8-11am); **pharmacy** Apotheke zur Gnadenmutter at Hauptpl. 4 (☎21 02; open M-F 8am-noon and 2-6pm, Sa 8am-noon, Su 9:30am-12:30pm); St. Sebastian **Hospital,** Spitalg. 4 (☎22 22); **emergency assistance** (☎144); and **Internet-Café,** Hauptpl. 8 (☎37 13; open Sept.-June M-Sa 8am-11pm, Su 10am-11pm; July-Aug. M-Tu and Th-Sa 9am-11pm, W and Su 3-11pm; €1.50 for 15min., €2.50 for 30min., €4 per hr.). The **post office** is downhill from the tourist office; turn right in front of Xing Long and head downhill. (☎25 51. Open M-F 8am-12:30pm and 2-6pm.) **Postal code:** A-8630.

🛏 ACCOMMODATIONS

Sportzentrum-Jugend und Familiengästedorf (HI), Erlaufseestr. 49 (☎26 69; fax 26 69 88). From the train station, face away from the tracks, turn left, and walk about 5min. (30-40min total). Colorful modern apartment-style rooms and lots of amenities make the walk worthwhile. Amenities include: **Internet** (coin operated), restaurant (8am-11pm), **climbing wall,** sauna (€8) and steam bath (€5.80), squash (M-F €4.35 per 30min., Sa-Su €5.45) and tennis courts (M-F €8.70 per hr.; rackets €2); bike rental (€3.50 per half day, €7 per whole day); and a fitness studio (€4.35). Room with 2-4 beds in winter €23, otherwise €21.50 per person; singles €27/€24.50. Under 3 nights €2.50 fee. MC/V. ❸

Pension Zechner, Wienerstr. 25 (☎60 40; fax 60 40 20). Head downhill from the tourist office and to the right. Small, bright rooms (all with bathroom), many of which have balcony for taking in the view. Common room with TV and small video library. Breakfast included. Singles €21.80, doubles €43.60; €22.53/€45.03 in winter. ❸

THE LOCAL LEGEND

THE "TEURO"

If everything seems more expensive in Austria than it was a few years ago, their new currency is at least partly to blame. Termed the "Teuro" by many Austrians, (punning on teuer, German for "expensive"), the Euro replaced Austria's Schilling on July 1, 2002. Though the transition was without major incident, it hasn't stopped people from grumbling. "It was bloody easy for the shopkeepers to change the prices," complains one Austrian expatriate. "They just rounded everything up." While most people were willing to pay a few extra cents here and there, some increases were harder to swallow. "In many places, they simply divided all the prices by ten and called that price in euros," explained a retired school teacher in Vorarlberg. What initially sounds reaonable seems outrageous once you realize the actual conversion rate was 13.7 Schilllings per Euro. Merchants who chose to divide by ten upped prices 37% literally overnight. "I guess we should consider ourselves lucky," a student buying soda said. "In Germany they used to sell Coke for DM1 in some places. Now it's €1, which is twice as much. And it's hurting those who can least afford it the most." Though the runaway inflation of the first few months has come to a halt, the budget traveler will notice that a euro just doesn't go as far as it used to.

Haus Zach, Wiener Neustädter Str. 29 (☎22 72), is slightly more rustic and lies on the edge of Mariazell. A 10min. walk past the tourist office up Wiener Neustädter Str. leads to this large white house with red flower window boxes in a field on the left. Large rooms and balconies with views of the valley create a peaceful atmosphere. Breakfast and TV included. Hall bathrooms. €15.50 per person, €3.50 fee for 1-night stays. ❸

🍴 FOOD

There is a **Billa** Supermarket on Wienerstr. 4. (Open M-W 8am-7pm, th 7:30am-7pm, F 7:30am-7:30pm, Sa 7:30am-6pm, Su 8am-4pm.)

Wirtshaus Brauerei, Wienerstr. 5 (☎25 23), occupying the oldest building in town, celebrates its age with home-brewed beer (large €2.75, small €2.10) and large pretzels (€1.25). Main dishes of schnitzel and sausage €7-9. Tours available M-W and F-Su, no groups on weekends. Open M-Sa 10am-midnight, Su 10am-2pm. MC/V. ❷

Hotel Goldener Löwe, Hauptpl. 1a (☎24 44), just downhill from the tourist office, lets you sit on the terrace overlooking Hauptpl. while sipping homemade mead (*Met,* €1.50), nectar of the gods. Serves Italian and Austrian dishes and fancy *Eis* concotions, but the real reason to visit is the **1st-floor bathrooms.** A rock- and plant-filled waterfall runs on the wall, a map of constellations lights up as you enter, and each stall is equipped with a 15min. hourglass. Open Tu-Sa 9am-7pm. ❸

Radlwirt, Wiener Neustädter Str. 6 (☎27 31), just up Wiener Neustädter Str. from the tourist office. Offers live music from the owner, whose keyboard is set up in the corner. Austrian dishes ranging from €7-9. Open 8am-10pm; hours may vary in winter. ❷

Goldenes Kreuz, Wienerstr. 7 (☎23 09), boasts simple, elegant decor including white tableclothes in the candle-lit interior. Enjoy fresh fish entrees and traditional dishes (€7-14). Open daily 11am-2pm and 6-10:30pm. ❸

👁 🏔 SIGHTS & OUTDOOR ACTIVITIES

BASILIKA MARIAZELL. Over the years, this town has welcomed millions of devout Christians who come to see the Madonna within the basilica. The building's black spires are visible from anywhere in town. EmprTheresaess Maria Theresa took her first communion in Mariazell and donated the silver and gold grille that encloses the Gnadenaltar (Mercy Altar) with the Madonna. There are 10-15 services a day for the flocks of pilgrims from Austria and eastern Europe. (☎ 259 50; www.basilika-mariazell.at. Open daily 6am-8pm. Free tours by appointment through the Superiorat, Kardinal-Tisserant-Pl. 1.) The church's amazing *Schatzkammer* (treasure chamber) holds former pilgrims' gifts, ranging from paintings and embroidery from the grateful cured to a pearl rosary given by Pope John Paul II upon his pilgrimage to Mariazell in 1983. Behind the church you'll find the *Kerzengrotte* (candle grotto), where you can buy a candle for €0.75. (Open May-late Oct. Tu-Sa 10am-3pm, Su 11am-3pm. €3, students €1.50, children €1.)

OUTDOOR ACTIVITIES. A cable car at Wienerstr. 24 zips to the top of the Bürgeralpe. (☎ 25 55. Every 20min. Jan.-Mar. 8am-5pm; May-Oct. 9am-5pm; Dec. 8am-4pm. Ascent €6.50, round-trip €9; children €5/€6.) Four ski lifts provide access to the nearby ski slopes and hiking trails. (Open Dec.-Mar. 8am-5pm. 1-day pass €23, children €11.50; 2-day €43, children €21.50.) For ski information, call the Mariazell tourist office or contact the **Ski- und Snowboardschule,** Hauptpl. 12. (☎ 27 20. Courses M-Sa 10am-noon and

1:30-3:30pm. 1-day course €28.) In warmer weather, wander Mariazell's hiking trails. Two types of maps *(€2.18 and €4.20)* are available from the tourist office. You might also consider taking a swim in the crystal clear **Erlaufsee,** a tiny lake surrounded by a white pebble beach. *(From the town center, take the Hans Wertnek Promenade (5km), or catch the city bus from the postampt to the Erlaufsee Herrenhaus stop. 10min., 7 per day May-Oct. 8am-4:45pm, €0.80.)*

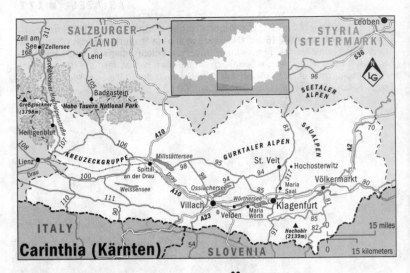

Carinthia (Kärnten)

CARINTHIA (KÄRNTEN)

The province of Carinthia covers the southernmost part of Austria, jutting between East Tyrol and Salzburger Land in the west and reaching into the Hohe Tauern National Park and the Glocknergruppe mountain range.

Carinthia is best known for its sunny climate, Italian architecture, and laid-back atmosphere, which combine to give the province a Mediterranean feel. Natives consider Carinthia a vacation paradise, thanks to its warm lakesides. There are nearly 200 lakes in the region, including the **Wörthersee, Ossiachersee, Faakersee,** and **Millstättersee.** In addition to the lakes, abbeys and castles dot the hillsides. If you're in Carinthia for awhile, consider investing in a **Kärnten Card,** good for up to two weeks of unlimited local transportation, free admission to over 100 area sights and museums, and discounts on many cable cars, boat cruises, toll roads, stores, and restaurants. (€32, ages 5-16 €13, under 8 free.)

HIGHLIGHTS OF CARINTHIA

Escape to **Velden,** on the warm, sunny shores of the **Wörthersee** (see p. 185).

Travel the (mini-) world in Klagenfurt's **Minimundus** amusement park (see p. 183).

Admire the view from the impressive medieval castle in **Hochosterwitz** (see p. 184).

KLAGENFURT   ☎ 0463

On the eastern edge of the idyllic Wörthersee, Klagenfurt (pop. 92,000) is a major summer destination for Austrian travelers. Austria's southernmost provincial capital now attracts thousands of Germanic tourists, who unwind in its beachfront suburbs on the lake. The Wörthersee is the warmest lake in the Alps, and serves as Europe's largest skating arena in winter. Italian Renaissance courtyards and espressos in outdoor cafés characterize the pace of life in and around Klagenfurt.

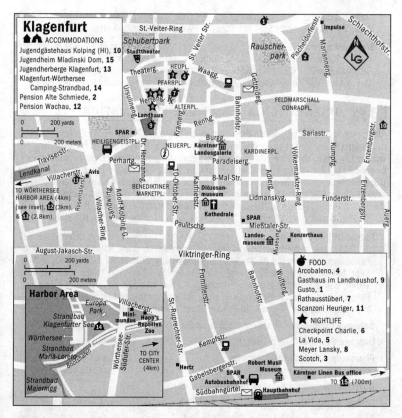

Klagenfurt

♠♣ ACCOMMODATIONS

Jugendgästehaus Kolping (HI), **10**
Jugendheim Mladinski Dom, **15**
Jugendherberge Klagenfurt, **13**
Klagenfurt-Wörthersee
    Camping-Strandbad, **14**
Pension Alte Schmiede, **2**
Pension Wachau, **12**

● FOOD
Arcobaleno, 4
Gasthaus im Landhaushof, 9
Gusto, 1
Rathausstüberl, 7
Scanzoni Heuriger, 11

★ NIGHTLIFE
Checkpoint Charlie, 6
La Vida, 5
Meyer Lansky, 8
Scotch, 3

TRANSPORTATION

Trains: Hauptbahnhof (☎17 17), at the intersection of Südbahngürtel and Bahnhofstr. Open daily 5:15am-7:30pm; after hours use the fare machine. To: **Graz** via Bruck an der Mur (3hr., 16 per day 1:48am-6:50pm, €27.70); **Lienz** (2hr., 5 per day 3:06am-8:51pm, €18.10); **Salzburg** (3½hr., 8 per day 3:06am-4:20pm, €26.10); **Vienna Südbahnhof** (4hr., 17 per day 1:48am-8:30pm, €24.80); **Villach** (30min., 2-3 per hr. 12:16am-11:42pm, €5.10); **Innsbruck** (5hr., 11 per day 3:06am-10:01pm, €37.30).

Buses: Autobusbahnhof (☎05 17 17, Central Bus info ☎01 711 01; www.oebb.at). Buses depart from the Autobusbahnhof to most destinations in Carinthia, including **Graz** (2½hr., 3 per day 8:10am-8:15pm, €14.90) and **Villach** (1¼hr., 7 per day 8:10am-6:15pm, €5.96). Ticket window open M-F 7:30-11am and 11:30am-3:30pm. Buy tickets either at the Autobusbahnhof ticket window or aboard the bus.

By car: Klagenfurt lies on A2 from the west, Rte. 91 from the south, Rte. 70 from the east, and Rte. 317 from the north. From **Vienna** or **Graz**, take A2 south to Rte. 70 west.

Public Transportation: Klagenfurt's **bus** system is punctual and comprehensive. The tourist office can provide a *Fahrplan* (bus schedule); the central bus station is at Heiligengeistpl. Buy single tickets (€1.50) or a 24hr. pass (€3.30) from the driver, or a weekly pass (€13) from a bus stop machine. *Tabak* kiosks sell cut-rate blocks of tickets. Illegal riders risk a €60 fine. City bus lines #40-42 leave from the train station.

Car Rental: Hertz, St. Ruprechterstr. 12 (☎561 47). Open M-F 8am-5pm, Sa 9am-noon. **Avis,** Villacherstr. 1c (☎559 38). Open M-F 8am-4:30pm, Sa 9am-noon.

Bike Rental: Impulse (☎51 63 10) has 6 stores, including the main store at Pischeldorfer Str. 20 (☎51 63 10; open daily 8am-6pm), Neuer Pl. 8 (☎537 22 23), and Campingpl. See (☎211 69). €4 per 5hr., €8 per day; mountain bikes €8/€14. Helmets €1-2. The tourist office distributes the pamphlet *Radwandern* detailing local bike paths.

◼️🛈 ORIENTATION & PRACTICAL INFORMATION

Alterplatz, Neuer Platz, and **Heiligengeistplatz,** the town's bus center, comprise the heart of the city and the center of tourist and commercial activity. They lie within the **Ring,** the inner district of Klagenfurt, the central commercial activity, bordered by St. Veiter Ring, Völkermarkter Ring, Viktringer Ring, and Villacher Ring. Streets within the Ring generally run in a north-south/east-west grid. **Villacherstraße** runs along the **Lendkanal** (canal), stretching 3.5km from the city center to the Wörthersee. To get to the center of the city from the station, follow Bahnhofstr. to Paradeiserg. and turn left; Neuer Pl. is two blocks down on the right.

Tourist Office: Gäste Information is on the first floor of the Rathaus in Neuer Pl. (☎537 22 933; www.info.klagenfurt.at). From the station, go down Bahnhofstr. and left on Paradeiserg., into Neuer Pl. The staff organizes daily tours of the *Altstadt*. (Open May-Sept. M-F 8am-8pm, Sa-Su 10am-5pm; Oct.-Apr. M-F 8am-6pm. 1½hr. tours July-Aug. 10am. Call 2 weeks in advance to arrange a tour in English.) The **Jugend Info** office, Fleischbankg. 4 (☎17 99), focuses on academic, social, and legal issues and has a knowledgeable staff. Open M-Th 7:30am-4pm, F 7am-12:30pm.

Currency Exchange: At the post office (exchange machine 24hr.) and its branches.

Luggage Storage: Only in **Lockers** (€2.50-3.50) during ongoing station construction.

Pharmacy: Landschafts-Apotheke, Alterpl. 32. (☎550 77). Open M-F 8am-6pm, Sa 8am-noon. Check any pharmacy window to find the 24hr. pharmacy on call that night.

Hospital: Klagenfurt Krankenhaus, St.-Veiter-Str. 47 (☎538).

Emergencies: Police ☎133 or 53 33, **Ambulance** ☎144, **Medical Assistance** ☎141.

Bi-Gay-Lesbian Organizations: Queer Klagenfurt, Postfach 146 (☎50 46 90). Hotline W 7-9pm. **AIDS-Hilfe Kärnten,** 8-Mai-Str. 19, 4th fl. (☎551 28; www.hiv.at.) Open M-Tu and Th 5-7pm.

Internet Access: Ringtone, Bahnhofstr. 55, 5min. from the station. Inexpensive international calls and Internet access, telephone cards, and digital computer services. (☎34 50 28.) Open daily 10am-9:30pm. **Internet Café,** on the 2nd floor inside the Sparkasse on Neuerpl. (☎58 88.) €3.70 per 30min. Open M-F 7:45am-3:30pm. **Sir Magic's Internet Pub,** Waagg. 10 (☎59 45 94; www.internet-cafe.at). €0.10 per min. Open M-Sa 10am-2am, Su 2-6pm.

Post Office: Main post office, Dr. Hermann Str. 4, off Neuer Pl. (☎55 65 50. Open M-F 7:30am-6pm, Sa 7:30am-11pm.) **Postal code:** A-9010.

🏠 ACCOMMODATIONS & CAMPING

For budget stays, two student dorms are converted to youth hostels during July and August. Be aware, however, that only Jugendherberge Klagenfurt offers dorm accommodations; for others, you'll pay considerably more for converted student rooms. The tourist office distributes the English-language *Hotel Information* and *You are Welcome* pamphlets, as well as the German lists of private rooms.

Jugendherberge Klagenfurt, Neckheimg. 6 (☎23 00 20; fax 00 20 20), at Universität-str., a 20min. walk from the Wörthersee and a 45min. walk from the city center. From the train station, take bus #40, 41, or 42 to "Heiligengeistpl.," then bus #10 or 11 to "Neckheimg." from stand #2. Although far from the city center, its proximity to the lake and bars in the university area make it worthwhile. Mostly spacious quads. All rooms have shower and separate toilet. Breakfast buffet (7-8:30am) and sheets included. Dinner €6. Kitchen, laundry, and sauna available. **Internet** €2.60 per 20min. Reception 7-11am and 5-10pm. Dorms €16.30; doubles €40. Non-members add €3. ❸

Jugendheim Mladinski Dom, Mikschallee 4 (☎356 51; fax 51 11). From the train station, turn right on Südbahngürtel, then right and through the underpass on St.-Peter-Str. Cross Ebentalerstr., follow the road that curves left and then to the right, and take the 1st left. Or take bus #40, 41, or 42 to "Heiligengeistpl.," then bus #70 or 71 (dir.: Ebental) to "Windischkaserne" from stand #13, and walk in the same direction (bus runs M-Sa until 6:57pm). This dorm becomes a B&B in summer, with large rooms including shower and bathroom. Parking and televisions available. Breakfast €2.50. Laundry: wash and dry each €2.80. Reception 6am-midnight. Open July 10-Aug. Singles €21.50; doubles €35; triples €41. Under 13 €10; under 7 €7. €1.50 per person per night cheaper for stays of 3 nights or more. ❸

Jugendgästehaus Kolping (HI), Enzenbergstr. 26 (☎569 65; fax 656 32). From the station, head down Bahnhofstr., right on Viktringer Ring, left on Völkermarkter Ring, right at Feldmarschall-Conrad-Pl. (which becomes Völkermarkterstr.), and right on Enzenbergstr. (20min.). A student dorm during the year, Kolping welcomes summer travelers, offering singles and doubles with gleaming bathrooms. A special deal with a nearby fitness center allows use of the facilities for €1.50. Breakfast included. Reception July-Aug. 24hr. Open early July-early Sept. Singles €29; doubles €46. Ages 10-15 €20/€40. €3 surcharge for 1-night stay. Members €3 discount. ❸

Pension Alte Schmiede, Pischeldorferstr. 8 (☎/fax 59 35 59). From the train station, turn right on Südbahngürtel, then left on Lastenstr. Follow Lastenstr. as it becomes Völk-ermarkter-Ring, then left onto Pischeldorferstr. (15min.). Singles and doubles, some with living room, couch, private balcony or terrace, and satellite TV. All rooms with bath. July-Aug. singles €28; doubles €60; Sept.-June €26-30/€48-60. Breakfast €3. ❸

Pension Wachau, Wilfriedg. 19 (☎217 17; office@pension-wachau.at). From Heili-gengeistpl., take bus #10 or 11 to Neckheimg., then walk back 2 blocks to Wilfriedg. and take a right. Tucked away in a residential neighborhood, Wachau offers comfortable rooms, all with TV and bath. Breakfast and evening snack included. Parking available. Reservations recommended. Singles €42, doubles €70. DC/MC/V. ❹

Klagenfurt-Wörthersee Camping-Strandbad (☎211 69; fax 69 93), on Metnitzstrand off Universitätsstr. From the train station, take bus #40, 41, or 42 to "Heiligengeistpl.," then bus #12 to "Strandbad Klagenfurter See." Turn left and walk 2min. The busy yet comfortable campsite is on the left, across the street from the Wörthersee. On-site grocery store, mini-golf, and beach. Late June-late Aug. €7 per person, ages 3-14 €2.20. May-late June and late Aug.-Sept. €4.40/€2.20; large caravan site €8; small site €4. Showers included. €1 per person per night tax. AmEx/MC/V. ❶

CARINTHIA

🍴 FOOD

With a few notable exceptions, restaurants in Klagenfurt are closed Sundays. The tourist office's *Sonntagsbraten* lists addresses and hours of cafés, restaurants, clubs, and bars that are open on Sundays. Every Thursday and Saturday 8am-noon, the compact **Benediktinerplatz** on the lower west side of the *Altstadt* welcomes a rickety market of fruits and vegetables. There is a **SPAR** on the corner of Bahnhofstr. and Miesstalerstr., and one near Jugendherberge Klagenfurt on Villacherstr. After 5:30pm, breads and sweets in the *Konditoreien* are 25% off. (Open M-Th 7:30am-5:30pm, F 7am-7pm, Sa 7am-5pm.)

Gasthaus im Landhaushof (☎50 23 63; fax 75 17), inside the courtyard of the Landhaus on Ursulineng. Savor hearty, tastefully presented meals in the courtyard in front of the Landhaus, or go inside and eat for cheap in 1 of 3 stylish dining rooms. Lunch *Menüs* run around €5.80. *Wienerschnitzel* €10. Open daily 10am-midnight, kitchen until 11pm (Su 10pm). AmEx/DC/MC/V. ❷

Rathausstüberl, Pfarrpl. 8 (☎573 47), on a cobblestone street near the Pfarrkirche, serves fresh Carinthian specialties like *Marillien-* or *Zweschgenknödeln* (apricots or plums baked into a shell covered in brown sugar and butter; €6.50-7.30) alongside favorites like *Spätzle* (€6.50). Enjoy beer (0.2L €1.50, 0.5L €2.70) and a full meal with the sociable local crowd. Open M-Sa 9am-11pm. MC/V. ❷

Gusto, St. Veiter Ring 51a (☎50 42 20), on the northeast corner of the *Altstadt*, is a great place for lunch, offering roast chicken, *Käsenudeln,* and other lunchtime *Menüs* for €4.70-5.90 in a location with a Van Gogh on the wall. With the exception of lunch, feels closer to an *Imbiss* than a full-scale restaurant. Open M-F 7am-7pm. ❷

Scanzoni Heuriger, Villacherstr. 11, just west of Heiligengeistpl. Under newly painted ceiling frescoes of commoners drinking wine, this restaurant and bar offers a range of filling Carinthian dinners (€5-7), like *Gulasch* and bread or *Schnitzel* and fries. Wine €2-4. Open daily 10am-midnight. ❷

Arcobaleno, Wienerg. 11, at the corner of Heupl., serves a large variety of *Eis* cream for €0.75 a scoop, and sundaes for €4.50-5.50. Droves of people wait for this tasty treat in almost any weather. Open M-Sa 10:30am-midnight. ❶

🎦 SIGHTS

Klagenfurt and its suburbs are home to no fewer than 23 castles and mansions; the tourist office's English brochure *From Castle to Castle* gives a suggested path. Another brochure, the German-language *Museumswandern,* gives addresses and hours for the city's 17 art galleries, 18 museums, and other attractions.

THE OLD TOWN. The *Altstadt* buildings display an amalgam of architectural styles: *Biedermeier,* Italian Renaissance, Mannerist, Baroque, and *Jugendstil.* At the edge of Alterpl. stands the 16th-century **Landhaus,** originally an arsenal and later the seat of the provincial coucil. The symmetrical towers, staircases, and flanking projections create an elegant courtyard; inside, 665 brilliant coats of arms blanket the walls. Artist Johann Ferdinand Fromiller took 20 years to complete these pieces. Ask at the ticket counter about guided tours, which last 20min. and include admission to the Provincia congress chambers. (☎57 75 72 15. Open Apr.-Oct. daily 9am-5pm. €2, students and seniors €1.)

A stroll through Kramerg., one of the oldest streets in Klagenfurt, leads past the bronze statue of the legendary **Wörther-See Manndl,** whose little keg incessantly spills water into the pool below. Continue on Kramerg. directly to **Neuer Platz,** a torrent of motion and activity. Empress Maria Theresa gazes regally over the eastern end. Despite her proud stance, a 60-ton copper half-lizard, half-serpent creature is not ashamed to spit water in her direction. This fountain represents the **Lindwurm,** Klagenfurt's heraldic beast.

CATHEDRAL. Rebuilt after Allied bombing in 1944, the modern exterior of the **Kathedrale** renders it almost indistinguishable from its surroundings on **Domplatz.** The cathedral's interior, however, is awash with high arches, crystal chandeliers, pink and white floral stucco, and a brilliant gold altar. Other ecclesiastical objects are on display in the tiny **Diözesanmuseum** next door, including the Holleiner Kreuz, dating from 1170, as well as the oldest existing stained-glass window in Austria—an 800-year-old sliver portraying Mary Magdalene. *(Lidmanskyg. 10, 2 blocks south of Neuer Pl., off Karfreitstr. ☎50 24 98. Cathedral open daily 6:30am-7pm. Free. Museum open M-Sa mid-June to mid-Sept. 10am-noon and 3-5pm; mid-Sept. to mid-Oct. and May to mid-June 10am-noon. €3, students and children €2.)*

LANDESMUSEUM. Klagenfurt's Landesmuseum (Historical Museum) was Emperor Franz Josef's favorite. It houses the Lindwurmschädel, the fossilized rhino skull discovered in 1335 that, three centuries later, inspired the *Lindwurm* statue at Neuer Pl. (see "Dragon's Tale," below). Other pieces include 18th-century musical instruments, huge crystals, and ancient Celtic and Roman artifacts. The Medusas at the corners of the fully intact 3rd-century Dionysus mosaic could take on a *Lindwurm* any day. *(Museumg. 2. ☎53 63 05 52; fax 63 05 40. Open Tu-Sa 9am-4pm, Su 10am-1pm. €3, students €2.)*

DRAGON'S TALE Once upon a time, Klagenfurt was harassed by a winged, virgin-consuming lizard—the *Lindwurm* (Dragon). This awful monster terrorized the area, preventing settlers from draining the marshes. Enter Hercules, who quickly dispatched the beast and saved the village. Centuries later, the "skull" of the slain beast was found, proving many an old wives' tale about the heroic founding of the town. The townspeople commissioned sculptor Ulrich Vogelsang to recreate the monster using its "skull" as the model. The statue of the *Lindwurm* on Neuer Platz became the town's symbol, despite the fact that, in 1840, scientists proved the skull belonged not to the beast, but to a prehistoric rhino. Klagenfurt's collective heart broke in 1945 when an Allied soldier climbed onto the *Lindwurm's* sensitive tail, snapping it in two. Today, stuffed animals reminiscent of Puff the Magic Dragon are for sale everywhere.

AMUSEMENT PARK. Don't miss Klagenfurt's most shameless concession to tourist kitsch, the **Minimundus** park, only minutes from the Wörthersee. If you choose the audio-guide version, Louis Armstrong sings *It's a Wonderful World* as you gaze at the world's most famous buildings and monuments. Artists have created intricate models of over 170 world-famous buildings and sights—all on a 1:25 scale. You'll be on eye level with the Parthenon, Big Ben, the Taj Mahal, and many more; some of the models took over three years to build. *(Villacherstr. 241. From the train station, take bus #40, 41, or 42 to "Heiligengeistpl.," then switch to bus #10, 11, 20, 21, or 22 (dir.: Strandbad) to "Minimundus." ☎21 19 40; fax 211 94 60. Open daily Apr. and Oct. 9am-6pm; May, June, Sept. 9am-7pm; July and Aug. 9am-10pm. €10, students €8.50, ages 6-15 €4.50. English guidebook €3, audioguide €2.)*

ZOO. To prevent the persecution of the *Lindwurm's* descendents, the **Happ's Reptilien Zoo** exhibits reptiles in their natural environments. Herr Happ has a loose definition of "reptile"—along with puff adders and iguanas, the reptile zoo features spiders, scorpions, guinea pigs, and fish. The accident-prone should perhaps avoid Saturday's 3pm piranha and crocodile feeding. *(Villacherstr. 237, next door to Minimundus. ☎234 25; fax 234 25 14. Open daily May-Sept. 8am-6pm; Oct.-Apr. 9am-5pm. €8.50, students and seniors €7.50, children €4.50.)*

🎵 NIGHTLIFE & ENTERTAINMENT

The best of Klagenfurt's nightlife rages in the pubs of **Pfarrplatz** and **Herrengasse**, located only a 5min. walk from each other. For the latest, read the tourist office's *Veranstaltung-Kalender* (calendar of events), available in English.

CARINTHIA

The tourist office has brochures listing concerts, gallery shows, museum exhibits, and plays. Get tickets from **Reisebüro Springer** (☎387 00 55). The *Jugendstil* **Stadttheater** is Klagenfurt's main venue for operas and plays: everything from Christopher Marlowe to Broadway musicals. (Box office ☎540 64. Open from mid-Sept. to mid-June Tu-Sa 9am-noon and 4-6pm. €3-40, students and seniors half-off.)

For dancing, try Pfarrplatz's **Scotch**, an after 11pm establishment with a cross-section of ages. Herrengasse's nightlife is around **La Vida**, Herreng. 5 (☎780 31 31), which provides a nice atmoshere and English-speaking hosts willing to offer advice to travelers. La Vida offers an outdoor garden atmosphere only a few steps away from an indoor bar section with lots of dancing. Nearby, **Checkpoint Charlie,** Herreng. 3 (☎412 47 65), has a mix of both young and middle-aged patrons, while **Meyer Lansky** packs a noisy crowd of 20-something revelers into a smoky interior.

■ OUTDOOR ACTIVITIES

On hot spring and summer days crowds bask in the sun and loll in the clear water of the Wörthersee. This water-sport haven is Carinthia's largest and most popular lake. The two **beaches** closest to Klagenfurt are **Strandbad Klagenfurter See** (www.happynet.at/stw/strandbad.htm; open 8am-8pm; €3, children €1.40, family €6.60; locker key deposit €5) and **Strandbad Maria-Loretto.** (Open in good weather daily May and Sept. 9am-6pm; June 9am-7pm; July and Aug. 9am-8pm. €3.50, ages 6-15 €1.70; after 2pm €2.70/€1.) Both are easily reached by public transportation. From the train station, take bus #40, 41, or 42 to "Heiligengeistpl.," then bus #10, 11, or 12 to "Strandbad Klagenfurter See." Both offer afternoon discounts. To get to Maria-Loretto, walk to the end of Metnitz Strand, and turn left onto Lorettoweg. Strandbad Maria-Loretto, around the corner of the lake on the southern side, is quieter than Strandbad Klagenfurter See. There are no lifeguards, so swim at your own risk.

To enjoy the water without getting (too) wet, rent a **rowboat** (€2 per 30min.), **paddle boat** (€3), or **motor boat** (€5.80) from **STW Boote** near the Strandbad Klagenfurter See. A *Radwandern* brochure, free at the tourist office, suggests **bike** tours, including one along a castle-church circuit. The Karawanken mountains to the south, such as the **Hochobir** (2139m), provide good **hiking,** but many are accessible only by car. Ask at the tourist office for details.

■ DAYTRIPS FROM KLAGENFURT

BURG HOCHOSTERWITZ

Hochosterwitz is just outside the town of Launsdorf, northeast of Klagenfurt and 10km east of St. Veit. Trains run to Launsdorf from Klagenfurt (30min.; 10 per day, fewer on Sa-Su, 3:42am-9:20pm; €9 round-trip). Walk 2km to the base of Hochosterwitz (you can't miss it), and 10min. more to the main parking lot and entrance kiosk. Drivers take Rte. 83 from Klagenfurt to St. Veit and switch to the district road to Hochosterwitz.

Dominating the countryside from the top of a steep hill, **Burg Hochosterwitz** is a striking testament to the erstwhile wealth and power of Carinthia's nobility. This is the stuff that medieval dreams are made of—a fortified wall winds around the hillside, culminating in a stocky castle with turrets and towers. The castle's elevation above pastures and crop fields make it even more imposing. It's been around since 1571, when Carinthian governor Georg von Khevenhüller bought the property and made extensive renovations. Irked by marauding Ottoman Turks, Georg constructed the 14 massive gates, each with its own nickname, to guard the road up to the castle using strategically designed shooting apertures. The path to the top commands postcard-worthy views at every turn, taking in town, country, and mountains beyond. (Open daily May-Sept. 8am-6pm; Apr. and Oct. 9am-5pm. €7, seniors €5, ages 6-15 €4, under 6 free. Groups of 10 or more €6. English brochure €3.)

A steep, 20min. walk along the outer wall, through gates and across drawbridges, takes you to the top of the hill. Or, take the **funicular** (€3 round-trip). A **restaurant** and a small **museum** filled with old paintings and a collection of medieval arms sit at the top. (Tours in German every 45min. Open same hours as castle. Free with castle admission.)

VELDEN ☎ 4274

Trains run from Klagenfurt to Velden (20min., 1-2 per hr., round-trip €8.40). To reach the town center from the train station, turn right on leaving the station, then left onto Birkenallee, marked with the sign "Zum See."

Dubbed the "Austrian Riviera," tiny Velden attracts loads of Austrian and German tourists, who head for the shores of the Wörthersee in summer. In mid-July, the town's main street rumbles with race cars, and there are nightly fireworks to music like Beethoven or the Beatles. The beaches are swamped with sunbathers, but the image of Velden wouldn't be complete without the golden *Schloß* (castle) reflecting onto the lake. To many Germans, its fame as the location of the soap opera *Ein Schloß am Wörthersee* is reason enough to visit.

LIGHTS OVER THE LAKE While its location on one of Austria's most picturesque lakes might be enough to attract its share of tourists, Velden isn't taking any chances. They have put the lake to even better use, pumping water straight from the Wörthersee and spraying it upwards, right in front of the castle, for spectacular light shows to the tune of pop, rock, and classical music three nights per week. Using an array of lasers, the water is lit and colored into spinning, psychedelic patterns as it shoots and twists into different shapes from the hoses that pump it higher than the *Schloß* itself. Best of all, these *Klangwelle* (musical waters) are free.

For the **tourist office,** Villacherstr. 19, turn right at the end of Birkenallee into Am Corso, then right on Villacherstr. It's on the left side of the road, in a shiny metal and glass building. A free 24hr. accommodations phone is outside. (☎21 03; www.velden.at. Open July-Aug. M-Th 8am-8pm, F-Sa 8am-10pm, Su 9am-5pm; May-June and Sept. M-Th 8am-6pm, F-Sa 8am-8pm, Su 9am-5pm.)

To get to **Jugend- und Familiengästehaus Cap Wörth ❸,** Seecorso 37-39, ask the bus driver to get off at "Cap Wörth," and then walk to the intersection of Süduferstr. and Strandcorso. This spa-type hostel is directly on the Wörthersee, with indoor and outdoor swimming, large dining room, volleyball field, a small restaurant and bar, and an expansive wooded campus. The rooms have lockers (keys provided), sliding wooden beds, and reading lamps. This is a gem of a hostel with tiles and walls colored in earthtones and wheelchair-accessible rooms with customized bathrooms. (☎26 46; www.oejhv.or.at. Reception until 11pm. €21.90 per person; singles €29.17; doubles €25.53. **Pension Teppan ❸,** Sternbergstr. 7, has comfy rooms on a hill above the town center. From the train station turn right, then left onto Birkenallee (marked with "Zum See" sign). Follow it to the end and turn right onto Am Corso. Turn right onto Kirchenpl., which becomes Kirchenstr. Pension Teppan is at the intersection of Kirchenstr. and Sternbergstr. (15min.). The owners lend **bikes** for free. (☎31 69; pension.teppan@utanet.at. Breakfast included. Open Apr.-Sept. Call ahead. €23.40, €22 for stays of more

CARINTHIA

than 2 nights.) **Camping Kofler ❶**, Klagenfurterstr. 62, is located on the water's edge, a 15min. walk from Velden. The campground offers both RV and tent space, water sports, restaurant, showers and toilets, and occassional live music from American musicians. (☎31 98; blueasianmusic@aon.at. Mid-July to mid-Aug. €15, children €12; mid-June to mid-July €12/€8; May to mid-June and mid-Aug. to Oct. €8/free. Electricity €4.)

Refuel after swimming at **Restaurant Aqua ❷**, Seecorso 3, with three levels of outdoor seating and deals like pasta (€7.20-12.80), salads (€2.80-8.70), and a Sunday buffet (€13.50). Located right on the beach (and near the light show—see "Lights Over the Lake," p. 185), so most of the clientele wear bathing suits. (☎517 71. Open high-season 7am-1am; low-season 9am-1am. AmEx/DC/MC/V.)

Beaches line Seepromenade and Seecorso. Crowds congregate at **Strandclub** (☎511 01; €5) at the tip of the lake. Smaller beaches include **Strandbad Leopold** (☎26 32; €3.30), **Strandbad Wrann** (☎27 70; €5.20, children €3), and **Strandbad Bulfon** (☎34 15; €7/€3.50). Each beach offers watery fun, but only Leopold gives refunds for bad weather. (Strandclub: rowboats €11 per hr., motorboats €14. Wrann: €3/€13.) There's also windsurfing, waterskiing, and sailing. Beachside activities include volleyball, ping pong, and mini-golf, depending on the beach. On non-beach days, bike along the lake for beautiful views. **Rent bikes** at **Impulse**, Villacherstr. 21, at the Agip Tankstelle next to the tourist office. (☎04272 24 82.)

THE DRAUTAL

Located only 20km from the Slovenian and Italian borders, and graced with a moderate climate and plentiful lakes, central Carinthia's Drautal (Drau Valley) feels decidely un-Teutonic. The **Drau river,** which winds through the area, makes water sports a substantial industry, and Mediterranean cultural influences abound, though the region's proximity to the Villacher and Gailtaler Alps provides ample opprtunity for alpine activities like skiing and hiking. The extensive Villach Highway Interchange provides easy access to the Drautal's lakes; the waters of the **Millstättersee, Ossiachersee,** and **Faakersee** glisten due to a unique mineral and metallic makeup that reflects startling blues, aquas, and greens. Villach's role as a transportation hub, with rail lines connecting to the city of Jesencie in nearby Slovenia and to Tarvisio on the Italian side of the border, supports a nacsent electronics industry that drives the region's economy.

VILLACH   ☎04242

Villach (pop. 58,000) is a lively city that quickly gives way to grassy, tree-lined suburbs. Italian and Slavic influences make the city multicultural and vibrant, catering to many different types of visitors. An important transportation hub to its southern neighbors, Villach is a pleasant place from which to spend a day exploring the nearby **Gerlitzen** (1911m) and **Dobratsch** (2166m) peaks, or as a base for trips to the castle **Berg Landskron,** or the **Ossiachersee** and **Faakersee** lakes.

▐▀ TRANSPORTATION

Trains run to: Graz (3½hr., 17 per day 4:15am-8:05pm, €21); Klagenfurt (35min., 37 per day 1:21am-9:56pm, €5.60); Vienna Südbahnhof (5-5½hr., 19 per day 1:21am-8:25pm, €37). A **free city bus** travels a circuit covering most of Villach. (Every 20min. M-F 8:40am-6:20pm, Sa 8:40am-12:20pm.) **Ferries** cruise up and down the Drau. (☎580 71; www.schifffahrt.at/drau; free with the Kärnten Card.) **Tour boats** cruise from Villach's Congress Center to Wernberg by Faakersee on the Drau or from one of eight ports in the Ossiachersee. (2-day round-trip €16, 2½hr. round-trip €10.50, 1hr. one-way €6.50.) Find **taxis** at the train station. (☎288 88.) Rent **bikes** at **Das Radl,** Italienerstr. 25. (☎269 54. €10 per day.)

◼︎🛈 ORIENTATION & PRACTICAL INFORMATION

Villach sprawls on both sides of the Drau River. The train and bus stations are both on Bahnhofspl., north of the town center. Bahnhofstr. leads from the station over a 9th-century bridge to **Hauptplatz,** the commercial heart of the city. Two sweeping arcs of stores flank Hauptpl., enclosed by a towering church at one end and by the Drau at the other. The Hauptpl. itself is crisscrossed by narrow paths.

To get to Villach's **tourist office,** Rathauspl. 1, from the station, walk to Bahnhofstr. over the bridge and through Hauptpl. to Rathauspl. The office is at the far end. (☎205 29 00; fax 205 29 99. Open high-season M-F 9am-6pm, Sa 9amnoon; low-season M-F 9am-12:30pm and 1:30-5pm.) The **regional tourist office** in St. Ruprecht (☎420 00; fax 420 00 42) offers up-to-date ski information. There are **ATMs** throughout the city. The station has 24hr. electronic **lockers** (€2-3). The local **hospital** (☎20 80) is on Dreschnidstr. The **police** headquarters are at Tralteng. 34. (☎203 30.) **Internet access** is available at **Ken-i-di,** Ledererg. 16. (☎213 22. Open Tu-Sa 6pm-2am, Su 8pm-midnight. €0.10 per min.) The main **post office** at the train station **exchanges currency.** (Open daily 7:30am-noon and 2-5:30pm.) **Postal code:** A-9500.

🛏 ACCOMMODATIONS

Despite the fact that Villach is not a top international destination for jet-setters and skiers, business travelers keep hotel prices higher than one might expect.

Jugendgästehaus Villach (HI), Dinzlweg 34 (☎563 68; jgh.villach@oejhv.or.at). From the train station, walk up Bahnhofstr., over the bridge, and through Hauptpl. Turn right on Postg., walk through Hans-Gasser-Pl., which merges into Tirolerstr., and bear right at St. Martinstr. Dinzlweg is the first street on the left (30min.). The hostel is tucked away past the tennis courts. Plastered with 1970s neon, it has 140 beds in spacious five-bed dorms, each with its own shower and toilet. Free sauna, music studio, TV room, **e-mail** kiosk, and foosball and table tennis. Lunch or dinner €5.81. Breakfast and sheets included. Key available with ID. Reception 7-10am and 5-10pm. Dorms €14.90; singles €22.17. DC/MC/V. ❷

Gästehaus Pirker, Rennsteinerstr. 21 (☎241 76), offers rooms with shower and bath in a 1950s ambience. Turn right out of the station, past the post office, and follow the ramp (Rennsteinerstr.) up to your right, over the train tracks, and around several sharp bends. Breakfast included. Singles €23.50; doubles €42; triples €63. ❸

Hotel Bacchus, Khevenhüllerg. 13 (☎06 99 12 49 67 54). From Hauptpl. facing the bridge on Bahnhofstr., it's the large park building with turrets one block to the right. Conveniently in the middle of town, the hotel lives a double life as a *Weinstübe* and restaurant. All Rooms with TV. Breakfast included. Singles €30-40; doubles €60-80. ❹

Romantik Hotel Post, Hauptplatz 26 (☎26 10 10; www.romantik-hotel.com), located in the central *Fußgängerzone,* is a pricey hotel in a former 16th-century city palace. Amenities include a fitness center and sauna. All rooms with TV, phone, mini-bar, and hairdryers. Singles start at €56; 1 double €72. AmEx/DC/MC/V. ❺

FOOD

Lederergasse overflows with small, cheap eateries, while **Hauptplatz** and **Kaiser-Josef-Platz** seat swankier patrons. There is a **SPAR Markt,** on Hans-Grasser-Pl. (open M-F 8am-7pm), and a **farmer's market** on Burgpl. (W and Sa mornings).

Trastevere, Widmanng. 30 (☎21 56 65; www.trastevere.co.at), serves fine Italian cuisine in an enclosed courtyard to scores of businessmen and families, many of whom are Italian visitors. Open daily 11am-2am; kitchen open 11:30am-midnight. ❷

Park Café, Moritzstr. 2 (☎27 77 01; office@parkcafé.at), across from the post office. For a glass of wine or light lunch with dozens of Villachers, away from the crowds on the patio, or in a charming 1930s-style smoking room. Wine and beer €1.80. Sandwiches €2-4. Café open M-Sa 7am-10pm; lounge open W-Sa 4pm-1am. ❶

Stern, Kaiser-Josep-Platz 5 (☎247 55; www.stern-villach.at). With a flair for combining the retro with the modern, Austrian specialties with Japanese sushi, and a restaurant with a bar, Stern boasts an unusual menu and a comfortable atmosphere for socializing. Breakfast €4-6. Lunch €4.90. Dinner €9-14. Open M-F 7am-midnight, Sa-Su 9am-midnight. Kitchen until 11pm. AmEx/DC/MC/V. ❸

Salud, Seilerg. 1 (☎269 35; www.salud.at). Near the tourist office in a small passageway off the *Fußgängerzone*. Decorated with colorful earthtones, tablecloth seating, and a lively bar, Salud offers Mexican dishes for about €8. Open Tu-Su 5pm-2am. ❷

Rainer Konditorei, Oberer Kirchenpl. 5 (☎243 77; www.rainer-villach.at), is a 140-year-old Villach tradition. Extensive menu with 50 dessert options. Open daily 10am-7pm. ❶

SIGHTS, ENTERTAINMENT, & OUTDOOR ACTIVITIES

DOWNTOWN. Any tour of Villach traverses **Hauptplatz,** the city's 800-year-old commercial center. The southern end of the square lives in the shadow of the mighty Gothic **St. Jakob-Kirche,** one of Villach's 12 churches. Raised on a stone terrace, this 12th-century church became Austria's first Protestant chapel in 1526. An ascent up the church's **Stadtpfarrturm,** the tallest steeple in Carinthia (94m), provides a view of Villach and its environs. (☎205 25 40. Open June-Sept. M-Sa 10am-6pm, Su noon-6pm; May and Oct. M-Sa 10am-6pm. €1.82, students €1. Free organ concerts in the church June-Aug. Th 8pm.)

The **Stadtmuseum,** Widmanng. 38, founded in 1873, has archaeological displays spanning six millennia, as well as art from the Middle Ages and the original Villach coat of arms from 1240. There is also a huge 3D model of Carinthia's landscape. (☎205 35 35 or 205 35 00; www.villach.at. Open May-Oct. daily 10am-4:30pm. €2.50, students €1.80, under 8 free.) Across from the museum is a glass **Holocaust Memorial** almost hidden by shrubbery. **Tierpark Rosegg,** Carinthia's largest animal park, maintains more than 350 animals of different species, including American Bisons and white wolves, within a lush environment. (☎745 23 57. Open daily Apr.-Nov. 9am-5pm; July-Aug. 9am-6pm.) Built for Madamme Lucrezia (Mozart's Italian lover), **Schloss Rosegg** boasts a kilometer of hedges that make Austria's largest maze when 1.5km cornstalks are added to it. Wax figures are also part of the castle's offerings. (☎72 30 09; www.rosegg.at. Open May-Oct. Tu-Su 10am-6pm. The labyrinth is closed when it rains.)

OTHER SIGHTS & FESTIVALS. Two blocks farther down Peraustr. looms the Baroque **Heilig-Kreuz-Kirche,** the pink edifice visible from the city bridge. Cool for car enthusiasts, the **Villacher Fahrzeugmuseum** is at Draupromenade 12 on the other side of the Drau. Two rooms crammed with vehicles give you a look at some 50s and 60s rides. (☎255 30 or 224 40; www.oldtimermuseum.com. Open daily mid-June to mid-Sept. 9am-5pm; mid-Sept. to mid-June 10am-noon and 2-4pm. €5.50, ages 6-15 €3.50.) On the first Saturday in August, the **Villacher Kirchtag** (Church Day), allowed by decree in 1225, helps the town celebrate its "birthday" with raucous revelry. (Admission €6.)

NIGHTLIFE. Villach's nightlife is clustered in several different locations, particularly near Seilerg.'s **Salud**, Seilerg. 1, and around Ledererg. near **Stern** (see Food, above). For a college-age crowd and alternative music, the **Pelican**, Rathausg. 3, is a 1min. walk from Salud. (☎06 76 35 38 51 53.) For something more sedate in a wine cellar atmosphere, head for **Per Du**, Ledererg. 29. (☎226 23. Open M-Th 5pm-2am and F 5pm-4am.) **Barsoho**, Freihausg. 13, attempts to conjure American-British trendiness. (☎247 55. Open daily 7pm-2am. AmEx/MC/V.)

OUTDOOR ACTIVITIES. Villach lies in a valley between the small but lovely **Ossiachersee** (8km from Villach) and the placid **Faakersee** (10km). Plenty of nearby terrain is ideal for **swimming, boating,** and **cycling.** Peaks near Villach make for good **hiking** and **skiing,** with winter resorts near each lake. At the corner of Austria and Slovenia, the Drei-Ländereck lifts offer additional slopes. (1-day ticket €22, 15 and under €13.)

SPITTAL AN DER DRAU   ☎4762

At the foot of the Goldeck Mountain by the Drau river sits the small city once known for its *Spittal* (hospital). People came from far and wide to find cures for their ailments. They still do, only now laughter is the best medicine at the *Komödienspiele* (comedy play festival) held at Schloß Porcia every July and August. Self-dubbed the Komödienstadt ("City of Comedy"), Spittal has seen its share of tragedy too, as the ghost at Schloß Porcia will attest. Along with its mascot, the tragi-comedic clown, Pierrot, Spittal embodies a healthy mixture of Mediterranean gaiety and Central European melancholy.

🖪🖥 TRANSPORTATION & PRACTICAL INFORMATION. Trains run frequently to Spittal an der Drau from: Klagenfurt (1-1½hr., every hr. 6:32am-8:51pm, €10.20-11.20); Lienz (45min.-1hr., every hr. 6:20am-9:17pm, €9.70-10); Villach (30min., 1-2 per hr. 5:20am-11:18pm, €5.90-6). **Lockers** are available at the train station (€2). To reach the town center from the train station, walk down Bahnhofstr. and cut diagonally across the park. The creamy white Schloß Porcia is at the end of the park and houses the **tourist office,** Burgpl. 1. (☎56 60; www.spittal-drau.at. Open July-Aug. M-F 9am-8pm, Sa 9am-noon; Sept.-June M-F 9am-6pm, Sa 9am-noon.)

🖪🖥 ACCOMMODATIONS & FOOD. The Jugendherberge Spittal (HI) ❷, Zur Seilbahn 2, is at the base of Goldeck Mountain. From the train station turn right and walk past the post office. Continue on Körnerstr, turn right on Ortenburger-str., walk under the train tracks, and make the second right onto Wiesenweg. Take a left through the parking lot and follow the signs to "Goldeck" (20min.). Rooms and hall bathrooms go for function over form. A solid restaurant is located on the ground floor. (☎32 52; stadionbuffet@aon.at. Breakfast included. Reception 8am-midnight. Call ahead. Dorms €9.50, without breakfast €7.50, with all 3 meals €29; singles €14.) For magnificent views, try **Jugendherberge Goldeck (HI) ❷.** Follow directions for the first hostel and take the cable car to "Mittelstation." (☎27 01. Breakfast included. Call ahead. Reception 8-9am and 5-9pm. Open Christmas-Easter and late June-late Sept. Dorms €15. Cable car €5.80; round-trip €6.20 with guest card. Last ascent 5:30pm.)

CARINTHIA

Eat like a Countess at **Schloß Café ❸**, Burgpl. 1, where a piece of *Spittaler Torte* runs €2.50. For a meal, try *Käsenudeln* or *Schnitzel*. Light lunch entrees are about €7, with daily specials €4.50-8. (☎47 07. Open M-F 7:30am-11pm, Sa 8:30am-9pm, Su 2-8pm; July-Aug. daily until midnight.) Hungrier folks will enjoy the filling food and expansive beer garden at **Das Gösserbrau ❷**, Villacherstr. 5, just on the other side of the river from the center of town. (☎23 83; fax 333 31. *Wienerschnitzel* with salad and fries €9, *Topfenstrudel* for dessert €2.50.) Despite the Donald Duck mascot, **Goldene Ente ❷**, Hauptpl. 20 heading toward the river from the town center, offers a wide-ranging Chinese menu. Most meals are around €7, with signature duck dishes €8.50-10. (☎351 21. Open daily 11:30am-3pm and 5:30-11pm.) Buy groceries at the **SPAR** supermarket inside the Gerngroß store, Neuerpl. 1. (☎42 78 70. Open M-F 8:30am-6pm, Sa 9am-5pm. AmEx/DC/MC/V.)

◎ SIGHTS. The rather plain facade of **Schloß Porcia** fails to prepare the eye for the delicate beauty of the Florentine Renaissance courtyard within. The arcades serve as a backdrop for the light laughter of Spittal's Komödienspiele in summer (see Entertainment, below). Spanish count Gabriel von Salamanca, who was also the Austrian imperial treasurer, built the castle in the 16th century. It eventually passed into the hands of the Austro-Italian Porcia family, but at least one Salamanca never left the castle: the ghost of Countess Katherina is said to inhabit its walls to this day. According to one story, the Countess laments the death of her beloved son; another says she's condemned because of very un-countess-like behavior, such as setting hounds on her subjects and reportedly murdering one of her maidservants for discovering her hidden stash of money. The castle also houses the **Museum für Volkskultur** (Museum of Folk Culture). Through creative displays, including a reconstructed 1900 classroom and rooms devoted to local mining and mountain climbing, this museum recreates Carinthian daily life, with explanations in English. Check out the great collection of carnival masks and *Bartl* costumes: in Carinthia, he's Santa's little helper, only he dresses like a devil, wears a sheep skin, and caries a willow switch to hit bad kids. The first floor ends with the richly decorated living room of Count Salamanca. (☎28 90; fax 56 50 61 56. Open mid-May to Oct. daily 9am-6pm; Nov. to mid-May M-Th 1-4pm. €4.50, students and seniors €2.25.)

◫ ENTERTAINMENT. During July and August, laughter fills Schloß Porcia's courtyard with the annual ▨**Komödienspiele** (Comedy Festival). Europe's greatest comedies are performed by the actors of Spittal's own Komödienschule. (School of Comedy. Tickets €22-29, standing room €6. Students 40% off. Box office in Schloß Porcia open every performance day 9am-7pm.) On the last weekend in June of every odd-numbered year, Spittal celebrates **Salamancafest.** 16th-century garb becomes standard, drawing the town back to the time of the aristocratic Salamancas who built Schloß Porcia. Food and drink stalls swarm the town center and street musicians add to the merry atmosphere. The highlight of the festivities, however, isn't so merry. The gruesome death of Countess Katherina's son is reenacted in an attempt to somehow appease the Countess.

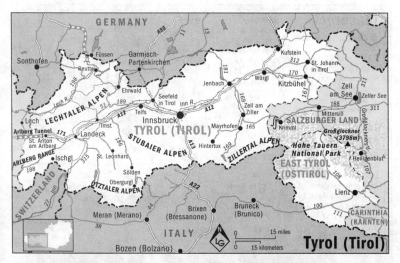

Tyrol (Tirol)

TYROL (TIROL)

The Hapsburgs fell in love with Tyrol, and it's not hard to see why. Few other regions so effortlessly blend culture, natural spectacle, and ultimate relaxation. Craggy summits rising in the northeast and south cradle four-star resorts and untouched valleys like the Ötztal and Zillertal. In eastern Tyrol, the mighty peaks of the Hohe Tauern range are protected as a national park. In the center of it all, stylish Innsbruck unabashedly flaunts Baroque façades and bronze statues before an appreciative audience of foreigners. The architecture blends seamlessly with impressive alpine backgrounds, showcasing why Tyrol has become one of the world's most celebrated mountain playgrounds.

HIGHLIGHTS OF TYROL

Gape at the world's largest jewel in **Innsbruck** (see p. 200).

Relive your Olympic dreams on the slopes in **Seefeld** (see p. 203).

Use **Sölden** as a base for exploring the dramatic **Ötztal Arena** (see p. 221).

INNSBRUCK ☎ 0512

Although the 1964 and 1976 Winter Olympics brought Innsbruck (pop. 128,000) international recognition, the mountain city has too rich a history to succumb to ski-resort status. Innsbruck boasts numerous intricate Baroque façades, the legacy of the Hapsburgs' prolonged stay here; beginning with Maximilian I, many Hapsburgs called Innsbruck home. Though the family is gone, the beauty that drew them here remains: the jagged ridge of the Nordkette peaks loom almost directly above the *Altstadt's* cobblestone streets. If the natural beauty, history, and the skiing aren't tempting enough, several quiet mountain suburbs offer the opportunity to enjoy Innsbruck away from the normal city bustle.

TYROL

TYROL

Innsbruck

🏠🏠 ACCOMMODATIONS
Camping Innsbruck
  Kranebitten, **21**
Gasthof Innbrücke, **9**
Hotel Charlotte, **22**
Hotel Fritz Prior-
  Schwedenhaus (HI), **2**
Jugendherberge
  Innsbruck (HI), **4**
Pension Paula, **3**
Technikerhaus, **15**

🍎 FOOD
Al Dente, **14**
Dom, **1**
Gasthof Weißes Lamm, **10**
Noi Original Thaiküche, **7**
Restaurant Zum Griechen, **5**
Salute Pizzeria, **17**
Theresienbräu, **20**
University Mensa, **16**

🍺 PUBS
Bacchus, **19**
Jimmy's, **18**
Hofgarten Café, **6**
Krah Vogel, **13**
Nacht Café, **12**
Treibhaus, **11**

Alpenzoo

Walterpark
Inn
Weyerburgg.
Herzog-Otto-Str.
Herreng.
Dom St. Jakob
Rennweg
Badg.
Pfarrg.
Hölblinghaus
Hofburg
Goldenes
Dachl
Maximianeum
Hofg.
Herzog-Friedrich-Str.
Hotel
Goldener
Adler
Kiebachg.
Rieseng.
Stadtturm
Hofkirche
Seilerg.
Schlosserg.
Stiftg.
Tiroler
Volkskunst-
museum
Marktgraben
Burggraben

Elisabethstr.
TO 4
(1.5km)

St. Nikolas
Rennweg
Hoher Weg
Inn
Kaiserjägerstr.
Falkstr.
Claudiastr.
Schillerstr.

Innstr.
Imdster.
Karl-Kapferer-Str.
Bienerstr.
Siebererstr.
Bus info center
Kochstr.

St.-Nikolaus-G.
Walterpark
Hofgarten

HÖTTING
Höttingerg.
Congress
Landestheater
UK
Kapuzinerkirche
Etzel Str.
Jahnstr.
Dreiheiligenstr.
Kettnerstr.
BRUCKEN-
PLATZ

Inn-
Brücke
Herzog-Otto-Str.
Hofburg
Universitätsstr.
Anreichstr.
Meinhardtstr.
Sillg.
Ingenieur
Weinhartstr.
König Laurin Str.
PRADL

Mariahilfstr.
see
inset
Burggraben
Tiroler
Landesmuseum
Ferdinandeum
Museumstr.
Defreggerstr.
Sill
Pradlerstr.
Körnerstr.
Stadt
Park
Amraserstr.

Höttinger Au
Inn
Herzog-Sigmund Ufer
Volksgarten
M-Preis
Maria-Theresien-Str.
Erlerstr.
Bubblepoint
Waschsalon
BOZNERPL.
Hertz

TO 15
(1km)
Universitäts-
brücke
Blasius-Hueber-Str.
Innrain
Burgerstr.
Kaiser Josef Str.
Stainerstr.
Meranerstr.
Brixnerstr.
Bruneckerstr.
Hunoldstr.
Sillufer
Anton Eder Str.
Anzengruberstr.

University
Library
Anichstr.
Landhaus
ÖAV
Adamg.
W-Greil-Str.
SÜDTI-
ROLERPL.
Haupt-
bahnhof
Südbahnstr.

TO HOMOSEXUELLE
INITIATIVE TIROL (2km)
Peter-Mayr-Str.
Speckbacherstr.
Maximilianstr.
Sport Neuner
M-Preis Triumphpforte
Salurnerstr.
Heiliggeiststr.
Denzel Cars

Schopfstr.
Fritz-Pregl-Str.
Andreas-Hofer-Str.
Templstr.
Müllerstr.
Michael-Gaismayr-Str.
Frauenzentrum
Innsbruck
Liebenggstr.
Leopoldstr.
WILTEN

Westfriedhof
Franz-Fischer-Str.
Stafflerstr.
Neuhauserstr.
Tschamlerstr.
Olympiabrücke
A12
Olympiastr.
Olympic Ice
Stadium

Egger-Lienz-Str.
Karwendel str.
Westbahnhof
Feldstr.
Anton Melzer Str.
Fritz Konzert Str.
Pastorstr.
Grassmayr
Bell-Foundry
Basilika
Wilten
Stiftskirche
Wilten

0   200 yards
0   200 meters

TO 21 (5km)
Autobahn A12

TO SCHLOß AMBRAS &
IN AMBRAS (2km)
22
A12

N
LG

✈ INTERCITY TRANSPORTATION

Flights: The airport, **Flughafen Innsbruck,** Fürstenweg 180 (☎225 25), is 4km from town. Shuttles to and from the main train station from the airport F 6-11pm, with service at 15min. intervals 6:51-8:30pm (€1.60). **Austrian Airlines** has offices in Innsbruck; call the airport info number and they'll transfer you. **Tyrolean Airways** (☎222 20) offers regional flights. **Trains** arrive at the **Hauptbahnhof** on Südtirolerpl., which is on bus lines A, DE, F, R, RR, S; night bus lines NL1, NL2, NL3 and NL4; trams #3, 6, and the **Stubaitalbahn.** The **Westbahnhof** and **Bahnhof Hötting** are cargo stations.

Trains: Hauptbahnhof, Südtirolerpl. (☎05 17 17). At least 1 ticket counter open M-Sa 6am-9:45pm, Su 6:30am-9:45pm. After-hours purchase is by machines (English and other languages available on touch-screen display). Trains to: **Munich** (2hr., 13 per day, €31.60); **Salzburg** (2½hr., 13 per day, €29.50); **Vienna Westbahnhof** (5½-7hr., 10 per day, €47); **Zurich** (4hr., 4 per day, €43.90).

Buses: BundesBuses leave from the station on Sterzingerstr., immediately behind and to the left of the Hauptbahnhof. (☎53 07) for Innsbruck buses, (☎56 16 16) for destinations in Tyrol but outside of Innsbruck.

By car: From the east or west take Autobahn A12. From Vienna, take A1 west to Salzburg, then A8 (in Germany) west to A93, which becomes A12 again in Austria. From the south, take A13 north. From Germany and the north, take A95 to Bundesstr. 2 east, which becomes Bundesstr. 177 east in Austria. The Austrian highway toll, "Vignette," for travel on Austrian highways, is available at gas stations. (€7.60 for 1 week, €21.80 for 2 mo.) If going to Italy on A13, the private road toll can be purchased when entering or by calling ☎520 12, ext 127 M-F 8am-1pm.

✦ ORIENTATION

Most of Innsbruck lies between the **Inn River** to the west and the train tracks to the east. The main street is **Maria-Theresien-Straße,** running north-south, at times parallel to both the river and the train tracks. Open only to taxis, buses, and trams, and crowded with tourists and cafés, Maria-Theresien-Str. runs between the *Altstadt* and Maximilianstraße, another big street. Take tram #3, or bus A to "Maria-Theresien-Str." to get to the *Altstadt* from the Hauptbahnhof; or exit the station, turn right onto Südtirolpl. and later Bruneckerstr., then left onto Museumstr. and continue straight ahead for 10min. Most sights are near the *Altstadt.* To reach the **university district,** near Innrain, continue down Museumstr. toward the river, curving left onto Burggraben, across Maria-Theresien-Str., and onto Marktgraben. The university itself is to the left down Innrain. Though Innsbruck is not particularly confusing (for an old, imperial European city), a color map available at the train station or at tourist offices is useful.

▐ LOCAL TRANSPORTATION

Public Transportation: Head to the **IVB** Office at Stainerstr. 2, near Maria-Theresien-Str., to pick up a local bus schedule. (☎530 17 99; fax 71 10. Open M-F 7:30am-6pm.) The main **bus station** is in front of the main entrance to the train station. Single-ride 1-zone tickets €1.60, 24hr. tickets €3.30; 4-ride tickets €5, week-long passes €10.10, from the office. Validate your ticket when you board the bus or risk a €55 fine. Bicycles, dogs, bags, and baby carriages are allowed free of charge. Most buses stop running around 10:30 or 11:30pm; check each line for specifics. 3 *Nachtbus* lines run after-hours every night; NL1, NL2, and NL3 go through Maria-Theresien-Str. and Marktpl. (every 30min., 11:39pm-5:09am) on their way to the Hauptbahnhof and beyond.

Taxis: Lined up at the Hauptbahnhof, or call ☎53 11, 17 18, 56 17 17, or 29 29 15. Approximately €10 from the airport to the *Altstadt*. A fee of €4.80 is applied for any distance up to the first 1.3km and €0.15 per m thereafter. On Su, holidays, and daily 10pm-6am the fee is €5.10.

Car Rental: Avis, Salurnerstr. 15. (☎57 17 54, mobile 0664 134 54 38). Open M-F 7:30am-6pm. **Hertz,** Südtirolerpl. 1. (☎58 09 01; fax 09 01 17). Open M-F 7:30am-6pm, Sa 8am-1pm. AmEx/DC/MC/V. **Denzel Drive** offers 3-day weekend specials for about €73. (☎58 20 60; www.denzeldrive.at.) Open M-F 8am-6pm.

Auto Repairs: ARBÖ (☎123). **ÖAMTC** (☎120).

Hitchhiking: While *Let's Go* doesn't recommend hitching, thumbers have been known to take bus C to "Geyrstr." and cross the parking lot of DEZ mall to the Shell gas station.

Bike Rental: Sport Neuner, Maximilianstr. 23 (☎56 15 01). Mountain bikes and helmets €20 per day, €16 per half day. Open M-F 9am-6pm, Sa 9am-noon.

🖪 PRACTICAL INFORMATION

TOURIST & FINANCIAL SERVICES

Innsbruck's tourist offices offer information on accommodations, sights, and transportation. Arrive early in the day to avoid lines during peak season. All offices offer the **Innsbruck Card,** which gives free access to dozens of local attractions and all public transportation for 24, 48, or 72hr. (€21, €26, or €31; children 50% off.)

Main Tourist Office, Burggraben 3 on the third floor (☎598 50; www.tiscover.com/innsbruck), is on the edge of the *Altstadt* just off the end of Museumstr. Tons of brochures, a city map (€1), and a helpful staff await. Open M-F 8am-6pm, Sa 8am-noon. The large glassed-in office on the ground floor is **Innsbruck-Information** (☎53 56; fax 56 14), which is allied with the tourist office but consists of a profit-maximizing consortium of local hotels. Nonetheless, this can be a valuable source of information when the tourist office is closed. Open daily 9am-6pm, currency exchange closes 5:30pm. **Branches** at the train station and major motor exits. **Jugendwarteraum** (☎58 63 62), in the Hauptbahnhof near the lockers, hands out free maps and skiing information. Open from mid-Sept. to June M-F 11am-7pm, Sa 10am-1pm.

Hiking information and Insurance: Österreichischer Alpenverein (ÖAV), Wilhelm-Greil-Str. 15 (☎595 47; www.alpenverein-ibk.at). The Austrian Alpine Union's Innsbruck area office provides fantastic advice and information on huts and hiking opportunities. Membership €55, students and seniors €40, children 6-18 €10.

Budget Travel: Tiroler Landesreisebüro, Boznerpl. 7, (☎59 88 50; fax 57 54 07), by Wilhelm-Greil-Str. Open M-F 9am-6pm. AmEx/DC/MC/V.

Consulate: UK, Kaiserjägerstr. 1 (☎58 83 20). Open M-F 9am-noon.

Currency Exchange: Good rates at the train station **post office** (see p. 195), and **Innsbruck-Information** (see above). Most **banks** are open M-Th 7:45am-12:30pm and 2:15-4pm, F 7:45am-3pm.

ATMs: Outside the train station, post office, and in front of banks throughout the city.

LOCAL SERVICES

Lockers: At the train station. €1.50-2.50 for 4hr. in electronic lockers.

Bookstores: Buchhandlung Tirolia, Maria-Theresien-Str. 15 (☎596 11; fax 58 20 50). 19 shelves of English-language classics and a large table with bestsellers. Open M-F 9am-6pm, Sa 9am-5pm. **Wagner'sche,** Museumstr. 4 (☎59 50 50; fax 595 05 38). Some bestsellers and classics. Open M-F 9am-6pm, Sa 9am-5pm.

Library: Innsbruck Universität Bibliothek, Innrain 50 (☎507 24 31), where it crosses Blasius-Heuber-Str. Take bus O, R, or F to "Klinik." Reading room open July-Aug. M-F 8am-2pm; Sept.-June M-F 8am-8pm, Sa 8am-6pm.

Religious Services: Catholic Mass in English at the Jesuit church in Karl-Rahnerpl. on Universitätstr. every Sa 6pm. List of services in other languages outside of St. Jakob.

Bi-Gay-Lesbian Organizations: Homosexuelle Initiative Tirol, Innrain 100 (☎56 24 03; fax 57 45 06). All meetings 8:30-11:30pm: mixed younger crowd M, lesbian night Tu, gay night Th, transgender night every other F. Call ahead to check about meetings. To attend the monthly party, call for information on location and time. **Frauenzentrum Innsbruck** (Women's Center), Liebeneggstr. 15 (☎58 08 39), runs a women's-only café for lesbians and straights M, W, F 8pm-midnight, and hosts discotheques and poetry readings. Office hours Tu 10am-1pm, Th 2-5pm.

Laundromat: Bubblepoint Waschsalon (☎56 50 07 14; www.bubblepoint.com), with 2 snazzy locations full of English-speakers at Brixnerstr. 1, and Andreas-Hofer-Str. at the corner of Franz-Fischer-Str. 7kg wash €4, dryer €1 per 10min. Soap included. **Internet** access €0.10 per min. Open M-F 8am-10pm, Sa-Su 8am-8pm.

EMERGENCY & COMMUNICATIONS

Emergencies: Police ☎133, headquarters at Kaiserjägerstr. 8 (☎590 00); **Ambulance** ☎144 or 142, **Fire** ☎122, **Mountain Rescue** ☎140.

Pharmacy: Apotheke St. Anna, Maria-Theresien-Str. 4 (☎58 58 47; fax 15 67.) Open M-F 8am-6pm, Sa 8am-noon. DC/MC/V.

Medical Assistance: Universitätsklink, Anichstr. 35 (☎50 40).

Internet Access: International Telephone Discount, Bruneckstr. 12 (☎59 42 72 61). Turn right from the Hauptbahnhof; it's on the left just past the end of Südtirolerpl. (€0.11 per min.). Reduced rates on international phone calls. Open daily 9am-11pm.

Post Office: Maximilianstr. 2 (☎500 79 00). Open M-F 7am-11pm, Sa 7am-9pm, Su 8am-9pm. Address *Poste Restante* to: Postlagernde Briefe, Hauptpostamt, Maximilian-str. 2, A-6020 Innsbruck. Additional branch next to the train station. Open M-F 7am-7pm; currency exchange until 5pm. **Postal code:** A-6020.

■ ACCOMMODATIONS

Although 9000 beds are available in Innsbruck and suburban Igls, cheap accommodations are scarce in June when the only hostel open is Jugendherberge Innsbruck. The opening of student dorms to backpackers in July and August alleviates the crush somewhat. Book in advance if possible. Visitors should join the free **Club Innsbruck** by registering at any Innsbruck accommodation. Membership gives discounts on skiing and ski buses (mid-Dec. to mid-Apr.), bike tours, and the club's hiking program (June-Sept.).

Hostel Fritz Prior-Schwedenhaus (HI), Rennweg 17b (☎58 58 14; www.tirol.com/youth-hostel). Take bus A or tram #4 to "Handelsakademie," continue to the end and straight across Rennweg to the river. This 95-bed hostel located in a cul de sac adjacent to the Inn River offers clean, spacious rooms. On summer weekdays, luggage may be stored at the front desk. Private shower and bathroom included. No door locks, but key for luggage closet available with deposit. Breakfast €4. Sheets €3.10. Laundry €5.50, soap included. **Internet** €0.10 per min. Wheelchair-accessible. Keys with ID deposit. Reception 7-9:30am and 5-10:30pm. Check-in before 6pm. Lockout 9:30am-5pm. Curfew 10:30pm, but upon asking for a key guests can stay out later. Open July-Aug. and Dec. 27-Jan. 5. Dorms €10; doubles €28; triples €41.25. ❷

TYROL

Jugendherberge Innsbruck (HI), Reichenauer Str. 147 (☎34 61 79; fax 61 79 12; www.youth-hostel-innsbruck.at). Take tram 3 to "Sillpark" from the train station (6min.) then bus O to "Jugendherberge" (6min.). With sleek glass-and-metal architecture and sliding doors, this 178-bed hostel resembles a high-powered corporation. Rooms with locking closets and shelves for belongings are well-maintained. TV and a small library. Bicycle rental €11 per day. Breakfast (7-8am), hall showers, and sheets included. **Internet** access €0.10 per min.; after 9pm €0.05 per min. Laundry (€3.30) until 10pm. Reception Sept.-June 5-10pm; July-Aug. 3-10pm. Check-in before 6pm. Lockout 10am-5pm. Curfew 11pm; key available. Quiet time from 10pm. 6-bed dorms €12.05 1st night, then €9.50; 4-bed dorms €14.80/€12.25; singles with shower €28; doubles with shower €40.80. Nonmembers add €3. ❸

Gasthof Innbrücke, Instr. 1 (☎28 19 34; www.innsbruck.nethotels.com/innsbruecke). From the *Altstadt*, cross the river at Innsbrücke; the Gasthof is at the corner. This 575-year-old inn has both a riverside and mountain view, giving it an unbeatable combination of price and location. Head downstairs for a drink at the *Innkellner* (beer €2-3). Breakfast and shower included. Parking €5. Singles €27, with shower and toilet €35; doubles €45/€54; triples €60/€70; quads with shower and toilet €110. MC/V. ❸

Pension Paula, Weiherburgg. 15 (☎29 22 62; www.pensionpaula.at). Take bus D to "Schmelzerg." and head uphill. Large, well-furnished rooms, many with balconies, for those who wish to escape the city rumble. Beautiful views across the valley. Breakfast included. Reservations recommended. Singles €26.50, with shower and toilet €33; doubles €45/€54; triples €60/€70; quads with shower and toilet €80. ❸

Hotel Charlotte, Phillipine-Welser-Str. 88a (☎34 12 70; www.tirol.com/hotel-charlotte-ibk). Take the #3 bus to "Amras," then walk onto the main road and follow the signs. A farm facing the hotel and the single-family houses nestled nearby lend a country feel to the surroudings, despite the proximity to the train station. TV, shower, and toilet in every room, semi-private and shared balconies, outdoor swimming pool, and parking lot. Breakfast included. Singles €47; doubles €72. MC/V. ❹

Technikerhaus, Fischnalerstr. 26 (☎282 11 00; fax 110 17). Take bus R to "Unterbergerstr./Technikerheim." This student housing complex isn't near the train station, but provides clean, well-appointed rooms during the summer crunch. Restaurant and 2 TV rooms. Breakfast and showers included. Reception 24hr. Check-in after noon. Checkout 10am. Open from mid-July to late-Aug. Singles €23; doubles €40; triples €55. With student ID €17/€35/€51. V. ❸

Camping Innsbruck Kranebitten, Kranebitter Allee 214 (☎28 41 80; www.campinginnsbruck.com). Take bus O from the "Landesmuseum" stop (near the train station) to "Technik" and then bus LK to "Klammstr." Walk downhill to the right, and follow the road. These pleasant grounds in the shadow of a snow-capped mountain include a playground for the young at heart. Restaurant with **Internet** access (€3 per 30min.) open 8-11am and 4pm-midnight. Showers included. Laundry €4. Reception Sept.-June 8am-9pm; July-Aug. 8am-11pm. If reception is closed, find a site and check in the next morning. €5, children under 15 €3.50, tents €3, cars €3. Tent rental €8. Electricity €3. Bicycle €5 per day. ❶

◖ FOOD

Gawking at the overpriced delis and *Konditoreien* on glamorous Maria-Theresien-Str. won't fill your stomach, so escape the *Altstadt* and its profiteers by crossing the river to Innstr., in the university district, where ethnic restaurants and cheap pizzerias proliferate. Those looking for inexpensive or late-night eats may actually find themselves pleasantly surprised (and filled) by the cheap, large kebab and pizza portions served in and around the Hauptbahnhof. A few more late-night pizza digs are near the station on Ingenieur-Etzol-Str.

Theresianbräu, Maria-Theresienstr. 51 (☎58 75 80), bills itself as the oldest private brewery, and its blacklit bar is built around 2 giant copper brewing kettles. The microbrew, a pleasant dark lager, is available 0.1 to 2.4L glasses (.5L stein €3.30) alongside traditional meals such as *Käsespatzl* (homemade noodles with cheese; €6.80) and *Gröstl* (roast potato, beef, and fried egg; €6.50). Chocolate fondue for 2 or more is available after 6pm (€6 per person). Frequent live music entertains a diverse crowd. Open M-W 10:30am-1am, Th-Sa 10:30am-2am, Su 10:30am-midnight. MC/V. ❷

Salute Pizzeria, Innrain 35 (☎58 58 18), on the side of the street farthest from the river. A popular student hangout with black and white pictures on the wall and what appears to be a tree growing in the middle of the floor. Walk up to the counter to order, then sit back and wait to enjoy some of the best and least expensive pizza in town. Make sure to get a seat quickly though; Salute's is never empty for very long. Pizza €3.05-7.85. Pasta €4.50-6.50. Salad €3-4.50. Open 11am-midnight. ❷

Noi Original Thaiküche, Kaiserjägerstr. 1, (☎58 97 77), cooks up a vast array of Thai soups (€4-8.40), and deliciously spiced dishes from the wok (€8-11) ranging from mild to flaming. Most tables are outside and come with umbrellas and neon green chairs. Inhale the sweet aroma drifting out of the kitchen while enjoying your meal. Open M-F 11:30am-3pm and 6-11pm, Sa 6-11pm. ❷

Dom, Pfarrg. 3 (☎93 53 99; www.domcafe.at). Located in the heart of the *Altstadt* and diagonally across from the cathedral, this restaurant café offers light fare, such as soups (€4), salads (€3.50-8.70), sandwiches (€2.40-4), and a wide selection of ice cream desserts (€2-4.30). The arched ceilings and red interior give this place the feel of a wine cellar but in the summer, most prefer to sit outside facing the *Dom.* **Internet** access available. Open daily 11am-1am. ❶

Al Dente, Meraner Str. 7 (☎58 49 47), offers a wide variety of dishes with a hip Italian flair, with the food prepared before your eyes. The young, lively crowd makes this a great place to relax between sightseeing stops. Scrumptious pasta €6.40-10.60. Open daily 11am-midnight; kitchen open until 11pm. AmEx/DC/MC/V. ❷

Restaurant zum Griechen, Innstr. 28 (☎29 15 37) is not to be confused with a mere kebab place. Gyros (€8) are on the menu, but souvlaki dishes—grilled meat with tomato sauce, rice, and vegetables—steal the show. *Fasoulada* soup (navy bean and tomato; €3), grilled fish (€8-13), and vegetarian options (€5.20-8) round out the menu. Open M-Tu 5pm-midnight, W-Su 11:30am-midnight. ❷

Gasthof Weißes Lamm, Mariahilfstr. 12 (☎28 31 56), on the second floor. A small dining area upstairs decorated with pictures of Greece serves a local crowd. Check out the daily *Tagesempfehlungen* (soup, entree, and salad €6.50-18). Soups €2.80-4. Meat dishes €8.70-18. Open M-W and F-Su noon-2pm and 6-10pm. MC/V. ❸

Shere Purjab, Innstr. 19 (☎28 27 55), is a small restaurant with scattered Indian decorations, serving some of the cheapest food around. Of the 3 daily *Menüs,* 1 is always vegetarian (soup, entree with basmati rice, and dessert €5.45), and loads of other vegetarian options are available (€2.20-8.50). Open daily 11:30am-2:30pm and 5:30-11pm. AmEx/D. ❷

University Mensa, Innrain 52, in the basement of the white building marked "Leopoldino-Francisca." Cheaper eats in Innsbruck are hard to come by. 2 daily *Menüs* (soup, entree, and salad €3.70-4.60). Open during the term M-F 9am-2:30pm; hot lunch 11am-1:30pm. Irregular hours in summer, closed mid-July to mid-Aug. ❶

MARKETS

M-Preis Supermarket has branches at Museumstr. 34, Innrain 15, Maximilianstr. by the arch, and across from the train station on the corner of Salurnerstr. and Sterzingerstr. Generally open M-F 7:30am-6:30pm, Sa 7:30am-5pm.

TYROL

Farmers' Markets at Franziskanerpl. (Th 9am-2pm), Sparkassenpl. (F 8:30am-2:30pm), St. Nikolaus-Brunnenpl. (Sa 8:30-11am), and the *Markthalle* near the river at Innrain and Marktgraben. Food, flowers, fungi, and fun, though the prices on some organically grown produce may cause shoppers to scramble back to the supermarket. Open M-F 7am-6:30pm, Sa 7am-1pm.

◉ 🏛 SIGHTS & MUSEUMS

Visiting many museums in Innsbruck in a short period is cheapest with the **Innsbruck Card,** available at museums, cable cars, and the tourist office. It allows entry into all museums, cable cars, buses, and trains (24hr. €21, 48hr. €26, 72hr. €31). A 2hr. **bus tour,** including the *Altstadt* and a visit to the ski jump, leaves from the train station. (June-Sept. noon and 2pm; Oct.-May noon; €13, children €6.)

THE OLD TOWN. The *Altstadt*, a cobbled mix of old buildings, churches, and museums on the river, is often crowded with tourists. Its centerpiece is the **Goldenes Dachl** (Golden Roof) on Herzog Friedrichstr., a shiny, gold-shingled balcony built to commemorate Maximilian I and Bianca Maria Sforza's marriage. Facing the *Dachl*, turn around to the left to see the cream façade of the 15th-century *Helbinghaus*, blanketed with a pale green, 18th-century floral detail and intricate pink stucco work. For a modest rooftop view of the city, climb the 148 steps in the graffiti-lined staircase of the 15th-century **Stadtturm** (city tower), across from Helbinghaus. (☎512 56 15 00. Open daily June-Sept. 10am-8pm; Oct.-May 10am-5pm. €3.50, students and seniors €2, under 15 €1.) The 15th-century **Hotel Goldener Adler** (Golden Eagle Inn) is a few buildings to the left. A marble slate testifies that Goethe, Heine, Sartre, Mozart, Wagner, Camus, and Maximilian were once there.

Innsbruck's most distinctive street is **Maria-Theresien-Straße,** which begins at the edge of the *Altstadt* and runs south. The street, lined by pastel-colored Baroque buildings, gives a clear view of the snow-capped Nordkette mountains. At the end of the street (away from the *Altstadt*) stands the **Triumphpforte** (Triumphal Arch), built in 1765 to commemorate the betrothal of Emperor Leopold II. Up the street, the **Annasäule** (Anna Column) commemorates the Tyroleans' victory on St. Anne's Day (July 26, 1703) after a bloody and unsuccessful Bavarian invasion during the War of Spanish Succession.

MAXIMILIANEUM. This small museum commemorates Innsbruck's favorite emperor, Maximilian I, and provides a solid introduction to local history. A 20min. video *(in 6 languages, including English)* details Maximilian's conquest of Europe from Portugal to Hungary which shaped the future of Innsbruck and Tyrol. The one-room exhibit next door contains artifacts from the film. *(Inside the building under the Goldenes Dachl. Open May-Sept. daily 10am-6pm; Oct.-Apr. Tu-Su 10am-12:30pm and 2-5pm. €3.63, students €1.45, seniors €2.90, families €7.27; headphones for commentary included.)*

CATHEDRAL ST. JAKOB. The unassuming gray facade of the *Dom St. Jakob* (remodeled 1717-1724) conceals a riot of pink and white High Baroque ornamentation within. *Trompe l'oeil* ceiling murals depict the life of St. James. The cathedral's prized possession is the (small) altar painting of *Our Lady of Succor* by Lukas Cranach the Elder. A 1944 air raid destroyed much of the church, but renovations have restored it to its former grandeur. *(1 block behind the Goldenes Dachl. Open daily Apr.-Sept. 7:30am-7:30pm; Oct.-Mar. 8am-6:30pm. Free.)*

HOFBURG. The Hofburg (Imperial Palace) was built in 1460 and remodeled between 1754 and 1770 under the direction of Maria Theresia. Imposing furniture, large portraits, and elaborate chandeliers fill the sumptuously decorated rooms. The biggest room is the Giants' Hall, a gigantic, two-story space with huge paintings of Maria Theresia and Francis I along the walls, as well as equally gigantic portraits of their 16 children. The White Room contains the portrait of Maria's youngest daughter, Marie Antoinette of France (with head, without cake). Don't miss the gilded "Augusta Family" tableau in the Audience Room, depicting the whole Hapsburg gang in big, round, gold medallions. *(Behind the Dom St. Jakob to the right. ☎58 71 86; www.tirol.com/hofburg-ibk. Open daily 9am-5pm. Last entrance 4:30pm. Call ahead for English tours at 11am, 2pm. Group tours (limit 35 people) €29.07. English guidebook €1.82. €5.45, students €3.63, seniors €4, children 6-14 €1.09.)*

TIROLER VOLKSKUNSTMUSEUM. Built between 1553 and 1563 as the "New Abbey," the Tiroler Volkskunstmuseum (Handicrafts Museum) was converted into a school in 1785 and then a museum in 1929. The exhaustive collection of home and farm implements, peasant costumes, and period rooms provides a dusty introduction to Tyrolean culture from the past fewl centuries. Included are butter churns, playing cards, tobacco pipes, and the *Brotgrammeln* tools used to break bread. Downstairs is a collection of incredibly detailed *Krippen* (nativity scenes) that depict Jesus and the Wise Men. *(At the head of Rennweg. ☎58 43 02; fax 02 70. Open M-Sa 9am-5pm, Su 9am-noon. €4.35, students €2.25, ages 7-16 €1.45.)*

HOFKIRCHE. The Hofkirche (Imperial Church) houses an intricate sarcophagus decorated with alabaster scenes from Maximilian I's life and the *Schwarze Mander*. Twenty-eight bronze statues of Hapsburg saints and Roman emperors line the nave. Dürer designed the statues of King Arthur, Theodoric the Ostrogoth, and Count Albrecht of Hapsburg, who pay their last respects to the emperor. Oddly, Maximilian's resting place is not in the Hofkirche, but in Wiener Neustadt, near Vienna; the elegant Silver Chapel holds the corpse of Archduke Ferdinand II instead. *(In the same building as the Volkskunstmuseum. Open M-Sa 9am-5pm; Su noon-5pm.)*

HOFGARTEN (IMPERIAL GARDEN). Walk through the lush, manicured grounds of the Hofgarten and admire the ponds, elaborately designed flower beds, lofty trees, and concert pavilion. A crowd sometimes shouts advice to chess players moving the 1m tall pieces. Walk farther for a lovely spot to escape the crowds of the *Altstadt*. *(Walk down Museumstr. toward the river, turning right onto Burggraben and continuing as it becomes Rennweg. Open daily 6am-10:30pm. Free.)*

LANDESMUSEUM. Originally opened in 1823 and reopened after renovations in May of 2003, the Landesmuseum (Regional Museum) boasts collections from prehistory to Roman times and the Middle Ages. Romanesque, Gothic, and Modern arts and craftworks form a highpoint of the gallery's display. *(Museumstr. 15. ☎594 89, ext. 9; www.tirolerlandesmuseum.at. Open June-Sept. M-Sa 10am-6pm, Th 10am-9pm; Oct.-May Tu-W and F-Su 10am-6pm, Th 10am-9pm. Library Tu-F 10am-5pm. €8, seniors and groups €6, children €4. Audio guide €2.)*

ALPINE ZOO. The Alpenzoo is the highest-altitude zoo in Europe and houses every vertebrate species indigenous to the Alps, including bears, *Baummarden* (pine martens), and golden eagles. Also of note is the bearded vulture in the zoo, with a 3m wingspan the largest bird species of the Alps. *(Weherfurgg. 37, near Schwedenhaus hostel, across the covered bridge: follow signs uphill 15min. ☎29 23 23; www.alpenzoo.at. A bus to the zoo leaves from in front of the Landestheater every hr. 10am-5pm in summer. €1.50, students and children €1, round-trip €2.60/€1.60. Open daily Apr.-Sept. 9am-6pm; Oct.-Mar. 9am-5pm. €5.80, students and seniors €4, ages 6-15 €2.90.)*

TYROL

CRYSTAL MUSEUM. Outside the city is the bizarre and entertaining **Swarovski Kristallwelten,** an unashamed plug for the decorative crystal figurines made in the nearby factory (the gift shop is nearly as large as the exhibits). Above the underground entrance, the fabulous **Giant,** a vine-covered face on a hillside, shares space with 3D modern art, and New Age installation pieces from artists like Salvador Dali, Andy Warhol, and Brian Eno. Make sure to go through the hand-shaped hedge maze in the park behind the Giant's head. *(Take bus #4125 from the bus station to "Wattens Kristallwelten," then walk a little further and take a left. Bus 35min., every 30min. 7:45am-8:22pm, €6.10 round-trip. ☎05224 510 80; www.swarovski-crystalworld.com. Open daily 9am-6pm. €5.45, groups €4.72, under 12 free.)*

⚠ OUTDOOR ACTIVITIES

HIKING. A ⬛**Club Innsbruck** membership lets you in on one of the best deals in Austria (see Accommodations, p. 195). The club's excellent and very popular **hiking** program provides guides, transportation, and equipment (including boots) free to hikers of all ages. Participants assemble in front of the Congress Center (June-Sept. daily at 9am), board a bus, and return from the mountain ranges by 4 or 5pm. The hike isn't strenuous, the views are phenomenal, and the English-speaking guides are qualified and friendly. There are a total of 40 different hikes, so many return the next day for new adventures. Free nighttime lantern hikes also leave Tuesday at 7:45pm; the 30min. hike near Igls culminates in a party with traditional Austrian song and dance, in which *everyone* ends up taking part (willing or not).

If you want to hike on your own, there are several options. For easier hikes, take the J-line bus to "Patscherkofel Seilbahnen" (20min.). The lift provides access to moderate 1½-5hr. hikes near the bald summit of the *Patscherkofel*, offering vistas of neighboring mountains, Innsbruck, and other towns far below. (☎37 27 34; fax 37 27 23 15. Open 9am-noon and 12:45-4:30pm. Round-trip €15, ages 16-18 €12, ages 7-15 €8; dogs €1.50).

For more challenging hikes, head to the lifts ferrying passengers up to the **Nordkette** mountains. The first lift, a short hike from the river and the Schwedenhaus, can also be reached by taking the J bus to "Hungerbergbahn." From here, a second lift leads to the Seegrube, just below the rocky walls of the peaks above. A third and final lift leads to the very top, at the Hafelekarspitze. From both the Seegrube and Hafelekarspitze, several hikes lead up and along the jagged ridges of the Nordkette, but be prepared: they are neither easy, nor particularly well-marked. Even if you don't go hiking, the trip up is worth it for the views. For those more interested in flying down mountains than climbing up them, Innsbruck-Information has a €95 **paragliding** package, including transport, equipment, and photos (or call **MountainFly,** ☎37 84 88).

WINTER ACTIVITIES. The Club Innsbruck membership also significantly simplifies winter **ski excursions.** Hop the complimentary club ski shuttle (schedules at the tourist office) to any suburban cable car (mid-Dec. to mid-Apr.). Membership provides discounts on ski passes. The **Innsbruck Gletscher Ski Pass** (available at all cable cars and at Innsbruck-Information offices) is valid for all 59 lifts in the region (with Club Innsbruck card 3 days €86, teens and seniors €68, children €51; 6 days €150, €120, €90). The tourist office **rents ski equipment** for the Intersport shop on the mountain (downhill €19-32 per day, children €9; cross-country €9, children €7; snowboarding €15 per day). The bus to the **Stubaier Gletscherbahn** for **summer skiing** leaves at 7:20 and 8:30am (☎05226 81 41; www.stubai.gletscher.com). Take the earlier bus—summer snow is slushy by noon. In winter, buses leave at 9:45, 11am, and 5pm (1½hr., last bus back 4:30pm, €10.90 round-trip). One day of winter glacier skiing costs €31.50; summer €21, ages 16-19 €14, ages 10-15 €11, under 10 free. Both branches of **Innsbruck-Information** offer summer ski packages (bus, lift, and rental €47).

For a one-minute thrill, summer and winter **bobsled** rides are available at the Olympic bobsled run in Igls (Bus J to "Patscherkofelbahn"; follow the signs). (May-Sept. ☎0664 357 86 07; fax 37 88 43. Rides Th and F after 4pm; the sled has wheels rather than runners. €22. Late Dec. to late Feb. ☎37 75 25; fax 33 83 89. Rides Tu 10am-noon, Th at 7pm. €30. Professionals pilot the 4-person sleds. Reservations required.)

♫ ENTERTAINMENT

At a corner of the Hofgarten, the **Congress Center** and **Tiroler Landestheater** (☎520 74) host various festivals and concert series in Innsbruck. In August, the **Festival of Early Music** features concerts by some of the world's leading soloists on period instruments at Schloß Ambras, Congress Center, and Hofkirche. (☎56 15 61; www.altemusik.at. Tickets €9-127.) The **Landestheater** also presents plays, operas, and dance most nights of the year. Recent productions have included Benjamin Britten's *A Midsummer Night's Dream*, Georges Bizet's *Carmen*, and Giacomo Puccini's *Turandot*. (☎52 07 44; www.landestheater.at. Concerts €6-49, standing room €4; plays €5-40, standing room €3; rush tickets available 30min. before the show to anyone under 21 and students under 27 for a 40% discount.)

The **Tyrol Symphony Orchestra of Innsbruck** plays Mozart, Beethoven, Stravinsky and more in the Congress Center from October to May. (☎58 00 23. Tickets for symphony concerts €25-39, master concerts €33-85; children and students under 27 30% off.) **Chamber music concerts** (€16-24) are held in the concert hall of the Tyrol Conservatory. (☎58 34 47; same discounts apply.) The Spanish Hall at Schloß Ambras holds **classical music concerts** most Tuesday nights in summer (€10-44; same discounts apply). In late June and mid-July world-renowned dancers—everyone from the Alvin Ailey Dance Troupe to the Sydney Ballet—come to the **International Dance Summer** in the Congress Center to perform in a range of styles. Varied workshops are also conducted throughout the three-week festival, held during the last week in June and the first two weeks in July. (☎57 76 77; www.tanzsommer.at. International Dance Packages include accommodation with concert admission and the Innsbruck Card; 1 night €59, 2 nights €121. Tickets for productions at Innsbruck-Information, Burggraben 3; €20-68.)

For something a little more dicey, check out **Casino Innsbruck.** In a massive complex in the Innsbruck Hilton, by Landhauspl. (☎593 50; www.casinos.at. Semiformal dress. Open daily from 3pm. AmEx/DC/MC/V.)

♥ NIGHTLIFE

Most visitors collapse after a full day of alpine adventure, but there's action a-plenty to keep party-goers from their pillows. Nightlife revolves around the area between the university quarter and the *Altstadt*. For the very latest club and rave events, stop by Treibhaus (see below) and pick up one of the fliers by the door.

▨ **Hofgarten Café** (☎58 88 71; www.hofgarten.at), inside the *Hofgarten* park. Follow Burggraben under the arch and past Universitätstr., pass the *Landestheater,* enter the park through the gate, and follow the path—you'll hear the crowd. By day, diners sip beers beneath a big white tent; by night, it's a relaxed, sprawling outdoor affair with 20- and 30-somethings. Screened from the noise of the city by the dense trees, it's easy to forget Innsbruck is out there and that there's a world outside the *'garten.* In summer, live music most Th. Snacks €2.50-8, beer 0.2L €1.60, 0.3L €4.40, 0.5L €3.10, liquor €2.80. Open daily 10am-4am, kitchen until midnight.

Treibhaus, Angerzellg. 8 (☎57 20 00). Turn right on Angerzellg. from Museumstr., and right again into the alley next to China Restaurant. Innsbruck's favorite place for everyone from jazz-inspired adults to teenage students, *Treibhaus* boasts an indoor café with sound-absorbing canvass and outdoor tent. Occasional live music. Food €2.10-5.80. Beer €1.80-3. Open M-Sa 10am-1am, Su and holidays 4pm-midnight.

Bacchus, 14 Salurnerstr. (☎94 02 10). Diagonally across from the casino; enter from the side of the building's driveway. This bar and discotheque, largely gay and lesbian, is on the lower level beneath a café bar. Mixed in ages, sexual orientation and gender, the discotheque really gets going with dancing around 2am, and caters to students, local *Innsbruckers*, and tourists alike. A friendly place with lots of lively conversation. Beer €2.60-4. Open M-Th 9pm-4am, F-Sa 9pm-6am.

Krah Vogel, Anichstr. 12 (☎58 01 49), off Maria-Theresien-Str. Blood-red walls and a student-aged crowd at the tables. There's a small patio in back, and the upstairs seating area opens up when it's crowded. Beer €2-3. Wraps and sandwiches €5-8. Open M-Sa 10am-2am, Su and holidays 5pm-2am; kitchen closes at 11:45pm.

Jimmy's, Wilhelm-Greil-Str. 17 (☎57 04 73), by Landhauspl. East meets West beneath the all-seeing eyes of the fluorescent Buddha (hanging on the wall). Not a nook left un-hip in this trippy world of brushed steel and rough hewn stone. 2 bars and a diverse menu, sporting dishes from all over the world. *Ciabatta* (filled bread pockets) €4-5.50. Mixed drinks €4-6.60. Beer €1.80-3.30. Open M-Th and Su 11am-1am, F 11am-2am, Sa 7pm-2am. Kitchen daily 11am-2pm and 6-11pm. DC/MC/V.

Nacht Café, Museumstr. 5 (☎57 68 26), near the tourist office. For the night owls who can never get enough partying, the *Nacht Café* offers loud dance music and green and blue lights glowing off the metallic surfaces all night, long after everywhere else is closed. Every night has its own "special" and a 2hr. Happy Hour 10pm-midnight. Beer €2.50-3.50. Snacks €3.50-11. Open 10pm-6am, but really stays open until everyone leaves, sometimes as late as noon. AmEx/DC/MC/V.

◪ DAYTRIPS FROM INNSBRUCK

SCHLOß AMBRAS

The castle stands southeast of Innsbruck, at Schloßstr. 20. Take tram #6 (dir.: Igls) to "Tummelplatz/Schloß Ambras" (20min., €1.60) or tram #3 from Maria-Theresien-Str., which leaves every 7½min. to the last station, "Ambras." Follow signs from the stops. Or, take the shuttle bus that leaves every hr. from Maria-Theresien-Str. opposite McDonald's. (Apr.-Oct every hr. 10am-5pm; €1.60, children €0.80; round-trip €2.20/€1.10.) Walk from the city only with a map, as the trail is poorly marked.

One of Innsbruck's most impressive edifices and museums is **Schloß Ambras,** a Renaissance castle built by Archduke Ferdinand II of Tyrol in the 16th century. He acquired vast collections of art, weapons, and trinkets—from Roman busts to the armor of Japanese shoguns.

The museum's inner courtyard includes a manicured garden and an outdoor café. Around the courtyard is the Hochschloß, which houses the famous Spanischer Saal (Spanish Room), with its Hapsburg coats-of-arms. Upstairs from the Spanish Room are the three floors of the Hapsburg Portrait Gallery (only open in summer), showcasing an assortment of famous rulers, including several popes, Hapsburg *Kaisers*, Napoleon Bonaparte, Catherine the Great, and Louis XVI and Marie Antoinette. (☎34 84 46; www.khm.at/ambras. Open Apr.-Oct. daily 10am-5pm; Dec.-Mar. M and W-Su 10am-5pm. Tours €2; reservations required for English tour. €7.50, students and seniors €3.50, children ages 7-18 €2.) After several hours in the castle, emerge and take a break in the gardens outside, which vary from manicured shrubs and modern sculptures to shady, forested hillsides. Keep an eye out for the peacocks.

STAMS

Frequent regional trains that head west towards Landeck stop in Stams (35min., €5.70). By car, take Autobahn A12/E60 or Hwy. 171 directly to the abbey.

Stift Stams is a magnificent onion-domed monastery 40km west of Innsbruck. Founded by the Tyrolean Duke Meinhard II in 1273, the cloisters were completely restyled in the 18th century. The 22 Cistercian monks who reside there allow several guided tours per day through the majestic **Basilika** and the heavily frescoed **Fürstensaal.** The basilica, restored for its 700th anniversary in 1974, features the masterwork of local artist Andreas Thamasch. Twelve of his gilded wooden statues line the walls of the basement **crypt** where Duke Meinhard and his wife are buried. Stift Stams contains many examples of stunning artwork, but travelers should note that it is the only tourist site in Stams. It is rather far from Innsbruck for those without a special interest in Rococo buildings or monasteries. (☎ 05263 569 72 or 62 42; www.stiftstams.at. Entrance to the cloisters only with the tour. Tours M-Sa every hr. Jan.-Apr. and Oct.-Dec. 9-11am and 2-4pm; May 9-11am and 2-5pm; June and Sept. 9-11am and 1-5pm; July-Aug. tours every 30min. 9-11am and 1-5pm. Tours Su only in the afternoon. €3.50, seniors €3, students and children €2.) A **museum,** also within the monastery, has a small collection of religious paraphernalia and art. (Open mid-June to Sept. Tu-Su 10-11:30am and 1:30-5pm. €4, seniors €3, students and children €2.)

NEAR INNSBRUCK

SEEFELD IN TIROL   ☎ 05212

After Innsbruck borrowed its smaller neighbor's terrain for skiing events during the 1964 and 1976 Winter Olympics, Seefeld became famous enough to lure celebrities and charge high prices for its snowy slopes. Some cities don't even have one five-star hotel, so Seefeld's five five-star hotels alongside its 26 four-star hotels are somewhat unique for the region, and indicative of the town's atmosphere and price levels.

■ **ORIENTATION & PRACTICAL INFORMATION.** To the the town center, go from the train station down Bahnhofstr., which becomes Klosterstr.; the **tourist office,** Klosterstr. 43, provides a list of accommodations. (☎ 23 13; www.seefeld-tirol.com. Open mid-June to mid-Sept. and mid-Dec. to Mar. M-Sa 8:30am-6:30pm; mid-Sept. to mid-Dec. and Apr. to mid-June M-Sa 8:30am-12:15pm and 3-6pm). Seefeld's main square, Dorfpl., and Innsbruckerstr. are on your left coming from the train station; to the right, Münchenstr. forms the other arm of the *Fußgängerzone.* **Internet access** is available at Hotel Bergland. **ATM** at Erstes Bank across from the station. The **post office** is on Klosterstr. one block past the tourist office. (Open M-F 8am-noon and 2pm-5pm). If you need storage for an hour or so, the tourist office is your best chance. For a **snow report,** call ☎ 37 90.

⭑⭒ ACCOMMODATIONS & FOOD. Seefeld has no hostel, making *Pensionen* and *Privatzimmer* the best budget options. Prices per person average €24-40 in the winter; €17-36 in the summer. Make reservations in advance.

The entire *Fußgängerzone* is stocked with rows of pricey restaurants, outdoor cafés, and bars, but there are very few reasonably cheap establishments. Try **Sportcafé Sailer ❷**, Innsbruckerstr. 12. This centrally located restaurant offers traditional Tyrolean specialties such as *Gröstl* (potatoes, bacon and eggs) and *Käserrahnspätzel* (fried onions with spices in a cream sauce) averaging €8-10, and soups for €3.80. Food is served in a Tyrolean atmosphere, with outdoor seating at the beginning of the *Fußgängerzone*. (☎200 51; www.sportcafésailer.at. Open summer and winter daily 11:30am-10pm; lowseason 11:30am-2pm and 6-10pm.) The **Albrecht Hat's Supermarket,** Innsbruckstr. 24, is located across from Sport Sailer just off Dorfpl. (Open M-Sa 8am-6:30pm, Su 10am-noon.)

⭑ OUTDOOR ACTIVITIES. The tourist office distributes *Seefeld A-Z*, a listing of season-specific activity calendars and local services. The tourist office runs an excellent summer **hiking** program of 5-7hr. hikes that wind through the surrounding countryside. (Hikes leave mid-June to mid-Sept. Tu and F 9:30am, W 8:30am. Register by 5pm the day before. €5 with guest card.) The **Kneipp Association Seefeld** (☎22 63) allows guest-card-holders for free on its weekly 3-5hr. outings, which depart from the train station Thursdays at 9:30am in summer and 11:30am in winter. To wander on your own, pick up hiking or biking maps (€4.50) at the tourist office.

For an impressive hike with several tricky ascents and less uphill hiking than you might expect, try the trails that leave from the **Roßhütte** (1760m) area, accessible with the **Roßhütte Bergbahnen,** including a funicular leading to the hut. Two gondolas climb still higher, to the **Seefelder Joch** (2064m) and the **Härmelekopf** (2045m). To get there, turn right out of the train station, and right again following the sign to "Roßhütte." (15min. walk. For all 3 gondolas buy the *Topkarte*—€14, youth €12.50, children €8.50. Funicular and 2 gondolas €14/€12.50/€8.50. Add up to €2 for visitors not staying in Seefeld. Open from late May to mid-Oct. 9am-5pm with rides every 30min. except 12:30pm.) From the *Seefelder Joch*, it's a 30min. hike to the **Seefelder Spitze** (2220m), with dazzling panoramas on both sides. Continuing farther down the other side of the mountain for about 45min., a narrow trail leads down through tight switchbacks and hugs precipitous limestone cliffs before slowly climbing to the arm below the **Reither Spitze** (2373m), a jagged pile of rock that is the highest mountain in the area. From here, finish the loop back down to the lifts, or undertake another 30min. scramble over steep and sometimes uncertain terrain to the peak, where an unobstructed 360° view of the Tyrolean Alps awaits. Often the "trail" is just a scramble over rock walls with red blazes painted on them. From the summit, there are two options: brave the path a second time or take the trail to the *Nördlinger Hütte* back towards the lifts. Views of the valley on the second route are tamer, but so is the path (4-5hr.).

Seefeld offers winter tourists two money-saving ski passes. The **Seefeld Card** is valid for Seefeld, Reith, Mösern, and Neuleutasch. (1-day pass €27.50, ages 16-17 €25, ages 5-15 €16.50.) The **Happy Ski Pass** is valid at Seefeld, Reith, Mösern, Neuleutasch, Mittenwald, Garmisch-Zugspitze, Ehrwald, Lermoos, Biberwier, Bichlbach, Berwang, and Heiterwang. (Pass available for 3-20 days and requires a photograph; 3 days €79, ages 5-15 €47.50, ages 16-17 €72.50.) Twelve different **sports equipment rental shops** lease alpine and cross-country skis, snowboards, and toboggans at standard rates. (Downhill skis with poles and boots €7.50-15, snowboards €14-23.) A free **ski bus** runs between town and the **Roßhütte** and **Gschwandtkopf** ski areas (daily, every 20min. 9:20am-4:40pm). For those who prefer their skiing on the level, choose from the 100km of *Langlauf* (cross-country) trails (map available at the tourist office). **Fun Factory**, Riehlweg 492 (☎50 90; fax 50 92) offers **snowrafting,** which entails sliding down the side of a mountain in a rubber boat (Tu and Th nights, €9.50 per trip), and tobogganing (W nights 8:30pm-midnight, €20). You can also rent toboggans from any ski shop for €4 per day.

EHRWALD   ☎05673

Ehrwald (pop. 2300m) located in Austria's *Wetterstein* area, lies on the Austrian side of the *Zugspitze* (2964m), which is Germany's highest mountain and Ehrwald's prize attraction. Despite this tourist magnet, Ehrwald remains a charming mountain town.

■⁊ TRANSPORTATION & PRACTICAL INFORMATION. All trains to and from Ehrwald pass through Garmisch-Partenkirchen in Germany. **Trains** run to Garmisch-Partenkirchen to Ehrwald (26min., 5:46am-7:59pm, €2.80) and Innsbruck (2hr., 5:45am-6:57pm, €9.70). By **car,** Autobahn A12 follows the Inn from Innsbruck to Mötz. Bundesstr. 314 runs north from Mötz to Ehrwald, close to Germany and Garmisch-Partenkirchen. Bundesstr. 198 runs along the Loisach river. The **tourist office,** Kirchpl. 1, is in the town center, a few steps beyond the church. (☎23 95; www.ehrwald.com. Open July-Sept. and Dec.-Mar. M-F 8:30am-6pm, Sa 9:30am-4pm; Oct.-Nov. and Apr.-June M-F only.) Services include: **currency exchange** at banks (open M-F 8am-noon and 2-4:30pm) and the post office; **ATM** at the **Bank für Tirol und Vorarlberg,** Kirchpl. 21a; **bike rental** at **Zweirad Zirknitzer,** Zugspitzstr. 16, across the tracks and up the hill. (☎32 19. €20 per day, children €10. Open M-F 8am-noon and 1-5:30pm, F 8am-noon and 1-3pm, Sa 10am-noon.) The **post office,** Hauptstr. 5, is on the right about 100m before the town center coming from the train station. (Open M-F 8am-noon and 2-5:30pm.) **Postal code:** A-6632.

■⊡ ACCOMMODATIONS & FOOD. Ehrwald is filled with fairly inexpensive guest houses. Pick up a **guest card** for discounts. **Gästehaus Konrad ❸,** Kirweg 10, is only a few minutes from the station; take the first right onto Kirweg. Each large room has a TV and a painting with alpine scenery. Step out onto the balcony for the real thing. (☎/fax 27 71. Breakfast included. June-Sept. dorms €16-18 per person; mid-Dec. to Apr. €20.50.) Camping is available at **Camping Dr. Lauth ❶,** Zugspitzstr. 34 if you're willing to walk about 25min. uphill. Head left out of the train station and turn left immediately. Take the right-hand fork past Zweirad Zirknitzer and continue uphill (ignore the "Leaving Ehrwald" sign). After the road curves left at the Thörleweg intersection, the well-marked campground is on the right. Pitch your tent in the shadow of the *Zugspitze* in a clean, inexpensive campground. Amenities include a restaurant (open 8am-midnight) serving breakfast for €5.80. (☎26 66; www.campingehrwald.at. Reception 8am-midnight. Laundry €3.60 for wash and dry. May-Oct. €7.50 per person, tax €1.41 per person; Nov.-Apr. €8, tax €1.80 per person. €7 per child, €4.36 per tent; electricity €2.20.)

The **Metzgerei Restaurant ❷,** Hauptstr. 15, has a surprising number of casual tables beyond its storefront meat counter. A no-brainer choice is one of the Tyrolean specialties with *Kraut* and potatoes (€4-6), though other entrees such as smoked bacon with bread (€8) show off the local cuisine equally well. Vegetarian meals are available for €6.40-7.20. (☎23 41. Open M-Sa 11:30am-8:30pm.) **Al Castagno ❸,** is an outdoor café with a penchant for all things yellow

TYROL

and an exhaustive menu. (Pizza €4.20-9.50. Pasta €6.30-9.80. Fish €18-20.20. Grilled steak and pork fillets €13-20. Kitchen 11:30am-2pm and 6pm-midnight.) If you're planning a picnic, try the **SPAR supermarket,** Hauptstr. 1, next to the post office. (Open M-Th 8am-7pm, F 8am-7:30pm, Sa 7:30am-5pm.)

🔄🚪📷 **SIGHTS, ENTERTAINMENT, & OUTDOOR ACTIVITIES.** The **Tiroler Zugspitzbahn** is Ehrwald's leading tourist attraction and an astounding feat of engineering. This cable car climbs to the 2964m summit of the *Zugspitze* in 7min. In fair weather, the observation station at the ride's end has a breathtaking view. Bring a sweater, even in summer. (☎23 09. Trains run mid-May to late Oct. and mid-Dec. to Mar. daily every 20min. 8:40am-4:40pm. €31, ages 16-17 €22, ages 5-15 €18.) The **Ehrwalder Almbahn** doesn't climb as high (1510m), but neither do the prices. (☎24 68. May 21-Oct. 18 8:30am-5:40pm; Dec.-Apr. 8:30am-4pm. €10, teens €9, children €5.) Buses leave from Kirchpl. for the *Zugspitzbahn* (10min., 7 per day 8:15am-5:10pm, €1.50) and the *Ehrwalder Almbahn* (5min.). Try Bergsport-Total, across the street from the tourist office. (Hikes €13-42, bike tours €14-18, climbing €100-130, rafting from €35.) The tourist office also sells hiking maps for €6.50 and provides information on hiking, fishing, swimming, boating, skating, climbing, tennis, river-rafting, paragliding, and kayaking.

For winter guests, Ehrwald offers the **Happy Ski Pass,** the only lift ticket offered for blocks of three days or more. It gives access to 143 lifts, 200km of ski runs, 100km of cross-country trails, and several winter sports arenas (see Seefeld, p. 203). For shorter ski trips, one- and two-day tickets are available for the "Zugspitzarena," the mountains by Ehrwald. (1-day pass €26.60-28, ages 16-17 €24-25.50, ages 5-15 €12.50-13; 2 days €50-52.50/€45-47/€29.50-31.) Shops in the main square and at lift stations rent ski equipment (€23-27 per day, €99-119 per week).

KITZBÜHEL   ☎05356

When Franz Reischer arrived in Kitzbühel in 1892, his 2m snowshoes and wild ideas about sliding down mountains stirred up a fair amount of skepticism. Two years later, the town held its first ski championship and everyone wanted a piece of the big-shoe action. The six peaks surrounding Kitzbühel were named the "Ski-Circus," and life in town was never the same. Now the annual **International Hahnenkamm Race** (Jan. 23-25, 2004), considered the "Wimbeldon of World Cup Skiing," attracts thousands of spectators to watch the world's finest get knocked over by the infamous first turn, known as the *Mäusefalle* ("Mousetrap"). When the snow melts, there are ample opportunities for hiking, cycling and swimming.

▎ TRANSPORTATION

Kitzbühel has two **train stations:** the **Hauptbahnhof,** Bahnhofpl. 2 (☎64 05 53 85 13), and the **Hahnenkamm Bahnhof,** which are one train stop away from each other. All **Buses** stop at the Hauptbahnhof and a few at the Hahnenkamm station. Kitzbühel lies on Bundesstr. 161 and is the east terminus of Bundesstr. 170. By **car** from Innsbruck, take Autobahn A12 east to Wörgl and switch to Bundesstr. 170. From Salzburg, take Bundesstr. 21 south to 305 to 178; at St. Johann in Tirol, switch to 161 south, which leads straight to Kitzbühel.

Trains: Trains leave to: **Innsbruck** (1hr., every 2hr., €12); **Salzburg** (2½hr.; 9 per day; €27.70 via Kufstein or €20.80 via Zell am See); **Vienna** (6hr.; 4:55am-7:30am; €41.50, or €44.50 via Zell am See); **Zell am See** (45min., every 2hr., €8.70).

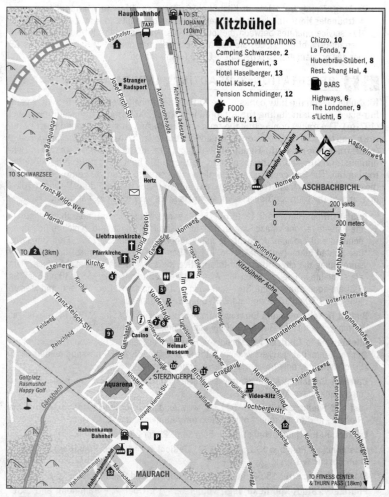

Kitzbühel

ACCOMMODATIONS
Camping Schwarzsee, **2**
Gasthof Eggerwirt, **3**
Hotel Haselberger, **13**
Hotel Kaiser, **1**
Pension Schmidinger, **12**

FOOD
Cafe Kitz, **11**

Chizzo, **10**
La Fonda, **7**
Huberbräu-Stüberl, **8**
Rest. Shang Hai, **4**

BARS
Highways, **6**
The Londoner, **9**
s'Lichtl, **5**

Buses: All depart regularly from the **Hauptbahnhof,** some buses also depart (less frequently) from the **Hahnenkamm** station. Destinations include Lienz, Kufstein and Wörgl; for a complete listing of train and bus routes (bus schedule available until sold out only), pick up the free *Fahrpläne Bus und Bahn*. A *Stadtbus* local line (€1.50 per ride) serves the city.

Taxis: In front of the Hauptbahnhof, or call ☎ 62 617.

Car Rental: Hertz, Josef-Pirchlstr. 24 (☎ 648 00; fax 721 44), at the traffic light on the way into town from the main station. Open M-F 9am-6pm, Sa 9am-noon. 20% discount with valid guest card. AmEx/DC/MC/V.

Bike Rental: Mountain bikes at **Stanger Radsport,** Josef-Pirchlstr. 42, for €22 per day 8am-6pm, or €16 per half-day noon-6pm. Open M-F 8am-noon and 1:30-6pm, Sa 9am-noon. DC/MC/V. Also at nearly any **Intersport** in town; ask for their 2004 rates.

Parking: There are 4 lots in Kitzbühel: **Griesgasse, Pfarrau, Hahnenkamm,** and **Kitzbüheler Horn.** The latter 2 are next to the major ski lifts. In winter a free park-and-ride service operates between the lots and lifts. Free parking at Kitzbüheler Horn and Pfarrau; 50% of the spaces are free at Griesgasse; pay parking at Hahnenkamm is €3 per day or overnight, €20 per week, €130 for the season.

■ ⁊ ORIENTATION & PRACTICAL INFORMATION

Kitzbühel lies on the hilly banks of the Kitzbüheler Ache (river), at the foot of several fair-sized peaks, including the Kitzbüheler Horn (2000m) and the Steinbergkogel (1971m). The tracks connecting the train stations form a sort of U around most of the town, and the stations are on opposite sides of the town. To reach the *Fußgängerzone* (pedestrian zone) from the Hauptbahnhof, head straight out the front door, down Bahnhofstr., and turn left at the main road. At the traffic light, turn right and follow the road uphill. The city center is a maze of twisting streets; if you get confused, look for the occasional *Zentrum* (center) signs to point you back to the middle. Be sure to pick up a map at the tourist office as soon as you can; it's easy to get lost at night.

Tourist Office: Hinterstadt 18 (☎62 15 50; www.kitzbuehel.com), near the *Rathaus* in the *Fußgängerzone*. Make sure to pick up a Kitzbühel guest card, which is free upon demand and provides discounts to many shops and services in town. From June-Oct. free **guided hikes** (with guest card, M-F 8:45am and Sa-Su on request) in the country surrounding the city and **guided informative tours** (M 10am) start at the office. Both are available in English. Open July-Aug. and Dec. 25 to mid-Mar. M-F 8:30am-6pm, Sa 8:30am-noon and 4-6pm, Su 10am-noon and 4-6pm; Nov.-Dec. 25 and mid-Mar. to June M-F 8:30am-12:30pm and 2:30-6pm, Sa 8:30am-noon.

Budget Travel: Reisebüro Eurotours, Rathauspl. 5 (☎713 04; fax 71 30 44), exchanges currency. Open M-F 8:30am-12:30pm and 3-6pm, Sa 8:30am-12:30pm.

Alternatives to Tourism: Ask Michael at Hotel Kaiser (see p. 209) about special offers for short-term backpackers working in the area, especially for EU passport holders. Non-EU citizens may only be able to receive a rate reduction.

Currency Exchange: At banks, travel agencies, and the post office. The post office and most banks have **ATMs** outside.

Lost and Found: ☎662 33 or 621 61, www.fundinfo.at or www.fundamt.gv.at. In the *Rathaus*, next to the tourist office. Open daily 8am-noon and 1:30-7pm.

Lockers: At the Hauptbahnhof. Open 5am-1am. €2 for 24hr.

Emergencies: Police ☎133, **Fire** ☎122, **Medical** ☎144, **Auto Repair** ☎123, **Mountain Rescue** ☎140.

Ski Conditions: ☎62 15 50 (in English or German). **Road Conditions:** ☎15 86.

Pharmacy: Stadt-Apotheke Vogl, Vorderstadt 15. Open M-F 8am-noon and 2:30-6:15pm, Sa 8am-noon.

Internet Access: Video-Kitz, Schloßerg. 10 (☎724 27; kitzvideo@kitz.net). On Jochbergerstr., head down the stairs in front to Schloßerg. They also rent videos. Internet €0.10 per min. Open M-Sa 11am-9pm, high-season also Su 2-7pm.

Post Office: Josef-Pirchlstr. 11 (☎627 12), between the stoplight and the *Fußgängerzone*. Bus schedules, fax, and copier (€0.20) inside. Open M-F 8am-noon and 2-6pm. **Currency exchange** open M-F 8am-noon and 4-5pm. **Postal Code:** A-6370.

⁊ ACCOMMODATIONS

Kitzbühel has almost as many guest beds (7678) as inhabitants (8625), but the only youth hostel is far from town and restricted to groups. The cheaper *Privatzimmer* and *Pensionen* generally run €15-22 per person; expect to shell out as much as €8 per person more during the winter. Be sure to call ahead in winter, as the ski races create a huge bed shortage. Cheaper lodging is also available by bus or train 6km away in **Kirchberg** (tourist office ☎05357 20 00), or in homes and farms in the country around Kitzbühel.

Hotel Kaiser, Bahnhofstr. 2 (☎647 09; mikedodemont@hotmail.com). Exit Hauptbahnhof facing away from the tracks; the hotel will be on left at the end of the street. Michael Dodemont (the English-speaking owner) and his staff, all former backpackers, are happy to greet road-weary travelers; if the hotel's 150 beds are full, Michael will try to help you find somewhere else to stay. School groups often book the hotel, and it is occasionally closed off-season, so call ahead. There's a terrace, billiards table, and inexpensive bar. Laundry service €5. Parking available. €15 per person in 4- to 6-bed dorms and doubles. Possible winter surcharges. Nov.-Dec. Michael offers €12 dorms for backpackers seeking local work. AmEx/DC/MC/V. ❷

Pension Schmidinger, Ehrenbachg. 13 (☎631 34; www.schmidinger.cc). From the *Innenstadt,* head south on Bichlerstr., which merges with Ehrenbachg. The 17 rooms are clean, have local craftsman-style woodwork, and are furnished with desk and TV. All rooms have newly tiled showers. Almost all are doubles, but if there is space lone travelers can have one to themselves. Breakfast included. Reception open about 8am-8pm. Summer rooms €27-35; winter €30-37. Discounts for longer stays. ❸

Hotel Haselberger, Maurachfeld 4 (☎628 66; haselberger@aon.at). Literally 1min. from the bottom station of the *Hahmennkammerbahn,* with the cables passing just inches from the windows. A full-service hotel with hunting lodge decor, Haselberger offers rooms with cable TV, phone and bath. Parking and breakfast included. Summer €35 per person; winter €44. AmEx/MC/V. ❹

Gasthof Eggerwirt, Gänsbachg. 12 (☎624 55; info@eggerwirt-kitzbuehel.at). Approaching town center from the station on Josef-Pirchl-Str., head down the stairs onto Gänsbachg. Mostly doubles; all with TV and bath. On-site restaurant. Breakfast and parking included. Summer €31-40 per person; winter €48-55. Add €5 for singles. MC/V. ❹

Camping Schwarzsee, Reitherstr. 24 (☎62 80 60; hotel.bruggerhof@camping.netwing.at). Take the *Stadtbus* (€1.50) from the train stations (7:20am-6:22pm, only 1 bus 8:07am-12:22pm). Showers included. Tents welcome. Reception 8am-5pm. €7.50, ages 2-12 €5.60. ❶

▐ FOOD

Local specialties include *Tiroler Speckknödel* (bacon-fat dumplings), served either *zu Wasser* (in broth) or *zu Lande* (dry, with salad or sauerkraut), and *Gröstl* (meat and potato hash topped with a fried egg). There is a **SPAR Markt** on the corner of Ehrenbachg. and Bichlstr. (Open M-F 8am-7pm, Sa 7:30am-1pm.)

Huberbräu-Stüberl, Vorderstadt 18 (☎656 77). In the center of town with a terrace that overlooks the street, Huberbräu offers quality *Wienerschnitzel* (€8.00) and Tyrolian *Gröstl* (€ 6.20). Or wash a *Blutwurst* (blood sausage) down with a Huberbräu and get change back from a ten. Closed end of May and beginning of June. Open M-Sa 8am-midnight, Su and holidays 9am-midnight. ❷

Chizzo, Josef Herold-Str. 2 (☎624 75). Skiers staggering off the Hahnenkamm lift can head straight to Chizzo. *Gulasch* with *Eierspatzl* (€12), and *Palatschinken* (currant crêpes) for dessert (€6.70). This restaurant-bar is filled with posters of every Kitzbühel ski race in the last 40 years. Open daily 11am-midnight. ❸

Cafe Kitz, Bichlstr. 7 (☎753 26). This small café boasts excellent *Tiroler Speckbrettl* (bacon, cheese, and pepper platter) and *Wienerschnitzel.* Enjoy friendly, prompt service while dining on the terrace in the shopping district along Graggaug. Most entrees €7-10. Open daily 10am-midnight. Reservations recommended in winter. DC/MC/V. ❷

Restaurant Shang Hai, Kirchg. 5 (☎621 78). Painted dragons and peacocks on the ceiling watch tourists eat fried rice (€7.20), *Verücktes Huhn* (Crazy Chicken; €9.90) and fish with bamboo shoots (€8.70). Chinese harp music reminds you this is a classy establishment. Open daily 11:30am-2:30pm and 5:30-11pm. AmEx/MC/V. ❸

La Fonda, Hinterstadt 13 (☎736 73). Straw hats, stucco walls, and Garth Brooks on the stereo: it's Tex-Mex done Austrian-style. Chicken wings, chicken curry, and nachos run €5.50-7. Despite crowds, La Fonda maintains a laid-back atmosphere. Take-out on request. Open daily June-Sept. 11am-2am; Dec.-Mar. 4pm-2am. ❷

🅾 🎵 SIGHTS & ENTERTAINMENT

Kitzbühel's church steeples define the town's skyline. The **Pfarrkirche** (parish church) and the **Liebfrauenkirche** (Church of Our Lady) lie in an ivy-cloaked courtyard surrounded by an old cemetery. Between the churches stands the **Ölberg Chapel,** dating from 1450, with frescoes from the late 1500s. The town itself is even older, having celebrated its 700th anniversary in 1971. The local **Heimatmuseum** (Regional Museum), Hinterstadt 34, celebrates this longevity with artifacts in Kitzbühel's oldest house, dating from the 12th century. Old rusty tools are displayed, including prehistoric mining equipment and the world's first metal bobsled into storage. Occasional special exhibits, like "The Magic of Tibet" (the only place in the world Tyroleans are willing to admit has better mountains) sometimes take the place of the regular displays. (☎672 74. Open June 21-Sept. 21 M-Sa 10am-6pm; Sept. 22-Dec 5 Tu-Sa 10am-1pm; Dec. 6-March 10 Tu-Sa 10am-1pm and 3-6pm. Adults €4, with guest card €3; children 6-18 €3; under 6 free groups €3.)

At the free **concerts** in the center of town, you might find anything from folk harpists to Sousa bands. Scheduled events include a March 2004 Jazz Festival and San Pellegrino Star Cup and in April 2004 a *Bridge-Turnier*. Current events available at tourist office. **Casino Kitzbühel** is near the tourist office. (☎623 00. W ladies' night, free glass of champagne; first F of each month men's night, free cognac. Semi-formal. 18+. No cover. Open July-Sept. 7pm-late.) At the end of July, the **Austrian Open** Men's Tennis Championship (Generali Open) comes to town, drawing such athletes as Austria's own Thomas Muster to the Kitzbühel Tennis Club. (☎720 76; www.generaliopen.at. Tickets ☎633 25.)

🎵 NIGHTLIFE

During the high tourist season (roughly mid-Dec. to Mar. and July-Sept.), Kitzbühel nightlife comes alive. Particularly during special events like the *Hahnenkamm* race (Jan. 23-26, 2003) and the *Generali Open* (last weekend in July), tourists pack the streets, looking for a place to party. With more than 30 bars in town, Kitzbühel is up to the challenge.

🏅 The Londoner, Franz-Reichstr. 4 (☎714 28). A staple for 27 years, The Londoner is the place to be. The bar has a huge list of specialities for €3, including the Slippery Nipple, Flugerl, and Kamikazi. Posters and pictures plaster the walls, and the liveliness of both staff and guests makes for an unbeatable party. During the famous Hahnenkamm race, the men's downhill stars take off their shirts and dance on the bar. Dec.-Apr. live bands all week; May-Nov. 2 times per week. Open Dec.-Apr. daily noon-4am; May-Nov. Su-Th 7pm-2am, F-Sa 7pm-3am.

Highways, Im Gries 20 (☎753 50). From the tourist office, turn right and exit under the arch onto Bichlst., left onto Graggaug., walk 2 blocks and turn left onto Im Gries. Home to crowds of teenagers in summer and tourists in winter, Highways serves pizza (€5-7) and sandwiches (€3-4), and offers an extensive drink menu (cocktails €7). Their loud music consists of 60s-90s hits, interspersed with occasional live acts. Open daily May-Oct. 9pm-3am; Nov.-Apr. 8pm-3am.

s'Lichtl, Vorderstadt 9. Christmas lights, small disco balls, and blood-red tablecloths give this place a funky feel. DJ plays today's hits. Beer €3, drinks €5. W 60s night. Open June-Mar. daily 9pm-3am. AmEx/MC/V, for bills over €20.

⚠ OUTDOOR ACTIVITIES

Few visitors to Kitzbühel remain at ground level for long. The Kitzbühel **ski area,** the "Ski Circus," is one of the finest in the world. Every winter since 1931, Kitzbühel has hosted the **Hahnenkamm Ski Competition,** part of the annual World Cup and considered one of the world's most difficult runs. The competition turns the town into a rollicking seven-day party. (☎ 735 55 for tickets. €4-15 per day.) For summer visitors, three- or six-day vacation passes can save a bundle of money. They're good for free lifts and *Aquarena* swimming pool (see below). They are available at all lifts. (3-day pass €35, children €19.50; 6-day €48, €26.50.)

SKIING. The best deal is the **Kitzbüheler Alpen Ski Pass,** which gives access to 260 lifts and 680km of skiing trails. (Good for any 6 days of the ski season. Dec. 20-Mar. €160, Dec. 5-19 and after Mar. 15 €139.5; ages 8-16 $128/€115.50. 1-day ski pass Adults €34/€29.50, children €27.50/€24. Passes grants passage on 64 lifts and shuttle buses that connect them. Lift ticket prices drop for multi-day purchases, from anywhere from 2-14 days.) Tickets for individual lifts, such as the **Gaisberg, Maierl I,** and **Obergaisberg,** are also available. Purchase passes at any of the lifts or at the **Kurhaus Aquarena,** which offers a pool, as well as a sauna and solarium at extra fees. (☎ 643 85; www.bergbahn-kitzbuehel.at. Open daily 9am-8pm. €8, children €5, with guest card €6.80/€4.50; free entry in winter with ski passes of 2 days or more, in summer with 3- or 6-day vacation pass.)

Rent skis at the Hahnenkamm lift or from a sports shop in the area. Try **Kitzsport Schlechter,** at Jochbergerstr. 7. (☎ 625 04; www.horsthoerl@kitzsport.at.). **Skiport Flori** (☎ 725 13; m.resch.kitz@aon.at), or **Skiverleih.** (☎ 654 96; josef-dagn@skischule-reith.at. Hours are generally M-F 8:30am-noon and 2:30-6pm, Sa 8:30am-12:30pm.) Lessons cost around €35 for a one-day group lesson. Ask at the tourist office about **ski packages:** special low-season deals on lodging, ski passes, and instruction. Week-long packages without instruction start at around €280 per person.

HIKING. More than 70 **hiking trails** snake up the mountains surrounding Kitzbühel. Among these are a variety of pleasurable day hikes, covering a wide range of difficulty levels. To avoid getting lost, pick up a free *Hiking Trail Map* at the tourist office which details trailheads, estimated hiking times, and difficulty ratings for 77 hikes.

Hausbergweg: trail #36 (5km, 5hr. round-trip). Follow the signs to "Hahnenkamm" the whole way up. Good for relatively advanced hikers. The Hausbergweg is a consistently steep trail that tracks staight up the spine of the Hahnenkamm. Grand views almost the entire way, particularly toward the top, make this trail well worth all the sweat. If you go, leave time for some reasonably priced, hearty Tyrolean cuisine at **Gasthaus Seidlalm** ❷ (☎ 631 35; open May-Oct. and Dec.-Easter daily 9am-6pm), on the side of the trail. The hike finishes at the top of the Hahnenkammbahn (see below) and provides access to other trails that go even farther and higher.

Seidlalmweg: trail #9 (about 10km, 2-5hr. round-trip). Somewhat less difficult than the Hausbergweg. There are a number of ways to hike this trail without going the whole 10km. The lower parts of the trail generally go through the forest, while the higher part that cuts across the mountains has the best scenery. Starting points are at the Hahnen-kammbahn parking lot and the parking lot near the Streifalm chair lift.

Schwarzseerundgang: trail #12 (3.2km, 1½hr. round-trip). A great choice for those who don't want to climb a mountain (or even part of one). A generally level, enjoyable hike along the lake on the outskirts of Kitzbühel. Trailhead near "Schwarzsee" bus or train stop.

For those with a bit more cash, cable cars do the climbing for you, and provide the same open vistas. You can take the **Hahnenkammbahn** to the top of its name-sake. During the summer the starting gate is open from 11am-3:30pm, allowing free access to see the course, albeit without the snow. (Open daily 8am-5:30pm; €14 up or round-trip, with guest card €13, children €8. Full-day summer pass for Kitzbühel's lift €24; 3-day €35; 6-day €48, children €26.50; all summer €113. The *Summerhit* special includes a 3-course meal and a ride on the Hahnenkamm for €20.) At the top of the Hahnenkammbahn is the **Bergbahn Museum Hahnenkamm,** which gives a history of winter sports in the area, and includes a larger-than-life ski simulator. (☎69 57. Open daily 10am-4pm. Free.) The **Kitzbüheler Hornbahn lift** ascends to the **Alpenblumengarten,** where more than 120 different types of flowers blossom each spring. (Open late-May to mid-Oct. 8:30am-5pm. Same prices as Hahnenkammerlift. Free tours July-Aug. 10am, 1:30pm.) The smaller **Gaisberg, Rest-erhöhe,** and **Streiteck** lifts also run in summer.

Guest card holders can take advantage of the tourist office's **hiking program.** Daily 3 to 5hr. hikes cover over 100 routes and are easy or moderate. (Mid-May to mid-Oct. M-F at 8:45am; call ahead for weekend hikes. Free with guest card, but doesn't include cable cars and taxi.) Contact **Mountain High Adventure Center** (☎/fax 05352 621 01; www.mountain-high.at) in neighboring St. Johann, for extreme activities like paragliding (€98, includes lift), skydiving (€189), rafting (€38), ballooning (€250), mountain biking (€19), and horse trekking (€16).

SWIMMING. The **Schwarzsee,** 2.5km from Kitzbühel, is famed for its healing mud baths. Float in the water and gaze at mountains above. *(See directions to Camping Schwarzsee; last bus back at 6pm. ☎623 81. Open 8am-6pm. €3, children €1; after 4pm €1/€0.50. Electric boat rental after 8:30am; €7 per 30min., rowboats €3.70.)*

▶ DAYTRIP FROM KITZBÜHEL

KUFSTEIN   ☎05372

Trains run from Kitzbühel with a transfer in Wörgl (1hr., 2 per hr. 4:56am-9:29pm, €7.50), and from Innsbruck (1hr., 2 per hr., €10.50). The station is on the west bank of the Inn river. Ticket office open M-F 5:35am-7:45pm, Su and holidays 7:30am-8:15pm.

A sleepy village along the swift-flowing Inn River, Kufstein retains much of the small-town atmosphere that some of its bigger and glitzier neighbors lack. The impressive 12th-century *Festung* (fortress) on a hill in the middle of town and the mountainous backdrop provide good reasons for a relaxing daytrip. The **tourist office,** Unterer Stadtpl. 8, just across the river from the train station, distributes free hiking, biking, and skiing maps, as well as a complete list of accommodations and restaurants. (☎622 07; www.kufstein.at. Open high-season M-F 8:30am-6pm, Sa 9am-noon; low-season M-F 8:30am-noon and 2-5pm.)

TYROL

The **Pension Striede ❸**, Mittendorfstr. 20, located a 5-10min. walk from Kuf-stein's center: from the station, cross the bridge and go straight, through Unterer Stadtpl. and then right onto Kinkstr.; after 5min. left onto Weissachstr. and then almost immediately a right onto Mittendorfstr. Offers 15 rooms equipped with TV, bath, and many with balconies. (☎622 16; www.striede.at. Parking available. Reception daily 8am-noon. Winter €24-27.25; summer €23-26 per person. Discounts for children. Reservations strongly recommended.)

Kufstein's main attraction is the **Festung** (fortress), which towers over the rest of the city. Climb to the fortress grounds via a wooden *Gangsteig* (covered staircase) or take a short cable car ride. Once within the *Festung*, you're free to walk around the stone ramparts and grassy knolls, many of which provide excellent views of the river valley below. At the top of the fortress, the **Heimatmuseum** (Regional Museum) features an assortment of prehistoric and early modern artifacts, rooms devoted to the lifestyles of locals in previous centuries, and a room with a model of the *Festung* and a history of its construction. Across from the *Heimatmuseum* is a tower containing the restored former city jail. (☎60 23 50. Open Palm Sunday to mid-Nov. 9am-5pm; mid-Nov. to Palm Sunday 10am-4pm. Entrance to fortress, museum, and cable-car ride summer €8, students €4.40; winter €7/€4. 1hr. tours in summer upon request €1.50.) The *Festung* also houses the 4037 pipes of the **Heldenorgel** (Heroes' Organ), the world's largest open-air organ, constructed in 1931 in honor of Austrian soldiers who died in WWI. An exhibit in the fortress near the pipes contains WWI artifacts including uniforms and grenades. The organ is played on the keyboard at the base of the fortress every day at noon, and during July and August again at 5pm. (€0.80 for auditorium seat; or stand a bit outside and hear the pipes nearly as well.)

For hiking, take the **Kaiserlift** into the mountains. Turn left at the end of Unterer Stadtpl., walk a few blocks, and follow the signs to the chairlift parking lot. The first lift goes to Duxeralm, the second to Brentenjoch. (Open daily 9am-4:30pm. Duxeralm ascent €4.35, children €1.35, round-trip €5.45/€2.90. Brentenjoch ascent €7.25/€2.90, round-trip €10.15/€4.35.) There are myriad mid-level **hiking trails** on the mountain. After Unterer Stadtpl., take Georg-Pir-moserstr. to Bachg. (turns into Schutzerstr.) to the trailheads. At the top near the Brentenjoch, the trails open up to breathtaking vistas. It is well worth going because the backside of Mt. Kaiser is visible above Duxeralm—just follow the signs to Berghaus Aschenbrenner and climb from there. (4-5hr. total hiking time without any chairlifts.)

ST. ANTON AM ARLBERG   ☎05446

Always one of the world's premier ski towns, St. Anton had the world's attention in 2001 when it hosted the world skiing championships. In anticipations of the event, the train station was moved to the other side of the valley and a glistening new conference center and sports complex were built. What has been constant both before and after this facelift is the yearly winter influx of tourists looking to hit the world-class slopes.

 TRANSPORTATION. St. Anton lies at the bottom of a steep, narrow valley, with neighboring **St. Jakob** and **St. Christoph** (both technically part of St. Anton) each a few minutes away. Several **train** routes connect St. Anton with major destinations including: Feldkirch (45min., every 2hr. 5:15am-11:59pm, €6.60); Innsbruck (1¼hr., every 2hr. 6:13am-12:45am, €12.80); Vienna Westbahnhof (6½-8½hr., 8 per day 6:13am-11:18pm, €52.50); Zurich (2½-3½hr., 7 per day 5:28am-7:59pm, €32.80). From late June to September and December to April, **Postbuses**

(☎05442 644 22) run from the Hauptbahnhof to: Lech (30min., June-Sept. 5 per day, 8am-5pm); St. Christoph (10min., June-Sept. 5 per day, 8am-5pm. €1.80); St. Jakob (5min., June-Sept. 12 per day 6:21am-6:35pm, €1.80). A **free town bus** leaves from the post office every 10 min. past the hour, 7:10am-6:10pm. Call for a winter bus schedule. Buses stop at the train station as well as the "Westterminal," the parking lot by the highway on the east side of town. A sign with a black eagle denotes the free city bus stops.

■■🛈 **ORIENTATION & PRACTICAL INFORMATION.** St. Anton's main road runs the length of the *Fußgängerzone*. The large wooden **tourist office,** across from the train station, provides information on St. Anton and the Arlberg region. Outside is a 24hr. accommodations board. (☎226 90; www.stantonamarlberg.com. Open May-late Nov. M-F 8am-6pm, Sa-Su 2-6pm; Dec.-Apr. M-F 8:30am-6:30pm, Sa 9am-noon and 1-6pm, Su 10am-noon and 3-6pm.) Services include: **currency exchange** at banks (M-F 8am-noon and 2-5pm); **bike rental** at **Intersport Arlberg** in the pedestrian zone (☎34 53; info@intersport-arlberg.com; open M-F 9am-noon and 1-6pm, Sa 9am-noon; 1 day €20-28, 1 week €99-139); **Internet** access at **Mailbox** near SportCafé Schneider (open July-Oct. noon-5pm; Nov.-Apr. 9am-9pm; €0.20 per min.), and at Soapbox (below; same prices); 24hr. **luggage storage** at the station (€2-2.50); **laundry** at **Soapbox,** Dorfstr. 61 (open M-F 9am-10pm, Sa 9am-noon); and **taxis** (☎231 50, 236 80). **Snow report** ☎25 65. **Police** ☎133 (town police ☎23 62 13 or 22 37), **ambulance** ☎144. To find the **post office,** exit the tourist office, turn right down the main road, right again opposite Hotel Schwarzer Adler, and then take a quick right after the bend to the left. (☎33 80. Open M-F 8am-noon and 2-5:30pm.) **Postal code:** A-6580.

🚪🍴 **ACCOMMODATIONS & FOOD.** During the ski season, prices double and rooms fill up well in advance, so make reservations early. Your best bet for an affordable winter lodging may be in **St. Jakob** (5min. by free city bus); check with the St. Anton tourist office. To get to **Pension Pepi Eiter ❸,** turn left from the tourist office and head uphill; after 300m, a green sign points the way. Pepi Eiter provides comfy beds and pine-panelled rooms with TV and a chocolate on the nightstand. (☎25 50 or 23 19. Breakfast and parking included. June-Sept. €18-20 per person; mid-Dec. to Apr. €36.) Four-star accommodations are nearly affordable in the summer. For the **Hotel San Antonio ❸,** Nassereinerstr. 38, from the *Fußgängerzone* head up Dorfstr. to Nassereinerg., then turn left onto Nassereinerstr. The hotel is on the right. Boasting a pizzeria (entrees €6-6.50), candlepin bowling, and huge, sunny rooms with living room and TV, San Antonio provides luxury for relatively little money. (☎34 74; fax 34 73 15. Breakfast included. Rooms June-Sept. €28-30; Dec.-Apr. €55-60.)

For a great meal at a low price, head to **Restaurant Grieswirt ❸,** between the *Fußgängerzone* and the post office. Well-prepared entrees (€6.90-10.61) and two daily *Menüs* including soup, entree, and dessert (€10.54-12, €1.45 more in winter) will leave you fully satisfied. (☎29 65; fax 200 56. Open daily June-Sept. 9am-9pm; Dec. to mid-Apr. 11am-10:30pm.) **SportCafé Schneider ❷,** Dorfstr. 19, is to the right down the *Fußgängerzone* from the tourist office. A cross between an Imbiss and a restaurant, SportCafé is perfect for a quick lunch or late dinner. They serve a small selection of soups and sandwiches (€3-5.20), spaghetti Bolognese (€6.90), and ice cream desserts (€3-4.70). (☎25 48. Open daily 9am-midnight.) The local **SPAR Markt,** Dorfstr. 62, is down the main road, 10min. away from the tourist office, just past the *Fußgängerzone*. (Open M-F 7am-noon and 2-7pm, Sa 7am-5pm.)

⚄ OUTDOOR ACTIVITIES. A century after the Ski Club Arlberg was founded, St. Anton's main draw is still its exceptional slopes. Some 262 trails cover the area, divided into 260km of groomed trails and some 185km of ungroomed ("deep snow") runs, all accessed by over 80 cable cars and lifts. **Ski passes** for the Arlberg region are sold at the ski lift stations (Galzigbahn, Rendlbahn, St. Christophbahn, and Nasserein-bahn), or at the ticket office in the *Fußgängerzone* behind the Hotel Post. (Half-day pass €29, ages 16-19 €26.50, ages 7-15 €17.50; 1-day pass €38.5/€35/€23; 7-day pass €202/€174/€121. Further discounts apply outside of peak season.) Those interested in St. Anton's free 4.2km **toboggan run** should call ☎235 20. There are two **ski schools** in St. Anton: **Ski School** (www.skischool-arlberg.com; open Su-F 8:30am-4:30pm, Sa 9am-noon and 1-5pm; offers half-day group lessons and private half-day lessons) and **Ski and Snowboard School St. Anton** (☎35 63, www.skistanton.com; open Su-F 8:30am-4:30pm, Sa 8am-5pm; gives half-day group lessons €57; half-day private lesson €150; 3-day "Snowboard College" lessons €147).

In the summer, St. Anton is a hiker's haven. Trails lead through the hills around town and the tourist office dispenses maps and directions. Once a week in July, the tourist office sponsors **wildflower hikes.** The easy **Rosannaschlucht hike** (3hr. loop) leads through the Rosanna gorge between St. Anton and Ferwall to the west, out to the emerald-green Ferwall See, and back on the hills on the other side of the river. Walk on the highway leaving St. Anton towards Lech, and look for the Rendl cable car on the left side of the road, where the trail begins. From there, the **Leutkircher Hütte** mountain hut is a 3hr. moderate hike. (☎05448 82 07. Open early July-late Sept.) For a great view from the roof of the Arlberg, take the series of three Galzigbahn lifts starting in St. Anton to the top of the 2811m Valluga. (Lifts in summer daily 9am-4:30pm. Round-trip €17.50.) A number of wonderful hikes through high Alpine country can be found in the neighboring resort towns of **Lech** and **Zürs.** Try the strenuous hike around the **Madloch** between the two towns, or the **Gipslöcher Naturlehrpfad,** which wanders through the a strange landscape of natural sinkholes on the mountainside above Lech. Inquire at the St. Anton tourist offices for bus schedules, and at the Lech tourist office for hikes. (☎05583 22 45; www.lech-zuers.at.) **Biking** in the Arlberg is arduous but rewarding; 150km of marked mountain bike paths await, including the popular Ferwall Valley and Moostal trails.

THE ZILLERTAL

When the fog descends on the small villages of the Zillertal (Ziller Valley) they may as well be cut off from the rest of the world. Squeezed between three mountain ranges, these towns are remote and peaceful year round. Boasting more trails than roads and a larger ski patrol than police force, the Zillertal is a great place for skiing and hiking. In March of 2001 the province of Tyrol listed three of the region's valleys as protected areas, and classified the region as the Alps High-Mountain Nature Park. While the Tuxertal, extending into the mountains from Mayrhofen, is not part of the park, it offers year-round skiing on the Hintertux Glacier.

⚏ TRANSPORTATION

Trains: The Zillertal can be reached by train from the north through Jenbach, at the head of the valley. Trains leave the Jenbach station (☎05244 62 54 63 85) for: **Innsbruck** (20-35min., 2-3 per hr. 4:31am-10:38pm, €5.30); **Vienna** (4.5-6.5hrs., 7per day

5:19am-7:50pm, €46.50); **Wörgl** (20min., 2-3 per hr. 5:19am-12:06am, €4.60). For travel to within the valley contact the **Zillertalbahn (Z-bahn),** an efficient network of private buses and trains connecting the villages. (☎05244 60 60; www.zillertalbahn.at.) The Z-bahn has 2 types of trains, the Dampfzug and the Triebwagen. The Dampfzug is an historic red steam train targeted at tourists; it costs extra and moves more slowly. The Triebwagen is a normal train, and has the same rates as the Z-bahn Autobus. One of either the Triebwagen or Autobus leaves daily every hr. 6am-9pm. Beyond Mayrhofen, travel is by bus only. Those planning to stay in the region for several days should consider the **Zillertal card (Z-card),** which covers all train and bus lines from Jenbach to Hintertux (except the Dampfzug). In the summer the card also includes mountain lifts other than the upper gondolas of the Hintertux Glacier.

Buses: If possible, travel to or from the Zillertal over the Gerlos Pass on A165 to Zell am Ziller. The road offers awe-inspiring vistas, curves, and creeks not to be missed. Transit through the valley this way is available by Zillertalbus (☎05282 22 11) from Zell am Ziller to Königsleiten (departs Zell 8:52, 11:10am, 1:30, 4:10pm; €4), and then a connection with the Postbus from Königsleiten to Krimml (☎0250 856 23 52; 9:50am, 5:05pm; €4). The road is also open to cars and bikes.

◪ HIKING & SKIING

The **Z-card** is valid on all summer lifts in the Zillertal, including those in Zell am Ziller, Fügen, Mayrhofen, Gerlos, and Hintertux Passes are available at tourist offices, lifts, or railway stations in Zell am Ziller and Mayrhofen, and may be used only once at each lift per day. Hiking without cable cars is also possible throughout the valley. Hiking between towns in the Zillertal Valley is an option for the hardy traveler. The Zell am Ziller **ski area,** recently connected to the Gerlos and Königsleiten ski areas, is the largest ski zone in Tyrol. The **Zillertal Super Skipass** covers lifts for the entire region, and is available at any valley lift station. (☎716 50; www.zillertalski.at. 4-day Super Skipasses not including the Hintertux Glacier €114, ages 15-18 €91, children €68; with Glacier €117/€94/€70.)

Located at the end of the the Tux Valley, **Hintertux** is an expensive, well-touristed town with year-round skiing on its famous glacier. Buses run from Mayrhofen to Hintertux, €6, 7:55am-5:50pm. (☎05287 858 04 10. **Summer skiing:** 1 day €28.50, ages 15-18 €23, children €17; 4 days €99/€79.20/€59.50; 10 days €201/€160.80/€120.60. **Winter skiing:** 1 day €34.50/€28.50/€21, 4 days €117/€94/€70, 10 days €243/€195/€146.)

ZELL AM ZILLER   ☎05282

Zell am Ziller (pop. 4000), 20km south of Jenbach, embodies picture-book images of Austrian mountain villages, with fields of tall grass and taller mountains embracing clusters of wood-shuttered alpine houses. Founded by monks in the late 8th century—hence the *Zell,* or chapel— Zell surrendered to materialism in the 1600s when it flourished as a gold-mining town. Today, this idyllic and unassuming village offers skiing and hiking without resort-town hype.

◪ TRANSPORTATION. Zell is at the north-central end of the Zillertal, between Jenbach and Mayrhofen. Those taking **ÖBB trains** should get off at **Jenbach** and switch to the private **Zillertalbahn** (**Z-bahn;** see above), which leaves from the front of the train station. Z-bahn trains and buses leave at least once per hour about 6am-9pm for Jenbach or Mayrhofen. Get to Zell am Ziller by **car** from the Inntalautobahn, taking the Zillertal exit and driving 24km on Zillertal-Bundesstr. 109.

⚡ 🛈 ORIENTATION & PRACTICAL INFORMATION. The center of town is **Dorfplatz**. Straight out of the train station down Bahnhofstr., Dorfpl. intersects both of Zell's main streets, Unterdorf next to the river, and Gerlosstr. by the train tracks. From the station, head right on Bahnhofstr., and turn right at the end to get to the **tourist office**, Dorfpl. 3a. Pick up a town map, hiking maps (€6.50-7.95), skiing information, and accommodations listings. There's a free reservations phone on the side of the office. (☎22 81; www.zell.at. Open M-F 8:30am-12:30pm and 2:30-6pm, Sa 9am-noon and 4-6pm, July-Oct. also Sa 9am-noon and 4-6pm. Dec.-Jan. also Su 4-6pm). Services include: **luggage storage** at the train station (daily 8am-noon and 2-5pm, €2.50); **taxis** (☎26 25, 23 45, or 22 55); **bike rental** at the tourist office (€15; mountain bikes only), the train station (€12, children €7.20), or at **SB-Markt Hofer,** Gerlosstr. 30, opposite the campground. (☎22 20. Open M-F 7:15am-noon and 2:30-6:15pm, Sa 7:15am-noon. Mountain bikes €14 per day, road bikes €9, children €5.) **Mountain rescue** or **police** ☎133; **ambulance** ☎144,. The **post office** at Unterdorf 2 **exchanges** money until 5pm and has an **ATM** in front. (☎23 33 11. Open M-F 8am-noon and 2-6pm.) **Postal code:** A-6280.

🛏 ACCOMMODATIONS & CAMPING. Many places offer decent rates, and good accommodations can be found without trekking too far from the town center. To reach **Haus Huditz ❷,** Karl-Platzer-Weg 1, cross the train tracks by the tourist office and continue onto Gerlosstr.; bear left onto Gauderg. at the Mode Journal building and look for Karl-Platzer-Weg on the left at the next fork in the road (10min.). The incredibly warm and friendly owner provides beverages, TV, down comforters, and balconies with mountain views, all at a reasonable price. (☎22 28. huditz.bern-hard@gutanet.at. Breakfast included. Shower €1. €14.60, in winter €16-17.) **Hotel Rosengarten ❸,** Rosengartenweg 14, has window boxes with beautiful geraniums and marigolds. Offers spacious rooms, all with shower and satellite TV. On-site sauna and café. (☎24 43; fax 244 34. Doubles with shower Apr.-Oct. €26; Dec.-Mar. €34.) **Camping Hofer ❶,** Gerlosstr. 33, offers just enough space for your tent a few blocks from the town center. Free bike tours, weekly hikes, a swimming pool, and a playground are all provided. There's a grocery store across the street. 'Fritz and Didi,' the house band, performs in the bar adjacent to the reception W nights. Showers are included. (☎22 48; office@campinghofer.at. Laundry €7. Reception Dec. 12 to Jan. 1 and July-Aug. 15 8am-10pm; May-June and Sept.-Oct. 9am-noon and 3-8pm. €4.50-5.20 per adult; €7-8 per campsite; €1 tax per person per night. Also offers rooms: doubles with shower €20-22.)

🍴 FOOD. Local specialties include *Käsespätzle* (baked noodles with cheese and onions, and sometimes wurst or eggs), *Zillertaler Krapfen* (crispy fried shells filled with potato and cheese) and *Tiroler Gröstl* (fried potatoes, onions and bacon with a fried egg on top). **SB Restaurant Zeller Stuben ❷,** Unterdorf 11, the cheapest place around, serves big buffet-style portions. Spaghetti (€4.50), *Gulaschsuppe* (€3), and almost nothing over €6.50. The somewhat less casual restaurant upstairs features 6-8 daily *Menüs* including soup, entree, and dessert for €6.50-14. (☎22 71. Children's and vegetarian menus available. Both restaurants open July-Oct. and Dec. 20 to mid-Apr. daily 11am-9pm.) Cross the river for **Pizza Cafe Reiter ❷,** Zelbergr. 4. Stay outdoors by the river or sit inside and watch continuous videos of paragliders (see Pizza Air, p. 218). The chef serves pizza (€5-10), pasta, and calzones (€7). (☎22 89. Open daily 11am-midnight.) Put the cherry on your night at **Café-Konditorei Gredler ❶,** Unterdorf 10, near SB restaurant. 1995 Confectioner of the Year Tobias Gredler whips up desserts for patrons to enjoy on the riverside patio. Banana chocolate torte actually looks like a banana, thanks to the yellow sugar and chocolate shell; the other 17 tortes (€2.50) are no less intricate or delectable. (☎248 90; www.torten.net. Open daily June-Oct. 10am-11pm; mid-Dec. to May 10am-6pm.) **SPAR Supermarkt** is around the corner from the tourist office, next to Intersport Strasser. (Open M-F 7:30am-12:30pm and 2-6:30pm, Sa 7:30am-1pm and 2-5pm.)

BRING ON THE BREW The residents of Zell am Ziller celebrate their local brewer with **Gauderfest** on the first weekend in May, when the whole town gets sauced in a 3-day celebration of cold, frothy beverages. The name "Gauderfest" is derived from the estate that owns the local private brewery. The Bräumeister's vats, Tyrol's oldest, concoct the beloved and potent Gauderbock especially for the occasion. The festival even has its own jingle: *Gauderwürst und G'selchts mit Kraut / hei, wia taut dösmunden / und 10 Halbe Bockbier drauf / mehr braucht's nit zum G'sundsein!* ("Gauder sausage and smoked pork with sauerkraut / hey, how good it tastes / and 10 pints of beer to go with it / what more could you need for your health!"). The festival's highlight is the **Ranggeln,** traditional wrestling for the title of "Hogmoar." There are also animal fights (attended by a veterinary surgeon) and customary activities like the **Grasausläuten** (ringing bells in order to wake the grass and make it grow). Revelry continues into the night with Tyrolean folk singing and dancing.

⚑ OUTDOOR ACTIVITIES. For skiing, Zell sells single day passes valid on the **Kreuzjoch-Rosenalm Königsleiten** and **Gerlosplatte,** 492 km of slopes served by 152 ski lifts. (1 day €32, ages 15-19 €25.60, under 15 €19.20; 3 days €87/€69/€52.20); and Super Skipasses for longer visits (without the Hintertux glacier 4 days €114/€91/€68; with glacier €117/€94/€70). Single-ride tickets are available for non-skiers who tag along to watch. (€5.40, round-trip €8.80; children €2.70/€4.40; discount with guest card.) Obtain passes at the **Kreuzjoch** (☎71 65), **Gerlosstein** (☎22 75), or **Ramsberg** (☎27 20) cable car stations. (All 3 lifts open 8:30am-5pm.) Info from the snowphone. (☎71 65 26; www.zillertalarena.at.) **Rent skis** at any of Zell's sporting goods stores. Try **Pendl Sport** at Gerlosstr. 3. (☎22 87; fax 39 17. Open M-F 8am-noon and 2:30-6:30pm, Sa 8am-noon, Dec.-Easter also Sa 2-6pm. DC/MC/V.) Prices average €16-20 for skiing gear, €24 for snowboards. Rent **toboggans** at the Gerlossteinbahn. (Open M-Sa 7:45am-9:15pm, Su 8:30am-4:30pm.)

Summer activities include **Nordicwalking,** a program of guided tours through the mountains. Early birds can join the "Sunrise Experience" (5am start) or "Peak as Goal" (8:30am for two peaks in one day), among other tours. (June-Sept. M-W. All free with **guest card** obtained by registering a day in advance with the tourist office as a guest at any Pension or hotel in town.) Much hiking around Zell am Ziller is lift-assisted. Two of the three ski lifts in Zell's vicinity offer **alpine hiking:** the **Kreuzjochbahn** (☎716 50; open 8:40am-12:10pm and 1-5:10pm; round-trip without guest card €9.20, with card €8.40; to Rosenalm €13.80/€12.60) and **Gerlossteinbahn** (☎22 75; open 8:30am-12:15pm and 1-5pm; round-trip €9.30/€8.40). The *Karspitz* (2264m) provides an ideal hiking goal; on sunny days you can see the entire valley and the waterfalls on the opposite ridge. From the Kreuzjochbahn top station, turn right and follow parth #11. At Grindalm, you have the option of heading straight towards Kreuzwiessenhut, and further to the peak. Take path #10 back to the lift.

Those preferring air travel to hiking on the ground should head to **Pizza Air,** the self-proclaimed "World's Smallest Airline." (☎22 89. Offers tandem flights from 5-25min. for €70-110.) For a down-to-earth look at Zell's history, take a tour of the nearby **gold mine.** The journey begins at a petting zoo and adjacent cheese factory before moving on to a 45min. hike to the mine entrance. (☎48 20; fax 32 72. May-Sept. 2hr. tours every hr. daily 9am-6pm. €10, ages 3-16 €5.)

MAYRHOFEN   ☎05285

At the southernmost end of the Zillertal, Mayrhofen draws flocks of travelers from afar who have come to see the Alps. The polished town is the center of tourist activity for the Zillertal, and therefore also the center for food, mountain schools, and nightlife. Four separate valleys (the **Zillergrund, Stillupgrund, Zemmtal,** and **Tuxertal**) converge on the town, providing endless opportunities for hikers and skiers. Mayrhofen residents walk the walk: native Peter Habeler and fellow Tyrolean Reinhold Messner completed the first oxygen-unaided ascent of Mt. Everest in 1978. Habeler now runs the town's alpine school.

◨◪ TRANSPORTATION & PRACTICAL INFORMATION. Mayrhofen is accessible via the **trains** and **buses** of the Z-Bahn from Jenbach (50min.-1hr., 27 per day 6:05am-9:05pm, €5.30) and Zell am Ziller (15min., 27 per day 6:43am-9:52pm, €1.80). The **train station** lies slightly northeast of town; to reach the center, walk uphill on the main road and turn left at the intersection. (☎623 62. Open M-F 8-11:45am and 12:30-5pm, Sa 8-11:45am and 12:30-4:10pm, Su 8:55am-3:30pm.) **Taxis** ☎633 64, 638 40, or 622 60. The **tourist office,** Dursterstr. 225, is in the lower end of town. Enter town from the train station, turn left on Hauptstr., then right onto Dursterstr. The office leads free **guided hikes and tours,** from valley tours to 5hr. hikes; transportation costs not included (€5-15). A 24hr. accommodations board is outside. Tours mid-May to mid-Oct. M-F; call ahead for details. ☎67 60; info@mayrhofen.at. Open M-F 8am-6pm, Sa 9am-noon, Su 10am-noon; July-Aug. also Sa 2-6pm.) Services include: **ATM** at Hypo-Tirol bank at the corner of Einfahrt Mitte and Hauptstr.; **luggage storage** at the train station (Open daily 7am-6:30pm, €2.10 per piece); **bike rental** at the train station (€12 per day, €7.20 for a half-day after 1pm). **Police** ☎133, **fire** ☎122, **mountain rescue** ☎140, **ambulance** ☎144. The **post office,** Einfahrt Mitte 434, is on your right on the way into town. (☎62 35 10. Open M-F 8am-noon and 2-6pm.) **Postal code:** A-6290.

▟◨ ACCOMMODATIONS & FOOD. Accommodations fill up quickly in Mayrhofen, so it's best to makes reservations in advance. To get to **Haus Woldrich ❸,** Brandbergstr. 355, take Einfahrt Mitte as it turns into Pfarrer-Krapfstr. until the sign for "Brandbergstraße." Turn right and it's the second house on the left. The guest house offers spacious rooms, some with balcony. (☎/fax 623 25. Breakfast included. Singles Apr.-Oct. €14, with shower €18-€20; Dec.-Easter €16/€20.) **Haus Andreas ❸,** Sportplatzstr. 317, a 5min. walk past the tourist office, offers 8 beds in blue and white decorated doubles and triples, all with balconies. (☎/fax 638 45. Breakfast buffet included. Closed May. €16-22.) **Hotel Pension Sieglerhof ❸,** Dursterstr. 226, provides a dark wood interior, TV in each room, and a swing set for the kids. Bar serves drinks after 5pm. (☎62 493; fax 62 49 37. Apr.-Nov. €17-19 per person, with bath €27-29; Dec.-Mar. €20-23/€30-33.) For **Camping Mayrhofen ❶,** Laubichl 125, head left from the station and away from town. At the first intersection turn right, then an immediate left onto Gemeindestr.; the campground is about 700m ahead on the right. Amenities include a heated pool, children's play area, and tent spots away from the RVs. (☎625 80; www.alpenparadies.com. Meals at the on-site restaurant around €8. Solarium €5, sauna €6. 10:30pm-6:30am no vehicles can enter. Open year-round, but limited service in Nov. Summer €5.50 per person, winter €5. Tax €0.65. Cars €2.50; tents and RVs €3.30.)

Mo's Esscafé and Musikroom ❶, Hauptstr. 417, is all about being American, even if much of the decor seems rather Cuban. The Mo burger (€4), nachos (€3) and "Real American Donuts" (€1.50) will fuel your belly. There's live music on weekends. (☎634 35; fax 63 43 54. Open Dec.-Easter Tu-Sa noon-1am, Su-M 4pm-1am; Easter-Dec. M-Sa noon-1am.) **Restaurant Manni ❷**, Hauptstr. 439, offers weekly specials (€8-12.50) like baked potatoes filled with sour cream and chicken strips and veggies, along with pizza (€12.50) and other standards. (☎633 01. Open daily 11am-midnight. AmEx/MC/V.) **Café Dengg ❸**, Hauptstr. 412, serves well-prepared dishes beneath an awning just down Hauptstr. (☎648 66. Spaghetti €6.80, pizzas €7-8. Open M-Sa 9am-11pm.) There's a **BILLA**, Am Marienpl. 346, left from Europahaus and then an immediate right onto Seigler (☎634 24), and a **SPAR Markt** on Hauptstr., right from Einfahrt Mitte. (☎639 10. Open M-F 7:30am-6:30pm, Sa 7:30am-6pm, Su 8am-noon.)

🄺 OUTDOOR ACTIVITIES. Mayrhofen has ample possiblities for hiking. The **Z-Card** (see p. 215) can be a great deal for those who prefer to ride lifts up into the mountains rather than hike uphill. The **Penkenbahn** gondola passes directly over the town on its way to the 1850m Penkenberg. (☎622 77. Open end of May to mid-Oct. daily 9am-5pm. €12.90, with guest card €11.80; children €7.20.) From there, follow path #23 uphill to the **Penkenjoch** (1½hr.) for panoramic views of the valley. The **Ahornbahn** lift takes passengers up to the vicinity of both easy and difficult hikes. (☎626 33 16. May 17-Oct. 12 every 30min. 8:30am-noon and 12:30-5pm. Same prices as the Penkenbahn.) For the **Edelhütte hike** (2-2½hr., moderate), exit the Ahornbahn, head left, and look for trail #42. Winding through scrub meadows and rocky areas before reaching the hut (2238m), the hike offers views of neighboring mountains and their snow aprons.

In winter, **skiers** and **snowboarders** flock to the Ahorn, Penken, and Horberg ski areas, all of which are covered by the **Ski Zillertal 3000** pass, along with neighboring villages Finkenberg and Tux. (1 day pass €32, youths ages 14-19 €26, children ages 7-13 €19.50, under 7 free; 3-day pass €87/€70/€52.50.) The pass includes transit on local ski buses. The **Zillertal Super Skipass** covers an even larger area (see p. 216). **Rent skis** at **Intersport,** Hauptstr. 415. (☎624 00; fax 624 00 15. Open M-F 8:30am-12:30pm and 2-6:30pm, Sa 8:30am-6pm, Su 8:30am-noon and 3-6pm.)

The **Cultural Countryside Walking Tour** leads uphill to a scenic location with two historic sites. Pick up a walking map from the tourist office for Steinerkogl and Emberg, and take the Postbus to Brandberg. Follow the map to Emberg's Bauernhof Hanserhof, a 500-year-old farm still in operation, and the Schrofenmühle, where a water-powered mill grinds grain the old-fashioned way. From this vantage point on the ridge you see the entire valley beneath including Mayrhofen and the Ahornspitze (2973m). **A bicycle path** runs along the length of the valley; bike maps are available at the tourist office.

Paragliders catch winds in surrounding valleys, or take a tandem flight with instructors at **Flugtaxi Mayrhofen,** Sportplatzstr. 300 (☎0664 205 50 11; from €55), or **Stocky-Air,** in the yellow gondola right next to the Penkenbahn lift. (☎0664 340 79 76. 7-8min. flight €55, 20-30min. €110.) Other "don't tell Mom" activities including rafting (from €29) and canyoning (from €27) can be found at **Action Club Zillertal,** Hauptstr. 458 (☎629 77; www.action-club-zillertal.at).

🄴 NIGHTLIFE. For aprés-ski action, head left from the tourist office and take the first right, stay left at the fork, and look for signs to **Scotland Yard,** Schelllingstrasse 372. The bar is a popular skier and snowboarder hangout, where both ski champions and locals mingle. Get there by 10:30pm in the winter, when this English-speaking establishment sometimes doesn't even have standing room. (☎623 39; www.scotlandyard.at. Beer about €3. Open daily 7pm-3am. MC/V.)

THE ÖTZTAL

Bending its way between hundreds of 3000m peaks on the Italian border, the Ötztal (Ötz valley) offers some of the wildest and most impressive scenery in the Tyrolean Alps. Tiny farms cling impossibly to mountainsides while rivulets carve through the rocks to silt-gray rivers. The 1991 discovery of a frozen man who lived 5000 years ago (nicknamed Ötzi), proves that visitors have been enjoying the breathtaking views for millennia. The area, known as the Ötztal Arena, is Austria's largest skiing and snowboarding center. There is also glacier skiing in summer, as well as some of the most awesome hiking outside of the Hohe Tauern. At the mouth of the valley, Bahnhof Ötztal sends **trains** to Innsbruck (30-45min., 5:27am-1:31am, €7.50) and St. Anton (1hr., 4:14-11:01am, €8.40). **Buses** pass through the Ötztal's main town of Sölden before forking into the narrow Gurgler and Venter ranges. The region is accessible by public transportation, although buses to the more remote towns run on reduced hours in the summer and fall.

SÖLDEN ☎05254

Wedged in the Ötztal 36km south of Bahnhof Ötztal, Sölden is ideal for exploring the razor-sharp, snow-streaked mountains on either side of the valley. Numerous area ski lifts serve eager skiers throughout the winter, when the town becomes a ski resort. In the summer, these mountains provide fantastic hiking as well as glacier skiing up high near all the 3000m peaks.

◨◪ TRANSPORT & PRACTICAL INFORMATION. There are several bus stops in town; the most centrally located is "Postamt." **Buses** arrive from Bahnhof Ötztal (1hr., every hr. 8:05am-7:15pm) before departing for Vent (30min., 5 per day 8:03am-4:40pm, €4) and Obergurgl (25min., every hr. 7:45am-7:15pm, €2.30). From the Post Office bus stop, turn left and cross the bridge in front of Hotel Tyrolerhof and keep walking straight to the **tourist office,** with two **Internet** terminals (€0.10 per min.). (☎510; www.soelden.com. Open M-Sa 8am-6pm, Su 9am-noon, summer also Su 2-6pm.) A 24hr. accommodations board and telephone is across from the

IN RECENT NEWS

SKI DESCENT?

The summer of 2003 brought a major heat wave to Europe, smashing records and renewing speculation of the potential impact of global warming. But there is reason for hope, spurred by the discovery of the 5000-year-old Ötzi, a frozen man uncovered as the glaciers in the Ötztal receded (see p. 221). This discovery has provided further evidence that temperatures have been getting warmer for millennia, and that the rise may not be due to human development. Scientific evidence suggests that we are still exiting the previous Ice Age, and that global warming will eventually yield to cooler temperatures and the start of the next Ice Age.

But such predictions have done little to dampen concern over the effect of climate trends on one of Austria's most precious industries—skiing. A *Kurier* article from August 9, 2003 reported that the Pasterze Glacier beneath the Großglockner (see p. 278) melts during the summer so fast that the water level in the nearby reservoir rises 1.4m each day. It has been estimated that the glacier today is only half as long as it was a century ago. Much like the Pasterze, many of Austria's skiable summer glaciers have taken a hit. None of the glaciers have been forced to close yet, but the trend is disturbing. Even if the climate change eventually reverses, Austria's ski industry may still have to deal with shorter-term consequences.

"Shell Tankstelle" bus stop. **E. T's Internet Café,** Hof 430 (☎ 0676 703 15 61) at the "Hotel Huberttus" bus stop, charges €0.10 per min. (Open daily noon–10pm.) **Rent bikes** at any one of the five sports shops in town (full day €16-18, weekend €25-28). The **post office** is at Hof 439. (☎ 22 66. Open M-F 8am-noon and 2-6pm, from mid-Jan. to Apr. also Sa 9-11am.) **Postal code:** A-6450.

▐▌▐▌ ACCOMMODATIONS & FOOD. Be aware that lodging prices rise significantly in winter. To get to **Haus Alpenrose ❸,** take the first right after the "Shell Tankstelle" bus stop. Proprietor Reinhard Schöpf has long been a local mountain guide and ski instructor—he can tell you where the best skiing and hiking can be found. All rooms come with TV, shower, and a balcony. (☎ 23 33. Mid-Dec. to Apr. €30-33 per person; July-Sept. €15-18; Oct. to mid-Dec. €22.) For a down-home family experience, try **Haus Wachter ❸.** Get off the bus at "Schmiedhofbrücke," cross the bridge, and turn right. If the Wachters and their two children don't charm you, the gigantic breakfast buffet will. Rooms include TV, balcony, and private bath. (☎/fax 24 23. June-Nov. €23-28; Dec.-Apr. €35-42; Christmas and Mardi Gras holidays €43.) To get to **IDEAL ❸,** Rainstadl 736, cross the bridge in front of Tyrolerhof and make a left in front of the tourist office, take the second right and walk to the mountain's base. This newly built house offers expansive views, and large furnished rooms with foyers and private bathrooms. (☎/fax 304 13; ideal@soelden.at. Summer €14-20, winter €35-42; children 20-60% discount.)

There are several restaurants in town; many close in summer. ▨**Hotel Stefan ❷** is located 30m from the Hochsölden chairlift, diagonally across from the SPAR. First, you'll notice the restaurant's waitresses (clad in medieval outfits); then quiet, romantic rooms with wood paneling; and finally, once the food arrives, some of the most flavorful traditional dishes in all of Tyrol. Try the *Schlutzkrapfen* (mushrooms, sauce, and breaded chicken; €7.10) or ask for the daily special. (☎ 22 37, fax 22 37 25. Open daily 11:30am-2:30pm and 6-10:30pm. AmEx/MC/V.) **Restaurant-Pizzheria Corso ❷,** across the bridge from the Hotel Liebe Sonne, serves pizza (€6.47-10.32) and pasta (€7.12-10.76) in an elegant, candle-lit atmosphere, with animal skin covers on benches. (☎ 24 98; fax 29 80. Open June-Apr. M-Tu and Th-Su noon-midnight.) For local fare in a farmhouse-like setting, head to **Die Alm ❷,** on the main road past the post office. Panelled floors and walls with sea-stained wood give the place a traditional feel. House specialties cost €6.58-9.87. (☎ 24 01; fax 35 35 14. Open daily 11:30am-11pm.) If the blaring oompah music and rustic agricultural implements at **Törggele Stub'n ❷** don't scream "Tyrol," then the menu will. Cheese dumpling soup (€4.50) and traditional Tyrolean *Käsespätzle* (€8.50) will satisfy your hunger. (Cross the bridge toward the tourist office; Törggele is on your right. ☎ 35 35. Open daily 11am-11:30pm.) Turn left from the post office for the **SPAR Supermarkt.** (Open M-Sa 8:30am-12:30pm and 2:30-6pm.)

▨ OUTDOOR ACTIVITIES. The high altitude of Sölden's skiing areas (1377-3058m) guarantees snow even in the summer. The **Gaislachkoglbahn,** whisking passengers up the 3058m Gaislachkogl in a twin-cable gondola is, according to Sölden's advertisements, "the largest and most modern continuous bi-cable overhead ropeway in the world." (Open late June to mid-Sept. and Dec.-Apr. Round-trip for non-skiers in winter and hikers in summer €18.50; ages 8-16 €9.50.) **Lift tickets** for the 32 cable cars and lifts that serve Sölden's slopes are sold at the Gaislachkoglbahn booth at the southern end of town. (Mid-Dec. to Apr. €36-38, ages 15-18 €29, under 15 €24.) There are ski and snowboard schools in and around Sölden, including **Sölden/Hochsölden** (☎ 23 64 or 25 46;

www.ski-soelden.com; 4hr. group lessons €46) and **Yellow power** (☎220 35 00; www.yellowpower.at; 4hr. group lesson €47-52). Ask at the tourist office about the 5.5km toboggan run, which has lighting for the evenings.

The area above Sölden between **Hochsölden** on the right (looking up) and the **Rettenbachalm** on the left is excellent for hiking. To get to Hochsölden, the best bet is to use the **Sesselift Hochsölden,** in the parking lot behind the Intersport down the road from the post office. (Open end of June to mid-Sept. daily 9am-noon and 1-4:15pm. Round-trip €7.50, ages 8-14 €4.50.) If you want to start on the Rettenbachalm side, a moderate trailhead is on the right of the post office (about 2hr. one-way). Plunging through the forest and briefly over a paved road, this trail ends facing the magnificent glacier in the distance beyond the Rettenbachalm. From there, several great hikes are worth trying:

Lehrpfad zur Hochgebirgsökologie (1hr. one-way). Cutting across the face of the mountain between Hochsölden and the Rettenbachalm, this easy trail remains flat the whole way, though never dipping below 2000m. It is mostly on the open mountainside just above tree level, affording uninterrupted, magnificent views of the mountains across the valley. Along the way, colorful signs in German explain the unique ecology of high alpine environments.

Schwarzkogel hike (2½hr. round-trip from the Rotkogelhütte). For those who have dreamed of climbing a mountain and planting a flag on the top, the 3016m Schwarz-kogel will not disappoint. Though fairly difficult, it is a popular climb for intrepid families and adventurous older couples. From the chapel above the Rotkogelhütte, it leads through a narrow, rocky pass to the Schwarzsee, a tiny blue glacial lake that remains partly frozen well into the summer. From there, cross ankle- to knee-deep snowfields and ascend the steep path to the summit, which holds stunning views of the Urfeld valley, dozens of glaciers, and mountains like the Wildspitze, Tyrol's high-est mountain (3774m). Sign the book in the metal stand before heading back.

◼ DAYTRIP FROM SÖLDEN

OBERGURGL ☎05256

Buses run from Sölden to Obergurgl (25min., 1-2 per hr. 7:42am-7:15pm, €2.50).

Tiny Obergurgl, Austria's highest village, is little more than a few hotels and guest houses, but you're not likely to stay on the ground long. The town is at the very end of the valley, and the burly Ötztaler Alpen loom directly above. The **tourist office** is in the same building as the bus stop. (☎64 66; www.ober-gurgl.com. Open July-Sept. M-F 8am-6pm, Sa 8am-4pm, Su 9:30am-noon; Oct. M-F 9am-5pm, Sa 9am-noon; Nov.-Apr. M-Sa 9am-5:30pm, Su 9:30am-noon; May-June M-F 9am-12:30pm and 1:30-5pm, Sa 9am-noon.) For the most chal-lenging **skiing**, head to the area above Hochgurgl (2150m), or above Obergurgl to **Hohe Mut** (2670m). Purchase **tickets** at lift stations. (1-day pass €37, ages 8-16 €24; 1-week €200/118. Children under 8 free.) **Snow report** ☎64 69.

In summer, the chair-lift behind the SPAR can carry you to the top of **Hohe Mut,** where the stunning view encompasses 21 glaciers and the seemingly endless peaks of South Tyrol. (Round-trip €11. Open late July-Sept. 9am-4:15pm.) The trails beyond the top provide some of the most spectacular hiking in all of Austria.

Rotmoosferner hike (2hr. to the Zirbenwald). From Hohe Mut, head straight back along the grassy ridge and follow signs to the "Rotmoosferner" glacier. This easy path remains nearly flat the entire way, keeping an altitude of roughly 2700m. In the sum-mer, hike earlier in the day, before the snow melts and you find yourself wading knee-deep. On the way back, consider bypassing the chair lift in favor of the trail leading down through the rocky glacial debris field below Hohe Mut and back to Obergurgl via the Zirbenwald (see below; 3hr. from the glacier back to Obergurgl).

Zirbenwald (3hr. round-trip). Walk down the main road in Obergurgl until it becomes gravel at the edge of town, and follow signs to the "Rotmoos Wasserfälle." This moderate hike climbs through a forest of dwarf evergreens that has been declared a "Naturdenkmal" (natural monument) by the province of Tyrol. The deepest and most dramatic gorge is also home to the Rotmoos waterfall, which plummets through a narrow opening to a small pool. After the waterfall, trail #5 leads off to the left and returns to Obergurgl through the higher sections of the Zirbenwald.

VORARLBERG

Austria's westernmost region, Vorarlberg, sits at the intersection of four nations and two currencies, making for a diverse and vibrant province. A broad representation of Vorarlberg can be found in cities like Feldkirch, which retains its medieval influences; Bregenz, an international magnet for the arts; and Dornbirn, the state's economic center and gateway to the pastoral Bregenzerwald. Bordered by the Arlberg range to the east, the Rätikon and Silvretta mountains to the south, and the Bodensee (Lake Constance) to the north and west, Vorarlberg's expression of itself is exemplified by the 1980s Baukünstler, local artists who merged traditional materials like wood into contemporary architecture.

The geography offers many outdoor options. From the tranquil Bodensee in the west, Vorarlberg is higher in elevation as you move south and east, rising through rolling hills to the imposing Arlberg range (passable only through the 10km Arlberg Tunnel) on the boundary with Tyrol. A number of hiking and skiing options exist, especially in the higher parts of the province. In addition, Vorarlberg's 161km network of cycling paths ranges from leisurely tours near the Bodensee to challenging climbs in the Alps. Cycling maps are available at bookstores and tourist offices. For more info, contact the **Vorarlberg Information Office** in Bregenz. (☎05574 425 25; www.vorarlberg-tourism.at.)

HIGHLIGHTS OF VORARLBERG

Watch world-class performers at the **Bregenzer Festspiele** (see p. 230).

See evidence of Vorarlberg's medieval past in **Feldkirch** (see p. 230).

Admire the works of painter Angelika Kaufmann in **Schwarzenberg** (see p. 234).

BREGENZ   ☎05574

Bregenz, the capital city of Vorarlberg, spreads along the eastern coast of the Bodensee, separated from four different countries by only a few kilometers. If it looks a little tired, it's because it was hosting a variety of tourists long before the invention of Eurail. First it was the Celts, and then the Romans, who established a camp called Brigitania on the site of the present-day city. Later the Irish missionaries Gallus and Columban dropped by and dubbed the shining lake surrounded by mountains "The Golden Bowl." Bregenz now plays host to travelers wandering along the lakeside or around the historic **Oberstadt**.

Bregenz

🏠🏔 **ACCOMMODATIONS**
Camping Lamm, **2**
Jugendgästehaus (HI), **3**
Kaiser Hotel, **8**
Pension Gunz, **4**
Pension Sonne, **7**

🍎 **FOOD**
China Restaurant Da-Li, **5**
Ikaros, **9**
König Pizza und Kebap, **6**
Wirthaus am See, **1**
Zum Goldenen Hirschen, **10**

💼 **PUBS**
Uwe's Bier-Bar, **11**

Footpath

🔁 TRANSPORTATION

Trains: Bahnhofstr. (☎ 675 50, 232 or 1810; information ☎ 05 17 17). To: **Feldkirch** (30-45min., 2-4 per day 5am-11:42pm, €4.50); **Innsbruck** (2¼hr., 8 per day 5am-9:45pm, €25.10); **Munich** (2½hr., 4 per day 9:20am-7:20pm, €34.20); **St. Gallen** (45min., 4 per day 10:40am-8:40pm, €10.30); **Vienna** (8-10hr., 5 per day 5am-9:45pm, €57); **Zurich** (1¾hr., 4 per day 10:40am-8:40pm, €25.70).

Regional Buses: BundesBuses leave from the train station to **Dornbirn** (30min., every 30min. 4:55am-6:55pm, €2.10), **Egg** (1hr., 1-2 per hr. 6:51am-6:51pm, €3.30), and other regional destinations.

Public Transportation: 4 bus lines run through the city. Day pass €2.

Taxis: ☎ 650 00, 866 88, or 718 00.

Parking: By the *Festspielhaus*. Open 8am-noon and 1-6pm. €0.50 per hr., €3.60 per day; 6pm-midnight €2.20 per hr. Public parking €0.35-0.70 per hr. in the city center and by the Pfänderbahn. Buy parking permits from one of the ubiquitous automats.

🔋 PRACTICAL INFORMATION

Tourist Office: Bregenz Tourismus und Stadtmarketing, Bahnhofstr. 14 (☎ 495 90; www.tiscover.at/bregenz). From the train station, face away from the lake, and turn left; it's the glass building on the right with the green "i" sign. The staff makes hotel reservations (€2.50), has *Privatzimmer* lists, gives out hiking and city maps, and provides concert info and free **Internet access.** Open M-F 9am-noon and 1-5pm, Sa 9am-noon; during the *Festspiele* M-Sa 9am-7pm.

Consulate: UK, Bundesstr. 110 (☎785 86), in neighboring **Lauterach.**

ATM: At the train station.

Lockers: At the train station, 6:30am-9:30pm (€2).

Internet Access: S'Logo, Kirchstr. 47 (☎441 91). €0.08 per min. Open daily 5pm-1am.

Post Office: Seestr. 5 (☎437 007), on Seestr. across from the harbor. Open M-F 8am-7pm (cashier closes at 5pm), Sa 8am-2pm. **Postal code:** A-6900.

ACCOMMODATIONS & CAMPING

With a half-dozen four-star hotels as well as reasonably-priced pensions, Bregenz can accommodate both affluent vacationers and backpackers. When the Festspiele comes to town during the last week of July and the first three weeks of August, prices rise and reservations far in advance become absolutely necessary.

Jugendgästehaus (HI), Mehrerauerstr. 5 (☎428 67; www.jgh.at). Cross the bridge that goes out of the train station and over the tracks and. Facing away from the tracks, walk left through the parking lot; it's the big, yellow-brick building on the left when you come out onto the street. This large, well-staffed hostel offers spic-and-span bunks in 2- to 6-person rooms, all with bathroom and shower. **Internet** access in café €2.60 for 40min.; ask for keycard at desk. Breakfast buffet and sheets included. Laundry €4. Free bike storage. Reception 7am-10pm. Lockout 10pm, open every half hr. until 2am. Checkout 10am. Dorms Apr.-Sept. €17; Oct.-Mar. €15. For singles add €7, for doubles €5. Oct.-Apr. €0.51 tax; May-Sept. €1.24. For 1- or 2-night stays, add €3. DC/MC/V. ❷

Pension Sonne, Kaiserstr. 8 (☎ 425 72; www.bbu.at). From the station, go right (facing the lake) on Bahnhofstr., then right on Kaiserstr. Rooms with wood floors and sink, located in the heart of the *Fußgängerzone*. The hallways' colorful rugs give the place an inviting atmosphere. Breakfast included. Reception 7:30am-7pm. Check-in after noon. Singles €30-36; doubles €52; triples €69; quads €81.40. Add €5-6 for rooms with bath. ❷

Pension Gunz, Anton-Schneider-Str. 38 (☎/fax 436 57), located 2 blocks behind the post office. This homey *Pension* and restaurant keeps tidy rooms. Breakfast included. Their restaurant serves fresh fish from the Bodensee, as well as daily *Menüs* for €5-10. Restaurant and reception 8am-8pm. Singles €31-33; doubles €54. AmEx/MC/V. ❷

IN RECENT NEWS

BURNING THE 9PM OIL

Foreigners in Austria have long had to adjust to the difference in store and bank hours. Traditionally, no retail or banking establishments are open on Sundays or after 6pm. But there are signs of change, for better or worse. In 2003, the Nationalrat (National Parliament) decided to liberalize the existing national laws governing hours of operation. According to an article in Austria's *Kurier* newspaper from July 9, 2003, the new law, on business days stores are permitted to stay open until 9pm and on Saturdays until between 5 and 6pm.

But the matter is not exactly settled; many of Austria's nine provinces are protesting, refusing to do away with an Austrian tradition. The *Kurier* also reported that in Vorarlberg the workers and employers entered into a joint agreement whereby stores will be open once per week until 9pm. Regardless of the law's eventual outcome and its effect on local businesses throughout Austria, tourists need not worry too much about getting what they need. Although buying groceries and renting bikes may still be more limited in hours than in the United States, businesses dealing primarily with tourists are allowed to keep extended hours due to a loophole in the law.

Kaiser Hotel, Kaiserstr. 2 (☎52 980; www.bbn.at/kaiser), slightly uphill from Pension Sonne. If you came to the Bodensee to splurge, this is the place. Marble staircase, oil paintings, and personal attention—it's a hotel fit for a Kaiser. Whirlpool bathtub, satellite TV, VCR, and minibar in each room. It also boasts one of the best café-to-bed ratios in all of Europe, with 3 different cafés open to the public. Nov.-Apr. singles €65; doubles €108. May-Oct. €80/126. During the Festspiele €123/192. ❹

Camping Lamm, Mehrerauerstr. 50-51 (☎717 01 or 745; fax 71 74 54), is 10min. past the youth hostel. Small, economical campground with adjoining restaurant/pension. Somewhat worn, with a bit of a hippie feel. Lamm has their own stables and will let kids ride the ponies. Moderate traffic noise. Reception 8-10am and 5-8pm, or inquire within restaurant. €3.50 per person, ages 6-14 €1.50; tents €2.60-3.30; cars €2.60; RVs €4.40-5.50; campers €3-3.60. Electricity €2.60. ❶

◉ FOOD

Markets fill up Kornmarktstr. Tu and F; there's a **farmer's market** Sa 8am-noon.

Zum Goldenen Hirschen, Kirchstr. 8 (☎428 15). Look for the restaurant with small stained-glass windows and a gold flying reindeer over the door near the *Fußgängerzone*. Dark furniture and a half-timbered style interior give an authentic feel to a place that has brewed its own beer and served local favorites like *Schweinenbraten* and *Sauerkraut* (€7-13) for over 300 years. Vegetarian menu available. Open M and W-Su 10am-midnight. AmEx/DC/MC/V. ❷

Ikaros, Deuringstr. 5 (☎529 54). Look for the blue-and-white-striped awning at the edge of Leutbühel in the *Fußgängerzone*. This exceptional café offers a little taste of the Mediterranean with a wide variety of Greek dishes, including lunch *Menüs* (€6 for appetizer and entree), salads, and main dishes (€3.50-8.50) served indoors to Greek music or outdoors by the street. Open M-Sa M-F 10am-2pm and 5pm-1am, Sa 10am-1am. ❶

China Restaurant Da-Li, Anton-Schneider-Str. 34 (☎534 14), near Pension Gunz, serves typical Chinese fare. Stop by weekday afternoons for some great deals: the *Mittagsmenü* with rice, spring roll, and main dish (€5), or the lunch buffet (€7). Nice atmosphere with neo-classical Chinese music and a plant-filled interior. Your reward for finishing your meal is a free shot of peach schnapps. Entrees €7-10. Open daily 11:30am-2:30pm and 5:30-11:30pm. MC/V. ❶

König Pizza und Kebap, Rathausstr. 6 (☎538 81), is open late, late, late. Serves some of the cheapest food in town in a squeaky-clean eatery with extensive bar options. Eat-in or take-out pizzas (€3.27-6), *Dönerkebaps* and veggie-*Kebaps* (€5.5-7.20). Open M-Th 11am-3am, F-Sa 10am-4am, Su 6pm-4am. ❸

Wirtshaus am See, Seepromenade 2 (☎422 10; www.wirtshausamsee.at). Walking along the promenade between the harbor and the floating stage, one can't help notice the crowds under the canopy at the Wirtshaus. Serving a variety of Austrian specialties under rows of decorative lights, it attracts a steady dinner crowd as well as those just interested in ice cream or beer. Meals average €12. With luck, you can hear the opera at the Seebühne. Open daily 10am-midnight, until 1am during the *Festspiele*. V/MC. ❸

◉ SIGHTS

On the hill above Bregenz looms the **Oberstadt,** or "upper city," a once-fortified settlement that contains many of the city's oldest and most attractive buildings. A short hike up Maurachg. from the *Fußgängerzone* are the towering walls, beyond which lie rows of pastel-painted, wood-beamed houses, many hundreds of years old. Some of them have incorporated fragments of the old city walls in their construction; others have extensive rose gardens or are painted with murals. The major landmark of the Oberstadt is the wooden **Martinsturm,** dating from the 13th century, which supports Europe's largest onion dome. The second and third floors of the tower house the **Vorarlberg Militärmuseum,** which chronicles in German every war the Vorarlbergers ever fought (including the notorious German Farmer's war of 1525). The third floor, overlooking the Bodensee and beyond, is not to be missed. (☎466 32. Open mid-Apr. to mid-Oct. Tu-Su 9am-6:30pm. €1, ages 6-14 €0.50.) Next door is the **Martinskirche,** filled with frescoes dating back to the early 14th century. Particularly noteworthy are the depictions of St. Christopher, the Holy Symbol of Grief, and the 18th-century Stations of the Cross. Across Ehregutapl. (with the fountain) from the Martinsturm is **Deuring Schlößchen,** a 17th-century castle that houses a decidedly non-budget hotel.

Shaded by overhanging trees and vines, Meißnersteige leads down from the corner of the castle to the bottom of the Oberstadt. Cross Thalbachg. and hike up Schloßbergstr. to reach **St. Gallus Pfarrkirche,** reputedly founded by medieval Irish missionaries, St. Gallus and St. Columban. The white-stucco sanctuary of the 11th-century church now glows with lavish gold ornamentation and a detailed ceiling fresco that dates from 1738. The shepherdess in the altar painting has the face of Maria Theresia, who donated 1500 guilders to the church in 1740. On the opposite side of the Oberstadt at the corner of Am Brand and Bergmannstr., the twin steeples of the imposing **Herz-Jesu Kirche** seem to breach the heavens. Built in 1907 and recently renovated in neo-Gothic style, the huge sanctuary's brick and wood furnishings bring out the Expressionist stained-glass windows.

Walking from the tourist office through the *Fußgängerzone* and away from the train station, you'll come across a large, imposing building covered with translucent gray tiles: the **Kunsthaus Bregenz.** The stark concrete interior, gleaming floor, and subdued lighting are slightly spooky, making this a perfect home for avantgarde exhibits of outlandish modern art. Exhibits rotate approximately every two months and range from installation art—one recent exhibit consisted of an indoor bog and boardwalk—to art by Jeff Koons and George & Gilbert. (☎ 48 59 40; fax 48 59 48. Open Tu-W and F-Su 10am-6pm, Th 10am-9pm. €5, students €3.50.)

⚠ OUTDOOR ACTIVITIES

There's no better place to stretch your legs than the **Strandweg** and **Seepromenade,** which follow the curve of the Bodensee from one end of town to the other. All along the waterfront, groomed paths, rose gardens, and strategically placed ice-cream stands surround playgrounds, a mini-golf course, and a human-sized chess board. For would-be mariners who like to steer themselves, **paddle-** and **motor-boat rentals** are available from the "Bootsmeiten" stand near Wirtshaus am See, next to the harbor. (Open 10am-twilight. €11-18 per 30min.) Several companies run ⚑**sightseeing cruises** on the Bodensee from the Bregenz Hafen (harbor), Seestr. 4 opposite the post office. (☎428 68; www.bodenseeschifffahrt.at.) Ferries run the 2½hr. length of the shimmering lake to the **Blumen Insel Mainau** (Mainau Flower Isle) on the German side, which features a Baroque castle and church, an indoor tropical palm house, a butterfly house, and gardens rife with orchids, tulips, dahlias, and 400 kinds of roses. (Ferries leave Bregenz July-Oct at 8, 9:10, 10:20, 11am and return at 6:25, 7:08, 7:55, 8:23pm. Admission to the island €10.50; round-trip ferry and admission €33.30.) An alternative 2hr. cruise will take you to the **Zeppelin-Museum** in Friedrichshafen, Germany, former home base of round-the-world Zeppelin flights. The museum provides a fascinating and well-designed look at an era when people thought large balloons filled with volatile gases were a good idea. Along with a mock-up of the Hindenberg's passenger cabin, it has a large exhibit of oil paintings and sculpture dating to the 15th century. (☎ +49 07541 380 11; www.zeppelin-museum.de. €6.50, seniors €5.50, students and children under 16 €3. Ferries leave Bregenz June-Aug. Tu-Su every 70min. from 8am; round-trip €18.80.)

The **Pfänderbahn** cable car leaves from the top of Schillerstr., uphill from the post office, and swings up the **Pfänderspitze** (1064m) for a panorama all the way to Germany's Black Forest. (☎42 16 00; www.pfaenderbahn.at. Every 30min. 9am-7pm. One-way €5.70, round-trip €9.80. Discounts for seniors and children under 19.) At the top of Pfänderspitze, there are nature trails in the free **Alpine Wildlife Park**, which pass enclosures housing native animals such as boars, mountain goats, and *Murmeltiere* (marmots). A 10min. walk from the top of the lift is the "Greifvogel," a 40min. **bird flight show,** which send birds of prey swooping across the mountainside. (May-Oct. daily 11am, 2:30pm. €3.90, children under 16 €2.)

🎵🎭 ENTERTAINMENT & NIGHTLIFE

The concrete monstrosity on the edge of the lake is not a ski ramp gone awry. It's the **Seebühne**, Europe's largest floating stage, and the centerpiece for the annual **Bregenzer Festspiele.** Every year from mid-July to mid-August, the Vienna Symphony Orchestra and other opera, theater, and chamber music groups come to town, bringing some 180,000 tourists with them. The main events are performances on the floating stage, drawing capacity crowds of 6800. In 2004, the floating opera will be Leonard Bernstein's *West Side Story*, with German dialogue and English lyrics (July 22-Aug. 22). The **Vienna Symphony Orchestra** will perform the score for two Kurt Weill operas playing in the Festspielhaus: *Der Protagonist* and *Royal Palace* (both July 21-Aug. 8). Dozens of other opera, music, and dance shows play throughout the *Festspiele*. For in-demand shows (usually weekend or high-profile productions), reserve tickets months in advance. Weekday performances, however, rarely sell out more than a few days before the show. (Tickets sales begin Oct. 2003. Postfach 311, A-6901 Bregenz. ☎40 76; www.bregenzerfestspiele.com. Seebühne seats €26-125; *Festspielhaus* €40-135; concerts €16-75. Students under 26 25% off, except for premieres. Standing room tickets available.)

There are several popular late-night student hangouts on and around Kirchstr. **Uwe's Bier-Bar,** Kirchstr. 25, is a popular bar with a young, lively crowd. (Beer €1.70-4. Open daily 7pm-1am, F-Sa until 2am.)

FELDKIRCH   ☎05522

Just minutes from the borders of Switzerland and Liechtenstein, Feldkirch (pop. 30,000) has served as a trade and transportation hub for centuries. More than any other city in Vorarlberg, Feldkirch's history remains vivid today—the triangular *Altstadt* is a maze of pastel Baroque buildings and medieval towers, lined by arcades that shelter shops and fruit stands. The city itself is compact, quickly fading into shady suburbs with cliffs and mountains rising nearby.

🚆 **TRANSPORTATION. Trains** depart from Feldkirch to: Bregenz (45min., 1-2 per hr. 5am-midnight, €5.70); Innsbruck (2hr., 5:25am-12:21am, €20.80); Salzburg (4¼hr., 7 per day 5:25am-12:21am, €41); Zurich (1½-2½hr., 6 per day 4:45am-9:04pm, €24.50). The Liechtenstein **bus** system runs to Schaan, near Vaduz (30min., every 30min. 6:05am-11:05pm, €1.40), with connections to Buchs and Sargans in Switzerland. Bus info at the tourist office or at ☎739 74 or 42 32 37 66 99 (Open M-Th 8am-12:30pm and 2-4:30pm, F 8am-noon.) **City buses** connect Feldkirch's subdivisions (€1, day pass €2). Buses stop at the train station and at the main bus stop, which can be reached by exiting the train station, walking away from the tracks, and turning left at the intersection. **Taxis** ☎17 18, 387 00, or 842 00.

⚠ PRACTICAL INFORMATION. Primary locations of interest in Feldkirch are clustered on the Ill river in the old city, a confusing warren of streets that makes a map necessary (free at the tourist office). To reach the city center, walk past the cemetery next to the station, stay straight, at Schlossgraben, the main busy intersection, cross over it, and after one block make a right onto Neustadt and a left at the main Cathedral. The **tourist office,** Schlosserg. 8, is in Palais Liechtenstein at the beginning of the city center, and distributes walking-tour maps, sells hiking maps for €5.75, and provides info about the city and its events. (☎734 67; www.tiscover.at/feldkirch. Open May-Sept. M-F 9am-6pm, Sa 9am-noon; Oct.-Apr. M-F 8am-noon and 1-5pm, Sa 9am-noon.) The **Sparkasse** just down the street from the tourist office has a computer kiosk on the first floor providing free **Internet access.** (Open M-Tu and Th 8am-noon and 2-4pm, W 8am-noon and 2-6:30pm, F 8am-4pm.) An **ATM** and the **post office,** Bahnhofstr. 31, are across from the station. (☎34 00. Open M-F 7am-7pm, Sa 7am-noon.) **Postal code:** A-6800.

▐▞ ACCOMMODATIONS & CAMPING. Feldkirch's tourist office maintains a short list of *Privatzimmer,* but if you can't find a spot in one of the places listed below, Feldkirch is an easy daytrip from Bregenz. **Jugendherberge "Altes Siechenhaus" (HI) ❷,** Reichstr. 111, Feldkirch's lone hostel, can be reached by Bus #2 and #60 to Götzis or by walking out of the station onto the main road, Bahnhofstr. (which becomes Reichstr.), turn right and walk 15-20min. The hostel may well be the most historic spot on your visit—it's a white 700-year-old brick-and-wood building that served as an infirmary during several plague epidemics. Today, it is preserved as a family-oriented hostel with clean rooms and modest beds. (☎731 81; fax 793 99. Wheelchair-accessible. Breakfast buffet (€4.50) features pickled fish, homemade sausage, and fresh cherries. Laundry €3. Sheets included, €1.50 discount if you bring your own. Hostel key available for €20 deposit or ID. Reception M-Sa 7am-10pm, Su 7-10am and 7-10pm. €16.20 per person; add €2 in winter.) Or try **Gasthof Löwen ❸,** Egelseestr. 20. Take bus #1 or 3 (dir.: Tosters) to "Burgweg," a leafy suburb of Feldkirch. From the stop, walk back and take the first right. The hotel has simple, quiet rooms. (☎728 68; loewen@gmx.at. Breakfast, shower, and TV included. Restaurant meals €9-14. Reception M 6:30am-noon, 3-5pm, 8-11pm; Tu-Su 6:30am-noon and 3-11pm. Singles €40; doubles €56-58; triples €72.) For cheap digs in an antique-filled setting, try **Gasthof zum Engel ❸,** 106 Liechtensteinerstr., in nearby Tsis. Take Liechtenstein Bus 70 or 71 to Tsis Letzestr. and walk two blocks. The painstakingly painted flowers on the woodwork make up for the peeling wallpaper, and your dresser just might date from the 19th century. (Singles €23; doubles €46.) For **Waldcamping Feldkirch ❶,** Stadionstr, take bus #1 (dir.: Gisingen) to "Milchhof," and follow the signs; it lies past the soccer field. Nicer than most, this campground offers camping under the pines, right next to the sprawling town swimming pool. (☎743 08; www.feldkirch.com/kkf/fbg3.htm. Laundry €3.50. Reception 8am-12:30pm and 2-10pm. July-Aug. €5.10 per person, children €2.95; cars €3.60; tents €4.35. Sept.-June €4.30/2.10/2.60/3.60. MC/V.)

◖ FOOD. Eateries line the streets of the *Fußgängerzone,* and with the convenient location come high prices. A few budget establishments are just outside the pedestrian area. Try **Pizzeria-Trattoria La Taverna ❷,** Vorstadtstr. 18, a busy restaurant near the river, offering an extensive menu with plenty of pizza (€5.10-7.20) and many varieties of pasta (€5.50 to 9.10), all in a candle-lit, wine-cellar interior. (☎792 93. Open daily 11:30am-2pm and 5pm-midnight.) Probably the only restaurant in all of Vorarlberg to specialize in salads, **Treff ❷,** Mühletorpl., is located just past the end of Vorstadt. Try the *Treffsalat* (€6.50)—beets, radishes, kidney beans, onions, and a half-dozen other veggies that give heft and color to the iceberg lettuce and grilled chicken. Mexican and seafood are also available with the same prompt service. (☎849 67. Open daily 10am-midnight.) Just across the Illsteg. bridge, **Element ❶,** Waltraud Hackspiel, down Vorstadtstr. and across Illsteg., is a trendy café in the shape of a glass cube. Its drawn shades and soft jazz give it a smooth appeal, and the river rippling outside adds its own music. Small meals and snacks cost €1.60-7. In summer, ice cream scoops are €0.80. (☎67 64 86 63 00. Open mid-Oct. to mid-Apr. M-F 7:30am-8pm.) An **Inter-SPAR** is on Neustadt, not too far from the Schatterburg, in the same complex as the Holiday Inn. (Open M-F 9am-7:30pm, Sa 8am-5pm.) Marktpl. hosts an **outdoor market** every Saturday morning March-November.

🔲🎵 **SIGHTS & ENTERTAINMENT.** Feldkirch's Gothic cathedral, the **St. Nikolaus Kirche,** forms one edge of the *Altstadt.* The cathedral received a face-lift in 1478 after a series of devastating fires. Frescoes of Feldkirch history and the coats of arms of local potentates adorn the 15th-century **Rathaus** on Schmiedg. At nearby Schloßberg. 8 stands the **Palais Liechtenstein,** completed in 1697. The palace once supported the royal seat of the Prince of Liechtenstein (see p. 316) but now houses the town library, tourist office, and city archives.

At the edges of the *Altstadt,* three towers of the original city wall remain: the **Katzenturm,** the **Pulverturm,** and the **Wasserturm.** Outside the *Altstadt,* one block toward the station on Bahnhofstr., lies the **Kapuzinerkloster** (Capuchin monastery), built in 1605. For a fantastic view of the *Altstadt,* hike up the staircase on Burgg. to reach the **Schattenburg,** Feldkirch's most impressive structure, dating from 1260. (Castle and café open Tu-Su 10am-midnight.) From the early 1200s until 1390, the castle was the seat of the Counts of Montfort, who dominated the Vorarlberg region. The town purchased the castle in 1825 to save it from demolition and converted it into the **Feldkirch Heimatmuseum,** which showcases the region's history, including an 800-year-old fresco, carved wooden furniture, coins from AD 69, and an armory full of old weapons. (☎/fax 719 82. Open Tu-Su 9am-noon and 1-5pm. €2.50, ages 12-18 and students under 26 €1.50, ages 6-12 €1.)

For those lucky enough to catch one, Feldkirch schedules a number of festivals and special events. Perhaps the biggest is the **Feldkirch Festival,** a music celebration that features opera and theater by such composers as Strauss, Haydn, and Mozart. (June 2-13, 2004; contact the Palais Liechtenstein, Schloßberg. 8. ☎829 43, www.feldkirchfestival.at.) Ask the tourist office for dates of the 2004 **Wine and Gaukler festivals** held in the Markpl. The annual **Christmas bazaar** brings crafts, candy canes, and carols November 28-December 24, 2004.

BREGENZERWALD

Spreading out to the south and east of Bregenz, the Bregenzerwald is home to many small towns and villages that preserve the rustic flavor of Vorarlberg's past. The villages dot the countryside's pastures and pine forests, and are coddled by steeply rising mountains, especially further to the southeast. Explore the Bregenzerwald by taking daytrips into the region from Bregenz or Dornbirn, or by staying in any of the more charming, rural towns in the *Wald* itself.

▐ TRANSPORTATION

Bregenz and Dornbirn both serve as good transportation hubs for the Bregenzerwald. Bundesstr. 200 heads generally southeast from Dornbirn with Egg and Au in its path. Public transportation in the Bregenzerwald is based around a regional network of **buses (Netz);** train service between the towns in the Bregenzerwald is limited. A **Tageskarte Euregio Bodensee** allows for unlimited travel by bus and train in the region. (1 day €20, ages 6-15 €10.)

⚑ ACCOMMODATIONS

Staying in the Bregenzerwald on the cheap is possible in most small towns. Huts dot the mountains; their telephone numbers are available at the tourist office and in the *Kumpass* Bregenzerwald/Westallgäu map/handbook available at newsstands as well as in the booklet distributed by all Vorarlberg tourist offices.

DORNBIRN ☎ 05572

Dornbirn (pop. 44,000), though not technically in the Bregenzerwald, is considerably larger and more industrial than its tiny woodland neighbors. Home of the Vorarlberg Institute for Architecture and influential in the acceptance of new architectural designs, the city is reaching out culturally. There are natural wonders just outside town, including a steep cave-like gully with a waterfall. Dornbirn's size and location make it a good launching pad for journeys to towns in the Bregenzerwald.

🚆🚌 TRANSPORTATION & PRACTICAL INFORMATION. Trains to: Bregenz (10-15min., 3-4 per hr. 5:28am-1:08am, €2.10); Feldkirch (20-30min., 2-3 per hr. 5:09am-12:18am, €3.30); Innsbruck (2¼hr., 7 per day 5:09am-9:52pm, € 23.50); Lindau (20min., 11 per day 5:28am-7:07pm, €3.30); St. Anton am Arlberg (1hr., 7 per day 5:09am-9:52pm, €6.60). The station has **lockers** (€2) and **luggage storage** (€2.10; M-Sa 6:30am-8:50pm, Su 7:30am-8:50pm). Regional **buses** depart from the parking lot at the train station and across the street. Line #38 runs to Schwarzenberg (7:20am-7:35pm) and line #40 to Egg (7:02am-10:35pm). Both stop in front of the Post Office, next to the Bahnhof. Day pass for all Dornbirn city buses €2. Exit the station and walk straight on Bahnhofstr. to reach the town center. The **tourist office,** Rathauspl. 1, is through Marktpl. and across Stadtstr., about 50m to the left. The tourist office has a list of accommodations pasted on the window and sells hiking maps for €6. (☎221 88; www.tiscover.com/dornbirn. Open M-F 9am-noon and 1-6pm, Sa 9am-noon.) **Internet** access is at **Netgate,** Bahnhofstr. 26, on the way to the town center. (Open M-F 10-7pm, Sa-Su 2-10pm. €1.20 for 15min., €5 per hour.) An **ATM** is located at the post office and across from the tourist office at **Raiffeisenbank,** which also **exchanges currency** for about €2 per $100 (open M-Th 8am-noon and 2-3:30pm, F 8am-noon and 2-4:30pm). The **post office** is next to the train station. (Open M-F 8am-noon and 2-6pm; exchange closes at 5pm.) **Postal code:** A-6850.

🏠🍴 ACCOMMODATIONS & FOOD. Most budget accommodations in Dornbirn are a fair distance from town. Try **Haus Ottowitz ❸,** Im Winkel 15. From Riedg., take bus #7 (dir.: Messegelände) to "Bürglegasse," walk uphill, and turn left onto Im Winkel. Reasonably-priced singles and doubles include TV, balcony, and views of Dornbirn and the Bodensee. The family includes daughters and dogs, giving the place a down-home feel. (☎330 25; angelika.ottowitz@vol.at. €20-25 per person; discounts for longer stays.) If you'd rather be closer to Dornbirn, **Gasthof zum Grauen Bären ❹,** 17 Dr. Anton-Schneidierstr., turn left from the train and follow Dr. Anton-Schneiderstr. for 15min, or take bus #3 to Eigenheim, and walk 2min. farther. It's a large, yellow building on the left side, boasting affordable rooms and a crowd of regulars who down Mohrenbraus in the adjoining *Biergarten.* (Breakfast included. All rooms with shower and TV. Singles €36; doubles €56.)

While *Menüs* are generally cheap and tasty, **⊠Extrablatt ❷,** the self-proclaimed café-bar at 4 Bahnhofstr. (on the way to Marktpl.) has turned them into an art form, serving €6.25 entrees pleasing to the eye and tastebuds. For those craving pizza, the house pizza is positively crammed full of ham, pepperoni, corn, green peppers, and onions on a thin, chewy crust (€7). Sit with the lunchtime and late-night crowds on the geranium-laden terrace or sip on an elaborate mixed drink (€3.8-6.30) while listening to classic American rock in the dimly lit interior. (☎255 68. Open daily 8am-1am.) Shoppers, businessmen, and occasional packs of soccer hooligans all converge on **Café Steinhauser ❷** and its wicker chairs for a shaded lunch in the Marktpl. Light Italian fare carries the day—mozzarella and tomatoes covered in basil (€6.50) and stuffed zucchini (€6.50) are attractive vegetarian options, while chicken cordon bleu and pork fillets satisfy carnivorous tastes. (Open M-Sa 9am-midnight, Su 2pm-midnight.) The huge **EuroSPAR** market, behind the church on Mozartstr., sells everything from bananas to flip-flops. (Open M-F 7am-7pm, Sa 7am-5pm.)

▥ MUSEUMS. The **Stadt Museum,** across from the church in the town center, has rotating exhibits on its first floor and historical artifacts on the floors above, dating from 800 BC to the 20th century. (☎330 77; www.dornbirn.at. Open Tu-Su 10am-noon and 2-5pm. €2.50, students and children €1.) Take city bus #5 to Gütle to get to the **Rolls-Royce Museum,** which displays the world's largest exhibit of Rolls-Royce cars, engines, and memorabilia. A local man with a great deal of money to burn "collected" the cars over several decades. The museum is at the same bus stop as the Rappenlochschlucht and two stops from the Karrenseilbahn (see Hiking, below); the three sites together make for a good day. (☎526 52; www.rolls-royce-museum.at. Open Tu-Su 10am-5pm. €8, seniors €7, children €4.) For a nature museums, try the **Inatura,** inside of Dornbirn's city garden. (☎232 35; www.inatura.at. Open M-W and F-Su 10am-6pm, Th 10am-9pm. €8, students and seniors €5.50, children €4.)

▧ HIKING. Though Dornbirn itself is mostly devoid of tourist attractions (unless you are an architecture buff), the hills and forest surrounding it are chock-full of great hiking trails. Be sure to pick up a map from the tourist office, as trails often cross over one another and it is easy to follow the wrong one. Take the bus to the last stop on #5 bus (dir.: Gütle) for the 1½hr. hike to the **Rappenlochschlucht,** which is a steep gaping cleft through a mountain ridge where a small waterfall reflects amazing sunrises and sunsets. For a pleasant view of the town, the valley, and the Bodensee, hop on the **Karrenseilbahn** cable car, which takes riders 1km above sea level. (Take bus #5, dir.: Gütle. Open summer daily 9am-11pm. Round-trip €8.20, youths €6.40, children €4.10.) From there, numerous hikes spread out over the countryside. One particularly nice hike circumnavigates the Staufenberg, offering views of the mountains and waterfalls from the shade of a pine forest. The highlight is crossing the cow pasture near Schuttanen, which can cause quite a bovine ruckus if you're not polite. From Karren, follow signs to Kuhberg (10min.), then to Staufenberg and Schuttanen. Exit the pasture through the turnstile, then keep right and follow signs to the Karrenseilbahn. (2½hr., moderate.)

SCHWARZENBERG   ☎05512

You'll get the impression that not much has changed in Schwarzenberg (pop. 1750) in the last few hundred years. Tucked in meadows cradled by a ring of mountains, it exemplifies the charms of the Bregenzerwald. Many of the houses are made out of wood from the nearby forests, using techniques that are centuries old.

🖃🔢 TRANSPORTATION & PRACTICAL INFORMATION. Bus #38 (every 30min. 8:10am-6:10pm, €2.70) and bus #40 (1-2 per hr. 7:02am-10:35pm, €2.70) both run from Dornbirn. Follow the main road downhill from the church and take the first right to the **tourist office**, which dispenses maps for hikes in and around Schwarzenberg. (☎35 70; fax 29 02. Open M-F 9am-7pm, Sa 10am-noon.) The **Raiffeisenbank,** uphill toward the Angelika-Kaufmann-Museum, has an **ATM.** (Open M, W, F 9am-noon and 3-6pm, Tu and Th 9am-noon, Sa 8am-noon) A **post office** is near the church. (Open M-F 8am-noon and 1:30-5pm.) **Postal code:** A-6867.

🏠🍴 ACCOMMODATIONS & FOOD. There are dozens of wooden guest houses in Schwarzenberg and the outlying regions. The tourist office can find inexpensive private accommodations. **Haus Feuerstein ❸,** Hof 20 behind the church near the town square, provides a hearty breakfast in a charming wood-panelled house, parts of which are over 200 years old. (☎20 39. €20-25 per person. €5.81 surcharge per night for 1- to 2-night stays and for singles.) For a warm meal, head 50m downhill from the town square to **Mesner Stüble ❷,** serving tasty *Gasthof*-style dishes costing €6.54-10.54. (☎20 02. Open Dec.-Oct. M-Sa 3pm-midnight, Su 10am-midnight.) Stock up on groceries at the local **SPAR,** downhill from the town square. (Open M-Th 7am-noon and 2:30-6pm, F 7am-6pm, Sa 7am-noon.)

🄶🎿 SIGHTS & OUTDOOR ACTIVITIES. The **Pfarrkirche** is an airy church with wrought-iron gravestones, unstained carved wood columns, and an altar painting by the town's most famous (sometime) resident, Angelika Kauffmann (1741-1807). Kauffmann was one of the few wealthy female painters of her age, and her work received great acclaim in England and Italy. The **Angelika Kauffmann Museum,** a 300-year-old wooden lodge a few minutes up the main road, houses a small collection of the artist's paintings and memorabilia, as well as rooms displaying woodworking tools and some wildly inflated currency from the Weimar Republic. (☎29 67 or 20 84. Open May-Sept. Tu, Th, Sa-Su 2-4pm; Oct. Tu and Sa 2-4pm. €2.50, ages 6-14 €0.70.) This year Schwarzenberg will host its eleventh annual **Schubertiade,** a celebration of the composer's works and the creative spirit of local talents, spread over several weekends during the year. Such weekends see multiple performances, from chamber concerts to poetry readings. Purchase same-day tickets at the **Angelika-Kauffmann Saal** near the tourist office. (☎05576 729 01; www.schubertiade.at. Apr. 29-May 2, May 20-23, June 10-27, Aug. 27-Sept. 12, 2004.)

Signs in the town center, across from the church, point the way to a variety of well-marked hikes and walks. If you have 3hr. to spare, try the easy-to-moderate loop up to the **Lustenauer Hütte.** When you come to the hillside town of Klausberg, bear right at each fork in the dirt road, and you'll be at the hut within 25min. From there, continue on the other well-marked side of the loop back to Schwarzenberg.

SALZBURGER LAND

The Salzburger Land derives its name from the German *Salz* (salt), and it was this "white gold" that drew Roman Emperor Claudius's attention to the region in the first century, inciting him to unite it with his Empire for the first time. Although tourism displaced the salt trade long ago, images of St. Barbara, the patron saint of miners, are everywhere. The province itself encompasses a section of the shining lakes and rolling hills of the Salzkammergut, where Salzburg and Hallstatt are among the more enticing destinations. Though mostly in the province of Upper Austria, the Salzkammergut it is accessible primarily through Salzburg.

HIGHLIGHTS OF SALZBURGER LAND

Satiate your sweet tooth with **Mozartkugeln** (see p. 245).

Hobnob with upper echelon musicians at the **Salzburger Festspiele** (see p. 253).

Get in touch with your animal instincts at the **Hellbrunn Zoo** (see p. 256).

SALZBURG ☎ 0662

Set against a backdrop of mountains and graced with Baroque wonders as befits the ecclesiastical center of Austria, Salzburg offers both spectacular sights and a rich musical culture. After spending a long day touring the Archbishop's magnificent constructions you can relax while enjoying Salzburg's musical tradition. Whether it's tourists singing songs, street musicians playing medieval ballads, or a famed soprano bringing the house down with the "Queen of the Night" aria, Salzburg resonates with sound. The city's adulation for homegrown genius Mozart and the arts in general reaches a dizzying climax every summer during the Salzburger Festspiele (see p. 253), when wealthy admirers the world over come to pay their respects to the musical elite. The Festspiele lasts for five weeks, during which time hundreds of operas, concerts, plays, and open-air performances dazzle the crowds. Salzburg's appeal comes not only from its architectural aesthetics, but also from its deserved reputation as an impeccably clean and very safe city, making it an enticing destination for any tourist—never mind that both Mozart and the von Trapps eventually left.

✈ INTERCITY TRANSPORTATION

Flights: The airport is **Flughafen Salzburg** (☎858 00; www.salzburg-airport.com), 4km west of the city center, with frequent connections to **Amsterdam, Innsbruck, Paris, Vienna,** and other major European cities. It is considerably cheaper, however, to fly into **Munich** (see p. 546) and take the train from there. If you do fly into or out of Salzburg, bus #77 (dir.: Bahnhof from the airport, dir.: Walserfeld from the train station) circles between the train station and the airport (15min., every 15-30min. 5:32am-11pm, €1.70). A taxi from the airport to the train station should cost roughly €11.

Trains: There are 2 train stations in Salzburg; the main passenger hub, the **Hauptbahnhof** on Südtirolerpl., is the 1st Salzburg stop for trains coming from Vienna, while the Salzburg Süd Bahnhof (the 1st stop when coming from Innsbruck) is primarily a cargo station. Trains from Hauptbahnhof to: **Graz** (4hr., 8 per day 5:24am-5:18pm, €36.50); **Innsbruck** (2hr., 11 per day 6:23am-12:45am, €29.50); **Klagenfurt** (3hr., 8per day 7:13am-9:18am, €26.10); **Munich** (2hr., 30 per day 4:27am-11:57pm, €25.80); **Vienna** (3½hr., 26 per day 2:18am-9:35pm, €36.50); **Zell am See** (1½-2hr., 17 per day 4:51am-9:18pm, €11.30); and **Zurich** (6hr., 7 per day 6:23am-12:45am, €65.20). For reservations dial ☎05 17 17. Regular ticket office open 24hr.

Buses: Leave from the bus depot in front of the train station. Get information at the Reisebüro am Bahnhof in the train station (☎05 17 17, M-F 9am-6pm). BundesBuses to **Mondsee** (1hr., every hr. 6:35am-10:20pm, €4.50); **St. Wolfgang** (1½hr., every hr. 5:50am-7:15pm, €7.60); **Bad Ischl** (1½-2hr., every hr. 5:50am-9:15pm, €8.30); and throughout Salzburger Land.

By car: From Vienna, exit at any of the Salzburg-West exits off Autobahn A1. Of these, the Salzburg-Nord exit is near Itzling and Kasern, and the Salzburg-Süd exit lies south of the city near Schloß Hellbrunn and Untersberg. A8 and E52 lead from the west into Rosenheim and then branch off to Munich and Innsbruck. A10 heads north from Hallein to Salzburg. From the Salzkammergut area, take Grazer Bundesstr. #158. Since public transportation is efficient within the city limits, consider the **Park and Ride**—park for free off the highway and take the bus into town. The most convenient lot is **Alpensiedlung Süd** on Alpenstr. (exit: Salzburg-Süd), but a bigger lot is open July-Aug. at the **Salzburger Ausstellungszentrum** and costs €1 per hr. (exit: Salzburg-Mitte).

SALZBURGER LAND

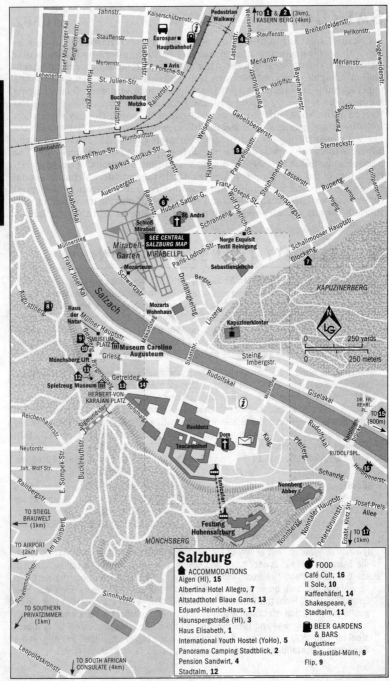

Salzburg

ACCOMMODATIONS
Aigen (HI), **15**
Albertina Hotel Allegro, **7**
Altstadthotel Blaue Gans, **13**
Eduard-Heinrich-Haus, **17**
Haunspergstraße (HI), **3**
Haus Elisabeth, **1**
International Youth Hostel (YoHo), **5**
Panorama Camping Stadtblick, **2**
Pension Sandwirt, **4**
Stadtalm, **12**

FOOD
Café Cult, **16**
Il Sole, **10**
Kaffeehäferl, **14**
Shakespeare, **6**
Stadtalm, **11**

BEER GARDENS & BARS
Augustiner
Bräustübl-Mülln, **8**
Flip, **9**

✈ ORIENTATION

Salzburg, just a few kilometers from the German border, covers both banks of the **Salzach River.** Two of Salzburg's three hills loom on the skyline near the river: the **Mönchsberg** over the **Altstadt** (old city) on the south side and the **Kapuzinerberg** by the **Neustadt** (new city) on the north side. The Hauptbahnhof is on the northern side of town beyond the Neustadt; buses #1, 5, 6, 51, and 55 connect it to downtown. From the bus, disembark at "Mirabellplatz" in the Neustadt or "Mozartsteg," a footbridge that leads to Mozartpl. in the Altstadt. On foot, from the train station to the Neustadt, turn left out of the station onto Rainerstr. and follow it all the way (under the tunnel) to Mirabellpl.

⊏ LOCAL TRANSPORTATION

Public Transportation: Get information at the **Lokalbahnhof** (☎44 80 61 66), next to the train station (when you exit the train station, turn left and after a few steps enter the doors on your left and head down the stairs). Twenty bus lines cut through the city, with central hubs at Hanuschpl. by Makartsteg, Äußerer Stein by Mozartsteg, and the Hauptbahnhof. Single tickets (€1.70) are available at machines or from the drivers; books of 5 (€7.00) are available at *Tabak* (newsstand/tobacco shops) and at the Lokalbahnhof ticket office. *Tageskarte* (€2.90) or *Wochenkarte* (€9) allow travel on buses within the city for a full day or week, and are available at machines, the ticket office, or *Tabak* shops. Punch your ticket to validate it when you board, or pay a €36 fine. Buses make their last run from downtown at 10:30-11:30pm, earlier for less-frequented routes. Check the schedule posted at stops. **BusTaxi** fills in when the public buses stop running. Meet it at the stop at Hanuschpl. or Theaterg. and tell the driver your destination. (S-Th 11:30pm-1:30am, F-Sat 11:30pm-3am. €3 for anywhere within the city limits.)

Parking: Consider the "Park and Ride" option (see By Car, above). Otherwise, try **Altstadt-Garage** inside the Mönchsberg (open 24hr.; €2.40 per hr., €14 per day); **Mirabell-Congress-Garage** in Mirabellpl. (Open 7am-midnight; €3.20 per hr., €15 per day); or **Parkgarage Linzer Gasse** at Glockeng. off Linzerg (open 7am-10pm; €1.80 per hr., €14.40 per day). Other lots are at the airport, Hellbrunn, and Hauptbahnhof.

Taxis: (☎81 11). Stands at Hanuschpl., Residenzpl., and the train station.

Car Rental: Avis, Ferdinand-Porsche-Str. 7 (☎87 72 78; www.avis.at).

Bike Rental: Top Bike Salzburg (☎062 72 or 45 56; www.topbike.at) at the train station and the Staatsbrücke. €13 per day, €41 per week, 10% off with Salzburg Card, 20% off at the train station with valid train ticket. Open daily Apr.-June, Sept., and Oct. 10am-5pm; July-Aug. 9am-7pm, except in bad weather.

Hitchhiking: While *Let's Go* does not recommend hitching, hitchers headed to Innsbruck, Munich, or Italy have been seen on bus #77 to the German border. Those bound for Vienna have been known to take bus #29 (dir.: Forellenwegsiedlung) to the Autobahn at "Schmiedlingerstr." or #15 (dir.: Bergheim) to the Autobahn at "Grüner Wald."

🖟 PRACTICAL INFORMATION

TOURIST & FINANCIAL SERVICES

Tourist Office, Mozartpl. 5 (☎88 98 73 30; www.salzburg.info), in the *Altstadt*. From the train station, take bus #5, 6, 51, or 55 to "Mozartsteg," head away from the river and curve to your right around the building into Mozartpl. On foot from the train station, turn left on Rainerstr., cross Staatsbrücke, and continue along the river's south bank to Mozartsteg (20min.). The staff has free hotel maps, lists available rooms, and offers the

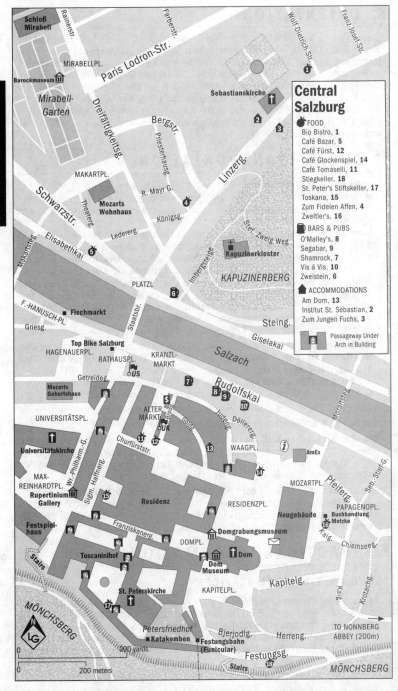

Central Salzburg

🍎 **FOOD**
Bio Bistro, **1**
Café Bazar, **5**
Café Fürst, **12**
Café Glockenspiel, **14**
Café Tomaselli, **11**
Stiegkeller, **18**
St. Peter's Stiftskeller, **17**
Toskana, **15**
Zum Fidelen Affen, **4**
Zweltler's, **16**

🍺 **BARS & PUBS**
O'Malley's, **8**
Segabar, **9**
Shamrock, **7**
Vis á Vis, **10**
Zweistein, **6**

🏠 **ACCOMMODATIONS**
Am Dom, **13**
Institut St. Sebastian, **2**
Zum Jungen Fuchs, **3**

Passageway Under
Arch in Building

Salzburg Card (see p. 247). Reservation service is €2.20, for 3 or more people €4.40, plus a 10% deposit deductible from the 1st night's stay. There are also guided tours of the city that leave from the tourist office daily at 12:15pm (€8, in German and English). Open daily 9am-6pm. There is another **branch** at the **train station** platform #2a (☎88 98 73 40; generally open daily 9:15am-8pm, though hours may vary).

Consulates: South Africa, Buchenweg 14 A-5061 Elsbethen-Glasenbach (☎/fax 62 20 35; www.south-africa-embassy.at). Open M-Th 3-5:30 pm. **UK,** Alter Markt 4 (☎84 81 33; fax 84 55 63). Open M-F 9am-noon. **US,** Alter Markt 1/3 (☎84 87 76; fax 84 97 77), in the *Altstadt.* Open M, W, Th 9am-noon.

Currency Exchange: Banks offer better rates for cash than AmEx offices but often charge higher commissions. Banking hours M-F 8am-12:30pm and 2-4:30pm. **Rieger Bank,** Alter Markt 15, has extended exchange hours. Open daily 10am-2:30pm and 3-8pm. The train station's exchange is open 7am-9pm. **Panorama Tours** offers bank rates with no commission; available only to guests taking their tour (see p. 251).

American Express: Mozartpl. 5, A-5020 (☎80 80; fax 808 01 78), near the tourist office. Provides all banking services and charges no commission on AmEx cheques. Holds mail for cheque- or card-holders, and books tours. Open M-F 9am-5:30pm, Sa 9am-noon (only for money or traveler's cheque exchange).

LOCAL SERVICES

Luggage Storage: At the train station. 24hr. small lockers €2, medium €2.50, large €3.50. At the tourist office on Mozartpl. €1, with a €5 key deposit.

Bookstores: Buchhandlung Motzko (Platz der Bucher), has 2 stores with English-language sections. Elisabethstr. 1 (☎883 31 10), near the train station, has a shelf of English books. Kaig. 11 (☎88 33 11 50), in the *Altstadt,* has a small selection of best-sellers. Both stores open M-F 9am-6:30pm, Sa 9am-5pm. **Buchhandlung Höllrigl,** 10 Sigmund Haffnerg., just beyond Café Tomaselli, is the oldest bookstore in Austria (opened 1594). There's an English-language section on the 2nd floor.

Bi-Gay-Lesbian Organizations: Homosexual Initiative of Salzburg (HOSI), Müllner Hauptstr. 11 (☎43 59 27; www.hosi.at), hosts regular workshops and meetings, and publishes a list of bars, cafés, and restaurants available at the main tourist office. Other resources include a library and a transgender group.

Laundromat: Norge Exquisit Textil Reinigung, Paris-Lodronstr. 16 (☎87 63 81), on the corner of Wolf-Dietrich-Str. Self-serve wash and dry €10 (including their soap, which patrons must use). Full-serve €14.20; clothes ready by 5pm if you bring them in early in the morning, otherwise pick them up the next day. Open M-F 7:30am-6pm, Sa 8am-noon.

Public Toilets: Look for the green WC signs located at most tourist sites. In the Festungs-bahn lobby, the Hanuschpl. fish market., and the *Altstadt* under the archway between Kapitelpl. and Dompl. Although these restrooms are free, it is polite to tip the attendant.

EMERGENCIES & COMMUNICATIONS

Emergencies: Police ☎133, Headquarters at Alpenstr. 90 (non-emergency ☎63 83); **Ambulance** ☎144; **Fire** ☎122.

Rape Hotline: Frauennotruf (☎88 11 00). Contact Dr. Andrea Laher.

AIDS Hotline: AIDS-Hilfe Salzburg, Gabelsburgerstr. 20 (☎88 14 88).

Women's Emergencies: Frauenhilfe Salzburg (☎84 09 00 or 84 42 69). Contact: Annemarie Schobesberger, Ulli Huber, Dr. Gertraud Hess, and Ulrike Klingeis.

Pharmacies: Elisabeth-Apotheke, Elisabethstr. 1a (☎87 14 84; fax 87 14 84-4), a few blocks south of the train station. Pharmacies in the city center are open M-F 8am-6pm, Sa 8am-noon; outside the center M-F 8am-12:30pm and 2:30-6pm, Sa 8am-noon. There are always 3 pharmacies open; check the door of any closed pharmacy for info.

Medical Assistance: call the hospital, **St. Johnnspital Landeskrankenanstalten Salzburg,** Müllner Hauptstr. 48 (☎44 820; a.burger@lks.at); or call the **Ärzte Bere-itschaftsdienst,** Dr. Franz-Renner-Str. 7 (☎141), F 7pm to M 7am.

Internet Access:

Internet Café, Mozartpl. 5 (☎84 48 22; www.cybar.at). €0.15 per min. 10min. minimum. Open daily Sept.-June 9am-11pm; July-Aug. 9am-midnight.

BIGnet.café, Judeng. 5-7 (☎84 14 70). 10min. €1.50, 30min. €3.70, 1hr. €5.90. Snack bar, funky music, and a total of 33 workstations make for great surfing. Open daily 9am-10pm.

Piterfun Internetc@fe, Ferdinand-Porsche-Str. 7 (office@piterfun.at). 15min. €1.80, 30min. €2.90, 60min. €5. Bright colors and loud techno give a rave ambiance. Directly across from the train station. Open daily 10am-10pm.

Post Office: At the Hauptbahnhof (☎88 30 30). Address *Poste Restante* to *Postlagernde Briefe,* Bahnhofspostamt, A-5020 Salzburg. Open M-F 7am-8:30pm (counter closes at 6pm), Sa 8am-2pm, Su 1-6pm. **Postal Code:** A-5020.

⛰ ACCOMMODATIONS

Salzburg offers a wide variety of hostels to host the flocks of tourists that pass through yearly. Most affordable accommodations are on the outskirts of town, easily accessible by local transportation. Ask for the tourist office's list of *Privat-zimmer* (private rooms) or the *Hotel Plan* for information on hostels. From mid-May to mid-September, hostels fill by mid-afternoon—call ahead. During the *Festspiele*, hotels fill months in advance, and most hostels and *Gästehäuser* are full days before. At HI hostels there is a €3 surcharge per night for non-members.

HOSTELS & DORMITORIES

Stadtalm, Mönchsberg 19c (☎84 17 29; www.stadtalm.com), towers over the *Altstadt* from atop the Mönchsberg. Take bus #1 (dir.: Maxglan) to "Mönchsbergaufzug," then walk down the street a few steps and through the stone arch on the left to the Mönchs-berglift (elevator), which takes you to the top of the mountain (9am-11pm; one-way €1.50, round-trip €2.40). At the top, climb the steps and follow signs for "Stadtalm." Or climb the stairs in Toscaninihof after the end of Wiener-Philharmoniker-G., turn right at the top, and look for the "Stadtalm" sign. Get a princely view on a pauper's budget at the most scenic hostel in Salzburg. Holds 26 in simple 2- to 6-bed rooms (including a room in the tower). Breakfast included. Showers €0.80 per 4min. Reception 9am-9pm. Curfew 1am. Open Apr.-Sept. Dorms €13. AmEx/DC/MC/V. ❷

Institut St. Sebastian, Linzerg. 41 (☎87 13 86; www.st-sebastian-salzburg.at). From the station, take bus #1, 5, 6, 51, or 55 to Mirabellpl. Cross the street and continue in same direction. Turn left onto Bergstr. and left at the end onto Linzerg. The hostel is through the arch on the left before the church. Smack in the middle of the Neus-tadt on the St. Sebastian church grounds, the buildings are dorms for female stu-dents during the school year but accept travelers of either gender year-round. Rooftop terrace with postcard views of the city. Breakfast, kitchen, and lockers included. Laundry €3, €4 with soap. Reception 8am-noon and 4-9pm. No curfew. Dorms €15, sheets €17; singles €21, with shower €33; doubles €40/€54; triples €60/€69; quads €72/€84. MC/V with stay of more than one night. ❸

International Youth Hotel (YoHo), Paracelsußtr. 9 (☎87 96 49 or 834 60; www.yoho.at), off Franz-Josef-Str. Exit the train station to the left down Rainerstr. and turn left onto Gabelsbergerstr. through the tunnel. Take the 2nd right onto Paracelsusstr. (7min.). *The Sound of Music* screens daily at 10:30am at the request of tourists. Filled with beer-sipping postcard writers, this hostel is a no-frills place to crash. There are no room keys for dorm rooms—lockers in the hall for €0.10-€1. Happy Hour in bar 6-7pm with 0.5L Stiegl €1.50, other brews €2.50. Breakfast €3-4. Dinner entrees (including veggie options) €5-6. Sheets €5 deposit. Front door locks at 1am, but you can ring the bell anytime. 6- to 8- bed dorms €15; 4-bed dorms €17; 2-bed dorms €20. €3 more for shower in room. MC/V. ❸

Haunspergstraße (HI), Haunspergstr. 27 (☎87 96 49; fax 88 34 77), near the train station. Walk out Kaiserschützenstr., which becomes Jahnstr. Take the 3rd left onto Haunspergstr. and walk one block to the hostel. It will be on the right-hand side on the corner of Stauffernstr. This student dorm becomes a hostel in July. Houses 90 in spacious 2- to 4-bed rooms. Breakfast and sheets included. All rooms have either a private shower or share it with 1 other room. All guests must leave €10 or other sufficient collateral to obtain their key (including a house key to the main door). Reception 7am-2pm and 5pm-midnight. Open July-Aug. 3. 4-person dorms €14.50; singles €19. MC/V. ❷

Eduard-Heinrich-Haus (HI), Eduard-Heinrich-Str. 2 (☎62 59 76; hostel.eduard-heinrich@salzburg.co.at). Take bus #51 (dir.: Salzburg-Süd) to "Polizeidirektion." Cross over Alpenstr., then continue down Billrothstr., turn left on Robert-Stolz-Promenade footpath, walk 200m, and take 1st right; the hostel is the big pink and yellow building up the driveway on the left. Near the Salzach Forest with enormous 6-bed rooms and lobbies on each floor with leather couches and a TV. Breakfast and lockers included. **Internet** access: 20min. €2.60, 40min. €4.40, 75min. €7.30. Reception M-F 7am-midnight. Sa-Su 7-10am and 5pm-midnight, with lockout 10am-5pm. No curfew, but ask about key deposit. Dorms €17.42; €20.42 with private bathroom. ❸

Aigen (HI), Aignerstr. 34 (☎62 32 48; hostel.aigen@salzburg.co.at). From the station, bus #6 or 51 to "Mozartsteg.," then bus #49 (dir.: Josef-Käut-Str.) to "Finanzamt." Walk 5min. in the same direction as the bus; it's on the right behind the hedges. Large hostel with clean, large, and simple 2-, 4-, and 6-bed dorms. Breakfast, shower, locker, and sheets included. Reception 7-10am and 5-11pm. No curfew. 2-person dorms €20.24, 4-person €17.42, 6-person €14.42. Singles €27.31. MC/V. ❸

PRIVATZIMMER & PENSIONEN

Privatzimmer and *Pension* accommodations in the center of the city can be quite expensive, but better quality and lower prices await on the outskirts, minutes from downtown Salzburg by train. Rooms on **Kasern Berg** are officially out of Salzburg, which means the tourist office can't recommend them, but the clean, comfortable rooms and bargain prices make these *Privatzimmer* a terrific housing option. However, keep in mind that these rooms are not in the city, so be prepared for quiet, rolling fields, and reliance on public transportation. Realize that these are people's homes, so be on your best behavior. Stays include a typical Austrian breakfast of rolls, meat, cheese, homemade jam, and eggs. All northbound regional trains run to Kasern Berg (generally 4min., every 30min. 6:17am-11:17pm, €1.60, Wochenkarte and Eurail valid). Get off at the first stop, "Salzburg-Maria Plain," and take the only road up the long hill, or call from the Hauptbahnhof and your host will pick you up at Maria Plain. All the Kasern Berg Pensionen are along this road, whose position on a hill above the city affords marvelous views of the valley below. Alternatively, take bus #15 (dir.: Bergheim) from Mirabellpl. to "Kasern," then continue straight up Söllheimerstr. and follow Wickenburgallee up the mountain (15min.). By car, exit A1 on "Salzburg Nord."

■ **Haus Lindner,** Panoramaweg 5 (☎/fax 45 66 81; www.House-Lindner.at). Head five minutes up the road from the train station and take a left at the top of the hill onto Panoramaweg. In her charming house at the top of the hill, friendly owner Matilda offers homey rooms, some with balcony for mountain views. The entire house is warmly decorated, with lots of flowers, vases, and statuettes. Breakfast served on a sunny terrace and in a room with satellite TV, available for guests' use during the day. Capacity of 15 people makes it the biggest in Kasern Berg. Families welcome. €15-16 per person. Credit cards accepted, but cash preferred. ❷

Haus Moser, Turnerbühel 1 (☎45 66 76). Climb up the steep hidden stairs on the right side of Kasern Berg road across from Germana Kapeller. If you have a heavy backpack, try the driveway entrance at beginning of Kasern Berg road. Charming, elderly couple warmly welcomes you into their home, offering comfortable rooms in this cozy, dark-timbered, antler-decorated home. 2 rooms have balcony. Free drinks, breakfast, shower, and laundry included. €15 for one night, €13.50 for longer stays. ❷

Haus Christine, Panoramaweg 3 (☎/fax 45 67 73; haus.christine@gmx.at). The house before Haus Lindner. Haus Christine has spacious, clean triples and quads with a country motif. Breakfast served on a lovely glass-enclosed patio overlooking the countryside. €14-15 per person. Credit cards accepted, but cash preferred. ❷

Germana Kapeller, Kasern Bergstr. 64 (☎45 66 71; www.germana.at). Lively, gregarious hostess Germana speaks English well and maintains traditional rooms with pleasant, vibrant colors. Some rooms have hand-carved furniture, and others have balcony. 2 terraces overlooking the valley for lounging. €15-17 per person. Reservations, made in advance by telephone or email, are preferred. ❷

Haus Seigmann, Kasern Bergstr. 66 (☎45 00 01). Clean rooms, some with balcony overlooking the valley, as well as 2 patios on the hillside where afternoon tea is served. Relax on the lounge chairs outside, in the TV room downstairs, or curled up in bed under a snug comforter. Small kitchen available for guests' use. About €15 per person (negotiable). Reservations recommended in summer. MC/V. ❷

The following *Privatzimmer* are on the southern edge of Salzburg, but are easily accessible by car and by public transportation. Take bus #1 to "Hanuschpl.," then bus #60 heading south. For House Ballwein, get off at "Gsengerweg" and for House Bankhammer get of at the next stop, "Marienbad."

■ **Haus Ballwein,** Moostr. 69a (☎/fax 82 40 29; haus.ballwein@gmx.net). Bright, spacious rooms with balcony looking out onto quiet fields and distant mountains make this the perfect reprieve from city life. Breakfast room with teapot collection hanging from ceiling. Rooms come with shower (in the hall for singles) and cable TV. Bicycle rental €7 per day. Singles €22; doubles €38-50. ❸

Haus Bankhammer, Moostr. 77 (☎/fax 83 00 67; helga.bankhammer@telering.at). This house has rooms with carved wooden beds and armoires. Doubles with bath. Breakfast of homemade strawberry-rhubarb jam and fresh milk from the dairy. Helga speaks fluent English and will do laundry for guests. Rooms €22-24 per person. MC/V. ❸

The following *Privatzimmer* are located in other parts of Salzburg.

Haus Elisabeth, Rauchenbichlerstr. 18 (☎/fax 45 07 03; info@haus-elizabeth.net). Take bus #51 to "Itzling-Pflanzmann," turn around and walk about 50m back, then head right onto Rauchenbichlerstr., over the footbridge, and continue along the gravel path sloping uphill to your right. Spacious rooms have TV, balcony, and sweeping city view. Breakfast buffet included in newly remodeled room. Refrigerators available for guest use. Singles with shower €26; doubles €44-50; one quad €80. ❸

Pension Sandwirt, Lastenstr. 6a (☎/fax 87 43 51). Exit the train station from the platform #13 staircase, turn right on the footbridge, right again at the bottom onto Lastenstr., and go behind the building with the Post sign (3min.). The hosts of this bed-and-breakfast (not a private home) speak excellent English and will let you do laundry for free. All rooms have TV. Breakfast included. Surprise: shower is actually *in* the bedroom. Singles €22; doubles €36, with shower €43; triples €51; quads €64. ❸

HOTELS

Am Dom, Goldg. 17 (☎84 27 65; bach@salzburg.co.at). This historic wood-panelled hotel is great if you are looking for clean, quiet accommodations in a wonderful location in the heart of the *Altstadt*. As its name implies, it is located just across the square from the *Dom*. Make sure to reserve a room ahead of time in the summer—this small hotel of only 14 rooms fills up fast. Singles €68; doubles €94. MC/V. ❹

Albertina Hotel Allegro, Glockeng. 4b (☎889 60; www.albertina-hotels.at). Turn off Schallmooser Hauptstr. where it says Linzer Parkgarage and turn right into Glockeng. Hidden behind a row of buildings on the Schallmooser Hauptstr., this stylish blue building is a delightful departure from the architecture surrounding it. The interior is well lit and decorated in swaths of bright color. Open July-Sept. Singles €46; doubles €72. ❹

Zum Jungen Fuchs, Linzerg. 54 (☎87 54 96). Just across the street from St. Sebastian, this small hotel is perfect for travelers on a budget who are tired of the bustle of hostels. Don't be discouraged by the tunnel-like hallways and drab reception area—the rooms are pleasant and large. Reservations required. Singles €27; doubles €36, €40 with shower; triples €48/€50. ❸

Altstadthotel Blaue Gans, Getreideg. 41-43 (☎84 29 91; www.blauegans.at). Take #1 bus directly to the back door of the hotel, or from Hanauer Platz take a left on Getreideg. The hotel is on the left. The Blaue Gans dates back hundreds of years, even if its decor does not. Each room in this cosmopolitan hotel has sleek furniture and a unique piece of modern art, as well as a TV. The hotel is home to minimalist sculpture and elaborate wall paintings. Singles €99-115; doubles €109-189. AmEx/MC/V. ❺

CAMPING

Panorama Camping Stadtblick, Rauchenbichlerstr. 21 (☎45 06 52; www.panorama-camping.at). Next to Haus Elisabeth (see above for directions) and run by her brother. By car, take exit "Salzburg-Nord" off A1. It's bring-your-own-tent (or RV) in this peaceful green yard with a view of the city. On-site store. Laundry €5. Shower included. Open Mar. 20-Nov. 11. €5.90, *Let's Go* readers €5.30; 2-person RV with fridge and stove €25; 4-person €36. Lots with parking and tent (including electricity) €3.20. ❶

🄵 FOOD & DRINK

With countless beer gardens and pastry-shop patios, Salzburg is a great place to eat outdoors. The local specialty is **Salzburger Nockerl,** a large soufflé of egg whites, sugar, and raspberry filling baked into three mounds to represent the three hills of Salzburg. If you order one be prepared to wait 20-30min. and pay around €10-12. Also make sure you have a friend to share it with—it's huge. Another regional favorite is **Knoblauchsuppe,** a rich cream soup loaded with croutons and pungent garlic—a potent weapon against unwanted admirers. During the first two weeks of September, local cafés dispense **Stürm,** a delicious, cloudy cider (reminiscent, aptly enough, of a storm) that hasn't quite finished fermenting.

There are probably more world-famous **Mozartkugeln** ("Mozart balls," hazelnuts covered with marzipan and nougat and dipped in chocolate) lining café windows than notes in all Mozart's works combined. A Salzburg confectioner invented the treats in 1890, but mass production inevitably took over. Although mass-produced *Kugeln* wrapped in gold and red are technically *echt* (authentic), try to find the handmade ones wrapped in blue and silver. Reasonably priced *Kugeln* are sold at the **Holzmayr** confectioners (€0.40 for gold, €0.65 for silver) or at Konditorei **Fürst** (€0.80 for silver), both on Alter Markt. Holzmayr serves many varieties including light and dark chocolate, original recipe, apricot "original recipe," and "diet."

In most cases, markets are open weekdays 8am-7pm and Saturday 8am-noon. Salzburg has many supermarkets on the Mirabellpl. side of the river but few in the *Altstadt*. **SPAR** is widespread, and a giant **EuroSpar** sprawls next to the train station bus terminal at Sudtirolerp. 11. (Open M-F 8am-7pm, Sa 7:30am-5pm). **Open-air markets** are held on Universitätpl. (M-F 6am-7pm, Sa 6am-1pm) and Mirabellpl. down into Hubert-Sattlerg. (Th 5am-noon).

RESTAURANTS

Zum Fidelen Affen, Priesterhausg. 8 (☎87 73 61), off Linzerg. This wood-paneled restaurant is popular with locals. Hearty, honest Austrian food keeps everyone coming back "At the Faithful Ape." Try the toasted black bread with various toppings or the farmer's salad (€10). Meals €8.50-17, beer €3.20. Open M-Sa 5-midnight. MC/V. ❸

St. Peter's Stiftskeller, St.-Peter-Bezirk 1/4 (☎84 12 680; www.haslauer.at). From Dompl., pass through the arch that leads to Franziskanerg. and take the first left. Tucked away in a courtyard at the foot of the cliffs, St. Peter's Stiftskeller is considered to be the oldest restaurant in Central Europe: when construction on the fortress began in 1077, this restaurant had already been in business for over 200 years. With traditional Austrian food, old-fashioned decor, and classical music, it lives up to its heritage. Most entrees around €18-20, but a few run cheaper, such as asparagus risotto (€12.50). Open daily 11am-midnight, during the *Festspiele* until 1am. MC/V. ❹

Stadtalm, Mönchsberg 19c (☎84 17 29). Even if you aren't staying in the Stadtalm youth hostel, you should consider making a trip to the Mönchsberg lift to eat at the delightful café of the same name. This casual spot features picnic tables situated under large sun umbrellas, teetering at the brink of the cliff. Enjoy chicken cordon bleu (€9.90), Greek salad (€5.90), or a glass of Stiegl (€2.70) while soaking up the amazing view of the *Altstadt*. Open Mar.-Oct. daily 10am-10pm. ❸

Zwettler's, Kaig. 3 (☎84 00 44), in the *Altstadt*. From the tourist office walk straight out to the back left corner of Mozartpl. to Kaig. Cozy wooden interior turns into a lively bar at night. Tasty *Spinatnockerl* (spinach baked into a pan with cheese and parsley) is out of this world at €6.70, or opt for the classic *Wienerschnitzel* (€9.70). For added excitement, local customers yell suggestions to the chef on the second floor. Open daily 6pm-1am; during the *Festspiele* 11am-2pm and 6pm-1am. AmEx/MC/V. ❷

Shakespeare, Hubert-Sattlerg. 3 (☎87 91 06; www.shakespeare.at), off Mirabellpl. This artsy, eclectic spot serves a variety of foods, from Italian and Austrian dishes to surprisingly good Chinese dishes. Large, spicy platter of Szechuan pork €9.40, spaghetti alla carbonara €6.90. Art exhibitions about twice every month in the back rooms. **Free Internet.** Open 8am-2am daily. Kitchen open until 11pm. D/MC/V. ❷

Stiegkeller, Festungsg. 10 (☎84 26 81). A short walk up the Festungsg. from the bottom of the Festungsbahn. The Stiegkeller has been a Salzburg tradition since 1492. With seating for 1600, there's plenty of room in this restaurant, both outside under shady trees and inside under imposing antlers. Dinner options include the good old standby *Schweinsbraten* (roast pork with sauerkraut and dumpling; €9.60), as well as perch fillet (€14.20) and salad with strips of roast turkey (€8.20). Open May-Sept. 11am-11pm. AmEx/MC/V. ❸

Il Sole, Gstätteng. 15 (☎84 32 84), just to the right of the bottom of the Mönchsberg lift. The wonderful aroma of fresh cooked pizza (€5.50-8.50) greets you as you enter this lovely Italian restaurant. While listening to soothing background music, enjoy lasagna (€6.50), or one of the many pasta dishes. Open daily 11:30am-2pm and 5:30-11:30pm. Closed on Tu in spring and fall. AmEx/MC/V. ❷

Bio Bistro, Wolf-Dietrich-Str. 1 (☎87 07 12). Walk down Linzerg. from the *Altstadt* and turn left onto Wolf-Dietrich. Inside this organic eatery and spice store you will find a world of aromas and a different vegetarian lunch *Menü* each day (€5), with soup (€2.50) and 3 kinds of salads (€3.50). Dinner *Menü* includes appetizer, main course, and dessert (€9.90). Takeout available. Open M-Sa 9am-9pm, Su 11am-9pm. ❷

Toskana, Sigmund Haffnerg. 11 (☎80 44 69 009), across from Sigmund Haffnerg. 16, through the iron fence and on the right. This college cafeteria is a good deal for penny-pinchers with 2 hot entrees (€3.50-4.25), served in a smoky courtyard just within the university grounds. Get there early, before ravenous students deplete the food supply. Open July-Aug. daily 9am3pm; Sept.-June M-Th 8:30am-5pm, F 8:30am-3pm. ❶

CAFÉS

Café Tomaselli, Alter Markt 9 (☎80 44 69 00), has been a favorite haunt for wealthier *Salzburger* since 1705. The interior glows with the light of the crystal chandeliers reflecting off the warm wood paneling and gold trim. Try the hot chocolate with rum (€4.20), which is guaranteed to warm your belly. Cakes about €3 on a mobile dessert counter. Kick back and sample the *Glühwein* (€4.25), *Grog* (€3.75), or *Tomaselliums Café,* a decadent concoction of mocha, original Mozart liqueur, whipped cream, and almond slivers (€5.70). Newspapers available for perusal. Open M-Sa 7am-9pm, Su 8am-9pm, during the *Festspiele* until midnight.

Café Bazar, Schwarzstr. 3 (☎87 42 78; www.café-bazar.at). From the *Altstadt,* cross the Makart bridge and turn left onto the foot path. The terrace in back provides a peaceful way to escape the crowds along the tree-shaded riverbank of the Salzach. Enjoy a light lunch for €4.10, or indulge in a dessert such as raspberry yogurt, *Sachertorte,* or *Mozarttorte,* for around €3. Open M-Sa 7:30am-midnight.

Café Cult, Hellbrunnerstr. 3 (☎84 56 01). Go into the Kunstlerhaus building and around to the back on the ground floor. This Mediterranean café is popular with the artistic set of Salzburg, but less so with tourists. Eat on the glass terrace by the river or on the trendy orange furniture. Meals €6.10-9.10. Open M-F 9am-11pm, Sa 8am-3pm.

Café Fürst, Brodg. 13 (☎84 37 59). Basically on Alter Markt, right across from Café Tomaselli. Savor a *Mozartkugel* (€0.80), or any one of a vast selection of candies (try the marzipan potato), chocolates, pastries, *Torte,* strudels, and cakes (around €2). Grab one of the sunny tables outside if you can. Branch in Mirabellpl. Open daily June-Sept. 8am-9pm; Oct.-May. 8am-8pm. AmEx/DC/MC/V.

Café Glockenspiel, Mozartpl. 1 (☎84 14 03). Near the tourist office, this place serves ice cream concoctions (€4.40-5.80) and cakes (€3.10). The restaurant ❸ upstairs serves good typical Austrian fair, ranging from *Bratwurst* (€6.60) to duck (€15.90). Vegetarian specials including tortellini and *Spinatspätzle.* Sit at a table on the square and listen to free concerts of light classical music each evening in July and Aug.—or just watch the flocks of tourists parade past the Mozart statue. Open daily Easter-Aug. 9am-11pm; Sept.-Easter 9am-7pm; during the *Festspiele* until midnight. AmEx/DC/MC/V.

Kaffeehäferl, Getreideg. 25 (☎84 32 49), from Hagenauerpl. facing Mozarts Geburt-shaus turn right down Getreidg. Walk 25m and turn left into the passage across from McDonald's. Unpretentious courtyard café provides a place to rest from the tourist rush of Getreideg. Coffee around €2.54, strawberry milkshake €2.80, Johannis juice €2.10. Open M-Sa 9am-7pm, Su noon-7pm.

◎ SIGHTS

Salzburg is a relatively small town with a disproportionate number of *Sehenswür-digkeiten* (points of interest). Whether you're into decadent floral gardens or centuries-old fortresses, Salzburg's got it. The tourist office sells the **Salzburg Card,**

START YOUR ENGINES...

At the end of May Salzburg shuts down in recognition of *Christi Himmelfahrt*, the Catholic holiday of the Ascension. Although the holiday is a celebration of Jesus' return to heaven, part of Salzburg's observance may seem surprising. At the end of May, antique race cars pour into Residenzpl., revving their engines and parading around town for three days. In 2003 the Gaisberg Race for classic motor cars, which ran from 1929 to 1969, was resurrected by a group of farsighted politicians and antique car lovers. The race is a "regularity contest," meaning that racers try to match their own times. The 8652m course runs from the city center to the Gaisberg, one of three hills overlooking Salzburg. In their cars, all models from 1910 to 1970, the beaming owners make the 672m climb. The event allows car collectors a chance to show off their babies, and gives Salzburg citizens and tourists the opportunity to gather in the *Altstatdt* and see some really cool cars. While admiring the competitors' automobiles, spectators enjoy the live music and the food stands set up around the edges of Residenzpl.

In 2004, *Christi Himmelfahrt* falls on Thursday, May 20. The festivities last for three days, through Saturday. For more information, check out the Gaisberg Race's site: www.src.co.at.

which grants admission to all museums and sights as well as unlimited use of public transportation, but it's a good deal only if you cram lots of sightseeing into a short period of time. (24hr. card €19., 48hr. €27, 72hr. €33; ages 7-15 half-price.)

FESTUNG HOHENSALZBURG

(☎84 24 30. Grounds open daily mid-June to mid-Sept. 9am-5:30pm; mid-Sept. to mid-Mar. 9am-4:30pm; mid-Mar. to mid-June 9:30am-5pm. If you walk up, entrance to fortress is €3.60, ages 6-15 €2, which allows only access to the perimeter of the castle; combo ticket includes fortress, castle interiors, and museums €7.20/€4.)

Built between 1077 and 1681 by the ruling archbishops, **Festung Hohensalzburg** was used as a refuge during religious wars. Looming over Salzburg from atop Mönchsberg, it has never been successfully attacked, making it the largest completely preserved castle in Europe. Nowadays, penetrating the castle walls is just a matter of a few euros.

FESTUNGSBAHN. The trail up to the fortress and the *Festungsbahn* (funicular) can be found at the far end of Kapitelpl. on Festungsg. The stairs require about 20min. of uphill walking. Because the ride ends inside the fortress walls, funicular tickets include entrance. *(☎84 97 50. Every 10min. May-Sept. 9am-9pm; Oct.-Apr. 9am-5pm. Ascent €5.60, children €3; round-trip €8.40/€4.50. MC/V.)*

FÜRSTENZIMMER. The trail up to the fortress will be worthwhile with a visit to the inner rooms of the castle, which contain formidable Gothic state rooms, the fortress organ (nicknamed the "Bull of Salzburg" for its off-key snorting), the archbishop's medieval indoor toilet, and an impregnable watchtower that affords an unmatched view of the city and surrounding mountains.

BURGMUSEUM. Inside the fortress, this museum exhibits findings from 16th-century excavations, stick figures displaying weapons used between 1300 and 1700, and a series of side-by-side timelines depicting the history of the Festung, Salzburg, and the world at large. Also notable are the music samples in the section on Turkish music from Austria.

RAINER MUSEUM. Exhibits here include objects of war from the 17th century to the present, including uniforms, books, weapons, and paintings. Don't miss the life-size model of an Austrian soldier in alpine uniform, complete with ice pick, hiking boots, and knee-length pants. The fortress also has a gift shop, café, restaurant, and a small marionette museum.

OTHER SIGHTS. From the fortress many footpaths spread out over the Mönchsberg, providing bird's-eye views of the city below. At times, the paths are framed by damp stone walls, many of which were originally parts of the city wall, dating back to the 13th century. From these trails, hikers can descend back to the *Altstadt* via the stairs or the **Mönchsberglift** (an elevator built into the mountain), which opens onto Gstätteng. 13. *(Operates daily 9am-11pm. €1.60, round-trip €2.60; children half-price.)* Down the hill and to the right of the fortress, **Nonnberg Abbey** (where the real Maria von Trapp lived) is still a private monastic complex and closed to the public. Persistent visitors can opt to tour the dimly-lit church in the complex and see the Romanesque wall paintings.

THE ALTSTADT

THE CITY CENTER. In the shadow of the hill-top fortress, arcade passages open up into tiny courtyards filled with geraniums and creeping ivy that lead, in turn, to the tourist-jammed Getreidegasse. The buildings here are the oldest in the city, some dating back to the 12th century. Many of the shops have wrought-iron signs dating from the Middle Ages, when the illiterate needed pictorial aids.

RESIDENZ (ARCHBISHOP'S RESIDENCE). The square on the far side of the cathedral is Residenzplatz, named for the magnificent Residenz of Salzburg's powerful Prince Archbishops. The ecclesiastical elite of Austria have resided here, in the heart of the *Altstadt*, since 1595; Mozart conducted symphonies within. An audio-guide offers commentary on the Baroque *Prunkräume*, massive state rooms decorated with immense ceiling frescoes and stucco work, gilded furniture, and 17th-century Flemish tapestries. The Residenz also houses a gallery (see p. 252). *(☎80 42 26 90. Open daily 10am-5pm. €7.30, students €5.50, children €2.50, audio guide included.)* Outside the palace, dead-center in Residenzpl. is a 15m fountain—the largest Baroque fountain in the world—featuring amphibious horses charging through the water (when the fountain works). Appropriately, *Fiaker* (horse-drawn carriages) congregate in the square. *(€33 for 30min. rides.)*

MOZARTS GEBURTSHAUS (BIRTHPLACE). The long red and white flag suspended from the roof of the **Mozarts Geburtshaus** is a beacon for music pilgrims worldwide. Although Mozart eventually settled in Vienna, his birthplace holds the most impressive collection of the child genius' belongings: his first viola and violin, a pair of keyboard instruments, and buttons from his coat. Several rooms also recreate life in Salzburg and Austria during Mozart's time, as well as what Mozart's young years as a traveling virtuoso must have been like. Come before 11am to avoid the tourists who crowd around the exhibits, blocking the prodigy's relics from all but the most persistent. *(On the 2nd floor of Getreideg. 9. ☎84 43 13. Open daily July-Aug. 9am-6:30pm; Sept.-June 9am-5:30pm. €5.50, students and seniors €4.50, children €2.)*

UNIVERSITY CHURCH. Behind Mozart's Birthplace is the Universitätskirche, one of the largest Baroque chapels in Europe, and designer Fischer von Erlach's masterpiece. Its distinctive dome stands watch over Universitätspl. and the daily farmer's market. Sculpted clouds coat the nave, while pudgy cherubim (lit by pale natural light from the dome) frolic all over the church's immense apse.

FESTSPIELHAUS. The Festspielhaus, once the riding school for the archbishops' horses, now houses many of the big-name events of the annual Festspiele. It has three separate performance spaces—the large Opera House, the small Opera House, and an open-air performance space. *(☎84 90 97. Down Wiener-Philharmonikerg. from Universitätspl. Tours daily July-Aug. 9:30am, 2, 3:30pm; June and Sept. 2, 3:30pm; Oct.-May 2pm. €5, ages 12 and under €2.90.)* Opposite the *Festspielhaus*, the Rupertinum

Gallery hosts temporary exhibits of modern painting, sculpture, and photography in a graceful building remodeled by Friedensreich Hundertwasser. (☎ 80 42 23 36. Open mid-July to Sept. Tu and Th 9am-5pm, W 10am-9pm; Oct.-mid-July Tu and Th-Su 10am-5pm, W 10am-9pm. €8, students €4.50.)

ST. PETER'S. The **Toscaninihof,** the courtyard of **St. Peter's Monastery,** hides the stone steps which lead up the Mönchsberg cliffs. The monastery itself, which was already standing when St. Rupert arrived in Salzburg in AD 696, is the oldest monastery north of the Alps. The **Stiftskirche St. Peter,** within the monastery, began as a Romanesque basilica in the 1100s and still features a marble portal from 1244. In the 18th century, the building was remodeled in Rococo style, with green and pink moldings curling delicately across the graceful ceiling and gilded cherubim blowing golden trumpets. (Open 9am-12:15pm and 2:30-6:30pm. Free.)

PETERSFRIEDHOF (CEMETERY). Petersfriedhof is one of the most peaceful places in Salzburg, partly because tour groups are denied entry. The tiny cemetery is filled with flower-covered graves, some dating back to the 1600s. In the middle is St. Margaret's Chapel, built between 1485 and 1491. (Continue through the arch to the right of the Stiftskirche St. Peter. Open daily Apr.-Sept. 6:30am-7pm; Oct.-Mar. 6:30am-6pm.)

KATAKOMBEN (CATACOMBS). Near the far end of the cemetery, against the Mönchsberg, lie the medieval catacombs. The part open to visitors consists of two rooms built into the rock wall above the cemetery. The old stone passageways will make you feel like a medieval monk, minus the robes. In the lower room (St. Gertrude's Chapel), a fresco commemorates the martyrdom of Thomas à Beckett. (Near the far end of the cemetery, against the Mönchsberg. ☎ 78 47 435. Open May-Sept. Su and Tu-Sa 10:30am-5pm; Oct.-Apr. W-Th 10:30am-3:30pm. €1, students and ages 6-18 €0.60.)

DOM (CATHEDRAL). Archbishop Wolf Dietrich's successor, Markus Sittikus, commissioned the baroque Dom in 1628. Mozart was christened here in 1756 and later worked at the cathedral as Konzertmeister and court organist. The cathedral boasts five organs which, when all played at once, create a phenomenal surround-sound experience. The original cupola was destroyed during WWII, but was repaired in 1959 to its previous condition. The square leading out of the cathedral, Domplatz, features a statue of the Virgin Mary. Around her swarm four lead figures representing Wisdom, Faith, the Church, and the Devil. (Across the square from Residenzpl., the cathedral is the large building with green domes. Free.)

MOZARTPLATZ. Mozartplatz is dominated by the **Neugebäude,** seat of the city government's bureaucracy. A 35-bell **Glockenspiel** atop the building rings out a Mozart tune (posted on the corner of the Residenz) every day at 7, 11am, and 6pm. The Hohensalzburg fortress's organ bellows a response. (To the northwest of Residenzpl.)

THE NEUSTADT

SCHLOß MIRABELL & GARDENS. On the bus and walking route into town, **Mirabellplatz** holds the marvelous **Schloß Mirabell.** The supposedly celibate Archbishop Wolf Dietrich had his own place in the Residenz (see p. 249), but he also had this Renaissance beauty built in 1606 for his mistress Salome Alt and their 10 children. He named the palace Altenau in her honor, but when the new archbishop Markus Sittikus imprisoned Wolf Dietrich for arson, he seized the palace and changed its name to Mirabell. The castle is now the seat of the city government, and some of the mayor's offices are open for public viewing. The palace hosts classical concerts in the evening, and fans swear that the Marmorsaal (Marble Hall) is one of the best concert halls in Europe. (Open M-F 8am-4pm. Free.)

Behind the palace, the delicately cultivated **Mirabellgarten** is a maze of flower beds and groomed shrubs. On the left side is a gigantic fountain with four sculptures representing Greek myths, including the rape of Helen and Pluto's abduction of Proserpina. Walk up the staircase by the smaller fountain directly in front of Schloß Mirabell to the **Dwarf Garden,** named for the vertically challenged statues that share the space with playful Salzburg toddlers. The statues' grotesque marble faces were supposedly modeled after the archbishop's court jesters.

From one of the hedge-enclosed clearings in the Mirabellgarten, you can see a tiny wooden shack called the **Zauberflötenhäuschen,** where Mozart allegedly composed *The Magic Flute* in just five months. It was transplanted from Vienna as a gift to Salzburg's conservatory for young musicians, the **Mozarteum,** which borders the gardens on Schwartzstr. 26-28. The Mozarteum was built for the Salzburg Academy of Music and Performing Arts, and there are regular performances in its concert hall (see p. 251). It is also known for its enormous **Mozart Archives.** *(☎88 94 013; fax 88 24 19. Open M-F 9am–noon and 2-5pm. Free.)*

MOZARTS WOHNHAUS (RESIDENCE). Mozart moved to the **Wohnhaus** at age 17 with his family from their house in the *Altstadt,* staying from 1773 to 1780. A somewhat helpful audio guide plays selections from Mozart's work as an accompaniment to exploring the displays, which feature some original scores from the maestro and old pianos he once played. *(Makartpl. 8. ☎87 42 27 40; fax 87 29 24. Open daily July-Aug. 9am-6:30pm; Sept.-June 9am-5:30pm. €5.50, students €4.50; audio guide included.)*

MONK-Y BUSINESS Legend has it that the robes of the *Kapuzinerkloster's* resident monks inspired the world's first cup of cappuccino. A café proprietor with an overactive imagination observed the pious gents on a noonday stroll and *voilà*—the world witnessed the birth of a drink with the rich coffee color of the monk's robes topped by white froth hoods. According to this theory, Italy's cappuccino is just a rip-off of the much older *Kapuziner,* still ordered in Austrian cafés today.

KAPUZINBERG & SEBASTIANSKIRCHE. At Kapuzinerberg's crest stands the simple **Kapuzinerkloster** (Capuchin Monastery) that Wolf Dietrich built in the late 16th century. Stations of the cross are represented by dioramas behind iron gates on the path up from town. The outlook point alongside the path offers a unique view of the city. *(From Mirabellpl., follow Dreifaltigkeitg. south to its intersection Linzerg.; head under the stone arch on the right side of Linzerg. 14 and follow the stone staircase up to the monastery.)* Farther down Linzerg. is the 18th-century **Sebastianskirche.** On the far side of the church lies the entrance to its Italian-style cemetery, with overgrown graves and fir trees. In the center, framed by arched walkways, stands the impressive mausoleum of Archbishop Dietrich, with skylights in the dome allowing light to reflect off the ceramic wall tiles. The tombs of Mozart's wife, Constanze, and father, Leopold, are also here on the path leading to the mausoleum.

THE SOUND OF MUSIC

In 1964, Julie Andrews, Christopher Plummer, and a squad of 20th Century Fox crew members arrived in Salzburg to film *The Sound of Music,* based on the true story of the von Trapp family. Salzburg has never been the same. The city encourages the increased tourism due to the film's popularity (although many *Salzburgers* themselves have never seen the film, and most who have dislike it). Three official companies run **Sound of Music Tours** in Salzburg, and many hostels and pensions work with one of them to offer discounts to guests. **Salzburg Sightseeing Tours** (☎88 16 16; fax 87 87 76) and **Panorama Tours** (☎87 40 29; fax 16 18) operate rival kiosks on Mirabellpl. and run remarkably similar programs. (Both €33, children €17. Tours leave from Mirabellpl. 9:30am, 2pm.) The renegade **Bob's Special Tours,** Rudolfskai 38, has no high-profile kiosk, but they do have a minibus. The smaller vehicle enables visitors to tour *Altstadt* locations that the big tour buses can't reach. (☎84 95 11; fax 84 95 12. Tours in summer daily 9am, 2pm; in winter 10am. €35, students €32.) All three companies offer free pick-up from your hotel. Tours last 4hr. and are generally worth the money if you're a big *Sound of Music* fan or if you have a short time in Salzburg and want an overview of the area. Another option is **Fraülein Maria's Bicycle Tours** (☎34 26 297), which start at the entrance to the Mirabellgarten behind the Hotel Bristol and cost only €16 for a three-hour trip, including the bike rental. (Mid-May to late Aug. daily 9:30am.)

You can save money and get closer to the sights by renting a bike and doing the tour on your own. Though Maria was a nun-apprentice in the film, in reality she merely taught at **Nonnberg Abbey,** high above the city near the Festung (see p. 248), which serves as a backdrop for the number in which a gaggle of nuns sing "How Do You Solve A Problem Like Maria?" The little gazebo where Liesl and Rolf unleashed their youthful passion is on the grounds of **Schloß Hellbrunn** (see p. 256). From the Hellbrun parking lot, head down Hellbrunner Allee. On the way, you'll pass the yellow castle used for the exterior of the von Trapp home (Maria sang "I Have Confidence" in front of the long yellow wall). It's now a dorm for music students at the Mozarteum. Continue along Hellbrunner Allee until it turns into Freisalweg. At the end of Freisaalweg, turn right on Akadamiestr., which ends at Alpenstr. and the river. The river footpath leads all the way back to Mozartsteg. and Staatsbrücke (1hr.). The back of the von Trapp house (where Maria and the children fell into the water after romping in the city) was filmed at the **Schloß Leopoldskron** behind the Mönchsberg, now a center for academic studies. Visitors are not permitted on the grounds, but to get a glimpse of the house, take bus #55 to "Pensionistenheim Nonntal," turn left on Sunnhubstr., and left again up Leopoldskroner Allee to the castle. Other filming locations scattered throughout Salzburg include the **Mirabellgarten** (see p. 250) and the **Festspielhaus** (see p. 253).

The von Trapps were married in the church at Nonnberg Abbey, but Hollywood filmed the scene in **Mondsee** instead (see p. 262). The sightseeing tours allow guests to stop in Mondsee for 45min., but the town is really worth a whole daytrip for its pastry shops and beautiful lake. **Buses** leave the Salzburg train station from the main bus depot (45min., every hr., €5.40).

To squeeze the last few euros out of starry-eyed tourists, the Sternbräü hosts a **Sound of Music Dinner Show.** Performers sing your favorite film songs while servers ply you with food. (☎82 66 17. May-Oct. the dinner starts at 7:30pm, the show starts at 8:30pm. Show and a drink €29.)

🏛 MUSEUMS

Although Salzburg's small, specialized museums often get lost in the shadow of the Festung, *The Sound of Music,* and the Festspiele, they are worthwhile attractions. In addition to the art museums, there are also private galleries on Sigmund-Haffnerg. that allow budget art viewing.

ART MUSEUMS. Museum Carolino Augusteum, named after Emperor Franz I's widow Caroline Augusta, houses local Roman and Celtic artifacts, including mosaics and burial remains, naturally preserved by the region's salt. The upper floors feature Gothic and Baroque art. (*☎62 08 08. From Hanuschpl., walk down Griesg. and turn right onto Museumpl. Open daily 9am-5pm. €3.50, students €1.10.)* The **Residenz Gallery,** in the *Residenz,* displays 16th- to 19th-century art, much of it religious work. *(Residenzpl. 1. ☎84 04 51. Open Apr.-Sept. daily 10am-5pm; Oct.-Mar. closed M. €5, students €4.)* The **Barockmuseum,** in the Orangerie of the Mirabellgarten, pays tribute to the aesthetics of 17th- and 18th-century Europe. *(☎87 74 32. Open Tu-Sa 9am-noon and 2-5pm, Su 9am-noon. €3.00, students, seniors, and ages 6-14 €1.50.)*

BEER MUSEUM. Stiegl Brauwelt (Brew World) is attached to the Stiegl brewery, close to downtown. Three floors showcase the history of beer-making and modern beer culture. Don't miss the *Brauwelt*, a two-story bottle pyramid. Two glasses of Stiegl beer, a *Brezel* (pretzel), and a souvenir beer glass cap the tour. *(Brauhausstr. 9. Take bus #1 to "Brauhaus" and walk up the street to the giant yellow building. ☎ 83 87 14 92; www.stiegl.co.at. Open Su-W 10am-4pm. €9.20, students €8.30.)*

OTHER MUSEUMS. The **Haus der Natur,** opposite the Carolino Augusteum, is an enormous museum (80 rooms) with everything from alligators and giant snakes to huge rock crystals and spinning planets. *(Museumpl. 5. ☎ 84 26 53 or 84 79 05. Open 9am-5pm. Reptile zoo open 10am-5pm. €4.50, students and children €2.50.)* Inside the main entrance to the *Dom*, the **Dom Museum** houses an unusual collection called the **Kunst- und Wunderkammer** (Art and Curiosity Chamber) that includes jewel-encrusted cups, prayer books bound in gold, and a golden dove made in the 13th century. In the main museum, the gigantic *Rupertskreuz* guards the back room. *(☎ 84 41 89; www.kirchen.net/dommuseum. Open mid-May to mid-Oct. M-Sa 10am-5pm, Su 1-6pm. €4.50, students €1.50. Guided tours Sa 10:30am €1.45.)* Between Residenzpl. and Dompl., the **Domgrabungsmuseum** provides a subterranean exhibit under the cathedral, displaying excavations of Roman ruins, some dating back to the 2nd century AD. *(☎ 84 52 95. Open May-Oct. W-Su 9am-5pm. €1.80, students €1.45.)* The **Spielzeug Museum,** near the *Festspielhaus*, features three floors of puppets, wooden toys, dolls, electric trains, and nifty pre-Lego castle blocks from 1921. *(Bürgerspitalpg. 2. ☎ 620 80 83 00. Open daily 9am-5pm. Puppet show Tu-W 3pm. €2.70, students €0.80.)*

🎵 ENTERTAINMENT

SALZBURGER FESTSPIELE

Max Reinhardt, Richard Strauss, and Hugo von Hofmannsthal founded the renowned **Salzburger Festspiele** (Festival) in 1920. Every year since, Salzburg has become a musical mecca from late July to the end of August. A few weeks before the festival, visitors strolling along Getreideg. may bump into world-class stars taking a break from rehearsal. On the eve of the festival's opening, over 100 dancers don regional costumes, accessorize with torches, and perform a *Fackeltanz* (torch dance) on Residenzpl. During the festivities themselves, operas, plays, films, concerts, and tourists overrun every available public space.

TICKETS. Information and tickets for Festspiele events are available through the Festspiele Kartenbüro (ticket office) and Tageskasse (daily box office) in Karajanpl., against the mountain and next to the tunnel. (Open M-F 9:30am-3pm; July 1-July 22 M-Sa until 5pm, and July 23-Aug. 31 daily until 6:30pm.) The festival prints a complete program of events that lists all concert locations and dates. The booklet is available at any tourist office (€1.50). Fans snap up the best seats months before the festival begins. To order tickets, contact Kartenbüro der Salzburger Festspiele, Postfach 140, A-5010 Salzburg (☎ 804 55 00; www.salzburgfestival.at), no later than the beginning of January. After that, the office publishes a list of remaining seats, which generally include some cheap tickets to the operas, concerts, and plays, as well as standing room places. These tickets, however, are gobbled up quickly by subscribers or student groups, leaving only very expensive tickets and seats at avant-garde modern music concerts. Middle-man ticket distributors sell marked-up cheap tickets, a legal form of scalping—try AmEx or Panorama Tours. Those 26 or younger can try for cheap subscription tickets by writing about eight months in advance to Direktion der Salzburger Festspiele, attn: Ulrich Hauschild, Hofstallg. 1, A-5020 Salzburg.

FREE EVENTS. The powers-that-be have discontinued hawking last-minute tickets for dress rehearsals to the general public. As an alternative, consider taking in the **Fest zur Eröffungsfest** (Opening Day Festival), when concerts, shows, and films are either very cheap or free. Tickets for these events are available on a first-come, first-serve basis during the festival's opening week at the box office in the Großes Festspielhaus on Hofstallg. The only other event visitors can always attend without advance tickets is *Jedermann*, the city's staging of Hugo von Hofmannsthal's modern morality play. The production occurs every year in front of the cathedral. At the end, people placed in strategic locations throughout the city cry out the eerie word *Jedermann* (everyman) which echoes all over town. Shouting contests determine which locals win the opportunity to be one of the ghostly criers. Standing-room for shows are available at the Festspielhaus.

CONCERTS

Even when the Festspiele is not on, Salzburg hosts many other concerts. The **Salzburg Academy of Music and Performing Arts** performs on a rotating schedule in the **Mozarteum** (see p. 251). The school often dedicates one cycle of concerts to students and reduces the ticket price. (For tickets to any of these concerts, contact Kartenbüro Mozarteum, Postfach 156, Theaterg. 2, A-5024 Salzburg. ☎87 31 54; www.mozarteum.at. Open M-Th 9am-2pm, F 9am-4pm.) The **Dom** also has a concert program in July and August. Five separate organs in the cathedral create a powerful effect. (€8.80, students €7.37, children free. Times vary—check the door for upcoming programs.) Other churches throughout Salzburg perform wonderful music during services and post information on other concerts, particularly near Easter and Christmas. The **5-Uhr Konzerte** (5 o'clock concerts) held at St. Peter's Monastery are performed by young musicians at low prices (€10, students €5).

For an enchanting (and expensive) evening, attend a **Festungskonzert** (Fortress Concert) in the fortress's ornate Fürstenzimmer (Prince's chamber) or Goldener Saal (Golden Hall). Concerts are year-round, mostly on Fridays and Saturdays, and include dinner at the fortress restaurant for a slight surcharge. Reservations are required for concerts. (For more information, contact Festungskonzerte, Anton-Adlgasserweg 22, A-5020 Salzburg. ☎82 58 58; www.mozartfestival.at. Open daily 9am-9pm. Tickets €29-36, students €20; with dinner €44-48, students €33.) A less tourist-oriented activity is the year-round **Salzburger Schloßkonzerte** in Schloß Mirabell. The box office is in Mozarts Wohnhaus. (☎84 85 86; www.salzburgerschlosskonzerte.at. Open M-F 9am-5:30pm.)

In July and August, **outdoor opera** rings out from the historical hedge-theater of Mirabellgarten. Tickets are available from the box office in Schloß Mirabell. (☎84 85 86; fax 84 47 47. Open M-F 9am-5:30pm. Free.) In addition, from May through August there are **outdoor performances,** including concerts, folk-singing, and dancing. The tourist office has leaflets on scheduled events, but an evening stroll through the park might prove just as enlightening. Mozartpl. and Kapitelpl. are also popular stops for talented street musicians and touring school bands, and the well-postered Aicher Passage next to Mirabellpl. is a great source of information for other upcoming musical events.

While it is possible to get tickets from each of the above venues at their own box offices, one convenient way of finding and getting tickets to a concert is to visit the *Altstadt* tourist office on Mozartpl. The Salzburg Ticket Service available there allows you to purchase tickets to numerous performing arts productions. (☎84 03 10 or 87 65 85; www.salzburgticket.com.)

THEATER, MOVIES, & GAMBLING

Next to Mirabellgarten, at the **Salzburger Marionettentheater** (☎87 24 06; www.mar-ionetten.at), handmade marionettes perform to recorded *Festspiele* operas. For information, contact Marionettentheater, Schwarzstr. 24, A-5020 Salzburg. (Box office open M-Sa 9am-1pm and 2hr. before curtain. €18-33. AmEx/MC/V.) Track down English-language **movies** with the film program in *Das Kino* newspaper. Cinemas rotate a few films each month and often show them in English with German subtitles. Win enough money to pay your concert ticket debt at **Casino Salzburg** in Schloß Klessheim. Slot machines, blackjack, roulette, poker, and much more await you. Ask at the tourist office about the free shuttle service from the city center. (☎85 44 55 or 85 48 58. Open from 3pm. 19+. Semi-formal attire required.)

☁ OUTDOORS

If you're overwhelmed by Salzburg's culture, you can turn to wonders of a different variety. Try an adventure tour with **Crocodile Sports**, Gaisbergstr. 34a (☎64 29 07; www.crocodile-sports.com)—they pick you up from your hostel for a day (or multiple days) you'll never forget. Adventures include **canyoning** (€45-132), **canoeing** (€36-210), **paragliding** (€115), and **rafting** (€36-124). The lower prices are generally for day or half-day trips; the larger prices correspond to those that are multi-day and include food and accommodations of some kind. Call ahead. You can now also take a 40-50min. boat trip with **Salzburg City Cruise Line** leaving from the Makart Bridge. The cruise, which runs up the Salzach past the city center and back, is a relaxing way to admire Salzburg's skyline. (☎82 57 69 12; www.salzburg-schifffahrt.at. Open Apr.-May and Sept. 10am-5pm; June-Aug. 9:30am-7pm with boats departing about every hour. €10, children €7.)

☁ NIGHTLIFE

Salzburg's daytime charm becomes nighttime boogie in its lively and varied nightlife scene. The more boisterous stick to the section of Rudolfskai between the Staatsbrücke and Mozartsteg, where a youthful crowd congregates in the street. Elsewhere, especially along Chiemseeg. and around Anton-Neumayr-Pl., you can throw back a few drinks in a more reserved *Beisl*. More refined, adult bars can be found along Steing. and Giselakai on the other side of the river.

☁ Augustiner Bräustübl-Mülln, Augustinerg. 4 (☎43 12 46). From the *Altstadt,* follow the footpath from Hanuschpl. downstream along the river, and after the next bridge (the Müllnersteg), take the stairs going up to your left. Cross the street, then continue to your right along the Müllner Hauptstr. Turn left when you get to Augustinerg., and head up under the archway. The entrance will be on your right. Serving home-brewed beer since 1621 in the halls of a former monastery, this gigantic complex seats 2800, split evenly between an outdoor *Biergarten* and 4 gigantic indoor halls. Beer €2.40-€2.70. To save a bit of cash, give your stein directly to the *Biermeister,* by the barrels. The stands outside the beer halls sell snacks. Open M-F 3-11pm, Sa-Su 2:30-11pm.

Vis à Vis, Rudolfskai 24 (☎84 12 90), in the shape of an arched stone tunnel with blacklight and blue neon. A sharply dressed crowd packs every nook around the couches and chairs. Open M-F 3-11pm, Sa-Su 2:30-11pm.

Shamrock, Rudolfskai 11 (☎84 16 10; www.shamrock.at). Built around part of the old city wall, this relaxed and friendly Irish pub has plenty of room—just keep going until you find a spot you like, or stay by the dance area in front to take in the nightly live music.

Also shows sporting events. Most drinks €2-4. Open Su noon-2am, M 3pm-2am, Tu-W 3pm-3am, Th 3pm-4am, F-Sa noon-4am. AmEX/D/MC/V.

O'Malley's, Rudolfskai 16 (☎84 92 63; www.omalleyssalzburg.com). Two bars ensure that you always have a drink (generally €4-5), while the wall decorations and music evoke the Emerald Isle. Packed with a mixed crowd of German and English speakers. Happy Hour 8-9pm all beer ½ price. Open June-Aug. Su-Th 6pm-2:30am, F-Sa 6pm-4am; Sept.-May Su-Th 7pm-2:30am, F-Sa 7pm-4am.

Zweistein, Giselakai 9 (☎87 71 79). The place to come for Salzburg's gay and lesbian scene. On weekends, this bar becomes crowded, serving liquor for around €4.60-6.40. The wall art changes monthly. Open M-W 6pm-4am, Th-Su 6pm-5am.

Flip, Gstätteng. 17 (☎84 36 43). Away from the hectic scene on Rudolfskai, this bar helps keep the Gstätteng. corner of Salzburg alive. The sloping stone roof in the back creates cave-like surroundings while you sip your cocktail (most around €5-6). Side corners allow for greater intimacy. Open daily 8pm-4am. AmEx/D/MC/V.

Segabar, Rudolfskai 18 (☎84 68 98). This busy bar along the strip on Rudolfskai packs in a young lively crowd on weekends with blasting music and TV, creating a crowded party scene. Cover €1.50. Drinks €1.10. Open Su-Th 8pm-2am, F-Sa 8pm-4am.

DAYTRIPS FROM SALZBURG

HELLBRUNN & UNTERSBERG

To reach Hellbrun, take bus #55 (dir.: Anif) to "Hellbrunn" from the train station, Mirabellpl., or Mozartsteg., 30min. down tree-lined Hellbrunner Allee (see p. 251).

LUSTSCHLOß HELLBRUN. Just south of Salzburg, this unforgettable estate was built between 1613 and 1615 at the behest of Archbishop Markus Sittikus. The sprawling complex includes a palace, fish ponds, flower gardens, and tree-lined footpaths. An audio tour leads through the small palace, which includes a "fish room" and a "bird room" devoted to paintings of the rare and exotic animals the Archbishop had collected at Hellbrunn as a sign of his power. Don't be surprised if you hear screams of surprised laughter from outside; Archbishop Markus amused himself by creating water-powered figurines and a booby-trapped table that could spout water on his guests. The tour of these *Wasserspiele* (water games) is a delight on a warm day. Prepare yourself for an afternoon of wet surprises, including a small crown suspended high in the air on a stream of water and a mechanical demon spouting water from his nose. *(Open daily July-Aug. 9am-10pm; May-June and Sept. 9am-5:30pm; Apr. and Oct. 9am-4:30pm. Castle tour, gardens, Wasserspiele, and Volkskundemuseum €7.50, students €5.50. In July and Aug. there is only an evening ticket for the Wasserspiele after 6pm; €7, students €3.50.)*

VOLKSKUNDEMUSEUM (FOLKLORE MUSEUM). On the hill above the manicured grounds sits the tiny hunting lodge Monats-schlössl (Little Month Castle), which was built when the Archbishop won a bet that he couldn't build a castle in a month. The castle now houses three floors of exhibits, including several *Salzburger Schönperchten*—traditional 2m-tall hats worn to scare away the demons of winter. *(☎82 03 72 49 21. Open Apr.-Oct. daily 9am-5pm.)*

STEINTHEATER & HELLBRUNN ZOO. Continue past the Monats-schlössl to the Steintheater where sheer rock faces form a natural theater. The first opera performance in the German-speaking world took place here in 1616. Near the castle also lies the enormous Hellbrunn Zoo, the modern-day descendant of the Archbishop's exotic animal collections. Residents include griffin vultures, wolves, leopards, red

SALZBURGER LAND

pandas, emu, and crowned cranes. The zoo prides itself on not caging animals—they put them instead behind fences with cliffs at their backs. There is also a petting zoo for kids. (☎82 01 76. Open daily June-Sept. 8:30am-6:30pm; Dec. to mid-Feb. until 4:30pm; mid. Feb. to May until 5:30pm. €6.50, students €4.70, children €3.30.)

UNTERSBERG PEAK. Bus #55 continues south from Hellbrunn (catch the bus at the main road) to the looming **Untersberg peak** ("St. Leonhard" stop), where **Charlemagne** supposedly rests deep beneath the ground, prepared to return and reign over Europe when he is needed. A **cable car** glides over the rocky cliffs to the summit. From there, the 30min. hike over the alpine ridge out to the Salzburger Hochthron provides unbelievable mountain scenery. (☎062 46 87 12 17. Open daily July-Sept. 8:30am-6:30pm; Mar.-June and Oct. 8:30am-5pm; Dec.-Feb. 9am-4pm. Roundtrip €17, €15 with Salzburg Card.)

THE SALZKAMMERGUT

Early summer brings tourists, bands of Austrian school children, and groups of elderly Europeans to the smooth crystal lakes and towering mountains of the Salzkammergut. Though the region takes its name from the salt mines that once financed Salzburg's architectural treasures, today it is the sunshine in summer and the fresh snow in winter that support the area. Though not technically in Salzburgerland, Salzburg is the hub for all transportation in the area.

If your trip allows only one stop in the Salzkammergut, make it Hallstatt, whose strikingly beautiful locale makes it worth more than a day's visit. After Hallstatt, the desirability of other destinations will depend on what you're seeking; you can find everything from posh spas to rustic hostels. For all the best bargains, pick up the ✿**Salzkammergut Card,** which provides 30% discounts on countless local sights and attractions (€4.90; available at local tourist offices. For information on the region, contact the Hotel Destination Salzkammergut, Wirerstr. 10, A-4820 Bad Ischl (☎613 22 69 09; info@salzkammergut.at).

F TRANSPORTATION. The Salzkammergut is easily navigable, with 2000km of footpaths, dozens of cable cars and chairlifts, and numerous hostels. Within the region, there is a dense network of **buses** that are the most efficient and reliable method of travel into and through the lake region, since much of the mountainous area is barren of rail tracks. When traveling by bus, be sure to plan your route in advance, as some connections run infrequently (dial ☎05 17 17 from Salzburg for complete schedule information). While *Let's Go* does not recommend it, **hitchers** from Salzburg have been seen taking bus #29 to Gnigl and coming into the Salzkammergut at Bad Ischl. **Bikers** should check out the 280km **Salzkammergut bike path,** which winds through many of the towns in the region. (Contact the Salzkammergut regional tourist office for more information on the route, or consult www.radtouren.at/english.) **Hikers** can capitalize on dozens of **cable cars** in the area before setting out on their own, though hiking from the base is almost always an option. Compared to the higher peaks in Tyrol and the Hohe Tauern, hiking here is generally easier. Ask for hiking maps at any tourist office. Reasonably priced **ferries** service each of the larger lakes (railpass discounts available on the **Wolfgangsee, Attersee,** and **Traunsee** lines).

F ACCOMMODATIONS. Hostels are common throughout the area, but you can often find far superior rooms in private homes and *Pensionen* at just-above-hostel prices. **Campgrounds** dot the region, although for a higher-altitude experience, the many **alpine huts** accessible from hikes are a better bet. Contact the **Österreichischer Alpenverein** (Austrian Alpine Club; ☎051 25 95 47) for info.

SALZBURGER LAND

HALLSTATT ☎ 06134

On the banks of the Hallstättersee, in a valley surrounded by the sheer cliffs of the Dachstein mountains, Hallstatt is easily the most striking lakeside village in the Salzkammergut. Declared a UNESCO World Cultural Heritage site in 1997, Hallstatt's perch on a mountainside assures that the lake dominates the horizon from nearly every vantage point. Hallstatt's salt-rich earth has helped preserve its archaeological treasures, which are so extensive that one era in Celtic studies (800-400 BC) is dubbed the "Hallstatt era." Tourists throng the narrow streets, but Hallstatt refuses to be corrupted. The town and area merit more than a daytrip; stay a night (or a week) in a room overlooking the beautiful clear blue lake.

⌐ TRANSPORTATION

From Salzburg, the **bus** (€12) is the cheapest way to get to Hallstatt, but it requires layovers in both Bad Ischl and Gosaumühle; buses run from Bad Ischl daily 6:50am-5:30pm, and the **bus stop** is at the edge of downtown on Lahnstr., across from the Konsum market. The **train station** is on the other side of the lake, but there is no staffed office to help travelers. A ferry shuttles passengers between the town and the station before and after each train (15min., 6:50am-8:15pm, €1.90). All trains come from Attnang-Puchheim in the north or Stainach-Irdning in the south. Outbound trains run to: Attnang-Puchheim (1½hr., every hr., €9.74); Bad Ischl (30min., €2.90); Salzburg via Attnang-Puchheim (2½hr., €17); Stainach-Irdning (50min., every other hr., €7.40). **By car** from Salzburg or the Salzkammergut towns, take Rte. B-158 to Bad Ischl onto Rte. B-145 to Gosaumühle, then B-166 to Hallstatt. Automobile access to Hallstatt is limited to the town's overnight guests May-October. Ample day **parking** lots are available near the tunnels leading into town (free for guests staying in town).

✴ 🛈 ORIENTATION & PRACTICAL INFORMATION

Hallstatt is on the Hallstättersee, a shimmering oasis at the southern tip of the Salzka-mmergut. To get to the **tourist office** from the ferry stop, face away from the lake and turn left, walking past the Gemeindeamt until you see the office on your right at Seestr. 169 (4min.). From the bus stop, face away from the lake and turn right, walking on the lake along Seestr. for 5min. The office will be on your left, and provides free maps and finds rooms. (☎82 08; www.tiscover.com/hallstatt. Open July-Aug. M-F 9am-5pm, Sa 10am-4pm, Su 10am-2pm; Sept.-June M-Tu and Th-F 9am-noon and 2-5pm, W 9am-noon.) When the office is closed, you can always consult the tourist computer at the bus station, which has information on activities and accommodations as well as a free reservations phone. Services include: **ATM** next to the post office; **laundry** at Hotel Grüner Baum, 104 Marktpl. (€11 for washing and drying service; inquire at reception); **public bathrooms** next to the tourist office and bus stop; and a **doctor** with an in-house **pharmacy** at Baderpl. 108. (Dr. Sonja Gapp, ☎84 01. Walk-in hours M-Tu 8am-noon, Th 5-7pm, F-Sa 8-11am.) **Internet** access (€5 per 20min.) and **bike rental** (€6 per half day, €11 per whole day) at the Hotel Grüner Baum. The **post office**, Seestr. 160 (☎82 01), is below the tourist office. (Open M-Tu and Th-F 8am-noon and 1:30-5:30pm, W 8am-noon.) **Postal code:** A-4830.

⌐ ACCOMMODATIONS & CAMPING

Gästehaus Zur Mühle, Kirchenweg 36 (☎/fax 83 18; toeroe.f@magnet.at). Walk uphill to the right of the tourist office, toward the short tunnel at the upper right corner of the square. The hostel is at the end of the tunnel, by the waterfall. Close to the city center with homey, wood-paneled 3- to 20-bed dorms. There are lots of English-speaking backpackers. Breakfast €2.50. Lunch and dinner available at the restaurant downstairs; see below. Showers included. Locker with €20 deposit. Sheets €2.50. Reception 10am-2pm and 4-10pm. Closed in Nov. Dorms €10. MC/V. ❷

Frühstückspension Sarstein, Gosaumühlstr. 83 (☎82 17). From the ferry landing, turn right on Seestr. and walk for 10min.; it will be on the right. Although the bathrooms show signs of wear, Frau Fischer's *Pension* offers glorious vistas of the lake and village as well as a beachside lawn for sunning and swimming. Carved and painted wardrobes. Breakfast included. Hall bathrooms and showers (showers €1 per 10min.). Singles and doubles €16 per person, with balcony €18; double with shower, bathroom, and balcony €25. ❸

Seehotel Grüner Baum, Marktpl. 104 (☎82 63; www.hallstatt.net/gruenerbaum). If you're tired of "water closets" that actually are closets, it's time for a soak in the tub in one of the enormous bathrooms at the Hotel Grüner Baum. This hotel has the best location in town—on the lake by the old market square. The building was once a salt trader's house and retains much of its historic feel. Pets welcome. Breakfast included. Closed Nov. to mid-Apr. Singles €50-70; doubles €85-160. AmEx/D/MC/V. ❹

Frühstückspension Seethaler, Dr.-F.-Mortonweg 22 (☎84 21; pension.seethaler@kronline.at). Turn uphill next to the tourist office and follow the signs; it will be on your right. All rooms have balcony, most with an amazing lake view. Breakfast in an antler-studded room included. Shower €1 per 8min. 4-bed dorms €18, with in-room shower and toilet €26; 2- to 4-person apartment with kitchen €26. ❸

Camping Klausner-Höll ❶, Lahnstr. 201. Exit the tourist office and walk past the bus stop on Seestr. for 10min. to this clean campground at the base of the mountains. (☎832 24; camping.klausner@magnet.at. Laundry €8. Open mid-Apr. to mid-Oct. Gate closed daily noon-3pm and 10pm-7:30am. €5.80, children 6-14 €3, tent €3.70, car €2.90, camper €4.50, trailer €5.80. Electricity €2.90. MC/V.

🍴 FOOD

While rooming in Hallstatt isn't pricey, eating is. The cheapest food is at the **Konsum** supermarket across from the bus stop (open M-Tu and Th-F 7:30am-noon and 3-6pm, W 7:30am-12:30pm, Sa 7:30am-noon).

THE LOCAL STORY

SALT OF THE EARTH

Dr. Fritz Eckart is the head of Hallstatt's archaeological excavations. He is also co-author of The EU Project Archeo-live *and* Archeological Inheritance of Hallstatt.

LG: How did you pick this career?
A: [At] college 50 years ago.
LG: What kind of [work] do you do?
A: My special area of study is salt mining—Austrian salt mining—and I've been studying the salt mines here in Hallstatt for 40 years.
LG: What would you say is the most important thing that you have found here?
A: Well, it's not just about finding things, but rather about history, interpretation. There are different locations in the mountain where we have found things. For example, there is a place from the 14th century where we can see how they extracted salt from the mountain at that time.
LG: How long has salt mining in Hallstatt been going on?
A: The oldest evidence we have found is from 7000 years ago, so 5000 BC.
LG: And the "man in salt" that was found here—his body is now missing, so how do you know how old he was?
A: Well, the place he was found tells us fairly exactly...probably at the time of the Hallstatt grave fields, between the 8th century BC and the 4th century BC. At that time, the "man in salt" was taken down into the valley and buried.

SALZBURGER LAND

Gästehaus zum Weißen Lamm, Dr.-F-Mortonweg 166 (☎83 11). Uphill behind the tourist office, serves large, tasty portions. Head downstairs to the "mountaineer's cellar" or to their outdoor patio for two daily *Menüs* (€8-9) for lunch and dinner, including soup, entree, and dessert. Open daily 10am-10pm, closed Tu in winter. Kitchen open 11am-3pm and 5-10pm. ❷

Gästehaus Zur Mühle (also see p. 258). Get pizzas (€5.80-7.30), salads (€2.20-6.80), and pasta (€5.80-6.90) at the pizzeria in the hostel. Sit out on the ivy-covered terrace and enjoy the view of the lake and the quiet of Hallstatt's back streets. Open Dec.-Oct. M and W-Su 11am-2pm and 5-9:30pm. MC/V. ❷

Bräugasthof at Seestr. 120 (☎200 12). From the tourist office, turn right and head down Seestr. for 3min. Nice weather merits a splurge on a Bräugasthof fresh fish entree, appropriate for its nice lakeside location. The chef cooks up lunch dishes for €9-13 and dinner for €10-16, including *Wildfish* fresh from the Hallstättersee (€14). Open daily 11:30am-3pm and 6-9pm. MC/V accepted in the evening. ❸

Bar Zimmermann, Marktpl. 59. For a late-night snack, try homemade pastries and savory treats (around €2.50) at this chic café right on Markpl. Open 9am-2am. ❶

👁 🏛 SIGHTS & MUSEUMS

Hallstatt packs a surprising number of attractions into a very small space. The tourist office sells a €3.90 English cultural guide, but strolling the steep twisting streets requires no plan. Be sure to get a guest card at your accommodation for discounts at many attractions, as well as entrance to the town by car.

CHURCH & CHARNEL HOUSE. The charnel house in the graveyard at the **Pfarrkirche** offers a fascinating (if slightly macabre) insight into the burial scene in Hallstatt. Within the parish charnel house (*Beinhaus* in German, literally "bonehouse") rest the bones of villagers from the 16th-century onward, the latest added in 1995. The Celts buried their dead high in the mountains, but Christians wanted to rest in the churchyard. Unfortunately, space on the steep hillside soon ran out, so the skulls and bones of the long deceased were transferred after 10 or 20 years to the charnel house. Each of 610 skulls was decorated with a wreath of flowers (for females) or ivy (for males) and inscribed with the name of the deceased and the date of death. The skulls were then stacked neatly on a shelf supported by leg bones. *(From the ferry dock, follow the signs reading "K.Kirche." Open daily June-Sept. 10am-6pm; Oct. and May until 4pm, Nov.-Apr. call ☎82 79 for an appointment. €1, students €0.40.)*

MUSEUMS. In the mid-19th century, archaeologists in Hallstatt unearthed a collection of artifacts, a pauper's grave, and the crypts of the ruling class—all incredibly well-preserved and circa 1000-500 BC. The **Prähistorisches Museum** and **Heimatmuseum,** across from the tourist office, exhibit some of these treasures, including coiled copper jewelry from the tombs and mines, costumes of the region, modern mining equipment, and local art. Renovations completed in 2002 add amusing multimedia effects to exhibits on the landslide of AD 350 and the fire of 1750. *(☎82 80 15; fax 82 80 12. Open Apr.-June and Sept.-Oct. daily 9am-6pm; July-Aug. daily 10am-7pm; Nov.-Feb. Su-Tu 10am-4pm. €6, students and children €3. AmEx/MC/V.)*

SALT MINES. The 2500-year-old Salzbergwerke, the oldest saltworks in the world. Nowadays they are heavily touristed. Fascinating guided tours (1hr., in English and German) include a zip down a wooden mining slide, a visit to an eerie lake deep inside the mountain, and a ride on a miner's train. Be sure to ask for a salt rock as a souvenir, or pick up the photo taken of you as you sped down the slide. *(☎200 24 00; fax 031 22. Open daily May-Sept. 9:30am-4:30pm; Oct. 9:30am-3pm.*

€14.50, students €8.70; children €7.25-€8.70, seniors €13.50. Reach the salk mines via either the cable car or the 1hr. hike (see below). To get to the cable car, turn right at the bus circle and follow the "Salzbergwerk" signs to Salzbergbahn. From the top of the cable cars it's a 15min. walk uphill. Trains run daily May-Sept. 9am-6pm; Oct. 9am-4:30pm. For the last tour, take the 4pm train; 2:30pm train in Oct. Tours every 15min. for €4.70, round-trip €7.90; children under 15 €2.80/€4.70. Combination train and tour €19.90, students €11.95, children €9.95-€11.95, seniors €7.90, children 4 and under not allowed.)

OUTDOORS

HIKING. Hallstatt offers some of the most spectacular day hikes in the Salzkammergut. They lead through forests where drops of water cling to the pine needles year-round, thanks to a climate very close to that of a temperate rainforest. The tourist office offers bike trail maps (€7.12) and an excellent Dachstein hiking guide, describing 38 hikes in the area (€5.80, available in English). Hike to nearby mountain huts (use the Dachstein hiking guide) or try one of the following hikes:

Salt mine (Salzbergwerk) hike (1hr.). Walk to the Salzbergbahn (see directions and info above) and head up on the road to the right, turning at the black-and-yellow "Salzwelten" sign. This well-paved, shady, steep hike leads to the salt mine tour, giving you increasingly elevated and astonishing views of the *Hallstätter See*. Halfway up, look for an entrance to the stone tunnel of the old mine named after Emperor Franz Joseph. Walking up the stairs to your left leads to an archaeological memorial path that provides information (in German) about the history of the burial field discovered there.

Waldbachstrub waterfall hike (1½-2hr.). From the bus station, follow the signs heading away from the lake to a light walk along a stream that leads to a clear, cold waterfall. For 40min. the path follows the sound of the rushing river along the "Malerweg." When you come to a sign reading "Waldbachstrub" make a detour (if you have sturdy shoes) to the "Gletschergarten" to see a fantastic array of riverbed formations created by glaciers during the last Ice Age. From the main trail, continue by following the "Waldbachstrub" signs for another 10min. to the magnificent double waterfall. To get back to Hallstatt, retrace your steps or turn left when you get to the bridge and make your way to the bus station.

Gangsteig (45min.-1½hr.), for experienced hikers only, is a primitive stairway carved onto the side of the cliff that is the Echental valley's right wall (the Waldbachstrub waterfall's valley). Completing the trail will take hiking shoes and a strong will to climb, but the work is worth it for the relatively low traffic and beautiful vistas of the valley. Follow the Waldbachstrub hike until 2min. before the falls, where "Gangsteig" is marked on the right. It's about another hour to the top.

WATER SPORTS & SKIING. For a view of the mountains from below rather than above, try a scenic boat trip around the lake with **Schiffrundfarten Hemetsberger.** Ferries leave from both ferry landings in town. (☎82 28. 50min., May to late-Sept. 11am, 1, 2, 3pm, in good weather or by appointment, €6.50.) **Boat rental** for two people costs €5.50 per 30min. for an electric boat, €4.50 for a paddleboat, and €4 for a rowboat from **Hallstatt Schmuck** near the ferry landing by the Marktpl. For **wild water canoeing,** contact Gasthof Zauner "Seewirt" (☎82 46). **Swimming** in the lake is free, but watch out—the water's cold. The best place to swim is the public park, which can be reached from the bus stop by heading away from town along the Seelände, the road closest to the water's edge.

Winter visitors can take advantage of Hallstatt's **ski bus** (free with snow gear, contact the tourist office for info), which runs to the Krippenstein and Dachstein-West Ski areas several times a day. Dachstein's lifts (3 cable cars and 6 lifts) run from mid-Dec. to May. Lift tickets cost €25.40 for adults, €14.50 for children, and €23.40 for seniors. The *Inneres Salzkammergut* also provides a 116km of cross-country ski trails. The tourist office provides ski maps.

☙ DAYTRIP FROM HALLSTATT

OBERTRAUN & THE DACHSTEIN CAVES ☎ 06131

To reach Obertraun from Hallstatt, take the bus from the Lahn bus station, on the lake near the Salzbergbahn at the western end of town. (8:50am-4:50pm, 7 per day, €1.70.) Stop at the cable car station, "Dachstein," for the ice and mammoth caves. Ride the cable car up 1350m to "Schönbergalm" for the ice and mammoth caves (every 15min. 8:40am-5:30pm, last trip for a tour at 4:15pm; round-trip €13, children €7.50). The Koppenbrüller cave is a 15min. walk from the bus stop in Obertraun. For all cave tours, wear good footwear and something warm—the caves hover near freezing for most of the year.

The magnificent **Dachstein Caves** are one more testament to the region's geological activity. The **Rieseneishöhlen** (Giant Ice Caves) are the primary attraction. Their amazing ice formations not only last year round, but continue to grow, even in the summer. The **Mammuthöhlen** (Mammoth Caves) are up on the mountain along with the ice caves. As the name implies, they have an explored length of over 60km. The **Koppenbrüllerhöhle**, a giant spring, is in the valley near the village of Obertraun. The tours, offered in English and German, are required and last 50min.; you'll be assigned to a group at the Schönbergalm station. *(☎ 84 00. Open May to mid-Oct. 9am-5pm. Admission to each cave €8, children €4.80; for both caves €12.30/€7.)* The Koppenbrüllerhöhle is more romantic than gigantic, and can be reached without cable car from the Obertraun bus or Koppenbrüllerhöhle train stops. *(Tours May-Sept. every hr. 9am-4pm. €6.80, children €4.10.)*

For a panoramic **hike,** try the **Karstlehrpfad** *(3-4hr., accessible from late June-first snowfall),* beginning from **Krippenstein,** the top station of the Dachstein lift. From there, follow the path below the Schutzhaus restaurant and go left at the split. From the peak you will be able to see the entire Dachstein plateau. The finish is at the bottom of the **Gjaidalm lift,** which returns to the Dachsteinbahn. *(Ticket for both lifts €18.50, children €11.50. Open daily 9am-5pm.)*

The town of Obertraun is a 1hr. walk from the caves. Buses are infrequent; make sure to check the schedule. The Obertraun **tourist office** is in the Gemeindeamt, Obertraun 180. From the train station turn right onto the main road and follow signs. *(☎ 351; fax 342 22. Open July-Aug. M-F 8am-noon and 2-6pm, Sa 9-11am; Sept.-June M-F 8am-noon and 2-5pm.)* An **ATM** is at the Volksbank directly next to the tourist office. **Post office,** Obertraun 94, is inside the Konsum market. *(☎ 382. Open M-Tu and Th-F 8am-noon and 2-5pm, W 8am-noon.)* Buy groceries at **Konsum market,** at the turnoff for the tourist office. *(Open M, W, F 7:30am-noon and 3-6pm, Tu and Th 7:30am-noon, Sa 7am-noon.)*

BAD ISCHL ☎ 06132

Bad Ischl (pop. 14,000) was a salt-mining town for centuries, until Dr. Franz Wirer arrived in 1821 to study the curative properties of the area's heated brine baths. He began to prescribe brine bath vacations in Bad Ischl for his patients. Seeking a cure for their infertility, Archduke Francis Charles and Archduchess Sophia journeyed to Bad Ischl and produced three sons, the so-called **Salt Princes.**

TRANSPORTATION

Only one train comes through the **train station** (☎24 40 70; desk open M-F 6:30am-6:35pm, Sa 8:05am-5:15pm), running between Attnang-Puchheim in the north (1hr., 5:05am-8:15pm, €6.50) and Hallstatt in the south (40min., 6:15am-6:05pm, €2.90). Trains go through these towns to Linz (€11.60) and Vienna (4hr., €30.50). **Buses** leave the station (☎231 13; desk open M-F 8am-4pm) for Salzburg (1½hr., every hr. 5:50am-10:50pm, €7.27) and St. Wolfgang (40min., every hr. 6:42am-6:15pm, €3.10). By **car**, Bad Ischl lies on Rte. 158 and 145. From Innsbruck or Munich, take A-1 East past Salzburg and exit onto Rte. 158 near Thalgau. From Salzburg, take Rte. 158 through St. Gilgen and Fuschl. From Vienna, take A-1 West to Rte. 145 at Regau.

ORIENTATION & PRACTICAL INFORMATION

Though Bad Ischl is one of the only towns in the Salzkammergut not on a lake, it lies at the junction of the **Traun** and **Ischl** rivers, which form a horseshoe around the city. The **tourist office** is on Bahnhofstr. 6. From the station, turn left on Bahnhofstr. The office has lists of *Pensionen* and *Privatzimmer* and an excellent free map. Also available are free guided tours (1hr.), leaving from the Trinkhalle on Sundays at 10am and Thursdays at 4pm. (Continue down Bahnhofstr. and it is on the left. ☎277 57. Open mid-June to Sept. M-F 9am-6pm, Sa 9am-3pm, Su 10am-1pm; Sept. to mid-June M-F 9am-5pm, Sa 9am-noon.) **Salzkammergut-Touristik,** Götzstr. 12, the regional tourist office, is also a great resource for information, places to stay, and bike rental (mountain bike €13 per day, city bike €10 per day). From the train station, turn right down Bahnhofstr. and turn left onto Götzstr., just before you get to the river. (☎24 00 00. Open daily 9am-8pm.) Services include: **ATM** at Oberbank on Franz Josef Str.; **lockers** at the train station (€2); **public restrooms** at the train station; **Kurapotheke** pharmacy, Kreuzpl. 18 (☎232 05. Open 8am-noon, 2-6pm, and for emergencies); and **post office**, down Bahnhofstr., on the corner of Auböckpl. by the Trinkhalle (open M-F 8am-6pm, Sa 9am-noon.) **Internet** access (€2.50 for 35min., €4.50 for 1hr.). **Postal code:** A-4820.

ACCOMMODATIONS

Every guest who stays the night in Bad Ischl pays a *Kurtax*, which entitles you to a guest card (June to mid-Sept. €1.50 per person per night; Oct.-May €1).

Jugendgästehaus (HI), Am Rechensteg 5 (☎265 77; fax 265 77 75). From the tourist office, walk left on Bahnhofstr., turn right on Franz Josef Str., and keep going until you see the *Jugendgästehaus* sign to the left, after the bend to the right. Minutes from the *Kaiser's* summer residence and almost directly in the city center, this clean, dorm-style hostel offers mostly quads, each with its own bathroom. Breakfast included. HI membership required. Reception 8am-1pm and 5-7pm. Quiet hour 10pm. Check-out 9am. Reservations recommended. €13 per person; singles €26.50; doubles €19.) MC/V. ❸

Haus Stadt Prag, Eglmoosg. 9. (☎/fax 236 16). From the train station, go left on Bahnhofstr., right on Franz Josef Str., and left on Kreuzpl. until it becomes Salzburgerstr.; follow the signs from there. This bright, well-maintained pension provides comfortable and spacious rooms with balcony decorated in the local style. Breakfast included. All rooms with bath and TV. Singles €30; doubles €56. MC/V. ❸

Villa Dachstein, Rettenbachweg (☎23 151; office@villadachstein.at.). From the train station, take a right on Bahnhofstr. and head straight. Immediately on the other side of the river, take a right onto the footpath, which heads steeply uphill after going under the railroad bridge. For a slightly nice stay this huge house not only has great views of Bad Ischl, but also offers clean, spacious rooms. 3 pointy towers lend the place lots of character. Breakfast included. €32-35 per person. ❹

Hotel Stadt Salzburg, Salzburger Str. 25 (☎235 64; stadt-salzburg@eunet.at). From the train station, head left down Bahnhofstr., right on Franz Josef Str., and then left through Kreuzpl. to Salzburger Str. At the higher end of the price spectrum, this 3-star hotel offers many services such as a sauna and terrace, TV, bar, and safe in each room. Catering to the fish-loving demographic, the hotel offers special fly-fishing programs. Breakfast included. Singles €42; doubles €70. MC/V. ❹

🍴 FOOD

Restaurants are tucked into every possible niche in the pedestrian zone. and *Eis* stands are practically more numerous than people. As an alternative to eating out, the **Konsum grocery store** is conveniently located at Auböckpl. 12, behind the Trinkhalle. (Open M-F 7:30am-6:30pm, Sa 7:30am-5pm). Browse at the **open-air market** held every Friday morning on Salinenpl.

Konditorei Zauner, Pfarrg. 7 (☎235 22). This crowded eatery is almost as famous as the *Kaiser* himself. Established in 1832, Zauner has an international reputation for heavenly sweets and *tortes*. Enjoy the old-fashioned atmosphere and treat yourself to their extravagant desserts (most around €2.80), *Eis* creations, or gourmet sandwiches (around €3). Open 8:30am-6pm. MC/V. ❷

Bistro Oriental, Kreuzpl. 13; at the turn-off, look to your left behind the building on Franz Josef Str. This tiny but modern café serves fresh and flavorful kebabs (€3.30), and is marked by friendly staff. Open daily 10am-10pm. ❷

Gasthaus Sandwirt, Eglmoosg. 4 (☎264 03), just up the street from Haus Stadt Prag. For good deals on a sit-down meal, come to this informal restaurant in a residential neighborhood perched on a hill at the edge of town; the extensive menu offers both Austrian and Italian dishes ranging widely from €4-20. For dessert, join in Bad Ischl's love for Kaiserin Elizabeth by ordering a *Coupe Sisi*—a sundae with vanilla, chocolate, and hazelnut ice cream doused in chocolate liqueur. (€4.30). Open daily 11am-1:30pm and 5-9pm, closed Th after 2pm. MC/V. ❷

China Restaurant Happy Dragon, Pfarrg. 2 (☎234 32), at the intersection of Pfarrg. and Wirestr., is one of the most pleasant places to eat along the river. Chinese standards go for around €7-8. Open daily 11:30am-3pm and 6-11pm. MC/V. ❷

Gasthaus zu Bürgerstub'n, Kreuzpl. 7 (☎235 68), just up the street from Bistro Oriental. The restaurant, secluded from the main street in a courtyard, offers traditional Austrian dishes in a relaxed setting. Try the house specialty featuring 3 different types of fillet (€12). Open 11:30am-3pm and 6-9pm; May-Sept. closed Su. MC/V. ❷

👁 SIGHTS

Other than the baths, Bad Ischl's main attractions are the Hapsburgs' cultural and architectural legacies, including the Kaiservilla and Pfarrkirche. For those eager to engage the outdoors, the Siriuskogl hike lets you see it all from above.

VILLAS. In 1854, Austria's last empress received the Kaiservilla as a wedding present from her mother-in-law. Though she didn't care for the place, her husband Emperor Franz Josef designated it his family's summer getaway. Enter the park and enjoy strolling the beautifully groomed grounds. Inside the villa, Franz Josef's vast collection of mounted chamois horns (over 2000) still graces the walls in his wing of the house. Also interesting is the desk where Franz

Josef signed the declaration of war against Serbia that led to WWI. Entrance is allowed only through a guided tour in German, with English text available. *(Just off Franz Josef Str.; tickets can be bought at the entrance to the park. ☎ 232 41. Open May to mid-Oct. daily 9-11:45am and 1-5:15pm. €9.50, children €4.)* Also within the Kaiserpark, you'll find the ivy-covered Marmorschlößl, which houses a Photo Museum of Hapsburg family photos and temporary exhibitions. *(☎ 244 22. Open Apr.-Oct. daily 9:30am-5pm. €1.50, children €0.70, family card €3.)* The Lehár Villa, Lehárkai 8, former summer home of Franz Lehár, longtime Bad Ischl native and composer of *The Merry Widow*, is worth a quick visit. From Bahnhofstr., continue straight until you hit the river and esplanade, then take Grazerstr. across the river and turn left. *(☎ 269 92. Open May-Sept. 9am-noon and 2-5pm. Obligatory tour €4.40, students and children €1.82.)*

PARISH CHURCH & ORGAN. The **Stadtpfarrkirche** houses gorgeous wall paintings and the magnificent late-Baroque **Kaiserjubiläumsorgel** (Emperor's Jubilee Organ). To get there, turn left out of the tourist office, then right onto Franz Josef Str.; the church will be on your left. Empress Maria Theresia had it built in place of the original Gothic building, whose tower still stands. Don't miss the ceiling frescoes depicting the life of St. Nicholas. The Latin inscription across the front of the church reads: "Due to the piety and generosity of the empress." Its open, light-flooded interior and acoustics are equally breathtaking. Check in front of the church for organ performance times (free).

SALT BATHS. Regardless of whether or not the **brine baths** that Dr. Wirer promoted really have curative powers, they certainly relieve stress. The bath facilities are mostly in the posh **Kaiser Therme**, a resort across from the tourist office on Bahnhofstr. 1. Splash around in the heated salt baths with whirlpool or consider relaxing in the spacious **sauna**. Massages, mud baths, and other services are more expensive but are sure to soothe both body and soul. *(☎ 23 32 40. Baths with whirlpool open 9am-10pm; €10, children €6. Sauna open Su-Tu 1:30-10pm; Tu men only; Th women only; €14 for 3hr., children €8 for 3hr. Massages, etc., M-Sa 8am-noon or by appointment.)*

▟ OUTDOOR ACTIVITIES

For hiking and biking, pick up free maps of local paths from the tourist office, though a more detailed biking map is available (€7.12). For a good place to start hiking, head to the summit of nearby **Mt. Katrin** (1544m). Get to the **Katrinseilbahn** cable car (☎ 237 88. 12min., one each hr., open mid-May to Oct. daily 9am-5pm; ascent €10.50, children €9) by taking a city bus (€2.90) from the train station (€1.30, day pass €2.20, family day pass €2.90) or by walking 30min. on the extension of Bahnhofstr. along the Esplanade, Kaltenbachstr., and Dumbastr. For a shorter Bad Ischl-based hike, try the **Siriuskogl hike,** which requires no cable car and rewards hikers with a wondrous panoramic view of Bad Ischl and its environs. To begin, exit the tourist office to the right, walk toward the train station, walk right across the river, and continue over the bridge on the right onto Grazerstr. Turn left onto Siriuskoglg., and follow the sign "Zum Siriuskogl." After passing through the outskirts of Bad Ischl, stick to the main trail to the top, about 30min. from the base. For refreshments, **Gasthaus Siriuskogl** is situated on the summit. (☎ 258 36. Open May-Oct. daily 10am-10pm.) In winter, Bad Ischl maintains an extensive network of **cross-country skiing** trails (free maps at the tourist office). The bus to the Katrinseilbahn also leads to trails around the Kaltenbach. 7km to the northwest of town is Rettenbach, a cross-country skiing area that is not accessible by bus.

🎵 ENTERTAINMENT

For the most up-to-date information on Bad Ischl performing arts events, pick up the brochure *Bad Ischl Events* from the tourist office. Free outdoor **Kurkonzerte** take place between May and October at the *Kurpark* along Wienerstr., or in the *Trinkhalle*, depending on the weather. The exact program of performances by the 20-piece *Kurorchestra* or quartet is posted weekly on kiosks, in the hotels, and at the *Kurhaus* itself. Every year in mid-August, the **Bad Ischler Stadtfest** brings a weekend of music—classical, pop, jazz, boogie-woogie, and oom-pah-pah. Immediately after the Stadtfest on August 18, the Bad Ischlers celebrate Franz Josef's birthday with live music on the Esplanade. In July and August, the **Bad Ischl Operetten Festspiele** celebrates the musical talent of composer Franz Lehás by regularly performing several operettas. Tickets are available from Büro der Operettengemeinde Festspiele, Kurhausstr. 8, A-4820 Bad Ischl. (☎238 39; www.operette.badischl.at. Open daily Aug.-June 9am-3pm; July 9am-6pm.) From May to October a **flea market** comes to the Esplanade on the first Saturday morning of the month. At Christmastime, Bad Ischl indulges in all sorts of Yuletide festivities, including a **Christkindlmarkt** (Christmas market), Advent caroling in the *Kurhaus*, tours of elaborate **Weihnachtskrippen** (nativity scenes) in the area, and horse-drawn sleigh rides (*Pferdeschliffen*).

🏔 DAYTRIP FROM BAD ISCHL

GMUNDEN   ☎07612

Only one train goes through Gmunden, running from Attnang-Pucheim in the north to Stain-ach-Irding in the south. The town is best done as a day (or slightly longer) trip from Bad Ischl (€5) or Hallstatt (€7.20). Within the city, the street car line runs from the train station to the lake (Franz Josef Pl.), with a stop at the ceramics factory. By car from Salzburg, take A1 east and exit onto 145 at Regau. From Vienna, take A1 west and exit onto 144 at Steyermuhl.

Situated at the edge of the clean and cold Traunsee, Gmunden is well known for its ceramics, castles, and beautiful mountain scenery. The city began as a Celtic settlement, and records of it date back to the year AD 909.

To get to the **tourist office** from the train station, take the street car to the end of the line. Continue in the direction of the street car and turn left at the next intersection. The tourist office will be on your right at Am Graben 2. (☎643 05; www.traunsee.at. Open M-F 8am-1pm and 2-6pm, Sa 9am-1pm.) For overnight stays, pick up a list of *Privatzimmer*; one good option is **Haus Reier,** Freyg. 20. Walk to the Grünberg *Seilbahn* and then continue 100m along Freyg. The house is on the right. (☎/fax 724 25. Singles €25.)

Gmunden is well known in Austria for its ceramics, especially for its green-and-white china pattern. Shops selling dishware and porcelain knick-knacks dot the town. The **ceramics factory** itself also has a large store selling its work and offers guided tours for groups upon request (*Keramikstr. 24. Take the street car to "Keramik." ☎786 39. Tours M-Th 9am-2:30pm, F 9am-noon; €3. Store open M-F 9am-6pm, Sa 9am-1pm*). Ceramic creations can be seen in many places around town, including the ceramic bells hanging in the town hall and the ceramic fountain in Rinnholz Square. The best place to see true masterpieces, however, is the **Galerie Schloß Weyer,** a museum dedicated to Meissner porcelain inside a small Renaissance castle. It has seven rooms full of delicate figurines, elaborate table services, and opulent oriental rugs. Head to the Grünberg *Seilbahn* and then continue on Freyg. for 300m. (*Freyg. 27. ☎650 18; fax 656 05 31. Open*

Tu-F 10am-noon and 2-5:30pm, Sa 10am-1pm.) The picturesque **Seeschloß Ort** is worth a visit for its unusual location out in the waters of the Traunsee. Walk down the Promenade away from the river, take the first street left, then follow the signs. Don't be surprised by tons of German tourists here—this castle is the location of an extremely popular German television show called "Schloßhotel Ort." Unfortunately, the castle is not actually a hotel, and you can't go inside any of its rooms. Marks on the walls show water levels in various floods. The ■**Museum of Historical Sanitary Objects** (nicknamed "Klo und So") offers a remarkable collection of sinks, toilets, and tubs. Highlights include a collapsible travel bidet and the bidet which belonged to Empress Elizabeth. This museum feeds into the *Volkskundemuseum,* a small exhibit of objects from the past, including umbrellas, pipes, and waffle irons. *(From Franz Josef Pl. continue in the direction of the street car and make a sharp left heading uphill before crossing the bridge. The museum will be on your right. ☎79 44 25. Open May-Oct. Tu-Sa 10am-noon and 2-5pm, Su 10am-noon. €3, students under 18 €1, family ticket €3.)*

There are several places to rent **boats** along the Promenade, including **F. Berger Bootverleih** or **Oberleitner.** *(Electric boat €6 for 30min., €10.50 per hr.; pedal boat €4.50/€7.50; row boat €3/€5.)* Be sure to take a ride on Europe's oldest paddle-driven **steamer,** *Gisela.* *(Tours leave from in front of the Rathaus, just beyond Franz Josef Pl. 50min. tours €7.50, children €5.50; 2½hr. €13.50/€10.50.)*

Gmunden's *Seilbahn* serves as a point of departure for several hikes. To get the cable car, head from Franz Josef Pl. past the *Rathaus* and across the bridge. When the road branches, head to the right and continue for 10min. on this street, making a left onto Freyg. The *Seilbahn* will be on the right. From the Grünberg, numerous trails branch off and lead throughout the nature preserve toward neighboring towns. Pick up a hiking map for free at the tourist office, or purchase a more detailed one for €2.20 at the gondola. *(Gondola open daily July-Aug. 9am-6pm; Apr.-June and Sept.-Oct. 9am-5pm. Round-trip €10.30, children €6; ascent only €7.20/€4.20.)* For a day hike, consider heading from the Grünberg down to Laudachsee and then back through the woods and fields to Gmunden via Franzl im Holz. This 2-3hr. hike offers you a wonderful view of the valley as well as a peaceful resting point at the Laudachsee. The trail is well marked and mostly flat or downhill.

GRÜNAU ☎07616

Sitting in the middle of the **Totes Gebirge** (Dead Mountains), Grünau is a tiny community with an incredible backyard ideal for hiking, skiing, boating, fishing, swimming, and relaxing. A small regional **train** runs to Grünau from Wels (1hr., 5:47am-8:48pm, €6.50) which can be reached via Salzburg, Linz, or Vienna. A **bus** runs frequently from Rathauspl. in Gmunden to the Grünau town center and train station (45min., 5:35am-5:20pm, €3.60). The **tourist office** is on the right across the street from the town center's bus stop. The staff gives free maps of Grünau and lists of pensions in the area. (Open M-F 9am-noon and 2-5pm, Sa 9am-noon.)

However, Grünau is best experienced from ■**The Treehouse ❷**, Schindlbachstr. 525, a backpacker's dream resort. Each room has its own bathroom with private shower and goose-down blankets. Call ahead and one of the staff will pick you up at the train station free of charge—otherwise it is more than an hour's walk left down Schindlbachstr. from the town center. While enjoying your relaxed stay, make yourself at home and take advantage of its many facilities: TV room with hundreds of English-language movies, book-exchange library, sauna, basketball court, pool tables, and tennis courts (all free of charge, equipment provided), plus

SALZBURGER LAND

two bars for nighttime revelry. **Internet** access is €0.10 per min. **Mountain bike** rental is €6 per day. (☎84 99; www.geocities.com/treehousehostel. Breakfast buffet included. 3-course dinner €6.90. 6-bed dorm €14.50 per person; doubles €37; triples €51.50; quads €66. AmEx/MC/V.)

To help its guests enjoy the mountains, the Treehouse staff organizes adventure tours including **canyoning** (€50, not in winter), **bungee jumping** (€95, only on weekends), and **horseback riding** (€9.50 per hr.). For **hiking,** a free map available at the tourist office or the Treehouse helps to navigate the mountains and three lakes in the vicinity. For a day hike, walk to the Kasberg (1500m, 7hr. round-trip) or for a half day to the Spitzplaneck (1617m, 4-5hr.). The more adventurous may try the longer, moderate hike to Große Priel (2515m), which can also be a two-day trek with a mountain hut stay (€10; ask the Treehouse staff for info.)

The winter **ski lift,** a 5min. walk from the hostel, is scheduled to become a cable car by the start of the 2004 ski season. The Treehouse loans snow apparel (jackets, snowsuits, gloves, etc.) to its guests for free. Overall in Grünau, there are 40km of slopes accessed by 14 lifts. Day ski-lift passes are €21, while ski and snowboard rental from the base runs €13. A ski school charges €41 per day for skiing lessons and €44 for snowboarding. (☎/fax 81 09. Open daily 9am-4pm.)

ST. WOLFGANG ☎06138

This rural lakeside village, once the site of mass pilgrimage, is now subject to mass tourism. Built in AD 976 by Bishop Wolfgang of Regensburg, the church on the Abersee (now the **Wolfgangsee**) first became popular after his canonization; present-day pilgrims are of the camcorder- and fannypack-toting variety. During the summer months, some 2000 visitors pass through St. Wolfgang, admiring the bright blue waters and striking mountain scenery, as well as the winding cobblestone streets and excitement of the Schafbergbahn.

▮ TRANSPORTATION

The town has no train station, but **buses** run every hour to and from Bad Ischl (40min.; M-F 5:05am-8:13pm, Sa starting at 6:02am, Su starting at 9:13am; €3) and from there you can catch a bus to Salzburg. The Wolfgangsee **ferry** (☎223 20) runs to nearby St. Gilgen (45min., 9:15am-3:15pm, €5) and Strobl (30min., 8:20am-7pm, €4; children are half price and Eurail is valid). From Vienna by **car,** take A1 West to Mondsee and head south through St. Lorenz and Scharfling. From Salzburg, take Rte. 158 east through Hof, Fuschl, and St. Gilgen.

▮ ORIENTATION & PRACTICAL INFORMATION

St. Wolfgang is a lovely place to get lost, which is fortunate, since street names are difficult to find and maps are as rare as they are indecipherable. There are three bus stops in town— "St. Wolfgang Au," "St. Wolfgang Markt," and "St. Wolfgang Schafbergbahn." For the town center get off at St. Wolfgang Markt and walk uphill, staying to the right at Pilgerstr. as you go around the bend. For those arriving via ferry, disembark at the St. Wolfgang Markt bus stop and head up the Promenade to the left for the town center. The main **tourist office,** Au 140, is a few steps away from the *St. Wolfgang Au* stop, but to get there from town walk 5min. uphill from the church on M. Pacher Str. (☎80 03; www.wolfgangsee.at. Open June-Sept. M-F 9am-7pm, Sa 9am-noon and 2-6pm; Oct.-May M-F 9am-noon and 1-6pm, Sa 9am-noon.) Services include: **ATMs** in the tourist office; **public bathrooms** near the bus stop "St. Wolfgang Markt" (€0.50); **pharmacy** Apotheke Zum Hl. Wolfgang near Hotel Peter on M. Pacher Str. (☎33 37. Open M-F 8am-12:30pm and 2:30-6pm, Sa 8am-noon, Su 9-11am, and anytime for emergencies.) **Post office:** from the church turn left toward the Schafbergbahn and the post office will be on the right. (☎22 01. Open June-Sept. M-F 8am-noon and 2-5pm; Oct.-May M-Tu and Th-F 8am-noon and 2-5pm, W 8am-noon; exchange closes at 5pm.) **Postal code:** A-5360.

ACCOMMODATIONS & CAMPING

With so many tourists passing through town, finding a bed can be tough. The tourist office provides a brochure listing hotels, *Pensionen,* and *Privatzimmer.*

Haus am See, M. Pacher Str. 98 (☎22 24), across the street from the tourist office. 40 beds in a sprawling old house on the lake. The bathrooms could use a renovation, but the rooms are clean and the view is fantastic (most rooms with balcony). Breakfast included. Hall showers. Parking available. Open June-Sept. Prices depend on balcony and view. Boathouse 5-person dorm €11 per person; singles €15-20; doubles €30-44; quads €59-88. Surcharge for one-night stays. ❷

Haus Reif, Sternalle 143 (☎/fax 22 15; margareta.reif@aon.at). From the bus stop "St. Wolfgang Markt," head downhill and take the first right at the flashing light. Haus Reif will be on your right—its beautifully manicured lawn and the verse painted above the front door make it easy to spot. Head up the small marble staircase to large rooms, all with toilet and balcony. Breakfast included. Singles €22-27; doubles €25-27. ❸

Strandhotel Margaretha, Margarethenstr. 67 (☎23 79; strandhotelf@wolfgang-see.com). Just beyond the Schafbergbahn outside of town, this luxurious hotel offers great opportunities to enjoy the scenery, including a lakeside deck and free use of the hotel's rowboat and bicycles. Doubles €42-80; singles available on request about €60 per night. All rates depend on view and time of year. AmEx/MC/V. ❹

Pension Raudaschl, Deschbühel Au 41 (☎25 61). From the tourist office, walk toward town past the parking lot and turn uphill at Hotel Peter heading toward the cluster of houses. This smaller *Pension,* on the way to the major hiking paths, offers 7 rooms with private wooden balcony and bath. Breakfast included. Open May-Oct. Singles €22; doubles €44. Add 20% for one-night stays. ❸

Camping Appesbach, Au 99 (☎22 06; fax 22 06 03), from the tourist office walk down M. Pacher Str. away from town for about 1km and then turn left onto Au. Use of the extensive beach and warm showers included. Open May-Oct. €4 per night for a space plus €5 per adult, €3 per child. ❶

FOOD

Most of St. Wolfgang's restaurants and *Imbiße* are rather expensive. Snack shacks selling sausages and hamburgers (€2-5) line M. Pacher Str. Sit down at **Gasthof Franz Josef ❷**, at the St. Wolfgang Markt ferry landing (when facing the church head downhill to the left), for vegetarian entrees, which run €5.50-€6.50. (Open Easter-Sept. 11am-9pm. MC/V.) Another good option is the **Zimmerbrau ❷** restaurant, Markt 89 (☎22 04), just downhill from the church on the street to the far left. Most dishes are €7-8, but some are less, such as the *Käsespätzle* with caramelized onions (€6.80) and sandwiches from €5.30. *Kondi-*

toreien also serve up a local specialty—*Schafbergkugeln* (about €1.70), a tennis-ball-sized hunk of milk chocolate filled with cream, spongecake, nuts, and marzipan. Pick one up at **Bäckerei Gandl**, Im Stöckl 84, across from the post office. (☎22 94. Open M-Sa 6:30am-6pm, Su 7am-1pm.) The **SPAR** on Pilgerstr. (when facing the church turn right toward the Schafbergspitze) sells standard groceries. (Open M-Tu and Th-F 7:30am-noon and 2-6pm, W 7am-noon, Sa 7am-6pm.)

👁 SIGHTS

WALLFAHRTSKIRCHE (PILGRIMAGE CHURCH). St. Wolfgang's main attraction, the **Wallfahrtskirche**, is in the Marktpl. The church's interior is unbelievably ornate. The altarpiece, completed by Michael Pacher in 1480 after a decade of labor, opens like a heavenly portal to reveal the coronation of Mary, complete with trumpeting angels. The Baroque Schwanthaler Altar, installed in 1676, was originally made to replace Pacher's, but the sculptor Thomas Schwanthaler bravely persuaded the abbot to leave Pacher's masterpiece alone. Together the altars almost overwhelm the church—don't miss smaller treasures like Schwanthaler's *Rosenkranzaltar* (Rose Garland Altar) or the St. Wolfgang memorial room. To see the breadth of St. Wolfgang's attractions in under 30min., take a carriage ride (25min., €19) from the church. *(Turn right out of the tourist office and head straight down the road, M. Pacher Str.)*

SCHAFBERGBAHN. St. Wolfgang's other major attraction is the **Schafbergbahn**, a romantic steam engine that slowly ascends to the summit of Schafberg. The railway was built in 1892, and Hollywood found it charming enough to merit a cameo in *The Sound of Music*, with the von Trapp children waving from the windows. From the top, dozens of trails wind down the mountain, leading to such nearby towns as St. Gilgen, Ried, and Falkenstein. Tickets for the 40min. ride run as steep as the mountain. *(☎223 20. May-Oct. every hr. 9am-6pm; ascent €13, half-way €10, round-trip €22; children 6-15 half-price. Eurail valid.)* If you must pay full price, you might as well take advantage of the special deal offered by the 🏨 **Berghotel Schafbergspitze** ➍ *(☎35 42; fax 354 24)*, a lovely mountain inn peeking over the Schafberg's steepest face. For €48 per person, you get a round-trip ticket on the railway, a room (with shower), and breakfast. Reserve in advance and purchase at the Schafbergbahn station.

🏔 🎭 OUTDOORS & ENTERTAINMENT

The clear and expansive *Wolfgangsee* is great for water sports. Facing the church, turn right and walk 10min. down Pilgerstr. for **public lake** access. **Waterskiing** is available through **Stadler** on the *Seepromenade* near the Schafbergbahn. (☎066 44 01 75 36; €10 per circuit.) Rent **boats** in town at the landing near Marktpl. and at the *Seepromenade*. (Motor boats €8 per 30min., €14 per hr.; pedal boats €8 per hr.) **Hiking** trails are clearly marked from town; maps from the tourist office cost €1.20-€6.40. Try **Vormauerweg** ("C," marked near Pension Raudaschl) to **Vormauerstein**, a 1450m peak overlooking the lake. Return over Aschau by Sommerauweg 28 to make a complete loop (4-4½hr.). **Bike rentals** are available from **Pro Travel Agency** by the *Markt* ferry landing (☎252 50. Open daily 9am-6pm. €9 per day. Lock and helmet included.) On a weekend evening in St. Wolfgang, catch a production of local composer Ralph Benatzky's operetta *Im Weißen Rössl* ("White Horse Inn") at Michael-Pacher-

Haus, the city theater. (☎80 03. Performed in German May 23-Sept. 12 F 8:30pm. Tickets available at the White Horse Inn, or from box office just prior to the show. €14, children €8.)

MONDSEE   ☎06232

This colorful one-street-town's position on the Salzkammergut's warmest lake makes it a relaxing getaway from the hustle and bustle of Salzburg. Mondsee (named "moon lake" after its crescent-shaped body of water) offers numerous hiking and biking opportunities as well as less strenuous amusement in the Schloß-galerie's art exhibits. The newly renovated Alpenseebad, where you can swim or laze on the sandy beach, is situated against a lovely backdrop.

TRANSPORTATION. Mondsee has no train station but is accessible by **bus** from Salzburg's Hauptbahnhof (50min., 1-2 per hr. 6:40am-8:30pm, €4.60) and from Vienna, Wien-Mitte (4hr., Apr.-Oct. M-Sa 7:30am, Nov.-Mar. M-F 7:30am). Buses run to St. Gilgen on the Wolfgangsee (20min., M-F 6:25, 8:40, 11:50am, 6:55, and 7:15pm, Sa 11:50am; €2.60). By **car,** take Autobahn A-1 or the more scenic Rte. 158 from Salzburg to St. Gilgen and then Rte. 154 along the lake to Mondsee.

ORIENTATION & PRACTICAL INFORMATION. To reach the **tourist office,** Dr.-Franz-Müllerstr. 3, head up the road from the bus stop, turn right onto Rainerstr., and continue to Marktpl. Turn right again; the office is on the left. A box in front of the office contains maps of Mondsee. (☎22 70; info@mondsee.at.org. Open July-Aug. daily 8am-7pm; June and Sept. M-F 8am-noon and 1-6pm, Sa 9am-noon and 3-6pm; Oct.-May M-F 8am-noon and 1-5pm.) **ATMs** are at the Volksbank by the tourist office, at the Raiffeisenbank on Rainerstr., and at the Salzburger Sparkasse on Marktpl. The **post office,** on Franz-Kreuzbergerstr., is across from the bus station. (☎266 50. Open M-Th 8am-noon and 2-5:30pm, F 8am-12:30pm and 2-5:30pm; exchange closes at 5pm.) **Postal code:** A-5310.

ACCOMMODATIONS. *Gasthöfe* and hotels crowd the area near Marktpl., and *Privatzimmer* hang *Zimmer Frei* signs. The tourist office lists available rooms.

Jugendgästehaus (HI), Krankenhausstr. 9, (☎24 18; jgh.mondsee@oejhv.or.at). Go up Kreuzbergerstr. from the bus station, right on Rainerstr., and left onto Steinerbachstr. After 150m, where the street branches, follow Krankenhausstr. around the bend to the left; the hostel is hidden off a driveway to the left. Slightly off the main drag, you can find a place to crash in this retro-styled hostel, with wood-paneling and orange and brown decor. The hostel serves lunch and dinner (€5) and has reading corners with newspapers and games. Often filled with groups, so call ahead. Breakfast buffet included. Reception M-F 8am-1pm and 5-7pm, Sa-Su 5-7pm. Check-in 5-10pm, check-out by 9am. Closed Jan. 15-Feb. 15. Dorms €13.80; singles with bath €27.30; doubles €31-€38.20; quads €56-€66.40. Non-members pay €3.50 surcharge. MC/V. ❸

Pension Klimesch, M. Guggenbichler-str. 13 (☎25 63). Walk toward the lake from the bus station, take a left onto Atterseestr., then a right onto Guggenbichler-str.; it will be to the left. This well-kept *Pension,* close to the lake, has 15 cheery rooms up a steep flight of stairs, common room with TV, and feather comforters. The friendly hostess offers a generous breakfast on her back patio, weather permitting. Breakfast included. Singles from €24-28; doubles €52. ❸

Hotel Leitnerbräu, Steinerbachstr. 6 (☎65 00; www.leitnerbräu.at). Heading up Rainer-str., turn left onto Steinbachstr. A typical mint-on-the-pillow, all-the-corners-tucked-in-perfectly kind of place. The friendly staff, soothing pale green decor, and unlimited use

SALZBURGER LAND

of their fitness room, sauna, and steam bath make a stay here truly relaxing. Breakfast and **internet access** included. Parking €8 per day. Whirlpool €8.70. Singles €68-81; doubles €110-148. AmEx/MC/V. ❸

◧ FOOD. Marktpl. is brimming with restaurants and *Gasthöfe* serving Austrian and Italian dishes. If you want the ingredients in a bag, the **Konsum,** across from Rainerstr. 15, sells food and develops pictures. (Open M-F 7:30am-7pm, Sa 7:30am-5pm.) A **farmers' market** comes to Marktpl. Saturdays May-September.

Jedermanns, Marktpl. 9. Serves regional specialties such as *Kaiserschmarren* (similar to French toast) as well as salads and pasta. Try the salmon fillet (€13.50). Cheaper entrees such as *Rindsgulyas* €6-8. Open daily 9am-11pm. Closed Nov. MC/V. ❷

China Restaurant, Rainerstr. 13, offers a lunch deal for the budget-conscious with hot-and-sour soup and an entree for €5. For dinner, it offers staples such as sweet and sour chicken ranging from €7-13. Open daily 11:30am-2:30pm and 6-11pm. MC/V. ❷

Blaue Traube, Marktpl. 1 (☎22 37), specializes in traditional Austrian food. Most entrees are €6-10; prices remain the same for the lunch menu, with a wide selection including dishes like *Mondseer Kasspatzen* with caramelized onion (€5.96). ❸

Krone Restaurant, 2 Dr. F. Muller Str. Directly across from the tourist office. The outdoor patio is ideal for a leisurely summer meal. Offers local and international food, including fillet of pork with vegetable risotto (€12.40) and Swiss-style sausage salad (€3.60). Open daily 11am-11pm; lunch menu 2-5:30pm. AmEx/MC/V. ❸

◩◪◩ SIGHTS, OUTDOOR ACTIVITIES, & ENTERTAINMENT. Mondsee is the lake resort closest to Salzburg and has remained one of the least touristed, despite tour buses that roll in to see the local **Pfarrkirche,** on Markatpl., site of the wedding scene in *The Sound of Music.* The church connects to the remains of a Benedictine monastery from AD 748, over which the *Schloß* (castle) was built. The completely-renovated *Schloß* houses businesses, bars, and the **Schloßgalerie,** which displays temporary art exhibits. (☎77 44. Open M-F 9am-3pm, Sa-Su 11am-6pm. Free.) The open-air **Freilichtmuseum,** on Hilfbergstr., features a 500-year-old smokehouse, dairy, and farmhouse. Play with antique farm tools and utensils. (Behind the church and uphill to the right. Open May-Aug. Su-Tu 10am-6pm; Sept.-Oct. Su-Tu 10am-5pm; Apr. and late Oct. Sa-Su only 10am-5pm. €2.20, children and students €1.10, seniors €1.90.)

In summer, the *Mondsee* waters buzz with activity, but not motor boats—private motors are banned to protect wildlife. The newly renovated **Alpenseebad,** down Kreutzbergerstr. from the bus station, is the main **public beach.** (☎22 91. Open in fair weather May-Sept. 9am-6pm. €4.40, children and students €1.80.) For waterskiers or wakeboarders, the **Wasserskizentrum** is inside the Seebad. (☎066 41 60 52 10. Rafting €10.20 per circuit, 2-person rafting same price; waterskiing €9.50 per circuit.) Rent a bike at **Velofant,** next to the Seebad. (Open May-Sept. daily 9:30am-5pm. Mountain bike €18 per day; road bike €13 per day). Or, rent a **boat** from Peter Hemetsberger at the **Kaipromenade**—just head down to the dock. (☎24 60. Rowboats and paddleboats €6 per 30min.; electric boats €8 per 30min.) He also offers *Mondsee Schifffahrten,* boat rides around the lake. (1hr.; 10:45am, 12:15, 1, 2, 3:30, 4:30, 5:30pm, or as requested. €6.90, children half price.) For **hiking,** you can pick up an extensive guide of day hikes at the tourist office. There's also a 2hr. hike around the Mondseeberg: start behind the Pfarrkirche to the right, at the sign for "Hochalm-Oberwang."

hot hotels
cool prices!
with up to 50% off hotels' standard rates in Europe!

why stay in a hostel when you can afford a quality hotel with ensuite facilities?

HotelConnect, the European Hotel Specialist, offers a great range of quality accommodation in 100 European destinations to suit any budget.

Booking is easy with **no booking fee** and offered through both our call centre and online.

hotels in Europe from:

€20

per person per night
including breakfast & taxes!
(based on a twin/double room)

book now at:
www.hotel-connect.com
0845 230 8888

Mondsee holds the **Mondseetage,** an annual classical music festival, from September 3rd to 11th *(tickets €36)*. Tickets can be ordered through the Mondseetage Bestellbüro *(☎35 44; www.mondseetage.com)*. Every year **Hugo von Hofmannsthal's** 1922 morality play, *Jedermann,* is performed (in German) at the open-air **Freilichtbühne** theater. *(☎066 43 38 74 97. Performances mid-July to mid-Aug. Sa 8:30pm. Tickets start at €11-13; advance tickets available at Foto Schwaighofer, Rainerstr. 12.)*

HOHE TAUERN REGION

The enormous **Hohe Tauern** range extends well into Carinthia, Salzburg, Tyrol, and East Tyrol. As part of the Austrian Central Alps, it boasts 246 glaciers and 304 mountains over 3000m in height. Between 1958 and 1964, large tracts of mountain land in Salzburg and Carinthia were declared preserves. An agreement signed by the governing heads of Tyrol, Salzburg, and Carinthia on October 21, 1971, made **Hohe Tauern National Park** the largest national park in all of Europe. Officially, the park encloses 29 towns and 60,000 residents, though most of the park territory is uninhabited. One of the park's most important goals is preservation, so there are no large campgrounds or recreation areas within its borders. The best way to take advantage of this rare circumstance is by hiking one of the numerous trails, which range from pleasant ambles to mighty summits attempted only by world-class mountaineers. The brochure *Natur Erlebnis* ("An Experience in Nature"), available at any park office and most area tourist offices, plots 84 different hikes and ascents on a map of the park and provides short descriptions of each hike.

Appropriately, the founding papers for the park were signed in **Heiligenblut**, the most central town for visitors. **Zell am See** and **Lienz**, on either end of the **Großglocknerstraße**, are two of the larger towns, while tiny **Krimml** offers famous waterfalls.

HIGHLIGHTS OF THE HOHE TAUERN REGION

Make the trip between Lienz and Zell am See on the **Großglocknerstraße,** the world's most exciting highway (see p. 225).

Sleep in the shadow of Austria's mightiest mountain, the Großglockner, in the tiny mountain town of **Heiligenblut** (see p. 227).

Go skiing in August on the glacier above **Zell am See** (see p. 238).

HOHE TAUERN NATIONAL PARK

Unlike national parks in other countries, the Hohe Tauern National Park is owned not by the government, but by a consortium of private farmers and members of the **Österreichischer Alpenverein** (**ÖAV**; Austrian Alpine Union). In 1914, the land enclosing the **Glockengruppe range** was actually for sale. Just as it was about to be sold to an individual who wanted to turn it into a private hunting ground, wealthy industrialist Albert Wirt bought it instead and donated it to ÖAV so that it could be enjoyed by all. The land remains privately owned and, with the exception of the park's mountainous center, many of its meadows and valleys are used for raising cattle or cutting timber. Farmers still herd their cattle over the same 2500m *Tauern* (ice-free mountain paths) once trod by Celts and Romans. The Glocknergruppe, in the heart of the park, contains Austria's highest peak, the **Großglockner** (3798m), as well as many lakes and glaciers. Besides the omnipresent Edelweiss, the park is also home to dozens of species of endangered alpine flowers (like the fiery *Almsrauch*, or "meadow smoke") as well as armies of marmots. The *Bartgeir* (bearded vulture) and the lyre-horned ibex were recently reintroduced after near extinction throughout Europe. A lazy drive—or a vigorous bike ride—down the Großglocknerstraße offers a beautiful, if summary, look at the peaks and valleys of the park. Rest stops dot the highway, providing vistas of valleys that can be explored only by foot.

Hohe Tauern National Park

ORIENTATION

The center of the park and BundesBus hub, above Heiligenblut, is **Franz-Josefs-Höhe** and the **Pasterze glacier** (see p. 226). Aside from the skiing and hiking opportunities on these mammoths, the main attractions in the park are the **Krimml Waterfalls** (p. 234), just west of Zell am See, and the **Großglocknerstraße** (see p. 225), a spectacular high mountain road that runs north-south through the center of the park, between Zell am See and Lienz, through the Franz-Josefs-Höhe.

TRANSPORTATION

Two **train** lines service towns near the park: one runs west from Zell am See along the northern border of the park, ending in Krimml (1½hr., 19 per day 6:06am-10:56pm, €6.80); another runs south from Salzburg to Badgastein in the southwest corner (1¾hr., 15 per day 7:13am-9:13pm, €11.10). The park itself is criss-crossed by **bus** lines, which operate on a complicated timetable, with some buses running infrequently and others changing schedules in early summer. Pick up a schedule in one of the tourist offices, then be sure to confirm with your driver (all of whom are experts on schedules) when the next bus to your destination departs. Bus routes from all directions go through the center of the park at Franz-Josefs-Höhe. Buses run to Franz-Josefs-Höhe from Lienz via Heiligenblut (1½hr., €7.20 total fare), and from Zell am See (2hr., 2 per day 9:20am-12:20pm, €10). Return trips run to: Heiligenblut (30min.; July 7-Oct. 7 M-F 9:30am, 12:06, 3:50pm, Sa 9:30am, 12:06pm, Su 12:06, 4:30pm; €3.60); Lienz via Heiligenblut (1½hr., 6-8 per day 6:19am-5:15pm, €7.20); Zell am See (2hr., 2 per day 11:45am-3:50pm, €10). Again, *check with your driver* before getting off the bus. It's either an 8km walk to Heiligenblut or an expensive cab ride if you miss the last ride. By **car** from Kitzbühel, take Bundesstr. 161 south to 108, which leads through the park. From Lienz, take Bundesstr. 107 or 108 north into the park. From Zell am See, take Bundesstr. 311 south to 107. In case of **breakdown,** call the ÖAMTC (☎120).

HOHE TAUERN

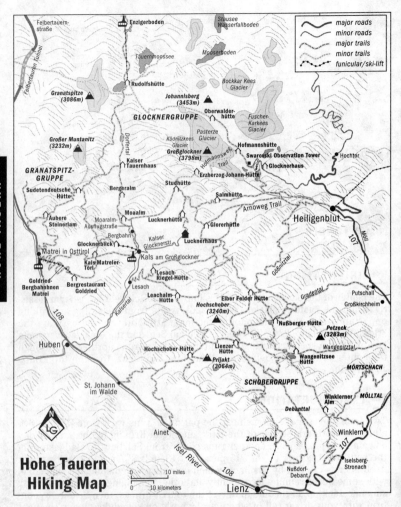

Hohe Tauern Hiking Map

PARK INFORMATION

Because the park is distributed over three different provinces, the network of tourist information is decentralized. Check www.hohetauern.org, or talk to the park service branch closest to you. The **Kärnten (Carinthia) Park Office** is in Großkirchheim (☎ 048 25 61 61; fax 61 61 16), the **Tyrol office** is in Matrei (☎ 04875 51 61; npht@tirol.gv.at), and the **Salzburg office** is in Neukirchen (☎ 06565 655 80; fax 65 58 18). There are also small offices scattered throughout the park.

ACCOMMODATIONS

Given that camping is forbidden in the park, visitors can either operate out of a nearby town or stay in any of numerous huts throughout the park. Zell am See and Lienz are solid, though large, bases for exploring the park; Krimml, on the park's northern border, and Heiligenblut, smack in the middle, are smaller and closer to the park. Mountain huts are excellent places to rest and investigate the surroundings. A caretaker, *Hauswirt*, provides food; bringing your own is frowned upon–if you do, make sure it's consumed elsewhere. A few *Hütten* are within a day's hike of Heiligenblut and provide intimate views of the Großglockner, including the **Salmhütte** (2644m, 6hr. hike from Heiligenblut; ☎04824 20 89; open mid-June to Sept.), and the **Glorerhütte** (2642m, 2hr. from Salmhütte; ☎0664 303 22 00; open late June to late Sept.). The **Erzherzog-Johann-Hütte** is the highest hut in the park, and is nearest the Großglockner peak. (3454m. ☎04876 85 00. Open late June to late Sept.; by guide only.) For a full list of huts pick up a *Hüttenführer* at any tourist office. For more info on huts, contact the ÖAV in Lienz (see p. 238). Camping in the park is prohibited.

OUTDOOR ACTIVITIES

The best **cycling** in the area is on the **Tauernweg** from Krimml to Zell am See (then on to Salzburg), giving glimpses of the Hohe Tauern to the south. Tourist offices and www.tauernradweg.com have more info on the route. Cyclists can also ride the grueling Großglocknerstraße, but be aware that since the National Park is foremost a preserve, bikes are not always allowed off the main highway.

Hiking trails head into isolated valleys from every road and town. With over 50 mountain huts in or near the park offering overnight stays, serious backpackers can lose themselves in the park for weeks at a time. To do so, pick up the *Hüttenführer* guide at any park office. The park's "An Experience in Nature" brochure suggests good hikes. Also essential are trail maps, which cost around €7.50 at any park office and give descriptions of popular hikes and cultural attractions along the trails. The National Park also leads daily guided tours along various trails (usually €6-10, depending upon transportation) detailed in the brochure. The program changes each summer, but generally includes hikes along the Geotrail Tauernfenster, the Pasterze glacier, and a wildlife trek. For Anglophones there is a good list and description of hikes on the park's web site, but the best idea is to purchase a topographic map of the area and talk to the local tourist office. For safety advice on hiking see Essentials, p. 28.

THE GROßGLOCKNER HOCHALPENSTRAßE

Each day more than 3000 visitors pack cars, motorcycles, and buses for a ride along the breathtaking **Großglockner Hochalpenstraße** ("Großglocknerstraße"),

> **! DRIVING SAFETY TIPS.** Many first-time drivers of the Großglocknerstraße are tempted to lean heavily on the brakes, which can lead to brake failure and overheating. Instead, shift to low gear, drive slowly, and never, ever pass anyone.

one of the most beautiful highways in the world. Skirting Austria's loftiest mountains, the Großglocknerstraße winds for 48km amid silent valleys, meadows of wildflowers, powerful waterfalls, and giant glaciers between Heiligenblut and Bruck an der Großglockner. **Bundesstraßen 311** and **197** connect the official parts of the road to the larger towns of Zell am See and Lienz, respectively. These two highways are often unofficially considered part of the Großglocknerstraße, and are generally included in bus tours, along with a stop at Franz-Josefs-Höhe.

The slow, steady climb is choked with motorists and cyclists soaking up the stupefying views. Although the entire length of the road is thrilling, there are several highlights. The climb as you approach the Hochtor (2505m, highest point on

HOHE TAUERN

A PRIEST, A SLOVENIAN, AND FOUR GUIDES WALK UP A MOUNTAIN...

It's not a joke, but rather the first expedition to reach the summit of the Großglockner, on July 28, 1800. Of the party of more than 60 intellectuals, well-to-do nobles, and locals hired to carry the baggage, only six reached the summit of the peak. At the top, they (and their compatriots at what is today the Kleinglockner peak and the Salmhütte) engaged in cutting-edge scientific research: some measured the blueness of the sky with a device called a cyanometer, others put air into jars for study back at sea level, and a few collected previously undiscovered varieties of moss. Their attempt to measure the elevation was fairly successful—their estimate of 3894m is only 96m higher than today's measurement of 3798m.

the Großglocknerstraße) takes you from abundant Alpine flora and fauna to frigid, Arctic-like environments that are always under 10°C (50°F) at night. On a clear day, time is best spent at **Franz-Josefs-Höhe**, enjoying the magnificent views. Don't miss the 1.2km Edelweißestraße spur, which runs by the **Edelweißspitze** (2571m).

Many visitors traverse the Großglocknerstraße in a **tour bus** or **rental car**, neither of which is recommended for those with light wallets or weak stomachs. **Public buses**, with their giant windows, serve as excellent tour buses at much lower prices (see p. 224), although their schedules can be inconvenient. If you only have one day, resist the urge to disembark at any of the smaller stops along the way–buses come so infrequently that you may be stuck for hours.

The full trip on Großglockner Hochalpenstraße, with scenic rest stops along the way, lasts about 2hr. (1hr. roundtrip driving time). Between Lienz and Zell am See, it's about 4hr. (3hr. total driving time). Drivers must pay **tolls** at Ferleiten on the Zell am See side, or Roßbach on the Heiligenblut side (€26 day, €32 for month pass; motorcycles €17/€22). Parking at Franz-Josefs-Höhe is free upon entry. There are also parking and scenic pull-off areas along the road.

Be aware that the road is open only 5am-10pm mid-June to mid-September and 6am-9pm in May and June, with last entry 45min. before close. Snowfalls dumping up to 4m of heavy snow on the road force the Großglocknerstraße to close entirely from October to April. For info on **road conditions** call the Großglockner Hochalpenstraßen Aktiengesellschaft (GROHAG; ☎ 0662 873 67 30; www.grossglockner.at). It is important to note that Großglocknerstraße is not part of the National Park, nor under its auspices. Be aware of this when asking park volunteers about the road, or road officers about the park.

⚠ ACTIVITIES ALONG THE GROßGLOCKNERSTRAßE

KAISER FRANZ-JOSEFS-HÖHE. Buses to Großglockner Hochalpenstraße from Zell am See, Lienz, and Heiligenblut finish their routes at Kaiser Franz-Josefs-Höhe, a large observation center stationed above the **Pasterze glacier.** Located on Gletscherstraße, an 8km spur off the Großglocknerstraße, the Kaiser Franz-Josefs-Höhe is packed with tour buses and camera-toting visitors spread over two levels of parking lots (with a free bus running between them every 10min.), but even they can't detract from the sight of the glacier's icy tongue extending down the valley. Unless it's shrouded in clouds, you can glimpse the towering summit of the Großglockner (3797m) on the left wall of the valley. Franz-Josefs-Höhe has its own **park office** at the beginning of the parking area, with a free mini-museum and Hohe Tauern information center. The staff also answers questions about availability and opening times of mountain huts in the vicinity. (☎04824 27 27. Open daily from mid-May to mid-Oct. 10am-4pm.)

GLACIER FUNICULAR AND OBSERVATION CENTER. The **visitor center,** near the parking lots, has three floors devoted to the first ascent of the Großglockner, the geology of the mountain, free educational films, and panoramic views with labels on each mountain. (Open daily 10am-4pm. Free.) Take the elevator next to the visitor center or the winding road to the **Swarovski Observation Center** for an even better view, as well as brief but fun exhibits on park wildlife and glacier formation. Binoculars are available for viewing the surrounding terrain. If you're lucky, you might see some ibex chewing the grass on the mountain behind you. (Open daily 10am-4pm. Free.) The nearby **Gletscherbahn funicular** ferries you down from Franz-Josefs-Höhe close to the glacier. (☎04824 25 02. Runs mid-May to late Sept. daily 9am-4pm. Round-trip €7, children €5.50.) Or, hike down yourself (see Hiking, below). Catch the glacier while you can—it is receding an average of 20m per year.

HIKING. On any hike in the park, make sure to dress in layers–you should be prepared for rapid temperature changes (as much as 20°F in an hour). Information on more difficult hikes can be obtained from the park office; make sure to purchase a detailed trail map of the area (ÖAV Map #40 €7.19). **Guides** are available for hiking, climbing, or ski touring. (Heiligenblut park office ☎04824 27 00; Heiligenblut Bergführerverein ☎04824 27 00.) For a moderate hike, try the ◼**Gletscherweg** (3hr.). Heading down to the glacier (or coming up from it), follow the "Gletscherweg" sign. This varied trail leads away from the Pasterze glacier through an area that in decades past was covered in ice. The large piles of rock and dust—debris left behind by the glacier—will make you feel like you're walking on the moon. Later highlights include a glacier-fashioned sand lake and the reservoir where runoff from the icy mass still collects. The whole Hohe Tauern panorama comes into view on the descent to the reservoir. The final hour is a stiff climb back to Franz-Josefs-Höhe, so be sure to rest every few minutes and drink plenty of water. Numerous other amazing hikes start at the Kaiser Franz-Josef-Höhe. The **Gramgrubenweg** reopened in 2003 after closing due to a Steinschlag (rock slide). The trail offers a great opportunity to hike and see some of the region's caves.

HEILIGENBLUT ☎04824

The most convenient accommodations for those wishing to explore Franz-Josefs-Höhe and the Hohe Tauern region are in Heiligenblut (pop. 1250), in the middle of the Großglockner Hochalpenstraße. As the town closest to the highest mountain in Austria, Heiligenblut is a great starting point for hikes. The center of town is low on a mountainside, with the rest spilling down to the Möll River. Mountains rise sharply on each side of the valley, wedging Heiligenblut into a narrow corridor that looks northward to the Großglockner. The town's name, which means "holy blood," derives from a legend about a Byzantine general named Briccius who died nearby in a snowstorm. He carried with him a vial supposedly containing a few drops of Christ's blood, now kept in a reliquary in the town church.

◼◪ **TRANSPORTATION & PRACTICAL INFORMATION. Buses** run to Heiligenblut from Franz-Josefs-Höhe (30min.; July-Sept. 4 per day 9:30am-5:45pm, May and Oct. 1 per day 4pm; €3.60), Lienz (1hr., 2-6 per day 6:19am-5:15pm, €5.90), and Zell am See (2½hr., 3 per day 9:20am-12:20pm, €11). The bus stop is in front of Hotel Glocknerhof. The **Kärnten tourist office,** Hof 4, up the street from the bus stop, dispenses information about accommodations, hiking, sporting activities, and park transportation. (☎20 01 21; www.heiligenblut.at. Open July-Aug. M-F 8:30am-6pm, Sa 9am-noon and 4-6pm; Sept.-June M-F 8:30am-noon and 2:30-6pm, Sa 9am-noon and 4-6pm.) The **National Park Tourist office,** behind Intersport, provides detailed information about hiking trails, maps, and mountain accommodations (open only summer months). An **ATM** is next to the tourist office at **Raiffeisenbank.** The **post office** with **currency exchange** is below the center of town at the bottom of the hill. Follow the main road past the chair lift. (☎22 01. Open M-F 8am-noon and 1:30-5pm. Exchange closes 4pm.)

⚑🖸 ACCOMMODATIONS & FOOD. To reach the **Jugendgästehaus Heiligenblut (HI) ❷,** Hof 36, take the path down from the wall behind the bus stop parking lot. Large, pleasant rooms, often with baths and showers, await you. (☎22 59; www.oejhv.or.at. **HI members** only; exceptions made depending on space. Breakfast included. Reception July-Aug. 7-10am and 5-10pm; Sept.-June 7-10am and 5-9pm. Lockout 10am-4pm. Curfew 10pm. Dorms €20, ages 19-27 €15, 19 and under €10; singles €27.27/€22.27/€17.27; doubles €23.63/€18.63/€13.63.) **Pension Bergkristall ❸,** Hof 71 on the uphill side of a U-curve on the street behind the tourist office, is one block from the cablelift and offers balconies and TV; some suites include living room, kitchen, and shower or bathtub. (☎20 05; fax 20 05 33. Breakfast included. Dec.-Easter €28; Easter-Nov. €21.80.) **Nationalpark Camping-Großglockner ❶,** Haderg. 11, across the Möll river, offers scenic campgrounds and a restaurant. (☎20 48; www.heiligenblut.at/nationalpark-camping. Laundry €3.70. Breakfast €8. Reception 8am-midnight. €5.90; children €3, cars and motorcycles €2.20. Electricity €2.20.)

Cheap eats are tough to come by in the center of town, as most restaurants are run by the big hotels. For affordable grub, head down the hill, cross the river, and turn left (15-20min.). **Gasthof Sonnblick ❷,** Hof 21, offers a classic ski-lodge atmosphere with daily dinner specials for €5.50-6.90. Eat to the backdrop of mountains and pastures while enjoying a decor that includes a pastiche of some 200 badges from fire departments around the world. (☎213 10; fax 213 15. Open daily 8am-9pm.) Lodged between the souvenir stores in the square in the center of town is **Dorfstüberl ❷,** Hof 4 (☎22 14), an outdoor café that serves pizzas (€7-9.20) alongside hearty meat entrees for €9-11. (☎20 19. Open daily 8:30am-midnight.) There is an **ADEG,** Hof 46, just a short ways up the road from the tourist office and across from the start of the Großglockner Hochalpenstraße. (☎22 14. Open M-Sa 8am-6pm, Su 9am-6pm; summer Su 8:30am-6pm, M-F 8am-6:30pm, Sa 8am-6pm.)

🕅 HIKING. The Heiligenblut hiker is a happy one, as almost any hike in the area brings amazing scenery. Before heading out, familiarize yourself with a hiking map, available at the Heiligenblut National Park office, the tourist office, or from many shops nearby. Hohe Tauern National Park officially exists only on the western side of Heiligenblut, across the Möll River from the church and tourist office. To get there, take the road out of Heiligenblut and descend the hill. Turn right, cross the river, and turn right again. Walk until you see hiking information signs on the left, or walk a bit farther to the parking lot for trails at the end of the road. The **National Park Office,** Hof 8, behind Intersport, can suggest routes and offer advice; they also have a small exhibit on wildlife and geology that will make your hike that much more educational. (Open daily 10am-5pm.)

🕅 Wirtsbauer Alm hike (4hr., moderate to difficult). From the parking lot, take the main trail past the signs to the Gössnitzfall. After some steady uphill climbing, the path leads to a meadow and a trail leading up the mountain on the left. Past the initial climb on this trail, the hike is mostly flat, cruising along wooded cliffs above the churning Gössnitz River. The Wirtsbauer Alm boasts magnificent views of the entire alpine valley and all the peaks nearby. The hike to **Elberfelderhütte** (☎22 85) is 4½hr. farther and is entirely above the tree line on a path that often skirts the cliff's edge, passing the 3 Langtal Lakes. Both the Wirtsbauer Alm and the Elberfelderhütte accommodate overnight stays (roughly July to mid-Sept.). Call ahead or ask the park office in Heiligenblut.

Salmhütte hike (day hike; moderate to strenuous). This is as close as you can get to the Großglockner peak without a professional guide. Hop on the bus toward Franz-Josef-Hohe to Glocknerhaus. Proceed downhill, cross the dams across Margaritze Lake, then follow the signs to Salmhütte along trail 741, the "Viennese Highway." The path climbs steadily for the next 1½-2hr. before leveling off at around 2450m, a ¼mi. above the valley floor. The 3 "sword peaks" tower over you; to the left is the fantastically green Leiterbach valley. You'll eventually reach the Salmhütte, which was built in 1799 by the first expedition up Großglockner and was, in fact, where most of them quit walking and went home (see p. 278). If you're more determined, continue another hour over increasingly rugged, difficult terrain past the ruins of the expedition's stone hut, following the cairns uphill to the **Hohenwirt glacier.** This is where you turn around and let the professionals continue on to Erzherzog Johann Hütte (it will take them about 2hr. to cover a ¼mi.). Return to the Salmhütte, then take the low road, trail 702b, back to Heiligenblut and enjoy close-ups of the valley and the marmots you towered above on the way out. (Glockneraus to Salmhütte 3hr.; roundtrip to glacier 2hr.; return to Heiligenblut 4hr.) ÖAV map #40 (Großglocknergruppe) is extremely useful.

Gössnitzfall hike (1hr., moderate). Hike begins shortly after the parking lot and continues off the main path, following the sign for "Aussichtspunkt Gössnitzfall." After 10-15min. of steep climbing, an 80m high waterfall appears. Continue to the top of the trail, where you can see the gushing beast in all its glory. The gorge surrounding it is twice as high and just as steep as the waterfall itself. The mist coming off the falls will cool you down, a fitting reward for your effort.

Großglockner (various times, extreme). The king of the Hohe Tauern (3798m) is only to be ascended from Heiligenblut after July 28 through the Leitertal. Climbing of this mountain is to be attempted by experienced hikers and *only* in the company of a guide. Inquire at the mountain hiking office. Generally speaking, Großglockner ascents are done in 1 of 2 ways:

Fürstbischof Salm Weg via **Salmhütte** (1½ days). The classic way to the top, passing over the Hofmannskees and the Meletzkigrat. Guides charge around €105 per person for 4-person groups, €120 for 3 people, €160 for 2 people, and €255 for a single person.

Fürstibischof Salm Weg over the Pasterze glacier. Prices per person: €110 for 4 people, €135 for 3, €175 for 2, €285 for 1 person.

⚑ OTHER OUTDOOR ACTIVITIES. Two skiing mountains, **Schareck** and **Hochfleiß**, rise from the valley's main station (☎022 88 18), middlestation (☎022 88 24), and Tauernberg station (☎22 88 15), and offer 13 ski lifts, challenging runs and open-bowl skiing. Passes available at the Seilbahn lift station past the tourist office. (www.skiheiligenblut.at. Access to ski areas in Ost Tyrol and Carinthia with the Gold pass, 1½-day min. €46 adults, age 15-18 €37, children under 15 €23.)

Bike and **ski** rental are available at **Intersport Pichler,** Hof 4, across from the tourist office. (☎22 56 45, intersport@heiligenblut.at. Open May-June and Sept.-Nov. M-F 9am-6pm, Sa 9am-4pm; July-Aug. M-F 9am-6pm, Sa 9am-4pm, Su 10am-4pm; Dec.-April M-Sa 9am-12:30pm and 2:30-6pm, Su 9am-noon and 3-6pm. Bikes €18 per day, €28 per weekend, €64 per week; skis €14-26 per day; snowboards €14-26 per day.)

HOHE TAUERN

ZELL AM SEE
☎ 06542

Surrounded by a ring of snow-capped mountains cradling a broad turquoise lake, Zell am See (pop. 9700) functions as a year-round resort for mountain-happy European tourists. The town's horizon is dominated by 30 peaks of the Hohe Tauern range, several of which are over 3000m tall. The town is a convenient base from which to explore these mountains on foot or skis. The cool blue lake calls just as enticingly to those who desire summer rest and relaxation, while visitors to the cobblestone town center wind through shops and cafés during the day and bars and dance clubs at night.

☐ TRANSPORTATION

Zell am See lies at the intersection of Bundesstr. 311 from the north and Bundesstr. 168 from the west. It's also accessible by Bundesstr. 107 from the south, which runs into Bundesstr. 311 north. From **Salzburg**, take Bundesstr. 21 south to 305 to 178; at **Lofer,** switch to 311 south.

Trains: The station (☎ 73 21 43 57) is at the intersection of Bahnhofstr. and Salzmannstr. Ticket counter open M 4:50am-7pm, Tu-Sa 6am-7pm, Su 7:15am-8:20pm. Trains arrive from: **Innsbruck** (1½-2hr., 3:45am-9:27pm, €19.60); **Kitzbühel** (45min., 7:17am-9:27pm; €8.70); **Salzburg** (1½hr., 1-2 per hr., €11.30); **Vienna** via Salzburg (5hr., 10:40am-10:56pm, €41).

Buses: BundesBus station on Postpl., behind the post office and facing the corner of Gartenstr. and Schulstr. Buy tickets from the driver or call (☎ 54 44). Open M-F 7:30am-1:30pm. Buses run to a variety of local destinations, including: **Krimml** (1½hr., 5:48am-8:49pm, €7.60); **Salzburg** (2hr., 5:35am-8:50pm, €9.90); **Franz-Josefs-Höhe** (mid-June to Sept. only; 7:20, 10:45am, 12:20pm; one-way €11.90, round-trip €17.10).

Taxis: At the train station, or call ☎ 680 90 or 741 11.

Parking: On Brucker-Bundersstr. between the tourist office and the post office, Magazinerstr. at the *Bahnhof*, between Saalfeldnerstr. and Lofer Bundesstr., by the *Hallenbad*, and underground at the post office. Above-ground parking €1.50 per hr., 3hr. max €2.50. Underground €1.40 per hr., €11.20 per day. Open 24hr.

Bike Rental: From **Base Camp,** Mobile Bike Rental (☎ 0664 343 38 71), and **Intersport,** Bahnhofstr.13 in the *Fußgängerzone* (pedestrian zone) or at the *Schmittenhöhe Talstation* (☎ 726 06). Prices average €20 mountain bike per day or €84 for 6 days, €10 city bike per day or €55 for 6 days: €15 per day, children €8 per day.

◪ ☐ ORIENTATION & PRACTICAL INFORMATION

Zell am See sits among several towns, all of which are huddled on or near the lake and are connected by bus or bike path. The closest town, Schüttdorf, is only a 15min. walk. Go to the right and up the hill from the train station to reach Zell am See's pedestrian zone.

Tourist Office: Brucker Bundesstr. 1a (☎ 770; www.europasportregion.info/en/sommer). From the station, turn right, take the left fork, go around the corner, and turn right again. Open July to mid-Sept. and mid-Dec. to Mar. M-F 8am-6pm, Sa 9am-noon and 4-6pm, Su 10am-noon; Apr.-June and Sept. to mid-Dec. M-F 9am-6pm, Sa 9am-noon.

Currency Exchange: At banks or the post office. Almost every bank has an **ATM.**

Luggage Storage: At the train station. €2.10 per piece, in the office next to the ticket window. Open M-Sa 6am-7:30pm, Su 7am-7:30pm. 24hr. electronic lockers and ski lockers €2.50.

Bookstore: Ellmauer Buchhandlung, Bahnhofstr. 1 (☎473 33; fax 47 33 32), has several racks of novels in the middle of the back room.

Weather conditions: ☎736 94 for *Schmittenhöhe* only. Regional conditions posted daily in English at the tourist information office.

Emergencies: Police, ☎133. **Mountain rescue,** ☎140.

Internet: Café Estl, Bahnhofstr. 1 (☎726 10; www.icak.at), has 4 terminals (€0.15 per min.). Open M-Sa 10am-10pm, Su 11am-8pm. **Schloß Rosenberg's** reading room, Brucker Bundesstr. 2 (☎065 427 6652). Open M 2-6pm, Tu-Th 10am-noon and 2-6pm, F 10am-noon.

Post Office: Postpl. 4 (☎73 79 10). Open M-F 7:30am-6:30pm, Sa 8-10am; early July to mid-Sept. and Dec. 25 to Easter Sa 8-11am. **Postal Code:** A-5700.

ACCOMMODATIONS

Zell am See has more than its share of four-star hotels (and prices), but it has not forgotten the budget traveler. Ask for a free **guest card** at your accommodation, which provides numerous discounts on activities throughout the city.

Pensione Sinilili (Andi's Inn), Thumersbacherstr. 65 (☎735 23). Take the BundesBus (dir.: Thumersbach) to "Krankenhaus" (€1.45, last bus 7:15pm). Turn left after exiting the bus, walk about 200m, and look for an old wooden sign on the left side of the street. If you call ahead, Andi will pick you up. On the north shore of the lake, this pension features simple furniture and an easy-going environment. The lived-in, down-home feel of the house gives it a charm most pensions lack. Andi, reared in Zell am See, knows everything about the town and can tell you what's worthwhile. Hall bathrooms and shower. Big breakfast included. Doubles, some with balcony, €30. ❷

Haus der Jugend (HI), Seespitzstr. 13 (☎571 85; fax 57 18 54). Exit the station facing the lake ("Zum See"), turn right, and walk along the footpath beside the lake; when the footpath ends, take a left onto Seespitzstr. (15min.). The footpath is deserted at night. You can also take the Stadtbus to "Alpenblick" (€1.50, last bus 7:45pm). This well-maintained hostel is group-oriented, providing rooms with bath and lakeside terraces. Other amenities include TV room with VCR, foosball table, and snack shop. Breakfast included. Lunch and dinner €5 each. Key deposit €20 or passport. €1 deposit for locking wardrobes in some rooms. Reception 7-9am and 4-10pm. Check-out 9am. Lockout noon-4pm. Curfew 10pm. Reservations recommended. 6-bed dorms €12.72; 4-bed dorms €13.81; doubles €14.53. 1-night stay add €1.45. Tax €0.84. MC/V. ❷

Landesberufschülerheim Zell am See (HI), Schmittenstr. 27 (☎/fax 470 36). From the Bahnhof, go past the tourist office and turn left onto Schmittenstr. just past the post office. Some of the spacious rooms have a couch or a living room with TV and VCR. Wardrobes can be locked with room key. Breakfast included. Lunch or dinner €5.10. **Bike rental** €10 per day. Reception 8am-10pm. 4-bed dorm €17.24; singles €19; doubles €38. 1-night stay add €1.45. ❸

Pension Herzog, Saalfeldnerstr. 20 (☎725 03; www.members.aon.at/pension.herzog). From the Bahnhof, turn right and go uphill, through and out of the *Fußgängerzone*, past Hotel Grüner Baum. This well-kept pension sits near the lake and a babbling brook. Plain, clean rooms with wood furniture. Shower and toilet in the hall.

HOHE TAUERN

Reception 7am-8pm. Check-out 10am. Rooms with private toilet and shower €25-28, private shower with shared toilet €19-22, shared toilet and shower €15-17. Singles €5 extra. ❷

Camping Seecamp, Thumersbacherstr. 34 (☎721 15; www.see-camp.at), in Zell am See/Prielau, can be reached by BundesBus (dir.: Thumersbach) to "Seecamp" (€1.40, last bus 7:15pm). Lakefront campground with restaurant, outdoor café, grocery. Kayak, sailing, surfing, and bike rental €11 per day. The winter ski shuttle has a stop here. Showers included. Reception M-Sa 8-11am and 4-6pm, Su 9-11am and 4-6pm. Check-out 11am. Car lockout noon-2pm and 10pm-7am. €7.20 per person, ages 5-15 €3.95; €0.90 tax per person. Tent €3.90; cars €2.50; motorbikes €1.50. Oct.-Dec. and May-June, prices 20% off. AmEx/MC/V. ❶

◧ FOOD

Zell am See lies in the Pinzgau region, where food is prepared to sustain the strenuous labors of farmers. Try the *Brezensuppe* (a clear soup with cheese cubes) as an appetizer and then *Pinzgauer Käsnocken* (homemade noodles and cheese, onions, and chives). Top it all off with *Lebkuchen Parfait* (spice cake), *Blattlkrapfen* (deep-fried stuffed pancakes), or *Germknödeln* (a steamed sweet roll served with poppy seeds, butter, and sugar). The grocery store **SPAR** is at Brucker Bundesstr. 4. (Open M-Th 8am-7pm, F 8am-7:30pm, Sa 7:30am-5pm.)

Ristorante Pizzeria Giuseppe, Kircheng. 1 (☎723 73), in the *Fußgängerzone*. From the station, walk past the church and go straight. Subdued lighting and tasteful decoration give this place a pleasant ambience. Plenty of vegetarian options and an extensive wine list. Pasta dishes €5.45-7.99; pizza €5.67-9.16; salads €3.63-7.19. Open Tu-Su 11:30am-11pm. DC/MC/V with €20 min. order. ❷

Fischrestaurant "Moby Dick," Kreuzg. 16 (☎733 20). The restaurant smells like what you might expect, but no matter. Try a double fishburger with potatoes and salad (€7.50), single fishburger (€1.90), or customize your own sandwich. Main dishes occasionally feature fish straight from the lake. Open M-F 9am-6pm, Sa 9am-2pm. MC/V. ❶

Kupferkessel, Brucker-Bundesstr. 18 (☎727 68, fax 72 76 86). As you exit the Bahnhof, turn left and follow the road as it curves uphill and dead-ends at the Kupferkessel. A converted gas station, different parts of the restaurant have unique atmospheres, from Japanese-influenced California kitchen-style (with seating surrounding the chefs) to an outdoor patio and bar. Try the vegetarian menu (€3.30-7.90) or the steaks (€9.20-14.90). Open M-Sa 11am-2am, Su 5pm-2am. AmEx/DC/MC/V. ❷

◉ ◪ OUTDOOR ACTIVITIES & SIGHTS

HIKING & ADVENTURE SPORTS. Though expensive, the **Schmittenhöhebahn** leads to many hikes. The BundesBus *(dir.: Schmittenhöhebahn/Sonnenalmbahn Talstation; 7min., 7:20am-5:50pm, €1.70 from post office)* goes to the lift, about 2km north of town on Schmittenstr. *(Lift runs mid-May to late Oct. daily 9am-5pm. One-way €10.20, with guest card €9.20; children €5.10. Round-trip €18.80/€16.90/€9.40.)* The lift station provides several brochures (with English translations) detailing hikes ranging from strolls to cliff-hangers. In the former category, the **Erlebnisweg Höhenpromenade** (1hr.) connects the top stations of the Schmittenhöhe and Sonnkogel lifts. Displays on history, nature, and ecology along the way. Guided hikes, free with a lift ticket, leave from the lower stations and have a variety of themes, including botanical hikes, forest walks, and children's hikes *(July-Oct. M-F)*. Contact the Schmittenhöhebahn Aktiengesellschaft *(☎78 92 12)* for details.

Independent of the downtown park, the Zell am See area provides many opportunities to work those calf muscles. Consider the **Pinzgauer Spaziergang,** which begins at the upper terminal of the Schmittenhöhebahn and is marked "Alpenvereinsweg" #19 or 719. It dips and climbs a bit at the beginning, but levels off high in the Kitzbüheler Alps. Most people take an entire day to hike along this trail, eventually taking a side trail leading to one of the valley towns west of Zell am See. From there you can take the bus back. For a shorter hike, walk up Mozartstr. until it ends, and follow the hiking trail. The **Kohlergrabenweg** is a 1hr. hike that gradually ascends through the forest to the Schmittenhohebahn lower station.

For **rafting** (€25-50), **canyoning** (€40-60), **paragliding** (€100), and **climbing** (€36) information, contact **Adventure Service,** Steinerg. 9 (☎735 25; fax 742 80), or **Base Camp,** Dreifaltigkeitsg. 6 (☎0664 253 03 81).

SKIING. Winter turns Zell am See into a ski resort. The **Zell/Kaprun Ski Pass** covers both Zell am See and nearby Kaprun; a free bus runs between the two every 30-45min. from late-December to late-March, as well as every 30min. between Zell am See and the Schmittenhöhebahn from late December to late April (1-day pass €34.50, ages 16-18 €31, ages 7-15 €17, under 7 free when accompanied by an adult.) Get a report in German on ski conditions in the Schmittenhöhe area (☎789 in English) or the Kitzsteinhorn-Kaprun area (☎(06547 86 21). The **Kitzsteinhorn** (3203m) and its glacier in Kaprun also offer **summer skiing.** Get there early on summer days to avoid skiing in slush. (Day passes €19.62, children €10.54.) Renting snowboarding or skiing gear runs €21.44 per day, available at **Intersport Bründl** on the glacier. (☎06547 83 88. Open M-F 8am-noon and 2:30-6:30pm, Sa 8am-6pm, Su 9am-11am and 3-6pm.) Intersport also has several other shops open in winter, as well as one near the top of Kitzsteinhorn, with a new cross-store return policy allowing you to rent from one store and then return or exchange at a different Intersport at no extra cost.

OTHER ACTIVITIES. Zell's buildings are clustered in the valley of the *Zellersee.* Stroll around the lake or get wet at one of the **beaches: Strandbad Zell am See,** near the center of town (walk down Franz-Josef-Str.), complete with platform diving and a waterslide; **Strandbad Seespitz,** by the Haus der Jugend; or **Thumersbacher Strandbad,** almost directly opposite downtown on the shore's other side. (Round-trip boat passage from the downtown park €4.10, children €2. Beaches open June-early Sept. 9am-7pm. €5.20 or €6.50 with guest card, ages 15-18 €3.80, ages 6-16 €3, under 6 free.) **Boat tours** depart from the Zell Esplanade, off Salzmannstr. (40min.; 13 per day 9:30am-5:30pm; €7.20, ages 6-14 €3.60.) Visit Strandbad Thumersbach Kurpark (☎723 55) for **water skiing.**

Around the cafés and shops in the middle of the *Fußgängerzone* of Zell stands the *Vogtturm,* Kreuzg. 2, a medieval tower that has housed the funky **Heimatmuseum** since 1985. Overflowing with exhibits, highlights include the toilet that Franz Joseph used at the Hotel Schmittenhöhe, an entire room devoted to the history of skiing in the area, stuffed birds, and a history of coinage in the *Pinzgau.* (☎86 43. Open June to mid-Oct. and mid-Dec. Tu and F 5-6pm. Free.)

◩ NIGHTLIFE

Those who want to get really hammered should try the local drinking game **Nageln,** in which drinkers compete to see who can drive a nail into a tree stump first—with the sharp end of a hammer. Somehow, you end up drunk.

Crazy Daisy's Bar, Brucker Bundesstr. 10-12 (☎725 16 59), across from the tourist office, is a fun though touristy joint featuring its own wacky, irreverent t-shirts and the aforementioned hammer-in-stump game. Also serves Mexican and American food. Hamburgers €7. In winter try the burritos (€8.72), salads €2.91-4.36, "breath-killer garlic bread" (€2.18.) Happy Hour in summer 8-10pm; in winter 4-6pm. Open summer 8pm-1am; winter 4pm-1am. MC/V.

Pinzgauer Diele, Kircheng. 3 (☎21 64), has 2 bars and a small dance area guaranteed to get you moving. Mostly an under-25 crowd. Mixed drinks €3.63-6.90, Beer €2.20-4.70. Cover €6.18. Open daily 10pm-3am.

Bierstad'l, Kircheng. 1 (☎72 36 33). 18-to-25-year-olds sample 33 different brews in stock. Creamy, dark *Hirter* €3.49. Open daily 8pm-4am.

⯈ DAYTRIP FROM ZELL AM SEE

KRIMML
☎06564

*The Pinzgauer Lokalbahn **train** comes only westward from Zell am See (1¾hr., 5:48am-6:49pm, €6.90; a steam train runs from July to mid-Sept. Su, €6.90; Eurail valid, 50% off for children 6-15.) **Bundesbus** lines run from Zell am See (1½hr., 11 per day 5:47am-8:55pm, €7.50) and Zell am Ziller (1½hr.; 8:52am, 1:32pm; €5.60) to the start of the falls (bus stop: "Maustelle Ort").*

Each year, over 400,000 visitors charge up the sloping path near Krimml to the Krimml Waterfalls–a set of three roaring cascades. The town itself is a small, sleepy Austrian mountain hamlet. The **tourist office,** Oberkrimml 37 is 2min. from the "Krimml Ort" bus stop; follow the road by the stop, then turn right down the hill in front of the church. (☎723 90; www.krimmls.at; Free 24hr. accommodation phone and computer. Open M-F 8am-noon and 2:30-5:30pm, Sa 8:30-10:30am.) There is an **ATM** at Raiffeisenbank across from the church. The **post office** next door to the tourist office offers good **exchange** rates. (☎72 01. Open M-Tu and Th-F 8am-noon and 2-5pm, W 8am-noon.) **Haus Mühlegg ❸,** Oberkrimmlstr. 24, is 5min. downhill along the road past **ADEG** and the sport shop: it's the brown farmhouse on the right, with flowers on every terrace. Large rooms with mountain views and homey decorations await. (☎74 59 or 73 38. €18.) **Gasthof Post ❸** is located across from the ADEG. The Steger Family's traditional home evokes real Austrian charm. A breakfast buffet is included. (☎73 58; www.salzburgerland.com/post. Sauna and whirlpool. €29-32; ages 5-12 50% discount, 12-14 20%.) Buy groceries at **ADEG** (☎74 59), up the hill from the tourist office on Oberkrimmlstr. (Open M-F 7:30am-noon and 2-6pm, Sa 7:30am-noon.)

Paid parking at the entrance of the waterfall can be avoided; Krimml offers free parking within walking distance. Ask the tourist office for details. Entrance to the falls costs €1.50 (children €0.50) 8am-6pm. The **OAV/National Park Information** stand, next to the ticket booth, offers maps, pamphlets, and German guides for €3.30-14. (☎72 12. Open May-Oct. M-Sa 11am-4pm.)

Dropping a total of 380m, the Krimml waterfalls taken together are the largest series of falls in Europe. The source of the waterfalls is the Krimml *Kees* (glacier), 20km up the valley above the falls. The upward-sloping **Wasserfallweg** (4km) is a wide hiking path that starts past the entrance booth. The first set of falls are accessible almost directly from the entrance It's 30min. from there to the second cascade, and an additional 30min. to the third. Alternatively, a **taxi service** transports paying customers to the second and third cascades. (☎72 81 or 72 28. €5.50 to 2nd falls, €7.70 to 3rd falls, €6.50 to Krimml Bahnhof.)

The first and most powerful cascade (65m) is visible almost immediately after the entrance; it kicks up a huge skirt of spray that douses rocks, plants, and those tourists who just have to get a liiiittle closer for the perfect picture. The second falls drop from a precipice named **Jagasprung** (Hunter's Leap). As legend has it, a poacher once jumped from here to the other side of the falls to elude his pursuers. The third set of falls (60m) is the most scenic—one long cascade from the upper river valley. The trail continues through the upper Ache valley; a further 30min. walk provides views of the towering **Dreiherrenspitze** (3499m) near the source of the waterfalls.

A little ways before the entrance to the waterfalls lies **WasserWunderWelt,** a new water museum/park with two floors of fun facts about water: everything you ever wanted to know about waterfalls, the Krimml waterfalls in particular. The Aqua-Park outside has games, including a gauntlet that blasts tourists with water when they step on the wrong tiles. (☎201 13; www.wawuwe.at. Open May-Oct. daily 10am-5pm, also mid.-Jan. to mid.-Apr. noon-9pm. €7, children €3.50.)

LIENZ ☎04852

Lienz is the primary city of East Tyrol (Osttirol), despite a population of only 12,000. The center bustles with businesses and cafés, but walk away from it for 5min. and you'd swear you were in a small mountain village. Walk 15min. out of town, and you'll find yourself in a valley surrounded by the Dolomites and the southern reaches of the Hohe Tauern National Park. Linz's proximity to both mountain ranges makes it a perfect base for exploring the countryside.

▐ TRANSPORTATION

Trains: Hauptbahnhof, Bahnhofpl. (☎05 17 17). Information booth open M 5am-6:55pm, Tu-F 6:20am-6:55pm, Sa 6:20am-6:55pm, Su and holidays 8:30am-6:55. Trains to: **Innsbruck** (3hr., 5 per day 4:42am-6:54pm, €17.60); **Spittal-Millstättersee** (Spittal an der Drau; 1hr., 17 per day 5:20am-8:19pm, €9.70-10); **Villach** (2hr., 6 per day 5:20am-7:23pm, €10.20).

Buses: BundesBus (☎649 44; fax 623 57). Buses leave from the Hauptbahnhof for destinations throughout the region. Lienz ticketing open M-F 8am-noon and 2-4pm, closed Sa-Su and holidays. Buses to: **Franz-Josefs-Höhe** (1½hr., 3-4 per day 8am-4:10pm); **Heiligenblut** (1hr., 2-12 per day 8am-7:20 pm, €7); **Kitzbühel** (2hr., 1-2 per day 5:45am-5:15pm, €12.40); **Zell am See** via Franz-Josefs-Höhe (2 daily 10am, 2pm). July 7-Aug 23 a **free Stadtbus** circles the city, making 14 stops before returning to station parking lot (every hr. 8am-7pm).

By car: Lienz lies at the junction of Bundesstr. 108 from the northwest, 106 and 107 from the northeast, and 100, which runs east-west. From Innsbruck, take Autobahn A-12 E to 169 south. At Zell am Ziller, switch to 165 E, and at Mittersill take 108 S to Lienz. From Salzburg, take Autobahn A-10 S to 311, and, just before Zell am See, switch to 107 S to Lienz.

Taxi: ☎638 63, 640 64, or 653 65.

Parking: At Europapl. €0.50 per hr.; max. 3hr.

Car Rental: OPEL, Kärntnerstr. 36 (☎623 35). Open M-F 8am-5:30pm, Sa 8am-noon.

Bike Rental: Trend Sport Wibmer, Egger-Lienz Pl. (☎623 35; fax 690 68). **Papin Sport** (☎0474/91 34 50; fax 04 740/091 37 14), in the train station's parking lot. Pick-up in Lienz with a return elsewhere €3 extra. €18 per day, children €12.

HOHE TAUERN

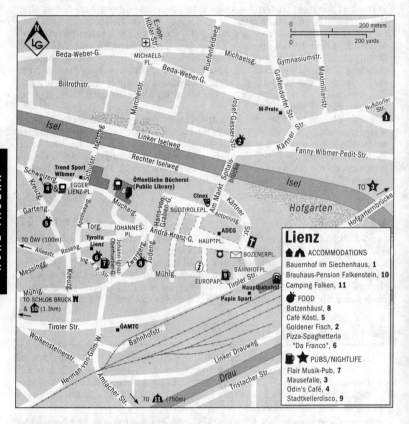

Lienz

🏠🏠 ACCOMMODATIONS
Bauernhof im Siechenhaus, 1
Brauhaus-Pension Falkenstein, 10
Camping Falken, 11

🍴 FOOD
Batzenhäusl, 8
Café Köstl, 5
Goldener Fisch, 2
Pizza-Spaghetteria
"Da Franco", 6

🍺⭐ PUBS/NIGHTLIFE
Flair Musik-Pub, 7
Mausefalle, 3
Odin's Café, 4
Stadtkellerdisco, 9

■🛈 ORIENTATION & PRACTICAL INFORMATION

The Isel River, which feeds into the Drau, splits Lienz. The Dolomites spread south into Italy, while peaks to the north rise toward the Hohe Tauern range. From the train station, the Hauptpl. and *Altstadt* are across Tiroler Str. and to the left through Boznerpl.

Tourist Office: Europapl. 1 (☎652 65; www.lienz-tourismus.at). From the station, turn left on Tiroler Str. and right on Europapl. **City tours** in German M and F 10am; call ahead for English. Open M-F 8am-7pm, Sa 9am-noon and 5-7pm, Su 10am-noon. **Igelsberg-Stronach Information Center** (☎641 17) has info on **national park tours.**

Currency Exchange: Best rates are in the **post office,** which has an **ATM** in front. Exchange open M-F 8am-7pm. ATMs also at the train station and banks.

Luggage Storage: In the train station. Small lockers €2, ski lockers €3.50. Luggage watch €2.10. Open daily 7:30-11:10am and 1:10-6pm; lockers 6am-9:30pm.

Hospital: Emanuel-von-Hibler-Str. 5 (☎60 60).

Emergencies: Police, Hauptpl. 5 (☎133), **Fire** ☎122, **Mountain Rescue** ☎140, **Ambulance and water rescue** ☎144, **Road service** ☎120.

Internet Access: At the **Bücherei** (public library; ☎639 72), inside the Franziskanerkloster on Mucharg. Open Tu-F 9am-noon and 3-6pm, Sa 9am-noon. €2 per hr. Also **Odin's Café**, Schweizerg. 3 (☎635 97). Open daily 4pm-2am. €0.10 per min., €3.80 per hr.

Post Office: Boznerpl. 1, at the beginning of Hauptpl. across from the train station. Open M-F 7:30am-7pm, Sa 8-11am. **Postal Code:** A-9900.

▐ ACCOMMODATIONS & CAMPING

Bauernhof im Siechenhaus, Kärntnerstr. 39 (☎621 88). From the station, turn right onto Tiroler Str. and walk across the Isel; take the 1st left and then an immediate right. Walk 1 block to Kärntnerstr. and turn left. This wood-beamed farmhouse was a home for the sick during the Middle Ages and now offers large rooms decorated with jigsaw puzzles. All rooms with radio, most with shower. Doubles €30; triples €45. ❷

Brauhaus-Pension Falkenstein, Pustertalerstr. 40 (☎622 70; fax 704), is run by the same folks who own the Gössler brewery next door, so expect fresh beer at the restaurant/*Biergarten* downstairs. Take the Lienz-Arnbach bus from the train station to Falkenstein (6:40am-6:10pm) or turn left on Tirolerstr., follow it as it turns into A-Eggerstr., then turn left on Pustertalerstr. and walk 10min. (20min. total). Rooms are large, with TV, couch, and shower. €27.50 per person. ❸

Camping Falken, Eichholz 7 (☎640 22; camping.falken@tirol.com), is across the Drau River. From the station, turn left onto Tiroler Str. and left at the ÖAMTC garage, then pass through the tunnel and over the Drau. Continue past the stadium, then turn left down the asphalt footpath (15min.). This site, encircled by fields and mountains, has a ping-pong table, soccer field, mini-playground, and store. Laundry €3. Car lockout 1-3pm and 10pm-7am in the bigger lot. Reception 8-10am and 4-8pm. Reservations recommended. July-Aug. €5.50, children €3.50; tent site €7; caravan site €9. Sept.-June prices €0.50 less. Showers €1. ❶

▐ FOOD

Calorie-laden delis, bakeries, and cafés lie in wait in Hauptpl. and along Schweizerg. in the heart of the city. A venture through the side streets off Hauptpl. will often unearth more substantial restaurants.

Pizzeria-Spaghetteria "Da Franco," Ägidius Peggerstr. (☎699 69). Head through Hauptpl. to Johannespl., turn left at Zwergerg., and continue down the small alley, then gradually bear right up onto Ägidius Peggerstr. Try terrific stone-oven pizzas (€5.30-9) and pasta (€5.50-9) in this restaurant established by Italians who decided to make it big up north. Open daily 11:30am-2:30pm and 5pm-midnight. AmEx/DC/MC/V. ❷

Batzenhäusl, Zwergg. 1a. The place with the giant coffee pot hanging from the sign offers great deals, like the *Wienerschnitzel* platter (€6.50), but the real attraction is the outdoor *Gastgarten* next to the old city wall. On weekends, the Batzbar fills with a diverse crowd and frequently has live music. Open M-Sa 10am-2am. ❷

Goldener Fisch (aka Fischwirt), Kärntnerstr. 9, (☎621 32; www.tiscover.at/goldener-fisch). Formerly a *Versteigerungsmarkt* (a cattle market), this restaurant offers excellent *Schnitzel* (€9) and 3 newly remodeled rooms as well as a popular outdoor patio environment. Open daily 7:30am-10pm. AmEx/DC/MC/V. ❸

Café Köstl, Kreuzg. 4 (☎620 12). In the *Altstadt,* this diner-style restaurant/bakery is good for a light lunch. Ham and eggs or *Bratwurst* run €2.50-4. Delectable ice cream sundaes are around €4. Takeout available. Open M-F 7am-8pm, Sa 7am-12:30pm. ❶

For those attempting to stay on a budget, there is an **ADEG Aktiv Markt,** in Hauptpl. open M-F 8am-6pm, Sa 8am-noon) and an **M-Preis** at 990 Beda Weberg. 1a. (☎72 66 70. Open M 7:30am-6:30pm, Tu-Th 7:30am-6:30pm, F 7:30am-7:30pm, Sa 7:30am-5pm.) The M-Preis is newly remodeled and offers comfortable seating across from the Fischwirt. There is a **Bauernmarkt** (farmer's market), on Südtirolerpl. (open Sa 9am-1pm), and a **Stadtmarkt** with farmers' goods on Messingg. (open F 2:30-7pm).

👁 🜂 SIGHTS & OUTDOOR ACTIVITIES

On a hill above Lienz, Schloß Bruck houses the **Museum der Stadt Lienz.** From the tourist office, turn right on Tiroler Str., following it as it becomes Albin-Eggerstr. and then Iseltalerstr. (20min.). The castle was built in the mid-13th century as the Count of Gorz's home and includes a small chapel whose walls and ceiling are adorned with frescoes. It now serves as a museum with rotating exhibits, including a recent one on hometown impressionist painter Albin Egger-Lienz (whose scenes of farmers at work have been popular in the area for 70 years), along with several works by Klimt and Rodin. A collection of Roman and pre-historic artifacts is also on permanent display. Climb the castle's tower for a regal view. (☎0625 80 83; www.museum-schlossburck.at. Open June 7-Sept. 14 daily 10am-6pm; Sept 15-Oct. 26 Tu-Sa 10am-5pm. €6, children €4.50, students €2.)

HIKING. Although outside the National Park, the Dolomites around Lienz afford excellent hikes. For information on hikes and huts, contact either the tourist office or Lienz's chapter of the **Österreichischer Alpenverein (ÖAV),** Franz-von-Defreggerstr. 11. (☎721 05. *Open F 3-5pm.*) Various day hikes leave from **Schloß Bruck.** *(Round-trips 1-7hr.)* Signs on the trail to the castle give hiking information.

Hochsteinhütte (4hr. to the hut, 7hr. round-trip). From Schloß Bruck, follow signs to "Hochsteinhütte" and keep going. This well-marked hike to the ÖAV-maintained hut is moderately steep and suitable for intermediate or seasoned hikers. The climb to the hut (2025m) gives the best views of all, with gorgeous panoramas of the Dolomites to the south and the Hohe Tauern range extending northward. Head for the hut's terrace, sit back, and enjoy the elevation with a glass of beer.

Böses Weibele (1½-2hr. out, 3hr. round-trip). Those with a bit more fortitude can continue past the Hochsteinhütte and head toward this peak, the highest around (2521m). Getting to the "Evil Wench" requires a mostly uphill trek completely above the tree line, making you feel like you're on top of the world. Depending on how late in the summer it is, you may have to ford a few streams of snow. Not for the faint of heart.

Waldehrpfad Hike (45min.). Follow the "Waldehrpfad-Leisach" signs near Schloß Bruck. A level, leisurely forest hike wanders past a number of signs (in German) offering fun facts about the forest or the species of various flora along the way. Most of the hike stays in the woods, but there are occasional views across the valley. Follow the white-and-red blazes and avoid trails that plunge downward. Eventually a sign for

"Lienz" appears: follow this path, which ends 20min. out of the town center (otherwise the hike continues, depositing you in nearby Leisach). From the bottom of the path, take a left onto the road, then a right onto Bundesstr. 100, and walk 15min. back to Lienz.

The Tristachersee (5km, 3hr. round-trip). Cross the bridge by the train station and follow Tristacherstr. The sparkling blue lake is at the base of the Rauchkofel mountain. Couch potatoes can enjoy the lake by riding the free ferry (hours vary).

Bäder- und Freizeitbus (Bath- and Leisure-Bus) from the *Dolomitenstation* across the Drau to "Parkhotel Tristachersee." (July-Aug. 9 per day 8:53am-6:46pm.)

SKIING. Lienz serves as an excellent base to attack the ski trails of the **Lienzer Dolomiten Complex.** (☎ 639 75; www.lienzerbergbahnen.at.) Two passes are available—one for the Lienzer Bergbahnen, the **Lienzer Pass,** and the other, the **Gold Pass,** for the entire region including the Lienzer Bergbahn's two peaks and 28 others. (*Gold pass 1½ day min. €46, ages 15-18 €37, children under 15 €23; Lienzer Pass €27/€22/€13.50.*) The **Skischule Lienzer Dolomiten** offers instruction in skiing. (*☎ 656 90; fax 672 62. €38, €9 for each additional person; group lessons €37 per 4hr., private snowboard lessons €38 per hr.*) **Joachim's Ski Shop** rents **skis** and **snowboards.** (*☎ 685 41; fax 642 03. Complete downhill equipment from €18-30 per day, children €8; snowboard €24/16.*)

OTHER ACTIVITIES. Swimming is at the **Dolomitenbad** waterpark, across the Drau on the way to the campground. (*☎ 638 20; Open M noon-9pm, Tu-F 9:30am-9pm, Sa-Su 9:30am-8pm. €4.50; students €3.30; seniors, children and the disabled €2.*) Rookie **paragliders** can call Bruno Girstmair, Beda Weberg. 4 (*☎/fax 655 39; brunoWgirstmair.com*), for tandem flights from the nearby peaks.

🎵 🖼 ENTERTAINMENT & NIGHTLIFE

For an age-diverse crowd of 17- to 50-year-old locals, students and tourists, head to the **Mausefalle,** Großglocknerstr. 4, in Nußdorf, the town adjacent to Lienz. (25min. walking along Tirolerstr., a €5 taxi may be the easiest way there from the city's center, or a 25min. walk toward Nußdorf along Tirolerstr. Oldies, disco, and rock will get you moving. You may want to warm up at **Flair Musik-Pub** located next to Da Franco's Pizzeria. Flair offers live music every weekend; 20-somethings dance to a range of genres including reggae, jazz, blues, and folk. (☎ 698 35. Beer €2. Open Su-Th 5pm-1am, F-Sa 5pm-6am.) Disco-lovers should get excited for the **Stadtkellerdisco,** Tiroler Str. 30, near Europapl., where two bars and a dance floor beckon. (☎ 62 85 24. Cover €3.50 includes 1 drink. W 9-11pm all drinks €1.60. Open daily 9pm-4am.) Next door to Pizzeria Da Franco is **Odin's Café,** Schweizerg. 3, which hops to loud rock and rap, lots of young locals, interesting special events (including a planned boat-burning on the river), and **Internet** access (€0.10 per min.) by the bar. (Beer and wine €1.50-3. Open daily 7pm-2am.) **Cinex Lienz,** Am Markt 2 (☎ 67 111), in the town center, shows mostly recently-released American **films** dubbed into German. (Shows 3pm-midnight. Tickets €5.50-8.)

The 3rd week of July brings out the street artists—musicians, actors, and the finest chalk-drawing guys in the world—for the **Straßentheater Festival** in the city center. This includes five nights of free performances. During the second weekend of August, Lienz's annual **Stadtfest** calls all the local *Musiktappelle* to bring out their horns and play the polka from 2pm to 2am, while everyone else makes merry and drinks like crazy. (Admission to town center €4.) The summer months also witness the reaffirmation of Tyrolean culture in a series of *Musiktanzabende*r (music and dance evenings). Watch as local men dust off their old *Lederhosen* and perform the acclaimed *Schuhplattler*—the age-old shoe-slapping dance. (June-Aug. occasionally F 8pm. Free.)

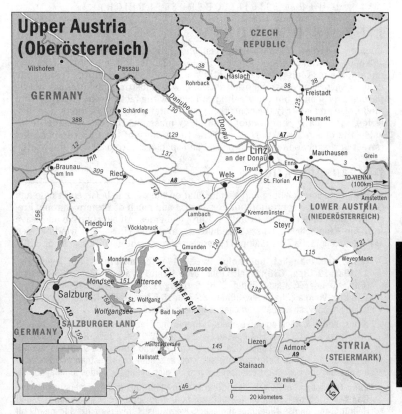

Upper Austria
(Oberösterreich)

GERMANY

CZECH
REPUBLIC

Vilshofen Passau

Rohrback Haslach
Danube 38 38
Schärding 130 (Donau) 125 Freistadt
388 129 127 Neumarkt
12 137 A7
Inn Linz
an der Donau Mauthausen Grein
Braunau am Inn 309 Ried A8 Wels Traun Enns 3
143 1 St. Florian A1 TO VIENNA (100km)
147 Friedburg Vöcklabruck Lambach Kremsmünster Amstetten
156 A1 A9 Steyr LOWER AUSTRIA (NIEDERÖSTERREICH)
1 Gmunden 120 115 Weyer/Markt
Mondsee Traunsee Grünau 121
Mondsee 151 Attersee 138
Salzburg St. Wolfgang
Wolfgangsee Bad Ischl 117
SALZBURGER LAND Liezen
GERMANY 159 Hallstättersee 145 Admont STYRIA (STEIERMARK)
Hallstatt A9
Stainach
146 0 20 miles
0 20 kilometers

UPPER AUSTRIA
(OBERÖSTERREICH)

The province of Oberösterreich (Upper Austria) is comprised of three regions: the **Mühlviertel,** in the northeastern corner; the **Innviertel,** covering the western half; and the **Salzkammergut,** the southwestern corner, encompassing the popular resort area. The charming streets of the provincial capital **Linz** mask the city's industrial soul; it is a major center of iron, steel, and chemical production, and home to many Danube port installations. The relatively flat terrain in Upper Austria makes for wonderful **bike** tours. Well-paved paths, suitable for cyclists of any ability, wind throughout the entire province.

HIGHLIGHTS OF UPPER AUSTRIA

Savor a jam-saturated **Linzer Torte** while relaxing in a garden café (see p. 296).

Peruse medieval manuscripts at the ornate library in **Kremsmünster** (see p. 300).

Soar like a bird at the Ars Electronica museum in **Linz** (see p. 298).

LINZ AN DER DONAU ☎ 0732

Located between Vienna to the east and Salzburg to the west, Linz (pop. 183,500) is often overlooked. The third largest city in the country, Linz was once home to Kepler, Mozart, Beethoven, Bruckner, and Hitler. Technologically, it surpasses Austria's other cities. Linz's industrial outskirts may not be particularly scenic, but the wealth produced by the factories has been used to modernize and gentrify the central city, with interesting shops, modern art galleries, cyber cafés, and a cool technology museum. The city's annual festivals—the classy Brucknerfest and the tomfoolery of the Pflasterspektakel (street performer's fair)—draw artists and spectators from all over the world.

⌐ TRANSPORTATION

Midway between Salzburg and Vienna, and on the rail line between Prague and Graz, Linz is a transportation hub for Austria and much of Eastern Europe. Frequent **trains** connect to Austrian and European cities. All **buses** arrive and leave from the **Hauptbahnhof,** where schedules are available. (Bus ticket window open M-F 7am-5:50pm, Sa 7am-1:20pm.) **Motorists** arrive via Autobahn West (A1 or E16).

Trains: Hauptbahnhof, Bahnhofpl. (☎517 17). To: **Innsbruck** (4hr., every 2hr. 12:19am-11:13pm, €38); **Munich** (3hr., every 1-2hr. 1:37am-10:29pm, €39); **Prague** (6hr., 4 per day 7:16am-5:55pm, €28); **Salzburg** (1½hr., every hr. 1:30am-11:13pm, €16.50); **Vienna** (2hr., every 30min. 3:43am-10:57pm, €25). Not all international trains run daily, so it's better to change trains in Vienna.

Ferries: Wurm & Köck operates boats in **Krems** and **Linz** (Untere Donaulände 1. ☎78 36 07; fax 771 09 09), and **Passau** (☎0851 92 92 92; fax 355 18). To **Passau** (5-7hr.; 2 per day 8am, 2:15pm; €21, round-trip €24) and **Krems** (Sa 9am). Boats dock in Linz at the **Donau Schiffstation,** and stop at a number of Austrian and Bavarian towns along the way. ½ price for seniors and children under 15. Ferries run May to Oct.

Public Transportation: Linz's public transport system runs to all corners of the city. Trams start at the Hauptbahnhof and run north through the city along Landstr. and Hauptpl. and across Nibelungenbrücke. Several buses traverse Linz, and nearly all pass through **Blumauerplatz,** down the block and to the right from the train station. A hub closer to the city center is **Taubenmarkt,** below Hauptpl. on Landstr. A ticket for 4 stops or fewer ("Mini") costs €0.70; more than 4 ("Midi") €1.40; and a day ticket ("Maxi") €2.90. Buy tickets from any machine, *Tabek,* at bus or streetcar stops and stamp them before boarding, or face a €36 fine. The tourist office sells a €3.50 combination ticket that includes a day ticket for tram #3 and a round-trip cable car ride to **Pöstlingberg.**

Taxis: At the Hauptbahnhof, Blumauerpl., Schillerpl., and Hauptpl. (☎69 69 or 17 18).

Parking: Free parking at **Urfahrmarkt** and at Stadion Parkpl. Ziegeleistr., beginning directly west from the train station. Limited parking zones are marked by blue lines; €.50 per 30min. Garages are located throughout the city (outside of the *Altstadt*). Depending on the location, prices range from €11.50-23 per day.

✴? ORIENTATION & PRACTICAL INFORMATION

Linz straddles the **Danube,** which weaves west to east through the city. Most of the *Altstadt* sights are near the southern bank, by **Nibelungenbrücke.** This pedestrian area includes the huge **Hauptplatz,** just south of the bridge, and extends down **Landstraße,** which ends near the train station. To get to the center of town from the train station take tram #3 to "Hauptplatz." The tourist office is extremely helpful, offering detailed pamphlets on dining and hotels in Linz.

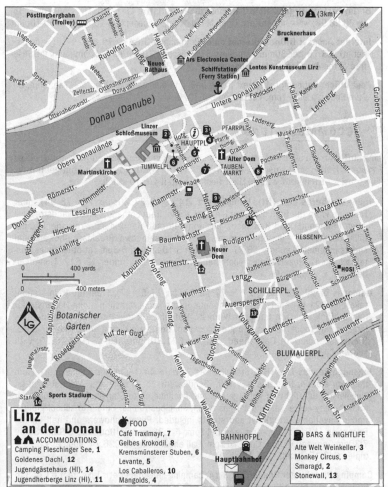

Linz
an der Donau

🔺🏠⛺ ACCOMMODATIONS
Camping Pleschinger See, **1**
Goldenes Dachl, **12**
Jugendgästehaus (HI), **14**
Jugendherberge Linz (HI), **11**

🍎 FOOD
Café Traxlmayr, **7**
Gelbes Krokodil, **8**
Kremsmünsterer Stuben, **6**
Levante, **5**
Los Caballeros, **10**
Mangolds, **4**

🍸 BARS & NIGHTLIFE
Alte Welt Weinkeller, **3**
Monkey Circus, **9**
Smaragd, **2**
Stonewall, **13**

Tourist Office: Hauptpl. 1 (☎ 70 70 17, ext. 77; www.linz.at), in the *Altes Rathaus* on the left side of the Hauptpl. The multilingual staff helps find rooms. Pick up *A Walk Through the Old Quarter* for a summary of the *Altstadt's* main attractions. The tourist office sells the **Linz City Ticket** (€20) which provides discounts at various sights around the city, including a voucher for a meal up to €10 at selected restaurants and a free ride on the Linz City Express. Open May-Oct. M-F 8am-7pm, Sa 10am-7pm, Su 10am-7pm; Nov.-Apr. M-F 8am-6pm, Sa-Su 10am-6pm.

Currency Exchange: Banks open M-W 8am-noon and 2-4:30pm, Th 8am-noon and 2-5:30pm, F 8am-2pm. **24hr. exchange machine** at the train station.

American Express: Bürgerstr. (☎ 66 90 13). Only acts as tourist agency; doesn't handle traveler's cheques. Open M-F 9am-5:30pm.

Luggage Storage: At tourist office, €1.

Bi-Gay-Lesbian Organizations: Homosexuelle Initiative Linz (HOSI), Schubertstr. 36 (☎60 98 98; www.hosilinz.at). Open M-F 4-10pm. Counsel M 8-10pm, Th 6:30-10pm.

Internet Access: BIGnet.internet.cafe, Promenade 3 (☎70 79 68 20 10; www.bignet.at). €3.70 per 30min., students 33% discount. Open daily 10am-midnight. Also **free** at the **Ars Electronica Museum** (see p. 298).

Post Office: Bahnhofpl. 11, next to the train and bus stations. Open M-F 7am-6pm, Sa 9am-6pm, Su 9am-1pm. **Postal code:** A-4020.

▚ ACCOMMODATIONS

Linz suffers from a lack of cheap rooms. The city is just urban enough not to allow *Privatzimmer*, so it's usually best to stick to the youth hostels and budget hotels. The tourist office staff will do their best to help if you're stuck.

Jugendherberge Linz (HI), Kapuzinerstr. 14 (☎78 27 20; fax 781 78 94), near Hauptpl. From the train station, take tram #3 to "Taubenmarkt," cross Landstr., walk down Promenade and Klammstr., and turn left onto Kapuzinerstr. This friendly, no-frills hostel offers 4- and 6-bed rooms, the cheapest in town. Breakfast, showers, and sheets included. Laundry €3.27. Reception 8-10am and 6-8pm (at other times hostel is locked). Reservations recommended. Dorms €15, under 19 €12. Non-members add €3. MC/V. ❷

Goldenes Dachl, Hafnerstr. 27 (☎77 58 97; fax 77 58 97). From the train station, take bus #21 to "Auerspergpl." Continue in the same direction along Herrenstr. for half a block and turn left onto Wurmstr. Hafnerstr. is the 1st right. The hotel has large, sunny rooms and is in a great location. Courtyard dining area. Only 17 beds. Breakfast included. Call ahead. Singles €21.80; doubles €37.80-40.70, with shower €43.60. ❸

Jugendgästehaus Linz (HI), Stanglhofweg 3 (☎66 44 34; jgh.linz@oejhv.or.at). From the train station, take bus #27 (dir.: Schiffswerft) to "Froschberg." Walk straight on Ziegeleistr., turn right on Roseggerstr., and continue on to Stanglhofweg. Although far from the city center, this hostel has clean, spacious rooms. Caters to school groups. Parking available. Breakfast and sheets included. Private showers and hall toilets. Reception M-Th 7:30am-4pm and 6-11pm, F 7:30am-12:30pm and 6-9pm, Sa-Su 7:30am-9am and 6-9pm. Curfew 11pm. Call ahead. Singles €26.74; doubles €38.95; triples €43.17; quads €60. MC/V. ❸

Camping Pleschinger See (☎30 53 14; camping-linz@utanet.at). Take tram #1 or 3 to Rudolfstr. and bus #33 to "Pleschinger See." On the Linz-Vienna biking path on Pleschinger Lake. Plenty of room to sunbathe and swim, with great views of the countryside. Open May to Nov. €4 per person, children €2.35. ❶

🍴 FOOD

Duck into the alleyway restaurants off Hauptpl. and Landstr. to avoid inflated prices, or seek out the supermarkets: **Billa,** Landstr. 44 (open M-W 8am-7pm, Th 7:30am-7pm, F 7:30am-7:30pm, Sa 7:30am-5pm) or **SPAR Markt,** Passage City Center, near the Jugendgästehaus (open M-F 7:30am-7pm). Linz's namesake dessert, the **Linzer Torte,** is rich and worth the price (usually €3). It's unique for its dry ingredients—lots of flour and absolutely no cream. The secret is in the red-currant jam filling, which slowly seeps through and moisturizes the crumbly crust. Below is a small cross-section of the eating experiences that Linz has to offer—pick up a *Gastronomie Verzeichnis* from the tourist office for a complete listing.

■ **Mangolds,** Hauptpl. 3 (☎ 78 56 88), is a vegetarian's paradise in a pleasant, central outdoor space. This cafeteria-style restaurant uses only the freshest ingredients in their fresh-squeezed fruit and vegetable drinks (€2.11) and extravagant salad bar with 40 different kinds of salad. Pay by weight. €1.16 per 100g; 30% discount after 6pm. Open M-F 11am-8pm, Sa 11am-5pm. ❶

Café Traxlmayr, Promenadestr. 16 (☎ 77 33 53). From Hauptpl., head down Schmidttor-str., and turn right onto Promenadestr. Chandeliers and marble tables adorn both the elegant interior of this Viennese-style café and its sprawling outdoor patio. For €4.50 you can nibble on rolls and jam, sip coffee from your own little pot, and watch people play chess, cards, and billiards through the afternoon. Try the *Palatschinken* (sweet crêpe filled with jam; €1.90) or the *Linzer Torten* (€2.20). Open M-Sa 8am-10pm. ❶

Gelbes Krokodil, Dametzstr. 30 (☎ 78 41 82), downstairs in the Moviemento Theater, pleases the young artsy crowd relaxing in its beautiful *Gastgarten*. Varying menu includes soups (€2.62), salads (€5.81-6.54), and vegetarian entrees (€5.81-7.27). Open M-F 11am-1am, Sa-Su 5pm-1am. ❷

Los Caballeros, Landstr. 32 (☎ 77 89 70; www.caballeros.at), in the commercial district, is a Mexican restaurant and bar with a large tequila selection and an excellent all-you-can-eat lunch *Menü* (€6.40). Ribs, wings, fajitas, and steak tacos €6-13. Drink your Corona (€4.20) indoors or in the courtyard. Open daily 11am-2am. MC/V. ❷

Kremsmünsterer Stuben, Altstadt 10 (☎ 78 21 22; fax 21 222). This quaint, luxurious restaurant offers gourmet Austrian cuisine in a sensuous environment of ornately carved chairs and oriental rugs. Reservations recommended. Main dishes include *Gulasch* and paella (€20-22). Open M and Sa 6-10:30pm, Tu-F 12-2pm and 6-10:30pm. ❹

Levante, Hauptpl. 13 (☎ 79 34 30; www.levante.at), has crowded outdoor seating on Hauptpl. (look for the bright yellow umbrellas) and authentic Turkish and Greek food at low prices. €3 sandwiches are a great deal. *Menü* €6.20. Falafel €3.20. Open daily 11:30am-11:30pm. AmEx/MC/V. ❷

UPPER AUSTRIA

⚇ SIGHTS

THE OLD TOWN. Start your exploration of Linz at **Hauptplatz,** where the green Pöstlingberg in the background. The city constructed the enormous plaza in the 14th and 15th centuries with the wealth of taxes collected on the salt and iron passing through town. The focus of the square is the marble **Trinity column,** commemorating the city's escape from the horrors of war, famine, and the plague. An octagonal tower and an astronomical clock crown the Baroque **Rathaus.** To date, only two people have ever addressed the public from its balcony: Adolf Hitler and Pope John Paul II. Free-spirited stargazer **Johannes Kepler** (the fellow who explained the elliptical orbits of the planets) completed his major work, *Rudolph Tables,* while living around the corner at Rathausg. 5. In 1745, Linz's first print shop opened there; today, it houses a pub.

CHURCHES. On nearby Domg. stands Linz's twin-towered **Alter Dom** (Old Cathedral), where symphonic composer Anton Bruckner played during his stint as church organist. *(Open daily 7am-noon and 3-7pm.)* To the south, the neo-Gothic **Neuer Dom** (New Cathedral) is the largest church in Austria. Its tower could have been the highest in the country, but regulation decreed no tower could outdo Vienna's

Stephansdom. *(Open daily 7am-noon and 3-7pm.)* **Martinskirche** is the oldest church in Austria. The central structure was erected during the late 8th century using debris from Roman ruins and is still intact today. *(To the left of the Schloßmuseum on Römerstr.)*

MUSEUMS. The ▧**Ars Electronica** bills itself as the "museum of the future." It's a bird, it's a plane, it's *you* strapped to the ceiling in a full-body flight simulator that sends you soaring over Upper Austria. After this not-so-natural high, head downstairs to the **CAVE,** an interactive 3-D room that sends you even higher to explore the outer reaches of space. Free **Internet** access with entrance. *(Hauptstr. 2, just over the bridge from Hauptpl.* ☎ *727 20; www.aec.at. Open W-Su 10am-6pm. €6, students and seniors €3. MC/V.)* The newly opened **Lentos Kunstmuseum Linz** is phenomenal, both in its architecture and its collections. On the edge of the Danube, the asymmetrical silver building is impossible to miss. The museum features 1500 works, featuring Chagall, Picasso, Matisse, Schiele, and Warhol. Sundays bring €10 jazz concerts and "cultural breakfasts." *(Ernst-Koref-Promenade 1. Call ahead for guided tours.* ☎ *70 70 36 00; www.lentos.at. Wheelchair-accessible. Open M, W, F-Su 10am-6pm, Th 10am-10pm. €6.50, students €4.50. Audio guides in English, €3. Call ahead for guided tours.)* The **Linzer Schloßmuseum** presents an eclectic collection of objects from the Middle Ages to the 20th century including one of Beethoven's pianos and an 18th-century pharmacy. Special exhibits on ground floor. *(Tummelpl. 10.* ☎ *77 44 19. Open Tu-F 9am-5pm, Sa-Su 10am-4pm. €4, students €2.20. English brochure available.)*

BOTANICAL GARDEN. For sheer olfactory ecstasy, visit the **Botanischer Garten's** renowned cactus and orchid collections. Take bus #27 (dir.: Chemie) from Taubenmarkt to "Botanischer Garten." *(Rosegerstr. 20-22.* ☎ *70 70 18 72. Open daily May-Aug. 7:30am-7:30pm; Sept. and Apr. 8am-7pm; Oct. and Mar. 8am-6pm; Nov.-Feb. 8am-5pm. €2, students and seniors €1, children €0.88.)*

URFAHR AND PÖSTLINGBERG. Cross Nibelungenbrücke to reach the left bank of the Danube. This area, known as **Urfahr,** was a separate city until Linz swallowed it up in the early decades of the 20th century. It boasts some of the oldest buildings in the city and a captivating view of Linz from the apex of the **Pöstlingberg** (537m). To reach the summit, take tram #3 to "Bergbahnhof Urfahr," then either hike 500m up Hagenstr. (off Rudolphstr., which is off Hauptstr. near the bridge) or hop aboard the **Pöstlingbergbahn,** a trolley car that ascends the summit in a scenic 20min. *(*☎ *78 01 70 02 or 78 01 75 45. Every 20min. M-Sa 5:20am-8pm, Su 11:40am-8pm. €2, round-trip €3.20, children €1/€1.60.)* The twin-towered **Pöstlingbergkirche,** symbol of the city, stands guard on the crest of the hill. Children of all stripes (whether they're age 5, 15, or 45) will love taking the "magic dragon" train, the **Grottenbahn,** into the fairy tale caves of Pöstlingberg. *(*☎ *34 00 75 06; www.linzag.at. Open daily May-Sept. 10am-6pm; Apr. and Oct.-Nov. 10am-5pm. €4, under 15 €2.)*

🎭 ENTERTAINMENT

From mid-Sept. to mid-Oct., the **Brucknerfest** brings a rush of concerts paying homage to native son Anton Bruckner at the **Brucknerhaus** concert hall. The opening concerts (the end of the second week in Sept.), billed as *Klangwolken* (soundclouds), include spectacular outdoor lasers, a children's show, and a classical evening with Bruckner's 7th Symphony broadcast live into the surrounding Donaupark for 50,000 fans. *(*☎ *77 52 30; www.brucknerhaus.at. Tickets €16-80, standing room about €8. Contact Brucknerhaus-kasse, Untere Donaulände 7, A-4010 Linz.)* During the third weekend of July, the city hosts **Pflasterspektakel,** a free, three day street performers' festival. Every few steps down Landstr. and Hauptpl., international artists perform Houdini acts, fire-eating, outdoor theater, bongo concerts, and punk rock before a young crowd.

NIGHTLIFE

The pulse of Linzer nightlife is at the **Bermuda Dreiecke** (Bermuda Triangle), behind the west side of Hauptpl. (head down Hofg. or follow the crowds of decked-out pub crawlers). This area is frequented by *Linzers* and tourists alike.

■ **Monkey Circus,** Spittelwiese, 6-8 (☎78 78 68; www.monkeycircus.at). A colorful blend of Mexican-inspired art, Monkey Circus is wonderful for either a late night meal (Chilled Mango Soup €7.90) or one of many colorful and creative cocktails (Ernest Hemingway €6.90). Friendly service complements eastern-influenced Mexican and American fare (starting at €5). Open daily 6pm-midnight. V. ❷

Alte Welt Weinkeller, Hauptpl. 4, (☎77 00 53), outside the Dreiecke, is an arcaded, Renaissance-era "wine and culture cellar" where you can soak up wine and spirits (most €3-6) and enjoy tasteful Latin music. In summer the rows of courtyard benches fill quickly. Tasty salads (€2.50-6). Open M-Sa 5pm-2am; kitchen 5:30pm-11pm. ❶

Smaragd, Altstadt 2, (☎79 40 60; www.smaragd.cc.). From Hauptpl., take Hofg. A café, bar, dance floor, and performance space, this complex draws eclectic locals seeking late-night revelry under the moon and stars of its walls. Have a bowl of chili con carne (€3.50) and wash it down with a Desperado (tequila beer, €3.60). The student crowd really cranks up the party around 2am. Tu-W live music, Th Fiesta Latina, F-Sa disco and DJs. Open daily 8pm-6am. ❶

Stonewall, Rainerstr. 22 (☎60 04 38; www.stonewall.at), is a bar during the week and a disco on the weekends. Attracts a largely gay and lesbian crowd, some of whom arrive in drag to dance among the miniature greek statues and life-size armor. Stonewall closes when everyone leaves, usually late. Enjoy a wide selection of beers, cocktails, and schnapps (€2.90-8.30). Open daily from 8pm. Dancing begins F-Sa 10pm. ❷

◪ DAYTRIPS FROM LINZ

MAUTHAUSEN

From Linz, take a train (transfer at St. Valentin; 45min, 4:43am-11:01pm, €5). However, the Mauthausen train station is 3km away from the camp. A special Oberösterreichischer Verkehrsverbund day pass (€7.50) covers this 3km by city bus, plus the round-trip train ticket from Linz. But coordinating the train and bus schedules can be tricky and frustrating. Instead, consider taking a cab (€1.50-2.50 per km). Or walk from the Mauthausen station through town and turn right after the Freizeitzentrum onto the signposted KZ Mauthausen path (45min.-1hr.). Maps available from the train station. By car, take Autobahn A1 (Vienna-Linz) at Enns. (www.mauthausen-memorial.at. Camp open daily Apr.-Sept. 8am-6pm; Oct. to mid-Dec. and Feb.-Mar. 8am-4pm. Admission until 1hr. before closing. €2, students and seniors €1.)

About 30min. down the Danube from Linz, the remains of a Nazi *Konzentrationslager* (KZ; concentration camp) stand in silent vigil. Unlike other camps in southern Germany and Austria, Mauthausen remains intact. Built by Dachau prisoners in 1938, Mauthausen was the central camp for all of Austria and administered 49 subcamps throughout the country. More than 200,000 prisoners passed through Mauthausen, mainly Russian, Italian, and Polish POWs, along with Austrian homosexuals and political criminals, Hungarian and Dutch Jews, gypsies, and Communists. Mauthausen was infamous for its **Todesstiege** (Staircase of Death), which led to the stone quarry where inmates were forced to work to exhaustion. The inner part of the camp is now a **museum** (☎07238 22 69), which displays haunting photographs of the once-packed camps—a striking contrast to the vast, grassy space that remains today. The barracks, roll-call grounds, cremation ovens, and torture rooms are also accessible. A free brochure or audio-tour (in English) walks you through the central camp. There is an exhibit on the history of the camp and video documentaries in several languages (45min.).

KREMSMÜNSTER

Trains go to Kremsmünster from Linz (45min., every hr. 7:40am-7:35pm, €5.60). From the station, follow Bahnhofstr. as it curves left, then right, then left again, and continue on Hauptpl. to Marktpl. The path to the abbey starts at the tourist office, Rathauspl. 1. (Tourist office: ☎07583 72 12; www.tiscover.com/kremsmuenster. Open Tu-F 9am-noon. Abbey: ☎07583 527 50; www.kremsmuenster.at/stift. Open daily 9am-noon and 1-6pm. Free. Fischkalter €1.10. Enter through the ticket office. 1hr. Kunstsammlung tours Apr.-Oct. 10, 11am, 3, 4pm; Nov.-Mar. 11am, 2pm, €4.80. 1½hr. Sternwarte tour May-Oct. 10am, 2pm. €5.10. Both tours include the Fischkalter.)

Kremsmünster's *Stift* (Abbey), 32km south of Linz, belongs to Austria's oldest order and dates from AD 777. Some 75 monks still call the abbey home. The abbey owns most of the land in the area, including 3800 hectares of woods and a wine-producing vineyard. Beneath the frescoed ceiling, the **library** has a few hidden doors, as well as two rows of books on every gold-encrusted shelf. Visitors are not allowed to handle the books, but guides will take out any volume and leaf through it on request. The **Kaisersaal**, built to receive imperial visitors, is a Baroque gallery with marble columns and ceiling frescoes. It feels as if you are being sucked into the scene above. Portraits of the Holy Roman Emperors (from Rudolf of Hapsburg to Charles VI) gaze down at you from the walls. The abbey's *Kunstsammlung* (art collection) tour covers the library, the Kaisersaal, several art galleries, and the **Schatzkammer** (treasury), which shelters a beautifully engraved golden chalice dating from the time of Charlemagne. The monks' collection of animal specimens is displayed in the seven-story **Sternwarte.** Also open is the **Fischkalter,** a series of pools set with pagan and pastoral statues spouting water, and wooden stag heads with real antlers.

ST. FLORIAN'S ABBEY

To reach the abbey from Linz Hauptbahnhof, take the bus (dir.: St. Florian Stift) to "Kotzmannstr." or "Lagerhaus" (30min., 6:20am-6:35pm, €2), then walk 15min. on Romantikstr. from either stop. The tourist office has info about the abbey and accommodation (Marktpl. 3 ☎/fax 07224 56 90). Tours of the abbey minus the Kaiserzimmer leave daily. (☎07224 89 02 10. Abbey open Apr.-Oct. €5.30, children €1.80. Tours 10, 11am, noon, 2, 3, 4pm. 20min. concerts May-Oct. Su-M and W-F 2:30pm; €2.40. Tour and concert together €6.80.)

The abbey of St. Florian, 17km from Linz, is Austria's oldest Augustinian monastery. According to legend, the martyr Florian was bound to a millstone and thrown in the Enns river. Although Florian perished, his stone miraculously floated and now serves as the abbey's cornerstone. The complex owes much of its fame to composer Anton Bruckner, who began his career here first as a choirboy, then as a teacher, and finally as a virtuoso organist and composer. His body is interred beneath the organ inside the spectacular, recently renovated church (the only part of the abbey accessible without a tour), allowing him to vibrate in perpetuity to the sound of his dearly-beloved pipes. The abbey contains the **Altdorfer Gallery,** filled with altarpieces by 15th-century artist Albrecht Altdorfer of Regensburg, an Old Master of the Danube school. Although they are works of art with balanced compositions and warm tones, these paintings also contain a political agenda. Notice that Altdorfer paints some of Christ's tormentors as Turks, the sworn enemies of the Austrian Empire. The 14 **Kaiserzimmer** (imperial rooms), built in case of an imperial visit, overwhelm visitors with Baroque splendor.

Salzkammergut

THE MÜHLVIERTEL

Stretching north and west from Linz, the Mühlviertel's shaded woodland paths and pastures are an increasingly popular hiking area. The region was once the stomping ground of the Celts, but in the Middle Ages Christians constructed churches out of supposedly Celt-proof local granite. This same granite filters mineral-rich waters and hot springs of the region, considered curative by some.

Along the old **Mühlviertel Weberstraße** (Weaver's Road), textile-oriented towns display their methods of linen preparation. The **Gotischestraße,** which winds past numerous examples of High Gothic architecture, and the **Museumstraße,** with numerous **Freilichtmuseen** (open-air museums). Poppies *(Mohn)* are another of the Mühlviertel's big selling points: products range from poppy seed oil to mouthwatering poppy seed strudels. Throughout this pastoral countryside, *Bauernhöfe* (farm houses) open their doors to world-weary travelers. Contact the **Mühlviertel Tourist Office** for brochures detailing trails and *Bauernhöfe*. (Blütenstr. 8, Linz. ☎0732 73 50 20; www.tiscover.com/muehlviertel.)

FREISTADT ☎07942

Freistadt, the largest town in the Mühlviertel, is an idyllic, compact village at the juncture of the **Jaunitz** and **Feldiast** rivers. Due to its strategic location on the Pferdeeisenbahn route, which connected the Babenberg and Hapsburg lands, Freistadt was a stronghold of the medieval salt and iron trade. Freistadt's pride and joy is the **Freistädter Brauerei,** a community-owned brewery that is still in operation but, unfortunately, no longer open to the public.

⌨🕿 TRANSPORTATION & PRACTICAL INFORMATION. Freistadt is accessible from Linz. The **Post Bus** leaves from Linz's main train station (1hr., every 1½hr. 6:20am-8:15pm, €5.80) and arrives at Böhmertor in Freistadt, just outside the old city walls. **Trains** also run from Linz (40min., 5:59am-6:59pm, €5.80), but they arrive 3km outside of town at the Hauptbahnhof, and require a taxi (€10). The tiny **tourist office,** Hauptpl. 14, has a free reservation service and provides info about nearby villages. (☎757 00; fax 757 00 20. Open May-Oct. M-F 9am-7pm, Sa 9am-noon; Oct.-Apr. M-F 9am-5pm). The **post office** is located on Promenade 11 at St. Peterstr. (Open M-F 8am-noon and 2-5:30pm, Sa 8-10:30am). **Postal code:** A-4240.

🕿⌂ ACCOMMODATIONS & FOOD. The **Jugendherberge "Speicher" (HI) ❶,** Schloßhof 3, is a walk around the corner from the tourist office to the red building next to Café Lubinger. Hand-painted stripes and silly cartoons decorate the walls, and the rooms are comfortable. There is also a roller skating rink. The proprietress, Margarete Hawel, will wait from 6-8pm to give you a key. If you don't arrive in time, call ☎732 68. (☎743 65. Breakfast and sheets €2.18 each. Hall showers and toilets. Kitchen facilities in youth center below. Call to let them know you're coming. Dorms €6, non-members €8.)

There are plenty of inexpensive meals in this budget-friendly town. **Café Vis à Vis ❷,** Salzg. 13, offers the local *Mühlviertler Bauernsalat* (farmer's salad; €5.30), and local *Freistädter* beer (€3.20). (☎742 93. Open M-F 9am-2am, Sa 5pm-2am.) Food is easy to find on Hauptpl. as well. The best ice cream in Freistadt is at **Café Lubinger ❶,** Hauptpl. 10 (soft-serve €1, scoops €0.60, less for each additional scoop). Pastries (€1.80) and a great breakfast selection round out the menu. (Open Su-M and W-Sa 8am-5pm.) The most convenient grocery store is **Uni Markt,** Pragerstr. 2, at Froschau behind the Böhmertor side of the *Innere Stadt.* (Open M-F 8am-6:30pm, Sa 7:30am-5pm.)

◪ SIGHTS. Wander around Freistadt's inner and outer fortifications and scan the horizon from its watch tower. The moat is gradually being drained and filled with grass to form a belt-like park around the town. Pick up *A Walk Through the Old Quarter* at the tourist office. The tower of Freistadt's remarkable 14th-century **Bergfried** houses the **Mühlviertler Schloßmuseum Freistadt,** Schloßhof 2, a regional museum that displays traditional tools and period pieces. (☎722 74. Admission with tour only; May-Oct. M-F 9, 10:30am, 2, 3:30pm; Sa 10:30am, 2pm; Su 2pm. Nov.-Apr. M-F 10:30am, 2pm; Sa-Su 2pm. €2.40.)

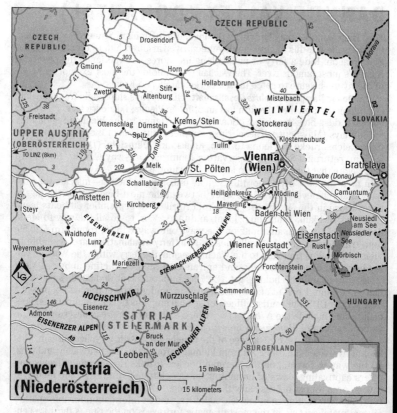

LOWER AUSTRIA
(NIEDERÖSTERREICH)

Surrounding Vienna, the province of Niederösterreich accounts for a quarter of Austria's land mass and 60% of its wine production. Castle ruins lie in the hills above medieval towns, while hikers and bikers enjoy the varied terrain, usually on daytrips from Vienna. The region's food provides another reason to visit: one local specialty, the Wienerwald cream strudel, is a sinful mixture of flaky crust, curds, raisins, and lemon peel.

HIGHLIGHTS OF LOWER AUSTRIA

Climb up to the ruins of Richard the Lionheart's prison, **Schloß Dürnstein** (see p. 308).

Marvel at **Melk's** big beautiful yellow Benedictine abbey (see p. 308).

Smell the roses, all 20,000 of them, in **Baden bei Wien's** rosarium (see p. 314).

DANUBE VALLEY (DONAUTAL)

The "Blue Danube" may largely be the invention of Johann Strauss's imagination, but the valley of this mighty, muddy-green river inspired him to create music for good reason. Ride a ferry or pedal along its shores to experience the beauty of Austria's most famous river. The **Wachau** region holds the most exemplary bends of the river—be sure to catch those between Melk and Krems.

The **Donau Dampfschifffahrts-Gesellschaft** (DDSG) runs ships daily from May-late Oct. along the Danube. The firm has an office in **Vienna,** I, Friedrichstr. 7. (☎58 88 00; www.ddsg-blue-danube.at.) Boats go from Vienna to the Wachau region only on Sundays (May-Sept.). These trips, complete with didactic commentary, run from Reichsbrücke in Vienna to **Tulln, Krems,** and **Dürnstein.** (Departing Vienna 8:45am, returning 8:45pm. Reservation required. One-way €16.50, round-trip €22). Note that they don't go to **Melk** and its monastery.

In fact, the best trip is not this Sunday cruise from Vienna—instead, take the ferry that runs every day of the week between the most beautiful towns on the river, those in the Wachau region. From April 30 to September 30 boats leave Krems at 10:15am, 1pm, and 3:45pm, and take 2¾hr. to go all the way to Melk, docking at Dürnstein and Spitz on the way (one-way €15.50, round-trip €20.50; bike transport is free but call ahead). **Rail/ferry combinations** are available in Vienna, including train fare to the Wachau region, the ferry within the Wachau valley between Krems and Melk, and entrance to the Benedictine abbey of Melk (€40). Eurail and ISIC holders get a 20% discount on travel, and families travel for half-price (min. 1 parent and 1 child ages 6-15; under 6 travel free with a parent). Contact the DDSG or tourist offices for special ship/bus ticket combinations. Specialty tours include the *Nibelungen,* which sails through areas described in the ancient saga and a *Heurigen* ride with a live *Liederabend* (evening song) trio.

Bicyclists should take advantage of the **Danube Cycle Path,** a cyclist's dream. This 305km riverside bike trail goes from Vienna, through the Wachau Valley and Linz, all the way to Passau, on the German border. It links the Danube villages and offers captivating views of crumbling castles, latticed vineyards, and medieval towns. Area tourist offices carry the route map. There is also information on the route at www.radtouren.at/english. Ask local tourist information for information on renting bikes. One of the most dramatic fortresses on the ride is the 13th-century **Burg Aggstein-Gastein,** formerly inhabited by Scheck von Wald, a robber-baron known to fearful sailors as **Schreckenwalder** (the terror of the woods).

KREMS & STEIN ☎02732

At the head of the Wachau region, the neighboring towns of Krems and Stein are surrounded by lush, green hills covered with terraced vineyards. Historically, Krems and Stein have shared a mayor to coordinate trade and military strategy on the Danube trading route, and through the years the towns have grown into each other's territories. Much of the region's wealth came from the tolls on this riverbend's traders—the Kremser Penny was the first coin minted by the Hapsburgs.

The stuccoed walls of Krems have pastel charm in a comparatively modern, shop-filled *Fußgängerzone.* Although Krems holds most of the sights, from art exhibits to sporting events, Stein has a gorgeous *Altstadt.* Its crooked, narrow, cobblestone passages twist and wind back on themselves, giving it an old-world feel. In the valley around the towns, vineyards produce 120 different wines. Head for **Steiner Kellergasse,** the high street in Stein, where *Heurigen* offer the local wines and great views of the **Stift Göttweig** (abbey) across the Danube. Tour buses often block the entrance to this street leading to the *Heurigen*—rich wine and the impressive panorama of the valley make it worthwhile for every tourist.

LITTLE OLD LADIES Lower Austria is packed not only with yellow remnants of the Hapsburg days, but also with a few reminders of prehistoric times. Krems is one of Austria's top archaeology centers, and its researchers have recently unearthed the remains of a 32,000-year-old hunting community settled in the Danube bend near a place now named Galgenberg. Among the usual shards of bone and clay animal figurines, archaeologists excavated eight pieces of slate which, when fitted together, form a well-endowed female statuette. Fanny von Galgenberg, named for the famous dancer Fanny Elßler, is Austria's oldest known work of art and the world's only known female sculpture from the Aurigae Period. Barely three inches tall and half an inch thick, the figure is engraved with sketches and positioned in a pose that classifies her as part of the archetypal prehistoric Venus figures, like her much younger sister and symbol of fertility, the *Venus of Willendorf*, who was found between Krems and Melk.

⌐ TRANSPORTATION

Many visitors arrive on bicycles, but the **train station** is a 5min. walk from Krems's *Fußgängerzone*. To get to the *Fußgängerzone*, exit through the front door of the Bahnhof, cross Ringstr., and follow Dinstlstr. Regional trains connect Krems to Vienna (Spittelau station; €11.50, 5:05am-10:05pm) via Tulln. A **bus depot** is in front of the station. Both buses and trains leave every 30min. for routes to Melk and St. Pölten. Krems lies along the **DDSG ferry** route from Passau through Linz and Melk to Vienna (see p. 308). The ferry station is on the riverbank close to Stein and the ÖAMTC campground, near the intersection of Donaulände and Dr.-Karl-Dorreck-Str. To reach Krems from the landing, walk down Donaulände, which becomes Ringstr., then left onto Utzstr. To reach Stein, follow Dr.-Karl-Dorreck-Str. and then take a left onto Steiner Landstr.

❋🛈 ORIENTATION & PRACTICAL INFORMATION

Stein is west of Krems, bracketed by Steiner Kellerg. and Steiner Landstr. The **tourist office** is housed in the Kloster Und at Undstr. 6. From the train station, take a left on Ringstr. and continue (15min.) to Martin-Schmidt-Str. Turn right and follow the street to the end; the office is across the street and to the right. The staff has information on accommodations, sports, and entertainment, as well as the indispensable *Heurigen Kalender*, which lists the opening times of regional wine taverns. Discmans are provided for self-guided walking tours (€6) and group guided walking tours in several languages leave for Krems or Stein. (1½hr.; €52 per group or €2.50 per person for groups larger than 20.) They also book hotel reservations. (☎826 76; fax 700 11; www.tiscover.com/krems. Open Easter-Oct. M-F 8:30am-6:30pm, Sa 10am-noon and 1-6pm, Su 10am-noon and 1-4pm; Nov.-Easter M-F 9am-6pm.) **ATMs** are along shopping streets. **Lockers** (€2) are at the train station. **Bike rental** is at **Radstudio Krems**, Hafnerpl. 5 (☎/fax 818 80. Open M-F 8am-noon and 1:30-6pm, Sa 8:30am-noon; €11 per day), and at **R&R**, Steiner Landstr. 103. (☎710 71. €10 per day.) **Public toilets** are at the train station, tourist office, and in the *Stadtpark*. **Currency exchange** is at the **post office** right off Ringstr. on Brandströmstr. (☎826 06. Open M-F 8am-noon and 2-6pm, Sa 8-11am.) **Postal code:** A-3500.

♜ ACCOMMODATIONS

No matter where you stay, ask your hosts for a **guest card** that grants a number of discounts. *Privatzimmer* are available on Steiner Landstr.

Radfahrjugendherberge (HI), Ringstr. 77 (☎834 52; oejhv.noe.krems@aon.at). Walk away from the tourist office and continue down Martin-J-Schmidt-Str. until making a left onto Ringstr. The hostel is clean and close-quartered, accommodating 52 in comfortable 4- and 6-bed rooms. Appropriately, it is packed with bicycling enthusiasts. Breakfast, lockers, sheets, and bicycle storage included. Reception 7-9:30am and 5-8pm. For advance bookings, call the central office in Vienna (☎533 53 53; fax 535 08 61). Open Apr.-Oct. Dorms €12.20; non-members pay €3.50 extra. €2.20 surcharge on stays less than 3 nights. Tax included. ❷

Baroque Bürgerhaus, Untere Landstr. 53 (☎/fax 761 84 or 740 36), in Krems's *Altstadt,* is filled with *Jugendstil* furniture and hand-painted wood. Open mid-June to mid-Sept. 2- and 3-bed dorms with shower €20. 3 nights or more €8 per person. Low-season €11/€7. 30% discount for children under 10. ❸

Hotel-Restaurant "Alte Post," Obere Landstr. 32 (☎822 76; fax 843 96). although more costly, Krem's oldest guest house will host you amid its dark velvet couches, embroidered curtains, and garden café. Rooms are medium sized. Breakfast included. Singles €27, with shower €47; doubles €50-70. ❹

ÖAMTC Donau Camping, Wiedeng. 7 (☎844 55), is on the grassy Danube riverbank near the highway. Located a 7min. walk from tennis courts, swimming pools, and a lake. Showers included. Special facilities for disabled guests. Reception 7:30-10am and 4:30-7pm. Open Easter to mid-Oct. €3.65 plus €0.76 tax, children €2.54. Tent spots €2.18-4.36; bring your own tent. Cars €3.65. Electricity €1.82. ❶

🍴 FOOD

The area around Krems's *Fußgängerzone* overflows with restaurants and streetside cafés. There are two **SPAR** markets one block from the train station on f Sparkasseng. and Obere Landstr. (Open M-F 7:15am-6:30pm, Sa until 5pm.)

Heuriger Hamböck, Steiner Kellerg. 31 (☎845 68), has a leafy terrace with a view of the town's spires and a restaurant decorated with old *Fässchen* (kegs), presses, and other vineyard tools. The owner gives free tours of the cellar, including a wine tasting. Wine starts at €1.50; snacks are €2.80-4. For a fragrant experience, try the sweet apricot and raspberry wine (€1). Open daily 3pm until everyone leaves. ❶

Café-Konditorei Hagmann, Untere Landstr. 8 (☎831 67), is known in Krems for its outstanding pastries and chocolates. Try the *Schokotorte* (€2.40) with a *Mokka* (€3) or grab a *Wachauer Kugel* (ball of chocolate and nougat; €0.80) for the road. Open M-Sa 7am-7pm, Su 1:30-6pm. ❶

Schwarze Kuchl (☎831 28), right next door to Hagmann, offers a salad buffet (small €2.76, large €4) and assorted goulashes (€3.56-6.40) in a pleasant, homey interior. Open M-F 8:30am-7:30pm, Sa 8:30am-5pm. ❷

Café Pizzini, Spänglerg. 4, serves pizza (€2.10) and other inexpensive Italian delicacies amid modern funky decor not often seen in the Wachau region. Open M-F 10am-7:30pm, Sa 10am-4pm. ❶

China Restaurant Tai-Yang, Obere Landstr. 5 (☎841 83), offers cheap, filling food at lightning speed. The lunch *Menü* (soup and entree with rice; €4.60) is popular with the tourist crowd. Open 11:30am-2:30pm and 5:30-11:30pm. AmEx/MC/V. ❷

👁 SIGHTS & ENTERTAINMENT

THE OLD TOWN. In Stein, medieval buildings line **Steiner Landstraße,** and stone steps tucked between houses lead to impressive views of the town and valley. Krems's *Fußgängerzone,* the center of mercantile activity, consists of Obere and Untere Landstr. The entrance to the pedestrian area is marked by the Steiner Tor; this section of town is a great place to meander past the city's architectural treasures. Markets line Obere Landstr., starting in Dominikanerpl., home of the **Dominikanerkirche,** now the Weinstadt Museum (see below). Farther down the pedestrian zone is **Pfarrkirche Platz,** home of the Renaissance **Rathaus** and the **Pfarrkirche,** with its piecemeal Romanesque, Gothic, and Baroque architecture. Once there, walk up the hill to the **Piaristenkirche** to see life-sized depictions of Jesus' crucifixion. At the end of the pedestrian zone stands the **Simandlbrunnen,** a fountain depicting a husband kneeling in front of his stern wife. The fountain commemorates the power and influence of women in Krems during the Renaissance, when they succeeded in shutting down the Simandl brotherhood, a fraternity of carousing and late-night debauchery.

KUNSTHALLE KREMS. Kunsthalle Krems has recently opened a new facility on the corner of Steiner Landstr. and Dr.-Karl-Dorreck-Str. The enormous exhibition hall has fascinating cultural and historical exhibits on rotation, often about postmodern or non-European art. Much of the art on display consists of caricatures and satire. (*Steiner Landstr. 3a. ☎ 90 80 10; www.karikaturmuseum.at. Wheelchair-accessible. Open daily 10am-6pm. €7.50, students and seniors €3.50.*)

WEINSTADT MUSEUM. Built in the Dominikanerkloster, the excellent Weinstadt Museum in Krems features a combination of paintings by the world-renowned Baroque artist Martin Johann Schmidt and, in the cloister cellars, archaeological treasures from the Paleolithic Era through the Middle Ages. The changing exhibits cover subjects ranging from local folklore to apocalyptic art. (*Körnermarkt 14. ☎ 80 15 67 or 80 15 72; fax 80 15 76. Open Mar.-Nov. Tu-Su 10am-6pm. €3.60, students and seniors €2.50.*)

> # HOLDING A GRUDGE
> Upon arrival in the Holy Land during the Third Crusade, England's King Richard the Lionheart threw the Austrian flag to the ground, deeply offending Leopold V, Duke of Austria. Needless to say, when the Holy Roman Emperor was short of cash and ordered Richard captured, Leopold was happy to help out. Richard's ship was wrecked en route to England, and he was forced to cross Austria. Despite his clever disguise (as a peasant), Leopold's men recognized him and locked him up in Dürnstein (giving Robin Hood time to flourish under evil Prince John). A legend arose in the 13th century about how Richard was found: Richard's faithful minstrel Blondel wandered through Austria, looking for his master by whistling a tune they had composed together. When the minstrel got to Dürnstein, Richard heard him whistling and whistled back the refrain. England sent representatives with 100,000 Marks for Richard's ransom, of which Leopold garnered 75,000. The pope excommunicated Leopold for imprisoning Richard, but Leopold consoled himself by building (among other things) the town of Wiener Neustadt with his new fortune.

WINE CELLARS. The **Heurigen** (wine cellars) are not to be missed. Plan carefully, however—they are only allowed to stay open for three weeks every two months from April to October. If you don't have time for any *Heurigen,* stop by the city-owned **Weingut Stadt Krems,** on the edge of the pedestrian zone. This winery lacks an attached restaurant, but it does offer free tours of the cellar and bottling center. The tastings after the tour usually seduce visitors into buying wine. (*Stadtgraben 11. Go to the end of Obere Landstr., through the gate, and to the right. ☎ 80 14 40; www.weingutstadtkrems.at. Open for tours M-F 8am-noon and 1-5pm, Sa 8am-5pm.*)

FESTIVALS. Krems is a happening festival town, celebrating everything from apricots to wine. Check with the tourist office for exhaustive info. Each year the **Donaufestival,** from mid-June to early July, brings open-air music and dancing, kicking off a summer of cultural activities including theater, circus, symposia, folk music, and even Korean drumming. From July 15 to August 15, Krems hosts a **Musikfest,** featuring a number of organ, piano, and quartet concerts in the Kunsthalle and various churches. Tickets are available at the tourist office. From late August to early November, Krems hosts the **Weinherbst,** which features wine tastings, culinary specialties, presentations, and folklore.

▶ DAYTRIP FROM KREMS

DÜRNSTEIN

Trains connect Dürnstein to Krems (20min., every hr. 6am-7pm, €1.89) and Vienna's Franz Josef Bahnhof (1hr. 15min., every 2hr., €10.68). To reach town, descend the hill, turn right, and pass through the underground walkway (5min.). Boats dock at the DDSG ferry station on the Donaupromenade, a riverside road with beaches and bike paths. To reach town, turn right on Donaupromenade and left on Anzugg., which intersects with Hauptstr.

Located a bend or two down the Danube from Krems, among deep green vineyards, this hilltop medieval village attracts tourists and locals alike with its mythical charm. A main draw is the hike up to the ruined castle where **Richard the Lionheart** was imprisoned after his capture on the way back from the Third Crusade in 1192 (see "Holding a Grudge," p. 207).

The relocated **tourist office** is in the same building as the Nah & Frisch grocery store. From the station turn right at the bottom of the hill; the green "i" is on the right. The office and the *Rathaus* (on Hauptstr.) provide lists of *Privatzimmer* and open *Heurigen.* (☎027 200; www.duernstein.at. Open M-Sa noon-7pm.)

Although Richard's capture was the last hurrah for the local Kuenringer dynasty, they continued to prosper on their home turf, building **Schloß Dürnstein.** This Baroque abbey, commissioned by the daughter of the penultimate heir to the throne in 1372, was dedicated to the Virgin Mary. Joseph II dissolved it at the same time he dismantled most of Austria's ecclesiastical institutions, but it has been well maintained nevertheless. You'll get mesmerizing views from the blue and white church steeple. Skeletons guard the elegant interior of the church from all sides. (Apr. 1-Oct. 31 ☎02711 375, Nov. 1-Mar. 31 ☎02711 227; fax 02711 432 yearround. Open Apr.-Oct. daily 9am-6pm. €2.20, with tour €3.65, tour for students €3.25 including free glass of wine on Th.)

MELK ☎02752

The sight of Melk's yellow monastery towering over the countryside is one of the most striking sights in Austria. The monastery was constructed in AD 994 as a Babenberg residence, but eventually it became the Benedictine monastery around which Melk formed. The monastery was renowned in the medieval world for its monumental library and learned monks; today, it is one of few ecclesiastical institutions that report directly to the Pope, with no bishop as middle-man. Below the abbey, the tiny town is a jumble of Renaissance houses, narrow pedestrian zones, cobblestone streets, old towers, and remnants of the medieval city wall.

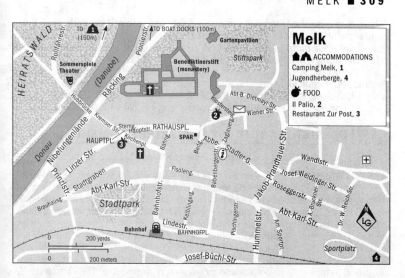

Melk

▲⛺ ACCOMMODATIONS
Camping Melk, **1**
Jugendherberge, **4**

🍴 FOOD
Il Palio, **2**
Restaurant Zur Post, **3**

🚃🛈 TRANSPORTATION & PRACTICAL INFORMATION

Trains link Melk to Vienna's Westbahnhof (1½hr., €12) via St. Pölten. Just outside the station's main entrance is the **bus depot**. Bus #1451 runs (slowly; 2hr.) from Melk to Krems (€6) and #1538 from Melk to St. Pölten (€3.30). Melk is at the end of the **DDSG ferry** route between Vienna and Passau (from Krems €15.50, round-trip €20.50; see p. 308). The **tourist office,** Babenbergstr. 1, has large **lockers** (€1) and bike racks, and makes free room reservations. (☎52 30 74 10; www.tidiscover.com/melk. Open May-June M-F 9am-noon and 2-6pm, Sa-Su 10am-noon and 4-6pm; July-Aug. M-Sa 9am-7pm, Su 10am-noon and 5-7pm; Sept. M-F 9am-noon and 2-6pm, Sa-Su 10am-noon and 4-6pm; Oct. M-F 9am-noon and 2-5pm, Sa 10am-noon.) **Currency exchange** and **luggage storage** (€3.50) are available at the train station. **Bicycle rental** is at Hotel zur Post, Linzerstr. 1. (☎523 44. €10 per day, €7 after 3pm.) The **pharmacy Landschaftsapotheke,** Rathauspl. 10, is next to the town hall. (☎235 15. Open M-F 8am-noon and 2-6pm, Su 8am-noon.) The **post office** is at Wienerstr. 85. (Open M-F 8am-noon and 2-6pm.) **Postal code:** A-3390.

🏠🍴 ACCOMMODATIONS & FOOD

To soak up the cozy atmosphere of Melk, stay in a *Pension, Privatzimmer,* or on a country farm (generally €12.50-26). There is a list at the tourist office. The **Jugendherberge ❷,** Abt-Karl-Str. 42, is 10min. from the train station. This clean hostel offers 104 beds in quads with private showers and hall toilets. Caters to bikers, families and school groups. (☎526 81; fax 542 57. Breakfast and bicycle storage included. Reception 8-10am and 5-9pm. Open Apr.-Oct. Dorms €12.66 including tax; 19 and under €9.90. €3 for non-members. €1.85 extra per night for stays less than 4 nights.) **Camping Melk ❶** overlooks the Danube next to the ferry landing. Walk on Rollfährestr for 20min. to get there. (☎532 91. Reception 8am-midnight. €2.60 per person; tents €2.60; cars €1.90. Showers €1.10. Tax €0.80.)

The vast majority of the restaurants and cafés are located on Rathauspl. Substantial meals can be found at **Restaurant Zur Post ❸,** Linzer Str. 1, whose bright yellow outdoor patio is full of relaxed locals and vacationers. Dishes include fried chicken (€10.20), and beef roast with onions (€11.20). (☎523 45. Open daily 10am-11pm.) Black lacquered wood and faux-Italian decor greet you at **Il Palio ❶,** Wienerstr. 3, home of fantastic ice cream concoctions. (☎525 10. Open daily 10am-close.) Stock up on food at **SPAR Markt,** Rathauspl. 9. (Open M-F 7am-6pm, Sa 7am-5pm.) There's an open-air **market** every W 8am-4pm on Rathauspl.

👁 🏔 🎵 SIGHTS, OUTDOORS, & ENTERTAINMENT

Melk's prime attraction is the impressive **Benediktinerstift** (Benedictine abbey).

BENEDIKTINERSTIFT. The monastery is huge—the secular wing alone was large enough to house Maria Theresia and her coterie of 300 on visits from Vienna. Today, this wing is filled with exhibits (mostly in German) and various Baroque optical tricks, including a portrait of Leopold II whose eyes follow you around the room and a flat ceiling that appears to be a dome when viewed directly beneath its center. The stunning library in the opposite wing is brimming with sacred and secular texts painstakingly hand-copied by monks. The two highest shelves in the gallery are fake—in typical Baroque fashion, the monks sketched book spines onto the wood to make the collection appear even more impressive. The church itself, maintained by 20 monks, is a Baroque masterpiece. Maria Theresia donated the

---

HIDDEN TREASURE The crown jewel of Melk's Benediktinerstift is unquestionably the Melker Kreuz, a bejeweled and gilded cross that contains a splinter believed to be a tiny fragment of the cross upon which Jesus was crucified. Crafted in 1363, the cross is two-faced: the "wealthy" side sparkles with diamonds, rubies, emeralds, and freshwater pearls from the Danube, while the "sacred" side depicts the crucified Christ and the four Evangelists at each of its rounded points. On two occasions, the cross has been stolen from the monastery, but each time has made its way back to the abbey by supernatural means (once by sailing itself back on a boat). Legend has it that anyone who opens the cross to look at the relic will be blinded by the holiness of the sight. For those brave (or foolish) enough to try, the cross can only be opened by simultaneously turning the aquamarine stones at the four corners of the cross.

---

two skeletons that adorn the side altars. They are unknown refugees from the catacombs of Rome, lounging in jeweled, embroidered outfits and thin veils over their gaping sockets. The greatest treasure of the monastery is the AD 1363 *Melker Kreuz* (Melk Cross), decorated with gold and jewels (see "Hidden Treasure," p. 310). The monks curate temporary exhibits of contemporary art. They even commissioned artist Peter Bischof to create new murals over weather-ruined frescoes in the interior of the main courtyard. You can also visit the monastery's small garden with its delicate pavilion containing frescoes of imaginary far-off jungles. (☎555 232. Open daily May-Sept. 9am-6pm; Oct. to early Apr. 9am-5pm. Tours 11am, 2pm; last entry 1hr. before closing. English guide book €3.50. Guided tours daily in German Nov.-Mar. every hr.; in English 3pm or by arrangement. €6.90, students €4.10, tour €1.60 extra; €1.09 extra for garden when combined with Stift.)

SCHLOß SCHALLBURG. 5km out of town is **Schloß Schallburg,** one of Austria's only well-preserved Romanesque castles. Romanesque, Gothic, Renaissance, and Mannerist influences converge in the terra-cotta arcades of the main courtyard. (☎02754 63 17. Open May-Oct. M-F 9am-5pm; Sa, Su, and holidays until 6pm. €6.50, students

€2.90. Call ahead for a tour.) The castle doubles as the **International Exhibition Center of Lower Austria,** which brings foreign cultures to life. In 2004, the main exhibit will focus on the political, artistic, and cultural histories of China. There is also a display on 100 years of Austrian radio and a small toy exhibit. (☎ 63 17. Exhibits in German. Shuttles leave Melk's train station daily 8:50, 9:40am, 1:15, 4:20pm. Return shuttles run 9:10, 9:55am, 1:30, and 4:30pm. Each way 15min., €2.50, students €1.50. You can also take 2hr. to hike to the complex; ask the tourist office for a map .)

OUTDOOR ACTIVITIES. A network of **hiking** trails winds through the wooded groves of the Wachau region. The tourist office provides a map that lists sights, paths, and information on the 10km Leo Böck trail, 6km Seniorenweg, and 15km Schallburggrundweg. **Cyclists** tour the Danube toward Willendorf on a former canal-towing path; the 30,000-year-old **Venus of Willendorf** is a voluptuous 11cm stone figure and one of the world's most famous fertility symbols, discovered there in 1908 (see "Little Old Ladies," p. 305). For a more sedate option, **ferries** travel across the Danube to **Spitz** and **Dürnstein,** for the local *Jause* (an Austrian version of British high tea). The returning ferry passes the **Heiratswald** (Marriage Woods)—Melk awards couples who marry here with a young sapling tree.

SOMMERSPIELE. The **Sommerspiele Melk** (Melk Summer Festival) comes to town from mid-July through mid-Aug. An open-air stage across the arm of the Danube provides the perfect setting for enjoying world-class theater (in German) on summer nights. Tickets are available at the Melk tourist office. (www.sommerspiele-melk.at. Performances mid-July to mid-Aug. Th-Sa 8:30pm. Tickets €17-35.)

ST. PÖLTEN ☎ 02742

St. Pölten (pop. 50,030) is worth a visit, even though it doesn't lie on the Danube. Its industrial heritage would hamper its present bid for tourism, if not for its shopping-oriented Baroque *Altstadt,* turn-of-the-century *Jugendstil* buildings, and the interesting modern architecture that has surfaced in recent years.

🛇🛈 TRANSPORTATION & PRACTICAL INFORMATION. The **train station,** on Bahnhofpl., sends trains to Vienna Westbahnhof (45 min., 3 per hr., €8). The **tourist office** is on Rathauspl. 1 at the end of Rathausg. They provide a list of accommodations, lead 1hr. **tours** of the inner city (call up to a week in advance), and rent **cassette tours** in several languages for €1.45. (☎ 35 33 54; www.st-poelten.gv.at. Open Nov.-Mar. daily M-F 8am-5pm; Apr.-Oct. M-F 8am-5pm, Sa 9am-5pm, Su and holidays 10am-5pm.) There is a free reservation phone just across Rathausg. from the tourist office. Other services include: **currency exchange** at **Bank Austria,** Rathauspl. 2 (☎ 549 19; fax 545 75); **bike rental** at the tourist office (€9.55 per day); 24hr. **lockers** at the train station (€3). **Internet access** is available at **M@trix,** Rennbahnstr. 29, at the edge of the Regierungsviertel. (☎ 22 640. Open M-Sa 10am-midnight. €0.07 per min.) The main **post office** is located at Daniel-Gran-Str. 13. (Open M-F 7am-8pm, Sa 7am-1pm.) **Postal code:** A-3100.

🛏🍴 ACCOMMODATIONS & FOOD. St. Pölten works well as a day trip, especially since the town does not have a youth hostel. You might consider staying in the hostels in **Krems** (see p. 304), **Melk** (see p. 308), or **Vienna** (see p. 89). The tourist office maintains a list of *Pensionen* and *Privatzimmer,* most of which are outside the city limits. If you're willing to spend a little money, there are some good options in town. The **Mariazellerhof ❸,** Mariazellerstr. 6, is just south of the Europapl. The hotel is the pink and blue building at the beginning of Mariazellerstr. (☎ 769 95; fax 769 958. Breakfast included. Reception M-Th 7am-9pm, F-Su 7-10am and 4-9pm. Singles €33-42; doubles €52-64.) **Stadthotel Hauser-Eck ❹,** Schulg.

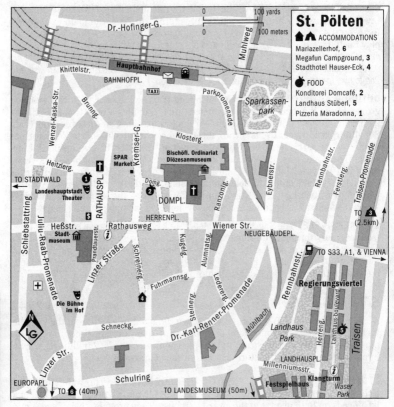

St. Pölten

🏠🏔 ACCOMMODATIONS
Mariazellerhof, **6**
Megafun Campground, **3**
Stadthotel Hauser-Eck, **4**

🍓 FOOD
Konditorei Domcafé, **2**
Landhaus Stüberl, **5**
Pizzeria Maradonna, **1**

LOWER AUSTRIA

2, in the pedestrian zone, is a green Art Nouveau building offering spacious rooms with floor-to-ceiling curtains, TVs, minibars, and sofas. (☎733 36; vfax 783 86; www.hausereck.at. Breakfast included. Singles €35-45; doubles €60-74. V.) The campsite **Megafun ❶**, Am Ratzersdorfer See, is on a small lake outside of town. Take bus #4, which leaves across the street from the train station, to "Unter-ratzersdorf Schule" (15min., every 30min., 5:45am-6:45pm, €1.50). Go down Ratzersdorfer Hauptstr., take a left onto Fritschstr. As it curves to the left, take a right onto E.-Werk-Weg, continue until you cross the stream, then turn left onto Bimbo-Binder-Promenade. The campground will be on your right (10min.) (☎25 15 10; fax 251 51 01 18. Reception 6am-midnight. €5 per person, children €2, RVs €5.50; tent €2.50; car €2. Tax €0.75 per person per night.)

St. Pölten's local specialties include oysters, fried black pudding, and savory Wachau wine. **Pizzerria Maradonna ❷**, Rathauspl./Heitzerlerg. 1, is tucked between the Stadttheater and the Franziskanerkirche. Enjoy one of the pasta dishes (€5.40-7.10) or their pizza *Menü* (€5.80) in a quiet corner of the square. (☎35 21 92. Open M-Tu 11:30am-2pm, W-Su 11:30am-2pm and 5:30-11pm.) The **Landhaus Stüberl ❷**, Landhausstr. 27, in the new government quarter, offers a great view of the Landtagschiff from its outdoor patio, and serves dishes like paella (€6.20), tacos (€5.90), and Greek salad (€4.50). (☎255 24. Open M-F 8am-10pm, Sa 9am-10pm, Su 9am-3pm.) **Konditorei Domcafé ❶**, Domg. 8, features fruit frappes (€2.60), salad buffet (small €2.80, large €4.35), and small pastries (€1.35-2.45). Eat in the popular outdoor seating area. (☎35 23 22. Open M-F 7am-7pm, Sa 7am-6pm.) There is a **SPAR** supermarket on Kremserg. 21. (Open M-F 7:30am-6:30pm, Sa 7:30am-5pm.)

◳ **SIGHTS.** The 13th-century **Rathausplatz** in the heart of St. Pölten was built on the site of a first-century Roman settlement. The building at Rathausg. 2 earned the name **Schubert Haus** due to Franz's frequent visits to the owners. A neo-Grecian Schubert likeness conducts above the door. Pass Dr. Karl-Renner-Promenade to see the only *Jugendstil* (Art Nouveau) **synagogue** in Lower Austria. Josef Maria Olbrich also designed a few other *Jugendstil* buildings in the *Altstadt*.

Herrenplatz has witnessed centuries of haggling at St. Pölten's daily market, inspiring the fountain *The Gossiping Woman*. Narrow alleys just after Wienerstr. 29, Herrenpl., and Domg. all lead to **Domplatz.** The remains of the Roman settlement of Aelium were discovered here when sewer installers tripped over Roman hypocausts (ancient floor heating systems). St. Pölten's **Dom** (cathedral) is still intact. It features gilded accents, which were added to transform the original Roman basilica into a Baroque church. (Open daily until 6pm. Free.)

The **Landesmuseum** ("Shedhalle"), Franz-Schubert-Platz 5, is St. Pölten's most interesting museum. Fascinating displays deal with the history, art, and nature of Lower Austria. Although small, the museum's exhibits have a well-presented modern feel. (☎908 09 01 00, fax 90 80 99. Open Tu-Sa 10am-5pm. Tours Sa, Su, holidays 11am, noon, 4pm; €2. Call ahead for tours in English. €7, students €5.) Also check out the **Stadtmuseum,** Prandtauerstr. 2, which has a thorough collection detailing St. Pölten's history, from pre-Roman times to the present. Its great attraction is its collection of elegant Art Nouveau paintings. (☎333 26 43 or 333 26 01. Open Tu-Sa 10am-5pm. €2, students €1.)

The **Regierungsviertel** (government quarter) is a futuristic collection of minimalist-style buildings. Its centerpiece is the Landtagschiff, a semi-circular building on the Traisen River. The lofty **Klangturm** (sound tower) was intended to provide contrast to the horizontal sweep of the other buildings. A viewing area at the top of the 80m high monolith is accessible by elevator (€1). The **Festspielhaus theater** and the interesting modern art give the area a lively atmosphere. Facing the solid rear wall of building 1a is Hans Kupelwieser's *Hohlkopfwand*, an array of several dozen identical silver heads stacked into rows.

◳ **ENTERTAINMENT. Die Bühne im Hof,** Linzerstr. 18, hosts modern theater and dance. (☎35 22 91; www.bih.at. Office open M-F 9am-5pm. Tickets €19-26; students and seniors 50% off.) **The Landeshauptstadt Theater,** Rathauspl. 11, stages traditional opera and ballet. (☎35 20 26; fax 35 20 26 52. Office open M-F 9am-5pm. Tickets €12-32; box office sells a few standing room tickets for €11 on performance evenings.) Neither theater has performances in July or August.

The **Festspielhaus,** Franz Schubert-Pl. 2, stages classical music and modern dance concerts. (☎908 08 02 22; www.festspielhaus.at. Ticket counter open M-F 9am-6pm and 1½hr. before performances. Tickets €3.50-43.) Ballet enthusiasts should check out the **Ballettkonservatorium St. Pölten,** the classical ballet school and training ground for the prestigious **Ballett St. Pölten.**

Seasonal festivities include the **St. Pöltner Festwoche,** which brings all kinds of events to local theaters and museums from mid-May to mid-June. In early July, the **St. Pöltner Hauptstadtfest** raises its tents, and the locals cut loose. From late July through early September the **International Culture and Film Festival** screens free flicks weekly. (www.st-poelten.gv.at, or call the tourist office at ☎35 33 54.)

BADEN BEI WIEN ☎ 02252

Surrounded by vineyards, dense woodlands, and sulfur springs, Baden is a great weekend spot for anyone looking to relax. Although primarily a day spa devoted to therapeutic massage and thermal bath treatments, Baden also offers a wide range of activities including fishing, bowling, tennis, golf, ice skating, and horseback riding. Plus, the city's expansive flower-filled **Rosarium**, its **Casino** (the largest in Europe), and the nearby **Wienerwald** (Vienna Woods) make Baden a veritable playground for people of all ages. Prices can be high, especially in the summer, so traveling to Baden as a daytrip (only 26km from Vienna) can be a good idea.

🖪🖻 TRANSPORTATION & PRACTICAL INFORMATION. The easiest way to get to Baden is by the **Badener Bahn**, a **tram** that runs from Vienna's Karlspl., beneath the Opera House, to Baden's Josefspl. (1hr., every 15min. 5am-10:30pm, €3.50.) **Trains** also travel frequently between Vienna's **Südbahnhof** and Josefpl. (outbound from Vienna 4:40am-11:15pm, inbound 4:16am-11pm; €5.) By **car** from the west, take Autobahn West to Bundesstr. 210 at "Alland-Baden-Mödling." From Vienna, take Autobahn South (Süd) and exit at "Baden." Baden's **tourist office,** Brusattipl. 3 at Leopoldsbad, is accessible from the Josefpl. station. Bear right toward the fountain and follow Erzherzog-Rainer-Ring to Brusattipl. The tourist office is at the end of the street. In summer, they offer **free tours** of the *Altstadt* (1½hr.; M 3:30pm, Sa 10am), the wine region (2hr.; W 3pm; make appointments in advance), and guided **hiking** tours (Tu and Sa 2pm). (☎ 22 60 06 00; www.baden.at. Open May-Oct. M-Sa 9am-6pm, Su and holidays 10am-1pm; Nov.-Apr. M-F 9am-5pm.) Services include clean, free **public toilets** at Brusattipl., the Rosarium, and the train station. **Police** ☎ 133, **medical emergency** ☎ 144. **Postal code:** A-2500.

🖪🖸 ACCOMMODATIONS & FOOD. The tourist office can give you a list of lodgings in Baden with prices and descriptions. **Pension Steinkellner ❸,** Am Hang 1, offers reasonably priced rooms in a typical Austrian *Gästehaus*, which is open throughout the year. It's a walk from the center of town (10min.), up Vöslauerstr. from Josefspl. and right at the 4th stoplight, but the proprietors will pick you up if you call ahead. (☎862 26; www.baden-bei-wien.at/steinkeller. Breakfast included. Singles €26; doubles €50; €2 extra per person for rooms with showers and toilets.) Closer to the *Altstadt* is **Pension Wienerstub'n ❸,** Weilburgstr. 19. (☎481 02; www.hotel-artner.at. Breakfast included. Singles €20-37; doubles €36-55.) For the ultimate in luxury, stay at the **Grand Hotel Sauerhof ❺.** This four star hotel is close to the baths and provides its guests with two restaurants, tennis courts, and a Beauty Farm. (Weilburgstr. 11-13, ☎41 25 10; www.sauerhof.at. Singles and suites €95-800; children under 12 free.)

Café Damals ❷, Rathausg. 3, in a cool, ivy-covered courtyard, is a popular local place for a satisfying lunch for only €6. (☎426 86. Wheelchair-accessible. Open M-F 10am-midnight, Sa 10am-2pm, Su 10am-7pm. AmEx/MC/V.) There are plenty of cafés along Hauptpl. and Pfarrg. For a side of history with your *Tafelspitz* (boiled beef), head to **Gasthaus zum Reichsapfel ❷,** Spiegelg. 2. Follow Antong. one block from Theaterpl.; the restaurant is on the corner. The oldest guest house in Baden, it has served hungry wayfarers since the 13th century. (☎482 05. Dishes €6-12. Wheelchair-accessible. Open M and W-F 5pm-11:30pm, Sa-Su 11am-2pm and 5-11pm. AmEx/MC/V.) **Billa,** Wasserg. 14 (open M-W 8am-7pm, Th 7:30am-7pm, F 7:30am-7:30pm, Sa 7:30am-5pm), and **SPAR,** Rathausg. 7 (open M-F 7:30am-6:30pm, Sa 7:30am-5pm), are grocery stores in the *Fußgängerzone;* there is also a **farmer's market** on Brusattipl. (Open M-F 8am-6pm, Sa 8am-1pm.)

◨ **SIGHTS.** Centered around Hauptpl., Baden's lovely *Fußgängerzone* features the striking Dreifaltigkeitsäule (Trinity Column), erected in 1718. The thermal baths that were Baden's biggest attraction in the days of Caesar Augustus are still the focal point of the city today. **The Strandbad,** Helenenstr. 19-21, lets you simmer in a hot sulfur thermal bath and cool off in room-temperature chlorinated pools. Children can play on the huge water slide and in the sand—a lifeguard is present, but parents should keep an eye on their kids as the beach is very large and usually crowded. (☎486 70. Open M-F 8:30am-7:30pm, Sa-Su 8am-6:30pm. M-F €5.60, after 1pm €4.80; Sa-Su €6.80/€5.60, student rate €2.90.) The **Kurdirektion** itself, Brusattipl. 4 (☎445 31; www.kurhaus-baden.at), is the center of all curative spa treatments, housing an indoor thermal pool open to all visitors (€8.60). The spa has water jet massage therapy (€23.40), sulfur mudpacks (€19.50), and massages (15min. €11.60, 50min. €37.10). A giant new spa complex, the **Römertherme Baden,** Brusattipl. 4, offers soothing luxuries all year long. (☎450 30; www.roemertherme.at. Open M-Su 10am-10pm. 2hr. soak €8.20, students €6.30.)

In addition to the baths, the **Kurpark** lies north of Hauptpl. via Maria-Theresia-G. On the southeast edge of the Wienerwald, this carefully landscaped garden is studded with statues. The imperial court gamboled here during the Congress of Vienna in the early 19th century. Another worthwhile site is the **Theresiengarten,** laid out in 1792, with a flower clock that has been ticking since 1929. Gaming aficionados might want to visit the **Casino.** (In the Kurpark. ☎444 96. Opens daily at 3pm. Semiformal dress required. 19+.)

The **Emperor Franz-Josef Museum,** Hochstr. 51, sits atop the Badener Berg at the end of the park (follow signs through the Sommerarena along Zöllner and Suckfüllweg) and holds exhibitions of folk art, weapons, religious pieces, and photography. (☎411 00. Open Apr.-Oct. Tu-Su 2-6pm.) The **Beethovenhaus,** at Rathausg. 10, is where the composer spent summers while composing the *Missa Solemnis* and much of his *Ninth Symphony.* The museum features his death mask and locks of his hair. (Open Tu-F 4-6pm, Sa-Su and holidays 9-11am and 4-6pm.)

◪ **ENTERTAINMENT.** Baden hosts a range of festivals, notably the **Beethoven Festival** in late September, which features performances by famous Austrian musicians and film screenings at the **Stadttheater.** For tickets, dates, and times, contact Kulturamt der Stadtgemeinde Baden, Hauptpl. 1, A-2500 Baden (☎86 80 02 31; fax 86 80 02 10); ticket orders by mail must be received by mid-August. From late June to mid-September, the **Sommerarena** in the Kurpark stages open-air performances of classic Viennese operettas. (Box office is on Kaiser-Franz-Ring-Str. in the Stadttheater. Contact: Stadttheater Baden Kartenbüro, Theaterpl. 7, A-2500 Baden. ☎485 47; www.stadttheater-baden.at. Open M-F 10am-6:30pm, Sa 10am-1pm and 5-6:30pm. €14-45, standing room €3.50.)

Baden blooms in the beginning of June with the **Badener Rosentage,** a multiweek celebration of roses. Most activities, including children's theater and puppet shows, are free; they take place throughout the Badener Rosarium. (Open daily 9am-7pm.) World-class **horse racing** occurs from June to the end of August, primarily on Th and Su; ☎887 73 for details. From September to early October, Baden hosts the **Grape Cure Weeks,** where local wineries gather on Hauptpl. to show off their grape juice (not wine). For details, stop by one of the wine taverns. (☎22 60 00. Stands open daily during the festival 8am-6pm.)

LIECHTENSTEIN

FACTS AND FIGURES

CAPITAL: Vaduz

CURRENCY: Swiss Franc (SFr)

POPULATION: 33,525

MAJOR EXPORTS: Dental products

FORM OF GOVERNMENT: Hereditary constitutional monarchy

LAND AREA: 160 sq. km

LANGUAGE: German

RELIGION: 80% Catholic, 7.4% Protestant, 12.6% other

GEOGRAPHY: Flat, river valley in west with two largest towns (Vaduz and Schaan); mountainous terrain in east

PHONE CODE	Country code 423; **international dialing prefix** 00.

EMERGENCIES	**Police** or **mountain rescue** ☎ 117, **Fire** ☎ 118, **Medical emergency** ☎ 144, **Roadside assistance** ☎ 140.

Liechtenstein

A recent Liechtenstein tourist brochure unfortunately mislabeled the already tiny 160 sq. km country as an even tinier 160 sq. m. Ironically, this is approximately how much most people see of the world's only German-speaking monarchy, as travelers usually pause only long enough in the capital city of Vaduz to buy the obligatory postage stamp and hastily record their visit in a passport. Most miss the alpine beauty of this tiny country altogether. Its ruling monarch, Prince Hans Adam II, is the first ruler to actually live in Liechtenstein since the present dynasty came to power in 1699. Liechtenstein's ties to Switzerland were established in 1923 with a customs and monetary union, replacing a similar agreement with the Austro-Hungarian empire from 1852 to 1919.

The lack of an army and independent foreign representation does not mean the Principality (*Fürstenturm*) of Liechtenstein is weak; the booming industries of dental manufacturing, banking, and tourism have brought considerable wealth. Nonetheless, many locals remain down-to-earth; old-fashioned huts in the more isolated regions are built at the same rate as ultra-modern buildings in Vaduz. Above the valley towns, cliff-hanging roads are gateways to what's truly worth visiting—the mountains above offer hiking and skiing without a touristy atmosphere.

VADUZ & LOWER LIECHTENSTEIN

Liechtenstein's capital is a town of tourists traveling in packs, furiously scrambling to find something worthy of a photo opportunity. Often they find nothing but the *Schloß* looming above town and the high prices looming in town. A handful of museums await the traveler here, but that's about it; Vaduz rarely requires more than one day. While campers and bikers might enjoy the surrounding countryside of Lower Liechtenstein ("lower" referring to the region's 500m elevation), others should consider heading for the hills in Upper Liechtenstein, particularly Malbun.

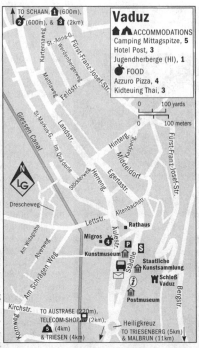

Vaduz

▲🏠 ACCOMMODATIONS
Camping Mittagspitze, **5**
Hotel Post, **3**
Jugendherberge (HI), **1**

🍴 FOOD
Azzuro Pizza, **4**
Kidteuing Thai, **3**

TRANSPORTATION. Although trains from Austria and Switzerland pass through the country, Liechtenstein itself has no rail system. Instead, it has a cheap, efficient **Post Bus** system. (Short trips 2.40SFr, longer trips 3.60SFr; students, children 16 and under half-price. Swiss-Pass valid.) A one-week bus ticket (10SFr; students, seniors, and children 16 and under 5SFr) covers all of Liechtenstein, as well as buses to Swiss and Austrian border towns. If you're planning on taking more than two rides, it's the best deal in the country. The principality is a 20-30min. bus ride from **Sargans** or **Buchs** in Switzerland and **Feldkirch** in Austria (3.60SFr). Keep a passport on you when traveling.

PRACTICAL INFORMATION. Liechtenstein's **national tourist office**, Städtle 37, one block up the hill from the Vaduz Post Bus stop, will stamp your passport with Liechtenstein's bi-colored seal (2SFr). It also gives advice on hiking, cycling, and skiing in the area and sells hiking maps for 8-15.50SFr. (☎239 63 00; www.tourismus.li. Open July-Sept. M-F 8am-5:30pm, Sa-Su 9am-5pm; Oct.-June M-F 8am-noon and 1:30-5:30pm, Apr. and Oct. also Sa 9am-noon and 1:30-5pm, May also Sa-Su 9am-noon and 1:30-5pm.) For **currency exchange**, try the **Liechtenstein Landesbank** next to the post office, or the **post office** in Schaan. The *Erlebnispass*, available at the tourist office and post offices, offers a variety of discounts for museums and transportation, but is worth it only for an extended stay. (2 days 24.12SFr, 6 days 42.21SFr.) **Free Internet** is available at **Telecom-Shop**, Austr. (Take bus #1 dir.: Sargans to "Rütti" from "Schaan/Vaduz." ☎237 74 74. Open M-F 9am-noon and 1:30-6:30pm, Sa 9am-1pm.) Rent **bicycles** at **Bike-Garage** in nearby Triesen. (☎390 03 90. Open M-F 8am-noon and 1:30-6pm, Sa 8am-2pm. 35SFr per day.) **Parking** is available on Aulerstr. across from the Old Castle Inn (1SFr per hr.) and also by the theater. For a **taxi**, call ☎373 29 52 or 392 22 22. For Liechtenstein's **hospital**, dial ☎235 44 11. The main **post office** is near the tourist office, has an amazing selection of stamps and sells tickets for the opera, theater and sporting events. (☎239 63 63.

FROM THE ROAD

A SIX-HOUR TOUR

Let's Go Researcher-Writer Tom Miller volunteered to supplement his job by going for a run—a long one. No stranger to marathons, Tom (having completed the 2001 Bay State marathon in 3hr. 13min. and the 2002 Boston marathon in 3hr. 40min.) was up for the challenge. Though he found it a fantastic way to see the countryside, Let's Go *does not necessarily recommend this mode of sightseeing for everyone.*

Though we joke about being able to see all of Liechtenstein in a day, it's actually possible to see the entire nation in a little under six hours. The LGT-Alpin marathon runs 42km from Bendern (outside of Schaan) to Malbun, in the southeastern corner of the country. My editor and I rearranged my entire schedule so I could run it.

It was worth it.

The course began in the relatively flat farmland near the Rhine. It was an unseasonably warm day—well over 80° F at 9:30am— and the smell of cow manure was overwhelming at times as we ran past farmers harvesting hay. Beginning in the capital city of Vaduz, the next 11km were entirely uphill, rising over 1000m. Most of us slowed to a walk early on, but the enthusiastic Liechtensteiners were out in force chanting, "Haub, haub, haub! Bravo!" as we lumbered past.

The course finally flattened out at about km 22, in the mountains

Open M-F 7:45am-6pm, Sa 8-11am.) **Postal code:** FL-9490.

▐▐ ACCOMMODATIONS & FOOD. Budget housing options in Vaduz are few and far between. Liechtenstein's sole **Jugendherberge (HI) ❷,** Untere Rüttig. 6, is in neighboring Schaan. From Vaduz, take bus #1 (dir.: Schaan) to "Mühleholz," walk toward the intersection with traffic lights, and turn left down Marianumstr. Walk 4-5min. and follow signs to this spotless pink hostel on the edge of a farm. Clean rooms, a large breakfast buffet, and a game room with a Nintendo make this a great place to stay. (☎232 50 22; www.youthhostel.ch. Dinner 12.50SFr. Laundry 6SFr. Reception 5-10pm. Check-out 10am. Curfew 10pm; key code available for late entry. Open Feb.-Oct. Dorms 30SFr; doubles 40SFr.) For convenience, budget-friendly **Hotel Post ❸,** Bahnhofstr. 14, is right by the Schaan Post Bus stop and train station, which can be a downside for light sleepers. Rooms are large, carpeted, and reasonably priced. (☎232 17 18. Breakfast included at the restaurant downstairs. Reception 8am-11pm. 50-60SFr.) For a night under the stars, try **Camping Mittagspitze ❶.** Take bus #1 (dir.: Sargans) to "Säga," cross the street, and walk toward the mountains on the street near the bus stop, following the signs. This country campground has great scenery and its own swimming pool. Reception is just past the two brooks. (☎392 26 86. Laundry 4.50SFr. Shower included. Reception June-Aug. 8-11:30am and 5-8:30pm; Sept.-May 7-8am and 5-6pm. 8.50SFr per person, tent 5SFr. Electricity 5.5SFr. Tax 0.60SFr per person.)

Eating cheaply in Liechtenstein is challenging, as most meals in the center of town will easily run 25-30SFr. **Azzuro Pizza ❷,** Aulestr. 20, sells take-out pizzas for 7-14SFr and kebabs for 9SFr. (☎232 48 18. Open M-Sa 8am-7pm, Su 8am-6pm.) **Kidteuing Thai ❷** offers duck curry, pad Thai and other Asian meals for 10SFr (11 Landesstr., #1: Falknis). Groceries are available at **Migros,** Aulestr. 20, across from the tour bus parking lot in Vaduz. (Open M-F 8am-1pm and 1:30-7pm, Sa 8am-6pm.)

◉ SIGHTS. The 12th-century **Schloß Vaduz,** regal home of Hans Adam II, Prince of Liechtenstein, presides over the town. You can hike up to the castle for a closer look; the 15min. trail begins down the street from the tourist office, heading away from the post office. The signs along the path offer lessons on Liechtensteinian government in German, French, and English. The interior of the ruler's residence is off-limits to the masses, except for a select group of rich politicians, retirees, and university students with excellent grades, who are all invited annually to visit the Prince, usually on New Year's Day. Across the street from the tourist office is the large modern building housing the **Kunstmuseum Liechtenstein,** Städtle 32. The museum shows modern art, works by Dalí, Kandinsky, and Klee, and some rotating special exhibits. The modern art exhibits, the bulk of the collection, are a mixed bag (including a few huge installation pieces like a giant white marble ball enclosed in glass). They are located next door to the prince's collection of Renaissance and Romantic masterpieces, including several Rubens. (☎235 03 00; www.kunstmuseum.li. Open Tu-W and F-Su 10am-5pm, Th 10am-8pm. 8SFr; students, seniors, and ages 10-16 5SFr.) Reproductions of the royal art collection often end up on postage stamps displayed in the small **Postmuseum,** Städtle 37, on the other side of the tourist office. (☎236 61 05; fax 236 61 09. Open daily Apr.-Oct. 10am-noon and 1:30-5:30pm; Nov.-Mar. 10am-noon and 1:30-5pm. Free.)

UPPER LIECHTENSTEIN

Just when it seems that the roads cannot possibly become any narrower or steeper, they do—welcome to Upper Liechtenstein. Even if you're only in the country for one day, take the short bus trip to **Triesenberg** or **Malbun** (30min. from Vaduz) for spectacular views of the Rhine valley below.

TRIESENBERG

Spanning a series of switchbacks and foothills 800m above the Rhine, the first town up the mountain (serviced by bus #10) is Triesenberg (pop 2600). Founded in the 13th century by Swiss immigrants forced to flee Valais due to religious intolerance, the **Walser Heimatmuseum** chronicles the history of these intrepid people (and of the entire region). With hundreds of artifacts from cowbells to axes to carvings in tree roots, it's worth a quick look. (Facing uphill from the bus stop, head to the left. ☎262 19 26; fax 19 22. Open Sept.-May Tu-F 1:30-5:30pm, Sa 1:30-5pm; June-Aug. also Su 2-5pm. 2SFr, children 1SFr.) The **tourist office** is in the same building as the museum and has the same hours, phone, and fax.

For great **hiking,** take bus #34 to "Gaflei." (20min., every hr.) Stunning views of the **Rhine Valley** await on a 1½hr., relatively flat hike through alpine meadows and forests. (From the parking lot exit, head toward the gravel path on the left toward "Silum" and then "Ob. Tunnel, Steg." At the end, walk through the tunnel, then down the road to Steg, where bus #10 runs to Vaduz or Schaan every hr.) Follow the signs for the **"Drei Schwestern"** (Three Sisters) for a really chal-

above Gaflei. Coming around the corner I heard dozens of bells tolling and wondered if a local church had decided to ring its bells for us. As I came around a hairpin turn, I found about 400 cows, all wearing bells. To my left I had a perfect view of the yellow-green rolling hills in the Rhine valley below and of the snow-covered peaks of the Alps straight ahead. A paraglider chose this moment to fly overhead and I wondered if I hadn't stumbled into a picture postcard by mistake.

The euphoria wore off in km 31-35, which were again steep uphills, this time over narrow, rocky paths. As one Liechtensteinian runner stumbled past me, he yelled out, "Hey Meester Meeler!" I had my name written across the back of my shirt, but couldn't figure out how he knew I was American. When I asked him in German how he knew, he said, "Because no one spells Miller with an 'i' around here."

The final 8km were all downhill as we circled the valley that contains Malbun at reckless speeds, winding our way toward the finish line on paths that would have alarmed even downhill skiers. I finished in 5 hr. 40min. and 40 seconds, about 2½ hr. behind the winner, having crossed the entire country and ascended 1800m in the process. I think the mountain goats were proud of us—they've been doing the same thing for years.

—Tom Miller, 2002

lenging hike (5½-6hr). The trail climbs up from Gaflei, up a couple of ladders, and across the craggy peaks that grace postcards in every kiosk in the country. From Drei Schwestern, head toward Sarojasattel and Planken, and take the bus back to Vaduz or Schaan. A variety of other shorter hikes (15min.-1hr.) are also marked from Gaflei.

MALBUN

Like a peninsula of green farmland surrounded on three sides by mountains, the village of Malbun sits high in an alpine valley in the southeastern corner of Liechtenstein. It is undoubtedly the coolest place in the principality, harboring approachable people, affordable ski slopes, and plenty of hiking. Inquire at the **tourist office** about their *Greifvogel* (raptor) bird shows. (☎263 65 77; www.malbun.li. Open June-Oct. and mid-Dec. to mid-Apr. M-Sa 9am-noon and 1:30-5pm.) During the winter, two chair lifts, four T-bars, and one ski school provide access to uncrowded slopes. (Day pass 37SFr, youths and seniors 31SFr, children 25SFr; 6-day pass 155SFr/127SFr/98SFr; low-season 136SFr/110SFr/84SFr.) Right in the middle of town, **Malbun A.G.** (☎263 97 70 or 262 19 15) offers one-day ski lessons (60-70SFr), three-day classes (130-160SFr), and private lessons (1 day 230SFr). **Malbun Sport** (☎/fax 263 37 55) rents **skis** and snowboards. (35SFr, children 13-18SFr. Cross-country skis 28SFr. Open M-F 8am-6pm, Sa 8am-5pm, Su 9am-5pm.) **Cross-country skiing** is available 2km away in Steg.

PLEASE DON'T EAT THE FLOWERS. Liechtenstein is particularly protective of its abundant wildflowers, which are protected by law—picking those violently purple gentians will result in a 500SFr fine. And just in case pine nuts straight from the tree sounds great, be aware that hemlocks are abundant in alpine regions. The "Tree of Death," as it is referred to on one nature trail, felled Socrates and will fell you, too, if you indulge in needles, bark, or pinecones.

During summer, the #10 bus from Vaduz (30min., every hr., 3.60SFr) takes hikers to Malbun. The most worthwhile hike is a round-trip hike to **Pfälzerhütte** (5hr.), the starting point of which is the top of the only chairlift open in the summer, the **Sareiserjoch**. (One-way 7.50SFr, round-trip 11.70SFr; students 5.90SFr/9SFr; ages 5-16 4.30SFr/6.40SFr. Open daily 8-11:50am and 1-4:50pm.) At the beginning of June, there is snow on one side of the trail, wildflowers on the other, and *Murmeltiere* (marmots) throughout. Cross the rocky final ascent to the peak of **Augustenberg** (2359m), Liechtenstein's second highest mountain, then descend a few hundred meters to the Pfälzerhütte (mountain hut). To get home, head toward Gritsch and then Tälihöhi, completing a near-circuit of the valley that encloses Malbun. **Renting a bike** from **Malbun Sport** (35SFr per day) is also a great way to see the countryside. Numerous bike paths in the area provide great opportunities to see wildlife. For some excitement, climb up and then ride back down on the steep, narrow road from Triesenberg to Malbun. For an easy but rewarding ride, try the **Fürstenweg** loop between Vaduz and Schaan. Start at the Alte Rhein bridge in Vaduz and follow the river. When you get to where the train tracks cross the river in Schaan, head right and away from the river. The route heads to the Kloster Dux (Dux chapel), then through the woods and up to Schloß Vaduz, and then back down to Vaduz.

The best place to stay for hiking and skiing access is **Hotel Alpen** (☎263 11 81; www.alpenhotel.li), near the bus stop and tourist office. The hotel has a restaurant, swimming pool, and a large common room with TV. Some rooms have cable TV, phone, and a stocked fridge, but you'll pay extra for the luxury. (Open mid-May to Oct. and mid-Dec. to Apr. Reception 8am-10pm. Summer 45SFr per person, with shower 60SFr, with bath 70SFr. Winter add 10SFr.)

SWITZERLAND

Switzerland, in addition to cheese and watches, has an amazing wealth of natural beauty. Hikers, skiers, bikers, and paragliders from all over the globe flock to the alpine nation to take advantage of its winding trails, challenging slopes, and jagged summits. However, the outdoors are far from Switzerland's only virtues—the country's urban centers are as fascinating to explore as the Alps that surround them. Besides being international hubs of commerce, trade, and diplomacy, cities such as Zurich, Geneva, and Lucerne are also cultural centers home to world-class concert halls, museums, and cathedrals.

Right in the middle of Europe, yet cut off from it by the Alps (crucial to the nation's much vaunted neutrality), Switzerland is a nation of fascinating cultural variety. Divided into German-, French-, and Italian-speaking regions, Switzerland retains much of the customs and cuisines of the nations it borders, yet informs and combines them with a flavor that is uniquely Swiss.

Against a backdrop of stark natural beauty, Switzerland is a country of comfort and calm, and a delightful country in which to travel. The Swiss have raised hospitality to an art, resulting in food and accommodations of consistently high quality. The country's efficient public transportation system makes it an ideal destination for independent visitors. Though Switzerland is not known for being affordable, budget travelers can generally find bargains, especially since many of the best attractions (like sunsets over mountain peaks) remain priceless.

BUILDING THE SWISS CONFEDERATION:

The Swiss confederation is made up of 23 cantons (states) and 3 half-cantons, having grown from the original three in 1291 (Uri, Schwyz, and Unterwalden). Today, the cantons, clockwise starting with Bern, the capital, are: Bern (incorporated 1353), Lucerne (1332), Obwalden and Nidwalden (1291, originally part of Unterwalden), Zug (1352), Uri (1291), Schwyz (1291), Zurich (1351), Schaffhausen (1501), Thurgau (1803), Appenzell (1501), St. Gallen (1803), Glarus (1352), Graubünden (1803), Ticino (1803), Valais (1815), Geneva (1815), Vaud (1803), Fribourg (1481), Neuchâtel (1815), Jura (1978), Solothurn (1481), Basel (1501), and Aargau (1803).

LAND

As visitors can attest, Switzerland is primarily a mountainous country. Although technically only one-seventh of the Alps lie within Switzerland's borders, no other country is as geographically defined by them. Nor does any other country contain as many of the range's highest peaks: eight of the ten tallest peaks in the Alps are either on Switzerland's borders or wholly within them. Accounting for 60% of Switzerland's total surface area, the Alps rise in central and southern Switzerland to form high, jagged peaks with serrated ridges and steep, narrow river valleys. The Alps were born during the Oligocene and Niocene epochs as the North African continental plate moved into the Eurasian plate, pushing up the ocean floor between. The northern and southern fringes are composed primarily of sedimentary rock such as limestone, marl, and dolomite, formed from ancient deposits on the ocean floor. The central spine of the Alps in central and southern Switzerland is made of hard metamorphic rock—gneiss, granite, and schist—molded in the intense heat and pressure as the plates came together. Thousands of years ago,

In AD 1050, the Archdeacon Bernard de Menthon founded a hospice in an a mountain pass in the Jungfrau region, and brought with him a breed of large, furry dogs of Gallic origin. In addition to providing shelter for passing merchants, Bernard and the monks working under him would venture into blizzards in search of stranded travelers. Though it is uncertain whether or not the dogs would accompany the monks on their rescue missions—early accounts relate that dogs were used to run an exercise wheel which would turn a cooking spit—by the time of Bernard's canonization, dogs bearing his name had become famous, and regularly patrolled the pass (now also named after Bernard).

Gifted with a fine sense of smell, a thick coat, an amiable attitude, and a neck just made to tie a barrel of brandy to, the St. Bernards made a name for themselves by saving over 2000 lives over several hundred years; in the 1810s, a single dog named Barry saved 40 lost travelers. Today, few St. Bernards still work as rescue dogs—smaller, lighter breeds less liable to sink in the snow have taken their place. The St. Bernard is now a popular household pet, and though it has entered the popular imagination through films like *Cujo* and the innumerable Beethoven movies, it will always have dignity as the alpine fixture it once was.

glaciers swept over the area, carving out the sharp ridges, chutes, cirques, and waterfalls that have made the Alps famous for rugged beauty.

Northern Switzerland is characterized by the Jura (Celtic for wood), the subalpine region comprised primarily of woodlands on limestone hills. The Jura once saw extensive ore mining and metal processing, but has more recently been promoted as a tourist destination with hiking, riding, and cross-country skiing. The renowned Swiss watchmaking industry comes from the Jura region. Glaciers passed through the valleys surrounding the Alps and the Jura, creating Switzerland's major lakes: Geneva, Constance, Neuchâtel, Lucerne, Maggiore, and Zurich.

FLORA & FAUNA

PLANTS

Much of Switzerland's botanical beauty is found in its large and varied forest. While beech and oak trees predominate in the deciduous woods of the Swiss midland and at lower elevations in the alpine valleys, spruce and fir occupy areas of higher altitudes. In the southern and eastern alpine interiors, forests of pine and larch provide a stark contrast to the palm trees along the shores of Lake Lugano.

Floral diversity abounds even in the harshest and rockiest areas of the Alps, with several species of wildflowers thriving in the midst of snowy conditions. **Edelweiss,** famous for its elusiveness (and for the *Sound of Music* song), has a felt stem and leaves and a distinctive cluster of fuzzy yellowish round balls in the center of its bloom. The **Lady's Slipper** is slightly iris-like in appearance, with a yellow bulb and maroon tendrils coming out from all around it. More conventional flowers such as **daisies, buttercups, bellflowers,** and **dandelions** also abound. Wildflowers begin appearing in late April and disappear at the end of October.

ANIMALS

Many of Switzerland's fauna are of the familiar barnyard and wildlife variety with an alpine twist. **Black squirrels** are plentiful, and **red foxes** and **hedgehogs** make an occasional appearance. Less recognizable animals include the **marmot,** a furry, cat-sized rodent that inhabits the Schilt and upper Sefinen valleys, and **tächis,** large black birds common around Mürren and Schilthorn. Normal deer abound as well as Switzerland's own variation, the **Gemse,** which tend to be smaller with miniscule horns and roam the Bernese Oberland. Many of these animal populations were once dwindling; the creation of a game preserve in Lower Engadine prevented the extinction of several alpine species.

The cow is an institution in Switzerland and one or more bovine encounters during a trip through the Alps is almost guaranteed. Often a herd of them will pass you as you are hiking; simply stand still and let them so that they don't start heading in the wrong direction. Swiss cows can be of the Simmentaler (light brown and white), Brown Swiss (solid gray-brown), or Holstein (black and white) varieties.

HISTORY

FROM CAVE MEN TO CELTS

The early Swiss established settlements only 30,000 years ago, after the end of the last glacial period. By 750 BC, the Celts dominated Switzerland. The artistic and warlike **Helvetians,** whose land extended across the alpine valleys of central Switzerland, gained notoriety for their (largely unsuccessful) attempts to invade Roman Italy in 222 BC and again as allies of Carthage between 218 and 203 BC (when they assisted Hannibal and his elephants in their famous crossing of the Alps). Julius Caesar halted the Helvetian attempts to advance into Gaul in 58 BC by crushing their tribes and colonizing their lands.

As Roman influence waned in the 5th century, the tribes settled permanently. **Burgundians** filled the west, merging peacefully with the Romanized Celts and absorbing their culture and language. The more aggressive **Alemanni,** a Germanic tribe, forced their own culture on the Celts of central and northern Switzerland, eventually pushing the Burgundians west to the Sarine River (which now stands as the border between German- and French-speaking Switzerland). Slightly less numerous, the **Rhätians,** an Etruscan people, populated the eastern Switzerland (now Graubünden), and their language, **Rhäto-Romansch,** a combination of Roman Latin and the Rhätian Tuscan dialect, is still spoken today.

ALEMANNI LEGACY (1000-1519)

It was the nonconformist Alemanni who set the stage for centuries of Swiss individualism and decentralized rule. The lack of strong Roman imperial control over the patchwork of states allowed for de facto political autonomy. This growing commitment to democracy caused the descendents of the Alemanni to clash with Holy Roman Emperor **Rudolf of Habsburg** when he attempted to take three of their communities (Uri, Schwyz, and Unterwalden—the "Forest Cantons") under his direct control in the late 13th century. In a secret pact, the three Forest Cantons decided to rebel and signed the **Everlasting Alliance** in 1291—an agreement that obligated the cantons to defend each other from outside attack. This moment is what the Swiss consider to mark the beginning of the Swiss confederation. The Everlasting Alliance also signaled the beginning of 350 years of struggle against the **Habsburg Empire.** In 1315, the Swiss and the Hapsburgs met at the Battle of Morgarten, resulting in Habsburg defeat.

Despite conflict between the Everlasting Alliance and the Habsburg Emperors, the three-canton core of Switzerland expanded over the next several centuries to include Bern, Lucerne, Zurich, Glarus, and Zug. Habsburg emperor Frederick II allied himself with Zurich, but by force of arms the other cantons forced Zurich to renounce its alliance and rejoin the Confederation. In another attempt to conquer the Swiss, the Hapsburgs enlisted the help of the "Swabian League"—a group of Southern German cities whose motto became "the Swiss, too, must have a master." The Swabian War (1499-1500) lasted less than nine months, but strong Swiss efforts engendered independence from the Holy Roman Empire.

REFORMATION TO REVOLUTION (1519-1815)

The lack of a strong central government to settle disputes between cantons of different faiths caused problems for the Swiss during the **Protestant Reformation**. As Lutheranism swept Northern Europe, radical theologian **Ulrich Zwingli** of Zurich spearheaded his own brand of Protestantism that stressed both the importance of laypeople reading scripture and a rejection of the symbols and gestures of Catholicism. In 1523, the city government of Zurich sanctioned Zwingli's proposed *Theses* and strengthened Zwingli's influence by banning Anabaptism and harshly punishing its followers. Meanwhile, in Geneva, French-born lawyer and priest **John Calvin** preached a doctrine of predestination: neither God's grace nor good works could get you into heaven, but leading a good life was an indication that you were destined for it. For a time he exercised a theocratic sway over Geneva and instituted moral reforms, turning the city into a shining example of Protestant social control. While Zurich and Geneva became strongholds of the Protestant movement, the Forest Cantons remained loyal to the Catholic Church. Religious differences, combined with tensions between urban and rural cantons, resulted in battle, climaxing with the defeat of the Protestants at Kappel in 1531 and the death of Zwingli. In the mid-16th century the confederation finally interceded, granting Protestants certain freedoms but prohibiting them from imposing their faith on others. The confederation managed to remain neutral during the **Thirty Years War**. In 1648 the **Peace of Westphalia** granted the Swiss official neutrality and a multi-national recognition of their independence from the Austrian Habsburg empire.

After two centuries of relative quiet, Swiss independence was challenged in 1789, when Napoleon's troops invaded Switzerland and established the **Helvetic Republic**. Rebelling against the French puppet government, the Swiss overthrew the regime in 1803. Napoleon's **Mediation Act** settled the anarchy that ensued and established Switzerland as a confederation of 19 cantons. After Napoleon's defeat at Waterloo, the Congress of Vienna added Geneva, Neuchâtel, and the Valais to the Confederation and (again) officially recognized Swiss neutrality.

DIPLOMACY: 1815 TO THE 20TH CENTURY

The establishment of neutrality meant Switzerland could turn its attention to domestic issues. Industrial growth brought material prosperity, but the era was far from golden. The **Federal Pact** of 1815 that replaced Napoleon's decrees again established Switzerland as a confederation of sovereign states united only for common defense—united foreign policy was still impossible. Because of logistical barriers (each canton had its own laws, currency, postal service, weights, measures, and army—not to mention language and religion) the inhabitants of different cantons regarded each others as foreigners.

In 1846, continuing religious differences led to the formation of a separatist defense league of Catholic cantons known as the **Sonderbund**. In July 1847, the **Diet,** a parliamentary body representing the other cantons, declared the Sonderbund incompatible with the Federal Pact and demanded its dissolution. A civil war broke out, ending with Protestant victory 25 days later. In 1848, the winning cantons wrote a new constitution, modeled after that of the United States, which guaranteed republican and democratic cantonal constitutions and set up an executive body for the first time. The central government then established a free-trade zone and unified postal, currency, and railway systems across all the cantons.

Now internally stable, Switzerland began to resolve international conflicts. The **Geneva Convention of 1864** established international laws for conduct during war. Geneva also became the **International Red Cross** headquarters. Swiss neutrality was tested in both the **Franco-Prussian War** and **World War I** as French- and German-speaking Switzerland had different loyalties. In 1920, Geneva welcomed the headquarters of the ill-fated **League of Nations,** solidifying Switzerland's reputation as the center for international diplomacy. At the onset of **World War II,** Switzerland mobilized 20% of its population for a defensive army. Fortunately, Hitler's plan to invade Switzerland was thwarted by Allied landings, distractions on the North African front, and the protective alpine border. The Swiss government, not eager to incur Germany's wrath, officially impeded passage through its territory, while Jews, escaping Allied prisoners, and other refugees from Nazi Germany found secret refuge in Switzerland. Aside from some accidental bombings in 1940, 1944, and 1945, Switzerland survived the war unscathed.

As the rest of Europe cleaned up the rubble of two world wars, Switzerland nurtured its sturdy economy. Zurich emerged as a banking and insurance center, while Geneva housed international organizations. Although Geneva became the focal point of international diplomacy, Switzerland remained independent in its diplomatic relationships, declining offers of membership to the United Nations, NATO, and the European Economic Community.

TODAY

1999 ELECTIONS

While Austria made international headlines when its far-right, anti-immigrant political party made gains in October 1999 elections, no one seemed to notice when a similar thing happened in Switzerland two weeks later. The far-right **Swiss People's Party** (*Schweizerische Volkspartei*) captured 23% of the vote, catapulting from 4th to 2nd among the country's four main parties. The party is strongly anti-immigrant: its members rallied behind the cry "Stop Asylum Abuse," a reaction to the influx of refugees pouring into Switzerland from Eastern Europe. After the election, Jörg Haider of Austria was one of the first to congratulate fellow business maverick and fast-talking far-right political-leader **Christoph Blocher,** the leader of the People's Party. The People's Party's jump of 7.9 percentage points since the 1995 elections is astounding because the percentage of the vote received by one party has almost never changed more than 1-2% between consecutive elections.

THE LOCAL LEGEND

Years ago, when woodsmen were bold and the Austrian Hapsburg sheriffs power-hungry (around 1307, if it happened at all), a particularly nasty Austrian named Gessler set a peacock-feathered hat on a pole and ordered every self-respecting Swiss passing through the town of Altdorf to kneel before it. One particularly rugged Swiss fellow named William, either because he wasn't aware of the ordinance, didn't like Austrians, or just nursed a hatred of everything haberdasher, failed to pay obeisance to the hat, and incurred Gessler's rather inventive wrath. Commanded to shoot an apple off his son's head, our William not only demonstrated his prowess at the bow, but immediately hefted another arrow and told Gessler that it had his (Gessler's) name on it. This stirring and entirely probable event went on to become a rallying cry for Swiss independance.

But that's not all. Besides conjuring the otherwise bland Swiss to feats of intrepid nation-building, William Tell has also has given fodder for Schiller to wax poetic on, Rossini to compose an operetta about (whence the famous overture), advertisers a ready-made trademark, and William S. Burroughs an occasion to shoot his wife.

One of the primary reasons for the agitation is the Swiss fear that Eastern European refugees are taking their jobs. One in every five people living in Switzerland is foreign, and while Switzerland rarely lets these immigrants become citizens, these extra job-seekers were criticized when unemployment rose in the recent recession. The Swiss panicked when the unemployment rate hit a high of around 5% in the mid-1990s, a rate still low by most other countries' standards. Recently, the immigration debate was particularly relevant because Switzerland accepted more Kosovar refugees proportional to its population than any other country. The Swiss have never been thrilled with immigration, and the recent influx has heightened such concerns.

SWITZERLAND'S INTERNATIONAL TIES

The People's Party was the only one of the four major parties that did not support Swiss membership in the **EU;** among the requirements for EU membership is that all members accept foreign workers from all other EU nations. Switzerland has historically resisted international organizations primarily because they threaten the Swiss people's fierce sense of independence from outside entanglements. In March 2002, Switzerland finally joined the **United Nations** in an initiative supported by the people and cantons.

During the Cold War, Switzerland's independence and stability were economically advantageous, helping its people attain one of the highest standards of living in the world. But as the rest of Europe has become more stable and integrated, Switzerland's independence has turned into isolation and has frequently excluded the nation from trade deals. Realizing this, the government offered the people the opportunity to join the **European Economic Area (EEA)**, the economic forerunner to the EU, in 1992. The people rejected the government's plan through a referendum in which 80 percent of the people turned out to vote (usual turnout for referenda is 35 percent). This vote precluded the chance to vote on EU membership.

After the 1992 vote, the government initiated bilateral negotiations with the EU to create closer ties and eventually move Switzerland toward membership. The People's Party was the only political party that did not endorse the new bilateral negotiations. The fear that Switzerland was moving toward isolationism was calmed, however, when in May 2000 two-thirds of the people voted to accept the bilateral negotiations between the EU and the Swiss government in a referendum.

The election results have threatened to shake up the careful political system of consensus that has developed over the last fifty years. The People's Party's gains led Blocher to request a second seat on the seven-seat Federal Council, the cabinet-like board that is the most powerful political body in the country. For the last fifty years the People's Party has held one seat, while the other 3 parties have each held 2 seats, a political arrangement known as the **magic formula.** This formula was carefully crafted so that the Federal Council fairly represented three major languages and two major religions.

PEOPLE

DEMOGRAPHICS

Switzerland is a culturally diverse nation, with people of German origin making up 65% of the population, French origin 18%, Italian 10%, and Romansch 1%. Other minorities, including mostly foreign workers from Eastern Europe, make up the other 6% of the population. Though heterogeneous in culture, the Swiss are rather homogeneous in character, generally described as gracious, proper, and hard-working. Most Swiss are active people, encouraged to venture outdoors by the alluring mountain landscape. Skiing and hiking are national pastimes, with more than 40% of the population regularly wandering through the countryside, a fact that perhaps accounts for the 80 year life expectancy rate. In general, the Swiss enjoy an incredibly high standard of living due to a strong market economy and a low unemployment rate of 1.9%. Literacy is virtually 100%.

A CRASH COURSE IN SWISS GERMAN

Though you'll most likely never need to speak Swiss German, it is a charming language that reflects the traditional character of Swiss culture. If you want to pick it up, start with basic practical terms that are nearly the same in all dialects, such as the days of the week: *Mäntig, Zyschtig, Mittwuche, Donschtig, Frytig, Samschtig, Sunntig*. Even if you haven't mastered these tongue-twisters, watch out when buying cereal—be sure to distinguish between *Müsli*, the famous granola, which literally means "little smashed-up things," and *Musli*, the common misspelling, which means "little mice."

LANGUAGE

When in Switzerland, try to speak as the Swiss do (whatever the language happens to be). Fewer people speak English in Switzerland than in many other European countries because of the number of languages that must be learned to get by within Switzerland. Thus, while many do speak English, you're always better off trying one of Switzerland's three and a half official federal languages first: German, French, Italian, and Romansch (which is only partially an official federal language). Each language spans a particular geographic region: **German** is spoken by 64% of the population throughout the bulk of central and eastern Switzerland; in western Switzerland, **French** is the language of choice for 19% of the Swiss, while 8% speak **Italian,** primarily in the southern Ticino region. **Romansch** is spoken by less than 1% of the population, but it has historical and ethnic significance after having survived for hundreds of years in the isolated mountain valleys of Graubünden (see p. 422).

German speakers beware: **Swiss German** (*Schwyzertüütsch*) is unlike any of the dialects spoken in Germany and Austria, nearly unintelligible to a speaker of High German (*Hochdeutsch*). Linguistically, Swiss German more closely resembles Middle High German, spoken in Germany 500 years ago. Geographic isolation led to the development of highly disparate dialects in each region. *Wallisertütsch*, spoken in the southern Valais region, is one of the oldest Swiss German dialects and hence one of the least comprehensible, even to German-speaking Swiss. On the other hand, *Bärntütsch* and *Züritüütsch*, spoken around Bern and Zurich respectively, are more regular, though there is no written standard of Swiss German. Although words like *chääschüchli* (cheesecake) and *chuchichäschtli* (kitchen cabinets) may sound harsh to Anglophone ears, most German-speaking Swiss prefer their dialect to High German. The Swiss will appreciate any effort you make to speak it, so take a breath and practice saying *Ufwiderlüge* (goodbye).

RELIGION

When the dust settled after the Protestant Reformation, Switzerland ended up almost evenly divided between Catholics (46%) and Protestants (40%), though Protestantism has been in slight decline since World War II. Other groups (primarily Jews and Muslims) and agnostics make up the remaining religious pref-

ON THE MENU

FONDUE, AT YOUR DISCRETION

Although known worldwide as a Swiss tradition, fondue is a complex cultural artifact. Here are a few things to keep in mind the next time you dive into a bowl of boiling cheese.

Firstly, fondue is no monolith. The most common form is a mix of two cheeses, the French-Swiss Gruyére and Fribourger cheeses, there are substantial regional variations. Likewise, *Kirsch*, the clear Schnapps that farmers still make in their backyards is added in quantities varying by canton, and each brew retains its own unique bite.

The eating of fondue is likewise a playground of cultural variety. In some circles, if you lose your bread somewhere in the pot, you have to kiss you neighbor; in others, you buy them a bottle of wine, or sing a song. As the meal winds to a close, a ring of cheese is inevitably found stuck to the bottom of the pot, burned to a crisp. In Basel, this is called the *Oma* (Grandmother), while in Wallis, it's simply know as the *gut* part. No matter how it is named, though, all Swiss cut up and eat the burnt cheese, sometimes with an egg or two on top. Regardless, you should only drink white wine or hot tea with fondue: if you're quaffing a cold beverage, the cheese forms a hard ball in your stomach and breeds indigestion. Most importantly, as any Swiss will tell you, fondue is best when shared.

erences. Switzerland has been a welcoming home to many of these religious minorities; Geneva, the "City of Peace," houses various international religious organizations representing 130 faiths, such as the World Council of Churches, the Baha'i International Community, the Lutheran World Federation, the Quaker UN Office, the Christian Children's Fund, and the World Jewish Congress.

CULTURE

FOOD & DRINK

Switzerland is not for the lactose intolerant. The Swiss are serious about dairy products, from rich and varied **cheeses** (see "Say cheese!," p. 329) to decadent milk chocolate—even the major Swiss soft drink is a dairy-based beverage, *rivella*. These divine bovine goodies are always available at local Migros or Coop supermarkets. As far as **chocolate** goes, the Swiss have earned bragging rights for their expertise: with the invention of milk chocolate in 1875, Switzerland was poised to rule the world. Today the country is home to some of the world's largest producers: **Lindt, Suchard,** and **Nestlé.** Visit the Lindt factory in Zurich or the Nestlé factory near Bulle to load up on free samples. **Toblerone,** manufactured in Bern, is an international favorite famous for the bits of nougat in creamy milk chocolate, packaged in a nifty triangular box. Chocolate comes in different cocoa concentrations—the higher the concentration, the darker and more bitter the chocolate.

Cheese and chocolate cravings satiated, one might desire a more substantial entree. Not surprisingly, Swiss dishes vary from region to region and what your waiter brings you is most likely related to the language he is speaking. An array of "typical" Swiss dishes might include the Zurich speciality, *Geschnetzeltes* (strips of veal stewed in a thick cream sauce), *Luzerner Chugelipastete* (pâté in a pastry shell), *Papet Vaudois* (leeks with sausage from Vaud), *Churer Fleischtorte* (meat pie from Chur), and Bernese salmon. Each region or town usually has its own specific bread; ask for it by name (e.g. when in St. Gallen, ask for *St. Galler-brot*) at the local market or bakery.

Switzerland's hearty peasant cooking will keep you warm through those frigid alpine winters. Bernese **Rösti,** a plateful of hash brown potatoes skilleted and occasionally flavored with bacon or cheese, is as prevalent in the German regions as **fondue** (from the French, *fondre*, "to melt") is in the French. Usually a blend of Emmentaler and Gruyère cheeses, white wine, *kirsch*, and spices, fondue is eaten by dunking small cubes of white bread into a *caquelon* (a one-handled pot) kept hot by a small flame. Valaisian **raclette** is made by cutting a special cheese in half and heating it until it melts; the melted cheese is then scraped onto a baked potato and garnished with meat or vegetables.

The world's chocolate experts would never neglect the lingering sweet-tooth. The Swiss are adept at the art of **confectionery.** Among the most tempting cakes are the *Baseler Leckerli* (a kind of gingerbread), *Zuger Kirschtorte* (cherry cake), Engadine nutcakes, the *bagnolet crème* of the Jura (eaten with raspberries and anise seed biscuits), soda rolls, *rissoles* (pear tarts), and the nougat and pralines of Geneva. *Vermicelli* (not the Italian pasta, but a dessert made of chestnut mousse) is popular all over Switzerland.

SAY CHEESE! While the words "Swiss cheese" may conjure up images of lunch-boxed sandwiches filled with a hard, oily, holey cheese, Switzerland actually produces innumerable varieties, each made from a particular type of milk. Cheese with holes is usually *Emmentaler*, from the valley of the same name near Bern, but nearly every canton and many towns have specialty cheeses. To name a few of the most well-known: *Gruyère* is a stronger version of *Emmentaler*; *Appenzeller* is a hard cheese with a sharp tang; *Tome* is a generic term for a soft, uncooked cheese similar to French *Chèvre*. In the Italian regions, cheese often resembles the *Parmigiano* from Italy more than the mountain cheeses of the alpine regions. As Swiss cheese standards are regulated by law, cheese in Switzerland is always of superb quality.

The Romans introduced **wine** to the region, but it was not until the 9th century that the beer-drinking laity pried it away from the clergy. Because today there is very little land available for grape growing, Swiss wines are in short supply and are thus more expensive than most imports. Both whites and reds are very good; the red Dole and the white Aigle are especially fine. A wine statute in 1953 imposed rigorous quality controls, and Swiss wine has retained its reputation.

Each canton has its own local **beer,** a popular beverage in German-speaking Switzerland. Beer is relatively cheap, often less expensive than Coca-Cola. Some notable brands include the dry, moderate tasting *Original Quöllfrische*, an organic lager from the Brauerei Locher in Appenzell (formerly the beer of choice on Swiss Air flights), the subtly licorice flavored *Dunkel Lagerbier*, from Stadt Bühler in Gossau, and *Chambière*, a mix of beer and sweet wine from Lucerne.

CUSTOMS & ETIQUETTE

When in Switzerland be punctual and mind your manners; remember to say hello and goodbye to shopkeepers and proprietors of bars and cafés, and always shake hands when being introduced. At mealtime, keep both hands above the table at all times, with the knife and fork "open" (apart from one another), unless you are completely finished with your meal. When dining in public, leave your fork and knife crossed in an "X" on your plate if you need to get up and do not want the server to clear your plate; when finished, place the knife and fork together in the lower right hand corner of your plate, pointing towards the center. And, though not uniform across the entire country, it is customary to greet friends or even acquaintances with a kiss on the cheek.

THE ARTS

While Switzerland is not known for erecting great monuments in the artistic canon, it does have a lively arts scene today. This scene is particularly visible in contemporary works by young Swiss artists at Zurich's cutting-edge **Kunsthaus** (see p. 395) or a night spent prowling the city's underground music scene.

ARCHITECTURE

Switzerland is home to impressive examples of various European styles, from Romanesque to Gothic to Baroque. The varying climate and distinctive building materials (stone, timber, clay) have engendered distinctive Swiss styles such as the Bernese farmhouse, the Engadine house, and the Ticino *rustico*. In recent years world-renowned architects such as Le Corbusier, Peter Zumthor, Maro Botta, and Herzog & de Meuron have given Swiss towns and cities a modern face and villages and bridges a contemporary makeover.

PAINTING & SCULPTURE

Early greats among Swiss painters include **Urs Graf** (ca. 1485-1529), a swashbuckling soldier-artist-poet skilled in court portraiture, and **Ferdinand Hodler** (1853-1918), a Symbolist painter who used Swiss landscapes to convey metaphysical messages. In the 20th century, Switzerland has been a primary space for liberal experimentation exemplified by the work of **Paul Klee,** a member of the Bauhaus faculty, and of the school of *der Blaue Reiter* (The Blue Rider) led by Kandinsky. Klee's delicate watercolors and paintings helped shape abstraction by calling dominant modes of artistic expression into question.

During the World Wars, Switzerland's art scene was energized by an influx of talented refugees, including **Jean Arp, Richard Hülsenbeck, Janco, Tristan Tzara,** and **Hugo Ball,** some of whom produced the **Dada** explosion in Zurich in 1916. Together they founded the "Cabaret Voltaire" and "Galerie Dada," short-lived centers of Dada activity (see p. 391). The Dada creed was to champion the irrational, by mocking order with chaos. Marginal participants in the Zurich Dada scene later developed into artists in their own right. **Jean Tinguely** created kinetic, mechanized Dada fantasies that celebrated the beauty (and craziness) of motion.

Between and after the wars, Switzerland continued to attract liberal artistic thinkers. The **Zurich School of Concrete Art,** which operated primarily between wars, combined elements of Surrealism with ideas from Russian Constructivism in an attempt to work with objects and environments to explore interactions between humans and space. The school included Paul Klee and **Meret Oppenheim** (a Surrealist famous for her *Fur Cup*), and its philosophy led sculptor **Alberto Giacometti** to play with spatial realities in his creations of the 1930s. Later, Giacometti rejected the premise of Surrealism in order to concentrate on a deep representationalism, creating small, exaggerated, slender figures like *Man Pointing*. After sitting out the Second World War in London and spending time in Prague, Austrian Expressionist painter **Oskar Kokoschka** moved to Switzerland in 1953, settling in Villeneuve. When Kokoschka died in 1980, his widow Olda found herself with an overabundance of pictures and subsequently founded the Foundation Oskar Kokoschka in the Musée Jenisch in Vevey (see p. 518).

LITERATURE

Though not particularly renowned for its native literary traditions, Switzerland has been home to many famous and talented writers. **Jean-Jacques Rousseau,** best known for his *Social Contract* (inspiration for the French Revolution) was born in Geneva in 1712. Rousseau always proudly recognized his Swiss background, despite the facts that he spent most of his time outside the country and that the Swiss burned his books. A more conventional Swiss resident, **Jacob Burckhardt** promoted a new history of culture and art from his Basel home in the late 19th century. His works include *History of the Italian Renaissance* and *Cicerone: A Guide to the Enjoyment of Italian Art.*

EXILES & EMIGRÉS

Ever since **Voltaire** came to Geneva in 1755 to do some heavy-duty philosophizing, Switzerland has been the promised land for intellectuals, artists, and soon-to-be-famous personalities. George Gordon, otherwise known as the opium-smoking Romantic **Lord Byron,** quit England in 1816 for Switzerland. Byron wrote "Sonnet on Chillon" while brooding on Lake Geneva; his contemporary **Percy Shelley** crafted "Hymn to Beauty" and "Mont Blanc" in the vale of Chamonix. His wife **Mary Wollstonecraft Shelley** came across some ghost stories while in Switzerland, which, heightened by Switzerland's eternal mist and craggy Alps, inspired *Frankenstein.* Speaking of ghosts, such geniuses as **Gogol, Dostoyevsky, Hugo, Hemingway,** and **Fitzgerald** still haunt the Geneva countryside where they wrote when they were in more solid form. **James Joyce** fled to Zurich during WWI and stayed to scribble the greater part of *Ulysses* between 1915 and 1919. Other great minds came from Germany, Austria, and Italy. **Johann Wolfgang von Goethe** caught his first distant view of Italy from the top of St. Gotthard Pass in the Swiss Alps. **Friedrich Schiller** wrote about the massive church bell in Schaffhausen before penning *Wilhelm Tell.* While on holiday in the Engadin Valley, **Friedrich Nietzsche** went nuts and produced his mountaintop tome *Thus Spoke Zarathustra.* **Richard Wagner** composed most of his major operas during his years with Nietzsche in verdant Switzerland. **Thomas Mann** also found refuge in Switzerland, using one of the Swiss Alps as the setting for his novel *The Magic Mountain.* More recently Switzerland has harbored writers and scientists from the former Eastern bloc, notably Russian author **Alexander Solzhenitsyn** and Czech novelist **Milan Kundera.**

The age of Romanticism found **J.J. Bodmer** and **J.J. Breitinger's** advocacy of literature in Swiss German in conflict with many of their German contemporaries who strove to standardize German through literature. The Swiss-born **Madame de Staël** (born Germaine Necker) was an important writer in her own right and the driving force behind Romanticism's spread from Germany to France. Switzerland produced a few Romantic authors as well, most notably **Gottfried Keller,** who penned a classic 19th-century German *Bildungsroman,* entitled *Der Grüne Heinrich.* **Conrad Ferdinand Meyer** was another highly influential Swiss poet, whose writings, which feature individualistic heroes, effectively unite characteristics of Romanticism and Realism.

Only in the 20th century has Swiss literature come into its own with such greats as **Hermann Hesse,** who wrote the masterpiece *Siddhartha* and received the Nobel Prize for literature in 1946. Hesse's works, including *Steppenwolf* and *Narcissus and Goldmund,* explore the duality of spirit and nature and the protagonist's journey to inner self. Writer and psychologist **Karl Gustav Jung** began as an acolyte of Freud but split off by 1915 when he wrote *Symbols of Transformation;* later he set a growing psychoanalytic practice in Zurich. Critics laud **Max Frisch** for his Brechtian style and thoughtful treatment of Nazi Germany; his most widely known works are the play *Andorra* and the novel *Homo Faber,* which was made into a film in the early 1990s. **Friedrich Dürrenmatt** has written a number of cutting, humorous plays, most notably *Der Besuch der Alten Dame* (The Visit of the Old Lady) and *Die Physiker* (The Physicists). Both Dürrenmatt and Frisch are critical of but loyal to their home country.

SWITZERLAND

MUSIC

The subversive artistic spirit of the late 20th century has generated a handful of musical groups that have their pulse on the sound of the 21st. Most of them produce alternative music aimed at teenagers and twentysomethings, but their experimentalism extends to all age groups, particularly in the swinging festivals that heat up the summer nights throughout Switzerland.

A sampling of currently popular bands might feature **Chitty Chitty Bang Bang,** a Franco-Swiss rock foursome which has self-produced two CDs. On another note, **Der Klang** has invented a French *chanson* style which has led them far from the well-trodden tracks of the genre. Popular not only in Switzerland but also in Germany and Japan, **Gotthard's** raw, bluesy vocals, hard-rock rhythms and plentiful solos recall the sound of Bon Jovi. A rock band with folk roots, Geneva's **Polar** has performed with the likes of Massive Attack and Fiona Apple. The phrase "Swiss hip-hop" may incur some skepticism, but Switzerland does hold its own with a handful of groups, including Lausanne's **Legal, Rade,** and **Osez;** Geneva's **Fidel'Escro;** Vevey's **CE-2P;** and Neuchâtel's **La Sorcellerie.** Crossing over another genre is the jazz musician **Erik Truffaz,** who learned his trumpet skills from the famed Miles Davis. His sound combines jazz with rap and drum'n'bass influences.

FILM

As in Austria, the Swiss government subsidizes many film projects in order to encourage the growth of a domestic film industry. Switzerland has produced a handful of pictures that have garnered recognition at various international film festivals. Its own annual Locarno Film Festival, with over 4000 film professionals representing 20 countries in attendance, is considered to be among the top six film festivals in the world.

The Swiss have also made their mark on American film industry. **Emil Jannings** won the first Academy Awards for Best Actor for his work in *The Way of All Flesh* (1927) and *The Last Commandment* (1928). Swiss American and Academy Award winner William Wyler directed numerous noteworthy pictures including *Ben Hur.* More recently, H.R. Giger served as art director and set designer for the intense and gripping films *Alien* and *Species.*

SPORTS & RECREATION

The active Swiss spend much of their leisure time doing athletics. Thus, it came as no surprise when in 1972 a federal law ensured government financial support for the promotion of sports. Exercise and sports are regarded as integral parts of life and there are numerous sports organizations throughout the country. Even the headquarters of the **International Olympic Committee (IOC)** are located in Lausanne.

With more than 50,000 kilometers of designated footpaths, **hiking** remains one of the most popular recreational activities. **Skiing** is also extremely popular; Switzerland is known for having some of the best slopes in the world. Two sports unique to the country are **Hornussen** and **Schwingen. Hornussen** involves an offensive team that uses long metal rods with wooden handles to knock a disc called the *hornuss* as far as possible down the field, while the defensive team uses a wooden shield to prevent the advance of the disc. If the disc lands on the field without being intercepted, the defense loses a point; if the defense knocks it down, they gain a point. **Schwingen** (see p. 389) is a type of Swiss wrestling in which each participant grabs the waistband of his opponent with his right hand and a band on his opponent's leg with his left hand in an attempt to throw him down and hold his back to the ground. The match is over once the wrestler loses both hand-holds or has both shoulder blades touching the ground.

HOLIDAYS & FESTIVALS

National holidays in Switzerland are almost all of Christian origin. Expect most establishments to be closed on Easter (April 11 in 2004), Christmas (December 25), New Year's Eve (December 31), and Good Friday (April 9), in some areas.

SWITZERLAND'S HOLIDAYS (2004)

DATE	NAME & LOCATION	DESCRIPTION
January 1	New Year's Day	Celebration of the new year.
March 1	Unabhängigkeitstag; Neuchâtel	Independence Day.
April 30	Walpurgis Nacht	Night before May 1, when witches dance on the Blocksberg in the German Harz mountain range.
August 1	Swiss National Day	Commemoration of the agreement made at the beginning of August 1291 between Uri, Schwyz, and Unterwalden.
September 16	Bettag/Jeûne	Swiss "Thanksgiving."
October 25	United Nations Day	Commemoration of the ratification of the UN charter in 1994.
December 31	Restoration	Celebration of the restoration of the oligarchic Republic after brief French domination.

ADDITIONAL RESOURCES

GENERAL HISTORY

Target Switzerland: Swiss Armed Neutrality in World War II (2000). Stephen P. Halbrook.

Swiss Banks and Jewish Souls (1999). Gregg J. Rickman.

Why Switzerland? (1996). Jonathan Steinberg.

FICTION

Siddhartha (1922) and Steppenwolf (1927). Hermann Hesse.

Daisy Miller (1878). Henry James.

Frankenstein (1818). Mary Shelley.

A Tramp Abroad (1879). Mark Twain.

TRAVEL BOOKS

The German Way: Aspects of Behavior, Attitudes, and Customs in the German-Speaking World (1996). Hyde Flippo.

Living and Working in Switzerland: A Survival Guide (2000). David Hampshire.

Trekking and Climbing in the Western Alps (2002). Hilary Sharp.

SWITZERLAND

FESTIVAL FEVER Back in the 70s, a handful of Swiss hipsters put a new spin on the timeworn tradition of celebrating the harvest or honoring a religious holiday with a rip-roaring raucous festival. What started as a small movement has grown to encompass more than a dozen festivals in nearly every part of the Swiss countryside. Thousands of people flock from festival to festival all summer long, following the sounds of jazz, blues, folk, rock, pop, soul, funk, hip-hop, drum 'n bass, house, and techno. Many of the festivals offer free campsites for all comers, and have cheap tickets. Listed below are the festivals not to be missed.

Bern, *Gurtenfestival*. This 3-day festival in mid-July attracts 15,000 visitors per day to the Gurten hill above Bern (5min. from town center). Features 2 stages, a half-pipe area, and a DJ area. Oasis featured in 2002. (www.gurtenfestival.ch.)

Winterthur, *Winterthurer Musikfestwochen*. This 17-day festival in late August exhibits over 100 acts of many genres. Open-air festival the last weekend. (☎(052) 212 61 16; www.winterthur.musikfestwochen.ch.)

Nyon (near Geneva), *Paléo Festival Nyon*. Switzerland's largest open-air music festival in late July wins the prize for diversity of acts, ranging from electric salsa, hip hop and reggae to trip hop, drum 'n bass, and electronic vibes, as well as rock, pop, blues, and even traditional French *chanson*. A free campsite offers sleeps for thousands of festival-goers. (☎(022) 365 10 10; www.paleo.ch.)

Le Lausanne/Pulley for the Noise, An alternative to alternative music festivals, this 3-day fest in early-August focuses on new up-and-coming groups as well as standbys like Sneaker Pimps and Hillbilly Moon Explosion. (www.fornoise.ch.)

St. Gallen, *Open-Air St. Gallen*. This weekend festival in late June combines crowd-pleasing favorites like the Underworld and Rage Against the Machine with many less mainstream bands. (☎(0878) 877 994; cwww.openairsg.ch.)

Zurich, *Streetparade*. For one day in early August more than 400,000 house and techno fans congregate on the streets of Zurich and stay to party afterwards. No invitation necessary. (www.street-parade.ch.)

Gampel (near Sion), is growing in popularity, attracting 30,000+ visitors each year because of appearances by big names such as The Cure and Papa Roach. (☎(027) 932 50131; www.openairgampel.ch.)

BERNESE OBERLAND

The Swiss are fiercely proud of the Bernese Oberland. When WWII threatened to engulf the country, the Swiss army resolved to defend the area to the death and were aided in their endeavor by the natural fortress of savage mountains. The jutting peaks now shelter a pristine and silent wilderness that lends itself to discovery through scenic hikes up the mountains and around the twin lakes, the Thunersee and Brienzersee. Not surprisingly, the area's opportunities for paragliding, mountaineering, and white-water rafting are unparalleled. As a consequence, the lakeside towns attract a young, international, and occasionally rowdy crowd. Just north of the mountains and lakes lies the exuberant Bern, Switzerland's capital and the metropolitan heartbeat of the region. Bern's wide streets buzz with activity, while hills in the background hint at the wilderness just a short train ride to the south.

The Bernese Oberland provides oodles of hiking opportunities, but plan your trips wisely: cable cars are expensive. Whenever possible, *Let's Go* lists hikes possible without mechanical assistance. Try to use a town or village as a hub from which to explore the surrounding area, or buy a regional pass. The 15-day **Berner Oberland Regional Pass** (240SFr; with SwissPass or half-fare card 192SFr) grants five days of unlimited regional travel and a 50% discount on the other 10. A eight-day pass (195SFr, with SwissPass 156SFr) includes three days of unlimited travel and a 50% discount on the other four days. Both are available at train stations.

HIGHLIGHTS OF THE BERNESE OBERLAND

Climb the Münster for the best view in **Bern** (p. 343).

Ski surrounded by natural grandeur on the awesome **Jungfraujoch** (p. 372).

Scream, soar, and hold onto your lunch as you paraglide over **Interlaken** (p. 357).

BERN
☎031

Though it borders the French-speaking part of the country, Bern belongs to German-speaking Switzerland. The Duke of Zähringen founded Bern in 1191, naming it for his mascot, the bear. It's been the capital since 1848, but don't expect fast tracks, power politics, or men in black—Bern prefers to focus on the finer things in life. Endless arcade-lined streets house to numerous shops and *Weinstubes*, inspiring the adage, "Venice is built on water, Bern on wine." The not-to-be-missed Rosengarten (Rose Garden) peers over the city, while the lush, green banks of the serpentine Aare provide respite for laid-back locals. Rebuilt in 1405 after a devastating fire, Bern's sandstone and mahogany buildings are dominated by the Bundeshaus and the Gothic Münster's spire. Such architectural marvels caused UNESCO to name the city a world treasure in 1983.

⊠ INTERCITY TRANSPORTATION

Flights: Bern-Belpmoos Airport (☎960 21 11), 20min. from central Bern and served by Air Engadina (☎08 48 84 83 28). Direct flights daily to **Amsterdam, Basel, Brussels, London, Lugano, Munich, Paris, Rome,** and **Vienna.** 50min. before each flight, an airport bus that guarantees you'll make it leaves from the train station in front of the tourist office (10min., 14SFr). Check at the tourist office for a current bus schedule.

Trains: In the station, the **domestic ticket counter** is upstairs (open daily 5:30am-9:45pm); **international tickets** can be bought at the ticket office upstairs (open M-F 7:30am-6:50pm, Sa 7:30am-4:50pm), or, if it's closed, at the domestic counter for

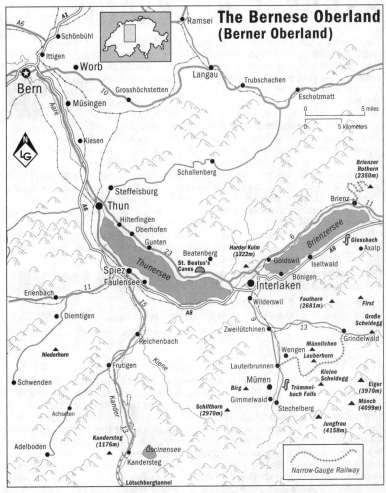

The Bernese Oberland
(Berner Oberland)

trips in the next 48hr. To: **Basel** (1¼hr., 4 per hr. 4:33am-11:52pm, 34SFr); **Berlin** (8hr., 14 per day 5:49am-11:17pm, 245SFr); **Geneva** (2hr., 3 per hr. 4:26am-11:24pm, 47SFr); **Interlaken** (50min., every hr. 6:22am-11:26pm, 23SFr); **Lausanne** (1¼hr., every 30min. 4:26am-11:24pm, 30SFr); **Lucerne** (1½hr., every 30min. 5:04am-11:21pm, 30SFr); **Milan** (3½hr., 6 daily 7:34am-4:22pm, 72SFr); **Munich** (6½hr., every hr. 5:49am-9:49pm, 117SFr); **Paris** (6hr., almost every hr. 5:49am-11:24pm, 109SFr); **Salzburg** (7¼hr., 2 per day 5:47am-9:49pm, 130SFr); **Vienna** (12hr., every hr., 5:47am-11:17pm, 157SFr); **Zurich** (1¼hr., every 30min. 5:04am-11:52pm, 45SFr). 25% reduction on all international fares for ages 26 and under.

By car: From **Basel** or the **north,** take A2 south to A1. From **Lucerne** or the **east,** take 10 west. From **Geneva** or **Lausanne,** take E62 east to E27/A12 north. From **Thun** or the **southeast,** take A6 north.

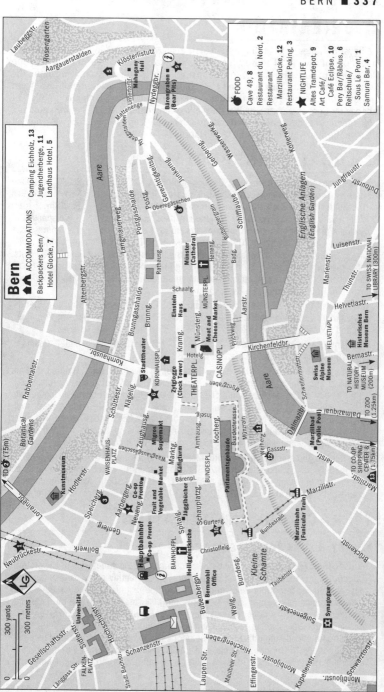

Bern

▲▲ ACCOMMODATIONS
Backpackers Bern/
Hotel Glocke, **7**
Camping Eichholz, **13**
Jugendherberge, **11**
Landhaus Hotel, **5**

🍴 **FOOD**
Cave 49, **8**
Restaurant du Nord, **2**
Restaurant
Marzilibrücke, **12**
Restaurant Peking, **3**
★ **NIGHTLIFE**
Altes Tramdepot, **9**
Art Café/
Café Eclipse, **10**
Pery Bar/Ráblus, **6**
Reitschule/
Sous Le Pont, **1**
Samurai Bar, **4**

⚡ ORIENTATION

Medieval Bern lies in front of the train station and along the Aare River, which cuts in and out of the city. The Kornhausbr. leads across the river to the north to the newer, less picturesque side of town. Staying to the south and venturing along the river walkways near Marzilibr. and Helvetiapl. is a favorite pasttime of locals and tourists alike. Bern is worth touring even on a rainy day, thanks to the 6km of arcades that cover the streets. **Warning:** Like many cities, Bern has a drug community; it tends to congregate around the Parliament park and Münster terraces, and, at night, in the stairways around the train station.

⊑ LOCAL TRANSPORTATION

Public Transportation: Bernmobil, Bubenbergpl. 5 (☎321 86 41 or 321 86 31; infotel 321 84 84; info@bernmobil.ch). A **visitor's card** from the Jurahaus ticket office entitles the holder to unlimited travel on Bernmobil routes. 24hr. pass 7SFr; 48hr. 11SFr; 72hr.15SFr. This pass is cheaper than the day pass alone (9SFr), which is dispensed at vending machines along with one-way tickets (1-6 stops 1.70SFr, 7 or more stops 2.60SFr; children always 1.70SFr; SwissPass valid). Buses run roughly 5:45am-midnight. **Nightbuses** called "Moonliners" leave the train station at 12:45am Th-Sa nights, also regularly 2-3:15am F-Sa nights, covering major bus and tram lines (5-20SFr; no reductions). The Bernmobil office has maps and timetables. Open M-W and F 6:30am-7:30pm, Th 6:30am-9pm, Sa-Su 7:30am-6:30pm.

Taxis: Bären-Taxi (☎371 11 11). **NovaTaxi** (☎331 33 13, www.novataxi.ch). Stands: Bahnhofpl., Waisenhauspl., and Casinopl. 6.80SFr base; 3.10SFr per km; 8pm-6am, Su and holidays 3.40SFr per km.

Car Rental: Avis AG, Wabernstr. 41 (☎378 15 15). **Hertz AG,** Kocherg. 1, Casinopl. (☎318 21 60). **Europcar,** Laupenstr. 22 (☎381 75 55).

Parking: At the **Bahnhof,** entrance at Schanzenbr. or Stadtbachstr, at **Parking Casino,** Kocherg. and **Metro,** on Waisenhauspl., as well as **City West,** Belpstr., runs 1.80-3.60SFr per hr. Day-permit parking discs available at the tourist office. Parking permits (9SFr) available at machines at tram stops. Note: all decks are underground; well-placed road signs throughout the city report how many free spaces remain and point the way toward the various decks. Many parking locations have spots on the first level that are well lit and reserved only for single women (*Frauenplätze*).

Bike Rental: The small blue **Bernrollt Kiosk** outside the train station and another at Kornhauspl. lends bikes for **free.** 20SFr deposit plus ID required. Bikes must be returned on the same day. Open daily May-Oct. 7:30am-9:30pm. Also try the luggage counter at the **train station.** (☎05 12 20 23 74. Open daily 7am-9pm. 30SFr per day.

⚡ PRACTICAL INFORMATION

TOURIST & FINANCIAL SERVICES

Tourist Office: (☎328 12 12; www.bernetourism.ch), on the street level of the station. Distributes city maps (1SFr) and *Bern Aktuell,* a bi-monthly guide to events in the city, and makes free room reservations. Pick up the restaurant guide called *Magenfahrplan,* which has a small, free version of the bulky map sold by the tourist office. For those who need a large fold-out map, the free blue-and-yellow *Bern: Plan/Map mit sofortiger Übersicht* is excellent and even includes bus routes. The 24hr. electronic board outside the office has a free phone line to hotels, computerized receipts, and directions in German, French, and English. Daily **city tours** available by bus (10am, 25SFr), on foot (2:30pm, 14SFr), or by raft (26.80-40.40SFr). Open June-

Sept. daily 9am-8:30pm; Oct.-May M-Sa 9am-6:30pm, Su 10am-5pm. **Branch office** at the bear pits (see p. 343) open daily June-Sept. 9am-6pm; Oct. and Mar.-May 11am-4pm; Nov.-Feb. F-Su 10am-4pm.

Budget Travel: STA, Zeughausg. 18 (☎312 07 24; www.statravel.ch). Sells ISICs. Open M-W and F 9:30am-7pm, Th 9:30am-8pm, Sa 10am-4pm. **Hang Loose,** Spitalg. 4 (☎313 18 18; www.hangloose.ch), has student airfares and ISICs. Open M-F 9am-6pm, Th 9am-8pm, Sa 9am-noon.

Embassies and Consulates: Nearly all foreign embassies in Switzerland are in Bern, southeast of the Kirchenfeldbr. A complete list of consular services can be found in the **Essentials** section (see p. 7).

FÜSSGÄNGER FRIENDLY The wide cobblestone streets of Bern unequivocally belong to the *Füssgänger* (pedestrian). Even in the sections of the *Altstadt* that do allow motor vehicles, most are forced to a slow crawl by the crowds of diners and merrymakers who own the streets. Along with pedestrians, the motorists in Bern have a more formidable obstacle: the city's ubiquitous 16th-century fountains. Most of the fountains, or *Brunnen*, are attributed to the sculptor Hans Gieng. The stone fountains have been restored repeatedly since the mid-1500s to maintain their gaudy color schemes (the city mascot, the bear, shows up in fire-engine red). Highlights include the Gerechtigkeitsbrunnen on Gerechtigkeitsg., in which Justice stomps on the Pope, Emperor, Sultan, and Mayor; and the *Kindlifresserbrunnen* ("Child-Devourer Fountain") at Kornhauspl., tastefully translated as "Ogre Fountain."

Currency Exchange: Downstairs in the station. No commission on traveler's checks. Cash advances on DC/MC/V. Western Union transfers daily 7am-7pm. Exchange open daily 6:30am-9pm. Automatic **24hr. currency exchange machines** at UBS across from the station at Bubenbergpl. 3, and at the Migros Bank, Aarbergerg. 20.

ATM: At the train station or at **Credit Suisse** (Kornhauspl. 7, M-F 8am-6pm; Bundespl. 2, M-F 8:30am-4:30pm, Th until 6pm) and **UBS** (Bubenbergpl. 3, Bärenpl. 8, M-W and F 9am-6:30pm, Th until 6pm).

LOCAL SERVICES

Luggage Storage: Downstairs in the train station. 24hr. Lockers 4-8SFr. **Luggage watch** at the Fly-Gepäck counter upstairs 7SFr. Open daily 7:30am-10pm.

Lost Property: Downstairs in station (open M-F 8am-6pm) and at Zeughausg. 18 (☎220 23 37; open M-F 8am-noon and 2-6pm).

Bookstore: JäggiBücher, Spitalg. on Bubenbergpl. 47-51 (☎320 20 20), in Loeb dept. store. 2 floors of books including English best-sellers and travel guides. Open M-W and F 9am-6:30pm, Th 9am-9pm, Sa 8am-4pm.

Libraries: Stadtbibliothek (Municipal and University Library), Münsterg. 61 (☎320 32 11), stacks books for the central library of the University of Bern and the city's public library. Open M-F 9am-5pm. *Medienraum* (on 2nd floor) with **internet** and general work spaces open M-Tu and Th-F 10am-9pm, W noon-9pm, Sa 8am-noon. **Swiss National Library,** Hallwylstr. 15 (☎332 89 11). Lending library and catalog room open M-Tu and Th-F 9am-6pm, W 9am-8pm, Sa 9am-2pm. Reading room open M-Tu and Th-F 8am-6pm, W 8am-8pm, Sa 9am-4pm.

Bi-Gay-Lesbian Organizations: Homosexuelle Arbeitsgruppe die Schweiz-HACH (Gay Association of Switzerland), c/o Anderland, Mühlenpl. 11, CH-3011 Bern. Headquarters of Switzerland's largest gay organization. **Homosexuelle Arbeitsgruppe Bern (HAB),** Mühlenpl. 11, Case Postal 312, CH-3000 Bern 13 (☎311 63 53) in Marzilibad,

THE LOCAL STORY

JUST YOUR EVERYDAY SOLDIER

Although hands-off when it comes to international politics, Switzerland maintains a military through mandating the compulsory service of every young Swiss male. Micha Zollinger, a 21-year-old from Laupen (near Bern), talked to Let's Go *about the Swiss military system and his unique experiences serving his country.*

In Switzerland, every male, from the age of 18 until he is 30, is required to serve in the military. It used to be till you were 42, but they shortened it a few years ago. When you turn 18, you go and take a bunch of tests. They test your physical skills, give you a physical check-up, and some psychological tests. About 15% of the guys tested are *untauglich*—unfit for military service from the beginning. They are people with some sort of health problem—asthmatics, people with knee problems, that sort of thing. They go straight into the *Zivilschutz* (civil guard). During the year, the *Zivilschutz* has maybe two or three meetings together, and does some work in the community.

The rest of the group has a few options. You can go into regular *Militärdienst* (military service), which is what most people do. First you start with four straight months of *Rekrutenschule*, a boot camp, basically. You stand in rows and practice saluting. You walk in lines. Then you stand around some more. You also carry a gun.

along the Aare. Hosts get-togethers W evenings, with coffee, drinks, and library access. **Schlub** (Gay Students' Organization), c/o Studentinnenschaft, Lercheweg 32, CH-3000 Bern 9 (☎371 00 87).

Laundromat: Jet Wasch, Dammweg 43 (☎078 743 92 09). Take bus #20 (dir.: Wyler) to "Lorraine." Wash 8kg for 6SFr, 5kg 4SFr; dry 4SFr for 1hr. Soap 0.80-1.20SFr. Open M-Sa 7am-9pm, Su 9am-6pm.

Public Toilets and Showers: McClean, at train station. 1-2SFr for toilets, 12SFr for towels, shampoo, and 20min. showers. Open daily 6am-midnight.

EMERGENCY & COMMUNICATIONS

Emergency: Police ☎ 117 and downstairs in the station, **Ambulance** ☎144, **Doctor** ☎311 22 11, **Rape Crisis Hotline** ☎332 14 14, **Mental Health Hotline** ☎ 143.

Pharmacy: In the station. Open daily 6:30am-10pm. **Bären Apotheke,** at the clock tower. Open M 1:45-6:30pm, Tu-W and F 7:45am-6:30pm, Th 7:45am-9pm, Sa 8am-4pm. AmEx/DC/MC/V. In the **Co-op Shopping Center** near Camping Eichholz. Open M-F 8am-6:30pm, Sa 8am-4pm. **24hr. pharmacy** call ☎311 22 11.

Internet Access: Stadtbibliothek, Münsterg. 61, offers Internet access for 4SFr per hr. in the *Medienraum* 1 floor up from the street. 2 terminals offer 10min. free surfing. Open M-Tu and Th-F 10am-9pm, W noon-9pm, Sa 8am-noon. **JäggiBücher,** Spitalg. on Bubenbergpl. 47-51 (☎320 20 20), in Loeb dept. store. 2 computers allow max. 20min. free, 4 more computers cost 5SFr per 30min. Open M-W and F 9am-6:30pm, Th 9am-9pm, Sa 8am-4pm.

Post Office: Schanzenpost 1, a block from the train station. *Poste Restante* to Postlagernde Briefe, Schanzenpost 3000, Bern 1. Open M-F 7:30am-9pm, Sa 8am-4pm, Su 5-9pm. At Bärenpl., open M-F 9am-6:30pm, Th 9am-9pm, Sa 9am-4pm. On Senftigenstr. near Camping Eichholz, open M-F 7:30am-noon and 1:45-6pm, Sa 8:30am-noon.

Postal codes: CH-3000 to CH-3030.

🏠 🏕 ACCOMMODATIONS & CAMPING

Bern has responded to the influx of backpackers during the busy summer months with several new hostels. The tourist office has a list of pricier private rooms.

🏚 **Backpackers Bern/Hotel Glocke,** Rathausg. 75 (☎311 37 71; www.bernbackpackers.com). From the train station, cross the tram lines, turn left onto Spitalg., continuing through Bärenpl. and the Käfigturm onto Marktg. Turn left at Kornhauspl., pass the Zytglogge clock tower, and then turn right on Rathausg. The hostel will be almost immediately on your right. A backpacker's dream—clean, new, and ideally located. Crowds of American backpackers ready to socialize fill the TV/lounge area that has CNN and a pool table. Room windows overlook a bustling street in the *Altstadt*. **Internet** (2SFr for 15min.) and free access to large, constantly-used kitchen. Laundry 6SFr to wash and dry. Sheets included. Reception 8-11am and 3-10pm. Strict 10am check-out (they come wake you up). Doors lock after 10:30pm, but your keycard provides 24hr. access. 4- to 6-bed dorms 29SFr; 2-bed single-sex dorms 39SFr; singles 60-75SFr; doubles 100-120SFr, with shower 130-150SFr. AmEx/DC/MC/V, 35SFr minimum. ❷

Jugendherberge (HI), Weiherg. 4 (☎311 63 16; info@jugibern.ch). From the station, cross the tram lines and go down Christoffelg. Take the stairs to the left of the park entrance gates and go down the steep slope, then turn left onto Weiherg., following the hostel signs. A friendly European and American crowd of backpackers and families makes use of this hostel. Conveniently near to the river and its restaurants, and clubs. Large common areas feature well-worn couches and TV with CNN, and picnic tables to watch life-sized chess matches on the patio. Wheelchair-accessible. **Internet** 1SFr for 4min. or 5SFr for 25min., half-price midnight-7am. Breakfast, lockers, and sheets included. Lunch 13SFr; dinner 12SFr. Laundry Wash 4SFr, dry 1SFr per 15min. Reception June-Sept. 7-10am and 3pm-midnight; Oct.-May 7-10am and 5pm-midnight. Check-out 10am. Reservations by fax and email only. Closed 2nd and 3rd weeks in Jan. Dorms 30SFr; overflow mattresses on the floor 22SFr. Singles from 44.30SFr; doubles 72-90SFr (reserve far in advance). Tax 1.30SFr. Non-members add 6SFr. MC/V. ❷

Landhaus Hotel, Altenbergstr. 4-6 (☎331 41 66; landhaus@spectraweb.ch). From the train station, turn left on Spitalg. and follow it all the way to Nydegg Kirche. Take the stairs down to the church, walk down the hill on Nydeggstalden, cross Untertorbr., and the hotel will be on your left. Though not entirely in the town, near the bear pits and the Altes Tramdepot. Partitioned bunks located above a stylish restaurant and bar along the Aare that provides cheap take-out. Employees are very busy in the restaurant during mealtimes. Internet 1.60SFr plus time used (ask at the reception). Free kitchen access. Breakfast 7SFr. Sheets 5SFr. Reception M-Sa 7am-10pm, Su 9am-6pm. Partitioned 6-bed dorms 30SFr; singles 65-

It's not uncommon to see a guy walking down the street with his gun. You can ask to not carry a weapon, if you don't want to.

There is a third option: the *Zivildienst* (civil service). It's only for people with serious theological, philosophical, or ethical reasons why they do not want to serve in the regular military. You write up a letter, a report really, explaining your reasons and why you don't want to do it. You send it in, wait two months, and then you get an interview. If you are citing religious reasons, you will definitely have a priest as part of your interviewers. If you have ethical or philosophical reasons, there will be a professor of philosophy. There are three interviewers, and they have nothing to do with the military; they're totally separate. Since my reasons are ethical, I had two professors and a stay-at-home mom; she was the head interviewer. If you get into the civil service, you have to serve 1½ times as long as those in the military service—12 months. They give you a huge book of all the options for work. You can work at homeless shelters, at government archaelogical digs, it's really a ton of options. You have to organize it all yourself—make phone calls, set up housing, everything. I worked for four months at a shelter for asylum-seekers and at one of the government youth hostels in St. Gallen.

Oh, and I forgot a fourth option. Some people *desertieren*—they desert. You spend three months in jail, and then have to pay a big income tax, much more than the civil guard, until you're 30. I wouldn't recommend that.

105SFr; doubles with linens and breakfast 95-135SFr, with bath 140-160SFr; triples 130SFr; 4-bed family room 140-160SFr. Towels 3SFr in dorms, included in other rooms. AmEx/DC/MC/V. ❷

Camping Eichholz, Strandweg 49 (☎961 26 02; www.campingeichholz.ch). Take tram #9 to "Wabern," backtrack 50m, and take the 1st right. Walk down Eichholzstr.; signs point the way (10min.). A riverside location opposite the zoo means that the site is often packed, though with a friendly crowd of families and students. On-site restaurant. Shopping center nearby has a post office, pharmacy, and grocery store (see Local Services above and Food below). Parking 2-3.20SFr. Laundry 5SFr. Reserve ahead. Reception 7am-10pm. Open Apr. 20-Sept. 6.90SFr per person, students 5.50SFr, children under 16 3SFr, tents 5-8.50SFr. Bungalow with very simple singles 21.90SFr; doubles 23.90SFr; and triples 31.90SFr. Electricity 3SFr. Showers 1SFr. MC/V. ❶

◘ FOOD

Almost everywhere with a name ending in "-platz" overflows with cafés and restaurants. *Die Front* (the Front), a row of restaurants along Bärenpl., fills up with locals and tourists at night, when restaurant owners spread an ocean of tables and chairs across the entire street. Food along *Die Front* is moderately priced, and nothing too special—the locale is perhaps better suited for people-watching. Wherever you are, try one of the city's hearty specialties: *Gschnätzlets* (fried veal, beef, or pork), *Suurchabis* (a sauerkraut), or *Gschwellti* (steamed potatoes).

■ **Restaurant du Nord,** Lorrainestr. 2 (☎332 23 38, fax 23 00), right across Lorrainebr., or take the #20 bus to "Gewerbeschule." An open and relaxed atmosphere where a diverse, alternative crowd smokes and socializes. Polo-shirt-wearing poets sit next to guitar-playing hippies in the outdoor seating draped with vines and Christmas lights. Try some of the more creative dishes like chicken and pasta with rosemary mustard sauce. Meat entrees 22-32SFr. Pasta plates from 17SFr. Special seasonal menus. Su night Indian specials. Beer from 4SFr. Open M-F 8am-12:30am, Sa 9am-12:30am; kitchen open M-Sa 11:30am-2pm and 6:30-10pm, Su 4-11:30pm. MC/V. ❸

Restaurant Peking, Speicherg. 27 (☎312 14 28, fax 311 69 94). Find the large tree-trunk fountain on Waisenhauspl. and turn left down Speicherg.; the restaurant is on your left. One of the best budget options in Bern: get a box of hot, tasty Chinese food and a cold canned drink to take away for 9.90SFr. Eat in the clean, brightly-decorated restaurant for a bit more (12-15SFr). Open M-Sa 11am-2:30pm and 6-11:30pm. ❷

Cave 49, Gerechtigkeitsg. 49 (☎312 55 92), is what the name implies: a sort of cave underneath the sidewalk. This quality Spanish underground tavern is frequented by a boisterous local crowd. Enjoy tortellini with parmesan (15SFr) or *chorizo* (paprika sausage; 6.50SFr). Beers from 3SFr, wine from 4SFr. Open Tu-Su 10am-12:30am; kitchen open 11am-2pm and 6-10pm. V. ❷

Restaurant Marzilibrücke, Gassstr. 8 (☎311 27 80). Turn right from the Jugendherberge onto Aarstr. and then again onto Gasstr. Divided into a classy restaurant and a more casual pizzeria, this classy joint overflows with couples, families, and small groups looking to enjoy the outdoor seating just steps from the Aare. Gourmet pizzas (15.50-25.50SFr) and a quality wine list (4.20-6.70SFr per glass). Reservations recommended. Open M-Th 11:30am-11:30pm, F 11:30am-12:30am, Sa 4pm-12:30am, Su 10am-11:30pm. Pizzeria open M-F 5:30-11pm, Sa-Su 4-11pm; kitchen open daily until 10pm, pizza available daily until 11pm. AmEx/DC/MC/V. ❸

MARKETS

Co-op Shopping Center, near Camping Eichholz after Dorfstr. on Seftigenstr., has a 24-hr. ATM, Swisscom payphones, and anything else you need. Wheelchair-accessible. Open M-Th 8am-7pm, F 8am-9pm, Sa 7:30am-4pm. MC/V.

Co-op Pronto, in the train station, stocks fresh fruits, breads, and basic groceries. Wheelchair-accessible. Open M-F 7am-10pm, Sa-Su 7:30am-10pm. MC/V. A more convenient location with shorter hours is on the corner of Neueng. and Bärenpl. Open M-Th 6am-7pm, F 6am-9:30pm, Sa 6am-4pm, Su 6am-6pm. MC/V.

Migros Supermarkt, Marktg. 46, also has a restaurant and take-away counters, including one with 4.80SFr sandwiches and a daily *Menü* (10-12SFr). Wheelchair-accessible. Open M 9am-6:30pm, Tu-W and F 8am-6:30pm, Th 8am-9pm, Sa 7am-4pm.

Fruit and vegetable markets sell fresh produce daily on Bärenpl. (May-Oct. M-F 6am-6pm, Sa 6am-4pm) and every Tu and Sa 7am-noon on Bundespl. A **meat and cheese market** fills Münsterg. every Sa 7am-noon. The off-the-wall **onion market,** which takes the city by storm every 4th M of Nov., is Bern's best-known festival.

◉ 🏛 SIGHTS & MUSEUMS

Bern is a walkable city, with major sights stretching along from the Parliament. Museums ring **Helvetiaplatz** near Kirchenfeldbr. (take tram #3, 5 or 19). If you are in town in late March, check out the annual **Museum Night Bern,** when area museums stay open from 6pm-2am and host bands, bars, and restaurants (Mar. 18-19, 2004).

THE OLD TOWN. The solid medieval architecture of Bern's *Altstadt* glows red with Swiss flags and geraniums. Behind church spires and government domes, the hills along the Aare river create a majestic backdrop—on a clear day, you can even see snowy peaks in the distance. The huge **Bundeshaus,** center of the Swiss government, dominates the Aare and glows at sundown. Free tours are offered of the **Parlamentsgebäude** (Parliament building). *(☎322 85 22. Wheelchair-accessible. 45min. tour every hr. M-Sa 9-11am and 2-4pm, except on holidays and during special parliamentary proceedings. English tours at 11am, 2pm. Call the afternoon before to confirm. Free.)*

From the state house, Kockerg. and Herreng. lead to the 15th-century Protestant **Münster** (cathedral). The late Gothic structure's highlight is the sculpture above the main entrance, which depicts punished sinners in gold. Notice how none of the buttresses along the church's sides are identical. Real detectives might find the stone inscription, made without an architect's approval by one of the church's construction workers, that reads: "We did the best we could." Climb the spiral stairs of its 100m spire, one of the tallest in Switzerland, for amazing area views. *(☎312 04 62. Open Easter-Oct. Tu-Sa 10am-5pm, Su 11:30am-5:30pm; Nov.-Easter Tu-F 10am-noon and 2-4pm, Sa 10am-noon and 2-5pm, Su 11am-2pm. Tower closes 30min. before the church. 3SFr, children under 16 1SFr. Church service Su 10-11:30am.)*

From the Bundeshaus, turn left off Kocherg. at Theaterpl. to reach the 13th-century **Zytglogge** (clock tower). At 4min. before the hour, figures on the tower creak to life with highly uneventful clanging and a couple of weak rooster squawks; the oohs and aahs of gathered tourists are more fervent, but quickly die down. *(Tours of the interior May-Oct. daily 4:30pm, also July-Aug. 11:30am 8SFr.)*

BEAR PITS. Across the Nydeggbr. on the right lie the **Bärengraben** (bear pits; see **Bären Brain,** p. 344). Descendants of the original Bern bear lounge lazily in stone-lined pits that date back to the 15th century. Tour groups and screaming kids provide the bears with hours of amusement and annoyance. During Easter, newborn cubs are publicly displayed for the first time. *(Open daily June-Sept. 9am-5:30pm; Oct.-May 10am-4pm. 3SFr to feed the bears.)* The tourist office at the pits presents **The Bern**

Show, a slickly choreographed multimedia recap of Bernese history that melds into an overly indulgent photo-montage. *(Every 20min. Alternately in German and English. Free.)* The path snaking up the hill to the left leads to the ◪**Rosengarten;** sit among the blooms and admire a stellar view of Bern's *Altstadt.* The garden, the fountains and flora of which are maintained by the city of Bern, is always open. Save your legs and take the #10 bus (dir.: Ostermundigen) to "Rosengarten."

KUNSTMUSEUM. Bern's Klee-crazed Kunstmuseum sprawls over three floors and boasts the world's largest Paul Klee collection: 2500 geometrically dreamy works, from his school exercise-books to puppets made for his son Felix to huge canvases. Works by current artists are displayed next to those of artists who inspired them. A smattering of big names are upstairs: Picasso, Giacometti, Ernst Kirchner, Pollock, and some Dada works by Hans Arp. The museum also has a chic café and screens art films. *(Hodlerstr. 8-12, near Lorrainebrücke. ☎ 328 09 11; www.kunstmuseumbern.ch. Information available in English. Open Tu 10am-9pm, W-Su 10am-5pm. Mandatory bag-check 2SFr deposit. Klee collection 7SFr,*

BÄREN BRAIN Bern's citizens have bears on the brain. The city's ursine mascot pervades even the most forsaken alleys in the form of statuettes, fountains, flags, stained-glass windows, and matchbox covers. Legend has it that Duke Berchtold V of Zähringen, founder of Bern, wanted to name the city after the first animal he caught when hunting on the site of the planned construction. The animal was a you-know-what, and Bern (from *Bären,* or bears) was born. The *Bärengraben* weren't built until the Bernese victory at the Battle of Nouana in 1513, when soldiers dragged home a live bear as war booty. A hut was erected for the beast in what is now Bärenplatz (Bear Square) and his descendants have been Bern's collective pets ever since.

---

students and seniors 5SFr. Entire collection 15SFr/10SFr. Under 16 free. Extra fees for temporary exhibitions.)

RIVER AARE. Several walkways lead steeply down from the Bundeshaus to the Aare; a cable car assists passengers on the way up (wheelchair-accessible; 6:30am-9pm; 1.10SFr). The riverbank is ideal for shady walks. On hot days, locals dive lemming-style from the bridges and ride its swift currents. Only experienced swimmers should join in, especially if starting farther upstream at Eichholz. Along the banks, numerous stone steps invite you to take the plunge. For a more languid afternoon, the **Marzilibad public pool** lies on the river 3min. to the right of the Jugendherberge. *(Open May-Aug. M-F 8:30am-8pm, Sa-Su 8:30am-7pm; Sept. M-F 8:30am-7pm, Sa-Su 8:30am-6pm. Safe 2SFr; lockers and showers available.)*

GARDENS AND ZOO. The **Botanical Gardens** of the University of Bern sprawl along the river at Lorrainebrücke. Exotic plants thrive alongside native alpine greenery. *(Take bus #20 to "Gewerbeschule." ☎ 631 49 44. Park open daily Mar.-Sept. 8am-5:30pm; Oct.-Feb. 8am-5pm. Greenhouse open daily 8am-5pm. Free.)* In a shaded area next to the river across from the campgrounds, the 24hr. park housing the **Dählhölzli Städtischer Tierpark** (Zoo) gives you the chance to animal-watch at night, too. The enclosures are small and mainly for young children. *(Tierparkweg 1. Walk south along the Aare or take bus #19 to "Tierpark." ☎ 357 15 15. Open daily summer 8am-6:30pm; low-season 9am-5pm. 7SFr, students 5SFr. Parking available.)*

BERNISCHESHISTORISCHES MUSEUM. This collection jams a wealth of artifacts and displays into the three open floors of the former castle (2 floors are under renovation until 2005). Bern's lengthy history is on display, from technology to religious art to 15th-century sculptural finds. The collection of oversized Burgundian tapestries is one of the museum's prized possessions. *(Helvetiapl. 5.* ☎ *350 77 11. Tours in German, French, English. Wheelchair-accessible. Open Tu and Th-Su 10am-5pm, W 10am-8pm. 13SFr, students 8SFr, school groups and children under 16 4SFr.)*

SWISS ALPINE MUSEUM. For those at all interested in geography, maps, and moutaineering, this museum is worth a visit. Intricate models of the Alps give a history of Swiss cartography and some information on Alpine exploration. The main floor is an array of topographical models of the country and offers info-stations with innumerable slides. The second-floor exhibit on mountain life may be more interesting—check out the devil masks used to protect against threats from the other world. *(Helvetiapl. 4.* ☎ *351 04 34; www.alpinesmuseum.ch. Signs in German, French, Italian, and English. Wheelchair-accessible. Open M 2-5pm, Tu-Su 10am-5pm. 7SFr, students and seniors 4SFr. Add 1SFr for special exhibits.)*

MUSEUM OF NATURAL HISTORY. Most people come to this bright, colorful museum to see Barry, the now-stuffed St. Bernard who saved over 40 people in his lifetime. Some of the other hyper-realistic dioramas, however, get a bit more intense—hyenas feed on zebra corpses, and more dynamic cousins of the *Bärengraben* bears fight over a recently killed moose. Very family- and school group-friendly. *(Bernastr. 15, off Helvetiapl.* ☎ *350 71 11. Open M 2-5pm, Tu and Th-F 9am-5pm, W 9am-6pm, Sa-Su 10am-5pm. 5SFr, students 3SFr, extra for temporary exhibits.)*

ALBERT EINSTEIN'S HOUSE. The humble home in which Einstein lived while developing his theory of relativity is now a mecca for physics lovers. Old pictures, letters, and even a copy of his school records line the walls. *(Kramg. 49.* ☎ *312 00 91. Open Feb.-Nov. Tu-F 10am-5pm, Sa 10am-4pm. 3SFr, students and children 2SFr.)*

🎵 ENTERTAINMENT

Bern's cultural tastes run the gamut from classical music concerts to late-night café bands. Events are well publicized on kiosks and bulletin boards. Publications like *Non-Stopp* and *Berner Woche* (the "Going Out" sections of two Bern newspapers) or *Gay Agenda* are available at the tourist office, along with the most informative and complete guide, the monthly **Bewegungsmelder,** which contains concert schedules and maps pointing out all event locations.

Operas and ballets are performed at the **Stadttheater,** Kornhauspl. 20. (☎311 07 77. Summer season runs from July to late August; for ticket info, contact Theaterkasse, Kornhauspl. 18, CH-3000 Bern 7. ☎329 51 15, theaterkass@stadttheaterbern.ch. Open M-F 10am-6:30pm, Sa 10am-4pm.) Bern's **Symphony Orchestra** plays in the fall and winter at the Konservatorium für Musik, Kramg. 36. (Tickets ☎311 62 21.) July's **Gurten Festival** has attracted such luminaries as Bob Dylan, Elvis Costello, Björk, and Sinead O'Connor. (www.gurtenfestival.ch. 1-day ticket 65SFr, 2-day 95SFr, 3-day 135SFr.) Jazz-lovers arrive in early May for the **International Jazz Festival.** (Tickets at any Bankverein Swiss branch; www.jazzfestivalbern.ch. About 16SFr.) Other festivals include the Bernese Easter-egg market in late March and the notorious **Onion Market** on the fourth Monday in November. The orange grove at Stadtgärtnerei Elfnau (take tram #19 to "Elfnau") has free Sunday concerts in summer. Additionally, **Mahogany Hall,** Klösterlistutz 18, (www.mahogany.ch), by the bear pits, is a popular venue for jazz, bluegrass, and folk.

From mid-July to mid-August, **OrangeCinema** (www.orangecinema.ch) screens recently released films, including many American ones, in the open air. Buy tickets at the tourist office in the train station or at the Orange Shop at Spitalg. 14.

▣ NIGHTLIFE

The fashionable folk linger in the *Altstadt*'s bars and cafés at night. An alternative crowd gathers under the gargoyles and graffiti of the Lorrainebr., behind and to the right of the station down Bollwerk. Grab the map in Bewegungsmelder, or check out www.cityhunter.ch for DJ schedules and to plan your evening.

Pery Bar/Räblus and **Kornhausplatz**, Schmiedenpl. 3 (☎311 59 08), off Kornhauspl. The area around the Kornhaus and this "see-and-be-seen" bar floods with a 20+ crowd and the local hockey team on weekends. Disco music spins inside, but everyone chats it up outside. The Räblus Restaurant serves lunch and dinner. Beers from 4.90SFr; wines from 5SFr. Bar open M-W 5pm-1:30am, Th 5pm-2:30am, F-Sa 5pm-3:30am.

Art Café and **Café Eclipse**, Gurteng. 6 (☎318 20 70). The Art Café is a café by day, and smoky bar by night. The decor sets a casually trendy tone that is overshadowed by neighboring pophouse, Café Eclipse. Tourists and a raucous 20+ crowd leaves little room to move on most weekend nights. Occasional live acts and DJs. Beers from 5SFr. Open M-W 7pm-12:30am, Th-F 7pm-3:30am, Sa 8pm-3:30am, Su 6pm-12:30am.

Reitschule, Neubrückstr. 8 (☎302 83 72). From the station, head down Bollwerk and turn right underneath the graffitied overpass. This spot is revered by left-wing locals and virtually legendary for its activist, alternative culture and laid-back atmosphere. Even if you aren't marching for the Red Party, you and your buddies are welcome to kick back on the patio with a beer and listen to the DJ spin hip-hop and who knows what. Loafers and a slightly seedier population emerge at night, so go with a group if you don't feel entirely at ease clubbing alone. Beers from 3.50SFr. *Menüs* 5SFr. Open daily 8pm-late.

Altes Tramdepot (☎368 14 15, www.altestramdepot.ch) across Nydeggbr. to the right of the bear pits. With the distillation chambers of its brewery in full view, the Tramdepot has a laid-back air for early evening beers and conversation. Brews on tap 4-4.30SFr. Open daily summer 10am-12:30am; winter 11am-12:30am.

Samurai Bar, Aarbergerg. 35 (☎311 88 03, www.samurai-bar.ch), is the heart of Bern's limited gay clubbing scene. Dance the night away to DJs Th-Sa. Open M-Th and Su 8pm-2:30am, F-Sa 8pm-3:30am.

THE THUNERSEE

From the Thunersee, the extensive forests and peaks off the Jungfrau seem deceptively accessible. Though the lake is in fact smaller than it looks, and the Jungfrau's proximity a trick of proportion, the region boasts larger-than-life charms of its own: the area is dotted with delightful castles, and the local mountains are often cloud-covered and snowy. The Thunersee's three significant towns, **Thun**, **Spiez**, and **Interlaken**, all lie on the main Bern-Interlaken-Lucerne rail line. **Boats** operated by the BLS shipping company (☎334 52 11; www.bls.ch) putter to the smaller villages between the Thun and Interlaken West railway stations (2hr., June 26-Sept. 26 every hr. 8:10am-11:35pm, special evening cruises available June-Dec.; Eurail, SwissPass, and Berner Oberland pass valid). A ferry day-pass good as far as **Brienz** (on the Brienzersee) costs 6.60SFr.

THUN ☎033

Known as the "Gateway to the Bernese Oberland," Thun (pop. 38,000) lies on the banks of the Aare River and the Thunersee. Ringed by castles of every imaginable size and color, this quiet town caused Johannes Brahms to observe that, "relaxing in Thun is delightful, and one day will not be enough." Though picturesque and historic, Thun is not stodgy. The Selve area offers everything from crowded discothèques and bars to a roller skating rink and an indoor racetrack.

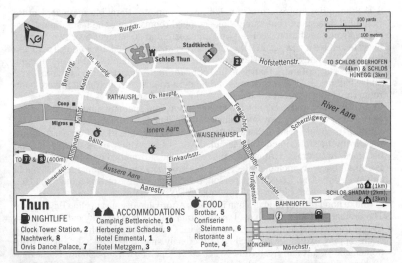

Thun

🎵 **NIGHTLIFE**
Clock Tower Station, 2
Nachtwerk, 8
Orvis Dance Palace, 7

🏠 **ACCOMMODATIONS**
Camping Bettlereiche, 10
Herberge zur Schadau, 9
Hotel Emmental, 1
Hotel Metzgern, 3

🍴 **FOOD**
Brotbar, 5
Confiserie
    Steinmann, 6
Ristorante al
    Ponte, 4

🔲 TRANSPORTATION

Trains to: Bern (every 30min. 5:12am-11:20pm, 13.40SFr); Interlaken East (every hr. 7:17am-11:47pm, 15.20SFr); Interlaken West (every hr. 6:43am-11:47pm, 14.20SFr); and Spiez (every 30min. 6:43am-12:52am, 6.60SFr). There is a rail information desk (open M-F 9am-6:30pm, Sa 9am-4pm). Boat landing (☎ 223 53 80) across the street and to the right of the station. **Boats** depart for: Faulensee (11SFr); Hilterfingen (5.60SFr); Interlaken West (20SFr); Oberhofen (6.60SFr); and Spiez (10.20SFr).

✴🔢 ORIENTATION & PRACTICAL INFORMATION

Thun is split by outflow of the Thunersee, and its *Altstadt* is situated on an island surrounded by the roaring waters of the Innare Aure and the Aussare Aure. Thun's main street is the tree-lined boulevard Bälliz, which changes to Einkaufstrasse halfway down the length of the island. The oldest squares and the castle (all hung with red-and-white flags) lie across the river from the train station on the Aare's north bank. Thun's **tourist office,** Seestr. 2, is outside and to the left of the station. (☎ 222 23 40; fax 83 23. Open July-Aug. M-F 8am-7pm, Sa 9am-noon and 1-4pm; Sept.-June M-F 8am-noon and 1-6pm, Sa 9am-noon.) Services include: **currency exchange** (M-Sa 6am-8pm, Su 6:30am-8pm) and **bike rental** (open M-Sa 8:30am-8pm; 30SFr per day). **Lockers** (4-6SFr) are at the station. **Free bike rental** at Waisenhauspl. next to the post office. (Open May-Oct. 7:30am-9:30pm, ID and 20SFr deposit required, bikes must be returned on the same day.) **Taxis** usually wait outside the station, or dial ☎ 22 22. **Parking** is available at the Parkhaus Aarestr. on Aarestr. (☎ 222 78 26; 1.50SFr per hr.; half-price nights and weekends.) Get **Internet** access at the Cipper Club (Bälliz 25). The **post office** is at Panaromastr. 1a, across from the station. (Open M-F 7:30am-7pm, Sa 8am-noon.) **Postal code:** CH-3601.

🏠🍴 ACCOMMODATIONS & FOOD

The **Herberge zur Schadau** ❸ packs 30 beds into five small rooms—there's a good chance you'll get to know your fellow hostelers quite well. Exit the train station, turn right, and walk 10min. down Seestr. (☎ 222 52 22. Breakfast included. Reception

8am-8pm, quiet hours 11pm-7am. 39SFr per person.) **Hotel Metzgern ❸**, Untere Hauptg. 2, has simple but sunny sink-equipped rooms above the restaurant downstairs. From the station, veer left on Bahnhofstr. and go straight over two bridges. Signs lead the way. (☎222 21 41; fax 21 82. Breakfast included. Reception Tu-Th and Su 8am-11:30pm, F-Sa 8am-12:30am. Singles, doubles, triples 62SFr per person; 55SFr for stays of more than 1 night; 50SFr for more than 1 week. Children 7 and under half-price. MC/V.) Spacious and modern rooms with sparkling private bathrooms are hidden within the unique exterior of **Hotel Emmental ❹**, Bernstr. 2. (☎222 01 20. Breakfast and sheets included. Reception 7am-2pm and 4pm-midnight. Apr.-Oct. 80SFr per person. Nov.-Mar. singles 70SFr, doubles 120SFr.)

Campers should head to **Camping Bettlereiche ❶**. Take bus #1 to "Camping" or turn right from the station and walk 45min. down Seestr., which veers sharply left and becomes Gwattstr. The campsite is near water and surrounded by hills. (☎336 40 67; fax 40 17. Showers included. Reception 8:30am-noon and 2-7:30pm, until 8:30pm in July-Aug. July-Aug. 7.60SFr per person, 8-10SFr per tent; Apr.-June and Sept.-Oct. 7.40SFr per person, 7-9SFr per tent. AmEx/MC/V.)

Unlike hotel rooms, food in Thun is cheap. Affordable restaurants line Bahnhofstr. The **Brotbar ❶**, Bälliz 11, is equal parts corner bakery and swanky café. Cross the river at Allmendbr. and turn right onto Bälliz. Order from a health-conscious menu while sipping exotic teas (3.60SFr), or a creamy smoothie (2.50-3SFr) made from homemade yogurt and fresh fruit. (☎222 22 21. Open M-W 7am-6:30pm, Th-Sa 7am-12:30am. Wheelchair-accessible.) Dine and feed the waterfowl at **Ristorante Al Ponte ❸**, Freienhofg. 16, at the foot of the Sinnebr. beside the river. Prices here are mostly in the teens; the *gnocchi al Arrabiata* is a good choice at 14.50SFr (Hours variable. Outside tables wheelchair-accessible.) For delectable pastries and sandwiches in a comfy corner tea room, try **Confiserie Steinmann ❶**, Bälliz 37, just past Brotbar. Enjoy mouth-watering *Thuner Leckerli* made from honey, lemon rind, and nuts (5 pieces 6SFr) or strawberry tarts for 3.50SFr. (☎222 20 47. Wheelchair-accessible. Open M 1-6:30pm, Tu-W and F 6:45am-6:30pm, Sa 6:45am-4pm.)

Both **Migros** and **Co-op** have markets and restaurants on Allmendstr. straddling the Kuhbr. (Both open M-W and F 8am-6:30pm, Th 8am-9pm, Sa 7:30am-4pm.) At the **open-air market** in the *Altstadt*, across the river from the train station, vendors hawk souvenirs, clothes, and produce (Sa 8am-noon). A **food market** covers Bälliz on Wednesdays and Saturdays 8am-2pm.

◉ SIGHTS

SCHLOß THUN. Thun's centerpiece, this castle looks down over the town from the top of the *Altstadt*. The castle houses a historical museum whose upper floors show off a collection of vicious weaponry, and a floor full of old folk instruments including Alphorns, accordions, and even a hammered dulcimer. The tower was the site of a gruesome fratricide in 1322, when Eberhard of Kyburg unsportingly defenestrated his brother Hartmann, but the windows now serve only to give visitors great views of the mountains surrounding Thun. Downstairs in the *Rittersaal* (Knight's Hall) the castle hosts classical music concerts June 7-25. (☎223 20 01. *From the station, bear left down Bahnhofstr. and go over 2 bridges, right onto Obere Hauptg., left up the Risgässli steps, and left again at the top; follow the signs to Schloß/Museum. Open Apr.-Oct. daily 10am-5pm. 6SFr, students 4SFr, children 2SFr, children under 6 free, families 12SFr. For concert tickets call* ☎223 25 30 *or contact the tourist office; tickets 30-50SFr.*)

SCHLOß SCHADAU. The pastel pink Schloß Schadau, in the peaceful Walter Hansen Schadaupark on the shores of the Thunersee, was built in the style of castles in France's Loire Valley. The castle houses a large gastronomy book collection and a fabulous **restaurant**. Hidden by the foliage, the nearby **Wocher Panorama** recreates the lake and its environs with a room-sized painting of the area. *(Seestr. 45; from the station, turn right and walk about 15min. ☎223 24 62. Panorama open May-Oct. daily 10am-5pm. 4SFr, students 3SFr, under 17 free.)*

SCHLOß HÜNEGG. Located in the wooded hills of Hilterfingen, Hünegg, the most elaborate of the Thunersee castles, houses displays of well-preserved and lavish *fin de siêcle* furnishings along with an 1863 drinking hall. Though left unchanged since 1900, the castle is very much in use—it even hosts the occasional birthday party. *(Bus #21 runs to Hilterfingen. Walk 100m back towards Thun; castle will be on the right. ☎243 19 82. Open mid-May to mid-Oct. M-Sa 2-5pm, Su 10am-noon and 2-5pm. 8SFr, students 7SFr, children 1.50SFr.)*

◤ OUTDOOR ACTIVITIES

The popular local half-day **hike** up **Heilingenschwendi,** the hillside above Thun on the lake's north shore, provides a view of the distant Jungfrau mountains. Past the casino and the village of Seematten, turn left, cross the river, and head up through the wooded ridge. Continue farther to the **Dreiländeregg** and **Niesenbänkli** for a panoramic view (3hr.). If you push on to the village of **Schwendi,** near the top, continue hiking a little farther to **Schloß Oberhofen** (see above), where you can catch bus #21 back to town. If the *Schlößer* stifle you, hit the water. There are numerous places to jump in, but the turquoise water is a little cold, so be prepared. The tourist office has information on **sailing, wind-surfing, river-rafting,** and **boat rental.**

◪ ◩ ENTERTAINMENT & NIGHTLIFE

Bälliz is lined with pricey drinking spots, most with outdoor seating. For a lower-key, cheaper evening, head to **Clock Tower Station,** Obere Hauptg. 89, just a few paces past the Risgässli steps that lead to Schloß Thun. Canadians will feel at home in this small, Canuck-themed sports bar, though the crowd is mainly composed of a loyal group of Thun locals. Grilled food served until 2am. (☎223 57 96. Open Tu-Sa 6pm-3:30am.)

The Selvereal part of town provides more lively entertainment and an energetic crowd. From the train station, go down Bahnhofstr., turn left on Aarestr. and keep going until it turns into Schiebenstr. and veers left. This strip is home to the **Thun Indoor Karting,** Scheibenstr. 37, an indoor race track where you can rent a car, safety equipment, and the track for an exhilarating race. (☎222 83 44. Open M 5-10pm, Tu 4-10pm, W-Th 4-11pm, F 4pm-1am, Sa 2pm-1am, Su 2-8pm. All equipment 25SFr, students who arrive before 8pm 17SFr.)

Many bars and clubs lie on the same street, including the very fashionable **Orvis Dance Palace,** Scheibenstr. 8, which features multiple stages for dancing and DJs spinning techno and house. A separate room has food, beer (5SFr), billiards, and a big-screen TV next to a quiet, cool-down bar. (☎222 27 55. 20+. Cover Th 5SFr, F-Sa 10SFr. Open Th 9pm-2:30am, F-Sa 9pm-3:30am.) Nextdoor **Nachtwerk** has a DJ on each floor: techno on the first, hip-hop on the second, and Top 40 on the third.

Thun's outdoor **festivals** juxtapose folk music and gunplay. Traditional festivals include the **Ausschiesset** (shoot out) among military cadets on the last Monday and Tuesday in September and the William Tell shoot honoring whoever takes the best shot at a model of Gessler. The *Altstadt* rocks with merry music in the **Festival of Barrel Organs and Ballad Singers** every July.

BRIENZ & THE ROTHORN ☎033

Attractions here include Switzerland's oldest cog railway, a parkful of traditional Swiss dwellings, and a reputation for wood-carving excellence draw visitors to Brienz. The tempo of life here is cued by the opaque green waters of the bordering **Brienzersee,** which move slowly below sharp cliffs and dense forests.

BERNESE OBERLAND

🖥️📶 TRANSPORTATION & PRACTICAL INFORMATION. Brienz makes an ideal daytrip from Interlaken by **train** (20min., every hr. 6:36am-10:35pm, 6.60SFr) or **boat** (1¼hr., every hr. 8:20am-5:32pm, 15.20SFr). Brienzersee cruises leave Interlaken's Ostbahnhof (June-Sept. every hr. 8:31am-5:40pm, Apr.-May and late Sept.-Oct. 4 per day 9:31am-2:31pm; Eurail and SwissPass valid). The station, dock, and Rothorn cog railway terminus are on the right boundary of the town, flanked on Hauptstr. by the post office, banks, and a supermarket. The Brienz-Dorf wharf bookends the town on the west end. The hostel and campsites lie a short walk along the lake east of the town proper. Brienz's **tourist office**, Hauptstr. 143, is across and left from the train station. (☎952 80 80; fax 80 88. Open M-F 8am-noon and 2-6pm, Sa 9am-noon and 4:30-6pm; July-Aug. M-F 8am-noon and 1-6pm, Sa 9am-12:30pm and 4:30-6pm, Su 4:30-6pm.) In addition to providing regional information, the tourist office also sells family passes that are valid for discount rides on boats throughout Switzerland (50SFr; using it, parents can travel half-fare, and accompanying children under 16 are free). The train station **exchanges currency** and has **lockers** (3-5SFr; both open daily 6:30am-9pm). **Police** ☎117; **ambulance** 144; **Rotbahn Pharmacy** across from Walz Tea Room. (Open M-F 8am-12:15pm and 1:30-6:30pm; Sa 8am-4pm). **24hr. emergency** ☎951 15 29. **Park** at the **Parkhaus Co-op** behind the Co-op on Hauptg. (1½hr. limit M-F 7am-7pm, Sa 7am-4pm; unlimited parking M-F 7pm-7am, Sa 4pm-7am.) The **post office** is next to the train station. (☎951 25 05. Open M-F 7:45am-6pm, Sa 8:30-11am.) **Postal code:** CH-3855.

🖥️📶 ACCOMMODATIONS & FOOD. The **Brienz Jugendherberge (HI) ②**, Strandweg 10, 400m west (left facing the lake) along the lakeside path from the train station, offers summer-camp-style bunks with doorstep access to the lake and a great view. (☎951 11 52; www.youthhostel.ch/brienz. Breakfast included. Dinner 11.50SFr. Kitchen facilities. Wheelchair-accessible. Reception 7:30-10am and 5-10pm. Open mid-Apr. to mid-Oct. Dorms 27.50SFr; doubles 62SFr.) **Hotel Garni Walz ④**, Hauptstr. 102, to the left from the station on the main road, offers centrally located rooms overlooking the lake, each situated atop a tea room. (☎951 14 59; www.firstweb.ch/walz-brienz. Breakfast included. High-season singles 95SFr; doubles 130SFr; triples 195SFr. Low-season singles 80SFr; doubles 100SFr; triples 135SFr. AmEx/MC/V.) For a luxurious getaway at a reasonable price, head farther down the street to **Seehotel Bären Brienz ④**. Wide hallways decorated with old jazz posters lead the way to spacious rooms with balconies overlooking the river. The top floor houses massage rooms and a comfortable deck. (Breakfast included. Wheelchair-accessible. Reception 7:30am-9pm. Check-out 11am. Singles 60-75SFr, with shower 65-84SFr; doubles 65-84SFr/84-98SFr; also available with small foreroom. AmEx/DC/MC/V.) Two campgrounds lie past the hostel on the waterfront. **Camping Aaregg ①**, past the other campsite along the waterfront, has an on-site restaurant. (☎951 18 43; www.aaregg.ch. Reception 8am-noon and 2-8pm. **Bikes** 30SFr per day, 15SFr per half day. Open Apr.-Oct. 9SFr per night, children 4.50SFr.; 14.20SFr per tent.) Alternatively, **Camping Seegärtli ①** is more secluded and offers free lake swimming and fresh bread at 8am. (☎951 13 51. Parking 15SFr. Reception 8am-7pm. Open Apr.-Oct. 15SFr per 1-person tent.)

Both the Seehotel Bären and Hotel Walz also have solid restaurants. In a quiet dining room, the **Bären ④** offers a vegetarian menu (15.50-23.50SFr), fish options (23.50-36.50SFr), or house specialities such as lamb filet for 32.50-38.50SFr. (Wheelchair-accessible. Open daily 7:30am-midnight. AmEx/DC/MC/V.) **Walz Tea Room ③** has a covered terrace with a view of the lake and the Axalphorn. The welcoming café offers a wide variety of salads (14.90-26SFr), omelettes (14-16.50SFr), and pastas (10.50-18.50SFr). The *Apfelstrudel* (2SFr) from the attached bakery is to die for. **Internet** access is also available for 5SFr per 15min. (☎951 14 59. Open daily 8am-

THE ALPHORN TREE If a Swiss pine tree looks suspiciously like an Alphorn, it's with good reason. Instead of growing perpendicular to the ground, the sturdy trees that cover the steep mountain sides of the Alps first grow straight out from the mountain and then curve upward towards the sun. For some, the gentle curve that develops in their trunks becomes the rounded bell of the alphorn. Stripped of its bark, cut in half, and hollowed out, the former tree is bound back together with wicker and fitted with a mouthpiece so traditional musicians can create melodies throughout the hills and valleys. Farmers have been playing Alphorns to call their cattle from the hills since the Middle Ages.

10pm. AmEx/MC/V.) **Restaurant Steinbock ❸**, farther along Hauptstr., provides outside tables and a warm wooden interior. The restaurant boasts an English-speaking staff and English menus. Options include Swiss-style macaroni with apple sauce (18SFr), and a filling house *Rösti* (19.50SFr) made of ham, cheese, tomato, bacon, and eggs. (☎951 40 55. Wheelchair-accessible. Open daily 8:30am-11:30pm. AmEx/ DC/MC/V.) The **Co-op** is on Hauptg. facing the station. (Open M-Th 7:45am-6:30pm, F 7:45am-8pm, Sa 7:45am-4pm.)

🏛 **MUSEUMS.** The **Freilichtmuseum Ballenberg** (Open-Air Museum), on Lauenenstr. in the nearby town of Ballenberg, is an 80-hectare country park dedicated to the preservation of Swiss heritage. Authentic rural Swiss houses are clumped by geographical region into 13 villages; most were transplanted when original locations. Many have live exhibitions of traditional trades, such as iron-smithing or cheesemaking. A new addition to the *Schokoladerei* provides **chocolate demonstrations** and **taste-testing**. The museum is worth at least a whole day's visit, so plan accordingly. (☎952 10 30. Open from mid-Apr. to Oct. 10am-6pm. 16SFr, with visitors card 10% off; children 8SFr; 2-day pass 28/14SFr. The park is a 1hr. walk from the train station, but a **bus** also connects the 2 every hr. 6:45am-5pm, round-trip 6SFr.)

Brienz is also the center of various cantonal wood-carving schools. The **Kantonale Schnitzlerschule** (Wood-Carving School; ☎951 17 51) and the **Geigenbauschule** (Violin-Making School; ☎952 18 61) both provide galleries that display their craft. Both centers lie on Schleeg., 400m from the station, in the western end of town. Home to 10 students, the Geigenbauschule houses a collection of antique instruments and a showroom of finished violins for a mere 5000SFr each. (Wood-carving school open M-Th 8-11:30am and 2-5pm, F 8-11:30am and 2-4:15pm; July to mid-Aug. and mid-Sept. to mid-Oct. M-F 8-11:15am. Violin-making school open Sept.-May M-F 8-11am and 2-5pm; June-Aug. call for opening hours. Both free.)

Additionally, the **Jobins Living Woodcarving Museum** lets visitors learn about the history of wood-carving, watch artisans at work, and try their hands at a work-in-progress public display; the emphasis, however, is less on demonstration than on encouraging. (☎952 13 00; www.jobin.ch. Open May-Oct. daily 8-11:30am and 2-5pm; Nov.-Apr. M-Sa 8-11:30am and 1:30-5pm. Admission 5SFr; guided tour 15SFr. AmEx/DC/MC/V.) Many local wood carvers also let tourists watch them work; contact the tourist office for a list. Bring your wallet if you're really interested—barely a museum, it is more a gallery and a store.

🥾 **HIKING.** Though superior hikes can be found around the Jungfrau, Brienz does offer several options in the way of hiking. The **Rothorn** (2350m) is the most accessible peak near Brienz thanks to the **Brienz Rothorn Bahn**. At 108 years, the Rothorn Bahn is the oldest cog steam railway in Switzerland. (☎952 22 22; www.brienz-rothornbahn.ch. Runs June-Oct. 1hr.; every hr. 7:39am-4:10pm, last descent 5:30pm; 44SFr, round-trip 68SFr. Bernese Oberland pass 22SFr/34SFr; with SwissPass 33SFr/57SFr.)

Getting off at **Planalp,** halfway up the mountain, allows medium-range hikes back down. Follow the railway down, turning left below Planalp to head through Baalen and Schwanden (3½hr.). From the summit, head east toward the lake and turn right at the Eiseesaltel, continuing down to Hofstetten, Schwanden, and Brienz (4hr.). Shelter is available at the **Hotel Rothorn ❸** on the summit. (☎951 12 21; fax 12 51. Breakfast included. Reception 8-11am and 2-5:30pm. 200m from hotel and bathrooms. Dorms 34SFr; singles 90SFr; doubles 140SFr.)

A bus from the station climbs to **Axalp** (8:15am-4:15pm, 9.20SFr) where you can hike to the **Axalphorn** (2321m) on the opposite side of the lake from Brienz by walking along either the east or west ridge (800m, half-day). As both trails are occasionally hard to make out, a map is a necessity (check the tourist office at Brienz).

Brienzersee's south shore is accessible by various boat services (check the tourist office). **Giessbach Falls,** with 14 cascades, is a 10min. ride from Brienz (6.60SFr) and a 1hr. ride from Interlaken. The walk to the falls passes a palatial hotel (15min.), also accessible by cable car from the dock (4.50SFr, round-trip 6SFr). From the hotel, a bridge traverses the river to the falls. A path to the left, along the streams, offers a view of all the waterfalls. At the top, a ridge walk leads to the right over the lake, and then down to the breezy lakeside village **Iseltwald** where a ferry travels to Brienz. (Mid-June to mid-Sept. every hr. 9:09am-6:12pm; mid-Sept.-Oct. 4 per day 11:40am-4:40pm. 9.20SFr.) Alternatively, for a low-key walk, turn right from the train station and take the footpath to the left toward the **Wildpark** and discover where the woodcarvers get their inspiration. (Always open. Free.)

INTERLAKEN ☎033

In AD 1130, two literal-minded Augustinian monks named the land between the **Thunersee** and the **Brienzersee** "Interlaken," or "between lakes." That land has grown from a collection of small medieval villages to a booming modern city. Geographically, Interlaken lies at the foot of some of the most famous mountains in Switzerland (the **Eiger, Mönch,** and **Jungfrau**), providing easy access to several natural playgrounds. Beneath the enchanting sight of the Jungfrau (4158m), the town spreads out around a large central green, the **Höhematte,** a popular landing pad for the hundreds of paragliders that drift down from the skies each day. Thanks to its mild climate and natural wonders, Interlaken has earned a deserved place as one of Switzerland's prime tourist attractions and as its top outdoor adventure spot.

▇ TRANSPORTATION

By **car,** Interlaken lies on A6. The city has two train stations. The **Westbahnhof** stands in the center of town bordering the Thunersee, near most shops and hotels; trains to Bern, Basel, and other western towns stop here. The **Ostbahnhof,** on the Brienzersee 1km from the town center, is cheaper for connecting to eastern towns. Both stations post hotel prices and offer courtesy phones for reservations.

Trains: The **Westbahnhof** (☎826 47 50) and **Ostbahnhof** (☎828 73 19) have trains every hr. to: **Bern** (6:39am-10:34pm, 24SFr); **Basel** (5:33am-10:34pm, 56SFr); **Geneva** (5:33am-9:35pm, 63SFr); **Lucerne** (5:33am-8:39pm, 26SFr); **Lugano/Locarno** (5:33am-4:37pm, 87SFr/76SFr); **Zurich** (5:33am-10:34pm, 62SFr). **Jungfraubahnen,** Harderstr. 14 (☎828 72 33; www.jungfraubahn.ch) runs all trains to the small towns on the way up to the Jungfrau. SwissPass valid for Wengen, Mürren, and Grindelwald; 25% discount at higher stops. Eurail 25% discount on the Jungfraubahnen. Trains leave June-Sept. every 30min., and Sept.-May every hr. from the Ostbahnhof to: **Grindelwald** (6:35am-10:35pm, 9.80SFr) and **Lauterbrunnen** (6:35am-10:35pm, 6.60SFr); with connections to **Kleine Scheidegg** (6:35am-4:35pm, 36.40SFr), **Mürren**

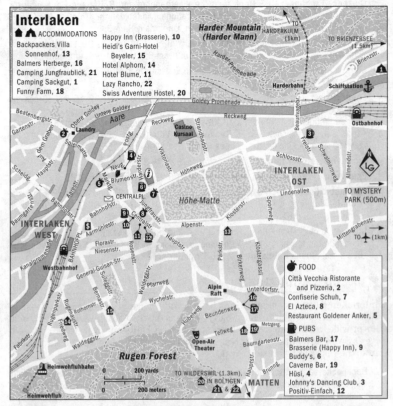

Interlaken

♦ ⚑ ACCOMMODATIONS
Backpackers Villa
  Sonnenhof, **13**
Balmers Herberge, **16**
Camping Jungfraublick, **21**
Camping Sackgut, **1**
Funny Farm, **18**

Happy Inn (Brasserie), **10**
Heidi's Garni-Hotel
  Beyeler, **15**
Hotel Alphorn, **14**
Hotel Blume, **11**
Lazy Rancho, **22**
Swiss Adventure Hostel, **20**

🍎 FOOD
Città Vecchia Ristorante
  and Pizzeria, **2**
Confiserie Schuh, **7**
El Azteca, **8**
Restaurant Goldener Anker, **5**

🍺 PUBS
Balmers Bar, **17**
Brasserie (Happy Inn), **9**
Buddy's, **6**
Caverne Bar, **19**
Hüsi, **4**
Johnny's Dancing Club, **3**
Positiv-Einfach, **12**

(6:35am-7:35pm, 16.40SFr), **Wengen** (6:35am-10:35pm, 12.40SFr), and the **Jung-fraujoch** (6:35am-3:35pm, round-trip 163.80SFr, 125.80SFr with Good Morning Ticket; see **The Jungfraujoch,** p. 362).

Taxis: Interlaken Ost, ☎822 80 80. **West,** ☎822 50 50.

Luggage: Lockers at train station 3SFr.

Parking: Parking is 7SFr per day at the train stations, behind the casino on Centralstr.

Bike Rental: At either **train station,** 30SFr per day; 23SFr per half-day. Open 6am-7pm. **Intersport Oberland,** Postg. 16, rents mountain bikes (☎822 06 61; fax 73 07). 30SFr, 20SFr per half-day; in-line skates 20SFr per day. Open M-F 8am-noon and 1:30-6:30pm, Sa 8am-noon and 1-4pm. AmEx/DC/MC/V. Some hostels also rent bikes or motor scooters.

Post Office: Marktg. 1 (☎224 89 50). From the Westbahnhof, go left on Bahnhofpl. Open M-F 8am-noon and 1:45-6pm, Sa 8:30-11am. **Postal code:** CH-3800.

🔢 PRACTICAL INFORMATION

Tourist Office: Höheweg 37 (☎826 53 00; fax 53 75), in the **Hotel Metropole,** has free maps and info. Open July-Aug. M-F 8am-6:30pm, Sa 8am-5pm, Su 10am-noon and 5-7pm; Sept.-June M-F 8am-noon and 1:30-6pm, Sa 9am-noon.

Currency Exchange: UBS Bank near the Westbahnhof and **Raiffeisen Bank** near the Ostbahnhof have **ATMs,** as do both train stations. Available in the **train station** (☎826 47 36), though rates are 1% better in town. Open daily 8am-6pm.

Bookstore: Buchhandlweg Krebser Haupt, Höheweg 11 (☎822 35 16). Best-sellers, phrasebooks, and travel books. Open M-F 8:30am-6:30pm, Sa 8:30am-4pm.

Library: Marktpl. 4 (☎822 02 12). Novels in English. Open M-Tu 3-6pm, W 9-11am and 3-7pm, Th 3-6pm, F 3-7pm, Sa 10am-noon.

Laundromat: Self-Service Wash & Dry, Beatenbergstr. 5 (☎822 15 66). Cross the bridge to the left of the Westbahnhof and take the 2nd right onto Hauptstr. The manager will do laundry for 12SFr per load. Open M-Sa 8am-noon and 1:30-6pm; Sa closes at 4pm. 24hr. self-service 6-8SFr. **Backpacker's Villa** (see p. 354) has self-service laundry (10SFr; soap included), as does **Balmers,** 8SFr (see p. 355).

Snow and Weather Info: For the Jungfrau, ☎828 79 31.

Emergencies: Police ☎117, **Hospital** ☎826 26 26, **Doctor** ☎823 23 23.

Pharmacy: Grosse Apotheke, Bahnhofstr. 5A (☎822 72 62), and **Pharmacie Internationale,** Höheweg 4 (☎828 34 34), both open M-Sa 7:30am-6:30pm, until 7pm in summer. AmEx/MC/V.

Internet Access: Many hotels, restaurants, and both train stations have quick access terminals but the best prices in Internet are found in the hostels: **Backpacker's Villa** has 5 computers; **Balmers** has 2 (10SFr per hr.).

ACCOMMODATIONS

Interlaken guest accommodations have a wide range of atmospheres. Those at Balmers and Funny Farm tend to party as late as the city will allow, while Backpackers provides a more low-key but lively social scene. Farther away from the city, Boltigen's Swiss Adventure Hostel creates its own community and offers guests a respite from the wild "spring break" crowds.

🏠 **Backpackers Villa Sonnenhof,** Alpenstr. 16 (☎826 71 71; www.villa.ch) diagonally across the Höhenmatte from the tourist office. This central but secluded, remodeled villa is friendly and low-key. Perfect after a tough day of backpacking, but still only a 3min. walk from the roaring nightlife of Balmer's and Funny Farm. Spacious rooms have wooden balconies with views of the Jungfrau and Harder Mann. Services include TV with CNN, movies on the villa's big-screen, mountain bike rental (28SFr per day; 18SFr per half day), laundry (10SFr per load, soap included), free phone for taxis, and **Internet** access (10SFr per hr.). The hostel also books **skiing, snowshoe treks, paragliding, skydiving,** and **bungee jumping.** Includes breakfast, kitchen, lockers, towels, sheets, and recreation and meditation rooms. Reception 7:30-11am and 4-10pm. Check-out 7-9:30am, but guests can leave luggage for a 2SFr deposit. No curfew. Call or arrive early in the morning to have a chance at a room. 4- to 7-bed dorms 29-32SFr; doubles 82-88SFr; triples 111-120SFr; quads 132-144SFr. 5SFr per person extra for Jungfrau view, balcony, and in-suite bathroom. AmEx/MC/V. ❷

🏠 **Swiss Adventure Hostel,** is an old hotel in the tiny town of Boltigen (☎773 73 73; info@swissadventures.ch). A free shuttle runs to and from Interlaken each day (40min.); call for times and availability. The Adventure Hostel has staked its place in this quiet valley as a sporty alternative to the party scene in Interlaken. A small adventure company running out of the hostel offers the same activities as Interlaken companies, but with a more personal touch: after your canyoning trip, you eat dinner with your trip leader. **Internet** access (15SFr per hr.), **mountain bike rental** (25SFr per day), a cellar bar and small dance floor (open 9pm-2am), TV, and restaurant (breakfast buffet 7SFr, dinner 12-18SFr, buffet most nights) with accomplished chef.

Check-in 10am-11pm. Spacious 4- to 10-bed dorms with bathrooms 20SFr; double with shower 70SFr; quad with shower 100SFr. Discounts for adventure program participants. AmEx/MC/V. ❷

Happy Inn, Rosenstr. 17 (☎822 32 25; www.happy-inn.com) lives up to its name with a friendly staff and simple style. From Westbahnhof, go left toward the tourist office and right onto Rosenstr. at the Centralpl. The multi-level building houses clean and spacious 4- to 8-person dorms with metal bunks and lockers, and is located above the **Brasserie,** a great bar. Free **parking** in back. Reception 7am-6pm. Call early for rooms. Check-out 10am. Breakfast 8SFr. Dorms 22SFr; singles 38SFr; double 76SFr. DC/MC/V. ❷

Balmers Herberge, Hauptstr. 23-25 (☎822 19 61; fax 823 32 61). Walk diagonally across the Höhenmatte from the tourist office and follow signs down Parkstr. Balmers runs a shuttle bus June-Aug. from both stations (every hr. 9-11am and 1-6pm). Switzerland's oldest private hostel (since 1945) is thoroughly American: it is a place to party, not relax. To enjoy the dorms or "Balmers tent" (a huge striped canvas bungalow with no insulation a few blocks from town), you must value camaraderie above comfort. Services include: **mountain bike rental** (35SFr per day), nightly movies, TV with CNN and MTV, a mini-department store (open 7:30am-8pm), safety deposit boxes (2SFr available 6:30am-noon and 4-10:30pm), and **Internet** access (20SFr per hr.). In winter, they offer **free sleds** and a 20% discount on ski and snowboard rental. After 9pm, activity shifts underground to the **Metro Bar.** (Beers 4.50SFr; Happy Hour 9-10pm, 3SFr. Open until 2am.) Breakfast included. Kitchen 1SFr per 20min. Laundry 8SFr per load. Reception summer 6:30am-noon and 4-10pm; winter 6:30-10am and 4:30-10pm. Check-out 9am. Lockout 9:30am-4:30pm. Sign in early, drop off your pack, and return at 4:30pm when beds are assigned (no reservations). Dorms 20-24SFr; doubles 68SFr; triples 90SFr; quads 120SFr. AmEx/MC/V. ❷

Funny Farm (☎652 61 27; www.funny-farm.ch), behind Hotel Mattenhof, down Hauptstr. from Balmers; reception is in the hotel. More frat house than youth hostel, this estate is very accommodating and hopping with people. Currently, Funny Farm offers tennis, basketball, volleyball, an enormous swimming pool with a climbing wall, adventure activities through Alpin Raft, an indoor nightclub with occasional live reggae, and an intense yard out back, complete with bar and volleyball court—in short, a playground for 20-somethings, and the scene of nightly parties. Breakfast included. Dorms 20-25SFr. ❷

Hotel Blume, Jungfraustr. 30 (☎822 71 31; www.hotel-blume.ch), toward the Westbahnhof from the tourist office, attracts guests with winding staircases and welcoming rooms in a building decorated with blue trim and Mexican art. Connecting doors and a central location make this an ideal option for families or groups of travelers. Breakfast included. Reception summer 6am-midnight; 7am-midnight. Check-out 11am. Singles 50-75SFr, with shower 75-85SFr; doubles 70-100SFr/110-150SFr; family room 150-200SFr. Ask about the unbeatable Jungfraujoch deal—165SFr per person for a double and ticket to the "top of the world." Reservations recommended. AmEx/DC/MC/V. ❸

Hotel Alphorn, Rugenstr. 8 (☎822 30 51; www.hotel-alphorn.ch). Turn right onto Bahnhofstr., left onto Rugenstr. and right again onto Rothornstr.; it's behind Hotel Eiger. Boasts newly remodeled doubles with clean beds, sparkling bathrooms with showers, and TVs with CNN. Breakfast included. Wheelchair-accessible. Singles 70-100SFr; doubles 90-150SFr. For slightly more, the 3-star **Hotel Eiger** in front has antique rooms with the same amenities, intricate wooden floors, and in-room tea and coffee. Singles 90-120SFr, doubles 130-180SFr; large triple 210SFr. Reception for both 6:30am-10:30pm. Check-out 11am. AmEx/MC/V. ❹

Heidi's Hostel (Heidi's Garni-Hotel Beyeler), Bernastr. 37 (☎/fax 822 90 30). Turn right from the Westbahnhof, go left on Bernastr. and walk straight for 300m (5min.). Friendly owners preside over a rambling old house decorated with sleds, bells, old photographs, carousel horses, and old furniture. Private rooms are available with bath and balcony.

Common room with TV, kitchen, and laundry (7SFr). **Bikes** 29SFr per day; tours 39SFr. Reception 7am-1am. Check-out 10am. Dorms 23SFr; 2- to 4-bed room 60-140SFr; doubles 80-90SFr; quad 135-160SFr; 8-person room 250SFr. MC/V. ❷

🏕 CAMPING

Camping Sackgut (☎079 656 89 58) is closest to town. Head toward town from the Ostbahnhof, turn right across the 1st bridge, and take another right onto the footpath or road. A few choice spots are available by the river, but most of the campground lies in an exposed grassy parking lot. Offers **Internet,** kitchen and laundry (4SFr). Reception 5-7pm Apr.-June and Sept.-Oct. 4.40SFr per person; 6-10SFr per tent; tent bungalow 65SFr, parking 3SFr. Electricity 3SFr. Trash 1SFr. ❶

Camping Jungfraublick (☎822 44 14; www.jungfraublick.ch). Take bus #5 from the Westbahnhof toward Widerswil, and continue 5min. past Balmers on Gsteigstr. This peaceful location has splendid mountain views and fairly extensive grounds. Open May-Sept. 6.80SFr per person, low-season 5.80SFr; tent 8-28SFr. Reception 8-10am and 4-6pm; summer 7-11am and 2-8pm. MC/V. ❶

Lazy Rancho (☎822 87 16; www.lazyrancho.ch). Head past Jungfrau Camping and left onto Lehnweg. This clean campground is equipped with a swimming pool, store, playground, kitchen, and laundry facilities (4-6SFr). Open mid-Apr. until mid-Oct. 5.50-6.90SFr per person, 3-4SFr per child; 7-10SFr per tent site. Electricity 4SFr. MC/V. ❶

🍴 FOOD

Interlaken has a wide range of restaurants, but, generally, the Balmers crowd eats at Balmers (*Bratwurst* and burgers under 10SFr), the hostel crowd eats at the *Jugendherberge* (12.50SFr), those at Backpacker's Villa cook their meals in the hostel's kitchen, and the Funny Farm folks eat from their renovated cable car (wraps 10SFr; burgers and fries 12-15SFr). Most of the restaurants listed here are on Marktg. Head up Aareckstr., the tiny street left from Westbahnhof, and turn left on Spielmatte. **Co-op,** across from the Ostbahnhof or behind the Westbahnhof, also houses a restaurant. (Open M-Th 8am-7pm, F 8am-9pm, Sa 7:30am-5pm; restaurant additionally Su 9am-5pm.) **Migros,** in front of the Westbahnhof also has a restaurant, and keeps the same hours.

Restaurant Goldener Anker, Marktg. 57 (☎822 16 72). This family-run restaurant has many traditional specialties and vegetarian dishes. The California salad (grilled turkey strips on lettuce and fresh fruit; 16.50SFr) is delicious. For dessert try the *Crêpe Normandy*—it's stuffed with apples and vanilla ice cream (8SFr). Frequently hosts live bands. Billiards available. Open M-W and F-Su 10am-12:30am. ❸

Confiserie Schuh (☎822 94 41), across from the tourist office, has been an Interlaken landmark since the 19th century. Among a wide array of goodies, chocolate medallions (1SFr) and strawberry tarts (5SFr) sell like mad in the summer. Open daily 8am-9pm. ❶

El Azteca (☎822 71 31), downstairs from Hotel Blume, serves up excellent Mexican. Select from a numerous options (12-20SFr) or choose one of the four daily lunch *Menüs:* Mexican (16.50SFr), international (15SFr), Swiss (14SFr), and vegetarian (14.50SFr), each served noon-1:45pm. Open daily June-Sept. M-Tu and Th-Su 7am-11:30pm; Oct.-May 8am-2pm and 6-11:30pm. Closed Jan. AmEx/MC/V. ❷

Città Vecchia Ristorante and Pizzeria (☎822 17 54), Untere G. 5. From Marktpl., follow Spielmattestr. across the river and turn left onto Untere G. Set off from the hustle of the main street, this upscale restaurant offers Italian specialties at reasonable prices. Pizzas (13-19.50SFr) and pastas (13-22SFr) both include a number of vegetarian options. Select from the seasonal menus (22-40SFr) and variety of fine Italian wines (3.50-6SFr per glass). Open Oct. 16-Mar. M and W-Su 10am-midnight; Apr.-Sept. 20 daily 10am-midnght. AmEx/DC/MC/V. ❸

OUTDOORS NEAR INTERLAKEN

> ❗ Interlaken's adventure sports industry is thrilling and usually safe, but accidents do happen. On July 27, 1999, 19 adventure-seeking tourists were killed by a flash flood while canyoning on the Saxeten river. Be aware that you participate in all adventure sports at your own risk, and if you don't feel comfortable doing something, don't do it.

ADVENTURE SPORTS. Interlaken's steep precipices, raging rivers, and wide-open spaces serve as prime spots for such adrenaline-pumping activities as paragliding, white-water rafting, bungee jumping, and canyoning (a sport in which wet-suited thrill-seekers rappel, dive, and swim through a canyon). **Alpin Raft** (☎823 41 00 or 334 62 02; www.alpinraft.com), the most established company in Interlaken, has qualified, personable guides, and promises that "unlike some first time experiences, this one will be great." All prices include transportation to and from any hostel in Interlaken: **paragliding** (150SFr), **canyoning** (110-195SFr), **river rafting** (95-109SFr), **skydiving** (380SFr), **bungee jumping** (125-165SFr), and **hang gliding** (180SFr). **Outdoor Interlaken** (☎826 77 19; www.out-door-interlaken.ch) offers **rock-climbing** lessons (89SFr per half-day) and **white-water kayaking** tours (155SFr per half-day). **Swissraft** in Boltingen offers similar adventures, as well as **hydro-speeding** (aided body-surfing down the river; 110SFr), and all-day combinations of multiple activities. (☎823 02 10; www.swissraft.ch.) **Skydiving Xdream** charges 380SFr per tandem jump. Stefan Heuser, the owner, has been a member of the Swiss skydiving team for 17 years, including two years as a coach, and has over 6000 jumps to his credit. Weekday jumps are from a plane (weekend ones from a helicopter) into waterfall-plentiful Lauterbrunnen. (☎079 75 93 48 34; www.justjump.ch. Open Apr.-Oct.)

The independent **Swiss Alpine Guides** (☎822 60 00; www.swissalpineguides.ch) lead full-day **ice-climbing** clinics (May-Oct., 150SFr), as well as full-day **glacier treks**, which journey to the other side of the Jungfrau (June-Oct. 120SFr). Interlaken's winter activities include skiing, snowboarding, ice canyoning, snow rafting, and glacier skiing. Contact the **tourist office** (☎826 53 00) for information.

HIKES FROM INTERLAKEN. The towns closer to the mountains offer longer, more strenuous treks, but Interlaken has a few good hikes of its own. The most-traversed trail climbs to the **Harder Kulm** (aka Harder Mann; 1310m). Only the Jungfrau can be seen from Interlaken itself, but from the top of this half-day hike, the Eiger and Mönch are also visible. This view is a striking mountain-scape, with the black face of the Eiger framed by the other two snowy masses. The easiest starting point is near the Ostbahnhof. From the Ostbahnhof, head toward town, take the first road bridge across the river, and follow yellow signs to "Harderkulm" that later give way to white-red-white *Bergweg* flashes on the rocks. From the top, signs lead back down to the Westbahnhof. A funicular runs from the trailhead near the Ostbahnhof to the top. (2½hr. up, 1½hr. down; May-Oct. daily 13.40SFr, round-trip 21SFr; 25% discount with Eurail/SwissPass.)

Flatter trails lead along the lakes that flank the city. Turn left from the train station, then left before the bridge and follow the canal over to the nature reserve on the shore of the Thunersee. The trail (3hr.) winds up the Lombach river, then through pastures at the base of the Harder Kulm back toward town.

⬛ NIGHTLIFE

If you still have energy at the end of the day, Interlaken provides plenty of options for its release. **Balmers** (p. 355) offers live music on most nights, most often reggae. (Beer 4.50SFr; bar open 9pm-1am.) The **Caverne Bar,** in the basement of the Mattenhof Hotel, in front of the Funny Farm, serves 3.50SFr beer and alternates between live music and techno. (☎821 61 21. Open W-Su 10pm-2:30am.)

If you're feeling adventurous, head beyond the hostel confines to one of the local hangouts. **Buddy's,** Höheweg 33, is a small, crowded English-style pub where the beer is only 3.50-5SFr. (☎822 76 12. Open daily 10am-12:30am.) **Johnny's Dancing Club,** Höheweg 92, located in the basement of the Hotel Carlton, is Interlaken's oldest disco and serves drinks from 6SFr. (☎822 38 21. Open Tu-Su 9:30pm-3am.) For smoky blues try **Brasserie,** Rosenstr. 17. (☎822 32 25. Beer from 3.20SFr. Open M-Sa 8:30am-12:30am, Su 3pm-12:30am.) **Positiv Einfach,** Centralstr. 11, is a dark cocktail bar complete with a "mood room" in the back. Mixed drinks 11.50-12.50SFr, but check for theme days, like Tuesday when almost everything is 6SFr. (☎823 40 44; www.positive-einfach.ch. Open 5pm-12:30am, F-Sa 5pm-1:30am.) **Hüsi,** Postg. 3, has a local feel; beers are 3-4.50SFr and pizzas are (14-20SFr) ordered specially from a neighboring pizzeria. (☎822 33 34; www.huesi.ch. Open Tu-Su 4pm-12:30a,; F-Sa 4p-1:30am.)

The apex of Interlaken's cultural life is the summer production of Friedrich Schiller's **Wilhelm Tell** (in German; English synopsis 2SFr). Lasses with flowing locks and 250 bushy-bearded local men wearing heavy rouge ham up the tale of the Swiss escape from under the Habsburg thumb. The showmanship is complete—20 horses gallop by in every scene, and a vaudeville-like stage around the corner from Balmers allows the cast to make real bonfires. (Shows from late June to mid-July Th 8pm; mid-July to early Sept. Th and Sa 8pm.) Tickets (22-38SFr) are available at Tellbüro at the tourist office. (☎822 37 22; fax 57 33. Open during run M-F 8am-noon and 1:30-5pm), or at the theater on show nights. Children under 6 not admitted. **Casino Kursaal,** between the Ostbahnhof and the tourist office, houses a newly opened casino and a stage for the **Swiss Folklore Show** in summer. (☎827 61 00; www.casino-kursaal.ch. Open Su-W noon-2am, Th-Sa noon-3am. Shows May-Sept. daily and Oct. M and Th 7:30pm; 20SFr. Include dinner at 7pm for 19-39.50SFr more.)

⬛ DAYTRIP FROM INTERLAKEN: ST. BEATUS' CAVES

To get to the caves, walk 15min. uphill from the Sundlauenen Schiffstation, a 30min. boat ride from Interlaken (every hr. 10:30am-5pm), or take bus #21 (9SFr round-trip from Interlaken Westbahnhof). You can also hike from Interlaken (2hr.) or Beatenberg (1hr.), just be sure to wear sturdy shoes; the path is rough at times. ☎841 16 43; fax 10 64. Caves and museum open Apr.-Oct. daily 10:30am-5pm. 16SFr, students 14SFr, children 9SFr.

At the **Beatushöhlen** (St. Beatus' Caves) in Beatenberg village, it is possible to spelunk through 1000m of glistening stalactites, waterfalls, and grottoes. There are several reflecting pools and neat geological creations including the limestone sculpture "Virgin with Child," formed by thousands of years of dripping water. At the entrance, a wax St. Beatus (the Irish hermit and dragonslayer) stares down some cavemen; at the exit, an iron dragon ambushes exiting spelunkers. Even on hot summer days, the cave stays a cool, constant 9° C. One-hour tours leave every 30min. from the entrance. Admission includes entry to the tiny **Caving Museum,** 5min. downhill, which chronicles the discovery and mapping of Swiss grottoes.

THE JUNGFRAU REGION

A few miles south of Interlaken, the hitherto-middling mountains rear up and become hulking white monsters. This is the Jungfrau Region, home of Europe's largest glacier and some of its steepest crags and highest waterfalls. In summer, the region's hundreds of kilometers of hiking consistently awe a steady stream of tourists with astounding mountain views, wildflower meadows, roaring waterfalls, and pristine forests. The three most famous peaks are the **Jungfrau** (4158m), the **Mönch** (4099m), and the **Eiger** (3970m)—in English, that's the Maiden, the Monk, and the Ogre. Natives say that the monk protects the maiden by standing between her and the ogre. On the other side of these giants, a vast glacial region stretches southward, where six major glaciers, including the **Grosser Aletschgletscher** (at 45km long the largest in Europe) converge at **Konkordiaplatz.**

■ **ORIENTATION.** The region is split into two valleys; the first gives access to the glaciers through the town of Grindelwald, while the second, the Lauterbrunnen, holds many smaller towns, including Wengen, Gimmelwald, and Mürren. The valleys are divided by an easily hikeable ridge; on the end closer to Interlaken is the Männlichen Peak. At the other end of the ridge, near the Jungfrau, is the train town of Kleine Scheidegg. Up above, and on either side of Lauterbrunnen, are cliff ledges on which the small towns of Wengen, Mürren, and Gimmelwald are perched; none are accessible by car.

■ **TRANSPORTATION & OUTDOOR ACTIVITIES.** The **Jungfraubahn** runs throughout the region and includes the cog-railways to the towns above Lauterbrunnen. Because of their proximity, hikes in different towns can frequently be combined, so check out hiking suggestions from other towns regardless of where you're staying. If you plan on doing any serious hiking, be sure to get a copy of the *Lauterbrunnen/Jungfrau Region Wanderkarte* (15SFr at any tourist office), which gives an overview of all of the hikes.

There are three main ski areas in the Jungfrau region: the **Mürren-Schilthorn** area, the **Kleine Scheidegg-Männlichen** area, and the **Grindelwald-First** area, with over 213km of downhill runs between them. The Mürren-Schilthorn area is much smaller than the other two. Day passes for the individual areas are 55SFr. Multi-day passes, which include transport on the Jungfraubahn, are only available for the whole region (all 3 areas). (☎828 72 33; www.jungfraubahn.ch. 2 days 118SFr, 7 days 312SFr, ages 16-19 94SFr/250SFr, children 6-15 50% discount.) Most towns have separate ski schools. For **snow information** and a **weather report,** dial ☎828 79 31.

GRINDELWALD ☎033

Grindelwald, launching point to the only glaciers in the Bernese Oberland accessible by foot, crouches beneath the north face of the Eiger—a difficult-to-conquer milestone in any climber's career. It is a cold-weather Shangri-la for outdoorsy types, though the tourism can become overwhelming at times.

■ **TRANSPORT & PRACTICAL INFORMATION**

The Jungfraubahn runs from **Interlaken's** Ostbahnhof (40min., 6:35am-10:30pm; 9.80SFr). Trains to the **Jungfraujoch** (see "The Jungfraujoch," p. 362) and **Kleine Scheidegg** (27SFr, 45SFr round-trip; Eurail or SwissPass 25% discount) leave from the Grindelwald station (every hr. 7:19am-5:19pm, 6:19pm in summer). There is also a bus from Balmers hostel in Interlaken (round-trip 15SFr). The **tourist office,** in the Sport-Zentrum 200m to the right of the station, provides a kiosk for hotel reserva-

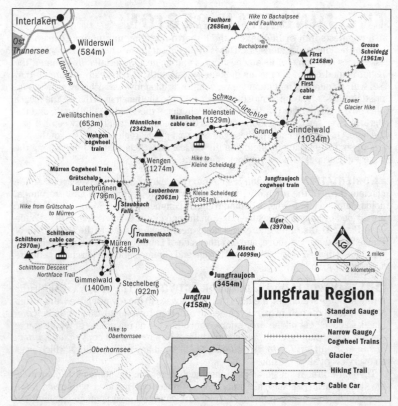

Jungfrau Region

Standard Gauge Train
Narrow Gauge/Cogwheel Trains
Glacier
Hiking Trail
Cable Car

tions, chairlift information, and a list of free guided excursions. (☎854 12 12; www.grindelwald.ch. Open July-Aug. M-F 8am-7pm, Sa 8am-7pm, Su 9-11am and 2-6pm; Sept.-June M-F 8am-noon and 2-6pm, Sa 8am-noon and 2-5pm.) Services include: **laundry** at **Wash & Dry** next to Da Salvi Pizzeria on Haupstr. (☎853 11 68; wash 4SFr, dry 1SFr per 10min.; open 24hr.); **weather forecast** ☎162; **medical assistance** ☎853 11 53; **police** ☎117; **emergency** ☎144. **Pharmacy Eiger** is right on the main street. (☎853 44 66; emergency also ☎425 68 84. Open M-F 8am-noon and 2-6:30pm, Sa 8am-noon and 2-5pm.) Access the **Internet** (15SFr per hr.) at the tourist office or **Ernst Schudel's Photo Shop,** across the street. (Open M-F 9am-noon and 2-6:30pm, Sa 9am-noon and 2-6pm.) The **post office** is opposite the station. (Open M-F 8am-noon and 1:45-6pm, Sa 8-11am.) **Postal code:** CH-3818.

▌ ACCOMMODATIONS & CAMPING

Hotel Hirschen (☎854 84 84; www.hirschen-grindelwald.ch), in the center of town. Turn right from the tourist office. Offers clean, bright rooms with comfortable beds and a bowling alley. All rooms have satellite-TV, telephone, and safe, and many have balconies. Breakfast and entrance to sports center swimming pool and ice-skating rink included. The hotel also offers currency exchange and **bowling.** Wheelchair-accessible. Reception 8am-10pm. Singles 90-135SFr; doubles 150-220SFr. ❹

Mountain Hostel (☎853 39 00; www.mountainhostel.ch) is a short train ride to Grund (3.80SFr) or a long walk from town. Turn right out of the Grindelwald train station, then immediately right on small trail towards "Grund." Go downhill; bear right at the Glacier Hotel. The bright blue hostel sits at the bottom of the valley. Renovated in 1996, the hostel has gleaming 4- and 6-bed dorms and a plush reception area with **Internet** (15SFr per hr.), TVs, foosball, and billiards. Breakfast buffet included. Sleep sack 5SFr. Laundry 12SFr. Outdoor cooking facilities 0.50SFr. Reception 8-11am and 3:30-9:30pm. Dorms 34SFr; doubles 88SFr. ❷

Jugendherberge (HI) (☎853 10 09; www.youthhostel.ch/grindelwald). Exit the train station and turn left. Go straight for 400m, then cut uphill to the right just before "Chalet Alpenblume" and follow the steep trail all the way up the hill (400m). It's a hike from town, but the enormous wooden chalet is beautiful. Wood-paneled living rooms have fireplaces and many rooms have balconies facing the Eiger. Laundry (5SFr), **Internet** (15SFr per hr.), TV and games room, and reduced entrance fees to nearby attractions. Buffet breakfast included. Lunch 8.50-11.50SFr. 3-course dinner 12.50SFr, vegetarian meals available on request. Lockers and sheets included. Wheelchair-accessible. Reception 7:30-10am and 3pm-midnight. No lockout. Open May-Oct. and mid-Dec. until Apr. Dorms 28-30SFr; 4-bed rooms 30-35SFr; doubles 35SFr per person, with toilet and shower 50.50SFr. Non-members add 6SFr per person. AmEx/DC/MC. ❷

Lehmann's Herberge (☎853 31 41). Follow the main street past the tourist office and take the first right (5min.). Enjoy the comfort of a renovated home as well as a hearty homemade breakfast (included). Reception 7am-10pm. Dorms and doubles 45SFr per person, after 1st night dorms 40SFr. ❸

Naturfreundehaus (☎853 13 33; www.naturfreunde.ch). Follow signs for Hotel Sonnenberg from the station and then walk 150m and turn right up the stairs (20min. from station). Offers a cozier alternative to the Jugendherberge. It's a hike to get here, but if you want the best views in town, this is the place. Wood-paneled walls and ceilings, large fluffy pillows and wooden closets add to the chalet-like atmosphere of the hostel. Laundry (4SFr; dry 3SFr), **Internet** (5SFr for 15min.), kitchen (2SFr.), and parking (5SFr) available. Breakfast 5SFr. Check-in until 10pm. Dorms 27SFr per person; children ages 6-12 18SFr; non-members add 5SFr. ❷

Gletscherdorf Camping (☎853 14 29; www.gletscherdorf.ch). Take a right from the station along the main road; at the ski school, take another right downhill and follow the path marked, sparingly, "Wandersteg." Follow the road. The small grounds are the closest campground, and have a phenomenal view. Showers included. Open May-Oct. Reception 8-10am and 5-8pm; come anytime. 6.90SFr per person, 3.50SFr per child; 6-12SFr per tent. Electricity 4SFr. ❶

FOOD

There is a **Co-op**, on Hauptstr. across from the tourist office (open M-F 8am-noon and 1:30-6:30pm, Sa 8am-6pm).

Hotel Eiger (☎854 31 31; www.eiger-grindelwald.ch), past the tourist office on the left, contains a variety of eateries. **Memory Bistro** (open 8:30am-11:30pm) and **Barry's Restaurant** upstairs (open 6pm-12:30am) offer cheap burgers (9SFr) and veggie *Rösti* (13SFr). Hosts yodelers and hand-organists for Swiss music night W. Later at night head across the hallway for the **Gepsi Bar.** Beers from 3.50SFr. Open 5:30pm-1:30am. ❷

Ye Olde Spotted Cat (☎853 12 34), on Hauptstr. just past Hotel Hirschen. Scratch a few wooden cats' heads and sip cheap beer (3.80SFr) at this old haunt of Winston Churchill. Open Su-M 11am-5pm, Tu-Sa 11am-12:30am; summer F-Sa until 1:30am. ❶

THE BIG SPLURGE

THE JUNGFRAUJOCH

The most arresting ascent in the Jungfrau region is up the Jungfraujoch, a head-spinning, breath-shortening, 3454m adventure on **Europe's highest railway.** Chiseled into solid rock, the track tunnels through the Eiger and Mönch mountains. Its construction was one of the greatest engineering feats of all time, requiring 16 years and 300 men. The line was to have gone even higher to the Jungfrau summit itself (4158m), but by 1912 the project was so over budget that the final 850m were left to mountaineers with crampons and ice axes.

Although not terribly difficult by Alpine mountaineering standards, the route up the eastern face from the Jungfraujoch is rated PD for "moderate." It involves some steep ice and snow climbing on a traverse near the summit, as well as some technical rock climbing at altitude. The first ascent was completed in 1812 by this route. Significantly harder mountaineering challenges exist on the Jungfrau's imposing north wall, which is almost 3000m high.

Thanks to the lack of pollution, the summit houses Europe's highest manned meteorology station and the Sphinx Laboratory for the study of cosmic radiation. Each year, half a million visitors explore the Ice Palace (free), a smooth maze cut into the ice. Enjoy the ice sculpture, but watch your footing on ice floors and don't sit too long on the ice bench!

Pizzeria Da Salvi (☎853 89 99), located in Hotel Steinbock at the base of the First Bahn (see Hiking, below), offers a hearty meal in a classy and romantic Italian atmosphere. Large pizzas (15-21SFr) and a gamut of pastas (16-18.50SFr) don't overshadow the variety of unique entrees (24-41SFr). Try the oven-baked lamb (31SFr) and select from a number of delectable ice cream creations for dessert (8-9.50SFr).Wheelchair-accessible. Open daily 11:30am-11:30pm. ❸

Restaurant Schmitte (☎853 22 02; www.hotel-schweizerhof.com.) Turn left from the train station on the main road (100m). A quiet setting for a luxurious meal; enjoy the risotto with truffles and tomatoes (25SFr; smaller portion 17SFr) or grilled sirloin tips (41SFr/30SFr) in one of the themed dining areas or among the fountains on the garden terrace. Wheelchair-accessible. Open daily 8am-10pm. AmEx/DC/MC/V. ❺

Tea Room Riggenburg (☎853 10 59), past the tourist office away from the station, offers soups, salads, lasagnas, pastas, and fresh-baked desserts in a typical tearoom fashion. Drink a huge hot cocoa (3.40SFr) or have a hearty *Birchermüsli* (7SFr) on the heated terrace. Open Tu-Sa 7am-10pm, Su 8am-6pm. ❶

◪ HIKING

Hiking possibilities in Grindelwald run the gamut from easy valley walks to challenges for top climbers. The greatest allure for the hiker is the proximity of glaciers. While most hikes are possible without the aid of expensive trains and cable cars, these means of transportation allow access to some fantastic hikes. The **First Bahn** leaves from the center of town and climbs the eastern side of the valley. (☎854 50 51; www.gofirst.ch. Runs 8:30am-4:30pm; 29SFr, round-trip 46SFr.) The **Männlichen Gondelbahn,** the **longest cable car route in Europe,** is on the other side of the valley. (☎854 80 80. Runs 8am-4pm, until 5:15pm in summer; 32.80SFr, round-trip 52.40SFr; 25% discount with SwissPass, 50% with Eurail.) The **Bergführerbüro** (Mountain Guides Office), located in the sports center next to the tourist office, sells hiking maps and coordinates activities like glacier walks, ice climbing, and mountaineering. (☎853 12 00; www.gomountain.ch. Open June-Oct. M-F 9am-noon and 2-5pm. 1-day activities 100-600SFr. Reserve ahead for multi-day expeditions.)

Lower Glacier (*Untere Grindelwaldgletscher,* 5hr. circular hike without funicular). Although it is conquerable in sneakers, this hike is moderately steep, and becomes steeper the farther the trail proceeds. To find the trailhead, walk up the main street away from station until signs point downhill to "Pfinstegg." Hikers can either walk the first forested section of the trail (1hr.), following signs up to Pfinstegg, or take a funicular to the Pfinstegg hut. (8am-4pm; July to mid-Sept. 8am-7pm. 9.80SFr.) From the hut, signs lead up the glacier-filled valley to "Stieregg," a hut that offers food.

The Faulhorn via the Bachalpsee (7hr.; shorter options available if cable cars are used). This is the most dramatic strenuous hike away from the glaciers. The HI hostel is the easiest starting point. Head uphill on the road (left at the Y) until signs lead upwards to Allflue, which provides clear views down into town. From Allflue, the trail leads uphill for more than 1hr. to Waldspitz. The final hike from Waldspitz to Bachsee and the Faulhorn travels through highland meadows (5hr.). On the way down, go to **Bussalp** (2hr.), where a bus goes back to Grindelwald. For those with a little less stamina and a bit more money, the **First Bahn** goes straight from town to a station only 1hr. away from the Bachsee, knocking 2-3hr. off the hike. Another level, easy 1hr. hike offering great views of the glaciers runs from the top of the First Bahn to Grosse Scheidegg, where it is possible to catch a bus to Grindelwald.

The Männlichen (1hr.). Access another easy (though more expensive) hike on the other side of the valley by taking the **Männlichen Gondalbahn.** From the Männlichen station, a quick circular hike scales the **Männlichen** peak, which divides Grindelwald from the Lauterbrunnen Valley, before continuing as a flat, 1hr. hike to Kleine Scheidegg and its intimate views of the Eiger, Mönch, and Jungfrau. Hop a train back to Grindelwald from here. This hike is easier (and free or at least with cheaper mechanical access) as part of the hike from **Wengen** (see p. 366).

LAUTERBRUNNEN   ☎ 033

The 72 waterfalls that plummet down the sheer walls of the narrow, glacier-cut valley give Lauterbrunnen its name, "loud springs." The town of Lauterbrunnen, which lies in the middle of the valley of the same name, adjoins Switzerland's highest waterfall, **Staubbach Falls** (280m), which inspired Goethe's poem "Song of the Spirit over the Waterfall" (later set to music by Franz Schubert). Mendelssohn composed some of his "Songs without Words" in Lauterbrunnen as well. Lauterbrunnen's abundant accommodations and easy accessibility by car and train make the town an ideal base for those hiking and skiing throughout the Jungfrau region, as well as exploring the mountain villages.

Outside, Siberian huskies pull lazy mountaineers across the snow on sleds for 10SFr. Budget sportsmen opt for free "snow-hurtling," i.e. sledding down bunny-level slopes on garbage bags (bring your own bag). If the weather is perfect, try the 30min., snowy trek to the Mönchsjoch climbing hut. For more passive entertainment, gaze out at the frozen expanse of the Jungfraufirm glacier gripping the backside of the mountain.

Trains start at Interlaken's Ostbahnhof and travel to either Grindelwald or Lauterbrunnen, continuing to Kleine Scheidegg and to the peak itself. The entire trip is expensive, but **"Good Morning"** ticket makes things cheaper (available for departures May-Oct. 6:30am; Nov.-Apr. 6:35 and 7:35am, returning before noon). All tickets are round-trip, and there is no way down from the top except by train. (Eurail or Swiss-Pass 25% off. From Interlaken Ostbahnhof 162.80SFr, "Good Morning" ticket 125.80SFr; Lauterbrunnen 145.60SFr/108.60SFr; Grindelwald 145SFr/108SFr; Wengen 134SFr/97SFr; Mürren 165.20SFr/128.20SFr.)

Call ☎ 828 79 31 for a **weather forecast** or use the cable TV broadcast live from the Jungfraujoch and other high-altitude spots (in all tourist offices and big hotels). Bring **winter clothing** and food—it can be 10°C (50°F) on a July day, and in winter alcohol thermometers crack and antifreeze freezes.

▛▜ TRANSPORTATION & PRACTICAL INFORMATION

Trains connect every 30min. with: Interlaken Ost (20min., 6:05am-10:05pm, 6.60SFr); Jungfraujoch (1¾hr.; 7:08am-4:10pm; round-trip 145.60SFr, "Good Morning" ticket 108.20SFr); Kleine Scheidegg (45min., 6:10am-5pm, summer until 6:05pm, 26.80SFr); Mürren (20min., 6:42am-8pm, summer until 9pm, 9.80SFr); and Wengen (6:10am-midnight, 5.80SFr). The **tourist office** 200m to the left of the train station provides binders of information about activities and large tables to plan your stay. (☎856 85 68; www.wengen-muerren.ch. Open Jan.-May and Oct.-Dec. M-F 8am-12:30pm and 1:30-5pm, Oct. also Sa 9am-12:30pm and 1:30-4pm; June and Sept. M-F 8am-6pm, Sa-Su 9am-12:30pm and 1:30-4pm; July-Aug. M-F 8am-7pm, Sa 9am-12:30pm and 1:30-5pm, Su 9am-12:30pm and 1:30-4pm.) Services include: **currency exchange** and small **lockers** and **luggage** storage (3SFr) at the station; **bike rental** at Bike Imboden (☎855 21 14) and **ski rental** at **Crystal Sports** (☎856 90 90). For **medical assistance** call ☎856 26 26; for **Internet** access visit the **Valley Hostel** (12SFr per hr.) or the Horner Pub (20SFr per hr.). The **post office** is across from the station. (Open M-F 7:45-11:45am and 2-6pm, Sa 7:45-11am.) **Postal code:** CH-3822.

▛ ACCOMMODATIONS

▩ **Valley Hostel** (☎855 20 08; www.valleyhostel.ch). Head left on the main street, past the Co-op on the left. The hostel is down a driveway on the left side of the street. Martha, the friendly owner, offers a pristine environment and a big kitchen. The large windows allow breezes to blow over the comfortable wooden bunks (with fuzzy, cow-patterned sheets) in the large, clean rooms, and give views of Staubbach Falls. Showers and sheets included. Laundry (10SFr) and **Internet** (4SFr per 20min.) open 8am-10pm. You can request fondue (in advance) for 16SFr. Reception 8am-noon and 2-9pm. Dorms 23SFr; singles 28SFr; doubles 56-64SFr. ❷

▩ **Hotel Staubbach** (☎855 54 54; www.staubbach.ch). Turn left on the main street, 400m from the station on the left. This was one of the oldest hotels in town until it was converted by Craig and Corinne Rochin-Müller into a pleasant and affordable bed and breakfast. Worn oriental rugs lead the way to multiple rooms—each is a little different but all are clean and comfortable with running water. The dark-paneled parlor comes equipped with games, comfortable couches, cable TV, and a kids' corner. Parking and breakfast buffet included. Wheelchair-accessible. Reception 8am-10:30pm. Check-in 3-10pm. Check-out 11am. Call early to reserve a room. Singles 55SFr, with shower 60SFr; doubles 80SFr/110SFr; 3- to 6-bed family suites 30-50SFr per person. Children in parents' bed 20SFr. 10SFr surcharge for 1-night stays. MC/V. ❸

Hotel-Restaurant Schützen (☎855 30 26; www.hotelschuetzen.com). Turn left on the main street, on the right. A slightly more expensive option, Schützen provides comfortable beds with shiny wooden headboards. Spacious rooms come fully equipped with telephones and couches; some rooms have balconies. Breakfast included. Reception 7am-midnight. Check-out 11am. Singles 60-100SFr; doubles 120-170SFr; triples 150-225SFr; quads 180-240SFr. ❹

Camping Schützenbach (☎855 12 68; www.schutzenbach-retreat.ch). Take a left on the main road, a left over the river by the church, and keep going down the street as it curves sharply to the right (15min.; follow the signs). This camping complex has several lodging options, and a small tasty restaurant and convenience store. Reception 7:30am-noon and 2-7pm. 6SFr, children 3SFr; tents 6-10SFr. Dorms 16.50SFr; doubles with sink 64SFr; 4-bed "tourist rooms" in barracks-like huts 28SFr per person. MC/V. ❶

FOOD

Crystal Restaurant ❸, on the main street, has a short menu full of Swiss classics. Try *Älpler-Rösti* for 15SFr, cheese fondue for 20.50SFr, or a daily *Menü* including salad and entree for 15-29SFr. A breakfast buffet is available for 14SFr. (☎856 90 90. Open daily 8-11am and 5:30-9pm.) **Horner Bar ❶**, farther down the street, has beer (3.20SFr), pizza (8SFr), and **Internet** access for 12SFr per hr. (☎855 16 73. Open 9am-12:30am, disco upstairs open evening-2:30am.) A **Co-op** is near the hostel on the main road. (Open M-F 8am-noon and 2-6:30pm, Sa 8am-noon and 1:30-4pm.)

OUTDOORS

Lauterbrunnen's best hike is the flat trail that leads up the valley (about 7km). The trail below leads to a number of hiking destinations. To reach the trailhead, follow the right branch of the main road as it leaves town (toward Camping Jungfrau). It dwindles slowly to a narrow path before becoming a dirt trail through the woods. **Crystal Sport** (☎856 90 90; www.crystal-lauterbrunnen.ch) rents hiking boots for 15SFr per day. (Open M-Sa 8am-noon and 2-6:30pm, Su 9am-noon and 4-6pm.)

HIKE DOWN THE LAUTERBRUNNEN VALLEY. The first, and hence most touristed, segment of the trail leads to the **Trümmelbach Falls.** These 10 glacier-bed chutes are the only drains for the glacial run-off of the Eiger, Mönch, and Jungfrau glaciers and pour up to 20,000L of water per second (45min.). An underground elevator takes visitors to just below the highest falls, and lets them descent through the cave-canyon via misty tunnels and small bridges. (Open daily July-Aug. 9am-5pm; May-June and Sept.-Oct. 10am-4pm. 10SFr; with Jungfrau region visitor's card 9SFr.) The falls can also be reached by **bus** from Lauterbrunnen (to "Trümmelbach"; every hr., 3SFr).

The flat and calm trail leading to the Trümmelbach Falls passes the Staubbach Falls, Spissbach Falls, Agertenbach Falls, and Mümenbach Falls. After the turn-off for the Trümmelbach Falls, the trail becomes less busy as it makes

---

SONGS OF THE WATERFALL From its most famous visitor, J.W. Goethe—who immortalized the valley's Staubbach Falls in his "Gesang der Geisten über den Wassern"—to lesser-known but fiercely loved painters, the Lauterbrunnen Valley has inspired poet and artist alike with its silvery cascades where "in comely waves of foam/It powders white/The smooth rock,/And lightly taken/Simmers in a haze." The last verse of Goethe's poem, possibly the most famous lines in German verse, "O mortal soul,/Thou are like water's image,/O human fate,/Thou resemblest the wind!" was set to music by Schubert when he visited the falls.

---

its way toward **Stechelberg,** passing even more waterfalls (1½hr.). Stechelberg, a tiny village with a small grocery store, is the last place to catch a bus back to Lauterbrunnen (4.40SFr). From Stechelberg, the trail climbs, entering the end of the valley, which is accessible only by dirt road. The trail runs through Stechelberg and its one road to the end of town. The **Schilthorn Bahn cable car** runs from Stechelberg to Birg (35.40SFr), Gimmelwald (7.80SFr), Mürren (15.60SFr), and the Schilthorn (52SFr). The trips to Gimmelwald and Mürren are free with SwissPass; Eurail offers a 25% reduction on all destinations. Gimmelwald and Mürren are carless by law. Leave cars at the parking lot near the cable car (day 5SFr, week 21SFr, mo. 30SFr).

Trachsellauenen, a two-building enclave 50min. from Stechelberg, is the next destination on the trail. This is the departure point for the trail leading into the **nature reserve.** A 2½hr. strenuous mountain hike leads to the tiny Oberhornsee, a lake which lies beneath the Tschingel glacier.

BICYCLING. Imboden Bike Adventures, on Lauterbrunnen's main street, rents mountain bikes for 35SFr per day, and lends out free maps and helmets. (☎855 21 14. Open daily May-Oct. 8:30am-6:30pm; Nov.-Apr. 9am-noon and 2-6:30pm. AmEx/DC/MC/V.) On the Mürren Loop, bike via funicular to Grütschalp (7.80SFr), pedal to Mürren and Gimmelwald, and roll downhill to Stechelberg and Lauterbrunnen.

WENGEN   ☎033

Wengen (pop. 1100) occupies a ledge on the cliff-curtained Lauterbrunnental. Accessible only by train, hotel golf carts and a few taxis provide all the transportation around the peaceful town. Despite its seclusion and emptiness in summer, Wengen retains a modern feel and attracts crowds of out-of-town skiers to its top resorts during the peak winter months. Because Eurail does not cover the train ride to Wengen, it is an ideal destination for summer travelers looking for a quiet break from the backpacker social scene of many nearby towns.

▐▚ TRANSPORTATION & PRACTICAL INFORMATION

Wengen is accessible by **train** from Interlaken Ost (45min., every hr. 6:35am-10:35pm, 12.40SFr) and from Lauterbrunnen (15min., every 25min. 6:10am-midnight, 5.80SFr). After stopping in Wengen, the train continues toward Kleine Scheidegg (7:25am-5:20pm, summer 7:25am-6:25pm; 21SFr) and the Jungfraujoch (7:25am-4:30pm; winter only until 2:30pm; 134SFr, morning ticket 97SFr). Cars can be parked in the Lauterbrunnen **parking garage** (8-16SFr per day depending on season and day of the week). The **tourist office,** right and then an immediate left from the station, offers **Internet** access (15SFr per hr.), doles out information on local hikes and sells maps for 4SFr or 15SFr. (☎855 14 14; fax 30 60. Open June-Sept. and Dec.-Apr. daily 9am-6pm. Other months vary, but generally closed on weekends.) Services include: **currency exchange, lockers** (3-5SFr), and hotel reservations at the train station. Facility contains a **pharmacy** (☎855 12 46) and **emergency** (☎280 55 40) services to the left out of the station and 2min. past the tourist office. (Open M-F 8am-noon and 2-6:30pm, Sa 8am-noon and 2-5pm in the summer, later in the winter). **Hospital** in Interlaken (☎826 26 26); **doctor** (☎856 28 28). **Internet** is at the station, tourist office, or at **Hot Chili Peppers** (5SFr per 15min.). The **post office** is next to the tourist office. (Open M-F 8am-noon and 2-6pm, Sa 8:30-11am.) **Postal code:** CH-3823.

▐▖ ACCOMMODATIONS & FOOD

Although not one of Switzerland's more glamorous ski resorts, lodging in Wengen does not cater to the budget traveler. Visitors get the best deal by staying in one of the hostels or hotels in Lauterbrunnen. The sole budget option in Wengen, **Mittaghorn ❷** lies down the hill on the outer edges of town. Follow the road past the Co-op under the railroad tracks as it makes switchbacks toward the large yellow building with the green shutters (10min.). Once a hotel and then a schoolhouse, this building is now an apartment with a mixture of rooms available from May to November. (☎745 58 50, 422 97 05, or 855 15 73; angelainthealps@hotmail.com. Kitchen, cable TV, BBQ and table tennis available. Beds or mattresses 28SFr.) On the way down the hill, turn right at the bakery for more luxurious accommodations at **Hotel Edelweiss ④**. This chalet-style hotel has pristine, bright wooden accommodations and a peaceful garden out front. Each spacious room comes equipped with shower and either a balcony or TV. Breakfast included. Reception all day. (☎855 23 88; www.vch.ch/edelweiss. June-Oct. 65-75SFr per person; mid-Dec. until Apr. 60-85SFr per person. MC/V.)

▣Ristorante da Sina ④, with its intimate, candle-lit tables and extensive wine selection (from 6SFr per glass), sits up the hill from Hot Chili Peppers (below). Most items are quite pricey, but you get what you pay for. There are some more affordable options: a large pizza margherita is 14SFr.; with added goodies like asparagus, artichokes, and spinach, it's 19SFr. Take-out and smaller portions (11-19SFr) available. (Open daily 11:30am-2pm and 6-11:30pm. AmEx/DC/MC/V.) **Hot Chili Peppers ❶**, left from the station past the tourist office, is centrally located and one of Wengen's main social highlights. This huge bar offers beer (3.50SFr) and snacks (mostly sandwiches; 7-9.50SFr) as well as **Internet** access (5SFr per 15min), billiards, and darts. (☎855 50 20; chilis@wengen.com. Open daily 8:30am-2am.) Next door is **da Sina's Pub**, which hosts a variety of discos, live music, and karaoke. (Beer 4SFr; 0.5L 6.50SFr. Happy Hour 9-10pm and midnight-1am involves 2 beers for 4.50SFr. Open 6pm-2:30am.)

A **Co-op** supermarket sits quite visibly opposite the station. (Open M-F 8am-12:15pm and 1:30-6:30pm, Sa 8am-4pm.)

⚡ OUTDOOR ACTIVITIES

Wengen's elevation above the valley floor puts it close to the treeline and provides spectacular views. The following 7hr. **hike** from Wengen traverses the ridge dividing the two valleys of the Jungfrau Region, above the tree line almost the entire time. Several cable car stops along the way can shorten the journey.

HIKE TO MÄNNLICHEN AND KLEINE SCHEIDEGG. (7hr.) The hike begins with an ascent of **Männlichen**. Walk up the main street, away from the tourist office, and towards the end of town; follow signs upward to "Männlichen" (red-and-white marked trail). The trail wanders upwards through a meadowed lane cleared by cows. As is true for the whole ascent of Männlichen, there are views of the glacier-laden side of the Jungfrau and the cliff-curtained Lauterbrunnen valley. Toward the top, be sure to turn left when another unmarked trail merges in. The climb to the Männlichen saddle steeply zigzags upwards for about 3hr. The cable car from Grindelwald stops at the saddle, a 15min. stroll from the peak, a vertical promontory with a 360° view of the Bernese Oberland. Walk back down to the Männlichen cable car station and restaurant, then follow the signs to **Kleine Scheidegg**. This highly populated trail curves, without climbing, around the contour of the ridge, all the while looking down on the Grindelwald valley and up to the towering Eiger, Mönch, and Jungfrau. It is possible to take the train from Kleine Scheidegg down to Wengen (21SFr) or Grindelwald (28SFr), or hike back to Wengen on a trail alongside the tracks (2hr.). For a quieter hiking option cross over the train tracks and follow the red-and-white trail. The trail passes the Mönch and Jungfrau as closely as is possible on foot, then swings toward Wengen (2½hr. downhill).

SKIING. The **Swiss Ski School**, beside the Co-op, is the cheaper of the town's two schools. (☎/fax 855 20 22; www.wengen.com/sss. 48SFr for a 3hr. lesson; 5 lessons for 199SFr. Open from late Dec.-early Apr. Su-F 8:30am-1:30pm and 3:30-6:30pm, Sa 8:45-11am and 4:30-7pm.) As its name suggests, **Privat Ski and Snowboard School**, offers lessons to smaller groups. (☎/fax 855 50 05 or ☎448 71 24; www.wengen.com/privat. 1-2 people 65SFr per hour; 3-4 70SFr per hr. Office open daily 5-6:30pm.) Every January, Wengen hosts the skiing World Cup's longest and most dangerous downhill race, the **Lauberhorn.** Hotels generally won't allow tourists to book rooms until about a week in advance so that they can guarantee a room for all the racers and support crews. The downhill course starts 2315m above Kleine Scheidegg, curls around Wengernalp, and ends at Ziel (1287m) at the eastern end of the village, a drop of nearly 1200m in 2½min.

MÜRREN ☎033

The quiet, car-free streets of Mürren (pop. 430) are frequented mostly by tractors and tourists. This gem of a town is lined primarily with hotels and guest houses that sprouted up when Mürren invented slalom skiing. Mürren's most popular attraction is the Schilthorn, which Hans Castorp scaled in *The Magic Mountain*, a novel by Thomas Mann, and which 007, the British secret agent James Bond, made famous with a ski scene in *The Spy Who Loved Me*. A multitude of hikes, a quiet and friendly atmosphere, and a stunning landscape make Mürren a destination in which travelers stay much longer than expected.

TRANSPORTATION & PRACTICAL INFORMATION

Mürren can be reached by **cogwheel train** from **Lauterbrunnen** (every 30min. 6:25am-8:30pm, 9.80SFr), or by **cable car** from Gimmelwald (7.40SFr) or Stechelberg (15.60SFr). Alternatively, **hike** from Gimmelwald (30min. uphill). From the station, the road leading into town forks in two; nearly everything, except the tourist office, is on the lower, left fork. The cable car is at the opposite end of town from the train station. The **tourist office,** in the sports center 100m from the station, off the right fork, has information about private rooms, hiking trails and skiing prices. (☎ 856 86 86; fax 86 96. Open July-Aug. M-F 9am-noon and 1-6:30pm, Th until 8:30pm, Sa 1-6:30pm, Su 1-5:30pm; Sept.-May M-F 9am-noon and 2-5pm; June M-F 9am-noon and 2-6:30pm.) There are **lockers** (2SFr) at the train and cable car stations. **Stäger Sport** across from the tourist office rents **hiking boots** for 12SFr and mountain **bikes** for 35SFr. (☎855 23 55. Open Dec.-Apr. and June-Oct. daily 9am-noon and 1:30-5pm.) **Police,** call ☎855 76 11; for **medical assistance,** ☎855 17 10. The Eiger Guest House provides **Internet** access (12SFr per hr.) all day, or try the **Feuz** souvenir shop down the main road (10SFr per hr. Open daily 11am-6pm). The **post office** is on the station side of the main street. (Open M-F 8:15-11:30am and 2:30-5pm, Sa 8:15-10:15am.) **Postal code:** CH-3825.

ACCOMMODATIONS & FOOD

Mürren's accommodations are quiet and comfortable in comparison to the alternatives down the hill in Gimmelwald (see p. 359), but they're also less fun. An enthusiastic British woman at the **Chalet Fontana** ❸ offers traditional Swiss lodging in seven private rooms with tea and coffee. (☎ 855 26 86 or 642 34 85. Breakfast included. Reservations recommended. Doubles 70-90SFr; triples 110SFr.) The **Eiger Guesthouse** ❸, across the street from the train station, is pristine and comfortable. (☎856 54 60; www.muerren.ch/eigerguesthouse. Breakfast included. Free access to pool and skating rink at Sports Zentrum and **Internet** access for 12SFr per hr. Reception M-F 8am-11:30pm, Sa-Su 8am-12:30am. Summer dorms 39-55SFr; doubles 100-120SFr, with shower 130-140SFr; 1-night stays 5SFr extra per person. Winter dorms 45-70SFr; doubles 110-140SFr, with shower 140-180SFr. AmEx/DC/MC/V.) The **Alpina Hotel** ❹, down the left fork in the main road, also provides its guests with access to the sport center pool and skating rink. The hotel offers chalet-style rooms with fluffy comforters and stunning balconies; ask for a view of the Eiger, Monch and Jungfrau. (Breakfast included. ☎855 13 61; www.muerren.ch/alpina. Singles 75-100SFr; doubles 130-170SFr. AmEx/DC/MC/V.)

Eating out in Mürren is pretty reasonable; almost all of the town's restaurants are in hotels. *Raclette* and an unobstructed view of the snow-capped mountains are available for 14.50SFr at **Alpina Hotel ❸**; try the house *Rösti* for 17SFr. (☎855 13 61. Wheelchair-accessible. AmEx/DC/MC/V.) The **Eiger Guesthouse ❸** also offers specialties such as fondue (20.50SFr; min. 2 people) or burgers (10.50-17.50SFr) and beer (5.20SFr for 0.5L). (AmEx/DC/MC/V.) **Tham Chinese Restaurant ❷**, down the left fork from the train station, serves cheap pan-fried noodles. Wonton noodles are 11.50SFr; vegetable fried rice is 12.50SFr. (☎856 01 10. Open daily June-Oct. 11:30am-9:30pm; Dec. 15-Apr. noon-11pm. Closed May and Oct. 20-Dec.15.)

Mürren's **Co-op,** which comes in handy for trips to nearby Gimmelwald, is 15min. down the right fork of the main walkway. (Open M-F 8am-noon and 1:45-6:30pm, Sa 8am-noon and 1:45-4pm.)

▧ HIKING

Mürren's location on the ledge above Lauterbrunnen makes it the ideal starting point for numerous higher-elevation hikes around the Lauterbrunnen Valley. From Mürren (1645m) the trails leading to Gimmelwald, Stechelberg, and the Trümmelbach Falls provide unparalleled views of the Eiger, Mönch, and Jungfrau. Ask at the tourist office for maps and suggestions.

Grütschalp (top of funicular from Lauterbrunnen) to Mürren (1-2hr.). A flat, 1hr. hike follows the train tracks to Mürren, and is well-touristed on sunny days. A more isolated mountain route takes twice as long, but has better views and less people. Both trails start across the tracks from the station balcony. A yellow sign to Mürren marks the easier trail, while the red-white-red "Mürren Höhenweg" sign marks the mountainous hike. After an initially steep ascent, the trail wanders through buttercup meadows that stretch before the rising peaks of the Eiger, Mönch, and Jungfrau. When the trail splits, head to "Allmenhubel," then down to Mürren.

Shark's Fin via Stechelberg and Obersteinberg (1½-5hr.). This hike is a steep descent from the Mountain Hostel in Gimmelwald that gives continual views of the sheer rock slabs lining the Lauterbrunnen Valley. It's a grand approach to the **Trümmelbach Falls** (1½hr.), with a return possible by cable car. Alternatively, for a challenging approach to the finish, hikers may take a trail that forks right 5min. after the river crossing on the Stechelberg path. This route crosses the river, climbing steeply and without pause along the flank of the unsettled Lauterbrunnen valley head. After passing **Obersteinberg hut** (1½hr. more), the trail tops out at Tanzboden (1978m) where there is an inspiring panorama of the wall leading to the Jungfrau, and then gradually descends to **Hotel Obersteinberg** (1778m), before continuing to the **Oberhornsee** (2065m, 2hr.).

Schilthorn descent (3-4hr.). For fit and experienced hikers. Head downhill along the secured ridge to **Roter Herd.** At the signpost, backtrack on the left toward the Schilthorn, then take the steep descent to the Rotstock Hut on **Poganggenalp.** Continue to **Bryndli** where a steep narrow trail connects to **Spielbodenalp.** From there a mountain road descends gently to Mürren. An ascent is a longer, harder alternative for those wishing to bypass the expenses of the cable-car. For a different route, head via Allmenhubel to Schilthornhutte for lunch (*Rosti* with *Bratwurst* 13SFr), and a break before the final steep climb to the Schilthorn.

⚠ OTHER OUTDOOR ACTIVITIES

UP THE SCHILTORN. The most popular journey this side of the Lauterbrunnen Valley is the short, albeit expensive, cable car trip to the *Schilthorn* (2970m) made famous by the exploits of 007 in *On Her Majesty's Secret Service.* (☎823 14 44;

www.schilthorn.ch. From Mürren 37.60SFr, round-trip 62.20SFr; morning ticket 46.80SFr round-trip.) The **Piz Gloria Restaurant ❸** spins at its apex. Settle down for a meal (entrees around 20SFr) and take in the 360° panorama from the Schilthorn station's deck. Bear in mind that there is very little to do at the top when it's cloudy (there tends to be clearer weather earlier in the morning).

The ski school has classes for downhill, slalom, and snowboarding. (☎/fax 855 12 47. 6 half-day group lessons run 135SFr. For ski pass information see the **Jungfrau Region** introduction, p. 359. The **Inferno Run** seeks volunteers every January (usually for 3 days from the 20th) for the Inferno downhill ski, which descends 2170m. The Inferno Triathlon is in August; the Mürren-Schilthorn stretch is last.

NEAR MÜRREN: 🎿GIMMELWALD   ☎033

Gimmelwald is a farming town of slightly over 100 people that was stopped in its tracks over 50 years ago when it was labeled an avalanche zone. The warning has not frightened away backpackers, who often outnumber the locals and inhabit the lower end of town. It retains the most secluded, rustic feel of any town in the Jungfrau. The lack of late-night hangouts has fostered a lively atmosphere at the hostel.

Splitting to the left after the post office, the lower road in Mürren leads downhill (30min.) to Gimmelwald, as does the **cable car** (to the right of the fork, 7.80SFr; Swisspass free, 25% off with Eurail) from either Mürren or Stechelberg (just up the valley from Lauterbrunnen). Gimmelwald has **no supermarket,** so stock up in Mürren. Fresh-baked bread (2.50-4.50SFr), fresh milk, and yogurt (both 1.20SFr) are available at Esther's Bed and Breakfast and the Mountain Hostel (see below).

All the beds in Gimmelwald lie along the small trail that rises from the cable car station. At the bottom of the trail, the social **Mountain Hostel ❷** is run by a laid-back couple, Petra and Walter, who offer a communal kitchen and access to life's essentials—fresh bread (3SFr), milk (2SFr), chocolate (2SFr), **Internet** (12SFr per hr.), billiards, and guitars. The hostel bar is also the local hangout, so every night sees a lively mix of traveler and villager alike relaxing at the bar, by the pool table, or on the benches outside. (☎855 17 04; mountainhostel@tcnet.ch. Showers 1SFr. Reception 8:30-11am and 5:30-10:30pm. Lockout 9:30-11am. Dorms 20SFr.) At **Hotel Mittaghorn (Walter's B & B) ❷**, at the trail's summit, host Walter makes *Glühwein* (mulled wine) and Heidi cocoa (with peppermint schnapps). He also cooks a three-course dinner for guests (15SFr) in *Edelweiss* suspenders. (☎855 16 58. Breakfast 12SFr. Showers 1SFr for 5min. Order meals in advance. Open Apr.-Nov. Old, wooden beds in the attic 25SFr; doubles 70-80SFr; triples 100SFr; quads 125SFr. Add 3SFr for a 1-night stay.) At **Esther's Guesthouse ❷**, a short walk up the street from the cablecar station, travelers can sleep in the hay in a barn or in a guest house with more comfortable rooms. (☎855 54 88. Kitchen access included. Breakfast 12SFr. Place in the hay 20SFr; singles 40SFr; doubles 80-95SFr; triples 100SFr; quads 160SFr.) The **Gimmelwald Guest House ❸**, directly across from the post office, provides the only conventional restaurant, serving *Bratwurst* with *Rösti* for 16.50SFr and other tasty country vittles. (Breakfast 12:30-2:30pm. Dinner served after 6:30pm; reserve early.)

WESTERN BERNESE OBERLAND

KANDERSTEG   ☎033

Kandersteg sits at the head of the Kander valley, which extends north to Spiez, and against the imposing peaks of the Doldenhorn (3643m) to the southeast and the Bonderspitz (2546m) to the west. It is also the northern terminus of the Lötschberg tunnel, the only connection between the Valais and Bern that doesn't make a large detour to the east or west. Short day hikes lead to isolated glacial lakes, mountain passes with views of the Bernese Alps, and some of Europe's largest glaciers. Slightly out of the way, and noticeably devoid of crowds of English-speaking backpackers, Kandersteg seems to have been overshadowed by towns nearer the Jungfrau, but as far as hiking goes, it can compete with them all.

TRANSPORTATION & PRACTICAL INFORMATION

Trains connect Kandersteg north to Spiez (30min., every hr. 5:23am-10:39pm, 16.20SFr) and then Interlaken Ost (1hr., 22SFr), or south to Brig (35min., every hr. 6:46am-12:38am, 18.80SFr). To reach the center of town, follow the road perpendicular to and right of the train station 75m until it meets the main road at the center of the village. The **tourist office,** left along the main road, offers **Internet access** (10SFr per hr.) and **hiking information.** (☎675 80 80; www.kandersteg.ch. Open July-Sept. and Jan.-Mar. M-F 8am-noon and 1:30-6pm, Sa 8:30am-noon and 1:30-4:30pm; Oct.-Dec. and Apr.-June M-F 8am-noon and 2-5pm.) The **Kandersteg Wanderkarte** (hiking map; 16.80SFr), an invaluable resource for any hike, is sold at the tourist office and at most stores. The tourist office also offers an online description of several hikes. Services include: **currency exchange, lockers** (4-5SFr), **luggage storage** (5SFr), and **bike rentals** (30SFr per day, 23SFr per half-day) at one counter of the train station (open daily 7:10am-7:30pm); **taxis** (☎671 23 77 or 07 93 33 39 33); **medical assistance** (☎675 14 24); **helicopter rescue** (☎14 14); **weather report** (☎162). A **post office** is next to the Co-op. (Open M-F 8-11:30am and 2:30-6pm, Sa 8-11am.) **Postal code:** CH-3718.

ACCOMMODATIONS

Kandersteg International Scout Center (☎675 82 82; reception@kandersteg.sout.org). Bus from the train station (5min., every hr. 7:20am-6:40pm, 2SFr) to "Pfadfinderzentrum," or head right on the main road until it goes under the railroad tracks and it's on the right (20min.). The Center's cheerful, multilingual volunteer staff prepares beds in the institutional chalet and some of the campsite. The area can often be overrun with groups of scouts, and the train runs audibly nearby, but various amenities compensate. The Center has extensive summer-camp-reminiscent facilities, and organizes a comprehensive array of outdoor activities, including **mountain biking** (35SFr per person), **canyoning** (86-110SFr), **rock climbing** (23-25SFr per person for a group lesson, just climbing without lesson 8SFr), and **river rafting** (46-69SFr), and offers discounts on train rides and nearby tourist attractions. Breakfast 6SFr, lunch 11SFr, dinner 13SFr; order in advance. Kitchen included. Bread, milk, and other staples available at the reception. Finnish sauna 9SFr. Sheets 3SFr. Laundry 6SFr. **Internet** access 2SFr per 15min. Reception M-Sa 8:15-11:45am and 2-5:30pm, Su 9:15-11:45am and 2-5:30pm; longer hours in summer. Call at least a week in advance for reservations. Bed in the chalet 21SFr, 16SFr for scouts; campsite 10.50/8.50SFr. ❷

Hotel Garni Alpenblick (☎675 11 29; www.aplenblick.be), left on the main road. Clean rooms complete with balconies, and comforters. TV room. Buffet breakfast included. Reception 8am-midnight. Check-out by noon. Reservations recommended. Rooms 48-58SFr per person, with shower 55-65SFr. AmEx/DC/MC/V. ❸

FOOD

Most restaurants in Kandersteg are in hotels, so don't be shy, but consider removing your hiking boots before dining. **Hotel Schweizerhof** ❸, on the riverfront in the town's center, is a gastronomic gem. The wooden-shingled pagoda on the edge of a

BERNESE OBERLAND

manicured garden is an ideal place to enjoy a variety of meals. Pastas run 12.50-17.50SFr, salads 7-18SFr, and traditional *Käseschnitte* goes for 13-17.50SFr. Follow any meal with a crêpe (7-15.50SFr) or one of the delectable ice cream options for 8-9.50SFr. (☎675 22 00. Wheelchair-accessible. Open daily 9am-7pm, until 10pm in good weather. MC.) The **Hotel Victoria Ritter ❸** serves elaborate Swiss specialties (18-33SFr) as well as different "Fitness" menus (23-28SFr) in a classy dining room. Try the *Bärner Gnusch*, a hearty one-pot mix of meats and vegetables (27SFr) or order from a variety of sandwiches for 8-17.50SFr. (Wheelchair-accessible. Open daily 9am-midnight; kitchen closes 10:30pm. Closed May and late Oct. until mid-Dec. AmEx/DC/MC/V.)

Pizzeria Antico ❷ (☎675 13 13), to the right on the main street, about 5min. past Hotel zur Post, offers varieties of pizza (11.50-20SFr) and numerous pastas (11-18SFr). (Wheelchair-accessible. Open noon-2pm and 6-9pm.) A **Co-op** is between the station and town. (Open M-F 8am-6:30pm, Sa 8am-5pm.)

◙ HIKING

Around Kandersteg, you'll pant up the mountain, then lose your breath again when you catch the views that await hikers. Some of the longest glaciers in Europe, most notably the **Kanderfirm,** are east of town, while the **Öschinensee** is surrounded by steep cliffs that rise to jagged peaks. The **Bergsteigschule,** a climbing school, also offers guided trips into the mountains. (☎675 80 89; www.bs-k.ch.)

Öschinensee (20min.-1½hr.). The most easily accessible trails in Kandersteg traverse the area around the spectacular Öschinensee. The **Öschinenseebahn** departs from near the tourist office and runs to trailheads. (Open daily May 8-June 15 and Sept. 16-Oct. 20 8:45am-5pm; June 16-Sept. 1 7:30am-6:30pm; Sept. 2-Sept. 15 7:30am-5pm. 12.60SFr, round-trip 17.10SFr, children 6.30SFr/8.60SFr.) From the top, a 20min. trail rolls to the edge of the blue lake bordered on all sides by sheer rock walls. The low pass that the trail crosses separates the Öschinensee from civilization. The **Öschinensee hut ❷** is a perfect base for exploration on the lake's shore. Its army camp beds adjoin a living room and TV room. (Breakfast included. Open daily May 8-June 15 and Sept. 16-Oct. 20 8:45am-5pm; June 16-Sept. 1 7:30am-6:30pm; Sept. 2-Sept. 15 7:30am-5pm. Dorms 35-40SFr; doubles 120-160SFr.) A small dock with paddleboats and rowboats allows excursions on the perfect calm of the lake. (Open May-Oct. and Jan.-Apr. Paddleboats 22SFr per hr., rowboats 16SFr per hr.)

Blümlisalp Glacier from the Öschinensee (3-4hr.). A steep, rocky trail (3hr.)—to be attempted only with hefty boots—shoots upwards from the cabin to **Fründenhorn hut ❷**. (☎675 14 33. Open June-Oct.; 25SFr per night, children 16SFr.) A longer, more gradual trail probes the glacial region between the Kandersteg Valley and the Jungfrau Region. A trail (4hr.) connects the Öschinensee to the **Blümlisalp hut ❷**, a stone fortress-like structure nestled beneath the Blümlisalp glacier. (Open late June until mid-Oct. 27SFr, children 15SFr.)

GSTAAD & SAANEN ☎033

At the juncture of four alpine valleys, Gstaad and its earthier sister, Saanen (combined pop. 6500), are at the heart of Swiss skiing country. Only a few kilometers apart, these two towns share little aside from their similar dark wood structures and chalet roofs. Saanen inhabits the mountainous scenery with contented ease, while Gstaad trades goats for Gucci—its five-star hotels and cardigan-draped tourists make it a glamorous gem surrounded by placid farmland.

▣ TRANSPORTATION

Gstaad is accessible by **train** from Interlaken (2hrs., every hr. 7:22am-8:40pm, 30SFr) or Montreux (1½hr., every hr. 6:30am-8:30pm and 9:30pm, 22SFr). Saanen can be reached from Gstaad by **train** (5min., every hr., 2.60SFr), **Post Bus** (10min.; almost every hr. M-Sa 6:35am-7:33pm, Su 7:50am-7:33pm; 3SFr) or a 40min. walk along the Yehudi Menuhin Philosophy Path (signs to Saanen lead the way from the station). **Buses** also run to Les Diablerets (50min.; every hr. 8:33am-1:33pm, also 3:50pm summer and winter high-season; 12.40SFr, half-price with SwissPass).

▣ ▣ ORIENTATION & PRACTICAL INFORMATION

Turn right from the train station to reach Gstaad's **tourist office,** and take the main road just past the railway bridge. Pick up a useful area map. (☎748 81 81, room reservations and package deals ☎748 81 84; www.gstaad.ch. Open mid-June to Aug. and mid-Dec. to mid-Mar. M-F 8:30am-6:30pm, Sa 9am-5pm, Su 9am-noon and 1:30-5pm; other times M-F 8:30am-noon and 1:30-6pm, Sa 10am-noon and 1:30-5pm.) Saanen's **tourist office,** labeled *Vehrkehrsbüro,* is on the main street. From the station go straight ahead, then right on the main road 70m. (☎748 81 60; saanen@gstaad.ch. Open M-F 8:30am-noon and 2-5pm, July to mid-Sept. and mid-Dec. to 1st week of Mar. also Sa 9am-noon and 2-5pm.) Gstaad train station services include: **currency exchange, Western Union services, ticket counter** (M-F 5am-9pm, Sa-Su 6am-9pm), **lockers** (3-5SFr), **luggage storage** (3SFr; M-F 5am-9:30pm, Sa-Su 6am-9:30pm), **bike rental** (30SFr per day, 23SFr per half-day; open daily 8am-noon and 1:30-6pm). At the Saanen train station, there is **ski storage** (1SFr deposit). Next door to the Saanen post office, the Saanen Bank **exchanges currency** and cashes traveler's checks; **ATM** also available. (Wheelchair-accessible. Open M-F 8am-noon and 1:45-5:30pm, Sa 8-11am.) **Taxis** (☎744 80 80). **Webmania,** across from the Co-op (☎744 29 65; open Tu-Sa 10am-1:30pm and 3-8pm, Su 3-8pm; 2SFr per 10min., more in evening) and **Café Pernet** (in front of Richi's Pub; open 8am-11pm; 5SFr per 20min.) in Gstaad provide **Internet access.** For **medical assistance**, call ☎744 86 86. Saanen has a **pharmacy,** the **Jaggi Drogerie,** right down the street from the tourist office on the corner. (☎744 13 21. Open M-F 8am-noon and 1:30-6:30pm, Sa 8am-noon and 1:30-4pm.) Gstaad's **post office,** to the left of the train station, has a **24hr. ATM** and Swisscom **payphones.** (Open M-F 8am-noon and 2-6pm, Sa 8:30-11am.) **Postal code:** CH-3780. Saanen's post office, 50m straight ahead of its train station on the left, has a **wheelchair-accessible payphone.** (Open M-F 7:45am-noon and 2-6pm, Sa 7:45-11am.) **Postal code:** CH-3792.

▣ ACCOMMODATIONS & CAMPING

Gstaad proper has few hotels for the budget-conscious, but the tourist office publishes a list of all the hotels and the cheaper *Privatzimmer,* which are farther from town. If you're looking to stay closer and don't mind splurging, a few hotels on the outskirts of town offer reasonable rates. From the tourist office, head right down the Promenade and in the direction of Gsteig. At the intersection next to the river, turn left. About a 10min. walk from Gstaad's center are two comparable hotels. **Sport-Hotel Rütti ❹** is farther down the road on the right and offers bright, spacious rooms right above a pizzeria. (☎744 29 21; www.sporthotel-ruetti.ch. Prices depend on season. Singles 95-133SFr; doubles 170-236SFr. AmEx/DC/MC/V.) Across the street, **Hotel Alphorn ❹** provides rooms with TV, minibar, and a family-friendly atmosphere. (☎748 45 45; www.gstaad-alphorn.ch. **Internet** 1SFr per 5min. Breakfast and tourist taxes included. Reception 7am-midnight. Check-in 2pm. Check-out 11am. Rates vary seasonally, with lowest prices Apr.-May and Oct. to mid-Dec. Singles 96-126SFr; doubles 172-272SFr. AmEx/DC/MC/V.)

The cheapest and most picturesque option in Saanen is the **Jugendherberge** ❷. From Saanen's station, go straight about 100m, turn right on the main street and walk 10min. till it dead-ends near the gas station. Cross over the busy road and follow hostel signs up the hill straight ahead, past the hospital and toward Hotel Spitzhorn. After 5min. uphill, the hostel will be on your left. Rustic rooms upstairs contrast oddly with the brightly colored kitchen, but the hostel offers **bike rental** (15SFr per day, 10SFr per half-day), TV and game room, and a decent library. (☎744 13 43; www.youthhostel.ch/saanen. Reservations recommended year-round. Breakfast and sheets included. Dinner 12.50SFr, lunch 9SFr. Laundry 11SFr. Reception 8-10am and 5-9pm, though you can obtain the access code if you'll be out late. Check-out 8-10am. Closed in Nov. Dorms 29SFr (ask for a balcony); doubles 78SFr; triples and quads available. Prices do not include tax (2.50SFr per night, 0.95SFr kids 12-16, under 12 tax-free. Children under 5 free.) Non-HI members 6SFr extra. Children 2-6 half-price, under 2 free. AmEx/DC/MC/V.)

Camping Bellerive ❶ lies just off the road between Gstaad and Saanen, a 15min. walk from both. From the Saanen train station, walk past the tourist office to the intersection and follow the camping signs. The site sits in a valley with quality mountain views. (☎744 63 30; bellerive.camping@bluewin.ch. Check-in 9-10am and 6-7pm, but you can arrive at any time. May-Oct. 8.80SFr per adult, 4.40SFr per child; 5.30SFr per tent. Nov.-Apr. 9.90SFr/4.40SFr/ 5.30SFr. 20% reduction May to mid-June and Oct. to mid-Dec. Electricity 2.70SFr.) The **Beim Kappeli** ❶, the Saanen campsite, is on the edge of town. Cross the tracks behind the station and head left along the river for a packed but friendly campsite next to the rushing water. (☎744 61 91; fax 61 84. Office open 6-7pm. 5.20SFr per person; 8SFr per tent; 15SFr per car. MC/V.)

🍴 FOOD

To get to **Richi's Pub** ❷, turn right from the Gstaad station. Chow down on a burger and a beer (14-18SFr), an omelette (12-18SFr), or soup and a salad (14SFr) on leather chairs in a no-frills environment. If you try the steak, you must choose one of three cuts: ladies', men's, or the Sitting Bull (36-54SFr). (☎744 57 87; fax 99 87. 18+. Open daily noon-12:30am.) Meanwhile, the front of the building houses **Café Pernet** ❷, which shares the same menu as Richi's but allows guests of all ages; **Internet access** is available at 5SFr per 20min. (Café open 8am-11pm.) **Apple-Pie** ❸, at the intersection past the tourist office on the left, serves tasty pizzas (14-21SFr) large enough for two, along with crêpes (10.40SFr) amidst cowbells and carved wood. (☎744 46 48; apple-pie@gstaad.ch. Ground level seating is wheelchair-accessible. Open daily 8:30am-11pm; kitchen open noon-10pm.)

In Saanen, try Swiss specialties like cheese fondue (21SFr per person) or sauteed veal with *Rösti* (15-19SFr) at the **Saanerhof Restaurant** ❸, across from the train station. (☎744 15 15; www.saanerhof.ch. English menu. Open M-F 7:30am-11:30pm, Sa-Su 7:30am-12:30am.) The **Co-op,** straight ahead from the Gstaad station and left on the main road, sells groceries and cafeteria meals (2.40SFr per 100g of salad; 6.50SFr for chicken nuggets, fries, and a drink) in a pleasant, well-lit atmosphere. (Wheelchair-accessible. Open M-Th 8am-6:30pm, F 8am-8pm, Sa 8am-5pm, caféteria only Su 9am-5pm. MC/V.)

⚠ OUTDOOR ACTIVITIES

ADVENTURE SPORTS. Three main adventure companies, **Alpinzentrum** (☎ 748 41 61; www.alpinzentrum.ch) in Gstaad, and **Swissraft** (☎ 744 50 80; www.swissraft.ch) and **Absolut Activ** (☎ 748 14 14; www.abslout-activ.ch) in Saanen, arrange adventure activities in the area in both summer and winter. All three companies, in addition to **H₂O Experience** (☎ 026 928 19 35) in Gstaad, lead **rafting** trips. (Alpinzentrum: 108SFr for 4hr., children 8-12 78SFr. H₂O Experience: 90SFr for 3hr., ages 10-15 70SFr. Swissraft: 105SFr for 3hr.; English-speaking guides. Absolut Activ: 98SFr for 4hr.) Absolut Activ also offers **skydiving,** Swissraft offers **ballooning,** and both have **canyoning** and **mountain biking** trips (60-370SFr). Alpinzentrum also offers **climbing, glacier tours,** and **jeep safari** (98-150SFr); there's even an organized team event where participants compete in traditional Swiss games (call ahead). Hans Büker's **Ballonhafen Gstaad** has been launching balloon excursions for over 25 years. (☎ 026 924 54 85; www.gstaadballon.ch. 285SFr for 40min., 85SFr for 2hr.) **Paragliding Gstaad** can also send you into the stratosphere. (☎ 079 224 42 70; www.paragstaad.com; 190SFr for a tandem flight.)

The tourist office publishes a guide of **mountain bike** trails and sells various maps of the area (8-15SFr). **Mountain bike rental** in Gstaad can be found at **Stauffer Radsport.** (☎ 744 42 61; 15SFr per hr., 38SFr per day). Go past the tourist office to the intersection at the river and head right on Geschwendstr. 10min. In Saanen, the family-operated **Reuteler Velos and Mofas** is just left on the main road and has about the same prices. (☎ 1744 51 33, fax 89 62; open M-F 8am-noon and 1:30-6:30pm, Sa 8am-noon and 1:30-5pm. AmEx/MC/V.) **Horse-trekking** (☎ 744 24 60; 40SFr per 30min. lesson) or riding in a **horse-drawn cart** (☎ 765 30 34; 1hr. ride 25SFr per person) are novel options. Ask about the *Easy Access* card at overnight accommodations or the tourist office. A two-night stay in the area makes you eligible for a cheap three-day pass to gondolas, admittance to pools, and discounts on guided adventures. It also gives free rides on the region's trains, some mountain railways, and Postauto buses; also a 40% discount on the gondola to Glacier 3000, the highest point in the area. (3-day pass 28.50SFr, children 15SFr; each additional day 9.50SFr.)

HIKING. The tourist offices have free hiking maps and descriptions of local hikes. A challenging panoramic hike up the Giferspitz horseshoe will take your breath away. From Gstaad station, turn right on the main road, left on the main road just before the river, and take the second big road on the right over the river (signs to "Bissen"; the turn is 1km from Gstaad). Follow the yellow *Wanderweg* signs for "Wasserngrat" up the hill to the top cable car station (1936m). The more fit and adventurous might continue to the Laünehorn (2477m) and, after a rocky scramble, farther to the Giferspitz (2541m), Gstaad's tallest peak. The path circles down to Bissen, but a bus can ease the descent. (1800m ascent. Perfect weather only. Allow 1 day.) A shorter, more accessible hike starts with a cable car ascent to Wispile and a 2-3hr. hike to Laünensee, a lake, and a waterfall nature reserve.

SKIING. In winter, Gstaad offers 250km of ski runs and 69 lifts. Experts will not be challenged but intermediates will find the runs ideal. Of the area's six sectors, #4 is the highest and contains the Tsanfleuron Glacier ("Glacier 3000"). The largest sector and the one most commonly used by skiers of moderate skill is #1. For information on opening times of the various lifts, runs, and mountains in the area, contact the Ski Gstaad Bergbahnenbüro (☎ 748 82 82; www.skigstaad.ch). The **Top Card ski pass** costs 50SFr a day for one sector. A two-day pass for 95SFr covers all sectors. A week of skiing costs between 167SFr and 278SFr, depending on age. **Season ski passes** (790SFr) from the Gstaad region allow skiing in Oberengadin/St. Moritz, Kitzbühel/

Tirol, Adelboden-Lenk, Alpes Vaudoises, Ordino-Arcalis, and Pal Arinsal (Andorra). The tourist office prints a sheet giving contact information and compares prices for all the **winter ski equipment rental** outlets in the area. **Ski and snowboard schools** include Alpinzentrum and Absolut-Activ (see Adventure Sports) in Gstaad, as well as Snowsports Saanenland in Saanen (☎744 36 65; www.snow-sports.ch). The **Gstaad Snowsports** company specializes in classes for children. (☎744 18 65, www.gstaadsnowsports.ch. Office open M-Sa 8am-noon and 2-6pm.) Consult the tourist office for details on heliskiing, curling, and skating. Finally, three snowboarding parks and a glacier offer year-round skiing. Summer runs are open June-early August daily 8:30am-2pm. Local boarders report that even in summer, the runs are of a fairly good quality—go in the morning for the best snow. **Summer ski rental** is at the top of the glacier. (☎024 492 33 77; www.glacier3000.ch. 20SFr snowsuit, 53SFr skis and boots. Shop open daily 8:30am-4pm.)

SPECIAL EVENTS. The **FIVB Beach Volleyball World Tour** rolls through town at the end of June (☎744 06 40; www.beachworldtour.ch. Free). The **Allianz Suisse Open Gstaad tennis tournament** brings professional-level claycourt action to Gstaad's city center. (☎748 83 83; for tickets ☎0900 61 62 63. Tickets 40-100SFr. July 3-11, 2004.) Combining high culture and grit, the Gstaad Polo Club hosts the **Cartier Polo Silver Cup** tournament in mid-August (☎744 07 41; www.pologstaad.ch). **Country Night Gstaad** is an orgy of country music in late September that brings in well-known mid-level artists like LeeAnn Womack, Mark Chesnutt, and Joe Diffie. (☎744 88 22; www.country-night-gstaad.ch. Tickets 55-125SFr.) The **Menuhin Festival Gstaad,** a late-summer event created by Gstaad resident and violinist Yehudi Menuhin, is a bit more refined. (☎748 83 33; www.menuhinfestivalgstaad.com. Usually mid-July through the 1st week of Sept.)

CENTRAL SWITZERLAND

With more hospitable, though less dramatic, terrain, Central Switzerland is considerably more populated than the mountainous cantons to the south. The greater population density and diversity brings a greater mass of cultural artifacts, as evidenced by innovative museums, enchanting castles, and medieval *Altstädte* in Zurich, Lucerne, and other towns along the shores of the region's lakes.

HIGHLIGHTS OF CENTRAL SWITZERLAND

Shock your artistic sense at Zurich's unconventional **Kunsthaus** (p. 389).

Bathe in multicolored light from the incredible stained-glass windows in Zurich's cathedrals, the **Fraumünster** and the **Großmünster** (p. 388).

Confront your mortality on the 660-year-old **Kapellbrücke,** Lucerne's famed, wooden-roofed bridge (p. 400).

Cruise the **Vierwaldstättersee** from Lucerne to Alpnachstad, where you can ascend the world's steepest cog railway to blue-shadowed **Mt. Pilatus** (p. 404).

ZURICH (ZÜRICH) ☎ 01

Battalions of briefcase-toting, Armani-suited executives charge daily through the world's largest gold exchange and fourth-largest stock exchange, pumping enough money into the economy to keep Zurich's upper-crust boutiques and posh restaurants thriving. But there is more to Zurich than money; the city was once the focal point of the Reformation in German Switzerland, led by the anti-Catholic firebrand Ulrich Zwingli. The 20th century brought an avant-garde artistic and philosophical radicalism that overwhelmed Zurich's Protestant traditionalism and attracted diverse and progressive thinkers. While James Joyce toiled away at *Ulysses* in one corner of the city, Russian exile Vladimir Lenin read Marx and dreamt of revolution in another. Meanwhile, a group of raucous young artists calling themselves the Dadaists founded a proto-performance art collective, the Cabaret Voltaire, promoting art that challenged traditional aesthetic norms. A walk through Zurich's *Altstadt* and student quarter will immerse you in the energetic youth counter-culture that spawned subversive thinkers, only footsteps away from the rabid capitalism of the famous Bahnhofstr. shopping district.

✈ INTERCITY TRANSPORTATION

Because PTT buses cannot go into Zurich proper, the easiest way into the city is by plane, train, or car.

Flights: Kloten Airport (☎816 25 00) is a major stop for **Swiss International Airlines** (☎084 885 20 00), which emerged from the merger between Swissair and Crossair. Daily connections to **Frankfurt, Paris, London,** and **New York.** Trains connect the airport to the Hauptbahnhof in the city center (every 10-20min., 5:02am-12:15am, 5.40SFr; Eurail and SwissPass valid), where trains arrive from all over Europe.

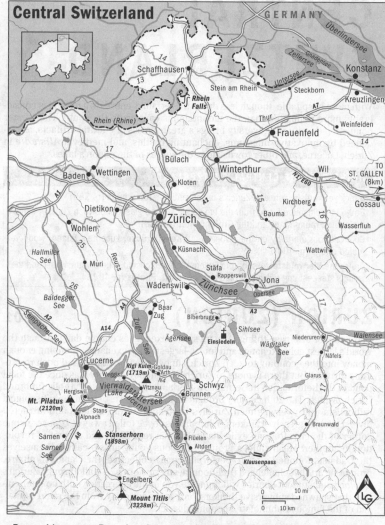

Central Switzerland

By car: A1 connects **Bern, Austria,** and southern Switzerland to **Zurich.** From **Basel,** A2 connects to Zurich. From **Geneva,** take A1 to Lausanne, A9 to Vevey, and A12 to Zurich.

Trains: Bahnhofpl. To: **Basel** (1hr., 1-2 per hr. 3:30am-2am, 30SFr); **Bern** (1¼hr., 1-2 per hr. 3:30am-2am, 45SFr); **Geneva** via **Bern** (3hr., every hr. 5:26am-10:04pm, 76SFr); **Lucerne** (1hr., 2 per hr. 5:35am-12:07am, 19.80SFr); **Lugano** (3hr., 1-3 per hr. 6:30am-10:07pm, 60SFr); **Milan** (4hr., every hr. 6:30am-10:07pm, 72SFr); **Munich** (5hr., every hr. 6:05am-10:33pm, 86SFr); **Paris** (5hr., every hr. 6:30am-midnight, 133SFr); **Salzburg** (5hr., every hr. 6:11am-7:10pm, 97SFr); **Vienna** (9hr., every hr. 6:07am-6:18pm, 124SFr); and **Winterthur** (25min., every 15min. 5:02am-12:15am, 10.60SFr). Under age 26 discount on international trains.

CENTRAL SWITZERLAND

Zürich

🍎 FOOD

Bodega Española, **20**
BQM Café and Mensa, **3**
Gran-Café, **14**
Infinito Espresso Bar, **7**
Milchbar Café, **23**
Outback Lodge, **26**
Raclette Stube, **6**
Restaurant Hiltl, **8**
Restaurant Mère
   Catherine, **21**
Sprüngli Confiserie
   Café, **22**
Zähringer Café, **9**

🏠⛺ ACCOMMODATIONS
Camping Seebucht, **28**
City Backpacker-Hotel Biber, **11**
Hotel du Theatre, **4**
Hotel Foyer Hottingen, **19**

Hotel Otter, **24**
Jugendherberge (HI), **27**
Justinus Heim, **1**
Leoneck Hotel, **2**
Martahaus, **5**

Zic-Zac
   Rock-Hotel, **18**
★ NIGHTLIFE
Bar Odeon, **25**
Barfusser, **10**

Cranberry, **15**
Double-U Bar, **13**
Nachtflug Bar, **12**
Oliver Twist, **16**
Öpfelchammer, **17**

TO MUSEUM RIETBERG
(1km), **27** (2km), &
28 (3km)

Ferries: Boats on the **Zürichsee** leave from Bürklipl. and range from a 1½hr. cruise between isolated villages (every 30min. 11am-6:30pm; 5.40SFr, children 2.90SFr) to a "grand tour" (4-5hr.; every hr. 9:30am-5:30pm; 20SFr, children 10SFr). Ferries also leave from the top of the Bahnhofstr. harbor (every 30min. 10:05am-9:05pm, 3.60SFr) for a cruise of the Limmat River. The Zürichsee authorities (☎01 487 13 33) offer themed tours—there's even a chance for an "Oldies Night" on the Zürichsee with 50s, 60s, and 70s hits (July-Aug. F 7:30pm, 22SFr) or a ride on the "Salsa/Merengue" boat (June-Aug. Su 7:30pm, 22SFr). In late Oct., the "Cheese Fondue Dreamboat" is added to the list (Tu and W 7:30pm, call for prices.) Eurail and *Tageskarten* valid on all boats.

⚡ ORIENTATION

Zurich sits in the middle of north-central Switzerland, close to the German border, on some of the lowest land in the whole country. Most of the activity within Zurich is confined to a relatively small, walkable area. The **Limmat River** splits the city down the middle on its way to the **Zürichsee**. On the west side of the river are the **Hauptbahnhof** and **Bahnhofstraße**. Bahnhofstr. begins outside the Hauptbahnhof and runs parallel to the Limmat River to the head of the Zürichsee. Two-thirds of the way down Bahnhofstr. lies **Paradeplatz,** the town center, under which Zurich's banks reputedly keep their gold reserves. **Bürkliplatz** is at the Zürichsee end of Bahnhofstr., and many grassy quais surrounding the lake provide a great spot for sunbathers to relax and runners to make them feel lazy. On the east side of the river lies the University district. Stretching above the narrow **Niederdorfstraße,** it pulses with bars, hip restaurants, and hostels. Stately bridges, offering elegant views of the stately old buildings that line the river, bind the two sectors together.

🚊 LOCAL TRANSPORTATION

Public Transportation: Trams criss-cross the city, originating at the Hauptbahnhof. Tickets for rides longer than 5 stops cost 3.60SFr and are valid for 1hr. (press the blue button on automatic ticket machines); rides less than 5 cost 2.10SFr (yellow button). Be aware, though, that the city is small enough that rides of more than 5 stops are unlikely. Purchase a ticket before boarding and validate it by inserting it into the ticket machine. Policemen will fine you (60SFr) if you travel as a *Schwarzfahrer* (Black Rider) and ride for free. If you plan to ride several times, buy a 24hr. **Tageskarte** (7.20SFr), valid on trams, buses, and ferries. *Tageskarten* are available at the tourist office, a few hotels and hostels, the automatic ticket machines, or the **Ticketeria** under the train station in Shop-Ville. (Follow the signs near the train station's escalators. Open M-Sa 6:30am-7pm, Su 7:30am-7pm.) The Ticketeria also offers 6-day cards (36SFr, under 25 27SFr). All public **buses, trams,** and **trolleys** run 5:30am-midnight. **Night buses** run from city center to outlying areas (F-Su 1-4am). **Night trains** have recently started running. Pick up a copy of *Nachtnetz* from the tourist office for specific timetables.

Taxis: ☎777 77 77, 444 44 44, or 222 22 22. **TIXI (Transportation Service for the Disabled),** Mühlezelgstr. 15 (☎493 11 44,; www.tixi.ch), requires reservations. Services include taxis as well as information on trains, trams, and other forms of transport outfitted for the disabled.

Car Rental: The way to rent cars is at the tourist office, which maintains a special deal with **Europcar** (☎804 46 46; www.europcar.ch) involving a free upgrade to a nicer car. Prices start at 149SFr for 1-2 days, 105SFr for 3-6 days. 20+. **Branches** at the airport (☎813 20 44; fax 813 49 00); Josefstr. 53 (☎271 56 56); Lindenstr. 33 (☎383 17 47). As a rule, try to rent in the city, as renting at the airport involves a 40% tax.

Parking: Metropolitan Zurich has many public parking garages, but prices are often high. Consider taking a tram or train to minimize time lost to traffic congestion (a real issue) and to cut down on parking expenses. If you choose to park, **Universität Irchel,** near the large park on Winterthurstr. 181, is the cheapest option (12.50SFr maximum); it and **Engi-Märt,** Seestr. 25, are both suburban lots. In the city, try garages at major department stores: **Jelmoli,** Steinmühlepl., **Migros Limmatplatz,** Limmatstr. 152, and **Globus** at Löwenstr. (All open M-F 8am-8pm, Sa 8am-5pm; prices vary but expect to pay 2SFr every 15min. during peak shopping hours.) City parking 2SFr for first hr.; "Blue-Zone" 24hr. parking 10SFr; suburbs 0.50SFr per hr.

Bike Rental: Bike loans are free at **Globus** (☎079 336 36 10); **Enge** (☎079 336 36 12); and **Hauptbahnhof** (☎210 13 88), at the very end of track 18. Passport and 20SFr deposit, same day return (open daily May-Oct. 7am-9:30pm.)

Hitchhiking: Though *Let's Go* does not recommend hitching and the practice is illegal on freeways, hitchers to Basel, Geneva, Paris, or Bonn often take tram #4 to "Werdhölzli" or bus #33 to "Pfingstweidstr." Those bound for Lucerne, Italy, and Austria report taking tram #9 or 14 to "Bahnhof Wiedikon" and walking down Schimmelstr. to Silhölzli. For Munich, hitchers have been seen taking tram #14 or 7 to "Milchbuck" and walking to Schaffhauserstr. toward St. Gallen and St. Margarethen, or taking S1 or S8 to Wiedikon and hitching at Seebahnstr.

🔁 PRACTICAL INFORMATION

TOURIST & FINANCIAL SERVICES

Tourist Offices: Main office (☎215 40 00; free hotel reservation service ☎215 40 40; www.zuerich.com), in the main station, offers concert, movie, and bar information, as well as helpful publications. *Zürich News* prints restaurant and hotel listings. German-language *ZüriTipp* provides tips on nightlife. The **electronic hotel reservation board** is at the front of the station. The tourist office will book hotel rooms during regular hours. (Open May-Oct. M-Sa 8am-8:30pm, Su 8:30am-6:30pm; Nov.-Apr. 1 M-Sa 8:30am-7pm, Su 9am-6:30pm. For bikers and backpackers, the **Touring Club des Schweiz (TCS),** Alfred-Escher-Str. 38 (☎286 86 86), offers maps and travel info.

IN RECENT NEWS

HIGH-PRICED ISLAND

Switzerland is pricey to travel through. Slightly less apparent, though, is the fact that it's also a pricey country to live in. A study in a 2003 issue of the *Neue Zürcher Zeitung* noted that Swiss citizens pay substantially more than consumers in other European nations when buying practically anything: 22% more for jeans, 105% more for half a liter of Coke, and nearly 300% more for fresh meat and fruit products, even those produced in Switzerland itself.

The Swiss have been slow to acknowledge that the high cost of living in Switzerland may in fact not be a sign of the nation's prosperity, but instead an impediment to its economic growth. But this is changing. "For a long time we excused the high prices, seeing them as only the natural result of the problem-free functioning of our official governmental services, the quality of our goods, or accordingly high loan rates," said Joseph Deiss, Chief Economic Secretary, in a statement on July 1, 2003. "We will not count those excuses anymore." Long referred to as *Hochpreisinsel Schweiz*, (the 'high-priced island'), Switzerland is now moving to plug vulnerabilities in its tourist industry, and is seeking to lure tourists from cheaper travel destinations in EU nations like Austria, Germany, and Italy with Regional discount packages and other measures. For now, though, still expect a stop in the Coop to dent your wallet.

Tours: The tourist office leads frequent tours: the "Stroll through the Old Town" (2hr.; May-Oct. M-F 3pm, Sa-Su 11am, 3pm; Nov.-Mar. W and Sa 3pm; Apr. 11am, 3pm; 20SFr); a trolley tour of major sites (2hr.; Nov.-Mar. noon and 2pm; Apr.-Oct. 9:45am, noon, and 2pm; 32SFr); and a 3hr. tour of the area surrounding Zurich (year-round daily 1pm, July-Sept. also Sa-Su 4:30pm; 45SFr). Special Christmas-themed tours added in the winter months. Tours available in 8 languages. Reduced prices for students and children ages 6-16 vary per tour and season.

Budget Travel: STA Travel, Leonhardstr. 10 (☎261 29 55). Open M-F 10am-6:30pm, Sa 10am-2pm. **Branch** offices at Bäckerstr. 40 (☎297 17 17). Student package tours, STA travel help, ISIC cards. Open M-F 10am-6:30pm, Sa 10am-4pm. Also at Örlikon, open M-F 9am-6:30pm, Sa 9am-2pm. **Globe-Trotter Travel Service AG,** Rennweg 35, fourth fl. (☎213 80 80; fax 213 80 88), specializes in overseas travel. Caters to individual travelers and arranges transport. Student discounts, tickets, and ISIC cards available. Open M-W and F 9am-6pm, Th 10am-6pm, Sa 9am-2pm; must have an appointment for Sa.

Consulates: UK, Hetibachstr. 47 (☎383 65 60). Open M-F 9am-noon. For visas and passports, UK citizens should contact the consulate in Geneva. **US Consulary Office,** Dufourstr.. 101 (☎422 25 66). Visas and passports available only at the embassy in Bern. Open M-F 10am-1pm. **Australian, Canadian, Irish,** and **South African** citizens should contact their embassies in Bern. **New Zealand's** consulate is in Geneva.

Currency Exchange: At the main train station. Cash advances with DC/MC/V with photo ID, 200SFr minimum. Open daily 6:30am-10pm. **Credit Suisse,** Bahnhofstr. 53, 2.50SFr commission. Open daily 6am-10pm. **Swiss Bank,** Bahnhofstr. 45 and 70, also charges 2.50SFr, and its ATMs take MC and Visa. Branches at Paradepl. and Bellevuepl. Both banks have currency exchange machines next to ATMs. Open M-F 9am-5pm. **ATMs** accepting all cards are everywhere in this banking capital.

LOCAL SERVICES

Luggage Storage: At the station 1 level below ground. Lockers 5SFr and 8SFr per day. 72hr. maximum. Luggage watch 7SFr at the *Gepäck* counter. Open daily 6am-10:50pm.

Bookstores: Orelli Fussli, Bahnhofstr. 70 (☎211 04 44), has an entire English bookstore right on busy Bahnhofstr. Also at Fusslistr. 4 (☎084 884 98 48). Open M-F 9am-8pm, Sa 9am-5pm. **Travel Bookshop,** Rindermarkt 20 (☎252 38 83; www.travelbookshop.ch), has a wide assortment of travel guides (including *Let's Go*) and maps. Open M 1-6:30pm, Tu-F 9am-6:30pm, Sa 9am-4pm.

Libraries: Zentralbibliothek, Zähringerpl. 6 (☎268 31 00). Open M-F 8am-8pm, Sa 8am-4pm. **Pestalozzi Bibliothek,** Zähringerstr. 17 (☎261 78 11), has foreign magazines and newspapers. Open M-F 10am-7pm, Sa 10am-4pm. **Internet** 1SFr per 10min.

Bi-Gay-Lesbian Organizations: Homosexuelle Arbeitsgruppe Zürich (HAZ), Sihlquai 67 (☎271 22 50; www.haz.ch), P.O. Box 7088, CH-8023, offers a library, meetings, and the free newsletter *InfoSchwül*. Open Tu-F 7:30-11pm, Su noon-2pm and 6-11pm. **Frauenzentrum Zürich,** Matteng. 27 (☎272 85 03), provides information for lesbians and a library of magazines and other resources.

Laundromat: Speed Wash Self Service Wascherei, Weinbergstr. 37 (☎242 99 14). Wash and dry 5kg for 10.20SFr. Open M-Sa 7am-10pm, Su 10:30am-10pm.

Public Showers and Toilets: At the train station 1 level below ground, **McClean Toiletten.** Toilets 1-2SFr. Showers 12SFr for 20min., including 2 towels and shower gel. Wheelchair-accessible. Open 6am-midnight. Clean enough to eat off the floor, though *Let's Go* does not recommend doing so.

Camping Supplies: TrottoMundo, Rindermarkt 6 (☎252 80 00; fax 252 01 82), located on the second fl. above Oliver Twist Pub. Sells hiking, trekking, and camping gear and travel books. Tents from 300SFr. Open M-F 9am-6:30pm, Sa 11am-4pm.

EMERGENCY & COMMUNICATIONS SERVICES

Emergencies: Police ☎117, **Fire** ☎118, **Ambulance** ☎144.

Medical Emergency: ☎269 69 69. **First Aid,** ☎361 61 61.

24hr. Pharmacy: Bahnhofpl. 15 (☎225 42 42; www.bahnhof-apotheke.ch).

General Crisis Line: Help-o-Fon, ☎157 00 57

Rape Crisis Line: ☎291 46 46.

Internet Access: The **ETH Library,** Ramistr. 101 (☎631 21 35, email info@library.ethz.ch, in the *Hauptgebäude,* has 3 **free** computers. Take tram #6, 9, or 10 to "ETH," enter the large main building, and take the elevator to floor H. Open M-F 8:30am-9pm, Sa 9am-2pm. Internet and more at **Quanta Virtual Fun Space,** Limmatquai 94 (☎260 72 66), at the corner of Mühlg. and the busy Niederdorfstr. Open daily 9am-midnight. Must be 16+ to enter. **Internet Café,** Uraniastr. 3 (☎210 33 11; fax 210 33 13), in the Urania Parkhaus. 5SFr per 20min. Open M-Sa 9am-midnight, Su 11am-11pm. **Telefon Corner,** downstairs in the station next to Marché Mövenpick, has 15 PCs. 6SFr per hr. Open daily 8am-10pm.

Post Office: Main office, Sihlpost, Kasernestr. 97, just behind the station. Open M-F 6:30am-10:30pm, Sa 6am-8pm, Su 11am-10:30pm. *Poste Restante:* Sihlpost, Postlagernde Briefe, CH-8021 Zurich. **Branches** throughout the city. **Postal code:** CH-8021.

☗ ACCOMMODATIONS & CAMPING

The few budget accommodations in Zurich are easily accessible by foot or via public transportation. Reserve at least a day in advance, especially during the summer.

Martahaus, Zähringerstr. 36 (☎251 45 50; www.martahaus.ch). Looking out of the station down Bahnhofstr. and at the large statue, turn left, cross Bahnhofbr., and take the second (sharp) right after Limmatquai at the Seilgraben sign. 3 walls and a thick curtain separate you from your neighbors, who are probably American college students. Clean beds and showers, large lockers, night-lights, and towels. Wheelchair-accessible. Airport shuttle every hr. after 6:20am, 20SFr. Breakfast 7:30-10am included. **Internet** access included. Laundry 10SFr. Lockers 2 or 5SFr deposit. Reception 24hr. Rooms usually ready between 1 and 2pm. Dorms 38SFr; singles 85-114SFr (varies if location is streetside or quiet-side); doubles 98/135SFR; quads 200SFr. AmEx/DC/MC/V. ❸ The owners of Martahaus also run the nearby **Luther Pension,** a **women-only** residence that shares reception with Martahaus and is cheaper (dorms 30SFr, singles 50SFr; breakfast included). Call Martahaus to reserve. ❸

Hotel Foyer Hottingen, Hottingenstr. 31 (☎256 19 19; www.foyer-hottingen.ch). Take tram #3 (dir.: Kluspl.) to "Hottingerpl." It's at the corner of Hottingenstr. and Cäcilianstr. Families and student backpackers fill this newly renovated house, only a block from the Kunsthaus. Sleek modern facilities, an in-house chapel, and an English-speaking staff make this hostel a good value, even though it is slightly removed from the main drag. Only women are allowed in the partitioned dorms during summer, but both sexes can rent other rooms. The dorm room has a balcony overlooking the city. Breakfast, lockers, and kitchen included. Laundry 5SFr. Wheelchair-accessible, including shower facilities. Breakfast 7-9:30am. Reception 7am-11pm. No lockout. Check-out 11am. 11-bed dorm 35SFr; singles 70SFr, with bath 105SFr; doubles 110SFr/150SFr; triples 140SFr/ 190SFr; quads 180SFr. MC/V. ❷

Justinus Heim Zürich, Freudenbergstr. 146 (☎361 38 06; justinuszh@bluewin.ch). Take tram #9 or 10 (dir.:Haldenegg) to "Seilbahn Rigiblick," then take the hillside funicular (by the Migros) uphill to the end. The hostel is across the street from the stop. Quiet, cheap, and relatively spacious private rooms in this house, which is home to students from the nearby university as well. Picturesque views of Zurich make the trip up the hill worthwhile. English-speaking staff. Breakfast and kitchen included. Laundry available; you pay for cost of electricity (0.50-1SFr). Reception 8am-noon and 5-9pm. Check-out 10am. Singles 35-50SFr, with shower 60SFr; doubles 80-100SFr; triples 135SFr/ 165SFr; all rates reduced for multiple week stays. V. ❸

The City Backpacker-Hotel Biber, Niederdorfstr. 5 (☎251 90 15; www.backpacker.ch/ city-backpacker). Cross Bahnhofbr. in front of station, then turn right onto Niederdorfstr. Tucked away down Schweizerhofg. (fright after Weingasse) and up 3 flights of spiral stairs, this high-traffic hostel is popular among students and those looking for a cheap place to crash. With bustling Niederdorf nightlife just outside the window, you may not even need to use your bunk-bed. Pick up a free copy of *Swiss Backpacker News* in the lobby. Kitchen included. Small lockers available, but bring a lock. Sheets 3SFr, towels 3SFr, blanket provided. Laundry next-day service 10SFr. **Internet** 12SFr per hr. Key deposit 20SFr or passport. Reception 8am-noon and 3-10pm. Check-out 10am and is strictly enforced. Reception watches bags. 4- to 6-bed dorms 29SFr; singles 66SFr; doubles 88-92SFr. All rooms non-smoking. MC/V. ❷

Hotel Otter, Oberdorfstr. 7 (251 22 07; www.wueste.ch), and the swanky **Wuste Bar** below it attract an eclectic and artsy student crowd. Hip and slightly unconventional, as evidenced by the creative decor of the individually-themed rooms (think "Purple" and "African Lodge"), Otter is an oasis for those not-so-starving artists. Floor bathrooms. Breakfast served from 9:15am (11am on weekends) until there is no more bread. Laundry next-day service 15SFr. TV, phone, fridge, towels, and sheets included. Sink in room. Parking nearby, open daily 6am-2am. Reception 8am-4pm in hotel, 4pm-midnight in bar. Check-out noon. Singles 100SFr; doubles 130-160SFr; apartment with shower and kitchen 180SFr. AmEx/MC/V. ❹

Jugendherberge Zürich (HI), Mutschellenstr. 114 (☎482 35 44; www.youthhostel.ch/zuerich). From the station, walk out past the fountain down Bahnhofstr. about 100m. On the right side of the street, take tram #7 (dir.: Wollishofen) to "Morgental" and walk 5min. back toward the Migros along Mutschellenstr. Pass a second Migros (on the right) and you'll see the gigantic hostel on the left. The hostel completed a huge expansion in July 2003, adding a 24-hr. snack bar, beer on tap, and a projector screen for movies and sporting events. A TV corner, small conference rooms, and a large common area make it a prime spot to catch up with other backpacking hostelers. Buffet-style lunch and dinner 12.50SFr. Breakfast and sheets included. Room equipped with sink. Ask for towels at reception. Lockers available for day storage and nightly, in-room storage (2SFr deposit). **Internet** 1SFr per 4min. Wheelchair-accessible. Reception 24hr. check-in 2pm. Check-out 10am. All prices per person: 6-bed rooms 35SFr; 4-bed rooms 37.50SFr; double with shower/bath 58SFr; single with shower/bath 99SFr. Under 6, half-price. Non-members add 6SFr. AmEx/MC/V. ❷

Zic-Zac Rock-Hotel, Marktg. 17 (☎261 21 81; www.ziczac.ch). Each room in this hostel is named after a singer or a band, but most decorations are limited to pictures of Elvis. This hotel's convenient locale is complemented by rooms with TV, phone, sheets, towels, and sink. Light breakfast 5SFr. Laundry same-day service 12SFr. Reception 24hr. Check-out 11am. Receptionist will watch luggage. Singles 75SFr, with shower 90SFr; doubles 120-135SFr/160SFr; triples 156SFr/168SFr; quads with shower 260SFr. ISIC 10% off. AmEx/DC/MC/V. ❹

Leoneck Hotel, Leonhardstr. 1 (☎254 22 22; www.leo-neck.ch). An obsession for cows and paint must have inspired this divinely bovine hotel, which sits above the appropriately named Crazy Cow restaurant. Serving a mixed crowd of families and business people, all rooms include bath, phone, TV, hair dryer, and of course, plenty of cows. Handpainted scenes of Swiss life adorn bathroom walls. **Internet** (5SFr for 15min.) and **currency exchange** available. Laundry next-day service available. Shuttle to airport hourly (6:15-10:15pm; 20SFr per person.) Some non-smoking rooms. Reception open 24hr. Singles 100-140SFr; doubles 150-185SFr; triples 185-240SFr; 4-bed family room 240-290SFr. AmEx/DC/MC/V. ❹

Hotel du Theatre, Seilergraben 69, Centralplatz. (☎267 26 70; www.hotel-du-theatre.com). Mainly geared toward businesspeople, this elegant and recently renovated hotel within view of the train station offers discounted rates on weekends. Modern facilities including keycard access, and high cleaning standards result in attractive rooms. All rooms, decorated with uplit scenes from classic movies on the walls and funky furniture, include bathroom, TV, phone, hair dryer, minibar, safe, and modem connection. Non-smoking rooms available. English-speaking staff. Breakfast 15SFr. Singles M-Th 150-220SFr, F-Su 135-180SFr; doubles 240-260SFr/195-210SFr. 2 mini-suites as well 290/235SFr. AmEx/DC/MC/V. ❺

Camping Seebucht, Seestr. 559 (☎482 16 12; www.camping-zurich.ch). Take tram #11 to "Bürklipl."; catch bus #161 or 165 to "Stadtgrenze" and it will be across from the Esso station. Lakeside location makes up for the trek. Market, terrace, café, and restaurant on-site. Reception M-Sa 7:30am-noon and 3-10pm, Su 8am-noon. Open May-Sept. 8SFr per person, 5SFr per child aged 4-16. 1.50SFr for tax. 12SFr per small tent, 14SFr per caravan. Showers 2SFr. ❶

◖ FOOD

Zurich's 1300+ restaurants cover every imaginable dietary preference. The cheapest meals in Zurich are available at *Würstli* stands for about 5SFr. For heartier appetites, Zurich prides itself on *Geschnetzeltes mit Rösti*, thinly-sliced veal (often kidney or liver) in cream sauce with hash-brown potatoes. Check out the *Swiss Backpacker News* (at the tourist office, Hotel Biber, and Martahaus) for info on budget meals in Zurich. Cheap kebab stands and take-out burger joints on Niederdorfstr. offer meals around 6SFr. The **Manor** department store off Bahnhofstr. 75 (corner of Uraniastr.) has a self-service restaurant on the fifth floor. (Open M-F 9am-8pm, Sa 9am-4pm.)

ON THE MENU

RACLETTE, ANYONE?

You can find it in Alpine huts, restaurants, packaged in TV dinners at the grocery store, and even on sale from street vendors at Basel's Herbschtmaess (fall festival). It's *raclette,* a Swiss culinary specialty originally from the Wallis region, which has now spread through the nation. *Raclette* is older than fondue—Alpine farmers were enjoying raclette well over 500 years ago. It is a dish that sprang from the mountain farmer's life, like many Swiss specialties, and therefore involves massive amounts of mountain cheese, along with a few home-grown vegetables.

A large amount of *Raclettekäse,* which melts more easily than regular cheese, is melted in a fondue-like set-up at the center of the table, with a fire blazing cheerily beneath. For the dishes and silverware, a *raclette* set (similar to fondue one) is used. Once the cheese is melted, it is ladled out to each person at the table. A few hot baked potatoes are given to each person, along with sour pickles *(Gurken)* and small, sweet onions *(Silberzwiebeln).* The dinner mixes the garnishes with the cheese and potatoes, adds some black pepper to taste, and enjoys the same, simple yet hearty meal that the Swiss have been enjoying year-round for centuries.

■ **Bodega Española,** Münsterg. 15 (☎251 23 10). Catalan delights served by charismatic waiters since 1874. The delicate but filling egg-and-potato tortilla dishes go for 15.50SFr, yummy *tapas* served all day for 4.80SFr. Wheelchair-accessible. Open daily 10am-midnight. Kitchen open noon-2pm and 6-10pm. AmEx/DC/MC/V. ❷

■ **Gran-Café,** Limmatquai 66 (☎01 252 31 19). Across the street from the rushing Limmat river, the outdoor seating for this popular restaurant is often filled on warm days. Enjoy the inexpensive *Menüs* (from around 13.80SFr) or try one of their tasty dishes (from 12.80SFr) while admiring the *Great Gatsby*-esque decor. Save room for one of the sundaes (6-8SFr). Open M-Th 6am-11:30pm, F 6am-midnight, Sa 7am-midnight, Su 7:30am-11:30pm. AmEx/MC/V. ❷

Restaurant Mère Catherine, Nägelihof 3 (☎250 59 40; www.commercio.ch). Hordes of locals find their way to this yuppie restaurant even though it is hidden away in a small street near the Großmünster, in a building constructed in 1565. Serving mainly Provençal French dishes (starting at 21.50SFr) with a lot of wine, this bustling place exudes ambience with a rushing fountain and shady outdoor seating to accompany your meal. On Sun., families with children can enjoy the Kid's Corner of toys and games. English language menu, children's menu. Vegetarian options. Daily fish specials from the Zürichsee. Wheelchair-accessible. Open Su-W 11:30am-10pm, Th-Sa 11:30am-10:30pm. AmEx/DC/MC/V. ❸

Restaurant Hiltl, Sihlstr. 28 (☎227 70 00; www.hitl.ch). Munch carrot sticks with the vegetarian elite at this swank restaurant, where the lack of meat makes things surprisingly cheap. Highlights include the all-day salad buffet (3.90SFr per 100g; 15SFr for large salad), and the Indian buffet at night (same price). No smoking. Open M-Sa 7am-11pm, Su 11am-11pm. AmEx/DC/MC/V. ❷

Raclette Stube, Zähringerstr. 16 (☎251 41 30). Serving a limited but high-quality menu of classic Swiss fare, this quaint, family-oriented restaurant opens onto the street and offers a good opportunity to lounge for an extended period of time surrounded by English-speakers. Large *raclette* appetizer 12.50SFr; *Fondue Käse* (cheese) 34.50SFr per person. *Fondue chinoise* (meat fondue) 39.50SFr per person. All-you-can-eat *raclette* 32.50SFr per person. Open daily 6pm to about 11pm. ❹

Outback Lodge, Stadelhoferstr. 18 (☎252 15 75; http://outback-lodge.ch). This Aussie-themed restaurant is located just after STA Travel in Stadelhofer Passage. The atmosphere gleans some authenticity from its cheap Foster's beer on tap (4.20SFr), and dishes like Kangaroo Island (29.50SFr) and Crocodile Dundee (34.50SFr) made from the real thing. Menu includes vegetarian options. 18+ after 6pm. Wheelchair-accessible. Open M-F 9am-midnight, Sa-Su 11:30am-2am. AmEx/MC/V. ❹

BQM Café and Mensa at Universität Zürich, behind Rämistr. 101. Take streetcar #6 to "ETH Zentrum" from Bahnhofpl. or take the red Polybahn uphill from Central Station. At the university's dining hall or the hip, student-filled BQM Café, sandwiches (3.50-6SFr), chips, and a beer (3.50SFr and up) make for a nice lunch break. The view from the open terrace, with the city's church steeples at eye level, makes the climb worthwhile. Closed during winter recess. Mensa open M-F 6:45am-7:45pm and every other Sa 11:30am-1pm. Café open M-Sa 11am-10pm. No smoking til 6pm. ❷

CAFÉS

■ **Sprüngli Confiserie Café,** Paradepl. (☎224 47 11), is a Zurich landmark, founded by one of the original Lindt chocolate makers who sold his shares to his brother. Women in matching red business suits assist customers in purchasing just the right chocolate from the confectionery. A chocolate heaven, the Confiserie-Konditorei concocts peerless confections and delicious desserts, including an eye-popping mocha sundae (10.50SFr) with homemade ice cream and sherbet, served on the Bahnhofstr. patio.

Pick up a handful of the bite-size Luxemburgerli for 7.90SFr per 100g. Lunch *Menüs* 19.50-25.50SFr. Wheelchair-accessible outdoor seating. Confectionery open M-F 7:30am-8pm, Sa 8am-4pm. Café open M-F 7:30am-6:30pm, Sa 8am-6pm, Su 9:30am-5:30pm. AmEx/DC/MC/V.

Zähringer Café, Zähringerpl. 11 (☎252 05 00; www.cafe-zaehringer.com), across the square from the library, at the end of Spitalg., above the *Altstadt.* Sip coffee, tea, or Italian soda with a hip young crowd, and fill your stomach with greasy goodness (*Rösti* topped with a fried egg 13.50SFr) or a variety of stir-fries (from 15.50SFr). Wheelchair-accessible. Open M 6pm-midnight, Tu-Th and Su 8am-midnight, F-Sa 8am-12:30am.

Milchbar Café, Kappelerg. 16 (☎211 90 13), right behind the Fraumünster. A cheap and highly frequented lunch stop among nearby business people, moms, and lunching friends. Simple *Menüs* (from 15.50-19.50SFr), inexpensive soups (4.80SFr), and a popular salad bar (3.30SFr per 100g) make Milchbar a convenient and pleasant place to eat between shopping and sightseeing. A full vegetarian menu is available. The proud staff make their own iced tea and highlight a different fruit-filled pastry each day. Open M-F 5am-6pm, Sa 6am-5pm.

Infinito Espresso Bar, Sihlstr. 20 (☎01 260 55 35; fax 01 260 55 34), is a chic and minimalist venue that serves a wide coffee selection and other yuppie drinks. Espresso from 4SFr, beers from 6SFr, sandwiches and snacks 4.50-9SFr. Open M-F 7am-10pm, Sa 8am-7pm. Prices for drinks increase about 1SFr after 8pm.

MARKETS AND BAKERIES

Two bakery chains, **Kleiner** and **Buchmann,** are everywhere in Zurich, offering freshly baked bread, sweets (whole apricot pies around 10SFr), and *Kuchen* (*Bürli* rolls 0.85SFr, *Chäschüchli* 2SFr) for reasonable prices. (Open M-F 6:30am-6:30pm.) The 24hr. **vending machine** in the Shop-Ville beneath the train station has pasta, juice, and other staples, but you may feel uncomfortable heading over there alone at night.

Farmer's Market, at Burklipl. sells fruit, flowers, and veggies Tu, F 6am-11am. At Rosenhof, fruit vegetables, and wares are sold Th 10am-8pm and Sa 10am-5pm.

Coop Super-Center, right on Bahnhofbr., is the Coop to end all Coops, visible from almost everywhere. Open M-F 7am-8pm, Sa 7am-4pm.

Migros, Stadelhoferpl. 16, right off Theaterstr. Open M-F 7am-8pm, Sa 8am-5pm. The adjoining restaurant has the same hours.

◉ SIGHTS

It's virtually inconceivable to start your tour of Zurich anywhere except the stately **Bahnhofstraße.** The famous causeway of capitalism has shoppers peering into the windows of Cartier, Rolex, Chanel, and Armani during the day but falls dead quiet when the shops and banks close at 6pm. At the Zürichsee end of Bahnhofstr., **Bürkliplatz** is a good place to begin exploration of the lake shore. The *Platz* itself hosts a colorful Saturday **flea market** (May-Oct. 6am-3pm). On the other side of the river, the pedestrian zone continues on Niederdorfstr. and Münsterg., and is made up of a wider range of shops from the ritzy to the erotic. From Niederdorfstr. turn right onto **Spiegelgasse,** Zurich's memory lane. Goethe, Buchner, and Lenin, who once lived on this street, are honored with commemorative plaques. A view of Zurich from overhead points to its three largest sights, **Fraumünster, Grossmünster,** and **St. Peterskirche,** all tightly packed and straddling the Limmat river.

FRAUMÜNSTER. This 13th-century cathedral's classic Gothic style is juxtaposed with **Marc Chagall's** not-so-classic stained-glass windows; the fusion attracts numerous admirers, religious and not. The five choir windows depict Chagall's personal interpretations of stories from the Old and New Testament. A more subdued window called "the heavenly Paradise" designed by Augusto Giacometti in 1930, decorates the northern transept. Outside the church on Fraumünsterstr., a mural decorating the courtyard's Gothic archway pictures Felix and Regula (the decapitated patron saints of Zurich) with their heads in their hands. If you get the feeling you're being watched, it's because floating sculptured heads peer from the corners and columns. (*Right off Paradepl. Open daily May-Sept. 9am-6pm; Oct. and Mar.-Apr. 10am-5pm; Nov.-Feb. 10am-4pm.*)

GROSSMÜNSTER. The twin Neo-Gothic towers of this mainly Romanesque church can best be viewed on the bridge near the Fraumünster. Considered to be the mother church of the Swiss-German Reformation movement begun by Zwingli, it has come to be a symbol of Zurich. The stained-glass windows, depicting the Biblical Christmas narrative, were designed in 1933 by Augusto Giacometti. Below the windows, one of Zwingli's Bibles lies in a protected case near his pulpit. Venture downstairs to the cavernous 12th-century crypt to see the forbidding statue of Charlemagne and his 2m-long sword. If you're feeling active, head up the many twisting stairs to the top of one of the towers: the climb is about 10min. and offers a great orientation to the city's major landmarks as well as shots of the Zürichsee. Guides to glance through or buy (.050SFr) are available in a variety of languages including English. (*Follow Niederdorfstr., which becomes Münsterg., to the end. Church open daily Mar. 15-Oct. 9am-6pm; Nov.-Mar. 14 10am-5pm. Tower open Mar.-Oct. daily 1:30-5pm; Nov.-Feb. Sa-Su 9:15am-5pm. 2SFr for entrance to the tower.*) In the same building is the small **Zwingli museum** and monastery. (*Open M-F 9am-4:30pm.*)

ST. PETERSKIRCHE. St. Peterskirche stakes its claim as the largest clock face in Europe. Find it near the Fraumünster, or just look up. (*Open M-F 8am-6pm, Sa 8am-4pm, Su 10-11am.*) Recently excavated Roman baths dating from the first century are visible beneath the iron stairway. (*Down Thermeng. from St. Peter's.*).

LINDENHOF. The original site of **Turricum,** namesake and birthplace of Zurich, the park provides refuge from the daily grind. It has a giant chess board and views of the river and the *Altstadt.* It attracts locals and tourists to lounge and admire the vistas. (*Follow Strehlg., Rennweg, or Glockeng. uphill to the intersection of the 3 streets.*)

GARDENS & PARKS. The lush, perfect-for-a-picnic **Rieter-Park,** overlooking the city, creates a romantic backdrop for the Museum Rietberg. (*Take tram #7 to "Museum Rietberg." Head in the direction of the tram to the first intersection. Turn right onto Sternenstr. and follow the signs to the museum uphill. Free.*) The **Stadtgärtnerei** attracts botanists and ornithologists alike to the moist Palmhouse/Aviary, which has artificial streams running through it. The Aviary houses 17 species of tropical birds, including two fantastically plumed green parrots and a mime bird, all of which whiz freely around the building. (*Sackzeig 25-27. Take tram #3 to "Hubertus" and head down Gutstr. ☎492 14 23; www.stadt-gaertnerei.ch. Open daily 9-11:30am and 1:30-4:30pm. Free.*) When the weather heats up, a visit to the bathing parks along the Zürichsee can offer a cool respite. Strandbad Mythenquai lies along the western shore. (*Take tram #7 to "Brunaustr." and walk in the same direction, cross to the left side of the street, and continue 2min. until you see a set of stairs. Signs hidden by the foliage lead the way. ☎201 00 00. Open daily June to mid-Aug. 9am-8pm; May and mid-Aug. to early Sept. 9am-7pm. 6SFr. Check out www.badi-info.ch for water quality information and other bathing locations.*)

ÜTLIBERG. The "top of Zurich," this is the king of picnic spots, with a view of Zurich's urban sprawl on one side and pristine countryside on the other. The flat walk from Ütliberg to Felsenegg is a peaceful escape from the city's bustle. From Zurich's Hauptbahnhof, take the train to "Ütliberg" (15min., every 10-30min., 14.40SFr discount with *Tageskarte*), then follow the yellow signs to Felsenegg (1½hr.). A cable car runs from Felsenegg to Adliswil, where a train returns to Zurich. *(Buy tickets at any train or cable car station or at most hotels; free with Eurail.)*

OTHER SIGHTS. The **Fluntern Cemetery** (Fluntern Cemetery) contains the graves of **James Joyce** and **Elias Canetti;** their graves are located at the top of the hill, accessed by the cemetery's central pathway. The **Zürich Zoo,** beside the cemetery, has over 250 animal species. Boasting one of the best bear enclosures around, the zoo is a much-frequented cultural treasure, entertaining school groups, families, and art students alike with the antics of its animals. The expansive Masoala Rainforest, a living biosphere of tropical life, just opened in 2003. Get there early to avoid long lines. *(Zürichbergstr. 221. Take tram #6 uphill to "Zoo." From the station, head uphill 100m to find the cemetery on your left; for the zoo, walk past the cemetery and the track, then about 200m more. ☎ 254 25 05; www.zoo.ch.. Open daily Mar.-Oct. 8am-6pm; Nov.-Feb. 8am-5pm. 18SFr; ages 6-16, students, seniors 9SFr; ages 6 and under free.)*

🏛 MUSEUMS

Zurich has channeled much of its banking wealth into universities and museums, which foster outstanding collections. The larger institutions hold the core of the city's artistic and historical wealth, but many smaller museums are equally spectacular. The tourist office in the main station offers a helpful listing of all the area museums' current exhibits. Colorful posters also coat the city, advertising upcoming museum events. During the first weekend in September each year, 30 of the city's 50+ museums are open from 7pm to 5am. Free entry into all museums listed (and some others) is available with the Zürich Card.

ART MUSEUMS

🖼 **KUNSTHAUS ZÜRICH.** The Kunsthaus, the largest privately-funded museum in Europe, houses a collection ranging from 21st-century American pop art to religious works by the Old Masters. Works by Picasso, van Gogh, Gaugin, Dalí, Rubens, Rembrandt, Renoir, and the largest Munch collection outside of Norway highlight a museum that, by itself, is a com-

NO WORK, ALL PLAY

DO YOU SCHWING?

A summer in Switzerland would not be complete without the institution that is the annual *Schwingfest*, an event dedicated to the arcane sport of *Schwingen*. A form of wrestling, *Schwingen* features two male *Schwingers* faced off in a Sägemuhlring (a ring of sawdust). The men wear leather overshorts with loops on the back which the other *Schwinger* must grip for leverage at all times. As a *Schwinger*, your goal in life is to throw your opponent down on his back, and to stay within the circle while doing so; matches last around five minutes.

The earliest known reference to the sport is a 13th-century stone carving in the cathedral of Lausanne, which depicts two overshort-wearing strongmen at loggerheads. The sport's origins lie in Alpine farming regions, where farmhands would compete to see who was the strongest, and everyone presumably wore suspenders. Today, the men are still distinguished by the roots of their training: *Sennen* are farmers and wear traditional blue workshirts; *Turnen are* gym-trained athletes and wear only white.

The *Schwingfest* itself includes more Swiss tradition than just wrestling. Normally, the playing of an *Alphorn* kicks off the first bout, and flag throwers, yodel choirs, and a beer-and-sausage tent provide entertainment on the sidelines. Check www.esv.ch for inforrmation on the *Fest* near you.

pelling reason to come to Zurich. The collection is continually expanding: a new wing devoted to Alberto Giacometti and artistic kin opened in May 2002. Future highlights include Georgia O'Keefe (fall-winter 2003), landscapes by legendary Swiss artist Hodler (Mar.-June 2004), a creative contemporary project by up-and-coming Swiss phenomenon Urs Fischer, and a major exhibit of Monet's garden works (Nov.-Feb. 2005). Renovations Feb.-Aug. 2004 will reduce the number of works on display, but not the variety. *(Heimpl. 1. Take tram #3, 5, 8, or 9 to "Kunsthaus."* ☎ *253 84 84; www.kunsthaus.ch. English audio tours and brochures available. Bag storage required. Call ahead for wheelchair-access. After 2005, fully accessible without prior arrangements. Open Tu-Th 10am-9pm, F-Su 10am-5pm. Admission 12SFr, students and seniors 6SFr; W free. Added charge (10-17SFr) for special exhibits. Free tours W 6:30pm, Sa 3pm.)*

■ **MUSEUM RIETBERG.** In confident contrast to the Kunsthaus, Rietberg presents an exquisite collection of Asian, African, and other non-European art, housed in two spectacular mansions in the Rieter-Park. Sprung from the well-known collection of Baron von der Heyt, the 50-year-old museum has firmly established itself as one of the best museums in Zurich. Park-Villa Rieter features internationally acclaimed exhibits of Chinese, Japanese, and Indian drawings and paintings. Villa Wesendonck stores most of the permanent collection of non-Western sculpture, with Bodhisattvas from India, China, Japan, Tibet, and Nepal. Renovations will close Park-Villa Rieter Spring 2004-2006, while Villa Wesendonck will remain open. *(Gablerstr. 15. Take tram #7 to "Museum Rietberg." See directions to Rieter Park ("Gardens and Parks," p. 388).* ☎ *202 45 28; www.rieterberg.ch.* ☎ *202 45 28; www.rietberg.ch. Villa Wesendonck open Tu-Su 10am-5pm. Audio guide (5SFr) and literature available in English and French. Wheelchair-accessible. Park-Villa Rieter open Tu-Sa 1-5pm, Su 10am-5pm. 6SFr, students 3SFr, under 16 free. Special exhibits and permanent collections 12SFr, students 6SFr. MC/V only at Wesendonck.)*

OTHER MUSEUMS

SCHWEIZERISCHES LANDESMUSEUM. Housed in a castle right next to the Hauptbahnhof, the Landesmuseum provides fascinating insights into Swiss history with its careful reconstructions and preservation of Swiss artifacts. The generic first floor contains medieval artifacts, but the castle rooms have 16th-century astrological instruments, Ulrich Zwingli's weapons from the Battle of Kappel (1531) in which he died, and a tiny bejeweled clock with a golden skeleton morbidly indicating the hour. Unique, creatively-presented special exhibitions change every few months. Check the web site for upcoming events. *(Museumstr. 2, next to the main train station.* ☎ *218 65 65. www.musee-suisse.ch. Wheelchair-accessible with assistance. Open Tu-Su 10:30am-5pm and public holidays. Entrance 5SFr, students and seniors 3SFr, under 14 free. Special exhibits around 5-10SFr. AmEx/DC/MC/V for 30SFr and up.)*

MUSEUM OF CLASSICAL ARCHAEOLOGY. As impressive as the collection of Greek and Roman vases and busts filling the first floor lecture hall is, it seems little more than a foil for the astonishing basement, which houses replicas of nearly every great statue of the ancient world from 800 BC on. *(Rämistr. 73. Take tram #6, 9, or 10 to "ETH." Coming to the city center, walk in the direction of the tram 3min. The main ETH building is on your left.* ☎ *01 257 28 20; www.archinst.uniz.ch. Wheelchair-accessible entrance on nearby Karl-Schmiedstr. Signs in German. Open Tu-F 1-6pm, Sa-Su 11am-5pm. Free.)*

MUSEUM FÜR GESTALTUNG (DESIGN MUSEUM). This museum's enormous spaces, adjoined to the School of Design, display student work, a collection of vintage advertisement posters, and temporary exhibits on subjects such as steam shovel art, female power stations, and giant corn. *(Ausstellungsstr. 60. Take tram #4 or*

13 to "Museum für Gestaltung" or walk 5min. from the main station. ☎ 446 22 11; www.museum-gestaltung.ch. Open Tu-Th 10am-8pm, F-Su 11am-6pm; graphics, poster, and design collections by appointment. Hall and gallery 10SFr, students 6SFr. Tours every W 6:15pm, Su 11:15am.)

LINDT AND SPRÜNGLI CHOCOLATE FACTORY. Visitors are welcomed into the company's one room exhibit on chocolate making and the history and tradition of the Lindt company with an open box of Lindt chocolate and a multilingual movie about chocolate machines. Your experience at the exhibit ends, appropriately,

DA, DA, DA The silent walls of Spiegalg. 3 in Zurich's *Altstadt* witnessed one of the most rebellious movements in the history of art and theater. The years between the World Wars offered no lull for the city's citizens, as a group of angry young artists spilled their creativity into the craziest forms of art. The result was Dadaism, an art that refused to be art, a style whose guiding principle was confusion and paradoxical humor. Dada's aim was to provoke a rude awakening from standardized thought and bourgeois preconceptions. Dada is said to have taken its name either from the French word for "hobby-horse," which Hugo Ball selected by sticking a pen-knife into a German-French dictionary, or from the refrain of two Romanian founders of the movement, who used to mutter, "Da, da" ("yes, yes" in Romanian). Distinguished painter/sculptor Alberto Giacometti entered the fray during a sojourn in Zurich—it is said that one day, he opened the door of Cabaret Voltaire, stepped out, shouted, "Viva Dada!" at the top of his lungs, and disappeared as promenadeurs on the Limmatquai stopped in their tracks. Lenin was also reputedly a fan of Cabaret Voltaire. Today Cabaret Voltaire is preserved in the entrails of the disco/bar Castel Dada.

with a free box of Lindt chocolate. Get bundles of chocolate at bargain prices at the end of the tour. All exhibits in German. *(Seestr. 204. Take train S1 (dir.: "Zug") or S8 (dir.: Pfäffikon) to "Kilchberg"(15min., 2 per hr. leave from the main station, round-trip 10.80SFr.) From the station, take the once-hourly bus #163 to "Lindt-Sprüngli" or walk down the sidewalk path to Seestr., where you continue in the direction of the train for 10min. The factory is on your right. ☎ 01 716 22 33. Open W-F 10am-noon and 1-4pm. Free.)*

MUSEUM BELLERIVE. Museum Bellerive specializes in constantly changing "out-of-the-ordinary" exhibits. The displays may sound tame, but the museum takes them in unexpected directions—one past exhibition included "Made in Japan" (a room full of plastic Japanese meals), another focused on the art of recycling. Through early January 2004, a "Picasso to Paladino" exhibit will fill the museum. *(Höschg. #3. Take tram #2 or 4 (dir.: Tiefenbrunnen) or bus #33 to "Höschg." and walk right; it's opposite the Zurich Ballet Academy. ☎ 383 43 76; fax 383 43 68. Closed between exhibits, so call ahead. Wheelchair-accessible. Open Tu-Th 10am-8pm, F 10am-5pm, Sa-Su 11am-5pm. 6SFr, students and children 3SFr.)*

♫ 🎭 ENTERTAINMENT & NIGHTLIFE

For information on after-dark goings-on, check **ZüriTipp** (www.zueritipp.ch) or the posters that decorate the streets and cinemas at Bellevuepl. or Hirschenpl. **Niederdorfstraße** rocks as the epicenter of Zurich's nightlife. Beware the deceptive and ubiquitous "night club"—it's a euphemism for strip club. Because of this, *women may not want to walk alone in this area at night.* On Friday and Saturday nights during the summer, Hirschenpl. on Niederdorfstr. hosts sword-swallowers and other daredevil street performers from around the world. Other hot spots include Münsterg. and Limmatquai, both of which are lined with cafés and bars that overflow with people into the wee hours of the morning. Beer in Zurich is pricey (from 6SFr), but a number of cheap bars have established themselves on Niederdorfstr. near Muhleg. If all else fails, go to the cinema. Most movies are screened in English with German and French subtitles (marked E/d/f). Films generally cost 15SFr and up, less on Mondays. After July 18, the **Orange Cinema,** an open-air cinema at Zürichhorn (take tram #4 or 2 to "Fröhlichstr.") attracts huge crowds to its lakefront screenings. To ensure a seat, arrive at least 1hr. before the 9pm showing (15SFr) or reserve a seat at the open-air ticket counter at the Bellevue tram station. Every August, the **Street Parade** brings together ravers from all over the world for a giant techno party (see "Festival Fever," p. 334).

🌑 **Double-U (W) Bar,** Niederdorfstr. 21 (☎251 41 44), on the first floor of Hotel Schafli. On the busy Niederdorfstr. main drag, this spot is popular with locals and students who crowd the terrace. Comes complete with palm trees and inflatable beer bottles. Beer (10SFr and up) and cocktails (14SFr and up) rise 2SFr in price after midnight. Wheelchair-accessible. Open Su-F 4pm-2am, Sa 4pm-4am. AmEx/DC/MC/V.

Nachtflug Bar, Café, and Lounge, Stüssihofstaff 4 (☎01 261 99 66; www.nacht-flug.ch), boasts a popular outdoor bar alongside **The Blue Monkey's** similar setup when the weather behaves. A flock of laid-back locals fill the Rosenhof alongside Hotel Biger's backpackers, college students, and the occasional live music. Wine from 7SFr, beer from 4.90SFr, and mixed drinks (12-16SFr) and a menu that also serves cold *tapas* and fresh-squeezed juices all day (6SFr). Low chairs and lots of pillows make this a comfortable place to see and be seen. Wheelchair-accessible via Niederdorfstr. Open M-Th 11am-midnight, F-Sa 11am-2am. Outdoor bar Th-Su 10pm-midnight.

Cranberry, Metzgerg. 3 (☎/fax 261 27 72), is a gay-friendly bar right off Limmatquai. A fashionable and somewhat artsy crowd packs this recently renovated space even at 9pm on a Thursday. With funky lights and a leather lounge upstairs, the bar serves up an endless selection of mixed drinks (9-14SFr). Wheelchair-accessible. Open Su-W 5pm-12:30am, Th-Sa 5pm-2am. AmEx/DC/MC/V.

Bar Odeon, Limmatquai 2 (☎251 16 50), Bellevuepl. This posh, artsy joint has served the likes of Vladimir Lenin, but is more commonly frequented by a relaxed, gay-friendly crowd. Great street-side seating. Beers from 6SFr. During the day, an ebullient crowd sips espresso, *aperos,* and enjoys desserts from 6.50SFr. Open Su-Th 7am-2am, F-Sa 7am-4am. AmEx/DC/MC/V.

Oliver Twist, Rindermarkt 6 (☎252 47 10; www.pickwick.ch), welcomes soccer fans, tourists, and other assorted ex-pats ready for an American brew in a pub atmosphere that's only somewhat contrived. Beers 6.50SFr and up; wine from 5.50SFr. Pub grub available noon-10pm. English breakfast (15.50SFr) available during major sporting events. Open M-Sa 11:30am-midnight, Su 1pm-midnight.

Öpfelchammer, Rindermarkt 12 (☎01 251 23 36). This popular Swiss wine bar (3-5SFr per glass) has low ceilings and wooden crossbeams covered with initials and messages from 200 years of merry-making. Those who climb the rafters and drink a free glass of wine from the beams get to engrave their names on the furniture. It's harder than it looks. Closed mid-July to mid-August. Open Tu-Sa 11am-12:30am. AmEx/DC/MC/V.

Barfüsser, Spitalg. 14 (☎01 251 40 64), off Zähringerpl., Europe's oldest gay bar, provides a lively spot to meet people and chat with the entertaining staff. Barfüsser specializes in sushi during the day, and serves it in an outdoor seating area (M-Sa 11:30am-10:30pm, Su 5-10:30pm). At night, cocktails (14-17SFr), wine (6-9SFr), and changing daily concoctions flow freely. Wheelchair-accessible. Open M-W 11am-1am, Th 11am-2am, F-Sa 11am-3am, Su 3pm-1am. AmEx/DC/MC/V.

🔢 DAYTRIP FROM ZURICH

EINSIEDELN
☎ 055

Trains leave Zurich for Wädenswil (toward Chur, 1-2 per hr. every 20min. 6:10am-10:16pm, 16.20SFr), where trains run to Einsiedeln (30min.).

Just an hour by train from Zwingli's Protestant pulpit in Zurich, the tiny town of Einsiedeln attracts pilgrims from all over Europe to its spectacular, massive cathedral and legendary Black Madonna. To find the **Klosterkirche** (cathedral), exit the station, cross the street to the left, turn right on the small lane behind "Doc Holliday's" restaurant, and turn left uphill on Hauptstr. From there it is a 10min. walk directly forward. Consecrated in 1735, the cathedral's Milanese exterior dominates the surrounding hills with its twin lemon-shaped domes. Endless frescoes by the Asam brothers line the interior; the ornate Baroque ceilings overflow with cherubs floating on a background of lavender, green, gold, and pink. After Vespers each day (except Sunday) from 4:30 to 5pm, the group of Benedictine monks who live and work at the monastery chant the "Salve Regina," which has been performed daily at the monastery since 1547. Visitors are welcome, but meditative silence and a ban on photography and videotaping are strictly observed. The 1m-high **Black Madonna** is the cathedral's centerpiece. Years of smoky candlelight and underground storage during the French invasion have darkened the figure. An Austrian craftsman once restored her natural color, but locals, refusing to accept the change, had painted her black again (*Klosterkirche* open 5:30am-8:30pm; for an extensive schedule of daily worship activities, visit the tourist office, www.kloster-einsiedeln.ch, or call ☎ 418 61 11. Bathrooms require a 50-cent coin. ½hr. tours of the grounds and monastic life were offered in Summer 2003 in several languages for 2SFr per person; inquire as to current price.) The **monastery** that stretches back from the cathedral offers 1.5 hour tours of its horse stables and renowned library every Saturday at 2pm. (18SFr; reserve and buy tickets at the tourist office. Conducted in German; tours in other languages available by appointment. 1hr. tours for 12SFr are offered M-Sa 2-3pm. Inquire at the tourist office for language and availability.) The gates to the monastery are usually open, and the pastoral grounds, protected by the crumbling walls of the monastery, are worth a stroll. Behind the monastery, short trails lead into the hills where its horses graze.

The town's **tourist office** sits below the cathedral at Hauptstr. 85, Klosterpl. (☎ 418 44 88; info@einsiedeln.ch). A helpful staff can book tours for you and advise you on **hiking** opportunities in the lush hills surrounding the cathedral, as well as provide a schedule of Klosterkirche **concerts,** services, and events. (Open M-F 10am-noon and 1:30-5pm, Sa 9am-noon and 1:30-4pm, Su and holidays 9am-noon.) A **24hr. ATM** and a Credit Suisse **bank** sit next to the tourist office. (Open M-F 8:30am-noon and 1:30-5pm, W until 6pm.) Limited **parking** is in front of the monastery; long-term parking in the nearby lot, with tickets bought at the tourist office. To reach the **police** station and lost-and-found office, call ☎ 055 418 74 44.

WINTERTHUR
☎ 052

Once the country home of eastern Switzerland's wealthy industrialists, Winterthur (VIN-ter-tur) today houses the fruits of their labor. The incredible array of museums—mostly endowed by those deceased wealthy industrialists—make it an excellent daytrip from Zurich.

☎ TRANSPORT & PRACTICAL INFORMATION

Trains run to Zurich (4 per hr. 6:22am-11:52pm, 10SFr) and connect there to Basel, Geneva, and St. Gallen (45min., 4 per hr. daily, 18.80SFr). Almost all buses to the museums leave from just right of the station. Winterthur's museums are closed Mondays. The **tourist office**, within the train station, provides brochures with excursion ideas and museum information. It offers free hotel reservations and a free but busy **Internet** terminal. (☎267 67 00; www.winterthur-tourismus.ch. Open M-F 8:30am-6:30pm, Sa 8:30am-4pm.) Next to the ticket counters in the information center, you'll find **currency exchange** (open daily 6am-8:30pm). Down the hall from the info center, there's **bike rental** (open M-Sa 8:30am-7:30pm, Su 9am-noon and 2:40-7:30pm; 30SFr per day, under 16 25SFr per day; add 6SFr if returning to another station), and **luggage storage** (7SFr; same hours as bike rental). There is a **pharmacy** in the station. **Lockers** with 24hr. access are also available in the train station (4-6SFr). **Post office** opposite the train station. (Open M-F 7:30am-7pm, Sa 8am-4pm.) **24 hr. ATM** available in the lobby. **Postal code:** CH-8401.

♨ ACCOMMODATIONS & FOOD

Budget accommodations are hard to find in Winterthur, although the city council is considering the construction of a large hostel. The only option in the way of youth accommodations is **Jugendunterkunft Winterthur ❷**, 18 Wildbach Str. From the train station, walk 7min. down Tecknikumstr. and turn right onto Zeughaus Str. After that turn, you'll immediately see a fork in the road; take the right fork (Wildbachstr.) and the hostel will be on the left at the next intersection. Student groups and traveling businessmen fill these simple, clean rooms. Spacious, lodge-style rec room and convenient location make this hostel an excellent value. Call ahead, because the staff never knows when the hostel will close. (☎267 48 48; fax 267 48 49. Breakfast 10SFr. English-speaking staff. Kitchen, TV room, sheets, and towels. Luggage watch during reception hours. Reception 7-10:30am and 4-9:30pm. Open Apr.-Sept. 3- to 4-bed rooms 30SFr; singles and doubles 38SFr per person.)

Food stands serve quick and cheap sandwiches throughout the downtown, particularly on Marktg. Locals on lunch break congregate at **Manta Sandwich-Bar ❷**, Untertor 17, near the train station. Filling gourmet sandwiches (tomato, mozzarella, and eggplant) go for 7-12SFr. (☎52 212 43 23; fax 52 212 43 18. Wheelchair-accessible. Open M-W and F 6am-6:30pm, Th 6am-9pm, and Sa 6am-5pm.) **Restaurant-Pizzeria Pulcinella ❸**, right off Marktg. on Metzg., is another local favorite. Eat in (pizza 14-20.50SFr) or take out for 5SFr less. (☎212 98 62. Open M-F 11:30am-2pm and 6-11pm, Sa 6-11pm. AmEx/DC/MC/V.) Fruit and vegetable **markets** invade the streets of the *Altstadt* on Tuesdays and Fridays from 6am-11am. A huge **Coop** supermarket is behind the post office, attached to the Manor department store. A **Migros** supermarket is on Marktg. and Unterer Graben in the *Altstadt*.

◉ SIGHTS

Since museums are Winterthur's biggest draw, two options save you time and money: buying a *Tageskarte* (7.20SFr) at the train station will get you to the museums via public transportation (biking is also a popular option), and a museum pass (20SFr for 1 day) will get you into them. If you do the math, the purchases are only worthwhile if you plan on visiting at least three of Winterthur's 16 museums.

OSKAR REINHART COLLECTION. Winterthur's most generous art patron was Oskar Reinhart, as the two museums housing his collection demonstrate. The smaller but more impressive branch of the collection is just outside of town in the ◼**Sammlung Oskar Reinhart am Römerholz.** Reinhart's gift to the Swiss Federation, the collection is valued at about 3 billion Swiss francs, and includes works by those who Reinhart considered the "fathers of modern art," like El Greco, Goya, Holbein, and Rubens. The museum also showcases 19th-century masterpieces by Cézanne, Renoir, Manet, van Gogh, and Picasso, including paintings of Arles by van Gogh, the year before he passed away. Stop to gaze into the soft eyes of the lady in Manet's *At the Café*. *(Haldenstr. 95. Take bus #10 to "Haldengut" (3 depart every hr. from the station 6am-7pm); turn left off the bus and head up Haldenstr. for a steep 10min. walk. The museum also sponsors a shuttle service, which runs from the train station to the villa (every hr. Tu-Sa 9:45am-4:45pm, 5SFr roundtrip). ☎ 269 27 40; www.kultur-schweiz.admin.ch/sor. English audio guides available for 5SFr. Parking is available right outside the museum. Wheelchair-accessible. Open Tu-Su 10am-5pm, Easter and Whit M. 8SFr, students 6SFr.)*

The larger collection is housed in the center of town at ◼**Museum Oskar Reinhart am Stadtgarten.** The museum focuses on the work of Swiss, German, and Austrian painters, particularly portraits. Glass steps lead to the remodeled fourth floor, which houses temporary exhibits. *(Stadthausstr. 6. Turn right out of the station, then go left on Stadthausstr. for 2 blocks. ☎ 52 267 51 72; fax 52 267 62 28. Open W-Su 10am-5pm, Tu 10am-8pm. 8SFr, students 6SFr.)*

TECHNORAMA. The **Swiss Technology Museum** houses a day's worth of interactive science experiments for kids from six to 60. Explore the amazing properties of water, the power of magnetism, or the magic behind optical illusions. Train lovers will appreciate the tin toy train collection of Dr. Bommer, considered one of the world's most impressive. Most displays are printed in German, French, Italian and English. Play a water-powered drum set, or test your hand-eye coordination in the jumbo-jet flight simulator. *(Technoramastr. 1. Take bus #5 (dir.: Technorama) to the last stop (3 per hr. when museum is open). ☎ 243 05 05; www.technorama.ch. Wheelchair-accessible. Open Tu-Su and public holidays 10am-5pm. 19SFr, students 15SFr, seniors 17SFr, ages 6-15 10SFr.)*

KUNSTMUSEUM. Winterthur's Kunstmuseum houses renowned Impressionist pieces, but its specialty is Modernist art by Arp, Kandinsky, Klee, Léger, and Mondrian. In the summer, the museum features rotating exhibits of contemporary art. *(Museumstr. 52. Turn left from the station, right on Museumstr., and left on Lindstr. ☎ 267 51 62; automated information 267 58 00; www.kmw.ch. Open Tu 10am-8pm, W-Su 10am-5pm. Prices hover around 10SFr, students 7SFr.)* The city library and the **Museum of Natural Science** are in the same building. **Internet** access available at the library. *(☎ 267 51 66; www.kmw.ch. Library open M 10am-6pm, Tu-F 8am-6pm, Sa 8am-4pm. Museum of Natural Science open Tu-Su 10am-5pm. Free. Internet access: first 15min. free, each additional 15min. 2SFr.)*

FOTOMUSEUM. Among Winterthur's smaller museums is the unique Fotomuseum, housed in a former factory. The museum, which serves as the center of the counter-culture crowd in Winterthur, features exhibitions of photography, lectures, and discussions. *(Grüzenstr. 44. Take bus #2 (dir.: Seen) to "Schleife." Follow the signs to the museum; at the fork in the road, stay right. ☎ 52 233 60 86; www.fotomuseum.ch. Open Tu and Th-F noon-6pm, W noon-7:30pm, Sa-Su 11am-5pm. 8SFr, students 5SFr.)*

STADTKIRCHE. While wandering around the *Altstadt*, visit the nearly hidden **Stadtkirche** (city church) on Kirchpl. The church was built in 1180, renovated in the late Gothic style between 1501 and 1515, and now blazes with Alberto Giacometti's stained-glass windows and Paul Zehnder's 1925 murals of brightly colored Bible stories. Check schedules at the church for frequent organ concerts of masterworks. *(Turn right off of Marktg. onto Unt. Kirchg. Open daily 10am-4pm.)*

LUCERNE (LUZERN)   ☎ 041

Nestled among the foothills of the Alps, Lucerne (pop. 60,000) lies at the end of a picturesque lake that has been praised by poets and composers. A panorama stretching from Mount Rigi to Mount Pilatus sets different moods for the city's skyline depending on weather, season, and time of day. Tours through one of the most engaging *Altstädte* in Switzerland, cruises on the placid **Vierwaldstättersee,** and hikes up the peaks of Mt. Pilatus and Rigi Kulm keep visitors enthralled for days. With so many tourist opportunities, Lucerne asserts itself as not only the capital of the canton, but as one of the most important cities in Central Switzerland. Nonetheless, after a few days, the local charm and the town's small size leave travelers feeling at home.

■✸ 🛈 ORIENTATION & PRACTICAL INFORMATION

The **Reuss River,** draining from the Vierwaldstättersee (Lake Lucerne), narrows steadily through the center of Lucerne. The train station, tourist office, and post office line the edges of Bahnhofpl. on the bank south of the Reuss, while the streets of the *Altstadt* twist through the northern bank. The **Kapellbrücke** in the east and the **Spreuerbrücke** in the west are the two ancient wooden bridges that span the Reuss, with three bridges between them.

TOURIST & FINANCIAL SERVICES

Tourist Office: In the train station (☎227 17 17; www.luzern.org). Offers free and informative city guide (with unwieldy map) and free hotel reservation service. Ask about the **Visitor's Card,** which, in conjunction with a hotel or hostel stamp, provides discounts (usually about 10-20%) at museums, bars, car rental, stores and more. The office also sells tickets for Mt. Pilatus, Rigi, and Titlis excursions, along with the **Tell-Pass** and tickets for the walking city tour (2hr.; May-Oct. daily 9:45am, Nov.-Apr. W and Sa 9:45am; 165SFr; tour departs from the tourist office.) The city tour may be combined with the new city train tour (35min.; hourly till 10pm; 8SFr, children under 12 5SFr, from the front of the Schweizerhof Hotel on Hirschmattstr.) in a combination ticket for 22SFr. Open May-Oct. M-F 8:30am-6:30pm, Sa-Su 9am-6:30pm; Nov.-Apr. M-F 8:30am-5:30pm, Sa-Su 9am-1pm. One **Internet** terminal in the office (4SFr for 10min.).

Budget Travel: STA Travel, Grabenstr. 8 (☎412 23 23; www.statravel.ch), offers ISICs, student travel deals, and discount flights. Open M-W and F 9:30am-6pm, Th 9:30am-8pm, Sa 10am-4pm.

Currency Exchange: At the station. Open May-Oct. M-F 7:30am-7:30pm, Sa-Su 8am-6pm; Nov.-Apr. M-F 8am-7pm, Sa-Su 9am-6pm. **Migros bank,** Seidenhofstr. 6, off Bahnhofstr., has an exchange machine. Open M-W and F 9am-5:15pm, Th 9am-6:30pm, Sa 8:15am-noon.

American Express: Schweizerhofquai 4, P.O. Box 2067, CH-6002 (☎419 99 00). Checks cashed. Travel services open M-F 8:30am-6pm, Apr.-Oct. also Sa 8:30am-noon. **Currency exchange** open M-F 8:30am-noon and 1:30-5pm, Sa 8:30am-noon.

LOCAL SERVICES

Luggage Storage: Downstairs at the station, window 24. **Luggage watch** 5SFr per item. Open 6am-9pm. Large **lockers** in a well-lit area with 24hr. access 8SFr.

English-language bookstores: Bücher Brocky, Güterstr.1. From the station take a right onto Iselquai, bear left on Werfstr., then right onto Güterstr. This massive warehouse of books has only a few English shelves, but the selection is unique and the price is right

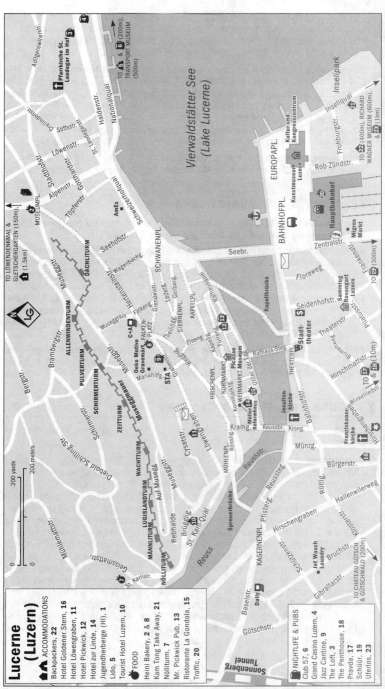

Lucerne (Luzern)

ACCOMMODATIONS
Backpackers, 22
Hotel Goldener Stern, 16
Hotel Löwengraben, 11
Hotel Pickwick, 12
Hotel zur Linde, 14
Jugendherberge (HI), 1
Lido, 5
Tourist Hotel Luzern, 10

FOOD
Heini Bakery, 2 & 8
Kam Tong Take Away, 21
Nölliturm, 7
Mr. Pickwick Pub, 13
Ristorante La Gondola, 15
Traffic, 20

NIGHTLIFE & PUBS
Club 57, 6
Grand Casino Luzern, 4
Jazz Cantine, 9
The Loft, 3
The Penthouse, 18
Pravda, 17
Schüür, 19
Uferlos, 23

Vierwaldstätter See
(Lake Lucerne)

Inselipark

Inseliquai

TO LÖWENDENKMAL &
GLETSCHERGARTEN (150m),
(1.5km)

Pfarrkirche St.
Leodegar im Hof

TO 5 & 6 (200m),
TRANSPORT MUSEUM
(500m)

Sommenberg
Tunnel

(1SFr for paperbacks). **Raeber,** (☎229 60 20), on Frankenstr. off Zentralstr. Sophisticated selection of English literature, travel books, and maps. **Free Internet** access for customers. Open M 1-6:30pm, Tu-F 8am-6:30pm, Sa 8am-4pm. For English magazines, check out the kiosk in the basement of the train station.

Bi-Gay-Lesbian Organizations: Homosexuelle Arbeitsgruppe Luzern (HALU; ☎360 14 60; www.halu-luzern.ch) publishes a monthly calendar of social events, available at the tourist office. Along with a library and a disco (see Nightlife, p. 403) HALU also runs **Why Not,** a discussion group for young gays, which meets regularly Tu and Th 7:30pm at local restaurants (www.whynot-luzern.ch). A discussion group for the young BGLT crowd meets Th 5-8pm at Zeughausg. 9, 6th floor. HALU also runs a lesbian information hotline and **Mona-Lila,** a women's discussion group (☎360 30 26; Tu 6-8pm).

Laundromat: Jet Wasch, Bruchstr. 28 (☎240 01 51), right off Pilatusstr. by the station. Wash and dry 16SFr. Open May-Oct. M-F 8:30am-12:30pm and 2:30-6:30pm, Sa 9am-1pm; Oct.-Feb. M-F 8:30am-12:30pm, Sa 9am-1pm.

EMERGENCY & COMMUNICATIONS

Emergency: Police ☎117, **Fire** ☎118, **Ambulance** ☎144, **Medical Emergency** ☎111, **Auto Emergency Service** ☎140, **24hr. pharmacy** ☎211 33 33.

Internet Access: The best deal, **Stadtbibliothek** (City Library) 1 floor up in the Bourbaki Panorama by the Glacier Garden provides access for 4SFr per hr. Open M 1:30-6:30pm, Tu-F 10am-6:30pm, Th 10am-9pm, Sa 10am-4pm. 10SFr deposit required. Wheelchair-accessible. **C+A Clothing** on Hertensteinstr. at the top of the Altstadt has 2 free terminals on its lower floor. 20min. time limit. Open M-W 9am-6:30pm, Th-F 9am-9pm, Sa 8:30am-4pm. Wheelchair-accessible. At the junction of Bruchstr. and Baselstr. the drink bar **Daily** offers **free Internet** with purchase of a drink. Beer 4SFr. Coffee 3.50SFr. Open 7am-midnight.

Post Office: Main branch on the corner of Bahnhofstr. and Bahnhofpl. Address *Poste Restante* to: Postlagernde Briefe, Hauptpost; CH-6000 Luzern 1. ☎229 95 23. Open M-F 7:30am-6:30pm, Sa 8-noon. **Postal code:** CH-6000.

▌ ACCOMMODATIONS & CAMPING

Relatively inexpensive beds are available only in limited numbers in Lucerne, so call ahead in order to ensure a roof over your head.

▨ **Backpackers,** Alpenquai 42 (☎360 04 20; fax 04 42). Turn right out of the station, following the lake around the corner past the Europapl. fountain. Cross the street and walk straight ahead through the tour bus parking lot to the concrete pedestrian bridge. When the walkway ends (10min.), follow the sidewalk straight ahead 5min. past the park. The hostel is at the end of the road on the right. The long walk can be annoying, but the path is lit. Dorm rooms with large balconies, a comfortable dining room, and tons of American college students make this hostel a pleasant spot. The store sells "survival kits" of pasta, sauce, and wine for 9SFr, and many use the 2 kitchens, each with a refrigerator, oven, and lots of cooking utensils. Tickets sold for cable cars on local mountains. Breakfast M-F 6:30-8:30am (7SFr). Bike rental 16SFr per day. Ping pong, badminton, roller blades, and scooters available. **Internet** 10SFr per hr., available when reception is open. Given time, the staff will wash, dry, and fold laundry for 8SFr. Towel 1SFr. Sheets included (sleeping bags strictly forbidden). Key deposit of 50SFr, passport, or driver's license. Reception 7:30-10am and 4-11pm. No lockout. 10am check-out is strictly enforced. 4-bed dorms 27SFr; 2-bed dorms 33SFr; 2SFr cheaper in winter. ❷

Tourist Hotel Luzern, St. Karliquai 12 (☎410 24 74; www.touristhotel.ch), on the *Altstadt* side of Spreuerbrücke. Attracting a pleasant international student crowd as well as families, the hotel offers cheap, clean rooms with views of the river at Mt. Pilatus. Very close to the *Altstadt's* center. Hertz car rental and Mt. Pilatus tickets available. Currency exchange available. **Internet** access 10SFr per hr. Breakfast included, served in a large common room with a view. Free luggage storage. Laundry 10SFr. Reception 7am-10:30pm. Check-out 11am. Lockers in dorms are small; bring your own lock. June-Nov. dorms 35-40SFr; doubles 98-112SFr; quads 180SFr-156SFr. Dec.-May dorms 33SFr and rooms 10-20SFr less. Add 10-25SFr per person for private shower. AmEx/MC/V. Traveler's checks accepted. Dorms must pay with cash. ❸

Hotel Löwengraben, Löwengraben 18 (☎417 12 12; www.loewengraben.ch). Until November 1998, Hotel Löwengraben was a prison providing full services to the miscreants of Lucerne. In only seven months the building was converted into a trendy hostel, dressed in black. The ground floor hosts a bar and several theme restaurants. Ask about daily events and tours. Löwengraben throws all-night dance parties (for guests only) every Sa during the summer, and also hosts a few city-wide events. Breakfast 11SFr. Dinner 18SFr. 24-hr. reception. Check-in after 3pm. Check-out 11am. Locked storage room for luggage. Quiet hours midnight-7am. Sheets included. 3- and 4-bed co-ed dorms, most with private showers and towels. 40SFr; single with shower 110-160SFr; triples 190SFr; quads 210SFr. Reduced rates in winter. AmEx/DC/MC/V. ❷

Hotel Goldener Stern, Burgerstr. 35 (☎227 50 60; www.goldener-stern.ch), From the station head left on Pilatusstr., turn right onto Hirschengr. and veer right onto Burgerstr. Simple rooms with large windows, TV and telephone. Public parking lot across from the hotel. Breakfast included. Reception 6am-midnight; Su until 10pm. Check-in M-Sa 11am. Check-out 10am. Singles 100SFr; doubles 150SFr, without shower 110SFr; triples 190SFr; quads 210SFr. Reduced rates in winter. AmEx/DC/MC/V. ❹

Jugendherberge (HI), Sedelstr. 12 (☎420 88 00; fax 56 16). During the day, take bus #18 to "Jugendherberge." After 7:30pm, take bus #19 to "Rosenberg" and walk along the direction of the bus route, turning right at the fork (5min.; follow signs). In a white concrete building, near the Rotsee, with a beautiful valley view. Beds have fresh sheets and night lights. Buffet breakfast, showers, lockers, and sheets included. Dinner 12.50SFr. Laundry service 15SFr. Reception Apr.-Oct. daily 7-10am and 2pm-midnight; Nov.-Mar. 7-10am and 4pm-midnight. Call ahead in summer. Dorms 31.50SFr, doubles 78SFr, with shower 108SFr. 6SFr extra for non-members. AmEx/DC/MC/V. ❷

Hotel zur Linde, Metzgerrainie 3 (☎410 31 93; fax 32 05), centrally located on Weinmarkt in the *Altstadt* above an Italian restaurant. Owner Alberino offers basic rooms with communal showers and toilet. Sinks in room. Reception M-Sa 11:30am-2:30pm and 6pm-12:30am. Check-out 10am. Singles 44SFr; doubles 88SFr. AmEx/MC/V. ❸

Hotel Pickwick, Rathausquai 6 (☎410 59 27; www.hotelpickwick.ch), centrally located in the Altstadt between the Kapellbrücke and Rathaus Steg bridge, Comfortable rooms. No breakfast, but bar and restaurant downstairs (see Food below). Reception in bar 11:30am-12:30am. Check-out 11am. Singles 75SFr, with shower 85SFr; doubles 95-105SFr/105-135SFr. Winter prices reduced. AmEx/MC/V. ❹

Lido, Lidostr. 8 (☎370 21 46; www.camping-international.ch), 35min. along Nationalquai, or take bus #6 or 8 (dir.: Würzenbach) to "Verkehrshaus." This campsite near the lake has all the amenities, including laundry (wash 2SFr; drying 1SFr), snack bar, and a variety of fresh baked breads on request (2.60-5.60SFr). Showers 0.50SFr per 3min. Reception and snack bar daily 8:30-11:30am and 3-8pm. Open Mar. 15-Oct. 7.70SFr per person, children 3.50SFr; tent and car 5SFr each. ❶

CENTRAL
SWITZERLAND

 FOOD

Markets along the river sell cheap fresh goods on Tuesday and Saturday mornings. Supermarkets and department stores offer the cheapest restaurant meals. A 24hr. vending machine is also available on the lower level of the main train station.

Mr. Pickwick Pub, Rathausquai 6 (☎410 59 27), in the *Altstadt* between the Kapellbrücke and Rathaus Steg bridge, offers some of the cheapest fare of the restaurants lining the *Reuss*. Order fish 'n' chips (15.50SFr) or an English chicken curry sandwich (6.50SFr) at the bar. BBC sports on the television. Hotel upstairs. Entrees 15.50-17.50SFr. Sandwiches 5.50-7.50SFr. Large selection of beer on tap and in bottles starting at 4.50SFr. (Guiness 5SFr.) Open 11:30am-12:30am. AmEx/DC/MC/V. ❷

Kam Tong Chinese Take Away, Inselquai 10 (☎218 58 50 or 532 31 54). Turn right in front of the station and right on Inselquai (10min. from Backpackers hostel) to reach this dim, red-paper-decorated eatery that serves large portions of cheap, tasty Asian fare and snacks to go. The sunny staff serves up most meals for 12-17SFr. Chicken with cashews 16SFr. Vegetable lo mein 12SFr. Wheelchair-accessible. Open M-W 9am-6:30pm, Th-F 9am-9pm, Sa 9am-4pm. ❷

Traffic, the train station caféteria, provides a large selection in a businesslike atmosphere that is surprisingly clean and pleasant. *Cordon bleu* with *rösti* is 10.80SFR, Asian stir-fry dish is 12.50SFr. Many *à la carte* items are also available (roll and coffee, 3.20FSr). Wheelchair-accessible. Open daily 6:30am-9:15pm. ❶

Ristorante La Gondola, Weinmarkt 3 (☎410 61 15), offers fine Italian cuisine in the heart of Lucerne's *Altstadt*. An efficient staff serves large pizzas for 13.50-26SFr and pastas 14.50-29.50SFr. Soups for 7SFr. Menu in English, and so is a lot of the converastion. Open M-Sa 11am-2:30pm and 6pm-midnight. AmEx/DC/MC/V. ❸

Nölliturm, St. Karlistr. 2 (☎240 28 66), on the *Altstadt* side of the Geissmatt bridge. Cheap, hearty Swiss specialties with bowling (20SFr per hr.; reserve in advance). *Rösti Bernois* (with bacon and onions) 15.50SFr. *Nölliteller* (selection of meats and cheeses) 13.50SFr. Open M and W-Su 8am-12:30am. AmEx/MC/V. ❷

Heini Bakery, at Löwenpl. and Falkenpl. (☎412 20 20), is locally famous for the 20 types of dense, flaky-crusted tarts it prepares each day (4.10-4.90SFr), good for meals or desserts. Also try the *Älplermakkronen* (Swiss mac 'n cheese, 13.30SFr) or the *Heini* plate with vegetable *Strudel* and salad (13.90SFr). Wheelchair-accessible. At Löwenpl., open M-F 6am-6:30pm, Sa 6am-5pm, Su 9am-6pm. At Falkenpl., M-F 8am-8pm, Sa 8am-6pm, Su 9am-6pm. AmEx/DC/MC/V only at Falkenpl. ❷

MARKETS

Migros, 2 locations: at the station, and at Hertensteinstr. 44. Both open M-W and Sa 6:30am-8pm, Th-F 6:30am-9pm, Su 8am-8pm. Restaurant in Hertensteinstr. location.

Müller Reformhaus, at the corner of Weinmark and Kornmarkt near the Picasso Museum, sells a large selection of organic foods. Open M and W-F 9am-6:30pm, Tu 8:30am-6:30pm, Sa 8:30am-4pm.

 SIGHTS & MUSEUMS

THE OLD CITY. The *Altstadt* is famous for its frescoed houses, especially those of Hirschenpl. and Weinmarkt. It is also known for the gorgeous bridges over the river. The **Kapellbrücke,** a 660-year-old wooden roofed bridge, connects the *Altstadt* to Bahnhofstr. It was accidentally set on fire by a barge in 1993, but proud citizens restored it within a few months. Over the years, its octagonal tower has served as a watchtower, jail, torture chamber, and guildhall. Further down the river, the **Spreuerbrücke** offers an image of what the *Kapellbrücke* looked like before the fire. Both bridges have painted triangle ceiling supports; those on the Spreuer allow you to confront your mortality in Kaspar Meglinger's eerie *Totentanz* (Dance of Death) paintings. On the hills above the river, the **Museggmauer** and its towers are all that remain of the medieval city's ramparts. They still define the city skyline, especially when illuminated at night. The *Schirmerturm*, *Männliturm*, and *Zeitturm* towers are accessible to visitors. *(Open in summer 8am-7pm.)* The **Zeitturm** (clock tower) provides a particularly pleasing panorama of the city, although closed windows and graffiti preclude photo-ops. *(From the station head left along the river and cross the Spreuerbrücke, the second wooden bridge. Walk left along St. Karli-Quai, turn right going uphill, and follow the brown castle signs.)*

■**PICASSO MUSEUM.** A stroll through the museum's three floors reveals an intimate and often funny side of Picasso's daily life, as captures in over 200 photographs by his longtime close friend David Duncan. Picasso is shown delicately sucking the last pieces of fish from a skeleton, trying his foot at ballet, and creating some of his finest works. A large collection of unpublished Picasso lithographs, drawings, and paintings are also on display. Guidebooks in English and French. *(Am Rhyn Haus, Furreng. 21. From Schwanenpl., take Rathausquai to Furreng. Next to the Rathaus. ☎410 17 73 or 410 35 33; fax 10 45. Open Apr.-Oct. daily 10am-6pm; Nov.-Mar. F-Su 11am-noon and 2-5pm. 8SFr, with guest card 6SFr, students 5SFr. Inquire about the Combination ticket with the Sammlung Rosengart.)*

■**VERKEHRSHAUS DER SCHWEIZ (TRANSPORT MUSEUM).** Climb into bigrigs and jet planes or go for a virtual reality ride, but make sure not to miss the train exhibits. Even the children's train chugging around the floor is an authentic steam engine. Learn about balloon flight and get a view of the city on the *Hiflyer*, or plan your next day in Switzerland on the largest aerial photograph of the country. Call ahead or pick up an exhaustive brochure with a schedule of special tours, lectures, and exhibitions, including a ride through the inner workings of tunnel construction. The museum also has a planetarium and Switzerland's only IMAX theater. *(Lidostr. 5. ☎370 44 44; www.verkehrshaus.org; IMAX reservations ☎375 75 75; www.imax.ch. Take bus #6, 8, or 24 to "Verkershaus" or walk along the Nationalquai for 20min. Wheelchair-accessible. Open daily Apr.-Oct. 10am-6pm; Nov.-Mar. 10am-5pm. Museum 21SFr, guest card holders and students 19SFr, children 6-16 12SFr, under 6 free, with SwissPass 16SFr, with Eurail 14SFr. IMAX 16SFr. Both 31SFr. Hiflyer daily 11am-5pm and night flights June-Aug. F-Sa 7-10pm. 20SFr, children under 17 15SFr, family 50SFr.)*

LÖWENDENKMAL AND GLACIER GARDEN. Danish sculptor Bertel Thorvaldesen carved the magnificent Löwendenkmal (Lion Monument), the dying lion of Lucerne, out of a cliff on Denkmalstr. The 9m monument honors the Swiss Guard who defended Marie Antoinette to the death at the Tuileries in 1792. Mark Twain described it as "the saddest and most moving piece of rock in the world." From the station, take bus #1 to Lowenpl., or walk across Seebrücke to Schwanenpl., follow Schweizerhofquai to the right, and turn left on Denkmalstr. The *Gletschergarten* (Glacier Garden), a lunar landscape of smooth sculpture-like rocks, lies up the stairs from the monument. A kitschy but interesting museum takes you through a mishmash of Lucerne history and leads to the disorienting *Spiegellabyrinth* (mirror maze) next door. The maze has been called "the finest mirror maze in the world today" by World Mazes Magazine, and they should know. (☎ 410 43 40; fax 43 10. Ask at desk for wheelchair-accessible entrance. Parking available. Open daily Apr.-Oct. 9am-6pm; Nov.-Mar. 10am-5pm; 9SFr, with guest card 7.50SFr, students 7SFr, children under 16 5.50SFr. AmEx/MC/V.)

RICHARD WAGNER MUSEUM. The famous composer's once-secluded lakeside home is now an exhibit of original letters, scores, and instruments. His years in Lucerne, the "Tribschen years" (1866-1872), were marked by productivity and personal happiness—it was here that he married Cosima von Bülow. (☎ 360 23 70. Wagnerweg. 27. Take bus #6, 7, or 8 to "Wartegg." or turn right from the station and follow directions to Backpackers. Walk 10min. past Backpackers hostel along the lake until you reach the small marina. Go past the marina building to the right and walk uphill on the wooded trail 5min., following the brown signs. Parking available. Open mid-Mar. to Nov. Tu-Su 10am-noon and 2-5pm. 5SFr, students and guest card holders 4SFr.)

KUNSTMUSEUM LUZERN. Housed within the futuristic Lucerne Culture and Conference Center, the Lucerne Museum of Art is home to temporary modern art exhibits. 2003 saw an array of unique creations, including a collection of "walk-in paintings," sculptures one could sit in, and a large exhibit exploring the "shifting boundaries of the self." (Europapl. 1, next to the train station. ☎ 226 78 00; www.kunstmuseumluzern.ch. Wheelchair-accessible. Literature in English. Open Tu-Su 10am-5pm, W and Th 10am-8pm. 10SFr, students and guest card holders 8SFr. AmEx/MC/V.)

SAMMLUNG ROSENGART LUZERN. The Rosengart Collection is the newest addition to Lucerne's cultural offerings. This three-story collection displays works of 20th century artists Mirò, Renoir, Kandinsky, Chagall, and Matisse. Bottom floors are dedicated to Picasso and Klee. Museum staff suggests visiting the Picasso Museum first, "to get to know him," then a visit to the Rosengart Collection. (Pilatusstr. 10, left from the train station. ☎ 220 16 60; www.rosengart.ch. Open daily Apr.-Oct. 10am-6pm; Nov.-Mar. 11am-5pm. 14SFr, students 9SFr, children 5SFr. Prices reduced by 2SFr with guest card. Inquire about Combi-ticket with the Picasso Museum.)

JESUITENKIRCHE. Left from the station down Bahnhofstr., after the Kapellbr. The twin steeples of the Jesuit Church are a well-known element of the Lucern skyline. Within the church, ornate pink-and-white frescoes and a massive front altar are accented by eight equally ornate side altars, all Baroque pieces telling a different Biblical story. (www.jesuitenkirche-luzern.ch. Open daily 7am-7pm.)

CHATEAU GÜTSCH AND GÜTSCHWALD. Head left down Bahnhofstr. until it becomes Baselstr. About 50m past the Daily Internet Café, take a left onto Gibraltarstr. and an immediate right onto Gütschweg. This takes you by foot (10min.) up the hill to Chateau Gütsch, a Cinderella's castle-hotel with gardens and fountains, though its main selling point is a great view of Lucerne below. An alternative to the top is to ride 15min. on the Gütschbahn funicular. (3SFr, children 2SFr; official transportation passes not applicable.) Check with the tourist office to see if tours of the grounds are available; the hotel was closed in summer 2003.

⚠ OUTDOOR ACTIVITIES

The cheapest option for getting out on the **Vierwaldstättersee** (Lake Lucerne) is to take one of the **ferries** that serve the tiny villages around the lake. Not only can you enjoy the magnificent scenery without exerting yourself, but you can also disembark at any one of the lakeside villages to explore further. The tourist office in the station has a much more user-friendly timetable than the one the ship office provides; it includes information on roundtrip tours ranging from one hour to five. In the shadows of Mt. Pilatus, the glass-blowers at **Hergiswil** have been creating works of art in their boiling-hot oven room since

1817. At the **Glasi Hergiswil** complex, stroll through the museum and exhibits devoted to glass musical instruments and physics experiments. Around the lake, glass art objects and water toys can entertain kids while adults sip beer from foot-tall Hergiswall glass flutes. (1hr. boat ride from Luzern, 10min. by train. ☎630 12 23; www.glasi.ch. Complex open M-F 9am-6pm, Sa 9am-4pm. Glass exhibitions M-F 9:30am-5pm and 5:30-6pm, Sa 9:30am-noon. Free) A short scenic hike at **Bürgenstock** via **Kehrsiten** (round-trip 2hr., 44SFr) is popular with families; visitors will find five of Central Switzerland's lakes at their feet. For an easy walk along the lake, get off the ferry at **Weggis** (round-trip 2hr., 23SFr). **SGV** boats depart from the piers in front of the train station (☎367 67 67; www.lakelucerne.ch; SwissPass and Eurail valid.) Catch one of the five steam ships still fully operational, the internal workings of which are displayed. On the **Wilhelm Tell Express,** a bugle-playing sailor may accompany your journey with a jaunty rendition of the famous Overture.

Lucerne's adventure provider **Outventure** (☎611 14 41; www.outventure.ch) provides outdoor thrills with local flair. This mid-sized company has grown from the original Mountain Guides Office to a full-service adventure company with **paragliding** (150SFr), **canyoning** (200SFr), **glacier hiking** (170SFr), and **bungee jumping** (160SFr). Outventure is a member of the Swiss Outdoors Association, a group which maintains safety and training standards. Daily shuttle from the tourist office at 8:30am. Book in advance. In winter, ski-loving locals flock to the Engelberg-Titlis slopes to snowboard, ski, and otherwise frolic on the glacier. A few slopes are open year-round. See **Engleberg-Titlis** below for more information.

ENTERTAINMENT

The city of Lucerne is alive with a full calender of concerts, festivals, and sporting events. Get a monthly schedule at the tourist office so you don't miss anything. In the third week of July, Lucerne attracts big names for its summer **Blue Balls Festival** (yup) and fall **Blues Festival** (second week in Nov.). In 2003, Roy Hargrove, Bonnie Raitt, Herbie Hancock, Cassandra Wilson, the Original Blues Brother Band, and Van Morrison all performed at Blue Balls. (☎/fax 227 10 58; www.blueballs.ch.) The **Lucerne Festival** runs mid-August to mid-September. The festival celebrates classical music but also features contemporary world music. (☎226 44 8; Lucerne Festival, P.O. Box, CH-6002 Luzern. Tickets 20-220SFr.) The **Nationalquai** is the scene for free summertime **Pavillon Musik** concerts, featuring brass and jazz bands playing Hollywood tunes, Gershwin, and Duke Ellington most Tu, F, and Su nights May-Sept. **Open Air Kino Luzern** (www.open-air-kino.ch), at the outdoor theater in the Seepark near Backpackers hostel Luzern, shows movies (15SFr), mostly in English, every night mid-July to mid-August. In mid-July, the International Rowing Regatta brings the world's most elite rowers and coxswains together for the **World Cup Finals** on the Rotsee. On Saturdays from 8am-noon, catch the **flea market** (May-Oct.) along Burgerstr. and Reussteg.

NIGHTLIFE

In Lucerne, the locals flock to clubs clustered around Pilatuspl. and down Pilatusstr. (the more modern section of town). Across the river and down Nationalquai, a few other spots around the Casino on Haldenstr. bustle with activity. **Uferlos,** Geissensteinring 14, a Saturday night-only disco in conjuction with HALU (see p. 398), is Lucerne's only self-proclaimed BGLT option. Check the monthly calender—the events range from women-only nights to themed parties.

Club 57, Haldenstr. 57, a 15min. walk down Haldenstr. from the Schweizerhofquai under the Carlton Tivoli Hotel, is replete with candle light and Moroccan red fabric pillows. During the week, 57 plays a hip mixture of jazz and funk; on weekends, DJs spin. ☎262 06 06. Beer 4-6SFr. Open 8pm-2:30am, F-Sa 8pm-4am.

The Loft, Haldenstr. 21 (☎410 92 44; www.theloft.ch), is a trendy new club with hip-hop in a cloud of smoke. Thursday is pure R&B; the Loft also hosts special DJs and theme nights constantly. Open W-Th 10pm-3am and F-Su 9pm-4am. No cover W and Su, Th 10SFr, F 12SFr, Sa 15SF; no cover until 11:30pm. Beer from 6SFr; Su women get 1 free drink. Across the street, the recently-opened **Grand Casino Luzern,** Haldenstr. 6 (☎418 56 56; www.casinoluzern.ch), offers poker, craps, and 218 slot machines. Minimum age 20. Bring a passport. Open daily noon-4am.

Jazz Cantine, Grabenstr. 8 (☎410 73 73). A product of the Jazz School of Lucerne, an almost daily stream of diploma concerts and jam sessions (usually starting at 7pm) grooves in front of a laid-back audience of locals. The outdoor seating is great people-watching, as tourists stream from nearby Löwenpl. Sandwiches 6-8SFr. Thai noodles 15SFr. Coffee 3.20SFr, beer 3.70SFr. Wheelchair-accessible. Open M-Sa 7am-12:30am, Su 4pm-12:30am; food served from 11:30am-2pm and 6:30-10pm.

Pravda, Pilatusstr. 29 (☎226 88 88; www.pravda.ch), jams to R&B, hip-hop, and house. On weekends an older, classier set kicks it with house spun by local DJs. Beer 10SFr, a wide selection of vodka 7.50-8SFr. 18+. 3SFr required bag/coat check. W-Th no cover, Fr.-Sa 20SFr cover. Open W 10pm-2:30am, Th 10pm-3am, F-Sa 10pm-4am.

The Penthouse (☎226 88 88; www.astoria-luzern.ch) is in the Hotel Astoria, seven floors up and eye-to-eye with Lucerne's steeples. The sleek rooftop bar waters a casual, international crowd. Beer (8SFr) and other drinks rise in price after 9pm. Every Thursday from 6pm is the "After-Work Party." DJs spin Th-Sa (no house or techno), and Su is the self-proclaimed "Chill-out Night." Wheelchair-accessible. 20+. No cover. Open Su-Tu 5pm-12:30am, W-Sa 5pm-2:30am. AmEx/DC/MC/V.

Schüür, Tribschenstr. 1 (☎368 10 30; www.schuur.ch), hosts a variety of themed nights and concerts, ranging from "Salsa Fest" to a "Pleasure HEADbangerparty." Follow Zentralstr. along the train tracks, turn left onto Lagensandbr. The club is on the left, on the other end of the bridge. Beer 5SFr. Open Th 8:30pm-2:30am, F-Sa 8:30pm-3:30am.

◗ DAYTRIPS FROM LUCERNE

Lucerne's most renowned daytrips are excursions to the mountains that haunt the city's skyline. The trip up is as memorable as the view from the top. Don't expect true Swiss countryside on these trips—you'll see few cows—but routes are well-touristed for good reason: Mt. Titlis is the highest point in central Switzerland, and Pilatus has the highest vista, though views from nearby Rigi are almost as rewarding. If you want to do two or more mountain excursions, consider the cost-effective **Tell-Pass.** One ticket grants the user two days of free travel, and half-price for another five (135SFr, 108SFr with SwissPass); the other ticket gives five days of free travel, plus 10 at half-price (184SFr, 147SFr with SwissPass). The pass is sold at the tourist office and at Pier 1. It is also valid for all cable cars, cogwheel trains, boats, buses, and regular trains in central Switzerland. One section of the Titlis route, however, is only half-price for Tell-Pass holders (25SFr).

MOUNT PILATUS

*The most memorable travel route begins with the 1½hr. boat ride from Lucerne to Alpnachstad, ascends with the steepest **cogwheel train** in the world (48° gradient), descends by cable car to Krienz, and takes the bus back to Lucerne (entire trip 3hr.;*

78.40SFr, with Eurail 43SFR, with SwissPass 40.60SFr). It is slightly cheaper if riding the cable car both ways. It is possible to cut down on the price by hiking: take the train or boat to Hegiswil and hike 3hr. up the hillside to Fräkmüntegg, a half-way point on the cable car (23SFr to Hergiswill, SwissPass and Eurail valid. 22SFr round-trip from Fräkmuntegg to the top). The hike offers constant views of the lake and Lucerne. In the summer, Fräkmüntegg operates central Switzerland's longest Rodelbahn course. For 7SFr, you can whizz down the hillside on a metal track, riding a plastic slide that achieves surprising speeds. Half the fun is being hauled back up to the top by a ski-lift type device. Wait a long time after the person ahead of you takes off before you slide down so that they do not slow you down in your descent. For more information on the Pilatus excursions, contact the Pilatus Railway ☎329 11 11; www.pilatus.com.

As hulking as the enormous dragons supposedly spotted here in the 15th century, **Mt. Pilatus** stretches 2132m (7000ft) to the top of Lucerne's southern sky.

I SPY The imposing facade of Mt. Pilatus has spawned numerous myths. The most oft-told, and the source of the mountain's name, says that the infamous Pontius Pilate was buried on the mountain. Each year on Good Friday, Pilate would emerge from the grave to wash his bloodied hands in the lake below. Any attempts to challenge Pilate's dominion brought storms of fury, so climbing the mountain was prohibited. In 1585, a priest and a few townsmen decided to test the story by going into the foothills and creating a ruckus. When there was no retribution, the spell was declared broken. Since then, there have been numerous Pilate sightings, so go at your own risk.

Numerous quick jaunts to the various craggy promontories are possible from the station and restaurant at the top. The easy and popular "Dragon Trail" tunnels in and out of the mountain and has displays that explain Mt. Pilatus's religious- and dragon-related history. The trip up the mountain—which, depending on your route, uses four different types of transportation—is at least half the fun.

ENGELBERG & MOUNT TITLIS ☎041

Take the train from Lucerne to Engelberg (1hr., 6:30am-11:32pm, 15.40SFr) and the cable car from Engelberg to Titlis. First ascent from Engelberg 8:30am, last ascent from Engelberg 3:40pm, last descent from Titlis 4:20pm; 76SFr, 60.80SFr with Eurail, 68.40SFr with Engelberg guest card, 57SFr with SwissPass; round-trip special 88SFr, 60.80SFr with Eurail, 57SFr with SwissPass. Guided tours available from Lucerne (including round-trip rail and Titlis fares 95SFr, same discounts). The mountain is completely wheelchair-accessible. AmEx/DC/MC/V accepted at ticket counter.

Near the small town of **Engelberg,** south of Lucerne, the world's first revolving cable car climbs to the crest of **Mt. Titlis** (3020m), the highest outlook point in central Switzerland. The ride gives views of the crevasses below and peaks above. If a revolving car at 10,000ft. gives you chills, don't worry—the cabin makes only one complete rotation during the trip. Stop halfway up (your ticket does not go bad) at Trübsee and stroll along the easy walking paths with rustic scenery, a gushing waterfall, and magnificent reflections of the mountains in the lake. Then continue to the summit, which has an active glacial outpost, with observation deck and restaurant, glacial grotto, free tube and scooter rides down an ice slide (the scooter is faster and more fun), and free guided **glacier hikes** to the peak of the mountain. (3hr. Late June to mid-Oct. Tu 9am. Reserve at the tourist office.) To avoid uncomfortably crowded cable car rides with lots of fellow travelers, plan your ascent and descent for off-peak hours—

ascend early in the morning (before 10 or 11am), and try to avoid the last two descending rides of the day. Wear layers and appropriate footwear. Titlis has snow year-round, and a few runs are maintained for skiing and snowboarding during the summer. Rentals are available at the Engleberg base station through the Solomon Snow Shop. (For winter activities, get the comprehensive *Winterfaszination* guide from the tourist office, which outlines the locations, prices, and opening hours of the region's slopes.)

Northeastern Switzerland

NORTHEASTERN SWITZERLAND

Encompassing the cantons of Schaffhausen, St. Gallen, Thurgau, Glarus, and Appenzell, Northeastern Switzerland contains some of the country's best-preserved towns. Stein am Rhein invites visitors to its medieval *Altstadt*, while Appenzell maintains the farmhouses and agricultural lifestyle that made Switzerland what it is. The region is also geographically diverse, with highlights including the waterfalls near Schaffhausen and mountains that surround Appenzell.

HIGHLIGHTS OF NORTHEASTERN SWITZERLAND

Experience Switzerland at its small-town quaintest in **Stein am Rhein** (see p. 411).

Sample **Appenzell's** uniquely pungent and potent local *Bitter* liqueur (see p. 417).

Go medieval while browsing priceless tomes in **St. Gallen's** *Stiftsbibliothek* (see p. 416).

SCHAFFHAUSEN   ☎ 052

In this region, the Untersee serves as the border between Germany and Switzerland. Schaffhausen, however, sits on the German side of the lake, the reason for the United States' accidentally bombing it during WWII. Remarkably, much of the medieval *Altstadt* survived the bombardment. Frescoes, architecture, and fountains dating to the 15th century decorate much of the Schaffhausen. The **Munot Fortress,** built in the 1500s, stands tall and valiant above the city. However, a complete absence of attacks proved it rather unnecessary, and the citizens apparently used the time spared from military operations to kick back—the local *Falkenbier* is reputedly the best in the canton. A mug or two of the bold brew will put you in a prime mood to enjoy Schaffhausen's ambience.

⊟ TRANSPORTATION. If you're in the mood for exploration, consider a **Tageskarte** (29SFr), which allows one day of unlimited travel on Bodensee area railways, waterways, and roadways. **Trains** depart from Schaffhausen to Kreuzlingen (50min., 1-2 per hr. 6am-11:05pm, 16.20SFr); St. Gallen (1½hr., 1-3 per hr. 5:45am-10:45pm, 26SFr); Winterthur (30min., 1-3 per hr. 5:27am-11:09pm, 17.20SFr); Zurich (25min., 1-3 per hr. 5:27am-12:18am, 17.20SFr). Numerous **ferries** traverse the Bodensee, departing from Schaffhausen (from Freiepl., below Festung Munot) to Konstanz and Stein am Rhein (4 per day, May 1-July 4 and Sept.-Oct. 5 9:10am-3:10pm, Jul 5-Sept. 7, 1 per day to Konstanz; 19.60SFr). **Parking** is in the garage off Rheinstr., in lots near the cathedral, off Moeratz, and behind the station on Spitalgasse (5SFr per day). **Maps** are available at main station.

PRACTICAL INFORMATION. The **tourist office**, Fronwagpl. 4, looks out onto the lively Fronwagpl. at the head of Vordenstr., to the right. From the station, head down Schwertstr. (the narrow street to the right of the post office), and turn right at the fountain in the main square. Walk through the main square and the office is just behind the second large fountain. The office gives city tours in German, French, or English. (☎625 51 41; www.schaffhausen-tourismus.ch. Open Oct.-May M-F 9:30am-12:30pm and 1:30-5pm, Sa 9:30am-1:30pm; June-Sept. M-F 9:30am-6pm, Sa 9:30am-4pm, Su (July and Aug. only) 9:30am-3:30pm. Tours Apr.-Oct. Tu, Th, Sa 2pm; 1hr. 12SFr, children 6SFr.) At the station are **currency exchange** (open daily 5:45am-8:10pm), **bike rental** (from 30SFr per day with photo ID, 25SFr with SwissPass; 6SFr extra to return bike at another station) and **luggage storage** (open M-F 8am-7pm, Sa-Su 9am-12:15pm and 1:15-6pm; 5SFr) on the far left side. **Lockers** cost 4-6SFr, with 24hr. access. **Energie Punkt** (Vorderg. 38; ☎052 635 11 00), right across from St. Johannkirche, offers two free **Internet** terminals. (Open M-F 9am-6pm, Sa 10am-2pm.) The **post office** faces the station on Bahnhofstr. (Open M-F 7:30am-6:30pm, Sa 8am-12:30pm.) **Postal code:** CH-8200.

⌂▢ ACCOMMODATIONS & FOOD. Jugendherberge Belair (HI) ❷, Randenstr. 65, lies in the newer (i.e. early 19th-century) section of Schaffhausen. Take bus #6 (dir.: Neuhasen SBB) to "Hallenbad" and find the hostel across the street from the bus stop (M-Sa 3 per hr. 6am-8pm). Once the rich family Maier hosted Japanese painters and writer Herman Hesse here; now, school groups and backpackers fill its shady paths and volleyball court. Two horses graze in the backyard. (☎625 88 00; www.youthhostel.ch/schaffhausen. Breakfast and sheets included. Kitchen available. Keys available. No smoking. Reception 8-10am and 5-9pm. Check-out 9:30am. Dorms 25SFr; singles 31SFr; doubles 63SFr; non-members add 6SFr. MC/V.) Those just seeking a restful night away from town should head to **Lowen ❹,** a small guesthouse just outside of Schaffhausen. Take bus #5 to the last stop, "Herblingen Hirschen" (dir.: Herblingen.) Facing the same direction, turn right and head uphill for 3min. The hotel is on your right. (☎643 22 08; call ahead to book one of the six rooms or have the tourist office do it for you. Breakfast, towels, and sheets included. Singles 75SFr; doubles 120SFr). **Camping Rheinwiesen ❶** stands at the edge of the Rhine, 2.5km from Schaffhausen. Take the train (dir.: Kreuzlingen) to "Langwiesen," and you'll be able to see the campground on the far left along the waterfront; it's about a 20min. walk from there. (☎659 33 00; www.campingtcs.ch. Apr. 27-Sept. 29 4.40SFr, children 2.20SFr; tents 5.50SFr. June 30-Aug. 31 6.40SFr, children 3.20SFr; tents 7.50SFr. Prices may vary; check web. AmEx/DC/MC/V.)

The Fronwagpl. comes alive during the day with outdoor cafés, inexpensive food vendors, restaurants, and live entertainment ranging from mimes to fire-breathers. The blue-shuttered **Restaurant Thiergarten ❸,** on Münsterpl. across from the Allerheiligen Monastery, offers a traditional Swiss appetizer, entree, or dessert from each of the nation's 26 cantons. Large portions of cheese from Appenzell (7.50SFr), Freiburg fondue (19.50SFr), or *Kässerösti* (hash browns drowned in cheese; 17.50SFr) from the Wallis region will fill you up. A changing array of ethnically-themed dishes ranging from Thai to Mexican round out the menu. (☎ 625 32 88; www.thiergarten.ch. Wheelchair-accessible. Children's menu available, as well as special group rates. Dish descriptions in English. Parking nearby. Open daily 9am-11pm. AmEx/DC/MC/V.) Health- and environmentally-conscious locals meet at **Zur Flamme ❷,** Vorstadt 9, a purely vegetarian and non-GMO establishment. (Open M-Sa 11am-2:30pm and 6-11pm. Closed M evening and Sa afternoons.) For take-out, try **Chinatown ❷,** Vorstadt 36, ideal for those wanting a quick bite of traditional Chinese take-out in sunny outdoor seating. Add 1-2SFr. for dining in. Dishes are 17.50SFr and under. (☎ 624 46 77; fax 47 44. Open daily 11am-11pm.) **Migros,** Bahnhofstr. 58, to the left of the station, has a restaurant as well. (Open M-W and F 8:15am-6:30pm, Th 8:15am-8pm, Sa 8am-4pm.) Stock up on produce at the **open market** (Tu and Sa 11am outside the Johannkirche) and at the **farmer's market** (F 9am-noon and 1:30-5:30pm, and Sa 8-11am; at the corner of Kirchhofplatz near Johannkirche). There's also **Aperto,** in the station, for basic conveniences. (Open M-Sa 6am-9:30pm, Su 7am-9:30pm.)

◎ SIGHTS. Throughout the *Altstadt,* Schaffhausen's classically Swiss streets, narrow and winding, are lined with frescoes, fountains, and woodcarvings. For impressive Renaissance-era murals, try the **Haus zum Ritter** (Vorderg. 65). A military installment dating from the 10th century, **Festung Munot** (Munot Fortress) now hosts tourists and a deer colony. After climbing a steep flight of stone steps from the town, you are treated to views of the Rhine and Schaffhausen's rooftops. The surrounding vineyard and Swiss rose garden (it blossoms in the summer) offer restful benches. (Turn right at the head of Schwertstr., then left onto Vorderg., continuing until you see signs to the fortress. Wheelchair-accessible, but steep. Open daily May-Sept. 8am-8pm; Oct-Apr. 9am-5pm. Free.) The nearby **Allerheiligen Monastery,** features the **Kloster Allerheiligen** (All Saints Monastery), whose hallways wind their way around a healthy herb garden and large enclosed courtyard. Within the cloister, you'll find the **Museum zum Allerheiligen,** which encompasses a **Natural History Museum** and exhibits by the **Kunstverein Schaffhausen** (Art Museum). This museum exhibits everything from stuffed boars to modern art, plus a display of Roman and German artifacts, and objects from the 11th-century abbey, including thousand-year-old illuminated manuscripts. (From the station, take Schwertstr. up to Vorderg., then turn right onto Münsterg. ☎ 633 07 77; www.allerheiligen.ch. Signs in German only. Open Tu-Su 11am-5pm. Free.) An old warehouse converted into four floors of permanent gallery space for 14 avant-garde artists, the **Hallen Für Neue Kunst** (Hall for Modern Art), is littered with massive, seemingly indecipherable shapes, colors, and sounds. (Baumgartenstr. 23, across the street from Kloster Allerheiligen. ☎ 052 625 25 15; www.modern-art.ch. Guidebook available in English. Open daily Tu-Sa 3-5pm, Su 11-5pm; tours Su 11:30am. 14SFr, students 8SFr.)

▶ DAYTRIP FROM SCHAFFHAUSEN

RHEINFALLS
The Rheinfalls are just a 10min. train ride from Schaffhausen. Take the train headed for Winterthur to Schloß Laufen am Rheinfall (2 stops on Schaffhausen). From the train

THE LOCAL LEGEND

NO E WILI

Around 1457, the people of Stein am Rhein broke free of their feudal landlords. The question then arose as to which larger group they would cast their lot with—would they join the Austrian Hapsburgs or the burgeoning confederation of city-state cantons then forming into Switzerland? The mean-spirited mayor of the town, Laitzer, opted for the former, and invited the Hapsburgs to take control of his town.

As the legend goes, one night, ships full of Hapsburg soldiers came sailing into the city. An apprentice working the graveyard shift at the bakery saw the lights along the Rhein. When the Austrians called on him to surrender, he responded with *"No e Wili"* ("just a moment"), and alerted everyone in the town to the impending invasion. The townsfolk somehow managed to fend off the Austrians, and later happily joined the new *Eidgenossenschaft* of Switzerland. To get rid of the bad Bürgermeister, they decided to make him "Drink the Rhein," i.e., be put in a sack and tossed into the river.

Though the story is probably a little apocryphal—it is a common *mordnacht* (murder night) narrative similar to that of Zürich—and was most likely invented by local Heinrich Waldvogel during the Depression, the event is re-enacted every few years by a cast of several hundred.

www.steinamrhein.ch. The next performance is in 2007.

stop, walk up the stairs to the left. At the immediate fork in the stairs, continue up to the right, walking through the village and following the signs to the falls. Take the left fork and walk downward to see the falls and avoid the 1SFr charge at the village entrance.

The **Rheinfalls** are one of Europe's largest sets of waterfalls, though their scope isn't nearly as grand as that designation might lead you to expect. Even though it is no Niagara, the falls still offer a grand display of natural power. Ample viewing spots give families and couples looking for a scenic, quiet daytrip, the chance to get within inches of the rushing water. The falls themselves are a mere 23m in height and gush at a rate of 650 c. m per sec. For a different perspective, boats, operated by **Rhyfall Mändli** (☎ 672 48 11) leave from both the Neuhausen and Schloß Laufen. Taking the short ride (less than 5min.) across the river from Scholß Laufen to Neuhausen expands your options to four different routes (Schloß Laufen has only one); one route drops you off at a rock outcroppings in the middle of the falls themselves. A panoramic viewing platform on the rock provides a close-up view, as the falls crash literally at your feet. (Open daily Apr.-Oct. 11am-5pm; May-Sept. 10am-6pm; June-Aug. 9:30am-6:30pm. 2.50-11SFr, children 1.50-5.50SFr.) A bridge over the falls leads to where, for 1SFr, you can follow winding stairs down the steep face of the hill to the foot of the falls.

In the turrets of Schloß Laufen, **Jugendherberge Schloß Laufen am Rheinfalls (HI) ❷** shelters backpackers and occasional student groups. Take the stairs to the left of the train station, then head right on the winding path. At the road, follow the signs to the falls. Once in the small plaza, the hostel will be on your right. Simple rooms recall the castle's 12th-century origins and offer splendid views of the Rhine. The welcoming couple running the hostel lives in one turret. Reserve a bed in advance because the hostel often fills up with school groups. (☎659 61 52; fax 60 39. Breakfast 7:30-8:30am included for dorms. Kitchen facilities 2SFr. Shower, sinks, and toilets on floor. Sheets provided. Small lockers for day storage. Reception 8-9:30am and 5-9pm. Check-out 10am. Open Mar.-Oct. Dorms 24SFr; quads 138SFr. Non-members add 6SFr.) The **Bannerstube ❷,** in the same building as the hostel, serves a number of reasonably priced dishes, including the acclaimed *Füürtopf à discretion*, an all-you-can-eat meat fondue buffet with salad and wine, 60SFr per person. The terrace has a fantastic view. Soups are 5.50-7.50SFr and pasta dishes start at 13SFr; steak entrees run 25-35SFr. (☎052 659 67 67; fax 052 659 61 95. Children's menu available. Open Mar.-Dec. daily 11:30am-11:30pm.)

STEIN AM RHEIN ☎ 052

The tiny medieval *Altstadt* of Stein am Rhein is postcard-perfect, its traditional Swiss architecture framed by gorgeous green hills and a flowing river. Tourists from nearby Germany and around the world fill the village each summer. Stein am Rhein will put your camera to good use: all the square's houses date back to the 15th century, and are marked by detailed façade paintings of the animal or scene after which each house was named. Beyond the town center, visitors enjoy ferries and the hospitality of local proprietors. As of late, Stein am Rhein has sacrificed some of its quiet and charm by allowing cars to course through the *Altstadt*.

❖❷ TRANSPORTATION & PRACTICAL INFORMATION. Trains connect Stein am Rhein to: Konstanz via Kreuzlingen (40min., 1 per hr. 6:24am-midnight, 9.80SFr); Schaffhausen (2 per hr. 5:28am-10:30pm, 7.20SFr); St. Gallen (1½hr. 1 per hr. 6:56am-5:56pm, 22SFr); Winterthur (45min., 1 per hr. 5:07am-11:07pm, 12.40SFr). **Buses** connect the city to small towns in the area and Germany. **Boats** depart four times per day for Schaffhausen (1¼hr., 19.60SFr), Konstanz (2½hr., 24SFr), and other Bodensee towns. (☎ 052 634 08 88; www.riverticket.ch.) An hour-long cruise on the **St. Georg Ferry**, named after Stein am Rhein's patron saint, costs 12SFr (ages 6-16 6SFr); tickets can be arranged through the Hotel Rheinfels. (☎ 741 21 44 www.rheinfels.ch. The ferry leaves from Schifflande about 3 times daily.)

To reach the city from the station, head straight out of the station onto Bahnhofstr., bearing first right on Wagenhauserstr., and then left on Charreg., which leads over a bridge and into the Rathauspl. in the *Altstadt's* center. Once you turn left and continue walking, Rathauspl. becomes Understadt, the town's main drag. **Parking** is available on all streets skirting the *Altstadt*, and along Hemishoferstr., off Untertor. (0.50SFr per hr., 3SFr per day) Stein am Rhein's **tourist office,** Oberstadt. 3, lies on the other side of the Rathaus. (☎ 742 20 90; fax 052 742 20 91. Open M-F 9:30am-noon and 1:30-5:30pm., July-Aug. also Sa 9:30am-noon and 1:30-4pm, Su 10:30am-12:30pm.) The station has **currency exchange** and **bike rental** (30SFr per day. Open Apr. 1-Oct. 15 M-F 6:15am-7:35pm, Sa 6:15am-6:35pm, Su 7:15am-7:35pm; Oct. 16-Mar. 31 M-F 6:15am-7:10pm, Sa 6:50am-12:10pm and 12:50-5:10pm, Su 8:15-11:35am and 12:50-6:35pm). Lockers 3SFr. **Internet** is in **Kiosk Charregass** (which also serves cheap pizza), Oberstadt 16, past the tourist office, coming from Rathauspl. It's at the end of the street on your right. (Open Tu-F 9am-6:30pm, Sa 9am-4pm; 6SFr per 30min.) Exiting the station, the **post office** is 200m to your right. (Open M-F 7:30-11am and 3-6pm, Sa 8:30am-10:30am.) **Postal code:** CH-8260.

❖❐ ACCOMMODATIONS & FOOD. The family-oriented **Jugendherberge (HI) ❷** is at Hemishoferstr. 87. From the train station, take the bus (#7349, dir.: Singen; M-F on the hr. 7am-10pm; Sa-Su every 1-2hr.) to "Strandbad" and head about 5min. farther in the same direction, walking directly on the road for the last few minutes (please be careful). The hostel is on your left. By foot, the hostel is an enjoyable stroll along the Rhine. Follow the directions to the *Altstadt;* once you cross the bridge, turn left and follow the river for 20min. The hostel fills up quickly, so call ahead. Though not ideally located, it has clean, if small, rooms (many of which overlook the Rhine), a game room, and a helpful staff. Get up early to avoid crowds and clogged showers. (☎ 052 741 12 55; fax 741 51 40. Breakfast, showers, and sheets included. Kitchen access 2SFr. Reception 8-10am and 5-10pm. Curfew 10:30pm; keys available. Open Mar. 1-Nov. Dorms 24.50SFr; doubles 60SFr; family rooms 30SFr per person. Children ages 6-16 accompanied by an adult half price. 3SFr low-season discount. Non-members add 6SFr. AmEx/DC/MC/V.)

THE HIDDEN DEAL

SLEEP IN STRAW

If crisply-made Swiss hotel beds and immaculate hostels have grown a little bland, consider making like Heidi (or Frankenstein's monster) and bedding down for a night in the comfortable straw of an authentic Swiss barn. Started in the Jura some ten years ago to provide novel, back-to-the-roots lodging for cost-conscious Swiss families on their vacations, the *Schlaf im Stroh* ('sleep in straw') program now involves some 240 farms in rural northeastern Switzerland, all of which set aside barn space for travelers eager for a different way to spend their night.

Though, as a rule, all *Schlaf im Stroh* plots are as well-tended and hygienic as everything else in Switzerland, bring bug spray to combat mosquitoes and a thick jacket to ward off any pre-dawn alpine chill. Call ahead to make sure there's space for you, and tell the host farmer about any allergies you may have (believe it or not, substantial accommodations can be made). Ammenities ranging from donkey rides to craft demonstrations vary from farm-to-farm, but the chances of a riveting Swiss sunrise are the same anywhere. For information on other *Schlaf im Stroh* barns, surf to http://www.abenteuer-stroh.ch/en/ or consult brochures available in regional tourist offices.

In the vicinity of Stein am Rhein, *Let's Go* recommends the *Schlaf im Stroh* barn run by Frau

The team of waitresses at the **Rothen Ochsen Wine Bar ❶**, Rathauspl. 9, are dedicated to preserving the tradition connected with their wooden hall, the oldest public house in the town, built in 1466. Though full meals are not available, their wooden seating and traditional Swiss oven keep the ambience decidedly from another century. (☎052 741 23 28; weinstube@rothenochsen.ch. Wheelchair-accessible outdoor seating. Open Tu-Sa 11am-11:30pm, Su 10:30am-6pm.) **The Spaghetteria ❷**, Schifflände 8, sits directly on the Rhine and serves cheap and tasty Italian fare to tourists, families with children, and locals alike (pasta dishes from 13SFr.). The restaurant's special is an all-you-can-eat spaghetti plate with a turntable of six different sauces (24.50SFr per person). (☎741 22 36; fax 741 51 56. English menu and children's menu available. Wheelchair-accessible. Open mid-Mar. to second Su in Nov. daily 9am-around midnight. AmEx/DC/MC/V.) **Café "Zur Hoffnung," ❶** Rathauspl. 21, satisfies a sugar craving with chocolate, fresh-baked pastries, two dozen cakes, and luck-bringing Steiner Scherben. (☎741 21 82. Open Tu-Sa 8am-6pm, Su 9am-6pm.) Picnickers fill their baskets at the **Co-op**, Rathauspl. 17, at the corner of Rathauspl. and Schwarzhorng. (Open M-F 8:30am-6:30pm, Sa 8am-5pm. AmEx/DC/MC/V.)

◗ ♫ SIGHTS & ENTERTAINMENT. The 12th-century establishment of the **Kloster St. George** first made Stein am Rhein prominent. You can reach the Benedictine monastery by heading up Chirchhofpl. from the Rathauspl. The rooms are preserved in their 16th-century state, just as the five-foot-tall monks (judging by the doors) left them, and the cloister exudes a perfect, ascetic peace. Among the ornate wooden engravings, try to find St. George. Less austere is the vibrant *Festsaal*, whose yellow-and-green-tiled floor is off-limits to feet. As lights are few and dim, try to go when it is bright outside for the best view of delicate paintings and engravings. (☎741 21 42. Open Mar.-Oct. Tu-Su 10am-5pm. 3SFr, students 1.50SFr.) Admire the stately **Rathaus** at the corner of Rhig. and Rathauspl.

Museum Lindwurm, Understadt 18, reconstructs 19th-century bourgeois domestic life with careful attention. Details like soil-covered boots in the farmhouse and a scratched chalkboard in the children's room provide a snapshot of daily living; and you can actually try out anything inside. (☎741 25 12. Exhibit placards in multiple languages, including English. Group tours available in English and French with prior reservation. Open Mar.-Oct. M and W-Su 10am-5pm. 5SFr, students 3SFr.)

A 30min. hike will take you up the mountain to a vantage point from the castle on **Hohenklingen.** To reach the trail, follow Brodlaubeg. out of town; signs point the rest of the way. When the trail meets the road near the top, the castle is on the left.

ST. GALLEN ☎ 071

Though it lacks the medieval charm of Schaffhausen, St. Gallen's easy access to Zurich, Germany, Austria, the Bodensee, and small mountain villages makes it a popular stopover for travelers. The relatively modern *Altstadt* livens on weekends when students from St. Gallen University descend from the hill. During the day, the *Altstadt* is also a window shopper's dream but a spender's nightmare. Beyond luxuries, St. Gallen has a few cultural gems to share—particularly the *Stiftsbibliothek*, the Baroque library named a World Heritage Treasure by UNESCO.

▐▀ TRANSPORTATION

Trains: To: **Appenzell** (30min., 1-3 per hr. 5:42am-11:40pm, 10.40SFr); **Bern** (2½hr., 4:36am-11:32pm, 63-65SFr); **Geneva** (4½hr., 4:36am-7:47pm, 94SFr); **Lugano** (4hr., 5:10am-7:02pm, 72-76SFr); **Munich** (3hr.; 4 per day 8:37am-6:37pm; 70SFr, under 26 51SFr); **Zurich** (1hr., 4:36am-11:42pm, 26-34SFr).

Buses: 2.20SFr, ages 6-16 1.30SFr; *Tageskarte* (day pass) 7SFr, ages 6-16 5SFr; 12 rides 22SFr. Buy tickets at each stop or on some buses; passes and *Tageskarten* available at large kiosks or **VBSG Transit Authority** across from train station.

Taxis: Sprenger AG, Rohrschacherstr. 281 (local ☎333 33 33, toll free 08 00 55 10 30).

Herold Taxi AG, Poststr. 11 (☎08 00 82 27 77).

Tixi, wheelchair-accessible taxis (☎244 14 34).

Car Rental: Herold Autovermietung AG, Molkenstr. 7 (☎07 12 28 64 28; fax 64 25). 77SFr per day, 195SFr per weekend. **Europcar,** Neumarkt 1, St.-Leonhardstr. 35 (☎222 11 14; fax 01 57). From 78SFr per day.

Parking: Neumarkt Parking Garage, ☎222 11 14, near the Neumarkt Supermarket on St. Leonhardstr. 5am-9pm 2SFr per hr., 9pm-5am 1SFr per hr. Open M-Sa 5am-12:30am. Park in one of the city's **blue zones** M-F for 5.50SFr per day, Sa-Su free.

Ullman, her son, Christian, and their amiable St. Bernard, Leila, who tends the chicken coop. Sleep earthly yet comfortably covered in fresh straw on a working farm that includes its own apple orchard, grazing cows and cheery barn wih a massive door.

Contact Fra Ullman through the Stein am Rhein tourist office. To get to her barn, ride the local train to the sleepy hamlet of Eschenz (pop. 1600). Press the button to signal that you want to get off—the train won't stop if you don't. From the station, make a left until you hit a bike path. Travel along the path and then follow the arrows on the Schlaf im Stroh signs. A stay with the Ullmans covers a 'farmer's breakfast' that often includes tea made from an on-premise lindenberry tree, and chocolate milk courtesy of the family's ever-obliging cows. Shower 2SFr. Guests 16+ 20SF; children 10-15 pay by the year; 10 and under 10SFr. Expect a 2-3SFr visitor's tax. For a small fee, the Ullmans will also groom your horse, if you have one.)

⚡ PRACTICAL INFORMATION

Tourist Office: Bahnhofpl. 1a (☎227 37 37; www.st.gallen-bodensee.ch). From the train station, walk to the left of the post office, crossing the street with the bus stop on your left. Pass the fountain on the left; the tourist office is on the right. Maps, brochures, and **city tours** available. (June 3-Sept. 30 M, W, F 2-4pm; 15SFr, museum admissions and juice included.) Special night tour around Christmas. Open M-F 9am-6pm, Sa 9am-noon. Phone calls taken M-F 8am-noon and 1:30-5:40pm, Sa 9am-noon.

Currency Exchange: At the station. Open M-F 9am-7pm, Sa 9am-5pm, Su 1-5pm. Services include **Western Union.**

Luggage Storage: At the station. Lockers with 24hr. access, 4-7SFr. Luggage watch 7SFr. Open M-F 8am-7:45pm, Sa-Su 9am-noon and 1:30-7pm. A few cheaper lockers (3SFr) stand at the Appenzeller/Trogen station, across from luggage watch.

Laundromat: Quick Wash, Rorschacherstr. 57. Take bus #1 to "Stadttheater" and on for 5min. Wash 6-7.90SFr, dry 1.80-3.80SFr. Open M-Sa 8am-10pm.

Internet Access: Media Lounge, Katherineng. 10 (☎244 30 90; fax 244 30 91). Facing away from the bus stop at Marktpl., cross at far right onto Katerineng. This hip lounge with pop music offers cheap **Internet** access. 2SFr minimum; after 10min. 1SFr per 5min., 12SFr per 1hr. Open M-F 9am-7 to 8pm, sporadic hours Sa-Su.

STA Travel: Metzgerg. 10, from Markpl. bus station walk to the left of Scala Kino down Metzgerg. STA Travel is on your right, across from Hotel Elite. Open M-F 9:30am-6:30pm, Sa 10am-2pm.

Post Office: On Bahnhofpl., across the street, to the left of the train station. Open M-W and F 7:30am-6:30pm, Th 7:30am-8pm, Sa 7:30am-4pm. **Postal Code:** CH-9001.

⛰ ACCOMMODATIONS

🏅 **Jugendherberge St. Gallen (HI),** Jüchstr. 25 (☎245 47 77; stgallen@youthhostel.ch). Next to the train station, you'll find the small Appenzeller/Trogener station with 2 tracks (#12 and 13). Take the orange train from track #12 (dir.: Speichen and Trogen) to "Schülerhaus" (10min., 2-4per hr. 5:32-11:32am, 2.60SFr). From the stop, walk uphill 6min. on the right, turn left across the train tracks at the sign for the hostel. You can see it at the bottom of the hill; walk another 2min. and the entrance is around the building on the left. This friendly hostel on a hill attracts an international student crowd. Though it's a bit of a hike to get here, the relaxing atmosphere and superb view make up for it. Well-equipped playroom. Extra perks include a breakfast room, terrace, barbecue pit, grassy lawn, library, board games, and TV room. Breakfast, sheets, and shower included. Dinner 12.50SFr. Lockers 2SFr deposit. Laundry 6SFr to wash, 4SFr to dry. Parking available. 1 room with wheelchair-accessibility. Reception 7-10am and 5-10:30pm. Call ahead. Check-out 10am. 24hr. keycard access. Quiet hours 10pm-7am. Closed Dec. 1-end of Feb. 6-bed dorms 27SFr; 4-bed dorms 32SFr.; 6-bed "family room" with toilet and shower 34SFr per person; singles 48SF; doubles 74SFr. Non-members add 6SFr. AmEx/DC/MC/V. ❷

Hotel Elite, Metzgerg. 9-11 (☎227 99 33; www.hotel-elite-sg.com), on the street by the bus station. Exit station and turn left, staying on the road closest to the train tracks. This road will become Bahnhofst. and then Marktpl. Turn left onto Metzgerg. directly opposite the bus stop. Located near the *Altstadt* and Marktpl., and within walking distance from Museumstr, this hotel offers simple rooms, most with a sink, TV, and chocolate on each pillow. Breakfast included. Doors lock and reception closes at 11pm. Check-out

11am. **Internet** available (10SFr. per hr.). Singles 67-75SFr, with shower 75-80SFr, with toilet and shower 93-110SFr; doubles with shower 124-134SFr, with toilet and shower 146-165SFr. Children 6-12 50% off, 12-16 30% off. AmEx/MC/V. ❹

Hotel Weisses Kreuz, Engelg. 9 (☎/fax 223 28 43; www.a-o.ch/9000-weisseskreuz). Follow directions to Hotel Elite; Engelg. is 1 street left from Metzgerg. Weisses Kreuz sits atop a lively and smoky bar run by a cheerful staff. Rooms are simple (and some cramped), but the location makes this hotel ideal for late-night pub crawlers in the Altstadt. Breakfast and hall showers included. Reception M-Sa 6:30am-2pm and 5-11pm, Su 9-11am. Lockout at 10pm; keys available upon request. Check-out 10am. All singles with shower 61SFr; doubles without shower 115SFr, with shower 135SFr. MC/V. ❸

Hotel am Ring, Unterer Graben 9, (☎223 27 47; hotelamring@bluemail.ch) Situated in a centrally located and historic building, the Hotel am Ring's rooms are as ornate and unique as the extravagantly decorated café downstairs. The owners of 30 yrs. present each guest with a small gift upon departure. Reception open 7:30am-1pm and 5-9:30pm. No lockout. Reservations by fax encouraged. All rooms with shower, toilet, and TV. Breakfast included. Singles 90SFr; doubles 130SFr; triples 180SFr. ❹

🍴 FOOD

Migros, St. Leonhardstr., 1 block behind the train station, has a buffet restaurant in a separate building behind the market. (Market open M-W and F 8am-6:30pm, Th 8am-9pm, Sa 8am-5pm; restaurant open M-W and F 6:30am-6:30pm, Th 6:30am-9pm, Sa 6:30am-5pm. Wheelchair-accessible.) A huge **public market** on Marktpl. bustles with fresh flowers, produce, bread, and meat. (Open M-Sa 8am-8pm.)

🍽 **Restaurant Scheitlinsbüchel,** Scheitlinsbüchelweg 10 (☎/fax 071 244 68 21). Follow the directions to the youth hostel. After walking uphill about 6min., turn right into a small parking lot instead of left at the youth hostel sign. As the road enters the woods, turn left onto the uphill trail and walk on a gradual uphill wooded path about 6min. When you reach the road again, go left and you will be able to see the farmhouse restaurant. The restaurant's terrace provides and amazing view of the surrounding countryside, St. Gallen, and even the Bodensee. Family-oriented in its style. Small cheese and meat plates 14-18SFr. Vegetarian dishes from 18SFr. Meat entrees 22-28SFr. Large ice cream desserts. The terrace is wheelchair-accessible. Garden room for large groups. Small playground for children. Open Tu-Su 9am until when everyone leaves. MC/V. ❸

Christina's, Weberg. 9 (☎223 88 08). Wooden tables and colorful walls provide a suitable backdrop for this bright, modern eatery. Weekly specials, American music, and a bar and dance club that opens up on the weekend (F-Sa 10pm-1am) make Christina's a favorite of locals and tourists alike. Fish lovers should try the homemade *Salmontatar*. Vegetarian and meat dishes from 18.50SFr. Soup or salad with lunch entree is 15-21SFr. Reservations suggested in the winter. Open M-Th 9:30am-11:30pm, F-Sa 9:30am-12:30am. AmEx/MC/V. ❸

Weinstube zum Bäumli, Schmiedg. 18 (☎071 222 11 74), offers Swiss dishes in an intimate setting where many locals sit for hours. Occupying one of the oldest buildings in St. Gallen, this quaint restaurant serves all the *Schnitzel* and *Wurst* you could want. Alternatively, try the traditional *Rösti* (36.50SFr) with fried potatoes, rice, or salad. Don't be shocked if the waiter puts down another plate when you're done with your main course—the restaurant offers a second round as part of your order. Open Tu-Sa 9am-11:30pm. MC/V. ❹

Roggwiller Confiserie and Tea Room, Multerg. 17 (☎222 50 92; www.roggwiller.ch), is a traditional confectionery and tea room. The small confectionery store sells rows of handmade sweets, including the shop's specialty, *St. Gallen Biber* (a combination of marzipan and gingerbread—ask for a sample). In the elegant pink velvet-and-mirrors tea room, couples and friends sip espresso and polish off tall sundaes and other specialty desserts. Teas, juices, and shakes from 4SFr. More elaborate ice cream dishes from 9SFr. Wheelchair-accessible. AmEx/MC/V. ❷

👁 SIGHTS

Aside from the aptly named Museumstraße, where St. Gallen's four museums are located, the city's main attractions are found within the grounds of the St. Gallen Abbey Precinct. Most noteworthy of these attractions are the magnificent *Stiftsbibliothek* and the Kathedrale St. Gallen. From the far left of the station, walk up Bahnhofstr. to Marktpl., then left on Marktg. to reach the abbey.

STIFTSBIBLIOTHEK. Anyone who loves books and medieval culture will marvel at St. Gallen's main attraction, the *Stiftsbibliothek*, the library of the Benedictine abbey at St. Gallen. You'll glide in on huge fuzzy gray slippers (provided by the library to protect the wooden-tiled floors) to a chorus of oohs and aahs at the library's lavishly carved and polished exotic wood shelves, filled with rows of centuries-old, gilt-spined books. The library maintains a collection of 140,000 volumes and 2000 manuscripts, 500 of which date from before AD 1200, including 3rd- and 5th-century texts from Virgil and early Bibles. Although the appearance of the resident death-blackened mummy might indicate otherwise, the *Stiftsbibliothek* is a living, lending library serving scholars from around the globe. (☎ 227 34 16; www.stibi.ch. Wheelchair-accessible. Pamphlets available in English though all displays are in German. Open Apr.-Nov. M-Sa 10am-5pm, Su 10am–4pm. Tours in German daily Apr.-May and Oct. 2pm; June, Sept. 10:30am, 2pm; July-Aug. 10:30am, 2, 3pm. English tours can be arranged through the tourist office. 7SFr, students 5SFr, under 16 free. AmEx/DC/MC/V.)

Other attractions of the abbey include the **Kathedrale St. Gallen,** a part of the abbey founded in the 8th century and renovated in the mid-18th. The cathedral, having undergone a massive renovation in 2003, now has large, clear windows that bathe the Baroque interior in light. The intricate carvings of the confessionals and the details of the murals are not to be missed. (☎ 227 33 88. Open daily 9am-6pm, except during Mass.) The abbey's bright courtyard is ideal for a picnic or sunbath. On the far side of the abbey from the library sits the smaller **St. Laurenzenkirche (Evangelical Church of St. Lawrence),** founded in the 9th century (at which point it was not Evangelical). Its interior showcases organ pipes and intricate wall patterning. On a sunny day, the stained-glass windows create shadows in the church that are worth a visit. Its ornate rooftop is also pretty. (Open M-F 9:30-11:30am and 2-4:30pm.)

MUSEUMSTRAßE. Two buildings side by side hold most of St. Gallen's museum-worthy relics. Though all the information is in German, impressive displays and varied themes make a trip to Museumstr. perfect for kids and adults on a rainy day. The small **Natural History Museum** (☎ 242 06 70; www.naturmuseumsg.ch) rotates thoughtful and interactive exhibits of all Mother Nature's creations. Housed in the same building, the four-room **Kunstmuseum** (☎ 242 06 71; fax 242 06 72) has a small collection that juxtaposes modern and traditional art, including works by Klee, Tinguely, and Picasso. St. Gallen's enormous **Historisches Museum** (☎ 242 06 42; fax 06 44) highlights traditional Swiss culture. Displays include ancient kitchens, an old barber shop, and children's toys. The **Ethnology Collection** (☎ 242 06 43; fax 06 44) presents various foreign cultures, carefully avoiding over-interpretation and allowing authentic artifacts to speak for themselves. (Museumstr. 32-50. From Marktpl., with your back to the bus stop, walk right on Bohl to get to Museumstr. All museums open Tu-F 10am-noon and 2-5pm, Sa-Su 10am-5pm. 6SFr, students 2SFr. 1 ticket grants admission to all 4 museums, except special exhibits in the Kunstmuseum.)

OTHER SIGHTS. For a view of the St. Gallen valley (and perhaps a glimpse of a few endangered species), visit the **Peter and Paul Wildpark**, on Kirchlistr. in Rotmonten. Take bus #5 (dir.: Rotmonten) to "Sonne." Walk in the opposite direction of the bus, turn left at the first intersection onto Kirchlistr. and walk uphill 20min. A well-tended trail leads through the park, ensuring that you don't miss the ibexes, which have made a comeback from near extinction. (☎ 222 67 92 or 244 51 13. Open 24hr. Free.) For a tamer excursion, explore the campus of the **St. Gallen University.**

🎵 🎭 ENTERTAINMENT & NIGHTLIFE

St. Gallen's *Altstadt* resonates with techno beats and the heavy clink of beer mugs. Head for the streets radiating out from Marktpl., which feature cheap, authentic bars frequented by local clientele. Clubs tend to be clustered together, particularly around Goliathg. and Brühlg.

Birreria, Brühlg. 45 (☎ 223 25 33). Homesick travelers longing for familiar alcohol will definitely find it here. With 240 types of beer, from a plain American Budweiser to the African Castle Lager, Birreria lets you take a barley trip around the globe without moving your lazy gut. Drink yours at the bar or take it with you for half-price. Open M-Sa noon-late, Su 5pm-late.

Seeger Bar, Oberer Graben 2 (☎ 222 97 90). A red velvet rope separates you from the passing cars and pedestrians at the Seeger Bar, where fashionable couples and groups go out for an early drink and to while away the hours. The **Seeger Lounge,** upstairs from the bar, is a more intimate setting, with silver velvet couches and pillows. Try the *Panache* (4.25SFr), a smooth, sweet beer with a squirt of lemon added. Open M-W 8:45pm-midnight, Th 8:45pm-1am, F-Sa 8:45pm-3am, Su 10pm-midnight.

La Boheme, Bohl 9. A hip and earthy 20-something crowd packs the bar to enjoy mixed drinks, beer, and an evolving wine list. Open M-Th 5pm-midnight, F 4pm-3am, Sa 1:30pm-3am, Su 7pm-midnight.

Each year, the **Stadttheater,** Museumstr. 24 (☎ 242 06 66; www.theaterstgallen.ch), in a fancy Art Nouveau building, hosts over 200 concerts and dramatic works by renowned artists and musicians. There are also several **movie theaters** at Marktpl. The largest is the **Scala Kinocenter and Bar** (☎ 228 08 60), on the corner of Marktpl. and Goliathg., with five screens. Every year in late July and early August, the **Open-Air Kino** at Kantonschulpark on Burggraben (www.open-air-kino.ch) screens mostly American films (15SFr).

The **Open Air St. Gallen Music Festival** (see "Festival Fever," p. 334) is the oldest open-air music festival in Europe, and features over 20 live bands performing in St. Gallen's field during late June or July. Past headliners have included Metallica, the Red Hot Chili Peppers, the Roots, B.B. King, and James Brown. Tickets sell for 142.50SFr for all of the festival's three days or 112.50SFr for just Saturday and Sunday. Bring a tent (showers and toilets available), or stay in St. Gallen and take the shuttle bus to the concert grounds. (☎ 084 880 0800; www.openairsg.ch.)

APPENZELL   ☎ 071

Appenzell, Switzerland's smallest canton, is world-renowned for its *Appenzeller Käse* (cheese) and its highly conservative people—women weren't allowed to vote until 1971. Its inhabitants maintain the traditional agrarian lifestyle, and herding animals is a common occupation. The canton is dotted with tiny villages, but the town of Appenzell is the gathering place for cantonal meetings and agricultural shows. Appenzell is best explored on foot: over centuries, local herdsmen have developed an extensive network of trails in the hills. These trails are frequented by herders in traditional garb and are sprinkled with *Gasthäuser* (guest houses).

FROM THE ROAD

ALPENBITTER, BITTE?

Appenzell locals are proud and devoted to the their unique regional liquor: Alpenbitter. A potent beverage flavored with anise and several dozen mountain herbs, it is a local favorite and a daily "medicine" to many a weathered Appenzeller man. I took the tour of the factory where the famous liquor was produced, thinking it would offer insight into the Appenzeller psyche and traditions, and perhaps get me a free shot.

The other Swiss on the tour kept to themselves, and the tour itself wasn't exactly enthralling, though the highlight, a cheesy 70's film strip, was amusing. Positing the question "What would the world be like without Alpenbitters?", it answered that, not surprisingly, a world without them was a world any true Appenzeller would not want to live in.

One woman on the tour came in late. When the guide informed her that the tour was only offered in Swiss German, she turned her nose to the air, and said, "I only speak French"—in French, of course. Later in the tour, she struck up conversation with me. I do not speak French, and made this clear in English and German. This did not make an impact, because she continued to address me in rapid French. Finally, I countered with the only French I could muster, saying "Je voudrai poisson"—I would like some fish. She turned her nose up again, and

TRANSPORTATION & PRACTICAL INFORMATION. The rattling *Appenzellerbahn* chugs between Appenzell and St. Gallen (45min., 2 per hr. 6:11am-10:46pm, 10.40SFr). From St. Gallen and Gossau, there is a regular **train** to Zurich (1hr., 32SFr). The train from St. Gallen continues from Appenzell to Wasserauen, a tiny hamlet that serves as a gateway to the Alpenteil valley and its hikes (10min., 3.80SFr). The Appenzell **tourist office**, Hauptg. 4, down Poststr. from the station and right at the intersection with Hauptg., makes hotel reservations, sells detailed hiking maps, and lists upcoming events. (☎788 96 41; www.myappenzellerland.ch. Open May to mid-Oct. M-F 9am-noon and 1:30-6pm, Sa-Su 10am-noon and 2-5pm; mid-Oct. to Apr. M-F 9am-noon and 2-5pm, Sa 2-5pm.) The tourist office also has information on free tours of the local Appenzeller Alpenbitter factory, in which the region's highly unique alcoholic drink has been made for over 100 years. The tour is only for those who understand Swiss German, are fervent enthusiasts of alcoholic beverages, or enjoy campy 70s-era filmstrips. Ask about the cheese factories that offer tours—one is in the town center, while a larger one in Stein is accessible by bus (10min., 1 per hr., 2.60SFr). **Internet** access is available at the library, or sporadically at the tourist office when the library is closed and they are not too busy. (5SFr per 30min. Library open Tu-W 2-5pm, Th 2-4pm, F 5-8pm and Sa 9:30-11:30am.) The train station offers **lockers** (3SFr) and **luggage storage** (5SFr). The **post office** is across the street from the train station. (Open M-F 7:30am-noon and 1:30-6pm, Sa 8am-noon.) **Postal code:** CH-9050.

ACCOMMODATIONS & FOOD. Picturesque lodgings await at ◙**Haus Lydia** ❸, Egggerstrandstr. 53. From the tourist office turn left onto Hauptg., turn left onto Gaiserstr. and walk up the bridge. Head uphill 5min. and turn right after the Mercedes-Esso station onto Eggerstrandenstr. (15min.). Alternatively take the train one stop toward St. Gallen to Hirschberg, turn right onto Hirschbergstr., again under the bridge and once more onto Eggerstrandstr. (3min.). The short walk is worth it. Run by a friendly and caring, English-speaking family, Haus Lydia is a traditional Appenzeller home with intricate wood-paneling, large rooms, Alpine views, and an elegant sitting room. The atmosphere provides an excellent way to experience Swiss family life. (☎787 42 33; www.haus-lydia.ch. Breakfast included. Reserve 2 weeks in advance. Singles 59SFr; doubles 88SFr.)

The ever-present aroma of Appenzeller cheese lingers around **Gasthaus Hof ❹**, on Landsgemeindepl. in the center of town. This bustling family-run hotel and restaurant provides guests with comfortable beds and crisp comforters in cozy, low-ceilinged rooms. (☎787 22 10; hotel_hof@hotmail.com. All rooms with shower and television. Breakfast included. Restaurant open 8am-10pm, reception open 7am-11pm. Reserve 1 week in advance from Aug.-Oct. 15. Singles 85SFr; doubles 130SFr; triples 180SFr; 4- and 5-person rooms also available. AmEx/DC/MC/V.) The tourist office also provides a list of **Privatzimmer**. The **Gasthöfe** (guest houses) that line the trail are comfortable overnight stops (see Hiking, below).

🛏**Restaurant Traube ❸**, Marktg. 7, near the Landsgemeindepl. in Hotel Traube, serves Appenzeller specialties by candlelight on traditional hand-embroidered placemats. *Appenzeller Chäshörnli* (macaroni and cheese) or *Käseschnitte* with ham, egg, or pineapple run 13-14SFr, while meat entrees cost 21-37SFr. Appenzeller beer is 2.60SFr. Desserts (6-10SFr) are elaborate; the *Coupe Denmark*, a vanilla ice cream dish, comes with your own pitcher of melted chocolate to pour on top. (☎787 14 07; www.hotel-traube.ch. Open Mar.-Jan. Tu-Sa 9am-midnight, Su 9am-10pm. AmEx/DC/MC/V.) The **Co-op** (with a pleasant restaurant) and **Migros** are across from one another on Zielstr. off Landsgemeindepl. (Both wheelchair-accessible. **ATM** nearby. Both open M-Th 8am-6:30pm, F 8am-8pm, Sa 8am-4pm.)

🔲 **SIGHTS.** The **Rathaus**, Hauptg. 4, houses the museum, town hall, cantonal library, and tourist office. The *Großratssaal*, with intricately carved wooden walls and 16th-century frescoes of giants supporting the central beam, is particularly remarkable. (Ask in the tourist office or in the museum to have a look inside.) Inside the *Rathaus* and the adjoining *Haus Buherre Hanisefs*, the **Museum Appenzell**, Hauptg. 4, chronicles local culture in displays of clothing and tools that weave throughout the wooden-raftered house; the exhibit also contains an old wooden prison cell. A video on hand embroidery (in English and German) is surprisingly captivating and exposes the harsh realities of often-idealized traditional Swiss life. (☎788 96 31. Open Apr.-Oct. daily 10am-noon and 2-5pm; Nov.-Mar. Tu-Su 2-5pm. 5SFr, students 3SFr, children under 6 free. Wheelchair-accessible.) Next door, the unassuming interior of **Pfarrkirche St. Mauritius** hides an impressive Rococo interior, complete with ceiling frescoes, 14 stained-glass windows, and a magnificent golden chandelier. (Open daily 7:30am-7pm.)

without a smile, walked away. Here I was, American and linguistically incompetent, bored with the tour and having just crippled my only chance at a sympathetic friend.

We proceeded on to the room containing the secret to every bottle of Alpenbitter brew: its 42 Kruueterlis, as the Swiss refer to them. These 42 herbs and spices give the drink its one-of-a-kind kick. The concoction is a secret recipe, so the herb room we were shown displayed only boxes and barrels of possible herbs used. The stench was far too great for my sensitive eyes. They began to water, and soon I was crying over the Kruueterlis and their pungency. I couldn't explain myself to the confused tour guide—how was I to tell her and a room of Appenzellers that their brew was disgusting and their Kruueterlis too strong? I left the room leaned on a distillation vat, my eyes burning.

The next thing I knew, the French lady was at my elbow, offering tissues and a pat on the shoulder. She talked a bit more in French, I thanked her in English, and we proceeded to have a broken conversation in German about just how gross we thought Alpenbitters were. Language suddenly wasn't a problem—the liquor had freed us from such petty constraints, and we proceeded to bond until the end of the tour over the distinctive taste that is Alpenbitters. The guide called me a "tuuefeli" (little devil) on my way out, but I left the factory bemused and somehow comforted. In a small town like Appenzell, cultural difference held much less sway than the disturbing aroma of the liquor.

HIKES IN THE APPENZELL REGION

Deep in the heart of the Alpstein, Appenzell offers great countryside hiking without the altitude or temperature extremes of the Zermatt or Ticino regions. The tourist office offers the **Panorama-Wanderkarte** (8.20SFr), a detailed map showing all trails and rest areas. A comprehensive topographical map is available at the bookstores. There are a number of themed hikes; acquire a *Wandern* brochure from the tourist office for further information. Hiking options range from easy strolls through pastures to strenuous overnight treks.

EASIER HIKES

Gontenbad Hike (2hr. round-trip). A relaxing walk known as the *Barfußweg* begins in the nearby town of Gonten (10min. by train from Appenzell; 3SFr). Stroll barefoot along a special trail over the meadows to Gontenbad (45min.), where you can rest and wash your feet (towels 2SFr) in the garden of the Bad Gonton Hotel and Restaurant before heading back to Appenzell (45min.).

Kapellenweg Hike (4-5hr. round-trip). The Kapellenweg provides a close look at local rural life by passing several country chapels. Cross under the train tracks, take a left, then a right at the major intersection to get to the trailhead; from there, brown "Kapellenweg" signs point the way. For the first 45min., the flat trail winds through local farms. For the adventurous, the trail veers from the paved road at times, leading through sheep and cow pastures. The trail splits in several places, but all paths eventually lead to the **Kapelle Maria** (1½hr.) and the larger and more ornate **Ahornkapelle** (2½hr.). The paved road is the easiest route to follow, passing a series of small painted Stations of the Cross. For a more challenging version of the hike (*sans* paintings, but with chapels), follow the "Kapellenweg" signs that lead uphill. Both trails lead back to Appenzell.

DIFFICULT HIKES

For more difficult hikes, start from tiny **Wasserauen,** the last stop on the Appenzellerbahn (10min. from Appenzell, 1-2 per hr., 3.80SFr). The best way to experience the area is to hike between guest houses. Several hikes listed below leave from the top of **Ebenalp Cable Car,** which is across the street from the small train station in Wasserauen. (Cable car runs 7:40am-7pm. 18SFr, round-trip 24SFr; stu-

---

MEADOW MEN Some local farmers spend the entire summer tending the livestock among the alpine meadows. Far from friends and family, these men look forward to the annual *Alpstobete* as a time to reunite with loved ones and celebrate the middle of summer. Originally held the Sunday after St. Jakob's Day (July 25), the patron saint of the Alps, locals don traditional garb of embroidered suspenders and brightly colored dresses to perform age-old courtship dances to folk music. Audiences of locals and tourists alike cheer on performers throughout the end of July, but in some locales festivals extend into mid-August. Ask at the tourist office for local festival dates.

---

dents 14SFr/18.50SFr; SwissPass or Eurail holders half-price. Reduced times due to renovations Nov. 1-Dec. 3 and Apr. 13-20; call ☎ 071 799 12 12 for schedules.) For those looking to travel and use cable cars daily, consider the **Appenzell Card,** which provides free access to three of the area's four cable cars (Säntis cable car not included) and bus and train lines as far as St. Gallen (31SFr, 3 days 52SFr, 5 days 84SFr; with SwissPass 22SFr/42SFr/68SFr). The **Berggasthaus Ebenalp,** 100m uphill from the top of the cable car, is a good base from which to explore the mountains, with more amenities than other guest houses. (☎ 799 11 94; www.ebenalp.ch. Breakfast included. Showers 4SFr. Optional sleeping bag 5SFr. Reception

7:30am-10pm. Reserve 2-3 mos. in advance for Sa stays. Open May-Nov. Dorms 28SFr; singles and doubles with sinks 52SFr per person. MC/V.) The last two hikes listed can be done without recourse cable cars.

Wasserauen to Wildkirchli (30min. round-trip). This quick, popular hike leads down from the Ebenalp (top station) through caves to the **Wildkirchli,** a 400-yr.-old chapel built into a cliff face and manned until recently by a hermit priest. **Berggasthaus Äscher ❷** lies just beyond Wildkirchli. At 150 yrs., Äscher is the oldest *Gasthaus* around. Tucked into the sheer cliff face at 1454m, 1 interior wall is the mountain. (☎799 11 42; www.aescher-ai.ch. Breakfast included. No showers. Reception 8am-midnight. Open May-late Oct. 27SFr per person, 20SFr for children under 12.)

Schäfler to Messmer (1½hr.). This exceedingly steep and rickety downhill trail leads from a *Gasthaus* called Schäfler to **Berggasthhaus Meßmer ❷**. A couple sections of the trail have a metal cable for balance, but this trail still should not be attempted after rain or snow. From Schäfler, follow the signs to "Meßmer," which will lead along a path called the Höheweg (30min.). The trail then turns left and descends even more steeply, for a view of the blue-green Seealpsee below. A steep uphill climb through cow pastures (10min.) leads to the final destination; the braying of livestock and clanging of cowbells signal the end. (☎799 12 55, winter ☎799 10 77; www.mesmer-ai.ch. Breakfast included. No running water, but a well outside. Reception 24hr. Reserve 1-2 mos. ahead for Sa-Su. Open May-late Oct. Dorms 24SFr, children under 17 17SFr.)

Seealpsee to Säntis (4hr.). The climb to **Säntis** (2503m), the highest mountain in the region, is a good hike from Seealpsee. From Seealpsee, hike to **Meglisalp** (1hr.), a cozy cluster of 6 farmhouses tucked beneath the peak. **◪Gästhaus Säntis ❷** is a great place to stay for a night with cows and the people who tend them. A local farmer calls out a prayer with a wooden megaphone every night for the benefit of neighbors and their cattle. (☎071 799 11 28; www.meglisalp.ch. Breakfast included. Reception 24hr. Reserve 1-2 weeks ahead. Open May-Oct. Dorms 31SFr; singles 52SFr; doubles 104SFr.) To get to Säntis from Meglisalp, head either to *Rothsteinpass* (more difficult) or *Wagenlücke* (easier), and then up to Säntis (both trips 3hr.). Both paths have snow through the end of June, and contain rock fields where the "trail" is rather do-it-yourself. Two guest houses sit on top of Säntis. **Gasthaus Säntis ❷** is older and more personalized. (☎071 799 11 60, winter 14 11; www.berggasthaus-saentis.ch. Breakfast included. Dorms 38SFr; singles, doubles, and 1 quad available, all 50SFr per person.) There are numerous routes from Säntis back to Wasserauen; the road-weary can take the cable car down to the **Schwägalp** and travel to Appenzell via Urnäsch. (Cable car every 30min. June 10-Oct. 26 7:30am-6:30pm; Oct. 27-Jan. 6 and Jan. 26-June 9 8:30am-5pm. 24SFr, 34SFr round-trip. Ages 6-16 are 12SFr/17SFr. Under 6 free. Yellow Postauto bus to Urnäsch behind the Berggasthaus Schwägalp, 30min., 1 per hr., about 5SFr; buy your tickets in Urnäsch. Train to Appenzell, 20min., 1-3 per hr. 6:14am-11:36pm, 5.80SFr; buy tickets at the magazine kiosk at the Urnäsch station.)

GRAUBÜNDEN

The largest, least populous, and most alpine of the Swiss cantons, Graubünden (*Grischuna* in Romansch) is made up of deep, rugged gorges twisting through snow-clad peaks and forests of larch and fir. The various towns ranging from the capital, Chur, to Portein (pop. 22) are scattered throughout the canton and seem dwarfed by the grandeur of their surroundings. The Swiss National Park in the Lower Engadine is the most tightly protected alpine landscape in Europe, and many communities, such as Zuoz and Scuol, are equally unspoiled. Glitzy St. Moritz and Davos have sprung up in the snowy mist as glamorous ski resorts.

As visitors travel from valley to valley, the language slips from German to Romansch to Italian, with a wide range of dialects in between. In addition to investing in a phrasebook, be aware that travel is not cheap in Graubünden. Buy the **Graubünden Total Regional Pass,** which allows three, five, seven, or 10 consecutive days of free travel on trains, buses, and cable cars in the region and a 50% discount on other days (140SFr, 190SFr, 240SFr, and 290SFr, respectively). The Regional Pass can be issued in Switzerland only from May to October, and is distributed by the **Rhätische Bahn** (**Viafer Retica** in Romansch), Graubünden's own train company. SwissPass and Eurail are also valid.

> **!** Plan your trip to Graubünden carefully—in ski season, calling ahead is a necessity. Also be aware that many establishments close for vacation in May and June.

HIGHLIGHTS OF GRAUBÜNDEN

Delve into the psychological underworld of Expressionist Ernst Kirchner at his eponymous museum in **Davos** (see p. 432).

Get wild in the winter in the secluded and seductively inexpensive **Arosa** (see p. 426).

Window-shop with the rich and famous in **St. Moritz** (p. 446).

CHUR (COIRA)   ☎081

Chur (pop. 32,000), the capital of Graubünden, has been inhabited for over 13,000 years, making it Switzerland's oldest settlement. Despite the area's rich history and diverse culture, Chur attracts few tourists and is a refreshing change of pace from the glitziness of nearby St. Moritz.

▌ TRANSPORTATION

Chur serves as a transportation hub for excursions into Graubünden. **Trains** connect to: Arosa (1hr., every hr. 5:35am-11:02pm, 13.40SFr); Basel (2¾hr., 1-2 per hr. 4:48am-10:16pm, 60SFr); Disentis (1¼hr., every hr. 6:15am-10:10pm, 25SFr) for the Furka-Oberalp line; St. Gallen (1½hr., every hr. 4:48am-10:16pm, 31SFr); St. Moritz (2hr., every hr. 5:10am-9:21pm, 38SFr); Zurich (1½hr., 1-2 per hr. 4:48am-10:16pm, 35SFr). Postal **buses** run to Ticino via Bellinzona (2½hr., 6 per day 8am-6pm, 50SFr).

Graubünden

TO ZÜRICH (100km)

Sargans

AUSTRIA

Bad Ragaz

Landquart

Schiers

Madrisahorn (2826m)

Küblis

Klosters-Dorf

Flims

Chur

Gotschnagrat (2285m)

Klosters-Platz

Scuol

Bonaduz

Parsenn

Verelna Tunnel

Guarda

Tarasp

Weisshorn (2653m)

Davos-Dorf

Davos-Platz

Piz Pisoc (3174m)

Arosa

Susch

Thusis

Alteiner Wasserfällen

Jakobshorn (2590m)

Zernez

Swiss National Park

Piz Nair (3010m)

Müstair

Tiefencastel

S-chanf

Munt La Schera (2587m)

St. Maria

Bergün/Bravuogn

Savognin

La Punt

Zuoz

Samedon

Inn

Splügen

St. Moritz

St. Moritz Bad

Pontresina

ITALY

Adda

Bivio

Silvaplana

Sils

Diavolezza (2973m)

San Bernardino Pass

Maloja

Upper Engadine Valley

Piz Bernina (4049m)

Soglio

Vicosoprano

N

Chiavenna

0   10 miles

0   10 kilometers

Tirano

GRAUBÜNDEN

⚡ PRACTICAL INFORMATION

Most directions begin at Postpl., which lies two blocks from the station on Bahnhofstr. Chur's **tourist office,** Grabenstr. 5, left on Grabenstr. off Postpl., makes hotel reservations (2SFr) and distributes guides to the city walking tours. (☎252 18 18; fax 90 76. Open M 1:30-6pm, Tu-F 8:30am-noon and 1:30-6pm, Sa 9am-noon.) Graubünden's **regional tourist office,** Alexanderstr. 24, on the second floor of the Media Café building, to the left of Bahnhofstr., stocks brochures and maps. (☎254 24 24; www.graubuenden.ch. Open M-F 8am-noon and 1:30-5:30pm.)

Train station services include: **currency exchange** (with Western Union services; open Su-F 6am-8pm, Sa 6am-7pm), **luggage storage** (7SFr; open M-F 7am-7:45pm, Sa 7am-7:15pm, Su 9am-noon and 1-6:45pm), kiosk for **hotel reservations** outside the train station, and **bike rental.** (30SFr per day, 23SFr per ½ day at baggage check; 6SFr to return bike to another station. Open M-F 7am-7:45pm, Sa 7am-7:15pm, Su 9am-noon and 1-6:45pm. General ticket counter open Su-F 5:45am-8:15pm, Sa 5:45am-7:15pm.) **Lockers** are at the station (2SFr); larger ones can be found at the Post Bus station above (3-5SFr).

Taxis are available at the train station and by calling **Taxi Rosamilia** (☎252 15 22) or A-ABA Taxi (☎284 55 55). A **pharmacy** is located on Bahnhofstr. near Postpl. open daily 9am-noon and 1:30-6:30pm.) The **police station** (☎081 254 43 41) is located in Karlihofspl.; head down Reichsg. until it turns into Süsswinkelg. on the left in the plaza. **Parking** (☎ 257 18 18 or 250 24 70) is located mainly down Graben-str. near Lindenquai. From Postpl., head right down Grabenstr. until it becomes Lindenquai; follow it along until you reach the Arosabahn train tracks. **Internet** access is available at **The Street Café,** Grabenstr. 47. (☎ 253 79 14; open M-Th 9am-midnight, F-Sa 9am-2am; 5SFr per 20min.). For the cheapest and quietest spot, try the **Kantonsbibliothek (library)** at Karlihofpl., 10min. down Reichsg. (Open Tu and Th 9am-5:45pm, W and F 9am-6:45pm, Sa 9am-3:45am. First 15min. free, 8SFr per hr. after that. Wheelchair-accessible.) **Laundry** (accompanied by pop music) is available at **Maltesen's Wash Self-Service,** Grabenstr. 49 in Malteserturm. (Open daily 9am-midnight. Wash 7-10SFr, dry 3-5SFr.) The **post office** is just right of the train station in the Post Bus station complex. (Open M-F 7:30am-noon and 1:30-6:30pm, Sa 8am-noon.) At Postpl., a secondary office offers better hours. (Open M-F 7:30am-6:30pm, Sa 8am-2pm.) **Postal code:** CH-7000/7002.

ACCOMMODATIONS

Budget options are hard to come by in Chur, and those that exist are rather spartan. The nearest hostel is in **Arosa** (see p. 428). **Hotel Drei Könige ❷** has been family-run since 1911. From the tourist office, head right down Grabenstr. and turn right on Reichsg. The "Backpacker's Lodge" is the attic, and is lined with beds eerily covered in plastic to avoid dust accumulation; the rafters outside are inhabited by constantly cooing pigeons. Despite its eccentricities, the hotel has a great breakfast, fantastic showers, a prime location, and a helpful staff. The restaurant downstairs offers a limited menu of Swiss classics, along with a "Backpacker's Special" dinner for 15SFr. (☎ 252 17 25; www.dreikoenige.ch. Breakfast and towels included. 24hr. parking 12SFr. Luggage storage and a safe for valuables available. Lodge is non-smoking. Dorm sheets 5SFr. Reception 7am-10pm. Check-out 11am. Dorms 25SFr; singles 50-70SFr, with shower 85-110SFr; doubles 100-120SFr/140-160SFr. AmEx/DC/MC/V.)

The **Post Hotel ❹,** Poststr. 11 off Postpl., is located in the pedestrian-only zone and is made up of plant-lined hallways and large, clean rooms. (☎ 252 68 44; www.comforthotelpost.ch. Breakfast, TV, and telephone included. Reception 7am-midnight. Check-out 11am. Doors lock at midnight; room keys will open the front door. Some non-smoking rooms. Wheelchair-accessible. Singles 75SFr, with shower 90-120SFr; doubles 120-150SFr/150-190SFr. AmEx/DC/MC/V.) **Camp Au ❶,** Felsensustr. 61, is a green and grassy campsite on the Rhine. Take bus #2 to "Obere Au" past the sports complex; it's on the left, on the gravel path. Equipped with kiosks and a restaurant, as well as toilets, dish-washing facilities, and waste disposal, Camp Au is a solid option. (☎ 284 22 83; www.camping-chur.ch. 6.60SFr per person, ages 6-12 3.30SFr; tents 6.20-17.70SFr. Electricity 3.30SFr. Showers 0.50SFr.)

FOOD & NIGHTLIFE

Wander around the squares of the old city to find a variety of cuisines, including Spanish, Thai, Greek, and lots of places serving good old *Rösti*. At nightfall, head down to Untereg. to try out Chur's developing bar and club scene.

Valentino's Grill, Untereg. 5 (☎ 252 73 22), the "1st Original Swiss Shwarma," right on Grabenstr. from Postpl. and left under the arches. Best budget option. Kebabs 8.90-9.90SFr. Falafel in pita 7.50SFr. Beer and wine from 3.50SFr. Open M 5-10pm, Tu-Th 11:45am-2pm and 5-11:30pm, F 11:45am-1:45pm and 5pm-2am, Sa noon-2am. ❶

Restaurante Controversa, Steinbruchstr. 2 (☎252 99 44; fax 99 43), on the corner of Grabenstr. and Reichsg. Filled with local couples, this spot's artsy decor, Louis XIV drapes, black coffee tables, and neon lights create a hip café ambiance in which to enjoy various pastas (14-19SFr), "dress-your-own-plate" meat dishes (28-32SFr), and the modest salad bar. Wine 4-8SFr. Wheelchair-accessible. Open mid-Aug. to mid-July M-Sa 11am-2:30pm and 5pm-midnight, Su 6-11pm. ❸

La Guajira Restaurante and Bar, Untereg. 16 (☎250 41 80). This charming hole-in-the-wall, draped with fishing nets and seahorses, is a new spot serving up fairly cheap Spanish dishes with a 20% student discount on all drinks. Tacos 7.40SFr. *Tapas* 10-14SFr. Chicken and rice with vegetables 15.50SFr. Beer from 3.50SFr. ❶

La Pasteria Otello, Ottopl. (☎250 55 15; www.otello.ch). From the station, turn left onto Ottostr. Secluded from the busy town center, this candlelit restaurant is perfect for an elegant night out. Pastas and pizzas are reasonable (14.50-22SFr), but fish entrees and specialties (24.50-39.50SFr) are a splurge. Adventurers can try the extensive fish and fowl menu, which includes ostrich (31.50-36.50SFr)—"It goes well with a light red wine," says owner Pepe. Wheelchair-accessible. Open daily 10am-midnight, with warm dishes available 11:30am-2pm and 6-10pm. AmEx/DC/MC/V. ❹

China Restaurant Han Kung, Rabeng. 6 (☎252 24 58; fax 31 98). Walk down Reichsg., then turn left onto Rabeng. before St. Martin's Church, to find a bit of China in Haus Pestalozza. Friendly staff and bright seating. 3-course lunch specials 15.50SFr. Open Tu-Su 11:30am-1:45pm and 6-9:45pm. AmEx/DC/MC/V. ❸

Street Café, Grabenstr. 47 (☎253 79 14). Filled with a young local crowd grooving to techno-jazz among mirrors, blue drapes, and exposed pipes. Beers from 3.90SFr. Panini sandwiches 10.50SFr. **Internet** 15SFr per hr. 18+ after 8pm. Open M-Th 9am-midnight, F-Sa 9am-2am. AmEx/MC/V. ❶

Q-Bar, near the laundromat on Grabenstr., with entrances on Untereg. and Engadinstr., spins house music for a mix of stylish locals in its decidedly sparse interior. Decorated only with furniture expressly designed for the bar, the blocks of chairs and couches are actually for sale. Beer from 4.50SFr, specialty drink of the day 12-14SFr. Open M-Th 4pm-midnight, F and Sa 2pm-2am. AmEx/MC/V. ❶

ON THE MENU

VELTLINER PIZZOCCHERI

Ask for it by name, and the locals will chuckle and understand what you've come for: the *Veltliner pizzoccheri* (felt-LEEN-ehr pit-TSOCK-ehr-ree) is the dish of the Veltlin (*Vattalina* in Romansch) region of Graubünden. Near the Engandines, the Veltlin area boarders Italy, and Italian influences have intermingled with local cuisine in delightful ways. The dish itself, like fondue and raclette, is a hot entree served mainly in the wintertime. *Pizzoccheri* (buckwheat noodles) and potatoes are cooked together with leafy green vegetables including green beans, spinach and kale. The dish is then flavored with butter, garlic, pan-seared onions, and fresh sage. The mix is then tossed together and baked, but only after being smothered in oodles of mountain cheese. The result is a Vattalina delicacy—a meal of Swiss heartiness, but with an Italian flair, all in one piping-hot pan.

Pizzoccheri can be had at many traditional restaurants throughout the region. At the Morteratsch Restaurant in the Veltlin, *pizzoccheri* (19.50SFr) is served even in the summer on a errace boasting spectacular views of the surrounding mountains and the Morteratsch glacier. (Take the train from Pontresina to "Monteratsch."; the restaurant is by the station. Wheelchair-accessible. Open daily 8am-midnight. ☎081 842 63 13; www.morteratsch.ch. AmEx/MC/V.)

IN RECENT NEWS

BUNA SAIRA!

Switzerland's oft-forgotten fourth national language, Romansch, is spoken only in the province of Graubünden, where it, German, and Italian are the official cantonal languages. Until about 1850, it was the most spoken language in the canton. By 1880, Romansch speakers dropped to 39.8% of the population, a percentage that kept dropping, finally leveling out around 22%. Today, in some small villages like S-chanf, Romansch speakers remain in the majority. Even in larger towns, like Chur, they form as much as a quarter of the population. The language is supported by the Swiss government, but its survival is threatened by the fact that at least four different dialects arose in isolated mountain villages.

A Romance language like French and Italian, Romansch is descended from Latin. Romansch didn't become a written language until the 16th century, when Biblical texts and historical ballads were first translated. In 1985, the Lia Rumantscha, a group dedicated to the preservation and proliferation of the language, succeeded in standardizing a common written language, called Grischuna, by drawing on several major dialects. Now, Romansch has a small literature of its own and translations of everything from the paperback bestsellers to Asterix comics. Its speakers support five different Romansch new-

👁 SIGHTS

Red and green footpaths throughout the town lead visitors past Chur's sights, most of which are located in the city's expanding car-free zone. The cavernous 12th-century **Kathedral St. Mariä Himmelfahrt** at the top of the old town is being restored until 2006 at a cost of nearly 1.5 million Euros. Only a small portion of its impressive Gothic and Romanesque interior is visible, with a small side chapel still open to the public. A display on the history of the church, its art and artifacts, and the restoration project, is translated into English. (From St. Martinspl., go left on Kirchg. and head up the stairs.) Downhill, the **Martinskirche** (St. Martin's Church, built in 1491) offsets the cathedral's looming presence with a simple interior dominated by a pipe organ and three Giacometti stained-glass windows.

Chur's **Bündner Kunstmuseum,** Bahnhofstr. 35, at the corner of Bahnhofstr. and Grabenstr., blazes with the art of the Giacomettis: Giovanni, Alberto, and Augusto. Works by Swiss artists Angelika Kauffman and Ferdinand Hodler occupy the ground floor, while modern exhibits enliven the black-and-white basement, a work of art itself. (☎257 28 68; info@bkm.gr.ch. Open Tu-W and F-Su 10am-noon and 2-5pm, Th 10am-noon and 2-8pm. 8SFr, students 6SFr, under 16 free. During the summer exhibition (usually late June to mid-Sept.), the museum open without an afternoon break. German tours of special exhibits Th 7pm. Ground and second floors wheelchair-accessible. 12SFr, students 10SFr.)

The **Rätisches Museum,** Hofstr. 1, houses a collection of tapestries, coins, and archaeological trivia that document the origin of "Rätia" and its development into current Graubünden. An English guide to the exhibits is available for 12SFr. (☎257 28 89. Open Tu-Su 10am-noon and 2-5pm. 5SFr, students 2SFr, seniors and groups 3SFr, under 16 free.)

NEAR CHUR

AROSA ☎081

A squeaking train ride from Chur (1hr.) twists and turns through rugged peaks and above lush valleys to reach the secluded town of Arosa. Bounded by two main lakes—Obersee by the train station, and Untersee below the town—Arosa's landscape is dominated by countless stony peaks including the 2653m Weißhorn. Offered the land for 55,000SFr in 1936, the president of Chur missed his chance, claiming that Arosa's heyday had passed; today, the area is a lucrative resort with a network of great skiing in winter and hiking in summer. Arosa remains accessible to budget travelers, thanks to well-equipped dormitories.

When planning your visit, be aware that Arosa lives by its seasons: *Winter* is from December to April, *Sommer* is from mid-June to mid-October, and the *Zwischen* or *Sonder* seasons are the weeks in between. Hotels break down the year further by defining low, middle, peak, and off-seasons. Be sure to call ahead to make sure your hotel, huts, and activities will be open during your stay.

The Arosa **All-Inclusive Card,** first offered in summer 2003, is free to travelers staying overnight in an Arosa hotel or hostel and 8SFr for daily visitors. The summer-only pass gives free access to pedal boats on the Obersee, the ice rink, the Weisshorn cable car, the Hörnli Express, and the Arosa bus system. A 5SFr deposit is required for the card, which can be returned at hotels, the post office, the train station, and the tourist office. Check out www.all-inclusive.ch.

🄴🄷 TRANSPORTATION & PRACTICAL INFORMATION

Arosa is accessible by scenic **train** from Chur (1hr., every hr. 5:35am-11:02pm, 13.40SFr). A **free shuttle bus** (summer every 30min., winter every 10min. 7am-7pm; 3SFr each way during the winter, free in summer with the Arosa Card) transports visitors in town, between ski lifts, and along the 10min. walk from the train station to the tourist office (stop: "Casino"). A **night bus service** operates late December-late April (1 per hr. 8pm-2am). The **tourist office,** right out of the station and right uphill 5min. on Poststr., arranges hiking trips and ski lessons for free. (☎378 70 20; www.arosa.ch. Open Dec. 7-Apr. 13 M-F 9am-6pm, Sa 9am-5:30pm, Su 4-6pm; Apr. 14-Dec. 6 M-F 8am-noon and 1:30-6pm, Sa 9am-1pm, June 29-Aug. 17 also open Sa 2-4pm.) While all parking on Arosa city streets is forbidden, **parking** is free in summer with the Arosa Card at the **Parking Garage Ochsenbühl** (winter 2SFr for 3hr., 1SFr per additional hr.). A strict traffic ban is imposed nightly midnight-6am, due to winter snow hazards, but also in summer to maintain quiet. The **train station** gives **currency exchange** at the ticket counter (☎377 14 90; www.rhb.ch; open daily 6am-9pm), **luggage storage** (M-F 6am-8pm, Sa-Su 6:30am-8pm; 5SFr), and **bike rental** (☎377 14 90; 30SFr per day, 23SFr per half-day). Electronic **lockers** that don't

spapers, TV news broadcasts, and 100 hours of radio time per week.

Although dependence on the German-speaking economy hinders the progress of Romansch, the Lia Rumantscha continues to fight for the advancement of the language, focusing primarily on the role on the government and schools. Today, many schools in Lower Engandine teach strictly in Romansch until students are 10 years old. At this time, students elect to continue their education in either German or Romansch, with continued study of the other language.

The German majority constantly encroaches on this small linguistic reserve, but the locals remain faithful to their rare heritage, slipping easily between German and Romansch as they move from home to school, books to magazines or even within the same conversation. Travelers can do their part to preserve the language and culture that accompanies it by responding in kind when they hear someone calling out, "Bun di!" (Hello!), "Grazia" (thank you), "Buna Saira" (good evening) or even "Tge bel che ti es!" (How beautiful you are!).

give change are available at the end of the station for luggage (3-5SFr) and skis (2SFr deposit). **Internet** access is available at café Bar Los, across the street from the tourist office. (15SFr per hour. Open summer 2pm-2am, winter till 3am.) Montana Apotheke on Oberseepl. is the **pharmacy.** (☎377 15 22. Open M-F 8 am-noon and 2-6:30pm, Sa 8am-noon and 2-4pm.) The **police station** on Poststr. also houses the lost-and-found office (☎378 67 17). **Express Taxi** almost always has a car or two at the train station. The **post office** is in the main square, right of the train station. (Open M-F 7:45am-noon and 1:45-6:30pm, Sa 8:30am-noon.) **Postal code:** CH-7050.

ACCOMMODATIONS

Most lodgings are near the tourist office. Reserve in advance during ski-season.

Haus Florentinum (☎377 13 97; www.arosabergbahnen.ch). Follow the right-hand sidewalk of Poststr. past the tourist office. Then make an extreme right and head uphill 10min. on Murasteig, the zig-zagging paved path. At the top, continue right toward Hotel Hohe Promenade, turn left at the gravel path for Pension Suveran, and right at the dirt path in front of the sign. Run by the ski-lift company Arosa Bergbahnen, Florentinum provides cheap and convenient housing in winter only (summer is reserved for groups). This enormous former convent in the woods is now a 150-bed party house with large lounges, balconies, and a chapel-turned-disco. Breakfast included. Dinner 15SFr. **Internet,** TV, ping-pong, and washing facilities available. Parking 7SFr per day. In the winter, 2-night min. stay on weekends. Reception open 8:30-11:30am and 4:30-10pm. Dec.-Apr. 2-night stay with 2-day ski pass 246SFr, under 19 231SFr; 6-night stay with 6-day ski pass 588SFr/551SFr. AmEx/DC/MC/V. ❷

Jugendherberge (HI), Seewaldstr. (☎377 13 97; www.backpackers-arosa.ch), past the tourist office down the hill (follow the signs), has a friendly English- and Russian-speaking staff. A good choice in summer, when lifts are not necessary for hiking (it is closer to the bottom of the valley, near the trails), this hostel attracts families, school groups, and the occasional sports team. Dorms have balconies overlooking the *Untersee* or the Engadine slopes. Breakfast (7-8am) and sheets included. Bag lunch 8.50SFr; dinner 12SFr. Showers 0.50SFr per 3min. In winter, a 2-night stay is required on weekends. Reception summer 7-10am and 5-10pm; winter 7am-noon and 4-10pm. Check-out 9am, strictly enforced. Curfew 10pm, 11pm in winter; key provided. Open June 15-Oct. 15 and Dec. 15-Apr. 15. Summer dorms 31.50-37.50SFr; doubles 70SFr. In winter required half-pension included; dorms 44SFr; doubles 108SFr. ❷

Pension Suveran (☎377 19 69 or 079 640 49 93; www.suveran.ch), on the way to the Haus Florentium above, is a quiet, homey, wood-paneled chalet. Breakfast included. Dinner on request 15SFr. Sinks in rooms. Toilet and shower on the floor. Reception 7am-9am. Check-in 3pm. Check-out 10am. Open July-Oct. and Dec. to mid-Apr. July-Oct. singles 42-52SFr; doubles 84-104SFr. Dec. to mid-Apr. singles 52-60SFr; doubles 104-120SFr. Add 10SFr per person in winter for stays shorter than 3 nights. ❸

Camping Arosa (☎377 17 45 or 079 611 30 59; sportanlagen@arosa.ch), downhill from the hostel. Cooking facilities available. The caretaker is on location 4:45-5:15pm, so payment is on the honor system. 9SFr per person, ages 6-12 4.50SFr, tents 4.50SFr. Electricity 3SFr. Showers 0.50SFr per 3min. ❶

FOOD

There are several quality food options in Arosa. **Le Bistro** ❹, in Hotel Cristallo on Poststr., has a French ambience, classic posters on the walls, and cushioned wicker seating, and draws a conservative crowd of couples and older families. Moderately high prices for dinner entrees like truffles and noodles (18.59SFr) and lasagna with Scottish lox (24.50SFr). Soups are 8.50-9.50SFr, and meat dishes around 38SFr. The lunch menu (daily noon-2pm; 15-22SFr) includes cold sandwiches and warm dishes like ravioli and *Bratwurst* plates. (☎378 68 68; www.cristalloarosa.ch. Wheelchair-accessible. Open Dec.-May and mid-June to mid-Oct. daily 9am-midnight, kitchen open noon-2pm and 6pm-midnight. Reservations suggested in winter. MC/V.) **Hotel Central Arve ❸**, Hubelstr., is down the hill from the tourist office just before the youth hostel on the right. The *Arvenstube* at the hotel serves season-specific *Menüs* for 16.50-20.50SFr in a causal and cozy den. The "soup trilogy" gets you a small portion of three different soups for 10.50SFr; the house speciality beef filet (29/38SFr) is prepared at your table. (☎378 52 52; www.arve-central.ch. English menu available. Parking available. Closed in May. Open daily 11:30am-2pm and 6-10pm. Reservations recommended for summer weekends and in winter. AmEx/DC/MC/V.)

At **Orelli's Restaurant ❷**, Poststr., down the hill from the tourist office on the left, hikers and families alike eat Swiss cuisine in a kid-friendly restaurant decorated with Mickey Mouse images. The thrifty can get the soup du jour and bread for 5-8SFr. A vegetarian *Menü* (15SFr), salad buffet (8-12SFr), and warm entrees (15-26.50SFr) like salmon fillet or risotto (both 16SFr) with mushrooms round out the options. English menu is available. (☎377 12 08; www.hotelorelli.ch. mid-June to mid-Apr. Su-Th 7:30am-9pm, F-Sa 7:30-10pm. MC/V.)

Get groceries at the **Co-op**, on Poststr. (wheelchair-accessible; open M-F 8am-12:30pm and 2-6:30pm, Sa 8am-4pm), or at **Denner Superdiscount** (which boasts a massive amount of chocolate), near the station (wheelchair-accessible; open M-F 8am-12:15pm and 2:30-6:30pm, Sa 8am-12:15pm and 1:15-4pm; open Sa in winter 8am-5pm; summer closed Th).

⚠ 🎵 OUTDOOR ACTIVITIES & ENTERTAINMENT

SKIING. Separate passes for the 15 ski lifts and cableways that hoist skiers to the 70km network of slopes in the Arosa-Tschuggen ski area B are available for tourists not staying in the dorms. The mountains are covered with slopes for all levels, but the easier paths are concentrated on the lower Tschuggen area. Ticket offices in Arosa (at the tourist office and at the main "Arosa Bergbahnen" office behind the train station) offer myriad passes. (Day, morning, afternoon, 1½-day, "choose-your-day" etc. 54SFr per day; 271SFr per week; 410SFr for 2 weeks. AmEx/DC/MC/V.) The smaller Tschuggen-sector day-pass is 30SFr. Children under 15 get a 50% discount; ages 16-19 and seniors get a 10-15% discount. Save 20% by going in the low-season (2nd week of Dec., first 2 weeks of Apr.) or in the first week of December, though only limited runs are open (20SFr for 1 day, children 15SFr).

HIKING. When the snow melts, it uncovers over 200km of flower-covered hiking paths. An **Alpine guide,** available through the tourist office, leads 8- and 10hr. hikes for fit hikers only. (July to mid-Oct. Tu, Th. 20SFr; 16 and under 10SFr.) Two cable cars operate in summer. The **Weisserhornbahn cable car,** above the train station, whisks travelers to the top of the Weisserhorn (2653m; every 20min. 9am-5pm). The summit allows views of the whole Engadine valley. The **Hörnli-Express** (free with Arosa Card; 16FSFr, round-trip 28SFr, day pass 32SFr) at the other end of town is accessible by bus. A 1½hr. hike follows the ridge between lifts; longer hikes wind into the valleys opposite the town. Most hikes that do not involve cable cars start from the Untersee (at the very end of the street on which the hostel is located). A number of hiking maps are available at the tourist office. The "Arosa und Umgebung" map (19.80SFr) comes with a list of suggested trails and lengths.

Alteiner Wasserfällen Hike (2hr. 1-way). This easy-to-medium trail begins at the Untersee and starts out flat, winding through the Hintern Wald and fields of wildflowers before crossing over a stream several times. At the end of a climb, the trail splits, leading to the Kleiner Wasserfall or the impressive Großer Wasserfall. Take the same path to Arosa. To lengthen the hike, climb along the steep trail from the waterfalls to the Atteinsee (5hr. round-trip). This continues to the other side of the ridge and on to Davos.

Ochsenalp to Tschiertschen Hike (5hr. round-trip). After first taking the Arosa bus to Prätschli or Maran, this hike of medium difficulty climbs along the Rot-Tritt trail 2hr. and peaks at Ochsenalp. At 1936m, Ochsenalp offers great views of the surrounding rocky peaks and is home to a traditional Alpine restaurant. The hike then winds down the other side of the mountain 1½hr. to the unpronounceable Tschiertschen. A bus from Tschiertschen to Chur leaves hourly, but check the schedule to be sure of any seasonal changes. Then ride the train from Chur to Arosa (1hr., 1 per hr., 13.60SFr).

OTHER ACTIVITIES. The Untersee's **free beach** is open daily from 10am to 6pm, while pedal boats are for rent on the Obersee. (10am-5pm. Free with Arosa Card; 9-12SFr per 30min, 12-17SFr per hr.) The outdoor **ice rink** is open November-April and hosts ice skaters, curling lessons, and hockey games. (☎13 77 17 45; sportanlagen@arosa.ch. Winter open daily 10am-5pm. Free entry with Arosa Card; skate rental 6SFr. Call ahead in July and Aug., because camps fill up indoor ice time.) A local horse owner gives **pony rides** for 10-18SFr per 30min. (☎377 41 96. July-Aug. M-F.) **Cheese tasting** is available at the Alpkäserei Maran (near bus stop at Maran). Contact the tourist office the day before by 5:30pm for reservations (June-Sept. Th. 1hr. long. 5SFr, under 12 free.) Don't miss the picturesque area of **Innerarosa**, the town only 20min. from the Arosa city center heading toward the Hörnli Express (by Arosa bus, just 5min.) There, the **Bergkirchli,** situated among lush green hills and Alpine flora, hosts regular organ concerts and traditional music nights. The **Arosa Jazztage** in mid-July grants free admission to local venues. The festival features New Orleans jazz played by a small number of international bands. For 10 days every mid-December, the **Humorfestival** gets Arosa laughing by hosting comedy shows performed by artists from all over the world. (Tickets 10SFr in afternoon, 35SFr in the evening; available at the tourist office. Ask for a schedule of English-speaking performers.)

DAVOS ☎081

Davos (pop. 12,000) sprawls along the valley floor under seven mountains laced densely with the wires of chairlifts and cable cars. Originally a health resort for consumptives, the city catered to such *fin de siècle* celebrity guests as Robert Louis Stevenson and Thomas Mann, who, while in Davos, wrote *Treasure Island* and *The Magic Mountain*, respectively. Davos now relies on its world-class skiing and classy resorts to lure visitors. An influx of tourists in recent decades has given the city an impersonal feel, but the thrill of carving turns down the famed run from Weißfluhgipfel to Kublis (a 2000m vertical drop) may compensate.

▣ TRANSPORTATION

Davos is accessible by **train** from Chur via Landquart (1½hr., every hr. 4:57am-10:08pm, 25SFr) or from Klosters (25min.; 2 per hr.; free with guestcard from either city, otherwise 8.60SFr) on the Rhätische Bahn lines. The town is divided into two areas, Davos-Dorf and Davos-Platz, each with a train station and linked by the 3km **Promenade**. Platz is the site of the tourist office, main post office, and most other places of interest to budget travelers. Dorf is closer to the quiet and picturesque Davosersee. A convenient system of **buses** (free with guest card or

2.70SFr) runs frequently between the two train stations and stops near major hotels and the hostel on the Davosersee. **Parking lots** line the Promenade and Talstr. (1-2SFr per hr.). Parking is also available at the train station (5SFr per day; additional days 3SFr.)

? PRACTICAL INFORMATION

The high-tech main **tourist office,** Promenade 67, in Platz, up the hill and to the right of the train station, caters mostly to those staying in hotels, but has free **Internet** access at one terminal and a weekly bulletin of events and general information. A smaller **branch office** sits across from the Dorf train station. (☎415 21 21; www.davos.ch. Both offices open Dec. to mid-Apr. and mid-June to mid-Oct. M-F 8:30am-6:30pm, Sa 9am-5pm. Platz location also open Su 10am-noon and 3-5:30pm. Both locations open mid.-Oct. to Dec. and mid-Apr. to June M-F 8:30am-noon and 1:45-5pm, though the Platz location doesn't take a midday break, Su 8:30am-noon.) The stations **store luggage** (3SFr), rent **lockers** (3-5SFr), provide **Western Union** services, and **currency exchange.** (Platz station open M-Sa 4:45am-10pm, Su 5:50am-9pm; Dorf station open daily 6:50am-7pm.) **Expert Roro,** in Dorf, Promenade 123, across from the blue-and-pink Hotel Concordia, offers **Internet** access at more terminals than the tourist office. (☎420 11 11. Open M-F 8:30am-noon and 2-6:30pm, Sa 8:30am-noon and 2-5pm. 5SFr per 20min., 12SFr per hr.) Closer to the Platz, the **Esso bar,** Talstr. 22, below the station houses an **Internet** café and bar with long hours. (☎413 12 83. Open 7am-2am. 14SFr. per hr.) **Laundry** available at self-service **Waschsalon,** Promenade 102, below the yellow-painted Walhalla Bar. (☎416 32 70. Open M-F 8am-8pm, Sa 9am-5pm. Wash 2-4SFr per load, dry 4-5 SFr.) The main **post office** is in Davos-Pl. at Promenade 43, in the shopping center across from the train station. (Open M-F 7:45am-6pm, Sa 8am-noon.) **Postal code:** CH-7270.

┏ ACCOMMODATIONS & CAMPING

In the summer, or for a more relaxing hostel atmosphere, head to Klosters (see p. 434). Always ask for the Davos **visitor's card,** which grants free unlimited travel on the city's buses and discounts on attractions, including 20% off cable car passes, 10% off ice skate rental, and 1.50SFr off hiking maps. The only **camping facility** in Davos was closed in 2003; the city hopes to have a new spot by summer 2004. Until then, the closest pseudo-campgrounds are at **Caravan & Mobilhome Rinerlodge** in nearby Rinerhorn on bus line #7 from the train station. (☎401 12 52, www.rinerhorn.ch. Breakfast, hot water, communal showers, and toilets provided. 26-32SFr per person.)

Jacobshorn Ski Mountain (☎414 90 20; www.fun-mountain.ch). The folks here have made their youth-oriented mountain accessible to travelers with 4 dorms for winter thrill-seekers, sold as a package with ski passes. All houses have plain white rooms and down quilts. Parking available for 10SFr per day. Reception open M-Th and Su 8-11:30am and 4-7pm, F 8:30-11am and 4-9pm, Sa 8-11:30am and 4-8:30pm. Check-out 10am. Call ahead for wheelchair-accessibility in Guest House Bolgenhof. Passes good only for Jacobshorn mountain; all 3 open Nov.-May. AmEx/MC/V. ❷

Snowboarder's Palace, Oberestr. 45-47. Located right above the main tourist office, the Palace has the most authentic ski-lodge appearance, with wooden balconies. 2- to 6-bed rooms. Breakfast included. 1-night, 2-day ski pass 135SFr, Sa-Su 185SFr; 6-night, 7-day ski pass 630SFr, whole region 700SFr.

Guest House Bolgenhof, Brämabülstr. 4A, is bland but convenient, right beneath the Davos-Pl. train station, next to Jakobshorn office near the ski lifts. Prices same as Snowboarder's Palace.

Snowboardhotel Bolgenschanze, Skistr. 1. The most hopping house is conveniently located over a bar oodles of post-skiing partying occurs. 18+. 2- to 5-bed dorms. Free **Internet** for guests. 1-night, 2-day ski-pass 125-135SFr, Sa-Su 175-185SFr; 6-night, 7-day ski pass 570SFr, whole region 640SFr.

Hotel Herrmann, Dorfstr. 23 (☎416 17 37; fax 35 73), behind the tourist office and to the right in Dorf, provides a peaceful respite for those looking to enjoy the resort town off the slopes. Fresh fruit upon your arrival, hardwood floors with rugs, and a bathtub on the floor make this spot friendlier than most. Parking 10SFr per day. Reception 7:30am-10pm. Open July-Oct. and Dec.-Apr. Winter singles with breakfast and dinner 92-110SFr, with shower 105-125SFr; doubles 164-200SFr/190-230SFr. Summer singles 60-65SFr/75-80SFr; doubles 100-110SFr/130-140SFr. MC/V. ❹

🍴 FOOD

Haven't had your *Rösti* fix yet? **Röstizzeria ❸,** in Dorf, Promenade 128, downstairs from the Hotel Dishma, can satisfy a craving with 15 variations (17.50-24.50SFr) and pizza (from 13SFr) in a dining room decorated with carved wood and fake grapevines. (☎416 12 50. Take most any bus to Dischmastr. Open daily 6am-11pm. AmEx/D/MC/V.) Alternatively, grab a Bud and a bar stool, American style, at **Café Carlos ❷,** Promenade 58, which is fittingly located in a mall opposite the main tourist office. This restaurant feeds a friendly local crowd with juicy American standards, including burgers and sandwiches from 14SFr and beers from 4SFr. (☎413 17 22. Wheelchair-accessible. English menu. Open daily except W in summer 10am-1am, winter daily 11:30am-10:30pm. AmEx/D/MC/V.)
Romeo & Juliá Belvedere Tratorria ❹, Promenade 89 (500m toward Dorf from Platz; bus stop: "Kirchner Museum"), lives up to its name in romance in the candlelit, wood-paneled five-star Hotel Steigenberger Belvedere. Enjoy a gourmet meal of homemade spaghetti with white truffle sauce and jumbo shrimp (31SFr). For those on a budget, moderately priced pasta and vegetarian dishes are just 15.50-22SFr. (☎415 60 00; www.davos.steigenberger.ch. Reservations suggested in summer; necessary 2-3 days ahead in winter. AmEx/D/MC/V.)
You cannot miss the enormous new **Co-op** (caféteria-style restaurant inside features weekly *Menüs* 10SFr) across from the Platz station. (Open M-Th 8am-6:30pm, F 8:30am-8pm, Sa 8am-5pm; restaurant open M-Th 8am-6:30pm, F 8am-8pm, Sa 8am-5pm, Su 10am-6pm.)

🏛 🎿 MUSEUMS & OUTDOOR ACTIVITIES

Although surprisingly small, Davos' rink holds the title of Europe's largest natural **ice rink** (22,000 sq. m). Located by the sports center between Platz and Dorf, it has figure skating, ice dancing, hockey, speed skating, and curling. (☎415 36 04. Open weather permitting Dec. 15-Feb. 15. M-W and F-Su 10am-4pm, Th 8-10pm. 5SFr, 4SFr with visitors card; skate rental 6.50SFr with 20SFr deposit.)
For joggers, birdwatchers, and aspiring windsurfers, the **Davosersee** is the place to be. A 10min. bus ride from the city, this lake claims to be "the windiest Alpine lake in the world." (Take bus #1 (dir.: Stilli) to "Flueelastr." and follow the yellow signs to the lake.) At the **Davosersee Surfcenter,** board rentals are 30SFr for 1hr., 60SFr for the day. (Open mid-June to mid-Sept. daily 11am-6:30pm, weather permitting.) Runners, strollers, and picnickers use the facilities around the lake.

KIRCHNER MUSEUM. The frosted glass structure opposite the Hotel Belvedere on the Promenade houses an extensive collection of artwork of Ernst Ludwig Kirchner, whose harsh colors and long figures reveal troubled visions. This seminal figure of 20th-century German Expressionism lived in Davos for 21 years before committing suicide after the Nazis dubbed his art degenerate. Curators oversee an ever-changing exhibit that places Kirchner's work alongside that of related artists. From December 2003 through April 2004, the museum will present *Ein Künstlerpaar*, a special exhibit on Kirchner and his wife. (☎413 22 02; kirchnermuseum@spin.ch. Take the bus to "Kirchner Museum." Open Dec. 25-Easter and July 8-Aug. Tu-Su 10am-6pm; Easter-July 7 Tu-Su 2-6pm. 10SFr, seniors 8SFr, students and children under 16 5SFr.)

SKIING. Davos provides direct access to two main mountains—the Parsenn and Jakobshorn—and four **skiing areas,** covering every degree of difficulty. Parsenn, with long runs and fearsome vertical drops, is the mountain around which Davos built its reputation. Unfortunately, Parsenn's fame has brought hordes of tourists. (www.fun-mountain.ch. Day pass 60SFr.) Jacobshorn has found a niche with the younger crowd since the opening of a snowboarding "fun-park" with two half-pipes (day pass 52SFr). The **Pischa** and **Rinerhorn** are smaller resorts within the Davos area. The **regional ski pass** covers all six mountains in the Davos-Klosters area, including unlimited travel on most transport facilities, and doesn't cost much more than individual tickets (2 days 121SFr, 6 days 279SFr). If you're going to be doing a lot of skiing in the area, a season **SnowPass** is available for all Graubünden slopes. (www.snowpass.ch. 1200SFr, under 17 900SFr.) Info and maps can be found at the tourist office. In addition to downhill runs, Davos boasts 75km of **cross-country trails** throughout the valley, including a night-lit trail. **The Swiss Ski School of Davos,** Promenade 157, offers lessons starting at 40SFr per half-day group lesson. (☎416 24 54; www.ssd.ch.) **Fullmoons,** Promenade 102, provides telemark lessons and tours. (☎/fax 240 14 77; www.fullmoons.ch. Half-day 170SFr.)

HIKING. One main ski lift on each mountain is open in summer, and many of the area's trails require these expensive lifts to bring hikers out of the dense valley. *Bergbahnen Sommer 2004,* an easy-to-read map and schedule of prices, operating hours, and hiking routes/lengths is free from the main tourist office.

Panoramaweg (2hr.). A relatively flat trail follows the contours of the broad hills above town, following views of the valley and the Swiss Alps. The route stretches from the Gotschnabahn (from Klosters) to Strelapass above Davos (5hr.). After the renovation, visitors will be able to easily traverse between the "Panoramaweg" stop and Klosters's cable car. (☎417 67 67; www.parsenn.ch.)

Davos-Platz to Monstein (5hr.). A more isolated and difficult hike into an adjoining valley that requires no cable car. Take Bus #8 from Platz to the trailhead at Sertig-Dörfli. Signs lead to "Fenezfurgga," which passes waterfalls and a valley that divides the Hoch Duncan and the Alpihorn. A stone wall separates the trail from the resorts beyond. The trek ends in Monstein, where buses connect to Glaris and then Davos.

KLOSTERS
☎081

Davos's sister resort, Klosters, lies across the Gotschna and Parsenn mountains. Though Klosters is 10min. from Davos by train, it is a world away in atmosphere. While Davos makes an extra effort to be cosmopolitan, Klosters capitalizes on its natural serenity and cozy chalets. Most ski packages include mountains from both towns, and Klosters's main ski lift leads to a mountain pass where one may ski to either town. Klosters also has better access to fantastic biking trails.

▐ **TRANSPORTATION.** Klosters-Platz and Klosters-Dorf are connected to Chur by **train** through Landquart (1¼hr., every hr. 5:19am-9:31pm, 18.80SFr) and St. Moritz (1½hr., every hr., 31SFr). The same line connects Klosters and Davos

(30min., every hr. 5:34am-11:32pm, 9.20SFr or free with guest card). Local **buses** run between Dorf, Platz, and the major ski lifts (1-6 stops 1SFr, 7-10 stops 2SFr, more than 10 stops 3SFr; guest card holders and children under 16 free).

7 PRACTICAL INFORMATION. Like Davos, Klosters is divided into Klosters-Platz and Klosters-Dorf, connected by bus and train; most activity occurs in Platz. Platz and Dorf both have tourist offices, but the main **tourist office** is in Platz right from the train station (follow the signs). Detailed area hiking (15.50SFr) and biking (7.50SFr) maps are available. **Currency exchange** is available on weekends. (☎410 20 20; www.klosters.ch. Open May-Nov. M-F 8:30am-noon and 2-6pm, Sa 8:30am-noon and 2-4pm; Dec.-April M-Sa 8:30am-noon and 2-6pm, Su 9-11:30am and 4-6pm; July to mid-Aug. Su 9-11am.) Services at the Platz station include: **tickets** and **currency exchange** (open daily 6am-8:30pm), **lockers** (2SFr), **luggage storage** (open 6am-8pm, pick up until 10:40pm; 3SFr), **scooter rental** (inquire for prices). **Internet** access in the **Silvretta Park Hotel**, Landstr. 190, is available 24hr. (Wheelchair-accessible. 15SFr per hr.) A **bike rental** service is at **Andrist Sport** on Gotschnastr. (☎410 20 80. Open M-F 9am-noon and 2-6:30pm, Sa 8am-noon and 2-6pm; closed W afternoons. 38SFr per day, 130SFr for 6 days. AmEx/MC/V.) Daily 24hr. **taxi service** is offered by **Cowboy's Taxi** (☎422 20 84 or 079 232 60 60; www.cowboys-taxi.ch). The **post office** is to the right of the station. (Open M-F 7:30am-noon and 1:45-6:15pm, Sa 8:30am-noon.) **Postal code:** CH-7250.

7 ⬛ ACCOMMODATIONS & FOOD. Jugendherberge Soldanella (HI) ❷, Talstr. 73, is a solid option. From the station, go left uphill past the Hotel Alpina to the church, then cross the street and head up the alleyway to the right of the Kirchplatz bus station sign. Walk 10min. along the gravel path and admire the views as you come upon this massive, renovated chalet with wood paneling, a comfortable reading room, and couches on a flagstone terrace. The owners are friendly English-speakers full of hiking suggestions and tips. (☎422 13 16; www.youthhostel.ch/klosters. Breakfast and sheets included. Dinner and lunch on request 12SFr. All rooms non-smoking. Reception 7-10am and 5-10pm. Check-out 10am. No lockout or curfew. Quiet hours 10pm-7am. Open late June to mid-Oct. and mid-Dec. to mid-Apr. Dorms 28SFr; singles 39SFr; doubles 70SFr, with sink 78SFr. Family rooms 38SFr per person, children 2-6 ½price. Tourist tax 2.70SFr per day June-Sept., 2.20SFr Oct.-May; 6SFr nonmember surcharge. AmEx/D/MC/V.)

Some great deals await in *Privatzimmer* from 25SFr; a list is available at the tourist office. The tourist office can offer details on **mountain huts** in the Klosters area. Two of them, the **Silvrettahütte** (2342m) ❷ and the **Vereina-Berghaus** (1945m) ❸ are serviced by shuttle buses transporting visitors to and from Klosters. (Silverettahütte: ☎422 13 06; www.sac-stgallen.ch. Breakfast 10SFr, breakfast and dinner 28SFr. Open mid-June to mid-Oct. and mid-Feb. to Apr. Hut 26SFr, SAC members 17SFr. Vereina-Berghaus: ☎422 12 16 or 422 11 97. Breakfast and dinner included. Open July to mid-Oct. Dorms 58SFr; doubles 156SFr.) For Silvrettahütte, **Taxi Helmi** provides access to Alp Sardasca, from which the hut is a 2hr. hike. Call ahead for reservations. (☎422 17 13; taxi_helmi@bluewin.ch. 1-way 60SFr, round-trip 26SFr for 4 people or more.) A **shuttle bus** for Vereina-Berghaus leaves from the sports store (see Outdoor Activities below; 24SFr round-trip).

Gasthaus Casanna ❸, Landstr. 171, offers Italian pasta specialties (16.50-18.50SFr) such as gnocchi with gorgonzola (17SFr) in a smoky den. (☎422 12 29; fax 422 20 29. Open M-F 7:30am-12:30am, Sa 9am-6pm.) **Chesa Grischuna ❸**, Bahnhofstr. 12, right from the station, provides a warm wooden interior decorated with rural antiques. Entrees are expensive (35SFr and up for meat dishes), but traditional Swiss specialties (*Rösti* with *Wurst* or bacon, egg, and cheese 17SFr) are reasonably priced. (☎422 22 22; www.chesagrischuna.ch. Open Dec. 16-Oct. 20 daily 7am-11pm, kitchen open 11:30am-2pm and 6:30-9:30pm. AmEx/D/MC/V.) **Hotel Rustico ❹**, Landstr. 194 past the Park Hotel, serves fish, vegetarian dishes, and other fresh entrees (avocado salad with *Zanderfilet* 25SFr) in a bright interior with colorful paintings of wildlife. (☎422 12 46. Open M-W and F-Su 11:30am-1:30pm and 6-9:30pm.) The **Co-op** has cheap groceries, and the restaurant upstairs has *Menüs* around 10SFr. (Wheelchair-accessible. Open M-F 8am-12:30pm and 2-6:30pm, Sa 8am-5pm; restaurant M-F 8am-6:30pm, Sa 8am-5pm.)

◪ OUTDOOR ACTIVITIES. Ski passes for the Klosters-Davos region run 121SFr for two days and 279SFr for six days (including public transportation). The **Madrisabahn** leaves from Klosters-Dorf (1-day pass 46SFr, 6-day pass 249SFr; ages 13-17 82SFr/187SFr; children 40SFr/93SFr). The **Grotschnabahn** gives access to Parsenn and Strela in Davos and Madrisa in Klosters (1-day pass 57SFr, 6-day pass 308SFr). The **ski school,** located in Klosters's tourist office, offers ski and snowboard lessons. (☎410 20 28; www.ssk.ch. Group lessons from 52SFr per day; call the day before to book private lessons at 310SFr per day.) **Swiss Ski and Snowboard School Saas,** operated out of Dörfji Sport at Landstr. 15, has cheaper instruction. (☎420 22 33. Open 8am-8pm. 70SFr per hr.; 285SFr per day.) **Bananas,** operated out of Duty Boardsport, Bahnhofstr. 16, gives snowboard lessons. (☎422 66 60; www.bananas.net. 70SFr per 4hr.; private lessons 80SFr per hr.; board and boots 31SFr per day.) **Ski rental** is available at **Sport Gotschna** across from the tourist office. (☎422 11 97. Open M-F 8am-noon and 2-6:30pm, Sa 8am-12:30pm and 2-6pm, Su 9am-noon and 3-6pm. Skis and snowboards 38SFr per day plus 10% insurance, 5 days 123SFr; boots 19SFr/69SFr.)

Summer cable car passes (valid on Grotschna- and Madrisabahnen) are also available (6-day pass 120SFr). On the green valley floor, hikers make a large loop, from Klosters's Protestant church on Monbielstr. to Monbiel. The route continues to an elevation 1488m and turns left, passing through **Bödmerwald, Fraschmardintobel,** and **Monbieler Wald** before climbing to 1634m and returning to Klosters via **Pardels.** Several adventure companies offer a variety of activities like **river rafting, canoeing, horseback riding, paragliding,** and **glacier trekking.**

LOWER ENGADINE VALLEY

The Engadine Valley takes its name from the Romansch name *(En)* for the Inn River, which flows through the valley and on through Innsbruck, Austria. The transportation line runs from Maloja at the far west end of the valley to Scuol at the far east, connecting all towns by train or short bus rides. The region is divided into the Upper and Lower Engadine, with the town of Brail, just west of Zernez and the Swiss National Park, on the border separating them.

The Lower Engadine valley represents Graubünden at its purest. Unaltered by the swift torrent of change brought by the ski industry elsewhere, the people maintain a strong connection to their land and culture. The Lower Engadine is a stronghold of the **Romansch language,** and nearly every sign is printed in it. The region may not be a skier's paradise, but **hikers** revel in the untouched alpine beauty of the **Swiss National Park.** Regional travel is easy with the **Lower Engadine Regional Pass,** which covers all trains and Post Buses (any 3 days in a 7-day period 50SFr, children 35SFr, any 7 days in a 14-day period, 70SFr/55SFr).

THE SWISS NATIONAL PARK

The Swiss National Park is 25% meadow, 25% forest, and 50% hard rock. The park may not test the hardcore hiker's most extreme will, but it does offer a chance to see plenty of wildlife, alpine flora, and gorgeous panoramas—ultra-strict conservation laws have left the scenery untouched by human hands. Though admittedly small (only 172 sq. km) relative to the American and Canadian connotations of "national park," the *Parc Naziunal Suizzer* is the oldest park in the Alps, and the most fiercely protected. The government's emphasis on preservation has paid tremendous dividends: last year, the park's animal population outnumbered its human visitors. Though a few well-traveled trails draw wildlife enthusiasts and hordes of hikers every summer, sightings of marmots, deer, ibexes, eagles, and bearded vultures (recently reintroduced) are still common.

✴ 🛈 ORIENTATION & PRACTICAL INFORMATION

The Swiss National Park is a kidney-shaped area of land stretching from S-chanf in the southwest to Scuol in the northeast. The wilderness extends southeast from the towns. Thick pine forests and rocky peaks are arrayed around glacial streams. **Munt La Schera** and Chamanna Cluozza, the one alpine hut in the park, lie in the center. The northern regions' grassland is a habitat of red deer and marmots.

Camping and campfires are prohibited in the park, as is collecting flowers, plants, or insects. A team of wardens patrols the park at all times, slapping fines of up to 500SFr on rule-breakers. The park's central office is in Zernez. The names of the park's geographical features are all in Romansch, and a glossary of terms can be found in the back of the park's official trail guide. A few common terms: **piz** and **munt** mean "point" and "mountain," respectively; **val** is "valley;" **ova** is "stream;" **pra** is "meadow;" and **chamanna** means "mountain hut." Bird-watching is best mid-June to mid-July; deer, chamois, and ibex are most active in September; deer buck for mates during October. The park is closed after the first snowfall (usually sometime between Oct. and Nov.) and reopens at the beginning of June.

🚌 TRANSPORTATION

The towns of Scuol, Zernez, and S-chanf lie just north of the park along the **Rhätische Bahn** train line. **Post buses** wind along the three major roads that skirt the park. The **Ofenpass** bisects the park from Zernez; nine parking lots sit along it at regular intervals. The buses make almost hourly stops at nearly all of the parking lots and other popular trailheads. If you plan on using them for more than three days, then buy a **Mehrfahrtenkarte**; cards are available at the Zernez train station or any bus, and provide six rides for 20% off. Roads from S-chanf and Scuol skirt the western and eastern edges of the park. The most manageable hike between the villages surrounding the park is from S-chanf to Zernez, and makes use of the Chamanna Cluozza hut as an overnight resting spot (see Hiking, below).

🏠 ACCOMMODATIONS

Camping is not allowed in the park, but Zernez, Scuol, and S-chanf have campsites outside the park boundaries.

Many hikes leave from around **Hotel Il Fuorn ❷,** on the Ofenpass, a bus ride from Zernez (20min., every hr. except noon 7:10am-7:10pm, 8.40SFr). A friendly crowd fills the hiker's lodge, which sits at the base of several peaks and wel-

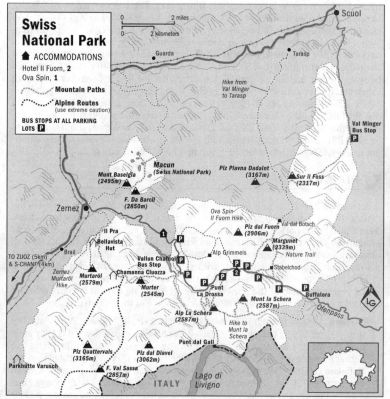

Swiss National Park

▲ ACCOMMODATIONS
Hotel Il Fuorn, **2**
Ova Spin, **1**

∿∿ **Mountain Paths**
∙∙∙∙ **Alpine Routes**
(use extreme caution)

BUS STOPS AT ALL PARKING LOTS P

Scuol

Guarda

Tarasp

Hike from
Val Minger
to Tarasp

Val Minger
Bus Stop P

Macun
(Swiss National Park)

Munt Baselgia
(2495m)

Piz Plavna Dadaint
(3167m)

Sur Il Foss
(2317m)

F. Da Barcli
(2850m)

Zernez

Ova Spin-
Il Fuorn Hike

Val dal Botsch

Il Pra

Bellavista
Hut

Piz dal Fuorn
(2906m)

Margunet
(2339m)

Nature Trail

TO ZUOZ (5km)
& S-CHANF (4km)

Brail

Vallun Chafuol
Bus Stop
Chamanna Cluozza

Alp Grimmels

Stabelchod

Buffalora

Zernez-
Murtaröl
Hike

Murtaröl
(2579m)

Murter
(2545m)

Punt
La Drossa

Munt la Schera
(2587m)

Ofenpass

Piz Quattervals
(3165m)

Alp La Schera
(2587m)

Hike to
Munt la
Schera

Parkhütte Varusch

Piz dal Diavel
(3062m)

Punt dal Gall

ITALY

F. Val Sassa
(2857m)

Lago di
Livigno

GRAUBÜNDEN

comes weary hikers with inviting foam mattresses on wooden bunks. Although across the street from showers and sinks, use of the hotel's facilities, along with the scenery, makes up for the inconvenience. Rooms in the hotel itself are spacious and comfortable. The food is delicious, though the menu is limited and pricey. (*Spätzle* 19.90SFr, *Rösti* 22.20SFr, spaghetti 14.80-17.80SFr.) But you don't have a lot of alternatives; the next restaurant is 10km away. (☎856 12 26; www.ilfuorn.ch. Breakfast included with rooms, 18SFr if you stay in dorms. Free **Internet** available in office upon request. Reception 7:15am-10pm. Check-in 2pm. Check-out 10am. Reserve in advance mid-June to mid-Aug. during peak hiking season, and Oct., when crowds fill the hotel to watch male deer buck for mates. Open May-Oct. Dorms 19SFr; singles 72-79SFr, with shower 103-111SFr; doubles 150/208SFr; triples 171-195SFr; quads 204-232SFr.) The straightforward **Naturfreundehaus Ova Spin ❷**, is before Il Fuorn from Zernez, just outside the western park boundary. (☎/fax 852 31 42. Dorms 15SFR.) **Wegerhaus Ova Spin ❸**, is slightly more modern and slightly more expensive. (☎/fax 856 10 52 or 079 406 73 33; www.stimer.ch. Dorms 20SFr.)

The **mountain huts** scattered near the park offer instant access to the forest. **Chamanna Cluozza ❷**, located in the western block of the park, can only be reached by hiking 3hr. from Zernez. It is the only mountain hut within park limits operated by the park. Along with a happy-but-tired hiker crowd, welcoming family staff members at the hut serve up piping-hot, filling meals at 1882m. (☎856 12 35; cluozza@hotmail.com. Breakfast 6:30-7:30am and dinner 6:30-8pm both 31SFr. You can order modest packed lunches the night before for 8 or 16SFr. Reception 7am-10pm. Open last week of June to mid-Oct. Rooms 27SFr, under 20 and students under 26 11SFr.) The **Parkhütte Varusch** ❷, just outside the southwestern border of the park, is a 1hr. hike from S-chanf. A solar-powered hut with rooms for two-ten people, the hut includes a garden restaurant. (☎854 31 22. Breakfast included; lunch and dinner available. Open May-Oct. Dorms 27SFr; under 16 23SFr; doubles 80SFr.) The **Bellavista hut** ❷ (2000m), a 1½hr. hike from Zernez along the trail to the Murtaröl and the Chamanna Chuozza, has five beds, a wood stove, a kitchenette, outhouse, and a clear view of Zernez and Piz Linard from the front porch. (☎856 17 21. Bring drinking water. Call 1 week in advance for reservations and to get the key. 20SFr. Sleep sack 5SFr. Summer beds 18SFr; winter 20SFr.)

 HIKING

A network of 21 hiking trails (80km) runs throughout the park, concentrated in the central 100 sq. km. Trails are clearly marked, and it is illegal to stray from them. Most hikes in the park involve a lot of elevation gain, occasionally into snow-covered areas. The **Parkhouse** in Zernez lists which trails are navigable, though they all almost always are. Available at the Parkhouse are fantastic trail maps (14SFr) and a somewhat helpful (but fairly hilarious) five-language trail description guide (10SFr, 20SFr for both map and guide). The Parkhouse also sells a geological map and a vegetation map of the park. Trails that require no mountaineering gear are marked with white-red-white blazes, but even some of them are tricky.

Buffalora (1968m) **to Munt la Schera** (2587m) **to Il Fuorn** (1794m) (5½hr.). With this hike, you get a lot of bang for your buck—it can be done in ½ a day and is fairly easy, save the Munt la Schera ascent (which can be easily deleted from the route if so desired). From the **Buffalora** bus stop, a wide cowpath (20min.) heads uphill to **Alp Buffalora** (2038m). The path then becomes deceptively steep through lightly forested cow pastures (30min.). A pleasant amble through flat, meadowy land encompasses most of the 1st 2hr. of this hike. The walk is worth it, however, as you are walking through a postcard-perfect view of the park's eastern range of rocky and snowy peaks. The climb to **Munt la Schera** passes through marmot country and finally reaches the windy, barren peak (1hr.). Glimpses of the **Lago di Livigno** resevoir and the **Italian Alps** complete the panorama. The descent down is through larch forest to **Alp la Schera** (2091m), a park ranger hut with drinking water. From here, one can decide to head south toward Italy to the **Vallun Chafuol**, traversing the Spöl many times and catching sights of waterfalls, or head back to **Il Fuorn** along the forested **God la Drossa** (both routes 2hr.; Vallun Chafuol is at the P3 bus stop).

Zernez (1471m) **to Chamanna Cluozza** (1882m) (3hr.). The way to Chamanna Cluozza is popular hike of easy-to-moderate difficulty. For the most part, the path is a wide, gravelly trail through the woods, leading through farmland, forest, meadows, and along a rocky ridge, with plenty of mountain views in the last half. It is a great introduction to the park and short enough for a leisurely pace. The trail begins across the wooden bridge over the Spöl river, 100m past the Park House. After a flat walk through a meadow, the path enters the forest, where it turns into an uphill climb. The path turns right at the Fritz Sarasin commemorative stone and quickly splits at **Il Pra** to **Cluozza** or **Bellavista** (1hr.). Take the left fork to Cluozza. From here, the trail opens up into the Cluozza Valley (2100m) and travels along a flat ridge (45min.). Afterwards, the A descent to the river offers an opportunity to linger in the **Il Grass** meadows to see the occasional ibex or red deer. After descending to the bridge over the **Ova da Cluozza** with **Piz Linard** in the background (45min.), a final climb awaits **Chamanna Cluozza** overnighters (30min.). With a set of binoculars, you can see tracks of the **Theropod** on the western flank of the Piaz dal Diavel. This 5m long herbivorous dinosaur roamed the area over 200 million years ago and left footprints 30cm across.

Chamanna Cluozza (1882m) **to Murter** (2505m) **to Vallun Chafuol** (1640m) (5hr.). A classic route for those who hiked to Cluozza the day before. The first 2hr. consist of a steep, zig-zagging ascent of 700m to the peak through the meadowy western face of Murter. Ibex and chamois populate these peaks and are especially active in the early morning around sunrise. The Murter summit provides glimpses of the blue-green Ova Spin resevoir below and the snowy peaks of the closed-off western portion of the park. A steep descent of 1000m on a rocky trail turns into a soft wooded trail, ending at the Plan Praspöl. From there, a ½hr. hike across a wooden bridge and up 80m more leads to P3 and Vallun Chafuol. The more motivated hiker can continue for another 2hr. over easy, wooded terrain past Alp Grimmels and on to Il Fuorn.

Zernez (1471m) **to Murtaröl** (2579m) **and back** (6hr.). This hike of moderate difficulty couples an ascent of over 1000m with a fair number of panoramic views as a reward. It begins at the same spot as the Chamanna Cluozza hike and follows the same trail until the path splits at Il Pra (about 1hr.); take the right-hand fork. After passing the Bellavista hut (see Accommodations, p. 436), the trail rises above the tree line and offers wide views of Zernez below. The path passes a set of stone walls (2300m), built during the 19th century in an effort to prevent avalanches, and offers a panoramic view of the Val Tantermozza (inaccessible to visitors) and the mountain chain that surrounds it. The **Murtaröl** crest (3½hr.), with views of the Engadine, Cluozza, and Tantermozza valleys, is only a short climb. Sometimes herds of chamois and ibexes are visible. The route back to Zernez passes bizarre rock formations before plunging into the forest to rejoin the original path at the point where it splits from the Chamanna Cluozza trail.

Val Minger to Tarasp (5hr.). Take the bus from Scuol (dir.: Scharl) to "Val Minger" (9.40SFr; with Eurail or SwissPass 4SFr). One of the more difficult hikes. From the bus stop, cross the bridge and turn left on the trail, which begins with a slow and steady climb up rocky stream beds. As you walk, turn around often for magnificent views of **Piz Pradatsch.** When the trail moves above the tree line it enters a half-pipe-shaped valley, at the end of which lies the solitary, majestic **Piz Plavna Dadaint.** The **Sur il Foss pass,** with its uniquely intimate view of nearby mountains, lies at the end of the valley. From Sur il Foss, a trail leads around the head of the valley to the **Val dal Botsch pass,** which then leads to Il Fuorn in the center of the park. This route is only safe in later summer, when the snow has melted, and even then should only be attempted with hiking poles and very sturdy boots. Check at the National Park House in Zernez for up-to-date conditions. An easier route leads right, toward "Tarasp Fontana." The initial descent can be tricky, depending on recent rock slides. The trail moves into a wide rocky plain, bordered by cliffs that create a visual tunnel, toward the mountain range over Scuol, and backward to Piz Nair and the peaks in front of it. The trail heads through the woods to **Tarasp,** where a bus returns to Scuol (every hr. M-F 6:13am-8:10pm, Sa-Su 8:10am-8:10pm; 4.60SFr).

Nature Route: P8 (1887m) **or P9** (1906m) **to Margunet** (2328m) **to Il Fuorn** (1794m) (3-3½hr). This is the park's only nature trail, with information about the surrounding flora and fauna provided in 5 languages, and an easier hike that still provides a summit of sorts from which to view the Val dal Botsch and Val da Stabelchod. From P8, the route goes through thick pine forest and then an overgrown meadow to the Stabelchod hut (1958m), a residence for park rangers (30min.). The trail then travels along a gorge and a rushing stream, climbing slowly to an outlook point before the 400m ascent to Margunet (1hr.). Marmot families and a recently re-introduced flock of bearded vultures are sometimes spotted on Margunet's eastern slope.

GRAUBÜNDEN

In July, some hikers spot the young, which are just learning how to fly during this time. Arriving at the Margunet panorama, the hike quickly descends on the other side of the saddle into the Val dal Botsch (1hr.). A fairly flat path leads back to the Ofenpass and finishes at the Il Fuorn estate.

P9 (1906m) **to Val Minger bus stop** (1794m) (7hr.). Due to the 800m rapid elevation gain over two ridges, plus the length of the Val Minger, this route is one of the more difficult hikes. As always, the reward is the views: summitting Marguent (2339m), Val dal Botsch (2677m), and Sur il Foss (2317m) provide views of the northern region of the park, including Piz Tavru (3168), its highest peak. This route follows the first half of the Margunet route, then continues north and climbs steeply up to the Val dal Botsch outlook point. From there, the path descends 400m over slippery scree (the bits of rock left behind by a glacier; pick your path carefully). It climbs again, though less steeply, to Sur il Foss. The descent from Sur il Foss lands in the Val Minger, a long stretch of relatively flat meadowland all the way to the bus stop. Val Minger is fairly dry in the summer, so bring plenty of water.

TOWNS NEAR THE NATIONAL PARK

TRANSPORT HUB: ZERNEZ ☎081

Zernez (pop. 1100) is the main gateway to the **Swiss National Park** and home to the headquarters of the park, the **National Parkhouse. Trains** depart for **Samedan** (30min., every hr. 5:53am-11:03pm, 13.40SFr) and **Scuol** (40min., every hr. 6:52am-10:49pm, 12.40SFr) with connections to the rest of Switzerland, including St. Moritz (45min., 16.60SFr). **Currency exchange** and **luggage storage** (3SFr) is available at the train station. (Open M-F 5:30-7:10am and 7:40am-8:10pm, Sa 5:30-7:10am and 7:40am-7:10pm, Su 7:40am-12:10pm and 1:40-6:10pm.) **Internet** access can be gotten at the tourist office (4SFr for 15min., 2SFr every 15min. after; printing and disk entry available). The **post office** is across from the train station. (Open M-F 8-11:30am and 2-6pm, Sa 8:30-11am.) **Postal code:** CH-7530.

From the train station, take the main road (Röven) to the left uphill 6min. to the **tourist office.** (☎856 13 00; fax 11 55. Open June-Oct. M-F 9am-noon and 2-6:30pm, Sa 9-noon and 2-5pm; Nov.-May M-F 9am-noon and 3-5pm.) The **National Parkhouse,** reached by walking from the station uphill 10min., then turning right after the tourist office and heading toward the park 10min. (follow brown signs for "Parc Nazinual Svizzer"), provides information about trail safety and has an extensive selection of maps and souvenirs. (☎856 13 78; www.nationalpark.ch. Open end of May-Oct. Tu 8:30am-10pm, W-Su 8:30am-6pm.) It also houses a small free **museum** about the park; the exhibit is mainly geared toward children. **Sport Sarsura,** in the same building as the tourist office, provides expensive outdoor gear. (☎856 14 34. Open M-F 8am-noon and 2-6:30pm, Sa 8am-noon and 2-5pm.) The **Co-op** is across the street from the tourist office. (Open M-F 8am-noon and 2-6:30pm, Sa 8am-noon and 2-4pm.) The tourist office lists **private rooms** from 25SFr. **Hotel Bär-Post ❷,** left and within sight of the main intersection past the tourist office, is a classy hotel that offers less classy rooms in a back building. The dorms are small and a bit damp. (☎851 55 00; www.baer-ost.ch. Breakfast 12SFr. Sleepsack 5SFr. Reception 9am-10pm. Quiet hours after 10pm. Open mid-Dec. to Oct. Dorms 18SFr. AmEx/DC/MC/V.) Just past the National Parkhouse, **Touristenlager Hummel ❶** offers lager-style accommodations with a spice-stocked kitchen and sitting room included. (☎856 18 74; fax 19 60. Sheets available on request. Dorms 15SFr; doubles 54SFr.) There is camping at **Camping Cul ❶,** across the train tracks from town, in a quiet spot by the river Inn. Turn right out of the station and follow the signs. (☎/fax 856

14 62; www.camping-cul.ch. Reception July-Aug. 8am-noon and 1-8pm; Sept.-June times vary. Open May-Oct. 15. 7SFr per person, children 4SFr; tents 6SFr, cars 5SFr; visitor and trash tax not included. MC/V.)

Grotia Pizzeria Mirta ❸, downhill around the corner from the bank at the main intersection, offers some of the best wood-oven pizza (14-18.50SFr) in Graubünden. (☎856 17 35. Open Tu-Su 8am-11pm; closed May and Nov. V.)

ZUOZ ☎081

Though located in the Upper Engadine, Zuoz's adherence to architectural and linguistic (Romansch) traditions, as well as the warmth of its citizens, mark it as a Lower Engadine town. Its position on the border of both regions makes it a good point from which to explore both sides of the Engadine Valley. Burned to the ground by residents in 1499 to keep it out of Austrian hands, Zuoz (pop. 1300) was rebuilt in the early 16th century and has changed little since. Ibex, pinwheels, and flowers float on the whitewashed walls of village houses, and a carved bear defends the fountains from bloodthirsty imperial Hapsburg troops.

F7 TRANSPORTATION & PRACTICAL INFORMATION. Zuoz is a **train** ride from St. Moritz (30min., every hr. 6:12am-11:22pm, 9.20SFr) via Samedan (20min., 5.80SFr); and Zernez (20min., every hr. 5:17am-10:26pm, 8.40SFr). The train station provides **luggage storage** (3SFr) and **bike rental** (30SFr per day, 23SFr per ½ day; open M-F 6:40am-6:30pm, Sa 6:40am-6pm, Su 8:10am-12:20pm and 1:40-5:30pm). **La Passarella,** which extends directly opposite the station (right off the Co-Op), leads to the main street in town, **San Basiaun,** which heads right and turns into Via Maestra. The **tourist office,** right on Via Maestra (5min.), provides guides to the local sights and suggests hikes. (☎848 986 946; www.zuoz.ch. Open June to mid-Oct. Sa 10am-noon and 4-6:30pm; Aug. to mid-Oct. Su 4-6:30pm; mid-Oct. to Nov. and mid-Apr. to May M-F 9am-noon and 2-5pm.) Zuoz has two **public telephones,** one at the station and one at the tourist offices. The **Kantonalbank,** past the tourist office, **exchanges currency** and has a 24hr. **ATM.** (Bank open M-F 8:30am-noon and 2-5pm.) The **post office** is in the train station. (Open M-F 8am-noon and 2:15-5:45pm, Sa 8-11am.) **Postal code:** CH-7524.

BOYS WILL BE BOYS
Zuoz takes pride in its unique holidays and traditional festivals. On March 1, the **Chalandamarz** engulfs Engadine as young boys wander from house to house, ring huge bells, and sing songs to drive off evil spirits and welcome spring. A statue commemorating the event stands in the town square. Originally a pagan fertility rite, the more peculiar **San Gian's Day** commemorates John the Baptist on July 24, when village boys spritz girls with water from Zuoz's fountains.

F◩ ACCOMMODATIONS & FOOD. The cheapest lodgings are located in the center of town at **Ferienlager Sonder ❷.** Head down Via Maestra from the tourist office and turn right onto tiny Chanels at the sign for "Ferienlager" for simple rooms in a 16th-century building with kitchen and ping pong. (☎854 07 73; www.engadina.ch. Dorms 23SFr; after 2 nights 20SFr.) At the 400-year-old **Chesa Walther ❸,** opposite Willy's Sports near the tourist office, very spacious rooms are comfortably decorated with plush red furniture and gold-trimmed mirrors. (☎854 13 64. Partial kitchen facilities 5SFr. Rooms with communal bathroom 40SFr.) The multi-lingual staff at **Hotel Steinbock ❸,** at the end of town away from the station (150m past the tourist office), offers cozy wood-paneled rooms in a friendly environment, though prices double in high season. (☎854 13 73; www.steinbock-zuoz.ch. Breakfast included. Reception 8am-midnight. Rooms high season 120SFr, low season 60SFr per person. MC/V.) The **Steinbock Bar,** within the hotel, is filled most nights with beer-sipping locals and becomes "the" hangout for the students from the local boarding school. (Open W-Su 7pm-1am. Pizza from 12SFr served till 11pm or midnight.

Restaurant Dorta ❸, from the station, left to the end of the parking lot, then again under the bridge, is farmhouse-turned-restaurant and bar that defines rustic. The barstools are tree stumps, and the 400-year-old door is held open with a rope. While locals chat in the candlelit bar, fresh flowers and an impressive menu of Engadine specialties await those eating dinner. *Zuozer Krautpizokel,* a large plate of *Spätzli* (German egg noodles) with ham, bacon, and cream sauce is 23SFr. Vegetarians can try the *Maluns,* shredded potatoes with applesauce and plum compote. (☎854 20 40; www.dorta.ch. Kids menu available. Open Dec.-Christmas and Easter-June W-F 6-10pm, Sa-Su 11:30am-10pm; Christmas-Easter and June-Oct. Tu-Su 11:30am-10pm. Kitchen open 11:30am-2pm and 6-10pm. Reservations recommended. AmEx/D/MC/V.) The popular **Dorta Bar** runs changing specials and ladies' nights. (Open W-Su 6pm-1am, also Tu in high-season.) **Café-Restorant Klarer ❹,** in the center of town, offers a variety of pastas for 14-20SFr along with lighter dishes with an Italian and French flair. At lunch, *Menüs* (20-25SFr) come with soup, salad, and the daily chef's special. Meat entrees (29-45SFr), like grilled Forelle with spinach (29SFr), are available in the evening. Fondue is 22SFr, *pizzoccheri* 16SFr. Wine enthusiasts can view the extensive cellar; ask the waiter for a quick tour. (☎851 34 34; www.klarerconda.ch. Wheelchair-accessible. Open daily 7:30am-11pm; May 7:30am-noon. AmEx/D/MC/V.)

The **Co-op** supermarket is opposite the station. (Open M-F 8am-12:15pm and 2-6:30pm, Sa 8am-5pm.) **Primo** is uphill from the tourist office. (Open M-F 8am-noon and 2-6:30pm, Sa 8am-noon and 2-4pm; closed Th afternoons.)

◎🅽 SIGHTS & HIKING. The small **Church San Luzius** on Via Maestra has sweet-smelling pine pews and Romansch hymnals with brilliantly colored stained-glass windows above the altar. The **prison tower** next door is preserved as the last prisoner left it—a dark, dank chamber, filled with terrifying implements of torture and chilling dungeon cells (descriptions only in German). Farther from the tourist office toward the station, on the corner of Via Dorta, lies the tiny **San Bastiaun** chapel with fading frescoes. (Ask the tourist office for the keys to all sights; hours are the same as those of the tourist office; San Luzi open sometimes without the key.)

Zuoz woos **bikers** with 37km of marked trails. **Rental** available at the train station or for less across the river at the **Inline Shop** operated by Willi Sport. (☎854 08 06; Open M-Sa 10am-12:30pm and 1-6:30pm, June and Sept. until 5pm. 25-29SFr per day; 18-20SFr per ½day.) For **hikers,** the National Park is right next door, but Zuoz offers a few distinctive hikes of its own. The **Via Segantini** eventually leads to the **Piz Bernina** (4049m). The path begins past the Hotel Engiadina, on Via Maestra. Turn right onto Chröntschet, then walk along the private driveway, which leads to the gravel path labeled "Castell." The path leads to the historic Alpenschloßhotel Castell; from there, follow signs for "Via Segantini." The easy trail leads from Zuoz to La Punt (2hr.) and Bever (4hr.), where the train runs back to Zuoz.

For a more rugged afternoon, the **Ova d'Arpiglia** leads to a crashing 20m waterfall. To find the trail, turn left from the train station and go through the underpass toward the river. Cross the river on the smaller bridge, head under the road, and turn left, following the yellow "Wanderweg" signs on the dirt road heading into the woods. Stay on the right side of the stream following

GRAUBÜNDEN

signs for "Mont Seja," to the waterfall. The path, replete with purple wildflowers, then climbs steeply to a green meadow to the right of the falls. It is known locally as the "Stairway to Heaven." Signs point the way from this picnic haven to Zuoz (round-trip 1½hr.).

UPPER ENGADINE VALLEY

About 350km of ski trails and 60 ski lifts crisscross the Upper Engadine Valley. Unlike Zermatt and Grindelwald, where Japanese and American tourists flock about, the Upper Engadine attracts mostly German, Italian, and Swiss visitors. Connoisseurs rate the downhill skiing in the Upper Engadine just below the Jungfrau and Matterhorn regions. The summer sun clears the snow from the region's ample hiking trails; the most unique hiking skirts the melting glaciers flowing down from **Piz Bernina** (4049m, the highest in the region) and its neighbors.

Ski, snowboard, and hiking equipment rental is available in multiple shops throughout the towns. Although not standardized, prices tend to be similar (skis 50-70SFr per day, ages 16-20 30-37SFr, ages 6-16 21-24SFr for top-of-the-line skis; snowbarods 28-38SFr; boots 9-19SFr. Some smaller shops rent basic skis from 28SFr). Ask at the local tourist office about **ski schools**—many have well-developed programs for children, including weekly races for novices on Alp Languard (Pontresina). Novices should head for Zuoz or Corviglia (St. Moritz), or Alp Languard (Pontresina); experts, for Diavolezza (Pontresina), Piz Nair (St. Moritz), or Piz Lagalb (Pontresina). One-day passes are available for each town. (St. Moritz and Celerina passes are sold together.) Prices range according to time in the season (40-61SFr, ages 16-20 36-55SFr, ages 6-15 20-30SFr; St. Moritz is the most expensive area.) Multiple-day passes are available only for the entire Engadine region—they're not much more expensive and cover most trains and buses as well (5-day pass 225-277SFr, youth 203-249SFr, children 114-139SFr). Cross-country fanatics should glide to **Pontresina,** where hundreds train for the grueling **Engadine Ski Marathon,** which stretches from Maloja to S-chanf. The race is on the second Sunday in March. (36th Annual Engadin Skimarathon. March 14, 2004. ☎ 081 850 55 55; www.engadin-skimarathon.ch for application/registration. 16+. Register by Feb. 1. Entry fee 80SFr.) The weekend before sees the 17km **Frauenlauf** solely for women. (5th Annual Frauenlauf. March 7, 2004. See above for registration; entrance fee 40SFr.) **Ski schools** in almost every village offer private lessons. (General information ☎ 081 830 00 00; www.skiengadin.ch.)

PONTRESINA   ☎ 081

Away from the bustle of the rest of the Upper Engadine, Pontresina is nestled in one of the highest wind-sheltered valleys of the region at the head of two major rivers. The resort has glitzy aspirations, with luxury hotels and a modern main street, but the proximity of three major peaks makes Pontresina a favorite mountaineering destination. Every morning, the famous Diavolezza glacier tour draws hordes of hikers. In winter, Pontresina becomes the cross-country skiing center of the Upper Engadine and offers a cheaper downhill alternative to St. Moritz.

⊟ TRANSPORTATION. Trains run to Chur (2hr., every hr. 5:49am-8:04pm, 38SFr) via Samedan and St. Moritz (10min., every hr. 6:52am-7:52pm, 4.60SFr). The **Engadin Bus** connects Pontresina to the villages of the Upper Engadine Valley all the way to Maloja. One route also runs from the left of the train station to the post office, the tourist office, and other important spots in town. (High season every 30min., low season every hr. 6:55am-8:36pm; 2.60SFr.)

⚠ PRACTICAL INFORMATION. Via de la Staziun winds over two rivers and uphill to the center of town (20min.). The **tourist office,** in the modern "Rondo" building where the Via de la Staziun meets the town, plans free excursions (see p. 446), gives hiking advice, provides information on weekly events, and finds private rooms from 28SFr. (☎838 83 00; www.pontresina.com. Open M-F 8:30am-noon and 2-6pm, Sa 8:30am-noon; mid-June to Sept. also Sa 3-6pm, Su 4-6pm; mid-Dec. to Easter also Sa-Su 4-6pm.) The **Ferienregion Engadin,** the regional tourist office, answers questions and offers information about the region via telephone. (☎842 65 73. Open M-F 8:30am-noon and 2-6pm, Dec. 25-Mar. and mid-July to mid-Aug. also Sa 9am-noon.) Services at the train station include: **currency exchange, luggage storage** (3SFr), **bike rental** (30SFr per day), and **lockers** (2SFr). (Station ☎842 63 37. Open high season daily 5:40am-7pm; low season M-F 5:40am-7pm, Sa-Su 6:40am-7pm.) **Internet** at the Hotel Post, uphill 5min. from the tourist office at Via Maestra 74. (Wheelchair-accessible. Open daily 8am-9pm. 8SFr per 30min.; disk entry and free printing.) **Taxi** with Berlina Taxi. (☎079 786 19 17. Free telephone at the station.) **Post office** 6min. uphill from the tourist office on the corner of Via Maestra and Via da Mulin. (Open M-F 7:45am-noon and 1:45-6:15pm, Sa 8:30am-noon.) **Postal code:** CH-7504.

⌂ ACCOMMODATIONS. The **Jugendherberge Tolais (HI) ❸,** in the modern, salmon-colored building across from the train station, is convenient for early-morning ski ventures and connections throughout the Engadine Valley in the winter. In summer, families and older hikers fill the six-bed dorms and use the sometimes less than pristine showers. Dinner is required and usually simple but decent; order the vegetarian entree for better quality and more creative dishes. The hostel also has a restaurant, ping-pong, swings, a large ski room, and a soccer field. (☎842 72 23; www.youthhostel.ch/pontresina. Breakfast, lockers, and sheets included. Buffet dinner 6:30-8:30pm included; later times and vegetarian options on request. Board less 7SFr if you do not want one meal. Laundry 10SFr. Free parking. All rooms non-smoking. Reception 7:30-9:30am, 4-6:30pm, 7:30-10pm, June and Oct. until 9pm. Doors lock 11pm; entrance code given. Quiet time from 10pm. Open Dec.-Apr. and June-Oct. 6-bed dorms 44SFr; doubles 138SFr; quads 220SFr; nonmembers add 6SFr, families add 12SFr total. Prices do not include tax. AmEx/D/MC/V.) In the heart of town (5min. uphill from the tourist office, across from Papeterie Schocher) at **Pension Valtellina ❹,** Mariuccia Della Briotta, a gentle Italian grandmother, furnishes her cozy, mountain-view rooms with warm down comforters. The Pension's triple has a balcony overlooking the Piz Bernina; pink bathrooms are down the hall. (☎842 64 06. Breakfast included. Open Dec. 26-May and June-Nov. Singles 52-60SFr; doubles 104-112SFr; triple 150-156SFr.)

The lovely **Camping Plauns ❶,** in Morteratsch (train dir.: Tirano; 3.80SFr), offers laundry (3-4SFr), a basic foods shop, and a grill after 5pm. Campers walk the 3km from the trail head above the train station to the Bernina Pass. (☎842 62 85; www.pontresina.com. Open June to mid-Oct. and mid-Dec. to mid-Apr. 8.50SFr; ages 12-15 5.50SFr, ages 6-11 4SFr; tents 9SFr; car 4SFr. Electricity 3-4:50SFr.)

◖ FOOD. The **Puntschella Café-Restaurant ❸,** on Via da Mulin off Via Maestra before the post office, is the birthplace of the **Engadiner Torte** (a local delicacy made from candied almonds, raisins, layers of cream and nut pureé, and crunchy crust; 4.20SFr). The bakery is filled with a dazzling array of glazed chocolate and fruit delicacies; the restaurant offers local specialties, pastas, and vegetarian dishes (entrees 13-24.50SFr). Locals fill the bar (beer from 3.80SFr), while families are welcomed in the red-velvet restaurant area. (☎838 80 30. Open daily June-Oct. 7:30am-10pm, Dec.-Feb. 7:30am-9pm. Closed May and Nov. AmEx/MC/V.) The **Pizzeria Sportpavillon ❷**, 400m downhill from the tourist office near the bus stop "Sportpavillon," looks out on tennis courts and Piz Bernina. The cheerful waitstaff in red bow ties and matching suspenders serves pizzas (13.50-19.50SFr, 10-11pm all pizzas 11SFr) and pasta from 14SFr. A family special (38SFr) is enough pizza for two adults and two children. (☎842 63 49. Kitchen open daily noon-2pm and 6-11pm. Reservations suggested 6-8pm.) **Pitschna Scena ❸**, downhill 5min. from the tourist office on Via Maestra and downstairs in the Hotel Saratz, is run by chic waiters dressed in black. *Pitschna* means "little" in Romansch; the restaurant and bar boast several different "little scenes." In the wood-paneled upstairs, get curried chicken with rice (24SFr) or a burger (18SFr). The uplit bar hosts a glitzy St. Moritz crowd in the winter, favored by young locals. In summer, a sportier crowd of hotel guests while away the hours with glasses of "the only Foster's on tap in Pontresina" (beer from 4SFr). Every Thursday in the summer, no-cover concerts fill the terrace until the wee hours, and the price of drinks goes up 6SFr. (☎839 45 80. Concerts start at 10pm; check www.saratz.ch for schedule. Open mid-June to Oct. and Dec.-Apr. daily 11am-midnight, later with special events. AmEx/MC/V.)

Cento Bar, 100m up the street from Tea-room Gianotti, is an earthy local hangout beneath the Hotel Müller. A laid-back setting with wool-covered benches and candle light, the bar fills up after 11pm, when local DJs spin a wide range of odd beats. (☎839 30 40; www.bar-cento-club.com. Beers 5-7SFr; mixed drinks 12-16SFr. Open Tu-Su 9pm until whenever.) The **Co-op** is at the corner of Via Maestra and Via da Mulin. (Open M-F 8am-12:15pm and 2-6:30pm, Sa 8am-5pm.)

◙ **SIGHTS.** In a well-preserved 17th-century farmhouse, the **Museum Alpin,** Chesa Delnon, up the street to the left of the tourist office, presents life in the Engadine as it used to be: full of bearded, pipe-smoking, wool-clad mountain men with picks and ropes. The brilliantly lit mineral collection is a museum highlight, as is the collection of over 100 stuffed Engadine-region fowl. (☎842 72 73. Open June-Oct. M-Sa 4-6pm, in bad weather 3-6pm. 5SFr, children under 16 free. A short English description of the displays is free.) At the highest point of the village, the bare exterior of the **Church of Santa Maria** conceals a number of well-preserved frescoes, including the 1495 **Mary Magdalene cycle.** Look closely at the back wall to see where the original frescoes from 1230 were painted over; don't go during a tour if you want to look around on your own—the church is very small. (Open June 10-28 M, W, F and July-Oct. daily 3:30-5:30pm. German tours W 5pm; also July-Aug. F 5pm. English guide 2SFr.) For an enchanting hour of music, attend the daily *Kurkonzerte* held in the **Taiswald** pavilion in the woods. (Concerts mid-June to mid-Sept. daily 11am-noon. Trail by train station; signs point the way.)

▚ **OUTDOOR ACTIVITIES.** In winter, Pontresina is a center for **cross-country skiing.** The youth hostel is the *Langlaufzentrum* (cross-country center); trails are not monitored by rescue personnel, and therefore free to all. The tourist office sells the helpful *Oberengadia Bergell* hiking and mountain biking map, which covers the Upper Engadine (15SFr). A number of trails stretch between the **Muottas Maragl cable car** (☎842 83 08; one-way 18SFr, round-trip 26SFr; base accessible by Post Bus, dir.: St. Moritz), the **Piz Languard,** and the cable car below it. The level "Hohenweg" rambles above the valley between the cable cars (4hr.). A more demanding route (1½hr.) leads from the Muottas Muragl to the **Alp Segantini,** where the painter Giovanni Segantini spent his last years. The trail then climbs to Piz Languard (3hr.), with photographic views up the snaking Morteratsch glacier to the 4049m **Piz Bernina.** To reach the Piz Languard more quickly, take the **Alp Languard chairlift** from town (☎842 62 55; 13SFr, round-trip 19SFr). From the top of the lift, follow signs to the steep 2½hr. hike to the peak and restaurant.

For more intimate contact with the surrounding five glaciers, it is possible to take the train (dir.: Tirano) to "Diavolezza" (6.20SFr) and then the cable car to the top of the Diavolezza glacier (call the region cable car office at ☎830 00 00 or 0844 844 944 with questions; www.bergbahnengadin.ch; Diavolezza costs 20SFr, round-trip 28SFr), which sits just above the valley between Piz Palu and Bernina. Bring sunglasses; the snow makes the view nearly blinding to the naked eye. The **Mountain Climbing School of Pontresina,** Switzerland's largest, leads a popular 4hr. hike down the Morteratsch glacier for sure-footed hikers. A more expensive glacier trek is also offered and requires pre-registration. (☎838 83 33; www.bergsteiger-pontresina.ch. Hikes daily July-Aug. 11am; Sept. to mid-Oct. every Su, Tu, W, F, 11am. Meet at the top of the cable car, or the bottom in questionable weather. 30SFr, ages 7-16 15SFr. Glacier trek 95SFr; 6hr.; special equipment provided. July-Sept. Th and Su, meet at 8am in the tourist office building.) Trails also attack the glacier from the bottom, which is significantly cheaper. Take the train from Pontresina (dir.: Tirano) to "Morteratsch" (3.80SFr) and walk up to and alongside the Morteratsch glacier. From the train stop it is a 30min. walk to the glacier and a 3hr. hike to the highest hut on the glacier. Signs mark the glacier's recession since the turn of the century. The tourist office has free beach volleyball and fishing, tours, and excursions, including botanical and wildlife observation excursions, and a guided trip to the Swiss National Park. (All available in English. Free only to those staying overnight in Pontresina; for day visitors, certain fees may apply.) For canyoning (170SFr), house running (rappeling frontwards; prices vary), or dog sled rides (winter only; 95SFr), call **Pontresina Events** (☎842 72 57 or 834 54 32; www.pontresinaevents.ch). For more moderately priced excursions, try **Fähndrich Sport** (part of Pontresina Events.) The company offers a weekly summer bulletin at tourist office, listing canoe trips, mountain biking, inline skating, nordic walking, and other activities that include transportation, equipment rental, and a guide. (☎842 71 55; fax 69 52. Reserve your spot the day before by 6pm 20-45SFr.)

ST. MORITZ ☎081

Chic, elegant, and exclusive, St. Moritz is one of the world's most famous ski resorts, but offers little of substance for the backpacker. A playground for the rich and famous, this "Resort at the Top of the World" will turn almost anyone into a window-shopper. As host to the Winter Olympics in 1928 and 1948, St. Moritz was catapulted into the international spotlight. Today it offers a wide selection of winter sports from world-class skiing and bobsledding to golf, polo, greyhound racing, cricket on the frozen lake, and *Skikjöring*—a sport similar to water skiing in which the water is replaced by snow and the motorboat by a galloping horse.

▐ TRANSPORTATION

Trains run every hour to: Celerina (5min., 4:56am-11:45pm, 2.60SFr); Chur (2hr., 4:56am-8:02pm, 38SFr); Pontresina (10min., 7:14am-8:20pm, 4.60SFr); Zuoz via Samedan (30min., 4:56am-8:02pm, 9.20SFr) Zernex (40min., 4:56am-9:13pm); Scuol-Tarasp (2¼hr., 4:56am-9:02pm). **PostAuto Buses** and the **Engadin Bus** provide similar routes and the only public access to the Engadine Valley west of St. Moritz. Buses depart from the station and run every hr. (6:38am-12:04am; add 5SFr after 9:36pm) to: Maloja (40min., 9.80SFr); Sils (20min., 6.60SFr); Silvaplana (15min., 3.80SFr).

Several scenic train routes originate in St. Moritz. The legendary **Glacier Express** covers the 290km to Zermatt in a leisurely 7½hr. (Departs Oct. 13-Dec. 12 dail, 9:02am, May 24-Oct. 12 9:25am; 131SFr; SwissPass valid, Eurail valid until Disentis), crossing 291 bridges and going through 91 tunnels. The **Bernina Express,** the only Swiss train that crosses the Alps without entering any tunnels, journeys to Tirano, Italy (2½hr.; every hr. 7:14am-4:45pm; 26SFr, Eurail and SwissPass valid).

🛈 PRACTICAL INFORMATION

The **tourist office,** Via Maistra 12, makes hotel reservations. Follow the signs from the top of Truoch Serlas across from the train station and turn right across the street and up the stairs after last sign. (☎ 837 33 33; www.stmoritz.ch. Open July to mid-Sept. and mid-Dec. to Apr. M-F 9am-6:30pm, Sa 9am-6pm, Su 4-6pm; May-June and Nov. M-F 8am-noon and 2-6pm, Sa 9am-noon. Questions answered by phone 1hr. before counter opens.) The **train station** (☎ 833 55 52 or 833 59 12) has **currency exchange, Western Union services, tickets,** and **information** (daily 7am-7pm). At a different counter are **luggage storage** (3SFr), a kiosk for **hotel reservations,** and **bike rental** (30SFr per day, 6SFr extra to return to a different train station; 23SFr per ½day). (Open daily 8am-noon and 1:30-5:30pm.) **Lockers** are 2SFr. Taxi services are available from **Erich's Taxi** (☎ 833 35 55). **Swisscom,** in the post office, on Via Serlas on the way to the tourist office, offers **Internet** access. (Open M-F 7:45am-noon and 1:45-6:15pm. 5SFr per 30min.) **Bobby's American Pub,** past Galerie Apotheke, has more terminals, two with disk entry (CD, floppy, zip). (15SFr per hr. Open daily noon-8pm.) **Post office,** at Via Serlas 23 wth Swisscom. (Open M-F 7:45am-noon and 1:45-6:15pm, Sa 8:30am-noon.) **Postal code:** CH-7500.

🛏 ACCOMMODATIONS

With a cappuccino maker in the main lobby, the **Jugendherberge Stille (HI) ❸,** Via Surpunt 60, provides luxury on a backpacker's budget. Breakfast and cafeteria-style dinner are required, which adds to the price, but the salad bar and all-you-can-eat entrees are worth it—and probably save you money, all told. Follow signs around the lake left of the station (30min.), or take the Ortsbus #3 (dir.: St. Moritz Bad, Signal) to "St. Moritz Bad, Sonne" (10min.; 2-4 per hr. 8am-8pm, after 9pm take the night bus dir.: Celerina-Samadan; 2.60SFr) and go left on Via Surpunt (10min.). Perks include: four-bed dorms, semi-private showers, a pool table (2SFr), ping-pong, a game room, **currency exchange** at the reception, **Internet** (4SFr per 15min.), children's playroom, and cheap **mountain bike rental** (15SFr per day, 10SFr after 4pm). The hostel can be overrun by sports teams in the summer; call in advance. (☎ 833 39 69; www.youthhostel.ch/st.moritz. Breakfast, dinner, lockers, and sheets included. Towels 3SFr with 10SFr deposit. Lunch 5-9.50SFr, order in advance. Laundry 4SFr wash, 3.60SFr dry. Reception daily June-Oct. 7-10am and 4-9:45pm; Dec.-Apr. 7:30-10am and 4-9:45pm; May and Nov. shortened hours. Check-out 9:45am. Door locked at 11pm; entrance code given. May-Oct. dorms 45.50SFr; doubles 117SFr, with shower 140SFr. Nov.-Apr. dorms 52SFr; doubles 130SFr-150SFr, with shower 170SFr. Nonmembers add 6SFr. AmEx/D/MC/V.) **Hotel Sonne ❹,** Via Sela 11 (take bus #3 to "St. Moritz Bad, Sonne"), offers luxury lodgings with spacious, clean rooms with private showers, balconies, safes, TVs, and minibars. (☎ 833 03 63; www.sonne-stmoritz.ch. Non-smoking floors. Breakfast included. Reception 6:30am-11pm. Check-out 11am. Apr. 21-Dec. 21 singles 95-105SFr; doubles 160-190SFr; triples 210-255SFr. Dec. 22-Apr. 12. 120-165SFr/ 190-230SFr/240-275SFr. AmEx/MC/V.) For **Camping Olympiaschanze ❶,** catch the Post Bus (dir.: Sils-Maloja) to "St. Moritz Campingplatz" (3SFr). This sprawling campground in the woods has a friendly atmosphere and features small picnic tables and weekend BBQs. (☎833 40 90; www.campingtcs.ch. Washing machine available. Reception 7:45am-noon and 2:30-8pm. Open mid-May to Sept. 5.20-7.20SFr per person, children ½-price; tent 6-7SFr; car 3SFr.)

■ FOOD

Restaurant Hauser ❸, on pl. da la Posta Veglia, a block downhill from the tourist office and across from the Schweizerhof Hotel, offers a diverse, relatively inexpensive menu (*Bratwurst* and fries 16.50SFr, tofu with Chinese vegetables 20.50SFr). For a culinary adventure, try the *Piöda* (Romansch for "hot stone"). Cooked right at the table, this house specialty comes in Aussie (ostrich and kangaroo), traditional (beef and venison), or vegetarian versions. In summer, the restaurant's large terrace hosts Sunday jazz brunches with live music; in winter, there is a giant outdoor "Roo Bar." (☎837 50 50; www.hotelhauser.ch. Open daily 8am-10pm; rotating specialty available 6-9:30pm; brunch Aug.-Sept. Su, call ahead; bar opens in Dec. daily 2pm-late.) **Acla ❺,** Via dal Bagn 54, in the Schweizerhof Hotel, has an intimate atmosphere for fine dining. Entrees (36-45SFr) include French duck breast with apricots. Pastas are 16-26SFr. (☎837 07 01. Reservations recommended. Open daily 11:30am-2pm and 6:30-8:30pm. AmEx/MC/V/DC.) For aprés-skiing action, head downstairs in the Schweizerhof Hotel and try out the three bars. The locals flock to the **Stübli,** which serves up filling hot meals like *raclette* (22.50SFr) to skiers, and offers relatively cheap beer on tap (from 4.50SFr); there is live music daily in winter. The **PianoBar** is just that, and the **Muli Bar** pays homage to country music. (☎837 07 07 or www.schweizerhofstmoritz.ch for all three. Beer from 4.50SFr, specialty drinks 6-7SFr. Open daily summer 8pm-2am; winter 4pm-2am.)

Get groceries at the **Co-op Center,** up from the tourist office or at Via dal Bagn 20, the main road between Dorf and Bad, on the way to the youth hostel. (Open M-F 8am-12:15pm and 2-6:30pm, Sa 8am-5pm. The location on Via dal Bagn is wheelchair-accessible, open over lunch time, and on F till 8pm.) The **After Hours** grocery store, Via Maistra 2, under the kiosk, is open 24hr. (In May and Nov. daily 6am-11pm. ☎834 99 00. AmEx/MC/V.) In late January, sample the culinary delights of the annual week-long **St. Moritz Gourmet Festival.** Sponsored by the World Gourmet Club, the event brings chefs from around the world, hosts classes, and offers package deals through St. Moritz Tourism. (Check www.stmoritz.ch. Jan. 26-31, 2004.)

▥ MUSEUMS & EVENTS

The **Giovanni Segantini Museum,** Via Somplaz 30, is a 15min. uphill walk from the "Aruons" stop on the #3 Ortsbus route. The walk is worth it—the domed structure on the hill is both a museum and a memorial that the art nouveau painter designed for himself before his death in nearby Maloja. The dome was made expressly to house the exhibit's highlight, the alpine trilogy "Life, Nature, and Death," (also known as "Becoming, Being, and Passing"). On its lower level, the museum displays two changing rooms full of Segantini originals. (☎833 44 54; www.segantini-museum.ch. English guidebook 10SFr. Open June 1-Oct. 20 and Dec.-Apr. Tu-Su 10am-noon and 3-6pm. 10SFr, students 7SFr, children 3SFr.) The **Engadiner Museum,** Via dal Bagn 39, between Bad and Dorf, is a rare example of Engadine *sgraffiti* architecture, where designs are carved into white plaster on the exterior of buildings to reveal a darker base color. The house features tiny doorways, beautiful *Chuchichästli*s (cupboards), and a macabre plague-era four-poster sickbed with a skeleton on the ceiling. The inscription translates, "As you are, I would like to be," in other words, still alive. (☎833 43 33. English guides 1SFr. Open June-Oct. M-F 9:30am-noon and 2-5pm, Su 10am-noon; Dec.-Apr. M-F 10am-noon and 2-5pm,

Su 10am-noon. Closed May and Nov. 5SFr, students 4SFr, ages 6-12 2.50SFr.) July brings the **Opern Festival** to the legendary Badrutt's Palace Hotel in St. Moritz. (☎833 01 10; www.opernfestival-engadin.ch. Tickets 90-170SFr.)

🔼 OUTDOOR ACTIVITIES

St. Moritz's **skiing** is world-famous. Two main areas, Corviglia and Corvatsch, are packed with easy runs, although tougher runs pepper each. The third area, Diavolezza, offers some more difficult slopes. (☎830 00 00 for regional ski packages; www.skiengadine.ch. Skiing day passes 49-61SFr, youth 16-20 45-55SFr, ages 6-15 26-30SFr. Equipment rental available at several shops throughout town.) The St. Moritz Sports Office, housed in the tourist office, has a listing of all major events throughout the year. Highlights in 2004 include: **World Bobsledding Championships** (Jan. 24-25); the annual **Polo on Snow** tournament, played on the frozen St. Moritz Lake (Jan. 22-25); and the 77th **White Turf: Running of the Horses,** a similar event where horses race across the ice (Feb. 1, 8, 15). Each year the 1.6km **bobsled** run from the '28 and '48 Olympics is rebuilt by 14 skilled laborers for the **Olympia Bobrun.** (☎830 02 00; www.olympia-bobrun.ch. Open Dec. 210SFr for 1 run, diploma, and photo; call ahead, as slots fill up quickly. No experience necessary.)

In the summer, visitors take advantage of the area by **hiking** (the tourist office sells a map for 17SFr). A flat trail cuts its way from St. Moritz to Pontresina (1½hr.). The trailhead is on the other side of the train station (the "See" exit), across the bridge. For a more demanding trip (3hr.), ride from St. Moritz up to **Piz Nair** for a rooftop view of the Engadine. (3075m. ☎833 43 44.) From here, a train goes to **Suvretta Lake** (2580m) in the shadow of majestic **Piz Julier** (3380m). Follow the Ova da Suvretta back down to the Signalbahn or St. Moritz (3½hr.). **The St. Moritz Experience** (☎833 77 14; www.stmoritz-experience.ch) provides **canyoning** (W, F; 180SFr) and **glacier adventures** (M, Th; 120SFr). Other summer activities include **river rafting** (☎861 14 19; www.engadin-adventure.ch; 85-95SFr per ½-day, 160SFr per day) and **horseback riding.** (☎833 57 33. 60SFr per hr., 90SFr per private lesson.)

ITALIAN SWITZERLAND (TICINO, TESSIN)

Ticino (*Tessin* in German and French), nestled below the Alps, is renowned for its mix of Swiss efficiency and Italian *dolce vita*—no wonder the rest of Switzerland vacations here. Ecologist and philosopher Luigi Ferrari notes, "In Ticino, I have found images straight out of history." Here, jasmine-laced villas painted bright colors and traditional stone huts replace the charred-wood chalets of northern Switzerland. The landscape charms with its tropical vegetation and emerald-green lakes. Bellinzona's pastel church façades spill out onto the cities' piazzas, and castles abound. Culture-seekers flock to the annual international film festival in Locarno. Farther south in the canton, the financial capital of Lugano and its gardened hostels serve as a center for budget travelers.

HIGHLIGHTS OF TICINO

Marvel at Marianne Werefkin's modern works in the **Museo Comunale d'Arte Moderna** in Ascona (see p. 464).

Make like James Bond and dive off the 220m Verzasca dam, the **world's highest bungee jump** (see p. 459).

Groove to bass-heavy beats at the **Bellinzona Blues Festival** (see p. 454).

Couldn't crash Cannes? Try the **International Film Festival** in Locarno (see p. 460).

BELLINZONA   ☎ 091

Three impressive **medieval castles** peer down ominously from the heights above Bellinzona (pop. 18,000), reminding visitors that the city was once a strategic Milanese fort guarding trade routes through the San Bernardino and St. Gotthard passes. Today, Bellinzona is the capital of Ticino, and is still an important crossroads for tourists heading to lake resorts farther south. The city has a modern quality missing in other Ticinese towns, making it a haven for lovers of art and architecture both classic and contemporary. Meanwhile, villas and vineyards in the surrounding hills cast a pastoral calm over the city, which is melodically disrupted every year by the beats of the **Bellinzona Blues Festival.**

⬜ TRANSPORTATION

Bellinzona is the main train hub for Ticino, with **trains** to: Basel (4hr., every 30min. 6:05am-8:36pm, 72SFr); Locarno (20min., 2 per hr. 5:38am-12:38am, 7.20SFr); Lucerne (2¼hr., 6:05am-9:06pm, 50SFr); Lugano (30min., every 30min. 5:06am-12:36am, 11.40SFr); Milan (2hr., every hr. 5:06-9:25pm, 29SFr); Rome (7hr., every hr. 6:46am-7:36pm, 90SFr); Zurich (2½hr., every hr. 6:26-9:25am and every 30min. 10:26am-9:06pm, 54SFr). Travelers under 26 save on Milan (23SFr) and Rome (68SFr). Trains to and from Geneva require a change in Domodossola, Italy (5½hr., 7 per day 8:07am-6:38pm, 94SFr), Zurich (5¾hr., 1-2 per hr. 6:26am-6:26pm, 111SFr), or Olten (6hr., 1-2 per hr. 6:05am-6:26pm, 101SFr). **Post Buses** leave from the station for Chur (Coira) via Thusis (3hr., every hr. 6:07am-6:07pm, 50SFr), San Bernadino (1¼hr., every hr. 6:07am-9:07pm, 19.80SFr), and elsewhere in eastern Switzerland. By **car,** arrive from the north on N2/E35 or N13/E43; from Lugano or the south on N2/E35 north; from Locarno or the west on N13.

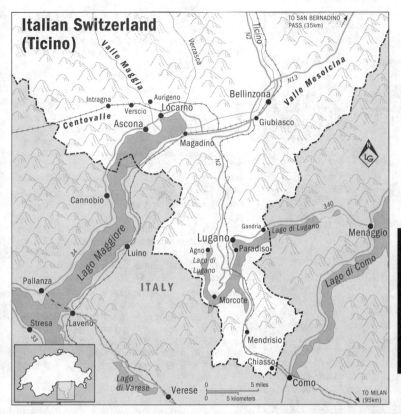

Italian Switzerland
(Ticino)

PRACTICAL INFORMATION

To reach Bellinzona's **tourist office** on Via Camminata 2 in Palazzo Civico, turn left from the train station and follow the main road past p. Collegiata; it's in the beautiful, old **municipal government** building. (☎825 21 31; www.bellinzona.ch. Open M-F 9am-6:30pm, Sa 9am-noon.) Services at the train station (open daily 6:10am-7:40pm) include: hotel reservations (free), **currency exchange**, **luggage storage** (5SFr at baggage check), **lockers** (3-5SFr), and **bike rental** (at baggage check; reserve ahead; 30SFr per day, 23SFr per half-day; additional 6SFr to return at another station); public **parking** at the station (1SFr per 30min.; 8SFr per day) or in the Colletivo at p. del Sole, off Viale Stazione to the right, down Largo Elvetica (open 24hr.; 7am-10pm 1SFr per 45min; 10pm-7am 1SFr per hr.); **taxis** ☎825 44 44 or 825 11 51. **Internet** at the **Bar Cervo** gets a crowd. (☎825 40 70. Open M-Sa 7:30am-8pm. 6SFr per hr.) The **Post Office**, via Stazione 18, left from the station, is open M-F 7:30am-6:30pm, Sa 9am-noon. **Postal code:** CH-6500.

ACCOMMODATIONS & CAMPING

Youth Hostel Montebello, Via Nocca 4 (☎825 15 22; www.youthhostel.ch/bellinzona), occupies the former Instituto Santa Maria just below the Castello di Montebello. Left from the station and then left onto Piazza Indipendenza. Although institutional in atmo-

THE LOCAL STORY

BUTTER AND LONG LIFE: THE ALPHORN

Dani Schlaepfer has been playing the alphorn, the traditional Swiss wooden instrument, for the last ten years as a part of the Spitzli Trio. The group is based in Urnaesch in the Appenzell region, famous for its reverence still today of traditional Swiss culture, as well as a population of cows that far outnumber the humans. He stopped during a concert in Schwaegalp, below Mt. Saentis, to talk with Let's Go.

LG: When did you start playing the alphorn?
A: I started when I was twelve. My father taught me.
LG: And his father taught him?
A: No, he just tried it—and ended up teaching himself.
LG: Tell me a little bit about the instrument itself.
A: Well, my alphorn is 2.5m long; it's a G flat. They come in all different keys—F, A sharp, A flat, etc. The difference in key is made by the difference in length of the horn. The horns are so long, they come apart into three pieces so that you can actually carry them around to practice and to different events.
LG: How are they made?
A: There are some alphorn factories now, where the entire instrument is made by machines. But I ordered my horn specially from a man who still does it all by hand. You have to wait 12-14 months for the horn to be made. They cos

sphere, and right beside the railroad tracks, this hostel offers large, sparkling rooms and museum-like charm. Laundry (6SFr), **Internet** (15SFr per hr.; 7.50SFr after midnight). Dinner 12.50SFr. Breakfast and sheets included. Wheelchair-accessible. Reception 8-10:30am and 3-10pm. Check-out 10am. Dorms 30-35SFr; 4- to 5- bed rooms 34-39SFr; singles 45-50SFr; doubles 80-90SFr. Non-members 6SFr extra. MC/V. ❷

Albergo Internazionale, p. Stazione (☎825 43 33; www.ticino.com/hotel-international), across from the train station. Here, a red-carpet-draped staircase leads to clean and cozy rooms with showers off wide hallways. Breakfast buffet included. Reception 8am-noon and 2-6pm. Singles 100SFr; doubles 130-170SFr. AmEx/DC/MC/V. ❹

Hotel Garni Moderno, Viale Stazione 17b (☎/fax 825 13 76). Go left from the station, right on Via Claudio Pelladini, and right on Via Cancelliere Molo. Offers rooms with plush carpeting, sinks, and large windows. Breakfast included. Reception in hotel café M-Sa 6:30am-10:30pm. Singles 55SFr; doubles 90SFr, with shower 120SFr. MC/V. ❸

Camping Bosco de Molinazzo (☎829 11 18; fax 23 55). Take bus #2 (dir.: Castione) to "Arbedo Posta Vecchia." (2.20SFr). The campground has laundry services (3-4SFr for washer and dryer) and a pool. Open Apr. until mid-Oct. Reception 9am-1pm and 4-10pm. 6.20-7.20SFr per person, ages 6-14 half-price; tent 6-7SFr; electricity 4SFr. ❶

🔆 FOOD

Bellinzona is full of cafés that serve hot and cold *panini* (sandwiches) for 5-10SFr, but, oddly, warm meals are hard to find. **Migros** is in p. del Sole, across from the Castelgrande entrance. (Supermarket open M-F 8am-6:30pm, Sa 7:30am-5pm; restaurant open M-F 7am-6:30pm, Sa 7am-5pm.) A huge **outdoor market** along Viale Stazione lays out everything from fruits and breads to incense and rugs (Sa 7:30am-noon).

Croce Federale, Viale Stazione 12 (☎825 16 67), offers Italian dining on a terrace overlooking the main road, in an ordinary dining room with a stone oven, or in a splendid back room decorated with floral watercolors. Enjoy pastas (13-19SFr), pizzas (11-18SFr), or meat entrees (25-33SFr) with an inexpensive bottle of local wine. Warm food served M-Sa 11:30am-2pm and 6-10pm; pizza 11:30am-11pm. ❸

Ristorante Corona, Via Camminata 5 (☎825 28 44), on the far end of town before p. Nosetto, also offers good Italian fare and the option of dining outside on a cobblestone street. Pastas in 2 sizes (10-16SFr), pizzas (11-16SFr) and daily *Menüs* (20SFr) available from noon-2pm and 6:30-10pm. Wheelchair-accessible. Open M-Th 7am-midnight; F-Sa 7am-1am. Pizzas available after 10pm. AmEx. ❷

Peverelli Panetteria Tea Room Pasticceria (☎825 60 03) in p. Collegiata off Viale Stazione, serves a large selection of teas (2.40-3.40SFr), *panini* (5-6SFr), and large pizza slices (4.50SFr). Wheelchair-accessible. Open M-F 7am-7pm, Sa 7am-6pm. ❶

👁 SIGHTS

Originally joined by stone walls, the three castles of Bellinzona became separate entities when the city joined the Swiss Confederation and the three original cantons Uri, Schwyz and Nidwalden each claimed one of the battlements as its own. Today the **Castelgrande, Castello di Montebello,** and **Castello di Sasso Corbaro** remain linked through their membership in the UNESCO World Heritage list and combined tourism. Tourists may buy a "3 Castelli" ticket (8SFr, students 4SFr), available at the castles, or a special excursion ticket from the train station that includes travel to and from various cities, lunch, and admission to the 3 castles. (Train tickets good for 3 days. Chiasso 30.40SFr, Locarno 22SFr, Lugano 25.40SFr.) For history buffs, the tourist office and castle museums also sell a fascinating guide detailing the war-filled history of Bellinzona (9SFr; available in English).

Rising 50m above the p. del Sole on a huge hunk of rock, the oft-renovated **Castelgrande,** accessible by the free elevator near p. del Sole or by the winding uphill paths from p. Collegieta and p. Nosetto, occupies a site inhabited since the Neolithic period (5500-5000 BC) and fortified since the 4th century. Construction on the current fortress began in the 13th century with the Milanese Visconti family; major changes were introduced between 1473 and 1486. The *bianca* (white) and *nera* (black) towers, rising 28 and 27m high respectively, date from the 13th and 14th centuries. The top of the **Tora Bianca** offers panoramic views of Bellinzona. The castle was renovated from 1984 to 1991, with an elevator, expensive courtyard restaurant, and museum designed to make it more hospitable to tourists. The **museum** exhibits unique painted panels from the house of a Bellizonan noble and a Swiss coin collection. (Open daily 10am-6pm. 4SFr, students 2SFr.)

The smaller but more satisfyingly dank **Castello di Montebello,** on the hill opposite Castelgrande, offers visitors working drawbridges, ramparts, dungeons, and views as far as Lake Maggiore on a clear day. The

3500 Swiss francs. He paints a scene from Swiss farm life on the top, and burns his name into the bottom, along with where it was made.

LG: What sort of events do you play?

A: Outside of practice with the trio three times a week, we play at a lot of traditional festivals and events throughout the year.

LG: What is your favorite event to play?

A: Definitely weddings. We do a lot of weddings. We play classic Appenzeller songs, but a large selection of church songs as well.

LG: Tell me a little bit about your clothing.

A: I am wearing the traditional Appenzeller dress from the 19th century. All of the embroidery is done by hand, along with the tanning of the leather for the belts and suspenders. The gold cows on the belt are also hammered out by hand.

LG: And what's with the earring?

A: All Appenzeller men wear this earring. I got mine when I was five. On the top, there's a horseshoe, which means good and long life. The thing that dangles down on the bottom is a *Rahmkette;* it's what the farmer uses to skim the cream off the top of the milk, which then is made into butter.

LG: Why are they together?

A: It's a symbol—it means that through butter, milk, the cows, and the ways of farming, you will enjoy a long and healthy life.

LG: Do you always wear this symbolic earring?

A: No; normally it is just a cow.

castle can be reached on foot from p. Collegiata up the slippery steps of Sallita alla Motta or by bus from Viale Stazione. The tower and former residential quarters now house a mildly interesting **archaeological and civic museum** containing vases, jewelry, and ceramics, as well as ancient bric-a-brac and ceremonial and military arms. (☎825 13 42. Open Feb.-Dec. Tu-Su 10am-6pm. Museum 2SFr, students 1SFr.)

A number of notable churches grace Bellinzona, tucked away among the villas and hotels. The gorgeous **Chiesa Collegiata dei SS Pietro e Stefano,** on the p. Collegiata, bears an early Renaissance facade flanked by trumpeting heralds. The breathtakingly ornate stone interior features numerous paintings and frescoes (attributed to Simone Peterzano), overhung by a gilded canopy. The *scagliola* (a painted plaster imitation of marble) pulpit that dates from 1784 and the holy water stoup, named the "Fontana Trivulziana" after a nobleman from Messocco who owned it in the 15th century, are other interesting features.

To reach the 16th-century **Chiesa di San Biagio** from the train station, walk 15min. to the left or take bus #4 to "Cimiterio"; cross under the railroad tracks, turn left up the stairs, turn left again, and follow the tracks 50m. The church exhibits a gigantic painting of St. Christopher on its exterior and a flock of saints on its columned interior. Tombstones and a beautifully carved granite font are displayed on the south and west walls. (Open daily 9-11am.)

⚠ OUTDOOR ACTIVITIES & ENTERTAINMENT

The **Ticino River** is perfect for idle strollers. A 45min. hike with grand views of Sasso Corbaro starts in Monti di Ravecchia, a short bus ride from Bellinzona. The trail begins at the hospital and follows an ancient mule path, leading to now-deserted **Prada,** an ancient trading post possibly dating from pre-Roman times.

Opera lovers with a bit of extra cash will relish the blockbuster productions of the Bellinzona **Open Air Opera** (end of July 2004) performed on the temporary stage within the Castelgrande grounds. Past years have featured productions such as *Aida* and *Nabucco.* (☎0848 80 08 00; www.ticketcorner.ch. Prices range from 70-140SFr; contact the tourist office or **Ticket Corner.**) The annual **Blues Festival** (July 1-3rd 2004) draws musicians from across southern America in late June. Past performers include Luther Allison and Joe Louis Walker (entrance 10SFr per night.)

LOCARNO ☎091

On the shores of **Lago Maggiore,** Locarno's (pop. 30,000) cypress and magnolia bask in warm breezes. This relatively unspoiled town has a tropical presence, perhaps because it gets the most sunlight in Switzerland—over 2200 hours per year. During its world-famous **film festival** each August, Locarno swells with people enjoying balmy evenings of *al fresco* dining beneath palm trees. All this worldly languor coexists in relative peace with the piety of worshipers in the churches of the **Città Vecchia** (old city). In addition to its self-contained charms, Locarno serves as an excellent starting point at the foot of the Ticinese hills for mountain hikes along the **Verzasca** and **Maggia valleys** or for regional skiing.

▣ TRANSPORTATION

"Holiday" passes offer free travel along the bus and train lines in the Lago Maggiore region. Available at the tourist office, the Travel Office at the train station, or at **Viaggi Fart** on p. Grand. (☎751 87 31; fax 40 77. 3-day pass 46SFr, children 23SFr; 1 week 66SFr/33SFr.)

Locarno

▲ ⌂ ACCOMMODATIONS
Delta Camping, **11**
Garni Sempione, **5**
Hotel Dell' Angelo, **8**
Palagiovani Youth Hostel, **4**
Pensione Città Vecchia, **2**

🍴 FOOD
Ristorante Contrada, 6
Ristorante
 Debarcadero, 7
Ristorante Manora, 1
Trattoria da Luigi, 3

🍸 NIGHTLIFE
Barspot, 9
Katjaboat, 12
Simba Bar, 10

ITALIAN SWITZERLAND

Trains: p. Stazione (☎ 743 65 64; rail info ☎ 0900 30 03 00). To: **Bellinzona** (25min., every 30min. 5:59am-1:09am, 7.20SFr), connecting north to **Lucerne** (2½hr., every 30min. 6:05am-9:06pm, 54SFr) and **Zurich** (2½hr., every hr. 6:26am-9:06pm, 58SFr). Trains go south to **Lugano** (50min., every 30min. 5:30am-12:05am, 16.60SFr) and **Milan** via Bellinzona (2hr., every hr. 5:06am-9:25pm, 34SFr). For **Geneva** (5¾hr., 90SFr), **Montreux** (4¾hr., 76SFr), or **Zermatt** (4hr., 84SFr), change trains in **Domodossola, Italy** (1¾hr., every hr. 7:55am-7:12pm, 41SFr).

Buses: Buses leave the train station or p. Grande for **Ascona** (#31, 15-min., every 15min. 6:23am-midnight), **Minusio** (5min., every 15min. 5:04am-11:46pm), and other nearby towns. Buses also run through the **San Bernadino Pass** to eastern Switzerland. Regional passes with **FART** (**Ferrovie Autolinee Regionali Ticinesi;** the local transport system) cost 46SFr for 3 days, 66SFr for 7.

Ferries: Navigazione Lago Maggiore, Largo Zorzi 1 (☎0848 81 11 22), conducts tours of the entire lake, all the way into Italy. A full day on the northernmost part of the lake costs 12SFr; for the entire Swiss side 22SFr. Sail to **Ascona** (15-45min., 9 per day 9:10am-5:15pm, day pass 12SFr) or **Brissago** farther south (1¼hr., 9 per day, day pass 21SFr). "Holiday" cards offer 50% off on Lago di Lugano (see above).

By car: Locarno is accessible from motorway A2 (Exit: Bellinzona-Süd).

Car Rental: Hertz SA, Garage Starnini SA, Via Sempione 12, Muralto (☎ 743 50 50). Small 4-person car 141SFr per day. Open M-F 8am-noon and 1:30-5:30pm, Sa 8am-noon. AmEx/DC/MC/V.

Taxi: Ask at the tourist office for a list or look for stations around town. **EcoTaxi** offers some of the best rates in town, and hybrid cars (☎ 08 00 32 13 21).

Parking: Metered parking on Via della Posta and major streets (1SFr per 30min.; max 1½hr.). The 24hr. parking garage, **Autosilo Largo SA** (☎ 751 96 13), beneath the *Kursaal,* accessible from Via Cattori, has the same rates 7am-10pm (half-price overnight).

Bike Rental: At the train station. Bikes 30SFr per day, 25SFr per half day. Open 8am-7pm. Call ☎ 743 65 64 to reserve. 6SFr fee for returning a bike to another station.

✦ ⓘ ORIENTATION & PRACTICAL INFORMATION

Piazza Grande, home of Locarno's International Film Festival, is the city's anchor; social life centers around its arcades. Just above p. Grande, the *Città Vecchia* is home to 16th- and 17th-century architecture. **Via Ramogna** connects the p. Grande to the train station. **Via Rusca** extends from its other side to the Castello Visconteo.

Tourist Office: Largo Zorzi (☎ 791 00 91; www.maggiore.ch), on p. Grande in the *Kursaal* (casino). Office makes hotel reservations. Open Nov.-Mar. M-F 9am-6pm, Sa 10am-6pm, Apr.-Oct. also Su 2:30-5pm.

Currency Exchange: Banks line p. Grande; open M-F 9am-4pm. Also, location at train station open daily 6am-7:30pm. **Western Union** at station open daily 9am-6pm.

Luggage Storage: At the train station, 7SFr. Open 6:50am-8:30pm. **Lockers** 4-7SFr.

Bookstore: Libriarte Internationale (☎/fax 743 03 33), p. Stazione 2, around the corner from the train station, houses maps, travel books, and a small selection of English novels. Open M-Sa 9am-6:30pm.

Internet Access: Visitors Center booth on Viale Balli (☎/fax 751 84 08), across the street and uphill from the dock (12SFr per hr.). Open June-Oct. M, F, Sa-Su 9:30am-6:30pm, W-Th 9:30am-noon and 5-7:30pm. **Rialto** (☎ 743 11 10) up Via Stazione from the train station. (Open M-F 11:30am-1am, Sa-Su 1:30pm-1am. 10SFr per hr.)

Emergencies: Police ☎ 117, **Fire** ☎ 118, **Road information** ☎ 021 163, **Weather** ☎ 021 162, **Medical Assistance** ☎ 111, **Ambulance** ☎ 144.

Post Office: p. Grande. Open M-F 7:30am-6:30pm, Sa 8:30am-noon. **Postal Code:** CH-6600.

▶ ACCOMMODATIONS & CAMPING

A display board outside the train station allows free phone calls to most of the city's hotels and pensions. Reserve everywhere a week in advance March through October; book six months in advance for a bed during the film festival.

Pensione Città Vecchia, Via Toretta 13 (☎ 751 45 54; www.cittavecchia.ch). From p. Grande, turn right onto Via Toretta. Because it boasts the best prices in town, it's usually full, though the convenient location comes at the price of occasional street noise. The co-ed rooms and bathrooms are simple but clean. Tiny breakfast 4.50SFr. Dorm sheets 4.50SFr. **Bike rental** 15SFr per day. Reception 8am-9pm. Check-in 1-6pm, call ahead if arriving after 6pm. Dorms 29-37SFr; doubles 70-80SFr; triples 120SFr. ❷

Palagiovani Youth Hostel (HI), Via Varenna 18 (☎ 756 15 00; www.youthhostel.ch/locarno). From p. Grande, turn right on Via della Motta. Take the left fork (Via B. Rusca) past p. San Francesco, then take V.S. Francesco, which turns into Via Varenna (HI signs point the way from Via Varenna on). High hedges and floral bushes conceal this sterile establishment. Most of the 2- to 6-bed rooms include balconies, sinks, and lockers. Huge buffet breakfast and sheets included. 3-course lunch and dinner 14.50SFr each. Other amenities include laundry (8SFr), towels (2SFr), **Internet** (15SFr per hr.), and **mountain bikes** (15SFr per day, 10SFr per half-day). The hostel can become overrun by families and school groups in July and Aug., so call ahead. Reception Nov.-Mar. 8-10am and 4-10:30pm; Apr.-Oct. 8-10am and 3-11:30pm. Dorms 32.5SFr, with shower and bathroom 37-39SFr; doubles 75SFr/118SFr. Non-members 6SFr extra. MC/V. ❷

Garni Sempione, Via Rusca 6 (☎751 30 64; fax 752 38 37). Walk to the end of the p. Grande, turn right onto Via della Motta, and then take the left fork onto Via B. Rusca. This small hotel ventures to take the outside inside with a variety of rooms leading from an enclosed courtyard. Wood paneling and tile along the walls and colorful comforters add to the atmosphere. Breakfast included. Wheelchair-accessible. Reception 8am-9pm. Check-out 11am. Singles 60SFr, with shower 65SFr; doubles 110SFr/120SFr; triples 150SFr/170SFr; quads 160SFr. Discounts for children. AmEx/DC/MC/V. ❸

Hotel Dell' Angelo, p. Grande (☎751 81 75; fax 751 82 56). On the far side of p. Grande. Winding marble staircases, and antique-decorated halls lead guests to clean and simple rooms. All rooms with TV and telephone, some with balconies. **Parking** 15SFr. Breakfast included. Wheelchair-accessible. Reception 7am-1am. Singles 70-135SFr; doubles 110-210SFr; triples 150-260SFr; quads 180-300SFr. Add 28SFr per person to include dinner and 45SFr for full board. AmEx/DC/MC/V. ❸

Delta Camping, Via Respini 7 (☎751 60 81; www.campingdelta.com). A 30min. walk along the lakeside to the right from the tourist office (turn left at the info map). Shuttle runs from the campground to Locarno daily 11am, 5pm. Shaded by birch trees, next to a golf course and rocky beach, this campsite has a restaurant (entrees 9.50-19.50SFr), supermarket, workout room, **Internet** access (5SFr per 30min.) and **bike rental** (20SFr per day, 12SFr per half-day). Of the 360 plots on this 5-star site, 72 have a waterside locations. Reception 8am-8pm, July-Aug. 18 until 10pm. 100SFr reservation fee July-Aug., 50SFr of which is returned. Open Mar.-Oct. Mar.-May and Oct. 11SFr per person, tent plot 21SFr, waterfront plot 31SFr, June and Aug. 19-Sept. 12SFr/26SFr/36SFr. July-Aug. 18 18SFr/37-47SFr/47-57SFr. Children 6SFr. Electricity 5SFr. ❶

🍴 FOOD

Though Locarno's restaurants are pricey, many offer *panini*, pasta, and pizza for 10-20SFr range, leaving room for *gelato*. Get groceries at **Aperto**, at the station (open daily 6am-10pm), or the **Coop** at p. Grande (open M-W and F-Sa 8am-6pm, Th 8am-9pm). A market fills the streets of the *Città Vecchia* (Apr.-Sept. Sa 9am-1:30pm).

Ristorante Debarcadero (☎751 05 55) on Largo Zorzi by the ferry dock, is one of the very few spots on the lake that's affordable. A crowd of tourists enjoys pizza (11.50-18.50SFr), homemade pastas (12.50-16.50SFr), frappes (8SFr), and beer (3.80SFr), accompanied by pop hits. For dessert try the *gelato* (3-5SFr). Daily *Menüs* arond 15SFr. Wheelchair-accessible. Open daily 9am-midnight. ❷

Ristorante Contrada, p. Grande 26 (☎751 48 15). This restaurant is a shrine to felines, which are artistically rendered in every medium on the walls. Terrace is ideal for people-watching. Pizza (11.50-19SFr) and pasta (13-22SFr) accompany *panini* (7-8SFr) on the menu. Wheelchair-accessible. Open daily 7am-midnight. AmEx/MC/V. ❷

Ristorante Manora, Via della Stazione 1 (☎743 76 76), left of the station, offers high-quality self-service and tons of options. Breakfast 5.50SFr. Pasta buffet 8.50-9.90SFr. Meat *Menüs* 10.50-16.50SFr. Wheelchair-accessible. Open Nov.-Feb. M-Sa 7:30am-9pm, Su 8am-9pm; Mar.-Oct. M-Sa 7:30am-10pm, Su 8am-9m. ❶

ITALIAN SWITZERLAND

Trattoria da Luigi, Via F. Balli 3 (☎ 751 97 46; fax 42 69), between p. Stazione and Largo Zorzi, offers a romantic dining experience with an arched skylight and flower-accented chandeliers. Although the entrees are pricey (29.50-34SFr), risottos and pastas such as spaghetti with tomatoes, broccoli, olives, and sardines (17.80SFr) are reasonable (16.50-18.50SFr). Open daily 9am-midnight. AmEx/DC/MC/V. ❸

👁 SIGHTS

For centuries, visitors have journeyed to Locarno solely to see the church of **Madonna del Sasso** (Madonna of the Rock), founded over 500 years ago when a Franciscan monk, Bartholemeo d'Ivrea, had a vision of Mary telling him to build a church high above the city. Its orange-yellow hue renders it immediately recognizable from anywhere in town. The church is accessible by a **funicular** that leaves from a small station just left of the McDonald's (every 15min. 7am-8pm, extended hours in summer; 6.60SFr round-trip, 5SFr with SwissPass, 4.50SFr one-way). A 20min. walk up the smooth stones of the Via al Sasso (off the Via Cappucini in the *Città Vecchia*), where capricious lizards scuttle across the path, also leads to the top. Funicular riders will miss the impressive stations of the cross sequencing Christ's passion that line the trail. A less religious but equally inspiring path heads past the turn-off along a shaded, tropical path to the back of the church. The open courtyard houses a series of life-size wooden niche statues depicting scenes of Christ, including a *Pietà*, a Pentecost, and a life-size, room-filling Last Supper from 1650. Bramartino's *Fuga in Egitto*, Ciseri's *Trasporto di Cristo al Sepolcro*, and a statue of Mary, sculpted for the church's consecration, adorn the **sanctuary.** Hundreds of silver heart-shaped medallions on the walls commemorate acts of Mary's intervention in the lives of those who have made pilgrimages here. Some of the hearts are accompanied by paintings and embroideries in silk.

The **museum** next door, in the oldest part of the complex, houses a collection of ancient reliquaries and pilgrims' souvenirs. The highlight of the museum is the second-floor collection of disaster paintings—near-drownings, fires, attempted murders, battles, train accidents, and lightning strikes—all commissioned by survivors of the events thanking the Madonna for answering their prayers and intervening to save their lives. Miniature body parts commemorate physical healings. (☎ 743 62 65; www.cappuccini.ch. Grounds open daily 6:30am-7pm. Museum open Apr.-Oct. Su-F 2-5pm. 2.50SFr, students 1.50SFr. English guidebooks for the entire complex are available at the devotions shop for 7SFr. Open daily 9am-7pm.) To reach the **Chiesa San Francesco** from p. Grande, turn right onto Via B. Rusca and left onto Via S. Francesca (wheelchair-accessible). The church was built in the 14th century on top of an older parish founded by the Franciscans shortly after the death of St. Francis of Assisi in 1226. The church displays faded frescoes, added during a 16th-century renovation, beneath its roof. Built of stones scavenged from a demolished castle, the exterior bears incongruous inscriptions from the material's original incarnation. A vanished cemetery, the only remnant of which is a curious skull-and-crossbones from the Orelli family monument, once surrounded the building.

Follow Via Marcacci from the p. Grande and turn left on Via Borghese to reach the cavernous **Chiesa San Antonio,** wheelchair-accessible, which presides over the outskirts of the *Città Vecchia*. (San Antonio is 1 block up from p. San Antonio.) Built between 1668 and 1674, it was renovated in 1863 after the roof and front façade collapsed, killing 45 people. Circular patches of sunlight illuminate a large fresco, *Cristo Morto* (Dead Christ) by G.A. Felice Orelli, which depicts Christ being taken off the cross.

A duke of Milan constructed the **Castello Visconteo,** down Via F. Rusca from p. Grande, in the 13th century, and you can now wander through dungeons and towers where soldiers poured boiling oil on attackers. The second floor houses an exhibit on the 1925 Treaty of Locarno, one of many ill-fated attempts to avoid another war. The medieval castle houses the **Museo Civico e Archeologico,** which exhibits Roman artifacts. (☎756 31 61. Open Apr.-Oct. Tu-Su 10am-5pm. 7SFr, students 5SFr, children 1SFr.)

⚑ OUTDOOR ACTIVITIES

ON THE LAKE. The deep blue water of Lago Maggiore is a delight to the eyes. A **ferry** ride to points on both the Swiss and Italian shores offers more intimate contact with the lake (see p. 455). The tropical **Isole di Brissago,** at the lowest point in Switzerland (193m), was cultivated in 1885 by a utopian-minded baroness hoping to create an earthly paradise. Exotic plants from four continents intermingle with delicate stands of bamboo, which conceal splendidly colored exotic birds. An early 20th-century villa occupies one end of the island. (☎791 43 61 or 00 91; www.isolebrissago.ch. Wheelchair-accessible. Open Mar.-Oct. daily 9am-5pm. 7SFr.) **Marco Brusa,** along the water towards Delta Camping, rents **boats.** (☎07 92 14 62 57. Pedal boats 15-20SFr per hr., 8-12SFr per 30min.; motor boats 45SFr, 25SFr). At **Bagno Pubblico La Lanca,** 2min. farther along the lake, it is possible to swim in the lake with swans and ducks for a few francs less. (☎752 12 95. Open 10am-7:30pm. 3SFr, children 6-15 1.50SFr.) Bathe for free at the **Fiume Maggia,** the rock-strewn artery that feeds into the lake.

VAL VERZASCA HIKE. To escape the city, head out on Post Bus #630 to **Sonogno** (1¼hr.; 7:37am-6:15pm; 16.60SFr, 33.20SFr round-trip) and hike amid the extraordinary peaks at the end of **Val Verzasca** (*val* means "valley"). From the bus stop, take the first left and follow the yellow signs to **Lavertezzo.** The mostly flat trail is marked by yellow signs with directions and town names, and white-red-white blazes. It passes through cool, shady glens and rocky riverbeds as it follows the Verzasca river through the valley. Close to **Lavertezzo,** the river eases its rapid pace, making swimming possible. Nonetheless, pick a swimming hole carefully, as the water can be quite cold and the undercurrents strong. Climb the **Ponte dei Salti,** a 17th-century double-arched bridge, and gaze into the clear green ponds. From Sonogno to Lavertezzo is a 6hr. walk, while Lavertezzo to Tenero requires another 5hr., but the Post Bus stops along the trail in the valley.

ADVENTURE SPORTS. The Verzasca Dam has allowed scores of visitors to break speeds of 100km per hr., courtesy of its famous **bungee jump,** the highest in the world. The 220m jump, conquered with panache by James Bond in *Goldeneye*, costs 255SFr the first time (with training, drink, and diploma) and 125SFr for subsequent leaps on the same day (195SFr for other days). Night jumps are possible. **Trekking Team** (☎0848 80 80 07; www.trekking.ch.), in addition to the Verzasca Dam jump, offers a 70m jump (125SFr first time, 75SFr for a second jump on the same day, then 90SFr), **canyoning** (100-210SFr), **snorkeling** (100SFr), and **spelunking** (98SFr, children 78SFr, students 48SFr) in **Centovalli.** The **Visitors Center** (☎751 84 08; www.visitorscenter.ch) on Vaile Bali, across the street and 25m uphill from the ferry dock, books the above activities with Trekking Team, as well as **skydiving** (385SFr for a jump from 3500m with a 30sec. free-fall), **paragliding** (165SFr), **windsurfing lessons** (60SFr per hr.), **waterskiing** and **wake boarding** (45SFr per 10min.), **rock climbing** (250SFr per day), rafting (65-105SFr per half-day, 150SFr for full day), and **sailing lessons** (190SFr, 2-4 people). **Bike rentals** 18SFr per half-day and 25SFr per day. (Prices get cheaper with successive days.)

🎵 🎭 ENTERTAINMENT & NIGHTLIFE

The lakeside **◼Simba Bar,** toward Camping Delta, appeals to Locarno's wealthier 20-something crowd. With its mesmerizing aquarium, hanging mirrors, and mosaic bar, along with lakeside views, Simba is happening. (☎752 33 88; www.bar-simb.ticino.ch. Beers for 4.50SFr; drinks 9-14.50SFr. DJ every night after 8pm. 18+. Open Apr.-Sept. daily 5pm-midnight; Oct.-Mar. Tu-Sa 5pm-midnight.) Along Via B. Luini four blocks from the lakeside, **Barsport** caters to a slightly older local crowd with pool, foosball, and a mix of techno and jazzy world music. (☎751 29 31. Beers from 3.70SFr; a dip from the Sangria bowl 4SFr. Wheelchair-accessible. Open Su-Th 8pm-1am, F-Sa 10pm-2am.) The **Katjaboat,** a yellow vessel that departs from the Hotel Rosa, down the Via Verbano from the ferry dock, is Locarno's Loveboat. For regular bar prices (mineral water 5SFr, beer 6SFr, gin 11SFr), the young-at-heart can enjoy a 40min. mini-tour of the lake with a soundtrack of sappy love songs. (☎079 686 39 90. Boat runs 10am-1am, departs about every 45min., though its schedule tends to be as free-spirited as its atmosphere.)

For 11 mid-summer days (Aug. 4-14 2004), everything in Locarno halts for the **International Film Festival,** one of the most important movie premiere events in the world. Unlike Cannes, no invitations are required. Over 150,000 big-screen enthusiasts descend upon the town, so book a room six months to a year ahead. The centerpiece of the festival is a giant 26m by 14m outdoor screen, the largest outdoor screen in Europe, set up in p. Grande for big-name premieres by the likes of Jean-Luc Godard, Woody Allen, Spike Lee, and Bernardo Bertolucci. Smaller screens highlight young filmmakers and groundbreaking experimentation. (☎756 21 21; www.pardo.ch. Unlimited access 270SFr. For daily ticket prices and more info, write to: International Film Festival, Via Luini 3a, CH-6601 Locarno.)

In the second half of July, Locarno teams up with Ascona to host **Ticino Musica,** a festival of classical music focusing on young musicians and students. It features concerts, operas, and master classes at several venues. Tickets (30SFr) are available at the tourist office and at the door of any event. Free events occur as well. (☎980 09 70; www.ticinomusica.com.)

AURIGENO ☎091

Nestled in the Valle Maggia ("magic valley"), Aurigeno offers its own charms with stone-shingled buildings and grapevines galore. An excellent side-trip from Locarno, this out-of-the-way village is a great place to enjoy traditional Swiss-Italian culture and a perfect spot to begin numerous hikes.

🚌 TRANSPORTATION & PRACTICAL INFORMATION

Take **bus** #10 from Locarno (30min., every hr. 7:02am-8:10pm and 11:35pm, 7.80SFr). The **tourist office** for the valley is at the bus-stop in Maggia next to the Coop. (☎753 18 85; fax 22 12. Open M-F 9am-noon and 2-5pm also June-Sept. Sa 9am-noon.) For **taxis,** call ☎079 423 69 7am-7pm; **police** ☎117, **ambulance** ☎144, **helicopter rescue** ☎14 14. The **post office,** on the main road between the towns, serves Aurigeno and Moghegno. (Open M-F 8-10:30am and 2:30-5:30pm, Sa 8-10am.) **Postal code:** CH-6677.

▲ ◖ ACCOMMODATIONS & FOOD

Accommodations in Aurigeno are scarce, but Maggia up the road offers more hotels. ◪**Baracca Backpacker ❷** (☎079 207 15 54) is an ideal starting point in Aurigeno. From the train station in Locarno, take bus #10 (dir.: Valle Maggia) to "Ronchini" (25min., every hr. 7:02am-8:10pm and 11:35pm, 7.20SFr). Cross the street and turn right from the bus stop; follow hostel signs through the forest over the bridge, and into the town (15min.); the hostel is beside the church. A young couple, Monika and Reto, create a homey environment with 12 beds, fresh herbs for cooking and a wood shop for tinkering. The office sells basic groceries (spaghetti 2SFr, tomato sauce 4SFr, wine 9.50SFr, milk 2SFr). Look in the games room at the best map in the area, and for multiple **hiking, biking,** and **swimming** suggestions. (**Bike rental** 10SFr per day. Sleep sack 2SFr per day. Reception 9-11am and 5-8pm. Open Apr.-Oct. Dorms 25SFr.) At the junction of the main road and the bridge, the Pedroni couple offers the opportunity of **Sleeping in the Straw ❷**. (☎753 24 62. Open May-Oct. 20SFr including breakfast.)

Trattoria Giovanetti ❶, in the center of town along the main road (2min.) is the closest thing to a restaurant in town, with cold plates of meats and cheeses (6-15SFr) and minestrone soup (6.50SFr). For warm meals, order ahead. (☎753 11 33. Open M-W and F-Sa 8:30am-11pm, Su 9am-11pm.) Opposite the Aurigeno/Mogheno bus-stop on the east side of the main bridge, the simple **Osteria del Ponte ❷** serves pastas and lasagna (10-13SFr) and beer (3.20SFr) by the stone hearth inside or on the balcony terrace overlooking the river and a local swimming hole. (☎753 31 95. Open M and W-Su 8:30am-midnight.) There are no grocery stores in Aurigeno, so stock up in Locarno or head to the **Coop** in Maggia. Baracca Backpacker provides two free bikes daily for grocery runs. (Open M-F 8:30-noon and 2-6:30pm, Sa 8am-12:15pm and 2-5pm; no lunch break from July until mid-Aug.)

◉ ⚠ SIGHTS & OUTDOOR ACTIVITIES

Just north of the bridge on the east side of the river lies one of Maggia Valley's oldest churches. View the frescoes and votive paintings of Giovanni A. Vanoni in the **Sanctuario Madonna delle Grazie.** (Open May-Oct. 15, Tu-Sa 2-4pm.) Vanoni's work is common throughout the valley and can be seen on buildings in Aurigeno as well as in grottoes along several forest paths. In late June and July the valley becomes alive with the sounds of blues during the **Vallemaggia Blues Nights.**

SWIMMING. Aurigeno's two best swimming options are a picturesque waterfall and a lagoon beind an old Roman bridge. For the former, head left from Baracca's toward town and take the left fork in the main road. Pass a large villa surrounded by a stone wall and go along a small path through the woods (5min.). In the summer, swimming at the falls is best in the early afternoon, when the sun's rays filter into the pool at its base. The sun makes the cold water more bearable. To swim, turn right from the hostel and follow brown signs to the Ponte Romana. This old Roman bridge is a wonder in and of itself, while the lagoon behind it provides a private swimming hole (20min.). The Maggia River also offers several swimming holes frequented by locals—ask at the hostel desk for recommendations.

HIKING. Though Auregino's hiking options are mild, it's easy to get lost. Maps are available at Baracca (24SFr) or the tourist office in Maggia (21SFr).

Passon della Garina (4-6hr. round-trip). Made famous by author Max Frisch, the hike over the Passo della Garina (1076m) into Loco in the neighboring Valle Onsernone offers amazing views for hikers. Head south along the main road and follow the signs

ITALIAN SWITZERLAND

toward Chiazza. The steep and narrow path follows traditional red-and-white signs to the pass (2hr.). At the pass, hikers have the opportunity to continue upwards along well-marked trails to the summit of Salmone (1559m) and an overview of Lago Maggiore (1hr.). Beyond the pass, the trail continues along to Loco (2hr.). To return, take a post bus from Loco to Cavigliano, Bivio Onsernone (4.60SFr), then the train to Ponte Brolla (2.60SFr). From Ponte Brolla, bus #10 from Locarno takes travelers back to Aurigeno (5.20SFr). The last bus from Loco runs at 5:05pm.

Giro Valle del Salto (1hr. round-trip). An easier hike begins from Maggia's main square (marked with red-and-white painted signs). Climb the flight of stairs to the Chapelle della Pioda (476m), which offers panoramas of the valley towns. Proceed into Valle del Salto (746m), then descend toward Maggia on the other side of the mountain. Stop in Braià along the way and view a chapel rich with frescoes by the Giovanni A. Vanoni.

BIKING. The 11km village tour through Maggia, Locano, Moghegno, and Aurigeno follows footpaths and side streets throughout the Maggia Valley. Those looking for a more challenging route should head toward Prato Sornica. This path starts at the ice rink in **Prato Sornica** and travels through neighboring villages. The moderate route is accented with a 260m technical climb from **Broglio** to **Monti di Rima,** providing a breathtaking panorama (14km).

ASCONA ☎091

In his memoirs of Ascona (pop. 5000), *The First Step into Wonderland*, Jacob Flach effuses, "Here lies a piece of the Mediterranean Sea embedded in rough mountains, a sun-bathed, blooming cape of the Côte d'Azure, a mile of the Riviera beach sprinkled with azaleas and carnations, and a good dose of the blue sky!" History buffs can trace the steps of leftist thinkers and Bohemian artists who tried, around the turn of the century, to establish a utopian community on the mountain above—a venture dubbed **Monte Verità** (The Mountain of Truth; see p. 463).

▐ ▍ TRANSPORTATION & PRACTICAL INFORMATION

Travel by **bus** #31 from Locarno (15min., every 15min. 6:23am-midnight, 2.60SFr) or by **ferry** (15-45min.; 9 per day 9:10am-5:15pm; day pass 13SFr, seniors 12SFr). The bus stops at "Ascona Posta" on Via Papio. Behind the bus stop the main road of the old city, Via Borgo, stretches to the lake. P. Guiseppe Motta, where the ferry docks, is lined with hotels and restaurants along the waterside. For **currency exchange** and access to an **ATM**, try any of the many banks along Via Papio. (All open M-F 9am-12:30pm and 1:30-4:30pm.) The **tourist office,** in the Casa Serodine behind the Chiesa SS Pietro e Paolo, provides a guide of the area sights and services in four languages and also **exchanges currency.** (☎791 00 91; www.maggiore.ch. Open Apr.-Oct. M-F 9am-6pm, Sa 10am-5pm; Nov.-Mar. M-F 9am-noon and 1-5pm.) A small train of cars leads **guided tours** of the town from the ferry docks. (☎079 240 18 00 or 859 29 57. 30min.; daily starting at 11am. 7SFr, children 3SFr.) Other local services include: **taxis** ☎791 46 46 or 41 41; **parking** at the **Autosilo** at the corner of Via Papio and Via Buonamno (1SFr for 30min., 18SFr per 24hr.) or down Via Papio in **parking garage** (☎751 17 07; 1SFr per hr., 18SFr per 24hr.); and **bike rental** at **Bike Cicli Chiandussi,** Via Circonvallazione 14, down Via Papio and right again before the Migros. (☎780 55 42 or 079 337 11 62. 20-25SFr per day; 15-18SFr per half-day. Open M and W-F 9am-noon and 2:30-6:30pm, Sa 9am-noon and 2-5pm. MC/V.) A kiosk across from the **post office,** 25m down from the bus stop, offers a list of hotels and free phone for reservations. (Open M-F 7:30am-noon and 1:45-6pm, Sa 8:30-noon.) **Postal code:** CH-6612.

ACCOMMODATIONS & FOOD

Few of the city's beds fall into the budget range (nearly everything boasts four or five stars). Luckily, Ascona is an easy daytrip from Locarno. Those who stay can try rooms above the **Ristorante Verbano ❸,** Via Borgo, near the modern art museum. The upstairs rooms are simple but clean, and are the only affordable choice downtown. (☎791 12 74. Breakfast included. Closed Su. 45SFr per person.) The tourist office has a list of *affitacamere* (private rooms).

Otello ❸, Via Papio 8, just downhill from the bus stop, offers a taste of Ticino with frescoed stone pillars and Mediterranean scenes along the walls. Choose from Italian pastas (13-22 SFr), or savor selected cheeses (9SFr) and a chocolate mousse (7SFr). Wines from 3.30SFr. (☎791 54 10. Open daily 11:30am-9:30pm. MC/V.) **Ristorante La Torre ❷,** p. Motta 61, offers prime views of the lake, but is famous for its whimsically decorated bowls of homemade gelato (10.50-10.80SFr). Pizza starts at 12.80SFr; daily *Menüs* 20SFr. (☎791 54 55; fax 792 27 97. Open daily 10am-midnight; closed Nov.-Dec. 20. AmEx/MC/V.) For groceries, look for the **Co-op's** orange sign shining down Via Papio from the bus stop. The **Migros** is 200m down the street. (Both open M-F 8:15am-12:30pm and 2-6:30pm, Sa 8:15am-5pm; Migros open from 8am.) A **market** spills onto the p. G. Motta (May-Oct. Tu 9am-4pm).

PARADISE LOST Around the turn of the 20th century, a distinctly left-of-center collection of anarchists, agrarians, artists, philosophers, nudists, writers, and vegetarians attempted to establish Utopia on the banks of the Lago Maggiore. Even political refugees, including Russian anarchist Michail Bakunin, sought refuge in Ascona in the late 1800s. In 1889, the Locarnese philosopher Alfredo Pioda proposed the establishment of a lay convent for international intellectuals to be named "Fraternitas" on La Monescia, the hill behind Ascona. Though his vision never came to fruition, thinkers seeking connections between humankind, nature, the world, and the universe came to La Monescia anyway. The hill was renamed "Monte Verità" ("mountain of truth") by Henri Oedenkoven and Ida Hoffman, a pair of free spirits who founded the "Co-operative Vegetarian Colony" there in 1900. Meanwhile, Ascona's reputation as a cultural center for the elite continued to grow, drawing the likes of D.H. Lawrence, James Joyce, Hermann Hesse, and Karl Jung (and, in the 20s and 30s, members of the German avant-garde and Dadaists like Arp and Segal).

SIGHTS

The Post Bus stop at the corner of Via Borgo and Via Papio, at the edge of the old city, leaves you within walking distance of all the sights and the waterfront. The *Città Vecchia* stretches from the lake to Via Papio with banner-hung streets and wrought-iron balconies. The sole remaining tower of the 13th-century **Castello del Ghiriglion,** 26 p.G. Motto, is at the eastern end of the boardwalk.

The **Chiesa SS Pietro e Paolo,** left from where Via Borgo intersects the lake, marks Ascona from the lake with its slender clock tower. The frescoes inside date from the 15th century; canvas paintings such as the "Crowning of the Virgin" (1617) above the altar date from the 17th century.

Banana trees and stone coats-of-arms frame the **Collegio Pontifico Papio's** 15th-century courtyard. From the tourist office turn right toward Piazetta S. Pietro, right again onto Contrada Maggiore, left at the Centro Culturale, and right onto Via Cappelle. Presiding over the still-operating Superior private school (est. 1399), the adjacent church of **Santa Maria della Misericordia** hides 15th-century frescoes by Seregnesi and Antonio da Tradate in a dim interior.

Private galleries lining the winding streets promote such artists as Marc Chagall and Georges Braque. **The Museo Comunale d'Arte Moderna,** Via Borgo 34, has an extensive permanent collection of works by Klee, Utrillo, Amiet, and Jawlensky, as well as moving and evocative temperas by Russian Marianne Werefkin that depict haunting mountain scenes and religious pilgrimages of rural Ticino. The museum frequently hosts temporary exhibitions of well-known artists from around the world. (☎780 51 00; www.cultura-ascona.ch. Open Mar.-Dec. Tu-Sa 10am-noon and 3-6pm, Su 4-6pm. 7SFr, students and seniors 5SFr.)

The **Museo Casa Anatta** immortalizes the dashed dreams of Ascona's utopian thinkers (without English labeling). Walk uphill along the winding Strada della Colina from the bus stop or follow the uneven stone stairs of Scalinata della Ruga off Via Borgo for a more direct, although steep, route. This fascinating museum contains photos of a 1930s nudist colony in Brissago, anarchist Ernsy Frick's collection of mystical minerals, and the costumes and crowns worn by members of the "individualistic cooperative." Don't miss the miniature model of one utopian architect's proposed Temple to the Land of Fidus, in which men would pass from the Room of Ambition to the Room of Love and worship a statue of the Woman of the Earth. (☎791 01 81; www.csf-mv.ethz.ch; www.centro-monte-verita.ch. Open Apr.-June and Sept.-Oct. Tu-Su 2:30-6pm; July-Aug. Tu-Su 3-7pm. 6SFr, students and seniors 4SFr.)

🎵 🍴 ENTERTAINMENT & NIGHTLIFE

In late June and early July, Ascona hosts the annual **New Orleans Jazz Ascona.** Musicians play on the waterfront among sculptures and in local cafés. (www.jazzascona.ch. Tickets 10SFr per night, 25SFr for 3 days, 75SFr for 10; children under 16 free.) The **International Horse Jumping Competition** (late July) and the **Settimane Musicali,** an international festival featuring classical music (late Aug. to mid-Oct.), are other opportunities for revelry. On the main street, **Bar Lago** hosts live pianists from countries such as Italy and Brazil, and also offers Latino disco music. (☎791 10 65. Drinks from 8SFr. Open daily 10pm-4am.) Catch a flick at the **Cinema Otello,** next to the restaurant of the same name on Via Papio. (☎791 03 23. Afternoon movies in English with German or Italian subtitles 14SFr; students 12SFr.)

LUGANO ☎091

Lugano, Switzerland's third-largest banking center, rests on Lago di Lugano in a valley between San Salvatore and Monte Brè peaks. Shady streets are packed with cobblestone piazzas, and visitors enjoy its seamless blend of religious beauty, artistic flair, and natural spectacle. There are two extraordinary youth hostels, both built from luxury villas, with swimming pools and magnificent gardens.

◨ TRANSPORTATION

Trains: p. della Stazione. Most destinations connect through **Bellinzona** (30min., every 30min. 5:30am-midnight, 11.40SFr). To: **Basel** (4-5hr., every 30min. 5:36am-8:12pm, 79SFr); **Bern** (1-2 per hr.) via **Olten** (5hr., 5:36am-7:47pm, 76SFr), via **Lucerne** (4¾hr., 5:36am-6:57pm, 56SFr), via **Zurich** (4hr., 5:57am-8:38pm, 87SFr); **Geneva** (1-2 per hr.) via **Olten** (7hr., 5:36am-5:36pm, 104SFr), via **Lucerne** (7hr., 5:36am-

Lugano

🛏🏠 ACCOMMODATIONS
Casa della Giovane, **4**
Eurocampo, **13**
Hotel Montarina, **10**
La Palma, **14**
Ostello della Gioventù, **1**
Pensione Selva, **2**

🍦 FOOD
Gelateria Arcobaleno, **12**
La Tinèra, **11**
Pestalozzi, **8**
Ristorante Manora, **5**
Ristorante Ticino, **9**
Taqueria El Chilichil, **7**
🍺 PUBS
Biblio-Café Tra, **3**
Mango Club, **6**

6:57pm, 104SFr), via **Zurich** (6¼hr., 5:57am-5:30pm, 118SFr); **Locarno** (1hr., every 30min. 5:36am-midnight, 16.60SFr); **Zurich** (3hr., 1-2 per hr. 5:57am-8:38pm, 60SFr); **Zurich Airport** (3¾hr., 63SFr). Trains connect south through **Chiasso** to **Milan** (45min.; every hr. 7:14am-9:48pm; 21SFr, under 26 16SFr).

Public Transportation: Buses run from the neighboring towns to the center of Lugano and also traverse the city. Schedules and ticket machines at each stop. 1.10-1.90SFr per ride, 24hr. "Carta Giorno" (day pass) 5SFr. SwissPass valid.

Taxis: ☎922 88 33 or 922 02 22.

Car Rental: Avis, 8 Via C. Maraini (☎913 41 51). **Hertz,** 13 Via San Gottardo (☎923 46 75). **Europcar,** 24 Via M. Boglia, Garage Cassarate (☎971 01 01).

Parking: Autosilo Comunale Balestra, off Via Pioda, on Via S. Balestra. 7am-noon and 2-7pm. 1SFr per hr., 12SFr for 5hr.; overnight parking (7pm-7am) 6SFr. Open 24hr.

Bike Rental: At the baggage check in the station (☎923 66 91). 30SFr per day; 23SFr per half-day. 6SFr to return at another station. Open 9am-6pm.

✈ 🛈 ORIENTATION & PRACTICAL INFORMATION

The 15min. downhill walk from the train station to the classically Italian Piazza della Riforma, the town's center, winds through Lugano's large pedestrian zone. For those who would rather avoid the walk, a funicular runs between the train station and the waterfront **Piazza Cioccaro** (1.10SFr, 5:20am-11:50pm).

Tourist Office: (☎913 32 32; www.lugano-tourism.ch). The office is across from the ferry station in the Palazzo Civico, Riva Albertolli, at the corner of p. Rezzonico. Free maps and **guided city walk** in English May-Oct. M 9:30am. Open Apr.-May and Sept.-Oct. M-F 9am-7:30pm, Sa 9am-5:30pm, Su 10am-4pm; July-Aug. M-F 9am-7:30pm, Sa 9am-10pm, Su 10am-4pm; Nov.-Mar. M-F 9am-12:30pm and 1:30-5pm.

Hotel Reservations: Kiosks outside the train station and tourist office list hotels and provide free reservations phones. Open Tu, W, Su 2-7pm; Th-Sa 11am-7pm; extended hours on request. Tourist office makes reservations (4SFr).

Consulates: UK, 22 Via Sarengo (☎950 06 06; fax 06 09). Open M-F 10am-noon.

Currency Exchange: Western Union in the station (☎923 93 26). Open M-Sa 7:10am-7:45pm, Su 8:30am-noon and 1:30-6:30pm. Banks open M-F 8:30am-4:30pm.

Luggage Storage: Lockers at station. 4-7SFr. Luggage watch 7SFr per piece. Open 24hr.

Lost Property: Check the *Fundbureau* (☎800 80 65) of the Polizei Communale, on the p. Riforma. Open M-F 7:30am-noon and 1:30-5pm.

Internet Access: Biblio-Café Tra, 3 Via A. Vanoni (☎923 23 05). From p. Dante, head down the Via Pretorio (15min.) and turn left onto Via A. Vanoni. Open M-Th 9am-midnight, F 9am-1am, Sa 5pm-1am. 2SFr per 15min. **Manor** in p. Dante has 4 terminals on the 3rd floor (10SFr per hr.). Open M-W and F-Sa 8:15am-6:30pm, Th 8:15am-9pm. 1SFr per 6min. **Burger King,** right from the tourist office, provides 30min. **free** with the purchase of a meal (10.90-12.60SFr). Open Su-Th 9am-midnight, F-Sa 9am-1am.

Bookstore: Melisa, 4 Via Vegezzi (☎923 83 43; fax 73 04). English-language books downstairs. Open M-F 9am-6:30pm, Sa 9am-5pm. AmEx/DC/MC/V.

Emergencies: Police ☎117, **Ambulance** ☎144, **Fire** ☎118, **Medical Services** ☎111, **First Aid,** ☎805 61 11. **Pharmacies** are throughout the city.

Post Office: Via della Posta, 2 blocks up from the lake near Via al Forte. Open M-F 7:30am-6:15pm, Sa 8am-12pm. traveler's checks cashed. Telephones, telegraphs, and faxes at the Via Magatti entrance to the PTT building. **Postal code:** CH-6900; **Post-lagerndebriefe** use CH-6901.

🛏 ACCOMMODATIONS & CAMPING

🏨 **Hotel Montarina,** Via Montarina 1 (☎966 72 72; www.montarina.ch). Walk 200m to the right from the station, cross the tracks, and go 50m uphill. Converted from a luxury villa, this palm-tree-enveloped, independent hostel attracts young families and students with its **swimming pool,** well-groomed grounds, ping-pong table, reading room, tiny kitchen, and terrace. Laundry 4SFr, soap 1.50SFr. **Internet** 10SFr per hr. Buffet breakfast 12SFr. Sheets 4SFr. Parking available. Reception 8am-10pm. Open Mar.-Oct. In July and Aug. call 2 weeks in advance for reservations. Dorms 25SFr; singles 70-80SFr; doubles 100SFr, with bath 120SFr. MC/V. ❷

🏠 **Ostello della Gioventù (HI),** Lugano-Savosa, Via Cantonale 13 (☎966 27 28; www.luganoyouthhostel.ch). Note: there are 2 streets called Via Cantonale, one in downtown Lugano and one in Savosa, by the hostel. Take bus #5 (walk 350m left from the station, past the parking lot, and cross the street to the bus stop) to "Crocifisso," and then backtrack and turn left up Via Cantonale. A former luxury villa, this sprawling family-run hostel has extensive gardens and a **pool** with waterslide, and unique, comfortable rooms in several different buildings. Kitchen access 1SFr (after 7pm only). Internet 5SFr for 20min. Breakfast 8SFr. Towels 1.50SFr. Parking available. Laundry 5SFr. Reception 7am-12:30pm and 3-10pm. Curfew 10pm; keys available on request for 20SFr deposit. Reserve ahead. Open mid-Mar. to Oct. Dorms 23SFr; singles 35SFr, with kitchenette 45SFr; doubles 60/74SFr; family rooms for 2-6 people 90-120SFr. Apartments for families (1 week min. stay) 100-170SFr per day. Lower rates for extended stays. MC/V. ❷

Pensione Selva, Via Tesserete 36 (☎923 60 17; villaselva@bluewin.ch). Take bus #4 (dir.: Ospedale; leaves opposite train station) to "Sassa," then walk along Via Gottardo for 250m and turn right on Via Tesserete. A path overhung with grapes seals this haven from the city noise and leads to the cozily romantic pension with an outdoor pool and terrace. Parking available. Breakfast included. Reception 8am-midnight. Closed Nov. Singles 49-58SFr, with shower 69-90SFr; doubles 98-110SFr/118-138SFr. ❸

Casa della Giovane, Corso Elvezia 34 (☎911 66 46; fax 66 40), across the street from Basilica Sacro Cuore. Take bus #5 (leaves opposite train station) to "Corso Elvezia." This modern peach and blue building provides rooms (most with balconies) for **women only.** The rooftop terrace allows for serious tanning. Breakfast 5SFr. Lunch or dinner 12SFr. Laundry 3SFr (bring soap). Reception 24hr. No curfew, but tell the receptionist when you'll be back. Reserve ahead. 4-bed dorms 20SFr. ❷

Camping: There are several campsites, 2 of which are in **Agno.** Check with the tourist office for a complete list. For **La Palma** ❶ (☎605 25 61; fax 604 54 38) or **Eurocampo** ❸ (☎605 21 14; fax 31 87), both lakeside, take the Ferrovia-Lugano-Ponte-Tresa (FLP) train to Agno (4.60SFr). From the station, turn left, then left again onto Via Molinazzo. La Palma open mid-Apr. to mid-Oct. 8.50SFr. Eurocampo open Apr.-Oct. 7.20SFr per person; tents 6-10SFr. All sites have showers.

🍴 FOOD

Outdoor cafés serving similarly priced Italian fare pepper the lakeside piazzas. **Via Pessina,** off p. della Riforma, livens up at midday. The multi-level **Migros,** 15 Via Pretorio, two blocks left from the post office down Via Pretorio, has a food court with slices of pizza from 2.90SFr and sandwiches from 2.50SFr. (Open M-W and F 8am-6:30pm, Th 8am-9pm, Sa 7:30am-5pm.) A **public market** on p. della Riforma sells seafood, veggie sandwiches (4SFr) and produce (open Tu and F 7am-noon).

La Tinèra, Via dei Gorini 2 (☎923 52 19), behind Credit Suisse off p. della Riforma, is a romantic, low-lit, underground restaurant, specializing in Lombard cuisine. Daily *Menü* 13-18.50SFr. Try the sausage with *risotto* (14SFr) or a vegetarian goulash (4SFr). Open M-Sa 8:30am-3pm and 5:30-11pm. AmEx/DC/MC/V. ❸

Gelateria Arcobaleno, Via Marconi 2 (☎922 62 18), beside the McDonald's on the waterfront, dishes out the most creative and unusual *gelato* desserts in town, as well as low-fat yogurt *gelato*. Menu includes *gelato* pizza (10SFr), *Spiedini* (fruit kebabs and yogurt; 2 for 22SFr), and the "Indonesia," a pineapple filled with yogurt gelato, fruit salsa, and whipped cream (11SFr). Scoop of ice cream 3.50SFr; 3 for 7.50SFr. Hot and cold sandwiches 5.50-8.50SFr. Open M-F 8:30am-1am, Sa-Su 9am-1am. ❷

Taqueria El Chilicuil, Corsa Pestalozzi 12 (☎922 82 26), down the Corsa Pestalozzi from the p. Indipendenza. Lively snack bar serves tacos, quesadillas (4.50-8SFr), and margaritas (7SFr, pitcher 38SFr). Happy Hour M-F 5-7pm (drinks 1-2SFr less). Wheelchair-accessible. Open May-Nov. M-Th 11:30am-11pm, F 11:30am-midnight, Sa-Su 7pm-midnight; Dec.-Apr. M-Th 11:30am-10pm, Sa-Su 5pm-midnight. ❶

Ristorante Manora, Manor Department Store in p. Dante, 3rd floor; entrance off Salita Mario e Antonio Chiattone also. Budget eaters can't beat this gourmet self-serve spot. Great selection and great atmosphere. Salad bar (4.50-10.20SFr), pasta (7.90-10.90SFr per plate), and beer (1.20-4.50SFr). Hot daily specials 10-15SFr. Wheelchair-accessible. Open M-Sa 7:30am-10pm, Su 10am-10pm. ❷

Pestalozzi, p. Indipendenza 9 (☎921 46 46), in the hotel. This non-alcoholic restaurant offers well-balanced, veggie-friendly menus (13-16SFr) and the option of a smoke-free dining room. Meat lasagna and mixed salad 12.50SFr. Open daily 11am-9:30pm; hot food served 11am-2:30pm and 6-9:30pm. MC/V. ❷

Ristorante Ticino, p. Cioccaro 1 (☎922 77 72; fax 923 62 78). This air-conditioned spot in the center of town offers an intimate setting with cozy booths for a special occasion. Choose from a variety of fish and meat entrees (22-38SFr) including chef recommendations such as Norwegian salmon (28SFr). Wheelchair-accessible. Open M-F 12-2pm and 7-9:30pm, Sa-Su 7-9:30pm. AmEx/DC/MC/V. ❹

🅖 SIGHTS

Frescoes of the 16th-century **Cattedrale San Lorenzo,** downhill from the train station, gleam with colors that are still vivid. The cathedral's plain outside hardly foreshadows the intricate interior beauty. Bernardio Luini's gargantuan fresco, **Crucifixion,** painted in 1529, rests in the **Chiesa Santa Maria degli Angioli,** right from the tourist office. The small 14th-century **Chiesa San Rocco,** two blocks to the left of the p. della Riforma, in the p. Maghetti, houses an ornate Madonna altarpiece and Discopli frescoes of saints being flayed alive and pierced with arrows. The national monument **Basilica Sacro Cuore,** on Corso Elevezia across from the Casa della Giovane (open M-F 7:45am-5:30pm, Sa-Su 10am-6pm), is more sparing. See hikers next to disciples in the frescoes ringing the altar. The **Museo Cantonale d'Arte,** 10 Via Canova, has a permanent collection of 19th- and 20th-century art including works by Swiss artists Vela, Ciseri, Franzoni, and Klee, and often replaces these with temporary contemporary art exhibits. (Across from the Chiesa San Rocco. ☎910 47 80; www.museo-cantonale-arte.ch. Wheelchair-accessible. Open Tu 2-5pm, W-Su 10am-5pm. Permanent collection 7SFr/5SFr; special exhibits 10SFr, students 7SFr. MC/V.) An elegant lakeside villa houses the **Museo delle Culture Extraeuropee,** Via Cortivo 24. An abundance of wood-carved masks, statues, and shields from distant lands adorn the villa's marble staircases and ornate windows. Italian captions tell the history behind the pieces. (On the footpath to Gandria in the Villa Heleneum. From the tourist office take bus #1 (dir.: Castagnola) to "San Domenica." Make a left U-turn to the street below. The Villa is 700m on the right. Or take the ferry to the Museo Helenum stop. (☎971 73 53. Open Apr.-Oct. W-Su 10am-5pm. 5SFr, students 3SFr.)

▲ OUTDOOR ACTIVITIES

PARKS & GARDENS. The **Belvedere,** on riva Caccia, is an enormous sculpture garden with an emphasis on modernist metalwork. Chess enthusiasts gather for open-air tournaments. The garden stretches along the lakeside promenade. The serene **Parco Civico** is dotted with flower beds. Small beaches offer direct access to the water. (Open daily Mar.-Oct. 6:30am-11:30pm, Nov.-Feb. 7am-9pm.)

BOATING. The dock for the **Societa Navigazione del Lago di Lugano** is across the street from the tourist office. (☎923 17 79; www.lakelugano.ch.) Tours of Lake Lugano pass tiny, unspoiled towns along the shore, including Gandria (11.60SFr, round-trip 19.20SFr), Morcote (16.60/27.40SFr), and Paradiso (3/5SFr). A "grand tour" of the lake in English (3½hr.) costs 32.60SFr, 19.60SFr with SwissPass; 62SFr/52SFr allows a week of unlimited lake travel. SwissPass is valid on all boats. Various points on the lake rent pedal boats (7-8SFr per 30min.). **Boat Saladin** across from the Chiesa Santa Maria degli Angioli, rents motor boats. (☎923 57 33. 40SFr per hr., 25SFr per 30min. No license required. Open Apr.-Oct. 9am-midnight.) **Bagno Pubblico,** on riva Caccia toward Paradiso, is good for a swim. (☎994 20 35. 4SFr, children 8-16 2SFr. Open daily May-June 14 and Sept. 9:30am-6:30pm; June 15-Aug. 9:30am-8pm.) A rope swing is near the Castagnola ferry stop.

HIKING. The tourist office and Ostello della Gioventù have topographical maps and trail guides (15SFr) into the Ticinese mountains. The most rewarding hike is to **Monte Boglio.** The 5hr. round-trip can be extended over two days by staying at the Pairolhütte (ask at hostels or tourist office). Reach the peaks of **Monte Brè** (933m) and **Monte San Salvatore** (912m) by funicular. Monte Brè is down the river to the left of the tourist office. (☎971 31 71. 13SFr, round-trip 19SFr; ages 6-16 6.50SFr/9.50SFr.) The San Salvatore funicular is 20min. from the tourist office, down the lake to the right in Paradiso. (☎985 28 28. 14-17SFr, round-trip 20-31.60SFr; ages 6-16 7-8.50SFr/10-15.80SFr.) Walks along the lake to the east provide access to some beautiful lakeside villages, including romantic **Gandria.**

ADVENTURE SPORTS. The **ASBEST Adventure Company,** Via Basilea 28 (☎966 11 14; www.asbest.ch.), based in the Hotel Continental, provides adventure opportunities. Most require group interest; lone travelers should call ahead. In winter, **snowshoe** and **ski** (full-day 90SFr) or **tandem paraglide** over icy crags (170SFr). **Canyoning** (from 90SFr) and **river-diving** (90SFr with appropriate training) are less chilling in Ticino, away from glaciers. In summer, **rock-climb** (90SFr) or **mountain bike.**

♫ ♞ ENTERTAINMENT & NIGHTLIFE

During the first two weekends in July, Lugano's **Festival Jazz** fills the p. della Riforma with free music. Past performers include Miles Davis and Bobby McFerrin. The looser **Blues to Bop Festival** (also free) celebrates R&B, blues, and gospel in late August by hosting international singers and local amateurs. The **Wine Harvest Festival,** in mid-October, drowns those fading summer memories. From late June to early August, **Cinema al Lago** shows international films on a large screen installed on the lake, nightly at 9:45pm; after July 15 9:30pm. (☎913 32 32; www.open-air-kino.ch. 15SFr, under 17 12SFr.)

The Latin American **Mango Club,** 8 p. Dante, mixes live salsa and techno in one of the premier clubs of Lugano. (☎922 94 38. 10SFr admission includes beer. Open W-Su 11pm-5am.) For a change of pace, head down the Via Pretorio from p. Dante and turn left on Via A. Vanoni for the **Biblio-Café Tra,** Via Vanoni 3. This laid-back café evokes a bit of leftist Spain with its shaded spot and battered wood tables on which subversive-types consume 3.60SFr beers. (☎923 23 05. **Internet** 2SFr per 15min. Open M-Th 9am-midnight, F 9am-1am, Sa 5pm-1am.)

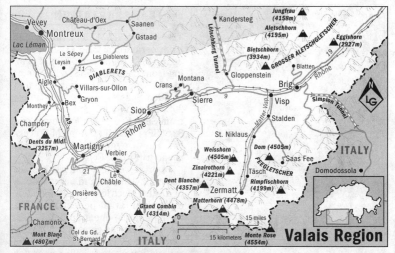

Valais Region

VALAIS (WALLIS)

The Valais area occupies the deep and wide glacial gorge traced by the Rhône river. The clefts of the valley divide the land linguistically: in Martigny and Sion, French predominates; in Brig and Zermatt, Swiss-German is used. Whatever the language, the towns share a common penchant for cheese and good wine, and make an industry of shuttling people to the snow-covered peaks on skis or on foot. Though mountain resorts can be over-touristed, the region's spectacular peaks and skiing, hiking, and climbing opportunities make fighting traffic worthwhile. Zermatt has the most to offer skiers and hikers, although some small towns have great appeal. Note: Eurail is not valid on the regional BVZ train line.

HIGHLIGHTS OF VALAIS (WALLIS)

Gorge yourself on breathtaking views in the hiker's paradise of **Zermatt** (see p. 471).

Combine world-class art with traditional alpine cow fights in **Martigny** (see p. 485).

Ski in the middle of summer on the slopes surrounding **Sion** (see p. 483).

ZERMATT & THE MATTERHORN ☎ 027

A trick of the valley blocks out the great alpine summits that ring Zermatt, allowing the Matterhorn (4478m) to rise alone above the town. Instantly recognizable and stamped on everything from scarves to pencils, the peak stands as a misshapen monolith that blazes bright orange at dawn and occasionally is clear of clouds long enough for the crowd to snap a picture. The Bahnhofstraße is populated in equal measure by ruddy outdoors-lovers and their shopping-bag-laden counterparts. The town keeps the peace with *Nachtruhe* (quiet hours) curfew after 10pm; raucous noise can result in a fine of 200-300SFr. A short hike or cable car ride best escapes crowds by leading to alpine meadows and splintered icefalls. Hiking, climbing, and skiing—some of Switzerland's best—are top reasons to make the trek to Zermatt.

VALAIS

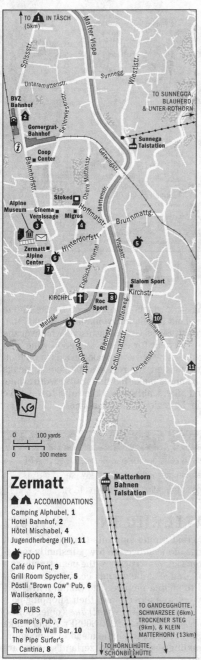

Zermatt

♠♠⚑ ACCOMMODATIONS
Camping Alphubel, **1**
Hotel Bahnhof, **2**
Hôtel Mischabel, **4**
Jugendherberge (HI), **11**

🍎 FOOD
Café du Pont, **9**
Grill Room Spycher, **5**
Pöstli "Brown Cow" Pub, **6**
Walliserkanne, **3**

🍺 PUBS
Grampi's Pub, **7**
The North Wall Bar, **10**
The Pipe Surfer's
Cantina, **8**

▐ TRANSPORTATION

The BVZ (☎ 921 41 11) runs **trains** from Zermatt to: Brig (1½hr.; 6am-9pm; 34SFr, round-trip 67SFr, if coming from Lausanne 73SFr/140SFr or Sion 47.20SFr/94SFr); via Visp and Stalden-Saas (1hr.; varying times; 29SFr, round-trip 58SFr; if coming from Saas Fee 41.40SFr, round trip 82.80SFr); Täsch (10min.; M-F every hr., Sa-Su every 20min; 7.80SFr, round-trip 15.60SFr).

To preserve the alpine air, Zermatt has outlawed **cars** and **buses**. Locals in toy-like electric buggies alternately dodge and target pedestrians. The town of **Täsch,** one stop before Zermatt, has **parking garages** for 7.50SFr per day; the large outdoor lot by the rail station costs 5-6.50SFr per day (and has a reservation board for hotels in Zermatt). Zermatt is accessible only by the **HGB** (Matterhorn Gotthard Bahn; www.mgbahn.ch) rail line (SwissPass valid, **Eurail not valid**). The station and tourist office have free phones to Zermatt's hotels and **hotel taxis,** which wait to round up guests after each train arrives.

🔲🄸 ORIENTATION & PRACTICAL INFORMATION

Most shops, services, and restaurants stretch along Bahnhofstr. from the train station to the Hotel Weisshorn and the Café du Pont. Halfway between these, Hoffmattstr. heads to the left. Beside the church, Kirchstr. slides down the hill and across the river.

Tourist Office: Bahnhofpl. (☎ 966 81 00; www.zermatt.ch), in the station complex. Distributes the free booklet *Prato Borni* that provides extremely detailed practical info for getting around the city, and the *Wanderkarte* hiking map (25.90SFr). Open mid-June to mid-Oct. M-F 8:30am-6pm, Sa 8:30am-6:30pm, Su 9:30am-noon and 4-6pm; mid-Oct. to mid-Dec. and May through mid-June M-F 8:30am-noon and 2-6pm, Sa 9:30am-noon; mid-Dec. to Apr. M-F 8:30am-noon and 2-6pm, Sa 8:30am-6:30pm, Su 9:30am-noon and 4-6pm.

Bike and Ski Rental: Julen Sport (☎967 43 40), on Hoffmattstr., rents skis and mountain bikes. (Open M-Sa 8:30am-noon and 2-6:30pm. 38-50SFr per day, 28-38SFr per half-day. AmEx/DC/MC/V.) Its companion, **Roc Sport** (☎967 43 40), on Kirchstr., rents the same equipment, but it's best to head straight to Julen. Rental prices for skis and boots are set throughout Zermatt (skis and snowboards 28-50SFr per day, boots 15-19SFr per day). Try **Glacier Sport** on Bahnhofstr. (☎967 27 19; open daily 8am-noon and 2-6:30pm), **Slalom Sport,** across the river on Kirchstr. (☎966 23 66; open M-Sa 8am-noon and 2-6:30pm), or **Bayard Sports,** directly across from the station (☎966 49 60; open daily 8am-noon and 2-7pm).

Currency Exchange: Free at the train station (5:45am-8pm). **Banks** are generally open M-F 9am-noon and 2:30-6pm.

Luggage: Lockers for ski equipment downstairs in station (15SFr), at end of the tracks (6-8SFr), or storage at the ticket counter (5SFr per bag). Open daily 5:45am-8pm.

Work Opportunities: The North Wall Bar, ☎966 34 12. (See p. 475.)

English-Language Library: Bahnhofstr. 32. In the English Church on the hill behind the post office. Small collection of used novels loaned on the honor system. Open M-Tu and Th-F 4-8pm.

Laundry: Waschsalon Doli (☎967 51 00), behind Swiss Souvenirs and across from the train station. 19SFr per load. Open M-Sa 8am-noon and 2-6pm.

Weather Conditions: ☎162 or check the window of the *Bergführerbüro.* **Winter Avalanche Information** ☎187.

Emergencies: Police ☎117, **Fire** ☎118, **Ambulance/24hr. Alpine Rescue** ☎144.

Pharmacy: Pharmacie Internationale Zermatt (☎966 27 27), Bahnhofstr. to right of station. Open M-Sa 8:30am-noon and 2-6:30pm, Su 11am-noon and 5-6pm. Emergency service for 20-30SFr surcharge depending on time.

Internet Access: Ask at the tourist office for a list of public access points. Most cost 15-20SFr per hr. **Stoked** (☎967 70 20), on Hoffmatstr. next to the tennis courts, charges 12SFr per hr.

Post Office: Bahnhofstr., in Arcade Mont-Cervin, 5min. to the right of the station. **ATM.** Open M-F 8:30am-noon and 1:45-6pm, Sa 8:30-11am. **Postal code:** CH-3920.

ACCOMMODATIONS & CAMPING

Climbers, hikers, and snowboarders raise the demand for budget beds in Zermatt. Finding a dorm bed on the spot can be tough in July and August, and mid-February through mid-March. Many hotels in winter and all chalets in summer only accept bookings for a week at a time. Some campers are thus tempted to sleep illegally in the wide-open spaces above town, a practice that can incur fines near of 300SFr.

Hotel Bahnhof (☎967 24 06; www.hotelbahnhof.com), on Bahnhofstr. to the left of the station, is a climber's hangout. Renovated rooms provide hotel housing at hostel rates. Ask for a view of the Matterhorn. No breakfast, but one of the few places with an extensive kitchen and large dining room. Laundry 6SFr. Dorms 30SFr; singles 59SFr, with shower 71SFr; doubles 86-96SFr; quads 172SFr. MC/V. ❸

Hotel Mischabel (☎967 11 31; www.zermatt.ch/mischabel), right off of Hofmattstr. This hotel creaks, but reassuringly. Straightforward TV room downstairs. The bedrooms, though plain, are not unpleasant. Breakfast included. Reception 7:30am-10pm. Check-out 11am. Open June 16-Oct. 20 and Dec. 16-Apr. 31. Singles, doubles, and triples 45-57SFr per person; singles with bath 55-67SFr. MC/V. ❸

Jugendherberge (HI), Winkelmatten (☎967 23 20; www.youthhostel.ch/zermatt). Turn left at the church, cross the river, take the 2nd street to the right (at the Jugendherberge sign) and the left fork in front of Hotel Rhodania. At this fully loaded hostel, tourists get all the goodies and a great deal, though the atmosphere is a trifle institutional. Unobstructed views of the Matterhorn from bedroom windows, friendly staff, a giant outdoor chess set, ping-pong, foosball, and **Internet** (5SF per 15min.) await. Breakfast, hearty dinner (including fondue on Su and vegetarian on request), and sleepsack included. Laundry 8SFr. Closed for renovations until mid-2004. Reception 7-10am and 4-10:30pm. Closed May. Dorms 48SFr; 2 doubles 116SFr. Non-members add 6SFr. AmEx/DC/MC/V. ❸

Camping Alphubel (☎967 36 35), in Täsch. From the station, cross the parking lot and turn right in front of the tourist offices past the river, then right across the railroad tracks. Caravaners and motorists can park their vehicles here. Showers included. Reception 8am-noon and 2-8pm. Open May to mid-Oct. 4.50SFr per person, ages 6-16 2.25SFr; 5SFr per tent, 5SFr per car, 6SFr per caravan; electricity 3SFr. Tax not included in price. ❶

Mountain Huts: The tourist office provides a list of private huts in the Zermatt area. A full day's hike from Zermatt, they offer a good deal for serious climbers and hikers. All huts are open July-Aug., are accessible to walkers if there's no snow, and include breakfast unless otherwise noted. Try **Schönbielhütte** (2694m; ☎967 13 54 or 47 62; 35.50SFr), **Rothornhütte** (3198m; ☎967 20 43 or 16 20; fax 16 39; 32SFr; see the Grandchild Hike, p. 478), the crowded **Gandegghütte** (3029m; ☎079 607 88 68 or 967 21 12; fax 967 21 49; 26SFr; no breakfast), or **Hörnlihütte,** also called **Berghaus Matterhorn** (3260m; ☎967 22 64; 43SFr; see Hörnlihütte Hike, p. 477). ❷

☐ FOOD

It's easy to find an inexpensive meal in Zermatt. Revellers flood the streets after dark, sipping whiskey to warm up following a day in the snow. The **Co-op** is across from the station. (Open M-F 8:15am-12:15pm and 1:45-6:30pm, Sa 8:15am-12:15pm and 1:45-6pm.) A **Migros** inhabits Hoffmatstr. across from the tennis courts. (Open M-F 8:30am-12:15pm and 2-6:30pm, Sa 8:30am-12:15pm and 2-6pm.)

Walliserkanne (☎966 46 10), Bahnhofstr., next to the post office, looks upscale inside, but offers filling Swiss fare at down-to-earth prices. The menu includes *Käseschnitte mit Schinken and Tomate* (toasted cheese with ham and tomato; 18SFr) and fondues (23SFr). *Menüs* (20-23SFr) with vegetarian options are also available. Additionally, Walliserkanne offers pizzas for take out (15-18SFr) from 11:30am-11pm. Open 9am-midnight. AmEx/DC/MC/V. ❸

Café du Pont, Kirchpl. (☎967 43 43). Zermatt's oldest restaurant tends to attract a similarly aged clientele. Multilingual menus burnt into slabs of wood hanging on the wall list stick-to-your-ribs Swiss dishes like *Raclette* (7.50SFr), *Rösti* (11-15SFr), and *fondue du Pont* (22SFr). The *Valais Platte* offers a sampling of regional meats (24SFr). Sandwiches 6.50SFr. Wheelchair-accessible. Open June-Oct. and Dec.-Apr. daily 9am-11pm; food served 11am-10pm. ❷

Pöstli "Brown Cow" Pub, Bahnhofstr. (☎967 19 31), is in the Great Swiss Disaster complex at the Hotel de la Post. The clientele of lively English-speaking locals comes for the whimsical cow-pattern decor and greasy-spoon food. Try the potato skins

(9.50SFr) or chomp on a burger (11-15SFr). In the summer cool off with a frappe (6.50SFr) or munch on one of the season's special salads (10-18SFr). Heineken 3.40SFr. Open daily 9am-2am. The rest of the complex offers a 3-story spaghetti factory with evening films and disco, a jazz bar with live music, an underground bar and disco, and a posh hotel. No cover. Discos open until 3:30am. ❷

Grill Room Spycher (☎967 77 41 or 20 41), across the river on Kirchstr. and left on Steinmattstr. Those looking to splurge and escape classic cheese-laden menus should head to the romantic Spycher. Wood ceilings and an abundance of greenery provide atmosphere for risotto with mushrooms (25SFr), duck in orange sauce (29SFr), or deer filet with brussel sprouts, chestnuts, and *spätzli* (36SFr). Wheelchair-accessible. Open June to mid-Oct. and mid-Nov. to Apr. daily 6-11pm. AmEx/DC/MC/V. ❹

🔍🎭 SIGHTS & ENTERTAINMENT

The **Alpine Museum,** near the post office, exhibits broken ropes, mangled shoes, and bashed-in lanterns found with the corpses of those who failed to master local peaks, as well as displays of the flora, fauna, and geology of the area. Special attention is given to the first ascent of the Matterhorn on July 14, 1865, when over half the team was killed on the way down. A haunting photograph is all that remains of one victim, Lord Alfred Douglas (the love of Oscar Wilde's life), whose remains were never found. Recovered remains of the Matterhorn's victims are buried in the cemetery next to the church with picks and ropes carved into their graves. The museum also displays two relief models: one of the Matterhorn, and the other of the mountain region around Zermatt. (☎967 41 00. Open June-Oct. daily 10am-noon and 4-6pm; July 10-Aug. 20 opens afternoons at 3pm; Dec. 20-May M-F and Su 4:30-6:30pm. 8SFr, children under 16 2SFr.)

The **Cinema Vernissage** (☎967 66 36), next to Julen Sports on Hoffmattstr., screens two or three nearly new releases per night (M-Sa), usually in English. **Casino Zermatt** (☎966 81 81) on Bahnhofstr. just before the church, offers American Roulette, Black Jack and Slots. There is no dress code, but you must be 20 to enter. August 15th brings the **Alpine Folklore Parade,** when locals take a break from their mountain chores and dust off their *Alphorns* and *Lederhosen.* The Roman Catholic church hosts **classical music concerts** (25SFr) in July and August.

🌙 NIGHTLIFE

▨ **The Pipe Surfer's Cantina,** on Kirchstr. (☎213 38 07; www.gozermatt.com/thepipe), before the river on the right, is the nightly site of the craziest beach party in the Alps. Owner Nikk, generous with the free shots (stop by in the afternoon for a 2-for-1 coupon or get one at the HI hostel), keeps customers rolling with his hilarious stories of late-night adventures and sound advice on everything Zermatt, and has recently altered the Pipe's image into that of a bistro, with excellent food and a still-lively clientele. The staff are all experts in something, providing a variety of adventure outings and good company (see Outdoor Activities, p. 476). Don't leave without downing a shot of Moo, the made-on-the-premises caramel vodka (6SFr). Frozen margaritas 6SFr, beer 4SFr or 0.5L 6SFr. Food served on request. In winter special Bum's Play plate includes beer and entree. Happy Hour daily 7-8pm. Open daily 3:30pm-2:30am.

The North Wall Bar (☎966 34 12). Take the 2nd right past the river on Kirchstr., en route to the youth hostel, to this English-speaking climber's haunt and workman's bar where skiing and mountaineering videos play every evening alongside the dart games. This is the place to scrounge a job in Zermatt—ask the staff, who also give hiking advice. The kitchen will serve you "the hottest pizza in the Alps" (12SFr, plus 1SFr per fancy top-ping; options include mussels, corn, broccoli, or egg). Beer, some of the cheapest in town, is 5SFr for 0.5L. Open daily mid-June to Sept. and mid-Dec. to Apr. 6:30pm-midnight; later in winter. Pizza served until 10pm.

Grampi's Pub, Bahnhofstr. 70 (☎967 77 75 or 417 99 85; fax 71 13), across from Pöstli Pub. This centrally located bar thumps with pop dance music. Draft beer 4SFr for 0.25L; bottled beer 6-8SFr; "lady killers" 11-13SFr. Open 8:30am-2am, downstairs bar until 4am (DJ 9pm-3:30am); upstairs Italian restaurant 6pm-2am; food until 1am.

🏔 OUTDOOR ACTIVITIES

The Zermatt Alpine Center, which houses both the **Bergführerbüro** (Mountain Guide's Office; ☎24 60; www.zermatt.ch/alpincenter) and the **Skischulbüro** (Ski School Office; ☎966 24 66; www.zermatt.ch/skischule), is past the post office from the station. Pick up detailed four-day weather forecasts, ski passes, and information on guided climbing expeditions. (*Bergführerbüro* open July-Sept. M-F 8:30am-noon and 3:30-7pm, Sa 3:30-7pm, Su 10am-noon and 3:30-7pm; late Dec. until mid-May daily 5-7pm. Ski school office closed in summer but reachable by phone.) Adventure-seekers looking to take home their vacation should contact the **Freeride Film Factory** (☎213 38 07), operated by the Pipe Surfer's Cantina. Skilled guides offer custom hiking, biking, and climbing expeditions for lower prices (160-250SFr) than the Ski School and also give you a 15-20min. videotape of your expedition. (See Pipe Surfer's Cantina, p. 475.) The highly recommended **Air Taxi Zermatt** (☎967 76 44) sends tandem-paragliders airborne at starting points from 2300m to 4100m (150-190SFr including transportation) and also offers a paragliding school for those with both time and money on their hands. The glitzier hotels have **swimming pools**; Hotel Christiania, Wiestistr., has the biggest one. Follow the right bank of the river to the left past the Rothorn/Sunnegga cable railway station. (Hotel ☎967 80 00. Pool access 10SFr, children 6SFr. Open M-Su 8-10:30am and 2-8pm; Th until 9pm. Sauna 20SFr.)

SKIING. Seventy-three lifts, 14,200m of combined elevation, and 245km of prepared runs make Zermatt one of the world's most extensive ski centers. Serious skiers will find challenges on **Europe's longest run**—the 13km trail from Klein Matterhorn to Zermatt. The town also has more **summer ski trails** than any other Alpine ski resort—36 sq. km of year-round runs between 2900 and 3900m. In the summer, the **Skischulbüro** (above) offers group five-day skiing (280SFr) and snowboarding (200SFr) classes. Individual, one-day, and summer ski/snowboard lessons available on request. **4Synergies** also offers ski instruction privately or in groups. (☎967 70 20; www.4synergies.com. Groups 95SFr per day, 410SFr for 5 days.) Meanwhile **Stoked Swiss Snowboard School** provides qualified instructors for downhill rides. (☎967 87 88; www.stoked.ch. Groups 50SFr for half-day; 200SFr for 5 half-days.) **Ski and boot rental** is standard throughout the area, as is snowboard rental (prices run 28-50SFr per day, 123-215SFr per week). Finding a reliable sports store is easy—just go for a brief walk on nearly any street. (Most shops open daily 8am-noon and 2-6:30pm. See **Orientation and Practical Information,** p. 472.) Zermatt's **ski passes** operate on a regional system during the **summer** (from the end of Apr.-Oct.). Passes are available for any of the regions (Matterhorn, Gornergrat, or Sunnegga complexes). The Matterhorn region costs 60SFr per day. The Klein Matterhorn/Trockener Steg sub-region is now combined with Italy's Mt. Cervinia (1 day 56SFr). From November to the end of April, a combined pass is available for all three regions (1 day 72SFr, 7 days 338SFr).

MONTE ROSA CONQUERS CELEBRITIES The Monte Rosa (the second highest mountain in Switzerland) has a long and illustrious career with glitterati. Leonardo da Vinci, staring up at it from the Italian side, thought it the highest mountain on earth. Among its unlikely conquerors have been Pope Pius XI, who pioneered a new route to the Grenzensattel in 1889 before donning the papal robes. A youthful Winston Churchill climbed Monte Rosa in 1894 before gaining his fame in more political ventures.

CLIMBING. The only company to lead formal expeditions above Zermatt is the **Bergführerbüro.** Groups go up the Breithorn (135SFr), Pollux (260SFr), and Castor (270SFr) daily in summer (see above). Prices do not include equipment, hut accommodations, or lifts to the departure points. For equipment rental, see **Hiking** below. Climbing the Matterhorn is expensive and requires a guide, perfect physical condition, a 4am start, and extensive rock-climbing experience (at least PD+).

HIKING. Outstanding walks into the world of glaciers and high mountains leave from Zermatt in every direction. Although most paths are well maintained and marked, a proper **topographic map** (25.90SFr from the tourist office) is essential for safety and enhances the experience. Also available at the tourist office (2SFr), and at some hotels for free, is a more basic map of hiking routes around Zermatt, which is more than sufficient for most day-hikers. Lifts and railways to the south and east can shorten difficult climbs. (25% discount on many lifts with SwissPass, **Eurail generally not valid.**) Prudent walkers come prepared (see Health, p. 19); Zermatt is particularly prone to sudden electrical storms. Check the weather forecast in the Bergführerbüro before departure. Hiking boots can be rented at **Matterhorn Sport,** Bahnhofstr. (☎967 29 56), which also rents out climbing equipment; **Glacier Sport,** Bahnhofstr. (☎967 27 14) across from Walliserkanne; or **Burgener Sport,** Bahnhofstr. (☎967 27 94) next to Grampi's Pub. (1-day rentals 14SFr; 7 days 52SFr; 14 days 80SFr. All stores open 8am-noon and 2-6:30 or 7pm.)

Hörnlihütte Hike (10hr. round-trip, 5hr. round-trip with cable car). The **Hörnlihütte** serves as the base camp for the most popular route up the Matterhorn and is a good platform for watching climbers claw their way up the ridge. The 1600m ascent to the hut is for the fit and well booted only (a walking stick is recommended); a **cable car** from the far end of town to the **Schwarzsee** via Furi (2584m) saves 900m of climbing. (Schedule varies throughout the year; ask the tourist office. 20.50SFr, round-trip 33SFr). Leave Zermatt along the left bank of the Matter Vispa. Approximately 2km from Zermatt, a wide track marked "Zum See, Schwarzsee und Hörnlihütte" leads down and left across the river. Follow the 3hr. path as it zigzags steeply up to the tiny Schwarzsee, passing gorges on the left. From the Schwarzsee, the path becomes rockier and wilder as it joins the true northeast ridge of the Matterhorn, climbing gently at first but ending in a merciless, exposed *arête* (sharp ridge) by the buildings at Hörnli. **Casual hikers *cannot* continue above the hut.** More than 500 people have died above this point, as a walk around Zermatt's cemeteries attest. For a different descent, bear right at the *Schwarzsee* to the Furgg cable car terminus and follow path to town. It traverses a steep cliff but is stable underfoot and has even closer views of the gorges carved by the **Gornergletscher.**

The Gornergrat (numerous hikes possible). The Gornergrat swarms with as many as 5000 visitors per day because it provides the best views of the Matterhorn. The **train,** which departs opposite Zermatt's main station (7am-11pm), ascends to the **Gornergrat** (3090m; 41SFr, round-trip 67SFr) via **Riffelalp** (2211m; 17.20SFr/32SFr), **Riffelberg**

OF SKIRTS AND MOUNTAINS In 1867, when most women were concerned with keeping a good house and finding a good man for whom to keep it, 18-year-old Félicité Carrel set her sights on loftier goals. She decided to be the first woman to ascend the infamous Matterhorn. With the help of the Maquignza brothers, who hoped to prove that anyone could climb the mountain, Félicité almost reached her goal. Unfortunately, a change in route along the way forced the climbers up a more difficult path that Félicité, in her required skirts (meant to hold down the wind) was not allowed to attempt. Instead, she waited for her companions 120m below the summit at a landmark that has been known since as Col Félicité.

(2582m; 27SFr/46SFr), and **Rotenboden** (2815m; 34SFr/58SFr), all of which are trailheads. From the Gornergrat, hikes descend to the wide, flat **Gornergletscher** and along the ridge toward the **Stockhorn** (3532m). A cable car traverses this distance (12SFr each way). Rotenboden is on the other side of Stockhorn. From Rotenboden, hikers can divert to the Monte Rosa hut (5hr. to the hut and back) by following the glacier. Each destination provides a closer encounter with the ice with the cost of losing a fraction of the panorama. Routes from the Riffelalp station descend to Zermatt by following the side of the mountain around to the *Grünsee*, facing the snout of the **Findelngletscher,** then crossing the river and returning to Zermatt by way of the **Moosjesee** and the **Leisee,** 2 small pools that provide a beautiful foreground to the Matterhorn.

Granny Hike; to Zmutt (1hr. round-trip). This easy hike offers the most dramatic encounter with the Matterhorn's north face. The path is wide, clear, and well marked. From Zermatt, follow Bahnhofstr. past the church, then follow the sign to the right. The steady slope climbs through the Arolla pines to the weathered chalets of the hamlet of Zmutt. The path, granting views of the Hörnli ridge and the Matterhorn, levels out as it continues through the meadows above a small reservoir. The Matterhorn's north wall, which drops 200m with an average gradient well over 45°, gradually comes into view above Zmutt.

Grandchild Hike (10hr. round-trip). If you want to make the Granny Hike more challenging (well worth the extra effort, since the views get drastically better as you ascend), the Grandchild Hike continues on to the **Schönbielhütte** (2694m; 4hr. from Zmutt). The hike becomes more difficult as it ascends past lakes and waterfalls at the outlet of the rock-strewn **Zmuttgletscher.** The Schönbielhütte is an ideal spot for lunchtime carbo-loading of pasta or *Rösti*, or an overnight stop. On the return journey, the valley frames the Rimpfischhorn (4199m) and Strahlhorn (4190m). The full-day hike is 25km, covering 1050m of gentle elevation.

SAAS FEE ☎027

Saas Fee, the "Pearl of the Alps," is one of Switzerland's most dramatic sites. The thirteen 4000m peaks that form a semicircle above the town peer down ominously. The glacial ice of the **Feegletscher,** "fairy glacier," comes so low that you can visit the frozen giant on a 30min. evening stroll. To protect its alpine glory, this resort town is closed to cars, giving electrically powered minivans and trucks free rein over the winding streets. Town officials prohibit disturbing "the fairy-like charm of Saas Fee" after 10pm (noisemakers fined 200SFr).

▐ TRANSPORTATION

A **post bus** runs (every hr. 5:35am-7:35pm) to Brig (1¼hr.; 17.20SFr; round-trip 34.40SFr) via Saas Grund (10min.; 3SFr/6SFr); Stalden Saas (40min.; 12.40SFr/24.80 SFr), connecting to Zermatt (41.40SFr/82.80SFr, reservations required);

and Visp (50min., 15.20/30.40SFr), where trains connect to Lausanne, Sion, and the rest of Valais. Reserve a seat on all buses starting at Saas Fee at least 2hr. before departure in the high season. Call ☎958 11 45 or drop by the bus station (open 7:30am-12:35pm and 1:15-6:35pm). **Parking** is available in the lot across the street to the right of the tourist office. (1 day 11SFr; with guest card after 2nd day 7.50SFr.)

✈ 🛈 ORIENTATION & PRACTICAL INFORMATION

The **tourist office,** opposite the bus station, dispenses seasonal information, hiking advice, and useful town maps. Outside, a kiosk provides hotel information and a free, direct phone for reservations. (☎958 18 58; reservations ☎958 18 68; www.saas-fee.ch. Open July to mid-Sept. and mid-Dec. to mid-Apr. M-F 8:30am-noon and 2-6:30pm, Sa 8am-7pm, Su 9am-noon and 3-6pm; closed Su in May.) The bus depot has small **lockers** (2SFr) and **luggage storage** (2SFr). For a **weather report,** call ☎162. In case of **emergency,** call ☎117. **Vallesia Apotheke** pharmacy is down the hill from the tourist office at the main street. (☎957 26 18. Open M-Sa 8:30am-noon and 2-6:30pm, Su 4-6pm; for emergencies call ☎079 417 67 18.) Call a **taxi** at ☎958 11 35 or 957 33 44. **Cyber Lion** in Haus Waldrain, left past the Migros, offers **Internet access** (☎947 39 61; www.cyberlion.ch; 5SFr per 20min.), or ask at Hotel Dom, on the main street past the church (☎957 51 01). There is a **post office** with public **fax** and **ATM** at the bus depot. (Open M-F 8:15am-noon and 2-6pm, Sa 8:15am-noon.) **Postal code:** CH-3906.

▌ ACCOMMODATIONS

Hotel Garni Bergheimat ❸, in the center of town, offers clean mid-sized rooms with showers at a reasonable rate. The rooms aren't exciting, but ask for a south facing window and the glacial views will be. (☎957 20 30; www.berghe-imat.ch. Breakfast included. 73-91SFr per person in winter; 570-69SFr in summer; 50SFr between seasons.) **Hotel Garni Feehof ❸** is right on the main street. Warm, wooden, and wonderful, nearly all the pine rooms have balconies and beds with enormous marshmallow-like down comforters. (☎957 23 08; fax 23 09. Breakfast and shower included. Reception 9-11am and 3-6:30pm. The hotel is fairly small, so be sure to reserve at least 2 weeks in advance in winter. Singles 38-62SFr; doubles 76-142SFr.) Travelers willing to sacrifice comfort can find bargains in hotel basements. **Hotel Garni Imseng ❷,** across the street from Feehof, has seven rows of 3-high bunks, with no space in between. However, the hotel is clean, frequently empty, and there is an impressive breakfast in the morning. Doubles upstairs in the hotel have TVs and leather couches but cost three times more. (☎958 12 58; www.saas-fee.ch/hotel.imseng. Breakfast and lockers included with dorms. All hotel rooms have satellite TVs, telephones, and a safe; most have balconies. Sheets 5SFr. Hotel is wheelchair-accessible, the dorms are not. Reception 8:30am-noon and 2-7pm. Dorms 35SFr; doubles 110SFr per person.)

    Mountain huts are a bold alternative to staying in Saas Fee proper. Breakfast is always included. The **Mischabel ❷** (3329m; ☎957 11 17; 28SFr, dinner available), **Hoh-Saas ❸** (3098m; ☎957 17 13; 36SFr), and **Weissmieshütte** (2726m; ☎957 25 54; 30SFr, dinner included) above Saas Grund are all accessible from July to September. It is a good idea to contact the hut caretaker about vacancies and opening hours before setting out. The Saas Fee tourist office (see Practical Information, above) and Bergführerbüro (see Hiking, p. 480 have more details.

🍽 FOOD

Spaghetteria da Rasso ❷, on the main street under the Hotel Britania, has a shady terrace where accordionists occasionally entertain the crowd. Two or more can try the house special with salad, unlimited pasta, and four different sauces for 25SFr per person. (☎957 15 26. Open M and W-Su late June to mid-Oct. 9am-11:30pm; mid-Oct.-Apr. 10am-11:30pm. AmEx/MC/V.) Though it's certainly not difficult to find Swiss specialties around town, the **Restaurant Chämi-Stube ❸** (☎957 17 47), a little farther down the hill from the church, is unique in the quiet, candle-lit atmosphere it offers. It serves a variety of *Rösti* for 14-16.50SFr, a Valaisian fondue for 25SFr, and, interestingly, tortillas for 17-28SFr. (Open Dec.-May and mid-June to Oct. 9am-11:30pm. Warm food 11:30am-2pm and 6-9pm. AmEx/MC/V.)

Most of Saas Fee's **supermarkets** in the center of town have the same hours. (M-F 8:15am-12:15pm and 2:15-6:30pm, Sa 8:15am-12:15pm and 2:15-5pm.) Every Thursday from mid-July to mid-August, there is a **Market** held on the main street of Saas Fee from 2-6pm.

🏔 OUTDOOR ACTIVITIES

SKIING. During the **summer,** two cable cars to **Felskinn** (3000m; 7:30am-4:15pm; 26SFr, round-trip 34SFr) and an underground funicular, the "Metro Alpin," farther to **Allanin** (3500m; 7:45am-4pm; an additional 26SFr, round-trip 34SFr) enable **skiers** to enjoy 20km of runs and a stupendous alpine view. In the winter, an immense network of lifts opens from Allanin (day ski passes 59SFr, children 35SFr; 6 days 27SFr/167SFr; 13 days 480SFr/288SFr). The **Ski School,** across the street from the church, offers group skiing and snowboarding lessons from mid-Dec. to April. (☎957 23 48; www.saas-fee.ch/skischool. Skiing 46SFr per 3hr., 172SFr per week; snowboarding 43SFr per 2hr., 158SFr per week. Slight reductions available in late Jan. Open M-F 8:30-noon and 2:30-6pm, Sa-Su 4-6pm.) In Saas Fee, many stores **rent skis.** Stores in the **Swiss Rent-A-Sport System** (look for the big red "S" logo) offer three grades of equipment (skis and snowboards 28-50SFr per day, 6 days 109-190SFr; boots 15-19SFr/56-80SFr). It is possible to call ahead and have equipment set aside prior to arrival; call or fax the main Swiss Rent-A-Sport outlet in town, **Anthamatten Sport Mode,** located across from the Spaghetteria. (☎958 19 18; fax 957 19 70. Open daily May-June and Sept.-Nov. 9am-noon and 2-6pm; July-Aug. 8:30am-noon and 1:30-6:30pm; Dec.-Apr. 8am-7pm. AmEx/DC/MC/V.)

HIKING. The **Bergführerbüro** (Mountain Guides' Office), housed in the same building as the ski school, leads climbs of varying difficulty levels to a number of 4000m summits. (☎/fax 957 44 64; www.rhone.ch/mountainlife. Open July-Apr. M-Sa 9am-noon and 3-6pm.) Day tours run 50-200SFr per person. Hikers have 280km of marked trails from which to choose. Maps at the tourist office are 7SFr, or ask for the free brochure with tour description. The **Saas Valley Hiking Pass** (171SFr, family rate 345SFr) provides access for one week to all cable cars and post buses in the valley and entrance to the ice pavilion at **Mittelallanin,** the **Bielen Recreation Center,** and other museums. The pass is available at the tourist office or any cable car station. Most lifts close from May to early June and from mid-October to mid-December.

Mischabelhütte Hike (full-day hike, 1550m ascent). A steep trail leads up to the **Mischabelhütte** (3329m), the best walking-accessible panorama of Saas Fee's natural amphitheater. From the pharmacy on the main street, turn right after the church and take the right fork after 100m. Check for snow cover before departing, as the last part of the hike is rocky and highly unpleasant with any hint of ice.

Glacier Hike (half-day hike). This lovely half-day voyage begins with a cable-car ride to **Plattjen** (2570m). From there a path leads to the right and then left after 5min. to views of the Dom and Lezspitze. From the summit, the trail descends for 15min., then heads left around the amphitheater, spiraling slowly down below the **Feegletscher.** The view opens up as the path drops to the **Gletschersee** (1910m) at the glacier tip. From there, the trail gently follows the left bank of the outlet stream back to Saas Fee.

Hannig Hike (round-trip 2½hr.). This easy walk from the church to Hannig follows a trail that begins level (30min.) and gets steeper as it moves into the woods. Follow the "Hannig" signs all the way. On the way up, there are opportunities for close encounters with goats and pigs as the path passes through the small farms on the hill. Stop at the Mannigalp hut for fresh milk and cheese from the cows and goats you saw along the way. After an hour, the path splits into the Hannig trail and the longer, more scenic Hannig Waldweg trail. From the restaurant at the summit, it is possible to continue the trail toward Melchbode and back to Saas Fee or take the **Sonnenbahn Hannig** cable car (15SFr adults, 7.50SFr children; 30% discount with Swiss-Pass) that descends to the Spaghetteria.

OTHER ACTIVITIES. The **Bielen Recreation Center,** next to the bus station, has an expensive but excellent **swimming pool** and **jacuzzi,** and also offers **massages,** indoor **tennis,** a **sauna,** and **badminton.** (☎957 24 75. Open daily June 1-9pm; July-Oct. 10am-9pm. 13SFr, children 8.50SFr, with guest card 12SFr.) The Mountain Guide Office organizes outings to a nearby gorge every Monday, Wednesday, and Friday in summer, and every Thursday in winter. Scuttle along water-carved rock faces (safety equipment 95SFr). **Feeblitz,** beside the Alpine-Express, offers a self-controlled roller-coaster ride. Riders control single cars that skate along a winding metal track down the mountain. (☎957 31 11. Open daily June noon-5pm; July and Aug. and Sa-Su in Sept. and Oct. 10am-6pm, Nov. F-Su 1-5pm, and Dec.-Apr. noon-6pm. 6SFr, under 16 4SFr, discount with visitors card.)

For two weeks in mid-August, Saas Fee hosts the **Musica Romantica** classical music festival, which brings artists from all over Europe. (www.saas-fee.ch/romantica. 25-65SFr symphony concert tickets, 16-40SFr recital tickets, 130-210SFr week-long ticket, 50% discount for children under 16.) Contact the tourist office for a list of performers and to purchase tickets.

BRIG ☎027

A simple town, Brig (pop. 11,500) aptly takes its name from the word for "bridge," providing access to the most famous resorts in Valais. Visitors can enjoy a quiet day visiting Brig's many churches and the *Stockalperschloß*, but the best reason to come is to catch a train or cable car to a nearby glacier or mountain peak.

▐ TRANSPORTATION & PRACTICAL INFORMATION

Brig is accessible by **train** from: Interlaken Ost via Spiez (1½-2hr., every hr. 5:33am-11:37pm, 40SFr); Martigny (50min., every hr. 6:54am-12:54am, 23SFr); Sion (45min., 2 or 3 per hr. 6:04am-1:09am, 17.20SFr). The **BVZ train** runs between Brig and Zermatt (1½hr.; every hr. 5:10am-7:23pm, June-Oct. extra trains and a bus at 8:25pm; 34SFr; Swisspass valid, no Eurail.) The last return train from Zermatt is June-Oct. 9:10pm (Nov.-Apr. 7:52pm). The **Post Bus** leaves for Saas Fee every hour

6:15am-8:15pm and returns 5:35am-7:35pm. Reservations required for return trips (1¼hr., 17.20SFr). The **train station** is open M-Sa 6:30am-8:30pm and Su 7:30am-8pm and offers **bike rentals** (30SFr per day, 21SFr per half-day), **luggage storage** (7SFr per bag), **lockers** (4-6SFr), and **currency exchange** (M-F 7am-7pm, Sa 7am-5pm and Su 8-11:30am and 1-5pm). The **tourist information office** is on the second level of the train station. (☎921 60 30; www.brig.ch. Open Oct.-June M-F 8:30am-6pm, Sa 8:30am-1pm; July-Sept. Sa 9am-6pm, Su 9am-1pm.) Other services are: **Internet,** at the Good Night Inn across the river from Sebastians Pl., (12SFr per hr.); **police** ☎922 41 60; **hospital** (emergencies ☎922 33 33); and **taxis** ☎0800 800 608. A **post office** across the street from the station is open M-F 7:30am-noon and 1:30-6:15pm, Sa 8-11am. **Postal code:** 3900.

ACCOMMODATIONS

For only a bit more than some hostels, **Pension Post ❷**, Furkastr. 23, right from the station onto Viktoriastr. and then left onto Furkastr., walk ahead 5min., offers one of the best deals in town. Spacious, high-quality, attractive rooms with clean inviting beds come with or without in-room showers. Sheets, towels, and breakfast included. (☎924 45 54; fax 45 53. Reception M-F 6am-11pm, Sa 7am-6pm. Dorms 35SFr; singles 40-50SFr; doubles 80-100SFr.) For those with a larger budget, **Hotel Du Pont ❸,** on the far side of Sebastians Pl., 5min. up Bahnhofstr. from the station, has aging but clean rooms in its old wing and luxurious doubles in the newer one. (☎923 15 02; dupont.brig@datacomm.ch. Singles 55-75SFr, with shower 95-130SFr; doubles 100-130SFr/150-210SFr. AmEx/DC/MC/V.)

   Camping Geshina ❶, just past the local swimming pool 15min. up Bahnhofstr. on Geshinaweg. off Neue Simplonstr., sports lines of trees between wheel-to-wheel RVs and arranges hikes or visits to cheese makers for its guests. (☎923 06 88; geshina@campings.ch. Reception 8:30am-noon and 4:30-8pm. Open Apr. 20-Oct. 14. 5.50SFr, children 3SFr; tents 5SFr.)

FOOD

The main street is dotted with high-priced hotel restaurants, but try **Walliser Weinstube ❷,** Bahnhofstr. 9, for Swiss classics at reasonable prices, including *Käseschnitte* for 14-17SFr and *Rösti* for 11-15SFr. (☎923 14 28; www.walliser-weinstube.ch. Open M-F 6:30am-11pm, Sa-Su 9am-midnight.) Past Sebastians Pl. on Alte Simplonstr., **Tea-Room Bistro Viva ❷** offers traditional fare in a non-traditional setting. Try the *Älpler macaroni* (12SFr) and apple *strudel* with ice cream (6SFr) in a modern room with that new-car feel. (☎924 56 03. Open Su 8:30am-1pm, M-F 7:30am-6:30pm.) **Molino Pizzeria Ristorante ❸,** is truly Italian, with Romanesque statues decorating the dining area, an ivy-covered terrace, and 14 kinds of pizza (15.20-25.50SFr), soups, and pastas. (☎923 65 56; fax 924 43 13. Open M-Sa 11:15am-2pm and 5:30-11pm, F-Sa until midnight, Su 11:15am-11pm.) **Migros,** left from station and across the street, has a grocery store and restaurant. (Store open M 1:30-6:30pm, Tu-F 8:15am-6:30pm, Sa 7:45am-4pm. Restaurant open M-F 7:30am-6:30pm, Sa 7:30am-4pm.) The **Coop** across the river from Sebastians Pl. on Gilserallee, offers cheap groceries and a bistro as well. (Open M 1:30-6:30pm, Tu-F 8am-6:30pm, Su 7:30am-4pm.) There's a **farmer's market** every Saturday from 8am-noon.

⚠ OUTDOOR ACTIVITIES

Brig provides easy access by bus or train to major ski areas including **Zermatt, Crans-Montana, Riederalp, Bettmeralp and Piesheralp, Rosswald, Belalp,** and **Saas Fee.** In the summer, head to one of the nearby towns for cable car access to the newly established **Aletsch Nature Reserve** and view 24km of flowing ice, the longest glacier in Switzerland. Cars aren't allowed beyond the border. Ask at the tourist office for more details about the reserve or for suggested **hikes.** Brig also lies just 2.5km from **Brigerbad,** home to Europe's first Thermal-Grotto pool and the largest **open-air thermal pools** in Switzerland. (Open May-Sept.) The last weekend in August brings the **Schäferwochenende Belalp,** during which a festival arises around the nearly 2000 sheep that are herded down from the hills. (☎921 60 40; www.belalp.ch.)

If you're spending the day in the city, visit the 17th century **Stockalperschloß** (Stockalper Castle) on Alte Simplonstr. The Baroque castle, impressive with its three towers, was restored between 1955 and 1961, and now houses a theater and art gallery in its cellars. Visit the museum across the street or walk around the rose garden and park on your own. (☎921 60 30. Open May-Oct. Tu-Su 9:15-11:30am and 1:15-4:30pm. Tours in German or by paper every hr. Open Oct.-May 9:30am-3:30pm; June-Sept. 9:30am-4:30pm. 5SFr, children 2SFr.) It's also nice to visit the **Kollegiumskirche** for a view of the town. Friday evenings in summer bring live music to Sebastians Pl. and occasional open-air movies free of charge.

SION ☎ 027

Surrounded by the glitz of winter-driven mountain towns, Sion, the capital of Valais canton, is a summer city. Behind the day-to-day business of the main streets lies the cobblestone-lined old city, overlooked by two looming hillside castles and exuding a refreshingly down-to-earth, sun-friendly environment. Additionally, Sion's size (large enough for an Olympic bid in 2006) and accessibility make it an ideal base for exploring all of Valais or for a momentary escape from the touring hordes.

E TRANSPORTATION. Trains pass every 30min. in each direction along the Rhône Valley, going west (4:52am-10:52pm) to: Aigle (35min., 17.20SFr); Lausanne (1¼hr., 27SFr); Martigny (15min., 9.20SFr); Montreux (50min., 21SFr); and east (6:04am-1:09am) to Sierre (10min., 5.80SFr) and Brig (30-45min., 17.20SFr). The **train station** is open M-Sa 6:30am-8pm, Su 6:50am-8pm. Switzerland's largest **Post Bus station** congests the square in front of the station with a blur of yellow buses. Ask about the Sierre-Sion Regional deal, offering three days of unlimited travel in the region over one week for 48SFr, children 38SFr. (☎327 34 34; www.poste.ch.)

◨⎘ ORIENTATION & PRACTICAL INFORMATION. Sion's main artery, ave. de la Gare, runs north up the hill from the train station, passing ave. du Midi on the right, to form the southwest corner of pl. de la Planta with r. de Lausanne. R. du Grand-Pont, a main thoroughfare of the old town, connects to the end of r. de Lausanne east of the plaza. The **tourist office,** off r. de Lausanne in pl. de la Planta, provides 2hr. **guided tours** and room reservations. (☎327 77 27; www.siontourism.ch. Open July-Aug. M-F 8am-6pm, Sa 9am-5pm; Sept.-June M-F 8:30am-noon and 2-5:30pm, Sa 9am-noon. Tours mid-July-Aug. Tu and Th 9:30am, additional group tours on request. 8SFr, children 5SFr.) The train station provides **currency exchange** when station is open (see times above), **lockers** (4-6SFr), and **luggage storage** (7SFr for 24hr.; open 6:45am-8pm). **Internet access** is cheapest at **NetOnline,** ave. de la Gare 39, a 5min. walk from the train station.

(☎321 33 11; www.netonline.ch. Open M-Th 11am-10pm, F-Sa 11am-midnight, Su 11am-7pm. 7SFr per hr.) In case of **emergency**, call ☎117, or ☎144 for an **ambulance**. For **pharmacy** call ☎111. The **post office**, pl. de la Gare, is to the left of the train station. (Open M-F 7:30am-6:15pm, Sa 8:15am-noon.) **Postal code:** CH-1950.

⌐ ACCOMMODATIONS & CAMPING. Sion's sole budget-friendly accommodation, the **Auberge de Jeunesse (HI) ❷**, ave. de l'Industrie 2, behind the train station, welcomes guests with brightly colored artwork. The building is vast and institutional, with clean bathrooms, little balconies, and lockers in every room. Rooms are often fully booked from June to September, so call ahead. Amenities include **bike rental** (15SFr per day; 10SFr per half-day), ping pong, pool, and foosball. (☎323 74 70; www.youthhostel.ch/sion. Breakfast included. Lunch on request 12.50SFr. Dinner 12.50SFr, reserve ahead. Kitchen facilities 2.50SFr. Reception 8-10am and 5-9pm. Keys on request. 4-bed dorms 28.80SFr; 3-bed dorms 32.80SFr; 2-bed dorms 35.80SFr. 6SFr surcharge for non-members. DC/MC/V.) Travelers seeking a cheaper bed should try villages outside Sion. In nearby **Pont-de-la-Morge,** singles run 40SFr, doubles 80SFr; in **Saint-Léonard** 50-70SFr/70-94SFr. Post Buses run to both towns.

Camping Les Iles ❶, rte. d'Aproz, boasts five-star riverside campsites 4km from town. Take a very short ride on Post Bus #2 to Aproz. (☎346 43 47; fax 68 47. Open Jan.-Oct. and the last 2 weeks in Dec. 8.40SFr, children 4.20SFr; tents 9SFr; low-season 6.60SFr/3.30SFr, 6SFr.)

▸ FOOD. Cafés and restaurants line the cobblestoned streets of the *vieille ville.* Unlike many cafés, the **Café des Châteaux ❸**, behind Hotel de Ville on r. des Châteaux 3, off r. du Grand Pont, is unpretentious and affordable. Swiss classics like *Raclette* (25SFr) and fondue (19-22SFr) are served alongside *escargots* (15SFr) and *tripe milanaise* (18SFr). (☎372 13 96. Wheelchair-accessible. Open M-Tu and Th-Sa 8am-midnight, Su 10am-midnight. MC/V.) For cheap and filling Turkish delights, head to ave. des Mayennets at ave. du Midi and grab a kebab and drink (7-13SFr) at **Kebab Istanbul ❷**. (☎323 79 05. Open M-Sa 10am-9:30pm, Su noon-9:30pm.) The menu at **Au Vieux Valais ❸**, on r. St. Théodule off r. de Lausanne (from pl. de la Planta, briefly follow r. de Lausanne as it enters the *vielle ville,* turn left on r. St. Théodule), is made for two. Try *potence flambée au whisky* (35SFr, with rice and house sauces) or the *fondue bourgnignonne* (32SFr), which comes with salad and potatoes. (☎322 16 74. Open M-F 9:45am-11pm, Sa 6-11:30pm; MC/V.)

Migros supermarket is in the Centre Commercial on ave. de France, one block left from the station, and on ave. Ritz, two blocks right from ave. de la Gare. (De France location open M 1-6:30pm, Tu-Th 8:15am-6:30pm, F 8:15am-7:30pm, Sa 8am-5pm; Ritz location open M 1:30-6:30pm, Tu-F 8:15am-noon and 1:30-6:30pm, Sa 8am-5pm.) The de France location also houses a Migros restaurant.

COWFIGHT For centuries, Valaisian breeders have raised cows in hopes of achieving success at the annual cow fights *(Combats de Reines),* a regional spectacle that is the source of much pride. The highest bovine reverence has been accorded to the *Heren* strain, valued for its fine milk, meat, and particularly mountain-adapted nature. *Heren* females have an aggressive streak that reveals itself in their violent eyes. When facing off, combatants exhibit a repertoire of well-documented moves and behaviors, from preliminary head movements and *escarpier* (pawing the ground), to head-on and lateral attacks. After a mighty struggle, whichever animal is not lying on the ground receives an extra-special bell and some salt from her owner, along with the distinction of being *la reine* (the queen), the true honor every virtuous cow desires.

☉ 🚶 SIGHTS & ENTERTAINMENT. Majestically perched on twin hills overlooking Sion are the **Château de Tourbillon** and the **Château de Valère.** The ave. des Châteaux leads upward to the castles from the *Hotel de Ville*, past **Château de la Majorie et du Vidomnat,** forking to the left toward Tourbillon and to the right to Valère. At night, the hillside castles are set ablaze with floodlamps. During the day, their looming presence is just as inspiring. Both offer panoramic vistas of Sion and its surroundings.

The **Château de Valère** houses the **Musée Cantonal D'Histoire,** which leads visitors on a tour through the historic building and through Swiss history from early Christian Europe until the present. Beyond the museum, the world's oldest working organ (c. 1390-1430) rests among the faded murals of the **Basilisque du Château de Valère** and can be heard at the annual organ festival every Saturday at 4pm in July and August. (Open daily June-Sept. 11am-6pm; Oct.-May Tu-Su 11am-5pm. Tours in French, English, and German from mid-Mar. until mid-Nov. every hour 11:15am-4:15pm except 3:15pm; additional 5:15pm tour June-Sept. Museum 6SFr, children 3SFr, families 12SFr; basilisque 3SFr/1.50SFr/6SFr; combined ticket 7SFr/4.50SFr/15SFr. Museum open Oct.-May Tu-Su 11am-5pm; June-Sept. daily 1-6pm. Basilisque open Oct.-May Tu-Sa 10am-5pm, Su 2-5pm; June-Sept. M-Sa 10am-6pm, Su 2-6pm.) To the north, the Château de Tourbillon is a much simpler edifice made up of old walls and ruins sitting atop a hill surrounded by terraced vineyards. Admission is free, and a brief hike to the hilltop rewards you with beautiful views and yards perfect for picnicking. At the bottom of the hill, the Château de la Majorie et du Vidomnat houses the **Musée des Beaux-Arts.** Fans of Valaisian art will enjoy the *fin de siècle* portraiture, the collection of 18th-century Valasian landscapes, and the scenes of rural life. (☎606 46 90. Open Tu-Su Oct.-May 1-5pm; June-Sept. 1-6pm. 5SFr, students 2.50SFr; families 20SFr; tours 8SFr.) Head up the hill 200m to the old **Sion jail** where the **museum** hosts intriguing temporary exhibits. (Open daily Oct.-May 1-5pm; June-Sept. 1-6pm.)

Summer evenings bring **free concerts** of classical music through the auspices of the **Academie de Musique** (☎322 66 52) and fusions of rock, funk, and jazz during **Festiv** (2nd weekend in June). **Open-air Cinema** occur during the last weeks of June and July.

The Valais canton produces some of Switzerland's finest wines. Most cafés have whitewashed terraces where patrons sip whites *(Fendant* or *Johannisberg)* and reds *(Gamay or Dole).* Consult the tourist office for organized **wine-tasting excursions** and a list of local cellars. A long-distance path through the vineyards, *le chemin du vignoble,* passes close to Sion and through wine-tasting territory. Always call before arriving at a cellar, and try to organize a group if you want the proprietor to be more welcoming. One *centre de dégustation* is **Le Verre à Pied,** ave. du Grand-Pont 29, which houses 150 wines from multiple sellers throughout the region. (☎/fax 321 13 80. Open daily 10:30am-1pm and 4-8pm or by reservation.)

MARTIGNY   ☎ 027

French-speaking Martigny (pop. 15,000) serves as one of the major access points to the jagged peak of Mont Blanc (4807m), which straddles the French and Italian borders and is the highest peak in the Alps. The oldest town in Valais, Martigny has long been the center of passages across the Alps, serving Hannibal, Caesar, Charlemagne, and Napoleon. The regional architecture thus displays a wide range of cultural influences: a medieval castle towers in the west while a Roman amphitheater stands in the east. Thanks to the **Fondation Pierre Gianadda,** Martigny is a center for modern art and classical music.

VALAIS

VALAIS

▐ TRANSPORTATION. Frequent **trains** west to Aigle (20min.; every 30min. 5am-8pm, every hr. 8-11pm; 9.80SFr); Lausanne (45-60min.; every 30min. 5am-8am, every hr. 8-11pm; 21SFr); and Montreux (30min.; every 30min. 5am-8pm, every hr. 8-11pm; 15.20SFr); and east to Sion (15-25min.; 3 per hr. 6:10am-9:10pm, 2 per hr. 9:10-12:54am; 9.20SFr). A private line travels to Châtelard (45min.; every hr. 6:42am-7:48pm, less often Sept. 15-Dec. 16 and Apr. 7-June 16; one-way 16.60SFr), where you change for Chamonix in France (one-way 12SFr, round-trip 15SFr), a starting point for the 10- to 14-day Mont Blanc circuit. The line goes to Orsières (30min., every hr. 7:12am-8:11pm, one-way 9.80SFr), where you change for a bus to Aosta in Italy via the St. Bernard Pass (1½hr., 8:35am and 5pm, one-way 19.80SFr). The **information office** is across the street from the station. (☎723 37 01. Open M-F 8am-noon and 1:30-6pm, Sa 8am-noon.) **Buses** run to Champex and the Col de la Forclaz pass, also starting points for Mont Blanc, through the **Post Bus** service (☎327 34 34). The station (open M-F 6:15am-8pm, Sa 6:15am-7:15pm, Su 7:45am-noon and 1:30-7:15pm; call ☎0900 300 300 for schedule information) has a **travel agency.** (Open M-F 9am-noon and 1:30-6pm, Sa 9am-noon and 1:30-5pm.)

▐▐ ORIENTATION & PRACTICAL INFORMATION. The **tourist office,** pl. Centrale 9, is straight down ave. de la Gare at the far corner of pl. Centrale. (☎721 22 20; fax 22 24. Open May-Sept. M-F 9am-6pm, Sa 8:30am-12:30pm and 1:30-5:30pm, Su 10am-12:30pm and 4-6pm; Oct.-Apr. M-F 8:30am-noon and 1:30-6:30pm, Sa 8:30am-noon.) In the train station, services include: **taxi** ☎722 22 00 or 21 17; **currency exchange, lockers** (3-5SFr), **luggage storage** (5SFr), and **bike rental** (30SFr per day, 23SFr per half-day). Emergency numbers: **police** ☎117; **ambulance** ☎144. The **hospital** (☎603 90 00) has a switchboard that connects you to the late-night doctor and pharmacy. **Internet** access (4SFr per 15min.) at **Cyber Café, Casino and Cinema,** on the right halfway between the station and pl. Centrale at r. de la Gare 27. (☎722 13 93. Open M-F 6am-midnight, Sa 7am-midnight, Su 9am-11pm.) The **post office,** ave. de la Gare 32, between the station and the tourist office, has a public **fax** and an **ATM.** (☎722 26 72. Open M-F 7:30am-noon and 1:30-6:30pm, Sa 8am-noon.) **Postal code:** CH-1920.

▐ ACCOMMODATIONS & CAMPING. Budget pickings are slim because travelers in Martigny are mainly business types. About a 5min. walk from the train station stands the **Hotel Grand-Quai ❹,** which offers long, carpeted hallways and sparse, clean rooms. Reservations suggested for the few single rooms. Breakfast included. (☎722 20 50 or 55 98; www.grandquai.com. From the train station turn left and go to r. du Simplon; the hotel is on the right. Singles 70SFr; doubles 100SFr; triples 130SFr.) **Auberge de la Poste ❸** provides lodgings for five individuals at the corner of Grand-St. Bernard and r. Du Levant. Rooms are comfortable and relatively clean, once guests get past the tilted floors. (☎722 25 17. Breakfast included. Floor bathrooms and showers. Open Tu-Sa 8am-midnight. Reserve ahead. Singles 45SFr; doubles 80SFr. AmEx/DC/MC/V.) **Camping Les Neuvilles ❶,** r. du Levant 68, packs its shaded plot with motor homes. From the station, head straight on ave. de la Gare, take the second left onto ave. des Neuvilles, and turn right onto r. du Levant. Amenities a store, laundry, a sauna (7SFr), miniature golf (5SFr, children 3SFr), and a solarium. (☎722 45 44; fax 35 44. Showers included. Reception 8am-noon and 2-8pm. 7.2SFr per person; tents 9SFr, cars and RVs 19SFr. Low-season 6.2SFr/7.5SFr; cars and RVs 14SFr. AmEx/DC/MC/V.)

▐ FOOD. Cafés crowd Martigny's tree-lined pl. Centrale, some with *Menüs* in the 15-25SFr range. For cheaper fare, **Lords' Sandwiches ❶,** ave. du Grand-St.-Bernard 15, on a continuation of r. de la Gare past pl. Centrale, serves 36 kinds of sandwiches (3.80-11.80SFr), including a bacon burger with fries, and the "Zeus," an overstuffed roast beef sandwich. Vegetarian options are limited, but the "Socrates," an affair involving tomatoes, mushrooms, and cheese, is a commendable alternative. (☎723 35 98. Open M-F 8am-10:30pm, Sa 8:30am-10:30pm.) **Crêperie Le Rustique ❶,** ave. de la Gare 44, lives up to its name with a dark wood interior and nature scenes painted on stucco. Enjoy savory crêpes (10-14.50SFr) or sweet ones (4.50-9.50SFr), washed down with a 3.50SFr mug of cider. Salads 3.30-12SFr. (☎722 88 33. Open M-F 8am-11pm, Sa 10:30am-midnight, Su 1:30-11pm.) For straightforward Italian food, try **Pizzeria au Grotto ❷,** r. du Rhône 3, off r. Marc-Morand to the left of pl. Centrale. Follow pizza (8-19SFr) with a monster tiramisu (5SFr) and gain a pound or two. (☎722 02 46. Open M-Th 8:30am-11pm, F 8:30am-midnight, Sa 10am-midnight, Su 10am-11pm. AmEx/MC/V.) Another Italian option, **Pizzeria d'Octodure ❷,** features a variety of pastas (13-18SFr) and brick-oven pizzas (8-18SFr) made in a semi-open kitchen. Follow ave. de la Gare, turn right on R. Marc-Morand, circle left around the church and three blocks down r. d'Octodure for tasty pizza in a classy setting. (☎722 08 08. Open daily noon-2pm and 7-11pm. MC/V.)

The immense **Migros** supermarket at pl. du Manoir 5, just off pl. Centrale, offers all that your picnicking heart might desire, while the popular park behind the market can provide the perfect outdoor dining setting. (Open M-Th 8:15am-6:30pm, F 8:15am-8pm, Sa 8am-5pm; Migros restaurant open M-Th 7:30am-6:30pm, F 7:30am-8pm, Sa 7:30am-5pm.) The **public market,** on ave. de la Gare mornings, sells edible and wearable goods. (Open Th 8am-noon.)

◪ **SIGHTS.** The **Fondation Pierre Gianadda,** r. du Forum 59, is Martigny's most engaging attraction. Head down the r. Hôtel-de-Ville behind the tourist office and follow the signs. The foundation displays the mildly interesting **Gallo-Roman Museum** as the permanent collection, while the central atrium and a barn-like building behind host blockbuster international traveling exhibitions. The special exhibits have included artists such as Chagall, Manet, Picasso, van Gogh, and da Vinci and tend to overshadow the rest of the museum. Downstairs, the entertaining **Automobile Museum** draws a crowd of its own with exhibits of more than 50 vintage cars (1897-1939), including a 1897 Benz, and a Delaunay-Belleville that belonged to Czar Nicholas II. The garden surrounding the foundation contains interesting Gallo-Roman remains and several modern sculptures, including some by Brancusi, Miró, and Rodin. Especially amusing are the bronze sculptures of giant body parts by César. Admission to the park is free on summer nights, when the entire palace is illuminated. Every year from April to October sees a fascinating exhibit on Leonardo da Vinci and his works in the **Vieil Arsenal,** located in the gardens behind the Museum. The exhibit includes over a hundred working models and facsimiles made from da Vinci's drawings. (☎722 39 78; www.gianadda.ch. Wheelchair-accessible. Open daily Nov.-June 10am-6pm and June-Nov. 9am-7pm. Guided tours W 8pm in French or by prior arrangement. 15SFr, students 13SFr, seniors 8SFr; family ticket 35SFr.) The foundation hosts classical music concerts, and also leads 1½hr. **guided tours** of Martigny that include the exhibits. (July 15-Aug. 15 10:30am, 2:30pm; Sept.-June by appointment for groups only. 80SFr plus museum entrance for 2hr.) If you want to explore on your own, the office distributes *Promenade Archaéologique*, a brochure detailing a walking tour of Martigny's Roman ruins. Past the railroad tracks, remnants of a Roman road point toward Britannia and, through the pass, Roma. Nearby, the grassy 4th-century **Amphithéâtre Romain** is the spectacular setting for the final contest of the Valais **cow fighting** season (see "Cowfight," p. 484).

VALAIS

Le Château de la Bâtiaz, a 13th-century castle, complete with dungeon and tower, once belonged to the bishops of Sion and is now a ruin. From the station, head along ave. de la Gare and turn right at pl. Centrale along r. Marc-Morand. The château is filled with relics from the Middle Ages, including a nail-covered chair and a "stretching" contraption. Climb the massive stone tower extending over an outcropping of bare rock for a bird's-eye perspective of the flat Rhône floodplain. (Open May 16-June 23 and Aug. 26-Oct. 12 F 4pm-midnight, Sa 10am-midnight, Su 10am-6pm; June 24-Aug. 25 also Th 4pm-midnight. Free.)

■ **FESTIVALS.** Martigny hosts the **Foire du Valais,** the trade fair of Valais, in a blue-and-yellow convention center October 3rd-12th; the fair allows local businessmen and farmers to offer everything from shoes to marble sculptures. The first weekend brings two days of all-day **cow fighting,** a must-see event. The **Foire du Lard** (Bacon Fair) has overtaken the pl. Centrale every first Monday in December since the Middle Ages. Traditionally, Valais mountain folk descended on Martigny to stock up on pork products for the winter. Now the festival has expanded to a large open-air market, but the pig still reigns supreme. Also keep an ear out for the **Folklore Festival** in July and August 2004, which will feature international music and displays.

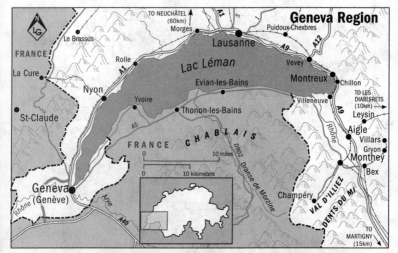

GENEVA & LAC LÉMAN

All around Lac Léman, hills sprinkled with villas and blanketed by patchwork vineyards sewn with garlands of ripening grapes seem tame and settled...until the haze clears. From behind the hills surge rough-hewn mountain peaks, and in that moment, the lake discards its pretty, cultivated urbanity for the energizing promise of unpopulated wilderness and wide lonely expanses. Many travelers suffer financial anxiety when they consider venturing to the refined Lac Léman region, since high prices are the general rule in tourist-infested Geneva, Lausanne, and Montreux. However, adventurers discover that towns along the lake abound with three of Switzerland's cheapest commodities: tranquility is just a short stroll along a tree-lined quai or into vine-laced hills, chocolate is available for a pittance nearly everywhere, and unforgettable views are, as always, free and plentiful.

HIGHLIGHTS OF LAC LÉMAN

Be moved to humanitarian action at **Geneva's Red Cross Museum** (p. 501).

Find radical inspiration at Lausanne's **Collection de l'Art Brut** (p. 509), then regain peace of mind on a pedal boat.

Tiptoe through the dungeon at Montreux's chilling **Chateau Chillon** (p. 515).

Meet thousands of cool cats in mid-July at the **Montreux Jazz Festival (p. 516)**.

GENEVA (GENÈVE, GENF) ☎ 022

As the most international city in Switzerland, Geneva is a brew of 178,000 unlikely neighbors: wealthy businessmen speed past young artists in the streets, while nuclear families share the sidewalks with dreadlocked skaters. Isolated from the rest of Switzerland both ideologically and geographically, Geneva has a sense of independence that unites the city's proudly eclectic group of citizens.

GENEVA

Geneva (Genève)

MUSEUMS
Musée d'Art Moderne et
   Contemporaire, **3**
Musée d'Ethnographie, **4**
Musée d'Histoire Naturelle, **6**
Red Cross Museum, **1**
Voltaire Museum, **2**

★ **NIGHTLIFE**
Au Chat Noir, **5**

rte. de Prégny

chemin de l'Impératrice

rte. de Lausanne

av. de la Paix

Palais des Nations
(United Nations)

Jardin
Botanique

av. de France

r. de Montbrillant

av. de la Paix

av. Blanc

r. de Lausanne

Parc Mon
Repos

r. du Valais

Lac Léman

r. du Vidollet

SEE CENTRAL GENEVA MAP

quai Woodrow Wilson

r. de Chateaubriand

Pâquis Plage

Genève Plage

r. de Lausanne

r. de Berne

r. des Alpes

quai du Mont-Blanc

Port Noir

PL.
DE TRIANT

ch. du Port-Noir

r.
Mont-Blanc

Pont du
Mont-Blanc

quai Gustave-Ador

**Parc des
Eaux-Vives**

PL. DE
MONTBRILLANT

quai Turrettini

quai des Bergues

**Parc la
Grange**

Le Rhône

quai de la Poste

r. du Rhône

quai Gustave-Ador

r. des Eaux-Vives

av. William-Favre

rte. De Frontenex

Stadium

r. du Stand

bd. Georges Favon

PL.
BEL-AIR

r. de Rive

r. de la Mairie

r. des Voilandes

rte. de la Gare-des-Eaux-Vives

r. des
Rois

PL. DU
CIRQUE

ROND-POINT
DE RIVE

r. 31-Décembre

av. de la Gare-des-Eaux-Vives

bd. de St. Georges

PL.
NEUVE

av. Pictet-de-Rochemont

r. de la Terrassière

**Gare des
Eaux-Vives**

OLD CITY

rte. de Chêne

r. de l'Athénée

r. Agasse

av. Th.-Weber

ch. de la Pte-Boissière

q. des Bains

av. de
Champel

PL. DES
PHILOSOPHES

bd. Helvétique

r. St-Victor

bd. des Tranchées

rte. de Malagnou

ch. de la Chevillarde

bd. des Philosophes

PL.
CLAPARÈDE

r. Michel-Chauvet

r. Crespin

av. Krieg

ch. Rieu

rte. de Malagnou

av. du Mail

bd. Carl-Vogt

q. Ernest-Ansermet

q. des Vernets

bd. du Pont d'Arve

r. Dancet

r. Prévost-Martin

av. de Champel

r. de Contamines

r. Bertrand

rte. de Florissant

ch. du Velours

Pont des
Acacias

quai Charles-Page

r. de Carouge

PL. DE
CHAMPEL

av. Peschier

av. Eugène-Pittard

Hôpital

av. Dumas

rte. de Florissant

PL. DES
AUGUSTINS

Université

r. Barthélemy
Menn

av. de Miremont

r. Ls-de-Montfalcon

r. Jacques-Grosselin

Pont de Carouge

PL. D'ARMES

r. St-Joseph

r. de l'Aubépine

av. de Champel

Capo-d'Istra

Pont de la
Fontenette

av. de Louis-Aubert

l'Arve

PL. DU
TEMPLE

PL. DU
MARCHÉ

Promenade des Orphelins

PL. DE
SARDAIGNE

r. de Veyrier

Pont du
Val d'Arve

CAROUGE

Vautier

Genevans have a long tradition of protecting their political and religious independence. As a strategic site, where the Rhône River flows out of Lac Léman, medieval Geneva fended off repeated attacks. In 1536 the city welcomed an unknown 25-year-old, John Calvin, and his version of the Protestant Reformation, voting en masse to convert. His fiery sermons (1536-1564) brought waves of persecuted French and Italian refugees to this "Rome of Protestants." Geneva waged a battle for freedom from the Catholic House of Savoy, whose duke sought to crush both Protestantism and Genevan democracy.

Over the next 150 years, Reformists' zeal occasionally took the form of authoritarian rule, exemplified by the burning of books by Rousseau and Calvin's detractors. Geneva's cosmopolitanism eventually won out, and it became a gathering place for aesthetes and free thinkers. Voltaire lived and worked in the Geneva area, and his compatriot Madame de Staël held salons in nearby Copped. In the early 19th century, mountain-loving romantics Shelley and Byron found inspiration in the city's surroundings. Lenin lived here in the early 1900s before being sent back to Moscow in a sealed train by German leaders hoping to disrupt the Russian government. Under the inspiration of native Henri Dunant, the **International Committee of the Red Cross** established itself in Geneva in 1864, and nations from around the world signed the peace-keeping First Geneva Convention. In 1919, Geneva's selection as the site for the **League of Nations** confirmed the city's reputation as a center for both international organizations and arbitrations. Geneva is still the European office of the **United Nations (UN)** and dozens of other international bodies, from the Center for European Nuclear Research to the World Council of Churches.

⊠ INTERCITY TRANSPORTATION

Flights: Cointrin Airport (☎717 71 11, flight information 799 31 11; fax 798 43 77) is a hub for **Swiss Airlines** (☎08 48 85 20 00). Bus #10 runs to the Gare Cornavin (15min., every 5-10min., 2.20SFr). The ticket dispenser requires exact change—large bills can be broken at the "change-o-mat" behind the escalator. For a shorter trip to Gare Cornavin, take the train (6min., every 10min., 4.80SFr). There are several flights per day to various international hubs. **Air France** (☎827 87 87) has 13 per day to Paris, and **British Airways** (☎08 48 80 10 10) has 9 per day to London.

Trains: Trains run approximately 4:30am-1am. There are 2 stations:

Gare Cornavin, pl. Cornavin, is the main station. To: **Basel** (2¾hr., every hr. 4:44am-10:44pm, 71SFr); **Bern** (2hr., every hr. 4:34am-10:34pm, 47SFr); **Interlaken** (3hr., every hr. 4:34am-9:30pm, 63SFr); **Lausanne** (40min., every 15-30min. 4:34am-12:21am, 18.80SFr); **Milan** (4hr., 8 per day, 81SFr); **Montreux** (1hr., 2 per hr. 5:16am-11:32pm, 29SFr); **Paris** (3¾hr., 10 per day 5:47am-10:23pm, 103SFr.); **Vienna** (10-12hr., 4 per day 6:30am-7:30pm, 189SFr); **Zurich** (3½hr., every 30min., 76SFr). To book a seat on long-distance or international trains, join the throng at the reservation and information counter. Open M-F 8:30am-6:30pm, Sa 9am-5pm. The 24hr. **rail information** number is ☎09 00 30 03 00 (1.19SFr per min.).

Gare des Eaux-Vives (☎736 16 20), on ave. de la Gare des Eaux-Vives (Tram #12, "Amandoliers SNCF"), connects to France's regional rail lines through **Annecy** (1½hr., 6 per day, 14SFr) or **Chamonix** (2½hr., 4 per day, 24SFr). The ticket machine at the station does not return change. Ticket office open M-F 9am-6pm, Sa 11am-5:45pm.

CGN Ferries: (☎312 52 23) connect Geneva to **Lausanne** and **Montreux,** departing from quai du Mont-Blanc. A round-trip ticket (54-74SFr, ages 16-25 half-price, seniors 20% discount) includes the option of returning to Geneva by train.

By car: Geneva is more accessible from **France** than from the rest of Switzerland. From the **west,** take A40, which continues on to **Lausanne** and **Montreux.** From the **south** take N201 north. From the **north,** take A40 from France or Switzerland. From the **east,** take A40 west. N1 is the best way to reach Geneva from Lausanne or Montreux. Route numbers are not always visible; follow signs for Geneva.

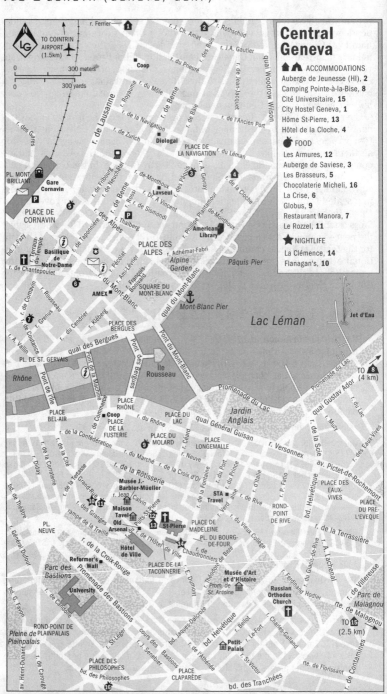

Central Geneva

■ ▲ ACCOMMODATIONS
Auberge de Jeunesse (HI), **2**
Camping Pointe-à-la-Bise, **8**
Cité Universitaire, **15**
City Hostel Geneva, **1**
Hôme St-Pierre, **13**
Hôtel de la Cloche, **4**

🍎 FOOD
Les Armures, **12**
Auberge de Saviese, **3**
Les Brasseurs, **5**
Chocolaterie Micheli, **16**
La Crise, **6**
Globus, **9**
Restaurant Manora, **7**
Le Rozzel, **11**

★ NIGHTLIFE
La Clémence, **14**
Flanagan's, **10**

✳ ORIENTATION

Straddling the Rhône as it opens into the Lac Léman, Geneva began as a fortified city on a hill, and the *vieille ville* (old city) overlooking the delta remains the city's heart. The *vieille ville* is characterized by labyrinthine cobbled streets and quiet squares centering around John Calvin's **Cathédrale de St-Pierre;** elsewhere, the city's esplanades coallesce into a more coherent grid. Across the Rhône River to the north, banks and five-star hotels gradually give way to lakeside promenades and various UN, Red Cross, and WTO complexes. Across the Arve river to the south lies the village of Carouge, home to many student bars and clubs (take tram #12 or 13 to "pl. du Marché").

▤ LOCAL TRANSPORTATION

Carry your passport at all times; the French border is never more than a few minutes away and buses cross it frequently. Ticket purchasing is largely on the honor system and some backpackers try to get away without paying. *Let's Go* does not recommend fare evasion; fines run 60SFr. The city is easily walkable, and renting a bike is a good way to get around as well.

Public Transportation: Geneva has an efficient bus and tram network. Major hubs are Gare Cornavin, Rd.-Pt. de Plainpalais, and pl. Bel Air (near the ponts de l'Ile). **Transport Publics Genevois** (☎308 34 34), next to the tourist office in Gare Cornavin, provides a free map of local bus routes called *Le Réseau*. Timetables cost 6SFr, and are not worth buying as buses run frequently and time-charts are posted at every stop. Open M-Sa 7am-7pm, Su 10am-6pm. Trips that stay within zone 10 (most of the city) cost 2.20SFr; 3 stops or fewer 1.80SFr. Full-day passes 6SFr for 1 zone, 12SFr for 4. SwissPass valid on all buses; Eurail not valid. **Buses** run roughly 5:30am-midnight. **Noctambus** (3SFr) runs 1:30-4:30am. Buy multi-fare and day tickets at the train station, others at automatic vendors at every stop. Stamp multi-use tickets at the automatic vendors before boarding.

Taxis: Taxi-Phone (☎331 41 33). 6.80SFr plus 2.90SFr per km. Taxi from airport to city around 30SFr, max. 4 passengers (15-20min.). There are also taxi phones located on select street corners.

Car Rental: Avis, r. de Lausanne 44 (☎731 90 00). **Europcar,** r. de Lausanne 37 (☎909 69 90). **Budget,** r. de Zurich 36 (☎900 24 00). All have offices at the airport; but beware of possible surcharges.

Parking: On-street 1SFr per hr. The garage (☎736 66 30) under Cornavin station (enter at pl. Cornavin) is a convenient option (7am-7pm 2SFr for 1hr., 4-6SFr for 2hr.; after 7pm 1sFr per hr.) **Garage Les Alpes,** r. Thalberg, is 2SFr per hr. M-F, 1SFr per hr. nights and Sa-Su. Per-hour prices decrease as time increases. Digital boards on highways and the main city streets list carparks and the number of vacant spaces remaining in each.

Bike Rental: Geneva is pedal-happy, with well-marked bike paths and special traffic lights. For routes, get *Itineraires cyclables* or *Tours de ville avec les vélos de location* from the tourist office. Behind the station, **Genèv' Roule,** pl. Montbrillant 17 (☎/fax 740 13 43), has free bikes available. 50SFr deposit and photo ID required; hefty fine if bike is lost or stolen. Slightly nicer neon bikes start at 5SFr per day. Open 7:30am-9:30pm. Genèv' Roule kiosks located at Bain des Paquis, pl. du Rhône, and Plaine de Plainpalais offer the same deals.

Hitchhiking: *Let's Go* does not recommend hitchhiking. However, travelers headed to Germany or northern Switzerland have been seen taking bus #4 to "Jardin Botanique." Those headed to France sometimes take bus #4 to "Palettes," then line D to "St. Julien."

GENEVA

🛈 PRACTICAL INFORMATION

TOURIST & FINANCIAL SERVICES

Tourist Offices: At information offices (marked by a blue lower-case "i" sign), the free must-haves are the city map and the booklet *Info Jeunes/Young People*. The **main office,** r. du Mont-Blanc 18 (☎909 70 00; wwww.geneve-tourisme.ch), lies 5min. away from Gare Cornavin toward the pont du Mont-Blanc, within the Central Post Office Building. English-speaking staff books hotel rooms (5SFr fee), offers **walking tours,** and provides information on just about everything. The office maintains a free direct phone line to Geneva hotels, as well as a board listing budget accommodations. Open July-Aug. daily 9am-6pm; Sept.-June M-Sa 9am-6pm. During the summer, head for Geneva's **Centre d'Accueil et de Renseignements (CAR;** ☎731 46 47), parked in pl. Mont-Blanc, by the Metro Shopping entrance to the Gare Cornavin. This office-in-a-bus is geared toward young people and posts a list of free musical and theatrical performances. Makes hotel reservations free of charge. Open mid-June to mid-Sept. daily 9am-9pm.

Budget Travel: STA, r. de la Rive 10 (☎818 02 00; www.statravel.ch). Student airfares and the like. Also home to an extensive travel bookstore. Open M 1-6:30pm, Tu-F 9am-6:30pm, Sa 9am-5pm. AmEx/MC/V.

Consulates: Australia, chemin des Fins 2 (☎799 91 00; fax 91 78); **Canada,** ave. de l'Ariana 5 (☎919 92 00; fax 92 77); **New Zealand,** chemin des Fins 2 (☎929 03 50; fax 03 74); **South Africa,** r. de Rhône 65 (☎849 54 54; fax 54 32); **UK,** r. de Vermont 37 (☎918 24 26; fax 23 22); **US,** R. Versonnex 5 (☎840 51 60; recorded information 51 61; fax 51 62). Call to schedule appointments.

Currency Exchange: ATMs offer the best rates and are easy to find in Geneva. There are a few at Gare Cornavin, at the top of the escalators from the platforms. For traditional service, Gare Cornavin has good rates and doesn't charge commission on traveler's checks. Advances cash on credit cards (min. 200SFr), and arranges **Western Union** transfers. Open M-Sa 6:50am-7:40pm, Su 6:50am-6:40pm. Western Union desk open M-Sa 7am-7:30pm, Su 7am-6:30pm. **Change Cite** r. du Mont-Blanc 21, (☎901 15 15) offers excellent rates, better than most banks in a convenient location, right by Gare Cornavin. No commission. M-F 8:30am-7pm, Sa 8:30am-5pm.

American Express: r. du Mont-Blanc 7, P.O. Box 1032, CH-1211 Geneva (☎731 76 00; fax 732 72 11). Mail held 2-3 months. All banking services; reasonable exchange rates. Hotel and train (50SFr) reservations and tickets for tours. Open Nov.-Mar. M-F 8:30am-5:45pm; Apr.-Oct. M-F 8:45am-5:45pm, Sa 9am-noon.

LOCAL SERVICES

Luggage Storage: Gare Cornavin. 6SFr per day. Open M-F 7am-7:30pm, Sa-Su 8am-12:30pm and 1:30-6:30pm. Lockers 4-7SFr. Open 4:30am-12:30am.

Lost Property: with the luggage storage (☎05 12 25 14 33). Open M-F 8am-2pm.

Bookstores: ELM (English Language and Media) Video and Books, r. Versonnex 5 (☎736 09 45; fax 786 14 29), has a quality range of new books and a book ordering service. Open M-F 9am-6:30pm, Sa 10am-5pm. AmEx/DC/MC/V. **Librairie des Amateurs,** Grand Rue 15 (☎732 80 97), in the vieille ville. Classy secondhand dealer. Open M 2-6pm, Tu-F 11am-6pm, Sa 2pm-5pm. **Payot Libraire,** r. de Chantepoulet 5 (☎731 89 50) and r. du Marché 16, is Geneva's largest chain of bookstores, with a broad and well-selected stock of English-language books. Open M 2-6:30pm, Tu-W and F 9am-6:30pm, Th 9am-8pm, Sa 9am-5pm. AmEx/DC/MC/V.

Library: American Library, r. de Monthoux 3 (☎732 80 97), at Emmanuel Church, just steps from the waterfront. Boasts 17,000 titles. 1mo. membership (35SFr) allows you to borrow books (6 max.) for 2 weeks. Small, eclectic collection of books on tape

(3SFr). Open Tu, Th, F 12:30-5pm, W 2-7pm, Sa 10am-4pm, Su 11:30am-1pm. **City Library (Bibliothèque de la Cité),** Pl. des Trois Perdrix 5 (☎418 32 22). Open Tu-F 10am-7pm, Sa 10am-5pm.

Bi-Gay-Lesbian Organizations: Diologai, r. de la Navigation 11-13 (☎906 40 40; www.hivnet.ch/diologai). From Gare Cornavin, turn left and walk 5min. down r. de Lausanne; turn right onto r. de la Navigation. Resource group with programs from support groups to outdoor activities. Publishes *Diologai,* a guide to French-speaking Switzerland's gay scene. Mostly male, but women welcome. Hosts W gatherings for gay men starting at 6pm; call ahead. **360°,** pl. Grenus 2 (☎741 00 70), publishes an eponymous magazine. Walk-in hours Su 4-9pm. **Gay International Group (GIG;** ☎789 18 69; gig@360.ch) is for international gay visitors or semi-permanents in Geneva, including Anglophones. Communal meals every 2-4 weeks. **Centre Femmes Natalie Barney** (women only), Chemin Chateau Bloch 19 (☎797 27 14), offers services similar to those at Diologai, but is smaller and lesbian-oriented. 24hr. answering machine with events listings; live operator W 6-8pm. **Lesbian International Group** is another support group (filozici@hotmail.com).

Laundromat: Lavseul, r. de Monthoux 29 (☎735 90 51 or 732 61 46). Wash 5SFr, dry 1SFr per 10min. Open daily 7am-midnight.

Public Showers: Point d'Eau, r. Chandieu 4 (☎734 22 40). Take bus #8 to "Cannonière" and turn right onto r. de Vermont; it's on the left. Free hot showers and personal hygiene center. Open M-F 3-7pm, Sa 10am-2pm. Additional location at r. de Fronteneux 48. Open M-F 9am-noon. **McClean,** at the train station, offers showers for 12SFr and toilets for 1-2SFr. Open daily 6am-midnight.

EMERGENCY & COMMUNICATIONS

Emergencies: Fire ☎118, **Ambulance** ☎144.

Police: r. de Berne 6 (☎117, non-emergency ☎715 38 50), next to post office.

Rape Crisis Hotline: Viol-Secours (☎345 20 20). Open M-Tu 2-6pm, W 4-8pm, Th 9am-1pm, F 9am-noon.

Late-Night Pharmacy: A revolving set of 4 pharmacies is open late (until 9 or 11pm) nightly. Consult the closest pharmacy or *Genève Agenda* for addresses and phone numbers.

Medical Assistance: Hôpital Cantonal, r. Micheli-du-Crest 24 (☎372 33 11). Take bus #1 or 5 or tram #12. Door #2 is for emergency care, door #3 for consultations. For information on walk-in clinics, call the **Association des Médecins** (☎320 84 20).

Internet Access: For less than the cost of doing laundry, **Connections Net World,** r. de Monthoux 58 (☎715 38 28), offers access to the Internet on 20 PCs. 3SFr per 30min., 5SFr per hr. Open M-Sa 9:30am-2:30am, Su 1pm-2am. Copier available. **Point 6,** r. de Vieux-Billard 7a, off r. des Bains (☎800 26 00). 5SFr per hr. Open daily noon-midnight.

Post Office: Poste Centrale, r. de Mont-Blanc 18, a block from Gare Cornavin in the stately Hôtel des Postes. Open M-F 7:30am-6pm, Sa 8:30am-noon. Address *Poste Restante* to: Genève 1 Mont-Blanc, CH-1211 Geneva. Another branch is located behind the train station at r. des Gares 10-16. 24hr. self-service; counters open M-F 7:30am-7pm, Sa 8:30am-noon; urgent mail counter open M-F 7am-10pm, Sa-Su noon-8pm.

▐ ACCOMMODATIONS & CAMPING

Geneva is a cosmopolitan city, and its five-star hotel system is geared toward the wealthy banker. Luckily for the budget traveler, however, the seasonal influx of university students and interns has created a secondary network of hostels, pensions, and university dorms moonlighting as summer hotels. The indispensable *Info Jeunes* lists about 50 options; *Let's Go* lists the highlights below. The tourist office publishes *Budget Hotels,* stretching the definition of "budget" to

120SFr per person. Even for short stays, make reservations. For longer stays, check *Tribune de Genève's* weekly supplement of apartment classifieds or the tourist office's board.

City Hostel Geneva, r. Ferrier 2 (☎901 15 00; www.cityhostel.ch). From the station, turn left onto r. de Lausanne, left onto r. de Prieuré, and right onto r. Ferrier. Only 5min. from the station, and on the way to International Hill, City Hostel offers snug, clean rooms and an excellent location. The small reception area overflows with friendly backpackers making use of the free nightly movies in the TV room. Beer and Swiss Army knives sold at the desk. Kitchen facilities, book exchange, a comprehensive listing of markets in Geneva, and **Internet** access (8SFr per hr.) are available. Lockers free. Sheets 3.5SFr; Laundry 8.5SFr. 6-night max. stay. Reception 7:30am-noon and 1pm-midnight. Check-out 10am. Single-sex 4-bed dorms 28SFr; singles 55SFr; doubles 80SFr. MC/V.❷

Hôme St-Pierre, Cour St-Pierre 4 (☎310 37 07; info@stpierre.ch). Take bus #5 to "pl. Neuve" or walk 15min. from the train station: cross the Rhône at pont du Mont-Blanc, then go up r. de la Fontaine toward pl. du Bourg-de-Four. Take the stairs up Passage des Degres-de-Poules (after Epicerie Pizzo), walk around to the front of the cathedral. It will be diagonally left with your back to the entrance of the cathedral. Ring the buzzer to be let in. Located in the heart of *vieille ville*, this 150-year-old "home" has comfortable beds, great location, and a convivial atmosphere. Beware, though, for the church bell tintinnabulates every 15min. Breakfast M-Sa, 7SFr. Lockers 5SFr. Reception M-Sa 9am-noon and 4-8pm, Su 9am-noon. Popular, so reserve ahead. Check-out 10am. Dorms 23SFr; singles 36-45SFr; doubles 50-60SFr. MC/V. ❸

Cité Universitaire, ave. Miremont 46 (☎839 22 11; fax 22 23). From the right of the station, take bus #3 (dir.: Crets-de-Champel) to the last stop; the Cité Universitaire is directly on your right. Institutional college housing in a modern tower has TV rooms, newspapers, a restaurant, a **disco** (all-night dancing Th and Sa, free to residents), ping-pong, tennis courts, a small grocery shop, and great views. Reception M-F 8am-noon and 2-10pm, Sa 8am-noon and 6-10pm, Su 9-11am and 6-10pm. Check-out 10am. Lockout 11am-6pm and curfew 11pm, dorms only. 4 dorms (July-Sept. only) 20SFr, lockers included; singles 49SFr; doubles 66SFr; studios with kitchenette and bathroom 75SFr. AmEx/MC/V. ❷

Hôtel de la Cloche, r. de la Cloche 6 (☎732 94 81; fax 738 16 12), off quai du Mont-Blanc across from the Noga Hilton. In this converted mansion with lofty ceilings, most rooms have a chandelier and TV, and some have antique mirrors and balconies. Ask for a lake view. Breakfast and showers included. Reception 8am-10pm. Reserve a month in advance in summer. Summer singles 65SFr; doubles 95SFr; triples 110SFr, with bath 130SFr; quads with toilet and shower 140SFr. Winter singles 50-70SFr; doubles 85SFr; triples 110SFr; quads 140SFr. AmEx/DC/MC/V. ❹

Auberge de Jeunesse (HI), r. Rothschild 28-30 (☎732 62 60; www.yh-geneva.ch). Walk 10min. left from the station down r. de Lausanne, then turn right onto r. Rothschild. Take bus #1 from the station (dir.: Wilson) to the end of the line. Comfortable bunks and lots of people to meet counterbalance the lack of atmosphere and the potentially long check-in lines. This hostel is mostly filled with large groups and middle-aged travelers. A bargain, as other amenities include a sizable lobby, a restaurant (dinner 11.50SFr, with dessert and drink 14SFr), kitchen facilities (1SFr per 30min.), TV room with CNN, a library, 3 **Internet** stations (7SFr per hr.). Complimentary breakfast, hall showers, lockers, and sheets. Laundry 6SFr. Special facilities for disabled guests. 6-night max. stay. Reception June-Sept. 6:30-10am and 2pm-1am; Oct.-May 6:30-10am and 4pm-midnight. Lockout in summer 10am-2pm, in winter 4pm. Curfew 1am, in winter midnight. Reservations recommended. Dorms 25SFr (31SFr non-members); doubles with toilet 70SFr, with toilet and shower 80SFr; quads 110SFr. AmEx/MC/V. ❷

Camping Pointe-à-la-Bise, Chemin de la Bise (☎752 12 96). Take bus #8 to "Rive" then bus E (north) to "Bise" and follow the "camping" signs for a 10min. walk down to the lake. The lakefront grounds, far from town, provide a free beach and a lively recreation area, as well as a calmer perspective on Geneva. Free showers. Reception 8am-noon and 2-9pm. Open Apr.-Sept. 6.20SFr per person, 0.50SFr tax per person, 9SFr per tent space. No tents provided, but beds 15SFr. 4-person bungalows 60SFr. ❶

🖸 FOOD

It's true that you can find anything from sushi to paella in Geneva, but ethnic foods can break the bank. Many supermarkets have cafeterias with some of the best deals available. *Info Jeunes* lists university cafeterias.

Boulangeries and *pâtisseries* offer gourmet food at budget prices—7SFr goes a long way when you combine a fresh loaf of bread with cheese and tomato from Migros or Co-op. There are extensive dining options in the *vieille ville* near the cathedral, but you'll pay for the location. In the Les Paquîs area, bordered by the r. de Lausanne and Gare Cornavin on one side and the Quais Mont-Blanc and Wilson on the other, a variety of ethnic foods can be found. Kebab stands are interspersed with Brazilian cafés, and the colorful neighborhood offers better prices than most. To the south, the village of Carouge is known for its lively student population and funky, chic brasseries. Dining on the waterfront will cost you; enjoy an ice cream cone at a lakeside café instead. Around pl. du Cirque and plaine de Plainpalais are cheap, student-oriented "tea rooms," offering bakery fare at good prices.

🖾 **Chocolats Micheli,** r. Micheli-du-Crest 1 (☎329 90 06), Take tram #13 to Plainpalais and walk up bd. des Philosophes until it intersects r. Micheli-du-Crest. Confectionery masterpieces abound in this exquisite Swiss chocolate store and café *par excellence*. The enticing aromas hanging in the air make choosing between the stacks of Swiss chocolate a true test of mental toughness. Open Tu-F 8am-7pm, Sa 8am-5pm. MC/V. ❶

Le Rozzel, Grand-Rue 18 (☎312 42 72). Take bus #5 to "pl. Neuve," then walk up the hill past the cathedral on r. Jean-Calvin to Grand-Rue. This Breton-style *crêperie* with outdoor seating on the most elegant street in the *vieille ville* serves large salty crêpes (4-18SFr), dessert crêpes (4.50-9SFr), and sangria (5SFr). A restaurant and café as well, Le Rozzel offers enticing elegant salads and meals such as Gaspach and demi-salad-nicoise for 15SFr. *Menü* available for 21SFr. Open M 7am-4pm, Tu-W 7am-7pm, Th-F 7am-10pm, Sa 9am-10pm. AmEx/MC/V.❷

Restaurant Manora, r. de Cornavin 4 (☎909 44 10), 3min. from the station on the right, in the Placette department store. This huge self-serve restaurant offers an incredible selection of fresh, high-quality food at excellent prices. Salads (from 4.50SFr), fruit tarts (3.20SFr), main dishes cooked on the spot (from 7.90SFr), and free tap water (a rare commodity in Geneva). Wheelchair-accessible. Open M-Sa 7:30am-9:30pm, Su 9am-9:30pm. ❶

La Crise, r. de Chantepoulet 13 (☎738 02 64). From the station, turn right onto r. de Cornavin and left onto r. de Chantepoulet. Eat in the middle of Mme. LeParc's kitchen for tasty meals at reasonable prices. Quiche and veggies 8.50SFr; soup 3.50SFr; beer or wine 3SFr; *plat du jour* with soup and salad 14SFr. A *Menü* offers great deals. Open M-F 6am-3pm and 5-8pm, Sa 6am-3pm. ❶

Les Brasseurs, pl. Cornavin 20 (☎731 02 06), diagonally left while exiting the station, serves a variety of *flammeküchen*, an Alsatian specialty similar to a thin crust pizza but topped with cream and onions instead of cheese and tomato sauce (11.60-23SFr). The main attractions, however, are the towers of beer brewed on location (starting from 31SFr for 2L) and made to share. The *flammeküchen* are served quickly, so be prepared to eat soon after ordering. Open M-W 11am-1am, Th-Sa 11am-2am, Su 5pm-1am. Kitchen open 11:30am-2pm and 6-10:45pm but *flammeküchen* available daily until midnight. ❷

Auberge de Saviese, r. des Pâquis 20 (☎732 83 30; fax 784 36 23). Take bus #1 to "Monthoux." Or from Gare Cornavin, turn left onto r. de Lausanne, then right on r. de Zurich, until you hit r. des Pâquis. Sip coffee (2.30SFr) in this English-friendly restaurant frequented by tourists. Excellent *fondue au cognac* (20SFr), *Raclette* with all the trimmings (31SFr), and classic regional perch (28SFr). Extensive selection of salads ranging from 14-20SFr. Open M-Sa 10:30am-3pm and 5pm-12:30am, Su 5pm-12:30am. AmEx/DC/MC/V. ❹

Les Armures, r. du Puits-St-Pierre 1 (☎310 34 42; fax 818 71 13), near the main entrance to the cathedral, in Hotel Les Armures. One small step up in price, one giant leap up in atmosphere. A huge plaque announces that President Clinton ate here, and for a small splurge you can too. Try to eat after sunset for the romance of the *vieille ville* at night. Good-sized fondue 24-26.5SFr; pizza 14-16.5SFr. Main courses run to 45SFr. Open M-F 8am-midnight, Sa 11am-midnight, Su 11am-11pm. AmEx/DC/MC/V. ❸

Globus, r. de Rhône 48, on the pl. du Molard. A self-serve establishment that offers fresh fruit, crêpes, and pressed-on-demand orange juice for those who are low on time. Other inexpensive gourmet delights here include fresh produce, a *fromagerie*, and still-swimming seafood. Daily specials from 11SFr. Open M-W and F 7:30am-6:45pm, Th 7:30am-8pm, Sa 8am-5:45pm. ❷

MARKETS

Co-op, Migros, Grand Passage, and **Orient Express** branches are ubiquitous. On Sundays, the few options include Gare Cornavin's **Aperto** (open daily 6am-10pm) and scattered neighborhood groceries and bakeries. **Public Markets:** Fresh fruits and cheese on **rue de Coutance,** M-Sa 8am-6pm. A produce market is located on **Rd-Pt. de Plainpalais** Tu and F 8am-1pm, Su 8am-6pm. In Carouge, the **pl. du Marché** offers a market W and Sa 8am-1pm. The **place de la Navigation** has markets Th and F 8am-1pm. **Marché des Eaux-Vives,** blvd. Helvétique, between cours de Rive and r. du Rhône, is a huge dairy, vegetable, and flower market. Open M and Th 8am-1pm. City Hostel Geneva posts information on all of the markets in its lobby; further information on markets can be found at the tourist office.

◎ SIGHTS

For centuries, Geneva was tightly constrained by a belt of fortified walls and trenches. By the mid-19th century, when the fortifications were finally removed, the city's most interesting historical sites had already been clustered in a dense, easily walkable space. The tourist office offers 2hr. **walking tours** in the summer on all things *Genevois* (Mid-June through Sept. M-Sa 10am; Oct. to mid-June Sa 10am. 12SFr, students and seniors 8SFr, children 6SFr. Recordings of the tours are available in winter for 10SFr plus 50SFr deposit.)

CATHEDRAL. The *vieille ville's* **Cathédrale de St-Pierre,** the heart of the early Protestant world, is as austere and pure as on the day Calvin stripped the place of its Catholicism. From its altar, Calvin preached to full houses 1536-1564; his chair from those days still remains. The brightly painted **Maccabean Chapel,** restored in flamboyant style, gives a sample of how the cathedral walls might have looked pre-Reformation. Perhaps the most striking part of the cathedral is the silver-plated organ that looms intimidatingly at the rear of the nave. The 157-step **north tower** provides a commanding view of the old town's winding streets and flower-bedecked homes. (*Open June-Sept. daily 9am-7pm; Oct.-May M-Sa 10am-noon and 2-5pm, Su*

11am-12:30pm and 1:30-5pm. Closed Su mornings for services. Tower closes 30min. earlier and costs 3SFr. July-Aug. bell-ringing Sa afternoon.) Beneath the cathedral rest the ruins of a Roman sanctuary, a 4th-century basilica, and a 6th-century church. This extensive **archaeological site** includes an ancient version of forced-air heating ducts. *(Open June-Sept. Tu-Sa 11am-5pm, Su 10am-5pm; Oct.-May Tu-Sa 2-5pm, Su 10am-noon and 2-5pm. 5SFr, students 3SFr. Free English audioguide available.)*

OLD CITY. Surrounding the cathedral are the medieval townhouses and mansions of Geneva's *vieille ville.* **Maison Tavel,** a fortified urban palace and Geneva's oldest residential building, is 1min. from the west end. The 14th-century structure now houses a municipal history **museum** by the same name (see p. 502). The **Old Arsenal** a few steps away has five cannons and a mural depicting the arrival of Huguenot refugees—and Julius Caesar. Across the street is the **Hôtel de Ville** (town hall), whose components date from the 15th through 17th centuries. World leaders signed the **Geneva Convention** (which governs the humane treatment of prisoners of war) here on August 22, 1864.

Beginning at the *Hôtel de Ville,* the narrow **Grand-Rue** is crammed with medieval workshops and 18th-century mansions, often with hastily added 3rd or 4th floors, the makeshift result of the real estate boom following the influx of French Huguenots after Louis XIV repealed the Edict of Nantes. Plaques commemorating famous residents abound, including one at #40 marking the birthplace of philosopher **Jean-Jacques Rousseau.** Antique shops and art galleries line the Grand-Rue, and night brings live jazz to the restaurants and cafés, whose open-air seating spills out into the cobblestone streets.

Head away from the *vieille ville* on r. de Chaudronniers to reach the nine glittering domes of the **Russian Orthodox Church,** on r. Töpffer, next to the Musée d'Art et d'Histoire. Step inside for the hauntingly lovely icons, stained glass, and opaque, incense-filled air. *(Photography, short skirts, and shorts are not allowed. Closed to visitors during the winter.)*

WATERFRONT. Descending from the cathedral toward the lake is akin to walking forward in time 600 years. The streets widen, buses scuttle back and forth, and every corner sports a chic boutique or watch shop. On the waterfront, the **Jet d'Eau,** down quai Gustave-Ardor, spews a spectacular plume of water 140m high. The sight, a tourist spectacle, was inspired by a faulty piping jet. The world's highest fountain keeps seven tons of water aloft from March to October, and is visible throughout the city.

The floral clock in the nearby **Jardin Anglais,** boasting 6500 plants and the world's largest second hand (2.5m), pays homage to Geneva's watch industry. The clock is probably Geneva's most overrated attraction and was once the city's most hazardous: almost a meter was cut away from the clock because tourists, intent on taking the perfect photo, continually backed into oncoming traffic.

The rose-lined quais lead to two fun-parks. **Pâquis Plage,** quai du Mont-Blanc 30, is popular with the *Genevois.* *(☎ 732 29 74. Open 9am-8:30pm. 2SFr.)* Farther from the city center, **Genève Plage,** on quai Gustave Ador, offers a giant waterslide, an Olympic-sized pool, volleyball tournaments, and topless sunbathing. *(☎ 734 26 82. 5SFr.)* The source of these waters, the Rhône, was consecrated by the pope during a particularly bad outbreak of the bubonic plague as a "burial" ground. Today, however, the lake and the river are crystal clear and free of bodies and pollution.

Ferry tours leaving from quai du Mont-Blanc provide views of Geneva. **Swiss Boat** *(☎ 732 47 47; 35min. 8SFr, children 5SFr; 1hr. 12SFr/7SFr; 2hr. 20SFr/15SFr)* and **Mouettes Genevoises** *(☎ 732 29 44; 45min. 8SFr, children 5SFr, seniors 6 SFr; 2hr. 20SFr/15SFr/15SFr)* narrate cruises in English. **CGN** provides a scenic cruise of the shores of Lake Geneva *(55min., 12SFr)* and has been sending cruises to lakeside towns, including Lausanne, Montreux, and the stupendous Château de Chillon, for the past 125 years. *(☎ 741 52 31 or 741 52 35. Round-trip 54SFr, Eurail and SwissPass valid.)*

ARTAMIS: GUERRILLA ARTIST COLONY What

do you do when you're a young artist in Geneva and have no place to work? If there are 300 others like you, you shut down the tourist industry until the city gives you a place of your own. That's what happened in the summer of 1996 when a group of artists staged a sit-in demonstration at pl. du Bourg-de-Four just below the Cathédrale de St-Pierre. They ripped up pavement, built bonfires, and confused tourists for six days until the city granted them an abandoned industrial park rent-free on the left bank, now called Artamis. (☎320 39 30; www.artamis.org.) You'll find it at quai de Rhône 14, on the #2 and 10 bus lines ("Palladium"). This ten-building complex displays high-quality graffiti and houses thriving art workshops, theaters, and fundraising facilities. There's an **Internet** café (5SFr per hr.), a movie theater (2SFr), and bars. Electronic music enthusiasts should stop by the Database Building, a recording studio where top house and jungle DJs in the area come to experiment. All facilities are open daily 4pm-2am.

PARKS & GARDENS. Geneva is bedecked with sumptuous gardens scattered strategically throughout the city. Below the cathedral on the r. de la Croix-Rouge, the **Parc des Bastions'** lovely expanse stretches from pl. Neuve to the pl. des Philosophes. **Le Mur des Réformateurs** (Reformers' Wall) displays a sprawling collection of bas-relief narrative panels, an array of multilingual inscriptions, and the towering figures of the Reformers themselves. As the largest statues (Knox, Beze, Calvin, and Farel) jostle each other for "leader of the Protestant pack" bragging rights, Cromwell and Rhode Island's Roger Williams trail behind. The imposing campus of **Geneva University** sits opposite the wall, with sunbathers in between.

Strolling north along the river quais brings you to the lush **Parc Mon-Repos** (off ave. de France) and **La Perle du Lac** (off ave. de la Paix), where panting joggers and playful kids stream along curvy paths painted in various floral hues and lined by massive, ancient trees. At the **Jardin Botanique**, situated along r. de Lausanne and opposite the World Trade Organization, basilica-shaped greenhouses contain a magnificent collection of rare and exotic plants. This garden is an exhibit in and of itself and merits at least one early morning walkthrough. *(Open daily Apr.-Sept. 8am-7:30pm; Oct.-Mar. 9:30am-5pm. Greenhouses Sa-Th 9:30-11:00am, 3-4:30pm. Free.)* Venturing farther uphill brings you to **Parc de l'Ariana,** where impressive grounds surround the UN building and the Ariana pottery museum. On the opposite (south) side of the lake, past the Jet d'Eau on quai Gustave-Ador, is **Parc la Grange,** features a garden of 40,000 roses, at their peak bloom in June. **Parc des Eaux-Vives,** next to la Grange, is the perfect spot for a picnic or an impromptu frisbee game.

INTERNATIONAL HILL. The garden-parks up the hill behind the train station offer spectacular views of Lac Léman with Mont Blanc in the background (see Jardin Botanique and Parc de l'Ariana, above). The **Museum of the History of Science** (see p. 502) lies in one park and the **World Trade Organization** lies in another farther north. For even better vistas, climb higher to Geneva's international city, where embassies and multilateral organizations abound. The one to visit is the **International Red Cross**, which contains its own museum (see below). Below it stand the European headquarters of the **United Nations**, filling the building that once sheltered the League of Nations. The guided tour of the UN is quite dull (typical title: "Peace: There is Room for All"), despite some art donated by all the countries of the world and an introductory video recapping the work of the UN in the past year. The constant traffic of international diplomats (often in handsome non-Western dress) provides more excitement than any tour. There's also a not-so-subtle display of Cold War one-upmanship: the armillary sphere depicting the heavens and donated by the US stands next to a monument dedicated to the "conquest of space" donated by the former USSR. *(Enter at the Pregny gate across from the Red Cross. Bring a photo ID. ☎917 48 96 or ☎917 45 38. Open July-Aug. daily 10am-5pm; Apr.-June and Sept-Oct. daily 10am-noon and 2-4pm; Nov.-Mar. M-F 10am-noon and 2-4pm. 8.50SFr, seniors and students 6.50SFr, children 4SFr, children under 6 free. 1hr. tours in any of 15 languages when requested by a sizable group.)*

🏛 MUSEUMS

Geneva is home to many exceptional museums. A handful of them are free.

RED CROSS MUSEUM. A visit to the ▨**International Red Cross and Red Crescent Museum** will etch the words of Dostoyevsky into your mind: "Each of us is responsible to all others for everything." The self-guided tour begins with these words and the ensuing passage through the museum's dark, black-walled rooms filled with spotlighted exhibits fixes them firmly on the mind. Built into a hillside, the museum employs still photographs and wartime film-clip montages to drive home its emotional narrative of historic humanitarianism. The stark, unadorned glass and steel building houses a maze of provocative and haunting graphics and audiovisual displays, all through the narrative lens of the life of Henri Dunant, the Red Cross's founder. Seven million file cards documenting the plight of some two million WWI POW's, including Charles de Gaulle, reside here. Displays in English, French, and German. *(Ave. de la Paix 17. Take bus #8 or F to "Appia" or bus V or Z to "Ariana." ☎748 95 11 or 95 28 or 95 25. Open daily except Tu 10am-5pm. 10SFr, students and seniors 5SFr, under 12 free. Self-guided audio tours 3SFr.)*

ART MUSEUMS. If you visit one art museum in Geneva, the ▨**Petit-Palais** should be it. This beautiful mansion has paintings, sculptures, and drawings by Picasso, Renoir, Gauguin, Cézanne, and Chagall. The inventive basement *salles* (rooms) present themed exhibits: the influence of primitive art on modern aesthetes, the nude female form, and radiant meditations on nature. *(Terrasse St-Victor 2, off blvd. Helvétique. Take bus #36 to "Petit Palais" or #1, 3, or 5 to "Claparède." ☎346 14 33. Open M-F 10am-6pm, Sa-Su 10am-5pm. 10SFr, students and seniors 5SFr, children under 12 free. V.)*

The **Musée Barbier-Mueller** has one of the world's most respected collections of African art; artifacts from the collection circulate the globe. Photographs of the objects in their original settings put the frequently changing exhibitions in context. There is rarely a crowd. *(R. Jean-Calvin 10. From Grand-rue in the vie-*

THE LOCAL LEGEND

CIRCUSES!!!

At some point in the film adaptation of Graham Greene's *The Third Man*, the villainous Harry Lime (played by Orson Welles) says: "In Italy, for 30 years under the Borgias, they had warfare, murder and bloodshed, but they produced Michelangelo, Leonardo da Vinci, and the Renaissance. In Switzerland they had brotherly love, 500 years of democracy and peace, and what did they produce? The cuckoo clock."

Well, Switzerland also has circuses. Lots of them. More than 20. The biggest, and perhaps the grandest, is Circus Knie, formally known as the National Circus of Switzerland. The Knies (who unabashedly refer to themselves as the 'dynasty Knie') have owned the world-class circus for exactly 200 years as of 2003. Made up of native Swiss, Poles and a cadre of Arabs, and under the auspices of March Schütz, a former banker turned circusateer, Circus Knie kicks around Switzerland sowing love, brotherhood and clowns from March to November. Though specializing in horse and rhino displays, the circus is constantly expanding itself: goats are being trained for the 2004 season. The repertoire also includes comedy: be prepared for hilarious jokes about Swiss-Germans if you're in the French region, and the reverse if you're in the German parts.

See www.knie.ch.

ille ville, turn onto r. de la Pélisserie and right onto r. Jean-Calvin. ☎312 02 70; musee@barbier-mueller.ch. Open daily 11am-5pm. 5SFr; children under 12, senior citizens, students, and the unemployed 3SFr.)

Featuring anything from creative artistry to the just plain weird, the **Musée d'Art Moderne et Contemporaire** displays the most avant-garde art in Geneva. If you want to see an "I am Still Alive" telegram exhibit, or huge, clear-plastic mattresses, this is the place to be. *(R. des Vieux-Grenadiers 10. Take bus #1 to "Bains." ☎320 61 22. Open Tu-F noon-6pm, Sa-Su 11am-6pm. 9SFr; ages 13-18, students, teachers, artists, and retirees 6SFr; children under 12, scholars, students of art, art history, or architecture, the unemployed, and invalids free. Mandatory lockers 2SFr.)* The museum also houses the **Jean Tua Car and Cycle Museum,** a collection of 70 cars, motorcycles, and bicycles, most pre-WWII. *(R. des Bains 28-30. ☎321 36 37. Open W-Su 2-6pm. 9SFr, students 7SFr, children 4SFr.)*

OTHER MUSEUMS. Maison Tavel near the Hôtel de Ville, acts as a storehouse for random artifacts typical of daily life in Geneva's past, including the 1799 guillotine from pl. Neuve, a collection of medieval front doors, wallpaper remains, clothing, and a vast zinc and copper model of 1850 Geneva that took 18 years to build. Guidebooks in nine languages available at the entrance. *(R. du Puits-St-Pierre 6. ☎310 29 00. Open Tu-Su 10am-5pm. Free, except for temporary exhibits.)*

The **Musée d'Ethnographie** has a small but varied collection, which includes Japanese Samurai armor, Australian aboriginal paintings, and a Bolivian mummy. *(Blvd. Carl-Vogt 65-67. Take bus #1 "Ecole-Médecins." ☎418 45 50. Open Tu-Su 10am-5pm. Permanent exhibits free. Temporary exhibits 4.50SFr, students 2.50SFr, children free.)*

Live boa constrictors and Janus, the two-headed turtle, greet you at the **Musée d'Histoire Naturelle** (Science Museum). The most frequent visitors to the museum are children on school trips, who come to see the extensive exhibits of everything from regional mammals and birds, stuffed and on display, to rocks, crystals and fossils from all over the world. Be sure to check out the Great Horned owl on display among a collection of other, more exotic birds. *(Rte. du Malagnou 1. Take bus #1 to "Museum." ☎418 63 00. Open Tu-Su 9:30am-5pm. Free.)*

Any *Candide* fan should make a pilgrimage to Musée Voltaire, located in the former home of the witty writer himself. Statues, paintings, and writing samples in this chandeliered townhouse. *(R. des Delices 25. Take bus #27 to "Délices". ☎344 71 33. Open M-F 2-5pm. Free.)*

🎵🎭 ENTERTAINMENT & NIGHTLIFE

There is enough to do in Geneva to keep even the most sophisticated traveler happy. *Genève Agenda*, available at the tourist office, is your guide to fun, with listings ranging from festivals to films (be warned—movies run about 16SFr).

FESTIVALS

Summer days bring festivals, **free open-air concerts,** and **free organ music** in Cathédrale de St-Pierre. (June-Sept. Sa 6pm, carillon performances Sa 5pm.) In July and August, the **Cinelac** turns Genève Plage into an open-air cinema that screens mostly American films. (☎840 04 04; www.cinelac.ch. Admission 16SFr.) Check the listings in *Genève Agenda* for indoor cinemas (films marked "v.o." are in their original language with French and sometimes German subtitles, while "st. ang." means that the film has English subtitles).

Geneva hosts the biggest celebration of **American Independence Day** outside the US on July 4, and a firework and party-filled celebration of **Swiss National Day** on August 1. The **Fêtes de Genève** in early August features international music combined with artistic celebration, and culminates in a spectacular fireworks display. **La Bâtie Festival,** a performing arts festival traditionally held from late August to early September, draws Swiss music lovers for a two-week orgy of cabaret, theater, and concerts by experimental rock and folk acts. (☎908 69 50; batie@world.com.ch. 10-32SFr; many events free; students half-price for the others.) **Free jazz concerts** take place in July and August in Parc de la Grange. Most parks offer free concerts; check at the tourist office for information. The best party in Geneva is **L'Escalade,** commemorating the dramatic repulsion of invading Savoyard troops. The revelry lasts for a full weekend in early December.

BARS & NIGHTCLUBS
La Jonction, at the junction of the Rhône and Arve rivers, accessible by the #2, 10-20, and the D buses (to "Jonction"), is the home of Artamis (p. 10) and casual bars and concert venues for rockers and ravers. **Place Bourg-de-Four,** in the *vieille ville* below the cathedral, attracts students and professionals to its charming terraces and more classy old-world atmosphere. **Place du Molard,** on the right bank by the pont du Mont-Blanc, has terrace cafés as well as big, loud bars and clubs. **Les Paquis,** near the Gare Cornavin and the pl. de la Navigation, is the red-light district, but also appeals to a less prurient appetite with its wide array of rowdy, low-lit bars, many ethnically themed. **Carouge,** across the river Arve, is a student-friendly locus of nightlife activity, the same place dissidents headed to party during Calvin's purification of the city. Some of Geneva's most popular nightlife is semi-underground. **Squats** have become a popular housing option for counter-cultural youth who prefer run-down housing to paying rent and living by rules. The authorities are quite aware of their existence, but rarely break up the parties. Information is generally spread word-of-mouth, but one more official squat is **Le Rhino,** blvd. des Philosophes 24, between Plainpalais and pl. Claparède, unmistakable given the oversized red rhino horn that graces it.

▧ **La Clémence,** pl. du Bourg-de-Four 20 (☎312 24 98). Directly behind the Cathedrale, walk from there or take bus #36 to "Bourg-de-Four." Generations of students have eaten at this famous chic bar, named after the bell atop the Cathédrale de St-Pierre. It offers quality food and drinks all day long and though it attracts a crowd at any given time, it tends to be particularly busy on weekends. Teen-Idol waiters cater to a chatty clientele of students and young professionals. Come for breakfast (croissant 1.30SFr, coffee 3.10SFr) or beer (3.80-7.20SFr). Open M-Th 7am-12:30am, F-Sa 7am-1:30am.

Flanagan's, r. du Cheval-Blanc 4 (☎310 13 14), off Grand-Rue in the *vieille ville*. Outside, a sign proclaims, "Irish Parking: All Others Will Be Towed"; inside, friendly bartenders pull a good beer and entertain well in this Irish cellar bar, though you'll be hard-pressed to find an Irish accent among the anglophones. If you're looking for a bar that isn't crowded, this is the place. Guinness 8SFr for a pint; 6SFr during daily 5-7pm Happy Hour. Open daily 5pm-2am.

Au Chat Noir, r. Vautier 13, Carouge (☎343 49 98). Take tram #12 to "pl. du Marché," turn left upon entering the square, and then left again on r. Vautier; the bar is on the right. The sensuously curved bar and dark red curtains set the mood in this popular jazz, funk, rock, salsa, and blues venue. Live concerts or DJs every night. Has a comprehensive collection of brochures upcoming concerts and shows. (10-15SRFr cover.) Beers 5SFr, sangria 6-8SFr. Open M-Th 6pm-4am, F 6pm-5-am, Sa 9pm-5am, Su 9pm-4am.

LAUSANNE ☎021

Two thousand years ago, Romans came to the little town of Lausanne on the shores of Lac Léman and found it so enticing that they stayed until the collapse of their empire. Later, the city inspired a different sort of visitor by welcoming vacationing novelists such as Dickens and Thackeray. T.S. Eliot managed to create the apotheosis of high Modernist pessimism here, writing *The Wasteland* near the

GENEVA

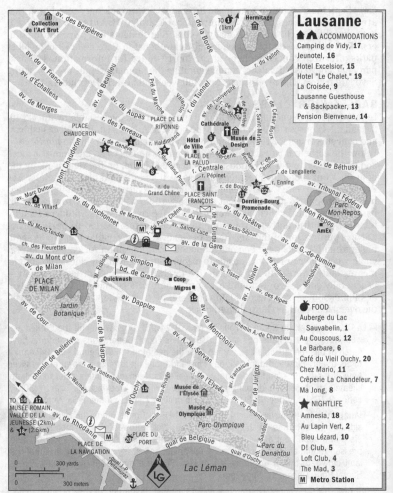

Lausanne

🏠▲ ACCOMMODATIONS
Camping de Vidy, **17**
Jeunotel, **16**
Hotel Excelsior, **15**
Hotel "Le Chalet," **19**
La Croisée, **9**
Lausanne Guesthouse
  & Backpacker, **13**
Pension Bienvenue, **14**

🍎 FOOD
Auberge du Lac
  Sauvabelin, **1**
Au Couscous, **12**
Le Barbare, **6**
Café du Vieil Ouchy, **20**
Chez Mario, **11**
Crêperie La Chandeleur, **7**
Ma Jong, **8**

★ NIGHTLIFE
Amnesia, **18**
Au Lapin Vert, **2**
Bleu Lézard, **10**
D! Club, **5**
Loft Club, **4**
The Mad, **3**
Ⓜ Metro Station

placid Ouchy shoreline and the medieval labyrinth of the *vieille ville*. Today, Lausanne's unique museums, distinctive neighborhoods, festivals, and magnificent parks make it worth a stay.

📧 **TRANSPORTATION**

Trains: pl. de la Gare 9 (☎ 157 22 22; 1.19SFr per min.). To: **Basel** (2½hr., every hr. 5:27am-9:27am, 63.6SFr); **Geneva** (50min., every 20min. 4:55am-12:46am, 18.80SFr); **Montreux** (20min., every 30min. 5:24am-2:29am, 9.80SFr); **Paris** (4hr., 4 per day 7:36am-5:52pm, 71SFr); **Zurich** via Biel (2½hr., 3 per hr. 5:27am-10:27pm, 65SFr).

Public Transportation: The 5-stop **Métro Ouchy** runs from the *vieille ville* to the Ouchy waterfront. The **Métro Ouest** runs west to the University of Lausanne and the Federal Institute of Technology. Both Métros run approximately M-Sa 5am-midnight, Su 6am-midnight. Buses cross the city roughly 6am-midnight (check bus stops for specific lines; the official city map also shows buslines). Exact change needed. 3-stop ticket 1.50SFr; 1hr. pass 2.40SFr; 24hr. pass 7.20SFr; ages 6-16 1.30SFr/4SFr. Métro free with Swiss Pass or Lausanne Pass.

Ferries: CGN, ave. de Rhodanie 17 (☎614 04 04). To: **Evian** (4:55am-12:15am; 16SFr, round-trip 27.20SFr); **Geneva** (3½hr.; 9:15am-5:15pm; 34.80SFr, round-trip 54SFr); **Montreux** (1½hr.; 4 per day 9:30am-6:05pm; 20.60SFr, round-trip 35.20SFr). Purchase tickets at dock. Eurail and SwissPass valid. Open M-F 8am-7:30pm.

Taxis: Available at r. Madeleine 1, pl. St. François, pl. de la Navigation, and in front of the station. Or call the **taxibus** (☎08 00 080 03 12) or **taxiphone** (☎08 00 81 08 10, 24hr. service).

Car Rental: Avis, ave. de la Gare 50 (☎340 72 00; fax 72 09). **Hertz,** pl. du Tunnel 17 (☎312 53 11). **Europcar,** ave. Ruchonnet 2 (☎323 91 52). **Lococar,** ave. Ruchonnet 30 (☎320 30 80).

Parking: Parking Simplon-Gare, r. du Simplon 2 (☎617 67 44), behind the station (entrance on blvd. de Grancy). 1SFr per 25min., overnight 1SFr per 100min. Open M-F 8am-7pm, Sa 8am-5pm. On city streets, white zones indicate free unlimited parking, while blue zones mark 1½hr zones. To park on the street, pick up a parking disc from the tourist office. Set the present time and the maximum stay time, and leave the disc displayed on the dashboard.

Bike Rental: (☎0512 24 21 62), at the baggage check in the station. 30SFr per day, 23SFr per half-day. 5SFr off with Eurail or SwissPass. Return bikes at another station for an additional 6SFr. Open 6:40am-7:40pm. Find bike rental starting from 10SFr at pl. du Port 6 (☎606 27 61), next to the Ouchy Métro exit.

⬛▚ ORIENTATION & PRACTICAL INFORMATION

Two-dimensional maps of Lausanne are confusing because the city is on a number of steep hills connected by vaulted bridges. The easiest way to explore the city is on the **Métro Ouchy,** a five-stop cog-rail subway system which runs from the waterfront up to pl. St. Francois. The Métro's Lausanne-CFF stop is across from the station and goes down to Ouchy (the neighborhood on the waterfront) or up to the vieille ville. Buses #1, 3, and 5 serve the station; most are routed to pl. St. François. Wheelchair-bound visitors should pay special attention to the city's terrain in planning their visits.

TOURIST & FINANCIAL SERVICES

Tourist Office: Main office (☎613 73 73 or 73 21; www.lausanne-tourisme.ch), in the main hall of the train station. Open daily 9am-5pm. **Branch office** across from pl. de la Navigation (M: Ouchy or bus #2: Ouchy). Pick up the *Plan Officiel* (map and public transportation guide) and *Welcome to Lausanne* (booklet listing cheap hotels and private rooms) for free. The staff sells **Lausanne Passes** for 15SFr (p. 505) and makes hotel reservations for 4SFr commission. Wheelchair-accessible. Branch office open daily Apr.-Sept. 9am-8pm; Oct.-Mar. 9am-6pm. Main office open 9am-7pm all year. AmEx/DC/MC/V.

Budget Travel: STA Travel, blvd. de Grancy 20 (☎617 56 27;www.statravel.ch), 2 streets downhill from the station past the overpass; turn right off of ave. d'Ouchy. Books student tickets, organizes group travel, and sells ISICs for 15SFr. Open M-F 9:15am-6pm, Sa 9am-noon.

Currency Exchange: At the station (☎312 38 24). Good rates. 2SFr commission. No commission on traveler's checks. **Western Union** transfers 7am-6:30pm. Cash advances with AmEx/DC/MC/V. Open 6:30am-7:30pm. **24hr. exchange machine** outside offers the same rates for the same commission.

American Express: ave. Mon Répos 14 (☎310 19 00; fax 19 19), across from parking garage. Cashes traveler's checks, sells airline tickets, and holds mail for 2 months. Travel services open M-F 8:30am-5:30pm; financial office open 2-5:30pm.

LOCAL SERVICES

Luggage Storage: At the train station. (☎0512 24 21 62). 7SFr per day. Open 6:40am-7:40pm. Lockers 5-7SFr per day.

Lost Property: At the train station with the luggage storage. Open M-Sa 6:40am-7:40pm.

Bookstore: Payot Libraire, pl. Pépinet 4 (☎341 31 31; fax 33 45), down r. Pepinet from Pl. St. Francois. Large Anglophone section with contemporary and classic fiction and some nonfiction. Open M 1-6:30pm, Tu-F 8:30am-6:30pm, Sa 8:30am-5pm.

Library: Cantonal and University Palais de Rumine, pl. de la Riponne 6 (☎316 78 80; www.unil.ch/BCU). Open for borrowing M-F 10am-6pm, Sa 9am-noon. Reading room open M-F 8am-10pm, Sa 8am-5pm. Borrowing card free with ID.

Laundromat: Quick Wash, blvd. de Grancy 44 (☎079 449 37 61), 2 streets downhill behind the train station; turn right. Wash and dry around 12-14SFr. Open M and W-Su 9am-8:30pm, Tu noon-8:30pm.

EMERGENCY & COMMUNICATIONS

Emergency: Police ☎117, **Fire** ☎118, **Ambulance** ☎144, **Crisis Line** ☎143.

24hr. Pharmacy: Call ☎111 to find out which pharmacy is open all night (they rotate). The pharmacy in the train station is open 6am-10pm everyday, all year.

24hr. Medical Service, at the hospital (☎314 11 11).

Internet Access: Quanta, ave. de la Gare 4, above the McDonald's and the Métro Lausanne-CFF stop, and across from the train station. 4SFr per 30min. Open M-Th and Su 9am-midnight, F-Sa 9am-1am.

Post Office: Centre Postal, ave. de la Gare 43b (☎344 35 13), on the right as you exit the station. Address *Poste Restante* to: 1000 Lausanne 1 Cases, CH-1001, Lausanne. Open M-F 7:30am-6:30pm, Sa 8am-noon. Express mail M-F 6:30am-10pm, Sa noon-4pm, Su 5-9pm. To dispatch your postcard from the site where Edward Gibbon wrote his *Decline and Fall of the Roman Empire,* visit **Poste St. François,** pl. St.-François 15 (☎344 38 31). Open M-F 7:30am-6:30pm, Sa 8am-noon. **Postal code: CH-1002.**

🏚 ACCOMMODATIONS & CAMPING

As the home of the world's oldest hotel school, Lausanne has a well-deserved reputation for service-industry excellence. It's a good idea to pick up the tourist office's list of cheap hotels, private boarding houses, and family *Pensionen,* since innumerable festivals, conferences, and congresses can make housing scarce. Owners generally prefer stays of at least three nights and often as long as a month. Travelers looking for apartments to rent can turn to the local paper *24 Heures,* which carries regular listings, or to big department stores' notice boards.

🏚 **Lausanne Guesthouse & Backpacker,** Chemin des Epinettes 4 (☎601 80 00; info@lausanne-guesthouse.ch). From the train station, head left downhill on ave. W. Fraisse. Take first right on Chemin des Epinettes. This elegant guesthouse has a convenient location and comfortable rooms which face the lake, as well as a flower-filled garden and an artistic lobby. Ask for a room with a balcony. Kitchen, BBQ grill, and lockers included; laundry 5SFr, night car park 10SFr. Key box available for late arrivals/early departures (1SFr). Reception 7am-noon and 3-10pm. At Backpacker: pillow, blanket, and sheets 5SFr. 4-bed dorms 29SFr per person. At Guesthouse: singles 80SFr, with bathroom 88SFr; doubles 86SFr/98SFr. MC/V. ❷/❹

Jeunotel (HI), Chemin du Bois-de-Vaux 36 (☎626 02 22; www.jeunotel.ch). Take bus #2 (dir.: Bourdonnette) to "Bois-de-Vaux." Cross the street and follow the signs. This large hostel is down a long concrete driveway on the right past the *Musée Romain de Lausanne-Vidy.* Courtyards with ping-pong tables, a bowling alley next door, a bar and a restaurant within the complex, and a backpacker crowd enliven it. Breakfast and sheets included. Wheelchair-accessible. Small lockers for personal things only. Parking available. Reception 24hr. Check-out 10am. Reserve in the summer. Single 53SFr, with shower 79SFr; doubles 41SFr, with shower 48SFr; triple or quad 31SFr (39SFr for non-members). Ask about monthly and group rates. AmEx/DC/MC/V. ❶

La Croisée, ave. Marc Dufour 15 (☎321 09 09; www.hotellacroisee.ch). 10min. from the train station. Walk up ave. du Ruchonnet and continue as it turns into ave. Marc Dufour. This youth hostel and 2-star hotel offers stunning views of Lac Léman, plus TV room, terrace, and cafeteria space. The dormitory quads offer in-room sinks and funky bunks. Breakfast buffet 7.50SFr; dinner around 17SFr. Some hall showers and bathrooms; some are within rooms. Pillow, blanket, and sheets 15SFr. Reception open M-F 7:30am-8pm, Sa 7:30am-noon and 4-7pm, Su 8am-noon. No curfew. Reservations recommended. 4- to 10-bed dorms 40SFr; singles 80-90SFr; doubles 130-150SFr. Children under 6 free, 6-11 50% off, 12-15 30% off. Special rates for extended stays. MC/V. ❸

Pension Bienvenue, r. du Simplon 2 (☎616 29 86), 5min. from the train station. Turn right out of the station, right onto ave. d'Ouchy, and right after the bridge. Or, more quickly, exit out the back entrance of the station, cross the street, turn left onto r. du Simplon, and it's 2 blocks farther on the left side of the street. **Women only.** This well-worn 27-room *Pension* has communal TV rooms and clean, comfortable rooms and beds. Breakfast included. Kitchen available. Laundry 3SFr. Hall showers and bathrooms only. Reception 9-11:30am and 5-8:30pm. 49SFr. Special rates for extended stays. ❸

Hotel "Le Chalet," ave. d'Ouchy 49 (☎616 52 06). Take Métro Ouchy to "Jordils" or bus #2 (dir.: Bourdonnette) to "Jordils." Built in 1877, this chalet has been run by the same welcoming matron since 1940. Travelers enjoy the personal touch and home-like atmosphere in the individualized rooms, each equipped with a sink. Literati occasionally visit the hotel, hoping to commune with the spirit of longtime guest August Strindberg in the evergreen garden. Breakfast 10SFr. Hall showers. Reception 8am-10pm. Singles 50-63SFr; doubles 92SFr. ❸

Hotel Excelsior, chemin du Closelet 6 (☎616 84 51; excelsior@fastnet.ch), 5min. from the train station. Turn right along ave. de la Gare, right on ave. d'Ouchy, and left after the bridge on Closelet. Spacious rooms balance the cramped, run-down hallways. Breakfast 9SFr. Parking 10SFr. Reception M-Sa 8am-10pm, Su 8am-noon and 7-10pm. Singles 65-90SFr; doubles 90-130SFr. AmEx/MC/V. ❹

Camping de Vidy, chemin du Camping 3 (☎622 50 00; www.campinglausannevidy.ch). Take bus #2 from M: Ouchy (dir.: Bourdonnette) to "Bois-de-Vaux." Cross the street and walk down chemin du Bois-de-Vaux past Jeunotel and under the overpass. The office is straight ahead across rte. de Vidy. Restaurant (May-Sept. 7am-11pm), supermarket, and playground. It's near a swimming pool and minutes from a lively public beach. Showers included. Reception daily Sept.-June 8am-12:30pm and 4-8pm; July-Aug. 8am-9pm. Wheelchair-accessible. 6.50SFr, students 6SFr, ages 6-15 5SFr; tents 8-12SFr. 1- to 2-person bungalow 54SFr; 3- to 4-person bungalow 86SFr. Electricity 3-4SFr. Tax 1.20SFr per tent, 1.30SFr per vehicle. ❶

🔾 FOOD

No visit to Lausanne is complete without a taste of Lac Léman's famous perch or *papet vaudois* (a local delicacy made from leeks, potatoes, cabbage, and sausage). Restaurants, cafés, and bars cluster around pl. St.-François and the *vieille ville*, while *boulangeries* sell cheap sandwiches on every street. Surprisingly fresh fare and crusty bread await at Métro stations. Numerous grocery stores, frequent markets, and abundant parks make for affordable and pleasant picnics. For crêpes, ice cream, and other sweet fare, there are a number of stands on the Ouchy waterfront, which are generally open from the morning well into the evening.

Le Barbare, Escaliers du Marché 27 (☎312 21 32), at the top of steps off the far right of the pl. de la Palud. Stop by this convenient (if oddly located) eatery for lunch or a mid-afternoon treat after trekking to the cathedral. Sandwiches from 5.50SFr. Omelettes 7.50-10SFr. Pizzas 12-16SFr. Try the *Chocolate Maison Viennois avec Chantilly,* a rich chocolate drink (5.20SFr), perfect as a reward for the uphill climb. Open M-Sa 8:30am-midnight. DC/MC/V. ❶

Crêperie La Chandeleur, r. Mercerie 9 (☎312 84 19). From pl. St.-François, head down the r. Pépinet to the pl. de la Palud; with your back to the Hôtel de Ville, r. Mercier is off the far right corner of the pl. de la Palud. Enjoy custom-made crêpes in a tea-room atmosphere. Try traditional (butter, sugar, or honey around 6SFr), ice cream (7.30-10.30SFr), or gourmet *flambées,* with choice of liqueur (8.30-11SFr). Open Tu-Th 11:30am-10pm, F-Sa 11:30am-11pm. DC/MC/V. ❶

Pizzeria Chez Mario, r. du Bourg 28. Head 5min. up r. du Bourg, which lies behind St.-François. Mario's offers undeniable atmosphere for those who want a bite of cheap pizza (from 13SFr) and who have never eaten in an alternatively-decorated restaurant filled with local teenagers. Open daily 11:30am-1am. ❷

Au Couscous, r. Enning 2 (☎321 38 40). From pl. St.-François, head away from the Zurich Bank sign and turn left up r. de la Paix to r. Enning. Inside this Tunisian/North African restaurant, red tablecloths, a mosaic-tiled floor, and sequined pillows are the backdrop for delicious alternative fare. Extensive, veggie-friendly menu (13.90-23SFr). Enjoy delicious couscous (23-24SFr) in an appropriate ambience. Open M-Tu 11:30am-2:30pm and 6:30pm-midnight, W-Th 11:30am-2:30pm and 6:30pm-1am, F 11:30am-2:30pm and 6:30pm-2am, Sa 6:30pm-2am, Su 6:30pm-1am. ❸

Café du Vieil-Ouchy, pl. du Port 3 (☎616 21 94). Take bus #2 to "Beau-Rivage," walk down the hill to the lake and turn left on r. du Port, on your left. This small lakeside café provides great view of both the lake and the chateau while you enjoy a *Rösti* platter (9-22.50SFr) or cheese fondue (21SFr). Savor a delectable *coupe maison* (9.50SFr) if you have room for dessert. Open Th-M. ❸

Auberge du Lac de Sauvabelin, at Lac Sauvabelin, 1018 Lausanne (☎647 39 29). Try this place if you've got a car, or take the infrequent bus #16 to "Lac Sauvabelin." An oasis far from the bustle of Lausanne, this classy, truly authentic Swiss restaurant sits directly on the lake and is next to a deer farm. Traditional Swiss fare (filet of perch 28SFr) served by waiters. Taste the high life with *escargot* (dozen 19SFr). MC/V.❸

Ma-Jong, Escalier du Grand Pont 3 (☎329 05 25). From the Lausanne-Flon Métro stop, walk up the incline; Ma-Jong will be on the right. cafeteria-style, pan-Asian dining in the tradition of Chinese streetside eateries. Specials from pad thai to roast duck are available for 15SFr (with salad and sometimes rice). For 20SFr, the Japanese fondue lets you simmer raw meat in a pot of heated boullion. Dim sum and sushi also offered. Take-out or eat-in. Open M-Th 11:30am-10:30pm, F-Sa 11:30am-midnight. ❸

MARKETS

Migros, ave. de Rhodanie 2 (☎613 26 60), right of Métro Ouchy stop or bus #2 stop "Pl. de la Navigation." Locations throughout city. Open M 9am-9:45pm, Tu-Su 8am-9:45pm.

Co-op, (☎616 40 66). From the train station, head downhill past the overpass; turn right onto blvd. de Grancy. Open M-F 8am-7pm, Sa 8am-5pm.

Aperto, at the train station. Open daily 6am-10pm.

Produce markets, at pl. de la Palud and the r. de Bourg behind the pl. St.-François. W and Sa mornings until around noon.

👁 🏛 SIGHTS & MUSEUMS

"In Lausanne, people are consuming culture as others swallow vitamins," a tourist brochure proclaims. Perhaps something was lost in translation, but nevertheless, 650,000 visitors flock to Lausanne's *vieille ville* and museums each year. For multi-day visits, the **Lausanne Pass** is a great deal, entitling visitors to museum discounts and free public transportation in and around Lausanne (15SFr for 2 days).

THE OLD CITY AND THE OLD CITY. The medieval town center is known as the *vieille ville*, but the true old city is on the waterfront, where archaeological digs have unearthed 2000-year-old remains of the *Vicus de Lousonna*. You can stroll through it and see the foundations of a temple, the remains of a basilica, a forum, a few villas, and the traces of a complete Gallo-Roman colony, now overshadowed by gigantic weeds. *(Take bus #2 to "Bois-de-Vaux" and follow signs.)* History buffs can poke around the **Musée Romain de Lausanne-Vidy,** the excavation site of a Roman house whose wall murals still retain their bright colors. Explanations in French. *(Chemin du Bois-de-Vaux 24, next door to the hostel. ☎652 10 84. Open Tu-W and F-Su 11am-6pm, Th 11am-8pm. Wheelchair-accessible. 4SFr, seniors 2.50SFr, students free.)*

In 1275 the Gothic **Cathédrale** was consecrated under Holy Roman Emperor Rudolph and Pope Gregory X. From pl. de la Palud, with your back to the Hôtel de Ville, head diagonally right and just off the plaza, climb the two series of medieval, covered stairs (*l'escalier du Marché*) which lead to the hilltop, where the cathedral's huge wooden doors open up into the hushed, vaulted space illuminated through stained-glass windows. At the south entrance, 2SFr lets you climb the main tower for an impressive view of the lake, the Alps and the surrounding rooftops. *(Cathedral open July to mid-Sept. M-F 7am-7pm, Sa-Su 8am-7pm; mid-Sept. to June closes 5:30pm. Church services Su 10am, 8:15pm. Free guided tours July to mid-Sept. 10:30, 11:15am, 3, 3:45pm.)*

The Renaissance **Hôtel de Ville** (city hall), with its bronze dragon roof, serves as a meeting point for guided **tours** of the town by local residents. *(On the pl. de la Palud, below the cathedral. Tours M-Sa 10am, 3pm. English available. 10SFr, seniors 5SFr, students free.)* Also below the cathedral is the majestic **Palais de Rumine,** which houses the Cantonal and University Library, as well as several small archaeological and zoological museums. *(On pl. de la Riponne. Open M-F 11am-10pm, Sa 7am-5pm, Su 10am-5pm.)*

ART MUSEUMS. The 🖾**Collection de l'Art Brut** is a must-see. The utterly original and unconventional gallery filled with disturbing and beautiful sculptures, drawings, and paintings by artists on the fringe–institutionalized schizophrenics, poor and uneducated peasants, and convicted criminals–started as an odd obsession of Jean Dubuffet. Today, the museum features unorthodox masterpieces: from a prison cell wall painstakingly carved with a broken spoon to intricate junk and sea-shell masks. Equally fascinating are the biographies of their tortured creators, most displayed in English and French and often accompanied by intense photographic portraits. Don't miss the unforgettable Henry Darger room, the fantasy world of a part-time janitor from Chicago who created an alternate universe on paper. *(Ave. Bergières 11. Take bus #2 or 3 to "Jomini." The museum is across the street. ☎647 54 35. Open Sept.-June Tu-F 11am-1pm and 2-6pm, Sa-Su 11am-6pm; July-Aug. open daily 11am-6pm. 6SFr, students and seniors 4SFr, under 16 free.)*

On a more conventional note, the **Musée de l'Elysée** houses an engaging series of diverse exhibits and photographic archives, ranging from 1820 prints to contemporary artistic endeavors in film. *(Ave. de l'Elysée 18. Take bus #2 to "Croix d'Ouchy" and go downhill, then left on ave. de l'Elysée. ☎316 99 11; www.elysee.ch. Open daily 11am-6pm. 8SFr, seniors 6SFr, students 4SFr.)*

North of the *vieille ville*, the **Hermitage** is a magnificent house given over to temporary exhibitions that vary from single artists and special themes to individual public and private collections. 2003 will bring works from French painter Derin from March-May and Kupka from June-October. *(Rte. du Signal 2. Bus #16 to "Hermitage" stops infrequently out front. ☎320 50 01. Open Tu-W and F-Su 10am-6pm, Th 10am-9pm. 15SFr, seniors 12SFr, students 7SFr, under 18 free. AmEx/MC/V.)*

MUSÉE OLYMPIQUE. This high-tech temple to Olympians opens with the words "Citius Altius Fortius" (faster, higher, stronger) and a tour through the museum brings these words to life. Displays in English and French detail the history of the Olympics and its athletes from antiquity to the present. An extensive video collection allows visitors to relive any highlight since the games were first filmed; and more recent events can be seen in the 3D cinema. On a busy day beware, though, for the exhibits are frequently swarming with kids. The museum is wheelchair-accessible via ave. de l'Elysée. *(Quai d'Ouchy 1. Take bus #2 or Métro: "Ouchy." ☎621 65 11. Open May-Sept. M-W and F-Su 9am-6pm, Th 9am-8pm; Oct.-Apr. Tu-W and F-Su 9am-6pm, Th 9am-8pm. 14SFr, students and seniors 9SFr, ages 10-18 7SFr, families 34SFr max. Audioguide available in 7 languages, 3SFr. MC/V.)*

MUSÉE DE DÉSIGN (MUSEUM OF DESIGN AND CONTEMPORARY APPLIED ARTS). Part contemporary, part traditional, this museum was once dedicated to the decorative arts, but now houses a well-chosen collection of modern, cutting-edge pieces. The overall effect is heady: exhibits of Egyptian and Chinese art in the basement, glass art on the top floor, and temporary exhibits in between. *(Pl. de la Cathédrale 6, next to the cathedral. ☎315 25 30; mu.dac@lausanne.ch. Open Tu 11am-9pm, W-Su 11am-6pm. 6SFr, students and seniors 4SFr.)*

WATERFRONT. A sign along the waterfront declares Ouchy to be "a free and independent community," and indeed its slower tempo, indulgent hotels, and eco-modern sculptures set it strikingly apart from the *vieille ville*. Ouchy's main promenades (the **quai de Belgique,** which turns into the **quai d'Ouchy,** and the **place de la Navigation**) are all excellent spots to exercise those calf muscles. The local word is that Lausanne's citizens have the best-looking legs in Switzerland, the hard-won prize of a life spent hiking the city's hills (*Let's Go* remains impartial). Several booths along the water rent out pedal boats (10SFr per 30min.) and offer water skiing or wake boarding on Lac Léman (30SFr per 15min.). See more of Ouchy's inhabitants at the **Bellerive Complex,** an extensive beach/park where locals let their children loose on the lawns while both men and women go topless and take in sun. *(Take bus #2 to "Bellerive" or walk down ave. de Rhodanie from Ouchy. Open mid-May to early Sept. daily from 9:30am until dark or rain. 4.50SFr, students and seniors 3SFr, under 17 2SFr; discount after 5pm. Lockers 2SFr.)*

PARKS & GARDENS. The Bellerive Beach is just one of Lausanne's many natural oases. East along the lake from Ouchy, the **park Olympique** and the **Parc du Denatou** offer more beautiful views of the lake and well-planned gardens. Farther west, at the **Vallée de la Jeunesse** rose garden, an unassuming path of wildflowers bends to reveal a spectacular display of 1000 bushes arranged in a terraced semicircle around a fountain, all to the tune of thousands of birds. *(Take Métro-Ouest to "Renens.")* More exotic birds trill from the aviaries of the downtown **Parc du Mon-Repos.** Centering around a small chateau where Voltaire wrote from 1755 to 1757, the park includes venerable trees, an orange grove, and a small stone temple. *(Take Bus #17 (dir.: Verdeil) to "Mon-Repos.")* The region's propensity to bloom is channeled at the **Derrière-Bourg Promenade,** where flowers depict events from the canton's history. *(Just off pl. St. François.)* The **Botanical Garden of Lausanne** is in one section of pl. de Milan-Montriond Park. Wander past rose bushes, herbs, and signs about local fauna, and visit the observation spot atop a hill next to the gardens for an unobstructed lake panorama. A sign names each peak visible across the water and the date on which it was first conquered. The surrounding neighborhood is charming and untouristed. *(Ave. de Cour 14. Just up the hill from the bus #1 stop "Beauregard." ☎616 24 09. Park open daily Mar.-Apr. and Oct. 10am-5:30pm; May-Sept. 10am-6:30pm.)*

🎵 🎭 ENTERTAINMENT & NIGHTLIFE

For every exhibit in Lausanne's museums, there are several performances in progress on stage and screen: the **Béjart Ballet, Lausanne Chamber Orchestra, Cinémathèque Suisse, Municipal Theatre, Opera House,** and **Vidy Theatre** reflect Lausanne's thriving cultural life. For information, reservations, and tickets, call Billetel (☎310 16 50). The **Festival de la Cité** (mid-July) brings the *vieille ville* to life with free theater and dance events. Swiss craftwork fills the **Marché des Artisans** in pl. de la Palud from 6am to 7pm on the first Friday of the month from March to December. **Lunapark** (amusement park) is at Bellerive from mid-May to mid-June.

SWISS GRACE. Founded in 1957 by Maurice Béjart, former dancer and choreographer of the Royal Swedish Ballet, the Béjart Ballet proudly holds a place as one of the world's most famous and innovative dance companies. Renowned for his unconventional style of choreography, Béjart frequently incorporates modern dance and acrobatics into performances by his classically trained ballet dancers. Pieces are known for their element of grand spectacle, and often include literature and multimedia elements. Fortunate to be directed by what some consider to be a living choreographic genius, the Béjart ballet regularly showcases new pieces by Béjart in their repertoire, and performs his epochal dance works like *Ninth Symphony of Beethoven, Le Flûte Enchantée,* and *Symphony for a Lonely Man.*

Lausanne is a clubber's dream and a penny-cruncher's nightmare. Bars and large, beauty clubs line the streets around pl. St. François. *Lausannois* party-goers fill the bars until about 1am (2am Sa-Su), and then move to the clubs where most stay until 4 or 5 in the morning. Unfortunately, the bus and the métro system stops running at midnight and cabs get expensive, especially if you're not staying near the city-center. On weekends, cover charges run 15-30SFr, and drinks inside many of the clubs aren't cheap either (it's not uncommon for mixed drinks to be over 20SFr). There is some solace: Lausanne now has a "Pyjama" bus service which runs from about 1:15am to 3:45am depending on the route (cost: regular fare plus a 2SFr supplement).

The Mad, rte. de Genève 23 (☎312 29 19). Exit the Lausanne-Flon Métro stop, go left, and then walk 3min. down rte. de Genève. A 5-floor warehouse discotheque splashed with bright colors and the slogan "Mad But Not Mad" crawling up its side. World-class

DJs spin trance W, house Th, and progressive stuff F-Sa. Beer 7.50SFr, mixed drinks 14-25SFr. Open W-Su 10pm-5am. Cover F-Sa before midnight 20SFr, after midnight 25SFr.

Loft Club, pl. Bel-Air 1 (☎311 64 00; www.loftclub.ch). Up the steps off the right hand side of rte. de Genève, heading toward The Mad. While other clubs may just be warming up, the hordes here have already fired up to the sounds of house, hip hop, or techno. So popular that a pat-down is required for entry. Cover 5-15SFr. W members-only night. Open W-Sa 10:30pm-5am.

Bleu Lézard, r. Enning 10 (☎321 38 30). From pl. St-François turn left to r. de Bourg, then head right past Au Couscous. Suits and students alike crowd this bistro, which is decorated by local artists. DJs or live music on weekends. Beer 3.50SFr, cocktails 13.50SFr. Vegetarian dishes 15-19SFr. Open Tu and Th 8pm-2am, W and Su 8pm-1am, F-Sa 6:30pm-2am. Kitchen open M-Sa 11:30am-2pm and 6:30-10:30pm, Su 10am-5pm and 6:30-10:30pm. AmEx/MC/V.

Amnesia, Off allée du Bornan in Esplanade des Cantons. Take bus #2 to "Theatre de Vidy" and walk toward the lake. Open F and Sa 11pm-5am. On the water. This upbeat, extremely popular club features a diversified atmosphere with several dance rooms and bars and an outside area with more music and drinks. The crowd is varied too, as a jeans and t-shirt crowd mixes with high-rollers coming in off yachts docked at the club's wharf. The club can be expensive, though, as there is a 15SFr cover on weekends, and most drinks are priced 20SFr and up.

Au Lapin Vert (☎312 13 17). On ruelle du Lapin Vert, off r. de l'Académie behind the cathedral, this upscale version of a hole-in-the-wall pub blasts English rock at a consistently local crowd of teenagers, college students, and young professionals. Friendly, young bartenders tend the pub's 2 bars. Beer 4SFr, mixed drinks 9-10SFr. Open Su-Th 8pm-2am, F-Sa 8pm-3am.

D! Club, ruelle de Grand Pont, entrance at pl. Centrale, attracts Lausanne's mature and well-dressed crowd with its wide range of music. Go left out of the Lausanne-Flon Métro stop, walk under r. de Grand Point bridge, and turn left. Open Th 11pm-4am, F-Sa 11pm-5am. Th Free, F-Sa cover 20SFr.

MONTREUX ☎021

Montreux feels like a resort past its heyday—one that could've been frequented by the elegant, Jazz Age characters of an F. Scott Fitzgerald novel. The grand hotels and lakefront promenade still emanate wealth and prestige, though the glitz has an air of pleasant decay to it. Still, music fans worldwide flock here in early July for the annual **Montreux Jazz Festival.** Not only a celebration of jazz, the festival attracts musicians of all genres and creates an ongoing, city-wide, all-ages party. Luminaries such as Neil Young, Bob Dylan, Stevie Ray Vaughan, and, most famously, Miles Davis have dropped in. Literary visitors have included Victor Hugo and Fitzgerald himself. Even further back in the area's literary tradition is Lord Byron's visit to the disturbingly beautiful **Château de Chillon,** a medieval fortress with a checkered history.

▐ TRANSPORTATION

Trains: ☎963 45 15, on ave. des Alpes. To: **Bern** (1½hr., 2 per hr. 5:39am-11:05pm, 37SFr); **Geneva** (1hr., 2 per hr. 5:39am-11:39pm, 26SFr); **Lausanne** (20min., 3-5 per hr. 5:29am-12:09am, 9.80SFr). **Direct trains** also go to **Aigle, Brig, Martigny, Sion,** and (literally) through the mountains to **Gstaad.**

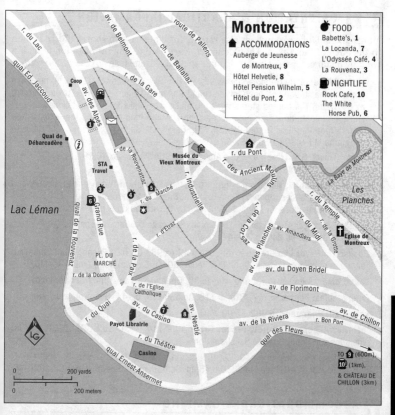

Montreux

🏠 ACCOMMODATIONS
Auberge de Jeunesse
    de Montreux, **9**
Hôtel Helvetie, **8**
Hôtel Pension Wilhelm, **5**
Hôtel du Pont, **2**

🍴 FOOD
Babette's, **1**
La Locanda, **7**
L'Odyssée Café, **4**
La Rouvenaz, **3**

🌙 NIGHTLIFE
Rock Cafe, **10**
The White
    Horse Pub, **6**

Local Transportation: A very helpful map, available at the tourist office in several languages, divides the area into bus zones; your fare is dependent upon the number of
zones you cross. 1 zone 2.20SFr, juniors (ages 6-20) 1.60SFr; 2 zones 2.80SFr/
2SFr; 3 zones 3.50SFr/2.50SFr; 4 zones 4.20SFr/3SFr. Day-pass 7SFr/5SFr; available at tourist office. SwissPass valid. Special late-night buses run during the Jazz
festival, tickets 2-4Sfr (buy at the back of the bus); SwissPass valid. Free buses run
from **Vevey** through Montreux to **Villeneuve** M-F 6pm-4am, Sa-Su noon-4am during
the Festival.

Boats: CGN, (☎963 46 55), on quai du Débarcadère next to the tourist office. To:
Geneva (4½hr.; 4 per day, 9:30am-4:50pm; 40.80SFr, round-trip 63.40SFr); **Lau-**
sanne (1½hr.; 5 per day, 9:30am-5:55pm; 20.60SFr, round-trip 35.20SFr); **Vevey**
(25min.; 6 per day, 9:30am-5:55pm; 9.20SFr, round-trip 16.60SFr). Rides to **Château**
de Chillon (7.60SFr, round-trip 13.80SFr) and **Villeneuve** (7.60SFr, round-trip
13.80SFr) available. Buy tickets at the quai or on board. Eurail and SwissPass valid.

Bike Rental: At the baggage check in the station. 30SFr per day, 23SFr per half-day;
6SFr charge to return bikes to other stations (including Aigle, Martigny, and Sion) by
prior arrangement. Open 7:30am-8pm. AmEx/MC/V.

✴ 🛈 ORIENTATION & PRACTICAL INFORMATION

Montreux and its surroundings rise rapidly from the eastern shores of Lac Léman to the edge of the Alps at Les-Roches-de-Naye Jardin. The train station is within walking distance of most sights. Hiking up r. du Marché leads to the *vieille ville*.

Tourist Office: pl. du Débarcadère (☎962 84 84; www.montreux.ch). Descend the stairs opposite the station and head left on Grand Rue for 5-10min.; the office is on the right, by the water. The harried staff shares the office with desks for festival tickets and bus and train information. Free hotel reservation service within Montreux. They offer 2 free maps. Open mid-June to mid-Sept. M-F 9:30am-6pm, Sa-Su 10am-5pm; late Sept. to early June M-F 8:30am-5pm, Sa-Su 10am-3pm.

Budget Travel: STA Travel, ave. des Alpes 25 (☎965 10 15; fax 10 19). Open M-F 9am-noon and 1:30-6pm. AmEx/MC.

Currency Exchange: No commission at the station. **Western Union** does transfers and credit card advances. Open 6:30am-8:45pm. **Banks** in Montreux are open M-F 8:30am-4:30pm. Some close for lunch, but the one by the station does not.

Luggage Storage: At the station. Lockers 4-7SFr, open 5:50am-8:45pm. Luggage watch 7SFr per bag. Open daily 6:30am-8:15pm.

Bookstore: Payot Libraire, ave. du Casino 42 (☎963 06 07). Friendly staff helps you search a multilingual stock. Open M-F 9am-6:30pm, Sa 9am-5pm. AmEx/DC/MC/V.

Laundromat: Salon-Lavoir, r. Industrielle 30. Open M-Sa 7am-7pm. 5SFr per load.

Emergencies: Police, ☎117. **Fire,** ☎118. **Ambulance,** ☎144. **Hospital,** ☎966 66 66.

Late-Night Pharmacy: ☎962 77 00.

Internet Access: Internet@Place, Grand Rue 114 (☎966 02 80). 15SFr per hr. includes soft drink. Open M-Sa 10am-8pm.

Post Office: ave. des Alpes 70. Exit the station, turn left. Poste Restante: Montreux 1, CH-1820 Montreux. Open M-F 7:30am-6pm, Sa 8am-noon. **Postal Code:** CH-1820.

🏠 ACCOMMODATIONS & CAMPING

Cheap rooms are scarce in Montreux and almost nonexistent during the jazz festival. Hotels and hostels are often full before May. Revelers frequently stash their bags in the train station lockers and crash on the lakefront, but the police will move lakeside sleepers out at 7am. Ask at the tourist office for the lists of *Pensions et Petits Hôtels* or studio apartments available during the festival. If you still can't find a room, try the hostel in Vevey (see p. 517; free shuttles to and from the festival) or in Gryon (see p. 522). Otherwise, take bus #1 to "Villeneuve," 5km away, to a handful of budget hotels, or commute from Lausanne or Martigny.

Auberge de Jeunesse Montreux (HI), passage de l'Auberge 8 (☎963 49 34; fax 27 29). Take bus #1 on Grand Rue (dir.: Villeneuve) to "Territet." Head up the street, take 1st right (r. du Bocherex), and go down the stairs (passage de l'Auberge); or walk 20min. along the lake past the Montreux Tennis Club. This modern hostel offers many conveniences, including a dining room, TV, and waterfront location, though it's far from Montreux proper. Light sleepers beware: train tracks run nearby. Wheelchair-accessible. Breakfast included. Dinner 12.50SFr. Lockers 2SFr deposit. Sheets included. Free parking nearby. Reception 7:30-10am and 5-10pm. Check-out 10am. Doors lock at 10pm but guests have access. Closed mid-Nov. to mid-Feb. 112 beds in 6- or 8-bed dorms. Dorms 30.50SFr; doubles 40SFr, with bathroom 42SFr. Non-members add 6SFr. AmEx/DC/MC/V. ❷

Hôtel Pension Wilhelm, r. du Marché 13-15 (☎963 14 31; hotel.wilhelm@span.ch). From the station, take a left at ave. des Alpes, walk up 3min. and take a left onto r. du Marché, uphill past the police station. Perched high above the nightlife of the waterfront in the *vieille ville,* you'll find a quiet, clean room and an accommodating staff. The Pension is a great place to relax and is a short walk from *Les Plances.* Breakfast included. Reception 7am-10pm. Closed Oct.-Feb. Singles 60SFr, with shower 70SFr; doubles 100SFr/120SFr. Cash or traveler's checks only. ❸

Hôtel du Pont, r. du Pont 12 (☎/fax 963 22 49), at the top of the *vieille ville.* From the station, go left on ave. des Alpes (3min.) and then left up r. du Marché. Continue uphill until it becomes r. du Pont; the hotel is on the left (enter through the café). Bright, large rooms with bathrooms and TVs, though it's a long trek to town. The distance may not be a bad thing, however; the trip comes with some views and some peace-and-quiet. Breakfast included. Dinner 18-25SFr. Reception M 7am-3pm, Tu-F 7am-midnight, Sa-Su 8:30am-midnight. Singles 70SFr; doubles 130SFr. Extra bed 40SFr. AmEx/MC/V. ❸

Hotel Helvetie, ave. du Casino 32 (☎966 77 77; www.montreux.ch/helvetie). From Grand Rue, take bus #1 (dir.: Villeneuve) to "Montreux." Rooms with TV, phone, and minibar located only a block from the casino. Private parking. Wheelchair-accessible. **Internet** 4SFr per 15min., 12SFr per hr. Breakfast included. Reception 24hr. Check-out noon. Singles 120-200SFr; doubles 160-250SFr. Children receive a discount when sharing a room with an adult: 0-6yrs. 50%, 6-12 yrs. 30%.❹

🍴 FOOD

Montreux is pricey and most establishments are well touristed. Markets with good prices abound on the Grand Rue and ave. de Casino. **Marché de Montreux,** pl. du Marché, is an outdoor food and flea market. (F 7am-1pm.) There's a **Co-op** at Grand Rue 80 (open M-F 8am-12:15pm and 2-6:30pm, Sa 8am-5pm), and numerous kebab stands lining the waterfront.

L'Odyssée Café, ave. des Alpes 17bis (☎961 38 46). Exiting the station, turn left on ave. Odes Alpes; walk for about 3-5min. Cheap café fare off a main road. Sandwiches 4.50-6.50SFr. Omelettes 7.50-12SFr. Daily *Menüs* 14.50SFr. Open M-F 7am-5pm. ❶

La Rouvenaz, r. du Marche, just off Grand Rue. This compact restaurant serves relatively cheap Italian food for a place with a lake view. Pizzas from 14SFr. Reasonably priced hotel rooms upstairs. MC/V. ❷

Babette's, Grand Rue 60 (☎963 77 96), downstairs from the station to the left. This casual restaurant serves crêpes of all types for lunch (11-14SFr) and dessert (7-10SFr). Has great location, but limited seating. Sandwiches to go 6-15SFr. Open daily 7am-7pm. ❷

La Locanda, ave. du Casino 44 (☎963 29 33), is a small restaurant with decor that works hard to be cozy. Large pizzas 15-21SFr. Salads 7-19SFr. Open M-Tu and Th-Sa 11:30am-3pm and 6:30pm-midnight, W 6:30pm-midnight. AmEx/MC/V. ❸

👁 SIGHTS

If you plan to visit more than three area museums, consider purchasing the Montreux-Vevey Museum passport (15SFr), available at the tourist office. The **Château de Chillon** is not only the main sightseeing draw in Montreux, but also one of Switzerland's most visited attractions. Take the CGN ferry from the quai de Débarcadère (13.80SFr round-trip) or bus #1 to "Chillon" from anywhere on Grand Rue or ave. de Casino (2.80SFr, ages 6-20 2SFr). Built on an island in the 13th century, Chillon is a fortress with all the comforts of any happy home:

prison cells, a torture chamber, an armory, and boobytraps to fend off attackers who get past the moat. From the dungeon comes the disturbing story of François de Bonivard, a priest who spent four years chained to a dungeon pillar in the 16th century for aiding the Reformation; he was freed in 1536 by Protestant soldiers who seized Montreux from the Catholic Duke of Savoy. Bonivard's captivity inspired Rousseau, Victor Hugo, and Lord Byron. Byron's poem "The Prisoner of Chillon" tells a romanticized version of Bonivard's plight. In the chateau you can see where Byron etched his name into a pillar, presumably to empathize with poor François. (☎966 89 10; www.chillon.ch. Open daily Apr.-Sept. 9am-6pm; Mar. and Oct. 9:30am-5pm; Nov.-Feb. 10am-4pm. 9SFr, students/seniors 7SFr, ages 6-16 4.5SFr, families 22SFr.)

From the museum, the *vieille ville* is just a few minutes up the r. du Pont. A refreshing world away from the bustle of the waterfront, the r. de Temple offers pure views and a quiet walk to the stone **Église de Montreux.** The **Musée du Vieux-Montreux,** r. de la Gare 40, on the outskirts of the *vieille ville*, chronicles Montreux's history from Roman times through its "colonization" by the resort industry in the late 19th century. The museum is a local-history buff's dream and has exhibits on everything from ancient local coins to a room filled with hundreds of thimbles. The list of the city's "illustrious guests" from over the years is also interesting. (☎963 13 53. Open Apr.-Oct. daily 10am-noon and 2-5pm. 6SFr, students and seniors 4SFr, under 17 free.)

🎵 ENTERTAINMENT

The **Montreux Jazz Festival** is world-famous for the exceptional musical talent it draws, and as one of the biggest parties in Europe. Starting the first Friday in July, everything in town is pushed aside for 15 days, and concerts occur practically nonstop. Past headliners have included B.B. King and Paul Simon. Demand has sent ticket prices into the stratosphere: individual tickets range from 79-119SFr. Standing room tickets run 49-79SFr. Write to the tourist office well ahead of time for information and tickets. The easiest way to purchase tickets in advance is at www.montreuxjazz.com. The **jazz hotline** in Montreux, run by the **Jazz Boutique** ticket sellers at Grand Rue 62, is active from mid-March through the summer (☎966 44 36). In Switzerland, buy tickets from **Ticket Corner** (☎848 80 08 00) and at the **Congress Center** in Montreux or visit www.montreuxjazz.com. Many events sell out before July, some as early as January. If you can find a room but no tickets, come anyway for the **Jazz Off,** 500hr. of free, open-air concerts by new bands and established musicians. The temporary **Jazz Café** near the mainstage is free for fans to spend entire nights partying.

From late August to mid-September, the **Montreux Voice and Music Festival** takes over with operas, symphonies, and classical recitals performed by musicians from as far away as Moscow and Memphis. Tickets to concerts in Montreux and Chillon range from 10SFr (student tickets) to 160 SFr (big names). Contact the **Office of the Classical Music Festival,** left of the Casino, at r. du Théâtre 5, 1st Floor, Case Postale 353, CH-1820 Montreux 2. (☎966 80 25; www.montreux-festival.com. Office open M-F 10am-1pm and 2-7pm, Sa 10am-1pm. Open for extended hours 2 or 3 weeks before the festival.)

🎭 NIGHTLIFE

Montreux caters to all tastes and personalities, from carefree campers to five-star fops. Don't worry about finding "the place to be" in this town—if you're by the water, especially in early July, you're there.

Casino de Montreux, r. du Théâtre 9 (☎962 83 83). From ave. du Casino, turn on r. Igor Stravinsky toward the lake. The newly renovated casino draws mobs to a ritzy interior and flashy slot machines. The charm of the original 1881 establishment (which helped launch the careers of Stravinsky and fellow composer Ernest Ansemet) is largely gone, but it's worth stopping by to cap off a day with video poker (M-Th 3pm-3am, F 3pm-4am, Sa-Su noon-4am) and *boule* (daily from 8:30pm). Closed for renovations; reopens Jan. 2003. 18+; bring your passport.

Rock Café, r. de l'Auberge 5 (☎963 88 88), up the stairs from the youth hostel. Its name and guitar-art may aspire to imitate the Hard Rock, but this neighborhood bar can't escape its more down-to-earth, grungy style. Loud music, young crowd, billiard room, video games, darts, and pinball. Convenient if you're staying in the Auberge du Jeunesse, but a trifle far from the rest of town. Beer 6SFr per pint; choose among bottles from 8 countries. Open Su-Th 5pm-midnight, F-Sa 5pm-2am. AmEx/DC/V.

The White Horse Pub, Grand Rue 28 (☎963 15 92). A sign on the door declares this an "authentic" English pub, but you won't find anything authentically English (unless crêpes and *caipirinhas* have become English cuisine). What you'll more likely find is a friendly, Francophone crowd watching sports on the multiple TVs. Sandwiches 7-9.50SFr. Fish and chips 15.50SFr. Pizza 11SFr. Beer 6.20-9.50SFr per pint. Pinball, darts, foosball, and arcade games in back. Open M-F 11am-1am, Sa 11am-2am, Su 3pm-midnight.

VEVEY   ☎021

The upside to its 20th-century decline is that Vevey has avoided the five-star stratification and crowding of nearby Montreux. As a result, it has a distinctly more local feel. Vevey experienced its heyday as a resort town back in the 19th century, when hordes of upper-class English made it a virtual colony of the Queen's empire, placing it in countless novels of society. Charlie Chaplin fled here from McCarthyism in 1953, and Jean-Jacques Rousseau, Victor Hugo, Fyodor Dostoyevsky, Henry James, Le Corbusier, and Graham Greene have all worked within Vevey's borders. The town remains handsome and well preserved, its central location along the shore of Lac Léman making it an ideal base for trips to neighboring Lausanne and Montreux.

▐▐ TRANSPORTATION & PRACTICAL INFORMATION

There are three ways to reach Vevey from Montreux: by **bus** #1 to "Vevey" (20min.; every 10min.; 2.80SFr, children 2SFr); **train** (5min., every 15-30min., 3SFr); or **boat** (20min., 5 per day, 9.20SFr). To get to the **tourist office** (Grand-Place 29) from the station, cross pl. de la Gare, go past ave. de la Gare, and turn left onto ave. Paul Cérésole. At the end of the road, cut across the parking lot toward the columned arcade; the office is inside. (☎962 84 74; www.montreux-vevey.com.) Open from late June to late Aug. M-F 9am-5:30pm, Sa 9am-6pm, from Sept. to mid-June M-F 8:30am-noon and 1:30-6pm, Sa 9:30am-noon.) **Lockers** (4-7SFr) and **bike rental** (open 7:30am-7:30pm; 30SFr, children 25SFr, 23SFr/18SFr per half-day) are available at the train station. **Internet** (12SFr per hr.) is available at **Cyberworld,** r. de Torrent 4/6. (☎923 78 33. Open daily 1pm-midnight.) In an **emergency,** call ☎117; **fire,** ☎118; **ambulance,** ☎144. The **post office** is across pl. de la Gare (open M-F 7:30am-6pm, Sa 8:30am-noon) and has a 24hr. **ATM. Postal code:** CH-1800.

▐▐ ACCOMMODATIONS & FOOD

Overlooking Grand-Place just off the waterfront is the ▨**Riviera Lodge ❷,** pl. du Marché 5. Head straight out of the station on the main road to the open square on the waterfront; the hostel is on the right, with 60 beds in bright, shiny rooms and modern, lavish facilities. The service here is unparalleled: be prepared for the deluge of information and advice on things to do in the region as soon as you check in. The reception desk shares the 4th floor with a terrace and is manned by owner François and his multilingual staff. Guests receive a pass for discounts and free activities in the Montreux-Vevey region, such as a ride up the Vevey funicular and free waterskiing. (☎923 80 40; www.rivieralodge.ch. Spotless kitchen. **Internet** 3SFr per 15min; 7SFr per hr. Sheets 5SFr. Laundry up to 7SFr. Reception 8am-noon and 5-8pm, extended during summer season. Call if arriving late. 4-, 6-, or 8-bed dorms 24SFr; doubles 80SFr. MC/V.)

Many family homes also house travelers; one is **Pension Bürgle ❸,** r. Louis-Meyer 16, off Grand-Place. Take the first right after the hostel; the Pension is on the right. The rooms, though old, are large; many have balconies and TVs. Pension Bürgle is also the area's only "green" hotel with wood and solar-power supplied heat. (☎/fax 921 40 23; www.vevey.ch/tourisme/pension-burgle.htm. Breakfast included. Dinner 12SFr. Hallway bathrooms and showers. Reception 7am-11pm. Reserve with 1st-night payment. 42SFr per person. MC/V.)

For cheap, fresh food, check out the comprehensive and bustling **produce** (and **flea**) **market** at Grand-Place (pl. du Marché; Tu and Sa 8:30am-noon). Do-it-yourself fare is available at **Migros** (open M 9am-6:30pm, Tu-W and F 8am-6:30pm, Th 8am-8pm, Sa 7:30am-5pm; restaurant opens 30min. earlier M-F) and the **Co-op** (same hours), across ave. Paul Cérésole off Grand-Place. Café-restaurants with *Menüs* for around 12-15SFr line Grand-Place, and various snack-huts line the lake-front quai's, but food is cheaper away from the lakefront. An **Aperto** stands next to the train station (open 6am-9:30pm).

🏛 MUSEUMS

Though not as thrilling as Montreux's Château de Chillon, the museums of Vevey are distinctive and well curated. For an excellent deal, pick up a **Montreux-Vevey Museum Passport** (15SFr), which grants entrance to eight museums in the two towns. Many of Vevey's museums can be reached via an eastward stroll along the lake toward the neighboring town of Tour-de-Peilz.

Musée Jenisch, ave. de la Gare 2(turn left onto ave. de la Gare after exiting the station and walk a block, on the left), displays well-constructed, temporary exhibits, filled with paintings and sketches by both well- and lesser-known artists, as well as a room of spontaneous watercolors and pastels by adopted citizen Oskar Kokoschka, who lived in nearby Villeneuve for his last 25 years. (☎921 29 50. Tours available. Open Mar.-Oct. Tu-Su 11am-5:30pm; Nov.-Feb. 2-5:30pm. 15SFr, seniors 12SFr, students 6SFr.)

The **Swiss Museum of Games,** at the end of Quai Roussy in the 13th-century Savoy Château de la Tour-de-Peilzs, is a shrine to the twin ideals of skill and luck. The Museum opens with "*jeu?*" ("game?") and though it never fully answers the question, it certainly shows you a lot of games. It houses a display of chess pieces, cardboard Cold War games, and Nintendo. Multilingual exhibits wax philosophical on the sociology of games (calling flirtation a game along with cow-tipping in rural America), but it's more fun just to play with the toys. (☎944 40 50. Open Mar.-Oct. 10:30am-noon and 2-5:30pm, Nov.-Feb. Tu-Su 2-5pm. 6SFr, students and seniors 3SFr, under 16 2.50SFr, free when accompanied by an adult. Tours 10SFr, students and seniors 7SFr, under 16 5SFr.)

The **Nestlé Alimentarium/Food Museum,** on the corner of r. du Léman and quai Perdonnet, three blocks from Grande Place, tells the story of food, from production to processing in the human body. Nestlé advertisements, an interactive kitchen, a 3D adventure through the digestive tract, and human-sized hamster wheels are some of the highlights of this child-friendly museum. A cafeteria featuring an international menu rotated every month or so (lunch 12SFr) is worth a taste. (☎924 41 11. Open Tu-Su 10am-6pm. 10SFr, students and seniors 8SFr, ages 6-16 free. Lockers for bags mandatory but free, 2SFr deposit.)

The **Swiss Camera Museum,** on ruelle des Anciens-Fossés 6, near the tourist office, features five floors filled with historic photographic equipment from daguerreotypes to early spy cameras and modern digital cameras. Though there are several hands-on exhibits, most displays are behind glass and only in French. The museum ends with several temporary exhibitions of photographs. (☎925 21 40. Open Mar.-Oct. Tu-Su 11am-5:30pm; Nov.-Feb. Tu-Su 2-5:30pm. 6SFr, students 4SFr, children free. Group tours 50SFr by appointment.)

NIGHTLIFE & ENTERTAINMENT

Nightlife options are slim in Vevey. If you're in the mood for a little craziness, head to nearby Montreux. In Vevey, right behind the Riviera Lodge at r. de Torrent 9, the **National** offers quiet meals (from 19SFr) and beers (from 3SFr) among funky decorations on a romantic candlelit terrace. (Open M-Th 11am-midnight, F-Sa 11am-2am, Su 4pm-midnight.) Across the street from the National at r. de Torrent 4-6 lies **Vertigo,** where drinks are served in a fashionable bar atmosphere.

The **Folklore Market** in pl. du Marché (open July-Aug.) allows sampling of all the local wine you can hold for only the price of the first glass, sometimes as low as 4SFr. Year-round, the **Winetrain** winds its way through 8km of villages and vineyards in Lavaux (every hr. from Vevey station 5:58am-10:08pm; take the "Puidoux-Chexbres" train; round-trip up to 10.40SFr, SwissPass and Eurail valid). The tourist office has a list of tasting venues, a map with directions to the wine centers, and a guide to six nearby hiking tours.

The summertime **International Comedy Film Festival,** dedicated to former resident Charlie Chaplin, features competitions by day and more accessible screenings by night. The **Theatre of Vevey,** r. de Théâtre 4 (☎923 60 55), produces live theater.

LES DIABLERETS ☎024

Drawing its name from *Quille du Diable*, the tower-shaped rock that looms over the town, Les Diablerets challenges the notion that evil spirits still lurk in the mountains above. Multiple paths throughout the rocky landscape and a skiable glacier welcome hikers, skiers, snowboarders, and adventure seekers year-round. In the early summer, the town is filled mainly with locals, but as July and August arrive, summer-skiing and extreme sports fill the village with vacationers. Come winter, the town (pop. 1300) holds its own the snootier stylings of local rivals Gstaad, Crans-Montana, and Verbier. A younger, more sports-driven crowd is the result.

TRANSPORTATION

Three public transport services connect Les Diablerets to the rest of Switzerland: the **train** down to Aigle (50min., every hr. 6:27am-9:28pm, 10.40SFr); the **Post Bus** over the mountains to Gstaad (via the Col du Pillon, summer 5 per day 9:39am-5:09pm, 12.40 SFr) or to Leysin (via train to Le Sepey; summer 10per day 6:27am-5:28pm, only 2 on weekends; 9SFr); and the **BVB bus** to the mountain town of Villars (via Col de la Croix, 35min., July 1-Sept. 16, 3 per day 10am-5pm, 11.40SFr).

GENEVA

Local buses provide access to the Diablerets glacier **cable cars,** which travel to Cabane (one-way 21SFr, round-trip 30SFr) and the glacier (34SFr, round-trip 49SFr). The first bus leaves at 9:39am and the last returns at 4:46pm. Plan accordingly or be ready for a 45min. walk. Train station attendants will watch your **luggage** in the small ticket room free of charge.

🖉 PRACTICAL INFORMATION

The **tourist office,** to the right of the station on r. de la Gare, publishes an impressive range of literature, including a list of activities. (☎/fax 492 33 58; www.diablerets.ch. Open July 7-Aug. 24 and mid-Dec. to Apr. 8:30am-6:30pm; May-June and Sept.-Nov. M-Sa 8:30am-12:30pm and 2-6pm, Su 9am-12:30pm.) Local services include **taxis,** ☎079 205 05 55; **emergencies,** ☎144; **ambulance,** ☎494 50 30; **police,** ☎492 24 88. **Internet access** at La Diabletine bar and tea room (☎492 13 55, 3SFr per 15min; open daily 8am-10pm); and **post office,** right of the train station (open M-F 8am-noon and 2:30-6pm, Sa 8-11am). **Postal code:** CH-1865.

> **WHAT'S IN A NAME?** Situated between the beautiful pastures of Anzeindaz and the green Vallée des Ormonts, the summit of Les Diablerets is said to have once hosted comparably lush fields. But according to local legend, the area has been barren and dangerous ever since the fated day a mean-spirited shepherd refused the mountain's benevolent aid. As a punishment, the mountain transformed the flowery pastures into the sea of solid glacier that still looms today. The shepherds who had brought their cattle to the area left, and the mountain became a playground for evil spirits. The valley people swore they heard spirits playing games, or "skittles," with the rocks high above. The rock tower at the southern end of the glacier became known as *Quille Du Diable* (Devil's Skittle), while the town adopted the name Les Diablerets.

🖉 ACCOMMODATIONS

The cheapest accommodations are on the outskirts of town.

Les Lilas, rte. du Col du Pillon (☎492 31 34; fax 31 57). Left out of the train station, after passing the Co-op, turn right on rte. du Pillon; Les Lilas will be on your left. Les Lilas sits above a restaurant and has a dim atmosphere created by the dark wood and low lighting, but the rooms themselves are well-kept and clean. Mid-sized double rooms come with full bathroom and TV, and most have balconies that offer beautiful views of the surrounding mountains. Breakfast included. Checkout 11am. Singles 85-90SFr; without bathroom 45SFr; doubles 115-150SFr. AmEx/Mc/V. ❹

Hotel Mon Abri, (☎492 34 81; www.monabri.ch), is on the rte. du Pillon past the Co-op. Mon Abri continues to be a mecca for hard-core snowboarders and skateboarders. In the summer Mon Abri hosts a massive skateboard camp to which young enthusiasts from all over Europe flock *en masse,* and in the months of Oct. and Nov. it offers snowboard rentals for top-of-the-line test gear. Other amenities include laundry (3SFr per kg), **free Internet,** a weekend bar and **disco,** beach volleyball courts, and **bike** rental in summer. Reservations recommended in high-season (July, Aug., Dec., Jan., Feb., March and Apr.). 48SFr per person; children 28SFr. Low season (May, June, Sept., Oct. and Nov.) 42SFr/20SFr. Dormitories 28SFr. ❸

Les Diablotins, rte. du Pillon, (☎492 36 33; www.diablotins.ch) is a big modern block popular with young snowboarding groups. From the station, turn right, bend left around the hairpin turn, and turn left along rte du Pillon at the top of the hill. Avoid the 30min.

uphill walk by calling from the station; the hostel will send a minibus. The 2- to 5-bed rooms are in good shape (all have private sinks and most have balconies) in spite of the thousands of schoolkids who tramp through the halls and shared showers each year. This mammoth institution has 4 dining halls, several lounges, a bar, and a **disco**—all segregated by age and noise-tolerance level. Breakfast included. Dinner 16SFr. Reception 8am-8pm. Reserve one week ahead in winter. Jan. 6-Jan. 17 54SFr, under 18 38SFr; Jan. 18-Feb. 7 60SFr/38SFr; Feb. 8-Apr. 3 64SFr/41SFr; Apr. 4-Dec. 25 35SFr/33SFr; Dec. 26-Jan. 5 67SFr/41SFr. Children under 16 30-50% discount. AmEx/MC/V. ❸

Camping La Murée, (☎079 401 99 15 camp.lamuree@swissfree.ch). Take the Aigle train one stop to "Vers l'Eglise," go left past the post office and church, and cross the railroad tracks to set up camp among the many RVs at this quiet site in a tiny valley town. Showers included. Reception 6-7pm. 4.80SFr per person in summer; 5.30SFr in winter. Summer 9SFr per car; winter 10SFr. Summer tents 9SFr; winter 10SFr. ❶

FOOD

Left at the intersection of r. de la Gare and rte. de Colde la Croix, or up the path behind the tourist office, **Pizzeria Locanda Livia** ❷ serves 24 kinds (15-20SFr, 2SFr less for miniature version), including a 4-cheese pizza with gruyère called *rêve de souris* (mouse's dream). Chinese food also available in the evening. (☎492 32 80. Open M-Tu and Th-Su 11:30am-2pm and 6:30-10pm. AmEx/DC/MC/V.) At **Le Muguet** ❶, on the right past the tourist office, try a dessert crêpe (5-9.50SFr) with *chocolat viennois* (4SFr), a dish of *crême de chantilly* (1.50SFr), or their sandwiches (3.50-8.50SFr) and tea or beer. (☎492 26 42. Open 6:30am-7pm; food until 5pm. MC/V.) For easy access to the good food, ask about renting the apartment upstairs (☎/fax 492 26 43; min. 1 week.) The **Co-op,** left on r. de la Gare from the station, is the perfect place to stock up on cheap cheese, wine, and bread. (Open M-F 8am-12:15pm and 2:30-6:30pm, Sa 8am-12:30pm and 2-5pm.)

OUTDOOR ACTIVITIES

SKIING. Les Diablerets' year-round skiing got better in 1999 with the completion of a **cable car,** which travels from the Col du Pillon above the village to Cabane, then to the glacier at Scex-Rouge. Diablerets day passes (39SFr), combined Diablerets/Villars passes (46SFr), Alpes Vaudoises transportation and lift passes (52SFr), and other **ski passes** are sold at the cable car's departure point. Book special hotel deals that include stay-and-ski passes, a fondue evening, tobogganing, curling, skating, and babysitting services at the tourist office. **Jacky Sports,** near the tourist office, rents **ski equipment.** (☎492 32 18; www.jackysport.ch. Open June and Oct.-Nov. 9am-noon and 2-6pm daily; closing times extended 30min. July 1-Sept. 9; Dec.-Apr. 8:30am-6:30pm. Skis and snowboards 28-50SFr per day, boots 15-19SFr; special rates for multi-day rentals. AmEx/DC/MC/V.) **Holiday Sport,** across from the tourist office, is another rental option (☎492 37 17; per day, skis 28-50SFr, boots 9-15SFr; snowboards 38SFr, boots 15-19SFr.) The **ski and snowboard school,** in the tourist office, can prepare you for the slopes. (☎492 20 02; www.diablerets.ch, 6 half-days 142SFr.) The **New Devil School of Snowboarding** can get the inexperienced ready for the mountains. (☎492 34 31 or 079 412 62 40. Open daily 8:30am-6:30pm. 2hr. lesson 44SFr.)

THE BIG SPLURGE

ROUGHING IT

If you feel the call to hike in the Alps, but the idea of living on power bars makes you queasy, never fear: Switzerland is a country in which rugged views can be had without forsaking creature comforts. Matt Tomlin's **Swiss Adventure Hike**, run out of the Swiss Alps Retreat in Gryon, treats gourmet-inclined hikers to a well-guided two-day sojourn in the Alps, and greases the trip with fabulous food and the promise of a hot bath at the end.

Guided by Monsieur Tomlin, an athletic American expatriate who came to Switzerland following the 1997 Tour de France, the first day of hiking leads to a traditional Alpine hut with views of Mt. Blanc and the Matterhorn. At night, courtesy of Monsieur Tomlin, you indulge in all the fondue, Swiss wine and chocolate that you can bear while watching the sun set over the surrounding snow- and granite-capped peaks. The next day, you head up the gorgeous Dantmarlces (3000m). The trip ends with a descent down along a river to thermal pools where you can ease your bloated stomach and tired legs with a long, soothing soak in the warmth and comfort of geothermally heated mineral water.

(Sign up at the reception desk of the Swiss Alps Retreat in Gryon. ☎ 02 44 98 33 21. www.gryon.com. Hikes leave weekly between mid-June and early October.)

HIKING & BIKING. Jacky Sports and Holiday Sports also rent **mountain bikes**. (Jacky: 35SFr per day, 5 days 110SFr; Holiday: 35-45SFr, 5 days 135-145SFr.) A good hike that can be done in several segments, depending on stamina, starts at the tourist office. Turn right across the river at the pharmacy, then right again so that you are facing the Sommet des Diablerets (3209m) and the glacier. The sides of the valley close in as the level riverside walk progresses and deposits you on the stage of a rugged 200m high amphitheater at **Creux de Champ**. (1hr., 160m ascent.) The path starts to climb steeply up the sides to the **Refuge de Pierredar** at 2278m. (3hr. above Les Diablerets, 1110m ascent.) The agile can then push up to **Scex Rouge** (2971m), the cable car terminus on the glacier, which affords an unforgettable alpine view. (1 day, high summer and perfect weather only; guide recommended for later sections of the hike.)

ADVENTURE SPORTS. Les Diablerets' adventure sports awaken the death wish within. **Mountain Evasion** (a perplexing misnomer) organizes **canyoning** (80-165SFr), **snow-shoeing** (25-70SFr), **rappeling** (85SFr), and **dirt biking** (35-70SFr), not to mention **luging** for 18SFr, or 36SFr for a nighttime descent with fondue. (☎ 492 12 32; fax 22 67.) Their office is in a little wooden shack along the river. Turn left across the river by the Co-op and the shack is on the right. (Open daily 8:30am-11:30am, 1:30pm-4:30pm, but best to call ahead. MC.) Left from the train station and past the post office along r. de la Gare, **Centre ParAdventure** offers **paragliding** (90-150SFr), **canyoning** (80SFr), and the new **Arapaho mud bike** (40SFr). (☎ 492 23 82 or 079 435 25 82; www.swissaventure.ch. Open daily 9-9:30am and 5:30-6:30pm. MC/V.)

GRYON ☎ 024

The tiny town of Gryon has experienced a population boom in recent years—from 800 to 1000. Rather than risk a greater unemployment rate, the proud locals have an ordinance which allows only one child from each family to stay in the town. The kids have a tendency to come back, though, drawn to Gryon's virtually untouched, tranquil mountain setting within reach of the Dents du Midi and the Les Diablerets glacier. Its main draw for world-weary travelers is undoubtedly its popular hostel, the ◪**Swiss Alps Retreat ❷**, housed in the Chalet Martin. From the station, follow the train tracks uphill; you'll see backpacker signs to your left. A gem even among Swiss hostels, the Swiss Alps Retreat has taken the "hostel" concept back to its roots and improved it with a hipper twist. New arrivals are immediately sucked into a bohemian, barefoot, Anglophone-with-any-accent backpacker community. Owners Bertrand and Robyn (along with a super-friendly young staff) provide backpackers a temporary family and activities from hiking to chocolate tasting. Happy to "take a vacation from their vacation," travelers passing through Gryon have been known to stay long and return often. In the nine years it took for the hostel to grow from four beds to 87, 10 couples who met at the Chalet Martin have gotten married. Amenities include discounted **ski rentals, Internet** access (10SFr per hr.), and **video/DVD rental** (2SFr/4SFr) from a small but entertaining collection. The main chalet features several homey common rooms, one of which provides a stereo and music for your listening pleasure, and funky wood-framed showers. Chalet Martin's real attraction, however, is its prime location for taking advantage of the outdoors. The hostel has daily sign-ups for **cheese farm tours, paragliding, thermal baths, guided overnight hikes,** and excursions (like a ski trip to Zermatt). They also lend maps to hikers and provide a 40% discount on ski rentals. (☎ 498 33 21; fax 35 31; www.gryon.com. Co-ed dorms and bathrooms. Large kitchen facilities available. Laundry 3-5SFr. For Christmas bookings check the web site. Check-in 9am-9pm. Call ahead. Dorms 18-25SFr; doubles 50-75SFr. Discounted prices for multiple night stays; 110SFr for full week. No credit cards.)

Reach Gryon by **cog railway** from Bex (30min.; every hr., last train 8:23pm; 5.80SFr, Eurail and SwissPass valid), which lies on the main rail line connecting the Lac Léman cities (Geneva, Lausanne, Montreux) to Aigle, Martigny, and Sion, or **by foot** from Villars (one stop farther on the cog rail; 45min. walk from the hostel). **Buses** connect to Villars, through Col de la Croix to Les Diablerets (35min., 3 per day 9:02am-4:20pm, 10.40SFr) and from there, a bus runs to Aigle (35min., every 1-2hr. 6:05am-7:45pm, 7.80SFr). The **tourist office,** in neighboring La Barboleuse, is uphill on the route de Villars, about 10min. from the hostel. (☎ 498 14 22; fax 26 22. Open M-Sa 8am-noon and 2-6pm, Su 9am-noon and 4-6pm.) To reach the **market** from the station, walk downhill on the road on the right instead of uphill (open M-F 7:30am-12:15pm and 2-6:30pm, Sa 7:30am-5pm, Su 8am-noon).

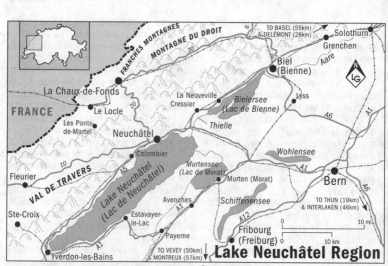

Lake Neuchâtel Region

LAKE NEUCHÂTEL REGION

Almost every town in the Lake Neuchâtel region can boast a sandy beach and clear view of the Jura mountains. As if this weren't enough, the region also produces some of the richest *Pinot noirs* and spritziest *Chasselas* of the country, a secret well kept by the Swiss. The good wine complements the easygoing spirit of the locals, who welcome tourists to their domain.

HIGHLIGHTS OF LAKE NEUCHÂTEL

Stroll through the lush vineyards of **Cressier** and sample the newest wine with fresh local cheese (see p. 528).

Weird yourself out at the eccentric **Château de Gruyères** (see p. 532).

Enjoy French-German fusion cuisine in the multilingual **Fribourg** (see p. 529).

NEUCHÂTEL   ☎ 032

Alexandre Dumas once said that Neuchâtel appeared to be carved out of butter, in reference to the unique yellow stone that characterizes many of the city's buildings. But the comment could easily be mistaken for a reference to the calorie-laden treats in local *pâtisseries*. Beyond tempting desserts, *Neuchâteloise* cuisine also prides itself on quality fondue, sausages, and fresh fish from the lake and nearby rivers. The town's winding streets exude historical charm and modern, student-oriented flair.

▊ TRANSPORTATION

Trains connect Neuchâtel to: Basel (1¾hr., every hr. 5:31am-10:24pm, 34SFr); Bern (45min., every hr. 5:15am-11:24pm, 17.20SFr); Fribourg via Ins-Murten (1hr., every hr. 5:34am-10:34pm, 18SFr); Geneva (1½hr., every hr. 5:57am-11:38pm, 35-40SFr);

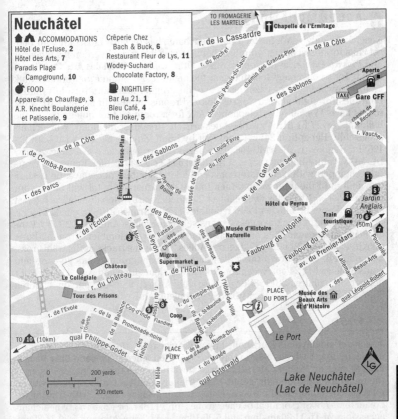

Neuchâtel

▲🏠 ACCOMMODATIONS
Hôtel de l'Ecluse, 2
Hôtel des Arts, 7
Paradis Plage
  Campground, 10

🍴 FOOD
Appareils de Chauffage, 3
A.R. Knecht Boulangerie
  et Patisserie, 9

Crêperie Chez
  Bach & Buck, 6
Restaurant Fleur de Lys, 11
Wodey-Suchard
  Chocolate Factory, 8

🍷 NIGHTLIFE
Bar Au 21, 1
Bleu Café, 4
The Joker, 5

and Interlaken via Bern (2hr., every hr. 6am-11:21pm, 38SFr). An underground **tram** called the *Fun'Ambule* travels from the bottom floor of the train station to the shore area, where you can catch **bus** #1 to the tourist office and Pl. Pury. **Ferries** provide service to Biel (2½hr., 3 per day, 27SFr) and Murten (1¾hr., 6 per day, 16.20SFr), departing from the Port de la Ville, just behind the post office (free with Eurail or SwissPass).

🔆 🛈 ORIENTATION & PRACTICAL INFORMATION

Neuchâtel centers on **place Pury**, a major square and the hub of every bus line. From pl. Pury, face the lake and walk two blocks to the left to find the **tourist office**, Hôtel des Postes (in the same building as the post office). City maps are free. Check out the *Terroir Neuchâtelois* guide for a listing of places that produce local goods. (☎889 68 90; www.ne.ch/tourism. Open July-Aug. M-F 9am-6:30pm, Sa 9am-4pm, Su 10am-4pm; Sept.-May M-F 9am-noon and 1:30-5:30pm, Sa 9am-noon.) The train station has **lockers** (4-6SFr) and **bike rental** (25SFr per day). Find **Internet** at **Shogun**, Faubourg du Lac 31. (☎721 21 01. 7SFr per hr.) **Police** ☎117, **hospital**, ☎722 91 11. The **post office** is open M-F 7:30am-6:30pm, Sa 8:30am-noon. **Postal code:** CH-2001.

☝ ACCOMMODATIONS

Neuchâtel's only youth hostel, Oasis Neuchâtel, has recently closed. If your budget calls for hostel prices, your best bet is to stay in nearby Yverdon-les-Bains, or find *Privatzimmer* at the tourist office. Otherwise, try **Hôtel des Arts ❹**, r. Pourtalès 3, for a convenient location near the nightlife. From the *Fun'ambule*, walk a block towards the city center on ave. du Premier-Mars and turn left onto r. Pourtalès for contemporary citrus-colored rooms filled with modern art. Most rooms have TVs, all have telephones. Ask for a room on the "quiet side" of the building. (☎727 61 61; www.hotel-des-arts.ch. Breakfast included. Wheelchair-accessible. Reception 24hr. Check-out by noon. Singles 87SFr, with bath 98-126SFr; doubles 112SFr/140-166SFr. 6-person apartments also available. AmEx/DC/MC/V.) Multi-themed rooms at the **Hotel de L'Ecluse ❺**, r. de L'Ecluse 24, come fully-equipped with clean bathrooms and a kitchenette. Follow ave. de la Gare downhill until the intersection, then follow the signs; the hotel will be on your right. (☎729 93 10; fax 93 20. Breakfast included. Nearby Globaline offers **Internet** access 7SFr per hr. Singles 135SFr; doubles 175SFr; triples 210SFr; quads 240SFr. Reductions for longer stays, less expensive on weekends. AmEx/DC/MC/V.) **Paradis Plage campground ❶** is on the lakefront in nearby Colombier. From pl. Pury, take tram #5 (dir.: Boudry) to "Bas des Allées." Cross the tracks at the tram crossing and walk 2min. down the gravel path. The campground rents go-carts and holds mail. (☎841 24 46. Reception 8:30am-9pm Mar.-June and Aug. 11-Oct. 9SFr per person, children 3SFr; 8SFr per site. July-Aug. 10 9SFr per person, children 3SFr; 15SFr per site. Electricity 3.50SFr per night. AmEx/D/MC/V.)

◘ FOOD

Neuchâtel may live off tourists in July and August, but the rest of the year it's a university town, which means there is cheap food aplenty. **Crêperie Chez Bach & Buck ❶**, ave. du Premier-Mars 22, across the street from the Jardin Anglais, near the underground tram exit, counters its friendly, laid-back atmosphere with an intensely detailed list of choices. Enjoy amazing sugar crêpes with fruit or ice cream for 3-7.80SFr, or meat or cheese ones for 6-11SFr. (☎725 63 53. Wheelchair-accessible. M-Th 11:30am-2pm and 5:30-10pm, F 11:30am-2pm and 5:30-11:30pm, Sa 11am-11:30pm, Su noon-10pm.) At **A.R. Knecht Boulangerie et Pâtisserie ❶**, situated on the corner of pl. des Halles and r. du Coq d'Inde, locals munch croissants stuffed with spiced ham (3SFr), fruit tarts (3.20-3.60SFr), and the *pain noix* (bread with nuts; 3.10SFr) while enjoying a vibrant atmosphere. (☎725 13 21. Open Tu-Sa 6am-6:30pm.) Further up the pl. des Halles, on r. des Moulins, the unassuming bistro **Appareils de Chauffage et de Cuisine ❸** serves a largely male clientele an affordable *plat du jour* for 16.50SFr. (☎721 43 96. Open M-Th 7am-1am, F 7am-2am, Sa 8am-2am, Su 7pm-1am.) This café is the main source of income for the **Centre d'Art Neuchâtel (CAN)** next door, an experimental art center. (☎724 01 60; www.can.ch/can.) Those desperately seeking Italian flavor should consider **Restaurant Fleur de Lys ❸**, on the second floor of r. de Bassinof off pl. Numa-Droz. *Fleur de Lys* offers over 50 kinds of pizza. (Pizzas 13.50-30SFr, pastas 16.50-21SFr. AmEx/D/MC/V.) Sample chocolates at the **Wodey-Suchard Chocolate Factory ❶**, r. du Seyon 5, directly behind the pl. Pury. (Open M 11am-6:30pm, Tu-F 6:30am-6:30pm, Sa 6:30am-5pm.) In the town center, **Migros**, r. de l'Hôpital 12, has groceries. (Open M-W 8am-7pm, Th 8am-9pm, F 7:30am-7pm, Sa 7:30am-7pm. MC/V.) Nearby, the **Co-op**, R. de la Treille 4, offers a similar selection. (Open M 1:15-6:30pm, Tu-W 8am-6:30pm, Th 8am-8pm, F 7:30am-6;30pm, Sa 7:30am-5pm.) There's an **Aperto** in the station. (☎721 20 41. Open daily 6am-10pm.)

◎ SIGHTS

Neuchâtel's cultural offerings are confined to an easily walkable area centering around pl. Pury. You can traverse the town in minutes, unless it happens to be the last weekend of September, when the three-day **Fête des Vendanges** (Wine Festival) occurs. On this weekend it can take hours to wade through throngs of carousers enjoying parades, jazz concerts, and wine feasts. A Swiss museum passport, available at many museums (30SFr), grants admission to most museums in Neuchâtel, La Chaux-de-Fonds, and neighbor La Locle.

THE OLD TOWN. The heart of town is the *vieille ville*, which is dominated by a cobblestone marketplace (pl. des Halles, one block to the right of pl. Pury) and home of the thrice-weekly market (T, Th, Sa 6:30am-noon). If you're up for meandering around town in a tourist train, hop aboard at the Jardin Anglais. (In English, French, and German, every 30min. after 2pm in the summer. 6SFr.)

CHURCHES, CASTLES, & DUNGEONS. From the pl. des Halles, turn left onto the r. de Chateau (marked by the red-faced clock, the **Tour de Piesse**) and climb the stairs on your right to reach both the **Collégiale** (a church) and the chateau which gives the town its name. Begun in the 12th century, construction of the church took so long that architectural styles changed from Romanesque to Gothic as it was built. The golden stars and blue skies of the vaulted ceiling arch harmoniously over stained-glass windows and faded wall murals that were reinstalled after the fervor of the Reformation died down. The garish **Cenotaph**, a sculptural composition of the Counts of Neuchâtel from 1372 on, all reverently looking skyward, was covered during the Reformation to prevent destruction and was recently restored. *(Open daily Oct.-Mar. 9am-6:30pm; Apr.-Sept. 9am-8pm. Concerts 6:30pm the last F of every mo. Free.)* Next door, the 12th-century **château** served as the seat of the Count of Neuchâtel during the Middle Ages. Look for splotches of red on the old outside walls, remnants of a fire in 1415 that literally baked the yellow stone. Today the bureaucrats of the cantonal government sit behind the striped shutters and flower boxes. A small garden connects the chateau to the **Tour des Prisons** (Prison Tower). The 125-step ascent allows you to examine the claustrophobia-inducing wooden cells used until 1848 and to enjoy a view from the top. *(On r. Jeanne-de-Hochberg. Open Apr.-Sept. 8am-6pm. 1SFr, coins only.)*

▨ MUSÉE D'HISTOIRE NATURELLE. The Musée d'Histoire Naturelle (Museum of Natural History) sits atop the r. des Terreaux, to the left off r. de l'Hôpital. This is a more innovative natural history museum than most, often featuring unconventional and hands-on exhibits about the Earth and its creatures. One exhibit is a digital experience that allows you to walk in scientists' footsteps to see how they discovered that crickets have memory. The museum also houses a fascinating room of illusions. *(R. des Terreaux 14. ☎717 79 60. Turn right from the pl. des Halles onto the Croix du Marché, which becomes r. de l'Hôpital. Open Tu-Su 10am-6pm. 6SFr, students 3SFr,)*

MUSÉE DE BEAUX ARTS ET D'HISTOIRE. The Musée de Beaux Arts et d'Histoire (Museum of Fine Arts and History) is an eclectic collection of paintings, weapons, and textiles telling the history of Neuchâtel, mostly in French. The curatorial staff gives presentations *(Tu 12:15pm)*. The uncanny 18th-century automatons created by Jacquet-Droz are the museum's pride and joy: two barefoot boys in velvet coats scribble away while a lady plays the harpsichord. Upstairs, the Art Nouveau cupola includes oil paintings (one of which portrays Neuchâtel as the "Intellectual Life"), stained glass, and sculpted angels that seem to fly out of the walls. *(From pl. des Halles, walk toward the lake and turn left onto esplanade Léopold-Robert 1.)*

☎ *717 79 20; fax 79 29. Wheelchair-accessible. Open Tu-Su 10am-6pm., from Easter to June 8 also M 10am-6pm. 7SFr, students 4SFr, under 16 free; free for everyone W. Automaton performances first Su of each month 2, 3, and 4pm.)*

OTHER SIGHTS. Further along r. de l'Hôpital, elegant gates and two alluring sphinxes invite a stroll into **Hotel du Peyrou,** which was once the home of Jean-Jacques Rousseau's friend and publisher Alexandre du Peyrou. Cheese enthusiasts can make a pilgrimage to the **Fromagerie Les Martel** (cheese factory) in neighboring Les Ponts-de-Martel for a tour and demonstration. *(Major Benoit 25, Les Ponts-de-Martel. 40min. bus ride from train station. ☎ 937 16 66. Open daily 8am-noon and 5-7pm. Free.)*

◆ NIGHTLIFE

A university crowd makes nightlife in Neuchâtel lively; the city is famous for its techno DJs. **The Joker,** Foubourg du Lac 14, has two dance clubs specializing in jungle music, with 3-5SFr beers. (☎ 724 48 48. Cover from 10SFr. Open F-Su 10pm-4am.) Just behind Joker is **Bar Au 21,** Faubourg de Lac 23. Nurture beers (2.20-7.80SFr) or long drinks (6-9SFr) under Pink Floyd posters or play foosball with a clientele younger than the bar's name suggests. (☎ 725 81 98. M-Th 7pm-1am, F 7pm-2am, Sa 5pm-2am, Su 5pm-1am.) A few doors down is the popular **Bleu Café.** You can catch a flick while enjoying a sandwich and drink for 20SFr. (Open M-Th 7:15pm-midnight, F 7:45pm-1am, Sa 4pm-1am, Su 4-9pm.)

◆ DAYTRIPS FROM NEUCHÂTEL

CRESSIER   ☎ 032

Trains run from Neuchâtel to Cressier, dir.: Biel (10min., every hr. 5:39am-11:22pm, 3.80SFr).

The sleepy medieval wine-making hamlet of Cressier is great for a daytrip. Built around a tiny château that houses the local government, the medieval village packs no less than seven **caves** (wine cellars) where friendly local vintners offer tours of their facilities and answer questions about grapes. The finale is *la dégustation,* sampling wines poured by the hands that make them. Choose from *chasselas, pinot noir,* or *l'oeil-de-perdrix,* or leave it to the expert *("Votre choix").*

Caves line the only main street. Of note is the particularly traditional and congenial *cave* of **Jean-Paul Ruedin,** rte. de Troub 4, around the corner from the train station. Jean-Paul is the 14th Ruedin son to operate the family vineyards since the first planted grapes in 1614. The *cave* Ruedin, whose white wine *(vin blanc)* has been honored by the *Gerle d'Or* (Golden Cellar) for several years, expresses a philosophical attitude towards the craft; the door declares, "*Aimer le vin c'est aimer la vie*" ("To love wine is to love life"). (☎ 757 11 51. Open Tu-F 8am-noon and 1:30-5:30pm, Sa 9-11:30am. Call in advance.)

Though sampling is encouraged, it is impolite not to buy afterwards. The cheapest bottles start around 9SFr; 4SFr more can buy a fresh baguette, cheese, and chocolate from the **Co-op** next to the church on r. Gustave Jeanneret. (Open M-Tu and Th-F 7:45am-12:15pm and 1:45-6:30pm, W 7:45am-12:15pm, Sa 7:45am-12:15pm and 1:30-4pm.) Take your bounty on a 10min. stroll into the vineyards for panoramic views of the valley by following yellow *tourisme pédestre* signs off r. de Chateau. A little extra effort brings you to tiny **Combe,** where the tinkling of cowbells accompanies the lake view.

FRIBOURG (FREIBURG)   ☎026

From the train station, modern Fribourg stretches out toward the river that surrounds the *vieille ville*. As the town runs down the hill toward the river, wide paved streets and concrete sidewalks lined by banks and businesses gradually meld into narrow cobblestones streets and alleyways lined by cafés and *pâtisseries*. Founded by the Zähringen dynasty in 1157, the *vieille ville* today exhibits beautiful and inspiring churches, monasteries, and convents, as well as views of the river and the chalky-white gorge that encircle the older part of town. Fribourg has a penchant for modern art, open-air shopping, and fine dining, but its most distinctive attractions stem from the quiet remnant of medieval religious fervor. Fribourg was an isolated bastion of Catholicism during the Reformation; even the local brew, Cardinal beer, celebrates a 19th-century bishop. Meanwhile, Fribourg bridges the Swiss linguistic divide: 30% of the population firmly count themselves *Freiburger;* the remaining 70% are *Fribourgeois*.

🚆🚌 TRANSPORTATION & PRACTICAL INFORMATION

Fribourg sits on the main rail line between Zurich and Geneva. **Trains** leave for: Basel (1¾hr., every 30min. 5:50am-11:16pm, 45SFr); Bern (25min., every 30min. 5:16am-12:16am, 12.40SFr); Interlaken (1½hr., every hr. 6:42am-9:46pm, 32SFr); Lausanne (50min., every 30min. 4:48am-11:47pm, 21SFr); and Neuchâtel (1hr., every hr. 4:33am-9:33pm, 18SFr). Fribourg's **tourist office** is at ave. de la Gare 1, 100m to the right of the station door. (☎350 11 11; www.fribourgtourism.ch. Open M-F 9am-6pm, Sa 9am-3pm; closed Oct.-May Sa afternoons.) **Exchange currency** at the train station (open 6am-8pm) or at one of many banks lining r. du Romont. Services at the station include: **lockers** (4-6SFr; open 5:10am-12:45am); **luggage watch** (7SFr per item; open M-F 7:30am-7:40pm, Sa-Su 8am-7:40pm); and **bike rental** (30SFr per day, with ID deposit). For a **taxi,** call ☎079 219 46 10. **Internet access** is available at **Cyber Atlantis,** r. de Lausanne 18. (8SFr per hr. Open M-Th 11am-6:30pm, F 11am-11pm, Sa 10am-11pm, Su 1-6pm.) The **post office,** ave. de Tivoli, is the skyscraper to the left of the station. (Open M-F 7:30am-6:30pm, Sa 8am-noon.) **Postal code:** CH-1700.

🏠 ACCOMMODATIONS

Auberge de Jeunesse (HI), r. de l'Hôpital 2 (☎323 19 16; fax 19 40). Head left out the train station on ave. de la Gare, which becomes r. de Romont; turn left onto r. de l'Hôpital. The entrance is at the far end of the building marked #2. If reception is closed, enter through the second door and leave your bags in the basement lockers (5SFr deposit). This converted hospital has long corridors and rooms in the basement. Bring earplugs—trains run nearby and the hallways echo. Breakfast, showers, and sheets included. Lunch and dinner (with early notice) 12.50SFr. TV room, laundry (3-5SFr), kitchen (6SFr per hr.), and ping pong available. Wheelchair-accessible. Reception 7:30-10am and 5-10pm. Check-out 10am. Doors are locked when reception is closed. Leave your passport as a key deposit. Open mid-Feb. to late-Nov. Reservations recommended. Dorms 30.65SFr, non-members add 6SFr. MC/V. ❷

Hotel du Musée, r. Pierre Aeby 11 (☎/fax 322 32 09), above a Chinese restaurant, is right near most of the sights. The reception is in the dining room. From the station, follow ave. de la Gare to r. de Romont to r. de Lausanne. Turn left up r. Pierre Aeby at the end of r. de Lausanne, by pl. Nova-Friburgo. The carpeted rooms are well-furnished and clean. Breakfast 10SFr. Reception 10am-2:30pm and 5-11:30pm. Reserve ahead. Singles 60SFr, with shower 70SFr; doubles 120/130SFr. AmEx/D/MC/V. ❸

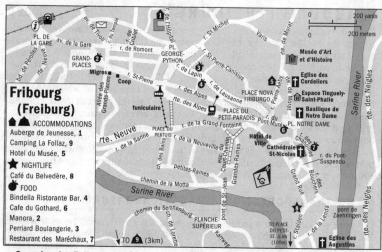

Fribourg (Freiburg)

▲▲ **ACCOMMODATIONS**
Auberge de Jeunesse, **1**
Camping La Follaz, **9**
Hotel du Musée, **5**

★ **NIGHTLIFE**
Café du Belvedère, **8**

🍎 **FOOD**
Bindella Ristorante Bar, **4**
Cafe du Gothard, **6**
Manora, **2**
Perriard Boulangerie, **3**
Restaurant des Maréchaux, **7**

Camping La Follaz (☎ 436 24 95). From the station, bus #1 to "Marly-Gérines" (2.80SFr). From the stop, backtrack across the bridge, take the first right, and follow the signs for 7min. Lakeside plots and showers. Reception 9am-10pm, but call ahead. Open Apr.-Oct. 5.30SFr per person; tents for 1-2 people 5.50SFr, for 4-6 7.50SFr. ●

🔲 FOOD

Small cafés selling quasi-Italian or Swiss-German dishes populate r. de Romont and almost every main street in the *vieille ville*. For kebabs, check out blvd. des Pérolles and other streets around the station. **Produce market** stand in pl. Georges Python between r. de Romont and r. de Lausanne (open Tu-W 7am-noon) and in pl. Hôtel de Ville (open Sa 7am-noon). The supermarket twins **Co-op** and **Migros** share the same street (r. St.-Pierre 6a and 2, respectively, by Grand-Places) and the same hours (M-W and F 8am-7pm, Th 8am-9pm, Sa 8am-4pm). This Co-op also has a restaurant. Migros has a second branch at Pérolles Centre, blvd. de Pérolles 21 (near the station), which houses a restaurant on the second floor, and large grocery with the same hours as above.

Café du Gothard, r. du Pont Muré 16 (☎ 322 32 85), by the Tilleul bus stop between the Hôtel de Ville and St. Nicolas. A friendly Francophone staff serves typical Swiss fare within the memorabilia-covered walls of this quirky restaurant. Veal sausage with *Rösti* and salad 14SFr; filet of perch 22SFr. ❸

Bindella Ristorante Bar, r. de Lausanne 38 (☎ 322 49 05). Inventive pasta made in-house (from 12.50SFr) and other Italian dishes served by ponytailed waiters. A small splurge to people-watch along the popular r. de Lausanne. Live jazz last Th of the mo. 8:30pm. Open M-Sa 9am-11:30pm, kitchen noon-2pm and 6:30-10pm. ❷

Restaurant des Marechaux, r. des Chanoines 9 (☎ 322 33 33), next to the cathedral, will satisfy Greek *gourmands* with large veggie-friendly plates and soothing Greek music in the background. Feast on *spanakopita* with *tzatziki* (9.50SFr) or *souvlaki* (26SFr) in an airy dining room overlooking the gorge. Open 5pm-midnight; kitchen 6-11pm. ❸

Perriard Boulangerie, r. de Lausanne 61 (☎ 322 34 89), will satisfy a sweet tooth with pastries and confectionery delights, such as *noisettines* for 5SFr per 100g and fresh breads for 1.50-3.20SFr. Wheelchair-accessible. Open Tu-F 7:30am-7pm, Sa 7:30am-6pm, Su 8am-6pm. ❶

Manora, in front of Grand-Places, is a self-service restaurant with high-quality selections of meat and produce, and worthy array of desserts and drinks. Together they make a fine meal for 8-15SFr. Wheelchair-accessible. Open M-Sa 8am-7:30pm, Su 9am-7:30pm. ❷

🔘 SIGHTS

THE OLD TOWN. From the station, head down r. de Romont, past pl. Georges Python, and along r. de Lausanne and its pink-bannered open-air shopping galleries. R. de Lausanne empties into pl. Nova-Friburgo, a busy intersection with a fine view of the **Hôtel de Ville** and its fanciful clock tower. Pantaloon-clad Renaissance automatons chime the hours. A fountain of St. George dominates the courtyard below, near the commemorative **Morat Linden Tree** (see "Death, a Maiden, and a Linden Tree," see below).

DEATH, A MAIDEN, AND A LINDEN TREE

Once upon a time (June 22, 1476) in a land far, far away (Fribourg), there lived an old man named Nicholas who declared that he would give his daughter Beatrice's hand in marriage to the man who proved himself most valiant on the battlefield. As the knights went off to fight Charles the Bold in Murten, Beatrice waved a linden branch at Rudolphe, her childhood love. Determined to win her hand, Rudolphe proved himself the bravest knight on the battlefield—at the cost of a mortal wound. Undaunted, he ran back to Fribourg, waving a linden branch and shouting "Victory!" When he finally reached Beatrice's balcony in pl. Hôtel de Ville, he collapsed. Beatrice ran to her love, who could say only "Homeland! Love! To Heaven!" before dying in her arms. The town planted the linden branch as a relic of the victory in the square. In 1984, a traffic accident uprooted the tree, but the town salvaged a shoot and replanted it in the original spot, where it flourishes today. In memory of the battle and of Rudolphe's plight, runners from Murten and Fribourg race between the two cities every October.

MUSÉE D'ART ET D'HISTOIRE. Off pl. Nova-Friburgo, r. Pierre Aeby leads to the Museum of Art and History. Skip the 18th-century portraiture—the haunting historical artifacts are the meat of the collection. Look for a number of the wood carvings of Geiler and Roditzer. The gleefully macabre, bejeweled skeleton of St. Felix, ca. 1755, is in itself a worthwhile reason to visit. The bust of Medusa is also worth a glance. Bring a mirror, or course. *(R. de Morat 12. ☎ 305 51 40. Wheelchair-accessible. Open Tu-W and F-Su 11am-6pm, Th 11am-8pm. 6-12SFr, depending on special exhibits'; students from 5SFr. MC.)*

JEAN TINGUELY-NIKI DE SAINT PHALLE MUSEUM. On the other side of the Église des Cordeliers from the Musée d'Art et d'Histoire, the museum showcases the work of avant-garde Fribourg native Tinguely and his wife, Saint-Phalle. Tinguely's work features bizarre, massive machines made out of rusty metal, while Saint-Phalle's work uses brilliant colors in curvaceous sculpture. *(R. de Morat 2. ☎ 305 51 70. Wheelchair-accessible. Open W and F-Su 11am-6pm, Th 11am-8pm. 5SFr, students 3SFr, children under 16 free.)*

MONASTERIES & CHURCHES. Peering from the hills above town are two tiny chapels. There are also a number of other churches worth seeing. At the **Église des Cordeliers,** part of a Franciscan monastery, the unassuming facade masks a colorful interior, featuring an elaborate altar that lies in star-studded darkness. *(From the Tinguely museum, backtrack on r. de Morat. Open daily Apr.-Sept. 7:30am-7pm; Oct.-Mar. 7:30am-6pm.)* Down the road is the **Basilique de Notre-Dame,** whose dim, incense-laden atmosphere contrasts sharply with the bright, ornate Église des Cordeliers, though its elaborate pulpit does add some elegance to its image. Across pl. Notre-Dame rises the bell tower of the **Cathédrale St.-Nicolas,** which shoots above the Fribourg skyline. It took over 200 years to erect the Gothic columns, now smoke-blackened, that shoot upwards into pointed arches and stained-glass windows. View the town from the 76m, 368-step **tower.** *(Cathedral open M-Sa 7:30am-7pm, Su 8:30am-9:30pm. Free. Tower open June-Oct. M-Sa 10am-noon and 2-5:15pm, Su 2-5:15pm. 3.50SFr, students 2SFr, children 1SFr.)* Although only order members have complete access to the 13th-century **Église des Augustins,** visitors can examine the monastery's huge altarpiece and the intricate altars around the sanctuary. *(From the cathedral, head downhill from r. des Chanoines to r. des Bouchers; take a right onto r. de Zähringen and a left onto Stalden. Take the steps of Stalden down to passage des Augustins and turn left.)*

🎵 🍷 ENTERTAINMENT & NIGHTLIFE

Fribourg's university, music conservatory, art groups, and civic institutions host several festivals throughout the year, including a **Carnival** (a Mardi Gras-type party in the *vieille ville,* February 21-24, 2004), an **International Film Festival** (mid-March), an **International Guitar Festival** (April 23-May 1, 2004), and an **International Jazz Parade** (July 2-18, 2004). There is also the **Belluard Bollwerk International** festival (late June to mid-July), a gathering of musicians, dancers, critics, scholars, and just about anyone else involved in the arts (☎ 469 09 00; www.belluard.ch). **Open-air cinema** runs from mid-July to mid-August, screening many American films (get advance tickets from the tourist office).

For a relaxed evening, try ◨**Café Belvedere,** Grand Rue 36, at the top of Stalden, which resembles an M.C. Escher drawing, with comfortably worn couches perfect for intimate conversation. Alterna-intellectuals lounge on terraces overlooking the gorge, sampling the wine of the month (3.50-5SFr) while listening to the pleasantly dippy music. (☎ 323 44 07. Open M-Tu 11:30am-11:30pm, W-Th 11:30am-12:30am, F 11:30am-3am, Sa 10:30am-3am, Su noon-midnight. Terrace closes at 11pm.)

🔆 DAYTRIP FROM FRIBOURG

GRUYÈRES ☎ 026

To get to Gruyères, buy a ticket (one-way 16.60SFr, round-trip 33.20SFR) at the train station in Fribourg and catch a bus from behind the station to Bulle. A 20min. bus ride will land you in Bulle, where you can catch a train to Gruyères (10min.). The last train from Gruyères is at 8:17pm, bus at 9:25pm. Buses and trains run approximately every hr.

Tiny medieval Gruyères (pop. 1600) carries a weighty reputation for its cheese, and it's unlikely that you'll find a cheesier town. The local tourist industry goes to absurd extremes (excessive flower boxes, hostesses in dubiously medieval garb, and suspiciously artificial-smelling smoke permeating a castle whose hearths have been bare and unlit for years), but the towering beauty of the surrounding mountains and the history of the town's buildings overcomes the kitsch. A chateau filled with contemporary art and the milky calm of working cheese dairies make this eccentric town well worth a daytrip. (☎ 921 10 30; www.gruyeres.ch. Open M and W-F 9:30am-noon and 1-5pm, Sa-Su 9:30am-5:30pm.)

La Maison du Gruyère, the cheese factory *par excellence,* is located directly across from the train station. Newly renovated, it draws crowds with a cheese-, chocolate- and wine-laden souvenir market, cheese-making demonstrations, and its own classic Swiss restaurant. (☎ 921 84 00; www.lamaisondugruyere.ch. Wheelchair-accessible. Open daily Apr.-Sept. 9am-7pm, Oct.-Mar. 9am-6pm. Cheese-making daily 9am-3pm. 5SFr, students and seniors 4SFr, family rate 10SFr. Audioguides available in 6 languages.)

The truly cheese-devoted can take a GFM bus to "Moléson-sur-Gruyères" to the **Fromagerie d'Alpage.** An anachronistic phenomenon, this 17th-century factory makes cheese the old-fashioned way, over a huge cauldron on the fireplace. After la Maison, you'll be amazed at the difference between new and old. (☎ *921 10 44. Open mid-May to mid-Oct. daily 9:30am-10pm, with demonstrations 10am, 3pm.)*

GOT MILK? Before most kids hear of watchmaking or political neutrality, they know about Swiss cheese. But the 84,000 tons of cheese Switzerland produces annually don't only consist of the familiar, hole-ridden variety. While most of it (56,500 tons) is the recognizable Emmental, 22,000 tons is Gruyère, a nutty-tasting cousin without any holes to speak of. The region has been making cheese since the 12th century. Two varieties of cows contribute their milk to the effort: *tachettée rouge* (red) and *noir* (black). Workers process 3 million kg a year by pouring it into large vats, where it is centrifuged, matured with bacteria, congealed with natural enzymes into a yogurt-like consistency, and heated to get rid of excess liquid. Each cheese round is then pressed into shape for 18hr. before it is stamped for quality and authenticity.

Gruyères's only major street, lined by flowerbox-adorned old houses and well-touristed restaurants, leads uphill past the town to the beautiful and bizarre **Château de Gruyères.** The castle was home to a series of earls from the 12th-16th centuries, but don't expect to be taken back to its earliest days when you walk in—the mismatched decor of each room reflects many different eras: medieval tapestries are juxtaposed with Louis XV chairs, and one room houses **Franz Lizst's** *pianoforte* (he lived here too). Only the dungeons remain of the original feudal castle—the living quarters burned to the ground in 1493 and were rebuilt as the first Renaissance castle in the Northern Alps. Some highlights are walk-in fireplaces, oddly-cobbled floors, and a room displaying dozens of antlers and stuffed game. Adding to the anachronistic confusion, the castle is also now home to the **International Center of Fantastic Art,** a elaborate sci-fi art collection scattered throughout the castle, including a tower of works by artist Patrick Woodroffe. Many rooms offer spectacular views of the **Jardin à la francaise** and the surrounding hills. (☎ *921 21 02. Open daily Apr.-Oct. 9am-6pm; Nov.-Mar. 10am-4:30pm. Last admission 30min. before closing. 6SFr, students 5SFr, ages 6-16 2SFr. Signs in German, French, and English.)*

If you're certain there's other life out there, further feed your obsession on the way back to town from the chateau at the eerie, freaky **H.R. Giger museum.** This out-of-this-world homage to the Academy Award-winning designer of Ridley Scott's *Alien* features many models of the chilling creature and items from Giger's private collection. There are alien sketches, alien paintings, and alien sculptures. Dark curtains hide a glowing red room filled with erotic aliens in compromising positions. (☎ *921 22 00. Open daily Nov.-Apr. 11am-5pm; May-Oct. 10am-6pm. 10SFr, students 7SFr.)* If you haven't gotten your extraterrestrial fix by the time you leave, the **H.R. Giger Bar** across the street offers an atmosphere that's just as wacked-out, but with a human touch: beer, as well as more exotic drinks. *(Open daily 10am-7pm.)*

NEUCHÂTAL REGION

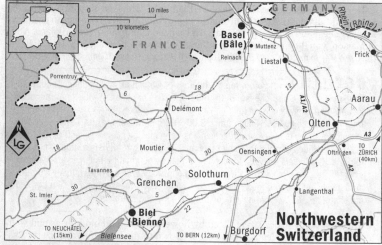

Northwestern
Switzerland

NORTHWESTERN SWITZERLAND

The cantons of Basel-Stadt and Basel-Land, Solothurn, and Aargau inspire peaceful contentment. Odds are, you'll be passing through anyway (Basel is a transportation hub for Germany and France) so why not slow down to enjoy subtle charms, excellent museums with a rich Humanist tradition, and delightful *Altstädte?* Despite their proximity to France, and the occasional French town name, the cantons of northwestern Switzerland are German-speaking.

HIGHLIGHTS OF NORTHWEST SWITZERLAND

Catapult yourself into wackiness at the **Museum Jean Tinguely** in Basel (see p. 541).

Gaze back in time from the top **St. Ursen Cathedral's dome** in Solothurn (see p. 542).

Sip the *Hell Spezial* with your pretzel in a Basel **Biergarten** (see p. 543).

BASEL (BÂLE)   ☎ 061

Basel sits on a spit of land that extends between France and Germany, with most of the city being no more than 15min. from either country. With the Rhine cutting through the heart of the city, it is split into two sectors: *Gross Basel* and *Klein Basel*, which share a healthy and historical love-hate relationship. Switzerland's third-largest city achieves what most modern cities lack—a balanced identity as both a home to modern industrial power and a bastion of old-world charm. The factories and office buildings on the outskirts of the city belong to global chemical giants that employ thousands of international workers. The city's medieval *Altstadt*, in contrast, is not contained in one specific district—buildings dating to the 12th century sprawl on both sides of the river and contain the living workings of a city: drugstores, boutiques, supermarkets, and the like. The University of Basel, one of the oldest universities in Switzerland and one of the few buildings miraculously untouched after the Thirty Years War, numbers Erasmus of Rotterdam, Bernoulli, and Nietzsche among its graduates. On the eastern riverbank, the **Münster** (cathedral) presides over the *Gross Basel Altstadt* in a towering conglomeration of red sandstone, stained glass, and sprouting spires. The most outstanding attractions of Basel are the 30 museums in the hilly streets of the elegant St. Alban district. Endless art fairs and festivals fill the calendar and the streets, but the biggest party of them all is Basel's **Fasnacht,** which rivals New Orleans' Mardi Gras in its glamour, atmosphere, and the locals' devotion to the event.

▐▀ TRANSPORTATION

The **Euroairport** (☎267 90 25) serves continental Europe, though most trans-continental flights are routed through Zurich. Shuttle buses run passengers between the airport and the SBB train station on the #50 line (daily 4:55am-11:30pm).

At the crossroads of Switzerland, France, and Germany, Basel has three **train stations:** the French **SNCF** station (www.voyage-sncf.com) is next door to the Swiss **SBB station** (www.sbb.ch) in Centralbahnpl.; trains from Germany arrive at the **DB station** (Badischer Bahnhof; ☎690 11 11; www.bahn.de), across the Rhine down Greifeng. City trams to town depart the SBB station (every 5min. M-F, every 15min. Sa-Su). **Buses** to Swiss, French, and German cities depart from respective stations. **Driving** from France, take A35, E25, or E60; from Germany, E35 or A5; from within Switzerland, Rte. 2 north.

> **Trains: SBB station** (☎157 22 22; 1.19SFr per min.), on Centralbahnpl. To: **Bern** (1¼hr., every hr. 5:50am-11:47pm, 34SFr); **Geneva** (3hr., every hr. 6:24am-8:44pm, 71SFr); **Lausanne** (2½hr., every hr. 5:50am-10:26pm, 60SFr); **Milan** via Lucerne or Bern (4½-6hr., every hr. 6:30am-3:10pm, 91SFr); **Munich** via Zurich or Karlsruhe (5¼hr., every hr. 7am-8:13pm, 116SFr); **Paris** (5-6hr., 12 per day 5:51am-12:28am, 69SFr); **Salzburg** via Zurich (7hr., 5 per day 5:51am-9pm, 122SFr); **Vienna** via Zurich (10-12hr., 5 per day 5:51am-9pm, 149SFr); **Zurich** (1hr., every 15-30min. 4:42am-midnight, 30SFr). Make international connections at the French (SNCF) or German (DB) stations. 25% discount on international trips for travelers ages 16-25.

NO WORK, ALL PLAY

IT'S FASNACHT — DO YOU KNOW WHERE YOUR WAGGIS ARE?

At exactly 4:00am on Monday, February 19th, 2004, every light in the city of Basel will be extinguished. The city will fall into momentary darkness, but instantly light will return—light from the lanterns of masked men and women playing instruments, holding flowers, and wearing wooden pointed shoes. It is *Fasnacht,* Basel's biggest party of the year, and the fancifully-dressed men and women are the *Waggis,* the soul of *Fasnacht.*

For the three days of the Carnival, which celebrates the coming of spring, the *Waggis* participate in countless parades, wandering the city giving flowers and gigantic lollipops to revelers who have purchased a carnival badge (*Plaket*), and shoving confetti down the shirts of those who haven't. Sponsored by *cliques*—professional guilds or groups of friends—the *Waggis* wear outfits in which every aspect is planned: the lantern is painted and inscribed with messages which poke fun at the year's scandals, the plaster mask is handmade, and the pointed, wooden shoes and costume carefully arranged. Also in the parade are *Alte Tante* wagons (horse-drawn carriages full of roses) and elite drum and fife corps.

Badges range in price from 10SFr for a standard "bronze" badge to 200SFr for artistically designed ones and are sold in the streets.

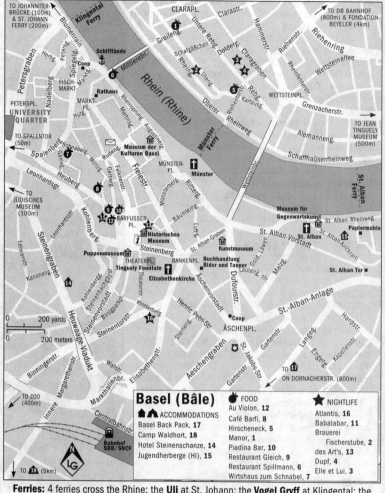

Basel (Bâle)

ACCOMMODATIONS
Basel Back Pack, **17**
Camp Waldhort, **18**
Hotel Steinenschanze, **14**
Jugendherberge (HI), **15**

FOOD
Au Violon, **12**
Café Barfi, **8**
Hirscheneck, **5**
Manor, **1**
Piadina Bar, **10**
Restaurant Gleich, **9**
Restaurant Spillmann, **6**
Wirtshaus zum Schnabel, **7**

NIGHTLIFE
Atlantis, **16**
Babalabar, **11**
Brauerei
  Fischerstube, **2**
des Art's, **13**
Dupf, **4**
Elle et Lui, **3**

Ferries: 4 ferries cross the Rhine: the **Uli** at St. Johann; the **Vogel Gryff** at Klingental; the **Leu** below the Münster terrace; and the **Wild Maa** at St. Alban (all M-F 7am-7pm, Sa-Su 9am-7pm; 1.20SFr, children 0.60SFr). Rhine **cruises** depart from Schifflände. (☎639 95 00: 2-4 per day Mar.-Oct. 20. Station open M-F 9am-12:15pm and 1-6pm, Sa 10am-4pm, Su 8am-3pm.) Enjoy "Samba Night" or another special Rhine cruise (varying times and prices; check at the station). Round-trip to Rheinfelden 45SFr, to Waldhaus 23SFr. Tickets available 30min. before departure. Reservations are recommended (☎639 95 00; www.portofbasel.ch).

Public Transportation: Trams and buses run 5:30am-12:30am. Most sights are within zone #10. 1-zone tickets 2.80SFr, day ticket 8SFr; ages 6-16 1.80SFr. Ticket machines at all stops sell tram tickets. Maps and timetables at tourist office or train station. Most have a wheelchair-accessible entrance. See www.bvb-basel.ch to print door-to-door itineraries and travel plans. ☎267 90 25 for further information.

NORTHWESTERN SWITZERLAND

Taxis: In front of the train station, or ☎271 11 11, 633 33 33, or 271 22 22.

Parking: Jelmoli, Rebg. 20. **Bahnhof SBB,** Güterstr. 2.50SFr per hr.

Bike Rental: At train stations. 30SFr per day. Open daily 6am-9:40pm.

◼◢ ◪ ORIENTATION & PRACTICAL INFORMATION

Basel sits in the northwest corner of Switzerland, so close to France that the Tour de France sometimes traverses the city. *Groß-Basel* (Greater Basel), where most sights are located, lies on the eastern bank of the Rhine; *Klein-Basel* (Lesser Basel) occupies the western bank. You can pick up a city map (0.50SFr) for motorists and pedestrians at either tourist office, but Basel's easy-to-use pedestrian tourist signs can help a lot, along with small, free tear-off maps available at the tourist office, hostels, and other sites. To reach **Marktplatz** on foot from the SBB and SNCF stations, cross the Centralbahnpl., go left on Elisabethenanlage, right down Elisabethenstr., and left on Freiestr. (20min.) From the DB station, follow Rosentalstr. (which becomes Clarastr., then Greifeng.) over Mittlere Rheinbrücke and around to the left on Eiseng. (15min.).

Tourist Office: Basel Tourismus, Steinenbergstr., in the Stadt Casino building on Barfüsserpl. (☎268 68 68; www.baseltourismus.ch). From the SBB station, take any tram headed to "Barfüsserpl." Guided walking tours are available (2hr., May-Oct. M-Sa 2:30, 15SFr). Hotel reservations 10SFr. Guide to the city 5.90SFr (German, French, or English). Buy a **Basel Card** and get the guided walking tour, admission to all Basel museums, ferries, and the zoo, as well as discounts for some restaurants, clubs, and taxis. Available at tourist office (24hr. card 25SFr, 48hr. 33SFr, 72hr. 45SFr). Open M-F 8:30am-6pm, Sa-Su 10am-4pm. **Branch office** (☎271 36 84; hotel@messe-basel.ch) at the SBB station has different Sa-Su hours: 9am-2pm.

Currency Exchange: The SBB station bureau, including a **Western Union,** offers currency exchange (2SFr fee) and cash advance with MC/V (min. 200SFr). Open daily 7am-8pm. A **24hr. currency exchange machine** sits next to their office.

Luggage Storage: At all stations. Lockers 5SFr, 24hr. access. Storage 7SFr per day. Open 6am-9:40pm.

Travel Agency: STA Travel, Freiestr. 15 (☎269 83 00; stabasel@statravel.ch). Open M-F 10am-6:30pm, Sa 10am-4pm.

Bookstores: Buchhandlung Bider und Tanner, Bankenpl., Äschenvorstadt 2 (☎206 99 99), is Basel's travel bookshop, with a room of well-selected English-language books. Open M-W and F 8:15am-6:30pm, Th 8:15am-9pm, Sa 8:15am-5pm.

Bi-Gay-Lesbian Organizations: Pick up a **doux bole** calendar with all of the month's events. **habs** (*Homosexuelle Arbeitsgruppen Basel*), Postfach 1519, CH-4001 Basel, is located on Lindenberg 23 and has general city info (☎692 66 55, info@habs.ch). **Rose,** a group for young people, meets at clubs and restaurants; call for exact times and locations (☎0848 80 50 80, www.rose.ch). **Arcados,** Rheing. 69 (☎681 31 32; www.arcados.com), at Clarapl. is a bookstore that has lots of information on BGLT bars, restaurants, and hangouts. Open Tu-F noon-7pm, Sa 11am-4pm.

Emergencies: Police ☎117, **medical** ☎144, **hospital** ☎265 25 25.

Hotlines: Helping Hand ☎143 for any crisis situation.

Internet Access: Domino, Steinenvorstadt 54. Arcade with an Internet coffee-bar upstairs. 10SFr per hr., after 6pm 12SFr per hr. Open M-Th 9:30am-midnight, F-Sa 9am-1am (summer Sa 10am-1am), Su 1pm-midnight. 18+. **Jäggi Bucher,** Greifeng. 3/5 has a **free** station (30min. limit). Open M, W, F 9am-7pm, Th 9am-8pm, Sa 9am-

5pm. **Mausklick,** Klingentalstr. 7, 10SFr per hr. Open M-F 7:30am-5pm. At **Manor,** Greifeng. 22, 5SFr for 30min. Open M-W and F 8:30am-7pm, Th 8:30am-9pm, Sa 8am-5pm.

Public restrooms and showers: In the station at McClean. 1-2SFr for toilets, 12SFr for 20min. shower, towels, and shampoo. Open daily 6am-midnight.

Post Office: Rüdeng 1. Take tram #1 or 8 to "Marktpl." and walk 1 block back from the river. Open M-W and F 7:30am-6:30pm, Th 7:30am-8pm, Sa 8am-noon. Poste Restante address: *Postlagernde Briefe,* Rüdeng., CH-4001 Basel 1. **Postal Codes:** CH-4000 to CH-4059.

▐ ACCOMMODATIONS & CAMPING

All accommodations in Basel offer a complimentary **Mobility ticket.** The ticket offers free use of public transport for the duration of your stay in zones 10 and 11 where most sights are located, and even the shuttle bus to the airport (normally 6.60SFr).

Jugendherberge (HI), St. Alban-Kirchrain 10 (☎272 05 72; www.youthhostel.ch/basel). Tram #2 to "Kunstmuseum." Turn right on St.-Alban-Vorstadt, then follow the signs, or walk 15min. from the SBB station down Äschengraben to St.-Alban-Anlage. At the tower, follow the signs down the hill. This hostel is a mecca for weary travelers, particularly those who don't mind the occasional cobweb. The institutional setup has lockers for every bunk, TV, and phones, but expect long waits for services. Breakfast and sheets included. Dinner and lunch 12.50SFr. **Internet** 5SFr for 25min., half-price after midnight. Laundry 7SFr. **Currency exchange** of euros and SFr only. Wheelchair-accessible. Reception Mar.-Oct. 7am-noon and 2-11:30pm; Nov.-Feb. 2pm-11pm. Check-out 7-10am. Reservations recommended. 8-bed dorms 30.50SFr; 6-bed dorms 31.50SFr; 4-bed dorms 32.50SFr; singles 80SFr; doubles 100SFr. Non-members add 6SFr. AmEx/MC/V. ❷

Basel Back Pack, Dornacherstr. 192 (☎333 00 37 or 076 538 37 19; www.baselbackpack.ch). Exit the rear of the SBB station, go up the stairs, and turn right onto the gallery that leads to Hochstr. Walk straight down Hochstr., then turn right on Bruderholzstr. Follow Bruderholzstr. until it intersects with Dornacherstr. Enter the gate at number 192 and walk all the way to the back of the building. Or ride tram #15 (dir.: Bruderholz) to "Bruderholzstr." Follow the signs on the building to the left to find the reception. Though slightly removed from the city center, Basel's newest (only independent) hostel is serviced by a convenient tram. Located in a renovated factory, Back Pack offers brand-new, clean facilities and a helpful staff. Color-coded rooms include matching lockers and extra-high IKEA bunk beds. Small on-site bar. Breakfast 7SFr. Sheets, showers, kitchen, and locker included. Laundry 8SFr. Online reservations possible. Reception 8am-1pm and 5pm-midnight. Check-out 11am. Dorms 30SFr; singles 80SFr; doubles 94SFr; triples 120SFr; quads 150SFr. ❷

Hotel Steinenschanze, Steinengraben 69 (☎272 53 53; www.steinenschanze.ch). From the SBB station, turn left on Centralbahnstr. and follow signs for "Heuwaage." Under the bridge, climb the ramp to Steinengraben and turn left. The monolithic building contains simple, well-lit rooms with fluffy covers and a classy breakfast area. Phone, TV, and balconies. Breakfast included. 24hr. reception. Singles 120-140SFr, under 25 with ISIC 60SFr per night for up to 3 nights; doubles with shower 180-210SFr/100SFr. AmEx/DC/MC/V. ❹

Camping: Camp Waldhort, Heideweg 16 (☎71 64 29), in Reinach. Take tram #11 to "Landhof." Backtrack 200m toward Basel, cross the main street, and follow the signs for a 10min. walk. Beautiful location in the middle of the woods, but far from Basel. Reception 8am-noon and 2-8pm. Open Mar.-Oct. 7SFr per person; 10SFr per tent. ❶

FOOD

Barfüsserpl., Marktpl., and the streets connecting them are full of cheap eats. Don't be alarmed by the local slang for the Barfüsserpl.—*Barfi* is no criticism of the food, just an abbreviation. A searchable index of many clubs and restaurants on the web, www.baselrestaurant.ch, also includes schedules of jazz nights, special events, and menus.

RESTAURANTS

Piadina Bar, Gerberg. 78, on the corner of Gerberg. and Barfüsserpl. This small wooden café serves fresh, tasty tortilla breads full of your choice of cheeses, meats, and vegetables (7.50-11.50SFr). Open M-Th 10:45am-midnight, F-Sa 10:45am-1am. ❷

Au Violon, im Lohnhof 4 (☎269 87 11; www.au-violon.com). Treat yourself to moderately priced gourmet food in this French brasserie on the *Barfi*. Before Gerberg., head left up the tiny Lohnhofgässlein and take the elevator at the top of the stairs to the 1st floor. The leafy terrace with fountain is the definition of pleasant in the summertime. Daily changing entrees like baked lox with olive oil and saffron sauce and vegetables, or veal cutlet with rosemary potatoes and green beans (28-32SFr). Salads 11-20SFr. English menu. Open Tu-Sa 11:30am-midnight. AmEx/DC/MC/V. ❹

Restaurant Spillman, Eiseng. 1 (☎261 17 60; fax 16 72), at the foot of Mittlere Rheinbr., near Schifflände. An upscale but unpretentious crowd sits above the rushing Rhine in this conveniently located restaurant with a pleasant terrace. Daily lunch *Menüs* starting at 17.80SFr, while most entrees are around 25-35SFr. If you feel like going all-out, try the Mediterranean-style king prawns (38.50SFr). Open M-Sa 8:30am-11pm; kitchen open 8:30am-9:30pm. AmEx/DC/MC/V. ❹

Wirtshaus zum Schnabel, Trillengässlein 2 (☎261 49 09; 49 92). From Marktpl., walk 1 block on Hutg. (by EPA) to Spalenberg.; turn left onto Schnabelg. In this corner terrace, Italian-speakers serve well-prepared German dishes to a family-friendly crowd. The Swiss oven in the corner and wood-panelling will have you hearkening back to your Alpine farming days, even if you don't really have any. Daily vegetarian *Menü* available. Pasta 12.80-19.80SFr, other entrees mid-20SFr. Open M-Sa 10:30am-till all the people leave (1:30 or 2am). AmEx/DC/MC/V. ❸

Restaurant Gleich, Leonhardsberg 1 (☎281 82 86). This casual restaurant serves an array of vegetarian dishes popular with locals, including a large salad buffet. Colorful, healthful dishes 13.50-23.50SFr. Open M-F 10:30am-9:30pm. ❸

Hirscheneck, Lindenberg 23 (☎692 73 33). Cross Wettsteinbr. and turn left onto Kartansg. An unabashedly left-of-center restaurant-bar where dreadlocks, piercings, and the hammer and sickle prevail. Features 2 vegetarian and organically grown dishes every day. *Menü* 12-18.50SFr. Open M-F 11am-midnight, Sa 2pm-1am, Su 10am-midnight; kitchen open M-F noon-2pm and 6-10pm, Sa 6-10pm, Su 10am-4pm. ❷

Café Barfi, Leonhardsberg 4 (☎261 70 38), to the right of Gerberg. from Marktpl. Mostly Italian pizzas and pastas with the unexpected samosas (6.50SFr) thrown in. Outdoor diners on this tiny, quiet side-street sometimes enjoy accordion serenades from street performers. Pasta 15.50-19.50SFr. Pizzas 16.50-20.50SFr. Homemade lasagna 19.50SFr. Open M-Sa 10am-11pm, Su 5-10pm. AmEx/MC/V. ❸

Manor, Greifeng. 22, and **Pfauen,** Freiestr. 75, are both quality, inexpensive self-service restaurants. Manor wheelchair-accessible. Both open M-W and F 8:30am-6:30pm, Th 8:30am-9pm, Sa 8am-5pm. Manor AmEx/DC/MC/V. ❷

MARKETS

Migros, SBB station. Wheelchair-accessible. Open M-F 6am-10pm, Sa-Su 7:30am-10pm.

Coop, at Schifflände tram stop and on Äschenpl. Wheelchair-accessible. Open M-W and F 7am-7pm, Th 7am-9pm, Sa 7:30am-5pm.

Public market, on Marktpl. An impressive array of fresh fruits, vegetables, cheeses, and baked goods every weekday morning. Open M-W until 5:30pm, Th-F until 1:30pm.

👁 SIGHTS

Marktplatz, which sits near the river at the culminating point of Freiestr. and other major shopping avenues, is the center of the *Altstadt.* The tourist office has a brochure outlining several well-marked walks through the city, following the historical lives of famous Basel residents, including Hans Holbein and Erasmus.

THE OLD TOWN. Erected in the early 1500s to celebrate Basel's entry into the Swiss Confederation, the very red **Rathaus** brightens Marktpl. with its blinding facade adorned with gold and green statues. Behind the Marktpl., cross the **Mittlere Rheinbrücke** and see life on the other side. Built in 1225, the bridge connects *Groß-Basel* to *Klein-Basel.* A block away from Marktpl. in the heart of the *Altstadt,* a colorful Gothic fountain livens up the **Fischmarkt.** Leading off of the Fischmarkt, the tiny **Elftausendjungfern-Gässlein** (Lane of 11,000 Virgins) is famous for St. Ursula's pilgrimage of girls to the Holy Land during the Children's Crusade. The medieval practice of walking this lane to recoup indulgences is now defunct, but people still stagger through after overindulging at nearby bars. For a contrasting aesthetic, walk from Marktpl. toward Barfüsserpl. onto Theaterpl. Here, the spectacular 🖾 **Jean Tinguely Fountain,** also known as the **Fasnachtsbrunnen,** captures a moment of modern chaos as iron sculptures spew water. The nearby **Elisabethenkirche** is an impressive structure and contains a café inside.

MÜNSTER (CATHEDRAL). Behind Marktpl. along the Rhine, the **Münster,** Basel's medieval treasure, stands on the site of an ancient Celtic settlement and a Roman fort. The red sandstone facade features hundreds of figures in various acts of piety ranging from trumpet-playing to dragon-slaying. Behind the altar, guilded Latin inscriptions memorialize the life of Erasmus, the renowned scholar and staunch Catholic who remained loyal to his faith even after his beloved Basel joined the Reformation in 1529. When he died, the city gave him a proper Catholic burial in its Protestant cathedral. Bernoulli, the mathematician who discovered the science behind flight, rests in the cloister among prominent Basler families. Also see the collection of Bibles in different languages. The **tower** holds the city's best view of the Rhine, Klein-Basel, and Black Forest. *(Open Easter-Oct.15 M-F 10am-5pm, Sa 10am-4pm, Su 1-5pm; Oct. 16-Easter M-Sa 11am-4pm, Su 2-4pm. Free. Tower closes 30min. before the church. 3SFr. Due to church policy (and past suicides), you must go up with another person. Services Sa 4:30pm, Su 10am.)*

UNIVERSITY QUARTER. The **University of Basel,** founded in 1406, is Switzerland's oldest university. Its library houses rare volumes by Erasmus, Luther, and Zwingli. The grounds are ideal for picnicking, napping, and tanning. Bargain-hunters flock here every Saturday morning for the **flea market,** which starts at 7:30am and lasts until early afternoon. Around the corner from the university library, the 700-year-old **Spalentor** (gate tower), one of the original city wall's three remaining towers and one of the most impressive gates in Switzerland, marks the edge of the *Altstadt. (Head down one of the tiny alleys off Fischmarkt to reach Petersgraben, which leads to Peterspl. and the University quarter.)*

ZOO. The Zoologischer Garten serves well as an excursion for the kids after a day of museum browsing, though animal enclosures are small and uninspired. But recent renovations have spruced up many exhibits. Restaurants, picnic areas, and ice cream vendors abound. *(Binningerstr. 40, a 10min. walk down Steinenvorstadt from Barfüsserpl. Follow signs along the wooden path, or take tram #1 or 8 to "Zoo Bachletten."* ☎ *295 35 35. Wheelchair-accessible. Open daily May-Aug. 8am-6:30pm; Sept.-Oct. and Mar.-Apr. 8am-6pm; Nov.-Feb. 8am-5:30pm. 14SFr, students and seniors 12SFr, ages 6-16 5SFr.)*

HIKING. Over 1200km of yellow-blazed trails crisscross the countryside around Basel. Take bus #70 to "Reigoldswil" where the **Gondelbahn** goes to the Jura mountain peak, "Wasserfallen" (937m). "Devil bike" (oversized mountain scooters) rental is available at the top. From the peak you can hike to Waldenburg (2½-3hr.), or to Jägerwegli (1½-2hr.). A steam engine will take you from Waldenburg back to Liestal where you can connect to Basel (1-3 per hr.).

᎙ MUSEUMS

Basel's 30 museums may seem overwhelming, but they are worth the time it takes to explore them. The **Kunstmuseum** is deservedly the most famous, but many of the more esoteric galleries are also fascinating. Subjects range from medieval medicine to mechanized mannequins. Pick up the comprehensive museum guide at the tourist office, or visit the web site, www.museenbasel.ch. A **Swiss Museum Pass,** valid for one month (all over Switzerland at participating museums) costs 32SFr. A **Basel Card** is good for all museums (see p. 537).

▓ MUSEUM JEAN TINGUELY. Noise and motion are the preferred modes of expression of the intriguing Swiss sculptor; the pink sandstone facade of this improbable homage to him hides endless amounts of interaction and chaotic entertainment. Tinguely's massive *Grosse Méta Maxi-Maxi Utopia* allows visitors to climb over and experience his crazy futuristic vision. *(Paul-Sacher Anlage 1. Take tram #2 or 15 to "Wettsteinpl." and bus #31 or 36 to "Museum Tinguely."* ☎ *681 93 20; www.tinguely.ch. Wheelchair-accessible. Open W-Su 11am-7pm. 7SFr, students 5SFr.)*

KUNSTMUSEUM (MUSEUM OF FINE ARTS). Despite being the first independent public gallery in Switzerland (opened in 1661), the Basel Kunstmuseum still retains its fresh perspective on art. A formidable marble structure, it houses extensive, outstanding compilations of old and new masters and temporary exhibits. The Picasso collection was begun when a resoundingly affirmative electoral referendum persuaded the city government to grant the museum money to buy two. Touched by such enthusiasm, the artist himself donated four more. *(St. Alban-Graben 16. Accessible by tram #2 or 15.* ☎ *206 62 62; www.kunstmuseumbasel.ch. Wheelchair-accessible. Open Tu and Th-Su 10am-5pm, W 10am-7pm. 10SFr, students 8SFr. Free 1st Su of the mo. Special exhibition rates usually 14SFr. Call ahead to ask about the occasional English guided tours and tours for those in wheelchairs. Includes entrance to Museum für Gegenwartskunst.)*

FONDATION BEYELER. As one of Europe's finest private art collections, the Fondation Beyeler includes works from dozens of major artists in an architecturally dynamic building. Picasso, Matisse, van Gogh, Warhol, and Cézanne top the list. The surrounding grounds are lush and were once wrapped in plastic by Christo. The outdoor lily pond is only matched by a massive Monet version within. *(Baselstr. 101, Riehen. Take tram #6 (dir.: Riehen Grenze) to "Riehen Dorf," then walk in the direction of the tram 5min. It's on the left after the "Kunstraum Riehen."* ☎ *645 97 00; www.beyeler.com. Wheelchair-accessible. Open daily 9am-6pm, W till 8pm. M-F 16SFr, Sa-Su 20SFr; students 5SFr; after 6pm 12SFr. Call ahead for exact dates. Tours of special exhibits in German, French, and English.)*

MUSEUM DER KULTUREN BASEL. A mansion topped by neoclassical friezes houses elements of non-Western cultures contrasting with its architecture. Stereotypical exhibits—check out the "American" kitchen. Particularly notable is the

New Guinea *Geisterhern* that stands three floors high. In the same building, you'll find the **Naturhistorisches Museum.** *(Augustinerg. 2. ☎266 55 00. Wheelchair-accessible. Both museums open Tu-Su 10am-5pm. 7SFr, students under 26 5SFr, under 16 free. Special rates for temporary exhibitions usually 14SFr. Free 1st Su of the mo. and Tu-Sa 4-5pm.)*

MUSEUM FÜR GEGENWARTSKUNST (MODERN ART). Find most of Basel's really modern art at this museum, largely composed of temporary exhibition spaces, between the youth hostel and the Rhine. *(St. Alban-Rheinweg 60. ☎206 62 62, www.mgkbasel.ch. Open Tu-Su 11am-5pm. Combined ticket with Kunstmuseum 10SFr, students under 25SFr. Special exhibition rates usually 14SFr, students 10SFr. Free 1st Su of every mo.)*

HISTORISCHES MUSEUM: BARFÜSSERKIRCHE. The church collection includes stained-glass windows emblazoned with cantonal coats-of-arms, stunning iconography, fine goldsmithing, and the oldest crosier city banner in Switzerland. The early Gothic church, with its pink stone columns and huge windows veiled in transparent linen, was converted into a museum in 1894. Downstairs, recreated rooms showcase medieval and Renaissance furnishings. *(Steinenberg 4, on Barfüsserpl. ☎205 86 00; www.historischesmuseumbasel.ch. Wheelchair-accessible. Open M and W-Su 10am-5pm. 7SFr, students and seniors 5SFr, under 16 and 1st of the mo. free.)*

OTHER MUSEUMS. The **Puppenhausmuseum (Toy Museum) Basel** holds four floors of toys (including over 2000 toy bears) and miniature model towns packed into display cases—this is one museum children adore. *(Steinenvorstadt 1. ☎225 95 95. Wheelchair-accessible. Open M-W and F-Su 11am-5pm, Th 11am-8pm. 7SFr, students 5SFr, under 16 free.)* Learn the art of paper-making at the **Papiermühle (Paper Mill)** and try your hand at the printing press. *(St. Alban-Tal 37. ☎272 96 52. Open Tu-Su 2-5pm. 9SFr, students 6SFr; family 22SFr.)* The **Jüdisches Museum der Schweiz** (Jewish Museum) contains small, well-organized exhibits on law, the observation of Jewish holidays, and other aspects of Jewish daily life. *(Kornhausg. 8. Take tram #3 to "Lyss." ☎261 95 14. Open M and W 2-5pm, Su 11am-5pm. Free.)*

🎵 🎭 ENTERTAINMENT & NIGHTLIFE

FESTIVALS. In a year-round party town, Basel's carnival, or **Fasnacht,** still manages to distinguish itself. The festivities commence the Monday before Lent with the **Morgestraich,** which has occurred annually for the last 600 years, a not-to-be-missed 4am parade that ends precisely 72 hrs. later with the **Gässle parade.** Fife and drum music plays to revelers in brilliant masks that lampoon the year's local scandals. Children wander the streets in costumes on Tuesday, and at night there is an exhibition of the lanterns (a feature of the parades) on Münsterpl., as well as concerts of local *Gugge* music. Spectators should purchase a carnival badge *(Plakete)*—it's not required, but the costumed *Waggis* aren't very nice to people who don't support the event. (Badges cost 10, 20, and 30SFr, up to 200SFr for specialty designs.) The tourist office provides lists of Basel's other cultural offerings— local favorites include **Jazz in the City,** when the city is covered with live jazz bands the second weekend in August, the **Klosterbergfest,** which fills the street with international bars, foods, and wares to raise money for Brazilian street children (last week in Aug.), and the 34th annual **ART Basel** fair, an early summer event that brings thousands to gawk at some of the most avant-garde art exhibited today. Basel's fall festival, the **Herbstmesse,** is Switzerland's oldest and largest outdoor market (late Oct.-early Nov.). The **Weihnachtsmarkt** at Christmastime is also an impressive display (last week of Nov. till Dec. 23rd).

BARS AND NIGHTCLUBS. A university town through and through, Basel's nightlife reflects the influence of student patrons. Start bar-hopping at **Barfüsserplatz,** where students sit at outdoor tables and drink wine on the steps of the Barfüsserkirche. When the bars close, kids in black often head for after-hours clubs, where things get rolling around 3-4am. Most places are 21+, but the crowds get younger on weekends. The two most popular local beers are **Warteck** and **Cardinal,** though the locally brewed **Üll** is also a favorite.

▨ Atlantis, Klosterberg 10 (☎228 96 96). From Bankenpl., it's off Elisabethenstr. to the right. One of the older bars in Basel's *Altstadt,* though you wouldn't know it by the crowd that lines up to get in on weekends. This multi-level, sophisticated bar sways to reggae, jazz, and funk. Bands or DJs play every night the Italian soccer team does not. Wheelchair-accessible in bar. Concerts around 35SFr. Club nights F-Sa, cover 15-25SFr. Open Tu-Th 11am-midnight, F 11:30am-4am, Sa 6pm-4am; kitchen open 11am-2pm and 6pm-2am. AmEx/MC/V.

Brauerei Fischerstube, Rheing. 45 (☎692 66 35). Cross Mittlere Rheinbr. and take the 1st right. This old-school *Biergarten* is adjacent to Basel's oldest brewery, crafting 4 of the best beers in town. The delectably sharp ▨ *Hell Spezial* goes well with the home-made pretzels. Stop by for an early evening Bier, 3-6.80SFr. Open M-Th 10am-midnight, F-Sa 10am-1am, Su 5pm-midnight; full dinner menu from 6pm. MC/V.

des Art's, am Barfüsserpl. 6 (☎273 57 37, fax 57 38), to the left of the Historisches Museum. For over 20 years, this classy café has turned into a hotspot at night, with its locally famous "after-work" party (Tu 5-8pm) and the largest humidor in Basel. Sink into one of the worn leather sofas or a movie theater seat, and you won't want to get back up. Piano player from 6pm on. Beer from 4.90SFr, wine 5-7SFr, cocktails 12-14SFr. Open Su-Th 11am-midnight, F-Sa 11am-3am; kitchen open 11am-2pm and 4-11pm.

Babalabar, Gerberg. 74 (☎261 48 49), to the left off Gerberg. from Barfüsserpl. Flash-ing lights and a smoky cloud serve to cover up the hot bodies at this trendy dance club. Go for techno nights or samba rhythms from the Latin-crazy DJ, and make sure to dress up. Cover Su-Th 7SFr, F-Sa 10SFr. Open summer M and W 9pm-1:30am, Th 10pm-2am, F-Sa 9pm-morning.

Dupf, Rebg. 43 (☎692 00 11). Cross Weittsteinbr. and left onto Rebg. This chic gay and lesbian bar welcomes a mixed crowd. Beers from 4.50SFr. Open daily 5pm-whenever.

Elle et Lui, Rebg. 39 (☎691 54 79). Dupf's bohemian next-door neighbor caters to a gay and lesbian clientele of all ages and tastes. Try the Caipirinha (14.50SFr) if you brought a friend to carry you home—it's 40% alcohol. Open daily Oct.-Apr. 4pm-3am; daily May-Sept. 6pm-3am.

SOLOTHURN   ☎032

Sandwiched snugly between the Jura mountains and the Aare River, Solothurn's charm rubs off on its inhabitants—the friendliness of shopkeepers and restaura-teurs is tangible. Annual film, classical music, and literature festivals attest to the town's love affair with culture. Citizens of Solothurn unleash their rambunctious side during the rowdy Winter Carnival. Although Solothurn lacks the major muse-ums and historical sights that would attract tourists for long visits, the Jura moun-tains offer endless biking and hiking prospects.

◪◪ TRANSPORTATION & PRACTICAL INFORMATION. Trains depart from Solothurn's main station at Hauptbahnhof for: Basel (1hr., 2-4 per hr. 5:50am-11:28pm, 23SFr); Bern (40min., 5 per hr. 5:18am-12:28am, 14SFr); Neuchâtel (45min., 2 per hr. 5:12am-11:50pm, 17.60SFr). For a map, or free room reserva-tions, head to the **tourist office,** Hauptg. 69. From the train station, take the under-pass toward the Zentrum and follow Hauptbahnhofstr. across Kreuzackerbr. up Kroneng. (☎626 46 46; www.solothurn-city.ch. Open M-F 8:30am-noon and 1:30-6pm, Sa 9am-noon.) **Train station** services include: **currency exchange, Western Union,** and **bike rental** (30SFr per day, 36SFr if returned to another station; both open M-F 6:10am-8:50pm, Sa-Su 6:30am-8:50pm); **taxis** ☎622 66 66 or 22 22; **lockers** (3-5SFr, 24hr.); and **luggage storage** (7SFr; open 6:30am-8:50pm). **Internet** is at

Tribe Music, Landhausquai 5, past the hostel on the right. (2SFr per 15min. Open M 1:30-6:30pm, Tu-W and F 10am-6:30pm, Th 10am-9pm, Sa 9am-5pm.) **Police** ☎117, **fire** ☎118, **hospital** ☎627 31 21. The **post office** is past the hostel on Postpl.; turn left off Kreuzackerbr., and onto Landhausquai. (☎625 29 29. Open M-F 7:30am-6pm, Sa 8am-noon). **Postal code:** CH-4500.

◪◪ ACCOMMODATIONS & FOOD. Overlooking the Aare River on the edge of the *Altstadt*, the **Jugendherberge "Am Land" (HI) ➋**, Landhausquai 23, is a slick, high-tech structure of glass and steel framed by the exterior of a 1642 schoolhouse. From the train station, walk over Kreuzackerbr. and take the first left onto Landhausquai (follow signs to "Landhaus;" street also labelled "Fischerg."). Amenities include a pool table, foosball, roof terrace, and music room. Beds can be close together in dorms, but a few are incredibly spacious. Request a river view. If you are staying here, save money and store your luggage in the free second floor lockers before sight-seeing, as opposed to the more expensive train station options. (☎623 17 06; fax 16 39. Breakfast and sheets included. Lunch and dinner 12.50SFr. Lockers 2SFr deposit. Wheelchair-accessible. Reception 7:30-10am and 4:30-10:30pm. Check-out 10am. 9-bed dorms 26.50SFr; 6-bed dorms and 5-bed dorms with sink 30SFr; doubles 86SFr; triples with toilet and shower 114SFr. Sur-tax 2SFr, 1SFr if under 16. Non-members add 6SFr. AmEx/DC/MC/V.) The **Hotel Kreuz ➌**, Kreuzg. 4, offers more privacy but less modernity. Go left off Kreuzackerbr. before the hostel. (☎622 20 20; kreuz@soluet.ch. Breakfast and hall showers included. Reception M-F from 11am, Sa from 9am. Spartan singles 50SFr, larger bed 60SFr; doubles 90SFr for 2 twin beds, 85SFr for 1 larger bed; triples 110-120SFr; quads 140SFr. Prices drop for multiple nights.) Higher prices at the **Zunfthaus zu Wirthen ➍**, Hauptg. 41, are worth it for a central location across from the Red Tower and spacious rooms with telephone and TV. (☎626 28 48; www.wirthen.ch. Breakfast included. Reception 6am-midnight. Check-in 2pm. Check-out 11am. Singles 83SFr, with shower 103SFr, with sitting area 135SFr; doubles 115SFr, with shower 138SFr. Children under 2 free; under 16 30SFr per night. MC.)

Pittaria ➋, at Theaterg. 12 (second left after the bridge from the station), is run by the beaming and talkative Sami Daher. A tiny operation decorated with a camel motif, this spot serves pitas stuffed with vegetables, chicken, and pork for 7-13SFr. (☎/fax 621 22 69. Open Tu-F 10am-9pm, Sa 10am-6pm.) The **Taverna Amphorea ➌**, Hauptg. 51 on Marktpl., serves large vegetarian-friendly Greek and Middle Eastern specialties for 13.50-26.50SFr in a simple restaurant near the cathedral. The menu changes daily, and there is outdoor seating in summer. (☎623 67 63. Open Tu and Th 11am-11:30pm, W 9am-11:30pm, F 11am-12:30am, Sa 9am-12:30am.) **Baseltor ➌**, Hauptg. 79, just past the cathedral on the left next to the tower of the same name, is a cooperative with a daily changing menu of creative Italian pasta and meat dishes, mostly organically grown; salads run 8-12SFr, entrees 19-28SFr. (☎622 34 22, www.baseltor.ch. Open M-Th 8:30am-11:30pm, F-Sa 8:30-102:30am, Su 5-11:30pm. Kitchen open noon-2pm and 6-10pm. AmEx/MC/V.)

The **Manor** grocery store/self-service restaurant is at Gurzelng. 18 to the left off Marktpl. (open M-W and F 9am-6:30pm, Th 9am-9pm, Sa 8am-5pm; AmEx/DC/MC/V), or try the **farmer's market** at Marktpl. (W and Sa 8am-noon). There is an **Aperto** at the train station. (Open M-Sa 6am-10pm, Su 7am-10pm. V.)

◪ SIGHTS. Solothurn's well-preserved Baroque architecture alone justifies a visit to the city. The **Red Tower** on the Marktpl. sports several clock faces and a macabre little skeleton. Built between 1762 and 1773 by a Ticino architect, the Italianate Baroque architecture of the **Kathedrale St. Ursen** dominates Solothurn's *Altstadt* at the end of the Kreuzackerbr. Massive for such a small town, the interior is also impressive and deserves a visit. The cathedral is dedicated to St. Ursus, the patron saint of Solothurn, who lost his head here for refusing to worship Roman gods. Its **tower** provides the *Alt-*

stadt's best view, although the 249 steps are spiralling and sometimes a tight squeeze. (☎ 622 37 53. Church open daily Easter-Oct. 8am-noon and 2-7pm; Oct.-Easter 2-6pm. Tower open M-Sa 9:30am-noon and 1:30-5:30pm, Su 1-5:30pm. Tower 2.50SFr, students 1SFr, children under 12 0.50SFr.) The four floors of the expansive **Museum Altes Zeughaus**, housed in a 1609 arsenal, holds row after row of gory instruments of death and battle paraphernalia ranging from medieval daggers and a room devoted to armor to WWII-era artillery. (Zeughauspl. 1, just uphill to the left of the cathedral. ☎ 623 35 28. Open May-Oct. Tu-Su 10am-noon and 2-5pm; Nov.-Apr. Tu-F 2-5pm, Sa-Su 10am-noon and 2-5pm. 6SFr, students 4SFr. English brochure free.) On the fringes of town, the rather dingy **Kunstmuseum,** Werkhofstr. 30, has an extensive collection of post-1850 Swiss works. The temporary exhibits tend to be more stimulating than the permanent collection. (☎ 622 23 07. Open Tu-F 10am-noon and 2-5pm, Sa-Su 10am-5pm. Free, but it is worth a few coins to see the Jean Tinguely collection box in action.) **Schloß Waldegg,** the local castle, is surrounded by fields of wheat and sunflowers that contrast with its French gardens. The castle looks over all of Solothurn and the surrounding area. (Take bus #4 (dir.: Ruttenen) to "St. Niklaus" (6 stops from the train station, 10min., 2 per hr.) and walk 10min. up Riedholzstr., the road at the intersection in the opposite direction of the bus. Wheelchair-accessible. Open Mar.-Oct. T-Th and Sa 2-5pm, Su 10am-5pm; Nov.-Dec. Su 10am-5pm. Parking available. 6SFr, students 4SFr.)

⚐ OUTDOOR ACTIVITIES. Marked **hiking** and **biking** trails lead through the Jura to nearby Altreu, site of the oldest and best-known stork colony in Switzerland (2hr., trailhead at the corner of Kroneng. and Ritterquai). The trek to the **Weißenstein Alpine Center** is more challenging and rewarding. (2hr., rail head at the corner of Wengisteinstr. and Verenawegstr.; follow the yellow signs to Weißenstein.) Take the chairlift (13SFr) down from Weißenstein and hop on a train (4.60SFr) in Oberdorf to return. **Boat tours** leave Solothurn for Biel and from there run to Murten or Neuchâtel. (Ferries run early May to mid-Oct. 2½hr.; 27SFr, round-trip 46SFr. SwissPass valid.) In the winter, **cross-country skiing** dominates the athletic scene. Weißenstein (1280m) has 7km of trails and chairlifts for downhill skiing on two small slopes best suited to beginners.

BROUGHT TO YOU BY THE NUMBER 11

Take a closer look while wandering through Solothurn's *Altstadt* and you'll notice a recurring numerical theme. The number of churches, fountains, and towers is eleven...as is the number of altars, bells, and steps in each flight of stairs in the St. Ours Cathedral! Even the two fountains outside the cathedral have 11 streams of water falling from one level to the next. The local beer? "Oufi" – "eleven" in Swiss German. It was in 1481 that Solothurn became the 11th canton to join the Swiss Confederation, and the town has made sure that its place in Swiss Confederate history is never forgotten...11th!

▣ ENTERTAINMENT. Various **festivals** enliven Solothurn. In 2004, the annual **Swiss Film Festival** will bring celluloid lovers to the city January 20-25. **Fasnacht,** is a week-long topsy-turvy carnival intended to drive away winter (Feb. 19-25, 2004). The party involves fantastical masks, raucous *Guggenmusik*, and renaming the town (temporarily) "Honolulu." Solothurn's version of this nation-wide event also includes the traditional and enigmatic *Chesslete* to begin the event. Swiss writers gather to read, drink, and sit on panels during the annual **literature festival** (May 21-23, 2004). Solothurn fans of opera enjoy the **Classic: Open Air Fest** in July (www.classic-openair.ch). The city's other big event is the **Jazz am Märetplatz** festival, in late August. Concerts fill the Marktpl. for three days, attracting jazz aficionados from far and wide.

Munich Region

MUNICH (MÜNCHEN)

Perhaps the only place in the world where *Lederhosen* and Gucci peacefully coexist, the city of Munich is both the sleek, modern capital of the German province of Bavaria and a bastion of antiquated regional ritual. Birthplace of the *Biergarten*, Munich's traditional merriment is in sharp contrast with the fragmented avant-garde attitude of Berlin, its long-time alter ego to the north. World-class museums, handsome parks and architecture, a rambunctious arts scene, and an urbane population conspire to create a city of astonishing vitality. *Müncheners* party zealously during *Fasching* (Jan. 7-Mar. 4, 2004)—Germany's Mardi Gras—and imbibe unbelievable quantities of beer during **Oktoberfest** (Sep.19-Oct.4, 2004).

PHONE CODES	The city code for Munich is 089. If calling Austria or Switzerland, dial 00 (int'l dialing prefix); then dial 43 (Austria) or 41 (Switzerland) before dialing the number.

▐ TRANSPORTATION

Flights: Flughafen München (☎97 52 13 13 for flight information, ☎97 52 13 13 for the main switchboard). S8 makes the 40min. trip between the airport and the Hauptbahnhof every 10min. €8 or 8 stripes on the *Streifenkarte* for 1; 2-5 adults can take a group rate for €15 (available at EurAide). A **Lufthansa shuttle bus** runs between the Hauptbahnhof and the airport (45min.), with a pickup at the "Nordfriedhof" U-Bahn stop in Schwabing. Buses leave from Arnulfstr., on the northern side of the train station, every 20min. 5:10am-7:50pm. Buses return from Terminal A *(Zentralbereich)* and Terminal D every 20min. 7:55am-8:55pm. One-way €9, round-trip €14.

Trains: Munich's **Hauptbahnhof** (☎22 33 12 56) is the transportation hub of southern Germany, with connections to: **Amsterdam** (9hr., 1 per hr.); **Berlin** (8hr., 1 per hr.); **Cologne** (6hr., 1 per hr.); **Frankfurt** (3½hr., 1 per hr.); **Füssen** (2hr., every 2hr.); **Hamburg** (6hr., 1 per hr.); **Innsbruck** (2hr., every 2hr.); **Paris** (10hr., 3 per day); **Prague** (7hr., 2 per day); **Salzburg** (1¾hr., 1 per hr.); **Vienna** (5hr., 1 per hr.); **Zürich** (5hr., 4 per day). For 24hr. schedules, fare information, and reservations (in German) call ☎01805 99 66 33. **EurAide,** located next to track 11 in the station, provides free train information in English and books train tickets. **Reisezentrum** information counters open daily 6am-10:30pm.

Public Transportation: MVV, Munich's public transport system, runs Su-Th 5am-12:30am, F-Sa 5am-2am. S-Bahn to the airport starts running at 3:30am. Eurail, Inter-Rail, and German railpasses are valid on the S-Bahn (S) but *not* on the U-Bahn (U), streetcars, or buses. Buy tickets (prices vary considerably) at the blue *MVV-Fahrausweise* vending machines and **validate them** in the blue boxes marked with an "E" before entering the platform. Payment is on an honor system, but disguised agents often check for tickets; if you sneak on or don't validate correctly, you risk a €30 fine. **Transit maps** and **maps of wheelchair-accessible stations** are at the tourist office or EurAide and at MVV counters near the subway entrance in the train station. *Fahrplans* (schedules) cost €1 at newsstands.

Taxis: Taxi-Zentrale (☎216 11 or 194 10) has large stands in front of the train station and every 5-10 blocks in the central city. Women can request a female driver.

☀ ORIENTATION

Munich's center is encircled by the main **Ring** and quartered by two thoroughfares which cross at the **Marienplatz** and meet the traffic rings at **Karlsplatz** (a.k.a. **Stachus**) in the west, **Isartorplatz** in the east, **Odeonsplatz** in the north, and **Sendlinger Tor** in the south. The Hauptbahnhof is west of Karlspl. East of the Isartor, the **Isar** river flows south-north by the city center. To get to Marienpl. from the station, go straight on Bayerstr. to Karlspl. and continue through Karlstor to Neuhauser Str., which becomes Kaufingerstr. before it reaches Marienpl. Alternately, take S1-8 (two stops from the Hauptbahnhof, dir.: Ostbahnhof) to Marienpl.

▐ PRACTICAL INFORMATION

LOCAL SERVICES

▨ **EurAide in English:** (☎59 38 89; www.euraide.de), along track 11 (room 3) of the Hauptbahnhof, near the Bayerstr. exit. *Let's Go* recommends that English speaking travelers go here first to buy train tickets, as EurAide is the English-speaking office of the Deutsche Bahn and books train tickets for anywhere in Europe at no extra charge. Tickets for the public transit system (at standard prices), maps of Munich (€1), and tickets for a variety of English walking, bus, and bike tours are also available. Drop in for sound advice and pick up a free copy of their brochure *Inside Track.* Open daily June-Sept. 7:45am-12:45pm and 2-6pm; Oct. 7:45am-12:45pm and 2-4pm; Nov.-Apr. 8am-noon and 1-4pm; May 7:45am-12:45pm and 2-4:30pm.

MUNICH

Munich (München)

⌂ ACCOMMODATIONS
Campingplaz Thalkirchen, **15**
Creatif Hotel Elephant, **4**
Euro Youth Hotel, **11**
Hotel Helvetia, **10**
Jugendlager Kapuzinerhölzl
   ("The Tent"), **1**

🍴 FOOD & DRINK
Café Ignaz, **2**
Dukatz im Literaturhaus, **6**
Weißes Bräuhaus, **13**

🍺 BEER GARDENS
Augustinerkeller, **7**
Hirschgarten, **9**
Hofbräuhaus, **12**

★ BARS
Bei Carla, **14**
Reitschule, **3**

★ NIGHTLIFE
Backstage, **8**
Kunstpark Ost, **16**
Soul City, **5**

Main Office: (☎23 39 65 00; www.munich-tourist.de), on the front (east) side of the train station, next to the SB-Markt on Bahnhofpl. Books rooms (for free with 10-15% deposit made to their office) and sells English city maps (€0.30). You can purchase the **München Welcome Card,** which offers free public transportation and reduced prices for 35 sights and services (single-day ticket €6.50, 3-day ticket €15.50). The English guide *Munich for Young People* (€0.50) lists beer gardens and gives tips on cycling, sightseeing, and navigating the public transportation system. Open M-Sa 9:30am-6:30pm, Su 10am-6pm.

Currency Exchange: ReiseBank (☎551 08 37; www.reisebank.de). In front of the train station on Bahnhofpl. Slightly lower processing fee than other banks. Open daily 7am-10pm. Or, around the corner from EurAide at track 11. Open M-Sa 7:30am-7:15pm, Su 9:30am-12:30pm and 1-4:45pm.

Luggage Storage: At the **train station** (☎13 08 50 36) and **airport** (☎97 52 13 75). Staffed storage room *(Gepäckaufbewahrung)* in the main hall of the train station. €1-3 per day. Lockers in main hall and opposite tracks #16, 24, and 28-36. €1-2 per day. Both open daily 4am-12:30am.

Laundromats: Waschcenter, Landshuter Allee 77. U1 to "Rotkreuzpl." Wash €3.50 (includes detergent), dry €0.50 per 15min. Open 24hr. **SB Waschcenter,** Paul-Heyse-Str. 21, near the train station. Right on Bayerstr., then left on Paul-Heyse-Str. for 1½ blocks. Wash €4, dry €0.60 per 10min. Open daily 7am-11pm, last loads 10pm.

Emergency: Police ☎110; **Ambulance** and **Fire** ☎112; **Emergency medical service** ☎192 22, home service 551 771; **Emergency road service** ☎018 02 22 22 22.

Pharmacy: Bahnhofpl. 2 (☎59 41 19 or 59 81 19), on the corner outside the train station. Open M-F 8am-6:30pm, Sa 8am-2pm.

Internet Access: Easy Everything, on Bahnhofspl. next to the post office. Open 24hr. Prices vary by time, but are always less than €3 per hr. Unlimited passes for periods of 24hr. (€4); 7 days (€7); or 20 days (€10). **Internet Café,** Marienpl. 20 (☎20 70 27 37; www.icafé.spacenet.de), serves cocktails and food all night. €1 per 30min. Open 24hr. **International Phone World,** Shillerstr. 8. From the Hauptbahnhof, walk half a block down Shillerstr. A wide variety of phone cards and phones for cheap international calls (€2.20 per min. to Australia, Canada and the US). Internet €1 per 20min.

Post Office: Bahnhofpl., 80335 Munich (☎59 90 87 16). The yellow building opposite the main train station exit. Open M-F 7:30am-8pm, Sa 9am-4pm.

TOURS

⚑ Mike's Bike Tours (☎25 54 39 88; www.mikesbiketours.com). Bike, swim, and down a few beers with English-speaking tour guides, picking up some creative Munich history along the way. If you only have 1 day in Munich, this tour should be at the top of your "to do" list. Tours leave from the Altes Rathaus in Marienpl. The 4hr., 6.5km city tour includes a *Biergarten* break and runs daily June-July 10:30, 11:30am, 3, 5:15pm (the 10:30am tour caters to families); Apr. 16-May and Aug. 11:30am, 4pm; and Sept. 1-Nov. 10 and Mar. 1-Apr. 15 12:30pm. €22. The 7hr., 16km tour has 2 breaks and stops at the Nymphenburg Palace and the Olympic Park. June-July daily 10:30am. €33. Prices include bike rental and rain gear. Historically oriented walking tours offered mid-Apr. to Oct. daily 10:45am, mid-May to mid-Aug. also 4:45pm. 10:45am tours meet in the tourist office at the train station; 4:45pm tours meet at the *Altes Rathaus.* Combo tickets available with Mike's Bikes Dachau tour (see p. 552).

The Original Munich Walks (☎55 02 93 74; www.munichwalks.com). Native English speakers give historical walking tours of the city with 2 different slants: the introductory tour of the *Altstadt* hits all the major sights (daily Apr.-Sept. 10am, May-Sept. also 2:30pm), while a more specialized tour traces the history of the Third Reich and sites of importance from that era (Jan. 11-Mar. and Nov.-Dec. 22 Sa-Su 2pm; Apr.-Sept. daily 3pm). Each 2½hr. tour is €10, students, €9, under 14 €5. Discounted combo tickets available for both the walking tours and the Munich Walks guided tour of Dachau (see p. 552). Both walking tours meet at the **EurAide** office next to track 11; bike tours leave from the Radius office opposite track 31—simply show up to participate.

ACCOMMODATIONS & CAMPING

Munich accommodations are usually expensive or booked; during Oktoberfest, they're just booked. In summer, call before noon or reserve a few weeks ahead.

■ **Euro Youth Hotel,** Senefelderstr. 5 (☎59 90 88 11; www.euro-youth-hotel.de). From the Bayerstr. exit of the Hauptbahnhof, turn left on Bayerstr., then right on Senefelderstr.; the hotel is on the left. Friendly, well-informed English-speaking staff offer loads of brochures and spotless, spiffy rooms. Sleek bar open daily 8pm-2am. Breakfast buffet €4.90. Wash €2.80, dry €1.30. Reception 24hr. Dorm beds €17.50; singles €45; doubles €24, with private shower, telephone and breakfast €36; triples €32; quads €21. Inquire about their new location on the S6 line, with 1500 beds and shuttle service to and from the airport. For reservations at either hotel, call the **central booking number** ☎59 90 88 71 or 59 90 88 72; fax 59 90 88 73. ❷

■ **Hotel Helvetia,** Schillerstr. 6 (☎590 68 50; www.Hotel-Helvetia.de), at the corner of Bahnhofspl., just beyond the Vereinsbank, to the right as you exit the station. The friendliest hotel in Munich. Over half of their beautiful rooms were recently renovated and outfitted with wood floors and oriental rugs. Free **Internet.** Breakfast included. Laundry service €6. Reception 24hr. Singles €30-35; doubles €40-55, with shower €50-65; triples €55-69; quads €72-90; 5-bed room separable into 2 rooms €90-112. Rates rise 10-15% during Oktoberfest. ❸

■ **Creatif Hotel Elephant,** Lämmerstr. 6 (☎55 57 85; www.munich-hotels.com). 300 yd. from the train station. From the Arnulfstr. exit, hang a quick right on Pfefferstr., turn left on Hirtenstr., and right on Lämmerstr. All newly renovated rooms with uniquely modern decor. Private baths, telephones, and TVs in all rooms. Free **Internet.** Reception 24hr. Singles €30-40; doubles €40-65; extra bed €10. ❸

■ **Jugendlager Kapuzinerhölzl** ("The Tent"), In den Kirschen 30 (☎141 43 00; www.the-tent.de). Streetcar #17 from the Hauptbahnhof (dir.: Amalienburgstr.) to "Botanischer Garten" (15min.). Follow the signs straight on Franz-Schrank-Str. and turn left onto In den Kirschen; The Tent is on the right. Night streetcars run at least once an hr. all night. Sleep with 250 fellow "campers" under a big tent on a wooden floor. **Internet** €1 per 15min. Bike rental €6 per day. Free city tours in German and English (W 9am). Free lockers. Laundry €2. Kitchen facilities available. Passport required as deposit. Reception 24hr. Open June-Aug. €8.50 gets you a foam pad, multiple wool blankets (use your sleeping bag too), bathrooms, a shower, and a rudimentary breakfast; actual beds €11. Camping available for €5.50 per campsite plus €5.50 per person. ❶

Campingplatz Thalkirchen, Zentralländstr. 49 (☎723 17 07; fax 724 31 77). U1 or U2 to "Sendlinger Tor," then U3 to "Thalkirchen," and change to bus #57 (20min.). From the bus stop, cross the busy street on the left and turn right onto the footpath by the road. The entrance is on the left. 550 sites on lush grounds on the banks of the river Isor. Jogging and bike paths nearby. TV lounge and restaurant. Wash €4, dry €0.25 per 6min. Curfew 11pm. €4.40 per person, €1.30 per child under 14. €3-4 per tent; tent rental €8 per night. €4.30 per car. Showers €1. Oktoberfest surcharge €3.60. ❶

FOOD

The **Viktualienmarkt,** south of Marienpl., is Munich's gastronomic center. (Open M-F 10am-8pm, Sa 8am-4pm.) For an authentic Bavarian lunch, grab a *Brez'n* (pretzel) spread with *Leberwurst* or cheese. Many reasonably-priced restaurants and cafés cluster on **Schellingstraße, Amalienstrße,** and **Türkenstrße.** Ride U3 or U6 to "Universität." Fruit and vegetable **markets,** many on Bayerstr., are common.

■ **Dukatz im Literaturhaus,** Salvatorpl. 1 (☎291 96 00). Any *Münchener* will tell you this is the place to see and and be seen. The home for small artists serves gourmet food (€6-8) to complement creative drink options (€2-4). Sip a cup of coffee and people watch—not only are entrees among the best in the city, they're also among the most expensive (€16-22). Open daily noon-2:30pm (Sa 3pm) and 6:30-10:30pm. ❹

Weißes Bräuhaus, Tal 7 (☎29 98 75), across from the McDonald's at the end of Marienpl. Traditional Bavarian restaurant brims with cheap, delectable dishes, many featuring meat and sausage specialties. Choose from 40-50 options on the daily menu (€3-17) served by waitresses in classic Bavarian garb. Open daily 8am-midnight. ❸

Café Ignaz, Georgenstr. 67 (☎271 60 93). U2 to "Josephspl.," then take Adelheidstr. 1 block north and turn right on Georgenstr. Earth-friendly café serves delicious food to a low-key clientele. Pasta, pizza, crêpes, quiche, and stir-fry dishes €5-9. Lunch buffet M and W-F noon-2pm (€5.50), brunch buffet Sa 9-11am, Su 9am-1:30pm (€8). Open M-F 8am-10pm, Sa-Su 9am-10pm. ❷

🔆 SIGHTS

MARIENPLATZ. Sacred stone spires tower above the Marienpl., a major S-Bahn and U-Bahn junction as well as the social nexus of the city. The plaza derives its name from the ornate 17th-century monument to the Virgin Mary at its center, the **Mariensäule,** built to commemorate the fact that the powerful Swedes did not destroy the city during the Thirty Years' War. At the neo-Gothic **Neues Rathaus,** the **Glockenspiel** chimes with a display of jousting knights and dancing coopers. According to legend, the barrel-makers coaxed townspeople out of their homes, singing and dancing, to prove that the Great Plague had passed. *(Daily 11am, noon, summer also 5pm.)* At bedtime (9pm), a mechanical watchman marches out and the Guardian Angel escorts the *Münchner Kindl* ("Munich Child;" a symbol of the city) to bed. On the face of the **Altes Rathaus** tower, to the right of the Neues Rathaus, are all of Munich's coats of arms since its inception as a city—with one notable gap. When the tower was rebuilt after its destruction in WWII, the local government decided to exclude the swastika-bearing coat of arms from the Nazi era. *(Tower open M-F 9am-7pm, Sa-Su 10am-7pm. €1.50, 18 and under €0.75, under 6 free.)*

RESIDENZ. Down the pedestrian zone from Odeonspl., the richly decorated Residenz, built from the 14th to 19th centuries, is the most visible presence of the Wittelsbach dynasty and the single best example of castle life available in the city. The Wittelsbach apartments and State Rooms are now the **Residenzmuseum,** a collection of European porcelain, and a 17th-century court chapel. The walls of the **Ahnengalerie,** hung with 120 "family portraits," trace the royal lineage. The beautifully landscaped **Hofgarten** behind the Residenz shelters the temple of Diana. *(Max-Joseph-pl. 3. Take U3-6 to "Odeonspl." ☎29 06 71. Open Apr. to mid-Oct. M-W and F-Su 9am-6pm, Th 9am-8pm; winter daily 10am-4pm. Last admission 30min. before closing time. German language tours meet just outside the museum entrance Sa 2pm, Su 11am; €6. €4, students and children €3.)* The **Schatzkammer** (treasury) contains jeweled baubles, crowns, swords, china, ivory work, and other trinkets from the 10th century on. *(Open same hours as Residenzmuseum. €4; students, seniors, and groups €3; under 18 free with adult. Combination ticket to Schatzkammer and Residenzmuseum €7; students and seniors €5.50.)* Across Max-Joseph Platz gleams the golden-yellow high Baroque **Theatinerkirche,** constructed by Ferdinand Maria from 1663 to 1669 in honor of their son's birth. The crypt houses the bronze coffins of the Wittelsbach clan.

FRAUENKIRCHE. The onion-domed towers of the 15th-century Frauenkirche are one of Munich's most notable landmarks and now the symbol of the city. Its towers (topped with their characteristic domes in the mid-16th century) offer travelers an elevator-accessible view of the old city. Inside is the final resting place of Kaiser Ludwig der Bayer. *(From the Marienpl., walk 1 block toward the Hauptbahnhof on Kaufingerstr. Towers open Apr.-Oct. M-Sa 10am-5pm. Free German language tour Apr.-Oct. at 2pm. €3, students €1.50, under 6 free.)*

MUNICH

ENGLISCHER GARTEN. Extending from the city center to the Studentenheim is the vast Englischer Garten, Europe's largest metropolitan public park. On sunny days, all of Munich turns out to bike, fly kites, play badminton, ride horseback, or sunbathe. A couple of beer gardens are on the grounds, as is a Japanese tea house, Chinese pagoda, and Greek temple. Nude sunbathing areas are designated **FKK** *(Frei-Körper-Kultur)* on signs and park maps. Consider yourself warned. Müncheners with aquatic daring surf the white-water rapids of the Eisbach, the artificial river that flows through the park. The stone bridge on Prinzregentenstr., close to the Haus der Kunst, is an excellent vantage point for these marine stunts.

SCHLOß NYMPHENBURG. After 10 years of trying for an heir, Wittelsbach elector Ferdinand Maria and his wife, Henriette Adelaide of Savoy, celebrated the birth of their son Max Emanuel in 1662 by erecting an elaborate summer playground. During his reign, Max extended the palace to its present proportions. Modeled after the French court, it is one of the most extensive and breathtaking complexes in all of Europe. The surrounding Park was added in 1715 and remodeled in the English style in the early 19th century. Present day visitors can marvel at the grandeur of the palace's two-story marble hall and electors' apartments, taking note of the many paintings of nymphs that are the palace's namesake. Of particular interest is King Ludwig I's **Gallery of Beauties,** paintings of women who caught his fancy (a scandalous hobby, considering many of the women were commoners). Look for the portrait of Lola Montez, a common theatrical dancer with whom Ludwig had obsessive affair well into his 70s. Then stroll through the gardens to the intimate manors housed on the grounds: the Amalienburg, Badenburg, Pagodenburg, and the Magdalen hermitage. Finally, visit the **Marstallmuseum** (carriage museum) to see how 17th-century royalty rode in style. *(Streetcar #17 (dir.: Amalienburgstr.) to "Schloß Nymphenburg." ☎17 90 80. All attractions open Apr. to mid-Oct. M-W and F-Su 9am-6pm, Th 9am-8pm; late Oct.-Mar. daily 10am-4pm. Museum and Schloß open Tu-Su 9am-noon and 1-5pm. Badenburg, Pagodenburg, and Magdalen hermitages closed in winter. Schloß €3.50, students €2.50. Manors €3, students €2. Marstallmuseum €2.50, students €2. Entire complex €7.50, students €6, under 15 free with adult.)*

DACHAU. The Third Reich's first concentration camp, Dachau opened in 1933 to house political prisoners on the former grounds of a WWI munitions factory. After Hitler visited the camp in 1937, it became a model for the construction of the 3000 other camps throughout Nazi-occupied Europe, as well as a training-ground for the SS officers who would work there. As the sign over the camp's only entrance—*Arbeit macht Frei* ("Work will set you free")—indicates, Dachau was primarily a labor camp: during the war, prisoners worked making armaments and performed various kinds of hard labor, often until they died. Those who volunteered for medical experiments in hope of release were frozen to death or infected with malaria in the name of science. Although Dachau has a gas chamber, for reasons that remain unknown it was only tested but never put into full use. The tightly-packed **barracks** once held the 206,000 men interned here; two have been preserved, but the rest have decayed down to their foundations. Walls, gates, and a crematorium were restored in 1962 as a chillingly sparse memorial to the victims; a museum further honors their memory. *(From Munich, take S2 (dir.: Petershausen) to "Dachau" (20min.; €4, or 4 stripes on the Streifenkarte), then bus #724 (dir.: Kraütgarten). Camp open Tu-Su 9am-5pm. 2hr. tours of the camp in English leave from the museum June-Aug. daily 12:30pm; Sept.-May Sa-Su 12:30pm. Tour is free; all donations go directly to the Holocaust Survivors' Association. English audio tour available. €2.50; children, students, and seniors €1.50. Museum guides available English €0.20; call ☎08131 17 41 for more information.)*

▥ MUSEUMS

Munich is a superb museum city and many of the offerings would require days for exhaustive perusal. The *Münchner Volkshochschule* (☎ 48 00 62 29 or 48 00 62 30) offers tours of many city museums for €6. The tourist office and many larger museums sell day passes for entry to all of Munich's state-owned museums (€15). All state-owned museums are free on Sunday.

▩ **PINAKOTHEK DER MODERNE.** The newest and largest addition to the art museums of Munich, this Pinakothek offers four museums in one. Art, works on paper, architecture, and design occupy the large building created by *Münchener* Stephan Braunfels. Lose yourself in the works of Picasso, Dalí, Matisse, Warhol, and others. *(Barerstr. 40. U2 to "Königspl." Take a right at Königspl., and a left after 1 block onto Meiserstr. Walk 1½ blocks to the museum.* ☎ *23 80 53 60. Open W and F-Su 10am-5pm, Tu-Th 10am-8pm. €5, students €3.50. Day pass for all 3 Pinakotheke €12.)*

▩ **ALTE PINAKOTHEK.** This world-renowned hall contains Munich's most precious art. Commissioned in 1826 by King Ludwig I, it houses works by Titian, da Vinci, Raphael, Dürer, Rembrandt, Rubens, and other European painters of the 14th through the 18th centuries. *(Barerstr. 27.* ☎ *23 80 52 16. Hours and prices same as Pinakothek der Moderne. Combination ticket for the Alte and Neue Pinakotheke €8/€5.)*

▩ **NEUE PINAKOTHEK.** A sleek space for paintings and sculptures of the 19th to 20th centuries: van Gogh, Klimt, Cézanne, Manet, and more. *(Barerstr. 29, next to the Alte Pinakothek.* ☎ *23 80 51 95. Open M and W-Su 10am-5pm, Tu 10am-10pm. Tour M noon. Same prices as the Alte Pinakothek.)*

GLYPTOTHEK. In 1825, Ludwig I assembled this museum, the realization of a dream to turn Munich into a "cultural work of such sheer perfection as only few Germans have experienced." It features 2400-year-old pediment figures from the Temple of Aphaea as well as Etruscan and Roman sculptures. *(Königspl. 3. U2 to "Königspl." Across Luisenstr. from the Lenbachhaus.* ☎ *28 61 00. Open W and F-Su 10am-5pm, Tu and Th 10am-8pm. Free tour Tu and Th 6pm. €3, students €2.)*

DEUTSCHES MUSEUM. One of the world's largest and best science and technology museums. Exhibits include the first telephone and the work bench upon which Otto Hahn split his first atom. The mining exhibit winds through a labyrinth of recreated subterranean tunnels. A walk through the museum's 50+ departments covers over 17km; grab an English guidebook (€4). They also have a planetarium. *(Museuminsel 1. S1-8 to "Isartor" or streetcar #18 to "Deutsches Museum."* ☎ *217 91; www.deutsches-museum.de. Open daily 9am-5pm. €7.50, students €3, children under 6 free.)*

▨ NIGHTLIFE

A nighttime odyssey begins at one of Munich's beer gardens or beer halls, and keeps flowing at cafés and bars, which, except on Friday and Saturday nights, shut off their taps at 1am. Then the discos and dance clubs suddenly spark, and throb relentlessly until 4am. The trendy bars, cafés, cabarets, and discos plugged into **Leopoldstraße** in **Schwabing** attract tourists from all over Europe. **Münchener Freiheit** (on the U3/6 line) is the most famous (and most touristy) bar/café district. Pick up *Munich Found, in München,* or *Prinz* at any newsstand to find out what's up. Munich's queer scene centers in the **Glockenbachviertel,** stretching from south of the Sendlinger Tor through the Viktualienmarkt/Gärtnerpl. to the Isartor. Pick up *Sergej,* Munich's gay and lesbian "scene magazine" at **Max&Milian Bookstore,** Ickstattstr. 2 (☎ 260 33 20; open M-F 10:30am-2pm and 3:30-8pm, Sa 11am-4pm), or at any other gay locale, for extensive listings of gay nightlife hotspots and services.

MUNICH

■ **Kunstpark Ost,** Grafinger Str. 6 (☎49 00 29 28; www.kunstpark.de). U5 or S1-8 to "Ostbahn-hof"; follow signs for the "Kunstpark Ost" exit, turn right onto Friedenstr. and then left onto Grafinger Str.; the Park is half a block down on the right. The newest and biggest addition to the Munich nightlife scene, this huge complex of 30 different venues swarms with young people hitting clubs, concerts, and bars and, of course, dancing the night away. Try the hip **MilchBar** (☎45 08 11 60; open M and W-F), with modern hits and old favorites; the psychedelic-trance **Natral Temple** (☎49 00 18 95; open F-Sa); the alternative cocktail and disco joint **K41** (☎49 04 21 60; Th 80s night); the very chill cigars-and-drinks mecca **Cohibar** (☎49 00 33 12; open W-Sa); or the risque South American rock bar **Titty Twister** (☎49 04 21 10; open W-Sa). Hours, cover, and themes vary—call the info and advance ticket number or check out the monthly magazine *Kunstpark* online for details on specific nights and specials.

■ **Reitschule,** Königinstr. 34 (☎33 34 02). U3 or 6 to "Giselastr." Above a club, overlook-ing a horseback-riding school. Marble tables and a sleek bar. In the summer, a back-yard beer garden teems with students crowding under straw huts and around rose-filled fountains. *Weißbier* €4. Breakfast served all day. Open daily 9am-1am.

Backstage, Wilhelm-Hale Str./Birketweg (☎126 61 00; www.backstage089.de). Streetcar #16 or 17 to "Stubenpl." or #18 or 19 to "Elsenheimerstr." "Underground" scene, playing hard core, indie rock, electronica, soul, and funk. Primarily local crowd. Check online or call for live concert listings. Open Su-Th 7pm-3am, F-Sa 7pm-5am.

Bei Carla, Buttermelcherstr. 9 (☎22 79 01). S1-8 to "Isartor," then walk 1 block south on Zweibrückenstr., take a right on Rumfordstr., turn left on Klenzestr., then another left onto Buttermelcherstr. This friendly lesbian café and bar is one of Munich's best-kept secrets. Women in their 20s and 30s flock here for pleasant conversation, a few cock-tails, and a round or two of darts. Open M-Sa 4pm-1am, Su 6pm-1am.

Soul City, Maximilianspl. 5 (☎59 52 72), at the intersection with Max-Joseph-Str. The biggest gay disco in Bavaria; music from 70s disco to Latin to techno. Straights always welcome. Beer €4 for 0.3L. Cover €5-13. Open W-Sa 10pm-late, Su 7pm-midnight.

BEER, BEER, & MORE BEER

The six great Munich labels are *Augustiner, Hacker-Pschorr, Hofbräu, Löwen-bräu, Paulaner,* and *Spaten-Franziskaner;* most restaurants will serve only one. The longest beer festival in the world is Munich's **Oktoberfest** (Sep.19-Oct.4, 2004) at Theresienwiese (U4 or U5).

■ **Augustinerkeller,** Arnulfstr. 52 (☎59 43 93), at Zirkus-Krone-Str. S1-8 to "Hacker-brücke." Walk left out of the station on the bridge and take a left on Arulfstr. Founded in 1824, Augustiner is viewed by many as the finest beer garden in town, with lush grounds, dim lighting beneath 100-year-old chestnut trees, and tasty, enormous *Brez'n.* The real attraction is the delicious, sharp Augustiner beer (*Maß* €5.70), which draws locals, smart tourists, and students. Food €2-14. Open daily 10am-1am; hot food until 10pm. Beer garden open daily 10:30am-midnight or 1am, depending on weather.

■ **Hirschgarten,** Hirschgarten 1 (☎17 25 91). Streetcar 17 (dir.: Amalienburgstr.) to "Romanpl." Walk south to the end of Guntherstr. and enter the Hirschgarten. The largest beer garden in Europe (seating 9000) is boisterous and always crowded. Families come for the grassy park and carousel, and to see the deer which are still kept on the pre-mises. Entrees €5-15. *Maß* €5.30. Open daily 9am-midnight; kitchen open 9am-10pm.

Hofbräuhaus, Platzl 9 (☎290 13 60), 2 blocks from Marienpl. Walk past the Altes Rathaus and take a left onto Sparkassenstr. Turn right onto Lederstr., and take your 1st left on Orlan-dostr.; the Hofbräuhaus is straight ahead. In 1589, Bavarian Duke Wilhelm the Pious earned his epithet by founding the Münchener Hofbräuhaus for the worship of Germany's most revered beverage. Though the Hofbräuhaus was originally reserved for royalty and invited guests, a 19th-century proclamation lowered prices of beer to "offer the Military and working classes a healthy and good tasting drink." 15,000-30,000L of beer are sold daily. Many tables are reserved for locals, and hundreds of *Münchener* keep personal steins in the beer hall's safe. Go in the early afternoon to avoid tourists, or in the evening to catch the true bustle of the beer hall. Live Blasmusik every day. *Maß* €6. *Weißwürste* €3.70. Open daily 9am-midnight.

APPENDIX

CLIMATE

Average Temperature	January		April		July		October	
	°C	°F	°C	°F	°C	°F	°C	°F
Geneva	0	32	9.5	49	19.5	67	10	50
Interlaken	0	32	10	50	19.5	67	11	51
Zurich	-1	30	8	47	18	64	8	47
Innsbruck	-2.5	28	9.5	49	18	64	9.5	49
Salzburg	-1.5	29	8	47	18	64	9	48
Vienna	-1	30	10	50	20	68	11	51
Munich	0.5	33	9	48	19	66	11	51

Although Austria and Switzerland are at about the same latitude as Newfoundland, their climates are considerably milder. In general, winters are cold and snowy enough for skiing, while summers are warm enough for outdoor cafés. July is usually the hottest month, with temperatures reaching 38°C (100°F) for brief periods, with generally cool evenings. February is the coldest, with temperatures down to -10°C (5°F). Mountainous areas of Austria and Switzerland are cooler and wetter the higher you get; as a rule, temperatures decrease about 1.7°C (3°F) with each additional 300m elevation. Snow cover lasts from late December to March in the valleys, from November to May at about 1800m, and year-round above 2500m. Switzerland's lake areas, in the temperate swath of plain that extends across from Lake Constance in the northeast through Zurich and Bern down to Geneva, are wet all year—don't forget your umbrella. For weather information on a particular city, check www.weatherlabs.com.

TIME ZONES

Austria and Switzerland both use Central European time (abbreviated MEZ in German), which is 6hr. later than Eastern Standard Time in the US and 1hr. later than Greenwich Mean Time. It is 9hr. earlier than Eastern Australia Time and 11hr. earlier than New Zealand Time. Austria and Switzerland use the 24hr. clock for all official purposes, so 19:30 is the same as 7:30pm.

HOLIDAYS & FESTIVALS

The *International Herald Tribune* lists national holidays in each daily edition, though the listing on www.holidayfestival.com is more complete and useful. If you plan your itinerary around these dates, you can encounter the festivals that entice you and circumvent the ones that don't. Many services shut down on holidays and could leave you strapped for food and money in the event of an ill-timed arrival. Note also that in Austria, the first Saturday of every month is *Langer Samstag* (long Saturday); most stores stay open until 5pm. In small towns, stores are often closed from noon Saturday until 8am Monday; remember this when stocking up on food for weekends. Check the individual town listings and the index for information on the festivals below.

BOTH COUNTRIES

DATE	FESTIVAL	REGION
January 1	New Year's	National
April 13	Good Friday	National
April 16	Easter Monday	National
May 24	Ascension	National
June 4	Whit Monday	National
December 25	Christmas	National

AUSTRIA

DATE	FESTIVAL	REGION
January 6	Epiphany	National
June 14	Corpus Christi Day	National
May 1	Labor Day	National
Late July to Late August	Salzburg Music Festival	Salzburg
August 15	Feast of the Assumption	National
October 26	Austrian National Day	National
November 1	All Saints' Day	National
December 8	Feast of the Immaculate Conception	National
December 26	Boxing Day	National

SWITZERLAND

DATE	FESTIVAL	REGION
January 2	Berchtold's Day	National
Early March	Fasnacht (Carnival)	Basel, Lucerne
Mid-July	International Jazz Festival	Montreux
August 1	Swiss National Day	National
December 26	St. Stephen's Day	National

MEASUREMENTS

Austria and Switzerland use the metric system. Unconventional local units for measuring wine or beer are explained in the text when necessary. Note that gallons in the US are not identical to those across the Atlantic; one US gallon equals 0.83 Imperial gallons.

MEASUREMENT CONVERSIONS

1 inch (in.) = 25.4mm	1 millimeter (mm) = 0.039 in.
1 foot (ft.) = 0.30m	1 meter (m) = 3.28 ft.
1 yard (yd.) = 0.914m	1 meter (m) = 1.09 yd.
1 mi. = 1.61km	1 kilometer (km) = 0.62 mi.
1 ounce (oz.) = 28.35g	1 gram (g) = 0.035 oz.
1 pound (lb.) = 0.454kg	1 kilogram (kg) = 2.202 lb.
1 fluid ounce (fl. oz.) = 29.57ml	1 milliliter (ml) = 0.034 fl. oz.
1 gallon (gal.) = 3.785L	1 liter (L) = 0.264 gal.
1 acre (ac.) = 0.405ha	1 hectare (ha) = 2.47 ac.
1 square mile (sq. mi.) = 2.59 sq. km	1 square kilometer (sq. km) = 0.386 sq. mi.

DISTANCE (IN KM)

Distances may vary depending on the type of transportation used and the route traveled. In certain cases, traveling through a neighboring country such as Germany or Italy can be the fastest route.

	Basel	Bern	Geneva	Graz	Innsbruck	Interlaken	Linz	Locarno	Lugano	Salzburg	Vienna	Zermatt
Basel												
Bern	71											
Geneva	187	129										
Graz	597	610	718									
Innsbruck	290	303	418	307								
Interlaken	98	43	230	581	278							
Linz	509	536	658	158	245	517						
Locarno	180	135	204	520	235	92	478					
Lugano	201	158	219	512	233	114	476	21				
Salzburg	410	433	554	200	137	412	108	370	369			
Vienna	658	684	801	138	383	661	151	615	608	249		
Zermatt	169	105	126	602	311	72	555	82	95	447	694	
Zurich	76	98	224	525	216	92	443	135	153	102	591	159

CITY PHONE CODES

CITY TELEPHONE CODES			
Basel	061	Liechtenstein	075
Bern	031	Locarno	091
Bregenz	05574	Lucerne	041
Geneva	022	Lugano	091
Graz	0316	Salzburg	0662
Innsbruck	0512	Vienna	0222
Interlaken	033	Zermatt	027
Lausanne	021	Zurich	01

LANGUAGE

Confronted with Switzerland's four official languages and the countless dialects of German spoken throughout Austria and Switzerland, many travelers feel somewhat intimidated by the thought of communicating. Each of the following phrasebooks is designed to help you master your most urgent communication needs in each of the major languages spoken in Austria and Switzerland. Each phrasebook is preceded by a pronunciation guide. Don't be afraid to attempt to use the phrases listed; with a little practice, they'll roll off your tongue.

The first, perhaps most helpful phrase a traveler should learn is "Sprechen Sie Englisch?," "Parlez-vous anglais?," or "Lei parla inglese?" (for use in the appropriate regions). Even if the person you ask doesn't speak English, he/she will appreciate your attempt to speak their language. Most younger Austrian and Swiss urbanites speak at least a smattering of English—usually much more—thanks to the establishment of English as a requirement for high school diplomas. Outside of cities and among older residents, however, the English proficiency becomes less reliable and you may have to rely on phrasebooks or an impromptu translation by the local tourist office.

If you're unsure in a foreign vocabulary, it's best to err on the side of formality. For example, it never hurts to use titles like *Herr* (Mr.) or *Frau* (Mrs.), the Italian *Signore* and *Signora*, or the French *Monsieur* and *Madame*. When in doubt, use the formal pronoun "you" (*Sie* in German, *Vous* in French, *Lei* in Italian) with the plural form of the verb. People will let you know when it's time to switch to more familiar language.

GERMAN PRONUNCIATION

In German, consonants are the same as in English, with the exceptions of C (sometimes pronounced *TS*, but almost never seen outside of diphthongs); J (pronounced *Y*); K (always pronounced, even before N); P (nearly always pronounced, even before F); QU (pronounced *KV*); S (pronounced *Z* at the beginning of a word); V (pronounced *F*); W (pronounced *V*); Z (pronounced *TS*). The ß, or *ess-tsett*, is simply a double S. An umlaut (Ä, Ö, Ü) theoretically blends the sound of the German vowel *E* with the umlauted vowel (sometimes written AE, OE, UE). Ä is pronounced like the e in "let"; Ö is pronounced as if you were saying "r" with the middle of the tongue rather than the front; Ü is pronounced as if you were trying to say "ooh" and the y in "you" at the same time. Pronounce SCH as *SH*. Rs are rolled with the back of the tongue. Unlike in much of Germany, CH in Austria and Switzerland is most often pronounced with the hoarse, throat-clearing sound that people often erroneously associate with High German. Vowels are as follows: A as in "father"; E as the *a* in "hay" or the indistinct vowel sound in "uh"; I as the *ee* in "cheese"; O as in "oh"; U as in "ooh"; Y similar to Ü; AU as in "ouch"; EU as the *oi* in "boil." With EI and IE, pronounce the last letter as a long English vowel.

FRENCH PRONUNCIATION

French pronunciation is more difficult than German, as many of the letters in a word are silent. Do not pronounce any final consonants except L, F, or C; an E on the end of the word, however, means that you should pronounce the final consonant sound, e.g., *muet* is mew-AY but *muette* is mew-ET. This rule also applies to plural nouns—don't pronounce the final S. J is like the S in "pleasure." R is rolled in the front of the mouth even more than in Austria. C sounds like *K* before A, O, and U; like *S* before E and I. A *ç* always sounds like *S*. Vowels are short and precise: A as the *O* in "mom"; E as in "help" (é becomes the a in "hay"); I as the *ee* in "creep"; O as in "oh." UI sounds like the word "whee." U is a short, clipped *oo* sound; hold your lips as if you were about to say "ooh," but say *ee* instead. OU is a straight *oo* sound. With few exceptions, all syllables receive equal emphasis.

ITALIAN PRONUNCIATION

Italian pronunciation isn't too complicated. There are seven vowel sounds in standard Italian: A as in "father," I as the *ee* in "cheese," U as the *oo* in "droop," E either as *ay* in "bay" or *eh* in "set," and O both as *oh* in "bone" and *o* as in "off." Save for a few quirks, Italian consonants are easy. H is always silent, R is always rolled. C and G are hard before A, O, or U, as in "cat" and "goose," but they soften into CH and J sounds, respectively, when followed by I or E, as in English "cheese" and "jeep" or Italian *ciao* (chow), "goodbye," and *gelato* (jeh-LAH-toh), "ice cream." CH and GH are pronounced like K and G before I and E, as in *chianti* (ky-AHN-tee), the Tuscan wine, and *spaghetti* (spah-GEHT-tee), the pasta. Pronounce GN like the NI in "onion," as in *bagno* (BAHN-yoh), the bathroom. GLI is like the LLI in *million*, so *sbagliato* ("wrong") is said "zbal-YAH-toh." If followed by A, O, or U, SC is pronounced as *SK*. *Scusi* ("excuse me") yields "SKOO-zee." When followed by an E or I, SC is pronounced SH as in *sciopero* (SHOH-pair-oh), "strike."

USEFUL PHRASES

ENGLISH	GERMAN	FRENCH	ITALIAN
Hello	Hallo	Bonjour	Ciao
Excuse me/Sorry	Entschuldigung	Excusez-moi	Scusi/Mi dispiace
Could you please help me?	Können Sie mir bitte helfen?	Est-ce que vous pouvez m'aider?	Potrebbe aiutarmi?
Good day	Guten Tag/Grüß Gott (Gruezi/Gruessach)	Bonjour	Buongiorno
Good morning	Guten Morgen	Bonjour	Buonagiorno
Good evening	Guten Abend	Bonsoir	Buona sera
Good night	Gute Nacht	Bonne nuit	Buona notte
Good-bye	Tschüß! (informal); Auf Wiedersehen! (formal)	Au revoir	Arrivederci/Arrivederla
yes/no/maybe	ja/nein/vielleicht	oui/non/peut-être	sì/no/forse
Please	Bitte	S'il vous plaît	Per favore/Per piacere
Thank you	Danke	Merci	Grazie
You're welcome	Bitte	De rien	Prego
Who?	Wer?	Qui?	Chi?
What?	Was?	Comment?	Cosa?
Where?	Wo?	Où?	Dovè?
When (what time)?	Wann?	Quand?	Quando?
Why?	Warum?	Pourquoi?	Perche?
My name is...	Ich heiße...	Je m'appelle...	Mi chiamo...
What is your name?	Wie heißen Sie?	Comment vous appellez-vous?	Come ti chiami?
Where are you from?	Woher kommen Sie?	Vous venez-d'où?	Di dove sei?
I'm from...	Ich komme aus...	Je viens de...	Sono di...
How are you?	Wie geht's?	Comment ça va?	Come sta (formal)/stai?
I'm fine.	Es geht mir gut.	Ça va bien.	Sto bene.
I'm not feeling well.	Mir ist schlecht.	J'ai mal.	Sto male.
I have a headache.	Ich habe Kopfweh.	J'ai mal à la tête.	Ho un mal di testa.
I need a doctor.	Ich brauche einen Arzt.	J'ai besoin d'un médecin.	Ho bisogno di un medico.
Leave me alone.	Lass mich in Ruhe.	Laissez-moi tranquille.	Lasciame in pace!
I'll call the police.	Ich rufe die Polizei an.	J'appelle la police.	Telefono alla polizia!
Help!	Hilfe!	Au secours!/Aidez-moi, s'il vous plaît.	Aiuto!
Stop/Enough!	Halt!/Genug!	Arrête!	Ferma!/Basta!
Do you speak English?	Sprechen Sie Englisch?	Parlez-vous anglais?	Lei parla inglese?
I can't speak	Ich kann kein Deutsch.	Je ne parle pas français.	Non parlo italiano.
I don't understand.	Ich verstehe nicht.	Je ne comprends pas.	Non capisco.
I understand	Ich verstehe.	Je comprends.	Ho capito.
Please speak slowly.	Sprechen Sie bitte langsam.	S'il vous plaît, parlez moins vite.	Parla più lentamente, per favore.
Excuse me?	Wie, bitte?	Pardon?	Come?
Please repeat.	Bitte widerholen sie.	Répétez, s'il vous plaît.	Potrebbe ripetere?
I would like...	Ich möchte...	Je voudrais...	Vorrei...
I'm looking for...	Ich suche...	Je cherche...	Cerco...
How much does that cost?	Wieviel kostet das?	Ça coûte combien?	Quanto costa?

ENGLISH	GERMAN	FRENCH	ITALIAN
Where can I buy something to eat/to drink?	Wo kann ich etwas zu essen kaufen/zu trinken kaufen?	Où est-ce que je peux acheter quelque chose à manger/à boire?	Dove posso comprare qualcosa da bere o mangiare?
OK.	OK/Alles klar.	D'accord.	D'accordo.
I don't know.	Ich weiss nicht.	Je ne sais pas.	Boh./Non lo so.
Where is the toilet?	Wo ist die Toilette?	Où sont les toilettes?	Dov'è il gabinetto?
Please	Bitte	S'il vous plait	Per favore
How do you say that in German?/French?...	Wie sagt man das auf Deutsch?	Comment ça se dit en français?	Come si dice...?
What does this mean?	Was bedeutet das?	Qu'est-ce que ça veut dire?	Cosa vuol dire questo?
Where is the phone?	Wo ist das Telefon?	Où est le téléphone?	Dov'è il telefono?
I am a student (male/female).	Ich bin Student/Studentin.	Je suis étudiant/étudiante.	Sono studente/studentessa.
student discounts	Studentenermässigungen	tarifs réduits pour les étudiants	sconto per gli studenti
No problem	Kein Proble	Ce n'est pas grave	Va bene

DIRECTIONS & TRANSPORTATION

(to the) right	rechts	à droite	a destra
(to the) left	links	à gauche	a sinistra
straight ahead	geradeaus	tout droite	sempre diritto
here	hier	ici	qui/qua
there	da	là-bas	li/là
far	fern	loin	lontano
near	nah	près de	vicino
east/west	Ost/West	est/ouest	ovest/este
north/south	Nord/Süd	nord/sud	nord/sud
I would like a ticket to...	Ich möchte eine Fahrkarte nach...	Je voudrais un billet à...	Vorrei un biglietto per...
Where is this train going?	Wohin fährt dieser Zug?	Quelle est la destination de la train?	Dove va questo treno?
Which bus goes to...	Welcher Bus fährt nach...?	Quel bus va â...?	Qual' autobus va a...?
When does the train leave?	Wann fährt der Zug ab?	Quand est-ce que le train part?	A che ora parte il treno?
Please stop.	Bitte halten Sie.	Arretez, s'il vous plait.	Ferma, per favore.
Where is...?	Wo ist...?	Où est...?	Dov'è...?
the train station?	der Bahnhof?	la gare?	la stazione?
the tourist office?	das Touristbüro?	le bureau de tourisme?	l'ufficio turistico?
the post office?	die Post?	la poste?	l'ufficio postale?
the old town?	die Altstadt?	la vieille ville?	il centro storico?
the hostel?	die Jugendherberge?	l'auberge de jeunesse?	il ostello?
a grocery store?	ein Supermarkt?	le supermarché?	il supermercato?
the bus stop?	die Haltestelle?	l'arrêt d'autobus?	la fermata dell'autobus?
one-way	einfache Fahrt	un billet aller-simple	solo andata
round-trip	hin-und zurück	aller-retour	andata e ritorno

TIMES & HOURS

At what time...?	Um wie viel Uhr...?	À quelle heure?	A che ora...?
What time is it?	Wie spät ist es?	Quelle heure est-il?	Che ore sono?
It is 5 o'clock.	Es ist fünf (5) Uhr.	Il est cinq (5) heures.	Sono le cinque (5).
It's early.	Es ist früh.	Il est tôt.	e anticipo/presto
It's late.	Es ist spät.	Il est tard.	e ritardo/tardi
opening hours	die Öffnungszeiten	Les heures d'ouverture	orari
daily	täglich	chaque jour	quotidiano
weekly	wochentlich	chaque semaine	settimanale
monthly	monatlich	chaque mois	mensile
today	heute	aujourd'hui	oggi
tomorrow	morgen	demain	domani
yesterday	gestern	hier	ieri
now	jetzt	maintenant	adesso/ora
immediately	sofort	tout-de-suite	subito
always	immer	toujours	sempre
except	ohne	sauf	ecceto
January	Januar	janvier	gennaio
February	Februar	février	febbraio
March	März	mars	marzo
April	April	avril	aprile
May	Mai	mai	maggio
June	Juni	juin	guigno
July	Juli	juillet	luglio
August	August	août	agosto
September	September	septembre	settembre
October	October	octobre	ottobre
November	November	novembre	novembre
December	December	decembre	dicembre
open	geöffnet	ouvert	aperto
closed	geschlossen	fermé	chiuso
morning	der Morgen	le matin	mattina
afternoon	der Nachmittag	l'après-midi	pomeriggio
evening	der Abend	le soir	sera
night	die Nacht	la nuit	notte
break time, rest day	die Ruhepause, der Ruhetag	fermeture	riposo
Monday	Montag	lundi	lunedì
Tuesday	Dienstag	mardi	martedì
Wednesday	Mittwoch	mercredi	mercoledì
Thursday	Donnerstag	jeudi	giovedì
Friday	Freitag	vendredi	venerdì
Saturday	Samstag	samedi	sabato
Sunday	Sonntag	dimanche	domenica
holidays	Ferien/Urlaub	vacances	giorni festivi

NUMBERS

No.	German	French	Italian
0	null	zéro	zero
1	eins	un	uno
2	zwei or zwoh	deux	due
3	drei	trois	tre
4	vier	quatre	quattro
5	fünf	cinq	cinque
6	sechs	six	sei
7	sieben	sept	sette
8	acht	huit	otto
9	neun	neuf	nove
10	zehn	dix	dieci
11	elf	onze	undici
12	zwölf	douze	dodici
13	dreizehn	treize	tredici
14	vierzehn	quatorze	quattordici
15	fünfzehn	quinze	quindici
16	sechzehn	seize	sedici
17	siebzehn	dix-sept	diciasette
18	achtzehn	dix-huit	diciotto
19	neunzehn	dix-neuf	dicianove
20	zwanzig	vingt	venti
21	ein-und-zwanzig	vingt et un	ventuno
30	dreißig	trente	trenta
40	vierzig	quarante	quaranta
50	fünfzig	cinquante	cinquanta
60	sechzig	soixante	sessanta
70	siebzig	soixante-dix	settanta
80	achtzig	quatre-vingt	ottanta
90	neunzig	quatre-vingt-dix	novanta
100	(ein)hundert	cent	cento
101	hunderteins	cent-et-un	centuno
1000	(ein)tausend	mille	mille

FOOD & RESTAURANTS

restaurant	das Restaurant	un restaurant	il ristorante
bar	die Bar	un Bar	il Bar
meal	das Mahl	un repas	pasto

water	das Wasser	l'eau	l'acqua
breakfast	das Frühstück	le petit déjeuner	la (prima) colazione
lunch	das Mittagessen	le déjeuner	il pranzo
dinner/supper	das Abendessen	le dîner	la cena
I am thirsty/hungry.	Ich habe Durst/Hunger.	J'ai soif/faim.	Ho sed/fame.
waiter(ess)	Kellner(in)/Herr Ober	serveur/euse	cameriere/a
Check, please.	Die Rechnung, bitte.	L'addition, s'il vous plaît.	Il conto, per favore.
Service included.	Bedienung inklusiv.	Service compris.	Servizio compresso.
I would like...	Ich hätte gern...	Je voudrais...	Vorrei...
It tastes good.	Es schmeckt gut.	C'est bon.	Tutto bene.
Do you have vegetarian food?	Haben Sie vegetarisches Essen?	Avez-vous de la nourriture vegetarienne?	Hai qualcosa vegeteriana da mangiare?
I am diabetic.	Ich bin Diabetiker.	Je suis diabétique.	Sono diabetico.
milk	das Milch	le lait	la latte
coffee	das Kaffee	le café	il caffè
beer/wine	das Bier/der Wein	la bière/le vin	la bierra/il vino
tap water	das Leitungswasser	de l'eau de robinet	acqua di rubinetto
bread	das Brot	le pain	il pane
vegetables	die Gemüse	le légume	le verdure
meat	das Fleisch	la viande	le carne
sausage	die Wurst	le saucisson	la salsiccia
chicken	das Huhn	le poulet	il pollo
pork	das Schweinfleisch	le porc	il maiale
cheese	der Käse	le fromage	il formagio
pasta	die Nudeln	les pâtes	pasta
dessert	der Nachtisch	le dessert	il dolce

MISCELLANEOUS WORDS & PHRASES

a single room	ein Einzelzimmer	une chambre simple	una camera singola
money	Geld	l'argent	gli soldi
hospital	das Krankenhaus	un hôpital	ospedale
sick	krank	malade	malato/a
smoking	rauchen	fumer`	fumare
good/bad	gut/schlecht	bon/mauvais	buono/cattivo
happy/sad	glücklich, froh/traurig	heureux/triste	felice/triste
hot/cold	heiß/kalt	chaud/froid	caldo/freddo
big/small	groß/klein	grand/petit	piccolo/grande
full/empty	voll/ leer	plein/vide	pieno/vuoto
dangerous/safe	gefährlich/sicher	dangereux/sûr	pericoloso/sicuro
Caution!	Achtung!/Vorsicht!	Attention!	Attenzione!
Fire!	Feuer!	Feu!	Fuoco!
May I buy you a drink?	Darf ich dir ein Getränk kaufen?	Je peux t'offrir quelque chose de boire?	Posso offrirti qualcosa da bere?
I'm waiting for my father/husband/ brother.	Ich warte auf meinen Vater/Mann/Bruder.	J'attends mon père/mon mari/mon frère..	Aspeto mio padre/il mio sposo/mio fratello

INDEX

MAP INDEX

MAP LEGEND

🏛 Museum	♠ Hotel/Hostel	▲▲▲ Mountain Peaks
✚ Hospital	✈ Airport	Mountains
Police	🚌 Bus Station	Glacier
✉ Post Office	🚃 Train Station	Cliffs
ⓘ Tourist Office	Ⓤ U-Bahn Station	Tunnel
$ Bank	⚓ Ferry Landing	Ferry Route
℞ Pharmacy	Bars	Funicular/Cable Car
■ Site or Point of Interest	✝ Monastery	🎭 Theater	Pedestrian Zone
⚑ Embassy or Consulate	Funicular/Cable Car	Mountain Pass	Stairs
Library	✝ Church	Mountain Hut	Footpaths/Trails
Internet Cafe	Gate or Entrance	Ski Resort	
P Parking	Castle	Waterfall	

Food & Drink
Coffee House
Nightlife/Clubs
Camping

Common Map Abbreviations:
Str. & -str.   Straße - street
Pl. & -pl.   Platz - square
G. & -g.   Gasse - lane
r.   Rue - street

576